A
DICTIONARY OF MIRACLES

A

DICTIONARY OF MIRACLES

Imitative, Realistic, and Dogmatic

WITH ILLUSTRATIONS

BY THE REV.

E. COBHAM BREWER, LL.D.

(The Fiftieth or Golden Year of his Authorship, 1884)

AUTHOR OF "GUIDE TO SCIENCE" (THREE HUNDRED AND EIGHTIETH THOUSAND)
"HISTORY OF FRANCE" (TENTH EDITION); "HISTORY OF GERMANY"
"THEOLOGY IN SCIENCE" (EIGHTH EDITION); "READER'S HANDBOOK" (THIRD EDITION)
"DICTIONARY OF PHRASE AND FABLE" (SIXTEENTH EDITION)
"RULES FOR ENGLISH SPELLING;" ETC., ETC.

PHILADELPHIA:
J. B. LIPPINCOTT COMPANY.

REPUBLISHED BY GALE RESEARCH COMPANY, BOOK TOWER, DETROIT, 1966

Library of Congress Catalog Card Number 66-29783

PAPER USED IN THIS EDITION IS
A FINE ACID FREE PERMANENT/DURABLE PAPER
COMMONLY REFERRED TO AS "300-YEAR" PAPER

TO

MRS. P. MILLS AND MRS. HENRY STORY

WHO FIRST TAUGHT HIM,

BY THEIR EXAMPLES,

WHAT TRUE BENEVOLENCE AND KIND-HEARTEDNESS

PRACTICALLY MEAN,

This Volume

IS

(WITHOUT EVEN ASKING PERMISSION, AND WHOLLY WITHOUT

THEIR KNOWLEDGE)

DEDICATED

WITH UNFEIGNED ADMIRATION,

BY THEIR NEIGHBOUR,

THE AUTHOR.

CONTENTS.

PART I.

MIRACLES OF SAINTS IN IMITATION OF SCRIPTURE MIRACLES.

PART II.

REALISTIC MIRACLES.

PART III.

MIRACLES TO PROVE CHURCH DOGMAS.

INTRODUCTION.

It is no part of this book either to maintain or to deny the historic truth of the miracles recorded, but simply to reproduce, in a compact and handy form, sufficient data to show a mode of religious thought. The truth or untruth of the statements has nothing to do with the subject, the only questions being, are the extracts here made fairly faithful, and do they represent the religious opinions of a large section of the family of man?

If a writer wished to show the religious opinions of the ancient Greeks and Romans, he would have nothing to do with the absurdity or wisdom of their myths, but only to collect them carefully, and reproduce them correctly. If, again, his object is to show the state of Assyrian art, his plain duty would be to reproduce, as faithfully as possible, the drawings to be found on Assyrian relics; but whether those drawings are in proportion or not, whether their perspective is correct or faulty, whether they are to be blamed or praised according to the rules of modern art, would be matters quite beside his business; and he would deserve the highest censure, if he omitted those specimens which seemed to him the most faulty, or attempted to improve others by correcting palpable errors. So, when a mode of religious thought is to be shown, the primary duty of the author must needs be to get together sufficient data, and leave those data to tell their own tale.

Obviously, it can matter very little whether the authors quoted from are good or bad historians, if the matter to be obtained from them is opinion and not history. An historian has to sift out facts, to pare down exaggerated statements, and discard obvious fables; but the interpreter of public opinion has no such task before him, and the very worst historian may be the best exponent of popular belief. Although, therefore, such a writer as Metaphrastês may be too credulous for sober history, he would be far more likely to give a faithful picture and presentment of the popular creed of his own period, than such a man as Alban Butler, who measures the saints of the primitive and middle ages by the standard of his own judgment, and produces a most distorted and garbled picture of the times. In fact, his *Lives of the Saints* is *Macbeth* without the dagger, the witches, and the ghost.

The study of legendary miracles opens a large and important field of inquiry, especially in this doubting age. How came the legends to be so exceedingly numerous, and how came the belief in them to be so firmly rooted and widespread? No doubt there is truth in what Gibbon says, "If the eyes of the spectators have sometimes been deceived by fraud, the understanding of the readers has much more frequently been insulted by fiction,"* yet to attribute the legends of the saints one and all to lying craft and ocular deception is simply absurd.

It seems to be a universal law in the history of man, whether considered as individuals or nations, that the dawn of intelligence is the dayspring of imagination. We find it so in children and in all uneducated classes. Hence the general belief in sorcery and the black arts, evil spirits and malignant influences. Hence, too, all early history is full of fable. Even Livy believed in a personal Romulus and Remus, a Numa and all the seven kings of Rome. Our own history, till quite recent times, was based on the fables of the early chroniclers; and Milton himself believed in the tale of Brute, the colony from Troy, and encounters with giants and magicians. The legends were not the inventions of the chroniclers, but traditions; they were the superstitions of a highly imaginative age; and the false etymology of names, with the highly figurative language employed, corroborated the error.† Superstition and fabulous tradition were further added to in the days of chivalry, when knights were called by the names of animals and flowers, when coat-armour became incorporated with family history, when sin, or what was deemed sin, was spoken of as a dragon, and a moated grange as an enchanted castle. With these and such-like elements of fable, it soon became impossible to disentangle fiction from fact, device from real achievement.

The language of the Church added no little to the same husbandry. Every sin, every heresy, every doubt, was believed to be the work of some demon. Sickness was produced by the indwelling of the same malignant spirits; so were storms and tempests, floods and fires, earthquakes and gales. Hence to cure a

* See IMPOSTURE, p. 180.

† Thus, speaking of St. Angel, Mgr. Guérin says (vol. v. p. 343), "On vit, dit-on, tomber des roses et des lis de sa bouche, pendant qu'il parlait."

So, again, when Mons. Breton, in his *Instruction sur le Sacré Cœur de Jésus*, seeks to prove the antiquity of this very modern "devotion," he says, "St. Thomas speaks of the *heart* of Jesus, full of charity to man. St. Bonaventure speaks of the *heart* of Jesus, as the source of grace. St. Bernardin says, Jesus shows us His *heart*, a furnace of love. Others speak of the *heart* of Jesus, as a place of refuge." How such figures of speech can justify the concrete "Sacré Cœur de Jesus" of Margaret Mary Alacoque must be left to Mons. Breton and his disciples. When, in *Prov.* xxiii. 26, it is said, "My son, give me thy heart," we should think it idiotic or childish to take this literally.

Surius, speaking of the princess Hedwiges, says "her goodness was a fountain from which all could draw water to their healing." Mgr. Guérin, in his life of St. Eutychus, says, "Quatre moines furent mordus par le serpent de la jalousie."

N.B.—Once again it must be insisted on that it is no answer to say the Life quoted is spurious, provided it is accepted by such compilers as the Bollandists, Mgr. Guérin, and other hagiographers of the [Roman] Catholic Church. In the acts of canonization may be found statements quite as marvellous as those which historical purists call spurious; and after all, spurious history is really a better index of popular credulity than any unvarnished statement of simple facts, which, of course, show no popular belief at all.

sickness was, in many cases, synonymous with casting out a devil; to break down a heathen altar was to dislodge a demon; to drain a flood was to overcome the evil one; and to combat a storm was to wage war with Satan. It is no part of the present volume to examine into the question whether such language has the sanction of Scripture or not; suffice it to say it accounts for much of what now appears, to Protestants at least, and still more to the minute exactitude demanded by modern history and science, as fabulous and false, but which was by no means so intended and so employed.

Far above all these sources of error was the dogma that God is glorified by miracles, and the more astounding the miracle, the more it exalted the power of the Almighty. Not only is God glorified by showing Himself the Master of nature, and unfettered by natural laws, but man is supposed to be honoured also, when delegated to be His fellow-worker. Hence the encouragement given by the religious world to those who avouched a share in such performances, and the eager willingness of all to believe every tale which magnified their faith and honoured its servants. When Placidus was dragged out of a river by Maurus, he told the abbot that he saw the hood of St. Benedict extended over him, as he was drawn from the water. Maurus modestly replied he had seen nothing of the kind; whereupon the abbot remarked, "It is plain, therefore, that the merits of Placidus exceed thine, my son; because he stands higher in God's favour than thou dost." This flattery paid to seers of visions and workers of wonders could not fail to have a very powerful influence on religious enthusiasts; they laid themselves open to delusion, and found ready hearers for every marvel.* If, instead of this adulation, all claims to the supernatural had been frowned down and discredited, as in Protestant countries at the present day, the supply of miracles, without doubt, would soon have ceased.

In corroboration thereof we may refer to the recent visions and miracles of Ballyraggett, in Ireland (1881). For a week or so the daily journals liked the novelty, and there were not lacking half-hour heroes who felt flattered to be paraded in print; but when the archbishop of Amiens set his foot on the whole affair, and frowned it down with unmistakable disapproval, the apparitions ceased, and a rumour got abroad that the visions were produced by reflecting-glasses. Whether this was true or not is of small moment, but it is quite certain that the apparitions ceased as suddenly as they rose. If, on the other hand, the authorities of the Church and the general public had encouraged the delusion, there can be little doubt it would have continued, and probably grown in intensity, to meet the craving of the public appetite. In this, as in everything else, the supply meets the demand: as long as wonders are required by the credulous, there will not fail those who are ready to supply them; but when the demand ceases, they become a drug not worth the trouble of production.

* They were also severely rebuked for doubting the truth of a miracle. Thus, when St. Hermeland professed to see events occurring eighty miles off, and some of the younger monks thought he was growing old and childish, they were brought to task for their want of faith, and severely punished.

Of course these remarks will be met with the retort, How could such men as the Gregorys, St. Jerome, St. Francis, St. Benedict, and many others, the very salt of the earth, whose names are justly held in the highest veneration, be supposed to lend themselves to palpable delusions? The reply is simply this: It was not miracles that made these men great, though the greatness of their names gave currency to the belief in miracles. But admitting they were deluded, they were not the first who have been deceived, or have deceived themselves, by a popular belief.* Take, for example, the spiritualists of the present day, who number in their ranks men and women of high education, honour, rank, fortune, and talent, mathematicians and theologians, politicians and historians; yet the scientific world will not admit their dogmas, and the religious world is more than half afraid of them. Take a far better case, that of witchcraft in the Middle Ages. Even bishop Jewell believed in it. Glanvil, the ecclesiastical writer, and one of the founders of the Royal Society, wrote a book to prove, "philosophically, theologically, and historically," that it is a sterling fact. Montesquieu was a believer in it. Addison and Blackstone only half doubted, and thought that such a power might have existed at one time. Pope Innocent VIII. published, in 1484, a bull, charging all true Catholics to search out, and put to death, "those who practised magic, sorcery, witchcraft, and enchantment." Alexander VI. (in 1494), Leo X. (in 1521), and Adrian VI. (in 1522) supplemented the bull of pope Innocent; and to come nearer home, the Scotch Assembly, between 1640 and 1649, passed no less than five Acts against witches and wizards, each one more stringent than the former. In fact, history teems with delusions, and neither talent nor integrity, rank nor education, piety nor single-mindedness, religion nor law, nor all of them combined, have proved a safeguard against them.

That some of the miraculous records in the lives of the saints are pure inventions is beyond a doubt. It would be mere waste of time to try any of them at the tribunal of experience or probability, but in some cases they are mixed up with history, and the historical part may be critically examined. If this part fails, the miracles interwoven with the history must fall at the same time. Take an example: Aurelian is said to have subjected St. Savinian, in Gaul, to sundry barbaric torments, and at last, on Jan. 29, A.D. 275, to have led forth a squadron of soldiers to seize him and behead him. How does this accord with plain history? In 275 Aurelian was not in Gaul at all, but somewhere between Byzantium and Heraclea; and on the very day named (Jan. 29) he was assassinated. Hence the persecution of this saint, and all the wonders connected with it, must be mythical. Other anachronisms are noticed in the body of this volume.†

* St. Gregory the Great (*Dialogues*, bk. ii.) gives a remarkable instance. While St. Benedict was building the monastery of Mount Cassino, the monks thought the kitchen was on fire, and ran to tell St. Benedict, but the saint soon proved to them that the fire was wholly in their own imaginations.

† Samuel Harsnet, afterwards archbishop of York, says (1604), "What people, but you [Roman Catholics] were ever so bewitched as to be borne in hand that a house was carried in the ayre from Palestina to Loretto; that a painted Image in a wall dothe worke as high miracles as wer ever per-

Another source of legendary myths was the habit of adaptation. It was customary in religious houses for some one to read aloud during meal-time, and a favourite amusement was to adapt some heathen tale and spiritualize it. Popular adaptations would be remembered, and handed down; and in time these traditions would be lifted into the national hagiography. Several of these adaptations appear in the body of this book.

Again,* the dogma that the end sanctifies the means, could not fail to be productive of immense mischief. It would matter little or nothing what deception was practised, provided men were persuaded thereby to abandon their idols and be baptized. Origen lays it down as an axiom that a "falsehood is quite lawful, when told to promote the cause of Christianity."

After all, by far the most fruitful source of hypothetical miracles, especially those connected with names of undoubted honesty and holiness, is the unhealthy and abnormal lives led by the saints; their unwholesome and insufficient food; the concentration of all their thoughts on one subject, and that a peculiarly sensational one; and the limit of their reading to the "lives of saints," crowded with miracles. These combined could not fail to produce disordered vital action and visceral disturbance, which would, of course, act upon the imagination, and fatally handicap the discernment of the mind. It is common sense which first gives way; and far short of lunacy or idiotcy the fancy may see things which are not. Macbeth was quite honest, when he told his wife he had seen a dagger in the air; and Hamlet, when he believed he had seen his father's spirit. This dagger and this spirit were realities to the seers, as much so as any of the ordinary phenomena of common life. Their troubled minds informed thus to their eyes, whereas in a healthy brain the eyes inform the mind. These visions are of such stuff as dreams are made of, but dreams are realities so long as the mental condition lasts which produced them. Without entering on the question of objective idealism, it is undoubtedly true in a very large sense that the mind

formed by the eternall Sonne of God; that the prints of St. Frauncis stripes, the tayle of our Saviour's asse, and the milke of our blessed Lady, are this day to be seen?"

* There cannot be a doubt that some men, either by legerdemain like Maskelyne and Cooke, or by bodily training like the yogis and fakirs of India, acquire an apparent power over the laws of nature, which to the uninitiated seems miraculous. Probably there is not a single "miracle of the saints" in all this book which they would not be able to imitate. Such things as "raising the dead" (p. 88), "healing diseases instantaneously," "floating in the air" (p. 215), "weighting articles so as to make them immovable, and releasing them as suddenly" (p. 160), "being apprised of events occurring many miles away, and guessing with marvellous accuracy future events" (called *yog-vi-dya*), are household tricks among Brahmins and Buddhists. Many an Englishman has seen them throw a rope into the air, climb up it, and suddenly disappear. Many an Englishman has seen a Brahmin stand on the bank of a river, render a pail of water quite immovable, and as suddenly release it. With magnetic or galvanic apparatus there is no difficulty in such a trick, but the Indian operator apparently has none. Many an Englishman has been told by an Indian of some event occurring miles away, which has proved correct. The "inexhaustible bottle" might pass for the multiplication of food to those ignorant of its *modus operandi;* and the common "mango trick" is every bit as amazing as any of the "tree and flower miracles" recorded of the saints. Photography, telegraphy, and chemistry have taught us to talk more modestly of the immutable laws of nature. They are immutable only till we know how to change them.

of every man creates its own creation. The child and the idiot see a crown of gold in a tinsel cap, and a banquet of kings in a few fragments of broken food. The savage sees a god in a block or stone. Bel was a vital deity to the wise Cyrus till Daniel disillusioned him. Men and women need not be lunatics or savages to see with the eyes of fancy or fashion. This sort of self-deception is quite compatible with honesty of mind, undoubted piety, irreproachable conduct, and intellect of the highest order; but it accounts for the singular fact that one person may see or hear what fifty other bystanders fail in doing, although the attention of all is equally directed to the same object. The brooding mind can create a pain in any part of the body, or inform the brain of anything it likes or loathes. This well-known pathological process will go far to account for the three subjects of this volume, that so many of the legends of the saints are IMITATIONS of Scripture stories; that so many are REALISTIC ILLUSTRATIONS of striking texts; and not a few are put forth to prove the DOGMAS of the [Roman] Catholic Church. Although, therefore, there may be some who will dislike to see the subject so anatomized and laid bare, it cannot be disputed that the subject is pathologically, theologically, socially, and morally one of the most important and interesting that can be ventilated.

The word "Saint" appended to living characters is acknowledged to be an anachronism, as canonization never took place till after death, sometimes after the lapse of a century or more; but the appendage is convenient for identification, and indeed in many cases a name would not be recognized without it. But St. Moses, St. Enoch, St. Abraham, St. David the sweet psalmist, St. Isaiah, and so on, strike strangely on the Protestant ear, and in such cases the prefix has been omitted.

It must be borne in mind that the fame now attached to *authors* was in the early and middle ages chiefly engrossed by saints. The profession of sanctity was the high-road to notoriety, and originality in this, as in authorship, was especially affected.

*** It is to be hoped that the novel rendering of "Samson and the Jawbone," "Joshua and the Sun," etc., will not be deemed out of place.

OBJECT OF THE BOOK.

THE object of this volume is to show by data alone a mode of thought which prevailed in Christendom for many centuries, and has not yet died out.* It was generally accepted in the early and mediæval ages that this earth is the kingdom of God and of His Christ, and that whatever opposed this reign is the work of Satan and his angels. Taking this as an admitted fact, it would follow as a natural consequence that law and medicine, science and literature, are merely handmaids of divinity. Law being legal divinity; leechcraft, medical divinity; the arts, scientific divinity; mathematics, magical divinity; astronomy, astrological divinity; and without divinity, even the beginning of wisdom could not exist.

Law was not trying offences by evidence, but by an appeal to God to defend the right. Hence some task was appointed, it mattered little what, and God was expected to make the guilty person fail in accomplishing it. So in medicine, cures were not effected by drugs and minerals, but by charms and amulets, pilgrimages and relics, the sign of the cross and the name of Jesus. It was not the experimental physician who cured the sick, so much as the priest, the delegate of God. Nor was it otherwise in science, where magic and astrology were mainly relied on; and as these were supposed by the clergy to be under the influence of Satan, science was not favoured by the Church. As the priest was the officer of God, his great aim was to sever himself as much as possible from earth—to stamp out every earthly wish, every earthly affection, every earthly ambition; and the more he succeeded in emptying himself thus, the more perfect was he, as the servant of God.

As the Bible was the only code and exemplar, the ambition of the religious was to imitate in all things the examples set before them there, hence the claim to miraculous powers, and hence the miracles ascribed to the saints are so often imitative of Bible ones. The first part of this volume is to show this; and the plan adopted is as follows. Some miracle of the Bible is taken as a text, and then from the various hagiographies are quoted corresponding examples. Thus, suppose the text is "Elijah fed by ravens," the following are considered parallelisms:—Auxentius fed by a pigeon prince Cadoc fed by a mouse; Catherine of Alexandria fed by a dove; St. Cuthbert fed by rooks; Dr. Moulins fed by a hen; an old hermit fed by a lion; Paul the hermit fed by a crow; St. Sorus fed by a stag; Wyat fed by a cat; and so on. If the text is "Elisha's axe made to float on the surface of the water," the following miracles are cited as parallels:—St. Benedict makes an axe-head, which has fallen into a lake, rise to the surface, and fix itself firmly into its haft again; St. Wulfran makes a silver paten, accidentally dropped into the sea, float on the surface till it is rescued.

The second part gives data illustrative of Scripture texts. Some text being taken, a number of miracles are set down to prove its literal truth. These are called in this volume "Realistic Miracles." For example: If the Bible says, "Thou hast hid these things from the wise and prudent, and revealed them unto babes," it must be shown that babes have been wise where wise men have failed. If the Bible says, "I will make a covenant with the beasts of the field," it must be shown by data that saints have actually entered into compacts with wild beasts. If it is said, "Thou wilt not suffer Thy holy one to see corruption," it must be shown that the bodies of saints do not decay like other bodies. If it is said, "Nothing shall by any means hurt you," it must be shown by examples that saints have been subjected to every sort of torment, and yet have received no hurt.

The third part consists of miracles to prove Roman Catholic dogmas. The whole is arranged in double alphabetical order; that is, each head is in alphabetical order, and each item under the head is in alphabetical order likewise. As, however, no conceivable plan could have been adopted to range data under heads, and yet give each name and subject a place easy to be found by every one, constant cross references are made, and an index, by double entry, is added, in which the names and particulars are arranged in strict alphabetical order wholly irrespective of the subject matter. Thus, if we have "Paul the hermit fed miraculously by a crow," we shall find

* See APPARITIONS, pp. xiii., 26, 476.

this, and all its congeners, under the head of "Elijah fed by Ravens;" but in the index under "Paul the Hermit," and under "Crow" also.

The arrangement under heads is valuable for two reasons; it shows at a glance what miracles are most frequently repeated, and also the shades of difference introduced; while the index facilitates references to any name or item which may be required, and adds to each head many fresh examples interlaced with other subjects.

A few passing observations have been occasionally introduced in small type; but as a rule comment has been avoided, and the data left to speak for themselves. It may appear like vanity to say that the reading required has been Gargantuan, but laborious as this has been, the arrangement has been far more difficult, especially in the second part. The book occupies entirely new ground, and however startling some of the examples may appear, they one and all go to make up an irresistible truth of enormous historical importance.

Without doubt, a book of this character must not be based on obscure writers, and authors out of date. The authorities here depended on are the highest possible: popes, archbishops, bishops, and abbots. First and foremost come the four series of the *Acta Sanctorum*, the first of which brings the lives down to 1753, the second to 1782, the third to 1826, and the fourth to 1855. This magnificent monument of industry and learning (of course in Latin) takes a very high position in the [Roman] Catholic Church; although certain Protestants doubt the judgment of some of the thirty-three collaborators. It is not, however, private judgment, like that exercised by Alban Butler, that is required in such a work, half so much as a fearless and faithful delineation of what Roman Catholics themselves now believe, and ever have believed; and this, no doubt, is broadly represented in the *Acta Sanctorum*. The next work relied on is the compilation of Mgr. Guérin, called *Les Petits Bollandistes* (in French). The first edition of this huge work was, I think, in 1864 or 1865; the one here used is the seventh edition, corrected, and dated 1880. The author is the chamberlain of pope Leo XIII., and the work is sanctioned and recommended by the two popes, Pius IX. and Leo XIII.; the three archbishops of Alby, Bordeaux, and Tours; and the nine bishops of Agen, Amiens, Angoulême, Langres, Mende, Nancy, Nantes, Poitiers, and Troyes (all between 1865 and 1879). The third staple work is called *The Lives of the Saints*, translated by Edward Kinesman in 1623. The original of these lives was issued *cum privilegio regiæ Majestatis* of Philip of Castille and Aragon; and Kinesman's translation has the following *approbatio* appended to it:—"Horvm Sanctorum Vitæ, ex alijs linguis in Anglicam à D. Edouardo Kinesman versæ, tutò & cum fructu edi possunt. Audomarop. 27 Maij M.DC.XXIII." (signed) *Joan. Floydus Soc. Iesu Theologus.* Numerous other writers are referred to, but the three works above named would have been all-sufficient except for one thing, and that is, to show that the statements of these writers are in perfect harmony with all other hagiographers who fairly photograph the pressure of the saints whose lives and acts they profess to delineate. We do not want to know how the saints fed and clothed themselves, retired from the world, and lived lives of seclusion, half so much as to know how their religious training and teaching affected their belief, their acts, their imagination, their status, their influence, their estimation in the eyes of the general public. What they thought about the gifts of the Spirit, the power of the Church, the gift of miracles, visions, angelic and Satanic agencies, deity, redemption, and the life to come,—we learn next to nothing of all this in such lives as those given by Alban Butler; but these are the points especially pronounced in the *Acta Sanctorum*, the *Petits Bollandistes*, and Kinesman; and this fidelity to the realities of life renders their works so exceedingly valuable as indices of modes of thought.

A few classical illustrations have been introduced, especially in connection with the *Gesta Romanorum*. It must be remembered that not only were heathen temples converted into Christian churches, heathen customs adapted to Christian ways, and heathen festivals changed to Christian memorials, but not unfrequently secular legends were spiritualized; and occasionally an historical tale, *nomine mutato*, has been made to do duty for an hypothetical saint.

Instead of quoting books by contractions, as *Not. Men. in Sac. S. Greg.*, or *L. de Glor. Mart.* 11, c. 101, the titles have been written out in full, because many of the books referred to are not well known to the general public. A list also of those most frequently referred to will be found pp. xxiv., xxv., where all necessary information respecting them has been given. Writers referred to only once or twice, breviaries, offices, and propres, have been omitted from this list, that it might not be pedantically swollen to a great length.

That no critic may refer to omissions it must be added that this volume contains exactly half the entire mass collected together; but this half will suffice for every useful purpose, and more can be furnished if more is required.

INFERENCES DRAWN FROM THE DATA CONTAINED IN THIS BOOK.

(Be it most distinctly understood that the author neither endorses nor condemns any one of these inferences. He simply states what the data given seem to teach.)

Acts of Merit.

Almsgiving, confession, penance, vows, communion, are acts of merit.

Absolution by a priest is a positive absolution, and not the mere heraldic announcement or declaration of God's covenant of grace.

The viaticum is an unspeakable benefit to the dying.

To die under an anathema or interdict is to die without hope, unless the curse is removed by the pope.

No salvation out of the Church of Rome.

Baptism.

Baptism is regeneration, and by baptism "sin is washed away." (See under "Savinian," p. 465.)

Celibacy.

It is one of the highest possible merits to remain single.

Chastity is one of the crowns of glory.

It is meritorious in married life to live in Platonic love only. (See THIERRY, p. 496.)

It is meritorious even to break off a marriage contract.

Charity.

Charity to the poor is certainly the most pronounced of all acts of merit.

When giving is indiscriminate it is always mischievous. "Sell all thou hast, and give unto the poor," does not mean give indiscriminately to all beggars, for many beggars are far from poor, and such giving is a great evil. In the *Lives of the Saints* we are not told that the saints visited from house to house, searched into the conditions of the neighbouring huts, and helped the deserving poor; but that the doors of the monasteries, and the cells of recluses, were daily beset with crowds of beggars, and food or alms was distributed promiscuously and often lavishly among them. Discreet almsgiving, no doubt, is an admirable Christian work, beyond all praise; but the indiscreet giving of money or alms to beggars is much to be reprehended.

Christ.

Christ not unfrequently visits the saints on earth, but generally in the form of an infant or little child. Sometimes in the guise of a beggar.

Crucifix.

The crucifix and the cross are not only remembrancers, but in some cases they act as spells. Occasionally they bleed, speak, move of themselves, and perform other acts of vitality.

Devils.

The world is divided into two unequal parts—the kingdom of God, and the kingdom of Satan. All that is not of the former belongs to the latter. The persecuted [Roman] Catholic Church is the kingdom of light; the persecuting world, the kingdom of darkness.

Every newly baptized person renounces the devil, and joins the army of Christ.

As Jews and Protestants, as well as Mahometans and heathens, belong to the kingdom of Satan, they are the natural enemies of the "Church of Christ;" and to destroy them, by craft, war, persecution, or in any other way, is as glorious as to trap a foe by ambush, or kill him in open fight. On the other hand, to persecute a [Roman] Catholic is to persecute Christ Himself, and to wage war against the kingdom of God.

Dreams.

God sometimes reveals His will by dreams or visions. Most dreams are visions.

Apparitions of saints are common.

Deceased saints may be invoked, and can accomplish, either directly or indirectly, what is required of them. Their tombs and relics possess miraculous virtues.

Duty to Saints.

Any injury done to a saint, or disrespect shown to one, is done or shown to Christ, and is generally punished forthwith.

It is meritorious for saints to injure and dishonour those who see not eye to eye with themselves, as Arians, Lutherans, Calvinists, and other "heretics."

For a Jew or "heretic" to injure a [Roman] Catholic is a sin; but for a saint to injure a Jew or "heretic" is meritorious, although often it is a hazardous civil offence.

Harsnet tells us that Cottam, Brian, and Campian, executed at Tyburn for treason in 1582, were canonized; because Elizabeth, whom they sought to dethrone and assassinate, was a Protestant.—*Popish Impostures*, p. 118.

Ecstasies.

The fifteenth, sixteenth, and seventeenth centuries were remarkable for ecstasies and visions; the third, fourth, and fifth centuries were remarkable for astounding "miracles" and marvels.

The earlier centuries abound with encounters with dragons; the latter centuries are more æsthetic.

Eucharist.

The elements of the mass are *bona fide* transubstantiated.

They are food, possessed with miraculous sustaining power. Hence Nicholas of Flue lived for twenty years on the bread administered to him daily in the Eucharist. Silvinus lived forty years on the same food.

God and Angels.

Saints have personal intercourse with God, Christ, angels, and the Virgin Mary.

Whatever opposes our abnegation and entire submission to God is from the personal interference of Satan and his demons.

Sickness, storms at sea, land tempests, earthquakes, hurricanes, and other "natural disturbances," are due to Satanic agency. Thus St. Geneviève is represented in Christian art with a devil [the wind] blowing out her candle, and an angel lighting it again.

All the laws of nature are wholly subservient to the will of God, and God can alter them locally without throwing the whole system of the world out of gear.

Health, fertility, good gifts, charity, benevolence, and all other Christian virtues, are due to the personal and active interference of good angels.

Guardian Angels.

Saints have one, two, or more guardian angels in constant attendance on them. Sometimes they become visible; sometimes they speak audibly; sometimes they hold sustained conversations. Rosana, afterwards called "Sister Humility," had two attendant angels in constant waiting, and used to address them familiarly by their names.

Hell.

Hell is a place of material fire. The punishment is incessant and everlasting. Satan is the prince of hell, demons or devils are his angels, who can assume any form to do his bidding.

Infants.

The lives of very little children are glaringly told from the standpoint of monks who know nothing about child-life. Their fasting from the breast, their voluntary seclusion, their fondness for church and prayer, their abstinence from all childish amusements and mirth, their ridiculous modesty, their prudery and priggishness, are dwelt on with lingering praise. Indeed, everything said about little children is unchildlike, and very much is utterly repugnant. Stealing money to give to the poor, secreting part of their food for the same object, even deceit of more open character still, are actually praised and held forth for imitation by Mgr. Guérin in the life of St. Monica and others. Such acts are worthy only of censure, and are not, as the pope's chamberlain expresses it, a "doux éclat de vertu naissante."

Light and Nimbus.

Those to whom Christ gives light within, often show it by radiant looks, luminous bodies, nimbus and glory.

This "light of life" acts upon the material body in some cases by neutralizing its gravity, so that a saint is sometimes buoyed up into the air like a balloon, and floats there sustained by nothing, unless it be the invisible hands of angels. Generally this legerity is ascribed to personal sanctity, which either etherealizes the body, or fills it with "spirit" to make it lighter than the lower strata of air.

Lives of Saints.

Self-denial, mortifications of the flesh, self-torment, suffering, martyrdom, all swell the merits of saints.

Generally the lives of saints may be called the romantic ideals of perfection, from a [Roman] Catholic point of view.* To most Protestants they will appear a sad waste of enormous force, and a total forgetfulness of that prayer of Christ, "I pray not that Thou shouldest take them

* See note, p. xxiii.

out of the world, but that Thou shouldest keep them from the evil." To live out of the world, cut off from all the society of man, hidden out of sight, seems to have been considered the highest perfection of human sanctity. Of course, such absolute seclusion is not now possible, at least in Europe.

Mgr. Guérin says of St. Lifard, "Il n'était plus que de corps sur la terre" (vol. vi. p. 429).

Merit.

It is possible to be meritorious, and even to accumulate merit.

Saints can transfer any part of their merits to others. (See IMPUTED MERIT, p. 204.)

The demerits of a sinner may be transferred to a saint, and balanced off.

Miracles.

It is a proof of merit to work a miracle.

It is meritorious in some measure to see miracles and believe in them. At any rate, it is a demerit not to see them, to doubt them, or disbelieve them.

Miracles can be performed by dead bodies, relics, and medals, as well as by living saints.

The miraculous power of saints seems to wax weaker as time rolls on. Many a saint whose dead body was honoured by hosts of miracles, passes out of mind in a few months, and all miraculous power ceases or is latent.

Monks and Nuns.

Monks and nuns, as a rule, are the elect and beloved children of God; certain of paradise, though not always without a term of purgatory.

The term of purgatory may be shortened by the prayers, gifts, and penances, either of one's self while living, or of some substitute, or by private help, or by Church offices after death.

Indulgences purchased by money help to shorten the term of purgatory, and in some cases to buy it off altogether.

To break a vow of monastic life, to forsake an "order," to return to secular life after having lived a "religious" one, is to be the child of the devil. Before such could be restored, they were sometimes, if not always, exorcised.

Mortification.

It is meritorious to torment the body in all possible ways; by filth, by ligatures, by standing for many years, by not lying down to sleep, by insufficient food, by unwholesome food, by scourging, by wearing iron, by wearing hair shirts, by never changing one's linen, by wallowing amongst brambles or in the mire, by going without shoes and stockings, by washing the skin with soot and water, by producing sores, and so on.

Those who torment themselves the most are the most meritorious.

It is a demerit to live, eat, sleep, drink, dress, and act, like other folks.

Eccentricity is much affected by saints. And that saint is lucky who can invent a self-mortification never thought of before.

Natural Solutions.

The constant repetition, with slight differences, of favourite "miracles" is proof positive against any natural solution. Thus, if one saint raises the dead, a hundred others do the same; if St. Antony makes a dead man speak, a score other saints do the same; if St. Denys carries off his head after death, so do many others; if the roast pullets of the alcaydê come to life, so did the fish and fowl of half a score more. Raising the dead, hanging clothes on sunbeams, turning water into wine, multiplying food, bringing water from dry ground, etc., are miracles of such constant repetition that the chief difficulty has been in selection. There can be no doubt that the miracles in mediæval and modern times too have been looked on as historic facts by the "faithful," and not as allegories; although in some cases, as, for example, encounters with dragons, it is possible that allegorical language has been misleading.

Obedience.

Blind obedience to superiors is the first law of piety. No matter how absurd the order, how revolting, how difficult, it must be obeyed without a murmur, or look of disapproval. We read of monks and nuns sent to a great distance daily to water a dry dead stick, and of others sent to kiss an open sore. In monastic and conventual life, even vows to God had to give way to the vow of obedience.

Odour of Sanctity.

Sanctity exhales a material perfume of great sweetness, perceptible to the senses. This sweet odour increases at death; and long after death—it may be weeks, months, years, or even centuries—the fragrance remains.

On the other hand, sin emits an offensive smell, equally perceptible to the senses; so that when one dies in sin, the very stench of the body proclaims it to bystanders.

Harsnet tells us that priests carried with them a divine odour quite recognizable. There may be some truth in this from their constant use of incense.

Perfection.

The perfection of a saint is when he has crushed out every natural affection, every earthly wish, every fleshly indulgence, every natural propensity, even love to father and mother. Nothing of earth, its loves, its hopes, its ambitions, its charms, must remain; the natural man must be clean swept out.

A saint should read no secular book, think no secular thought, hope no secular good. He should eat and drink the least possible quantity, and that of the most unpalatable sort. He should sleep as little as possible, and that on the most uncomfortable bed. He should wear as little as possible, and that of the most unbecoming and uncomfortable kind. He should wholly unfurnish the body, and empty it to receive the new or spiritual man.

Punishments.

It is wrong in civil magistrates to punish crimes by imprisonment, and a merit to release those who are imprisoned. The release of persons from prison is one of the most favourite "miracles" of saints.

All punishment should be left to God and His Church.

The Church, in the person of the pope, may issue anathemas, publish interdicts against whole nations for the offences of an individual, release subjects from allegiance, dethrone princes, organize wars against "heretics" and infidels, annul marriages, propagate new articles of faith, grant indulgences, open heaven or shut out therefrom, canonize saints, authenticate relics and miracles, determine what is heresy and orthodoxy, and *ex cathedrâ* speak with an infallible voice. Some of this power claimed may be restrained by the civil arm, but nevertheless the might and not the right of the civil arm is obeyed.

Purgatory.

Purgatory is for the remnant of sins not absolved or balanced off during life.

The term of purgatory can be shortened by the prayers of survivors, by masses for the dead, or even at the option of some saint in light. In the life of Benedicta we are told that the Virgin Mary, at the prayer of Benedicta, delivered "a thick cloud of souls" from purgatory, and took them up to paradise.

Relics.

Relics can be authenticated by any Church dignitary, such as pope, abbot, or bishop. They can even be multiplied or done in *replica*.

Relics possess miraculous virtues, and these virtues are transferable, either by touch or inoculation.

The size of a relic is of very small importance; a fragment, a little filing, a crumbling dust, is all-sufficient.

As a magnet can make a magnet, so a relic can make a relic.

Sacraments.

Baptism is "le sacrement de la régénération."—*Les Petits Bollandistes*, vol. vi. p. 612.

Eucharist is a *bona fide* sacrifice, and it is called "The Sacrifice of the Mass," The sacred water is called "The Creator," and partaking thereof "receiving thy Creator."—*Vies des Saints*, vol. vi. p. 623.

Saints.

Saints, after death, have the power of aiding their votaries—of interceding for them before the throne of grace, of curing diseases, and of visiting earth.

The Virgin Mary is the highest of all saints, the most powerful, and the most merciful.

The saints in paradise take an interest in the saints militant. They like to be invoked, like to be patronized, like to be honoured, like to be flattered, and even to be dressed up and decked with jewels.

Salvation.

Salvation is the reward of merit; hence the common termination of saintly biographies: "He was called to heaven to receive the reward of his merits" (see *Les Petits Bollandistes*, vol. vi. p. 90): "Godivin fut appelé dans le ciel pour y recevoir la récompense de ses vertus." Hundreds of similar examples occur in the *Acta Sanctorum* and other lives of saints.

Satan.

Satan can assume any shape; and he

often appears in the guise of an angel, man, or one of the lower animals.

Angels can also assume any shape, but generally appear in angelic form, arrayed in white, or in the form of human beings.

Christ, two or three times, is represented under the resemblance of a stag or hind.

Angels, at the death of a saint, often appear in the form of pigeons or butterflies, and probably the birds and beasts which have not unfrequently brought food to saints may be angels; still it is undoubtedly true that the general manifestations of angels are either angelic or human.

Scripture.

The words of Scripture are to be taken literally, and not in any case figuratively. Hundreds of examples are given in proof of this statement. If Christ said, "Faith can remove mountains," He did not only mean great moral difficulties, but material substances also. If the psalmist says, "The Lord is at my right hand, I shall not be moved," he must be understood to mean, not only that his faith and confidence could not be shaken, but that no human power should avail to move his body. If Jesus, speaking to His disciples, says of the bread He held in His hand, "This is My body," He meant what He said to be taken literally, though His body at the time was before them in perfect manhood.

Seven.

The reader will be struck by the perpetual recurrence of the number seven. Seven joys, seven sorrows, seven virtues, seven almost everything. (See, amongst other legends, that of St. Isumbras, p. 210.)

Sickness.

Sickness, as a rule, is the work of the devil, and exorcism cures the sick. Death, as a rule, does not seem to be attributed to Satan; though falls, shipwrecks, slips of the foot, tumbling downstairs, injury or death from falling chimneys, trees, and walls, are all ascribed to Satanic malice.

Sign of the Cross.

The signing the sign of the cross with the finger or otherwise acts as a charm or talisman to drive away or ward off devils, sickness, floods, storms, darkness, or other evils supernatural or natural. Eusebius is referred to for the antiquity of the custom (*Ecclesiastical History*, bk. iii. ch. 13), and in ch. i. of the same book he says that Julian (331–363), though an apostate, by making the sign of the cross in a fright, drove away the devils which his enchanters had evoked.

Soul.

The soul may become visible at death, and is often seen making its way out of the mouth of saints, either like a dove, a beam of light, or some other material object.

It is carried by angels to heaven, or by devils to hell, unless it is doomed for a certain term to purgatory.

Virgin Mary.

The Virgin Mary is more honoured by the French than by any other nation.

She is made the hypothetical ideal of perfection: beauty, chastity, love, mercy, tenderness, sinlessness, and what not.

We say "hypothetical," because there is not one iota of history to support this extravagant idea; nevertheless, hagiographers vie with each other in painting the rose, and adding perfumes to the violet.

N.B.—In Mgr. Guérin's *Hagiography*, we have one Christ, one Jesus Christ, and one Saviour; but 1911 Notre Dames or Virgin Marys.

LIVES OF SAINTS. A better example of the extravagant praise bestowed on saints need not be sought than that given to Antony of Padua; and that the reader may judge fairly, the extract shall be given in the identical words of his best biographer:—

"On ne sait où s'arrêter dans cette longue suite de prodiges; il faudrait pour être complet, prendre la vie du saint jour par jour, depuis sa naissance jusqu'à sa mort. Tout ce qu'il y a au monde de plus grande et de plus admiré des hommes, tout ce que Dieu entassa jamais de faveurs sur la tête de ses plus chers enfants, zéle et foi des apôtres, patience des martyrs, sagesse des docteurs, éloquence des pères de l'église, courage des confesseurs, pureté des vierges, piété des anges, il a tout rassemblé en lui dans une magnifique harmonie. Ajoutez à cela les miracles les plus étonnants, les prodiges les plus éclatants accomplis en presence de milliers de spectateurs, les hérétiques confondus et convertis, les pécheurs effrayés et repentants, les tyrans domptés ou contenus, les démons expulsés, des extases merveilleuses, des visions sublimes, des entretiens de tous les instants avec les puissance de ciel, la vie éternelle devinée et connue par avance, voilà quel fut Antoine, voilà ses titres à l'admiration et au respect des siècles."—L'abbé Guyard, *Life of St. Antony of Padua*. (Appendix to p. xx., LIVES OF SAINTS.)

CHIEF AUTHORITIES CITED IN THIS BOOK.

It would be mere pedantry to make a catalogue of all the works consulted in the compilation of this book; but a brief account of some of the most important may be both acceptable and useful.

ACTA SANCTORUM (Latin, 57 vols., folio). This great storehouse of hagiography is based on the *Acta Sincera* of Héribert Rosweyde, on which he had laboured for twenty years; he died in 1629, before his work was printed. Father John Bolland (1596-1665) was entrusted with Rosweyde's collections, and associated with himself several others, the principal of whom were Henschen and Papebröch; these, with ten others, brought the work down to 1753 in thirty-two folio volumes, and ended SERIES I. The abolition of the order of Jesuits in 1773 put an end to the work for a time, but in 1789 it was taken up again, and John Limpen, with six others who had assisted in the first series, carried the work down to 1782, when SERIES II. closed with the death of Ignatius Huben of Antwerp. A third series was begun after the dispersion of the Jesuits, and five new volumes were added by John Baptist Fonson and four others, bringing SERIES III. down to 1826, and completing the fifty-third volume. In 1837 a new society of Bollandists was organized under the patronage of the Belgian government, when Joseph van der Möre and six others continued the lives to 1855. In 1854 this new society published the fifty-fourth volume in two parts, and three more have been published since, continuing the lives to 1855. Probably the fifty-seven volumes contain at least thirty thousand saints. That the work is crammed with miracles may be readily admitted, but as an index of religious thought and belief it is wholly unrivalled, and its value beyond all price. It has been nearly five hundred years in hand; thirty-three collaborators have been employed upon it, and it runs to about fifty thousand folio pages. The market value is about £130.

January contains two vols., February three, March three, April three, May seven, June six, July seven, August six, September eight, October five, November and December the other seven.

LES PETITS BOLLANDISTES (in French, 17 vols., large octavo, average 700 pp. a volume; part in a larger type containing 52 lines in a page, and part in a smaller type containing 64 lines to the page. The mere index of the names occupies 370 pp., so that it cannot contain less than nineteen or twenty thousand saints). This huge work is by Monseigneur Paul Guérin, chamberlain to pope Leo XIII. My edition, the seventh, was published in 1880, and contains letters of recommendation and unqualified praise from the three archbishops of Alby, Bourdeaux, and Tours, and the nine bishops of Agen, Amiens, Angoulême, Langres, Mende, Nancy, Nantes, Poitiers, and Troyes, all between the years 1865 and 1879. To these high authorities may be added the sanction of two popes, Pius IX. and Leo XIII. The authority of this work is, therefore, beyond all question. None can say it is obsolete and out of date, nor can any one insinuate that it does not represent the religious opinions of the most educated classes of the Roman Catholic Church of the present hour. Price 30 francs 50 cents each vol.

LIVES OF THE SAINTS, by Edward Kinesman. In one vol., quarto. My copy is defective, only going to Dec. 26, pp. 1036, to which is added a supplement of 80 pp., date 1623. This book, without doubt, is very rare, but was issued with this *approbatio:* "Horvm Sanctorum Vitæ, ex alijs linguis in Anglicam à D. Edouardo Kinesman versæ, tutò & cum fructu edi possunt. Audomarop. 27 Maij M.DC.XXIII." (signed) *Joan. Floydus Soc. Ie.u Theologus.* The *privilege* to publish the supplement is by patent from "Philippe par la grace de Dieu, Roy de Castille, d'Arragon, de Leon," etc., and signed *De Groote*, 1625. The lives are very excellent, far less crowded with the marvellous than either of the Bollandists, but as far as possible removed from the dishonest *couleur de rose* of Alban Butler.

SAMUEL HARSNET (afterwards archbishop of York). "A Declaration of Egregious Popish Impostures to withdraw the harts of his Maiesties Subiects from their allegeance, and from the truth of Christian Religion professed in England vnder the pretence of casting out of deuils." *London*, 1604, small 8vo, pp. 284. This very rare old book was well known to Shakespeare, who often quotes from it. Its authority is beyond all question—the cases quoted being direct from the

"Records of Her Majesty's Commissioners for Causes Ecclesiastical," and all still extant. This odd little volume cost me £3.

GOLDEN LEGEND (The), by James of Voragine, or Varagine, archbishop of Genova (1230–1298), compiled from the *Epitomy of the Lives of the Saints* by Bartholomew of Braganza, in 1270; the *Speculum Historiale* of Vincent of Beauvais, in 1264; he *Legendary* of Peter of Chiozza; the *Bible of the Poor* by James of Hanapes; and the *Historical Summary* of Antony of Florence. Father Bollandus says, "I cannot approve of all that is written in the *Golden Legend*, but much of it is undoubtedly taken from sources of unexceptionable authority; and it is most unjust to condemn the book wholesale." As this book is only cited to furnish parallel examples or to supply some striking allegory, its *authority* is only supplementary, and the extracts taken from it have been made for the purposes above stated. As the Apocrypha may serve to confirm when it runs parallel with canonical Scriptures, but has no authority of itself, so the *Golden Legend* is excellent in corroboration of standard *Lives*, but has no weight in deciding points *sub judice*.

The 101 other works consulted in Greek, Latin, French, and English, from Alban Butler to Baring-Gould, and from Gregory the Great to cardinal Wiseman, I forbear to mention. I had prepared a list, but have suppressed its publication at the last minute, fearing it might savour of vanity. This, however, I will dare to add: I have always gone to the best sources, and have endeavoured to represent every case honestly and without exaggeration. Without doubt I have much abbreviated, but I have never mutilated or misrepresented, to the best of my knowledge.

ECCLESIASTICAL SYMBOLS EXPLAINED.

(i.) *Crosses on Tombs* (*seven crosses, five crosses, one cross*). Seven crosses mark the tomb of a bishop, five of a priest, and one of an ordinary Christian. There are seven sacraments, each of which derives its value from the cross of Christ. Only a bishop can administer all the seven sacraments, and only a bishop can impart to the faithful the graces which proceed from the seven virtues of the cross. A priest can impart to the faithful five sacraments, and his tomb bears five crosses. An ordinary Christian has but one cross on his tomb, to indicate his faith and hope in the cross of Christ.

Ecclesiastical Crosses—

† The Latin cross.

+ The Greek cross.

✠ The Maltese cross.

× St. Andrew's cross.

‡ The Lorrainese cross.

⊤ The Tau or Egyptian cross. Tertullian says, "Hæc est litera Græcorum τ, nostra autem ⊤, species crucis."

☧ Constantine's cross: X P Chr[ıstos].

I.H.S. or I.H.S. The Church anagram.

Gk. Ιησους 'Ημετερος Σωτηρ.
Lat. Jesus, Hominum Salvator.
Eng. Jesus, Heavenly Saviour.
Ger. Jesus, Heiland Seligmacher.

B

The sign of the cross is made by carrying the right hand to the forehead, the stomach, the left shoulder, and the right shoulder, thus forming a Latin cross, ⁘

(ii.) *Crowns.* Any virtue or merit of supereminent degree is supposed to be rewarded with a crown. Some saints have only one crown; others have two, three, or more. Two of the most exalted crowns are Martyrdom and Virginity; but Humility, Learning, Glory, etc., are also crowns. Thus we are told that St. Peter of Ravenna received at death the "triple crown of Virginity, Doctorate, and Martyrdom" (*de la Virginité, du Doctorat, et du Martyre*).—*Les Petits Bollandistes*, vol. v. p. 83. St. Cecilia, we are told, received the two crowns of Virginity and Martyrdom. Others received the three crowns of Martrydom, Virginity, and Glory; or Virginity, Humility, and Glory. St. Angelus (1225) received the three crowns of Virginity, Preaching, and Martyrdom.—*Les Petits Bollandistes*, vol. v. p. 344.

(iii.) *The Three Theological Virtues.* Faith, hope, and charity.

(iv.) *The Four Attributes of Glorified Bodies.* Subtility, agility, luminosity, and immortality.—Mgr. Guérin, *Vies des Saints*, vol. ix. p. 559.

(v.) *The Four Cardinal Virtues.* Fortitude, justice, prudence, and temperance.

The following seven have been also suggested:—Conscientiousness, courage, justice or justness, modesty, reverence, and sympathy. (See THE SEVEN VIRTUES.)

(vi.) *The Four Symbols.* There are four symbols or formularies acknowledged in the [Roman] Catholic Church.

1. The Symbol of the Apostles, called by us "The Apostles' Creed," because each of the twelve clauses is attributed to one of the apostles.

2. The Symbol of Nice, called by us "The Nicene Creed," because it was formulated in the famous Council of Nice, in A.D. 325. This creed was especially directed against Arianism.

3. The Symbol of Constantinople, so called because it was formulated at the Council of Constantinople, A.D. 331. It is the same as the Nicene Creed, with one exception, viz. the Holy Ghost "proceeding from the Father and the Son." In the [Roman] Catholic Church this is the creed recited by the priest in mass.

4. The Symbol of St. Athanasius, called by us "The Athanasian Creed," supposed to formulate the teaching of Athanasius against Arianism. It did not exist till A.D. 670, nearly three centuries after the death of Athanasius, who died A.D. 373.

(vii.) *The Four Vows of the Order of St. Francis of Paula.* Poverty, chastity, obedience, and the quadragesimal life [or Lenten fast].

(viii.) *The Five Christian Verities.*

1. The Child Jesus, conceived in the womb of the Virgin Mary, and called Jesus, was verily and indeed the Son of God, and the Second Person of the Trinity.

2. This Jesus is true God, one with the Father and the Holy Ghost.

3. The two perfect natures coexist in one only Person. The divine nature received from God the Father; the human nature from His mother Mary.

4. All that pertains to the Person of Christ as a substance is *unique;* but all that pertains to His nature is *double.*

5. The Virgin Mary is veritably and properly the mother of God.—Mgr. Guérin, *Vies des Saints*, vol. iii. pp. 625, 626.

(ix.) *The Seven Corporal Works of Mercy.* To bury the dead, clothe the naked, feed the hungry, give drink to the thirsty, to harbour the harbourless, visit the imprisoned, and administer to the sick.

(x.) *The Seven Spiritual Works of Mercy.* To admonish sinners, to bear wrongs patiently, to comfort the afflicted, counsel the doubtful, forgive offences, instruct the ignorant, and pray for the living and the dead.

(xi.) *The Seven Deadly Sins.* Anger, covetousness, envy, gluttony, lust or luxury, pride, and sloth.

In *Gal.* v. 19–21 St. Paul enumerates seventeen sins, and ends with "and such like." Pride and sloth are omitted in St. Paul's list. The small capitals given below are the synonymous words in the "seven deadly sins."

Adultery (LUST), drunkenness (GLUTTONY), emulations (COVETOUSNESS), envyings (ENVY), fornication (LUST), hatred, heresies, idolatry, lasciviousness (LUST), murder, revellings (GLUTTONY), seditions, strife (ANGER), uncleanness (LUST), variance, wrath (ANGER), witchcraft.

(xii.) *The Seven Gifts of the Holy Ghost.* Counsel, the fear of the Lord, fortitude, piety, understanding, wisdom, and knowledge.

The distinction between *understanding, wisdom,* and *knowledge* is not very plain, but they are three degrees: (1) understanding, (2) wisdom, and (3) knowledge.

Philip said to the eunuch, "Understandest thou what thou readest?" The very first step in religion is to *understand* what it is that God has revealed.

The next step is wisdom. "The fear of the Lord is the beginning of wisdom." This is an advance on understanding. The wise man not only understands what the Bible teaches, but honours that understanding by "fearing God and keeping His commandments." Wisdom, therefore, is understanding carried into practice.

Knowledge is one step higher still. "I know whom I have believed, and am persuaded that He is able to keep that which I have committed unto Him." A child may be *wise* unto salvation, but only the "man in Christ Jesus" can know the length and breadth, the height and depth, of God's love, which is the fruit of long experience.

Samuel could be taught by Eli to understand the priestly duties; when a mere child he was wise in his duties; but he was a prophet taught by experience before he knew the whole will of God.

(xiii.) *The Seven Joys of Mary.* The Annunciation, the Visitation, the Nativity, the adoration of the wise men, the presentation in the temple, finding Christ amongst the doctors, and the Assumption.

(xiv.) *The Seven Sorrows of Mary.* Simeon's prophecy, the flight into Egypt, Christ missed, the betrayal, the crucifixion, the taking down from the cross, and the Ascension when she was left alone.

It will be observed that the "resurrection" is omitted from the "Joys of Mary," to make room for the "assumption."

(For "the seven sorrows of Christ," see art. CHRIST'S SORROWS," p. 382.)

(xv.) *The Seven Orders of the Anglo-Saxon Church.*

1. The OSTIARY, a kind of sexton, whose duty was to ring the bells and keep the church doors.

2. The EXORCIST, whose office was by certain prayers to cast out devils.

3. The LECTOR or "Reader," who read the lessons at church.

4. The ACOLYTH or "Acolythist," who attended on the officiating priest, holding the candles while the Gospel was read and during the celebration of mass.

5. The SUBDEACON, who prepared the holy vessels and attended the deacon at the altar.

6. The DEACON, who assisted the priest, laid the oblations on the altar, baptized children, and gave the Eucharist to the laity.

7. The PRIEST or "Presbyter," who preached, baptized, and consecrated the Eucharist. Bishops and archbishops were merely higher grades of priests.

(xvi.) *The Seven Sacraments.* Baptism, confirmation, the Eucharist or Lord's Supper, penitence or repentance, holy orders, marriage, and extreme unction. Of these, confirmation and holy orders are restricted to bishops. Baptism may be performed, in emergency, even by laymen and women.

(xvii.) *The Seven Sorrows of Mary.* (See under THE SEVEN JOYS OF MARY.)

(xviii.) *The Seven Spiritual Works of Mercy.* (See THE SEVEN CORPORAL WORKS OF MERCY, p. xxvi. col. 1.)

(xix.) *The Seven Virtues.* These are the contraries of the seven deadly sins, viz.: 1. Brotherly love (opposed to envy or hatred); 2. chastity (opposed to lust); 3. diligence (opposed to sloth); 4. humility (opposed to pride); 5. liberality (opposed to covetousness); 6. meekness (opposed to anger); and 7. temperance (opposed to gluttony and self-indulgence). (See THE FOUR CARDINAL VIRTUES.)

(xx.) *The Eight Canonical Hours.* These consist of four great and four little ones (the great ones are in capitals).

MATINS, about midnight. On festivals and Sundays they consist of three psalms, three anthems, and three lessons.

LAUDES, sometimes immediately after matins, consist of five psalms, two or more capitules or Scripture extracts, prayers, and canticles.

Prime (the first hour of the day), *i.e.* six o'clock in the morning.

Tierce (the third hour of the day), *i.e.* nine in the morning.

Sexte, midday (the sixth hour of the day).

Nones (before vespers), three o'clock in the afternoon (the ninth hour of the day).

VESPERS, about three p.m. They consist of five psalms, a capitule or Scripture extract, a hymn, the *Magnificat*, one or more anthems, and prayers.

COMPLINS, after vespers, consist of confession, one lesson, three psalms, one anthem, one hymn, one capitule or Scripture extract, one short "response," the *Nunc Dimittis*, and prayers.

There are no complins in the Greek Church.

N.B.—Sometimes Matins and Laudes are joined together, and then the canonical hours may be called seven, instead of eight.

(xxi.) *The Ten Virtues of the Virgin.*

1. Chastity, because Mary is the queen of virgins.

2. Prudence, shown at the Annunciation.

3. Humility. Even when chosen for the mother of the Messiah, she called herself "the handmaid of the Lord."

4. Faith. Mary believed and doubted not what the angel announced.

5. Piety, shown by her retirement, silence, and submission.

6. Obedience, in submitting to the will of God.

7. Poverty, in despising all the grandeur and wealth of the world.

8. Patience, in bearing the pain of her travail.

9. Charity, in offering the sacrifice of her Son for the salvation of man.

10. Compassion, in that a sword pierced her own heart out of compassion to her Son.

(*For this I am indebted to the kindness of the editors of the "Oracle," Aug.* 25, 1883, p. 543.)

[I must take this opportunity of thanking the learned conductors of this excellent weekly for several acts of courtesy, and ever-ready help in this and some other of my books now in preparation. I would have written the name "Oracle" at the foot of some other articles, but I fear they would be hardly recognized.]

(xxii.) *The Twelve Articles of the Symbol.* (That is, the twelve articles of the Apostles' Creed. Said to have been suggested by them in a grotto of Mount Olivet before their final separation.)

PETER—1. I believe in God the Father Almighty, Maker of heaven and earth.

JOHN—2. [And] in Jesus Christ, His only Son, our Lord.

JAMES, SEN.—3. Who was conceived of the Holy Ghost, born of the Virgin Mary.

ANDREW—4. Suffered under Pontius Pilate; was crucified, dead, and buried.

PHILIP—5. He descended into hell.

(From the Creed of Aquilia.)

THOMAS—6. The third day He rose again from the dead.

(Augustine is the authority. Ascribed to Thomas because he required sensible proof of the Resurrection.)

JAMES, JUN.—7. He ascended into heaven, and sitteth on the right hand of God the Father Almighty. (See p. 252.)

MATTHEW—8. From thence He shall come to judge the quick and the dead.

NATHANAEL—9. I believe in the Holy Ghost.

SIMON—10. The Holy Catholic Church; the communion of saints.

(Added in the sixth century.)

MATTHIAS—11. The forgiveness of sins.

JUDE—12. The resurrection of the body, and the life everlasting.

(The latter part of this symbol St. Augustine attributes to St. Cyprian's time, 200–258. The former part, he tells us, was added in his own time, 354–430.)

"Was crucified, dead, and buried." The word *dead* does not stand in the early forms of the creed, nor in the Oriental form. It is a comparatively modern introduction, and is certainly of very doubtful grammatical construction. "Mortuus est," he died, not *was dead*. We should hardly say, "Charles I. was beheaded, dead, and buried."

The creed is given substantially by Tertullian (160–248). Is referred to by Irenæus (130–200), by Origen (185–253), by Gregory of Neocæsarea (202–270), and by Lucian the martyr (*–313). It was summarized by Ignatius (*–115).

The twelve apostles were anciently delineated, each holding a banderole, on which was inscribed the words of the symbol ascribed to him.

Mr. Walcott, in his *Sacred Archæology* (1868), does not in all points agree with Mgr. Guérin, the chamberlain of pope Leo XIII., in his ascriptions of the several symbols. Thus Mr. Walcott gives *Andrew*, and Mgr. Guérin gives *James the Elder*, for the third symbol. Mr. Walcott gives *Thomas*, and Mgr. Guérin gives *Philip*, for the fifth symbol. Mr. Walcott gives *Nathanael* or *Bartholomew*, and Mgr. Guérin, on the authority of St. Augustine, gives *Thomas*, for the sixth symbol. Mr. Walcott also divides the symbols somewhat differently.

⁂ When St. Peter of Ravenna was murdered, Mgr. Guérin says, "Il récita le premier article du Symbols des Apôtres;" and, dipping his finger in his own blood, he wrote upon the ground, "Credo in Deum" (*Vies des Saints*, vol. v. p. 83). St. Catherine of Siena with her blood wrote the same words, and died (ibid., p. 135).

(xxiii.) *The Twelve Fruits of the Holy Ghost*. Nine of these are given in *Gal.* v. 22, 23. The three in italics are not in St. Paul's list. (1) *Chastity;* (2) faith or fidelity; (3) gentleness; (4) goodness; (5) joy; (6) long-suffering; (7) love or charity; (8) meekness; (9) *modesty;* (10) *patience;* (11) peace; and (12) temperance or continence.

(xxiv.) *The Twelve Numeric Remembrancers.*

Come tell me, truly tell, what truth
  Abides in number *one?*
In number one is UNITY,
  Which dwelleth all alone.
What's brought to mind by number *two;*
  Say truly, if you can?
The HYPOSTATIC UNION
  Of Christ, both God and man.
Come tell me, truly tell, what truth
  Abides in number *three?*
The Father, Son, and Holy Ghost,
  That mystic TRINITY.
Come tell me, truly tell, what truth
  Will number *four* afford?
The great EVANGELISTS, who wrote
  Of Jesus Christ the Lord.
Come tell me truly to what thought
  Should number *five* be guide?
The WOUNDS of CHRIST in hands and feet,
  And in His piercèd side.
And number *six*, what mystic truth
  Do wise men find therein?
As six, six, six, is Satan's mark,
  Six is the badge of sin.
Seven tells us of the DYING WORDS
  Christ uttered on the cross;
And of the *Holy Spirit's gifts*,
  To which all else is dross.
Tell me to what the wise in heart
  Say number *eight* alludes?
Those sacred maxims of the Lord,
  Called the BEATITUDES.
What truth when number *nine* we see
  Should we remember most?
The ORDERS it should call to mind
  Of all the HEAVENLY HOST.
What should we call to mind whene'er
  We think of number *ten?*
The TEN COMMANDMENTS of the law
  By God to sinful men.
Number *eleven*, what event
  Does that recall, I pray?
The true apostles of the Lord,
  When one had fallen away.
Now, last of all comes number *twelve*,
  And what should that recall?
The APOSTOLIC COLLEGE when
  Completed by St. Paul.

E. COBHAM BREWER.

Matthias was not called by Christ, as the college of the apostles were.

(xxiv.) *The Fifteen Mysteries.* There are fifteen mysteries: five joyous, five dolorous, and five glorious.

1. *The Five Joyous Mysteries* are these: (1) The annunciation and conception of the Word in the Virgin's womb; (2) The visitation and influence of grace on John the Baptist, who "leaped in the womb;" (3) the birth of Jesus at Bethlehem; (4) the purification and offering made by Mary in the temple; and (5) Christ's visit to the temple at the age of twelve years, when He was found by His mother among the doctors.

2. *The Five Dolorous Mysteries* are these: (1) The agony of Christ in the olive garden; (2) the scourging; (3) the crowning with thorns; (4) the burden of

the cross borne to Calvary ; and (5) the crucifixion.

3. *The Five Glorious Mysteries* are these: (1) The Resurrection; (2) the Ascension; (3) the descent of the Holy Ghost on the day of Pentecost; (4) the assumption of the Virgin, body and soul, to heaven; (5) the consummation of her glory by her triple coronation of Grandeur, Power, and Goodness.

(xxv.) *The Ladder which reaches to Paradise.*

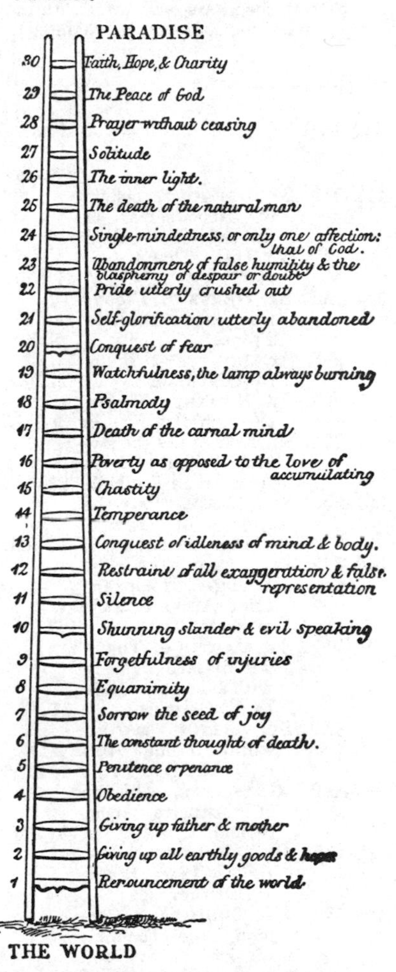

This ladder drawn by St. John, surnamed Climacus (A.D. 525), is very instructive, and lets in a flood of light.

(xxvi.) *A Rosary.* A rosary is either a sacred office in honour of the Virgin Mary; or a string of beads, fifteen of which are larger than the rest. The fifteen large beads are to tell off the *Pater Nosters*, and 150 other beads to tell off the *Ave Marias.*

The *office* called a rosary begins with making the sign of the cross thrice: (1) to ward off the devil; (2) to implore the help of the Holy Trinity; (3) to bring to mind the cross of man's salvation.

After crossing, "The Belief," called *The Apostolic Symbol* (or Symbol of the Apostles), is repeated.

Then follows the Lord's Prayer; and "Hail, Mary!" is thrice repeated: once because God is her Father [father-in-law], once because Christ is her Son, and once because the Holy Ghost is her Spouse.

These being done, the rosary proper begins. It consists of fifteen decades or dizains divided into threes: five recounting the *Joyous* mysteries, five the *Dolorous* mysteries, and five the *Glorious* mysteries (see xxiv.). These parts are called decades or dizains, because with each mystery "Hail, Mary!" is repeated ten times. That is, fifty times in the three Joyous Mysteries, fifty times in the Dolorous Mysteries, and fifty times in the three Glorious Mysteries; altogether 150 times.

As each mystery begins with a *Pater Noster*, it follows that in the fifteen mysteries the Lord's Prayer is repeated fifteen times.

For the proper recitation of the "Rosary" it is not enough to repeat the fifteen decades. There must be a meditation on the mystery in honour of which the recitation is about to be made; a prayer for the special grace appropriate to that particular mystery, and the doxology.

The Greater Rosary takes in all the fifteen mysteries.

The Lesser Rosary takes in one of the three decades.

St. Dominic is supposed to have introduced the Rosary Office.

(xxvii.) *Tonsure.*

St. Peter's tonsure. This tonsure was quite round the head; to resemble the Lord's crown of thorns. This is the tonsure adopted by the Roman Catholic clergy.

St. Paul's tonsure. In this tonsure the whole head is shaved. This is called also "the Oriental tonsure."

Simon Magus's tonsure. A semicircle

shaved from ear to ear above the forehead, but not reaching to the hinder part of the head, on which the hair was allowed to remain. This sort of tonsure is that of natural baldness.

Tonsures are mentioned by St. Dionycius the Areopagite, who died A.D. 95 (*De Hierarchia*, p. 2); by St. Anicet (A.D. 150–161), in a letter contained in *Patrologia Græca*, vol. v. col. 1129. And they were general in the fourth and fifth centuries.—Bede, *Church History*, bk. v. ch. 22. See also Mabillon's preface to his *Acta Sanctorum St. Benedicti in Sæculorum Classes Distributa*; Fluery *Histoire Ecclésiastique* (20 vols. in quarto), bk. xxxix.

(xxviii.) *Monumental Figures.*

Monumental figures in armour represent *knights*.
- with crosier, mitre, and pontificals, *bishops*.
- with hands on the breast and a chalice, *priests*.
- built into the wall, *founders*.
- east of the altar, and elevated, *saints* and *martyrs*.
- east of the altars, and level with the pavement, *holy men* (not sainted).

THAUMATURGISTS.

The present number of saints is, at least, thirty thousand, three-fourths of whom were martyrs or ecclesiastics.

Of craftsmen, the most numerous have been whitesmiths.

Of the thaumaturgists, twenty-one are almost unknown.

Of saints, forty-nine have died a martyr's death in infancy; but there are several infant martyrs not known even by name.

Thaumaturgists (from B.C. 1567 to A.D. 1850).

From the Old Testament the greatest wonder-workers are Moses, Jannes and Jambres, and Elisha.

Dositheus, who taught Simon Magus, was a great thaumaturgist; and Simon Magus is called in *Acts* viii. 10 the "Great Power of God."

(A most graphic account of his imitative ascent of Elijah in the chariot of fire, is given from P. Francs in *Notes and Queries*, Dec. 8, 1883, pp. 441, 442. It was in the presence of Nero and an immense crowd. He applied to himself many of the words uttered by the Lord, such as, "Behold, I go to the Father. . . . I will prepare a seat for you at the foot of my throne. Thence will I pour out upon my elect of my celestial treasures." And again. "Verily, verily, I say unto you, whoso believeth in me shall not see death; for in me is eternal life. And again, "Remember that your eyes have seen the Word of God. I am the Beautiful One, the Paraclete, the Omnipotent, the great Pan, the Divine All." The multitude accepted him as the "Great Power of God," bowed themselves in awe before him, and kissed the hem of his garment.)

A.D.		Fête-day.
3–98.	APOLLONIUS of Tyana. (Life by Philostratos.)	
205–270.	ST. PLOTINUS, and several other philosophers of Alexandria. (Porphyry, *Vita Plotini*, A.D. 301.)	
212–270.	ST. GREGORY, bishop of Neocæsarea, in Cappadocia. Called "The Thaumaturgist"	17 Nov.
3rd cent.	ST. DENYS or Dionysius, patron saint of France	9 Oct.
283.	ST. QUINTUS of Æolia, in Asia Minor ...	2 Mar.
303.	ST. ROMANUS of Antioch, martyr ...	9 Feb.
311.	ST. ASCLEPIAS the Sabine. Martyred at Antinoe, in Egypt ...	23 Jan.
301–390.	ST. MACARIUS the Elder, of Egypt. Solitary of Scetê ...	15 Jan.
310–395.	ST. MACARIUS the Younger, of Alexandria. Also a solitary of Scetê	2 Jan.
316–397.	ST. MARTIN of Tours, who divided his cloak with a beggar. (Life by N. Gervaise) ...	11 Nov.
410.	ST. TITUS, martyr, while Rome was under the Goths ..	16 Aug.
330–448.	GERMANUS, bishop of Auxerre (confessor)	31 July
412–485.	ST. PROCLUS. Marinus, *Vita Procli*, 5th century	24 Oct
436–523.	ST. BRIGIT of Ireland, the thaumaturgist. Her cell was called "Kill Dara"	1 Feb.

A.D.		Fête-day.
570-667.	**St. Linus**, pope and martyr	23 Sept.
668.	**St. Cuthbert**, the British thaumaturgist	20 Mar.
7th cent.	**St Jonas**, priest of St. Sabas, in Palestine. Honoured by the Greek Church	21 Sept.
8th cent.	**St. Hesychius**, solitary of St. Andrew's, in Bithynia. Honoured by the Greek Church ...	6 Mar.
8th cent.	**St. John**, bishop of Polybote, in Asia	5 Dec.
851.	**St. Isaac** of Cordova, martyr	3 June
800-856.	**St. Aldric**, bishop of Mans	7 Jan.
1091-1153.	**St. Bernard** of Clairvaux, thaumaturgist of the West	20 Aug.
1110-1170.	**St. Isidore** of Madrid, farm labourer. Honoured at Madrid. (Life by John of Damascus) ...	10 May
1170-1221.	**St. Dominic**, founder of the Dominicans	22 Jan.
1182-1226.	**St. Francis** of Assisi, founder of the Franciscans ...	4 Oct.
1182-1257.	**St. Hyacinth**, thaumaturgist of the 13th century ...	16 Aug.
1195-1231.	**St. Antony** of Padua, apostle and thaumaturgist. He preached to the fishes ...	13 June
1347-1380.	**Ste. Catherine** of Siena. (Not the one famous for the wheel)	30 April
1357-1419.	**St. Vincent Ferrier**, a Spanish Dominican ...	5 April
1416-1507.	**St. Francis** of Paula, founder of the Minims ...	2 April
1506-1552.	**St. Francis Xavier**, apostle of the Indians	3 Dec.
1538-1554.	**St. Charles Borromeo**, archbishop of Milan	4 Nov.
1576-1660.	**St. Vincent de Paul**, founder of the Lazarists and of the Sisters of Charity	19 July
1623-1662.	**Blaise Pascal**, mathematician and philosopher.	
1727-1779.	**Joseph Gassner** of Bratz, in the Tyrol; who treated all diseases as demoniacal possessions, and therefore exorcised the sick.	
1802.	**St. Filumena.** Called the thaumaturgist of the 19th century	10 Aug.
1794-1849.	Prince Alexander of Hohenlohe.	

Neither the birth nor death date is known of the following thaumaturgists:—

St. Aninas, an Asiatic anchorite. In Greek Menology ...	17 Feb.
St. Attalus the thaumaturgist. Honoured by the Greeks	6 June
St. Eustratius of Nicomedia. Honoured by the Greeks	6 June
St. Euthymius the thaumaturgist, bishop of Madytes, on the Hellespont ... 2 and	18 April
St. Felix. Honoured at Spoleto	16 June
St. George the Young. Honoured at Constantinople	23 Mar.
St. Illyrius. Honoured by the Greek Church	3 April
St. Jasimus. Honoured by the Greek Church	4 Feb.
St. Maurus. (Not the great Maurus of Glanfeuil.) Honoured at Sopeto ...	16 June
St. Memnon, the hegumen. Honoured by the Greeks ...	28 April
St. Peter, bishop of Argos ...	3 May
St. Peter of Gallia Cisalpina.	
St. Philotheus, founder of the monastery of Mermecium, on the Bosphorus	15 Sept.
St. Ritza of Coblentz	30 Aug.
St. Sebastiana. Honoured by the Greek Church ...	7 June
St. Stephen, the thaumaturgist, of the laura of St. Sabas, in Palestine	13 July
St. Tharasius of Lycaonia. (Not the patriarch of Constantinople)	25 Feb.
St. Theocleta. Honoured by the Greek Church ...	21 Aug.

Fete-day.

St. Zanaïs, the thaumaturgist of Constantinople ... ... 6 June

It will be seen that the great miracle-workers have continued uninterruptedly even to our own days. The miracles of prince ALEXANDER of HOHENLOHE, bishop *in partibus* of Sardinia, made a great noise in 1820–1821. He healed by prayer only, but it was essential for success that the sick person should pray simultaneously with him. Distance was of no consequence.

APOLLONIUS of TYANA raised the dead; healed the sick; cast out devils; freed a young man from a lamia or vampire of which he was enamoured; prophesied; saw at Ephesus the assassination of Domitian at Rome; and filled the world with his fame. He was a Pythagorean. Philostratus wrote his life.

ST. FILUMENA was wholly unknown till 1802; but since then her ghost has told the story of her life. According to this authority, she was born at Rome, in the reign of Diocletian, and her father was a prince. Diocletian wanted to marry her, but she told him she was the spouse of Christ, and the tyrant murdered her. L'abbé Migne says, "Ces révélations particulières paraissent reunir tous les caractères d'une source divine."—*Encyclopédie Théologique*, vol. xli. p. 719.

N.B.—One thing is very striking, and seems to demonstrate the low opinion held of miracles, and that is, that so many thaumaturgists are almost unknown. Neither the place of their birth, the field of their operations, the nature of their miracles, nor even the dates of their birth and death, are known. It looks as if a thaumaturgist held a place no better than a religious conjuror.

Child-Martyrs canonized (49 in number).

Fête-day.

ABUNDIUS of Aquileia, martyred under Diocletian ... ... 23 Aug.

ACHAS, honoured at Thourot, in Flanders; martyred 1220 ... 11 June

AGAPIUS, FIDELIS, and THEOGONIUS, three brothers, all martyred at Edessa, under Maximian ... ... 21 Aug.

(Their mother, St. Bassa, saw her children murdered first, and was then beheaded herself.)

ANDREW, crucified by Jews at Inspruck ... ... 12 July

ANDREW, martyred in Japan, 1622 ... ... 2 Oct.

ANTONY, THOMAS COZAKI (and 25 others), martyred in Japan, 1597 ... ... 5 Feb.

(Canonized by Urban VIII.)

ANTONIUS, martyred at Capua, A.D. 302 ... ... 3 Sept.

BRIXIUS, martyred at Esch, in Belgium ... ... 12 Nov.

CANDIDUS (an infant), martyred at Rome ... ... 1 June

CELSUS, martyred with his mother at Antinoe, in Egypt, A.D. 313 9 Jan.

CLAUDIUS, DIONYSIUS, HYPATIUS, and PAULUS, all martyred the same day at Byzantium, under Aurelian, A.D. 273. They were first cast into a furnace, which rain extinguished, and they were then beheaded ... 3 June

CONCORD and THEODORE, martyred with their father, St. Zeno, at Nicomedia, in Bithynia, under Diocletian, 303 ... ... 2 Sept.

CRESCENS (an infant), son of St. Euthymius, martyred by Turpilius, under Diocletian, in the Via Salaria of Rome 14 Sept.

CYRIACUS and THEODULUS, two brothers, sons of St. Exuperius, martyred in Pamphylia, under Diocletian ... 2 May

CYRIL, martyred at Cæsarea, in Cappadocia, under Decius ... 29 May

HUGH of Lincoln (1244–1255), crucified by Jews ... ... 27 Aug.

(Joppin and his accomplices were first torn limb from limb by horses, and then gibbeted.)

INNOCENT, martyred under Diocletian and Maximian ... 23 Aug.

JOHN, PETER, and SERAPION, three brothers, sons of Marcellin, the military tribune, martyred at Tomes, in Pontus ... ... 27 Aug.

JUSTUS of Auxerre, martyred at Beauvaisis by order of Rictiovarus, prefect of Gaul, under Diocletian, A.D. 287 18 Oct.

JUSTINIAN, son of St. Martial of Limoges ... ... 16 July

LUDOVIC VON BRUCK, crucified by Jews ... ... 30 April

LYCARION, a Greek child ... 8 Feb.

MAJORIC, martyred in Africa, by Huneric, king of the Vandals, A.D. 484 ... ... 6 Dec.

MAXIMUS, martyred at Carthage ... 17 and 23 Aug.

MERENDIN, martyred under Diocletian and Maximian ... 23 Aug.

MICHAEL of Hettengen, flayed alive, at the age of three years, by Jews, 1540 ... 26 Mar.

PAULILLUS, martyred in Africa, by Genseric, king of the Vandals ... ... 13 Nov.

PRILIDIAN, martyred at Antioch, under Decius, A.D. 250 ... 24 Jan.

RICHARD, crucified by Jews at Pontoise, 1182, March 25 25 and 30 Mar.

RODOLPH, martyred by Jews at Berne, Switzerland, 1287 ... 17 April

RUFINUS, SILVANUS, and VITALICUS, martyred at Ancyra, in Galatia ... ... 4 Sept.

SIMEON NOE of Prague, martyred by his own father, a Jew, 1694. (Not canonized.)

Fete-day.

Simon, martyred at Trent, in the Tyrol, 1472 ... ... 24 Mar.

(His name stands in the Roman Martyrology.)

Theodulus, a Greek child ... 28 Oct.
Urban, martyred at Antioch, under Decius, A.D. 250 ... 24 Jan.
Werner, martyred by Jews, at Oberwezel ... ... 18 and 19 April
William of Norwich, crucified by Jews, 1137 ... ... 24 Mar.

Of crucifixions by Jews, Hugh of Lincoln, Richard, and William of Norwich rest on legal authority. In Rymer's *Fœdera* are several documents relating to Hugh of Lincoln, and eighteen of the richest Jews of London were put to death for "taking part" in this murder. *The Prioress's Tale* of Chaucer, modernized by Wordsworth, has this for its subject.

Richard also marks an epoch in French history, as this alleged murder determined king Philippe to expel all Jews from his dominion the same year. Richard's body was preserved in St. Innocent's, Paris, and many miracles are ascribed to it.

William. On the spot where this murder is said to have been committed, a church was erected, called "William in the Wood." And we are told that his body was signalized by many miracles. It was placed in the cathedral, and the name inserted in the English calendar.

Rodolph was buried in Berne Cathedral, and his name is entered in several martyrologies.

Saints of the Nineteenth Century.

The following have been canonized during the present century:—

Columba. The very existence of this martyr was unknown till 1819, when her body was discovered in the cemetery of St. Calepode. Canonized by Gregory XVI.

Filumena. The existence of this person was wholly unknown till three tiles were discovered, in 1802, in the cemetery of St. Priscilla (see p. 22). Her ghost revealed her antecedents. Her body was removed to Naples in 1805, and was honoured by so many miracles that she was called "The Thaumaturgist of the Nineteenth Century." In 1852 Pius IX. granted great indulgences to those who honoured this new saint (p. 476).

Gerard Majella of Naples, died 1755, and the miracles which honoured her tomb caused her canonization by Pius IX. in 1847.

Hereneta. Her body was recently found in the catacombs of Rome, and her canonization was authorized by Gregory XVI. in 1841.

Mary Clotilde de France, died 1802. Was beatified 1808.

Ursie. Her body was recently found in the cemetery of St. Calixtus, and her body was removed to Bordeaux in 1842, when her canonization was authorized by Gregory XVI.

Canonization not yet fully consummated (1884) :—

Agolin of Sommariva. Canonization not yet complete (1884).

Benedicta (1648-1718). Mgr. Barnadou, bishop of Gap, is still collecting materials for her canonization (1884).

Camille Gentili (15th century). Her "cult" was authorized by Gregory XVI. in 1841.

Francis Xavier Joseph Mary Bianchi, died at Naples in the "odour of sanctity" in 1815, aged 71. His beatification is still in process at Rome (1884).

Gaspard del Buffalo, born at Rome, died 1837. Gregory XVI. introduced a decree for his beatification, but it is still *sub judice* (1884).

Joseph Mary Pignatelli of Saragossa, died in the "odour of sanctity" in 1811, aged 74. Several years ago the procedure of his beatification was introduced at Rome, but is not yet fully consummated (1884).

Mary Frances des Plaies de Notre Seigneur of Naples (1715-1791). Her beatification is still under consideration (1884).

Nicholas Molinari, bishop of Bovino, in Naples (1708-1792). The process of his canonization was commenced in 1831, but is not yet completed.

Paul de la Croix, founder of the Passionists, died at Rome in the "odour of sanctity" in 1775. Pius VI. introduced the cause of her beatification, but it is still incomplete (1884).

Pompilio Mary de St. Nicholas Pirotti of Benevento, died at Campo in 1756. Ferdinand II. of Naples interested himself in his canonization, which still goes slowly on at Rome (1884).

Theresa Margaret du Cœur de Jesus of Arezzo, died in the "odour of sanctity" in 1770. The cause of her beatification at Rome is nearly complete.

Vincent Mary Strambi of Civita Vecchia, died 1824. The process of her canonization is considerably advanced.

Vincent Morelli, archbishop of Otranto, died 1812, aged 71. The cause of his beatification is going on (1884).

Vincent Romanus of Naples, died 1831. The process of his beatification has commenced at Rome.

Tonquin swarms with martyrs of the nineteenth century. They were especially numerous in the year 1838. There have been above fifty since 1815.

THE FATHERS OF THE CHURCH.

The twenty-two Fathers of the Greek and Latin Churches, in chronological order, are: 1. Justin (103–167); 2. Irenæus, bishop of Lyons (130, 177–200); 3. Athenagoras (*flourished* 117); 4. Clement, or Clemens, of Alexandria (*died* 220); 5. Tertullian, a Latin Father (160–240); 6. Origen, a Greek Father (185–253); 7. Cyprian, bishop of Carthage (200, 248–258); Lactantius (*died* 325); 9. Hilary of Poitiers (*bishop* 350–367); 10. Athanasius, bishop of Alexandria (296, 326–373); 11. Basil *the Great*, bishop of Cæsarea (329, 371–379); 12. Cyril of Jerusalem (315, 348–386); 13. Gregory Nazianzen, bishop of Carthage (329, 380–390); 14. Gregory, bishop of Nyssa (332–396); 15. Ambrose, bishop of Milan (340, 374–397); 16. John Chrysostom (347–407); 17. Jerome (345–420); 18. Augustine, bishop of Hippo (354, 395–430); 19. Cyril, bishop of Alexandria (*bishop* 412–444); 20. Theodoret, bishop of Tyre (387–458); 21. Pope Leo I. *the Great* (390, 440–461); 22. Pope Gregory I. *the Great* (544, 590–604).

In *alphabetic* order: Ambrose, Athanasius, Athenagoras, Augustine, Basil, Chrysostom, Clement, Cyprian, two Cyrils, three Gregorys, Hilary, Irenæus, Jerome, Justin, Lactantius, Leo I., Origen, Tertullian, and Theodoret.

Chief works. AMBROSE: *De Officiis Ministrorum; De Virginitate;* Letter to Valentinian; the Ambrosian ritual, used in Milan. [The *Te Deum* is usually ascribed to him, but it was probably a century later.]

ATHANASIUS: Bible Commentaries; Apology to the emperor Constance; and a host of works against Arianism. [The Athanasian Creed embodies the anti-Arian dogmas of this Father.]

ATHENAGORAS: *Legatio pro Christianis* (addressed to the emperor Marcus Aurelius); Treatise on the Resurrection. ["The Romance of True and Perfect Love" has also been ascribed to him, but without sufficient authority.]

AUGUSTINE: *De Civitate Dei*, in 22 books (his great work); *Retractationes*, in two books; Confessions, in 13 books (containing an account of his conversion); A Treatise on Grace and Free Will; Soliloquies (with his own soul); Exposition of St. John's Gospel; Commentary on the Psalms; 363 Sermons; 270 Letters; etc.

This is not the St. Augustine sent to England by Gregory the Great to convert the Anglo-Saxons.

BASIL: The *Hexameron*, or six days of creation (his great work, in Greek); Lectures on secular authors; Homilies; Discourses; A Treatise on Asceticism; Scripture Commentaries; a vast number of Letters; etc.

CHRYSOSTOM: Homilies (his best work); Treatises on the Priesthood; Providence and Virginity; five Liturgies; Discourses, Commentaries, and Letters.

CLEMENT or CLEMENS: *Protrepticus* (an exhortation to the Gentiles); *Stromata* (a recital of Christian and philosophic thoughts); *Pedagogus* (on Christian morals).

CYPRIAN: *De Lapsis* (in the Decian persecution); On the Unity of the Church; *De Disciplina Virginum; De Gratia Dei; De Idolorum Vanitate;* Orations; Letters; etc.

CYRIL of Alexandria: The Treasure (against the Arians); Commentaries on St. John; sixty Letters; etc.

CYRIL of Jerusalem: Eighteen treatises addressed to catechumens on Scripture doctrines, and five addressed to the newly baptized on *rituals*, as baptism, chrism, and the Lord's Supper.

GREGORY Nazianzen: Fifty-three Sermons; a poem on the Vicissitudes of Life; 155 other poems; 242 Letters; etc. [The dramatic poem on "The Passion of Christ" has also been ascribed to him.]

GREGORY of Nyssa: *Macrinia* (a dialogue of the Soul and Resurrection in Greek, his chief work); Treatises on the Deity of the Holy Ghost, on Destiny, on Virginity, and on Christian Perfection; Homilies on Ecclesiastes and on Solomon's Song; Orations; Discourses; Panegyrics; Funeral Orations; Lives of Saints; Letters; etc.

GREGORY I. the Great: Exposition of Job (his great work); The Sacramentary; The Antiphonary (or Gregorian chants); Dialogues; Letters; etc.

HILARY: On the Trinity; Treatise on the Synods; Commentaries on St. Matthew, the Pauline Epistles, and the Psalms; Christian Poesy.

IRENÆUS: Against Heresies, in five books (Greek); etc.

JEROME: Translation into Latin and a continuation of "Eusebius;" Translation of the Bible into Latin (his great work); etc.

JUSTIN: Two Apologies for the Christians; Dialogues with the Jew named Tryphon. [His "Monarchy of God" is lost.]

LACTANTIUS: Divine Institutions, in seven books (Latin, his chief work); The Work of God, the Wrath of God; The Death of Persecutors. [The poem in Latin verse called "The Phœnix" is also attributed to him.]

ORIGEN: *Tetrapla* and *Hexapla* (editions in Greek of the Old Testament, his chief works); Apology for Christianity, against Celsus, in eight books; On Martyrdom; On Prayer; On the Resurrection. The [*Philosophoumena*, a Refutation of Heresies, has been ascribed to him, but without sufficient foundation.]

TERTULLIAN: His Apology (is his great work); Against the Jews; Proscriptions against Heretics; On the Soul; Against Marcion, in five books; etc.

THEODORET: A Church History, in five books, from 325 to 429; A Biography of Fifty Recluses; A Treatise on Providence; A History of Heresies; *Eranistes* (a dialogue against Eutychianism, *i.e.* the dogma that the human nature of Christ was absorbed in His divine nature).

DATES OF ECCLESIASTICAL CUSTOMS, DOGMAS, TITLES, ETC.

IN reading the lives of saints, I have met with the following dates, which cannot fail to be useful, as they are not to be found in any book with which I am acquainted, in a compact form suited for easy reference.

A.D. introduced in the eighth century. Legalized in the tenth century.

ADMONITIONS, or threats of excommunication, introduced 1181.

ADORATION OF THE HOST imposed by the Fourth Lateran Council, 1000.

ADVENT SUNDAY appointed 1000.

ALL SOULS' DAY appointed 998.

ALTARS in churches always made of wood in the first three centuries; early in the fourth century stone altars were occasionally introduced; and in December, 506, it was declared by the Council of Albon that stone is the only proper material for church altars. In England stone altars were exchanged for wooden communion tables (after the practice of the first three centuries) in 1550; and in Jan. 31, 1845, stone altars were declared by the Court of Arches to be illegal in the Church of England. This declaration was confirmed March 21, 1857, by the Privy Council.

ANATHEMAS in use 387. The synod of Pavia, in 850, determined that all who refused to submit to "discipline" should be anathematized (see *Rom.* ix. 3; *Gal.* i. 8, 9).

ANGELUS, a prayer to the Virgin commencing with these words, *Angelus Domini nuntiavit Mariæ*, recited thrice a day at the sound of a bell. Instituted by Urban II. in the Council of Clermont, 1095. Reorganized by John XXII., and announced by a bell, in 1316. Ordered by Louis XI. to be repeated daily at noon in 1472.

ANNUNCIATION. First mention of the festival is by Gelasius in 492.

APOSTLES' CREED received into the Latin Church in its present form in the eleventh century; but a formula somewhat like it existed in the second century; items were added in the fourth and fifth centuries, and verbal alterations were made even later.

(The notion that it was composed by the apostles is quite mythical.)

ASHES. (See HOLY ASHES.)

ASCENSION DAY first commemorated A.D. 68.

ATHANASIAN CREED received into the Western Church in 670.

(Adopted in France 850; in Spain and Germany a century later; in England before 1000. Athanasius lived 296-372.)

AURICULAR CONFESSION imposed by the Fourth Lateran Council, 1215.

BELLS said to be introduced into churches by Paulinus, bishop of Nola, 400, but this probably is a century too early. Used in France 550. One brought from Italy by the abbot of Wearmouth in 680. Pope Sabinian enjoined that every hour should be announced by sound of bell in 600, that due preparation might be made for the *horæ canonicæ*.

(Bede, who died in 735, makes mention of bells in England.)

Baptism of Bells introduced by John XIII. (965–972). They were first exorcised, and blessed with salt and water; then sprinkled within and without with the aspersoir; then anointed seven times in the form of crosses (thrice outside with oil for the sick, and four times inside with the holy chrism); then named after some saint; and lastly incensed and marked with a cross.

Bells were known to the Chinese B.C. 2262. They were used in the monasteries of Thibet long, long before the Christian era. They were common among the Indians, Egyptians, Jews, Greeks, and Romans.

BELL, BOOK, and CANDLE; this mode of excommunication existed in the eighth century.

BELL. The Angelus first rung in Italy in 1316; in France May 1, 1472.

BREVIARY attributed to Gelasius I. in 494. Modified in 1080.

CANDLES were first used in places of public worship, because Christians had to celebrate their mysteries in caves, catacombs, and dark underground secret places, to escape persecution.

CANON OF SCRIPTURE completed 494.

The Council of Laodicea (360–364) determined the canon of the New Testament Scriptures, but rejected the Apocalypse. The Apocalypse was admitted 494.

The Old Testament, as we have it, was not completed before B.C. 130, but there was a compilation in existence B.C. 285. The Apocryphal books were declared uncanonical in the fifth century. There was a Septuagint version B.C. 277.

CANONIZATION. First instance by John XVI., who canonized Uldaric, bishop of Augsburg, Jan. 30, 993. Bishops and popes mutually canonized till 1160, when Alexander III. restricted the prerogative to the pope. The canonization made at Rouen, in 1153, was the last which was made by bishops without the pope.

CARDINALS (The Sacred College of) instituted in 817; their right to elect the pope established by Nicholas II. 1059; red hat given by Innocent IV. at the Council of Lyons in 1245; title of *Eminence* accorded by Urban VIII. in 1630.

CELIBACY OF THE CLERGY. *Marriage forbidden* by the Council of Nice, 325; of Orange, 441; of Arles, 452; of Angers, 453; of Tours, 461; of Nantes, 465; of Rome, 721; of Worms, 868; of Augsburg, 952; of Poitiers, 1000; of Rome again, 1074; of Placentia, 1095; in London, 1125; in Denmark, 1180; finally, by the Council of Trent, in 1563.

Allowed by Jovinian in 400; by the archbishop of Seleucia, in 499; by Trullan Council in 692; by Council of Toledo, 701–710; maintained at Milan till 1080; in England, Normandy, and Brittany till after 1100; in Liege till 1220.

CHRISTIANS. Name given in Antioch to the followers of Christ about A.D. 41.

CHRISTMAS DAY (Dec. 25) introduced at Antioch 375.

COMMUNION in one kind enjoined in 1263.

CONFESSION once a year enjoined by the Lateran Council in 1215.

CROSS (The sign of the), as a curative symbol, was common in the fourth century, as Eusebius tells us from his own personal knowledge; but from the monumental inscriptions of the Catacombs it may be inferred that it was rarely, if ever, used in the first two centuries. It is, however, well known that the cross itself is not exclusively a Christian symbol, as the Spaniards found it an object of religious veneration in both South and Central America. In the Middle Ages the sign of the cross was used as a charm or amulet, and even to the present is so used by many [Roman] Catholics.

CRUCIFIX. Its general use enjoined in the Sixth Œcumenical Council, held in 680. Decreed by Benedict XIV. to be necessary to every altar in 1754.

DIVINITY OF CHRIST strenuously insisted on in the fourth century.

EXCOMMUNICATION in the Christian Church is a continuation of the Jewish practice. The Jews had three degrees of excommunication, called *Niddui*, *Cherem*, and *Anathema Maranatha*. The first was exclusion from the synagogue for thirty days. The second was exclusion from the synagogue and "boycotting" the offender for thirty days. The Anathema Maranatha included the loss of civil rights, and was accompanied with terrible curses. Gregory VII., in 1077, assumed the right of excommunicating sovereigns, and releasing subjects from their allegiance.

EXTREME UNCTION introduced by Felix IV. (525–530). The allusions to anointing with oil in Origen, Chrysostom, Cæsarius of Arles, and Innocent I., etc., refer to the unctions of baptism and confirmation (*James* v. 14, 15).

FASTS. Montanus, who flourished 170–212 ("the Paraclete"), introduced fasting as an inhibition upon the faithful. Wednesdays to commemorate the day when Christ was betrayed and taken prisoner, and Fridays to commemorate His crucifixion. The Lenten fast was fixed at the

Council of Orleans in 541. In England ordained by Act 2 and 3 Edward VI. c. 19, 1549.

*** Saturday and Sunday are non-fast days. The one in commemoration of the finished work of creation, the other in commemoration of the Resurrection. (Yet we find Saturday frequently held as a fast-day by the saints, in memory of the entombment.)

FESTIVALS: John Baptist, Paul, Peter, Stephen, all introduced in the fourth century.

FILIOQUE introduced into the Nicene Creed in 830. The *Missi* of Charlemagne pressed the pope to declare any one who rejected the new dogma "salvus esse non potest;" but Leo III. refused to do so.

FUNERAL ORATIONS. The first was June 5, 1382, pronounced over Andrea Contarini, the doge. The first in France was in 1389, over the constable Dugueslin.

HOLY ASHES. Gregory the Great (590–604) introduced the practice of sprinkling the ashes on the first of the four days added to Lent by Felix III. in 487. The ceremony of distributing them was introduced March 28, 1091, by the Council of Benevento.

HOLY BREAD. Bread blessed by the priest and distributed on Sundays and other fête-days, was first introduced in 655 at the Council of Nantes.

HOLY OIL in *extreme unction* is based on *James* v. 14; *Mark* vi. 13; but it was not formally ordained till the Council of Trent, 1545-1563.

HOLY OIL in *chrism* was first used about 1541.

HOLY WATER introduced by Leo (682-683). First used in exorcisms by Alexander II., 1070. For this purpose it is still kept in Roman Catholic countries.

Used in exorcisms by the Indians, Persians, Tibetians, and Mexicans.

IMMACULATE CONCEPTION made a dogma of the Church by Pius IX. in 1854.

INDULGENCES. First bestowed in 1002 by Ponce, bishop of Arles, to those who aided him in building his monastery. In 1087 Victor III. promised indulgences to those who took up arms against the Saracens. The first plenary indulgence, extending over "this life and the life to come," was given by the Council of Clermont in 1095, in favour of Crusaders.

INFALLIBILITY OF THE POPE first claimed in 750.

INQUISITION established in 1232.

INTERDICTS. An ecclesiastical interdict was laid on a parish in his diocese by Hincmar, bishop of Laon, in 870. One was laid on France by Gregory V. in 998. Very rare till 1073, in the pontificate of Gregory VII.

KISSING THE POPE'S TOE introduced in 708. Abolished by Clement XIV. in 1773.

LENTEN FAST (a tithe of the year, or thirty-six days) introduced in the fourth century. Felix III., in 487, added four days. The number forty fixed by the Council of Orleans 547.

MATTHEW. The first two chapters do not occur in the Ebronite copies, said to be the "original Hebrew."

MARK. The two oldest Greek MSS. terminate this Gospel with ver. 9, chap. xvi. See "New Version." The last eleven verses were introduced subsequently.

MONASTIC ORDERS. The monastic system originated with Pachomius in Egypt (320–330). Introduced into Palestine by Hilarion in 328; at Rome by Athanasius in 340; into Gaul by Martin of Tours in 370. Paul the first hermit 251.

Annunciades, an order for women, established by Joan, daughter of Louis XI. and wife of Louis XII., in 1501; in England in 1105.

Augustines, established by Alexander IV. in 1256; in France in 1596.

Benedictines, established in 529.

Bernardines, established in 1113.

Brothers of Charity, founded by Vincent de Paul in 1617. *Sisters of Charity* in 1634.

Camaldules (Reformed Benedictines), introduced by Romuald in 1010.

Cappucines (Reformed Franciscans), by Matthew Baschi in 1528.

Carmelites, established in 1171. Confirmed by Honorius III. in 1224. *White* Friars.

Carmes, founded by Albert, patriarch of Jerusalem, in 1209. Confirmed by Honorius III. in 1227. Barefooted Carmes founded by St. Theresa in 1562.

Carthusians (Reformed Benedictines), by Bruno in 1057.

Clarisses, an order for women, founded by St. Francis in 1224.

Cordeliers, founded by St. Louis in 1215.

Doctrinaires, founded by Cæsar de Bus in 1592.

Dominicans, founded by Dominic in the Albigensian war, 1215. First Dominican convent built in 1218. *Black* Friars.

Feuillants (Reformed Benedictines), by John de la Barsière in 1580.

Franciscans, founded by Francis d'Assisi in 1209. Confirmed by Innocent III. in 1215. *Grey* Friars.

Récollets in 1525; Picpus in 1530; Tiers Ordre de la Pénitence in 1595.

Geneviève (Monastery of St.), founded by Eugenius III. in 1148.

Canons Regular of St. Geneviève established in 1615.

Hospitallers, founded by St. John of Jerusalem in 1099.

Jesuits, founded at Rome by Ignatius Loyola of Spain in 1538. Confirmed by the Bull of Paul III. in 1540.

Lazarists, founded by St. Vincent de Paul in 1624. Confirmed by Urban VIII. in 1631.

Mercy (Order of), for the redemption of Christian captives, founded in 1218. Confirmed by Gregory IX. in 1235.

Minims, founded in Calabria by Francis of Paula in 1454. Confirmed by Sixtus IV. in 1474. Introduced into France in 1621.

Mission (Priests of the), same as Lazarists (*q.v.*).

Oratory (Congregation of the), founded by Philip of Neri in Rome in 1558. Confirmed 1575. Introduced into France in 1611. Introduced by Newman into England in 1847.

Premonstratensians (Canons Regular), introduced by Norbert into Laon in 1119; established in England in 1140. Reformed in 1573.

Templars (Knights), founded in 1128. Suppressed in 1312.

Teutonic Knights, or "Chevaliers of the Virgin Mary," founded by Frederick, duke of Swabia, in 1190. Confirmed by Celestine III. in 1192. Suppressed by Napoleon in 1809.

Theatines of the Hermitage, founded by Ursula Benincasa in 1524. Confirmed by Urban VIII. in 1624. Introduced into Paris by cardinal Mazarin in 1644.

Trappists (Reformed Benedictines), founded in Normandy by Rotrou, count of Perche, in 1140. Refounded by L'abbé de Bouthillier de Rancé in 1663.

Victor (Canons Regular of St.), established in Paris by William de Champeaux in 1113.

Visitation (Congregation of the), founded by the baron of Chantal in 1610. Confirmed by Urban VIII. in 1626.

Monseigneur. At first applied to all saints and all knights. Up to 1789 accorded in France to princes of the blood, princes of the Church, and high functionaries. In 1830 restricted to princes of the blood, archbishops, bishops, and cardinals. Bishops in England were barons in 1072, and all rectors were knights, and had the title of "Sir."

Nicene Creed, up to the paragraph "I believe in the Holy Ghost," introduced in 325; the rest in 391 (except the word "dead").

Office of the Virgin, appointed to be read daily by the clergy, in the Council of Clermont in 1095.

(This was the council that determined on the first crusade.)

Paintings known in churches in 394, but not generally approved of.

Pilgrimages. Common to almost all nations. Herodotus speaks of a pilgrimage of virgins to make offerings in the temple of Delos. Kœmpfer speaks of pilgrimages to the temple of Isis, in Japan, to obtain remission of sins and indulgences. In China they are common; in India, Arabia, and Thibet. The Saracens made pilgrimages. In the Christian Church they were known in the fourth century; and were common in the eleventh century (from 1050).

Pope. Title first given to all bishops. Adopted by Hyginus in 138. Restricted to the bishop of Rome in 400 by the Council of Toledo; again in the Council of Clermont in 1095. In 506 Enodius established the dogma that every pope is *ex officio* "holy." Sergius II. was the first pope who changed his name, on his election, in 844. Stephen III., in 1161, was the first pope to enter St. John Lateran on a litter borne by men

(Gregory the Great, in 604, was the first to subscribe himself "Servus Servorum.")

Prayers for the Dead. The Parsees repeat prayers for the dead for three successive days, and that uninterruptedly. This is the time when the soul of the deceased is supposed to be undergoing examination for its past life. The prayers are again renewed on the thirtieth day, and continue occasionally for a year. If the prayers are neglected on the fortieth night, the soul will remain unprotected till the resurrection. In Thibet a vast number of prayers are said for the dead. They are repeated every third day for a year.

In the Christian Church. Eusebius

informs us they were introduced about 190; but in mediæval times the first sure instance is that for the doge Andrea Contarini, June 5, 1382.

Prayers for souls in Purgatory, enjoined in 1000. Rejected in England in 1553.

Prayers to the Virgin Mary and to Saints, introduced by Gregory the Great in 593.

Praying with the face to the East, introduced by Boniface II. in 532.

Prayers of the forty hours, in memory of Christ in the tomb, established by Joseph of Ferne in 1556.

PROCESSIONS. Religious processions common in Egypt, India, Thibet, Greece, Rome, etc.

In the Christian Church Sunday processions were instituted by Agapetus in 585.

Of St. Mark, by Gregory the Great, in 590.

Of the Purification, by pope Gelasius, in 494.

Of the Holy Sacrament, in 1320.

Prohibited in Italy in 1865.

To make a list of all religious processions would require more space than can be here spared. The whole subject is treated of fully in *Des Processions de l'Église, de leurs Antiquités*, etc., 1713.

PURGATORY. Children, among the Jews, recite for a year a prayer, called *Kadis*, for the soul of a deceased father. The Mussulmans teach there is a place called *Araf*, between paradise and hell. The dogma was suggested in 407 by St. Augustine. Inculcated by Gregory the Great in 593. Received in England in 690; but rejected in 1553.

RELICS (Veneration of) introduced in the fourth century. Traffic in them forbidden by Theodoret in 386. Veneration of relics condemned by Vigilantius about 400–410. The Council of Saragossa in 592 enjoined that all relics should be tested by fire, to ascertain if they are genuine. Spurious relics manufactured before 600. Veneration of them enjoined by the Council of Trent, Dec. 25, 1563. Importation into England prohibited in 1606.

ROGATION DAYS introduced by Mamercus, bishop of Vienne, in 474. Prescribed by the Council of Orleans in 511. Established by Leo III. in 801.

SACRAMENTS.

Baptism, *Matt.* xxviii. 19.

Confirmation introduced in 190.

Eucharist, *Matt.* xxvi. 26, etc.

Penance introduced in 157.

Orders, no date known.

Marriage made a sacrament by Innocent III. in 1199.

Extreme Unction common in 550. Decreed to be a sacrament by Eugenius IV., at the Council of Florence, in 1439.

SACRAMENT (Festival of the Holy) introduced in 1246. Confirmed by Urban IV. in 1264.

SACRED HEART OF JESUS. This festival was introduced in 1732.

"SERVUS SERVORUM," style adopted by Gregory the Great (590–604).

SIGN OF THE CROSS. (See CROSS.)

STATIONS. Either the spots where a procession stops to make certain prayers, or the time of its stopping. In the Way of the Cross there are fourteen stations. Also the weekly fasts of Wednesday and Friday are so called.

STATUES, even of Christ, unknown till the fifth century.

SUNDAY appointed the Christian sabbath in 321.

(Sir William Domville says, "History does not furnish us with a single proof or indication that Sunday was at any time observed as the Lord's day previously to the sabbatical edict of Constantine in 321.)

TIARA. Hildebrand (1073–1085) wore a royal crown with this legend, *Corona regni de manu Dei.* Boniface VIII. (1294–1303) added a second crown, with the legend, *Diadema imperii de manu Petri.* John XXII., in 1314, added a third crown, to indicate that the pope is supreme: (1) in spiritual power; (2) in temporal power; (3) in ecclesiastical power both over the Church militant and the Church triumphant.

(Or, as some say, to indicate supremacy in the three parts of the world—Europe, Asia, and Africa.")

TRANSUBSTANTIATION declared to be a tenet of the Church in the Second Council of Nice, 787.

Denied by Rabanus Maurus about 850; by Lanfranc about 1070. Made a dogma of the Church in the First Lateran Council, 1215; and confirmed by the Council of Trent, 1551.

VIRGIN MARY, first honoured in the fifth century. Prayers addressed to her in 593. Office of the Virgin enjoined by the Council of Clermont, in 1095, to be recited daily by the clergy.

(For festivals of the Virgin Mary, see pt. iii. p. 517. Her perpetual virginity was wholly denied in 382.)

INSTRUMENTS OF TORTURE.

Armentarium. The only mention of this instrument of torture I have been able to discover is by Verinus and Armenius, priests of St. Stephen pope and martyr. Speaking of Christantianus, they say, "He was hung on the armentarium, but the crotch broke asunder, his bonds were unloosed, and the torches which were lighted to burn his sides were quenched." Armentarius is a

"herdsman," and armentarium the peg, pin, or crotch, on which he hangs the collars, yokes, and heavy harness of the oxen used in ploughing. Christantianus was drawn up by ropes, fastened round his legs and hands, till his feet were off the ground, and then his sides were singed with lighted torches. Primus was "hoisted by pulleys" to some such projecting beams, and burned with torches also. After he had hung awhile, he was let down, and molten lead poured down his throat.

Probably, instead of torches, a fire would be sometimes lighted under the feet. This sort of torture is still resorted to by some of the Indian tribes.

BASTINADO. According to Baronius, the bastinado was performed thus by the Romans: The tribune first touched the victim with his baton, and if he was a free man, all the soldiers in the camp ran upon him with staves and stones, beating him, for the most part, till he fell dead. If the victim was a slave, the soldiers used leaded knouts or flagra (p. xliv.) instead of sticks. No one was suffered to live in Rome after being bastinadoed; so that if perchance he survived the punishment, he was outlawed.

BOOTS. This instrument of torture consisted of a pair of iron boots, into which the legs of the victim were thrust up to the knees. Iron wedges were loosely inserted between the legs and the walls of the boots. A question was then asked the victim; and if not answered satisfactorily, two inquisitors (one to each boot) drove home with a sledge-hammer one of the iron wedges. Again the question was put, and if the answer was still unsatisfactory, another wedge was driven into each boot; and this was repeated, till the legs of the victim were crushed to a pulp. Dr. John Fian of Saltpans, near Edinburgh, was thus infamously tortured in the reign of James I. (See p. 342.) Bishop Burnet, in the *History of his Own Times*, and sir Walter Scott, in his *Old Mortality*, speak of this instrument of torture. Sometimes the boots were made of wood instead of iron. Bishop Burnet speaks of a case (it was a lad in Orkney, 1596) in which fifty-seven wedges were struck home. In 1583 queen Elizabeth ordered Father Holt, a Jesuit, to be "put to the boots."

St. Sergius was tortured by boots studded with sharp spikes, and made to run in them beside the emperor's chariot.

BULL'S HIDE. In this torture the victim, being enclosed in a fresh bull's hide, was placed in the blazing sun, when the hide gradually shrank, stiffened, and squeezed the victim to death. (See ST. CHRISANTUS, p. 403.)

BURNING METAL. Helmets of red-hot iron or brass were sometimes placed on the head of victims. This was a torture to which Savinian was subjected (p. 408). St. Thomas had plates of burning metal laid on his naked body (p. 408). Every one will remember the lines at the close of Goldsmith's *Traveller:* "Luke's iron crown, and Damien's bed of steel." The former was Luke Dosa, the Hungarian traitor, who was forced into a chair of red-hot iron for a throne, and then crowned with a burning metal crown. The earl of Athol, one of the murderers of James I. of Scotland, was also put to death with a red-hot iron crown. Francisca says usurers in hell are stretched on tables of red-hot brass (p. 412).

It was not Luke, but his brother George, who was subjected to the punishment referred to by Goldsmith. Zeck the Hungarian was similarly tortured. For "bed of steel," see CATASTA.

CALTROP. The caltrop was an instrument with four iron points, three of them, disposed in a triangular form, being on the ground, the fourth pointed upwards. Used in war to lame the feet of an enemy's cavalry.

CATASTA, OR IRON BED. The catasta was an iron bedstead, not of one sheet of metal, but with cross-bars like a gridiron. Under the bedstead fires in brasiers were placed, and the victim was roasted alive.

CHEVALET, OR EQUULEUS. The chevalet was a kind of gibbet, furnished with screws and pulleys for racking the victim by stretching each individual limb. The victim was fastened by the hair to the uppermost beam, and the whole body tightly bound in a bent condition to the chevalet. He was thus raised on a sort of gibbet, and was wholly unable to move hand, foot, or head; and every limb was racked. In order still further to intensify the agony, a fire held in a brasier was set under each of the feet. St. Jerome speaks of this instrument of torture (*Letter* 49), "Crines leguntur ad stipitem, et toto corpore ad equuleum fortius alligato, vicinus pedibus ignis apponitur, utrumque latus carnifex fodit." So that while the victim was thus tortured, "the executioner kept digging into the sides of the sufferer." Ammianus Marcellinus (bk. xviii.) says, "Quanquam incurvus sub equuleo staret, pertinaci negabat instantia." So that it appears the head was poked forward as it would be in the pillory, but was held in its position by the hair.

COLUMBAR. Columbar, *i.e.* the pigeon-holes, was a pillory with three holes, one

for the neck and two for the hands. The Greek pillory had five holes, one for the neck, two for the hands, and two for the feet. It was called the Pentesuringos (πεντεσύριγγος).

FIDICULÆ. The fidiculæ were probably iron hooks, with which the body of a victim suspended on a chevalet was torn and lacerated.

FORK, or PATIBULUM. The patibulum was an instrument shaped like a fork or ≺ placed round the neck of slaves and criminals of low degree. The two hands were bound fast to the prongs, and the patibulatus was flogged through the streets to the place of execution. "Patibulum appensos statim exanimat, crux autem suffixos diu cruciat."—Isidore.

The *Furca Ignominiosa* was used for small offences, and consisted simply in carrying the furca, more or less weighted, about the city.

The *Furca Pœnalis* was a much more severe punishment, as in this case the "patibulatus" or "furcatus" was whipped round some stated place, while his hands were bound to the fork.

The *Furca Capitalis* was having the hands fastened to the fork, and being scourged to death.

HURDLE (in Latin, "Crates"). The hurdle was not unlike our hurdles. The victim was laid on his back on the ground under a hurdle, and stones were piled thereon, till the sufferer was gradually crushed to death.

IRON VIRGIN (The). A hollow wooden figure, representing a woman of Bavaria. It opened like a cupboard, and the front of it was studded with long sharp spikes. The victim was placed in the figure, and then the front or lid was gradually closed upon him. The spikes were so arranged as to pierce the eyes and least vital parts; but when quite closed the victim was crushed, and lingered in horrible torture till actual agony exhausted his vital powers.

KOBILA. Two boards, one above the other; the head of the victim being bound to the higher board, the feet to the lower one, and the hands made to embrace the kobila by bonds. The bare back of the sufferer is thus hollowed, and in this state the public scourger administered 101 lashes, unless the victim died before the complement of blows had been given. (See ST. AUDALDUS, p. 403.)

NERVUS, the stocks, a wooden frame in which the feet of slaves were thrust and fastened. Like the compedes, it was sometimes made to move so as to stretch the legs further and further apart, till the thighs were out of joint.

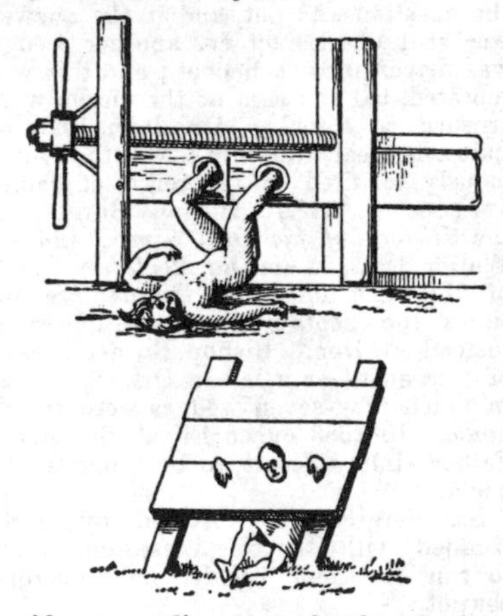

Also an ordinary stocks for the head and hands.

THE QUESTION. The instrument called "the question" was an iron frame with bars as sharp as scythes running across it; and underneath it a fire was kindled, which made the metal red-hot.

Examination by any sort of torture was

called "examination by the question;" and to be put to "the question," means to be put to torture for the purpose of extorting evidence from an unwilling witness, of forcing a confession of guilt, or of compelling a person to unsay something.

RACHENTEGES. This instrument of torture was fastened to a beam, and had a sharp iron to go about a man's neck and throat, so that he could in no wise sit, or lie, or sleep, without bearing the entire weight of the iron.

RACK. There were great varieties of racks, the most common being the horizontal rack, the vertical rack, and the roller rack.

(1) The first of these is the ordinary rack, made familiar to us by the Inquisition. It consisted of an oblong horizontal frame, on which the accused was stretched, while cords, attached to the legs and arms, were gradually strained by a lever or windlass. The wrists and ankles were generally dislocated, sometimes the shoulders and thighs.

(2) In the vertical rack the sufferer was raised to an upper beam, by a rope passed under his arms, bound behind his back. Being thus raised, heavy stones were attached to his feet, and then the hoisting rope being suddenly loosened, the victim fell with a jerk to within a few inches of the earth.

(3) The roller rack was a rack with a roller charged with spikes, over which the sufferer was drawn backwards and forwards.

SPANISH DONKEY (in Italian, "Cavaletto"). This was a wooden machine of torture, which was a species of impalement. The victim was made to sit on a sharp-pointed conical box, and in order to give weight to his body, and force the point of the seat further in, heavy weights were attached to the hands and feet of the sufferer. Not unfrequently fires were lighted under the feet to increase the agony, and sometimes the skin was lacerated with iron hooks or currycombs. One of these implements is still shown in the old fortifications of Nuremberg castle.

STRADDLES (in Latin, "Compedes"). Straddles were two blocks of wood set in a frame. Each block opened like stocks to admit one of the victim's feet, and when shut the feet were fast and astride. In some cases the blocks moved gradually further and further apart till the thighs were out of joint.

> In hoc barathrum conjicit
> Truculentus hostis martyrem,
> Lignis que plantas inserit
> Divaricatis cruribus.

That is, "In this dungeon the truculent enemy cast the martyr, and set his feet in wooden straddles, the thighs being stretched asunder." (See NERVUS.)

THUMBSCREW. The thumbscrew was much used by the Inquisition in Spain.

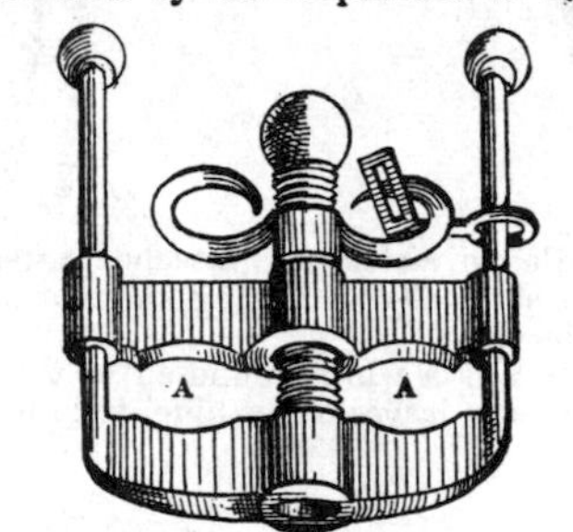

The thumbs were placed in the parts marked A A, and the screw was turned.

WHEEL. The trochos was a Greek instrument of torture. We read of Ixion, in hell, being chained hand and foot by Hermês to a wheel, which rolled incessantly in the air of the lower regions; but the ordinary torture-wheel had six spokes, into which the head, arms, and legs were interlaced and bound. The wheel was then whirled round with great rapidity, till the victim lost either consciousness or life.

The *Catherine Wheel* was a much more complex machine, devised by Maximinus II. for the torture of St. Catherine of Alexandria. The limbs were interlaced between the spokes as in the Greek trochos, but as the wheel revolved, it was met by several other wheels turning in different directions, some having keen sharp edges like razors, some teeth like saws, some fish-hooks or graters. These several wheels played on the body in turns, cutting it, sawing it, tearing it with hooks, grating the fresh wounds, and lacerating the flesh in every conceivable manner.

WHIPS AND SCOURGES; SCORPION, etc. No. 1 is a scourge called in Latin "Flagrum." It consisted of a short

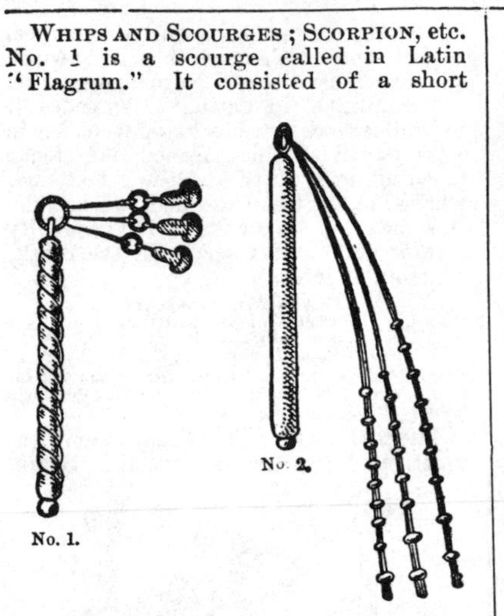

handle, to which was attached three or more short chains, having knots of metal at the end.

No. 2 is a whip composed of three or more long lashes of ox-hide, with bullets of lead fastened to them. Called in French *lanières plombées*. The scorpion mentioned by Rehoboam (1 *Kings* xii. 11) was a whip with leather thongs set with sharp iron points or nails, called in Latin *horribilia*.

Mgr. Guérin tells us this "lanière plombée" is the Russian *knout*, which A. de Lamothe, in his *Martyrs of Siberia* (ch. xii.), describes thus: "Le *knout* est une longue et étroite lanière, recuite dans une espèce d'essence, et fortement enduite de limaille métallique. Ainsi préparée, la lanière acquiert une dureté et une pesanteur extrêmes. Mais avant qu'elle ne se durcisse, on a le soin de replier sur eux-mêmes les bords, amincis à dessein, et qui forment de cette façon une rainure dans toute la longueur de la courroie, termin e par un petit crochet de fer. Si le bourreau sait son métier, le supplicié perd connaissance au troisième coup, et expire après le cinquième." The reader will instantly see that the knout is a modification of No. 2.

Respecting the scorpions, Mgr. Guérin says (vol. vi. p. 586), "Ils étaient des batons chargés de nœuds, et armés par le bout de crochets de fer. Ils rompaient les os des patients, entraient bien avant dans leur chair, et en enlevaient des morceaux à chaque coup; ce qui leur occasionnait une douleur incroyable."

PART I.

MIRACLES OF THE SAINTS,

ANALOGOUS TO

SCRIPTURE MIRACLES OR SECULAR STORIES

DICTIONARY OF MIRACLES.

Aaron's Rod becomes a Serpent.

EXOD. vii. 10–12. Aaron cast down his rod before Pharaoh, and before his servants, and it became a serpent. The magicians of Egypt, they also cast down every man his rod, and they became serpents.

EXOD. iv. 1–4. The Lord said unto Moses, What is that in thine hand? And Moses said, A rod. And the Lord said, Cast it on the ground. And he cast it on the ground, and it became a serpent; and Moses fled from before it. And the Lord said unto Moses, Put forth thine hand, and take it by the tail. And he put forth his hand, and caught it, and it became a rod in his hand.

The thong of a whip converted into a serpent (A.D. 303). St. Pelerin concealed himself near a fountain, where, being discovered by the Intaranians, he was made a captive. As he did not go along fast enough for their liking, one of them lifted up his whip to strike him, but the thong of the whip instantly slipped from the handle, turned into a serpent, and fled to the fountain, where it was soon lost to sight in the fissures of a rock.

F. Meyniel, curé of Bouhy, writing to Mgr. Crosnier, vicar-general of Nevers (Aug. 12, A.D. 1857), says, "Il est un fait constant et avéré qui ne doit laisser aucun doute sur la vérité du fouet transformé en serpent." In proof of this the vicar-general adds, There is a family in Entrains, descended from the very man whose whip was changed into a serpent, and all the members of this family, from that time to this (303–1857) "portent sur leur corps le stigmate du crime de leur ancêtre, c'est-à-dire un serpent qui les enlace." He furthermore adds, The very name of this family is a living proof of the fact, or rather I should say of the miracle, stated above.

The curé of Bouhy speaks very positively, but still it would havé been more satisfactory if he had told us how he came to know that all the descendants of this Intaranian for more than 1550 years were marked with a whip on their bodies, and also how the name of his family (which he does not give) can possibly be "une preuve vivante de ce fait, ou plutôt de ce miracle."

Abraham promised a Seed.

GEN. xv. 1–5. The word of the Lord came to Abram in a vision, saying, Fear not, Abram: I am thy shield, and thy exceeding great reward. . . . And [God] brought him forth abroad, and said, Look now towards heaven and tell the stars, if thou be able to number them; and He [the Lord] said, So shall thy seed be.

St. Eugendus, abbot of Condat (fifth century). At the age of six years God came in a vision to Eugendus, as he sat at the door of his house, facing the east. And the Lord, pointing to the sky, told the lad to count the stars if he was able, and then added, "So shall thy seed be." God then unrolled before the child the map of the future, and showed him a swarm of disciples. While Eugendus was still gazing with wonder on the innumerable crowd, the heavens opened, and a ladder like that which Jacob saw, was let down to earth, and angels appeared to be ascending and descending thereby, and ever as they moved they sang, "I am the way, the truth, and the life." This vision the child told to the very person who wrote his life, and who took down these words from the mouth of Eugendus himself. This is the disciple which testifieth of these things, and wrote these things, and he knows that his testimony is true. —Pragmacius, a disciple of St. Eugendus. See also *Lives of the Saints of Franche-Comte*, by the professors of the college of St. F. Xavier of Besançon.

This prophecy does not seem to have been very satisfactorily fulfilled. Eugendus died A.D. 510. A village grew up around the monastery, and in the following century received the name of St. Claude. The name of Eugendus does not appear to have survived, and a doubt exists whether it was Eugendus or Oyendus. The abbey was at one time famous, but now the inhabitants of St. Claude do not reach 7000. The chief industry of the people is the manufacture of clocks and toys.

Abraham offering up his Son Isaac.

GEN. xxii. Abraham, at the command of God, laid his only son, Isaac, upon the altar, which he had made, intending to offer him up in sacrifice to Jehovah, when his hand was stayed by a voice from heaven: Abraham, Abraham, lay not thy hand upon the lad.

neither do thou anything unto him, for now I know that thou fearest God. And Abraham saw a ram caught in a thicket by the horns, and he offered it up as a burnt-offering instead of his son.

Agamemnon offering up his daughter Iphigenia. When the Grecian fleet, on its way to Troy, was detained at Aulis by adverse winds, Agamemnon was commanded by the prophet Calchas to appease the wrath of Diana by offering to her in sacrifice his only daughter, Iphigenia. The damsel was bound to the altar, and Calchas had made ready the knife, when the damsel was spirited away by Diana herself; and Calchas, seeing a stag, took and offered it up in sacrifice, in lieu of the king's daughter.—Euripides, *Iphigenia in Aulis.*

> Not unlike to him [Jephthah]
> In folly, that great hero of the Greeks,—
> Whence on the altar Iphigenia mourned
> Her virgin beauty.
> Dante (Carey's), *Paradise* v. (See JEPHTHAH.)

Ahab covets Naboth's Vineyard.

1 KINGS xxi. Naboth the Jezreelite had a vineyard in Jezreel, hard by the palace of Ahab, king of Samaria. And Ahab said to Naboth, Give me thy vineyard, that I may have it for a garden of herbs, because it is near unto my house, and I will give thee for it a better vineyard, or will give thee the worth of it in money. But Naboth said to Ahab, The Lord forbid that I should give unto thee the inheritance of my fathers. Then Ahab went to his house, heavy and displeased, and laid him down upon his bed, and turned away his face, and would eat no bread. When Jezebel discovered the cause of this ill-humour, she accused Naboth of treason, and he was stoned to death. Naboth being dead, Ahab took possession of the vineyard, but Elijah said to him, Hast thou killed, and also taken possession? Thus saith the Lord, In the place where dogs licked the blood of Naboth, shall dogs lick thy blood, even thine.

The empress Eudoxia covets and takes possession of the vineyard of a widow (about A.D. 400). There was a law in Constantinople that if the emperor or empress set foot on a plot of ground, and took a fancy to it, the owner must part with it at a valuation, provided the person who fancied it had partaken of its produce. The empress Eudoxia one day went into the vineyard belonging to the widow of Theognostês, greatly admired the site, plucked a few grapes, and demanded to have the vineyard, according to the law. St. Chrysostom interfered on the widow's behalf, and Eudoxia forbade the archbishop ever again to set foot in the royal palace. The fête of "The Exaltation of the Cross" was close at hand; and when it arrived, the emperor Arcadius and his nobles entered the cathedral as usual, and departed when the service was over. St. Chrysostom now ordered the doors to be closed and bolted; but scarcely was this done, when the empress Eudoxia, with her suite, came to the church and demanded admission. The doorkeepers replied, they had strict injunctions not to open the doors to any one; whereupon the empress ordered one of her soldiers to burst the doors open with his battle-axe. As the man raised his arm to give the blow, it became paralyzed, and the axe fell to the ground. The empress, greatly alarmed, returned home, and St. Chrysostom, coming out to the man, said, "Let be, suffer thus far;" then, making a short prayer, he healed the withered arm. St. Chrysostom was exiled for this offence. —Socratês, *Ecclesiastical History*, bk. vi. chap. 16.

Lucretius covets the vineyard of St. Beatrice (A.D. 300). Lucretius, deputy of Diocletian, coveted the vineyard of St. Beatrice, which he wanted to join to his own lands, and he contrived the matter thus:—He summoned St. Beatrice to appear before him, and accused her of being a Christian. Beatrice confessed the charge, and Lucretius ordered her to prison, where, during the night, she was secretly strangled. On the death of Beatrice, the deputy took possession of the vineyard, and solemnized the event by a grand feast; but when the mirth was at the highest, a woman entered the banquet-hall, with a child in her arms. The suckling instantly said, with a loud voice, which was heard by all the guests, "Lucretius, thou hast put Beatrice to death, and taken possession of her vineyard sinfully; therefore, the devil shall take possession of thee." The words were no sooner uttered, than Lucretius began to roll his eyes, and contort his face most hideously. This continued for the space of three hours, and then he died.—Edward Kinesman (1623), *Lives of the Saints* (July 29).

A anias and Sapphira.

ACTS v. 1–10. Ananias and his wife sold a possession, and, keeping back a part of the purchase price, Ananias offered the rest to the apostles, pretending it was the whole. St. Peter said to him, Ananias, why hath Satan filled thine heart to lie to the Holy Ghost? While the possession remained, was it not thine own? and after it was sold, was it not in thine own power? Ananias hearing these words, fell down, and gave up the ghost. About three hours after, Sapphira came in; and Peter asked her if they had sold the land for so much; and Sapphira said, Yea, for so much. Peter then reproved her, and she also fell down dead.

The archbishop of Ravenna is struck dead for lying (A.D. 1150). Huntfrid, archbishop of Ravenna, was a most abandoned prelate, living a licentious life with harlots. He was anathematized by the pope in the Council of Verceil. The emperor ordered him to appear at Augsburg, to render up the preferments he had obtained by simony, and to make confession of his sins that he might receive absolution. As Huntfrid lay at the pope's feet, Leo IX. said to him, "May God give you absolution according to the measure of your sincerity." The archbishop now rose to his feet, with a smile of mockery; whereupon the pope, in tears, said to those standing by, "Alas! this wretched man is on the brink of the grave." The same day Huntfrid was taken ill, and scarcely had he entered his palace at Ravenna, when he fell down dead.—Wibert, *Life of St. Leo IX.*, bk. ii. chap. 7.

The bishop of Sutri tried by false testimony to justify himself of simony, and fell dead at the feet of pope Leo IX. (A.D. 1049). The bishop of Sutri being accused of simony, was arraigned by pope Leo IX., when he denied the charge, and brought up false witnesses to support his defence; but at the very moment of the lie, he fell down dead at the pope's feet, as Ananias fell at the feet of the apostle Peter.—Wibert, *Life of St. Leo IX.*, bk. ii. chap. 3.

Another instance. In the same visitation, pope Leo IX. went to Mayence, where Sibichon, bishop of Spire, was charged with simony, and for having broken his vow of celibacy. Sibichon boldly denied the charges brought against him, and volunteered to purge himself by the ordeal of the body and blood of Christ. In punishment of "this sacrilege," his jaw became paralyzed, and remained so till he died.—Migne, *Dictionary of the Councils*, vol. ii. col. 877.

Angel of Death sheathing his Sword.

1 CHRON. xxi. 14–27. So the Lord sent pestilence upon Israel. . . . And God sent an angel to destroy the people. . . . And David lifted up his eyes and saw the angel of the Lord standing between earth and heaven, having a drawn sword in his hand, stretched out over Jerusalem. . . . And he said unto God . . . Let Thy hand, I pray Thee, be on me, but not on Thy people. . . . And the Lord commanded the angel, and he put up his sword again into its sheath.

St. Gregory the Great and the St. Angelo. When Gregory the Great was consecrated pope, a terrible pestilence was devastating Rome. Gregory forthwith organized a grand religious procession, in the forefront of which was borne a painting of the "glorious Virgin," the work of St. Luke, still preserved in the church of Santa Mari Maggiore. As the procession moved on, a thick cloud of corrupt air was seen to fly before the painting, and angels were distinctly heard, singing, *Regina Cœli lætare; Alleluja!* Pope Gregory, we are assured, distinctly saw an angel above the castle put up his bloody sword into its scabbard; and the castle, which before was called the "Moles Adriani," has ever since been called the "St. Angelo."—Edward Kinesman (1623), *Lives of the Saints*, p. 185.

Angel Visitants.

GEN. xix. 1–3. *Lot entertains two angels.* There came two angels to Sodom at even; and Lot sat in the gate of Sodom: and seeing the angels, rose up to meet them, . . . and they turned in unto him, and entered his house, and he made them a feast, and did bake unleavened bread, and they did eat.

GEN. xviii. 1–8. *Abraham entertains three angels.* The Lord appeared unto Abraham in the plains of Mamre, as he sat in the tent door in the heat of the day. And Abraham lift up his eyes, and, lo, three men stood by him: and when he saw them, he ran to meet them from the tent door, and bowed himself toward the ground, and said, My Lord, if now I have found favour in thy sight, pass not away. . . . Let a little water . . . be fetched, and wash your feet, and rest yourselves under the tree; and I will fetch a morsel of bread, and comfort ye your hearts. After that ye shall pass on. . . . And he hastened into the tent unto Sarah, and said, Make ready quickly three measures of fine meal, knead it, and make cakes upon the hearth. And he ran unto the herd, and fetched a calf tender and good, and gave it unto [his] young man, who hasted to dress it. And Abraham took butter, and milk, and the calf dressed, and set them before [the three angels], and stood by them under the tree [while] they did eat.

JUDG. xiii. 3–20. An angel appeared to Manoah and his wife, and promised them a son. And Manoah entreated the heavenly visitant to wait while a kid was dressed: but the angel declined to eat anything, so Manoah offered the kid unto the Lord, and as the smoke of the burnt offering ascended towards heaven, "the angel ascended also in the flame of the fire."

An angel teaches St. Anthony the Great how to make mats from palms (A.D. 251–356). Besides cultivating his garden, St. Anthony used to make mats. One day, being very low spirited, because his manual toils prevented him from passing more time in divine contemplation, an angel came to him, and showed him how to make mats from palm leaves. The heavenly visitant repeated his visit frequently, and said on leaving, "Do this, and thou shalt be saved." From that day St. Anthony did what the angel had taught him to do, and found it easy to keep his heart with God while his hands were well employed. So true is it that useful toil strengthens the body and invigorates the mind, but idleness ruins both.—*Les Petits Bollandistes* (1880), vol. i. p. 429.

As whatever tempts man to evil was esteemed in the early and Middle Ages a devil, so whatever aided man in the right way was considered an angel. The angel that taught St. Anthony mat-making is an example; but St. Gregory the Great, in his *Dialogues* (bk. ii.), gives a still more striking example. He says, "Two angels, in the form of two young men, showed St. Benedict the way from Subiaco to Mont Cassino, a distance of eighteen leagues. Similarly two angels guided St. Aldegundis in her flight from home." (See WALKING ON THE SEA.)

Angels chant to St. Ignatius (A.D. 107). Eusebius of Cæsarea, Socrates, and Baronius all say that St. Ignatius established the custom of chanting the Psalms antiphonally, and that the idea was suggested to him by two choirs of angels which appeared to him when he was bishop of Antioch, and in this manner chanted the praises of the Holy Trinity. Ignatius said the Church militant on earth ought to imitate the Church triumphant in heaven, and accordingly he introduced the singing in his church by alternate choirs. In Christian art the saint is represented with a harp, listening to angels on each side of him, singing antiphonally.

Angels visit St. Martin. Angels used to visit St. Martin as guests, and hold familiar converse with him. One day two of his disciples heard conversation going on in St. Martin's cell, although they well knew no living being could possibly be there with him. When the monks met at night as usual, the two disciples begged their superior to inform them who it was he had been talking with, and he said he would do so, if they would promise on their part to tell no one what he was about to reveal. This they readily agreed to do, and St. Martin told them he had received a visit in his cell from the Mother of God, St. Agnes, and St. Thecla. He furthermore said that sometimes St. Peter and St. Paul vouchsafed to be his guests.—Sulpicius Severus, *Life of St. Martin.*

We are told in the *Acta Sanctorum* (Bollandists), vol. i. June 2, that Erasmus, the recluse of Mount Liban, used to entertain angels (A.D. 301).

Jesus Christ and His angels consecrate the monastery of Meinrad (Sept. 14, A.D. 948). The following is recounted in the bull of confirmation by Leo VIII., and has been corroborated by succeeding pontiffs from Leo VIII. to Leo XIII.; so that no [Roman] Catholic can doubt its exact "historic truth." Eberhard built a church and monastery on Mount Etzel, in honour of St. Meinrad, and dedicated it to the Virgin. On Sept. 14, A.D. 948, Conrad, bishop of Constance, came to consecrate it, accompanied by the bishop of Augsburg and a large number of pilgrims. At midnight preceding the 14th, as Conrad, the monks, and pilgrims were at prayer in the nocturne, all of a sudden the dead silence was broken by a sweet melody. On raising his eyes, the bishop of Constance saw a choir of angels, and noticed that they chanted the very psalms and hymns set down for the morrow. Jesus Christ, arrayed in violet, then appeared, and celebrated the Dedicatory office. Beside him were St. Peter, St. Gregory, St. Augustine, St. Stephen, and St. Laurentius. In front of the altar sat the "Queen of Heaven on a throne of light." The angel choir continued singing, but modified the *Sanctus* thus: "O God, whose holiness is revealed in the sanctuary of the glorious Virgin Mary, have mercy on us! Blessed be the Son of Mary, who has come down hither, and lives for ever and ever." In the *Agnus Dei* they thrice repeated: "O Lamb of God, who hast mercy on those that believe in Thee, have mercy upon us! O Lamb of God, who hast pity on sinners who believe and hope, have mercy upon us! O Lamb of God, who givest peace to the living and the dead, who reign with Thee everlastingly, grant us Thy peace!" Jesus Christ then said, "Peace be with you," and the angels responded, "The Saviour is borne on the wings of the Seraphim; the Saviour descends to the depths of the abyss." Before this service was over, the time appointed for the consecration was fully come, and the crowd without became impatient, wondering why the doors were not thrown open. At length one went, and told them the reason. The church was soon filled, expecting the service to begin, but a mysterious voice repeated thrice these words: "Forbear, forbear! the church has been consecrated already." All fell to the ground on hearing these words, and felt assured that the church had indeed been consecrated by Christ and his angels. Conrad, bishop of Constance, who himself witnessed this ceremony, recorded it in writing. The calendars of Einsiedeln, which go back to the remotest ages of the Christian Church, record the same on the 14th of September, called "The Miraculous Consecration;" and the service appointed for that day is annually performed with great solemnity and pomp. The people call the fête *Engelweihe* (the Angelic Consecration). Sixteen years afterwards, the bishop of Constance, the bishop of Augsburg, and a host of princes both lay and ecclesiastic, accompanying the emperor Otto and his empress Adelaide to Rome, were present while the above narrative was repeated to pope Leo VIII. They all gave their attestations in writing, and the pope issued a bull on the subject, beginning thus: "We, Leo . . . make known to all the faithful, now and to come, that our venerable brother Conrad, bishop of Constance, has sworn to us in the presence of our dear son the emperor Otto and of the empress Adelaide, and many of the high princes of the land, that on the 14th of September, A.D. 948, he went to the hermitage of Meinrad, for the purpose of consecrating a church dedicated to the incomparable Mother of God, always a virgin." . . . Then follows verbatim what has been already recited; and, in conclusion, the pope forbids any bishop from that day forth for ever to consecrate the church, thus consecrated by Jesus Christ and his angels. The pilgrims and ecclesiastics present at the "miraculous consecration," spread abroad the news on their return to their respective abodes, and the fame of Meinrad's hermitage drew pilgrims to the spot from every part of the Christian world. It would far exceed the limits of this book to set down all the miracles said to have been performed at this hermitage, but it must not be omitted that the thousandth anniversary was celebrated on March 9th, 1861, when many miracles, attested by the best possible authority, were performed. (See BLINDNESS, A.D. 1843; PARALYSIS, 1850; HALT, 1861.)—R. P. Dom Charles Brandes, *Life of St. Meinrad* (copied by Mgr. Guérin in his *Petits Bollandistes*, vol. i. pp. 524–526).

This "Miraculous Consecration" of St. Meinrad's hermitage and church has the highest sanction that the [Roman] Catholic Church can give. It is no legend, but is set forth as an indisputable "fact." The dishonesty of Alban Butler cannot be better shown than by his entire omission of so all-important a Saint as Meinrad; and his entire silence about the "Miraculous Consecration." Even Baring-Gould, who gives the life of Meinrad, and is far more exact than Butler, omits this important event altogether.

Angels carry Souls to Paradise. (See SOUL OF MAN.)

LUKE xvi. 22. It came to pass that the beggar died, and was carried by angels into Abraham's bosom.

The soul of St. Barbara carried by angels into heaven. St. Barbara was beheaded by her own father, and as her head fell to the ground her soul was carried by angels into Abraham's bosom. —Peter Galesinus, *Apostolic Protonotary.*

St. Fructuosus and two others carried by angels to paradise (A.D. 259). St. Fructuosus and his two deacons, Augurius and Eulogius, were burnt to death by the command of Gallienus, in Tarragon. Babylas and Mygdonius, domestics of the governor, and also the daughter of Emilian the governor, affirm that they distinctly saw the three martyrs ascending to heaven, escorted by a host of angels carrying crowns. Emilian could see nothing of the kind, although his attention was directed to the spot by his daughter. "Il ne vit rien, son infidélité l'en rendant indigne."—*Les Petits Bollandistes* (7th edit. 1880), vol. i. p. 505.

The soul of St. Paul the hermit carried by angels to paradise (A.D. 341). St. Antony left St. Paul the hermit to fetch a cloak; and on his return, saw amidst a host of angels, prophets, and apostles, the spirit of the hermit, shining like the sun and white as driven snow, buoyed upwards, till the clouds received it out of sight. St. Antony, who was over ninety years of age, used to tell how he ran the rest of the way, or "rather flew as a bird," and entering the hermit's cave saw there the lifeless body. He wrapped it in the cloak, and would have buried it, but had no spade. Man's extremity is God's opportunity, for while Antony was pondering the matter over in his mind, lo! two lions came running to the cave. Antony trembled with fear, but the wild beasts showed by unmistakable signs that they meant him no harm. They went to look at the dead body, and then retreated to a small distance, and proceeded to scratch a deep hole in the earth. When the hole was large enough and deep enough for a grave, the industrious beasts, twisting their tails around the dead body, carried it to the hole, and covered it with earth. Having finished their task, they went mournfully to St. Antony, licked his hands and feet, and lowered their heads for a blessing. Antony gave them a blessing, and the lions slowly and mournfully returned to their forest lair.—St. Jerome, *Vita S. Pauli, Eremitæ*, A.D. 375.

The executioner saw the soul of Peter the exorcist carried up to heaven. When St. Peter the exorcist and St. Marcellinus were beheaded, the executioner declared he saw their souls, arrayed in white, borne up to heaven by the hands of angels.—Archbishop Ado, *Martyrology*.

The soul of St. Siviard carried to heaven by St. Peter and St. Paul (A.D. 687). À sa mort [*i.e.* St. Siviard], un des frères vit sa sainte âme, toute brillante de lumière, entre les princes des apôtres, St. Pierre et St. Paul, qui la conduisaient au ciel.—*Les Petits Bollandistes*, vol. iii. p. 89.

St. Titus carried at death by angels to paradise. When St. Titus died, Peter de Natalibus tells us "he saw angels descend from heaven in a glorious train to fetch home his immortal soul, and the face of the dead saint was radiant at their approach." The body of St. Titus was kept for a time in the cathedral of Gortyna, but is now among the "sacred treasures" of St. Mark's, in Venice.—Baring-Gould, *Lives of the Saints*, vol. i. p. 56.

Angels, in the form of butterflies, carry the soul of St. Vincent Ferrier to paradise (A.D. 1419). At the moment of the decease of St. Vincent Ferrier, the windows of his chamber flew open of their own accord, and a crowd of winged creatures, no bigger than butterflies, very beautiful and purely white, filled the whole house. As the saint gave his last sign, these winged creatures suddenly disappeared, leaving behind them an exquisite perfume. Every one was convinced they were angels, who had come to carry in triumph the soul of the saint to the paradise of God.—*Les Petits Bollandistes*, vol. iv. p. 240.

Angels entertained unawares.

HEB. xiii. 2. Be not forgetful to entertain strangers: for thereby some have entertained angels unawares.

GEN. xviii. 3–33. Abraham in the plains of Mamre entertained three strangers, and discovered that his guests were three angels sent by God to overthrow the cities of the plain.

GEN. xix. 2, etc. Lot entertained two strangers, which proved to be two angels sent to deliver him from the destruction of Sodom.

St. Cuthbert, entertaining strangers, entertains an angel unawares (seventh century). Eatas, abbot of Mailros, being called to govern the new abbey of Rippon, took Cuthbert with him, and committed to him the very difficult task of entertaining strangers. Once at least, in the execution of this office, St. Cuthbert had the honour of entertaining an angel, who, in return of his hospitality, left on the table three loaves of bread, of such exquisite whiteness and taste, there could be no doubt of their being "bread from heaven."

This was not the only time, by many, that he enjoyed the good offices of angels, for he often saw them, often conversed with them, and was often fed by them. Before he entered the priory of Mailros, he was healed by an angel of an abscess in the knee, which prevented his walking; and on his return from Rippon to Mailros, he was, contrary to all expectation, cured by an angel of the plague.—Bede, *Church History*, bk. iv. chap. 27–32; *Acta Sanctorum*, March 20.

Angels have Charge of the Saints. (See SUSANNA AND THE ELDERS.)

PSALM xci. 11. He shall give His angels charge over thee, to keep thee in all thy ways.

PSALM xxxiv. 7. The angel of the Lord encampeth round about them that fear Him, and delivereth them.

GEN. xix. 16. When God was about to destroy Sodom, His angels took Lot, and Lot's wife, and their two daughters by the hand, and led them beyond the city that they might be safe from harm.

DAN. iii. 28. When Shadrach, Meshach, and Abednego were cast into the fiery furnace by order of Nebuchadnezzar, the Lord sent an angel "to deliver His servants who trusted in Him."

DAN. vi. 22. When Daniel was cast into the lions' den, king Darius next morning went to the cave, and said, O Daniel, servant of the living God, is thy God . . . able to deliver thee from the lions? And Daniel replied, O king . . . my God hath sent His angel, and hath shut the lions' mouths, [so] that they have not hurt me.

MATT. xviii. 10. Take heed that ye despise not one of these little ones; for I say unto you, that in heaven their angels do always behold the face of My Father which is in heaven.

St. Euphrasia protected by angels from the malignity of Satan (A.D. 412). St. Euphrasia was, on one occasion, pushed by the devil into a pond, but her good angel held her above water, till assistance came from the convent, and she was drawn out.

On another occasion the devil pushed her from a third-story window to the ground, but she was neither hurt nor bruised; for God gave His angels charge concerning her, to keep her in all her ways.—Surius, *Lives of the Saints*, vol. ii.

Angels charged to keep St. Francis of Paula in all his ways (A.D. 1416–1507). While St. Francis of Paula offered himself a living sacrifice to God, holy and acceptable, the Almighty exempted him from the ills that flesh is heir to. He always went barefooted over burning sands, cold snow, sharp stones, rugged rocks, gnarled roots, prickly thorns, and defiling mud; but hundreds testify that burning sands distressed him not, the sharpest stones wounded him not, the roughest rocks bruised him not, ice and snow chilled him not, thorns and briars pricked him not, and defiling mud soiled him not, because God gave His angels charge concerning him, to keep him in all his ways. Though he was always handling tools to assist his workmen, his hands were as delicate as if he had confined himself to his books. Though he never changed his habit, night or day, it had no disagreeable smell, but exhaled, on the contrary, a delightful odour. Though he practised austerities almost incredible, his face was never pinched, but plump and rosy, his eyes brilliant, his countenance serene and benevolent, and even in old age he was neither wrinkled nor grey-headed. He was an Adam, and this earth was a paradise, where he talked and walked with God and His angels.—Antonio Staramella, *Letter to Pope Leo X.*

An angel had charge of St. Francisca, to keep her in all her ways (1384–1440). God had given St. Francisca a guardian angel not only to keep her from the power of evil spirits, but also to guide her in all her ways. The angel never left her for a single moment; and sometimes, by special favour, her eyes were opened to see him face to face. She says he was of incredible beauty, his countenance being whiter than snow and redder than the blush rose; his eyes were always uplifted towards heaven; his long curly hair was in colour like burnished gold; his robe, which extended to the ground, was sometimes white, sometimes blue, and at other times a shining red. From his face proceeded a radiance so luminous, she could see to read her matins thereby even at midnight. Her ghostly father commanded her to show him this angel, so she took the angel by the hand, and introduced him. Her father confessor, speaking thereof in the monastery, said, the proportions of the angel introduced to him by St. Francisca were those of a child five or six years old.—From the *Acts of her Canonization*, May 29, A.D. 1606.

St. Marcellinus, bishop of Embrun, being pushed down a steep rock, is borne in the arms of angels (A.D. 370). The Arians were especially embittered against St. Marcellinus, bishop of Embrun, because they knew him to be their most formidable opponent. One day, a number of these "heretics" seized him, and, carrying him to the top of a steep rock, pushed him down; but angels had charge of him, and bore him in their arms to the bottom, so that he received no sort of injury.—Mons. Depéry, *Hagiographie de Gap.*

Angels bear up in their hands the infant Marianne de Jesus (A.D. 1618–1645). The reader must be warned beforehand that the following "historic fact" is recorded, for the edification of the Church, by no less an authority than the chamberlain of pope Leo XIII., and the book it is extracted from is of the nineteenth century (7th edit. 1880). Dom Jerome of Quito died while his daughter Marianne was a babe in arms. The mother, to solace her grief, retired from Quito to a country house, and carried her baby in her arms, riding on a mule. A brook or rivulet had to be forded, and as the water was much swollen, the mule stumbled, and the child was jerked from the mother's arms. Of course, the mother thought the babe had fallen into the stream, and as it could not be seen there, she supposed it had been carried away by the rapid current. Judge, however, of her surprise when she discovered that her babe was suspended in the air by the invisible hands of angels, and had never touched the water.—*Vies des Saints*, vol. vi. p. 230.

The chamberlain gives us his authority—J. F. Godescard, who died in 1800, the translator of Alban Butler into French. The reader will not need to be told that the above is not taken from Butler. No; it is given as a continuation of Ribadeneira, who died in 1611, about seven years before this wonderful child was born.

Angels sent to give Consolation. (See HARM, etc.; and HAPPY IN SUFFERING.)

MATT. iv. 11. After the temptations we are told that the devil left Jesus, and angels came and ministered unto Him.

LUKE xxii. 43. In His agony in the garden, Christ prayed, saying, Father, if Thou be willing, remove this cup from Me: nevertheless not My will, but Thine, be done. And there appeared an angel unto Him from heaven, strengthening Him.

Angels sent to console St. Andeol in his terrible tortures (A.D. 208). When the emperor Severus was on his way to Great Britain, he stopped at Bergoïate, and, observing a great concourse of people, asked the reason. He was informed they had assembled to hear St. Andeol preach about the crucified Jesus, and he ordered him to be sent for. After trying various means to make the saint renounce his faith, and finding all his efforts ineffectual, he handed him to the torturers, who at a given signal threw him on the ground, tied ropes to his hands and feet, and by means of pulleys stretched the tendons to their very utmost, and then scourged him with rods charged with points of iron. This over, they tore his flesh from head to foot with red-hot iron hooks, and, while the body was bleeding, bound it on a wheel, beneath which was a fire fed with oil. Andeol betrayed no sign of pain, but said, as the wheel turned slowly round, "Blessed be the name of God, and my Saviour Jesus, who have thought me worthy to suffer thus. Leave me not, O my Saviour, nor suffer me for any pains of death to fall from Thee." Severus, who was present all this while, "despairing, but not vanquished," now ordered the martyr to be taken to prison, and reserved for other tortures on the morrow. At the suggestion of Cericius, tribune of the Roman legions, the suffering saint was thrust into the crypt of the temple of Mars, on the bank of the Rhone. At midnight, the guards were greatly alarmed by seeing this souterrain brilliantly illuminated, and hearing thousands of voices in mysterious colloquy with the prisoner, or singing celestial music. They heard these words amongst others—"Courage, dear brother; to-morrow thou shalt be with us in paradise." They then applied healing balm to his wounds; and, when he was brought the next day to the tribunal, the emperor was amazed to find him in perfect health and joyous spirits. "Off with his head," roared Severus in a fury, "or the magician will corrupt the whole city!" A soldier, armed with a sword made of some very hard wood, such as those used by gladiators in the arena, cleft the head of the martyr "in the form of a cross;" and so he died.—Bollandists, *Acta Sanctorum*, vol. i. pp. 38, 39, May 1.

This extract has an antiquarian interest. It shows that the swords used by gladiators were not of metal, but some hard wood; and furthermore, that Roman soldiers, in some cases at least, were armed with these swords. We are told by antiquaries that in the early ages the Roman swords were made of brass (or a mixed metal), and in later times of iron, but neither Adams nor Rich mentions the wooden sword.

St. Concord, in torture, consoled by an angel. St. Concord was condemned by Torquatus, governor of Umbria, to be beaten with clubs and then hung on "the little horse" (see CHEVALET), a kind of rack. As he was led back to prison, heavily laden with chains on his hands and neck, he sang praises to God on the way. At night the angel of the Lord stood by him and said, "Fear not, beloved one, but play the man; for I am with thee. The God of Israel is thy strength; His rod and His staff shall comfort thee."—See Baring-Gould, *Lives of the Saints* (January, p. 5).

St. Euphemia in torture visited by an angel. St. Euphemia, in the reign of Diocletian, was martyred by Priscus, proconsul of Chalcedon. She was first impaled on the eculeus, or equileus (*q.v.*), by which all her limbs were pulled out of joint; then she was lashed to the wheel; but God sent an angel to comfort her, and he not only broke the wheel, but also slew the officers who were torturing her. The friends of the officers, greatly enraged against Euphemia, now kindled a huge fire, and cast her into the midst of it; but again the angel interposed and quenched the fire, so that she received no harm. Being taken from the fire she was cast to the lions, which mercifully killed her, but neither devoured her body, nor so much as mangled it.—Ado (archbishop of Vienne), *Martyrology*.

St. George of Diospolis comforted, in torture, by an angel. After St. George had been racked on the wheel, by order of the emperor Diocletian, it was thought by the tormentors that he was dead; and Diocletian, who was present, said scoffingly, "George, where is now thy God? Why does He not help thee?" So saying he left the dungeon, and went to the temple of Apollo to pay his adorations. Scarcely had he passed the prison gate, when a loud peal of thunder was heard, and a voice came from the cloud, saying, "Fear not, O man of God, for I am with thee. Stand fast in the faith, and many shall be brought to the knowledge of God by thy example." Then appeared to the martyr an angel, who loosed him from the wheel, healed his wounds, and bade him proceed without delay to the temple of Apollo and show himself to the emperor.

Diocletian was thunderstruck at seeing him, and could scarcely believe his eyes; but the empress Alexandra and the two chief captains of the imperial guard were converted to the faith, saying, "No other god can deliver after this sort."—Pasicrates (an intimate friend of St. George, and an eye-witness of his sufferings).

St. Julian comforted by angels. In the great persecution of Diocletian, St. Julian was seized, and subjected to most cruel tortures. Between which the governor Marcian ordered him to be laden with chains and dragged about the city. In one of these parades the martyr was led past the school where the governor's son, Celsus, was placed, and the boys were turned out to see him pass. As he came down the street, Celsus cried aloud, "I see angels comforting him, and holding out to him a crown of glory." This vision had such an effect upon the lad, that he ran up to the martyr and kissed his feet. Marcian was furious, and ordered both Julian and Celsus to be thrust into a noisome dungeon; but the dungeon was instantly redolent of celestial odours, and illuminated with a divine light, so that the keepers marvelled greatly, and became converts to the new faith.—The Bollandists, *Acta Sanctorum.*

The writer says, "We set down what we ourselves saw with our own eyes."

St. Lawrence, under torture, strengthened by an angel. St. Lawrence was racked on the catasta (*q.v.*), in which the limbs are drawn back and then pulled out of joint. Romanus, a Roman soldier, who witnessed the torture, went up to the martyr and said, "Lawrence, I see a most beautiful young man standing beside thee, and wiping off the blood and sweat as they fall from thee in thine agony. It is a blessed angel, Lawrence, sent from heaven to comfort and strengthen thee. There is no god like thy God, and I am resolved that thy God shall be my God, and Him only will I serve." When the martyr was taken from the rack, Romanus brought water, and was baptized by him. —Edward Kinesman (1623), *Life of St. Lawrence*, p. 605.

Christ and seven angels come to console the brothers Mark and Marcellian (A.D. 288). Mark and Marcellian were twins, of noble family and great wealth. They were both married and had families. Being converts of Sebastian, they were kept prisoners in the house of Nicostratus, and condemned to death unless they recanted. Thirty days' respite was accorded to them, during which interval their parents, wives, and children implored them to relent. They were furthermore promised high state offices and large rewards; but St. Sebastian, on the other hand, exhorted them to remain faithful unto death, when they would receive a crown of glory and everlasting life. After St. Sebastian had finished his exhortation, Christ Himself with seven angels descended into the prison, gave St. Sebastian the kiss of peace, and said to him, "Good and faithful servant, thou shalt be ever with Me." Zoe, the wife of Nicostratus, had been dumb for six years, and was a great invalid. She saw the light and the angels; and, falling at the feet of St. Sebastian, indicated by signs her wish to be baptized. St. Sebastian said to her, "If your wish is sincere, Jesus Christ will make you whole;" and immediately her speech returned to her, and her health was re-established. Nicostratus, seeing this miracle, was converted also, and said to Mark and Marcellian, "You are free to depart, and if the emperor insists on punishing me for this breach of duty, I will gladly lay down my life for your sake." Sebastian told Nicostratus to bring into the chamber all his other prisoners, and Claudius the jailer brought in sixteen malefactors heavily laden with chains. Sebastian addressed the assembly, and all were converted and baptized. At the end of the thirty days the converts were brought before Chromacius the prefect, when Chromacius and his son became converts. The end of this long story is this: Zoe was hung to the branch of a tree, and a fire was kindled under her feet; so she died, and her body was cast into the Tiber. Nicostratus and five others were drowned in the Tiber. Mark and Marcellian were nailed head downwards to a post, and stabbed with lances till they were dead; when their bodies were buried in a sandpit two miles from the city. The son of Chromacius was thrown into a ditch and buried alive. Chromacius resigned his office and retired to Campania. As for St. Sebastian, being bound to a post, a company of archers discharged their arrows at him. It was supposed he was dead; but when the widow of Castulus went at night to bury him, she found him still alive, took him home, and in a few days he completely recovered. The Christians wished him to secrete himself, but he boldly went into the temple of Jupiter, and accosted the emperor Diocletian as he was about to enter. "O emperor," he said, "your pontiffs deceive you. They invent many charges against us Christians: but know, O emperor, the Christians are your best subjects, who never cease praying for your conversion." Diocletian was thunderstruck at being thus addressed by a man he supposed to be dead; but, recovering from his surprise, he said, "What! is it you, Sebastian? I thought my archers had done their duty better." "Emperor," replied Sebastian, "Jesus Christ has spared my life a little while, that I may be a witness to the people of the true faith and of thy cruelty." "Off with the wretch," cried Diocletian in rage; "off with him to the hippodrome, and there scourge the life out of him." So he was scourged to death, and his body cast into the city sewer.—The abbot Corblet, *Hagiography of Amiens.*

An angel sent to console St. Meinrad tormented with devils (797–861). When St. Meinrad retired to his hermitage in Mount Etzel, he was beset by a band of black demons so thick and numberless that they shut from his sight the light of day. They rounded in his ears the most terrible threats, whirled about him in the most frightful postures, assumed the most hideous forms conceivable, and made such an uproar it seemed as if all the trees of the forest were being blown down with a crash. St. Meinrad remained calm, intrepid, and prayerful. Suddenly an angel descended, its face radiant, its countenance benignant. Smiling on the hermit, it said to him, "Courage, Meinrad, and trust in God; those that set their love on Him, He will deliver. Those that call on Him, He will answer." So saying, he drove the devils into the abyss, and they never after returned to trouble the man of God. —R. P. Dom Charles Brandes, *Life of St. Meinrad.*

St. Sergius in torture visited by an angel. Sergius was primicetius or chief secretary of the emperor Maximian; but when Maximian learnt that he was a Christian, he plucked from him his gold chain, and, stripping him of his robes, had him arrayed in woman's garments. After sundry other torments, his feet being thrust into shoes studded with sharp spikes, he was chained to the imperial chariot, and made to run nine miles. Blood gushed from his feet along the road, and the agony was indescribable; but at night an angel came to comfort him and heal his wounds. Next day he was again subjected to the same torture, and again the angel came to heal his wounds. The tyrant, seeing himself thus foiled, commanded his victim to be beheaded. As the martyr knelt before the headsman, he heard a voice from heaven inviting him to paradise, and congratulating him on his victory; and saw a company of shining ones with golden crowns in their hands waiting to receive him, as soon as he had sealed a life of holiness with a death of glory.—Edward Kinesman (1623), *Lives of the Saints*, pp. 816–818.

Mention is made of St. Sergius in the Second Nicene Council, Act v.

St. Theodorus of Heraclea consoled in torture by an angel (A.D. 319). When Licinius was informed that his general Theodorus was a Christian, he sent for him, and invited him to accompany the court to a grand sacrifice. Theodorus begged to see the gods before he adored them; and the emperor, thinking he had won back his brave soldier, commanded the priests to take the idols to his house. No sooner were they left, than Theodorus broke them up, and distributed the gold and silver, of which they were made, to the poor. The emperor, of course, was mad with rage, and sent officers to punish him. They first laid him face downwards on the ground, and gave him five hundred lashes on his back, with whips made of bulls' hide; then, turning him round, administered fifty more. After this, they pummelled him with flagra or leaden plummets (see FLAGRUM), tore his flesh with hooks, and cauterized the wounds with torches and hot irons. Being well-nigh dead, the martyr was sent to prison to be reserved for fresh tortures. Here he was kept five days without food or water, and was then fixed to a gibbet, while men employed for the purpose stuck him constantly in all the most sensitive parts of the body, stoned him, and insulted him in every imaginable way. When Licinius thought he was dead he left him, intending next morning to cast the body into the sea. At midnight an angel appeared to the martyr, healed his wounds, and said to him, "Rejoice, Theodorus, for Christ is with you, and will never leave you or forsake you. Fight the good fight and faint not, for great will be your reward in heaven." Next day the emperor sent two centurions to take down the body and cast it into the sea; but to their amazement they found the gibbet empty, and Theodorus in perfect health. The miracle was without gainsaying, and both the centurions were converted, with eighty of the men under them. Licinius, being informed of the affair, sent Sextus, the proconsul, with three hundred soldiers to behead the centurions and their eighty converts; but no sooner did this new company reach the spot, than they also were converted. The whole populace now took the side of Theodorus against the emperor, and shouted, "Long live the God of the Christians! The Lord He is God, and there is none else!" They would have deposed Licinius, but Theodorus forbade them, saying, "Vengeance belongeth unto God, and the wrath of man worketh not the righteousness of God." Theodorus was now carried in triumph through the city, and as he passed the state prison the chains of the prisoners fell off, the gates flew open, and the prisoners were free. Licinius, fearing a sedition, sent men to behead Theodorus; so he died, and his body was taken to Heraclea, and buried there.—Augard, *Life of St. Theodorus of Heraclea.*

Alban Butler gives a very expurgated account of this saint, and says, "The Greek Acts of his martyrdom, under the name of Augarus, are of no authority;" but a far better authority than Alban Butler, viz. Mgr. Guérin, chamberlain of pope Leo XIII., flatly contradicts this assertion, and tells us, "Le martyre de saint Théodore fut écrit par un auteur nommé Augard, qui s'y trouve présent, et qui fut prié par le saint même de l'écrire, et de faire porter ses reliques à Euchaïte pour les ensevelir dans l'heritage de ses ancêtres; et d'ordonner que, quand lui-même mourrait, on le mît dans son sépulcre à sa gauche."—*Vies des Saintes*, Feb. 7.

Angels sent to succour St. Venantius in his terrible tortures (A.D. 250). St. Venantius, having reproved Antiochus for worshipping false gods, was given over to the governor's soldiers, who were commanded "de lui faire endurer tous les supplices imaginables." They first tied the young man to a post, and scourged him with such savage cruelty, that he must have died, if an angel had not come from heaven, to loose him from his bonds, and drive away the butchers; but the soldiers, instead of being touched by this marvel, only returned to their task with greater savagery. They hung the young martyr to a tree by his feet, and burned him all over with flaming torches; then, forcing open his mouth, tried to suffocate him with the smoke of the stinking brands. Anastasius, the cornicular, who was present, saw an angel, robed in white, untie the saint from the tree, and heal his wounds. This vision caused his conversion, and, being baptized by Porphyry, he died a martyr. Antiochus, supposing Venantius to be dead, was not a little surprised to hear the way he had been delivered. Still hoping to bend his "obstinacy," because he was so young, he commanded him to be brought before him again; but neither threats nor promises had the least effect, so the governor ordered him back to prison, and sent a soldier, named Attalus, to try and win him over by guile. Attalus pretended he had himself been a Christian, and had given up the substantial good things of this life, for the shadowy promises of the life to come; but it did not pay, and he had returned to his senses. The saint saw at once through the artifice, and told Attalus so. Antiochus, still more angry at this miscarriage, had Venantius again brought before him, broke all his teeth, tore his gums from the jaws, and then bade his soldiers cast him into the city sewer, expecting he would soon be suffocated. Here, however, an angel came to him, drew him out, and healed his wounds, that he might be prepared for still greater triumphs. The prefect, in the mean time, died suddenly, crying with his last breath, "Venantius's God is the only true God, and those of Rome are no gods." When Antiochus was told this, he exclaimed, "The fellow will corrupt half Camerino. Take him," he added to his soldiers, "and cast him to the lions." So he was cast into the amphitheatre; but when the lions saw him, they lay fawning at his feet like lambs, and he stood in the arena, preaching the gospel of grace to the spectators, and converting many. Nothing could exceed the fury of Antiochus when he heard this, and he commanded his officers to drag the incorrigible wretch over thorns and brambles. This was done with such barbarity for two days, that he was more than half-dead; but again an angel came and healed his wounds, and again he was taken before the governor. "Cast him from the rock," roared Antiochus, "and break every bone in his skin." This punishment, however, was equally futile as the others, for angels bore him in their hands, and not a hair of him was hurt. "Away with him! away with him!" cried the governor; "let me see his face no more. Drag him a thousand paces beyond the gates over the rocks, and have done with him." The men were so exhausted with this task that they fainted with fatigue, whereupon Venantius, making the sign of the cross upon a large rock, there issued from the ground a spring of delicious water. This rock and this spring still exist to attest the truth of the miracle, and in the church of Camerino there is a carving of the saint, commemorating the event. Hundreds were converted on seeing these things, and many of them suffered for their faith with their lives. At length Venantius died; but, as he gave up his spirit, the earth quaked, thunder and lightning terrified the people, and Antiochus, fleeing from the city in affright, died miserably. The body of Venantius was buried with great honour, and the money of Camerino was stamped with his image and superscription.

This certainly is a most marvellous story, but Cardinal Baronius tells us all that is false or overstated in some accounts has been eliminated from this account by the Church, and that what is here recorded may be depended on as simple unvarnished truth. His words are, "Il est vrai, que les Actes de St. Venant, martyr, qu'il a vus à Camerino, sont remplis de choses apocryphes; mais l'église en a retranché les mensonges, et ne nous en a donné que ce qu'elle a jugé être conforme à la vérité."—*Remarques.* He has not told us how the Church was inspired to know better than the people of Camerino, among whom the martyr lived, suffered, and died. As far as one can judge with private judgment, nothing in the original history could possibly be too hard to be believed, if what remains is indeed "retranched from all falsehood," and made "conformable to simple truth."

Angels sent to comfort St. Vincent in his torture (A.D. 304). After being put to the "question" (*q.v.*) St. Vincent was carried back to his dungeon, and laid on broken potsherds; but God sent angels to comfort him, and his cell was illuminated with light from heaven. Then his bonds fell from him, and the broken potsherds seemed a bed of roses and other fragrant flowers.—Metaphrastês (from the original Acts by the Notaries of the Church).

Angels' Food given to Man.

Psalm lxxviii. 25. Man did eat angels' food.

Angels' food given by the Virgin Mary to St. Avoya, or Advisa (A.D. 234). St. Avoya, being taken captive by the Huns, was confined in prison, because she refused to marry her captor; but Christ, whom she had chosen for her Spouse, illumined her prison with celestial light, and sent an angel to tell her her martyrdom was deferred, that by suffering she might win a brighter crown of glory. The Saviour also told her that the Virgin Mary would be her foster-mother as long as she remained in prison. Accordingly, this Mother of God and Queen of Heaven sent to her every week three loaves of bread, kneaded by the hands of angels. The whiteness of this bread exceeded infinitely that used in the palace of her father Quintian, a petty king of Sicily, and its sweetness exceeded in delicacy and flavour any food made by mortals. In Christian art, St. Avoya is represented as receiving angels' bread, from the hand of the Virgin, through the iron grating of a prison cell.—Arthus du Moustier, *Martyrologe des Saintes Femmes.*

St. Clara has angels' food given to her (A.D. 1346). Meditating one day on the Saviour's fast, St. Clara resolved to drink nothing for forty days. When brought to the brink of the grave by this abstinence, a cup of gold, filled with a celestial beverage, was brought to her from heaven, and drinking therefrom her thirst was entirely assuaged. Jesus Christ Himself brought her, at night, a sweet drink which sufficed for the last twelve years of her life, during all which time she drank nothing except the wine of the Eucharist, accomplissant ainsi les paroles du prophète Jérémie, "Il y aura des personnes qui ne pourront plus boire de vin, ni d'eau; et qui n' auront soif que de l'Agneau sans tache."—*Les Petits Bollandistes*, vol. ii. p. 440.

Melancthon's story about angels' food Melancthon used to assert that he "knew of a surety the following fact":—A woman of Cignea sent her son in midwinter to fetch home her cattle feeding by the woodside. The boy did not return, and three days afterwards was found sitting in an open place of the wood where there was no snow. He did not know that three days had well-nigh passed since he left home, but said he was waiting for the night to come. When asked if he had eaten anything, he replied, "There came a man to me who gave me bread and cheese." Now follows the marvellous inference of Melancthon, who naïvely remarks, "This man who gave the boy food was undoubtedly an angel, for no human creature could have supplied him with bread and cheese in such a place in the middle of winter." It is a pity to be so prosaic as to ask why it was impossible for some rustic to give the poor boy food. The boy certainly thought his good Samaritan was a man, and probably you and I think so too. The story is told in Turner's *History of Remarkable Providences* (1697).

Annunciation.

(See Barren Women; Mothers; etc.)

LUKE i. 28-33. The angel Gabriel was sent from God to a city of Galilee, named Nazareth, and said to Mary, Hail, thou that art highly favoured, the Lord is with thee; blessed art thou among women. And, behold, thou shalt bring forth a son, and shalt call his name JESUS. He shall be great, and shall be called the Son of the Highest.

LUKE i. 11-14. An angel appeared to Zacharias, and said to him, Fear not, Zacharias: for thy prayer is heard, and thy wife Elisabeth shall bear thee a son, and thou shalt call his name JOHN. And thou shalt have joy and gladness, for many shall rejoice at his birth.

JUDGES xiii. 2-5. The angel of the Lord appeared to the wife of Manoah, and said to her, Thou shalt conceive, and bear a son. No razor shall come upon his head, for the child shall be a Nazarite unto God, and he shall begin to deliver Israel out of the hands of the Philistines.

Annunciation of an angel to the mother of Eucher (A.D. 687). While the mother of Eucher was in the church at Orleans, where she had gone to spend the day in prayer, a venerable man, clothed in white, said to her, "God be with you, thou well-beloved of the Lord. Thou art carrying in thy womb a son, which God has elected from all eternity to be the bishop of this city Orleans." The woman knew it was an angel who had spoken to her, and prayed that God would bless the child about to be born.—*Les Petits Bollandistes*, vol. ii. p. 603.

Anointing the Sick with Oil.

JAMES v. 14, 15. Is any sick among you? let him call for the elders of the Church; and let them pray over him, anointing him with oil in the name of the Lord, . . . and the Lord shall raise him up; and if he have committed sins, they shall be forgiven him.

MARK vi. 13. They cast out many devils, and anointed with oil many that were sick, and healed them.

St. Melanius anoints with oil king Eusebius and Aspasia (sixth century). Eusebius, king of Vannes, having made an incursion into Comblessac, put out the eyes and cut off the hands of a large number of the inhabitants. The night following, he was tormented with intolerable pains, which his physicians were wholly unable to assuage. Soon afterwards his daughter, Aspasia, suffered convulsions so violent that they were ascribed to demoniacal possession. St. Melanius was sent for, and said, "O king, this affliction is not unto death, but is sent in chastisement, and to lead you to repentance." Then, anointing the king three times with holy oil, he was restored to perfect health. After which Melanius went to Aspasia, prayed over her, and she also was cured. In reward of these services, the king gave St. Melanius all the land of Comblessac in support of his monastery of Platz.—Gui Alexis Lobineau, *Histoire des Saints de Bretagne* (1724).

Apparitions.

MATT. xxvii. 52, 53. The graves were opened; and many bodies of the saints which slept arose, and came out of [their] graves, and went into the holy city, and appeared to many.

1 COR. xv. 3-8. Christ died for our sins, . . . was buried, and rose again the third day: . . . and was seen of Cephas, then of the twelve: after that, he was seen of above five hundred brethren at once; . . . then of James; then of all the apostles. And last of all he was seen of me also.

ACTS x. 30-32. Four days ago I was fasting until this hour; and at the ninth hour I prayed in my house, and, behold, a man stood before me in bright clothing, and said, Cornelius, thy prayer is heard. . . . Send therefore to Joppa, and call hither Simon, whose surname is Peter; . . . who, when he cometh, shall speak unto thee.

ACTS i. 10, 11. While they looked steadfastly towards heaven, two men stood by them in white apparel, and said, Ye men of Galilee, why stand ye gazing up into heaven? This same Jesus, which is taken up from you into heaven, shall so come in like manner as ye have seen Him go into heaven.

MATT. xxviii. 2-6. Behold, there was a great earthquake: for the angel of the Lord descended from heaven and rolled back the stone from the door, and sat upon it. His countenance was like lightning, and his raiment white as snow; and he said to the women, Fear not: for I know that ye seek Jesus, which was crucified. He is not here: for He is risen, as He said.

DAN. x. (Too long to transcribe.)

ACTS xvi. 9. A vision appeared to Paul at Troas in the night. There stood a man of Macedonia, and prayed him, saying, Come over into Macedonia, and help us.

Without passing any opinion on the Biblical apparitions, every one knows that either a defect of blood (*anæmia*), or a superfluity thereof (*hyperæmia*), will account for almost all visions of ghosts. The unhealthy diet of the saints would be amply sufficient to make the following apparitions veritable *truths* to the seers, but simply the effects of diseased function, from anæmia or hyperæmia, in the eye of a skilful medical man. The ghosts seen by Hamlet were of the former character, those seen by Macbeth of the latter. The mind or thought of the seer for the most part determines the form assumed in apparitions. There cannot be the slightest doubt about the truth of ghosts and apparitions; but at the same time the cause is well known. They are not the dead revisiting the earth, but the natural exhibits of an over-excited brain; and remember it is the brain that sees, and not the eyes. The eyes act as a telegraphic clock to set force in motion, but that force can be set in motion without the clock in fifty ways.

The ghost of an abbot appears to St. Peter Celestine (1221-1296). St. Peter Celestine, being at Faifola, had great qualms of conscience about his worthiness to administer the holy sacrament, and had made up his mind to abandon the priestly office; but the abbot of Faifola, who had recently died, appeared to him, and told him it was God's will he should continue to say mass. "As to the scruple of merit," said the ghost, "who, I ask, is worthy to administer a service so august? The angels themselves are not. Sacrifice, sacrifice, my son, but always with fear and reverence." Celestine told his confessor what the ghost had said to him, and the confessor exhorted him to obey the heavenly vision, lest haply he should be found fighting against God.

Another instance. After this vision, in 1251, Celestine retired to Mount Majella with two disciples. Here, for three years, a mysterious dove, whiter than snow, used to light on his oratory; the sound of celestial bells was often heard, especially at the elevation of the host, and not unfrequently voices were heard singing in the air. When his new church was dedicated, St. Peter Celestine saw angels, clothed in white raiments, and heard them say, "Let us go to the dedication;" and while he was celebrating the office, one of the angels let fall upon his shoulders a garment like their own.—*The Admirable Life of St. Peter Celestine*, pope. (From the press of the Celestines, Bar le Duc.)

St. Agatha appears to St. Lucy, and heals Eutitia. Eutitia, the mother of St. Lucy, being afflicted with a bloody flux which no medical skill could cure, was induced by her daughter to visit the relics of St. Agatha in Catanea. When Eutitia and her daughter reached the tomb, Lucy prayed that the saint would vouchsafe to intercede for her mother, that she might be cured of her infirmity. While still in prayer, St. Agatha stood before her. She was accompanied with a heavenly host of angels, and said to the damsel, "Sister Lucy, why ask of me what you can yourself give unto your mother? Make your petition to God, for be assured if He loves me, He no less loves you also. If He will hearken to my prayers, so will He unto thine. If I am honoured as a saint here in Catanea, you shall be honoured as a saint in Syracuse." When Lucy had seen the vision, she rose from her knees, and found her mother perfectly restored. They gave thanks to God and St. Agatha, and then returned, filled with joy, back to their home again.—Ado (archbishop of Vienne), *Martyrology*. (See also Bede.)

Apparition of St. Agnes to her mother (A.D. 304). St. Agnes was brutally murdered, at the age of thirteen, by a Roman prefect, because she refused to marry his son. Eight days after her death she appeared to her mother, encompassed by a band of angelic virgins. She was dressed in a robe of gold cloth, studded with precious stones; on her head she wore a garland of pearls and diamonds, and in her arms she carried a lamb whiter than snow. She went to her mother and said, "Weep not for me, dear mother, as for the dead; but rather rejoice with exceeding joy that I reign with Christ in the kingdom of heaven." So saying she vanished out of sight, accompanied by her attendant virgins.—Mgr. Guérin (chamberlain to pope Leo XIII.), *Life of the Saints*, vol. i. p. 511.

An angel appears to St. Eleutherius, and brings him a pardon for king Clovis. When Clovis won the great victory of Tolbiac he was guilty of many barbarities, and Eleutherius met him at the door of the church, as he was about to enter to return thanks to God. "Seigneur king," said the bishop, "I know why you have come hither." Clovis protested he had nothing in particular to say to the bishop. "Say not so, O king," replied Eleutherius. "You have sinned, and dare not avow it." Then the king, bursting into tears, implored the bishop to entreat God's pardon for him. Eleutherius spent the whole night in prayer, and next day, at the celebration of mass, just as the host was elevated, a brilliant light filled the church, and an angel came to the bishop and said, "Eleutherius, thou servant of the living God, thy prayers are heard." So saying he placed in his hands a writing, which was a pardon of the king's sins. Clovis, being thus absolved by God Himself, rendered humble and hearty thanks to the Almighty, and made many magnificent gifts to the church at Tournai.—*Les Petits Bollandistes*, vol. ii. p. 601.

Mgr. Guérin subjoins this excellent remark: "The bold remonstrance of Eleutherius, the repentance of the king, the angel bringing a pardon from heaven, whether true or not, form an admirable picture of the popular mode of thought at the period."

Three angels appear to St. Nicholas de Flue (A.D. 1417–1487). While St. Nicholas de Flue, called by the Germans brother Klaus, was engaged on his house affairs (for he had a wife and ten children), three men of venerable mien addressed him: "Tell us, Nicholas," said one of them, "will you place both your body and soul under our charge?" "I can place them," he replied, "only under the charge of the Lord God Omnipotent. I have long wished to live to Him alone." The three strangers looked at each other and sighed. "If," said the first speaker, "you will give yourself body and soul to God, I will promise you, when you are seventy years old, you shall be taken from the troubles of this world; and as you have carried the cross with patience, you shall bear a banner in the army of God." So saying, the three men vanished from his sight.—Henry de Gundelfingen, *Life of St. Nicholas de Flue* (1488).

The apparition of St. Bacchus appears to Sergius. St. Bacchus was beaten to death by lashes made of ox sinews, but after death appeared to his companion Sergius to exhort him to remain steadfast in the faith, nothing doubting. He shone with celestial glory and brightness, and spoke of the joys unspeakable which God had prepared for him, in recompense of the light afflictions which he had endured for Christ's sake upon earth. He earnestly entreated Sergius to bear patiently the martyrdom which awaited him, looking forward to the recompense of reward.—E. Kinesman, *Lives of the Saints* (1623, Oct. 9).

St. Barbara brings the eucharist to Kostka (1550–1568). While Stanislaus Kostka was preparing for his admission into the Society of Jesus, he was prostrated by a violent and dangerous sickness, which reduced him to such extremity that his physicians gave him over. The young man was sore afflicted, not from any fear of death, but because he had no means of receiving the holy sacrament, as his hostess was a "heretic." In this perplexity he earnestly commended himself to St. Barbara, praying with great fervour that he might not die without partaking of the blessed eucharist. As he lay awake upon his bed at midnight, St. Barbara came to him, with two angels bearing the holy elements of bread and wine. The sick man received "his Saviour" from the hands of St. Barbara, assisted by the angels, and from that moment began to amend.

A similar story is told of him somewhat later on. He happened one Sunday to enter a Protestant church in which the sacrament was administered. He had entered it by mistake, supposing it to be a [Roman] Catholic church; but when he perceived he was in communion with heretics, he prayed God to pardon him and assist him in his difficulty. His prayer was heard as before; and God sent an angel of surpassing beauty to administer to him the sacred elements.—Peter Ribadeneira, *The Flower of the Lives of the Saints.*

In reading the lives or acts of the saints one thing is very striking, and that is the constant repetition of the same miracle. Thus in Theodosius the Cœnobiarch his special miracle was the multiplication of food; in Stanislaus Kostka it is the eucharist; in St. Antony the Great it is contests with Satan; in others the multiplication of food; and so on.

This is exactly what might be expected, on the solution suggested p. 15, viz. that each saint's idiosyncrasy determined the special mode or fashion of the illusion, while the fact of some sort of illusion was due simply to anæmia or hyperæmia.

St. Barnabas says where his dead body is to be found. Barnabas the apostle, after being stoned to death, was thrown into a fierce fire, that his body might be consumed; but the fire had no effect upon it, and St. Mark, carrying the dead body beyond the gates of the city wall of Cyprus, buried it. There it remained till A.D. 485 (that is, 433 years), when, Nicephorus Callistus assures us, the ghost appeared to Antemius, bishop of Cyprus, and told him where his body was to be found. The bishop went to the spot indicated, and found the body, with the original MS. of St. Matthew's Gospel, the very MS. written by the hand of the evangelist himself. Both relics were taken to Constantinople, according to the ghost's request; and a church was built in Cyprus on the site where these treasures were discovered.—Nicephorus Callistus (died 1350), *Church History.* (See also Metaphrastês, *Lives*, etc.; St. Isidore, *Lives of the Holy Fathers*, ch. lxxxii.; Sigisbert, *De Viris Illustribus*, ch. xvii.; Bede, *Retractations*, at the end of the "Acts of the Apostles," ch. iv.; etc.)

This MS. ought to determine once for all the questions respecting St. Matthew's Gospel, such as (1) in what language was it written, Hebrew or Greek? (2) is the Gospel which now goes by the evangelist's name the same as the "Original MS.," or greatly interpolated? (3) are any or all of the doubtful parts in the MS.; if so, which are there and which are not? If the MS. found is genuine, it should settle all these questions; if not, it is altogether a gross and egregious fraud.

St. Benedict appears to Bruno (Leo IX.) and cures him of a toad's venom (A.D. 1002–1054). Bruno, while at school, went to visit his parents, and while asleep, a toad jumped on his face, "sucked his breath," and injected its poison into his mouth. The boy woke with pain, jumped out of bed, and called for help. No one came to his call, and in the morning his face, throat, and breast were swollen to an extraordinary degree. Several remedies were tried, but for two months the boy hung on a thread between life and death. At length the apparition of St. Benedict appeared to him. He held in his hand a crucifix, with which he touched the boy's mouth, and all the other parts affected by the poison. No sooner was this done than the swellings subsided, and the boy felt better. In a day or two the imposthumes behind the ears broke, discharged a large quantity of corrupt matter, and the restoration to health was then only a matter of time. Bruno always attributed his cure in this case to St. Benedict.—Wibert, *Life of St. Leo IX.*

One thing may be taken for granted, that the toad and St. Benedict had an equal share in this malady and cure.

The ghosts of St. Dominic and of Thomas Aquinas lift St. Andrew Avellin on his horse (A.D. 1608). Riding on a hired horse one day to visit the prince Stigliano, St. Andrew Avellin was thrown on the edge of a sharp stone and greatly hurt. His feet got entangled in the stirrups, and the horse, terrified, ran off, dragging the ecclesiastic along the stony road. In this predicament the ghosts of St. Dominic and Thomas Aquinas came to his help, extricated his feet, wiped the blood from his face, healed his wounds, and set him on his horse again.—Mgr. Guérin, *Vies des Saints*, vol. xiii. p. 305.

The ghost of Andreas Bobola requests to be made patron of the college of Pinsk (April 19, A.D. 1702). The Jesuit college of Pinsk was threatened with destruction by the Cossacks of the Ukraine. And while the superior was pondering under whose protection to place the college, the ghost of Andreas Bobola appeared to him. It was dressed in the costume of the college, and said, "You are in want of a patron and protector; why not choose me? I am Andreas Bobola, put to death by the Cossacks in 1657, and you will find my body buried in your college." The rector searched the crypt of the college, but could find no such name as "Bobola;" so a night or two afterwards the ghost appeared to him again, and told him to look on the right-hand side of the high altar; and there, sure enough, was found a coffin bearing the name of "Andreas Bobola." When the coffin was opened the grave-clothes fell to powder, but the body was entire, though "wounded with a thousand wounds." The blood from the wounds was still fresh, the skin was soft, the flesh flexible, and the odour sweet and agreeable. "Ce fut ainsi que Dieu, par les plus éclatants miracles, préserva lui-même à jamais de l'oubli la mémoire de son serviteur."—R. P. Olivaint, *Notice Historique sur le Bienheureux André Bobola de la Compagnie de Jésus.*

The murder of Bobola was so horrible that it must be given in the *ipsissima verba* of the biographer. "Les Cosaques l'attachent à un arbre, et l'accablent de coups. Ils lui passent ensuite une corde au cou, et l'attachent derrière leurs chevaux, le conduisent à leur chef, à Ianow. Les réponses calmes que le martyr fait à ces barbares l'irritent et il reçoit pour punition un grand coup de sabre sur la tête. La main qu'il avait instinctivement levée en l'air fut presque détachée du bras, mais le préserva d'une mort infaillible. Alors les soldats se mirent de la partie. L'un lui arracha un œil, les autres le conduisirent chez un boucher où ils allumèrent des torches, et lui brûlèrent différentes parties du corps en lui demandant de renoncer à sa foi. Sur son refus, on l'étrangla à demi avec de jeunes branches vertes tordues à l'avance; on lui fit une tonsure en lui enlevant la peau de la tête; on le frappa au visage de façon à lui casser les dents. Sous l'horrible et dérisoire prétexte de lui faire une chasuble, on lui arrache la peau du dos. On essuie avec une torche de paille le sang qui coule à flots de cette plaie atroce; et pour achever de faire un monstre de cet homme dont l'aspect épouvante même ses bourreaux, on lui enfonce des roseaux sous les ongles, afin de leur donner l'apparence de griffes. Après lui avoir ensuite coupé le nez et les lèvres, on le jette sur un tas de fumier. Le bienheureux n'était plus qu'une masse de chair informe et repoussante. Deux heures après, le capitaine, passant par là, l'acheva d'un coup de sabre 16 mai, 1657."

(Bobola was beatified by Pius IX. in 1853.)

Jesus Christ appears in person to Augustine, and gives him the name of "The Great Father" (A.D. 354–430). Jesus Christ appeared in person to St. Augustine, afterwards bishop of Hippo, and addressed him as "The Great Father." The special occasion was while he was entertaining a number of poor folk as his guests. One of the guests said to the saint, "Magne Pater Augustine, gaude, quia Filium Dei hodie in carne videre et tangere meruisti." Having so spoken, he disappeared.—St. Augustine, *Confessions.*

Christ appears to St. Catherine of Siena, and gives her a betrothal ring (A.D. 1317–1380). One day, in the eve of Lent, when all the Christian world seemed mad with folly, Catherine was alone in her cell, and cried aloud in fervent prayer, "O Saviour, give me grace that nothing may separate me from Thy great love." A voice—it was that of her celestial Spouse—replied, "Be at peace, Catherine; I will never leave thee nor forsake thee." With these words the cell was filled with heavenly visitants. There was Mary, patroness of all virgins both in heaven and earth; John the evangelist, with the eyes of an eagle and the purity of a dove; St. Paul the victorious; the learned and angelic Dominic; and king David, the model of penitent love. The Virgin, placing the right hand of Catherine in that of her Son, asked Him to give her His mystic ring. The ring was of gold, with a large diamond, and four precious stones around it. The Saviour placed the ring on the maiden's finger, saying, "I, thy Creator, with My Father which is in heaven—I, thy Redeemer and thy Spouse—will preserve thee pure, till that day when I come to claim thee as My heavenly bride." The vision then vanished, but the ring remained on the saint's finger. She, however, alone could see it; to all others it was invisible.—Raymond of Capua (her confessor), *Life of St. Catherine of Siena.*

As the ring was wholly subjective, the creation of her own brain, and not objective, of course it was visible to herself alone, but to her it was as real as the dagger seen by Macbeth in the air.

Christ appears to St. Catherine of Siena to comfort her (A.D. 1317–1380). St. Catherine of Siena was subject to fits of great despondency, followed by ecstasies. In one of these desponding fits the Saviour appeared to her, nailed to a cross, as He was on Calvary. "Where wert Thou, Saviour," cried St. Catherine, lovingly, "while my spirit within me was so utterly cast down?" "In thy heart, beloved one," replied Jesus; "ravished by its fidelity. There was I to sustain thee in the battle, and to save thee in the great water-floods."—Raymond of Capua (her confessor), *Life of St. Catherine of Siena.*

Jesus Christ and His apostles show themselves to St. Clara (A.D. 1346). Jesus Christ one night appeared to St. Clara. He was seated on His throne of glory, surrounded by John the Baptist and the apostles, and He showed St. Clara the wound in His side.

On another occasion, as she was praying before an image of the crucified Saviour, the image said to her, "I can refuse you nothing. Feel assured that those whom you love are written in the Lamb's Book of Life."—*Les Petits Bollandistes*, vol. ii. p. 440.

Christ, as a beggar, appears to the mother of Columba (A.D. 1493). When Columba left her home clandestinely, being persuaded to do so by the ghost of St. Dominic, her mother was greatly distressed, and her cries brought together the neighbours to condole with her. On going over the house, they were amazed to find the door of Columba's chamber had not been opened. While this search was going on, a beggar presented himself, approached the disconsolate mother, and said, "Woman, I see your heart is very sorrowful." "How so?" she replied. "I can see it," said the stranger; "but, believe me, that which has occurred, has happened by the will of God. Your daughter has leaned on a staff that can never break. Be comforted, for you will soon see the hand of God in this affliction." "Après ces paroles," ajoute le Confesseur de Colomba, "cet homme disparut, et je soupçonne qu'il n'était rien moins que le Seigneur Jésus, qui dans sa compassion, avait voulu fortifier et consoler cette pauvre mère."—Father Sebastian of Perouse (Columba's confessor), *Life of Columba of Rieti.*

This anecdote is very suggestive, and shows how ready the confessor was to see a miracle, and deem it nothing extraordinary. There is nó reason why this beggar should not have been a human being, but a thousand why it should not be Jesus Christ.

Christ appears to the forty martyrs in prison (A.D. 320). The forty martyrs were forty Christian soldiers of different countries in the "Thundering Legion." The command of the emperor Licinius sent to Agricola, governor of Lesser Armenia, for all his army to offer sacrifice, being communicated to the 12th or Thundering Legion, then lying in Sebastê, the forty Christian soldiers firmly refused so to dishonour Christ; and, after being punished for insubordination, were sent to prison. Here, at night, Jesus Christ Himself came to them while they were at prayer, and said to them, "He that believeth in Me, though he dies, yet shall he live; and whosoever liveth and believeth in Me shall never die. Fear not them that can torment the body only, but know this: to him that overcometh will I give to eat of the tree of life which is in the midst of the paradise of God."—*Acta Sanctorum.* (This memoir is by Metaphrastês. See the three *Discourses* of St. Gregory of Nyssa, vol. ii. p. 203; vol. iii. pp. 499, 504.)

Jesus Christ and the Virgin often appeared to St. Lutgardes (A.D. 1246). St. Lutgardes was brought up in the convent of St. Catherine, near St. Trond, in Brabant; but she had no true religious feeling till Jesus Christ appeared to her in person, and, opening His breast, said to her, "Look here, Lutgardes, how ought you not to love Me? Leave the vanities of the world, and you shall find in Me the delights of divine love." These words pierced the young maiden like an arrow, and wrought a total change in her. She now lived a life of such penitence and prayer, that the other inmates of the convent said her fervour must soon burn itself out. This made her very sad; but the Virgin Mary came to console her, and said, "Feel assured, my daughter, that those whom my Son have once received will never fall from grace." From this hour Lutgardes grew daily in greater familiarity with Christ. One day Christ asked her what wish He should accomplish for her, and she replied, "Give me Your heart." "Nay," said Christ, "rather give Me thine." "Take it, Lord, and purify it with the fire of Thy love," said Lutgardes; and an exchange of hearts was made between them. "Il se fit une union si étroite et si parfaite de l'esprit créé avec l'esprit incréé, que Jesus était toujours dans Lutgarde, et que Lutgarde était toujours hors d'elle-même pour ne vivre qu'en Jésus et pour Jésus."—Thomas de Cantimpré, *Vie de St. Lutgarde.*

Christ Himself appears to St. Honoré, and administers to him the eucharist (sixth century). St. Honoré, on one occasion, went to St. Acheolus to assist in saying mass in the chapel of the Virgin, when Christ Himself appeared to him visibly, in human form, and administered to him the holy elements with His own hands, "lui accordant ainsi la même grâce qu'il avait faite aux Apôtres, le soir de sa Passion." In memory of this event, a divine hand is blazoned in the arms of the abbey of St. Acheolus.—*Les Petits Bollandistes*, vol. v. p. 576.

Christ appears to a priest, and bids him take food to St. Benedict, afterwards patriarch of the Western monks (A.D. 494). A holy priest of Mount Preclaro, about four miles from Subiaco, was just about to eat his Easter dinner, when Christ stood before him and said, "A servant of Mine is dying of hunger in a cavern, while you are about to indulge yourself on these dainties." The priest, hearing these words, rose at once, and, taking with him the food prepared, was conducted by the hand of God to the rocks near Subiaco, some fifty miles from Rome, and came to the cavern occupied by St. Benedict, and subsequently called "The Holy Grot." He found the saint, told him "God had sent him with food," and reminded him that Easter Day was no fast-day in the Church. So the two prayed and ate together; and, after a day of devout communion, the priest returned to his parish and St. Benedict to his cavern.—St. Gregory the Great, *Dialogues*, bk. ii. ch. i.

Christ crucified appears to St. Rosa of Viterbo (1235–1252). One day Jesus Christ appeared to St. Rosa, suspended on His cross, His hands and feet nailed, His head crowned with thorns, His face black and blue, His limbs dislocated, His flesh torn off to the bone, and His body covered with blood and sweat. St. Rosa screamed, shuddered, and fainted. When she came to herself she was still unable to speak for some time, and could only gaze on the victim before her. Her veins swelled, her nerves twitched, her heart beat high, and she seemed in a terrible agony. Instinctively she beat her arms against each other, tore her hair, and, seizing a stone, struck herself on the breast and shoulders; blood gushed from her mouth, and she cried aloud, "O my Jesus, why art Thou reduced to this pitiable state? What inhuman monsters could have used Thee thus? Why—oh, why art Thou so cruelly mangled, so cruelly nailed to the cursed tree?" "'Tis My love, My burning love for man," He answered. "Your love for man!" she exclaimed; "then Your love for me has brought You to this pass. My sins—ah, miserable me!—my sins have done all this." She shrieked, she stamped, she tore her hair, she struck herself, and broke one of her bones with the stone.—L'abbé Barascud, *Life of St. Rosa of Viterbo.*

Christ and many saints in glory appear to St. Vincent Ferrier. In 1396 St. Vincent Ferrier fell ill, and every one thought he would die. The crisis occurred on Oct. 3, the vigil of the fête of St. Francis. Then was fulfilled the saying that is written, "When thou thoughtest thyself on the point to die, then thou didst rise as the star of the morning." All of a sudden the sick-chamber was filled with light of celestial splendour, and the Saviour of the world, accompanied by a multitude of the heavenly host, and with the patriarchs St. Dominic and St. Francis, presented Himself to the sick man, and said to him, "Vincent, rise up safe and sound, and go forth to preach against sin. For this end have I chosen thee. Warn sinners to be converted, for the kingdom of heaven is at hand." The Saviour then told him three things: first, that He would confirm him in grace, that his preaching might have free course and abound; secondly, that he should come out unscathed from all persecutions; and thirdly, He gave him special directions how to exercise the apostleship committed to his charge. Then touching the saint's face with His right hand, He said, "O my Vincent, rise;" and with these words the vision vanished. The sick man felt that he was restored to health, and his heart was full of heavenly consolations.—Peter Ranzano (bishop of Lucera), *Life of St. Vincent Ferrier.*

This apparition recounted by Father Ranzano, the most ancient of the biographers of St. Vincent Ferrier, is substantially repeated by the saint himself in a letter addressed to pope Benedict XIII., A.D. 1411.

Apparitions of Christ and of the Virgin Mary to St. John-Joseph of the Cross (A.D. 1654–1734). St. John-Joseph had frequent ecstasies, in which state he was dead to the outer world, neither seeing, hearing, nor feeling, but resting immovable as a statue, with his face burning bright as a live coal, and a nimbus surrounding his head. In one of these transports the Virgin appeared to him, and conversed with him. One Christmas Eve "l'enfant Jésus descendait dans ses bras, et y restait plusieurs heures de suite." (See St. Cajetan, St. Coletta, pp. 25, 28.)—Cardinal Wiseman, contributed to Migne's *Démonstrations Evangéliques*, vol. xvi.

Sundry apparitions to Philip of Neri (A.D. 1515–1595). One Christmas Eve Christ showed Himself to Philip of Neri, in the form of a little child upon the altar. The beauty of the vision was surpassing thought. Philip often saw in the host a multitude of angels, and all the glory of paradise. He twice saw the Virgin Mary; once when she held up the roof of the church at Vallicella, which threatened to fall upon the congregation; and once, about a year afterwards, when he was sick, and she came to cure him.—*Bull of Canonization by Gregory XV.*

There is a painting of the Virgin Mary holding up the roof of the church at Vallicella.

Apparitions of Christ to St. Theresa (A.D. 1515–1582).

(1) As the love of St. Theresa for God and Christ increased, the malignity of Satan to her increased also. She stated her case to five or six masters, who told her to take more food, to associate more with the sisterhood, and to shorten her religious exercises. She followed this advice for three years, but in this period the Saviour often came to console her; and one day said to her, "Fear not, my daughter; it is I who speak. I will never leave thee, nor forsake thee." These comforting words banished her doubts; and, no longer fearing the devil, she defied him, saying, "Come on now, with all your legion. As Christ is with me, I care not who may be against me." Though Christ sometimes showed Himself to her in a sensible form, He more frequently manifested Himself to her spiritual eyes. Her confessor and superior, still believing these visitations to be Satanic, told her, when they appeared again, to make the sign of the cross, to turn her back, to quit her oratory, and change her place. She did as she was told; but Christ, far from thinking her rude and unloving, only loved her the more, and said to her, "You have done well, my daughter, in obeying your directors; but be assured it is I Myself who appear to you, and honour you with My presence." For two years the Saviour never left her side, but was ever with her to instruct, console, and fortify her. After the two years were ended, the whole Trinity abided with her for fourteen years, in a visible form—at least, so far as the immortal can be visible to a mortal. She was also visited by the Virgin Mary, St. Joseph, St. Peter and St. Paul, St. Dominic, St. Francis, St. Catherine, St. Clara, ten thousand martyrs, and many other saints of both sexes.

(2) On one occasion God the Father appeared to her, and said, "My daughter, I have given to you My Son, the Holy Ghost, and the Blessed Virgin; what more can I give?" On another occasion, Jesus Christ appeared before her, and, putting His right hand, printed with the nail, into her hand, said, "See this nail-print. It is the sign of My marriage contract with you. Ere long you shall be My bride, and nothing shall separate you from the love of God your Saviour." So full was her heart that she cried aloud, "O God, enlarge my heart, or it will burst with love."

(3) When St. Theresa founded the monastery of Seville, Jesus Christ came to visit her, and said, "Thou knowest, daughter, there is a marriage contract between thee and Me. Thou art Mine, and I am thine."

(4) One day St. Theresa knelt in prayer before a picture of Christ, beseeching her heavenly Spouse to save her from ever offending Him, in thought, word, or deed. From this moment the Lord Jesus held fellowship with her; often talking with her face to face, speaking in human speech in her own mother tongue.

(5) Theresa being on one occasion at her devotions, the Lord appeared to her with St. Peter and St. Paul. He first showed her His hands, which shone with celestial splendour; He then revealed His face; and continued with her for the space of three days.

(6) Being at mass on St. Paul's Day,

Christ manifested Himself to her in His human form, but His body was glorified. This intercourse continued for three years, when a seraph came with a flaming dart and pierced her to the heart. The pain of this wound never left her to the hour of her death.—John (of Jesus Maria), *Life of St. Theresa.* (She left her autobiography, which was carried to the year 1580, that is, within two years of her death.)

St. Filumena, a nineteenth-century saint, asserts her identity. St. Filumena was wholly unknown till A.D. 1802, and where she lived, when she lived, what she did, and how she died, are wholly unknown. Never mind. In 1802 a grave was found in the cemetery of St. Priscilla, and near it were three tiles, containing these "words," in red letters—

LVMENA	PAXTE	CVMFI

By changing the position of the tiles we get PAXTE CUMFI LUMENA, and by separating the letters into words, we get PAX TECUM FILUMENA. That this is the correct rendering there can be no doubt, for the "virgin martyr" herself told a priest and a nun so in a dream. She told them she was called "Filumena" because she was "Fi[lia] Lumena," the daughter of the "Light of the World." * In confirmation of this revelation, when the bones were carried to Magnano, the saint repaired her own skeleton, made her hair grow, and performed so many other miracles, that those who doubt the statement of the "virgin martyr" would not be convinced even if they themselves had dreamt the dream.

The ghosts of St. Hilary, St. Martin, and St. Agnan appear to St. Leontius to announce his death (A.D. 550). St. Leontius lived in the town of Mentenay, and was abbot of the monastery there. While he was still far from old age, the ghosts of St. Hilary, St. Martin, and St. Agnan appeared before him, as he was lying on his wretched pallet in the baptistery, and said to him, "Yet within three days, and we will come to carry you to paradise." On the third day they came again, and said, "All things are ready; hasten to the feast." St. Leontius requested a reprieve of three days, that his dead body might be wrapped in a robe which had been promised him. The delay was accorded him, and he instantly sent his nephew to a noble dame to say, "Our father Leontius is about to quit this world, and has sent me for the mortuary robe." "Fool that I am," said the dame, "it is not ready; but our good father is still hale, and has many days before him. Tell him I will send the robe in three days." In three days the robe arrived. In three days the good abbot died. In three days the same three saints came, and carried his soul to paradise.—*Ancient Breviary of Troyes.*

The ghost of St. John of Beverley confirms the claim of Edward I. to the lordship of Scotland. Edward I. founded his claim to the lordship of Scotland on these four pleas: (1) Ancient chronicles, which state that the Scotch kings paid homage to the sovereigns of England from time immemorial. Extracts in proof are given from St. Alban, Marianus Scotus, Ralph of Diceto, Roger of Hoveden, and William of Malmesbury; (2) old charters of Scottish kings, as those of Edgar, son of Malcolm, William, and his son Alexander II.; (3) papal rescripts, as those of Honorius III., Gregory IX., and Clement IV.; (4) "The Life and Miracles of St. John of Beverley." The extract referred to in the last plea runs thus: "In the reign of Adelstan, the Scots invaded England, and committed great devastation. Adelstan went to drive them back, and, on reaching the Tyne, found that the Scots had retreated. At midnight the ghost of St. John of Beverley appeared to Adelstan, and bade him cross the river at daybreak, for he should assuredly discomfit the foe. Adelstan obeyed the vision, and reduced the whole kingdom to subjection. On reaching Dunbar in his home march, Adelstan prayed that some lasting sign might be vouchsafed him to satisfy all ages that God, by the intercession of St. John of Beverley, had given to England the kingdom of Scotland. Then struck he with his sword the basaltic rock near the coast, and the blade sank into the solid stone "as if it had been butter," cleaving it asunder an ell or more. As the cleft remains to the present hour, none can doubt or dispute the justice of the plea.—Rymer, *Fœdera,* vol. i. pt. ii. p. 771.

The ghost of St. John Nepomuck pleads the cause of a woman unjustly condemned. A lady of noble birth was unjustly cast in a lawsuit, and memorialized the emperor Leopold. She put her memorial on the altar of St. John Nepomuck, while she attended mass; and, after the service was over, she found her document had

* The final *a* is simply the affix of "Lumen," taken as a female name.

disappeared. Four days afterwards the lady put another memorial on the same altar; and, when she returned to take it up, discovered in its stead her original paper, signed with the emperor's name, reversing the sentence. This schedule had gone from Prague to Vienna and back again in four days, which was impossible, except by miracle. On further inquiry it was found that St. John Nepomuck, who had been some time dead, had pleaded her cause, and obtained the emperor's signature to the remonstrance.—*Acta Sanctorum* (Bollandists), vol. v. p. 600.

The ghost of St. Martin appears to Hervēus of Tours (A.D. 1021). Hervēus, having restored the grand basilica of Tours, prayed St. Martin to celebrate the day of opening with some great miracle. St. Martin appeared to him and said, "My very dear son, what you ask you shall receive, and more too; but as for miracles, those already wrought will suffice for the present. Now is the reaping time, and your prayer should not be for miracles to convert souls, but for converted souls, fit for God's garner. As for me, I will not cease to pray God on your behalf. Many are too much attached to the things of this world, and my prayers have obtained (with great difficulty) the salvation of some of these. In regard to yourself, my dear son, finish the work you have taken in hand; and believe me when I say, that it is a work most pleasing and acceptable to God." When the clergy were assembled for the dedication of the church, Hervēus repeated to them the words of the apparition.—L'abbé Rolland (honorary canon of Tours), *Life of Hervēus.*

The archangel Michael appears to St. Hubert of Brittany (A.D. 714). After the death of his parents, St. Hubert longed to join them in paradise; and one day while he was in his garden (since called St. Hubert's garden), he knelt on a stone, and prayed God to take him to Himself. The archangel Michael was instantly at his side, told him his prayer was heard, and that God would remove him from earth to heaven within three days. His joy was boundless, but when he told his vision to the monks, sorrow filled their hearts.—*Acta Sanctorum* (Bollandists), vol. viii. May 30.

St. Michael appears to the bishop of Siponto. By "the apparition of St. Michael," the [Roman] Catholic Church means his appearance to the bishop of Siponto, when he commanded him to build a church and dedicate it to St. Michael. The legend is this: In the pontificate of Gelasius I. there was a man named Gargano, very rich in cattle, who happened to lose a bull. After long search, Gargano came to a cave, which the men with him refused to enter; but one of them shot an arrow into the cave, and the arrow, after penetrating the cave, returned back to the shooter. This seemed very strange; and the bishop of Siponto, who was one of the searchers, prayed and fasted for three days, that the mystery might be revealed to him. At the expiration of that time St. Michael appeared, and informed him that he (St. Michael) was himself in the cave when the arrow was discharged therein, and that it was he who had turned it back again by his own hand. He then commanded the bishop to build a church on the site of this miracle, and dedicate it to "St. Michael and all angels." The bishop then entered the cave, and found it fitted up like a beautiful chapel; so he celebrated mass in it, and many miracles made it noted. Subsequently a church was built on the site, called Mount Gargano, from Gargano, the farmer whose bull was lost, but the name was changed to St. Angelo's Mount, from the "apparition of St. Michael." This mount is in the Capitanate, near Manfredonia, in the kingdom of Naples.—Edward Kinesman (1623), *Lives of the Saints*, p. 311.

St. Januarius appears to an old man according to a compact. A certain old man requested St. Januarius to leave him some memento of his martyrdom, which Januarius promised to do. After he was beheaded, the saint made his appearance to this old man, and gave him the napkin wet with blood, which had been bound over his eyes at execution. The old man showed the napkin to the officers, who recognized it, and vouched for its identity.

At the very hour of execution, the devil seized Timotheus, the governor of Beneventum, who had ordered Januarius to be put to death, and, after tormenting him, killed him, and cast him into the bottomless pit.

The mother of Januarius saw in a vision the death of her son, and thanked God that he was deemed worthy of a martyr's crown.—*The Roman Breviary and Martyrology.*

St. Peter appears to St. Amandus, and assigns him work in Gaul (A.D. 594–684). While St. Amandus was waiting for a "call," he was shut up in a cell on the ramparts of Bourges. Here St. Peter appeared to him, surrounded with a great light. His face was that of an old man, but it was encompassed with a glory. "Amandus," said the apostle, "God desires you to go to the Gauls, and has promised you a great harvest of souls." Amandus obeyed without delay, and settled in the pays de Gand.—Menjoulet (vicar-general of Bayonne), *St. Amand, Apôtre des Basques.*

St. Peter appears to St. Peter Nolasco (A.D. 1189–1256). St. Peter Nolasco, founder of the Order of Mercy, had always a great desire to go to Rome, to render homage to the tomb of his namesake. It was his intention to go barefoot; but one day, as he was making arrangements for this pilgrimage, the "prince of the apostles" came to him, and said thrice, "Peter, as you have not been to see me, I have come to see you." Lifting up his eyes, he beheld the apostle in the very state in which he was crucified. "Peter, said he, "all the good wishes of saints are not accomplished in this life. I wished to die with my head downwards, to make it known that superiors should conform their spirits and their thoughts to the necessities of their inferiors, in imitation of our Master, who bent His head to my feet when He condescended to wash them." From this day forth Nolasco did something every day in imitation of St. Peter, and sometimes got a monk to tie him by his feet to the head of his bed. When, however, his spiritual father was told thereof, he strictly forbade it, as dangerous to health, if not hazardous to life.—R. P. F. Zumel, *Life of St. Peter Nolasco* (in Latin).

Apparition of St. Philip of Neri to dame Drusina Fantina, and to Leonard Rouel (died 1595). After death, Philip of Neri appeared to several persons; for example, to dame Drusina Fantina, who, having fallen from a considerable height, had her skull severely fractured, and her body much bruised. In a moment, the ghost of St. Philip was at her side, to comfort her and restore her to health.

Another example, is his presence to Leonard Rouel, while at the point of death. St. Philip came to his bed, and merely said, "My son, go in peace," when the dying man rose from his bed in perfect health.—*Process of Canonization.* (This "Process" is crammed with miracles, some during the life of the saint, and some after his death.)

The ghost of St. Thomas of Canterbury appears to St. Catherine of Bologna (A.D. 1413–1463). One day St. Catherine, weary of work, fell asleep in her prayers, when St. Thomas of Canterbury appeared to her, clad in his pontifical robes, and told her that she was not to wear herself out, even with prayer and good works; that she was now to relax a little, that she might renew her strength, and return with more vigour to her duties. He then gave her his hand to kiss, and vanished from her sight.—Paleotti (of the Order of St. Francis), *Life of St. Catherine of Bologna.*

The ghost of St. Vaast extinguishes a fire (sixth century). Some years after the death of St. Vaast, bishop of Arras and Cambrai, a fire broke out in the house where he used to dwell, and threatened to destroy the whole town of Arras. A woman named Abita invoked the name of the deceased prelate to assist in putting out the conflagration. Whereupon she saw St. Vaast in the midst of the flames, commanding them to cease their ravages. Wonderful to relate, not only the chamber once occupied by the bishop was wholly uninjured, but the very bed and bedclothes were untouched. This "miracle" increased the honour in which the name of the late prelate was held.—Surius, *Lives of the Saints*, vol. i. (1570).

The Virgin Mary appears to St. Agnes of Mount Pulciano (A.D. 1274–1317). When St. Agnes was only fourteen years old, the Virgin Mary appeared to her, and gave her three little stones of great beauty, saying to her, "My child, before you die, you will build a monastery in my honour. Take these little stones to remind you that this religious house must be founded on the faith and confession of the high and indivisible Trinity." *

Another instance. On Assumption Eve the Virgin Mary brought to Agnes the infant Jesus, and placed Him in her arms. Agnes, beside herself with joy, took from His neck a crucifix studded with pearls. In Christian art, the infant Jesus is represented giving her the cross, as He leaves her arms.

The Virgin Mary appears to St. Bont (A.D. 623–710). On the eve of the As-

* Some time afterwards, an angel reminded Agnes of these three stones, and told her the time was fully come when she ought to begin the convent. He said she was to build it on the site where she was attacked by the rooks (see DEVIL ASSUMES, etc.), that she was to dedicate it to "The Holy Trinity and the Incomparable Virgin," and that it was to be of the Order of St. Dominic.—Raymond of Capua, *Life of St. Agnes.*

sumption, St. Bont determined to pass the whole night in St. Michael's Church. While he was deep in prayer, the Virgin Mary appeared before him in great light, accompanied by a host of saints and spirits of the just made perfect. These heavenly visitants forthwith got all things ready for celebrating mass; and, when all was in order, the Virgin was asked who was to officiate. She replied, "St. Bont, who is already in the church." On hearing these words, St. Bont leaned against one of the church pillars to hide himself, whereupon the stone pillar became instantly plastic, and the impression of the saint's body was left in it as an intaglio, which may be seen by any who choose to look for it. The angels soon found the bishop, and led him to the Virgin, who commanded him most graciously to "offer up the divine sacrifice." St. Bont instantly arrayed himself in his sacerdotal robes, and went to the altar. The saints assisted, and the angels took part with them in chanting the service. When mass was finished, the Virgin gave St. Bont a chasuble, and told him to take care of it as a pledge of her favour. This chasuble, a fine delicate material, remained at Clermont till 1793, when it was destroyed accidentally by fire.—*Les Petits Bollandists* (7th edit. 1880), vol. i. p. 361.

The Virgin Mary appears to St. Cajetan of Thienna (A.D. 1547). One Christmas Eve, while St. Cajetan was in the Basilica Liberienne, meditating on the Incarnation, the Virgin Mary appeared to him, and placed the infant Jesus between his arms. It is thus he is often represented in Christian art. (See ST. JOHN-JOSEPH, ST. COLETTA, pp. 21, 28.)—*Les Petits Bollandistes*, vol. ix. p. 393.

The Virgin Mary appears to St. Cyril, general of Mount Carmel (A.D. 1224). St. Cyril, afterwards general of Mount Carmel, greatly distressed at the heresies which had corrupted the Church, wished to withdraw himself entirely from the society of man, that he might have only God to do with. While revolving this matter in his mind, the Virgin Mary came to him, with a face majestic and brilliant as the sun, and said to him, "My son, if you would avoid the heresies of the Greeks, seek an asylum on Mount Carmel, and follow the course which shall be shown you there." In obedience to this vision, St. Cyril sold all his possessions, gave the money to the poor, and started for Syria. At Jerusalem he met St. Brocard, prior-general of Mount Carmel, who took him to his cell, and the Virgin Mary again came to him, and told him it was here he ought to dwell, if he would escape the perils of heretical doctrines; so next day he entered the brotherhood as a novitiate.

Another appearance. When St. Cyril was made general of Mount Carmel he found the place almost a desert, but the Virgin came to him for the third time, and said, "Ere long many persons of rank will join the order, and affiliated monasteries will arise in all directions, to the glory of God, and advantage of the Church." This prophetic promise was most amply redeemed.—*Les Petits Bollandistes*, vol. iii. pp. 200-202.

The Virgin Mary and St. Joseph appear to St. Theresa (A.D. 1515-1582). While St. Theresa was building a convent, the Virgin Mary and St. Joseph appeared to her, and promised assistance; by their aid she overcame every obstacle, and brought her work to a successful issue. By the same divine assistance she was enabled to build fifteen religious houses, all well known in Spain.—John (of Jesus Maria), *Life of St. Theresa.*

The Virgin Mary appears to St. Julian, bishop of Cuença, on the day of his death (Jan. 28, 1207). St. Julian, being sick unto death, was laid in ashes on the floor of his cell. Presently the Virgin Mary, surrounded with angels and a company of virgins, entered the cell, singing these words: "Lo! here the man of God, who lived not unto himself, but to the Lord! Allelujah!" Then came the Virgin forward and said to him, "Beloved of my Son, take this lamp, the symbol of virginity, so well guarded by thee throughout all thy life, and enter into the joy of thy Lord." The words were scarcely uttered, when a palm branch proceeded from his mouth, whiter than snow. Up, up it shot, with marvellous rapidity, till it reached the sky, and its top was hidden out of sight. When it pierced the sky, celestial music was distinctly heard. So died St. Julian, bishop of Cuença, Jan. 28, 1207.—*Acta Sanctorum* (Jan. 28). This life was abridged from the Bollandists by P. Giry. The chamberlain of pope Leo XIII. repeats the above in his *Vies des Saints* (7th edit. 1880), vol. ii. p. 90.

One is tempted to believe that the incidents above recorded must be allegorical, but they are given by the authors referred to above as historic facts, and not the slightest hint is made to lead the reader to suppose otherwise.

The Virgin and Child appear to Stanislaus Kostka (sixteenth century). During sickness, and towards the close of his life, the Virgin Mary appeared to St. Stanislaus Kostka. She had her Child in her arms, and regarded the sick man with the sweetest graciousness. When she vanished, she placed the Child on Kostka's bed, and left Him there. From this moment he began to amend, at which the physicians marvelled; but he went on gathering strength daily, till he was wholly convalescent.—Peter Ribadeneira, *The Flower of the Lives of Saints.*

The Virgin and Child appear to Jeanne Marie de Maillé (A.D. 1332–1414). When Jeanne Marie de Maillé was only eleven years old, the Virgin Mary, bearing the infant Jesus on her left arm, appeared to her. In her right hand she carried a vessel filled with drops of the Saviour's blood, and sprinkled some of it on the young girl, who from that moment was more vividly alive to the mysteries of the cross, and the atoning sufferings of Christ. From that day Jeanne Marie carried in her bosom a crucifix painted on parchment, which she often wept over.—L'abbé Rolland, *Life of Jeanne Marie de Maillé.*

Apparition of the Virgin to several children in Pontmain (Jan. 17, 1871). The last apparition of the Virgin Mary, if we except that of Ballyraggett, in Ireland, in 1881, was at the close of the Franco-Prussian War, Jan. 17, 1871. This case is recorded at length by Mgr. Guérin in his *Vies des Saints*, vol. i. pp. 444–450, and is certified by M. Léon Guiller, secretary of the bishop of Laval, who writes this declaration:—(1) We decide "que l'Immaculée Vierge Marie, Mère de Dieu, a véritablement apparu, le 17 Janvier 1871, à Eugène Barbedette, Joseph Barbedette, Françoise Richer, et Jeanne Marie Lebossé, dans le hameau de Pontmain." (2) In consequence of this apparition he says, "Nous autorisons dans notre diocèse le culte de la bienheureuse Vierge Marie, sous le titre de Notre Dame d'Espérance de Pontmain. (3) Nous avons formé le dessein d'élever un sanctuaire en l'honneur de Marie sur le terrain même duquel Elle a daigné apparaitre." Mgr. Guérin's narrative is "imprimée avec la permission de Mgr. l'évèque de Laval;" and Mgr. Guérin is himself "Camérier de sa Sainteté Léon XIII." This, therefore, has the highest sanction which the Catholic Church can give. It was previously submitted to certain "Docteurs-Médicens appelés à émettre leur jugement sur les circonstances." Also to a commission "de théologiens chargée d'étudier le fait précité au point de vue de la théologie." It was demonstrated by them that the apparition could not be attributed "ni à la fraude ou à l'imposture, ni à une hallucination, ni à un état maladif des organes de la vue chez les enfants, ni à une illusion d'optique." Who were the persons who saw the apparition? Let us see what the chamberlain says. Eugène Barbedette was the second son of a small farmer living in the village of Pontmain, in the diocese of Laval. He was twelve years old, and his brother Joseph was ten. The other two were children from neighbouring cottages, called in to witness the sight. The parents of the children, the pastor of the village, Sister Vitaline, the abbot Guérin, all present, could see nothing, nor could any of the neighbours of outlying villages who flocked to the place. Only the children mentioned, a sick child, and a babe in the arms of its grandmother, saw the apparition. Let us now see what it was these children saw. It was a bright starlight night,* crisp and frosty, when Eugène Barbedette declared he could see, just above the roof of the opposite cottage, the Virgin Mary. She was very tall, robed in blue, and her robe studded with stars. Her shoes were also blue, but had red rosettes. Her face was covered with a black veil, which floated to her shoulders. A crown of gold was on her head, but a red line was observed to run round the crown, symbolical of the blood shed by Christ for the sins of the world. Beneath her feet was a scroll, on which was written these words: "Mais priez, mes enfants, Dieu vous exaucera, en peu de temps mon fils se laisse toucher." The persons present sang a canticle, the Virgin beat time with her hand, and when the canticle was finished the vision vanished piece by piece. As we have already observed, only children saw the vision, the oldest being twelve years of age, and the youngest an infant in arms. Many men and women, from the abbot and pastor, the nuns and parents of the children, to the neighbours all around, looked in the direction indicated, but saw nothing unusual. Well, says the chamberlain in concluding his narrative, "pour se manifester aux hommes, la Sainte Vierge a choisi des yeux simples. Semblables à

* The moon was full on the 6th.

des eaux troublées, les ames pécheresses eussent mal réfléchi sa céleste image."

This is no legend of antiquity, no story from books, no hearsay incident; it occurred in 1871, was searched into by men of science and theologians, abbots and nuns, pastors and people. The chamberlain of pope Leo XIII. wrote the narrative, the bishop of the diocese was satisfied with the evidence, and even ordained an annual "commemoration" to be observed in perpetuity; yet, I suppose, few Protestants will feel satisfied, with all this array of testimony, that any "miraculous vision" appeared at Pontmain. One thing is quite certain, the children did not all see alike; for while Eugène and others spoke of the vision as that of the *Virgin*, another child, three years old, called it *Jesus*, "en souvenir du beau portrait que sa mère lui avait fait du divin Enfant." Whether a fact or not matters little; the narrative so attested and so related proves to demonstration that the "mode of thought" so prevalent in the Middle Ages has not yet died out, and that is all this book is concerned with.

The Virgin Mary espouses St. Robert of Champagne before he was born (A.D. 1017). St. Robert of Champagne was the founder of Molesmes and of Cîteaux. The Virgin Mary, a little before his birth, appeared to his mother Ermengarde, and presented her with a gold ring, saying, "I wish the son which you now carry in your womb to be betrothed to me, with this ring, as my spouse." Hence St. Robert was always called the "Spouse of Mary." (See ST. HERMANN.) —Guy de Molesmes, *Life of St. Robert* (also *Acta Sanctorum* by the Bollandists, April 29).

The Virgin Mary appears to St. Henry Suzo (A.D. 1365). One morning, as St. Henry Suzo was singing *Maria, stella maris*, the Virgin Mary came to him and said, "The more you love me on earth, the more I shall love you in heaven; and the more your heart is joined to mine, the more unitedly shall you reign with me in the kingdom of my Son."

In the time of the carnival, angels descended into his cell, singing, "Surge, illuminare, Jerusalem, quia venit lumen tuum, et gloria Domini super te orta est."—Pustet of Ratisbonne, *The Life and Writings of Henry Suzo, surnamed "Amandus."*

The Virgin Mary appears to St. Veronica, at Milan (A.D. 1497). Veronica wished greatly to become a nun, but was disqualified because she was unable to read. To remedy this obstacle, she toiled in her peasant's hut long into the night over her alphabet and spelling; but found her labour great, and her progress extremely slow. One night, when quite disheartened, the Virgin Mary appeared before her. She was arrayed in dazzling blue, the colour of a summer sky. "My child," she said, "trouble not yourself with scholarship. The disciples of Christ are not the great scholars, but the humble minded; not those who know most, but those who believe most. Know, child, that not many wise men after the flesh, not many mighty, not many noble, are called, that no flesh may glory in God's presence. Let me give you three words, and ponder them in your heart—*Faith, Hope, Charity*, the greatest of which is charity." So saying, the holy mother vanished from sight, and Veronica, not long after, was admitted a sister in the convent of St. Martha, in Milan.—Isidore of Isolani, *Life of St. Veronica of Milan* (1518).

The Virgin Mary takes St. Hermann for her spouse, and gives him the name "Joseph" (A.D. 1230). One night, while St. Hermann was in prayer, the Virgin Mary appeared to him, at the foot of the high altar. She was accompanied by two angels of extraordinary beauty, and, calling to St. Hermann to approach, she vowed at the altar to take him for her spouse. While on earth, he was to represent Joseph, the spouse which she had on earth; and in heaven, he was to reign with her as her equal. St. Hermann modestly resisted, but the two angels assured him that such was the will of God, and that he must no longer resist the high honour of accepting the name of "Joseph the spouse of Mary." He had no choice but to submit, and was ever after so called. Even his biographers from this point of his life call him "Joseph the spouse of Mary, the mother of the King of kings."—*Life of St. Hermann of Steinfeld* (Bollandists), April 7.

Mgr. Guérin, referring to this espousal in his *Vies des Saints*, vol. iv. p. 276, says, "Une si admirable prérogative, que nous ne trouvons point avoir été accordée à d'autres saints, lui procura," etc. The chamberlain perhaps forgot St. Robert. While he was still in the womb the Virgin said to his mother, "Volo filium quem gestas in utero ex isto mihi annulo desponsari" (*Vita* i.) (I wish to take for my spouse the son about to be born, and here is the espousal ring).

The Virgin Mary lifts young Hermann into the gallery of Cologne cathedral (A.D. 1230). One day when Hermann, still a boy, entered Cologne cathedral, he saw in the gallery which runs between the choir and the nave, the Virgin Mary, the four evangelists, and the infant Jesus, conversing together in a most charming group. He longed to join them, but there was no ladder, and the gallery was locked. Presently the Virgin said to him, "Hermann, come up hither!" He tried to do so, but was unable; whereupon the divine mother, stretching out her hand, lifted him into the gallery, and set him next to her Son. Here he had the honour of passing several hours in this divine society, which filled his soul with grace and sweetness. That this was not a dream or vision, but an actual and material fact, is manifest by a wound which he received from a nail in the balustrade. At night the Virgin lifted the boy down again, and he returned home to his parents.—*Acta Sanctorum* (Bollandists), April 7.

The Virgin Mary places the infant Jesus in the arms of St. Catherine of Bologna (A.D. 1413–1463). The Saviour and His mother often appeared to St. Catherine of Bologna, and manifested towards her the most tender affection. One day the Virgin placed in the arms of the saint the infant Jesus. The sisters of the convent knew that God had vouchsafed to St. Catherine this favour, by her countenance, and the sweet odour which issued from her. She was also favoured by the three Persons of the Trinity, who explained to her this august mystery.—Paleotti (of the Order of St. Francis), *Life of St. Catherine of Bologna.*

The Virgin Mary places the infant Christ in the arms of St. Coletta (A.D. 1380–1447). To recompense St. Coletta for her tender devotion to the sufferings of the Saviour, the Virgin Mary placed between her arms the body of Jesus, all bloody, as if just taken from the cross. From this moment she daily felt at midday the pangs of Calvary. (See St. Cajetan, p. 25.)—*Acta Sanctorum*, vol. i. March, p. 553.

Father Ignatius, in his *Histoire des Maïeurs d'Abbeville*, p. 814, gives an engraved tablet from the church of St. Giles, Abbeville, with the following inscription:—

Sta. Colette, Vierge,
Priant la Très-sainte Mère de Dieu d'intercéder pour
Les Pécheurs envers son Fils,
Elle luy apparut tenant son petit enfant Jésus
Tout sanglant dans un plat, et luy dit:
Comment prierai-je, mon fils, pour ceux qui te
Démembrent par leurs offences.

The Virgin Mary places the infant Jesus in the arms of St. Hermann (A.D. 1230). The Virgin Mary, having taken St. Hermann for her spouse, and changed his name to Joseph (p. 27), enacted with him the early scene of Christ's childhood, to give reality to this espousal. Thus, as Joseph her real spouse nursed the child Jesus, the Virgin gave to Hermann the infant Jesus to nurse. As Joseph carried the infant Jesus into Egypt, the Virgin gave the infant Jesus for Hermann, her second spouse, to carry. The biographer says, "We find no other saint enjoyed the prerogative of being the accepted spouse of the Mother of God."—*Life of St. Hermann of Steinfeld* (Bollandists), April 7.

The souls of the dead appear to Henry Suzo (A.D. 1365). The souls of the dead used to come to Henry Suzo in the form of angels, and talk to him about heaven and hell. Amongst others, the soul of Eckard visited him, and told him, saying, "I am in heaven, in joy unspeakable and full of glory, being transformed to the likeness of God Himself." Henry asked him what state on earth should be cultivated in order to arrive at such blessedness. The soul of Eckard replied, "Renounce self, and confide blindly on God. Count everything that happens as sent by God, and nothing as sent from man, except as the messenger of God. Be patient, be loving even, to those who spitefully use you and persecute you. Try to be perfect, as your Father in heaven is perfect." Henry asked another soul what state on earth is the most lamentable, and it answered, "To be abandoned by God, and to live to please one's self rather than to please God."—Pustet of Ratisbonne, *The Life and Writings of Henry Suzo, surnamed "Amandus."*

The above instances are not a hundredth part of those I have met with in my reading, but with those inserted in pt. iii. will amply suffice to show the prevalency of this especial hallucination; for I suppose no one who reads this book will consider these apparitions to be objective and not subjective.

There can be no doubt that the seers of the apparitions set down in this group actually saw what they described, as a traveller actually sees a lake in a desert when he looks only on a mirage. It is not the sight that is deceived in these cases; the whole fault lies in the judgment or mental inferences, which do not take into account all the facts involved. A right judgment which takes in the whole case forms a realistic inference, but a faulty judgment which has not exhaustively sifted the subject forms a delusive inference. The traveller who sees a lake in a mirage, and the saint who sees the apparition of Christ, the Virgin, or some saint, honestly sees the phenomena, but his mental inferences are incorrect, because they do not take into account all the facts involved. Let the traveller tell his vision to a natural philosopher, and the seers of apparitions tell their visions to a medical man, and the former would instantly be told his lake was a mirage, and the latter would be told their apparitions were abnormal functional action arising from diseased action.

Mr. Green, in his *History of the English People*, speaking of St. Dunstan, says, "A traveller coming in his white mantle over the hills to tend Cuthbert, who had injured his knee, seemed to the lad to be an angel. The boy's shepherd life carried him to the bleak uplands, and here meteors plunging into the night became to him companies of angelic spirits carrying the soul of Aidan to heaven" (pp. 24, 25).

Apparitions to give Directions about their Dead Bodies.

The ghost of Patroclos appears to Achillês, to request that his body may be buried. Patroclos was killed in battle by Euphorbus and Hector. At night, while Achillês slept, the ghost of his friend came to him and said, "What! can you sleep, while your best friend lies in death uncared for? Haste, and give me burial, that I may pass the gates of Hades.

Thou art thyself about to die under the walls of Troy, and refuse not my last request. Bury not my bones apart from thine, but let us both be laid in one common tomb." To this Achillês answered, "I will perform minutely all thou hast enjoined." Then, trying to embrace his friend, the ghost slipped from his touch, and vanished out of sight.—Homer, *Iliad*, bk. xxiii. vers. 65, etc.

To Protestants the extraordinary care taken by Christians to bury the dead, to collect the bones and ashes of martyrs for interment, and the frequent apparitions of the deceased to secure for themselves the honour due to their dead bodies, are matters of wonderment; but with [Roman] Catholics "the burial of the dead" is the highest "corporal work of mercy" (see Intro.), and this will fully account for the numerous miraculous appearances in defence of this dogma. In Egypt not to be buried was infamy; the Greeks and Romans looked on the burial of a dead body as essential to its happiness in the world of shadows.

John the Baptist reveals the place where his head was buried. St. Jerome tells us that the disciples of John the Baptist buried the headless body in Sebaste, in Samaria, between Elias and Abdias. He adds that many miracles testified how highly God honoured the great forerunner of the gospel, for many who were sick were cured by the sacred relic, and many who were possessed were exorcised by it.

Ruffinus, in his *Ecclesiastical History*, informs us that Julian the Apostate, being annoyed by these constant miracles, had the body disinterred and burnt to ashes; but that certain Christians secreted some of the bones, and sent them to Philip, bishop of Jerusalem, and Philip sent them to the patriarch of Alexandria.

This is repeated in the *Tripartite History*.

The same historian (Ruffinus) tells us that Herodias buried the head of the Baptist in the palace of Herod, and there it remained hidden, till John the Baptist himself told some religious men where to find it. These men went to the place indicated, and found the decapitated head wrapped in the same garment of camel's hair which the prophet was accustomed to wear in the wilderness.

Simeon Metaphrastês and many others repeat this story, but none tell us how the camel-hair garment got there. It cannot be supposed that it was put on the charger when the head was handed to Salomê, nor can it be supposed that Herodias sent for it out of any reverence or superstitious regard for it. These "little" difficulties constantly crop up in these histories of the saints. However, John the Baptist himself told the "finders" that the head was his, and what better authority can be required? If he had told you or me, should we not believe him?

The ghost of St. Angelus gives directions about his funeral to the archbishop of Palermo (A.D. 1225). St. Angelus was murdered by some assassins of count Berenger at Alicata, in Sicily, May 5, A.D. 1225, and his ghost appeared the same day to the archbishop of Palermo, informing him that he was gone to heaven, and requesting him to see that his dead body was properly interred in the very spot where he was murdered. The archbishop complied with this request, and made a funeral for the martyr consistent with his saintly reputation.—Mgr. Guérin, *Vies des Saints*, vol. v. p. 344 (7th edit. 1880).

St. Eleutherius appears to St. Thecla to give directions about his relics (ninth century). One night St. Thecla saw a venerable old man come to her; he was of majestic port and great gravity. His hair was quite grey, and his clothing shone like the sun. It was St. Eleutherius, bishop of Tournai three centuries ago. Calling St. Thecla by her name, he bade her call on Heidilon, the then bishop, and tell him to go to Blandain, and take his relics from the grave, which he would find close by the altar of St. Peter. The aged Thecla, thinking this vision might be only a dream, prayed that God would make known to her His will on the subject. St. Eleutherius appeared to her a second and a third time, when, no longer doubting the mission, she went to the bishop of Tournai, and told him what had passed. Heidilon received the communication with great joy, made it known to his principal clergy, and appointed a day to carry out the saint's request. Having called together many prelates, abbots, and other clergymen, they went in grand procession to Blandain, and raised from the earth the relics of the ancient bishop of Tournai, according to his bidding. Many miracles solemnized the event; amongst others, the venerable Thecla, whose sight was dim with age, recovered the quick vision of her younger days.—L'abbé Destombes, *Vie des Saints de Cambria et d'Arras*.

St. Fructuosus appears to his brethren to command them to restore his ashes. St. Fructuosus, bishop of Tarragona, in Spain, after his martyrdom appeared to his brethren, and requested them to restore his ashes, which they had taken away as relics, that all might be laid in one place.—*Acta Sanctorum* (Jan. 21).

Gamaliel tells Lucian the monk where to find the body of St. Stephen and others (A.D. 415). In the [Roman] Catholic Church, Aug. 3 is dedicated to the discovery of the bones of St. Stephen, the first martyr, 415 years after he was stoned to death. It cannot but be interesting to know how these bones were identified, and as such high authorities as St. Augustine, Orosius, and a dozen others vouch for the truth of the following "facts," the mouth of gainsayers must be stopped. The subjoined account is epitomized from the Rev. Alban Butler's *Lives of the Saints*, vol. ii. pp. 183–186.

The place of the burial of St. Stephen, the first Christian martyr, was wholly unknown till the year A.D. 415, when it was revealed to a priest named Lucian, "while sleeping in his bed in the baptistery of Caphargamala, in the diocese of Jerusalem."

On Dec. 3, A.D. 415, at about nine o'clock at night, Lucian saw a tall, comely old man, with a long white beard, and a gold wand in his hand. He was clothed in a white robe edged with gold, and thickly covered with crosses. This venerable apparition having informed the monk that he was Gamaliel, who had instructed Paul the apostle in the law, bade him go without delay, and tell bishop John to open certain graves in the vicinity, and he would find the relics of Stephen the first martyr, Nicodemus who came to Jesus by night, himself, and his younger son Abibas.

As Lucian did not obey the order, the ghost repeated its visits on the two succeeding Fridays; and Lucian, no longer in doubt, went to the bishop and revealed to him the vision. The bishop ordered search to be made amongst a heap of stones in the neighbourhood, but a monk named Migetius said the "tombs" were at Debatalia, and were those of an old man, a young man, and two others. Thither, therefore, the searchers went, and found the four bodies, as Migetius had said. The four bodies were deposited in four coffins, and the names on the coffins were CHELIEL, NASUAM, APPAN, and DARDAN. There could not be a shadow of doubt that these names stood for "Stephen, Nicodemus, Abibas, and Gamaliel." True, they are not much alike, but that is of small moment; there were the four bodies, and they must be the four which the vision spoke to Lucian about in the baptistery.

The bishop John had brought with him two other prelates, and on opening the coffin of Cheliel the "odour of sanctity" was quite perceptible; and the identity of Cheliel with Stephen was still further confirmed by the number of miracles performed by contact with the body. So Lucian and the three bishops were fully satisfied, and as they lived only 415 years after the death of Stephen, it is manfestly unreasonable for persons living 1500 years later to doubt such respectable authority.

But to continue. Bishop John claimed Cheliel's relics for the church of Jerusalem, and the three other coffins were left at Caphargamala. Now occurred another miracle to make assurance doubly sure. When Cheliel's (*i.e.* Stephen's) relics were taken from the "place of the four tombs" to Zion Church, at Jerusalem, "a heavy rain fell." This extraordinary "miracle" removed every vestige of doubt.

Butler tells us that this account is given by Lucian himself; that Lucian's letter was translated into Spanish by Avitus, a friend of St. Jerome, and was attested by Chrysippus, a priest of Jerusalem, the two chroniclers Idatius and Marcellinus, Basil bishop of Seleucia, St. Augustine in his *City of God*, and many others. The discovery was made Dec. 3, A.D. 415, and therefore "the Invention of St. Stephen" is held on Aug. 3. They must be hard indeed to convince who doubt such a logical sequence of evidence as this.

The whole tale occurs also in Kinesman's *Lives of the Saints* (1623), where the "letter" of Lucian is given *in extenso*. The names in the letter are those mentioned above, and, to remove all doubt, Kinesman's narrative is avouched by John Floyd, pp. 560–564.

Nicodemus and Gamaliel are respectable names, but no care seems to have been bestowed upon their relics. There was something ungrateful in this neglect, seeing it was Gamaliel who revealed the locality of the relics, although it must be confessed he was not quite exact; and had it not been for the monk Migetius the bodies would not have been found. Probably in these discreditable days some may be found who think Migetius should have been asked if he knew anything about "the vision."

St. Hilary of Poitiers directs that a new tomb be made for him (A.D. 507). St. Hilary was deposited at death in a marble sepulchre between his wife and daughter, in the basilica of St. John and St. Paul, outside the city walls of Poitiers. This was A.D. 367. In the fifth century this church was entirely destroyed by the Goths and Vandals, and the sepulchre of St. Hilary was lost amidst the ruins. In 507 a ball of fire was observed to rise from the *debris* and move towards Clovis, who was encamped hard by. No further notice was then taken of the "meteor," for next morning was fought the great battle of Vouglé. Not long after the battle St. Hilary appeared to the abbot Fridolin, the head of a monastery close by Poitiers, told him where his body was lying, and directed him to build a new tomb for it, with the assistance of Clovis and the bishop of Poitiers. The abbot obeyed, and when the tomb was ready, a grand ceremony was arranged for the interment. The body had been sought out previously and laid for the nonce in the crypt of the new church, but on the day appointed the crypt was brilliantly illuminated and filled with a most delightful odour, and lo! the dead body raised itself, and was carried "no doubt by invisible angels," and laid in the new tomb.—Pierre Damien, *Sermon on St. Hilary of Poitiers.*

St. Januarius tells his disciples to hunt up his missing finger (A.D. 305). When St. Januarius was executed, one of his fingers was cut off; and while the Christians were burying the body, his ghost appeared to them, and told them to go in search of the missing finger. By the guidance of the Holy Spirit they found it, and buried it with the rest of the body.—Edward Kinesman, *Lives of the Saints*, Sept. 19, p. 742 (1623).

St. Longinus gives instructions to a poor blind woman about his head (first century). Longinus, the Roman soldier who pierced the side of Jesus with his spear, afterwards became a disciple, and was beheaded in Jerusalem. The decapitated head was taken to Pilate, and Pilate had it exposed over the gates of the city, after which it was cast into a sewer. Now, there lived at the time in Cappadocia, a poor old blind woman who had an only son, and this son led her by the hand to Jerusalem, under the hope that she might there recover her sight; but no sooner had she set foot in the holy city than her son died. She now saw in a vision Longinus come to her. He commanded her to go in search of his head, which was covered with silt, and told her the moment she touched it she would recover her sight and see her son. Encouraged by this vision, she started on her search, found the head in a public sewer, and recovered her sight. The night following, Longinus appeared to her again, and showing to her her son in glory, said to her, "Weep not for one in glory; but now take my head and place it in a coffin with your son, and cease not to praise God in His saints." So the woman buried the head and body of her son together in the village of Sardial, where Longinus was born.—*Acta Sanctorum* (Bollandists), March 15. (This is the subject of the one hundred and twenty-first figure of the *Greek Menology.*)

St. Lucian the Syrian tells Glycerius where to find his body (A.D. 312). St. Lucian was cruelly martyred by the Emperor Maximinus. After death, a heavy stone was tied to the right hand, and the body tossed into the sea. Fourteen days later the ghost of St. Lucian appeared to Glycerius, and told him, if he went to such and such a place, he would find the martyred body. Glycerius went with several companions to the place indicated, and there found a dolphin bringing the dead body on its back. The dolphin landed it safely and then died. This "fact" is mentioned in the hymn of St. Lucian, at one time sung by the [Roman] Catholic Church on Jan. 7, St. Lucian's Day. Two of the lines run thus—

> A dolphin brought to land the treasure,
> And died from its excess of pleasure.

No corruption had passed on the body, though it had been mutilated by torture, and afterwards tossed about in the deep sea for fourteen days; but the right hand had been wrenched off by the weight of the stone attached to it. This relic was, however, given up by the sea a few days later, and being laid near the corpse became miraculously united to it, so that the entire body, safe and sound, was restored to the disciples. Helena, the mother of Constantine, on her return from Jerusalem, built a city on the spot of sepulture, and called it Helenopolis. The place was previously called Drepan.—Bollandus, *Acta Sanctorum*, vol. i. Jan. 7.

St. Maura and St. Britta give directions about their dead bodies. One day a man observed a strange light burning on a spot where popular tradition gave out that two virgins were buried. On approaching the light, it was found to proceed from a wax candle of marvellous whiteness. After standing in admiration at the phenomenon for some time, the man went and spoke of it to others. Soon afterwards two ghosts appeared to him. They were two virgins, who told him they were buried in the very spot where he had seen the candle burning, bade him clear away the brambles and nettles therefrom, and afford their bodies a decent burial. The man went about his business next day, and thought no more of the apparition; but when night came on the two ghosts appeared to him again, and told him he should certainly die before the year was out, unless he obeyed their behests. Greatly alarmed at this threat, the man chopped away the brambles from the spot, and, having dug a few feet in depth, found two graves on which were great drops of perfumed wax. He cleared the graves, and built a little oratory over them. When his oratory was finished, he asked Euphrasius bishop of Tours to come and consecrate it, but the bishop wrote word back, "I am very aged, and as the weather is cold and stormy I dare not venture out." At night, the two virgins appeared to Euphrasius, and said to him, "Bishop, wherein have we offended you, that you refuse to consecrate the oratory raised over our bodies? Go, in the name of God, and perform the service required of you." Next day the bishop started on his mission. The rain ceased, the sun shone bright, the weather was delightful, and the bishop enjoyed his trip. He often spoke about the two ghosts, and used to say one was large and the other small, both were whiter than snow, and they told him their names were Maura and Britta. They are still venerated in Tours, and their fête is held annually on Jan. 28. The place where this occurred was then called Arciacum, but is now called Sainte Maure.—*Les Petits Bollandistes*, vol. ii. pp. 78, 79.

St. Sebastian gives directions to a certain dame to bury his body in the catacombs. (A.D. 288). The emperor Diocletian ordered St. Sebastian to be beaten to death in the Roman hippodrome; and that his body might not fall into the hands of the Christians, he commanded it to be thrown into the common sewer. But St. Sebastian's apparition appeared to a holy dame, and told her that his body was not washed away, seeing it was caught on a hook. He then directed her to rescue it, and bury it in the catacombs, near the entrance, at the feet of the two apostles St. Peter and St. Paul. The dame did as the ghost enjoined her, and continued thirty days in prayers for the dead, after her work was done.—The abbot Corblet, *Hagiography of Amiens.*

St. Vincent informs a widow where to find his body. St. Vincent was martyred A.D. 303. His relics are preserved in Lisbon to this day, and his "bloody stole" is still exhibited in the church of St. Vincent, in Paris. It cannot fail to be interesting to trace out these valued relics, especially as each adventure is set down with most marvellous minuteness, by [Roman] Catholic writers of undoubted repute. Well, we are told that after great tortures the saint was removed by Dacian, the Roman proconsul of Spain, from his bed of torture to a soft pallet, on which he died. This was not done in mercy to the victim, but with a view of prolonging his slow martyrdom; and Dacian, angry that his victim had escaped his grasp, had the dead body thrown "into a stinking ditch full of the offscouring of the city, not far from the gates." Here it was left unburied to be devoured by wild beasts and birds of prey; but God sent a raven to watch over it, and this raven kept off the wolves and all other creatures that attempted to molest it. Dacian, being told of this extraordinary "fact," had the body wrapped in an ox-hide, heavily weighted with stones, and cast into the sea. Eumorfius was employed to execute this order, and he carried the body several furlongs from shore, before he cast it overboard; when, however, he reached land, there was the body safe enough, lying on the sands. Metaphrastês tells us that the sea, more merciful than man, rolled sand over the body and buried it. Not long afterwards, the ghost of the saint appeared to a widow, and told her where he was buried; so the widow went to the spot indicated, found the body, and carried it to Valencia. Here a church dedicated to the saint was built, and the body magnificently enshrined. In 713, the Saracens destroyed the city, and Habbaragman, king of Cordova, ordered the relics to be burnt; but somehow the body of the saint escaped, and was carried to Cape St. Vincent, where those who carried it thither intended to form a colony. Here they built a little chapel, and interred the body in a hole under the chapel floor. In the reign of Alonso Henriquez of Portugal, A.D. 1139, four kings made war on Portugal, and Alonso, having defeated them, adopted "the quoin for his device." In this battle of the four kings, some Christian slaves were taken prisoners of war, amongst whom were some from the Cape St. Vincent, who told the king about the saint's body; so Alonso sent a ship to the cape to fetch it away. It was brought safely to Portugal, and in 1147 deposited in the great church at Lisbon.

Here we have the utmost minuteness of dates and names, although, it must be confessed, the adventures are most romantic. The body was cast into the city stew and guarded by a raven; it was then carried several furlongs from shore and cast into the deep sea, being first sewed in a sack and well weighted with stones;

being drifted ashore it was buried by the action of the waves in the sand of the seashore. St. Vincent's ghost told a respectable widow where to find the body, and the widow carried it to Valencia. Some four hundred years afterwards Valencia was taken by the Moors, who burnt all the Christian relics; but the body of St. Vincent escaped, and was carried by some refugees to Cape St. Vincent, where it was buried beneath a chapel. Another period of four hundred years rolled by, when Alonso Henriquez, being told of the body by some prisoners of war, removed it to Lisbon. The Portuguese are satisfied that the body they have is that of St. Vincent, who died in 303, and Jan. 22 is set apart in honour of this wonderful saint.—Edward Kinesman (1623), *Lives of the Saints*, pp. 76-83.

Kinesman tells us his authorities are St. Isidore, Prudentius,* Beda, and Metaphrastes; but many others have written the life of this favourite saint. Alban Butler adds "that this account of St. Vincent is recorded by unexceptionable vouchers in Bollandus, p. 406; and that Thomas ab Incarnatione, in his *Ecclesiastical History* (1759), has a full and particular account of the whole." This history is comparatively modern, but Mgr. Guérin, in his *Vies des Saints* (7th edit. 1880), is still more near our own times, and he repeats the same (vol. i. p. 539, etc.). If great names, minute dates, and historic facts suffice, I know no tale better fortified than this of St. Vincent.

The following authors have written the praises of St. Vincent:—St. Augustine, St. Bernard, St. Isidore, St. Leo (pope), Metaphrastês, Prudentius, etc. All writers of martyrologies; and many others.

Charles the Bald gave the bishop of Besançon two of the vertebræ of St. Vincent, A.D. 876.

St. Germain de Prés was built by king Childebert in honour of St. Vincent, and he gave to it an arm of the holy martyr.

The Church du Mans had the head of the martyr till the revolution, when it was lost.

The dames religieuses du Charme have two bones of the saint, one of the arm and another of the leg.

The heart was preserved in a silver reliquary in Dun-le-Roi, Berry, till 1562, when some Calvinists stole the reliquary and burnt the heart.

Vitry le François still possesses the forearm, which was brought from Spain by king Childebert.—Mgr. Guérin, *Vies des Saints*, vol. i. pp. 540, 541.

* Mgr. Guérin tells us the widow's name was Ionique. He also says the sack weighted with stones "nageait sur l'eau comme une éponge." The waves, he tells us, did not scatter sand over the body, but "creusèrent une fosse, et le couvrirent du sable de la mer pour lui donner la sépulture, jusqu'à ce qu'il plût à Dieu d'en disposer autrement."—Prudentius, *Sermons*, 274-277.

An old missal of Constance, printed 1504, contains this proverb on Jan. 22—

Vincenti festo, si sol radiat, memor esto;
Tunc magnum fac vas, quia vitis dabit tibi uvas.

If St. Vincent's Day be fine
'Twill be a famous year for wine.

Appearances soon after Death.

1 COR. xv. 4-8. [Christ was dead, and buried, and rose again the third day], and was seen of Cephas; then of the twelve; after that, He was seen of five hundred brethren at once; then of James; then of all the apostles; and last of all by me also.

Appearances of St. John-Joseph of the Cross after death (A.D. 1734). Scarcely had John-Joseph given back his soul into the hands of God than he began to manifest himself in his spiritual state. At the very hour of his death he appeared to Diego Pignatelli, duke of Monte Leone, while he was walking about his private apartment. The duke had seen him at Naples, a day or two before, sick almost to death, but he now appeared in perfect health, and was encircled in light. Greatly astonished at the spectacle, the duke said, "Father John-Joseph, is that you? I am glad you have so quickly recovered." The saint replied, "I am both well and happy," and then vanished. His grace then sent to Naples to make inquiries, and was informed that John-Joseph departed this life at the very hour he manifested himself to the duke.

John-Joseph manifested himself in a manner still more remarkable to Innocent Valetta. While Innocent was asleep, he felt his arm pulled, and heard himself called aloud by name. He woke in a fright, and perceived a cloud of glory, in the midst of which stood a "religious" of the Order of St. Peter of Alcantara, considerably advanced in age. Valetta could not recognize the face of the apparition in consequence of the numerous rays of light which dazzled his eyes. The apparition asked Valetta if he recognized him, and Valetta answered, "No." "I," said the apparition, "am John-Joseph of the Cross, just this moment delivered from the bondage of the flesh, and now on my way to paradise, where I will never cease to intercede for the house of Innocent Valetta. If you would like to see my mortal remains, you will find my body in the infirmary of St. Lucy of the Mount." So saying he vanished away, leaving Valetta filled with grief and great joy. Valetta hastened to St. Lucy of the Mount, and there found a great crowd, who announced the death of the saint, and were not a little amazed on hearing that Valetta had just seen him. This account was given to the council by Innocent Valetta himself, some thirty years after the decease of the saint, when the process of his canonization was being drawn out.

Three days afterwards John-Joseph appeared to Father-Buono, a monk of his own order, and bade him tell the superior to have the *Gloria Patri* chanted before the altar of the Saint-Sacrament, to render thanks to the Holy Trinity for the favours bestowed on him.

A few days later he appeared to Mad. Mary Anne Boulei de Verme, who greatly desired spiritual comfort.

After that, the baron Bassano, who was confined to his bed with a mortal sickness, was favoured with a visit from the saint, and was not only cured of his malady, but lived many years afterwards; and when at last he died, it was of a complaint far different from that which St. John-Joseph had miraculously cured. Sending for Father Buono, the baron recounted to him how St. John-Joseph had formerly cured him.—Cardinal Wiseman, communicated to Migne's *Démonstrations Evangéliques*, vol. xvi.

Army of Martyrs.

REV. vi. 9. I saw under the altar the souls of them that were slain for the Word of God, and for the testimony which they held.

REV. xx. 4. I saw the souls of them that were beheaded for the witness of Jesus, and for the Word of God, and which had not worshipped the beast, neither his image.

The following articles are interesting because they are martyrs in groups.

The four crowned (Nov. 8, A.D. 304). In the reign of Diocletian four Roman citizens were scourged to death with whips loaded with plummets of lead, and were buried on the Lavian Way, three miles from Rome. Pope Melchiades put them in the catalogue of martyrs, but, not knowing their names, called them "The Four Crowned," and appointed Nov. 8 as their fête-day. Afterwards (we are not told when) their names were revealed to a holy man (we are not informed how or to whom). They were Carpophorus, Severianus, Severus, and Victorinus.—Ado (archbishop of Trèves), *Martyrology;* Bosio, *Subterranean Rome* (1632), bk. iii. 8.

*** Other four martyrs were the illustrious Roman knights, Basilidês, Cyrinus, Nabor, and Nazarius, in the reign of Diocletian. They were scourged with scorpions (*q.v.*) by the prefect Aurelian, and after eight days were executed, June 12, A.D. 303.

The five image-makers, martyrs (Nov. 8, A.D. 304). During the persecution of Diocletian five carvers were put to death, for refusing to make idols. They suffered on the same day as "The Four Crowned" (*q.v.*), were buried in the same cemetery, their remains were translated by Leo IV. into the same church, and they are honoured on the same day Their names are: Castorius, Claudius, Nicostratus, Simplicius, and Symphorianus.—Bosio, *Roma Sotterranea*, bk. iii. 8 (1632).

The five Minorite friars, martyred Jan. 16, 1220. Five Minorites were sent by St. Francis to preach to the Mahometans of the West. They preached first to the Moors of Seville, but were banished from Spain. Passing into Morocco, they preached there the doctrine of the cross, and were again banished; but they returned, were scourged, and burning oil mixed with vinegar was poured on their wounds. The king then caused them to be brought before him, and clove their heads asunder with his scimitar.—Alban Butler, *Lives of the Saints*, Jan. 16.

These names, according to the Roman breviary, are: Acursius, Adjutus, Berard, Peter, and Otto.

The seven martyrs of Persia (A.D. 341–380). Sapor, king of Persia, was the most bloody of all the persecutors of the Christian Church. Sozomenês, in his *Church History*, reckons the number of martyrs in this reign at 16,000, but some writers set it as high as 200,000. The "seven martyrs of Persia" were: Azadê, Acepsimas, Joseph, Aïthala, Tarbula, Millês, and Barsabias.

AZADÊ was the first to fall. He was Sapor's chief eunuch; and the king was so distressed at his death, that he sent an edict to all the provinces, to confine the persecution to bishops, priests, and monks.

ACEPSIMAS was an Assyrian bishop, eighty years of age; JOSEPH, a priest of Bethcatuba; AÏTHALA, a deacon of Bethnuhadra.

Acepsimas being first scourged, his joints were pulled the wrong way till he died under the torture. Joseph was treated in the same manner, but, being younger and stronger, survived, and died in prison six months afterwards. Aïthala, after the most atrocious tortures, was executed.

TARBULA was the sister of St. Simeon, archbishop of Seleucia. Being tied to one post by the neck, and to another by the feet, she was cut asunder with a saw.

MILLÊS was once a soldier in the Persian army; but left the service, and was appointed bishop of a small Persian city. Being brought before Horsmida, he so provoked him by his plain speaking, that the judge leaped from his tribunal, and killed him on the spot.

BARSABIAS was bishop of Susa. His legs were first broken off at the knees, then at the thighs. His arms were next lopped off, then his ribs broken, his ears cut off, and his eyes knocked out, after which he was beheaded.—Assemani, *Acts of the Oriental Martyrs*, p. 66.

The seven martyrs of Samosata (Dec. 8, A.D. 297). In A.D. 297 the emperor Maximian, returning victorious from Persia, celebrated the quinquennial games at Samosata, near the Euphratês; and commanded all the inhabitants to repair to the temple of Fortune, in the middle of the city, to assist in public supplications and sacrifices. Two of the chief magistrates, Hipparchus and Philothëus, had embraced the Christian faith for three years; and five intimate friends, James, Habibus, Lollianus, Paragrus, and Romanus, young nobles, and senators, had only just become Christians. The emperor, being informed that the two magistrates had absented themselves, sent for them, and asked why they had not obeyed his command; being told they were Christians, he ordered them to be beaten, and put in prison. In the mean time, the other five nobles were also apprehended, and put in chains till the end of the festival. At the close of the festival, they were all brought again before the emperor, and as they proved obdurate, cords were put across their mouths and they were led away to crucifixion. A reprieve for a few days was granted, that the two magistrates might make up their public accounts; after which they were suspended on seven crosses. Hipparchus, a very old man, soon died; James, Lollianus, and Romanus expired the next day; the other three, being still alive, were then taken down, and nails were driven into their heads. The emperor commanded their bodies to be thrown into the Euphratês, but one Bassus, a rich Christian, having bribed the guards to give them up, buried them in his own farm.

The acts of these seven martyrs were written by an eyewitness; and his narrative is contained in Stephen Assemani's *Acta Martyrum*, vol. ii. p. 123.

(There are also the seven virgin martyrs of Ancyra, capital of Galatia. Their names were: Alexandria, Claudia, Euphrasia, Julietta, Matrona, Phaina, and Tecusa. May 18, A.D. 303.)

The ten martyrs of Crete (Dec. 23). In the persecution of Decius, Crete greatly suffered, but the ten martyrs of Crete were Agathopus, Bassilidês, Cleomenês, Eunicianus, Euporus, Evarestus, Gelasius, Saturninus, Theodulus, and Zolicus. Being apprehended, they were dragged on the ground, beaten, stoned, and spit upon. Their trial took place on Dec. 23, and they were ordered to offer sacrifice to the Cretan god Jupiter, whose festival it was. They replied, "We are no strangers to Jupiter. We can show you his grave. He was a native of Crete, the tyrant of his country, and a man abandoned to every filthy lust. Those who worship Jupiter as a god, ought to follow his example." Then were they, some of them, racked and torn with iron nails, so that the ground beneath was covered with great gobbets of flesh. Others were punctured all over with sharp stones, reeds, and stakes. Others were beaten with heavy plummets of lead. The martyrs bore it all without a murmur, and the proconsul, tired out, ordered their heads to be cut off. The fathers who composed the Council of Crete in 558, writing to the Emperor Leo, say that, through the intercession of these martyrs, their island has hitherto been preserved from heresy.—*Creta Sacra*. (Their martyrdom is given by Metaphrastês, Surius, Lipoman, and others.)

The twelve brothers, martyrs (Sept. 2, A.D. 258). The twelve brothers were natives of Adrumetum, in Africa; after suffering grievous torments for the faith, they were sent to Benevento, in Italy, where they suffered martyrdom, in the persecution of Valerian.—Baronius, *Roman Martyrology*.

Their names were: Arontius, Donatus, Felix (two), Fortunatus, Honoratus, Januarius, Repositus, Sabinianus, Satyrus, Septimius, and Vitalis.

The eighteen martyrs of Saragossa (A.D. 303). Engracia was the daughter of a Portuguese princess, engaged in marriage to a duke of Gallia Narbonensis. Her father sent her with a companion named Julia, and sixteen nobles, to her betrothed, and the brilliant cortége stopped at Saragossa in the house of Lupercus, her uncle. While here, Engracia was witness to one of the Christian butcheries of Diocletian and Maximian; and, with heroic zeal, she went to Dacian to plead on behalf of her co-religionists. She told Dacian her name, her rank, and her mission; but the monster, instead of being moved to pity, commanded the beautiful young princess and all her suite to be cast into prison. Engracia was first beaten with clubs; then tied to the tail of a horse, and dragged through the streets of the city; next day her body was torn with iron combs with such brutality, that some of her bowels were torn out and a part of her liver; her left breast was then cut off, and the knife cut so deep that her heart was laid bare; she was then taken back to prison, and died. Her companions were all beheaded.

The eighteen martyrs who suffered with Engracia were Julia her friend, Lupercus her uncle, and the sixteen nobles: Apodemus, Cecilianus, Evotius, Felix, Fronto, Martial, Optatus, Primitivus, Publius, Quintilian, Saturninus (four of the name), Successus, and Urban.

N.B.—In the persecution which followed, the number that fell is unknown. They are celebrated on Nov. 3, under the title of "The Innumerable Martyrs of Saragossa."—Tamayus-Salazar, *Spanish Martyrology*.

The nineteen martyrs of Gorcum (July 9, 1572). Nineteen priests and religious men were taken by the Calvinists in Gorcum, and, after suffering many insults, were hanged at Bril on account of their religion. Of these, eleven were Franciscan friars, called "Recollects," of the convent of Gorcum, one was a Norbertin, two were Dominicans, one was a canon regular of St. Austin, three were curates, and one a secular priest.—William Estius (Douay, 1603). See also *Batavia Sacra*, pt. ii. p. 174.

Franciscans: Antony of Hornaire, near Gorcum; Antony of Werden; Cornelius of Dorestate (a lay brother); Godfrey of Merveille; Jerome of Werden; Nicaisius Johnson of Heze; Peter of Asca (a lay brother); Nicholas Pick; Francis Rhodes of Brussels; Theodorick of Embeden; and Wilhadê, a Dane.

The other eight were: Godfrey Dunen of Gorcum, a curate; John Helvarenbeck, a Norbertin of Middleburgh; John, a Dominican of Cologne; James Lacop, a Dominican of Munster; John Oosterwican; Nicholas Poppel, a curate; Leonard Vechel, a curate; and Walter, a secular priest of Heinort, near Dort.

The twenty-six martyrs of Japan (Feb. 5, 1597). St. Francis Xavier arrived in Japan in 1549, and baptized many. In 1587 there were in Japan above a quarter of a million Christians; but in 1588 the emperor Cambacundono commanded all Jesuits to leave Japan within six months; many, however, still remained in the island. Tagcosama renewed the persecution; and, in 1597, twenty-three men and three boys who acted as acolytes were martyred. They were put to death at Nangasaqui, in the following manner:—Twenty-six crosses were planted in a row, about four feet asunder; the martyrs were fastened to these crosses by cords and chains about their arms and legs, and an iron collar about their necks. The crosses were then lifted up, and planted in holes prepared to receive them. By each cross stood a spearman, who thrust his spear into the left side of the victim, immediately the cross stood upright; and the victim soon died.—Alban Butler, *Lives of the Saints*, Feb. 5.

Besides these canonized martyrs there were many others who suffered martyrdom in Japan, notably the twenty-five who were fastened to stakes and burnt alive, Sept. 2, 1622. Of these, Spinola is the most noted. (For the twenty martyrs of Nicomedia, see Index.)

The forty martyrs of Acquigny, in Normandy (fourth century). Not much is known of this army of martyrs, but in Acquigny is a black stone, kept in a glass case, containing the following words:—"HIC EST LOCUS MARTYRUM, ET RELIQUÆ SS. MARTYRUM MAXIMI ET VENERANDI, ET SOCIORUM EORUM TRIGINTA ET OCTO." The tablet is not dated. Maximus and Venerandus were natives of Italy, born somewhere in the neighbourhood of Mola. They went into Gaul to preach to the barbarians there, and being seized at Acquigny, near Evreux, were put to death, it is supposed from the tablet, with thirty-eight companions or converts. Maximus and Venerandus, we are told, were buried near the spot of their execution, and in 960, some six hundred years afterwards, their bodies were discovered by Amalbert, and deposited in a chapel built by Robert I. duke of Normandy.—L'abbé Lebeurier, *Notice sur la Commune d'Acquigny*.

The time between the death and discovery would carry us back to Edward I., or even to the grant of Magna Charta, and no one knows who Amalbert is. Suppose a certain Mr. Smith were to say he has found the bodies of two of the barons who were present at the signing of Magna Charta, or even two of the "rebels" who were cut down by Richard II. in Wat Tyler's gang, we should certainly demand very strong proof.

The forty martyrs of the Thundering Legion (A.D. 320). Licinus gave an order for all his army to offer sacrifice. The 12th or Thundering Legion was at the time lying at Sebastê, in Lesser Armenia, and in this legion were forty Christians. When they heard of the imperial order, they told the governor Agricolaus that their religion forbade them to offer sacrifice to idols. Being punished for insubordination they were imprisoned; and as they still refused to obey the imperial edict, Agricolaus condemned them to death. The cold in Armenia is very severe, especially in March; and towards the end of winter, when the wind is north, the frost is almost unbearable. Now, under the walls of Sebastê, there was a large pond, which at the time was frozen over, and the judge ordered the insubordinate soldiers to be exposed naked on the ice of this pond; but, under the hope that their sufferings might induce them to change their minds, he commanded warm baths to be placed on the margin, to which any of them might go if they relented. When brought from prison, they went joyfully to the pond and stripped themselves without a murmur. Most writers say that the ice was broken, and they stood in the water; but St. Basil and St. Gregory of Nyssa affirm that they lay on the surface of the lake for three days, and all their limbs, one after another, were mortified by the frost. While thus exposed they made this prayer: "Lord, we are forty who have engaged in this combat; grant that we may be forty crowned, and that not one be wanting of that sacred number." One of the number, unable to bear the horrible suffering, ran to the baths; but, "as the devil always deceives his votaries, no sooner had he entered it than he died." This apostasy greatly afflicted the martyrs; but they were quickly comforted by seeing his place filled up. The sentinel was warming himself near the bath at the time, and saw a number of spirits descend from heaven on the martyrs to comfort them. They had warm garments and crowns in their hands. He counted the crowns and found the number was only thirty-nine; so, throwing off his clothes, he ran to the pond, crying, "I also am now a Christian." Then was heard the prayer, "Grant there may be forty crowned, and that not one be wanting of that sacred number." St. Ephrem says, "Thus was heard the prayer, though not in the manner it was imagined, and we ought to adore the impenetrable secrets of the Almighty. As Matthias took the place of the reprobate Judas, this sentinel was numbered with the thirty-nine in lieu of the apostate coward."—St. Ephrem, *Oration on the Forty Martyrs*, vol. ii. (The martyrdom of these forty will be found in all hagiographies.) See especially St. Basil, *Homily* 20, vol. i. p. 452; St. Gregory of Nyssa, *Discourses*, vol. ii. pp. 499–504; Cullistus, *Church History*, bk. xiv. ch. 10; Tellemont, *Memoirs serving for the Ecclesiastical History of the First Six Centuries*, vol. v. p. 518; Ruinart, *Acts of the First Martyrs*, p. 523.

The names of these forty martyrs are: Acacius, Aëtius, Alexander, Angias, Athanasius, Caius, Candidius, Chudion, Claudius, Cyril, Domitian, Ecditius, Eunoicus, Eutyches, Eutychius, Flavius, Gorgonus, Helian, Helius, Heraclius, Hysichius, John, Leonce, Lysimacus, Meliton, Micallius, Nicholas, Philoctimon, Priscus, Quirion, Sacerdon, Severian, Sisinius, Smarigdus, Theodulus, Theophilus, Valens, Valerius, Vibian, and Xanthus.

The forty-eight martyrs of Lyons (A.D. 177). Eusebius, in his *Church History*, gives an account of the martyrs of Lyons, and mentions some of their names. There is an inscription above a prison door in Lyons, running thus: "The church of Lyons has always venerated this cavern, as the prison where St. Pothin (its first bishop) was shut up with forty-eight Christians, and where he won the crown of martyrdom." Gregory of Tours and Ado, archbishop of Trèves, completed the list given by Eusebius. As the lists contain only forty-eight names, the bishop Pothin must be included in the words "fut enfermé avec quarante-huit chrétiens." There were twenty-seven men and twenty-one women. Of these, twenty-four were Roman citizens, and were beheaded; six were exposed to wild beasts; and eighteen died in the dungeon.

(1) Those who died in the dungeon were: Apollonius, Arescius, Cornelius, Gramnitus, Geminianus, Julius, POTHIN (the bishop, aged ninety), Titus, Zolicus, Zozimus; Æmilia, Alumna, two named Antonia, Julia, Justa, Pompeia, and Trophima.

(2) The twenty-four Roman citizens, beheaded, were: Alcibiadês, Comminus, Geminus, Macarius, October, Philommus, Primus, Silvius, Ulpius, Vettius Epagathus, Vitalis, Zachariah; Æmilia, Albina, Biblis or Bibliada, Grata, Helpis (also called Amnas), Julia, Materna, Pompeia, Posthumiana, Quinta, Rhodana, and Royala.

(3) The six exposed to wild beasts were: Alexander of Phrygia, Attalus of Pergamos, Muturus a neophyte, Ponticus a youth, Sanctus deacon of Vienne, and Blandina a female slave.

See *Saint Pothin et ses compagnons martyrs*. Also André Gouilloud, *Origines de l'Église de Lyon*; and D. Meynis, *Grands Souvenirs de l'Église de Lyon*.

St. Simeon, archbishop of Seleucia, with a hundred other Christians put to a martyr's death by Sapor, king of Persia (April 17, A.D. 345). St. Simeon, archbishop of Seleucia, being seized by order of Sapor, was brought before the shah, who gave him the choice of offering adoration to the sun or being put to death. St. Simeon refused to worship the creature instead of the Creator. He was beheaded, and a hundred other Christians with him. Of these, five were bishops, several were priests or deacons, and the rest laymen.

A day or two before, Guhsciatazadês, chief of the eunuchs, and first noble of the kingdom, had been beheaded for avowing himself a Christian.—Assemani, *Acts of the Martyrs of the East*, vol. i. p. 1.

The 120 martyrs of Hadiabena, in Persia (A.D. 344). In the fifth year of the persecutions in Persia, king Sapor being in Seleucia, 120 Christians were arrested; among which were nine virgins, several priests, and a large number of the inferior clergy. They remained six months in filthy dungeons, till the end of winter. Jazdundocta, a wealthy lady of Hadiabena, supported them all the time. They were ultimately beheaded, and Jazdundocta employed men to embalm their bodies and bury them.—Assemani, *Acts of the Martyrs*, vol. i. p. 105.

The 275 martyrs of Persia (April 9, A.D. 362). The Persians took by siege the castle Bethzarbe, on the Tigris, massacred the garrison, and led away nine thousand captives, among which were three hundred Christians. When they arrived on the confines of Assyria, the option was given to these Christians either to adore the sun or suffer death. Twenty-five saved their lives by abjuring the Christian faith, but the remaining 275 witnessed by their blood a good confession.—Alban Butler, *Lives of the Saints*, April 9.

The 6666 martyrs of the Theban Legion. The emperor Maximian had a legion of 6666 Christians, commanded by St. Maurice. This legion was raised in the Thebaïs of Egypt, and had been baptized by Zabdus, bishop of Jerusalem. When Maximian was on his march to Gaul to put down a rebellion, this legion formed part of his army. Halting at Agaunum, the emperor ordered that the gods should be propitiated with sacrifice. St. Maurice and his Christian legion refused to be present at this heathen ceremony, and Maximian, considering their absence an act of mutiny, ordered the legion to pass under the yoke, and every tenth man to be cut down. The survivors still refused to be present at the sacrifice, and the emperor commanded them to be decimated again; and when the residue still remained persistent, Maximian sent the other legions to hew them all to pieces.

The 6666 martyrs were buried in pits; but three hundred years afterwards their ghosts appeared to bishop Theodore, and told him where they lay. Theodore commanded the bodies to be disinterred, and sent their relics to sundry countries, where shrines or churches were erected to their honour. Divers miracles, we are assured, have fully attested the favour with which God has regarded this army of martyrs. In the vestry of Toledo, in Spain, is shown the head of St. Maurice, colonel of the legion.—Usuard (died 1475), *Martyrology*; Metaphrastês (tenth century), *Lives*, etc.; Antonius (died 1586), *Chronicon*; and many others.

St. Ursula and her eleven thousand virgin martyrs (A.D. 237). St. Ursula, the daughter of Dianotus, a British king, was sought in marriage by Holofernês, a heathen prince. Dianotus consented to the alliance, but Ursula made it imperative that the prince should be baptized, and that three years should elapse before the marriage was consummated. During these three years Ursula was to travel with her eleven maidens, each attended with a thousand companions. The conditions being accepted, St. Ursula, with her suite, set sail, reached Cologne, and proceeded thence to Rome. Having visited the tombs of the apostles, Ursula, with the eleven thousand virgins, returned to Cologne, and fell into the hands of Attila and the Huns, by whom all were put to the sword, except Ursula, who was reserved as a prize for Attila. Subsequently Ursula also was put to death. God heard the voice of the martyrs crying from the ground, and sent a host of angels to smite the Huns, as the angel of death once smote the army of Sennacherib. The inhabitants of Cologne, being thus miraculously delivered from its invaders, built a church in honour of the virgin martyrs, and called it St. Ursula's. The bones of the martyrs, piled together in the wall, are still shown to visitors through glass windows; but, undoubtedly, many of the bones shown are those of men and boys.

Another version makes the tale a Christian parallel to the "Rape of the Sabines" in Roman story. Thus Geoffrey of Monmouth, in his *British History*, bk. v. ch. 15, 16, tells us that Maximian, the British king, having conquered Armorica, now called Brittany, gave it to Conan Meriadoc, his nephew. Being almost depopulated by war, Conan wished to find wives for himself and his soldiers, and induced Dianotus, brother and successor of Caradoc, king of Cornwall, to assist him. Dianotus himself had a daughter, named Ursula, and her he promised to Conan for wife. He then summoned together all the chief men of his kingdom, and by their means got together eleven thousand maidens, all of whom, with his daughter Ursula, he shipped to Conan. Scarcely were the transports in the open sea, when contrary winds arose, drove them to Zealand and Holland, and thence to the mouth of the Rhine. Here a piratic force under Melga and Guanius, consisting chiefly of Picts and Huns, coasting about those parts, stumbled on the transports, and determined to take the maidens to themselves; but Ursula and the eleven thousand resisted the indignity. The pirates, infuriated at this resistance, fell on the women like wolves, and put them to the sword. Cordula escaped, but, being caught the next day, was put to death also. The bodies of the martyred virgins were afterwards carefully gathered together, and taken to Collen [Cologne], where was erected a famous nunnery, but many were distributed, as holy relics, in other parts of Christendom. The slaughter of the eleven thousand is said to have occurred Oct. 21, A.D. 237.

No saints in the calendar have received more notice than St. Ursula and her virgins. The oldest account is given by Gaufrid bishop of St. Assaffe [Asaph]. Cardinal Baronius, and William Lindan bishop of Ruremund, took their accounts from the book of the Welsh bishop Gaufrid, preserved in the Vatican library. St. Ado, archbishop of Trèves, in his *Martyrology*, gives the following names as the most noted of the virgins: Ursula, and Cordula who escaped but was afterwards captured and put to death, Britula, Clementia, Grata, Gregoria, Mardia (or Martha), Palladia, Pinnosa, Rabacia, Saturia (or Saturnia), Saturnina, Saula, and Sentia.

Wandalbert, who died about A.D. 590, gives an account of St. Ursula and her maidens; so does Sigelbert in his *Chronicle* (twelfth century); Rogerius Cisterciencis, Richardus Præmonstratensis, Claudius de Rola, Bonfinius in his *History of Hungary*, Petrus de Natalibus, Polidore Virgil in his *History of England*, and Laurentius Surius (1570) in his *Lives of the Saints*, where the most detailed account is to be found.

Aureola or Glory. (See LIGHT, pt. ii.)

EXOD. xxxiv. 29-35. When Moses came down from the mount with the two tables of testimony, "the skin of his face shone . . . and the children of Israel were afraid to come nigh him . . . [so] he put a veil upon his face."

MATT. xvii. 2. When Jesus was transfigured "His face did shine as the sun."

REV. x. 1. I saw another mighty angel come down from heaven . . . a rainbow was upon his head, and his face was as it were the sun.

ACTS vi. 15. All that sat in the council, looking steadfastly on Stephen, saw his face as it had been the face of an angel.

Many of the following sights of glory and luminous phenomena may be satisfactorily ascribed to morbid action in the encephalic sensory ganglia connected with the optic nerves, arising from derangement, centric or eccentric, of the circulation of the blood within the brain, or from over-tension of the brain or eye nerve-tissue. Every one knows that in vertigo, for example, flashes of light before the eyes are as common as aerial sounds and buzzings in the ears.

The face of St. Ælred in infancy cast a shadow (1109-1166). The following I give in the exact words of Mgr. Guérin, as I fear any translation would be considered apocryphal: " Lorsqu'il reposait, enfant, dans son berceau, son parent [Guillaume] s'approchant pour le considérer, fut tout à coup saisi de respect et d'admiration, car il vit la figure du petit enfant briller comme le soleil; elle rayonnait d'une telle lumière, que Guillaume en approchant sa main, elle faisait de l'ombre, et il se voyait dans ce visage comme dans un miror."—*Les Petits Bollandistes* (7th edit. 1880), vol. i. p. 286.

The expression "elle faisait de l'ombre" can only mean that William's hand threw a shadow on the child's face which shone like the sun; but how an opaque body can throw a shadow on a luminous one is certainly a new phenomenon in optics. Think of your hand, held before a burning lamp, throwing a shadow on the flame.

The aureola of St. Africus, bishop of Comminges (sixth century). One day when St. Africus was celebrating mass, an aureola or crown of fire encircled his head, "quam qui sanctissimæ synaxis digni erant, conspiciebant; indignis autem non aspectabilem" (only the holiest of the congregation could see it, to the rest it was not visible).—L'abbé Servières, *Saints du Rouergue*.

Agbarus and the painter. Agbarus, hearing of the fame of Jesus, sent an artist to take the likeness of the divine Redeemer. When the artist saw Jesus and looked on His face to draw it, he found it was so radiant with divine splendour, and so dazzling in brightness, that he could not bear to fix his eyes on it, and he told Agbarus that no art could depict such brightness any more than it could paint the glory of the sun.—Nicephorus Callistus, *Ecclesiastical History*.

The face of St. Antony of Padua seemed to Ancelinus like the face of an angel. When St. Antony of Padua reproved Ancelinus, tyrant of Padua, for his misdeeds, all expected that the tyrant would command his instant execution. What was their amazement when they beheld Ancelinus run towards the man of God, fall at his feet, and promise amendment! Ancelinus told his court that he saw a divine splendour come from the face of St. Antony, which he was afraid to look upon, and his heart within him lost its courage.—Edward Kinesman (1623), *Lives of the Saints*, p. 369.

The body of St. Arsenius seems to be on

fire (A.D. 450). A brother, to whom God had revealed some of His most chosen disciples, went to the cell of St. Arsenius, and looking through the window saw the saint, as it seemed, all on fire. "C'était l'ardeur dont son âme était saintement embrasée dans l'oraison, que Dieu voulait lui manifester par ce prodige."—Michael Ange Marin, *Lives of the Fathers of the Eastern Deserts.*

It is said of St Radegonda (sixth century) "Après sa mort, son corps brilla d'un éclat extraordinaire."—*Les Petits Bollandistes*, vol. v. p. 515.

The face of St. Eleutherius encircled with a glory (A.D. 531). When St. Eleutherius returned to Tournai, after his miraculous release from prison, as he descended St. Andrew's Mount (then called the Sacred Mount), holding aloft the precious relics, two distinct circles of glory encompassed his head, and all the people shouted. On his march towards the church a number of sick folk were healed of their infirmities, the dumb spake, the deaf had hearing restored, and many a cripple leaped for joy.—*Les Petits Bollandistes*, vol. ii. p. 601.

The face of St. Epiphanius luminous in infancy (A.D. 438). Epiphanius was the son of Marus and Focaria of Pavia, and was so called because a luminous glory surrounded his face when he was first put into his cradle.—Ennodius, *Life of St. Epiphanius of Pavia.* (This life is inserted in the *Acta Sanctorum* by Bollandus.)

Mgr. Guérin, in his *Vies des Saints*, says of St. Epiphanius, "La lumière éclatante qui parut sur son corps, après son décès, fut une marque de la gloire de son âme" (vol. i. p. 518).

The face of St. Francis Hieronimus too dazzling to be looked on (A.D. 1642–1716). Cardinal Wiseman says that St. Francis Hieronimus had frequent ecstasies; and one day, when he was exhorting the people to the communion, his face actually burned with light; in fact, like the face of Moses, "éblouissait les yeux de ceux qui le voyaient."

(St. Francis was canonized in 1839.)

St. Francis of Paula environed with an aureola in the form of three crowns (A.D. 1416–1507). One day, as St. Francis of Paula was praying at the foot of the high altar, while all the monks were present, two priests and a brother from another monastery saw him environed in light, and having on his head three crowns of glory, like the pope's tiara.

At another time, according to the memoirs of John de Milazza, one of his disciples, the archangel Michael appeared to him in great glory, and presented to him a cartouch environed with rays, "comme une gloire de saint sacrement," and containing the word CHARITY, in letters of celestial gold, on an azure field. St. Michael told him to adopt this device in his order.—*Acts of Canonization*, etc. (Father Giry).

The face of St. Oringa shone at death with celestial light (A.D. 1310). St. Oringa was born at Santa Croce. Occasionally she fell into ecstasies, and saw into futurity. She died at the age of seventy, of paralysis, and "her face shone with a celestial light, as it had been the face of an angel."—*Acta Sanctorum* (reprinted from *The Life of St. Oringa*, by Silvanus Razzi).

Whenever St. Philip of Neri received the sacrament his face became luminous (A.D. 1515–1595). In the sacrament of the mass, when the hand of St. Philip of Neri touched the chalice, his face glowed with mysterious light. And at the elevation, his soul became so ravished that he could not lower his arms. Sometimes he was actually lifted off the ground in these ecstasies. So also in prayer, not only was his face luminous, but real sparks of fire flew from his eyes.—Father Antony Galonio, *Life of St. Philip of Neri.*

During the sacrifice of the mass the face of St. Samson seemed on fire (A.D. 565). While offering the sacrifice of the mass, after his consecration as bishop of Dol, near St. Malo, all the assistants remarked that the face of St. Samson was on fire; that flames of fire burst from his mouth, ears, and nostrils, and a luminous glory encircled his head with rays like those of the sun. His biographer adds, it was no unusual thing to see angels at his side, while he was serving at the altar. —Dom Lobineau, *Lives of the Saints of Brittany.*

The face of Francis Xavier flashed with brightness (A.D. 1506–1552). Cardinal de Monte told pope Gregory XV. that flashing flames of heavenly brightness were often seen in the face of St. Francis Xavier while in communion with God in prayer, showing not only the fire of his own devotion, but kindling a new fire of devotion in those who saw it.—*Speech at the Canonization of Xavier*, Jan. 19, A.D. 1622.

The face of St. Yves of Auteuil encom-

passed with an aureola (A.D. 1040–1116). The love of God in the heart of St. Yves shed a divine light on his face; so that, many a time and oft, a luminous glory was seen round his head, especially when he was administering the divine mysteries.—L'abbé Sabatier, *Saints de Beauvais.*

Milton says—

A thousand liveried angels lackey [the pure-minded],
Driving far off each thing of sin and guilt . . .
Till oft converse with heavenly habitants
Begin to cast a beam on the outward shape . .
And turns it by degrees to the soul's essence,
Till all be made immortal.

Comus.

A celestial light surrounds the head of the venerable Antony Mary Zaccaria of Cremona (A.D. 1502–1539). When Antony Mary Zaccaria offered up mass for the first time, a celestial light encompassed him, and a multitude of angels formed a circle round him, assisting him in the august sacrifice. This was known to all in Cremona, and the young priest was called "The Man with the Angel," or "The Angel of God."—R. P. Teppa, *Life of the Venerable Zaccaria.*

The veiled prophet of Khorassan. This is only a tale, but the tale exhibits a very general belief. The story says that Mokanna imitated Moses by wearing a veil over his face when he appeared before his deluded followers. He gave out that he did so, because his face was so dazzling, that no one could look thereon and live. The real truth was this, his face was so hideous and so disfigured with scars, that he wore a veil to hide its repulsive ugliness. Thomas Moore has a poetical version of the legend in his *Lalla Rookh.*

Balaam's Counsel to Balak.

Numb. xxxi. 16, and v. 8. Balaam was sent for by Balak, king of Moab, to curse the people led by Moses in the wilderness; but the prophet told Balak that God would not curse the people so long as they remained faithful to Him. He added, however, if they can be enticed to idolatry, that then God's anger would be roused, and the people would be destroyed. The question was, how could this infamous hint be carried out? Balaam was ready with an answer; the Moabitish women, he said, were to be used for the purpose of enticing the people to sin. Let them be sent amongst the Israelites to hold dalliance with them, and allure the people to worship the Moabitish god Belphegor.

Then (ch. xxv.) was God's anger kindled against Israel; and Moses said to the judges, Slay ye every one that has joined in sacrifice to Baal-peor. Scarcely had he spoken, when Phinehas saw one of the Israelites with a Midianitish woman, and he slew both the man and woman with a javelin. So the plague was stayed.

King Antiochus tries to entice the Hebrews to sin. Antiochus, who succeeded Alexander the Great in Greece, made war on the Hebrews, took the city of Jerusalem, ransacked the temple, and laid the country waste. Following the example of Moab, he tried to entice the people from their allegiance to God, and commanded them, on pain of death, to eat swine's flesh, and to sacrifice to the Greek idols. Mattathias, the Jewish priest, one day saw a Hebrew approaching an altar with the intention of offering sacrifice, and thrust him through with his sword, so that he died. Antiochus insisted that Mattathias should himself offer sacrifice to Zeus; but the priest threw down the altar, and then exhorted all who were on the Lord's side to follow him to the mountain outside the city. Hither many resorted, and there they fortified themselves. Ultimately the numbers greatly increased, and they made themselves masters of Jerusalem. —*Maccabees.*

Balance of the Sanctuary.

Dan. v. 27. Thou art weighed in the balance, and found wanting.

Job xxxi. 6. Let me be weighed in an even balance, that God may know mine integrity.

The Chapel of the Balances, in Brittany. The abbot of Soissons, in his *Annals of the Diocese of Brittany*, tells us there was in Brittany a "Chapel of the Balances," in which persons who came to be cured miraculously were weighed, to ascertain whether their weight diminished, when prayer was made by the monks in their behalf. St. Quirinus and St. Arsacius both speak of a man weighed in a scale against the bread and cheese which he gave in alms to the poor. At Kierzy Church there was a similar "balance." In the life of St. Hubert of Brittany, the Bollandists tell us of a stranger who was making the foundation of a house, when the devil lifted him up and threw him into a deep pit. He was drawn out more than half dead, and had a black mark on his forehead. Being taken to the Chapel of the Balances, he was weighed, having been sentenced to give the monks as an offering as much wax to make into candles as would weigh down his own body. On p. 63 will be found the account of Peter the banker, who dreamed he was weighed against his alms to the poor, and was so terrified at the results that he became a converted man.

*** Rohese, the mother of Thomas Becket, used to weigh her boy every year, on his birthday, against the money, clothes, and provisions which she gave to the poor.

Barren Women the Mothers of Children.

1 Sam. i. 10–28. Hannah, one of the wives of Elkanah, had no child, and was very sorrowful. In the bitterness of her soul she went to the temple, and prayed. And she vowed a vow, and said, O Lord of hosts, if Thou wilt indeed look on the affliction of Thine handmaid, and give unto her a man child, then will I give him unto the Lord. Eli, supposing her to be drunk, said to her, How long wilt thou be drunken? Put away wine from thee. And Hannah answered, No, my lord . . . I have drunk neither wine nor strong drink, but have poured out my soul before the Lord. . . . Then Eli said, Go in peace: and the God of Israel grant thee thy petition that thou hast asked of Him. In due time a son was born, and after it was weaned, Hannah brought her offering to the temple.

Luke i. 1–13. Zacharias the priest had no child, and both he and his wife Elisabeth were well stricken in years. While he was burning incense in the temple, an angel appeared to him and said, Fear not, Zacharias: for thy prayer is heard; and thy wife Elisabeth shall bear thee a son, and thou shalt call his name John.

Gen. xvi. 1; xvii. 1, 15, 19; xviii. 9, 10. Sarai, Abram's wife, bare no children. And when Abram was ninety-nine years old, God said to him, As for Sarai, thy wife, thou shalt [no longer] call her name Sarai, but Sarah. . . . And I will bless her, and give thee a son of her, . . and thou shalt call his name Isaac.

The countess of Toulouse becomes a mother through the intercession of St. Foi (A.D. 1006). William Taillefer, count of Toulouse, married Arsinda of Anjou in 975, but, having no child by her, he lived in adultery with a married woman. Arsinda was very unhappy, and prayed earnestly that her reproach might be taken away; she also made a pilgrimage to St. Foi d'Agen. Here, at night, St. Foi appeared to her, and bade her consecrate on St. Saviour's altar, in the monastery of Conques, the rich bracelets she was then wearing. "I will," said the countess, "but obtain for me a son." "I will intercede on your behalf with Jesus Christ," said St. Foi, and vanished from her sight. Next morning the countess went to Conques with a grand cortége, and was greeted on her way by all the gentry of the neighbourhood. On reaching the monastery, she was directed to the altar of St. Saviour, and presented the bracelets; they were of gold tissue, artistically wrought, and enriched with precious stones. The countess remained in the monastery till Easter, and then returned to Toulouse. The same year she brought forth her firstborn child, and called his name Raymond. Not long after she had a second son, which she called Henry.—Salvan, *History of the Church of Toulouse.*

St. Nicholas promises Amata of St. Angelo a son. Compagnone and Amata were wealthy Christians of St. Angelo, in the territory of Fermo, but they had no children. So they besought St. Nicholas to obtain for them this favour of the Lord, vowing, if he did so, that they would call the child after the name of the saint. While they were in the church of St. Nicholas, in the city of Bari, in Puglia, the saint appeared to them, and assured them they should have a son which should be a blessed servant of God. In due time the child was born, and they called its name Nicholas.—St. Antony (archbishop of Florence), *Chronicon.*

Paphnucius of Alexandria promised a son. In the reign of Theodosius II., son of Arcadius, there lived in Alexandria a rich nobleman named Paphnucius, who had no child. He and his wife gave largely to the religious houses to obtain their intercession with God that this reproach might be removed from them, and that a child might be given them. In time a daughter was born, whom they named Euphrosynê. The child grew up a rare beauty, and at the age of eighteen her father betrothed her to a young man of fortune and family; but, like Samuel, she was God's child, and the Lord had said to her, "I betroth thee unto Myself for ever; yea, I betroth thee unto Myself in righteousness, in lovingkindness, and in mercy. I betroth thee in faithfulness; and thou shalt know the Lord." * While the wedding was pending, Euphrosynê secretly left her father's house, and, assuming male attire, entered a monastery under the name of "Brother Emerald." She soon distinguished herself by her devotion, gentleness, and patience, so that her fame spread abroad. Having lived secluded for twenty years, her father went to the monastery to bespeak the prayers of "Brother Emerald" that he might find his daughter. She bade him remain where he was for three days, at the expiration of which time she revealed herself to him and died. Her death was greatly deplored, and the monastery ap-

* Hosea ii. 19, 20.

pointed the anniversary to be kept in perpetuity as the "Fête of St. Euphrosynê." In Christian art St. Euphrosynê is represented with the clothes of a man lying at her feet, because, like St. Hildegonda, St. Marina, St. Palagia-Margaret, St. Theodora, and others, she so disguised herself.—*Acta Sanctorum*. (Metaphrastês wrote her life.)

Montanus assured Emilius and Celinia, well stricken in years, of a son. Montanus wept himself blind, bewailing the sins of the people of France, and ceased not day or night to importune God to visit the people and pardon their transgressions. At length his prayers were heard, and God assured him that a child should shortly be born, whose name would be Remigius, who should go forth in the power and spirit of Elijah, and should turn many of the disobedient to the wisdom of the just. Montanus went immediately to the house of Emilius, the person referred to by the angel, and told him that his wife Celinia should bear a son. Emilius laughed and said, "Shall a child be born to him that is fourscore years old; and shall Celinia, who is also well stricken in age, have a child, when it has ceased to be with her after the manner of women?" Montanus said to him, "Why dost thou laugh? Is anything too hard for the Lord? Verily, at the time appointed, Celinia shall have a son. And when the child is born she shall anoint my eyes with her milk, and my sight shall be restored to me." It all fell out as Montanus had said. The child was born, and was named Remigius or Remi; and Celinia having anointed the eyes of Montanus with her milk, his sight was restored. St. Remi grew up in the spirit and power of Elijah, as the angel of the Lord had said.—Flodoart, *Histoire de l'Église de Reims*, bk. i.

St. Hilarion obtains a child for a woman barren fifteen years. One day a woman came to the young hermit Hilarion, who made signs for her to go away; but she said to him with many tears, "O servant of the living God, pardon my boldness, for my sorrow is very great. Shun me not, but take pity on my grief. Remember, a woman was thy mother, and a woman was the mother of our blessed Saviour." Hilarion could not withstand these words, and asked his petitioner what she wanted, and why she wept. "Thy servant," she replied, "has been married fifteen years, but has no child. And my husband threatens to divorce me unless I bear him children." Hilarion, moved to pity, prayed for the woman that God would grant to her what her heart desired, and she left the cell. After a year had passed, the woman returned with an infant son in her arms, and said to the young hermit, "Behold the child of thy prayers!" And Hilarion blessed the child, and the name of the Lord. This is the first miracle of this holy saint. The life of St. Hilarion is in the *Ecclesiastical History* of Nicephorus Callistus (died 1350).

St. Theodosius promises a son to a barren woman (A.D. 423–529). A woman who never had any but dead children, cast herself at the feet of St. Theodosius, and implored him to take pity on her, and said, if through his intercession she brought forth a living child, she would call him Theodosius, in honour of the saint. Theodosius prayed on her behalf, and the woman had the desire of her heart, and brought forth a son, and called his name Theodosius.—*Les Petits Bollandistes* (7th edit. 1880), vol. i. p. 274.

St. Peter Thomas obtains a child for a barren woman by prayer (died A.D. 1366). Par ces prières, St. Pierre Thomas obtint un fils à un des seigneurs de la province d'Arcadie.—*Les Petits Bollandistes* (7th edit. 1880), Jan. 6.

St. Simeon Stylites obtains children for two queens (fifth century). St. Simeon obtint un fils à la reine des Ismaélites qui était stérile; et une fille à la reine des Sarrasins qui était dans la même peine.—*Les Petits Bollandistes*, vol. i. p. 144.

St. Polyeuctus obtains a child for Paul and Denysa (A.D. 1376). Paul was a noble and rich Armenian living at Melitena. Their sole grievance was that they had no child. They had recourse to prayer, and, to make their prayers more efficacious, implored the intercession of Polyeuctus. Their prayers being now accepted, Polyeuctus said to them, "Courage, Paul; God will give you a son, and you shall call his name Euthymius, to mark the sweetness of his disposition. From the day of his birth, the persecutions of God's people on earth shall entirely cease." And so it was, for the child was born at the death of Valens, when the forty years' persecution of the Roman emperors ceased, and were never afterwards repeated.—Cyrillus, *Life of Euthymius*. (See Surius, and the annotations of Bollandus.)

Bibliomancy, Belomancy, etc.

Numb. xxvii 21. Eleazar the priest shall ask counsel after the judgment of Urim before the Lord.

Ezek. xxi. 21. The king of Babylon stood at the parting of the way, at the head of two ways, to use divination. He made his arrows bright.

Hosea iv. 12. My people ask counsel at their stocks, and their staff declareth unto them.

Bibliomancy is consulting the Bible or some other book to discover the issue of a future event. It is done by opening the book at random, and the first passage your eye or finger lights on is the response. If Virgil is the book employed, the consultation is called "Sortes Virgilianæ;" if Homer, it is "Sortes Homericæ."

Belomancy is divination by arrows. A number of arrows containing responses are shot off, and the one which flies furthest is considered to be the true response. This method of divination was common with the Chaldæans, Arabs, and others.

Rhabdomancy or divination by sticks. Three sticks, one inscribed "Yes," the other "No," and the third with no inscription, being put into a bag, were drawn by lot. If "Yes" was drawn, the answer was favourable; if "No," it was unfavourable; if the third stick was drawn, the fates refused to give any answer. Another plan of consulting one's stick is explained by Rabbi Moses Samson, who says, a stick is stripped from top to bottom of half its bark, and hurled twice into the air: if it falls the first time with the peeled side uppermost, and the second time with the bark side uppermost, it is a good sign; if the reverse, it is a bad omen; if both alike, it is a mixed omen, partly good and partly bad.

The Scythians and Alains employed willow and myrtle branches.

The Betjuans, a tribe of South Africa, divine by sticks, and also by dice, which they carry on a strap about the neck. By the throw of these sticks or the dice they infer the future good or evil which awaits them.—Lichtenstein, *Travels in South Africa.*

The ancient Germans used to cut off the branch of some fruit tree, and then divide it into several pieces, each piece being marked with a separate character. The sticks were then tossed into the air, and the paterfamilias read the fortune of the consulter from their position, in much the same way as a fortune-teller reads a person's fortune by a pack of cards.

Mr. Berridge consulted the Bible to know if he should marry. Mr. Berridge, writing to the countess of Huntingdon, says, "Eight or nine years ago, having been grievously tormented by my housekeeper, I thought I would take a Jezebel to wife, but resolved to take advice of the Lord first. So, falling on my knees with the Bible in my hands, I prayed earnestly; then letting the Bible drop, the first verse I lighted on was (2 Esdras x. 1), 'When my son was entered into his wedding chamber he fell down, and died.' Not quite satisfied, it occurred to me that this verse was in the Apocrypha; so I fell on my knees again, and prayed the Lord not to be angry with me if, like Gideon, I requested a second sign, and that from the canonical Scriptures. This time the verse lighted on was (Jer. xvi. 2), 'Thou shalt not take thee a wife, neither shalt thou have sons and daughters in this place.' I was now fully satisfied, and have remained single."—*Life and Times of the Countess of Huntingdon.*

Heraclius consulted the Bible lot in his Persian expedition. Heraclius, in his war with Chosroes, king of Persia, consulted the Bible Urim, to ascertain where he should take up his winter quarters; and his finger touched the word "Illyricum" (Rom. xv. 19).—*M. Fleury.*

While writing this last sentence, the fancy came into my head to try what the "Sortes Sanctorum" would say respecting the publication of this book, and my finger lighted on these words, "Take heed now that ye fail not to do this" (Ezra iv. 22). The words are pertinent, at any rate.

The response given to Charles I. and lord Falkland by the "Sortes Virgilianæ." Certainly the most remarkable instances of bibliomancy on record are those recorded of Charles I. and lord Falkland, mentioned by Dr. Wellwood. While at Oxford, lord Falkland, to amuse the king, proposed to try what Virgil would tell them of their future destinies. The king, of course, tried first, and set his finger on the *Æneid*, bk. iv. vers. 881–893, the gist of which passage is, "Civil wars shall break out, whereby the king shall lose his life." Falkland tried to laugh the matter off, and said, "I will now show your majesty how ridiculously the 'lot' will foretell my fate;" and so saying he opened the book and laid his finger on *Æneid*, bk. xi. vers. 230–237, the lament of Evander for the untimely death of his son Pallas. In 1643 lord Falkland was shot through the body at the battle of Newbury, and Charles, like Evander, lamented his untimely death. Every one knows of the civil wars in the reign of Charles I., and how the king was brought to the scaffold, and was beheaded.

The emperor Gordianus tries his lot by the "Sortes Virgilianæ." Gordianus, who reigned only a few days, wishing to see what Virgil would say respecting his future lot, opened the *Æneid* and laid his finger on bk. vi. ver. 869, "Fate only showed him on the earth, but suffered him not to tarry."

The emperor Severus tries his fate by the "Sortes Virgilianæ." Severus the Roman emperor, consulting the "Sortes Virgilianæ" on his future destiny, lighted on *Æneid*, bk. vi. ver. 851, "Forget not, O Roman, to rule thy people like a king."

Blindness miraculously cured.

Matt. xx. 30. Behold, two blind men sitting by the wayside, when they heard that Jesus was passing by, cried out, saying, Have mercy on us, O Lord, Thou Son of David. . . Jesus called them, and said, What will ye that I do for you? They say to Him, Lord, that our eyes may be opened. So Jesus had compassion on them, and touched their eyes: and immediately their eyes received sight, and they followed Him.

MARK viii. 22–25. At Bethsaida they bring to Jesus a blind man, and besought Him to touch him. And Jesus took the blind man by the hand, and led him out of the town; and when He had spit on his eyes and put His hands upon him, He asked the man if he saw ought. And the man answered, I see men as trees, walking. After that Jesus put His hands again on the man's eyes, and made him look up: and his sight was restored, so that he saw everything clearly.

MARK x. 46–52. This is the case of blind Bartimæus.

ACTS ix. 17, 18. Ananias, putting his hands on Saul, said to him, Brother Saul, the Lord that appeared to thee in the way hath sent me that thou mayest receive thy sight. And immediately there fell from his eyes as it had been scales, and he received sight forthwith.

A blind man cured by a pilgrimage to the tomb of Agricolus (A.D. 580). A man named Salomon, a native of Touraine, who had been stone-blind for ten years, was told in a dream to go to Boulogne, to a place where he would find a monastery in honour of St. Marcellus. The voice told him, if he prostrated himself there at the tomb of St. Agricolus, which was in the abbey, he would receive his sight. Salomon obeyed the voice, and had not made half the journey when his sight was in part recovered, and no sooner had he knelt at the tomb of the saint than he saw everything distinctly; and he returned home without needing the aid of a guide.—Baillet, *Legendary of Autun; History of Châlon*. St. Gregory of Tours calls this saint Aregle (3 *syl.*).

A blind man cured by bathing his eyes in water used by St. Amandus for washing his hands (A.D. 594–684). When St. Amandus was on the point of leaving Gascony, a blind man offered him water in a basin to wash his hands. The bishop gave directions for this water to be saved, and taken to the cathedral; then, sending for the blind man, he said to him, "My son, if you have faith moisten your eyes with this water in which Amandus the servant of God hath washed his hands. I am persuaded through his merits you will receive your sight." The blind man obeyed, and the moment he touched his eyes with the water his sight was restored. The report of this miracle spread like wildfire; but when search was made for the saint, he was nowhere to be found, being far on his way to the province of Bourbonnais, to a place where now stands Ville de St. Amand.—Menjoulet (vicar-general of Bayonne), *Saint Amand Apôtre des Basques*. (See ST. MAYEUL, p. 46.)

The same is said of St. Eustadiola (seventh century) in the *Propre de Bourges*. A blind man, we are told, was cured by the water in which St. Psalmodius had washed his hands (*Les Petits Bollandistes*, vol. vii. p. 60). Several other examples might be added.

St. Ausonius cures the blind beggar of Angoulême (first and second centuries). A blind man, well known in Angoulême, where he lived on charity, was taken before St. Ausonius; and, throwing himself at the saint's feet, he said to him, "Ausonius, thou servant of the living God, I know that thy prayers will open mine eyes." "Be it unto you," said Ausonius, "according to your faith;" and immediately his eyes received their sight. As he was very poor and almost naked, Ausonius gave him alms also.—*Acta Sanctorum* (Bollandists), vol. v. May 22.

St. Barnard, archbishop of Vienne, cures a blind man (A.D. 810). One day a blind man said he wanted to see St. Barnard. Those who heard him laughed at him, but he placed himself on the stairs of a chapel, saying, "If I can but touch him, I shall receive my sight and see him." At this moment a cry of joy announced the arrival of the saint, and the blind man threw himself at his feet. The archbishop, lifting his eyes to heaven, said to him, "Thy faith has given thee sight: give God thanks;" and immediately the blind man saw clearly.—Mgr. Depéry, *Histoire Hagiologique du Diocèse de Belley*.

St. Bridget and the blind girl (A.D. 436–523). A blind girl named Daria came to St. Bridget, and prayed her to give sight to her blind eyeballs. St. Bridget said a benediction, and Daria received her sight. By the preaching of the saint Daria was converted, and then entreated St. Bridget to restore her blindness again, saying "the light of the body impeded the light of the soul." So St. Bridget closed her eyes again in darkness, according to the request of the blind girl.—*Les Petits Bollandistes*, vol. ii. p. 184.

St. Frodobert gives sight to his mother. When Frodobert was a mere child he cured his mother's blindness, as, in the fulness of love and pity, he kissed her darkened eyes, and signed them with the sign of the cross. Not only was her sight restored, but the historian adds, "it was keener than ever."—Lupellus, *Life of St. Frodobert* (seventh century).

St. Geneviève restored sight to a woman struck blind (A.D. 422–512). One day a woman, out of curiosity, went to the cell of St. Geneviève to see how she passed her time there. No sooner did she peep through the window than she was struck with blindness. Her blindness lasted all Lent, when St. Geneviève took pity on her, made the sign of the cross upon her eyeballs, and immediately their sight was restored.—*Les Petits Bollandistes* (7th edit. 1880), vol. i. p. 96.

In the legend of Lady Godiva of Coventry, who rode naked through the town to mitigate certain imposts on the people, a tailor, named Tom, determined to take a peep at the lady as she rode past, but his curiosity was punished by loss of sight. It does not appear from the story that "Peeping Tom" ever recovered his sight again.

St. John of Egypt cures a blind woman with holy oil (A.D. 305–394). The wife of a senator of Egypt, having lost her sight, incessantly urged her husband to take her to St. John, the Egytian hermit. The senator, who well knew that the saint never admitted a woman into his sight, went to St. John and told him his errand. The saint gave the senator a little holy oil, and directed that the eyes of the lady should be anointed therewith. This was done, and the cure was instantaneous and complete.—Ruffinus, *Lives of the Fathers*, bk. ii.

St. Lawrence cures a blind man. St. Lawrence, being on Mount Celion, in the house of Narcissus, cured a blind man by making the sign of the cross. The house of Narcissus stood in the fish-market, and was a well-known place of resort with all Christians.

Another instance. When St. Lawrence was put in prison by Hippolitus, he found in the dungeon a fellow-prisoner, named Lucillus, who had lost his sight by continually weeping at the misery of his long confinement. St. Lawrence promised to restore his sight if he would become a Christian. Lucillus gladly made the promise, and St. Lawrence restored sight to the blind eyeballs by making on them the sign of the cross. When this miracle got noised abroad, many blind persons, both male and female, flocked to the prison, and St. Lawrence healed them. Hippolitus, seeing these miraculous cures, was himself converted, and he with all his house, to the number of nineteen, were baptized.—Edward Kinesman (1623), *Lives of the Saints*, pp. 599–608.

(St. Lawrence is put in the canon of the mass.)

The martyrdom of this saint (says Kinesman) is most certaine, being written by the notaries of Rome, and accepted of many saints that doe recount it, as St. Ambrose, St. Leo, St. Augustine, St. Isidore, Prudentius, and others, from whom this account has been collated, p. 599.

St. Ludger cures Bernlef of his blindness (A.D. 809). While St. Ludger was in Fositeland, and was the guest of a noble lady, blind Bernlef was presented to him. He was greatly liked by the people, because he sang to them about the combats of kings, or told them about the times gone by. St. Ludger told Bernlef to meet him on the morrow in a place which he mentioned; and immediately the saint saw the blind man coming he dismounted from his horse, heard his confession, made the sign of the cross upon his eyes, and asked him if he could see. The blind man saw first the hands of the bishop, then the trees and roofs of the neighbouring cabins, then everything around him. Bernlef was afterwards baptized, and used to sing to the people the psalms of David.—*Les Petits Bollandistes*, vol. iv.

St. Macarius gives sight to a blind hyena. One of the strangest miracles connected with blindness is that ascribed to St. Macarius of Alexandria (A.D. 394). In Christian art this saint is portrayed with an hyena and its cub as his companions. The story is as follows:—One day an hyena brought her cub to St. Lawrence, and laid it at his feet. Macarius, astonished at the act, examined the whelp, and found that it was blind. He touched the eyes with his finger, and immediately the creature received its sight. Next day the grateful dam brought a sheepskin to the hermit's cell as a free-will offering, and Macarius wore it ever after till the day of his death, when he gave it to St. Melania.—Baring-Gould, *Lives of the Saints* (Jan., p. 33), 1877.

St. Martin restores Paulinus's eyesight. St. Martin cured Paulinus, over whose eyes was grown a thick film, which not only deprived him of sight, but also put him to great pain. St. Martin merely wiped the man's eyes with a napkin, and a perfect cure was instantly effected.—Sulpicius Severus, *Life of St. Martin.*

St. Mayeul, abbot of Cluny, cures a blind man with the sign of the cross (A.D. 906–994). One day as St. Mayeul was in Notre-dame du Puy-en-Velay, a blind man came and said, "I have received a revelation from St. Peter, that I shall recover my sight, if I bathe my eyes with the water in which your honour has washed your hands." The abbot severely reprimanded the man, and sent him away.

Finding on inquiry that the man had been begging his servants to give him some of this water, he strictly forbade their doing so. The blind man, not discouraged, waited patiently, watching on the road the abbot's return from Puy; and, when he came to Mont-Joie, took hold of the horse's bridle, and swore not to leave go without obtaining his demand. So saying, he poured water into a basin which hung on his neck, and handed it to the saint. The abbot dismounted, blessed the water, and, dipping his fingers into the basin, made the sign of the cross on the sightless eyes, and prayed the "Mother of Mercy" to take pity on the man. "All right!" cried the man; "I can see plainly!" "Then go," said the abbot, "and thank the Mother of Mercy who has vouchsafed to take pity on you."—*Les Petits Bollandistes*, vol. v. p. 463. (See p. 45.)

Blindness (1843) *cured by a visit to St. Meinrad's hermitage.* The following is a faithful translation from the German of the abbot Ganeval:—"My father, Claud Alexis Ganeval, merchant of Levier, chief city of the canton in the 'Departement du Doubs,' having exhausted all the resources of science and art to effect the cure of Frances Caroline, his youngest daughter, aged three years, and stone-blind for above a year, was taken by her father to the hermitage of St. Meinrad, the last week of March, 1831. The father, as a pilgrim, entered the Chapel of the Virgin at five o'clock in the morning, and besought the Virgin to take pity on his child. Instantly the child received her sight, and her eyes were so beautiful as to attract a crowd of strangers. The child died in 1843. Thousands of persons who knew the merchant and his daughter can attest this miracle, but it will be sufficient to give one name only, that of Sa Grandeur Monseigneur Caverot, bishop of St. Die."—*Les Petits Bollandistes*, vol. i. p. 526.

Blindness cured by kissing the feet of St. Melanius's dead body (A.D. 530). When the body of St. Melanius was carried in grand procession through Rennes, a woman who was stone-blind approached the bier, and falling to the earth kissed the feet of the dead saint. Immediately her sight was restored, and she gave to the Church, as a thank-offering, all her heritage.—Gui Alexis Lobineau (a contemporary), *Histoire des Saintes de Bretagne*, 1724.

Mondana, mother of St. Sacerdos, recovers her sight at the death of her son (A.D. 720). Mondana, the mother of St. Sacerdos, had been blind some years before her son's death, but being told that his dead body was on the river Dordogne on its way to Calviac, she went to meet the mournful procession; and God, wishing to testify His love for the deceased saint, restored her sight. Thus was it that St. Sacerdos raised his father to life to bestow on him the Viaticum; and his sainted name restored, at his funeral, sight to his blind mother, "Heureux le père, heureuse la mère d'un tel fils!"—Pergot, *Life of St. Sacerdos, bishop of Limoges.*

St. Odilo restores a nobleman's eye which had been knocked out (A.D. 962–1049). A branch of a tree, having struck a nobleman, knocked out his right eye. St. Odilo, abbot of Cluny, being applied to, effected a perfect and instantaneous cure by signing the sign of the cross over the injured part.—*Acta Sanctorum*, vol. i. Jan. 1.

St. Placidus cures a blind man. St. Placidus, being in Capua, healed a blind man by making the sign of the cross upon his sightless eyes.

In Sicily he restored sight to one who had been blind for eight years.—Laurentius Surius, *Lives of the Saints* (1570).

St. Thierry, the son of a peasant, cures king Thierry, the son of Clovis, of partial blindness (sixth century). The sanctity of St. Thierry reached the ears of the king, whose name was Thierry, one of the four sons of Clovis. The king, being nearly blind, sent for the abbot, received him with great honour, and told him his only hope was in the prayers of the saint, and if they failed him he must lose his eyesight. The abbot fell prostrate to the earth and prayed; then, rising to his feet, signed, in the form of a cross, the eyes of the king with holy oil, in the name of the Father, and of the Son, and of the Holy Ghost; whereupon the king "reçut au même moment une parfaite guérison, et recouvra entièrement la vue."—Billy (almoner of the abbey of St. Thierry), *Life of St. Thierry.*

St. Thuribius cures a blind dumb man (second century). Savina, the wife of Caïanus, was a Christian, and disciple of St. Thuribius; but her husband, a devoted partisan of the national religion, which was idolatry, confined her in a sort of domestic prison, and used all his influence to drive St. Thuribius from Mans, where he was bishop. In punishment of this offence, God struck Caïanus both blind and dumb. He now released his wife, and got her to intercede with the bishop. Savina implored St. Thuribius to cure her husband, and the bishop, offering prayer on his behalf, obtained the petition he desired. When Caïanus recovered his speech and sight, he requested to be received into the Christian Church, and was duly baptized.—*Les Petits Bollandistes*, vol. iv. p. 441.

Two blind men cured by St. Ubaldus (A.D. 1084-1160). A man who had been blind for four years, recovered his sight by merely kissing the hand of St. Ubaldus. Another, who had been blind for ten years, recovered his sight by simply invoking the saint's name.—L'abbé Hunckler, *Les Saints d'Alsace.*

St. Valentine cures the blind daughter of judge Asterius (A.D. 268). St. Valentine was brought before Asterius, the Roman judge, to be examined and punished for heresy. When he entered the court he prayed aloud that Christ, the true Light, would give him light what to say. Said Asterius, "What is that you say? How can Jesus Christ, the malefactor, be the true Light?" "He is not only the true Light," answered Valentine, "but the only Light that lighteth every one who cometh into the world." "If so," said the judge, "let me see the proof, and I will believe. I have a daughter who has been blind ever since she was two years old. If your Christ will give light to her eyes, I will believe Him to be what you say He is." The damsel was brought to St. Valentine, who put his hands on her eyes, and said, "O Jesus Christ, who art the true Light, give light to this Thy handmaid." While he still spake, the eyes of the damsel were opened, and she saw plainly. Asterius, his wife, and daughter threw themselves at the feet of the holy man, and entreated to be received into the society of the faithful. Whereupon St. Valentine instructed them what to do, and baptized Asterius and all his house, consisting of forty-six souls.—*Les Petits Bollandistes*, vol. ii. p. 511.

St. Virgil, bishop of Arles, cures a blind man (A.D. 610). A man who had been blind for fifteen years induced a subdeacon, named Fulgence, to conduct him to the porch of the basilica of St. Stephen's. "There," said he, "I shall be sure to find his reverence, when he comes from matins." When St. Virgil left the church, the blind man threw himself on his knees, and implored the bishop to intercede for him in prayer. The bishop, touched by this naïve confidence, implored God to restore his sight, and, making the sign of the cross on the man's eyes, their speculation returned, and he saw plainly. St. Virgil said to him, "See you tell no man;" but the man was too full of joy to remain silent, and ere the day was over the whole city knew of the miraculous cure.—*Martyroogy of France, Revised and Augmented.*

Instances of the cure of blindness by saints or their relics are so numerous in the *Acta Sanctorum*, that they lose all interest.

Blindness from Birth miraculously cured.

John ix. 1–38. Jesus saw a man which was blind from his birth, and He spat on the ground, and made clay of the spittle, and anointed the eyes of the blind man with the clay, and said to him, Go, wash in the pool of Siloam. So he went and washed, and came [back to Jesus] seeing. The neighbours and they which had seen him [before], said to him, How were thine eyes opened? He answered, A man called Jesus made clay, and anointed mine eyes, and said to me, Go to the pool of Siloam, and wash; so I went, and I received my sight. Then they brought to the Pharisees him that aforetime was blind, and the Pharisees asked him how he had received his sight. He said to them, He put clay upon mine eyes, and I washed, and do see. They say to the man again, What sayest thou of Him who opened thine eyes? The man said, He is a prophet. Then said they, Give God the praise. We know this man is a sinner. The man answered, Whether He be a sinner or not, I know not: one thing I do know, that whereas I was blind, now I see. Then said they to him again, What did He to thee? How opened He thine eyes? The man answered them, I have told you already, wherefore would ye hear it again? Will ye be His disciples? Then they reviled him and said, Thou art His disciple, but we are Moses' disciples. We know that God spake unto Moses, but as for this fellow, we know not from whence He is. The man answered, Why, herein is a marvellous thing; ye know not whence He is, and yet He hath opened mine eyes. Since the world began it has not been heard that a man has opened the eyes of one born blind. If this man were not of God' He could do nothing [of the kind]. The Pharisees said, Thou wast altogether born in sins, and dost thou teach us? And they cast him out [or excommunicated him].

St. Pantaleon cures a man that was born blind. This miracle and the incidents connected with it closely resemble the case mentioned in the Gospel of St. John (ch. ix.). While St. Pantaleon was talking with his father, a man who had been blind from birth entered the house. He had already spent largely upon physicians, but had received no benefit from them. Pantaleon said to the blind man, "What will you give me if your sight is restored?" "All that I have left," said the blind man. St. Pantaleon said in reply, "Give some of your substance to the poor, and I will give you sight, in the name of the Lord." Then touched he the eyes of the blind man, calling on the name of Jesus; and forthwith his eyes were opened, and his sight was perfect. The physicians were greatly amazed, and asked the man who had given him sight. The man replied, "Pantaleon." Thereupon the physicians, out of malice, accused Pantaleon of treason, for giving sight to an enemy of the emperor. Maximianus arrested the man who had been born blind, and demanded of him how Pantaleon had cured him. The man replied, "He called on the name of Jesus, and touched mine eyes." "Who do you say cured you," demanded the emperor; "Esculapius or Christ?" The man made answer, "The physicians called on Esculapius, but my sight was not restored; St. Pantaleon called on the name of Jesus, and now I see." The emperor remarked, "If the fellow has received his bodily sight, he must be blind in understanding to say such things." The man answered boldly, "Surely they must be blind in understanding who can see this miracle and not confess that Christ is God." "Dost thou reprove us, fellow?" said the emperor, in great wrath. "Lictors, take him hence, and put him to instant death."—Simeon Metaphrastês (tenth century), *Lives*, etc.

St. Maur gives sight to Linus, who was born blind (A.D. 512–584). A man named Linus, who was born blind, lived twelve years in the porch of St. Maurice (Agaunum), in the Alps. When he heard that St. Maur was about to enter the church, he cried aloud, "Thou servant of the living God, have mercy on me!" St. Maur stopped, and asked the man what he wanted of him. "That I may receive my sight," said the blind man. St. Maur then touched the sightless orbs, making as he did so the sign of the cross, and immediately his eyes were opened. The man, overwhelmed with joy, followed St. Maur into the church, and chanted the holy service, which he had learned by heart by living so long in the porch. Faustus, who tells this story, assures us that he was told it by the man himself, and adds that the man, from the time he received his sight, consecrated himself to the service of the altar, and survived to a very advanced age.—Faustus (one of St. Maur's companions), *Life of St. Maur*.

St. Odilo gives sight to a man born blind (A.D. 962–1049). St. Odilo, abbot of Cluny, gave sight to the son of one of his tenants, blind from his birth.—*Acta Sanctorum*, vol. i. Jan. 1.

Blindness from Demoniacal Possession cured.

Matt. xii. 22. There was brought to Jesus a man possessed with a devil, blind and dumb; and He healed him, insomuch that the blind-dumb man both spake and saw.

St. Remi exorcises a blind man (A.D. 449–545). St. Remi on one occasion was at Calmaciacum, where was a man possessed with an evil spirit which made him blind. The saint prayed fervently, and, the evil spirit departing, the man received his sight.—Edward Kinesman, *Lives of the Saints* (Oct. 1).

It will be remembered that the disciples (John ix. 2), when they brought a certain blind man to Jesus, asked this question, "Who did *sin*, this man or his parents, that he was *born* blind?" They ascribed blindness to sin, and all sin was supposed to be from the devil. Hence to cast out the devil, or to forgive sin, was an effectual cure of its fatal consequences.

Blood and Water from a Wound.

John xix. 34. When Jesus was on the cross, one of the soldiers with a spear pierced His side, and forthwith came there-out blood and water.

St. Cant, St. Cantian, and St. Cantianilla, martyrs (A.D. 290). Cant, Cantian, and Cantianilla were the two sons and daughter of the race of Anicius, and near relatives of the emperor Carin. They were put to death for being Christians by the command of Diocletian and Maximian. When their heads were cut off by the executioners, the blood which flowed from them was the colour of milk. Mgr. Guérin adds, "On en voit encore les traces de nos jours, sur la pierre placée au lieu de leur martyr." Their lives were written by John Chauvin; and Pierre le Gendre has composed an heroic poem in Latin, on their martyrdom, entitled "Cantias" (seventh century). The following is almost a literal translation of the opening verse:—

Champions by the headsman smitten,
  Over death and hell victorious,
God your names with saints hath written
  Kings and priests, enthroned and glorious.
All your combats now are ended,
Low the tyrants laid, all their wrath expended.

A remarkable combination of initial letters. Cant, Cantian, Cantianilla; Carin's children; chronologer Chauvin; canticle "Cantias;" Christians.

Milk flowed from the neck of St. Catherine (Nov. 25, A.D. 310). St. Catherine was tied to a wheel, but the machine broke. She was then beheaded; but instead of blood, milk flowed from the wound. After her head had fallen to the sword of the executioner, angels came and carried her body to Mount Sinai, where they buried it.—Metaphrastês (died 911), *Lives*, etc.

Milk instead of blood flows from the wounds of Secundina (A.D. 257). When St. Secundina was accused of magic on account of her miracles, the voices from heaven which attested her acceptableness with God, and the power of her prayers, her guards told her either to sacrifice to the gods of Rome, or to prepare herself for the vengeance of the law. She replied she would not sacrifice to gods which were no Gods, and as for preparation, her Saviour had already prepared everything for her. The guards roughly stripped her, tore her body in a most ghastly manner, and finally cut off her head. But what struck her persecutors was this: instead of blood gushing from her wounds, a liquor white as milk and of an enchanting odour oozed gently from her body, diffusing delicious coolness and medicinal balm. At length the loud voice of an angel, audible to all, exclaimed, "Come, beloved! The Spirit and the Bride say, Come! Receive the crown prepared for you from before the foundation of the world!"—*Les Petits Bollandistes*, vol. ii. p. 247.

Milk, instead of blood, flows from the wounds of seven holy women (A.D. 316). Seven women who followed St. Blaise after his cruel scourging, were seized by the order of Agricola, governor of Cappadocia, and, being tied to posts, were lacerated from head to foot with iron combs. "Mais, O puissance infinie du Dieu vivant!" instead of blood, milk flowed from their wounds, and angels came from heaven to console them and heal their wounds, saying, "Fear not, but bear thus much for Christ's sake. To those who overcome will He give crowns of glory." Agricola, seeing himself foiled, commanded the women to be cast into a fierce fire, "mais elles en furent retirées par la main du Tout-Puissant, sans en avoir été atteintes." The governor then ordered them to be beheaded, and they died praising God, who thought them worthy to suffer death for His sake. —*Les Petits Bollandistes*, vol. iii. p. 228.

A Bone of Him shall not be broken.

PSALM xxxiv. 19, 20. Many are the afflictions of the righteous: but the Lord delivereth him out of them all. He keepeth all his bones: not one of them is broken.

JOHN xix. 33-36. When the soldiers came to Jesus, and saw that He was dead already, they brake not His legs: but one of the soldiers with a spear pierced His side, and forthwith came there-out blood and water. These things were done that the Scripture should be fulfilled, A bone of Him shall not be broken.

Dr. John Jahn, in his *Archæologia Biblica*, p. 296, says, "When there was not a prospect that the victims crucified would die on the day of crucifixion, the executioners hastened the extinction of life by kindling a fire under the cross so as to suffocate them with the smoke; or by letting loose upon them wild beasts; or by breaking their bones upon the cross with a mallet; or by piercing them with a spear."

In regard to the spear the doctor says, p. 298, "In order to ascertain whether Jesus was really dead, or had only fallen into a swoon, a soldier thrust his lance into His side (undoubtedly his *left* side). If Christ had not been already dead, a wound of this kind would have put an end to His life, as has been shown both by the physician Eschenbach and by Gruner. The part pierced was the *pericardium*, hence the lymph which accompanied the blood. Eschenbach, *Opuscula Medic. de Servatore non apparenter, sed vere mortuo.* Gruner, *Dissertatio Inaug. Medica de Jesu Christi morte vera, non synoptica* (1800)."

The bones of the forty martyrs, though beaten by mallets, were not broken (A.D. 320). Agricola, governor of Lesser Armenia, having exposed the forty martyrs quite naked for three days and three nights on the ice of a frozen pond, during the severe frosts of March, commanded the victims to be beaten with mallets that their bones might be broken, and their death accelerated. They were still alive when the officers drew up the waggons to the edge of the pond, and when they saw the waggons they sang, in the words of the psalmist, "Our soul is escaped as a bird out of the snare of the fowlers: the snare is broken, and we are escaped, because our help is in the name of the Lord" (cxxiv. 7, 8). They were all placed in the waggons except Melito, the youngest of them, who was less exhausted than the rest. The mother of Melito was present, and when she observed that her son was left behind, she carried him herself to one of the waggons, saying, "Go, go, my son, with your companions, that you may present yourself with them before the throne of God." Their bones being beaten with mallets, the victims were cast into a fierce fire and burnt to cinders, after which the ashes were collected together and thrown into the river. But "the Lord did wonderful things: though beaten with mallets, their bones were not broken; though their ashes were tossed into the river, they were not dispersed; but the faithful were enabled to collect them, and they are still preserved as sacred relics." St. Gregory of Nyssa says, "There are but few countries in the whole Christian universe that do not possess some of these precious ashes." In France, Paris, Lyons, Reims, Bourges, Vienne, etc., all possess some of them.—*Vitæ Sanctorum.* (The memoir is by Metaphrastês.)

Book written Within and Without.

REV. v. 1–5. I saw in the right hand of Him that sat on the throne a book written within and without. . . . and I saw a strong angel proclaiming with a loud voice, Who is worthy to open the book? . . . And no man in heaven, nor in earth . . . was able to open the book, nor to look thereon. And I wept because no man was found worthy to open and to read the book. . . . And one of the elders said to me, Weep not: behold, the Lion of the tribe of Juda . . . hath prevailed to open the book.

A book written within and without handed to St. Ephrem (A.D. 378). An old man was in the spirit, and behold! a company of angels descending from heaven, holding a book written within and without; and they said among themselves, "To whom shall we present this book?" One suggested one person, and another another, as worthy to receive it. The angels, having examined into the merits of the persons named, said with one voice, "It is true they are all saints and servants of God, but none of them is worthy to receive the book." Other names were then spoken of, but the angels cried with one accord, "The book must be given to Ephrem only, the humble of heart." And to him they handed it. The old man then hastened to the church where Ephrem was about to preach, and when he heard him he said, "The words of his lips are those of the book, written by the hand of the Holy Ghost."—St. Gregory of Nyssa, *Panegyrics.*

Bound by the Devil.

LUKE xiii. 11–16. There was a woman which had a spirit of infirmity eighteen years, and was bowed together, and could in no wise lift up herself. When Jesus saw her, He called her to Him, and said unto her, Woman, thou art loosed from thine infirmity; . . . and immediately she was made straight. [When the ruler of the synagogue expressed his indignation that this cure was effected on a sabbath day, Jesus said], Ought not this woman, whom Satan hath bound, lo, these eighteen years, be loosed from this bond on the sabbath pay?

St. Donatus, bishop of Arezzo, looses a governor's son, bound by the devil. The governor of Apronianus went to St. Donatus and St. Hilarian, and besought them to heal his son who was bound by the devil. The holy men commanded the devil to depart; and as he went out he yelled with a loud shriek, "Donatus turneth me out of house and home;" but immediately he was gone out the young man was loosed of his infirmity, and his father received him perfectly restored.—Bede, *Church History* (A.D. 734). The acts of St. Donatus are mentioned in almost all Roman martyrologies.

St. Hilarion looses a charioteer, bound by the devil. There was at Gaza a charioteer bound by the devil, in such sort that only his tongue was left free. Being brought to St. Hilarion, he said to the man, "Believe in the Lord Jesus, and He will loose thee of thy bonds." The man answered, "Sir, I believe that God has given thee power over unclean spirits, and to heal all manner of diseases." Then said Hilarion, "My son, be it unto thee even as thou wilt;" and immediately he was made whole, both in mind and body.—St. Jerome, *Vita Sancti Hilarionis* (A.D. 390).

Bowed by Infirmities. (See CRIPPLE.)

LUKE xiii. 11–13. There was a woman which had a spirit of infirmity eighteen years, and was bowed together, so that she could in no wise lift up herself. When Jesus saw her, He said to her, Woman, thou art loosed from thine infirmity. And He laid His hands on her: and immediately she was made straight.

Blithmund, bowed by infirmity, cured by St. Valery (A.D. 614). Blithmund, the son of illustrious parents, was paralyzed from birth, so that he could not stand upright, but his body was bowed together. The parents, having exhausted all medical skill without receiving any benefit, carried the child to Leuconaus, in Picardy, where was a monastery presided over by St. Valery, and earnestly implored the saint to take pity on the child. St. Valery prayed, and then taking the child by the hand, and stroking it from head to foot, the body was made straight, and delivered to its mother.—St. Attalus (a contemporary), *Acts of St. Valery.*

Brazen Serpent.

NUMB. xxi. 4–11. When the children of Israel came to Edom, they began to weary of their wanderings, and said to Moses, Why have you brought us up out of Egypt to die here in the wilderness? God was angry at their murmuring, and sent fiery serpents among the people, which bit many, and many died. So the people repented, and implored Moses to intercede for them. Moses did so, and God said to him, Make thee a brazen serpent, and raise it on a pole in the sight of all the people, and say unto them, Whoever looks upon the serpent shall live. Moses did as the Lord commanded; and it came to pass, if a man bitten by a serpent looked on the brazen serpent, the bite was cured, and the man lived.

Alexander the Great and the burning candle. Alexander the Great placed a burning candle in the hall of his palace, and made proclamation by heralds throughout Macedonia, that "any one guilty of treason should receive free pardon if he came into the hall boldly while the candle was burning, but those who feared to come, or neglected to do so, should suffer the extreme penalty of the law." Many believed the proclamation, came, and went away free; they were courteously received, well treated, and went home penitent; but others feared or neglected to do so, and suffered ignominious deaths.—*Gesta Romanorum*, xcvi.

A Roman custom in sieges. The Romans had an ancient custom, when a city or castle was besieged, of burning a lighted candle, and as long as the candle lasted they were willing to receive overtures of peace; but immediately the candle was burnt out, the time of grace was over.—*Gesta Romanorum*, xcviii.

The modern custom is to fix a time for overtures, and to begin active operations at the expiration of the time fixed. Thus, in the recent Egyptian war (1881), Admiral Seymour gave Arabi the Egyptian rebel a stated time within which he would make terms with him; Arabi did not capitulate within the time fixed, and the British admiral instantly opened fire.

MacIan of Glencoe (1692). William III. gave the Jacobites of Glencoe to the end of December, 1692, to make their submission, but those who failed to do so were to suffer the death of rebels and traitors. MacIan was prevented by a heavy fall of snow from arriving within the appointed time, and Sir John Dalrymple (the master of Stair) sent Captain Campbell to put the chief, with thirty glenmen, to death.

Sir John is generally blamed for this severity, but in rebellion, treason, and war, no margin must be given, no excuse for disobedience should be admitted. Suppose, in the case of the brazen serpent, one of the sufferers had said, "The brazen serpent exposed to the full sun is so dazzling that it would blind me to look at it," his excuse would not have exempted him from the penalty of disobedience; nor would it be otherwise if he had said, "I was going to look, but night closed in and prevented my seeing it." Many a case may appear hard, but the mischief would be enormous if excuses were accepted.

Brought Him.

JOHN vii. 44–47. Some of them would have taken Jesus, but no man laid hands on Him. Then came the officers to the chief priests and the Pharisees, who said, Why have ye not brought Him? The officers answered, Never man spake like this man. Then said the Pharisees, Are ye also deceived?

Pastor Jaenick's anecdote. The following is a marvellous parallel, and has the merit of being historical.

Pastor Jaenick related the following fact to a company assembled in the house of Mr. Elsner. While Voltaire was in Berlin, a pious clergyman in one of the churches of that city protested strongly against "that viper, and enemy of all godliness." Frederick the Great, thinking himself insulted by this language, sent one of his generals to arrest the clergyman, and lodge him in the state prison of Spandau. The general went accordingly, and said to the clergyman, "What is it you said in your sermon to affront his majesty?' Whereupon the good man spoke to the general with so much fervour and power, that the officer returned to the king without executing the order. When Frederick said, "Why, general, how is it you are back so soon?" the general replied, "I could not hurt a hair of that good man if it were to cost my life." Whereupon the king replied, "Then go back, and tell him not to meddle with the subject again." Next Sunday the clergyman again exhorted his congregation to beware of the leaven of unbelief, and the king sent another of his generals to take the contumacious orator to Spandau, adding he was not to enter into conversation with him. The roads being bad, travelling was slow work, and the general expressed his regret at the task imposed on him. On this hint the clergyman spoke earnestly of Christ crucified, and the great danger of indifference and infidelity. The general was melted, he had no heart left him to carry out his commission, and when half-way to Spandau ordered the driver to turn the horses and drive back to Berlin. Having set down his prisoner at his own door, the general went to the king and said, "Your majesty may order me on any other service, but I cannot fight against God. I would not, to save my life, hurt a hair of that good man. In fact, I could not if I would."—Henderson, *Memorials of John Venning.*

The captain of the galleys, with a company of soldiers sent to arrest Francis of Paula, falls down before him in reverence (A.D. 1416–1507). Ferdinand I., king of Naples, so hated St. Francis of Paula, that he sent one of his captains, with a company of soldiers, to arrest him. This news threw the whole city into consternation; and the chief citizens of Naples tried to dissuade the officer from laying hands on so holy a man. The captain paid no heed to this remonstrance, but proceeded to execute the king's order. St. Francis, in the mean time, entered the cathedral as usual, and placed himself on his knees before the high altar. The captain and his band entered the church, but failed to see the saint, because God had rendered him invisible. At length he came forward, and said to the captain, "Whom seek ye?" The captain, instead of arresting the saint, fell at his feet, and begged pardon for having undertaken his commission. St. Francis raised him from the ground, and said, "Go and tell the king that unless he, the queen, and the princes amend their lives, the vengeance of God will fall upon their house." The message being reported to the court, the king was alarmed, and ceased from all further persecution.—Father Giry, *Acts of Canonization*, etc.

Budding Rod.

NUMB. xvii. When the election of a high priest was made, the twelve tribes took each a rod, and wrote "every man's name on his rod," and God said the man of His choice should be indicated by the budding of the rod which bore his name. When Aaron was chosen high priest the twelve tribes took twelve rods, and the tribe of Levi wrote on their rod the name of Aaron, and this was the rod which budded; so Aaron was appointed high priest.

The Virgin Mary given to Joseph by the lot of the budding rod. When Mary was of marriageable age, the young men of Judah, who were of the lineage of David, took each a rod, and deposited them in the temple, with the understanding that he was to have her to wife whose rod budded. The rod of Joseph budded, and Mary became his espoused wife.—Edward Kinesman (1623), *Lives of the Saints*, p. 191.

The stick of St. Desiderius throws out leaves (A.D. 253). The bishop of Langres being dead, the Church assembled in the oratory of St. John the Evangelist to select a successor, and God told them He had chosen Desiderius for that high office. No such person was known to any of them, and they sent to Rome for information. As the deputation were returning home, they saw near Geneva a labourer named Desiderius, driving a cart, and asked him to come and speak to them. When he dismounted, he stuck his stick into the ground; but judge of their amazement when they saw the stick shoot forth leaves and blossoms in great abundance. It was enough. The sign was indisputable, and Desiderius the labourer was elected bishop of Langres. —L'abbé Mazelin, *Saints de la Haute Marne.*

St. Orens accepted the bishopric of Auch, because his stick budded (fifth century). St. Orens, a solitary living in the cleft of a rock, was chosen bishop of Auch. When the deputation waited on him he declined the honour, and, taking up his staff, was about to leave the cave, but his staff rooted itself in the solid rock, and threw out leaves and branches. St. Orens, considering this miracle an undeniable indication of the will of God, went with the deputation, and no sooner did he set foot in the city, than all the sick were instantly restored to health, no matter with what malady they were afflicted. His biographer remarks, "ce second miracle acheva de lui gagner les cœurs."—Monlezun, *Histoire de Gascogne.*

Arnaud Colomiez tells us that at death a voice from heaven said to him, "Orens, Je t'accorde tout ce que tu me demandes en faveur de ceux qui se recommanderont à toy, lesquels invoquants ton secours en toutes les infirmités, tribulations d'esprit, nécessitez, et angoisses en seront délivrez, et ne manqueront jamais de biens temporels en leur besoin."—*La Vie du Glorieux St. Orens, Évesque d'Auch.*

St. Paul chosen bishop of Trois-Châteaux by the budding of a dry stick (fifth century). Paul of Reims, in Champagne, was the son of poor Christian parents, and followed agricultural pursuits. As he was ploughing one day, a deputation from Trois-Châteaux presented themselves before him and asked his name. "I am called Paul," he replied. "Then you are the person we seek," said the deputation. "The Church at Trois-Chateaux has chosen you for their bishop." "Chosen me for a bishop?" exclaimed Paul. "Get away with you; I certainly am not the Paul you are seeking for. You see I am only a common labourer." "We see," said the deputation, "that you are a ploughman; but Amos of Tekoa, the prophet, was a herdsman, and St. Peter, the prince of the apostles, was but a fisherman. God is no respecter of persons, and you, Paul, are the person chosen to be our bishop." Paul could not be persuaded that some mistake had not been made, and, picking up a dry stick, thrust it into the ground, saying, "When this dry stick buds and brings forth flowers I will believe you, and not till then." What, however, was his astonishment when he beheld the stick covered with leaves and flowers. The deputation was overjoyed. They saw at once that God Himself confirmed their choice, and Paul could no longer refuse to follow them.—L'abbé Nadal, *Hagiographic History of Valence.*

An annual festival is kept in Trois-Château on Feb. 1, in commemoration of the budding stick of bishop Paul, the ploughman; when a stick, called *aiguillado*, decorated with ribbons, leaves, and almond flowers, is carried in procession.

The reader, of course, will be reminded not only of Amos of Tekoa, the herdsman, but of Cincinnatus, in Roman story, called from the plough to be dictator of Rome. The tale of Abdolonymus the gardener is not quite so familiar, but those who have read Quintus Curtius (iv. ch. i.) will remember that Alexander chose this poor man to be king of Sidon.

The oven peel of St. Honoré's nurse becomes a mulberry tree (seventh century). When the nurse of St. Honoré heard that he was made a bishop, she was putting bread into an oven, and stood stupefied with amazement. "I don't believe it—I don't believe it!" she exclaimed, and sticking the peel, which she held in her hand, into the ground, she added, "When that takes root, I will believe my boy is made a bishop." No sooner had she spoken, than the peel became a mulberry tree, full of leaves and fruit. In reference to this "miracle," St. Honoré is represented in Christian art with a peel, and hence the rhyme—

Saint Honoré
Dans sa chapelle
Avec sa pelle
Est honoré.

—L'abbé Corblet, *Origine du Patronage Liturgique des Boulangers.*

Au xvi. siècle, on montrait encore ce mûrier dans l'ancien logis paternel du saint évêque.—L'abbé Corblet.

Pope Urban's budding staff and Tannhäuser. The following is only a tale, but it is of the nature of a legend. The ritter Tannhäusen was a German knight, who won the love of Lisaura, a Mantuan lady. Hilario the philosopher often conversed with him on supernatural subjects, and promised that Venus herself should be his mistress if he had courage enough to enter Venusberg. Tannhäuser had no lack of courage, and accordingly started off at once on the mysterious journey. Lisaura being told thereof, killed herself. At Venusberg the ritter gave full swing to pleasure; but after a time returned to Mantua, and made his confession to pope Urban. His holiness said to him, "Man, you can no more hope for pardon than I can expect this staff to put forth buds." So Tannhäuser fled in despair to Venusberg again. Meanwhile the pope's staff actually did bud, and Urban sent in all directions for the ritter, but to no purpose. He was nowhere to be found, and never again showed his face on this earth.—Tieck, *Phantasus.*

This tale is an allegory, designed to show the boundless mercy of God—"All manner of sin and blasphemy shall be forgiven unto men;" yea, even if they have lived to pleasure in the city of Venusberg. Tannhäuser is the penitent, whose better conviction is choked by the weeds which spring up with the good seed. He quits pleasure for a season, but finding his sudden repentance a matter of suspicion, falls back again into the world. Urban is a warning to ministers not to measure God's infinite love and mercy by the finite scope of their own judgments. Forbear to judge; leave that to God.

A dead elm, touched by the bier of St. Zanobi, bursts into full foliage (A.D. 407). The bier of St. Zanobi happened, in passing, to touch an elm tree, dead and withered to the roots from old age. The moment it did so the whole tree burst into leaf, and was covered with flowers. This tree was looked on by the people with such reverence, that every one coveted a piece as a charmed relic, and the tree ere long was wholly cut away. A marble pillar was then erected on the spot, with an inscription stating what has been said above. When the bier reached the doorway of St. Saviour's Cathedral, it (the bier) became immovable, and no power of man could force it further on, till bishop Andrew promised to found twelve chaplains to chant the praises of God in the chapel designed for the dead saint.—John Tortel (archpriest of Arezzo), *Life of St. Zanobi* (1433).

This weighting of coffins, pillars, beams, and so on, is so common, and apparently so senseless, that even Mgr. Guérin, chaplain to pope Leo XIII., is struck with it; and in apology says, "Notre intention n'est pas d'imposer une croyance aveugle en faveur de tel ou tel de ces *faits* en particulier, mais de renvoyer à l'histoire de la translation de sainte Philomène la thaumaturge de notre épique. On y verra, qu'en plein xix. siècle, s'est opéré plusieurs fois, en présence de milliers de témoins, ce *miracle de l'immobilité.*" (This was in 1802.)

Burning Bush.

EXOD. iii. 1–6. Now Moses kept the flock of Jethro his father-in-law, priest of Midian: and he led the flock to the back of the desert, and came to the mountain of God, even to Horeb. And the angel of the Lord appeared to him in a flame of fire out of the midst of a bush: and he looked, and, behold, the bush burned with fire, and the bush was not consumed. And Moses said, I will now turn aside, and see this great sight, why the bush is not burnt. And when the Lord saw that he turned aside to see, God called unto him out of the midst of the bush, and said, Moses, Moses. And he said, Here am I. And the Lord said, Draw not nigh hither: put off thy shoes from off thy feet, for the place whereon thou standest is holy ground. And Moses hid his face; for he was afraid to look upon God.

A burning church not injured by the fire (A.D. 1230). A great fire broke out in Cologne, which burnt down many houses. St. Hermann went to render assistance, and saw a church, wholly enveloped in flames on every side, yet not injured in the least. While gazing at this strange spectacle, he observed the Lord Jesus suspended on His cross on the roof of the church; and immediately perceived that the flames had forborne to injure the sacred edifice, out of respect to the sacred passion and crucifixion of the Lord. In fact, the flames durst not touch the building which was thus protected. This conviction was confirmed, on noticing that the cross multiplied itself, in order to protect those parts of the church which the flames from time to time threatened most. This marvellous sight filled his soul with this sacred reflection: The best way of keeping the heart from being consumed by earthly passions is to impress on the memory the image of Christ crucified.—*Life of St. Hermann* (Bollandists), April 7.

The burning thorn-bush in the suburbs of Châlons (March 24, A.D. 1400). March 24, 1400, a shepherd on the farm of Sainte Marie, and another from Courtisol, near Châlons-sur-Marne, while keeping sheep not far from the chapel of St. John the Baptist, observed, at a little distance from where they stood, a brilliant light in the midst of a great thorn-bush. The sheep in alarm ran away; the lambs only ventured to approach the bush!! Curious to know the cause of this extraordinary light, the two shepherds were drawing near, when they were so dazzled by the light that they swooned, and were a long time before they came to themselves. When they did so, they found the cause of this brilliant light was an image of the Virgin Mary holding her Son in her arms!! The light grew stronger after sunset, and crowds ran to see it from all the neighbourhood; and, as the place is elevated, the burning bush was seen for ten leagues round. When the phenomenon ceased, the bishop of Châlons, at the head of his whole chapter, the neighbouring clergy, and an enormous crowd of the inhabitants, went in procession to the bush, and found it covered with green leaves, notwithstanding the flames which had been seen in the midst of it. The image was still in the bush, and was carried with reverence to the chapel of St. John the Baptist.

The image is nineteen inches in height, of grey earth, tolerably modelled, and painted throughout. In the Revolution it was placed under the care of the curé de l'Epine, and therefore escaped demolition. The bush was cut down to give place to the church, and no one knows the exact spot where it stood, but it is supposed to have been where the altar is placed.—Mgr. Guérin (chamberlain of Leo XIII.), *Vies des Saints* (7th edit. 1880). *Extrait d'une notice sur Notre-Dame de l'Epine* by the curé of the place.

Notre-Dame des Miracles at Mauriac (A.D. 507). One dark night Theodechilde, daughter of Clovis, noticed in Montselis' forest a brilliant light, which shone among the trees, but injured them not. The night following it appeared again. Greatly astonished at this strange phenomenon, she went to the spot, and found, in the very centre of the light, a wooden image, as black as coal, representing the Madonna and her Infant. Theodechilde at once commanded a chapel to be built on the spot, and there she deposited the image. So numerous were the miracles which proceeded therefrom, that a town, named Mauriac, sprang up in the vicinity, and the chapel was called "Notre-Dame des Miracles." The miracles were for the most part the ordinary ones, of sight to the blind, hearing to the deaf, speech to the dumb, casting out devils, and curing paralytics; but the following is less common. One morning two men, in strange costume, were found at the chapel doors, fast asleep. On waking, they were evidently puzzled to make out where they were, and how they got there. Their tale was that they were two slaves from Spain, who prayed to Notre-Dame des Miracles to deliver them, and while they slept, the Virgin must have carried them from their prison in Spain, and deposited them in Mauriac, where they were found. "Tel est le fait raconté dans l'office même (i.e. *Propre de St. Flour*), et que confirment les chaines subsistantes qu'on porte en procession devant la statue miraculeuse."—Mgr. Guérin, *Vies des Saints* (7th edit. 1880), vol. v. p. 424.

The "chains" carried in procession can be no confirmation of this strange tale, any more than the stone encased in the coronation chair is a proof of Jacob's dream in Bethel.

Camels' Hair Raiment.

Matt. iii. 4. John the Baptist was the son of prayer. St. Luke says that Zacharias and his wife Elisabeth were both righteous before God, walking in all the commandments and ordinances of the Lord blameless; but they had no child, because Elisabeth was barren, and they were both well stricken in years. One day, as Zacharias was executing his official duties, an angel appeared to him and said, Fear not, Zacharias: for thy prayer is heard; and thy wife Elisabeth shall bear thee a son, and thou shalt call his name John. And thou shall have joy and gladness; and many shall rejoice at his birth, for he shall be great in the sight of the Lord.—This same John came preaching in the wilderness of Judæa, and had his raiment of camel's hair, and a leathern girdle about his loins, and his meat was locusts and wild honey.

Baron de Tott tells us that the Tartars to the present day cover their wooden huts with a coarse cloth made of camel's hair.—*Memoirs*, pt. ii. p. 50. Sir J. Chardin says that the modern dervishes wear garments made of camel's hair, girt about the loins with a leather girdle, and that sometimes they feed on locusts, which John the Baptist made his usual fare.—Note on 1 Sam. xxv. 4.

⁂ Probably the "cilice," or hair shirt worn by the saints, was more or less in imitation of the Baptist, but it must be borne in mind that raiments made of goats' or horses' hair were not uncommon among the Hebrews, and had no reference whatever to penance.

St. Genulph, like John the Baptist, was the son of prayer, and had his raiment of camel's hair (third century). Genitus and his wife Aclia were both pious Christians, who walked in all the commandments and ordinances of Christ blameless; but they had no child, because Aclia was barren, and they were both well stricken in years. One day, having prayed with more than usual earnestness that God would vouchsafe to give them a son, a voice said to them, "Fear not: for your prayers are heard; and Aclia shall bear a son, and ye shall call his name Genulph. And ye shall have joy and gladness in him; yea, and many shall rejoice in his birth, for he shall be great in the sight of the Lord." In due time the child was born, and at the age of five years was given to St. Sixtus, to be brought up in the fear and admonition of the Lord. This same Genulph, like John the Baptist, had his raiment of camel's hair, which he wore always, except when he celebrated the "Holy Mysteries," on which solemn occasions he arrayed himself in the finest linen and most costly robes, brilliant with gold and precious stones. In the territory of Cadurci (*Cahors*) he preached the Word, and exhorted all men to repentance and faith. The fame of his sanctity drew many unto him, and he performed many miracles in the name of Jesus Christ.—Bollandus, *Acta Sanctorum*, vol. ii. p. 83, etc.

Cauldron Innocuous. (See FIRE INNOCUOUS.)

HEB. xi. 32-34. The time would fail me to tell of those who through faith stopped the mouths of lions, quenched the violence of fire, escaped the edge of the sword, and out of weakness were made strong.

ISA. xliii. 2. When thou passest through water, I will be with thee; and through rivers, they shall not overflow thee. When thou walkest through fire, thou shalt not be burned; neither shall flame kindle upon thee.

The following are varieties of the tale told of Shadrach, Meshach, and Abednego (Dan. iii.), *q.v.*

St. Boniface, after numerous tortures, is ordered to be thrown into boiling pitch, but escapes unhurt (fourth century). The emperor Diocletian appointed Simplicius to stamp out Christianity in Cilicia. Amongst many others, St. Boniface was brought under his jurisdiction. He was first hung with his head downwards, and his flesh torn from his bones by iron hooks; in his horrible torture he uttered not a groan. He was then taken down, and, after an hour's respite, sharp spikes were driven up his nails; but still he suffered in silence. The governor, irritated beyond measure at this apparent insensibility, now ordered his myrmidons to force his mouth open, and pour into it hot molten lead. At this the crowd became so furious, that they took up stones to throw at the governor, who fled for his life. Next day Simplicius again took his seat on the tribunal, and commanded the saint to be thrown head foremost into a cauldron of boiling pitch. St. Boniface made the sign of the cross, the cauldron broke into fragments, and the boiling pitch burnt terribly the executioners, but never touched the saint at all. Simplicius, out of patience, then ordered the saint's head to be cut off. As this was done the earth quaked, and all present thought the world was come to an end.—*Acta Sanctorum* (Bollandists), vol. ii. May 14.

Archbishop Ado gives a different version of the last incident. He says that Simplicius caused the martyr's head to be held in a cauldron full of seething pitch, oil, and resin; but the martyr not only received no injury therefrom, he did not even suffer the slightest pain.

St. Cecilia exposed in a dry cauldron set over a huge fire, and yet unhurt. After the martyrdom of her husband Valerian, the Roman governor Almachius commanded his officers to place St. Cecilia in a dry cauldron, and place the cauldron over a fierce fire, till his victim was dried to a cinder. St. Cecilia was in the cauldron a day and a night, yet "felt no woe;" yea, she declared afterwards, that she found her dry bath "delightfully refreshing." An executioner then came with orders to cut off her head. Three times he cut across her neck with his sword, but still left it dangling on her bosom by the skin. For three days the saint lived in this state. Many came to visit her, and she spoke to them words of consolation and good hope. Among others came Urban, and "the blessed martyr" gave to him full directions for the conversion of her house into a church. When she had completed her directions, she rose to her knees in prayer, and in this posture fell asleep in Jesus.—Simeon Metaphrastês. (See Chaucer, *Canterbury Tales:* "The Second Nun's Tale.")

St. Cyprian and St. Justina unharmed in a cauldron of seething pitch. In the reign of Claudius II. of Rome, St. Cyprian and St. Justina were first torn from head to foot by hooks and harrows, and then set naked in a cauldron full of seething pitch, tallow, and other matters. But, by the grace of God, these holy martyrs felt no discomfort in their bath; and, being taken out uninjured, they were both beheaded.—Bede (A.D. 734). See also St. Gregory Nazianzenus, *Orations against Julian*, 18 (A.D. 363).

St. Erasmus, bishop of Campania, set in a cauldron of boiling pitch without injury (A.D. 301). St. Erasmus, in the reign of Diocletian, was first beaten with staves, then bastinadoed with knotty clubs, and then plunged into a cauldron filled with pitch, oil, and resin. The cauldron was set on a huge fire till the mass seethed; and yet the saint received no harm, for the very fire was in league with him. Being taken from the seething pot, he was led back to prison and laden with chains; but God sent His angel to deliver him. Afterwards he fell into the hands of Maximian, who put on him a corselet of red-hot iron; but this also did him no harm, and again he was taken back to prison. The God who delivered him before sent another angel to lead him out of prison, and take him to Campania. A third time was he apprehended, and this time he was martyred, but we are not told how.—Ado (archbishop of Vienne), *Martyrology*.

St. John the Divine cast into a cauldron of burning hot oil. When St. John the Evangelist was ninety years old, the emperor Domitian commanded him to be cast into a cauldron of boiling hot oil. The place appointed for this torture was a large open field before the Latin gate. A huge cauldron was prepared and filled with oil, pitch, and resin, which were melted over a fire of wood; and an enormous crowd assembled on the spot to see the spectacle. The evangelist, no doubt, was scourged first, according to the usual custom, and was then led forth into the field. More fire was piled up, and the cauldron began to seethe and overflow; then was he taken up, and let down into the midst of the boiling mass. The flames were so fierce and high as wholly to conceal the martyr, but the crowd distinctly heard a voice singing in the cauldron. Every one was amazed, and waited impatiently to see the end. More and more fuel was piled on the fire, till the heat was unbearable for many yards' distance, and still the voice was heard singing hymns of praise. At length the fire burnt out, and the multitude crowded to the cauldron, when, lo! there sat the aged apostle in the midst, wholly uninjured. The oil, the resin, and the pitch had all boiled away, the cauldron was quite dry; but there sat the evangelist, not a hair of his head injured, but his face beaming like the sun, and his aged body actually invigorated. The officers lifted him out of the cauldron, and led him back to prison.

This tale is told by St. Jerome, who lived A.D. 345–420, *In Jovianum*, i. p. 14; by Tertullian, who lived 160–240, *Proscriptions against Heretics*, ch. xxxvi.; by Eusebius, who lived 265–338; and has been repeated in almost all *Lives of the Saints*.

St. Lucy, being set in a cauldron of molten lead, receives no harm therefrom. St. Lucy, by the order of Diocletian and Maximian, was plunged up to her neck in a cauldron full of boiling pitch and molten lead. Here she remained for many hours, but received no sort of harm. Being taken out, she was haled by the hair through the streets, laden with gyves and fetters. As she was dragged past the door of Germinianus, a noted image-maker, all the idols in his warehouse fell to the ground, and were broken to pieces. This was the cause of his conversion, and he was beheaded with St. Lucy the same day.—Simeon Metaphrastês (died 911), *Lives of the Saints*. (See also Zonaras and Evagrius.)

Chains falling off Prisoners.

ACTS xvi. 25, 26. When Paul and Silas were at Philippi they were cast into prison. but at midnight they prayed, and suddenly there was a great earthquake, and immediately every man's bonds were loosed.

ACTS xii. 7. When Peter was cast into prison by Herod, an angel came to him, and "his chains fell off from his hands."

At a glance from St. Benedict of Mount Cassino, the bonds of a prisoner are broken (A.D. 480–543). A Gothic soldier cruelly tormented a peasant for money. The peasant said he had given all he possessed into the keeping of St. Benedict. Whereupon the Goth bound him with strong cords, and made him walk in front of his horse, and conduct him to the abbey. They found the abbot alone, reading; and the Goth, in a bullying tone, cried aloud, "Up, up, I say! give this fellow the money he has left with you." The saint, quite imperturbable, went on reading, but in a few minutes glanced at the peasant. The instant his eye was fixed on the captive, the strong cords broke like tow, and left the man free. The Goth was frightened, and throwing himself at the feet of the man of God, implored his pardon. St. Benedict never spoke a word, but went on with his book. After a few minutes' silence, the saint very quietly said to one of the brothers, "Give them to eat, and let them go." The bully was thoroughly cowed, and the peasant's money remained in safe custody.—St. Gregory the Great, *Dialogues*, bk. ii.

Chains of St. Chrisantus crumble into dust. When St. Chrisantus was cast into prison by the Roman tribune, he was loaded with gyves and fetters, and the floor of the prison was covered with foul and stinking things; but, in the sight of the officers, the irons which they had used to bind him with turned to dust, and the stench which filled the cell was converted into a fragrant perfume.

Verinus and Armenius, priests of St. Stephen, pope and martyr, wrote the *Life of St. Chrisantus;* and Metaphrastês expanded it. Chrisantus is mentioned in the *Roman Martyrology;* in the *Martyrology* of Usuardus; and in Surius, *Lives of the Saints*, vol. v.

St. Eleutherius released from prison by an angel (A.D. 531). A contagion having broken out in Tournai, the people ascribed it to St. Eleutherius, the despiser of their gods. A company of soldiers was sent, therefore, to apprehend him, and he was cast into prison. At night the angel of God came to him, his chains fell off, the prison doors opened of their own accord, and the angel conducted him to Blandain. The governor of Tournai, convinced by this miracle that the Christian's God is the one true God, prayed St. Eleutherius to return to the city. This did he, and the same day the saint received into the fold 11,000 souls by baptism.—*Les Petits Bollandistes*, vol. ii. p. 600.

Chasm filled up.

Mettius Curtius, B.C. 362. We are told in Roman story that a vast chasm, from some unknown cause, appeared in the Roman forum, and the soothsayers declared it would never be filled up, till Rome threw into it its best treasure. Mettius Curtius said, Rome's best treasure is a self-sacrificing devoted patriot; and mounting on his charger he leaped into the gulf, which immediately closed over him.—Valerius Maximus, *De Factis Dictisque Memorabilibus* (in nine books).

A gully and bog filled up by the body of St. Leo (third century). St. Leo, passing by the temple of Fortune, at Patara, in Lycia, saw it illuminated with lanterns, and broke as many as were within his reach. The governor ordered him to be brought before him, and asked why he had profaned the temple, and dishonoured the emperor. St. Leo replied that Fortune was no deity, and added, "There is but one God, the Creator of heaven and earth." The governor said, "You are not here to preach Christianity, but to answer your indictment." As Leo persisted in disavowing the gods, the governor ordered him to be scourged, and then to be dragged over rocks and stones till he was dead. After death, his body was thrown from a precipice into a deep chasm or gully, the bottom of which was a dangerous bog, and immediately the chasm closed upon it, and the bog became firm ground, over which persons could walk without the least danger.—Bollandus, *Acta Sanctorum*, vol. ii. February. (Alban Butler gives the life of St. Leo, with but little mutilation.)

Christ accused of Satanic Influence.

MARK iii. 22–30. The scribes which came down from Jerusalem said [of Christ], He hath Beelzebub, and by the prince of the devils casteth He out devils.

St. Maur accused of sorcery (512–584). After St. Maur had done many wonderful works at Glanfeuil, the devil inspired three artisans to accuse him of sorcery, giving out that he had come there only to make his fortune by deluding the people with false miracles; but God signally punished these calumniators. The devil entered into them all, and tormented them with excruciating tortures, under which one of the three died. St. Maur, instead of rejoicing, prayed earnestly that God would pardon them. His prayer was heard, for God not only drove out the devil from the possessed, but also raised the dead man to life. St. Maur then bade them leave the neighbourhood, lest their presence should keep alive in memory the miracle which had been wrought.—Faustus (a companion of St. Maur), *Life of St. Maur*

Christ as a Child.

[In the *Lives of the Saints* the favourite apparition of Christ is in the form of a little child. It was as a little child that He appeared to St. Alexander, St. Anthony, St. Augustine, St. Bernard, St. Opherus, St. Peter of Alexandria, and hundreds of other saints.]

Christ appears, as a little child, to St. Alexander and Balbina (A.D. 118). Pope Alexander I., in the reign of Hadrian, converted Hermês the governor and all his house, to the number of 1500 souls. Complaint being made to the emperor Trajan that Alexander and Hermês were greatly perverting the people, he sent Aurelian to investigate the matter, with full power of acting at discretion. Aurelian committed Alexander to prison; but Hermês, being a man high in dignity and honour, he placed in the house of Quirinus the tribune, as a prisoner on his parole. The tribune tried to persuade Hermês to abandon a religion which only led to dishonour and death; but the governor replied, "I once thought like you, but pope Alexander made me wise unto salvation." Quirinus said, "I wonder if the man you refer to is the Alexander I have under me in the common jail?" "Yes," replied Hermês, "that is indeed the man; and if he liked he could, with the help of Jesus Christ, free himself from bondage, and either come to me or go elsewhere." Quirinus laughed outright at this, and said, "If Alexander can quit his cell, and come hither without my permission, I will believe that Christ is God indeed." "Be it so," said Hermês. Then Quirinus departed, and set double locks on the prison doors, and a double guard to keep watch over both his prisoners. Hermês, by the medium of prayer, communicated to Alexander this conversation with the tribune, and presently there appeared before him a little child about five years old, who said to him, "Alexander, arise, and follow me." "As the Lord liveth," replied Alexander, "I will not go with thee, except I first hear thee repeat the *Pater Noster*." The child repeated the prayer, and, taking the prisoner by the hand, led him to the room where Hermês was in custody. When the tribune returned, and found Alexander and Hermês together, he was dumfounded; but after his first astonishment was abated he said, "I am ready to be baptized, for none of our Roman gods can do after this sort." After more conversation he said, "I have a daughter, an only child, grievously afflicted with an incurable quinsy; heal her, and I will bestow on you half of all my goods." "Bring her to my cell," said St. Alexander, and the damsel was taken to his cell. "Now take this chain," said Alexander, "with which I was bound, and hang it about her neck." The father took the chain, and hung it round the neck of his daughter, and she was cured in a moment. In the mean time, the holy child, which had delivered Alexander from prison, appeared again in the cell, and said to the maiden, "Balbina, Christ hath made thee whole, and desires to have thee for His bride." When Quirinus saw the vision of the child Jesus, he fell at the feet of Alexander, and cried, "My lord, depart out of this place, lest I be consumed." Alexander then bade Quirinus to assemble before him all his prisoners, and when he had done so, the saint preached to them Christ and Him crucified. His words went home to their hearts with power of the Holy Ghost, and all were converted. Quirinus supplied all the prisoners with white robes, as was the custom with catechumens, and they were baptized. (See PETER THE HOLY EXORCIST, p. 91.) — *Life of Pope Alexander I.* (from the public registers).

Christ, as a child, appears to St. Andrew Corsini (A.D. 1302-1373). When the clergy of Fiesolê chose St. Andrew Corsini for their bishop, he was nowhere to be found. Having been informed of the election, he had fled to Certosa, south of Florence, to compel the synod to make another choice. Another council being called, just as some other name was about to be proposed, a little child, apparently three years old, entered the assembly, and said, "Andrew Corsini is God's choice. You will find him at his orisons in Certosa." At the same moment a little boy in white appeared to St. Andrew, and said, "Fear not, Andrew, for I am with you, and Mary will be thy protector and helper." The call could not be resisted. As St. Andrew went on his way to Fiesolê, he met the deputation, and they entered the church together.—Surius, *Lives of the Saints* (6 vols. fol. 1570).

Christ, as a little child, often visited St. Antony of Padua (A.D. 1195-1231). Christ often went into the cell of St. Antony of Padua, in the form and likeness of a little child, and conversed freely with him.—Edward Kinesman (1623), *Lives of the Saints.*

Christ, as a child, appears to St. Cuth-

bert when quite a boy (seventh century). When Cuthbert was only eight years old, and was playing with his companions, a child some three years of age came to him, and begged him to spend his time more profitably. Cuthbert took no notice of this remonstrance, and the child, throwing itself on the ground, began to cry so bitterly, that Cuthbert and his companions ran to comfort it. The little child then said to Cuthbert, "Why, O holy priest and prelate, do you indulge in follies unsuited to your dignity and your order? It is not consistent for you to play with children—you whom God has elected to teach even the most advanced in wisdom and in years." Cuthbert, amazed at these words, was instantly changed in the spirit of his mind, and the little child, which before seemed an infant not exceeding three years of age, suddenly appeared before him as a man of full and perfect stature. —Bede, *Church History*, bk. iv. ch. 27–32.

Alban Butler refers us to all the usual authorities and yet omits this tale, which is given by all the best authorities.

Christ, as a child, appears to St. Emiliana of Florence (A.D. 1246). St. Emiliana had a most earnest desire to see Jesus Christ at the age of three or four years; and one day, as she was abed, very ill, she saw an infant child of that age in her chamber. The child was admirably beautiful, and played before her bed. Emiliana thought it was an angel, and said to it, "My dear child, have you nothing better to do than to waste your time in sport?" The child answered with a sigh, "What would you have me do instead?" "I should like you," said St. Emiliana, "to speak to me of the great God." The child replied, "In speaking of God one can only speak in praise, and it is not well to praise one's self." So saying, the child vanished from her sight.—A. Stolz, *Acta Sanctorum* (May 19).

Christ, as a little child, appears to St. Oxanna (A.D. 1449–1505). The good angel of Oxanna, of Mantua, conducted her, when only six years old, into heaven, and showed her the glory of the saints. When she returned to earth, she vowed herself to God without reserve, and forthwith Jesus Christ came to her, in the form of a little child of ravishing beauty, with long curling blond locks, but wearing a crown of thorns, and carrying on His shoulder a heavy cross. Stretching out His arms to Oxanna, He said to her, "My dear Oxanna, I am the Son of Mary. If you follow Me, you must suffer much, as I also suffered, and was made perfect with sufferings." Thus saying, He vanished, and the little girl was left with a heart brimful of divine love.—L'abbé Chapia, *La Vie d'une Sainte pour chaque Jour de l'Année* (June 18).

Christ appears, as a little child, to St. Veronica of Milan. On the octave of Corpus Christi, A.D. 1487, during mass in the cathedral church of Milan, Veronica, gazing intently on the holy elements, saw the form of Jesus Christ as a little child, surrounded by adoring angels. On her return to the convent she asked the sisters if they also had seen the vision, but none of them had done so.—Baring-Gould, *Lives of the Saints* (Jan., p. 197).

When Macbeth was about to murder Duncan, he saw a dagger in the air; but if the vestibule had been full of men and women, none would have seen the phantom. Again, in the banquet hall he saw the ghost of Banquo sitting on the vacant chair, but no one else saw it. Brutus, before the battle of Pharsalia, saw the ghost of Cæsar; and again, at Philippi. Veronica no doubt saw the child Jesus, as Macbeth saw the dagger, and Brutus the ghost of Cæsar, but that is no proof that the child Jesus was there in a bodily form. She was quite honest and truthful, but her mind informed her sight, not her sight her mind. Many a ghost tale may be equally true, and to the seer the vision is a reality, because the flow of blood in the nervous centres of the head is abnormal, being either in excess or in defect. Every medical man knows that visions of all sorts are common enough in such cases. Be it distinctly understood there is no deception in the sight-seer, but only disease.

Christ consorting with Sinners.

MATT. v. 11. The Pharisees said to the disciples, Why eateth your Master with publicans and sinners? When Jesus heard that, He said to them, They that be whole need not a physician, but they that be sick.

St. Martin accused by the devil of consorting with sinners. The devil reproved St. Martin because he received, "upon penance," those who had committed very heinous sins, and even those who had denied the abounding mercy of God, saying that God would not pardon them. St. Martin replied, "The physician visits the sick to heal them; and if thou, miserable wretch, didst but know thy sickness, wished for pardon, and would repent, I would pray the forgiving God to have mercy even on thee."—Sulpicius Severus, *Life of St. Martin.*

Christ enters, the Doors being Shut.

JOHN xx. 19. The same day at evening, while the doors were shut where the disciples were assembled, came Jesus, and stood in their midst.

St. Clara leaves her cell, the door being locked on her (A.D. 1346). The sisters one day locked St. Clara in her cell to prevent her returning to her retreat in the walls of the town, where she was accustomed to task herself beyond her strength by penances; but although there was no means of exit or entrance, she left her cell while the door was still locked. —*Les Petits Bollandistes*, vol. ii. p. 439.

St. Francis Hieronimus enters and leaves the chamber of Cataldo, when the doors are shut. When Cataldo was dying, St. Francis Hieronimus went in and out of the chamber while the doors remained shut. It is also said that he was often in the room, wholly invisible to any one but the dying man.—Cardinal Wiseman. (St. Francis was canonized in 1839.)

St. Paul of the Cross departs from a house when the doors are shut. St. Paul of the Cross came to Perugia, and being taken by the parish priest for a vagabond, was locked up in a secure place, the plate of the house being first well secured. Next morning the priest sent his sister to unlock the door and give the vagrant his breakfast; but what was her amazement, on opening the door, to find the room empty. The door certainly had been well locked, and the priest himself had kept the key. The window also was secured with iron bars, between which no human creature could possibly pass. There was no way of exit except by miracle. That alone could solve the mystery. As Christ entered the room where the disciples were assembled when the doors were shut, so St. Paul of the Cross had left the room in which he had been locked when the doors were shut.—Father Pius, *Life of St. Paul of the Cross.*

Christ identifies Himself with His Disciples and with Objects of Charity.

Matt. xxv. 40. Verily, I say unto you, Inasmuch as ye have done it unto one of the least of these My brethren, ye have done it unto Me.

Acts ix. 4. When Saul went to Damascus to persecute the Christians there, Christ said to him, Saul, Saul, why persecutest thou Me? [not, Why persecutest thou My disciples? but Me].

Christ restores to St. Catherine of Siena a crucifix which she had given in charity to a pauper (A.D. 1317–1380). One day a poor man asked alms of St. Catherine, who was greatly distressed, because she had nothing to give him. Happening to cast her eyes on her rosary, she saw there her silver crucifix, which she handed to the beggar. At night, while she was in prayer, the Saviour appeared to her, holding in His hand the crucifix, now beautifully studded with precious stones. "Do you recognize this crucifix, My daughter?" asked Christ. "Yes," said Catherine; "but it is infinitely more beautiful than it was this morning.' "This morning, Catherine, you gave it Me, in pure love," said the Saviour; "at the day of judgment I will restore it to you as you now see it." So saying, He vanished from her sight.

Another instance. On one occasion St. Catherine gave to a beggar the only robe she had preserved; and next day the Saviour appeared to her, wearing this robe thickly sown with pearls and gold.—Raymond of Capua (her confessor), *Life of St. Catherine of Siena.*

Brother Giles, at the bidding of St. Francis of Assisi, gives his cloak to a beggar (A.D. 1272). Giles was the first disciple of St. Francis of Assisi. When he went to join the saint, he met him on the road, and implored that he might be admitted into his society. As they journeyed on together, they encountered a beggar, and St. Francis told Giles to give the beggar his cloak. Giles instantly obeyed, and the beggar rose to the clouds in the sight of them both. Then Giles felt deeply how blessed is blind obedience.—*Acta Sanctorum* (Bollandists), April 23.

We have another anecdote of a similar character told of Brother Giles, but without the sequel. Going on a pilgrimage, barefooted, without purse, food, or a second cloak, he met a poor man in rags. Giles cut off half his own cloak and gave it to the beggar, and for twenty days went on his journey, exposed to all the changes of the weather, his only raiment being half a cloak. (See St. Martin, p. 62.)

St. Hubert, a monk of Brittany, has Christ for his guest (A.D. 714). St. Hubert, the son of pious parents, entered the monastery of St. Peter, in Brittany, in 670, and was ordained priest when only twenty years old. Three pontiffs were told by angels to go to Brittany to assist in the ceremony. At dinner, a beggar sat himself at table with the high and honoured guests, and after Hubert had given him food he vanished. The nobles, prelates, and other guests looked at each other in wonder, and recognized at once that the beggar was Christ Himself who had honoured their table.—*Acta Sanctorum* (Bollandists), vol. vii. May 30.

We see in this the readiness of the "faithful" to believe in the miraculous. There is no shadow of proof that this beggar was anything more than a human being. Another thought suggests itself. Is it possible that the word "angels" is used in the same sense as in the Revelation, where the *ministers* of the Asiatic Churches are called "angels;" or does the word mean simply *messengers?* That the word was generally considered to mean "spirits from heaven" there can be no doubt, but the original biographer may have simply adopted a term of Biblical authority, without the least intention of misleading.

St. Gregory the Great, feeding the poor, had Christ for his guest (A.D. 540–604). The charity of St. Gregory the Great was most exemplary. At every meal he had some beggars at his table. One day before the meal began he wished to give a beggar some water to wash in, but while he was absent the beggar vanished. During the night the Saviour came to him, and said, "Ordinarily you receive Me in the poor who assemble at your board, but to-day you received Me personally." [Membra prius quasi me suscepisti, sed hodie me.]

Another instance. On another occasion St. Gregory commanded his almoner to bring twelve poor men to his table, but when he sat down he noticed there were thirteen guests. He called his almoner and told him he had exceeded the number; but the almoner replied, his holiness had commanded him to furnish twelve guests, and twelve only were assembled. St. Gregory saw at once there was some mystery, and kept his eye upon the thirteenth. He observed that the figure and countenance of this guest was constantly changing: at one time he looked like a child, then a young man, and last of all as a very old man. After the meal was over he called the mysterious stranger to him, and asked his name. "Why would you know my name?" said the stranger; "it is unutterable. I am an angel, sent by God, to tell you how highly He approves of these acts of charity." Gregory now fell at his feet with his face to the earth, and said, "If God approves of such small services, I can well conceive how He will approve of greater. And henceforth I will increase my charities a hundredfold." And so he did. (See St. Julian, next col.)—John the deacon, *Life of St. Gregory the Great* (twelfth century), written at the express command of pope Leo VIII.

St. John of St. Facond gives the best of his coats to a beggar (A.D. 1430–1479). St. John of St. Facond was a native of Sahagun or St. Facond, in Spain, and was a very great saint. One day a naked beggar met him, and asked alms in the name of God. John had on two garments, and gave the better of them to the beggar. At night he received a celestial visit sc extraordinary, that his whole heart and soul seemed filled with ineffable delight. "God only knows what I felt," said John, "but such a fulness of joy I never felt before, and its remembrance will abide with me for ever."—*Acta Sanctorum* (Bollandists), vol. ii. p. 616, June 12.

St. Julian, bishop of Cuença, entertains Christ amongst his pauper guests (A.D. 1207). St. Julian, bishop of Cuença, was accustomed to give dinner to several paupers every day. On one occasion there appeared at his table one more meanly clad than the rest, but his face and bearing showed he was no mean person. St. Julian took him aside, after the meal, and inquired into his antecedents; when the pauper replied, "My dear Julian, I thank you for your hospitality to the poor, and promise you eternal life. Be well assured that whatever you do to the least of these My brethren, ye do unto Me." So saying, He vanished from human sight, and St. Julian knew it was the Lord. (See St. Gregory.)—Bollandus, *Acta Sanctorum*, Jan. 28 vol. ii.

St. Martin parts his cloak with a beggar St. Martin, at the age of eighteen, while serving in the Roman army, was stationed at Amiens during a very severe winter One bitterly cold day, when many perished with cold, marching through the city they came upon a poor naked beggar shaking and pinched. Martin, like al the other soldiers, was in armour, bu over his steel he had a large military cloak. As none of his companions took notice of the beggar, Martin cut his cloak in two with his sword, and gave half o it to the beggar, the other half he threw over his shoulders as a scarf. Some o his companions laughed at him, bu others felt ashamed that with large means they had not relieved the vagrant At night, Christ showed Himself to Marti in a vision. He was dressed in the parte cloak, and asked Martin if he recognize the garment, adding, "What is done t the poor in My name is done unto Me. Martin now resolved to be baptized, t leave the army, and devote the rest c his life to the service of Christ.

Another example. This act was repeated with modifications, when St. Martin wa bishop of Tours. Being about to sa mass, a poor naked man asked alms c him, and St. Martin bade his archdeaco go and buy a garment for the vagrant

The archdeacon was so long gone, that Martin took off his own garment and gave it to the man. The archdeacon returned after a time, bringing a cheap, coarse, scant garment, which the bishop put on, and proceeded to say mass. As he elevated the host his arms were quite bare, but angels covered them with plates of gold. Hence arose the custom in some churches of putting maniples of silk or other delicate textures over the alb. (See BROTHER GILES, p. 61.)—Sulpicius Severus, *Dialogues*, ii.

(Fortunatus says the bare arms of the saint were covered with emeralds, and that the word "chapel" is derived from this little *cape* or *capella*.)

Peter the banker and his dream (A.D. 619). St. John, patriarch of Alexandria, used to tell the following anecdote as a veritable fact. Peter the banker was governor of all Africa. He was immensely rich, but so niggardly that he was nicknamed "Peter the Miser." One day a poor man, watching his opportunity, applied to him for bread, at the very moment the baker was delivering bread at his gate. Peter was present, as usual, to see the tale of bread delivered, and the beggar craved a loaf, pleading hunger. The banker was very savage, but, unable to refuse the man, flung a loaf at his head, with an oath. The beggar picked up the loaf, and showed it to his companions as a curiosity. Two days afterwards the banker fell ill, and saw in a vision the Ethiopians collecting into a scale all his misdeeds and shortcomings, and into the other scale his one act of charity, the loaf flung at the beggar with a curse. It was a frightfully light weight, and Peter woke in alarm. He now resolved to increase his credit, and give largely to the poor. Accordingly, next day he gave his coat to a naked beggar, bidding him keep it for his use. The beggar, however, immediately sold the coat, and the banker felt greatly annoyed. On his way home, Jesus Christ Himself met Peter; He was clad in the very garment given to the beggar, and He said, "Peter, what you give to the poor in My name, you give unto Me. Seek neither gratitude nor glory in this world; your reward is in the world to come." So saying, He vanished out of sight. The miser was now thoroughly converted, and not only gave all that he had to the poor, but himself also to the service of Christ.—Leontius (bishop of Naples), *Life of St. John the Almoner.*

St. Philip Berruyer, archbishop of Bourges, and his valet strip themselves to clothe two naked beggars (A.D. 1264). One day in midwinter, as Philip Berruyer, archbishop of Bourges, was visiting his diocese, a beggar more than half naked asked alms of him. The archbishop, retiring out of sight, stripped himself of his under garments, and gave them to the beggar. He had not gone far before another pauper accosted him, worse clad than the former. The primate, turning to his valet, asked him to assist in clothing this miserable creature; and the valet, desirous of imitating his master, stripped off his under garments, and gave them to the beggar. This occurred in the vicinity of Vierzon, in Berri.—*Les Petits Bollandistes* (A.D. 1880), vol. i. p. 243.

St. Zita lends her master's cloak to a poor man, who proves to be Christ or an angel (A.D. 1218-1278). St. Zita was a servant-maid in the family of Signora Fatinelli. One Christmas night, when the cold was intense, and Zita was about to go to church, her master offered to lend her his cloak, but told her to take care of it, and not leave it behind. "Never fear, sir," she replied; "I will take the greatest care of it." At the church door, Zita saw a poor man more than half naked, shaking with cold. "What's the matter, friend?" said Zita. The poor man touched the cloak, and looked wistfully into Zita's face. It was too much; the poor girl took off the cloak, and, casting it round the beggar, said to him, "Here, take this cloak till the service is over, but be sure to give it me back, for it is not mine." After the service, she went to look for the beggar, but he was nowhere to be found, and with fear and trembling Zita returned home. Her master was very angry; but in the midst of his scolding the beggar was seen coming up the steps. He gave Zita the cloak, thanked her for the loan of it, and vanished out of sight. Every one said the beggar was either Jesus Christ or an angel, and ever after the church door, where Zita encountered him, was called "The Angel's Door."—*Acta Sanctorum* (Papebroeck, the Bollandist), April 27 p. 497.

Churlishness.

1 SAM. XXV. Nabal was a very rich man, and when David was a fugitive in Padan, he sent ten young men to Nadab to assist him with a gift, but Nadab replied churlishly, Who is David? and who is the son of Jessē? Shall I take my bread, and my water, and my flesh slain for my shearers, and give to men

whom I know not? So the young men returned and told David. And David was very angry, and would have fallen on the possessions of Nadab and taken them by force, but Abigail (Nadab's wife) appeased his wrath with a timely present and soft words.

Isa. xxxii. 7, 8. The instruments also of the churl are evil. . . . But the liberal deviseth liberal things; and by liberal things shall he stand.

Matt. v. 42. Give to him that asketh thee, and from him that would borrow of thee turn not thou away.

The governor of Bayeux punished for his churlishness (fifth century). When St. Germanus of Scotland was in France, he passed from La Hogue to Bayeux. Here he sent to the governor for a supply of food for himself and his companions, but the request was churlishly refused. Whereupon all the wine-tubs in the governor's cellar "se trouvèrent épuisés jusqu'à la dernière goutte." The contrary happened to another gentleman, named Gantius, who readily answered his appeal—"il reçut, pour sa récompense, une abondante bénédiction sur toute sa famille;" but the historian does not particularize the nature of this blessing. —Corblet, *Hagiographie d'Amiens.*

St. Antony punished for churlishly refusing Macarius a palm-branch (A.D. 306-395). One day St. Antony had collected some beautiful palm-branches, and Macarius asked him to give him one. "Thou shalt not covet thy neighbour's goods," was the churlish reply, and immediately all the branches withered and dried up, as if they had been passed through the fire. St. Antony, amazed at this miracle, confessed that Macarius was beloved of God, and was a chosen vessel of His Anointed.—*Les Petits Bollandistes* (1880), Jan. 2.

A sister of Pharaïldis refused to give alms of bread, and all her bread became stones. A woman begged bread for a hungry child of a sister of Pharaïldis, but she replied, "I have none to give you; in fact, there is none in the house." The poor woman became more urgent, but the sister persisted that there was none in the house. Then said the woman, "If there is any in the house, may St. Pharaïldis change it into stone." There were loaves in the house, and they were all converted into stones. In commemoration of this miracle, St. Pharaïldis is represented in Christian art with loaves of bread.—Baring-Gould, *Lives of the Saints*, vol. i. pp. 60, 61.

Cloak-raft.

2 Kings ii. 8. Elijah took his mantle and, wrapping it together, smote the waters, and they were divided hither and thither, so that they two went over Jordan on dry ground.

St. Bernardin makes a ferry-boat of his cloak (A.D. 1380-1444). St. Bernardin, having to pass a river in order to get to Mantua, where he was about to preach, could not induce the boatman to ferry him across, because he had no money. In this dilemma he threw his cloak on the surface of the river; and, without so much as wetting it in the least, sailed on it across the stream.—Barnaby of Siena (a contemporary), *Life of St. Bernardin.*

St. Francis of Paula sails on his cloak over the straits of Messina (A.D. 1416-1507). When St. Francis of Paula was about to visit Sicily, he stopped a few minutes at the ferry opposite the pharos of Messina. The straits of Messina, every one knows, are famous for the Gulf of Charybdis and the rock called Scylla. The poets used to say, if a navigator was lucky enough to escape the dangers of the gulf, he was almost sure to run foul of the rock. Well, being on the spot, St. Francis asked a ferryman to take him and his companions across for nothing. The ferryman laughed at the request, and seemed inclined to strike the saint. St. Francis made no more ado, but simply threw his cloak in the sea, and, jumping on it, bade his six disciples follow his example; and all seven sailed on this cloak across the strait. The sea trembled, but the saint did not tremble; the waves respected and the winds obeyed him. Scylla and Charybdis, which threatened nobler barks with destruction, honoured this novel bark, "et l'on dit même que, depuis ce temps-là, la mer y a été plus calme." The seven voyagers reached Messina in safety, where an enormous crowd was assembled, and received the saint as if he had been an angel sent from heaven.

This marvellous tale is attested in the acts of his canonization by many witnesses. The ferryman's name was Peter Colossus. We are told he acknowledged his fault in refusing to ferry the saint over the strait, and used to go to the church at Messina every day to bewail his folly, which deprived him of the honour of giving passage to so great a man.

St. Isidore's wife crossed the river Xamara on a cloak. St. Isidore's wife was accused to him of infidelity, and said to her husband, "I perceive, my beloved, by your countenance that this slander distresses you; but I am innocent. In proof whereof I am ready to pass over this river, the Xamara, trusting to God to clear me of this foul imputation." So saying, in the presence of her husband, several ecclesiastics, and hundreds of her neighbours, she spread her cloak upon the river, sat down upon it, and crossed over and back again in perfect safety, without even being wetted.

This life of St. Isidore, in Spanish, is vouched for by the highest authority; and Philip of Castile and Aragon gave letters-patent to John Heigham to print and publish it. The "letters" are signed by Da Groote, and the book was printed at Brussels, June 18, 1625.

It seems to me that the incident would prove the woman's "lightness," if it proved anything.

St. Raymund of Pennaforte sailed some 160 miles on his cloak (A.D. 1275). King James was living in adultery with a lady of the court, and refused to dissolve the union, at the earnest entreaty of St. Raymund. The man of God declared that he would no longer abide in the court, a witness to such an open violation of God's law; but the king strictly forbade any shipper, under pain of death, to convey Raymund across the water in his vessel. In this dilemma the holy man spread his cloak upon the water, and jumping thereon, held up on his staff one corner of the cloak for sail, and in this way was wafted to Barcelona, a distance of fifty-three leagues. On reaching shore he drew his cloak after him, found it was not even damp, and threw it across his shoulders. This "miracle" had so great an effect on the king, that he instantly dismissed his paramour, and lived a life more in accordance with Christian decency. (This incident is mentioned in the bull of his canonization, 1601.)—Leandre Alberti's *Life of St. Raymund.* (The miracles of St. Raymund fill sixteen folio pages of the Bollandists.)

Cloudy Pillar.

PSALM xcix. 7. [God] spake to them in the cloudy pillar.

EXOD. xxxiii. 9. It came to pass, when Moses entered into the tabernacle, the cloudy pillar descended, and stood at the door of the tabernacle, and the Lord talked with Moses.

EXOD. xiv. 19, 20 When Moses and the children of Israel came to the Red Sea, the angel of the Lord, which went before the camp of Israel, removed and went behind them, and it was a cloud of darkness to Pharaoh and his host, but gave light by night to Moses and the Israelites.

St. Cadoc and the band of robbers (sixth century). When a band of robbers came to pillage Llancarvon, in Wales, St. Cadoc went against them with his monks, harping and singing. As they drew nigh, St. Cadoc and his monks were bathed in celestial light, but the robbers were enveloped in such thick darkness that they turned back, and left the monastery unmolested.—Rees, *Lives of the Cambro-British Saints.*

God speaks to St. Basilissa out of the fiery pillar (A.D. 313). The emperor Maximinus II. renewed in the East the persecution set on foot by his predecessors Diocletian and Maximian, and the saints had a fearful looking forwards before them. It was at the beginning of this reign God told Basilissa that her husband Julian would pass through much tribulation before he entered into glory, but that she herself would be taken from the evils coming on the saints. Basilissa, who was the superior of a large convent, told her "daughters" what had been revealed to her, and exhorted them to purify themselves, and trim their lamps, that they might be ready to meet the Bridegroom at whatever hour He might come. As she thus spake the ground shook under her, and a pillar of fire appeared, from the midst of which the voice of the Almighty spoke, saying, "All these virgins, Basilissa, of which you are the superior, are beloved of Me. Come, ye blessed, and enjoy the kingdom prepared for you from the foundation of the world." This warning was not in vain, for Basilissa and all her saintly daughters, to the number of a thousand or thereabouts, died within six months; and scarcely had they been gathered into God's garner, when the fire of persecution broke out with great vehemence, and Julian, with most of his companions, witnessed the faith with their blood.—*Les Petits Bollandistes* (7th edit. 1880), vol. i. p. 235.

Cock Crow.

MATT. xxvi. 75. And Peter remembered the word of Jesus, which said, Before the cock crow, thou shalt deny Me thrice. And he went out, and wept bitterly. (Mark says, "Before the cock crow twice," etc.)

Torello the hermit called to repentance by the crowing of a cock (A.D. 1282). Torello of Tuscany was brought up by pious parents in the fear of the Lord, and in youth was a model of piety; but his father dying when he was budding into manhood, he was led astray by evil companions, and lived a most dissolute life. One day while he was playing at bowls, a cock jumped on his shoulder and began to crow. It seemed to Torello to say, "It is time to shake off the sleep of sin." This it did thrice. and Torello was so profoundly impressed, that he immediately quitted his companions, went straight to the abbey of St. Fido, and with tears in his eyes begged to be admitted as a lay brother. The request was granted, and Torello soon showed himself so exemplary in all Christian duties, that "sa vie sainte lui mérita les faveurs célestes."—*Les Petits Bollandistes* (7th edit. 1880), vol. iii. p. 461.

Compacts with Satan. (See Devil defeated.)

Matt. viii. 28-32. When Jesus was come to the country of the Gergesenes, there met him two possessed with devils, coming out of the tombs, exceeding fierce, so that no man could pass by that way. And, behold, they cried out, saying, What have we to do with Thee, Jesus, Thou Son of God? art Thou come to torment us before the time? Now there was a good way off from them a herd of swine feeding; so the devils besought Him, saying, If Thou cast us out, suffer us to go away into the herd of swine. And Jesus said, Go. And when they were come out, they went into the herd of swine; and, lo! the whole herd of swine ran violently down the steep into the sea, and perished in the waters.

Giles of Portugal makes a compact with the devil (A.D. 1190–1265). [We have all read about men making compacts with the devil, and the tale of Dr. Faustus has been repeated in prose, verse, and drama times out of mind; but this biography of Giles of Portugal is given in all good hagiographies, not as a tale, but a serious historic fact. It stands in the *Acta Sanctorum* of the old Bollandists, and is repeated as authentic history by Mgr. Guérin, chamberlain of pope Leo XIII., in the *Petits Bollandistes* (1880). Pope Benedict XIV. gives his sanction to the story, and the ancient journal of the kings of Portugal makes mention of this son of Vagliaditos, counsellor of his Majesty Sancho I. of Portugal.

These remarks are necessary to show that what follows is accepted, not as a mere tale or legend, but as a serious and undoubted historic fact.]

Egidius, or Giles, was the son of a Portuguese magnate, and, being the third son, was, according to Portuguese custom, destined for the Church, and in due time was admitted into the university of Coimbra. Here he greatly distinguished himself, and ultimately started for Paris to study medicine. On his road thither a person of tall stature and large bone accosted him. "Seignior," said the stranger, "good day. You have a long journey before you." "Yes," said Giles; "I am going to Paris." "Exactly so," said the stranger; "to study medicine, if I mistake not." Giles, greatly surprised that this stranger should know so much about him, expressed his astonishment; but the stranger remarked, "Oh, I know all the secrets of men's hearts, and can teach you to do the same, if you are willing to learn." The bait was too tempting to be rejected by a young student, and he at once closed with the offer; whereupon the devil took him up as easily as if he had been a straw, and carried him to a high mountain, which opened of its own accord, and admitted both into an enormous cavern. Here Satan presented Giles with a schedule containing the terms of the contract. Satan was to teach Giles all the sciences known to man, and give him wealth as much as he desired, and Giles was to consign his soul to Satan, both in this life and in that which is to come. Having agreed to the bond, he opened a vein and signed it with his blood. He remained in the cavern seven years, learning diabolic secrets, and was then set at liberty to enjoy amongst men his wonderful knowledge, and give full fling to his passions. Amidst all his carnal affections and diabolic pursuits, he never forgot the Virgin Mary, and was constantly repeating his *Ave Maria;* for, amidst all his wealth and honour and self-indulgence, he was far from happy. One day, when the devils were more pressing than usual, he cried aloud, "Mary, save me!" The devils fled in affright, and voices in the air cried, "Allelujah! thou art saved!" Egidius now burnt all his books, broke his alembics, and went to Valence, where he entered a monastery of the Dominican order, and for seven years was distinguished for his fastings, long prayers, silence, tears, and penances, whereby he won the esteem of all the brothers; and one night, while he was at prayer, the Virgin Mary brought him back the compact which he had signed. From this moment he was noted for his ecstasies, his miracles, and his preaching. After being looked on as the first of men, the honour of his order, and the favourite of the Virgin, he died the death of the righteous, in A.D. 1265. (See St. Theophilus breaks his Compact with Satan, p. 94.)

St. Gregory "Thaumaturgus" gives Satan a diploma. St. Gregory, surnamed

"Thaumaturgus," cleared the temple of Apollo of "a huge company of devils;" and when, next morning, the heathen priests were about to enter for their daily administration, they were met at the doors with the most hideous yells; the devils clamouring, "We cannot enter with you now, because Gregory has driven us out." They then told the priests which road the thaumaturg had taken, and where they would find him. So the priests and devils started together, and soon overtook him. Like the image-makers of Ephesus, they heaped abuse on him for spoiling their craft, and taking away their gains. St. Gregory answered them mildly, and asked for a writing tablet. When it was handed to him, he wrote on it these words: "Gregory to Satanas, ENTER;" and, handing it to the priest of Apollo, told him to lay it on their altar, and with this diploma the devils returned into the temple, and the priests continued to give responses as before.—St. Gregory of Nyssa, *Lives of Saints* (A.D. 330–396).

This is one of the most marvellous stories in the legends of the saints, and it is most perplexing to understand in what the merit of the act consists. Certainly the licence given to the devil was not for the glory of God, and it looks very like a compromise with evil, to save personal inconvenience.

St. Wodoal suffers the devil to abide in the river Aisne (A.D. 700). St. Wodoal was a native of Ireland, who went to Gaul, where he was generally called St. Voué. At the time when he lived the devil possessed great power at Soissons, and carried off a thirteenth part of all those who passed down the "rue du Mont-Revers." St. Wodoal, resolved to put an end to this frightful state of affairs, marshalled the people, and commanded them to pass him one by one. The first twelve passed, and nothing occurred; when the thirteenth came up, Satan put in his claim, but St. Wodoal cried aloud, "Avaunt thee, Satan! Off with thee to hell, thy own abode." Forced to obey, the devil besought the saint not to cast him into the pit, but to grant him a dwelling-place less wretched; so St. Wodoal told him he might betake himself to the river Aisne, below the Tower Lardier. Ever after, a priest used to go every year to conjure the devil not to quit the tower. (Un prêtre alla tous les ans conjurer le démon dans cette tour, où il avait établi sa résidence.)—L'abbé Pécheur, *Annales du Diocese de Soissons*.

Constantine and Asoka (the parallelisms between them). (See CROSS IN THE SKY.)

Asoka, king of Megadha, the prototype of Constantine. The resemblance between Buddha and Christ, Buddhism and Christianity, Asoka and Constantine, is so marvellous, that though history is proverbially known to repeat itself, yet no repetition of all history is more striking than this. Buddha, we are told, had an immaculate conception and miraculous incarnation. Buddha was said to be omniscient. Buddha worked miracles. Buddha had to struggle with the power of evil in the jungle of Uvuvela. Buddha was visited in infancy by wise men. The number in the case of Christ is not given, but those that visited Buddha were five. Continuing this repetition: Constantine lived about three hundred years after Christ; Asoka lived about three hundred years after Buddha. Before the battle of Rubra, the Christian religion had been run down by frightful persecutions; but Constantine, after his conversion, became its nursing father, and the religion of Christ spread rapidly in all directions. So Asoka, king of Magadha, began by being a relentless persecutor of the Buddhists; but, being converted "by a miracle," he became a most zealous defender of the Buddhist faith. Like Constantine, he built religious houses, endowed viharas or monasteries; and, under his fostering care, Buddhism spread rapidly in all directions.

The life and gospel of Buddha may be seen in Mr. Rhys Davids' *Buddhism*. Eugène Burmouf and Professor Wilson fix the advent of Buddha B.C. 600.

Consumed but not diminished.

(See ELIJAH AND THE WIDOW OF ZAREPHATH.)

1 KINGS xvii. 14. Thus saith the Lord God of Israel, The barrel of meal shall not waste, neither shall the cruise of oil fail, till the day that the Lord sendeth rain upon the earth.

The candles burnt on the tomb of Eucher diminished not (A.D. 738). The body of St. Eucher was deposited in the abbey church of Orleans, and it was observed that the candles which burnt on his tomb diminished not in burning, and that the oil of the lamps multiplied itself sensibly, and cured many afflicted with sundry diseases. —*Les Petits Bollandistes*, vol. ii. p. 605.

The candles set before the Lady at Arras never diminish. "The candles that burne before the blessed shrine of our Lady at Arras, doe burne without wasting or diminution, without receaving any addition of matter to feede and preserve the light."—S. Harsnet (afterwards archbishop of York), *Popish Imposture* (1604), p. 105.

The candles burnt by St. Grandé before the image of the Virgin wasted not (A.D. 1546-1600). John Grandé was a native of Carmona, in Andalousia. He was an acolyte in the parish church, whose duty was to light the candles on the Virgin's altar. He used in boyhood to prostrate himself so long before the image, that the sacristan scolded him for wasting the candles by his long prayers. "Blame me not," said the boy; "do you not see that the candles, though they burn, diminish not?" The sacristan took minute observation, found it was even so, called others to witness, and the boy was accounted a young saint.—*Les Petits Bollandistes*, vol. vi. p. 434.

The lamp of St. Geneviève in St. Denis burns perpetually, but the oil is not diminished. Mgr. Guérin, chamberlain of pope Leo XIII., tells us there is a lamp in St. Denis's Church before the shrine of St. Geneviève, the oil of which is always consumed but never diminished in quantity. This standing "miracle" is still more noteworthy, in that the priests constantly take of this oil for remedial purposes.—*Les Petits Bollandistes*, vol. i. p. 100.

The wax candles of St Hermann, though consumed, diminished not (A.D. 1230). When St. Hermann said mass he was generally in an ecstasy, and remained in silent prayer long after others; sometimes for three hours or more. Complaints were made against him for needlessly wasting the wax candles; but it was proved beyond a doubt, that however long he remained ravished in communion with his God, the wax candles never burnt further than if they had been used for thirty minutes. Another thing was also proved beyond a doubt, viz. that although his infirmities were very great, they all left him the moment he ascended the altar.—*Life of St. Hermann* (Bollandists), April 7.

St. Lidwina gives divers gifts which were not diminished by being consumed (A.D. 1380-1433). St. Lidwina was very charitable, and her Spouse, Jesus Christ, wishing to show the world how greatly He approved of her liberality, made her gifts self-renewing. Thus, when she gave a fore-quarter of beef to thirty poor families, they fed daily on the meat, but the quantity never diminished. When she put a little wine in a bottle for a poor epileptic woman, the wine increased and filled the whole bottle.

One of her brothers, who had charge of the family, died in debt. Lidwina, having some money for alms, put it into a purse, and told one of her relatives, named Nicholas, to pay off the debts. The whole amount of money that Lidwina put into the purse was eight francs; but, after paying all the debts, the purse contained above forty francs, which was distributed to the poor. The family called the purse *La Bourse de Dieu.*—*Life of St. Lidwina.* (Her life was compiled by John Gerlac her cousin, and John Walter her confessor.) See *Acta Sanctorum* by the Bollandists, April 14, vol. ii. p. 287.

It is not according to our notions of honesty for Lidwina to pay off her brother's debts with alms-money. If secretaries of religious or charitable societies did so in England, I suspect our magistrates would be down upon them pretty severely.

Conversions in Large Numbers. (See in Index.)

After the three years' ministry of Christ, with twelve apostles and seventy disciples as fellow-workers, and the power of miracles possessed by all, we read (Acts i. 15), "The numbers of names together were about an hundred and twenty [converts]."

After the preaching of Peter and the apostles on the day of Pentecost, we read (Acts ii. 41), "And the same day there were added unto the disciples about three thousand souls."

Isa. lx. 8. Who are these that fly as a cloud, and as doves to their windows?

Conversions by St. Vincent Ferrier (A.D. 1357-1419). Let no one feel astonished that the preaching of St. Vincent Ferrier was with such power of the Holy Ghost, that whole nations were born in a day. Thus we read of eighteen hundred Moors and Turks being converted by him; of twenty-five thousand heretics and schismatics being won by him to the true faith; of countless thousands of peasants, ignorant of true religion as the heathen, taught the way of salvation more perfectly; of idiots and children taught to make the sign of the cross, and to repeat the Lord's Prayer, the Creed, the *Avê*, and the *Salvê regina*, and even to invoke the all-hallowed names of Jesus and of Mary. He won from their evil ways more than a hundred thousand evil livers; he made many and many women of shameless character sinless as the saints in light; finally, preaching at Tortosa against Benedict XIII., the schismatic pope, he won over queen Margaret, widow of don Martin, king of Aragon, who entered into the convent of Barcelona, and there ended her days in the practice of true humility and repentance.—Mgr. Guérin (1880), *Vies des Saints*, vol. iv. p. 230.

Cornelius the Centurion.

Acts x. 1-6. There was a certain man in Cæsarea, called Cornelius, a centurion of the Italian band, a devout man, and one that feared God. He saw in a vision evidently, about the ninth hour of the day, an angel of God, saying to him, Cornelius, thy prayers and thine alms are come up for a memorial before God. Now send men to Joppa, and call for one Simon, and he shall tell thee what thou oughtest to do.

An angel appears to St. Patrick. St. Patrick, in his *Confession*, says, "I was profoundly ignorant, and hated study from boyhood. A free and open life in the fields was my delight. But being made a captive, and sent to keep sheep, a desire of prayer came over me, and I passed whole days, and sometimes whole nights, in communion with God. Six years was I in captivity, yet was I happy. One night an angel of God appeared to me and said, 'Maun, thy prayers and thy fastings have come up for memorials before God. You shall return soon to your own land, for the days of your captivity are drawing to a close.' I now fled, and arrived at the coast, where I found a ship in which I embarked, and arrived in time at my native land."—*Acta Sanctorum* (Bollandists), vol. ii. March 17, pp. 533-535.

Cripples healed. (See Bowed with Infirmities.)

Acts xiv. 8-10. There sat a certain man at Lystra impotent in his feet, being a cripple who never had walked. The same heard Paul speak. And Paul, steadfastly beholding him, and perceiving he had faith to be healed, said with a loud voice, Stand upright on thy feet. And the cripple leaped and walked.

Acts iii. 2-8. A certain man lame from his mother's womb was laid daily at the gate called Beautiful to ask alms of them that entered the temple. Seeing Peter and John about to go into the temple, he asked alms. Peter said, Silver and gold have I none, but such as I have give I thee. In the name of Jesus Christ of Nazareth rise up and walk. Immediately his ankle-bones received strength, and leaping up he stood, and walked, and entered with Peter and John into the temple, walking, and leaping, and praising God.

Matt. xv. 30, 31. Great multitudes came to Jesus, having with them those that were lame, maimed, and many others, and cast them down at the feet of Jesus; and He healed them: insomuch that the multitude wondered, when they saw the maimed whole, and the lame walk; and they glorified the God of Israel.

St. Ambrose of Siena, born a cripple, was an Adonis afterwards (A.D. 1220-1286). When St. Ambrose of Siena was born he was a fearful object; his arms were glued to his sides, his legs to his thighs, and his face was so dark and out of proportion that his mother was horrified. He was confided to a wet nurse, named Flora, who covered up the child's face when she took it abroad, to conceal the little deformity from public gaze. When a year old the child's delight was to be in St. Madeleine's, the neighbouring church, and to hear the monks chanting the different services. He would cry to be carried there, and was inconsolable when taken away The monks and their assistants noticed this with curiosity and surprise. One day, as the child was in the chapel, he drew his arms, hitherto glued to his side, out of his swaddling-clothes, and lifted them towards heaven, saying quite distinctly three times, "Jesus, Jesus, Jesus." On hearing these exclamations many ran to the spot, drew off the swaddling-clothes, and found, not only the arms free, but the legs straightened, and the face so beautiful and fair that they deemed it the face of an angel. The nurse was overjoyed, and the mother gave large alms to the church. Till the age of seven his amusements were cutting out crosses, dressing oratories, singing hymns, and joining religious processions. He would never go to sleep without a Virgin to cuddle; and a book with the pictures of saints was an endless delight to him.—Le R. P. Jean Baptiste Feuillet, *Année Dominicaine*, vol. iii. March 26.

St. Anthony of Padua restores a man's leg which had been cut off (1195-1231). A man in the confessional told St. Anthony of Padua that he had kicked his mother; whereupon the saint said to him sharply, "The foot that could kick one's mother ought to be cut off." The man on his return home actually cut off his foot. When St. Anthony was told thereof, he ordered the maimed man to be brought to him, and, making the sign of the cross on the mutilated limb, the foot was restored again. (See St. Peter of Verona, p. 71.)—Edward Kinesman (1623), *Lives of the Saints*.

St. Augustine cures and restores the leg of Innocentius. While St. Augustine was in Carthage, he lived in the house of Innocentius, a deputy lieutenant, who was laid up of a sore leg. One part of the limb had been cut off, and the surgeon was preparing to take off the whole leg to prevent the spread of the gangrene to vital parts. St. Augustine prayed, and the leg was not only instantly healed, but even the amputated part was restored.—Possidius (bishop of Calamentia), *Life of St. Augustine.*

Catherine Vial, a cripple, healed miraculously in the chapel of Laus (A.D. 1665). Many miracles being reported to be wrought in the chapel of Laus (2 *syl.*), the vicar-general of the diocese, accompanied by several distinguished gentlemen, went to examine into the matter. While this examination was going on, Catherine Vial, a dreadful cripple, was brought to the church. Her limbs were entirely withered, and so folded back that they seemed stuck to her body. No sooner had she entered the chapel than she was completely cured; and when, in October, a month afterwards, a procession was formed to thank the Virgin, Catherine Vial, the late cripple, carried the banner. The vicar-general, who was a personal witness of the miracle, made the *procès-verbal*, and had it signed by eye-witnesses.—Mgr. Guérin (chamberlain of pope Leo XIII.), *Vies des Saints*, vol. v. p. 222.

Giovanna Maronis, a cripple, was cured at the tomb of St. Charles Borromeo (July 19, A.D. 1604). Giovanna, daughter of Giovanni Baptista Maronis, citizen of Milan, had from her birth her legs and feet so paralyzed that she could in no wise use them. The joints of her knees were out of place, and she could twirl her legs this way or that, like ropes, toss them over her shoulders, and turn them about just as she pleased. When this sad cripple was four years old, her mother took her to the tomb of St. Charles Borromeo, and made her prayer to the saint. While she was still praying the child was cured; and she ran home leaping and skipping, like any other robust and healthy child, full of animal spirits.—*The Bull of Canonization.*

Margarita Montis, a cripple, cured by being laid on the tomb of St. Charles Borromeo (June 29, A.D. 1601). Margarita, daughter of Angello Montis, of Milan, was born a cripple. Her legs were twisted together, so that the soles of the feet were turned upwards, and the insteps were turned under. When this sad cripple was five years old, her mother carried her to the tomb of St. Charles Borromeo, and craved his help, offering at the same time a wax candle to the saint. When the sick child set light to the candle her right foot was set straight and put in its place. After a time she went a second time, and lighted another candle, whereupon her left leg was set straight also. Both were now of one length, both were quite sound and well-formed; but to the day of her death she carried a slight mark or scar to keep fresh in her memory the miracle by which she was made whole.—*The Bull of Canonization.*

Peronne Rault, a cripple, healed by the intercession of St. Francis of Paula, in 1661. Peronne Rault of Calais was a dreadful cripple who went on crutches, and also required the help of an attendant. Many of her bones were out of joint, and one of her legs was six inches shorter than the other. She got worse instead of better, and for the last three months could only be moved about in a wheel-chair. This pitiable object resolved to keep a neuvaine in the chapel of St. Francis of Paula, in order to obtain his intercession. The royal physician strongly dissuaded her, and assured her that nothing could be of the least service to her. However, so fixed and so resolved. On the fourth day of the neuvaine, the octave of the saint's fête, after mass, the girl was seized with a sudden pain and extraordinary weakness, during which she felt her bones moving about, her muscles stretching, and a humour spreading all over her limbs. She heard a cracking noise as the bones got fitted into their sockets and her limb lengthened. Presently she found herself entirely healed; and, after a second mass of gratitude, she left her crutches, walked home without assistance, and lived a fairly long life. Her crutches were long suspended in the chapel in remembrance of this miraculous cure. The bishop of Boulogne "fit faire une information juridique de ce grand événement, et, après avoir reconnu que c'était un véritable miracle, il en permit la publication, et une reconnaissance solennelle par un *Te Deum.*"—*Les Petits Bollandistes*, vol. iv 169, 170.

St. Gudula heals the cripple child of a poor woman (A.D. 712). One frosty morning St. Gudula, on leaving church, saw a poor mother carrying on her back a dumb child, who was also a cripple. The boy was bowed double, and could not even feed himself. St. Gudula, fastening her eyes upon the group, took the cripple in her arms, and prayed God to have mercy on him. Immediately his stubborn joints became supple, his back straightened, and, his tongue being loosed, the child cried out aloud, "See, mother, see!" and he leaped, and ran, and skipped, rejoicing in his new-found strength. St. Gudula begged the woman to tell no one, but she published it abroad, and all knew that it was St. Gudula who had wrought the miraculous cure.—Hubert (1047), *Life of St. Gudula.*

St. Laumer heals a cripple (sixth century). Par la virtu du saint sacrifice de la messe, St. Laumer rendit l'usage parfait des jambes à un enfant qui était extremement boiteux.—*Les Petits Bollandistes*, vol. i. p. 472.

The cripple Pancrace Schafhauser cured by St. Meinrad (1861). The following is a letter, written March 9, 1861, from Brunschofen, near Wyl, in the canton of St. Gall:—

"It gives me unspeakable pleasure, my dear uncle, to communicate to you the following news, which has filled the whole canton with joy. A child of the canton of St. Gall, eight years old, named Pancrace Schafhausen, was a cripple, wholly bedridden. His limbs were twisted the wrong way, and when he moved, he crawled about on all fours. Dr. W——, of Wyl, attended him, but pronounced the case hopeless. He was taken to Einsieden, and made his petition to the Virgin on the 6th March, at eight o'clock in the morning. The same hour the child rose up, and stretching forth his hands, exclaimed, 'Mother, see here; I can walk now!' Many saw him, and all cried with one voice, 'A miracle! a miracle!' Dr. W—— visited the child, and was astonished beyond measure when his patient ran to him and grasped his hands, saying, 'Doctor, doctor, I can walk now!' 'Incredible!' cried the doctor. 'I can scarcely believe my eyes!' But young Pancrace walks daily to school, and plays about like other children."—R. P. Dom Charles Brandes, *Life of St. Meinrad.*

St. Peter of Verona restores a man's foot which had been cut off (A.D. 1206–1252). One day a man came to St. Peter of Verona, and, in his confession, acknowledged he had kicked his mother. St. Peter reprimanded him severely, and said, "The foot which could do that ought to be cut off." The penitent, on leaving the confessional, went and cut off his foot. When St. Peter heard what the man had done, he went to him, and, making the sign of the cross, restored the foot to its original state.—*Acta Sanctorum* (Bollandists), April 29.

The identical tale is told of St. Antony of Padua (1195-1231), see p. 69. (See index, ST. ELIGIUS.)

St. Odilo, the cripple healed by the Virgin Mary. When a little boy, Odilo was a perfect cripple, destitute of all power in his limbs, so that he could not move without help. One day his nurse left him with her bundles on the porch of St. Mary's Church, while she went to buy food. By some means the child contrived to crawl into the church, and even to touch the altar vestments. The Virgin took pity on him, and condescended to intercede on his behalf. His nurse was greatly alarmed on her return, in not finding the child where she had laid him; and, entering the church, what was her astonishment at seeing him scampering about the aisles, hiding behind the pillars, and immeasurably joyous in his new-found strength! Jotsald tells us, "lest this incident should be thought incredible, I must inform you that I heard it from those to whom St. Odilo himself was wont to relate it."—*Acta Sanctorum*, vol. i. Jan. 1.

Cripples healed at the tomb of St. Rieul. St. Rieul, bishop of Arles and Senlis, died A.D. 130, and many miracles were performed at his tomb. A poor cripple from Auxerre, being carried to Senlis, and laid on the tomb of the saint, was instantly cured, and went into the church leaping and shouting for joy. So perfect was the cure, that the man walked back to Auxerre without fatigue.

A lame man from Gâtinais, and a poor girl from Senlis, so crippled in all her limbs that she moved about trailing her legs after her, were both completely healed in the same manner.—L'abbé Corblet, *Hagiographie du Diocèse d'Amiens.*

All who have read Boccaccio's *Decameron* will remember that Novel 1 (Second Day) is the story of three mimics, who wanted to get into a crowded church at Triers to see the body of Arrigo the new saint. To accomplish this one of them, named Martellino, feigned to be a helpless cripple, whom the other two had brought thither to be cured. Room was soon made for the party, and Martellino was laid on the dead body of Arrigo. Presently the mimic began to stretch his fingers, then his arms and legs, and at last jumped up as effectually cured. The crowd shouted, "A miracle! a miracle!" but it was only a well-played trick. The sole merit of this tale is to show that such tricks were sometimes played, for otherwise the story would be wholly without point. Of course, the obvious reply is, that the very existence of a counterfeit is proof positive of a reality. This, however, is not correct. A counterfeit may be only an imitation of a popular belief, true or untrue, as one in the reign of James I. might pretend to be a witch, as witches were then a popular belief, and one in our days might pretend to spiritism amongst those who believe in such a power.

Cross in the Sky. (See SAUL'S CONVERSION, article "Procopius.")

MATT. xxiv. 30. Then shall appear the sign of the Son of man.

DAN. vii. 13. I saw in the night visions, and behold, one like the Son of man came [in] the clouds of heaven.

Achaius, king of the Scots, and Hungus, king of the Picts, see a cross in the sky. A St. Andrew's cross appeared in the clouds to Achaius, king of the Scots, and Hungus, king of the Picts, the night before their engagement with Athelstane. As they won the victory, they went barefoot to the kirk of St. Andrew, and vowed to adopt his cross as the national emblem.—J. Leslie, *History of Scotland.*

A cross in the sky appears to Alonzo before the battle of Ourique (A.D. 1139). As Alonzo was drawing up his men in battle array against the Moors, the figure of a cross appeared in the eastern sky; and Christ, suspended on the cross, promised the Christian king a complete victory over the infidels. After the battle, Alonzo assumed for the royal device, on a field argent five escutcheons azure, charged with five bezants, in memory of the five wounds of Christ.

The emperor Constantine sees a cross in the skies. Constantine was on his march against Maxentius, who had declared war against him, and was at Rome with an army much superior in numbers. The emperor had marched from the Rhine, through Gaul, and was going to Rome by the way of Verona. He had passed the Alps, and was marching with part of his army towards Rome, when, a little before midday, he and those with him saw a bright cross of light in the clouds. In the night following, Christ appeared to him in his sleep. He had a cross in his hand, and commanded Constantine to have a standard made like it. Next morning the emperor gave orders for such a standard to be made, and called it the *Labarum.* It was a gilt pole with a cross-bar. The top of the pole was surmounted with a gold crown, set with precious stones, and in the midst of the crown were two Greek letters, *Chi* and *Ro* (X, P), arranged thus ☧. From the cross-bar hung a purple veil, spangled and dazzling. The emperor selected fifty of his best men to carry and guard this banner. The battle was fought in the Quintian fields, near the Milvian bridge. The foe was utterly defeated, and Maxentius drowned in the Tiber, Oct. 27, A.D. 312. Constantine now entered Rome in triumph, and always ascribed his victory to the cross. Philostorgius, describing the heavenly cross, says it contained in Greek words and letters this inscription "By this conquer" ('Εν Τούτῳ Νικᾶ).—Gibbon, *Decline and Fall*, ch. xix., *note;* Alban Butler, *Lives of the Saints*, Sept. 14, *note.*

ΕΝ ΤΟΥΤΩ ΝΙΚΑ

* * * *

Respecting the "Labarum," the accounts given somewhat differ. The Roman *vexillum*, or cavalry flag, was a small square piece of cloth fixed on a cross-bar at the top of a pole. It is said that Constantine preserved this general arrangement, but on the little flag devised a cross from opposite corners, and set a Greek P (= an English R) at the centre, where the cross lines cut. Below the little flag he also attached a small cross-bar, which, with the pole, represented a Latin cross. The cross or X = the Greek letter Ch., which, with the centre letter R, would form the monogram Chr. = Christ.

A cross seen in the sky soon after the inauguration of St. Cyril (A.D. 386). St. Cyril wrote a description of this meteoric phenomenon to the emperor Constantine, and his letter is inserted in the works of Sozomenês, Theophanês, Eutychius, John of Nice, Glycas, and others. On May 7, about nine in the morning, a vast luminous body, in the form of a cross, appeared in the heavens, just over the holy Golgotha, reaching as far as the holy Mount of Olivet (about two miles). This was seen not by one or two persons only, but by the whole city, and it continued for several hours, the light from it being more brilliant than that of the sun. "The whole city found in this phenomenon the truth of the Christian doctrine, to which the heavens bore visible witness."—Dr. Cave, *Life of St. Cyril*, vol. ii. p. 344.

How this meteoric phenomenon should be a proof of the doctrine of the cross, I am at a loss to imagine. I myself saw a very unusual phenomenon in the sky, Nov. 17, 1848, and sent an account to the papers. "The sky overhead seemed in flames, and bands of various colours of great brilliancy rose from the horizon to the north star, forming a luminous arch. This magnificent appearance lasted in full splendour from seven till ten at night." If the cross in the sky was a proof of the Christian doctrine, this arch or crescent might be claimed as a proof of the Turkish religion.

A cross in the sky seen when Julian attempted to rebuild the temple. When Julian recalled the Jews, and employed them in rebuilding the temple, the work was arrested by fire from the ground, earthquakes, and lightnings. Then we are told that crosses were miraculously attached to the garments of the Jews engaged in the building, and a luminous cross, enclosed in a circle, appeared in the clouds.—St. Gregory of Nazianzen, *Oration* iv., *against Julian.*

(Theodoret tells us that the crosses miraculously attached to the garments of the Jews were black; St. Gregory says they were luminous. The solution given by Mgr. Guérin is this, that the crosses were of a phosphoric nature, black in daylight, but luminous in the dark.)

A cross in the sky seen at Migné, in the diocese of Poitiers (Dec. 17, 1826). Dec. 17, 1826, at Migné, in the diocese of Poitiers, at the close of the jubilee, while a cross was being planted in the cemetery, a luminous cross was seen in the clouds by some three thousand persons. The sun had set about an hour and a half. The length of the heavenly cross was forty feet, and the cross-bar between three and four feet. The whole crowd was seized with admiration, and instantly fell on their knees; some wept, some raised exclamations of wonder or delight, and others lifted their hands to heaven, invoking the Saviour. Mgr. de Bouillé, bishop of Poitiers, published an account of "this miraculous apparition," and received two briefs from pope Leo XII. upon the subject. He also sent to the church of Migné a gold cross enclosing a piece of the true cross, and accorded plenary indulgence to all those who visited the church. The bishop fixed the third Sunday of Advent for the annual celebration of the phenomenon.—Mgr. Guérin, *Vies des Saints* (1880), *note*, vol. iii. p. 487.

Surely there is no reason for supposing this vision miraculous. As I was travelling from London to Nottingham, March 26, 1882, I was for a long time puzzled at seeing in the air, some hundred feet or more from the train, what seemed to me a gigantic carriage moving with great rapidity. After a little reflection I thought of the spectre of the Brocken in the Hartz mountains, and had no doubt that the spectre carriage was the one I was riding in, greatly magnified. We are told they were planting a cross in the cemetery when the spectre cross appeared in the air.

St. Ouen sees a cross in the skies (A.D. 646). When St. Ouen, on his return journey from Spain, was in the midst of the country not far from Louviers, his mule stopped short and refused to move. Astonished at this unusual behaviour, St. Ouen lifted up his eyes to heaven, and there saw, above his head, a luminous cross very brilliant, the light of which shone all around. God told St. Ouen, at the same time, that He had destined the spot for His service, and wished to be honoured there. So St. Ouen traced a cross on the ground, and left some relics there. He then continued his journey, and the mule made no further resistance. All that night a pillar of fire, reaching

from earth to heaven, and more brilliant than the sun, appeared on the sacred spot, and all the inhabitants saw it. It was here that St. Leufroi, about a century later, built a church and a monastery, but St. Ouen had erected a wooden cross on the spot, which went by the name of "La Croix St. Ouen."—L'abbé Pécheur, *Annales du Diocèse de Soissons.*

A cross in the sky seen by Waldemar II. of Denmark. Waldemar II. of Denmark is said to have seen a fiery cross in the sky, betokening his victory over the Esthonians, A.D. 1219. The king, like Constantine, adopted the cross as a standard, which was called the Danebrog or Danish Cloth, and instituted the Order of Danebrog in commemoration of this vision.

This legend is differently told in some Scandinavian chronicles. It is said that the Danes lost their royal banner in the fight, but another dropped from the sky to supply its place. It was a red flag with a white cross. Immediately this banner fell into the hands of the standard-bearer the army rallied, and won a signal victory. Those who explain legends tell us that the Danebrog was a consecrated banner sent to the king by the pope. Whatever its origin, it was long used as the royal standard.—Drs. Chrichton and Wheaton, *Scandinavia*, vol. i. p. 257.

The emperor Augustus sees a Virgin and Child in the skies. Suidas tells us that, about the time of the Nativity, the famous oracle of Apollo of Delphos became mute, and gave no more responses. Augustus, demanding a reason for this silence, was told by a priest it was because a Hebrew child was born, who was the master of the gods, and he had commanded them to confine themselves to the infernal regions. Nicephorus adds, that Augustus, on his return to Rome, erected an altar in the Capitol with this inscription: "ARA PRIMOGENITI DEI." Mgr. Guérin, chamberlain of pope Leo XIII., tells us (*Vies des Saints*, vol. xiv. p. 453), D'autres auteurs écrivent que le même empereur aperçut dans les nues une vierge tenant un enfant entre ses bras.

Cutting a Whetstone with a Razor.

Tarquinius Priscus of Rome wished to double the number of tribes; but when he proposed his plan to the senate, it was resolutely opposed by Attus Navius, the augur, who said the number was fixed by the gods to three, and that no human power could alter it. The king indignantly replied, "What! do you pretend to read the mind of the gods, who cannot so much as read the thoughts of a man? Tell me, if you are really so very wise, whether I can do the thing I am now thinking of." "Yea, O king," replied the augur, "thou canst." "Ha! ha!" rejoined Tarquin, "I have you there. I was thinking if I could cut in twain that whetstone with a razor." "Cut boldly, O king," said Navius, "and it is done." It is said that the king cut the whetstone, and had the good sense to give up his projected change in the constitution. A statue was erected in the comitium on the steps of the senate-house, the place where this "miracle" was wrought, and beside the statue the whetstone was preserved.

This need in no wise be a miracle. I have often cleft a block of ice on a glass dish by touching the block with an ordinary sewing needle, and tapping the needle on the head with the handle of a penknife.

Albert d'Ogna cuts through an anvil with a reap-hook (A.D. 1279). Albert d'Ogna was a farm labourer, and being one day employed as a supernumerary in the harvest-fields, the regular farm servants were jealous of him, because he worked faster than they did. In order to impede him, they placed an iron anvil in his walk; but when Albert came to the spot, he went on reaping, and cut the anvil in twain with his reap-hook, just as if it had been a wisp of straw. In allusion to this miracle, Albert d'Ogna is represented with a reap-hook in Christian art. —*Acta Sanctorum* (Bollandists), May 13, vol. ii.

Daniel accused of Prayer.

DAN. vi. 4, 5. The presidents and princes sought to find occasion against Daniel concerning the kingdom; but they could find none occasion nor fault, forasmuch as he was faithful, neither was there any error or fault found in him. Then said these men, We shall not find any occasion against him, except we find it against him concerning the law of his God. [They then accused him of praying three times a day to God, and he was cast into the den of lions.]

St. Isidore accused of prayer. St. Isidore was a farm labourer, who roused the jealousy of his fellow-workmen by going to mass every morning before he began his daily labour; so they accused him to the farmer of coming late to work of a morning, and of wasting his time in prayer. The farmer resolved to watch him; and if he found him neglecting his duty, to rebuke him sharply or dismiss him. Early one morning, soon afterwards, the farmer went into the field which Isidore had been set to plough, but was amazed to find *three* ploughs at work instead of one; two were guided by angels, and the third by Isidore. Instead of less work being done than he expected, there was fully thrice as much done, and done admirably well. The farmer was delighted, and falling down at his servant's feet, craved his pardon for giving ear to false reports. Isidore replied, "Master, no time is ever lost by prayer, for those who pray are workers together with God." So the farmer departed, ashamed of his suspicion, and full of reverence to his holy labourer. As soon as the farmer was departed, the angels returned to their ploughs.—*From the Spanish.*

David and the Draught of Water.

2 SAM. xxiii. 15–17. David, fighting against the Philistines, became so parched with thirst, that he cried out, Oh that one would give me drink of the water of the well of Bethlehem, which is by the gate! And three mighty men broke through the host of the Philistines, and brought water to the king. Nevertheless David would not drink it, but he poured it out unto the Lord.

St. Thomas Aquinas and the fish (A.D. 1274). In his last illness Thomas Aquinas stopped at the castle of Maganza, the seat of his niece Francisca. He had quite lost his appetite, but one day expressed a wish for a little piece of a certain fish which he named. This fish was not to be found in Italy; search, however, was made for it in all directions, and the dainty was procured. When cooked and brought to the dying man, he refused to eat it, but gave it as an offering to the Lord.—Alban Butler (1745), *Lives of the Saints.*

Sir Philip Sidney and the draught of water. In the battle of Zutphen, Sir Philip Sidney, being severely wounded, suffered greatly from thirst; whereupon one of the host went and fetched him a little water in a helmet, at the hazard of his life. Sir Philip took the helmet, and as he was raising it to his lips, noticed a private lying beside him, who eyed the helmet with greedy eyes. "Poor fellow," said Sir Philip, "thy necessity is greater than mine;" and he passed the helmet to the dying man.

A similar anecdote is told of Alexander the Great in the desert of Gedrosia. Quintus Curtius calls it "loca deserta Susitanorum."

Edward I. of England on one of his Welsh campaigns, refused to drink of the one and only cask of wine which had been saved from marauders. "It is I who have brought you into this strait," said he to his thirsty fellow-soldiers, and I will have no advantage of you in meat and drink."

David in the Cave of Adullam (1 Sam. xxii. 1, 2).

David saved by a cobweb. We are told in the Talmud, that when David, in his flight from Saul, took refuge in the cave of Adullam, a spider spun its web over the mouth of the cave. When Saul came up and saw the cobweb, he passed on, fully persuaded that no one had recently entered that cave, or else the web would have been broken.

St. Felix saved by a cobweb (third century). In the persecution which broke out again, soon after the death of Decius, St. Felix fled; and, being closely pursued by officers sent to apprehend him, he crept through a small hole in a ruin. The officers came to the spot, but seeing a cobweb spun over the hole, they passed on, assured in their own minds that Felix had not gone that way. St. Gregory says, "This was the Lord's doing. He sent a little spider to drop his lines, and lace them together with the utmost rapidity over the place through which his servant had escaped."* Felix, finding among the ruins an old wall half dug, hid himself there for six months, and was fed daily by a devout Christian woman. In Christian art, St. Felix is sometimes represented with a spider spinning its web.—St. Gregory of Tours, *De Gloria Martyrum*, bk. i. ch. 104.

Mahomet saved by a cobweb. When Mahomet fled from Mecca, like David, he hid in a cave, and a spider wove its net over the entrance. When the Koreishites came up and saw the cobweb, they passed on, feeling quite certain that no one could have recently entered the cave, or the cobweb would have been broken.

Dead hearing, speaking, and moving.

John v. 25. Verily, verily, I say unto you, the hour is coming when the dead shall hear the voice of the Son of God.

Heb. xi. 4. He [*i.e.* Abel] being dead yet speaketh.

John xi. 43, 44. Jesus cried with a loud voice, Lazarus, come forth. And he that was dead came forth, bound hand and foot with grave-clothes.

Luke viii. 54, 55. Jesus took her by the hand, saying, Maiden, arise. And her spirit came again, and she arose straightway.

* Would St. Gregory extend this remark to Mahomet, "the false prophet," who was saved in precisely the same manner as the "true saint"?

Luke vii. 14, 15. Jesus came and touched the bier. And he said, Young man, I say unto thee, Arise. And he that was dead sat up and began to speak.

Acts ix. 40. Peter, turning to the dead body, said, Tabitha, arise. And she opened her eyes: and when she saw Peter, she sat up.

1 Sam. xxviii. 11–20. The woman said, Whom shall I bring up [from the dead] unto thee? And Saul said, Bring me up Samuel. And Samuel said to Saul, Why hast thou disquieted me, to bring me up [from the grave]? And Saul answered, I am sore distressed, etc.

A dead man declares that St. Antony's father was not guilty of his death. While in Padua, it was revealed to St. Antony that his father was in danger of being put to death in Lisbon for manslaughter. An angel transported St. Antony from Padua to Lisbon, when his father's trial was on; and the saint ordered the dead man to be brought into court. He then asked the dead man, "Is it true that my father is guilty of thy death?" "Certainly not," said the dead body; "the accusation is false and malicious." The judges, on hearing this positive declaration from the dead man himself, discharged the prisoner at once, and St. Antony was retransported to Padua the same night by the same angel. (See St. Macarius, etc., p. 77.)—Edward Kinesman (1623), *Lives of the Saints.*

Basil, a monk, joins the singing after he was dead. St. Theodosius, the Cœnobiarch, having made a large sepulchre for the general use of the monastery, remarked, "The tomb is now finished, but who of us will be the first to occupy it?" Basil, falling on his knees, prayed earnestly that he might be allotted that honour, and within forty days he died, without pain or disease, as one taketh rest in sleep. For forty days afterwards St. Theodosius used to see the dead monk still occupying his usual place whenever the brethren joined together in singing praise to God. Only Theodosius saw the ghost, but Aëtius distinctly heard its voice. Theodosius prayed that others beside himself might see Basil's apparition, and God opened the eyes of all the brethren, and all saw it. Aëtius, in the fulness of his joy, ran to embrace the ghost, but it vanished, saying as it departed, "Stay, Aëtius. God be with you, my father and brethren. Me shall ye see and hear no more."—*Roman Martyrology.* (Cave tells us this life was written by Theodore, bishop of Pera.)

Two dead nuns rise from their graves and rush out of church. Two ladies of high birth inmates of a Benedictine convent, were accustomed to treat the rest of the sisters with extreme contempt, as being of inferior clay to themselves. St. Benedict admonished them of this unseemly pride, and, as they did not amend, threatened to excommunicate them. Soon after this they both died, and were buried in the church. When the deacon said to the ordinary, "Let those who are excommunicated depart hence," the nurse saw the two dead ladies leave their tombs, and fly out of the church. This occurred several times; and the nurse, calling to mind the threat of excommunication made by the abbot, told him what had occurred. Then St. Benedict took an offering, which he presented to God for the deceased; after which their souls were laid, and slept in peace.—St. Gregory the Great, *Dialogues*, bk. ii.

A woman named Catherine, being dead, told St Francis Hieronimus she was in hell-fire (A.D. 1707). When St. Francis Hieronimus was preaching in Naples, a woman named Catherine made herself conspicuous by interrupting him. The preacher took no notice of her at the time, but a few days afterwards, passing her house, found it closed. Asking the neighbours the reason, he was told that Catherine had died suddenly that morning. "Dead?" cried the saint. "What! is she dead?" and he requested leave to see her. The permission was granted, and, going into the chamber, he found the body swathed and laid out in the usual manner. The room was full, but great silence was observed. "Catherine," said Hieronimus, "say, where are you?" Twice he asked the question, but there was no answer. At the third time the eyes of the corpse opened, the lips trembled, and a feeble voice, which seemed to proceed out of the ground, replied, "In hell—in hell." All present were horrified, and rushed out of the room. "In hell? in hell?" cried the saint. "Great God, how terrible! In hell? in hell?" This scene produced an immense impression, and many sinners were brought by it to repentance.—Cardinal Wiseman. (St. Francis was canonized in 1839.)

This may be very graphic and sensational, but a tolerable ventriloquist could have made it appear that the four words came from under the floor; and one can hardly imagine that Cardinal Wiseman believed they proceeded from the dead soul in the bottomless pit.

St. Catherine of Bologna nineteen days after her death opens her eyes and speaks (A.D. 1463). Nineteen days after her burial, St. Catherine of Bologna was disinterred, and placed in a coffin. A crowd of persons came to look on the corpse, and were struck with the joy expressed in her face, and the saintly odour which came from the body. Amongst others, Leonora Poggi, a girl of eleven years old, came to look on the body, and forthwith the dead saint opened its eyes, and making a sign with its hand, said to the young girl, "Leonora, come hither." Leonora came up closer. Then St. Catherine added, "You will be a sister in this convent, where all will love you, and you shall be the guardian of my body." Eight years afterwards, Leonora refused the hand of a wealthy suitor, took the veil, was appointed guardian of St. Catherine's body, and lived in the convent fifty-five years.—D. Paleotti (of the order of St. Francis), *Life of St. Catherine of Bologna.*

Euphrosina answers from the grave the question of St. Donatus. Eustasius, receiver-general of the revenues of Tuscany in the reign of Julian, being called away on a journey, left the public money which he had collected in the hands of his wife Euphrosina, who, for better security, buried it in the earth. She died suddenly, and no one knew where she had hidden it. Eustasius was almost beside himself, fearing to be charged with embezzlement. In his perplexity he asked advice of St. Donatus, bishop of Arezzo; and the holy man, going to the grave of Euphrosina, said with a loud voice, in the hearing of many, "Euphrosina, let us know where thou hast put the public money." The woman answered from the grave, and told the bishop where it was hidden. St. Donatus went with the receiver-general to the place indicated, and there found the money without difficulty.—Edward Kinesman (1623), *Lives of the Saints*, p. 591. (He tells us he compiled the life of St. Donatus from Bede and other martyrologies.)

Relics join St. Gregory of Langres in singing (A.D. 541). One night a deacon watched St. Gregory of Langres, and saw him rise from his bed, and leave his dormitory at midnight. The deacon followed him unobserved, and saw him enter the baptistry, the door of which opened to him of its own accord. For a time dead silence prevailed, and then St. Gregory began to chant. Presently a host of voices joined in, and the singing continued for three hours. "I think," says St. Gregory of Tours, naïvely, "the voices proceeded from the holy relics there preserved; no doubt they revealed themselves to the saint, and joined him in singing praises to God."—Baring-Gould, *Lives of the Saints*, Jan., p. 59.

Qy. Had echo nothing to do with it?

The dead body of St. Injurieux moves out of his own grave to repose in that of his wife Scholastica (A.D. 388). Injurieux, a noble senator of Clermont, in Auvergne, married Scholastica, but from the day of their espousals they loved each other only with Platonic love, and mutually vowed to live together in chastity. St. Gregory of Tours tells us that Scholastica died first, and Injurieux, standing over her tomb, said, "I thank Thee, O God, for the loan of this treasure, which I return to Your hands, without spot, even as I received it." The dead wife, smiling at these words, replied from the grave, "What need to speak of such matters, which concern no one but ourselves?" Scarcely was the wife buried, when the husband died, and was buried in a separate grave, at some considerable distance from that of his deceased wife. Next day it was found that Injurieux had left his own grave to repose in that of Scholastica. He was not disturbed, but to the present hour the senator and his wife are called the "Two Lovers."

This tale is told by several writers besides Gregory of Tours in his *History of the Francs*, bk. i. ch. 42. Guerrier de Dumast has made it the subject of a poem, called "The Tomb of The Two Lovers of Clermont" (1836).

At the command of St. Macarius a dead man acquits an accused monk of any share in his murder (A.D. 304-394). A very similar tale to that of St. Antony and his father (p. 75) is told of St. Macarius of Egypt. One of the brothers of his own monastery was accused of murder, and as both accusers and defendant spoke with great positivity, St. Macarius took them to the grave of the deceased, and, speaking with a loud voice, said to the dead man, "The Lord Jesus Christ commands you to state whether this man, now accused of your murder, really committed the crime or not?" The dead man resolutely answered, "No, he is innocent, and had no hand at all in my death." "Who, then," asked Macarius, "is the guilty party?" The dead man replied, "It is not for me to accuse; suffice it to know that the accused man is innocent. Leave the guilty in the hands of God. Who can say whether the All-merciful may not take pity on his soul and lead him to repentance?"—Mgr. Guérin, *Les Petits Bollandistes*, vol. i. Jan. 2.

This is related by the chamberlain of pope Leo XIII And his book, which has passed through seven editions, is avouched by a host of cardinals, archbishops, and bishops, all between the years 1873 and 1880. A similar answer is given by a child just born, when asked if a certain deacon was its father. (See BABES, pt. ii.)

The dead body of Maria Madalena di Pazzi turns itself round (A.D. 1607). When Maria Madalena di Pazzi was dead, her body was wrapped in a tunic, a scapular, and a mantle of black taffeta. It was placed in the church, for the satisfaction of the seculars, with the face towards the sacristy; but the corpse turned its head the other way, because "en cet endroit il y avait un homme débauché dont elle ne put souffrir les regards, même après sa mort."—*Les Petits Bollandistes*, vol. vi. p. 173.

St. Melor, after his head was cut off, spoke to his murderer (A.D. 411). St. Melor was the son of Melian, duke of Cornwall; and his usurping uncle, Rainald, sent Cerialtan to cut off his head. While the murderer was carrying the head to his employer, he was so parched with thirst that he exclaimed, "Oh for a drop of water! I am dying with thirst." The head of the murdered prince, which was in his hand, made answer, "Cerialtan, strike the ground with your stick." This he did, and water immediately gushed forth to allay his thirst. Rainald received the boy's head with delight, but, dying within three days, the head was sent back to be buried with the trunk; and both were preserved at Amesbury, in Wiltshire, as holy relics.—Baring-Gould, *Lives of the Saints*, Jan., p. 44.

St. Patrick commanded that the dead should be asked if they deserved to have a cross raised over their graves (A.D. 373-464). St. Patrice commande à la mort de rendre ses *victimes*, afin que leur propre bouche proclame devant le peuple la vérité des doctrines qu'il leur annonce; ou bien il s'assure si son ordre de planter une croix sur la tombe des chrétiens, et non des infidèles, a été fidélement exécuté, en interrogeant les morts eux-mêmes, et en apprenant de leur bouche s'ils ont mérité ce consolant hommage.—Mgr. Guérin (chamberlain of pope Leo XIII.), *Vies des Saints*, vol. iii. p. 476 (1880).

At the command of St. Paul, bishop of Trois-Château, his predecessor declared from his grave that a Jew was making a false claim (fifth century). When Paul was inaugurated bishop of Trois-Château, as he was returning from the council, a Jew came up to him, and demanded payment of a sum of money lent, as he said, to Paul's predecessor, whose name was Torquat. In order to ascertain whether the claim was just or not, St. Paul, arrayed in full episcopal canonicals, went to the tomb of the late bishop, and, touching it with his pastoral staff, commanded Torquat to inform him whether the loan spoken of had been repaid or not. A voice from the grave immediately replied, "I repaid the Jew his loan, and he knows it." Many heard the reply, and could testify that these things are true, for they know that they are true.—L'abbé Nadal, *Hagiological History of Valence.*

St. Rheticus, when dead, speaks to his buried wife (A.D. 334). St. Rheticus died May 15, A.D. 334. After the corpse had been washed and shrouded, it was laid on the bier. Next morning, when the bearers attempted to lift the bier, they found it quite immovable. Not all their combined force was able even to stir it. All the mourners were stupefied, but an old man called to mind a promise which Rheticus had made to his wife, when she was dying, that he would rejoin her in the grave. Immediately this new arrangement was made the bier became quite light, and when it was set down at the grave of his deceased wife, the dead man sat up and said, "Do you remember, my dear wife, the request you made me on your death-bed? Here I am to fulfil my promise. Make room for me whom you have so long expected." At these words the deceased wife, who had been so long dead, revived, and, breaking the swaths which bound her, stretched forth her hands, made signs of approval, and beckoned to her husband to come and lie beside her. (*Deprensa est lævam protendens fœmina palmam, invitans socium gestu viventis amoris.*) The corpse was lowered, the grave shook, the deceased woman manifested every sign of joy, and the two lay in peace, waiting the resurrection of the just.—L'abbé Migne, *Appendix ad opera Juvenci, Patrologia*, vol. xix. p. 381 (1850).

St. Severinus asks a dead priest if he would like to return to life. St. Severin watched all night by the bier of Silvinus the priest. And at early dawn he bade the dead man, in the name of God, speak to the brethren. Silvinus opened his eyes, and St. Severin asked him if he had any wish to return to life. The dead man answered fretfully, "Keep me no longer here, nor cheat me of that everlasting rest which those who sleep in the Lord enjoy." Then, closing his eyes, he slept again the sleep which knows no waking.—Eugippius, *Life of St. Severin* (A.D. 511).

At the command of St. Stanislaus, one Peter, who was dead, rose from his grave and went into the law-court to certify the sale of an estate. St. Stanislaus, bishop of Cracow, in Poland, bought an estate of one Peter for the Church, but took no acquittance. Peter died three years afterwards, and his heirs claimed the inheritance. As St. Stanislaus had nothing to show in proof of his right, he was condemned to restore the estate to the plaintiffs. The saint now fasted and prayed God to defend his cause; then, going to the tomb of the dead man, he touched the body with his pastoral staff, and commanded it to arise. The dead man instantly obeyed the summons, and followed the bishop into the king's court. Stanislaus then said to the judge, "Here, my lord, is Peter himself, who sold me the estate. He has come from the grave to vindicate the truth." Peter confirmed the statement of the bishop in every particular, and judgment was reversed. St. Stanislaus now asked Peter if he would like to remain alive for a few years; but Peter replied he would rather return to his grave. He was in purgatory, he said, but had almost purged away his sins, and was in near prospect of paradise. So he returned to his tomb, where he decently composed himself, and yielded up his breath a second time.—Ribadeneira, *The Flowers of the Saints.*

Dead raised to Life again (with an account of human hibernation, etc.).

(See Elisha and the Moabite.)

Mark v. 35–42. Jairus, ruler of the synagogue, besought Jesus to heal his daughter, but a messenger told Jairus he need not trouble the Master, as the damsel was dead. Jesus said to the ruler, Be not afraid, only believe; and going to the ruler's house, he took the damsel by the hand, and said, Talitha cumi; and straightway the maiden arose and walked, for she was of the age of twelve years.

Luke vii. 11–15. When Jesus came to Nain, a dead man was being carried to his grave. It was an only son, and the mother was a widow. Jesus went to the bier and said, Young man, I say unto thee, Arise. And he that was dead sat up, and began to speak; and Jesus delivered him to his mother.

JOHN xi. 1–44. Lazarus died and was buried; and his two sisters told Jesus. Jesus went to the grave where Lazarus had been laid for four days, and when the stone at the mouth of the vault was rolled away, He said with a loud voice, Lazarus, come forth! and he that was dead came forth, bound in his grave-clothes; and Jesus said to the standers-by, Loose him, and let him go.

2 KINGS iv. 28–37. The son of a Shunammite woman, who had shown kindness to Elisha, died, and the mother besought the aid of the prophet. Elisha went into the chamber where the dead child was, shut the door, and prayed unto the Lord. Then he went and lay upon the child, putting mouth to mouth and hands to hands, and the flesh of the dead child waxed warm. Then the prophet walked to and fro for a time; and the child sneezed seven times, and opened his eyes. Elisha then bade Gehazi to call the mother, and when she came, he said to her, Take up thy son; and she took him up, and went out.

St. Amandus restores to life a man executed for brigandage (A.D. 594–684). While St. Amandus was at Tournai, the governor, Dotton, sentenced a brigand to death; and so well was the sentence deserved, that the whole court exclaimed with one voice, "Away with him, away with him! he is not fit to live!" St. Amandus entered the court at this moment, and implored the governor to accord to him the life of the prisoner; but Dotton told him it could not be, and the executioners hung the criminal, and watched him till he was dead. Amandus at night cut the body down, and conveyed it to his cell, when he fell on his face and implored the Lord of life to give back to this wretch his departed spirit. All at once the brigand raised himself, opened his eyes as if from a deep sleep, and seemed bewildered to find himself in the cell of the travelling bishop. Next morning St. Amandus called for water, washed the wounds of the resuscitated man, and having healed them all, bade the man return home and sin no more. Soon the noise of this miracle spread in all directions, and crowds flocked to the saint for baptism. All Gand was converted, and in an incredible short time two monasteries arose, one at Gand and the other on Mont Blandin. Truly a whole people was born in a day, and the name of the Lord was magnified. —Menjoulet (vicar-general of Bayonne), *Saint Amand, Apôtre des Basques.*

Peter Armengol was suspended six days on a gallows, and yet was taken down alive (A.D. 1304). Peter Armengol was a converted captain of a band of robbers, who spent his life in redeeming Christians made captives by the Moors. Hearing of the captivity of eighteen young men, he agreed with the Moors for their ransom, and gave himself up as a hostage till the money arrived. He had many opportunities of preaching Christ crucified during his captivity, and not a few were converted by him. This greatly annoyed the Moslems, who pretended that the time of payment had expired, and hung him on a gibbet. He had been suspended for six days, when William Florentin arrived with the ransom-money, and was extremely distressed to hear of the fate of his dear companion; but what was his amazement, as he stood under the gibbet, to hear himself addressed with these words: "Dear brother, weep not; I am alive; the Virgin Mary has kept me all these days." Florentin cut him down in the presence of many spectators, and the ransom-money was laid out in redeeming twenty-six more Christian slaves.—*Acta Sanctorum* (Bollandists), April 27.

St. Attalus raised two dead persons to life again (A.D. 627). Ariowald, king of Lombardy, was an Arian, and orthodox Christians were taught not to salute heretics. One day a monk of the Bobbio monastery, passing the king, neglected to salute him, and Ariowald employed an assassin to waylay the monk and murder him. This was done, but St. Attalus restored the dead man to life, and the devil, seizing the murderer, put him to horrible torments, from which Attalus alone was able to deliver him.

Another monk, employed to root out the residue of paganism in Tortona, was seized by the natives, who threw him into the river, and piled huge stones over him. St. Attalus drew him from the water safe and sound, but his persecutors all met with violent deaths.—Jonas (a Scotchman and disciple of St. Attalus), *Life of St. Attalus.*

St. Avitus, abbot of St. Mesmin, raises one of his disciples from death (A.D. 530). St. Avitus was in the habit of retiring from time to time into a thick forest near his abbey. One day a religious, in his suite, died on the road, but besought his companions not to bury him till the abbot had seen him. One of the companions ran into the forest to announce the death to Avitus, and to tell him that the body had been carried into the church. Avitus instantly went to the church, and prostrated himself in prayer. Then rising to his feet, he commanded the dead man to awake from the dead. The dead man could not resist, and giving his right hand to the abbot, he came from the bier, and immediately took part with the rest in chanting the service. This "miracle" made a great sensation; and St. Lubin, bishop of Chartres, assures us he was told it by the very man who was resuscitated.—*Les Petits Bollandistes*, vol. vii. p. 110.

This looks very like a case of epilepsy.

St. Benedict, abbot of Mount Cassino, restores to life a lad frightfully mangled by the fall of a wall (A.D. 480–543). While St. Benedict was building his monastery at Mount Cassino, he observed the devil busy at work also, and knew mischief was at hand. He accordingly called out aloud to the workmen, "Be on your guard, my brethren, for the devil is among you." Then the fiend, out of pure malice, knocked down a part of the wall, which fell on a young novice, the son of a nobleman; and not only killed him, but crushed him most horribly. The monks were greatly grieved, and the abbot told them to carry the dead body into his cell. It was impossible to carry the body in their hands, because it was so mangled; so they put it in a sack, and picked up carefully all the pieces. When they were brought into the cell, St. Benedict locked the door, prayed fervently, and lying on the dead body, put his mouth to the child's mouth. Presently the flesh of the young novice began to wax warm, the separate pieces drew together, the crushed parts assumed their normal condition, the young man sneezed, opened his eyes, stood upon his feet. The resuscitation was complete, as complete as if the accident had never happened; and St. Benedict, to prove his perfect triumph over Satan, bade the novice return to his work, and help to restore the wall which had fallen upon him. —St. Gregory the Great, *Dialogues*, bk. ii.

St. Benedict of Mount Cassino resuscitates the child of a peasant (A.D. 480–543). A peasant, having lost his only son, brought the dead body to Mount Cassino, and requested St. Benedict to restore it to life. Turning to his monks, the patriarch said, "Let us retire; these peasants seek of us feeble creatures acts which pertain to apostles only. Let us retire, my brothers." Still the parents of the child ceased not their entreaties, and said they would not leave till the saint granted their petition. St. Benedict could resist no longer. So, placing himself beside the dead body, and lifting his hands to heaven, he said, "Lord, regard not my unworthiness, but behold the faith of this Thy servant, who implores the resuscitation of his child. If, Lord, it seems good in Thy sight, let the soul and the life return to this dead body." Immediately the dead body began to stir; the abbot took the hand, life was restored, and the child was delivered to his father in perfect health. (See St. Severin, p. 78.)—St. Gregory the Great, *Dialogues*, bk. ii.

St. Coletta, or Nicoletta, raised a large number of the dead (1380–1447). St. Coletta resuscitated many dead bodies. For example, four grandees, who survived for many years. Many hundreds of children, still-born. A child which had been buried. A nun of Poligny, which had died without absolution; this woman was called back to life to make her confession, and receive supreme unction, after which she was restored to the grave again.—Douillet, *Vie de St. Collette.*

St. Cyril, general of Mount Carmel, restores to life a man recently cured of blindness (A.D. 1191). St. Cyril gave alms to a blind man, and as soon as the man knew who had given him the money, he laid the coin upon his eyes, and received his sight. What is still more remarkable is, that his soul was enlightened at the same instant, and he begged to be admitted into a religious house as an inmate. He was refused, because the prior was not at home, fell sick, and died within three days. Let Mgr. Guérin tell the rest:—On fit ses funérailles, et, quoiqu'il y eût longtemps qu'il fût étendu dans sa bière, et reconnu pour mort, étant tout près d'être mis en terre, il se releva, et dit à haute voix, "Que les prières de Cyrille l'avaient ressuscité, de même que ses mérites lui avaient rendu la vue du corps aussi bien que de l'âme.' —Mgr. Guérin, *Vies des Saints*, vol. iii. p. 201.

St. Dominic restores to life the son of a Roman matron. The son of a Roman matron died while his mother was listening to a sermon by St. Dominic The dead body was taken to the monk, and laid at his feet. The "blessed father," moved with compassion, made on the lad the sign of the cross, and taking him by the hand, the dead child rose, stood on his feet, and returned home in perfect health.

St. Dominic restores to life a carpenter

killed by a fall into a pit. A carpenter, working in the convent of St. Sistus, fell into a pit, and the earth falling on him crushed him to death. St. Dominic ordered him to be dug out, prayed over him, and he returned to life wholly unhurt.

St. Dominic restores to life Neapolion, killed by a fall from his horse. The nephew of cardinal Stephen, whose name was Neapolion, being thrown from his horse, had his neck broke, and was killed. St. Dominic, going to the spot of the accident, prayed thrice, saying the same words; then, taking the young man by the hand, he said with a loud voice, "Neapolion, I say unto you, in the name of Christ, Arise." Forthwith he arose, and St. Dominic led him to his uncle.—Edward Kinesman (A.D. 1623), *Lives of the Saints*, pp. 573, 574.

St. Eleutherius kills, and restores to life, the daughter of the governor of Tournai (A.D. 531). The daughter of the governor of Tournai, a pagan, conceived a violent affection for the young Eleutherius, and one day went to Blandain to make the avowal to him. "Unhappy woman!" said Eleutherius; "did you never hear how Satan tempted the Saviour, and He repelled him? In the name of the blessed Trinity I now command you to retire, and never again to come into my presence." On hearing these words the maiden fell dead, as if struck by a flash of lightning. The father was greatly distressed, and promised to become a Christian if his daughter was restored to life. Eleutherius fasted and prayed for many days; then, going to the maiden's grave, he bade the bystanders roll away the stone, and cried thrice with a loud voice, "Damsel, I command you, in the name of Christ, Come forth;" and she came from the tomb in the sight of all, and was baptized.—*Les Petits Bollandistes*, vol. ii. p. 600.

St. Francis of Paula raises his nephew from the dead (A.D. 1416-1507). Nicholas d'Alesso, the nephew of St. Francis of Paula, often expressed an ardent desire to be a monk, but his parents would not give their consent. While still young, he fell ill and died; and his dead body was taken to his uncle's church to be buried. The funeral service was finished, and the body was about to be lowered into the grave, when St. Francis, "qui avait en ses mains les clefs de la vie et de la mort," stopped the bearers, and taking the dead body in his arms, carried it into his chamber; and the same night, after many prayers and tears, it was restored to life. The mother came next day to weep over her lost child, when St. Francis asked her if she felt resigned to the will of God, and if she would now consent to her son entering upon a religious life. "Alas!" cried the mother, "he is past my consent now, and is in the hands of God. It is too late, too late now; I shall never again see my Nicholas either a secular or a religious." "You consent, then," said St. Francis; and so saying, led the mother into his chamber, and showed her the young man living. Nicholas took the habit of the order, and lived in his uncle's monastery for many years.—*Authentic Relation made in Consistory upon the Acts of his Canonization* (compiled by Father Giry).

We all remember the supposed death and burial of Juliet, who wanted to have her own way against her parents' wishes.

The son and daughter of king Brendin restored to life by St. Fursy (A.D. 650). King Brendin of Ultonia [Ulster] had a son and daughter, twins, who died the same day. Brendin was not able to bury them, because the Irish were cannibals, and would have disinterred the bodies to eat them; they were therefore thrown into the sea, but were washed ashore near the hermitage of their cousin, St. Fursy. The time when this occurred happened to coincide exactly with the hour that St. Fursy, according to his wont, was passing along the coast to church, and he saw his two cousins lying naked before him. He was greatly distressed, and said, "O merciful Lord, grant that the spirits of these my dear cousins may return into their bodies." His prayer was granted, and the two cousins rose joyously to their feet; but, being naked, they were ashamed. St. Fursy had pity on their shame, and clothed them both in suitable raiments. He then threw a stick into the sea, and told his cousins to follow it, nothing doubting. The rest must be told in the words of Mgr. Guérin, or no English reader will believe what follows has been accurately stated. "Or, écoutez une chose," says the chamberlain of pope Leo XIII., "écoutez une chose qui doit émerveiller, et qui doit être racontée pour la gloire de Notre Seigneur: le bâton s'en alla devant comme s'il eût eu de l'entendement. Les enfants marchèrent [on the surface of the sea] hardiment à sa suite dans le sillage qu'il traçait, jusqu'à ce qu'ils arrivèrent en leur pays, et reconnurent leur gens."—*Les Petits Bollandistes* (7th edit. 1880), vol. i. p. 401.

We are told, in a note by Mgr. Guérin, that the life of St. Fursy was written in 665 by a contemporary, and was published by Surius, vol. i. p. 259, etc. It was repeated by J. Bolland (Jan. 15), and by Mabillon, vol. iii. p. 299, etc. The venerable Bede, in his *Church History*, bk. iii. ch. 19, gives an abstract of the life; but the best life is by the abbot Corblet, *Hagiographie du Diocèse d'Amiens*, vol. ii. p. 260. With such high authority who can doubt the "sober facts" here set down?

Irish cannibals two centuries after the death of St. Patrick!!

St. Francis Hieronimus raises a dead infant to life (A.D. 1642–1716). A poor woman lost her infant child, twelve months old; but not having money enough to bury it, she placed it near the confessional of Father Francis. When the saint entered the church, he knew by inspiration where the child was lying, and told Mary Cassier to go and take charge of it. Mary instantly obeyed; but, on lifting up the covering, she exclaimed, "My father, the child is dead." "No, no, Mary," he replied; "behold, it sleepeth." So saying, he made the sign of the cross on the child's forehead, and applied some holy water to its lips. Forthwith the child opened its eyes, and began to breathe. "Go, and call the mother," said St. Francis. The woman at first refused to come, and, when she saw a living child, would not believe it to be her own. Soon, however, the child recognized its mother, and her joy was complete.—Cardinal Wiseman. (St. Francis was canonized in 1839.)

St. Galla restores to life a maiden declared to be dead. One day a handmaid, who waited on St. Galla, going to fetch water, fell, and hurt herself so severely that all thought she was dead. Galla ordered the maiden to be taken into her cell, and, kneeling in prayer, she cried aloud, "O Lord, heal her!" The words were hardly uttered when the handmaid rose; and all who saw it exclaimed, "See, what mighty power the Lord and Saviour hath committed to His saints!"—*Les Petits Bollandistes*, vol. ii. p. 199.

St. George of Cappadocia calls a dead man from his grave. Diocletian, by the advice of Athanasius, a magician, gave St. George a deadly poison, but it did the saint no harm. When the emperor expressed surprise, St. George said to him, "The God whom I adore can not only preserve life, He can also restore it." "This is it," rejoined the emperor: "if, now, one came from the dead, we should believe." St. George replied, "Then follow me," and led the way to a cemetery filled with graves. Standing before one of them, he prayed that God would show forth His power to confound gainsayers. Immediately the cave where he stood opened, and one came forth with his grave-clothes; and, falling at the feet of St. George, returned him humble and hearty thanks. The emperor declared it was the work of necromancy, but Athanasius, the magician, replied, "Not so, my sovereign liege; none but the great God can do after this sort."—Pasicrates (an intimate friend of St. George, and eyewitness of his deeds).

St. Gildas the Wise restores to life Trifina, about to be a mother (494–570). Trifina, daughter of Guerech, was demanded in marriage by Conomor, who had been married often before, but always killed his wives as soon as they conceived. As he was a very powerful monarch, Guerech durst not refuse him, and so Trifina became his wife. When she was about to become a mother, Conomor murdered her, as he had murdered his other wives. St. Gildas heard of this brutal act, and raised the princess to life again. In time the child was born. It was a boy-child, and was named Trech-meur (Death-won).—*Les Petits Bollandistes*, vol. ii. p. 106.

At the invocation of St. Godard a procession of dead men walked through the cathedral of Hildesheim (A.D. 1038). This marvellous story must be given in the *ipsissima verba* of Mgr. Guérin, chamberlain of pope Leo XIII. He prefaces the anecdote with the words, Though many miracles are ascribed to St. Godard, bishop of Hildesheim, the following most strikes the imagination of the masses, and serves as a characteristic of our saint in Christian art. "Il avait excommunié certains de ses diocésains: or, un jour qu'il se préparait à célébrer les saints mystères, il les vit entrer dans l'église, en dépit de l'excommunication. Invoquant le pouvoir de Dieu, il ordonna aux morts de se lever de leurs tombeaux, et de donner l'exemple de l'obéissance aux transgresseurs de ses ordonnances. Ceux-ci, soulevant le couvercle de leurs sépulcres, organisèrent une procession, et sortirent de l'église."—*Vies des Saints*, vol. v. p. 324 (7th edit. 1880).

St. Hilarion restores to life the three sons of a nobleman. A noble lady, returning from a visit to St. Anthony with her three sons, came to Gaza, where all her sons sickened and died. The mother, beside herself with grief, went to the cell of St. Hilarion, accompanied with two handmaids, and said to him, "O man of God, have pity on me for Christ's sake! O man of God, look on my misery and pity me! O man of God, come with me to Gaza, I implore you; come with me, and restore me my three sons who are lying dead. Come, O man of God, and God will be magnified in thee." St. Hilarion replied that he never left his cell. Whereupon the mother, frantic with grief, fell at his feet, weeping most bitterly. "O servant of the living God, give me back my sons!" she cried, "give me back my sons! O servant of the living God, give me back my sons!" Her two handmaids added their voices, and wept also. Hilarion was no stock or stone, and could resist no longer. He went to Gaza as the sun was setting, called on the name of the Lord, said to the mother, "The Lord killeth, and maketh alive; He bringeth down to the grave, and bringeth up." Then lifting up his eyes to heaven, uttered a short prayer, and the three sons who were dead arose, and were led to their mother.—St. Jerome, *Vita St. Hilarionis Eremitæ* (A.D. 390).

St. Hilary restores to life an unbaptized infant (fourth century). St. Hilary, after his return from exile into Phrygia, was received in Poitiers with unbounded joy, and commemorated his return with this miracle. An infant died before baptism, and St. Hilary, moved to compassion at the grief of the parents, restored the child to life; it was then baptized, and "newness of life was given to its soul." This miracle is memorialized by sculpture still extant in Poitiers cathedral.—Dom Coustant, *Vita Sancti Hilarii, Pictaviensis.*

St. James of Tarentaise induces by his tears a dead man to return to life (fifth century). After one of his missionary tours, St. James of the county of Tarentaise went to visit the grave of a very dear friend who had died during his absence. The saint wept so bitterly over the grave, that the dead man could not resist the force of his deep, deep grief; and as Lazarus came from the grave at the voice of Christ, so this friend returned to life at the tears of St. James.—Gui of Burgundy (afterwards Calixtus II.), *Life of St. James of Tarentaise.*

St. Julian restores to life the son of Anastasius (A.D. 117). When St. Julian went to Mans, what greatly contributed to the conversion of the people was the following "miracle." The son of Anastasius, one of the chief citizens, died, and the father said to Julian, "If, now, you could raise this lad from death, I would confess Jesus Christ, whom you preach, to be the true God, and would renounce at once the gods which I now worship." St. Julian went to the dead body, took it by the hand, and raising his eyes to heaven, implored Him who raised Lazarus from the dead to do the like in this case, to the end that this resurrection of the body might be the spiritual resurrection of a great multitude. Forthwith the lad who was dead arose, and his parents received him in their arms with unspeakable joy. Anastasius and all his house being then baptized, the name of the Lord was magnified.—D. Piolin, *Histoire de l'Église du Mans* (10 vols.).

St. Julian restores Jovian to life (A.D. 117). When St. Julian was in Champagne, he met a funeral procession conducted by the druids. The person who was carried to his grave was one Jovian, a young man of the chief family in the neighbourhood. St. Julian addressed himself to the father, and asked whether he would confess Jesus Christ to be the true God, if through His name the young man was restored to life. Then raising his eyes to heaven, he prayed, and as he prayed the young man revived, and cried with a loud voice, "The God of Julian is indeed the true God." Then, turning to his father, he said, "We have been worshipping demons all this while. I saw them with these eyes in hell, where they suffer ineffable torments." The fame of this miracle soon got noised abroad, and multitudes were baptized into the new faith.—D. Piolin, *Histoire de l'Église du Mans.*

In this narrative we are forcibly struck with its want of harmony with druidical times. It breathes throughout of Roman Catholic times and dogmas, and if we omit the word *druids*, would be far more in accordance with the twelfth or thirteenth century than with the second.

St. Julian, bishop of Mans, restores to life the son of Pruila Leguilla of Gaul (A.D. 117). While St. Julian was in Gaul, he entered the house of Pruila Leguilla, who was a pagan, and had asked him to be her guest. Just as he entered, the son of his hostess died. Never mind, he abode in the house notwithstanding. The saint passed the night in prayer, and next morning presented the young man alive and well to his mother. The whole house and many of the neighbours who witnessed the miracle were immediately baptized, confessing the God of Julian to be God indeed.—D. Piolin, *Histoire de l'Église du Mans.*

Laban returns to life to receive the Viati-

cum (seventh century). While St. Sacerdos was at prayer with his monks, a messenger arrived, to announce to him the death of his father Laban. At the time, Sacerdos was so absorbed in prayer that he did not hear what the messenger said. When he came to himself, and understood that his father was dead, he went with all haste to the house of mourning, and learnt to his great grief that Laban had died so suddenly there had been no opportunity of giving him the Viaticum. Kneeling at the bedside, in the presence of all assembled, Sacerdos took the hand of the dead man, and called him twice by his name. At the voice Laban sat up, as if aroused from sleep, and looking on the bystanders said, "I died at the second hour of the day, but have returned to life, in virtue of the merits of my son." Sacerdos then administered to him the Viaticum, and asked for his blessing. Laban, having blessed his son, rendered back his soul to God a second time.—Pergot, *Life of St. Sacerdos, Bishop of Limoges.*

Marianne de Jesus of Quito raises the dead (A.D. 1618–1645). (1) Jane was confided by her mother to the care of her aunt Marianne of Quito, and one day, while the child was playing with the mules, she received a severe kick, which fractured her skull. Marianne ordered the child to be brought to her cell, and praying over it, she healed the wound instantaneously, so that none could tell where the fracture had been made. (See Zanobi, p. 86.)

(2) An Indian, in the service of donna Geromine where Marianne lived, jealous of his wife, dragged her to a wood, strangled her, and threw the dead body over a precipice. Marianne saw the whole in a vision, sent a man to the place where the body lay, and told him to bring it to her room secretly. When this was done, Marianne rubbed the dead body with some rose-leaves, and almost instantly the woman "a recouvré la vie, la santé, et les forces."—Mgr. Guérin, *Vies des Saints*, vol. vi. 233.

St. Martin restores to life a catechumen. A young man of Poitiers, who was a catechumen, died suddenly; and just as the body was about to be buried, St. Martin arrived. He entered the chamber where the body was laid out, sent all away, and shut the chamber door. He remained in prayer for the space of two hours, when he that was dead began to revive. Life came back at first very gradually, but ultimately the catechumen left the chamber wholly restored to his usual health.

St. Martin restores to life a man who had hanged himself. St. Martin restored to life a man who had hanged himself. The dead man not only received newness of life to his body by the prayers of the saint, but what is far better, his mind was delivered from that despondency which had driven him to commit this great crime, and he was restored to a sound mind in a sound body.

St. Martin restores to life the son of a poor widow. When St. Martin was bishop he restored to life the son of a poor widow of Chartres. He prayed, and the dead man lived again, to the great joy of his mother.—Severus Sulpicius, *Dialogues.*

St. Martin used to say to his disciples, "Before I was made a bishop I restored two dead men to life, but since my elevation only one. So God gave me a double measure of His grace when I was nothing; but when He bestowed on me honours, He diminished His gift of grace.

St. Melanius restores to life the son of an old man. One day an old man of Vannes besought St. Melanius to resuscitate his son, who had just died. The holy bishop, turning to the crowd and those carrying the bier, said, "Ye men of Vannes, what is the good of showing you the power of God by signs and wonders, unless ye believe?" Some of the followers replied, "Be assured, O man of God, if you raise this man from the dead, we will all believe that the God you preach is the Lord indeed." Then Melanius laid his crucifix on the dead man's breast, and said, "In the name of Jesus Christ of Nazareth, young man, I say unto you, Arise." And immediately he who was dead arose; and all the whole country received baptism, and professed the catholic apostolic faith.—Dom Lobineau, *Life of St. Melanius.* (Lobineau was his contemporary.)

Martin, a monk of Pomposa, raised to life for three days. Martin, one of the brothers of the monastery of Pomposa, died some three or four leagues away from home, and his body was carried to Pomposa for interment. When the body was being lowered into the grave, signs of life were observed, and suddenly the dead man called aloud for St. Guido, the abbot. The abbot asked Martin whence he came, what he had seen, and what had caused his return to life. He replied, "I have seen hell, a place of indescribable horrors, where I saw many of my kinsmen and acquaintances. As I looked on them with consternation, St. Michael appeared to me, and gave me a little honey to taste. It was of extraordinary sweetness; and he commanded me to return to my body for three days." Brother Martin lived for three days, and the taste of that honey never left him. At the end of the three days the abbot gave him his blessing, and he died in peace.—*Acta Sanctorum* (Bollandists), March 31.

St. Philip of Neri raised Paul Fabricius from the dead. Paul Fabricius, of the house of the Massimi, died without the consolation of seeing Philip of Neri, whom he had greatly desired to see. When St. Philip arrived, he called Paul Fabricius to life again. The resuscitated man made his confession to the saint, and then died a second time; preferring to go to heaven and be with Christ, than to remain on earth exposed to temptations, and in danger of falling from eternal grace.—Father Antonio Galonio, *Life of St. Philip di Neri.*

St. Poppo restores to life a shepherd mangled by a wolf (A.D. 978–1048). While St. Poppo was on his way to the emperor Henry, he sat down to eat his breakfast; but scarcely was he seated, when he saw a wolf steal from a thicket with a shepherd in its mouth. Rising on his feet, St. Poppo vowed he would not touch food till he had rescued the shepherd. Guided by the blood, he tracked the wolf to a swamp, and found the man horribly mangled and quite dead. Falling on his knees, St. Poppo prayed, and the dead man came to life, and partook of the saint's breakfast. The shepherd carried to the grave a scar on his neck of the wolf's teeth. Everheilm informs us he was told this anecdote by St. Poppo himself; and in memory of this "miracle," the town of Stavelot, of which he was abbot, has a wolf in its arms.—Bollandus, vol. iii. p. 251, etc. (This life was written by Everheilm.)

St. Servasius delivered from the Huns (A.D. 384). As St. Servasius was journeying from Liége to Rome, he fell into the hands of the Huns, who were ravaging Italy. They threw him into a deep ditch till they made up their minds what to do with him. At midnight, the Huns were much alarmed by seeing a great light in the ditch, and resolved to set their captive free; but greater still was their amazement when they saw that the light proceeded from the face of their captive, and that an eagle hovered over him, covering him with one wing while he slept, and fanning him with the other. Many of the Huns were converted when they saw these marvels, and St. Servasius was set at liberty at once.—Father Giles Buchère, *Gestes des Évèques de Tongres*, etc., ch. iv.

St. Severin restores a woman to life (A.D. 482). A woman, having died after a long illness, was laid at the door of St. Severin's cell. "What is it that you want?" asked the saint; and the people replied, "We have brought this woman here that you may restore her to her family." "Who am I," said the saint, "that I should make alive whom the Lord hath taken away?" "We know," rejoined the people, "that God heareth you, and if you ask, He will deny you nothing." Then the saint prayed, and the woman, being restored to life, went about her daily work. "Know ye," said Severin, "this miracle is not due to my merits, but to your faith. Only believe, and nothing is impossible with God." (See St. Benedict, p. 80.)—*Les Petits Bollandistes*, vol. i. p. 219.

St. Severus raised to life a dead man, in order to confess him and absolve him (sixth century). While St. Severus was pruning his vine, he was sent for to confer the sacrament of penitence on a dying man. He did not go immediately, and when he reached the house the man was dead. St. Severus was horrified; threw himself on the earth; accused himself of mortal sin; and said he was worse than a murderer, as he had murdered the man's soul. All of a sudden the dead man began to breathe again, he sat up, and received the sacrament. St. Severus wept with joy, and thanked God. The man lived seven days, and then died again in a better hope of a joyful resurrection. (See Laban, p. 83.)—*Propre de Trèves.*

St. Valery raises to life a man who had been hanged (A.D. 619). When St. Valery of Luxeul was at Gamaches, a nobleman named Sigobard had just condemned a man to death, and the sentence was immediately executed. St. Valery saw the man suspended by the cord, and hastened to the gallows. The executioners drove him back; but, paying no attention to them, he cut the man down, and laying himself on the body, face to face, and hand to hand, he prayed God to restore the man to life. His prayer was heard; the man revived, and stood on his feet full of strength and vitality. St. Valery now supplicated Sigobard to let the man go; but he refused, and ordered the fellow to be hanged again. Valery expostulated, and said, "You have already punished him with death for his offences, and cannot in justice punish him twice for the same crimes. God has given him a new life, and in this new life he is yet innocent." Sigobard, seeing the force of the appeal, set the man free, and he lived many years. A chapel stands on the spot where this occurred.—Besançon (1854), *Les Saints de Franche Comté*.

St. Vincent Ferrier raised a dead man to life again (A.D. 1357-1419). St. Vincent Ferrier, preaching one day at Salamanca to many thousands of people, stopped short suddenly, and then, to the amazement of all, exclaimed, "I am the angel spoken of by St. John in the Apocalypse—the angel which was to preach to all peoples and nations and tongues, and to say unto them, Fear God and give Him honour, for the day of judgment is at hand." Then, seeing the vast assembly astonished, he said again, "I am the angel of the Apocalypse, and will prove it. Some of you go to St. Paul's gate, and you will find a dead man borne on men's shoulders to his grave. Bring him in hither, and you shall hear the proof of what I tell you." Some did as the saint commanded, and set the bier in a position to be seen by all. St. Vincent then bade the dead man return to life, and when he sat up, he asked him, "Who am I?" The man replied, "You, Father Vincent, are the angel of the Apocalypse, as you have already told this vast assembly." St. Vincent then asked if the man preferred to die or live. "To live," he replied. "Then be it so," said the saint, and the man lived for many years.—Mgr. Guérin (chamberlain of pope Leo XIII., 1880), *Vies des Saints*, vol. iv. p. 240.

St. Vincent Ferrier restores to life a Jew, who forthwith becomes a convert (A.D. 1357-1419). Abraham Ezija of Andalusia, a very rich Jew, went once out of curiosity to hear St. Vincent Ferrier preach; but not liking his discourse, he rose in anger to leave the church. The people at the door opposed his passage. "Let him go," cried St. Vincent; "come away all of you at once, and leave the passage free." Just as the Jew was leaving, the porch fell on him and crushed him to death. Then the saint, rising from his chair, knelt in prayer, and resuscitated the dead man, in the name of Jesus of Nazareth. The first words the Jew spoke when he came to life were these: "The religion of the Jews is not the true faith; the true faith is that of Christians." Being baptized, Ezija, in memory of this event, established a pious foundation in this church. (See DEVILS RECOGNIZING, "That which Ambrose preaches is true.")—Peter Ranzano (bishop of Lucera), *Life of St. Vincent Ferrier*.

St. Wulfran restores to life a lad named Ovon, who had been sacrificed to the gods of the Frisons (A.D. 647-720). The Frisons offered human victims to their gods, and these victims were selected by lot. One day the lot fell on a lad named Ovon, and St. Wulfran entreated king Radbod to forbid the sacrifice. Radbod replied that he durst not interfere with the laws of the land, and accordingly, Ovon was hanged on a gibbet and strangled, in the presence of a great multitude. St. Wulfran now prayed the Lord to magnify His name in the midst of this crowd of idolaters, that the people might be turned from the error of their ways, to serve the living God. Two hours after the execution the rope broke, and Ovon fell to the ground. St. Wulfran, running up, said with a loud voice, "Ovon, I command you, in the name of Jesus Christ, stand up." The lad stood up. His life was restored, and, what is more, spiritual life was given him at the same moment, and many of the Frisons were converted. —L'abbé Corblet, *Hagiography of the Diocese of Amiens*.

St. Zanobi, bishop of Florence, raises five persons from death to life (A.D. 407). (1) The first person was the son of a Gallic lady, passing through Florence to Rome. She left her sick son in the charge of Zanobi, hoping he would be well by the time she returned; but on the day of her return he died. As he was her only child, her grief was very great, and she implored Zanobi with many tears to restore him to life. Zanobi, by his prayer and the sign of the cross, restored him to life, and handed him to his mother. (See MARIANNE DE JESUS, p. 84.)

(2) The second instance was that of a young man whom Zanobi encountered in the faubourgs of Florence. He was being carried to his grave. The parents said to the saint, "You have had compassion on a stranger, and have given her son to her from the dead; you cannot refuse the same grace to one of your own people." Zanobi came up, touched the dead man, raised his eyes to heaven, and immediately life returned to the inanimate body.

(3) The third case was that of Simplicius, an envoy of St. Ambrose, who fell from his horse down a precipice, and was frightfully mangled. Zanobi not only restored his life, but rehabilitated the body so entirely that no vestige of the accident was discernible.

(4) The fourth instance was the infant child of a noble family, who had been run over by a carriage, while playing before St. Saviour's Cathedral. It so happened that St. Eugenius and St. Crescentius were present at the time, and joined Zanobi in prayer for the resuscitation of the child. Their prayers were heard, and the child was restored to perfect health, as if the accident had never happened.

(5) The fifth case was the father of St. Eugenius, who had died in mortal sin without the sacraments. Zanobi, moved to pity at the grief of Eugenius, told him to sprinkle the dead body with holy water. This did he, and the dead man was restored to life.—John Tortel (archpriest of Arezzo), *Life of St. Zanobi* (1433).

Simon Magus volunteered to be buried, and said he would rise again on the third day. Simon Magus volunteered to be buried alive, and declared he would rise again on the third day. His disciples buried him in a deep trench, but to this day, says Hippolytus, "they await his resurrection."—Milman, *History of Christianity*, vol. ii. p. 51, note.

An attempt to explain this phenomenon in some cases.

No miracle in hagiography is more common than that of resuscitating the dead. It is spoken of in so off-hand a manner in many cases, that it presumes familiarity. The examples given above stand out from the ordinary run by some speciality, or by some marked resemblance to Scripture incidents. Other examples might have been added to an almost indefinite amount. It would be childish to set down all these phenomena to imposition on the part of the operator or saint, but at the same time it cannot be denied that the resuscitation of the dead was at one time, and is still in the East, one of the commonest frauds of beggars and charlatans! (See ST. GREGORY'S ROCHET.)

It is well known that one mode of extorting money in Hindûstan is by feigning death. The imitator is laid on a light native bed, and wounds, sores, and bruises are neatly painted on the body. Confederates bring the apparently dead body where they hope to excite sympathy, tell their tale of woe, and collect what money they are able for funeral expenses. Lieutenant Bacon * assures us, if the trick is new to the beholders, "an ample shower of coins will be given," and the moment the money has been picked up the party decamps. He tells us he was once staying at a house when such a "dead man" was brought in. So well was the trick played, that although a wound was given by a spectator with a billiard cue, yet no indication of pain was manifested. Lieutenant Bacon, being suspicious, poured scalding hot water on one of the feet, when the "dead man" started up, and made off with all possible speed. Probably some of the numerous instances of resuscitation recorded may be referred to this category; and it can well be imagined how the trick would be vastly more dramatic, if the body was laid at the feet of some saint, whom it would be good policy to flatter by making him the instrument of an apparent miracle.

Voluntary asphyxia and death. Professor Huxley tells us a man may voluntarily produce asphyxia and "death" with the help of the diaphragm, as follows:—"If, the lungs being distended, the mouth and nose are closed, and a strong expiratory effort is then made, the heart's action may be stopped. And the same result occurs if, the lungs being partially emptied, and the nose and mouth closed, a strong inspiratory effort is made."—*Elementary Physiology*, p. 102. Lieutenant Boileau, in his *Narrative of a Journey in Rajwarra* (1835), tells us of men who by long practice acquired the power of "holding their breath for a considerable time, first suspending it for a short period, say while one could count fifty, and gradually increasing the interval to two or more hundreds, as pearl-divers do." One man he mentions possessed the power of shutting his mouth, and stopping the interior opening of the nostrils with his tongue. He tells us that the West Indian slaves, when suffering under the lash, sometimes kill themselves thus.

A fourth means of suspending animation is by mesmerism. A fifth by anæsthetics, such as chloroform, ether, etc. A sixth by hypnotism, which produces stupor simply by acting on the nerves through the eyes. It differs from mesmerism, in that no "animal magnetism" is infused. Epilepsy may be added, and various forms of asphyxia.

The following extract from Paulinus, the deacon and biographer of St. Ambrose, is to the same point. Speaking of the Arians, he says, "They calumniated the miracles of St. Ambrose, and stoutly maintained that he hired persons to feign themselves blind, and lame, and dead, that when they were brought to him he might have the credit of miraculously healing them." The remark is suggestive, even if we acquit the archbishop of complicity. Most certainly, if the dogma that "the end justifies the means" is admitted, even deception may be meritorious; and indeed is so, when thereby the power of the Church and "the glory of God" are supposed to be magnified.

St. Servan's dead bird. The following anecdote further elucidates the same point. St. Servan had a pet robin which was wont to feed out of his hand and perch on his shoulder; and when Servan chanted the psalms, his little redbreast would flap its wings and chirp most lustily. The boys under him, jealous of one Kentigern, the favourite pupil of the old saint, one day wrung the robin's neck, and laid the charge on Kentigern. Kentigern cried bitterly when he heard the bird was dead, and taking it up, signed it with the sign of the cross, praying earnestly that God would restore it to life. When St. Servan returned from church, the robin hopped to meet him as usual, flapping its wings and chirping joyously.

This is recorded as a "miracle," but it by no means needs be so. I myself once had a favourite canary very tame indeed; but one day, being frightened by the sudden entrance of strangers, it flew into the garden, and took refuge in a tall lime tree. Several neighbours came to help me to recapture my little favourite, and one of them, without my knowledge, threw a small stick at it, knocked it on the head, and it fell down on the ground. All thought the bird was dead, and a medical gentleman, who happened to be in the house at the time, pronounced it "undoubtedly dead." However, I laid it in wadding near the fire. For several hours no sign of life appeared, but next day the bird was alive, and lived many years afterwards.

Restoration of life by Semiramis. This legend is a manifest fraud, and yet may be typical of other legends. At the village of Ara, the king of Armenia inspired Semiramis, queen of Assyria, with a fatal passion, but he refused an alliance of marriage; so the queen declared war against the Armenians, but strictly enjoined her soldiers on no account to injure the young king. Notwithstanding this injunction, the king was mortally wounded in the battle, and the queen obtained possession of the dead body, intending to restore it to life by magical incantations. It is needless to say that her incantations were powerless; but she induced one of her favourites to personate the dead king, and then gave out that she had restored him to life by the special favour of her gods, who "had licked his wounds and cured them." In corroboration of this "miracle," the village where this happened was ever after called Lezk (*Licked*).—*The Constantinople Messenger*, June 15, 1881.

Simulated deaths. That fraud very early had crept in is not left to conjecture, we have the strongest and clearest evidence possible. Take, for example, the case of St

* *First Impressions and Studies from Nature in Hindûstan.*

Epiphanius (310–403). He is represented in Christian art as causing the actual death of an impostor who feigned himself dead, and his accomplice is represented as demanding of the saint his restoration to life. This was in the fourth century, and without the possibility of a doubt the fraud was neither new nor unknown. In this case Epiphanius is represented as having detected and punished the fraud, but this appears to be exceptional, and it is no great demand on human vanity to believe that hundreds would be willingly or unwillingly imposed upon, laying the flattering unction to their souls that God is glorified by the miraculous gifts of His saints.

The following cases of voluntary hibernation are to the same point:—

Human hibernation, or simulated death by a Hindû fakir. The fakir Harodas had frequently exhibited his voluntary power of hibernation to the natives; but in the following instance, quoted by Dr. Braid, it was exhibited to European officers before the maharajah and his principal sirdars. Harodas previously prepared himself by "forcing his breath into his brain; whereupon the lungs collapsed, and the heart ceased to beat." Being ready, he was put into a linen bag sealed by the maharajah's private seal, and the bag containing the fakir was deposited in a deal box, which was locked, sealed, and buried in a deep grave. Earth was piled over the box several feet deep, and was well trodden down. Sentries were now set to watch the spot all day and night, and the man remained thus buried in the earth for six weeks. After the expiration of the forty days the box was disinterred, the eyes and mouth of the fakir were moistened, and the man revived. The case is related by captain W. G. Osborne in the book entitled *The Court and Camp of Runjeet Singh* (1840). It occurred at Lahore in 1837.

Dr. Braid mentions other instances, and Meric Casaubon, D.D., gives several examples in his *Treatise concerning Enthusiasm, as an Effect of Nature, but mistaken by many for Divine Inspiration or Diabolical Possession.*

The case of Harodas is well known, and rests on undoubted authority, such as that of sir Claude Martin Wade, acting political agent at the court of maharajah Runjeet Singh, at Lahore; and vouched for by sir C. E. Trevelyan, Dr. J. M. Honigberger, formerly physician to Runjeet Singh, and by general Ventura.

Human hibernation, or simulated death among the Hindûs. Colonel Fraser states that the following case of simulated death was officially reported to the Indian government by an engineer officer. He says it occurred in the presence of himself and another officer, at the court of Runjeet Singh, the Lion of Lahore. The faster was a Hindû fakir, who objected to "die and be buried" till commanded by Runjeet Singh. The fakir was a lean, middle-aged man. After bathing he was wrapped in a light warm cloth, his tongue was drawn back to the gullet, and he was laid on his back on a hard litter with a mat under him. Meanwhile slabs of stone were prepared and fitted together, and on them he was laid. He was then hermetically built in with solid masonry, for he was anxious no opening should be left, lest the ants should get at him. The tomb of masonry was bound round with tape, and sealed with the rujput's signet, which was handed to the officers. Six weeks afterwards the seals were broken, and the tomb opened. The body was found in the same position, but was somewhat leaner. The man's tongue was then drawn forwards, and warm milk being poured in small quantities down his throat, he revived in about an hour. This is a more recent case than that of Harodas.

Lieutenant Boileau's case of voluntary hibernation. Lieutenant Boileau, in his *Narrative of a Journey in Rajwarra* (1835), tells us of a man, about thirty years of age, who travelled about the country to Ajmeer, Katah, etc., and allowed himself to be buried for weeks, or even months, by any person who paid him handsomely. For some days before his inhumation he abstained from all food except milk, that he might not be inconvenienced by the contents of his stomach. His powers of abstinence were wonderful, and it is said his hair ceased to grow. This man was put to the test at Pooshikur by an officer, who suspended him for thirteen days enclosed in a wooden box, open to inspection on all sides. The result proved to demonstration that the man was not an impostor. The same man was buried in a walled grave covered with large stone slabs, and strictly guarded. He was exhumed after being interred for ten days, in the presence of credible witnesses. The appearance of the body was as follows:—"Eyes closed, hands cramped and powerless, stomach shrunken, teeth jammed together so fast it was needful to employ an iron instrument to open the mouth that a little water might be poured down the throat. He revived gradually, and spoke in a feeble voice, as if weak; but so far from being distressed in mind from his long interment, he said he was quite willing to be buried again, and that for a twelvemonth, if desired."

A case of voluntary human hibernation recorded by Mr. Braid. Mr. Braid mentions a case of voluntary human hibernation made under the direct superintendence of a British officer. A period of nine days was stipulated for on the part of the devotee; but was reduced to three at the desire of the officer, who feared he might incur blame if the result proved fatal. The appearance of the body when first disinterred was quite corpse-like in every respect. No pulsation at the heart could be detected, and no respiration was perceptible. The means of restoration employed were chiefly warmth to the vertex, and friction to the body and limbs.—*Observations on Trance, or Human Hibernation* (1850).

Colonel Townshend had the power of voluntary hibernation. Colonel Townshend and Phul, rajah of Puttiali, in the Punjaub, had the power of voluntary hibernation. Colonel Townshend could "die" whenever he pleased, as many persons can faint at will. His heart would cease to beat; there was no perceptible respiration; the body became cold and rigid, the eyes glassy, and the features cadaverous. The colonel would continue "dead" for several hours, and then revive. Dr. Cheyne, who gives an account of this strange power, says that colonel Townshend told him "he could expire whenever he liked, and by an effort of his own will come to life again." On one occasion he performed the experiment in the presence of three medical men, one of whom kept his hand on the colonel's heart, another held his fingers at the colonel's wrist-pulse, and the third held a mirror before the colonel's mouth. They found all traces of pulsation and respiration ceased entirely, and really believed that the colonel had actually died; but he revived in due time, to the amazement of all.

Deaf made to hear.

MARK vii. 32–35. They bring unto Jesus one that was deaf, . . . and He put His fingers into his ears, . . . and looking up to heaven, He sighed, and saith, Ephphatha (that is, *Be opened*); and straightway his ears were opened.

St. Geneviève cures a lawyer who had been deaf for four years (A.D. 422–512). An advocate of Paris, who had been quite deaf for four years, applied to St. Geneviève for a cure of his infirmity. The saint made the sign of the cross on his ears, and forthwith he heard plainly.—Bollandus, *Acta Sanctorum* (Vita Genovefæ), vol. i. Jan. 3.

The cure of the deaf is too common a miracle in hagiography to have the least interest, and of course deafness and dumbness are so easily assumed if an impostor has any object in view to be gained thereby

Dearth forestalled.

GEN. xli. Joseph, having forewarned Pharaoh that seven years of plenty would be succeeded by seven years of dearth, lays up corn to provide against famine.

St. Remi in Reims follows the example of Joseph in Egypt, and forestalls a dearth (sixth century). When St. Remi was well stricken in age, it was revealed to him in a dream that certain years of plenty would be followed by a dearth; so he stored up corn in Celtum against the years of famine. The villagers, supposing he was going to make a market of his corn to their great loss, set fire to his granaries. While the fires were still blazing, the old primate made his appearance on the scene, and said to the people, "Be sure of this, that God will not forget to punish those who have done this mischief;" and immediately the peasants who had fired the granaries became humpty—a mark which God set on all their posterity also. Archbishop Hincmar naïvely remarks, "I, the author of this *Life of St. Remi*, can vouch for the truth of this miracle, for I have often seen the peasants of Celtum, some of whom have certainly crooked backs."—Hincmar (archbishop of Reims), *Life of St. Remi.*

The logic of the archbishop is not very strong. St. Remi died in 545, and Hincmar in 882. He does not tell us who kept the genealogy of the peasants for the three centuries intervening between St. Remi and himself, nor does he so much as say that the villagers told him that the fathers and grandfathers of these deformed peasants were humpty, but simply, "I have often seen deformed persons in Celtum, and God, three hundred years ago, punished some of the natives of this place with deformity, so the deformed persons I have seen must be the descendants of those whom God punished, and hence the corn collected by St. Remi was really destroyed, and the workers of the mischief were really punished." Q.E.D.

Delilah.

JUDGES xvi. 4–20. Samson fell in love with Delilah, who was enticed by the Philistines to betray him. So Delilah said to Samson, Tell me, I pray thee, the secret of thy strength, and whereby thou mayest be bound to afflict thee. Samson replied, if he was bound with seven green withs, he would be no stronger than another man. Delilah procured the withs, bound him, and called forth the Philistines, who were lying in wait to take him prisoner; but Samson broke the withs as tow, and the Philistines did not dare to molest him. Delilah chid the strong man for his deception, and coaxed him again to tell his secret. Said Samson, If I were bound with new ropes, I should be powerless as other men. So Delilah procured new ropes and bound him; but when the Philistines entered, he broke the ropes as he had snapped the withs, and the Philistines laid no hands on him. Again Delilah asked him wherein his strength lay, and how he might be bound; and she told him he had mocked her, and had told her what was not true. Samson now told her, saying, If you were to weave seven locks of my hair with a web, I should lose all my strength. So Delilah fastened his hair with a pin, and cried, The Philistines be upon thee, Samson. And he awoke, and went away with the pin of the beam, and with the web. How canst thou say thou lovest me, said Delilah, and yet mock me thus? And she pressed him day after day, and urged him, till his "soul was vexed unto death." So at last he told her that he was a Nazarite, and consequently his hair had never been cut, and so long as this was the case his strength would remain unabated; but if he broke his vow and his hair was shorn, he would lose his strength, and be no better than ordinary men. Then Delilah watched her opportunity, and one day, when he fell asleep with his head in her lap, she cut off his seven locks of hair, and called for the Philistines to come and bind him. So they bound him, put out his eyes, and sent him to grind in the prison-house of Gaza.

Jonathan, the youngest son of king Darius, wheedled out of his three talismans by a woman. Darius, on his death-bed, bequeathed his kingdom to his eldest son, his personals to his second son, and three magical gifts (a ring, a necklace, and a piece of cloth) to the youngest. Jonathan being, at the time of his father's death, too young to be entrusted with these magical treasures, they were given to his mother to take care of for him. When Jonathan became a young man, his mother gave him one of the three talismans, viz. the ring, which had these two virtues—it rendered the wearer invisible, and supplied him with everything he wanted. On handing it to the young prince, she said to him, "Wear it, my son, but beware of the wiles of women." So Jonathan went into the wide world, and fell in love with a Delilah. The woman, greatly amazed at his inexhaustible wealth, wheedled the secret out of him, and induced him to give the ring into her keeping, lest he should lose it. The love-sick youth did so; but when he wanted it again to supply his necessities, she swore that some one had stolen it. Being in great destitution, he returned to his mother, and told her of his loss. "My son," she said, "I cautioned you against the wiles of women, but it is of no use fretting over spilt milk." She then gave him his second treasure, the magical necklace, the virtues of which were the same as those of the ring—it made the wearer invisible, and supplied all his wants. Jonathan took the necklace, and went his way as before. When his old flame saw he was as well off as ever, she soon returned to him again, and ultimately coaxed him out of the necklace; and when asked to return it, with small ingenuity of invention she insisted that it had been stolen, like the ring. Jonathan told his mother of this second loss, and she sharply rebuked him before handing to him his third gift, a piece of cloth, which would transport those who sat on it, in a moment, to any place they liked. Again his Delilah joined him, and was told of the virtues of the rug. Then, sitting beside him on the magic cloth, she wished to be transported to the middle of a desert, and while the young prince was asleep, drew the cloth from under him, transported herself back, and left Jonathan in the desert. As Samson recovered his strength, and brought down destruction on the Philistines, so prince Jonathan recovered his three talismans, and saw his deceitful mistress die in excruciating agony.—*Gesta Romanorum*, cxx.

Delivered from Prison. (See Paul and the Jailer.)

Acts xii. 3–10. Herod, having seized Peter, put him in prison, and delivered him to four quaternions of soldiers to keep him; intending after Easter to bring him forth to the people. Peter therefore was kept in prison: but prayer was made without ceasing of the Church unto God for him. And when Herod would have brought him forth, the same night Peter was sleeping between two soldiers, bound with two chains: and the keepers before the door kept the prison. And, behold! the angel of the Lord came upon him, and a light shined in the prison: and the angel smote Peter on the side, and raised him up, saying, Arise up quickly. And his chains fell off. And the angel said to him, Gird thyself, and bind on thy sandals. And so he did. And the angel said to him, Cast thy garment about thee, and follow me. And he went out, following the angel. When they were past the first and second ward, they came to the iron gate that leadeth to the city, which opened to them of its own accord: and they went out, and passed on through one street; and forthwith the angel departed from him. Peter then went to the house of Mary, the mother of John Mark, where many disciples were gathered together.

St. Apollo and others delivered from prison by an angel (A.D. 395). St. Apollo went with his monks to visit his brother, who was imprisoned for conscience' sake in Upper Egypt, in the days of Julian the Apostate. The tribune happened to enter the prison while these monks were there, and ordered the gates to be shut upon them, vowing he would enlist the whole lot in the imperial army. At night, while engaged in prayer, an angel came to them, bearing a lamp, opened the prison doors, and led them forth, bidding them flee into the desert. They obeyed the voice of their divine deliverer, and all of them escaped from further molestation.—Palladius, *Historia Lausiaca.* (Palladius was a personal friend.)

St. Felix delivered from prison by an angel (third century). St. Felix, being seized, was heavily laden with iron chains, and cast into a dungeon strewed with broken crockery, into which no ray of light could enter. At midnight an angel entered the dungeon, and bade Felix depart, and search for Maximus, bishop of Nola, who was dying of cold and hunger in the mountains. Immediately his chains fell off his neck, hands, and feet; the doors opened of their own accord; and, guided by the angel, Felix was brought to the hiding-place of the aged bishop, whom he found utterly exhausted, speechless, and apparently dying. St. Felix moistened the lips of the old prelate with wine, forced a little food down his throat, and chafed his frozen limbs. By slow degrees Maximus revived, and then Felix carried him home on his shoulders, and put him under the charge of a good old woman to take care of him. In A.D. 251 the Church had rest for a while by the death of Decius. In Christian art, St. Felix is represented with an angel striking off his chains; and sometimes as bearing Maximus, the aged bishop, either on his shoulder or in his arms.—St. Gregory of Tours, *De Gloria Martyrum*, bk. i. ch. 104.

St. Germanus of Scotland obtains the release of twenty-four prisoners (fifth century). When St. Germanus was at Bayeux he asked the governor to release his prisoners, and was refused. So he left the town in anger, and striking his feet against the city-wall to shake off the dust of his shoes, he kicked down a large part of the rampart into the foss. However, his anger being over, he returned to the city, and raised a dead man to life. These miracles induced the magistrates to relent, and they gave him the prisoners he demanded, to the number of twenty-four.—Corblet, *Hagiographie d'Amiens.*

St. Joseph of Arimathæa delivered from prison by an angel (A.D. 33). Gregory of Tours and Boronius, in his *Annals*, vol. i., tells us that the high priest was so angry with Joseph of Arimathæa for entombing Jesus, that he arrested him and put him in prison. On the day of the resurrection, an angel released Joseph from prison; and when the Jews reproached the guard for allowing the body of Jesus to be stolen from the tomb, they replied, "Do you deliver into our hands Joseph, and we will deliver into yours Christ; but as you cannot give into our hands the friend of Christ, we cannot give into yours the Son of God."—Baronius, *Annals*, vol. i.

St. Julian of Antioch released from prison by an angel (A.D. 313). The governor Marcian had confined St. Julian and his own son Celsus in a noisome dungeon; but at midnight, one Antony, with seven of his scholars, entered the prison. Presently an angel made its appearance, and bade all of them follow him. He led them through the prison, and they came to the great iron gates, which opened to them of their own accord, and they passed through.—*Acta Sanctorum* (Bollandus), vol. i. Jan. 9.

Peter the Holy Exorcist and Marcellinus delivered from prison by an angel. In the reign of Diocletian, Peter the Holy Exorcist was apprehended in Rome by judge Serenus, laden with fetters, and locked in a dark dungeon with bolts of iron. Artemius, the prison-keeper, had a daughter possessed with an evil spirit, and Peter said to him, "If you would believe on Jesus Christ the Son of God, your daughter would be made whole, Artemius." The prison-keeper laughed at the remark, and replied, "If your God cannot deliver you from prison, Peter, how should He be able to deliver my daughter from the power of Satan?" Peter said, "The God I serve can do both one and the other." "I will put Him to the test this very night," said Artemius. "So be it," replied Peter. "This night, then," continued the keeper, "I will put you into the inner dungeon, lock and bolt the door myself, double the chains that hold you, and double the watch also; then, if your God can deliver you, I will believe in Him." "Be it so, Artemius," said Peter. At midnight, lo! Peter, notwithstanding the precautions employed, left his dungeon, and presented himself before the jailer and his wife Candida. He was clad in white, and carried in his hand a cross. When Artemius and his wife saw Peter, they fell at his feet and exclaimed, "Truly there is but one God who can do after this sort, and that is the Lord Jesus Christ whom you serve." Peter then commanded the devil to come out of Paulina, the jailer's daughter, and forthwith she was made whole. Above three hundred persons witnessed these miracles, and all of them received baptism, and continued steadfast in the faith to their lives' end. Then Artemius delivered Peter from his chains, and took him into his own house. When the knowledge of these things came to the ears of the judge, he commanded that Peter should be sent again to the dungeon, and his feet made fast in the stocks. A priest, named Marcellinus, was also a prisoner in the same cell. At night an angel came into the dungeon while they were praying, and delivered them both. Being set free by the angel, Peter and Marcellinus went to the house of Artemius the jailer, where the new converts were met together, and tarried there certain days, instructing them more fully in the way of Christ. Ultimately, Peter and Marcellinus, Artemius and his wife Candida, were all beheaded. The executioner declared, when he cut off the heads of Peter and Marcellinus, that he distinctly saw their souls, arrayed in white, borne up to heaven by the hands of angels. (See ALEXANDER and HERMES, p. 59, almost identical.)—Ado (archbishop of Trèves), *Martyrology*. (Bede has written the lives of these two martyrs. See also L'abbé Daras, *Vies des Saints.*)

St. Peter II., archbishop of Tarentaise, miraculously delivers three prisoners (A.D. 1103-1174). While St. Peter, the archbishop of Tarentaise, was at St. Claude, a crowd pressed upon him to obtain some of the graces which he so freely bestowed. Amongst others appeared three strangers, who came to thank him for delivering them from prison. "We were shut up in prison," they said, "in Lausanne. Here the recital of your virtues and miracles arrested our attention, and led us to repentance. We invoked your name, as one would invoke a saint in heaven. You appeared to us in our cell, broke our chains, gave us your hand, and led us out of prison without being seen by any one, or disturbing the guard on watch."—Geoffrey (abbot of Hautecomb), *Life of St. Peter II.*, etc. (written nine years after his death by order of pope Lucius III.).

St. Peter does not seem to have known what the prisoners tell him. It appears that, being invoked, his "double" went to Lausanne, just as the duplicate of St. Werulus went to Mussy to deliver a child from a house on fire.

Robert de Sillé delivered from prison by the Virgin Mary (A.D. 1356). When Jean le Bon, king of France, fell a captive into the hands of the Black Prince, the sieur Robert de Sillé was also taken prisoner, and the English demanded three thousand florins for ransom-money. As his wife, Jeanne Marie de Maillé, could not raise this sum, she prayed earnestly to the Virgin to come and help her. Her prayer was heard, and the Virgin Mary, entering the cell of Robert, broke off his chains and set him free.—Père de Boisgaultier (her confessor), *Life of Jeanne Marie de Maillé.*

Ordinary history says simply that he broke from prison and made his escape.

The prison walls of Rennes fall down when the dead body of St. Melanius passes by (A.D. 530). When the dead body of St. Melanius was carried in grand procession through Rennes, the chanting was heard in the prison, where twelve thieves were confined. The thieves joined in the chant, and the prison walls, though built of stone and very stout, were rent from the top to the bottom. The thieves being thus released invoked the mercy of God, and were numbered with the elect.—Dom Lobineau (a contemporary), *Life of St. Melani* (or Melaine).

Demoniacs possessed with Spirits of Truth.

MARK iii. 11, 12. Unclean spirits, when they saw Jesus, fell down before Him, and cried, saying, Thou art the Son of God. And Jesus straitly charged them that they should not make Him known.

MARK v. 2-13. When Jesus came to the country of the Gadarenes there met Him a man with an unclean spirit, who had his dwelling among the tombs; and when he saw Jesus afar off, he ran and worshipped Him, and cried with a loud voice, What have I to do with Thee, Jesus, Thou Son of the most high God?

LUKE iv. 33-35. In the synagogue there was a man which had a spirit of an unclean devil, and he cried with a loud voice, Let us alone, Thou Jesus of Nazareth. I know Thee who Thou art; the Holy One of God.

The devil tells Mme. de Bermond why he hates her. Mme. de Bermond was especially obnoxious to the devil. On one occasion she found herself unconsciously in the presence of a demoniac, and the demon tried to leap on her, crying with a loud yell, "Off, off! you burn me!" Mme. de Bermond, quite fearless, went up to the demoniac, and spat in his face, to show her contempt. The demon, furious, said to her, "I will direct all my efforts and all my craft against thee and thy hated daughters, even more than against other religious orders." "Why so, wretch?" demanded Mme. de Bermond. "Why?—ask me why?" screamed the foul fiend; "because the instructions which you give to these children wean them from me and mine. So, look out, I say, for my hatred and rage shall be employed to the utmost, to keep children from joining the Ursulines."—*Les Petits Bollandistes*, vol. vi. p. 338.

Demoniacs reveal the place where St. Solemnius was buried (A.D. 509). St. Solemnius assisted St. Remi in the baptism of Clovis, and died at Maillé in the year 509. He was buried where he died, in the crypt of the church dedicated to the Holy Virgin. This church was destroyed by pagans, and the body of the bishop, by the close of the century, was wholly forgotten. The subject cropped up suddenly by some curious phenomena which excited public attention. It was observed that every Sunday night a mysterious light was seen on the top of the mountain where the church of the Holy Virgin used to stand, and while men were speculating on the cause of these mysterious flames, two demoniacs from the basilica of St. Martin came to the mountain, crying out, "Here rests Solemnius, in a crypt below. Open up the tomb, and honour the friend of God according to his deserts. Do this, and your country will reap the benefit." The people accordingly took spades and opened the earth, till they uncovered the crypt and found the tomb, which the demoniacs declared to be that of Solemnius. The truth of the matter was proved by the many miracles performed by the relics thus discovered. In the eleventh century it was determined to remove the body to Chartres, but on arriving at Blois, the body was deposited for a night in St. Peter's chapel there, with the intention of renewing the journey on the morrow; but when the bearers next morning attempted to lift the coffin, it was found to be so heavy that no human strength could move it. This miracle was considered to be a plain indication of the will of God that the body was to remain where it was. So the old chapel of St. Peter of Blois was rebuilt, and dedicated to St. Solemnius. In 1568 the Huguenots burnt the body, but some of the bones being rescued were carried to Chartres, and the head was preserved in St. Mary's of Blois, till the time of the revolution. Even to the present day September 25 is observed as the anniversary of the saint's death.—Dupré, *Notices sur les Saintes de Blois*.

Possessed by a cat. The following is taken from the *North China Herald*, Nov. 1, 1881. It is very generally believed in China that if any person kills an animal from wantonness or cruelty, the soul of the dead animal will take possession of the murderer's body till the guilt has been expiated. An instance of this is said to have occurred recently at Yangchow. It is as follows:—"A man and his wife had a favourite cat, and this cat gave birth to three kittens. Like most other domestic animals, this feline family had its thievish propensities, and was constantly stealing sundry titbits which the servant girl had put aside for her own private eating. At last the girl got so exasperated that she killed both cat and kittens, one after another, in different ways. In a short time the girl was taken violently ill, mewing and scratching like a cat, and displaying all the symptoms of rabies. Her mistress, suspecting the true cause of the girl's attack, apostrophized the dead mother-cat, demanding why it had come to haunt the body of the girl. The cat, speaking through the girl's mouth, then recounted the ill treatment it had received, and said how its little ones had been killed. One had been drowned, another worried by a dog, and a third burnt to death. All this was said by the girl herself, in the character of the cat. At last the girl died in convulsions, at the feet of her mistress." Stories of this description are firmly believed in by the Chinese.—*Notes and Queries*, July 29, 1882.

Devil defeated. (See COMPACTS WITH SATAN.)

EPH. vi. 11–13. Put on the whole armour of God, that ye may be able to stand against the wiles of the devil. For we wrestle . . . against principalities, against powers, against the rulers of the darkness of this world, against spiritual wickedness in high places. Wherefore take unto you the whole armour of God, that ye may be able to withstand in the evil day, and having done all, to stand.

ROM. v. 20. Where sin abounded, grace did much more abound.

MARK iii. 28. Verily I say unto you, All sins shall be forgiven unto the sons of men, and [all] blasphemies wherewith soever they shall blaspheme.

Peter denied Christ, even with cursing and swearing, but Peter was a chosen vessel unto honour.

Saul was called to be the apostle Paul while in the very act of breathing out threatenings and slaughter against the disciples of the Lord.

LUKE x. 18. I beheld Satan as lightning fall from heaven.

JOHN xii. 31. Now shall the prince of this world be cast out. (See also xvi. 11.)

REV. xii. 9. The great dragon was cast out, hat old serpent, called the devil, and Satan, which deceiveth the whole world, was cast out, and his angels with him.

The devil put to flight by St. Benedict with a whip (A.D. 480–543). A certain monk felt an irresistible aversion to the long mental prayers of the Benedictine monks, so when the psalmody and office were finished, he used to steal out of the oratory and go to active work. The superior had often admonished him, but all to no purpose, so at last he took him before St. Benedict. The refractory brother promised amendment, but his resolution lasted only two days, and the superior again complained to the abbot. St. Benedict appointed Maur to be his companion, and when prayer-time arrived, the brothers said to the superior, "Look there; do you see that little black imp which keeps pulling at the cloke of Maur's companion?" "No," said the superior. "Then we will pray that God will open your eyes." In two days the superior saw the imp pulling the monk by the sleeve. St. Benedict followed with a whip, and flogged the monk till he scourged the offending Adam out of him. The cure was quite effectual, for never more did the imp return to tempt the monk, and the monk no longer shirked his religious duties.—St. Gregory the Great, *Dialogues*, bk. ii.

St. Dunstan and the devil (A.D. 925–988). St. Dunstan was not only a theologian and statesman, he was also a good painter, architect, and musician, a founder of metals, and skilled workman in gold and silver. One day, while he was occupied on some work in silver, the lyre suspended on the walls of his cell began to play spontaneously, as if struck by the hands of angels. The tune it played was the *Magnificat*.*

On another occasion, while working at his forge, the devil, that enemy of all good men, kept wandering round the anvil, hindering Dunstan in his work. Dunstan, greatly annoyed, took his tongs, red hot out of the furnace, and seized the intruder by the nose. Father Cahier tells us of "une vieille chappe conservée en Angleterre, où ce fait est représenté."—Mgr. Guérin (chamberlain of pope Leo XIII.), *Vies des Saints*, vol. vi. p. 20.

* Probably this lyre resembled in its mechanism a musical snuff-box.

, Dr. Freeman probably refers to this legend, when he says (*Old English History*, p. 164), "Many strange stories are told of [St. Dunstan], especially one very silly one." To this I cannot agree. Those who study the lives of the saints will know, that whatever impeded good work was called *a devil*, whether dog or horse, wind or accident, man or what not. A loafer loitering about the smithy would, in the language of the times, be called a devil, and it is quite in character with St. Dunstan to turn him out with his red-hot forceps or tongs.

St. Patrick drives away the demons that tried to oppose his landing in Ireland. When St. Patrick went to Ireland, the devils, knowing he would be a formidable adversary, formed a ring round the island to keep him off; but the saint raised his right hand on high, made the sign of the cross, and they fled. We are told that he alone could see the infernal cohort.—Jocelin (twelfth century), *Life of St. Patrick*.

St. Theophilus breaks his compact with the devil (sixth century). Mgr. Guérin, from whom the following narrative is abridged, introduces the life of St. Theophilus with these words: "Nous l'avouons, ce sera avec plaisir que nous écrirons ici l'histoire de St. Théophile, pénitent, puisqu'elle fera parfaitement connaître au lecteur combien la sainte Vierge est miséricordieuse envers les pécheurs, et combien elle a de pouvoir pour les retirer des abîmes de l'enfer, où ils seraient précipités par leurs vices, et par la violence des tentations." From these words we infer that, in the opinion of the chamberlain of pope Leo XIII., the narrative which ensues is strictly historical. And as his work is highly commended by the chief dignitaries of the [Roman] Catholic Church, we may conclude that there is nothing in the narrative out of harmony with their faith. And, thirdly, as the seventh edition bears the date of 1880, no charge of obsoleteness can be laid against it.

In A.D. 538 Theophilus was treasurer of the Church of Adna, in Cilicia, and discharged his duties so honourably that he was elected bishop, but declined to accept the office.

Now came a great change. He was slanderously accused to the new bishop, deprived of his office as treasurer, and retired into private life, boiling with anger and longing for vengeance. A certain Jew, who lived by sorcery, happened to reside in the neighbourhood, and, working on the evil spirit of the man, induced him to make a compact with the devil. To this end he had to abjure the Christian faith, deny Christ and the Virgin, and sign the compact with his blood.

In the mean time, the new bishop having discovered that the charge against the late treasurer was false, reinstated Theophilus, declared him innocent of every charge brought against him, and heaped honour upon honour on him. Theophilus now bitterly repented of his compact with the devil, and prayed for forgiveness. The "Holy Spirit advised him to apply to Mary, the fountain of mercy," and to Mary he cried for mercy. Forty days he made his supplication, with fasting and penance, when "the mother of God" vouchsafed to appear to him, robed like a queen, full of majesty, but with displeasure plainly marked upon her face. "Why, wretch," she said, "do you address yourself to me? Would it not have been bad enough if you had insulted me, but must you blaspheme my Son also? I can well pardon offences, but blasphemy against my Son is far more heinous." Theophilus pleaded hard for mercy, spoke of the Ninevites who obtained mercy, of Rahab and David, of Peter and Paul, of Cyprian too, who practised the black art, and was yet a martyr and a saint. The holy Virgin, touched with his contrition, bade him confess his sins, and then promised to bring back word what Christ said on the subject. Next night she returned, told Theophilus that his prayers and tears were accepted, and if he continued faithful to the end her Son would give him eternal life. Theophilus now implored that the contract he had signed might be restored to him; and in three days he found it on his breast, as he was getting out of bed. It was Sunday; he went to early prayers, and gave the document to the bishop, telling him the whole story. The bishop heard him, absolved him, and made the confession the subject of his sermon. The peroration of this discourse was a masterpiece of eloquence, setting forth the boundless mercy of God, the resistless intercession of the Virgin Mary, and ever abiding hope of the true penitent that all sins shall be forgiven unto the sons of men, and all the blasphemies wherewith soever they shall have blasphemed, for where sin hath abounded, grace hath much more abounded. The bishop then bade Theophilus approach the altar, and receive his God; but Theophilus would not rise from the ground till the bishop had burnt the contract.

"Qui n'admirerait ici les merveilles de la divine Providence; et qui ne craindrait, voyant jusqu'en quel abîme peut tomber un homme accablé de tristesse, et emporté par la tentation? Mais qui ne bénirait à jamais la bonté de Dieu de nous avoir donné une très-puissante médiatrice en la sainte Vierge, Mère de Miséricorde, et asile assuré de tous les pécheurs qui l'invoquent avec un désir sincère de se convertir!" (See GILES OF PORTUGAL, p. 66.)

This story is told in a "Vitrail de Laon," in a "verrière de Beauvais," and in a "petit tympan" of Notre Dame de Paris. "On voit [at Notre Dame] à la linge inférieure le désespéré qui s'abouche avec un magicien puis avec un démon. Près de là il se prosterne devant une image de Marie, et obtient que le diable soit forcé de se dessaisir du billet signé par lui. Au sommet le pénitent fait l'aveu de son crime, et prie l'évêque de lire devant tout le monde la cédule accusatrice. (Le Père Chahier a reproduit ce tympan, A.D. 1854.)"—*Vies des Saints*, vol. ii. pp. 253–256.

Devil full of All Mischief.

In the first chapter of the Book of Job, Satan is represented as the instrument of all his evils, the loss of his flocks and herds, the death of his children, the destruction of his houses and barns, and the frightful boils and blains with which his body was afflicted.

MARK ix. 22. Ofttimes the evil spirit hath cast him into the fire, and into the waters, to destroy him. (See also 1 Chron. xxi. 1.)

St. Euphrasia ill treated by the devil (A.D. 412). The devil, being unable to attack the soul of St. Euphrasia, tried to disqualify her body from performing her daily tasks. With this object in view, one day, as the young maiden went to draw water from a pond, the devil pushed her in, and she would certainly have been drowned, if her good angel had not held her above the water till assistance came from the convent. Hearing her cry, several of the sisters ran to the pond, and drew her out. "O Satan," said she with a smile, when safely landed, "I pray the Lord Jesus Christ that you may never triumph over me."

Another time, in cutting wood, she cut her foot with the bill-hook, and the pain was so great that she fainted. Some of the sisters came, and carried her into the convent. When she came round, she returned to her task, being resolved to fight with her great adversary as long as life remained to her.

Another time, Satan pushed her from a third-story window to the ground; but by the guardian care of her good angel, she was picked up safe and sound.

On one occasion, while cooking vegetables, the evil spirit overturned on her the boiler full of boiling water. The sisters fully expected she would be scalded most terribly; but Euphrasia protested to them that the water felt quite cold, and had not hurt her in the least.

*** Mgr. Guérin remarks, "L'epoux céleste permettait que le démon éprouvât ainsi la personne de sa bien-aimée, afin de la rendre plus illustre, et de nous donner à connaître que le démon ne peut rien contre ceux qui sont secourus et fortifiés de sa main toute-puissante."—*Les Petits Bollandistes* (7th edit. 1880), vol. iii. p. 391.

These are good examples of the "mode of religious thought" at the time. We should call these "accidents," or the "results of carelessness, clumsiness, or want of skill." Euphrasia call them "the works of the devil."

As St. Germanus of Scotland was crossing the Channel, the devil tried to drown him (fifth century). When St. Germanus crossed over to France the second time, the devil mounted the poop while the saint was asleep, and so overweighted the vessel that it nearly heeled over. Germanus, being roused from his sleep, saw the cause of the mischief in a moment, made the sign of the cross, the vessel righted, and the devil was tipped "dans les abîmes de l'enfer."—Corblet, *Hagiographie d'Amiens.*

Devil taking Men up into the Air.

MATT. iv. 5, 8. The devil taketh Jesus up into the holy city, and setteth Him on a pinnacle of the temple.

Again, the devil taketh Jesus up into an exceeding high mountain. [When the devil left, angels came and ministered to Jesus.]

Satan carries up Sister Benedicta to inaccessible rocks, church spires, and other lofty eminences (A.D. 1643–1718). Sometimes the devil would set Sister Benedicta on the top of an inaccessible rock, and leave her there; but her guardian angel always helped her down again, and carried her safely home. More than twenty times, the foul fiend left her on the roof of the chapel of Notre Dame de l'Erable, but her angel not only lifted her down, but also opened the chapel doors, that she might there recite her rosary with him. Once she was left for two whole days "sur le roc, où l'aigle niche, où Satan l'avait rudement laissée tomber."—Mgr. Guérin (chamberlain of pope Leo XIII.), *Vies des Saints*, vol. v. pp. 226, 227.

(Mgr. Barnadon, bishop of Gap, is collecting such data as these to effect the canonization of Sister Benedicta, 1883.)

The devil carries St. Gertrude von Oosten up into the air (A.D. 1358). The devil was not likely to witness the extraordinary virtues of St. Gertrude von Oosten without jealousy, but being wholly unable to trouble her thoughts with vile suggestions, he carried her up into the air, and then left hold of her, so that she fell violently through the air to the ground. No doubt she would have been dashed to pieces, if God had not given His angels charge concerning her, to bear her in their hands.—*Vita Sanctorum*, Jan. 6.

Devils assume Divers Forms.

GEN. iii. The devil assumes the form of a *serpent*, or entering into the body of a serpent employs that animal as his agent. In Rev. xii. 9 he is called "that old serpent, the devil, which deceiveth the whole world."

1 PET. v. 8. He is likened to a *lion*. The apostle says of this wicked spirit, "As a roaring lion he walketh about, seeking whom he may devour."

REV. xii. 7. He is represented as a *dragon*. "There was war in heaven: Michael and his angels fought against the dragon."

ISA. xxvii. 1. He is called *leviathan*. "In that day the Lord shall punish leviathan, that crooked serpent."

LUKE x. 18. The Lord says, "I beheld Satan, as *lightning*, fall from heaven."

He hides himself in maniacs, epileptics, and other diseased folks. Sometimes assumes the semblance of an angel of light. Sometimes enters into the bodies of prophets to make them prophesy falsely. Whatever tempts to sin is called his work, whether lying, covetousness, anger, or any other evil; nay, more, whatever opposes or prevents religious duties is ascribed to diabolic agency. Thus we read: "Quelquefois il a excité des tempêtes, et fait paraître en l'air des nuages noirs et épais, prêts à se résoudre en pluie et en grêle, afin que le monde qui était au sermon, en pleine campagne, se retirât promptement, et allât chercher un abri dans les maisons. Il a pris aussi la figure de chevaux fougueux qui semblaient venir fondre sur l'auditoire, pour en troubler l'attention et interrompre le saint au milieu de son discours."—Mgr. Guérin (chamberlain of pope Leo XIII.), *Vies des Saints*, vol. iv. p. 234.

The devil, disguised as an anchorite, tempts St. Vincent Ferrier (A.D. 1357–1419). On one occasion the devil, disguised as an anchorite, accosted St. Vincent Ferrier, and said to him, "I am an old anchorite living in the deserts of the Thebaïd. When young I lived a merry life, but that did not hinder my arriving at great purity as I grew older. Let me advise you not to enfeeble your strength, which will be required for preaching. Remember that discretion is the mother of all virtues. Take an old man's advice, and remember that a fire which burns too fiercely soon burns itself out." The temptation was doubtlessly plausible, but St. Vincent saw through it, and said to the tempter, "Avaunt, Satan! I wish to give my youth, as well as my old age, to God. Remember thy Creator in the days of thy youth, while the evil days come not, nor the years draw nigh when thou shalt say, I have no pleasure in them." And so the tempter left him.

Another instance. Not long afterwards, the tempter appeared before St. Vincent again. This time he had taken the guise of an Ethiopian, and threatened him with war to the death. St. Vincent merely replied, "Satan, He who has commenced a good work in me will give me courage to proceed. In Him is my trust."—L'abbé A. Bayle, *Life of St. Vincent Ferrier* (1855).

The devil, in the guise of a blackbird, appears to St. Benedict (A.D. 480–543). When St. Benedict, afterwards abbot of Mount Cassino, first retired to the cavern in Subiaco, some fifty miles west of Rome, Satan resolved to stamp out at once one who would otherwise prove a great enemy to his kingdom upon earth. With this object in view he transformed himself into a blackbird, and began to flutter round the hermit; sometimes approaching so near, that Benedict might have caught it easily if he had put out his hand. The young solitary, however, being suspicious, made the sign of the cross, and this showed him that his suspicion was well founded, for the bird instantly disappeared.—*Acta Sanctorum* (Bollandists), March 21.

The devil assumes the guise of a black horse to disturb the congregation assembled to hear St. Peter of Verona preach (A.D. 1206–1252). The devil was very angry because such vast crowds gathered together to hear St. Peter of Verona preach. One day, when the crowd was greater than usual, the devil, in the form of a black horse, rushed into the midst, stamping upon many, and frightening more. The saint simply made the sign of the cross, when the phantom vanished, and all the people saw it permeate the air like smoke.—*Acta Sanctorum* (Bollandists), April 29.

A devil, which assumes the part of a brawler, cast out by St. Giles. One Sunday at church, a man possessed with a devil made such a brawling noise that the voice of the preacher could not be heard. St. Giles prayed, and, the devil going forth, the man remained to the end of the service peaceable and devout.—Gilbertus (bishop of Carnotum), *Life of St. Giles* (abbot).

The devil, in the guise of a bull, tries to kill Catherine of Sweden (fourteenth century). St. Catherine of Sweden was the daughter of prince Ulpho, and was sent in early childhood to be brought up in the nunnery of Risburgh. One night, while the abbess was at matins, the devil, assuming the form of a bull, tossed the child out of its cradle, and left her half dead in the middle of the chamber. The abbess, on her return, picked up the child, and the bull said to her, "Oh that I had accomplished my work, which I assuredly should have done, if God had permitted me."—Ulpho (a Brigittine friar), *Life of St. Catherine of Sweden* (written thirty years after her death, A.D. 1411).

Dativus, running away from the abbey of Lauconne, is accosted by the devil in the guise of a demoniac (A.D. 480). Dativus, one of the monks of Lauconne, in the Jura, being seduced by the devil, determined to quit the abbey and return to the world. With all his worldly goods packed in a bundle, and thrown over his shoulder, he started for Tours. He came to the basilica of St. Martin with the intention of offering there a morning prayer, but was accosted at the door by a demoniac, who said to him, "Dativus? Why, it is our monk of the Jura, I declare! Good day, my good fellow; I am very glad you are now one of us." Dativus trembled to find himself thus recognized, and thinking himself mocked by the demon, sighed bitterly; and, after having prayed for a few minutes, hastened back to the monastery, imploring to be admitted again.—St. Gregory of Tours, *Lives of the Fathers*, ch. i.

I think the "devil" in this story is simply the personification of the monk's own thoughts.

Devils in the guise of dogs attack St. Peter the apostle. Samuel Harsnet, afterwards archbishop of York, says: "Thyræus doth tel it out of one Martinus a saint, that Simon Magus the sorcerer sent unto Peter the apostle certaine devils in the likenes of dogges, to devoure him. The apostle being taken on a suddaine, not looking for such currish guests, consecrates for the nonce some morsels of bread, and throwes them to the dogge-devils, and by the power of that bread, they were all put to flight."—*Popish Impostures*, pp. 97, 98.

The devil, in the form of a dog, visits St. Stanislaus Kostka. When St. Stanislaus Kostka was preparing himself for admission into the society of Jesus, he was visited with a dangerous sickness; at the beginning of which the devil appeared to him in the guise of a great black dog, horrible and fearful to behold. The foul fiend took the sick man thrice by the throat, trying to throttle him; but Stanislaus, with the sign of the cross, not only resisted him manfully, but even drove him away, and he never again disturbed this faithful soldier of Christ Jesus.—Peter Ribadeneira, *The Flower of the Lives of the Saints* (2 vols., fol.).

The devil, in the form of a dragon, tries to destroy St. Martinian's cell (A.D. 830). St. Martinian, at the early age of eighteen, became a hermit, and lived in the vicinity of Cesarea. The devil, jealous of his virtue, sought to frighten him with visions, noises, and apparitions. On one occasion, this enemy of all righteousness assumed the form of a dragon, and began scratching at the foundations of St. Martinian's cell, in order to destroy it and the hermit within. St. Martinian was at his orisons at the time, and said to the dragon-formed devil, "Your labour is in vain. You cannot frighten me while I have Christ at my side." At the word Christ, the devil fled in a whirlwind, crying, "Wait a bit, Martinian; I will make you submit yet, and drive you from this cell." Martinian was not easily frightened, and remained in his hermitage, doing battle with the devil, for five and twenty years.—Metaphrastês (a personal friend of St. Martinian), *Lives of Saints.* (Also in Joseph Assemani, *Universal Calendar*, vol. vi. p. 145, etc.)

The devil, under the form of an Ethiopian, asks pardon of St. John of Egypt. Devils used to torment St. John of Egypt at night, and appear to him under divers sensible forms, and ask pardon for disturbing him. On one occasion, when the saint had fasted two whole days, the devil, disguised as an Ethiopian of hideous look, threw himself at his feet, and said with insulting mockery, "Pardon me, I pray, for having troubled you to carry me through this long fast." St. John now saw that his fast was simply a temptation.—Cassian, *Fathers of the Desert.*

True or not, this certainly is a very sensible story. It is to be feared that many a fast has more of vanity than holiness to its support.

The devil, in the guise of a gentleman, visits St. Andrew Corsini (1302-1373). When St. Andrew Corsini entered the order of Carmelites, in Tuscany, he was made porter, or doorkeeper. One day, at dinner-time, a knocking was heard at the outer gate, and Andrew, opening the little wicket, saw a well-dressed gentleman with several attendants, who exclaimed imperiously, "Open the gate, caitiff, and that immediately. Your father sent me to you with a message, and I have no time to waste on beggars." Says Andrew, "I open to no strangers without permission. You say you come from my father, but I never set eyes on you before." "Don't stand prating there, but open the gate; I have something important to communicate, which the prior must not hear." Andrew, on hearing this, made the sign of the cross, and the tempter disappeared like a flash, leaving behind a filthy smell of fire and brimstone. Andrew thanked God, who had given him grace to resist the wiles of the devil, and felt the truth of that divine injunction, "Resist the devil, and he will flee from thee."—Surius, *Lives of the Saints* (6 vols., fol.), 1570.

Devils assume the form of jonchets to frighten St. Catherine of Sweden in childhood (fourteenth century). When Catherine, daughter of prince Ulpho of Sweden, was seven years old, she had a game of jonchets (or knucklebones) with other girls of the same age. The children went on playing, to the neglect of their religious duties; but the Spouse of the Church, who intended to make Catherine a saint, left not this dereliction of duty without due correction. At night, certain devils, in the form of jonchets, appear to the child, and whip her so severely, to wean her from her childish sports, that she never afterwards would play jonchets with her companions.—Ulpho (a Brigittine monk), *Life of St. Catherine of Sweden* (A.D. 1411).

This seems a most marvellous story. Why should these devils wish to wean the child from her sports, and whip her so severely for not being a better Christian? One would think they would have encouraged her to live more and more to the world and its vanities, and not have driven her to deny herself these pleasures. Devils, "in the form of jonchets," look like a childish dream, and the "whipping" seems like the reproof of conscience for having neglected duty for play.

Devils, in the guise of rooks or crows, annoy St. Agnes of Mount Pulciano (A.D. 1274-1317). One day, in her ninth year, St. Agnes proposed to her companions a pilgrimage to Mount Pulciano. The proposal was joyfully accepted; but as the party approached the ramparts of the city, a number of rooks attacked St. Agnes furiously with their beaks, claws, and wings. The young girl, with great presence of mind, invoked the name of Jesus, and the whole flock flew away. The biographer says, "No doubt these rooks were an army of demons, lodging in the contiguous house, which was a public brothel; and the presence of this 'angelic child' troubled the evil spirits."—Raymond of Capua, *Life of St. Agnes.*

The devil, in the form of two worms, comes out of the ears of Jean de la Roque (fifteenth century). Jean de la Roque was a nobleman and an ecclesiastic of Corigliano, who led a most scandalous life. He was on his road to Spezzia to meet a harlot, when St. Francis of Paula was told about it by revelation. The saint instantly sent a porter to lay hold of the young man, bring him to the convent, and lock him up. This was done, and Roque was furious, vowing vengeance, and making all the noise he could. When he was tired of beating the door and calling out, he threw himself on the floor, utterly exhausted, and fell asleep. Then St. Francis quietly entered the chamber, and waking the young man, said to him very coldly, "How now, friend; what thinkest thou? Pull from your ear that which torments you so." The young man, not knowing whether he was asleep or awake, put his hand to his right ear, and drew from it a hideous hairy worm of monstrous size. Then putting his hand to his left ear, he drew from it another worm of the same sort. The devil being thus taken from him, the young man returned to himself. All his base lust was gone, and throwing himself at the saint's feet, he prayed that he might be admitted as a disciple. He remained in the monastery till 1520, when he died. This was twelve years after the death of St. Francis himself.—*Acts of his Canonization* (compiled by Father Giry).

The devil, in the form of a monk, and in the form of a young woman, tempts St. Ambrose of Siena (A.D. 1220–1286). "Une fois qu'il n'avait pas voulu se trouver à des noces où on l'avait invité, ce monstre infernal, l'ennemi de notre salut lui apparut en form de religieux, et, sous prétexte de l'entretenir de quelque discours spirituel, il lui releva jusqu'au ciel l'état du mariage, afin de lui donner envie de s'y engager. Une autre fois, il se fit voir au milieu d'un bois, sous la figure d'une jeune fille d'une beauté ravissante, qui implorait son assistance; mais le saint jeune homme, découvrant le piége caché sous ces artifices, se munit l'une et l'autre fois du signe de la croix, et aussitôt ces spectres et ces fantômes disparurent."—Le R. P. Jean Baptiste Feuillet, *Année Dominicaine*, vol. iii. March 26.

This extract throws a flood of light upon the Satanic legends of the early and middle ages. Every thought and wish of evil, every one who tempts to evil, everything that allures (the lust of the eyes, the lust of the flesh, and the pride of life), being considered "a phase of Satan." helps to unravel many a tale which otherwise seems astounding. The words spoken by any tempter are to be accounted the words of the devil, and hence the exclamations of idolatrous priests are called those of the devil. Some might call this personification a figure of speech, but to [Roman] Catholics it is a veritable reality, and an important element in their hagiography.

The devil assails St. Pascal Baylon under divers forms (A.D. 1540–1592). The celestial favours shown to St. Pascal made the devils mad with rage, and they beset him in divers ways. Sometimes they rushed upon him in the form of lions and tigers, seeking to devour him; sometimes they tried to scare him by assuming horrible shapes; sometimes they beat him till all his body was black and blue, and his shrieks were heard through the whole house; but the saint, well accustomed to these attacks, was never alarmed. Then, changing their tactics, the devils suggested to him sentiments of vanity, or appeared under the guise of celestial visitants or guardian angels, sometimes as St. Francis of Assisi, and sometimes even as the Virgin Mary, in order to stir up his vanity, in making him believe he was a great saint, honoured by the visit of angels. When Pascal discovered this artifice, the devils tried another tack, and offered to impress upon his body the marks of the divine wounds, and made crosses of blood all over his body; but Pascal, discovering this ruse also, said to the foul fiend, "You ravening wolf, how dare you take on yourself the clothing of a lamb? Off with you!" And the fiend, terrified at these words, fled.—*Acta Sanctorum* (Bollandists), vol. iv. May 17.

A devil, which assumes the character of a ravenous young man, is cast out by St. Macarius (A.D. 304–394). One day an Egyptian woman brought to St. Macarius her son, and told him the young fellow was possessed of a ravenous devil. "He eats," she said, "every day a sack of corn made into bread,* and drinks proportionately! When I have no more food," she continued, "he seizes anything he can lay his hands on, and devours it. What, however, is very strange, whatever he eats se résout en fumée, qu'on voit sortir de son estomac." The mother, in great distress, prayed Macarius to do something for her. The saint asked what quantity of food would she consider reasonable. The woman replied,

* A sack of flour = 280 lbs., will make 360 lbs. of bread; that is, ninety quartern or 180 two-pound loaves.

"Ten pounds a day." "That is too much," rejoined Macarius; and then, turning to the young man, he commanded him to fast for seven days, and ever after to limit himself to two pounds* a day, which he was not to take from his mother, but to earn by the labour of his own hands.—*Les Petits Bollandistes* (1880), vol. i. Jan. 2. (This tale is told by Palladus as a fact.)

The devil assumes the form and takes the place of St. Leufredus. The monks of La Croix were extremely fervent, and most of them rose before matins, and passed an hour or more in private meditation. Generally St. Leufredus was the first at church, but one day affairs of the monastery detained him, and the devil took his place. As the fiend had assumed the dress and form of Leufredus, the monks saluted him. The devil took the abbot's chair with great mock modesty, and seemed very devout. All went smoothly till one of the brothers, who had just left the saint in his room, was amazed to see his double in a chair at the altar. At this moment God told St. Leufredus what had happened, and he went with all haste to the church; but before he entered he marked the doors and windows with the sign of the cross. When he entered, the devil was furious with rage, and, being unable to make his escape either by the doors or windows, ran up the bell-ropes, and escaped through the belfry.—Mgr. Guérin (chamberlain of pope Leo XIII.), *Vies des Saints* (7th edit. 1880).

Devils cast out.

1 Sam. xvi. 23. And it came to pass, when the evil spirit from God was upon Saul, that David took a harp, and played with his hand: so Saul was refreshed, and was well, and the evil spirit departed from him.

Matt. viii. 16. When even was come, they brought unto Jesus many that were possessed with devils: and He cast out the spirits with His word.

Matt. viii. 28. When Jesus was come into the country of the Gergesenes, there met Him two possessed with devils, coming out of the tombs, exceeding fierce, so that no man could pass that way. [Jesus delivered the man, but allowed the devils to enter into a herd of swine.]

Mark says of this man that he had often been bound with fetters and chains, but the chains were plucked asunder, and the fetters broken in pieces by him (ver. 4).

Matt. xvii. 14–18. There came to Jesus a certain man, kneeling down to Him, and saying, Lord, have mercy on my son: for he is lunatick, and sore vexed: for ofttimes he falleth into the fire, and oft into the water. Then Jesus rebuked the devil; and he departed out of him: and the child was cured from that very hour.

A child employed by a priest to exorcise a devil (1600). "You must be enformed of a farre greater foyle sustained by the devil at the hands of a young child, by the vertue of a holy candel holden in his hand. Heare the miraclists report in his owne gracious idiome: 'Sara [Williams] being set on a chaire, shee raged more then ere shee did before, especially at the presence of an infant holding a holy candell, crying oft with terrible voyce and countenance, *I will eate thee.* But the childe nothing abashed thereat, was brought to hold the candell to her nose, in order to put the devil to silence.'" To this Harsnet remarks, "O catholicam fidem! O fidem catholicam! that hast such a check and soveraignty over all the powers of hel, as that thy priests leade about devils after them, as men doe beares, and enduest thy young infants with such heroic magnanimitie, as that they dare play the devil, and crie aloud, 'Jack devill! Ho devill! Blow out the candell, devill!' and the devill stands like a mute on a blacke sanctus, not daring to speake a word."—Samuel Harsnet (afterwards archbishop of York), *Popish Impostures* (1604), p. 107.

A devil, through fear of the priest Dibdale, sneaks out of Trayford's ear. Samuel Harsnet, afterwards archbishop of York, says of Hilcho, the devil which possessed William Trayford, the manservant of Edmund Peckham, that when Dibdale the priest drew near, "finding his corner too hot he [the devil] would fain have come out at Trayford's mouth; but peeping out, and finding the priest's mouth somewhat too near, he suddenly drew back again, and was fain to slip out closely at his right ear." Dibdale the priest did not know this; but Sara, a maidservant in the same house, saw the attempt of the devil to come forth; saw his "bandie backe againe;" saw his going out at the man's ear, in the shape of a mouse; and discovered that the true cause why the fiend did not make his exit through the man's mouth was on account of the nearness of the priest's mouth to that of the possessed.—*A Declaration of Popish Impostures*, pp. 67, 68 (1604).

It was supposed that priests exhaled through their whole bodies the odour of sanctity; and as their bodies were the temples of the Holy Ghost, that their breath was imbued with the Divine Spirit within them.

* The allowance of a British soldier is one pound of bread and three quarters of a pound of fresh meat.

St. Euphrasia casts out a devil from a nun in the same convent (A.D. 412). The abbess of a convent in the Thebaïd, having remarked the great power which St. Euphrasia had over devils, commanded her to pray for one of the sisters who was possessed. Euphrasia, of course, obeyed, and said to the demoniac, "May the Saviour Jesus Christ who made you heal you." At the word the impure spirit came out of the sister, making terrific bellowings, and foaming horribly at her mouth.—Surius, *Lives of the Saints*, vol. ii.

St. Gall, a native of Ireland, casts out the devils of Bregentz (A.D. 646). While St. Gall was at Bregentz, he heard the mountain demon cry out to the demon of the lake, "Come to my rescue, that we may chase this stranger hence; for he has broken my idols, driven me from my temple, and is weaning the people from my service." The demon of Lake Constance made answer, "I suffer the same as you, dear mountain spirit; for this stranger has devastated my dominions also, and I can do nothing against him, for he has always the name divine in his mouth, and laughs at my snares." St. Gall cried aloud, "In the name of Jesus Christ, I adjure you to quit this neighbourhood, and do no harm to any one." Then was heard on the mountains a great roaring and groaning; it was the expression of rage made by the demons on being evicted. When St. Gall heard it, he thanked God and took courage.—*Vie des Saints de Franche-Comté*, by the professors of St. Xavier's college at Besançon.

St. Galla casts out the devil from a man who had insulted her. The devil entered into a man who insulted St. Galla while visiting the sick and needy. On her way home she observed the insolent writhing in convulsions; and, stopping before him, she said, "O God, have mercy on him, for he is made in Thy likeness. O Lord, have mercy on him, for he knew not what he said. O Jesus, Saviour of sinners, have mercy on him, for Thou didst die for him." Then made she the sign of the cross, and cried with a loud voice, "Thou unclean spirit, I command thee, in the name of the Father, Son, and Holy Ghost, come out of him, and enter no more in." On hearing these words the demoniac wallowed in the dust, the devil came out of him, and left the man peaceful and in his right mind.—*Les Petits Bollandistes*, vol. ii. p. 200.

St. Gregory the Great evicts a devil from his horse (A.D. 540-604). St. Gregory excommunicated a Roman knight for adultery, and the knight in revenge applied to magicians to encompass the pontiff with enchantment. Hearing that St. Gregory was about to take a journey, these magicians sent an evil spirit into his horse, commanding the demon to throw the pontiff, and then trample him to death. When the pontiff mounted, his horse reared and started, and behaved in such an unusual manner, that St. Gregory discovered it was possessed. So, making the sign of the cross, he drove the devil out of the horse. The magicians being struck blind, repented, abandoned their magic, and received the sacrament of baptism. St. Gregory baptized them, but declined to restore their sight, lest they should return to their diabolical arts and lose their souls.—John the deacon, *Life of St. Gregory the Great* (twelfth century). Written at the express command of pope John VIII.

St. Laumer evicts a devil by the sign of the cross (sixth century), St. Laumer, by the sign of the cross made with holy oil, delivered a man possessed with a devil, so furious that it was necessary to constrain him with chains.—*Les Petits Bollandistes*, vol. i. p. 472.

St. Marcellinus casts out a devil from a man who struck him with a whip (A.D. 374). The emperor Constantius was an Arian, and hearing that Marcellinus, bishop of Embrun, had opposed the doctrines of Arius in several councils, sent to arrest him. The myrmidons of the law came upon him unawares; and one of them, lifting his hand to strike the bishop about the face with a whip, found his arm paralyzed; and he rolled on the ground, gnashing his teeth. Marcellinus went up to the man, and the devil in him cried out, "Marcellinus, is it not enough that you have driven us from the coast of Africa, but you must come to Gaul also to trouble us?" "Silence!" cried the saint; "and come out of him, thou foul and unclean spirit." The demon durst not disobey, and the man, being restored to his right mind, lamented his crime, craved to be baptized, and bowed his heart to the yoke of Christ.—Mgr. Dépery, *Hagiographie de Gap*.

Marwood exorcised by the touch of Campion's halter (A.D. 1602). Campion, a Jesuit, was hanged at Tyburn for treason; but as queen Elizabeth was a Protestant, his death was called a martyrdom by those of his own order. It so happened that one Marwood was pronounced by Father Edmunds to be possessed, and after sundry attempts had been made to exorcise him, one of the standers-by touched his mouth with the halter. Says Harsnet, the devil "teares it with his mouth, bites it with his teeth, and spits upon it amaine." Says Edmunds, "Thou wicked fiend, tell true, what is the cause thou art so cruelly tormented with this rope, who doost not care for the potentest thinges that are in the world?" The devil in Marwood made answer, "Jerusalem knowes whose halter it is. Tiburne (the place where Father Campion receaved his crowne of martyrdome) is wel acquainted with it." On this Edmunds calls aloud to the standers-by, "Beare witnes, my maisters, of Father Campions most glorious martyrdome, whose smallest cord hath cast the devil into such an heate." To this Harsnet subjoins, "See heere three most grave and authentike witnesses of a Romish saint, viz. Jerusalem, Tyburne, and the devil."—*Popish Impostures*, pp. 84, 85.

St. Paul the Simple exorcises a demoniac (fourth century). One day a young man possessed of a devil very fierce and obstinate was brought to St. Paul the Simple. The young man uttered most horrible blasphemies, and tore every one who approached him. The saint prayed long and fervently, but in vain. Then calling to mind the words of Christ, "Howbeit this kind goeth not out but by prayer and fasting," he vowed to touch no food and drink no water till the man was made whole. "Et aussitot, comme si Dieu eût craint de déplaire à une personne qui l'aimait avec tendresse, et qui lui était si chère, le possédé fut delivré."—Roman martyrology (March 7). See also *Vies des Pères des Déserts d'Orient*.

St. Sulpice the Pious evicts the devil from the Gour de l'Yèvre (seventh century). Near Vierzon is a river, called Yèvre, at one time noted for a very dangerous gulf. In heathen times it was held sacred; but at the introduction of Christianity the "devil made his abode there, and watched day and night to spite the obnoxious race of Christians, and drag all he could into the abyss." St. Sulpice went in grand pomp to the borders of the river, threw into the gulf a little holy oil and chrism, and ever after the gulf has been perfectly safe, insomuch that fishers are wont to fish there.

We are told many wonderful tales of this "Gour de l'Yèvre." One is that it has no bottom; another, that it boils and bubbles on all the fêtes of the Virgin; another, that the fish always swim about in it so as to describe a cross. We are further told that the sound of church-bells may be distinctly heard in the water; and that one day a diver, named Perlas, saw at the bottom of the river a beautiful church full of the most costly articles; that he heard there the tinkling of a little bell, and saw the image of the holy Virgin.—Raynal, *Histoire du Berri*, vol. i. p. 267.

"Hoc quoque prætereundum non est, quod Virisionensi in territorio gurgitum quem olim pagani lustralem habuerant, quemque ob hoc in christianorum invidiam ita pessimus obsidebat dæmon, ut siquis eo transisset, suffocatum præcipitaret ac perderet. Injecto vir Dei chrismate, quod modica diluerat aqua, Elizel prophetæ usus benedictione, meabilem esse reddiditatque piscabilem."—*Nov. Bibl.*, ii. 42.

St. Victor de Plancy exorcises a thief (sixth century). One day St. Victor the hermit of Saturniac, in the diocese of Troyes, sent some labourers to sow wheat, when one of them purloined two bushels of the seed. Instantly he was possessed by a devil, who made smoke and fire issue from the mouth of the thief. St. Victor took pity on the man, and making on him the sign of the cross, the devil left him. The man, fully aware that the calamity had fallen on him because of the theft, confessed his sin with many tears, and made restitution.—St. Bernard, *Sermon on the Fête-day of St. Victor* (Feb. 26).

St. Zeno exorcises the daughter of the emperor Gallienus (third century). The daughter of the emperor Gallienus was most grievously tormented by the devil; and one day, when she was well-nigh suffocated, she cried aloud, "I can never be relieved of this torture but by Zeno." The devil added, "And I will never quit my abode here unless compelled to do so by Zeno." The emperor, touched by the sufferings of his daughter, sent for the saint, and immediately he entered the chamber, the devil cried out, "Zeno, you are come to drive me out, for here I cannot abide in the presence of thy holiness." "In the name of the Lord Jesus Christ," said the saint, "I command thee to quit the body of this young maiden." The devil came out, but said as he left the chamber, "Goodbye, Zeno; I am off to Verona, and there you will find me on your return." The emperor, in gratitude, took the royal crown from his head, and put it on Zeno's, saying, "This crown cannot be set on a worthier brow." Zeno sold the crown, that he might distribute the money to the poor, and Gallienus ceased to persecute the Church of Christ.—Peter and Jerome Ballerini, *Life of St. Zeno, Bishop of Verona* (compiled from his own writings and other monuments).

Exorcism by burning a picture of the devil. The fifth canon given by Mengus in his *Fustus* is by drawing a picture of the devil and burning it. "Exorcista projiciat imaginem pictam in ignem." This was tried on Sara Williams, and is thus reported by Harsnet: "The priest having placed Sara in a chayre, he cõmaundeth the devill to tell his name. The devill answered Bonjour, and began to make a shew of speaking French. The exorcist then reviling the devill, and calling him *asne* (in French), the devill exclaimed, 'I am no asse, and I will not be mocked.' Now, when Maho [the devil] trifled, and mocked the priest, and would by no dint of adjuration be brought to tel his name, the exorcist caused to be drawne uppon a peece of paper the picture of Vice in a play, and the same he caused to be burned with halowed brimstone. Whereat, the devill cryed out, as beeing grievously tormented."—S. Harsnet (afterwards archbishop of York), *Popish Impostures* (1604), p. 113.

Exorcism by nicknaming and blackguarding the devil (1600). Mengus wrote a book called *A Club for Exorcising Demoniacs.* The way of blackguarding the devil is his *fourth canon*, and runs thus: "If after masse has been celebrated, and the possessed has been signed with the five crosses, sprinkled with holy water, and there have been invocated over her the name of the Father, sonne, and Holy Ghost, the devill still shews himselfe refractarie, and will neither depart, nor tel his name,—then you must come upon him with as many nicknames as you can possiblie devise, and thou shalt say: 'Heare thou sencelesse, false, and lewd spirit, maister of devils, miserable creature, tempter of men, deceaver of bad angels, defrauder of souls, captaine of heretiques, father of lyes, bestial ninnie, drunkard, infernall theefe, wicked serpent, ravening wolfe, leane hunger-bitten sow, seely beast, truculent beast, cruell beast, bloody beast, beast of all beasts the most bestiall, Acherontall spirit, smoakie spirit, Tartareous spirit, and so on, I command thee to tel me thy name, and to depart hence into thyne owne place.'"—S. Harsnet (afterwards archbishop of York), *Popish Impostures* (1604), pp. 112, 113.

Mengus's *Fustus*, or Devil-mastix, is in Latin, and that the reader may know the fidelity of Harsnet's translation, the original Latin is here subscribed: "Audi igitur insensate, false, reprobe: dæmonum magister, miserrima creatura, tentator hominum, deceptor malorum angelorum, fallax animarũ, dux hæreticorũ, pater mendacij, fatue, bestialis, insipiens, ebriose, prædo infernalis, serpens iniquissime, lupe rapassime, sus macra, famelica, immundissima, bestia scabiosa, bestia truculentissima, bestia crudelis, bestia cruenta, bestia omniũ bestiarũ bestialissima, spiritus Acherontine, spiritus fuliginose, spiritus Tartaree . . ."

Devils recognizing Persons.

MARK i. 23–26. There was in the synagogue a man with an unclean spirit; and he cried out, saying, Let us alone; what have we to do with Thee, Thou Jesus of Nazareth? art Thou come to destroy us? I know Thee who thou art, the Holy One of God. And Jesus rebuked him, saying, Hold thy peace, and come out of him. And when the unclean spirit had torn him, and cried with a loud voice, he came out of him.

A devil yells out, "That which Ambrose preaches is the truth." A man possessed of a devil was a great calumniator of St. Ambrose, but God caused him to retract his calumnies, and the man yelled out amidst a crowd of people, "That which Ambrose preaches is the truth, but that which Arius preaches is false." Some Arians, hearing these words, threw the man into a pond, and he was drowned. (See ST. JULIAN RESTORES JOVIAN TO LIFE, p. 83; VINCENT FERRIER RESTORES A JEW TO LIFE, p. 86.)—Paulinus, deacon and biographer of St. Ambrose.

If it is true that the "devil is a liar, and the father of lies" (John viii. 44), his testimony against Arianism is not worth much.

St. Hilarion recognized by an evil spirit. When St. Hilarion passed from Africa to Cycile, there met him in the mountain a man possessed with an evil spirit, who cried out, "Let us alone, Hilarion; art thou come hither to torment us? We know thee who thou art, the servant of God in Cycile." Thus was made known the presence of this holy saint; and diseased persons from every part came to him to be healed of their infirmities. St. Hilarion, seeing he could not remain in that place unknown, went to Dalmatia.—St. Jerome (A.D. 390), *Vita St. Hilarionis Eremitæ.*

Devils recognize St. Marculphus in the court of king Childebert (A.D. 558). While St. Marculphus was living in his solitude.

God sent an angel to bid him go to Childebert I., king of France, and demand of him a place named Nanteuil for a monastery. Marculphus went forthwith to Paris, and reached the city while the king and queen were attending mass. He entered the chapel, and retired out of sight, but some demoniacs, being present, cried with affright, "Marculphus, thou servant of the living God, have pity on us, for thy presence is torture to us." These screams amazed the king and his court, and Childebert sent to find out to whom the devils referred. Marculphus being thus discovered, and brought before the king, told him the object of his coming, and who had sent him. Childebert readily gave what was required, and promised to assist in building the monastery; but requested Marculphus to exorcise the demoniacs. Making the sign of the cross, the saint commanded the evil spirits to come out. This they did, but left the men half-dead. However, in a few minutes they came to themselves, and arose in perfect health.—*Acta Sanctorum* (Papebroch the Bollandist), May 1.

Devils tell Half-truths.

MATT. iv. 6. When the devil quoted Psalm xci. 11, 12, to Jesus in the temptation, he omitted half verse 11. The whole verse runs thus: "He shall give His angels charge over thee, *to keep thee in all thy ways.*"

The devil tells St. Antony truths which are half falsehoods (fourth century). St. Antony said one day to his disciples, "I heard lately a great knocking at my cell door, and going to see who was there, found a man so prodigiously tall that his head reached the skies. I demanded who he was; and he made answer, 'I am Satan, and am come to ask you why all Christians speak so ill of me.' I replied, 'With good reason, Satan, because it is by you they are tempted to sin.' Satan said, 'But I ought not to be charged with the sins of man, seeing every one is a free agent and can do as he likes. It is not I who should be blamed if simpletons bite at my bait. It is man who makes war with man; it is man who wrongs his neighbour; it is man who builds cities, and dwells in them without God in the world. Only in deserts can saints and hermits be found, who sacrifice themselves to serve the Lord.' I was delighted to hear the father of lies compelled for once to speak the truth, although I knew what he said was half a lie. When, at last, I made the sign of the cross, and pronounced the name of Jesus, the phantom vanished from my sight."—*Les Petits Bollandistes* (1880), vol. i. p. 427.

In order to see this fallacy, take a very simple case. A child, no doubt, is free to do what is told him, or to abstain from doing it; but if a stronger mind and older person tempts the child to do wrong, the tempter deserves the greater blame. The tempter practises on the child's ignorance, inexperience, and weakness; sometimes on his fears, his natural passions, and his hopes; but who would exonerate the tempter, because the child is, in a sense, a free agent, and does what it is told, and even likes to do it?

The devil tells St. Maur "a lie which is half a lie" (512–584). When, in his old age, St. Maur retired from the active duties of Glanfeuil, one night the devil came to him and said, "You have been a long time toiling to drive me and my fellows out of this country, but don't suppose you have trampled us in the dust. You will yet live to see your work come to naught. I tell you, of all these monks which you have gathered together, scarcely one will escape from our hands." So saying, he left the man of God to meditate on what he had been told. St. Maur was greatly distressed, and prayed earnestly that God would avert so intense an evil. Whereupon, an angel came and said, "Fear not. Why art thou so cast down? Trust in God. The devil has spoken a truth which is half a truth, and a lie which is half a lie. The truth is that a plague shall desolate thy house; but thy brethren shall be gathered into the bosom of Abraham, and dwell for ever in paradise." St. Maur felt comforted, and warned his brethen of the impending evil. In due time the plague came, when one hundred and sixteen of the monks fell victims to the scourge, and not long after St. Maur also was gathered to his fathers, at the age of seventy-two.—Faustus (a companion of St. Maur), *Life of St. Maur.*

Devils tormented before their Time.

MATT. xxviii. 28, 29. When Jesus came to the country of the Gergesenes, there met him two possessed with devils, who cried out, saying, Jesus, Thou Son of God, art Thou come hither to torment us before the time?

A devil speaks to St. Victor of Plancy before he was born (sixth century). While St. Victor was still in his mother's womb, a devil publicly cried out to him, "Victor, thou holy one of God, why do you torment us even before you are born?"—Le sieur des Guerrois, *Histoire Ecclésiastique.*

Diana of Ephesus (the image which fell from Jupiter).

ACTS xix. 35. When the town-clerk had appeased the people, he said, Ye men of Ephesus, what man is there that knoweth not how that the city of the Ephesians is a worshipper of the great goddess Diana, and of the image which fell down from Jupiter?

Many cities have boasted of statues of gods sent directly from heaven. The *Palladium* of Troy was an image of Pallas Minerva said to have fallen from heaven. Numa's *Ancilia* (or sacred shields) descended from heaven. Herodian tells us that the Phenician statue of the sun was a large stone, circular below, and conical. It was quite black, and was said to have fallen from heaven. Without doubt it was a meteorite, like the Diana of Ephesus. The ancient Mexicans worshipped a similar meteorite.

An image of the Virgin in Avignonet sent down from heaven (A.D. 1283). In consequence of disputes between the "orthodox" party and the inhabitants of Avignonet, where the "heretics," called Albigenses, abounded, the parish, after most horrible slaughter, was laid under an interdict, and the church shut up for forty years. Alexander IV. removed the interdict, and the same day the church doors opened of their own accord, and the bells rang all day and night spontaneously. These "facts" are stated in a bull of Paul III., dated Rome, 1537, and still shown to any visitors who wish to see it. The unpardonable sin of the Albigenses was their denial that the Virgin Mary was the mother of God; so, when the interdict was removed from Avignonet, there was an especial significance in the following "miracle." The inhabitants rose one morning and discovered that an image from heaven of the Virgin Mary had been set up in the church porch. "Quel artiste avait conçu et exécuté cette belle œuvre? Quelle main l'avait déposée là? On était passé cent fois par jour, et pendant de longues années, sur la place occupée par la merveilleuse image. Cette apparition fut, comme un avertissement du ciel. Il était évident que Marie voulait être honorée là où l'on avait vomi contre elle les plus abominables blasphèmes, et rehausser par un miracle le mérite des défenseurs de son culte, et de sa divine maternité." The inhabitants of Avignonet were at once convinced that this image came from heaven, and demanded that a day should be consecrated as an annual memorial of the gift. The demand was approved of by the pope, and confirmed "par plusieurs souverains pontifes, enrichie d' indulgences." The day is called "La solennité de Notre Dame des Miracles," and is held the first Tuesday of every new year. — Mgr. Guérin (chamberlain of pope Leo XIII.), *Vies des Saints*, vol. vi. p. 298.

If the chamberlain of pope Leo XIII. and several popes maintain that this sculptured image fell or was brought from heaven, can we be surprised that the Ephesians worshipped a meteoric stone as a goddess, which they dubbed Diana?

Dido and the Bull's Hide.

When Dido came to Africa she bought of the natives "as much land as could be encompassed with a bull's hide." The agreement being made, Dido cut the hide into thongs, so as to enclose sufficient space for a citadel, which she called "Byrsa," the hide.

> Mercatique solum facti de nomine Byrsam,
> Taurino quantum possent circumdare tergo.
> Virgil, *Æneid*, i. lines 367, 368.

The Yakutsks. The Yakutsks granted the Russian explorers as much land as they could encompass with a cow's hide; but the Russians, cutting the hide into thin strips, covered with it land enough for the town and fort which they called Yakutsk.

(Our term "hide of land" has no connection whatever with the tales about Byrsa and Yakutsk. In Saxon English *hydan* (to hide or conceal) gives *hydels* (a den), *hyddern* (a hiding-place), and a *hýd* is the covering which hides the animal. A hýd or hide seems to have been used for a manor-house as well as a den; and a hide of land means as much land as would suffice to maintain the *hide* or *manor-house*. The exact quantity was determined by local usage; in some cases it was sixty acres, in some eighty, and in others as much as a hundred acres went to the hide. When a person was created a knight, his overlord gave him ten hides of land to cover the expenses of military service. In later times persons possessing ten or more hides of land were compelled to be knights.)

Pepin d'Heristal gives Rigobert as much land as he could walk over in a given time (A.D. 650-743). Pepin d'Heristal, one day hunting, came to the cell of St. Rigobert, who received him courteously, and set before him the best repast his cell afforded. Pepin was so pleased with the hermit, that he offered to give him whatever he asked for. Rigobert asked Pepin to bestow on him as much land as he could walk over while his highness took his midday nap. The request was granted, and the footprints of the saint remained in the land unobliterated. The grass which grew on this plot of land never withered. The frost of winter pinched it not, the heat of summer parched it not, and no lightning ever seared it.—Bollandus, *Acta Sanctorum*, vol. i. Jan. 4.

Diseases of All Sorts cured.

MATT. iv. 23. Jesus went about Galilee . . . healing all manner of sickness and all manner of disease among the people.

St. Clare, abbot of St. Ferréol, cures divers diseases (seventh century). (1) The superior of Santa Blandina being, as was supposed, at the point of death, St. Clare entered the sick-room, touched the hand of the dying man, and in the presence of the whole house he sat up, restored to perfect health.

(2) At another time St. Clare cured the colic, from which one of the brothers was suffering, merely by signing the sufferer with holy oil.

(3) Once when the river Rhone was full to overflowing, one of the monks of St. Ferréol fell into the river, and was in imminent danger of being carried away by its current, which is exceedingly rapid. St. Clare made the sign of the cross, and the river lifted the man upon the bank, and he returned to the abbey wholly without injury. — *Les Petits Bollandistes*, vol. i. p. 31.

(See PRAYER, "Isidore buoyed up by the water of a well;" and WATER OBEDIENT.)

St. Clara heals all manner of diseases by the sign of the cross (A.D. 1193-1253). St. Francis d'Assisi once sent to St. Clara a sick man to heal. She made on him the sign of the cross, and he recovered forthwith. This happened not to this man only, but to many. In fact, all who had infirmities resorted to the convent of St. Clara, and she healed them with the sign of the cross.—*Life of St. Clara* (written by the express order of pope Alexander V.).

St. Lawrence, by laying his hand on her forehead, cures Cyriaca of headache. St. Lawrence lodged for a time on Mount Celius with a widow named Cyriaca, who entertained all Christians that wanted refuge. Cyriaca had a violent chronic headache, which greatly distressed her; but St. Lawrence, laying his hands on her forehead, and calling on the name of Jesus, completely cured her, and the pain never more returned.—*From the Public Registers.* (This saint is in the canon of the mass.)

St. Marculphus cures the son of Genais, who had been bitten by a wolf (A.D. 558). A seigneur, named Genais, came to Nanteuil with his son, who had been frightfully bitten by a wolf. His whole body was lacerated, and his death expected every minute. St. Marculphus, touched with pity, perfectly healed all the wounds simply by the sign of the cross.—*Acta Sanctorum* (Papebroch the Bollandist), May 1.

St. Marculphus is very celebrated in France, because by him was accorded to the kings of France "the gift of healing scrofula;" hence called "the king's evil." (See Benedict XIV. *On the Canonization of Saints*, bk. iv. ch. iii. No. 21.) We are told that Henri IV. cured fifteen hundred in the year 1609; Louis XIV. cured two thousand in the garden of St. Remi's abbey in 1654; Charles X., as late as 1825, "touched" many. Edward the Confessor left the same "gi.t" to his successors in England, and Dr. Samuel Johnson, in 1712, was "touched" by queen Anne when he was only thirty months old. The Scottish kings also "touched;" and Shakespeare, in his *Macbeth*, makes Malcolm say he had often seen the good king do this "miraculous work" on "strangely visited people, all swoln and ulcerous," and adds—

> "'Tis spoken,
> To the succeeding royalty he leaves
> The healing benediction."

Carte, the historian, tells us of a young man named Lovel who was cured by the Pretender, which would be quite fatal to the theory that the virtue is communicated to kings with the anointing oil at their coronation.

St. Placidus, by laying his hand on Zoffa's head, cures his headache. Zoffa, chief secretary of the Church at Capua, was a martyr to headache, and entreated St. Placidus, then only twenty-five years old, to lay his hand on him and cure him. Placidus, out of diffidence, wished Zoffa to apply to St. Benedict, alleging that he was himself too young to work miracles. The bishop Germanus, who was present at the time, bade the young man do what was asked; accordingly, he laid his hand on Zoffa's forehead, and prayed that God would vouchsafe to restore His servant to health and ease. Immediately the headache went away, and never again returned.—Laurentius Surius (1570), *Lives of the Saints.*

St. Sebastian cures gout by baptism. Tranquillinus was bowed together with gout, which had drawn one side of his body quite awry. When, however, St. Sebastian baptized him, he was instantly made whole. He came to the saint halting painfully on crutches, but quitted his presence leaping joyfully and needing no support.

Another example. When Cromatius, governor of Rome, who suffered from the some infirmity, saw the cure wrought on Tranquillinus, he also went to St. Sebastian, and promised to become a Christian, if the saint would release him from the gout to which he had been a martyr for many years. While he was still speaking, an angel came, and said, "Cromatius, Jesus Christ hath sent me to thee, that all thy limbs may be restored to thee whole and sound." In a moment the governor, who before could scarcely put his feet to the ground, leaped up in perfect health. Then, falling at the feet of St. Sebastian, he entreated that both he and his son Tiburtius might be baptized. That very day, not only the governor and his son, but all his house, including slaves, to the number of fourteen hundred souls, were added to the Church. After his baptism the governor gave liberty to all his slaves, and half his goods he distributed to the poor.—Edward Kinesman (1623), *Lives of the Saints*.

Doves. (See SOUL.)

MATT. iii. 16. Jesus, when He was baptized, went up straightway out of the water: and lo, the heavens were opened unto Him, and the Spirit of God descended like a dove, and lighted on Him.

A dove brings Albert d'Ogna the Viaticum (A.D. 1279). When Albert d'Ogna was at the point of death, as the monk delayed to bring him the Viaticum, a dove flew to him, holding it in its beak.—*Acta Sanctorum* (Bollandists), May 13.

A dove brings a veil to St. Aldegundis when she becomes a nun (630–689). St. Aldegundis, daughter of prince Walbert of Hainaut, made a vow to be the spotless bride of Christ, and when prince Eudo pressed his suit of marriage, she fled to the monastery of Hautmont and told her tale. The reverend fathers highly commended her, and advised her at once to take the veil of virginity, which she readily consented to do. So they proceeded to the ceremony forthwith; but when they were about to present the veil, they found they had none at hand, for the veil with other vestments had been left on the altar of St. Vaast. It was a fatal mishap, and would have obliged them to defer the service; but, in the very midst of their perplexity, they saw a dove bringing a veil in its beak. Carrying it to St. Aldegundis, the dove dropped it over her head. Nothing could be better. Every one was ravished at the spectacle, and all agreed that St. Aldegundis had sacrificed herself to perpetual virginity with the palpable approval of God.—L'abbé Delbos, *Life of St. Aldegundis*.

The Holy Ghost, like a dove, descends on St. Ambrose of Siena (A.D. 1220–1286). The Holy Ghost, in the form of a dove, was often seen to descend on the head of St. Ambrose of Siena, in Tuscany, while he was preaching. This gave his words such power, that not only were hardened sinners pricked to the heart, and the most obstinate softened, but even the wise ones whose wisdom was not seasoned with grace learned humility, and felt that, after all, the love of God is the beginning of true wisdom.—Le R. P. Jean Baptiste Fouillet, *Année Dominicaine*, vol. iii. March 26.

The Holy Ghost, like a dove, descends at birth on the head of St. Austrebertha (630–704). St. Austrebertha was the daughter of prayer, and her name was given her by the angel who announced to her parents that God had heard their prayer, and would give them a child "who would be the mother of many." At the moment of her birth the chamber was filled with a heavenly odour, and a white dove which hovered awhile above the house flew into the chamber, and settled on the head of the infant.

As Austrebertha grew to years of discretion, one day a veil fell from heaven on her head while she was looking in a fountain in her father's garden. She knew this was a call from God for her to take the veil, and dedicate herself to His service.—Surius, *Lives of the Saints*, vol. i.

A beam of fire and a dove appear when St. Basil is baptized. When St. Basil came to the river, he stripped, and went down straightway into the water, where Maximus, bishop of Jerusalem, baptized him. And there descended on him a beam of light from which flew a dove. The dove touched the water with its wings, and then flying upwards straight into the clouds, was lost to sight. This was seen by all those who were present at the time.—Edward Kinesman (1623), *Lives of the Saints*, p. 374.

The Holy Ghost, in the form of a dove, descends on St. Braulio (died 646). The Holy Ghost, wishing to sanction the doctrines propagated by St. Braulio, bishop of Saragossa, descended on his shoulder in the visible form of a dove, and seemed before all the people to whisper in his ears the words he uttered, according to that promise, "It shall be given you in that same hour what you ought to say."—St. Ildefonsa, *Book of Illustrious Men*.

A dove rests on the head of St. Briocus (sixth century). While Briocus of Cardigan was receiving the communion for the first time, a dove white as snow settled on his head, and the abbot knew that the young boy was a chosen vessel of honour.—Dom Lobineau, *Lives of the British Saints*.

The Spirit of God sits, as a white dove, on the head of St. Catherine. As St. Catherine of Siena refused to wear fine clothes, and deck herself bravely according to her station in society, her mother relegated her to the kitchen. One day her father, having occasion to go into the kitchen, saw his daughter at prayer, and on her head sat brooding a dove whiter than snow. Immediately he entered the dove flew away, and he asked Catherine what dove it was he saw sitting on her head. "I know of no dove," she replied. So the father knew it was the Holy Ghost.—Laurentius Surius (1570), *Lives of the Saints.*

Catherine of Racconigi receives celestial wine from a dove (A.D. 1486-1547). Catherine of Racconigi was the daughter of poor parents, but from infancy showed great veneration for the Virgin Mary. When she was only five years old, a dove, white as snow, flew into her chamber, and lighted on her shoulder. Thinking it might be the devil, she made the sign of the cross, and cried out, "Jesus, Jesus!" Then a ray of light came from the dove's beak and entered her mouth, and she heard these words: "Take, my little daughter, and drink this wine; by virtue of which you will never thirst again, but will feel thy hunger and thirst for the love of God grow daily stronger in thy soul." When she had tasted the wine, she found it of heavenly sweetness, and forthwith there appeared to her a lady clad in a white robe and black mantle. "Let the name of my Son be always in thy heart, my child," said the lady. "Who are you?" asked Catherine; "and how came you here, seeing the door is shut?" "I am the mother of Jesus," she replied, "and I wish you to give yourself wholly to my Son." "Where is your Son?" inquired the child. "You shall see Him soon," said the lady; "but as delicate plants die from cold, so love in the heart dies without grace. Give thyself to my Son, and His grace shall abide with you for ever." "Poor as I am, what have I to give?" asked the child. "Thy heart, my daughter; give Him thy heart," said the lady, and vanished out of sight.—*Les Petits Bollandistes*, vol. x. p. 508.

A dove brings a phial of holy oil for the baptism of king Clovis. When Clovis was baptized, the church and all its approaches were so densely crowded it was impossible to move about; but when the king approached the font, it was discovered that the holy oil had been forgotten. It would have been most unseemly to have detained the king while one of the priests wormed his way through the crowd to the vestry and back again, so St. Remi besought the Lord to pardon the neglect, and to send help in this time of need, lest His holy servants became a byword, and His sacrament a jest of the scornful. While still he prayed, lo! a dove entered the church through an open window, carrying in its bill a phial of holy oil, which it placed in the hands of the officiating prelate, and then flew away. St. Remi gave hearty thanks to Almighty God for His timesome gift, and anointed the king with oil from paradise. When the phial was opened, and the body of the king was anointed, the perfume which filled the church was ravishing, and none could doubt that St. Remi's God was indeed the God of gods and King of kings.—Hincmar, archbishop of Reims (died 882), *Life of St. Remi.*

A dove lights on the head of St. Dunstan (A.D. 925-988). St. Dunstan poured out all the vials of his wrath on forgers and false moneyers, because the injury they did was immeasurable. One day, even on the feast of Pentecost, he made one of these forgers a public example; and "God showed, by a miracle, that He approved thereof;" for while Dunstan was saying mass, a dove lighted on his head, remained there till the sacrament was over, and then flew to the tomb of the late archbishop Odo.—Osbert of Canterbury, *Life of St. Dunstan.*

A dove lighting on the head of St. Fabian, he was chosen bishop (A.D. 236-250). Fabian, a Roman soldier, happened to enter the church at Rome the very moment the synod was met together for the election of a pope to succeed Anteros. No candidate had at present been nominated, and the electors were in doubt whom to choose. Suddenly a dove flew down through the louvre of the catacomb, and, fluttering about for a few moments, lighted on the head of Fabian. It was a repetition of the descent of the Holy Ghost on the head of Jesus at the river Jordan, and all the assembly cried at once, "He is worthy! he is worthy! he is the elect of God!" and he was accordingly led up to the episcopal chair, and seated thereon. A souvenir of this incident is preserved in the catacombs; and Bosio found at Aringhi a bas-relief in which the papal chair was surmounted with a dove. Fabian was the first layman ever elected pope, and his life certainly justified the choice, for no man more "worthy" ever ruled the church. (See St. Severus, p. 110.)—Eusebius, St. Jerome, Paul

Orosius, and Chrysostom in his *Annals of Alexandria*, all mention this incident.

"He is worthy!" were the words used at the election of bishops, in much the same way as "God save the king!" is shouted in regal elections.

St. Georgia of Clermont, in Auvergne, was honoured at death by a large flight of pigeons (sixth century). The one desire of St. Georgia's life was to mortify her body, "pour en faire un reliquaire de la virginité." When her body, "plus pur qu'un beau lis," was carried to the grave, a great flight of pigeons, "whiter than cygnets," followed the funeral procession and settled on a roof till the funeral service was over, when they flew upwards straight into heaven, and were lost to sight. "C'était, sans doute, une legion d'anges descendus du ciel pour honorer les obséques de cette épouse de Jésus Christ qui avait vécu dans une pureté semblable à la leur."—Jacques Branche, *Saincts d'Auvergne*.

This is a suggestive example of an inference drawn according to a preconceived notion, and may help to explain some of the phenomena called miracles in the lives of the saints. Whether these pigeons were angels or not rests solely on the *sans doute* of Messire Branche.

A dove was seen whispering to St. Gregory the Great his inspired writings (A.D. 540–604). Sabinian, the successor of St. Gregory, said that the great pontiff had wasted shamefully the finances of the see, and left an empty exchequer behind. This charge so irritated the people, that they collected together the writings of the saint to burn them. Many were thrown into the bonfire, but his *Dialogues*, and some other of his writings, were saved by Peter the deacon, who declared he saw a dove whisper in the ear of St. Gregory the words of his inspired writings, and that to burn his books would be to burn the inspired words of God. These words completely changed the mind of the people; and the pontiff who a little before was regarded as a prodigal, was now esteemed an inspired saint. In allusion to this story, painters in Christian art represent a white dove near the ear of St. Gregory the Great, to signify that the Holy Spirit inspired his writings.—John the deacon, *Life of St. Gregory the Great*. (Written in the twelfth century by order of pope John VIII.)

Peter the deacon is the person introduced in the four books of Dialogues as the interlocutor of St. Gregory. The other writings of St. Gregory extant are (1) his *Pastoral*, in four parts; (2) his *Sacramentary*, a missal and ritual of the Church of Rome; (3) *Homilies on Job*; (4) *Letters*; (5) an *Exposition of the Book of Canticles*; and (6) *Fugitive Pieces*. All his works are collected by Mons Migne in his *Patrologia*.

A dove sits on the head of St. Hilary to indicate that God had chosen him for the archbishopric of Arles (A.D. 401–449). St. Hilary attended the death-bed of St. Honorat, archbishop of Arles, and fearing lest he should be chosen his successor, fled and hid himself in a desert. Castus, the governor of the city, tracked him, and sent a troop of his militia to bring him back. When placed before the convocation he protested against being elected, but a dove, whiter than snow, descended and sat on his head. All the assembly considered this a direct indication of God's choice, and Hilary could no longer resist. He was only twenty-nine years old at the time, but his extreme youth only rendered his great virtues the more conspicuous.—Honorat (bishop of Marseille), *De Viris Illustribus*, ch. ix.

The soul of Julia, in the semblance of a dove, leaves her body (fifth century). St. Julia was crucified by Felix, governor of Corsica; and as she died, her soul, under the figure of a dove, ascended to heaven. In Christian art she is represented with a dove coming out of her mouth.—Dom Ruinart, *Acts of St. Julia*.

When Erasmus died (A.D. 301), his spirit flew from his body in the form of a dove of brilliant whiteness.—*Acta Sanctorum* (Bollandists), June 2.

When St. Medard died, two doves came from heaven (A.D. 545). When St. Medard died, just before he was placed in his tomb, two doves descended from heaven, and a third, whiter than snow, came out of the saint's mouth. The two doves were angels, and the third dove was the soul which they had come to accompany to heaven.—*Acta Sanctorum* (Bollandists), vol. ii. June 8.

There is something very noteworthy in this extract. St. Medard had been dead some days. He died at Noyon, and had been carried on men's shoulders to Soissons; so that the soul must have remained all this time in the dead body. It is quite certain, therefore, that life and soul are as independent as soul and body are. It is also certain that the soul does not always leave the body at the moment of death. Of course, I mean these inferences must follow from this story.

The Holy Spirit, in the likeness of a dove, descends on St. Maurilius (A.D. 426). While St. Martin was consecrating Maurilius bishop of Angers, a dove whiter than snow lighted on his head, and remained there till the service was over. St. Martin declared, to his personal knowledge, that not only did he see the Holy Ghost descend, as a dove, on the head of the new bishop, but he beheld a whole company of angels present at the ceremony.—*Acta Sanctorum* (Bollandists), Sept. 13.

Doves sent to point out a site for a new monastery, projected by Peter the hermit (A.D. 1098). Peter the hermit was promised, by the lords of the Apennines, the means of building a monastery. He laid the foundation, and raised the walls some six feet from the ground, when the Virgin, displeased that he had not first consulted her, overthrew the whole in one night. The hermit was stupefied, and instituted a religious procession to appease God and the saints. When the procession reached Vallombrosa, a flock of doves picked up some grains of wheat, and dropped them on the ground in advance of the procession, so as to form the words AVE, MARIA. St. Peter, concluding that this was the spot which the Virgin Mary had selected, built his monastery there.—*Acta Sanctorum*, vol. ii. April 12, pp. 101, 102.

A beam of light from heaven rested on the head of St. Remi when he was chosen bishop of Reims. When the people of Reims wished to make St. Remi their bishop he refused the office, because he was only twenty-two years old; but the people persisted in their choice. While the variance still continued, a great beam of light burst from heaven, and rested on St. Remi's head, a holy dew bathed him with divine baptism, and an odour sweeter than any earthly fragrance filled the place of the assembly. The people could no longer doubt that God Himself had confirmed their choice, and even St. Remi durst no longer resist, lest haply he should seem to be fighting against God.—Hincmar (died 882), *Life of St. Remi.*

When St. Samson was elected bishop, a dove rested on his head (A.D. 565). When St. Samson was elected bishop of the ancient see of Dol, near St. Malo, immediately he was seated on the throne, a white dove, "luminous and visible to all the congregation," settled on his head, and remained there till the close of the service, unscared even by the noise and movement of the crowd.—Dom Lobineau, *Lives of the Saints of Brittany.*

St. Severus of Ravenna and the dove (A.D. 389). On the death of Apollinarius, the Christian community of Ravenna fasted three days, and then assembled in the church to select a successor. A dove, whiter than snow, perched on the head of Severus, and the assembly said at once that Severus was the elect of God. A few, however, shocked at his rags and tatters, drove him out of the church. The same prodigy occurred the next day, and again the day following. Resistance was no longer possible, and Severus was consecrated to the high and holy office. (See A DOVE LIGHTING ON ST. FABIAN, p. 108.)—*Les Petits Bollandistes* (1880), vol. ii. p. 205.

A dove lights on the head of St. Yves (A.D. 1253–1303). On one occasion, when St. Yves was saying mass, a dove, all shining, lighted on his head, then flew to the high altar, and almost immediately disappeared.

Another example. Another day, as he was dining with a large number of the poor, a dove entered the room, fluttered round him, and then lighted on his head; nor would it fly away till St. Yves had given it his blessing.—Dom Lobineau, *Lives of the Saints of Great Britain.*

Mahomet's dove. A dove was taught by Mahomet to pick seed placed in his ear. The bird would perch upon the prophet's shoulder, and thrust its beak into his ear to find the seed; but Mahomet gave out that it was the Holy Ghost, in the form of a dove, come to impart to him the counsels of God.—Dr. Prideaux (1697), *Life of Mahomet* (see also Raleigh's *History of the World*, bk. i. chap. i. 6).

St. Peter Celestine, pope (1221–1296), had also a dove that pecked his ear, and was supposed to be whispering to him the inspirations of heaven. In Christian art he is often drawn with a dove whispering in his ear.—Mgr Guérin, *Vies des Saints*, vol. vi. p. 26.

Dragons subjected or subdued.

MARK xvi. 17, 18. These signs shall follow them that believe . . . they shall take up serpents.

LUKE x. 19. Behold, I give you power to tread on serpents and scorpions.

PSALM xci. 13. Thou shalt tread upon the lion and adder: the young lion and the dragon shalt thou trample under feet. Because he hath set his love upon Me, therefore will I deliver him.

ACTS xxviii. 1–8. When Paul was shipwrecked, and cast on the island of Melita, the people showed him and his companions no little kindness. As it was wet and cold, Paul assisted in gathering sticks for a fire, when a viper, warmed by the heat, fastened on his hand. The barbarians instantly said among themselves, No doubt this man is a murderer, whom, though he hath escaped the sea, yet vengeance suffereth not to live. Paul shook the viper into the fire, and when the people saw he suffered no harm from the venomous beast, they changed their minds concerning him, and said, He is a god.

REV. xii. 7, 8. And there was war in heaven: Michael and his angels fought against the dragon; and the dragon and his angels fought, but prevailed not.

ISA. xi 8, 9. The sucking child shall play on the hole of the asp, and the weaned child shall put his hand on the cockatrice' den.

ISA. xiii. 21, 22. Wild beasts of the desert shall be there; and their houses shall be full of doleful creatures [*ochim*]; and . . . satyrs shall dance there; and the wild beasts of the islands shall cry in their desolate houses, and dragons in their pleasant places.

Bel and the dragon. There was a great dragon which they of Babylon worshipped; and king Cyrus said to Daniel, "Wilt thou say that this is of brass? Lo! he liveth, he eateth, and drinketh. Thou canst not say that this dragon is no god, therefore worship him." Then said Daniel to the king, "I will worship the Lord my God, for He is the living God. But give me leave, O king, and I will slay this dragon without either sword or staff." The king said, "I give thee leave." Then Daniel took pitch, and fat, and hair, and did seethe them together, and made lumps thereof. This he put into the dragon's mouth, and so the dragon burst asunder. And Daniel said, "Lo! these be the gods you worship."—*Apocrypha: Bel and the Dragon,* 23–27.

A hippocentaur and satyr are seen by St. Antony the hermit (A.D. 342). St. Jerome gives the following, not as a poetical fancy, but a sober historical fact. Antony, thinking he was the only hermit in the world, was told in a vision that he was neither the only nor yet the oldest anchorite, for one was living older and better than he, whom it was his bounden duty to hunt up. He was ninety years old at the time, and knew neither the name nor the whereabouts of this hermit; but at break of day he took his staff, and began his journey, fully believing that God who sent the vision would also guide him in the right path. Scarcely had he started when he saw a hippocentaur (half a man and half a horse), and crossing himself he cried aloud, "Ho, there! where dwells this man of God that I am to find out?" The monster muttered, "How should I know anything of the barbarian?" yet he pointed out the road, and flew on as if he had wings. St. Jerome naïvely adds, no doubt it was the devil who assumed this guise to frighten the saint.

St. Antony was astonished but not alarmed, and walked on till he met a satyr, a creature partly human, but not wholly so. He was very diminutive in size, but strong; his nose was hooked, and horns grew out of his forehead, as in a goat. Antony was amazed, but the creature tried to win his confidence by offering him dates. Antony fell into conversation with his strange companion; and the creature told Antony he was what men call a satyr, and was sent by his fellows to meet Antony, to entreat his prayers, and learn from him something about the Saviour of the world. After a little further discourse the satyr set off running, and fled out of sight swifter than a stag.

So passed the first day of his journey. The second dawned, but still he knew not whither he was to go. On, still on he trudged, wearily, heavily, till nightfall, when he fell to the earth in prayer, and continued so till break of day. He now saw a she-wolf, panting with thirst, creeping down the slope of a high mountain. He followed the creature with his eye, and saw it enter a cavern in the side of the mountain. Thither went Antony; and, coming to the place, found a deep cavern, dark and intricate. Wholly without fear he entered; and, having penetrated about half-way, saw a distant light. To make a long story short, here dwelt the hermit he was in search of; he was called Paul the Eremite. They met, saluted, and conversed. Next day Paul prayed his brother hermit to go and fetch St. Athanasius's cloak to wrap round him, and while he was gone on this errand, Paul died.

The life of St. Paul, the first hermit, by St. Jerome, has never been doubted, and is certainly authentic.

St. Bernard of Menthon subdues the dragon of the Alps (A.D. 923–1008). Richard de la Val d'Isère, the successor of St. Bernard of Menthon, often called the "Great," says he was himself eye-witness of the following miracle. St. Bernard left at the bottom of the Alps the bishop, clergy, and procession, which had followed him thither; and with nine pilgrims ascended the mountain, where was the brigand Procus, called the "Giant," and worshipped as a god. St. Bernard and his companions came up to the giant, and saw hard by a huge dragon ready to devour them. Bernard made the sign of the cross, and then threw his stole over the monster's neck. The stole instantly changed itself into an iron chain, except the two ends held in the saint's hands. "C'est ainsi qu'un zèle accompagné de la prière et de la confiance en Dieu désarme l'enfer." The nine pilgrims killed the dragon, and the two ends of the stole are preserved in the treasury of the abbey of St. Maurice-en-Valais. It is from this event that St. Bernard, in Christian art, is represented holding in hand a chained devil. The body of this monster was buried in a cave near the monastery, and not long since a stone was disinterred bearing this inscription: "CI-GIT UN MAGICIEN, APPELÉ PROCUS, MINISTRE DU DÉMON."

St. Caluppa of Auvergne puts to flight two dragons (A.D. 576). St. Caluppa constructed for himself an oratory in Auvergne, where one day two enormous dragons encountered him. The larger of the two lifted up its head with open mouth against the face of the saint, as if it was going to say something, but Caluppa, horror-struck, was unable to move hand or foot, and stood stupefied. So the two remained for several minutes; at length the saint recovered himself sufficiently to make the sign of the cross, on his face, and, speech returning, he said to the dragon, "Are not you the serpent who appeared to Eve in the garden of Eden? Avaunt! the cross of Jesus Christ is your destruction." Then the dragon slunk away, and hid itself in the earth. In the mean time the other and smaller beast rolled itself round the legs of the saint, but Caluppa, taking courage by his victory, said, "Off, Satan! Touch me not; I am the servant of Jesus Christ." At these words this dragon also rolled away, and never afterwards was the saint annoyed by dragon or serpent.—St. Gregory of Tours, *History*, bk. v. ch. 9.

St. Domitian delivers Huy from a formidable dragon (A.D. 560). St. Domitian was bishop of Maestricht, and is noted for having delivered the inhabitants of Huy from a formidable dragon, which caused most frightful ravages. In Christian art, St. Domitian is represented with a dragon at his feet; and a yearly procession is still made to the fountain where the dragon was slain.

This looks extremely like an allegory. Domitian killed the dragon of idolatry, by baptizing the people in the fountain.

St. Eutychus extirpates the serpents of Castoria (A.D. 540). The neighbourhood of Castoria was greatly infested with serpents; but Eutychus prayed that God would extirpate them, and they were all destroyed by lightning. "They are well dead," said St. Florent, "but who shall remove them out of our sight?" "I will send a cloud of birds to devour them," said the Lord. And it was so.—Gregory the Great, *Dialogues*, bk. iii. ch. 15.

St. Fronton commands a dragon to die (A.D. 74). St. Fronton of Lycaonia, quitting Beauvaisis, came to Soissons, and here he was informed of a hideous dragon which committed great havoc, and spread terror through all the neighbourhood. The Christians of Soissons implored him to kill the monster, so he proceeded at once to Nogeliac, the dragon's haunt. As St. Fronton approached, the dragon retreated, evidently afraid. On went the saint fearlessly; the dragon stopped, raised its head, uttered an indescribable but frightful hissing noise, and its whole attitude spoke mischief. "In the name of Jesus Christ," said St. Fronton, "I command you to die." The words fell like a thunderbolt, and the monster died on the spot. The people of the country, amazed at the "miracle," demanded to be baptized, and numbers were added daily to the Church.—Pergot, *Life of St. Front* (or Fronton).

This is manifestly an allegory. The dragon dies at the words (or preaching) of St. Fronton, and when the dragon is dead, the people are baptized. No further hint is required.

St. George of Lydda kills a dragon (A.D. 280-303). St. George, the patron saint of England, is not George of Cappadocia, the Arian bishop of Alexandria, as Gibbon says, but St. George of Lydda, the son of wealthy parents, his father being in the imperial service. At the age of seventeen St. George entered the army of Diocletian, and was raised to the rank of military chiliarch or tribune of the imperial guards; but when Diocletian began his persecutions against the Christians, St. George sold all his goods to give in alms to the poor, liberated his slaves, and boldly rebuked the emperor for his cruelty. This drew upon him the anger of the emperor, and he was beheaded, April 23, A.D. 303. St. George is the patron saint of soldiers, and is honoured in the Greek Church as a "Great Martyr." He was the first patron saint of Genoa. In the crusades, he was a great favourite with our own kings; in 1322, it was determined by the National Council, held at Oxford, to keep April 23 in his honour; and in 1330, when Edward III. instituted the Order of the Garter, St. George was selected as its patron and protector. Jean Darche, in her *History of St. George*, published in 1866, has devoted above a hundred pages to the Story of the Dragon, and considered it an historical fact.

The tale of the dragon given in Percy's *Reliques*, III. iii. 2, is not told of St. George of Lydda, the patron saint of England, but of St. George of Coventry, called the son of lord Albert. This St. George was stolen in infancy by the "weird lady of the woods," who brought him up to deeds of arms. His body had three marks, viz. a dragon on the breast, a garter round one of the legs, and a blood-red cross on the right arm. When St. George of Coventry grew to manhood, he fought against the Saracens. In Libya he heard of a huge dragon to which a damsel was daily given for food; and it so happened that when he arrived, the victim was Sabra, the king's daughter. She was already tied to the stake when St. George came up. On came the dragon; but the knight, thrusting his lance into the monster's mouth, killed it on the spot. Sabra, being brought to England, became the wife of her deliverer, and they lived happily in Coventry till death.

This tale is comparatively modern; certainly not earlier than the second half of the fourteenth century. George of Lydda died in A.D. 303, and was at death under twenty-three years of age.

Many, like Gibbon, insist that our patron saint is George of Cappadocia, who died A.D. 361, and certainly was no saint. His father was a fuller, and, according to St. Gregory of Nazianzen, the son distinguished himself, in early age, as a parasite of so mean a type that he would sell himself for a cake. By these arts he obtained the contract for supplying bacon to the troops; but he fulfilled its terms so ill, that he with difficulty escaped being torn to pieces by the soldiers. He then fled to Alexandria, where he entered the public service, embraced Christianity, and finally became Arian bishop of that city. On taking possession of his see, he joined the hue and cry against the Trinitarians, but was obliged to flee for his life. Ultimately, the people rose up against him, dragged him out of the prison to which he had fled for refuge, paraded him through the streets on the back of a camel, and, after tearing him to pieces, burnt his remains.

It must be remembered, first, that this account is drawn up by his enemies the Trinitarians, who thought nothing too bad to say against the Arians, and would not admit any good at all in them. Secondly, the persecutors who tore George of Cappadocia to pieces were set on by the Trinitarians, who tried to justify themselves by vilifying the Arians, whom they hunted down. Nothing in all history is more deplorable than this long religious contention between the Arians and Trinitarians. It would be flattery to call it disgraceful; it was infinitely worse. Of course, Papebroch and Heylyn deny that this Arian bishop is St. George of England. (See *Acta Sanctorum* and *History of St. George*.)

It is very difficult to get the story of the dragon to fit on the young soldier; and if the Arian bishop is fathered with it, the dragon must mean the Trinitarians; but in that case the dragon slew St. George, and not St. George the dragon. The legend of George and the dragon seems like a crusader's tale tacked on the life of the crusaders' patron and protector. The reason why St. George took so high a place with the crusaders is this: When the Christian army was before Antioch, his ghost came to their aid, and the success of the siege was always ascribed to this saint by Godfrey of Bouillon. Hence the European choice of the young military martyr. This devotion was confirmed by the apparition of St. George to Richard Lion-heart, assuring him of victory. In Christian art, St. George is represented on horseback tilting at a great dragon. Jean Darche, in his *Vie de St. George* (published 1866), has given above a hundred pages to prove that this dragon was a real animal, but Alban Butler, in his *Lives of the Saints*, says, "The dragon is only an emblematical figure of the devil, which St. George overcame by his faith and fortitude." If so, there is no special propriety in the emblem; for all the thousands and tens of thousands of saints did the same, or they were no saints at all. Indeed, a very large part of hagiology is only a repetition of this conflict, described by Bunyan as a battle between Christian and Apollyon. If St. George is simply meant for an emblem of a young Christian, the dragon may be an emblem of the temptations which beset him; but if he was a young soldier, who died at the early age of twenty-three, it is no less than ridiculous to make him the typical hero of the Christian athlete fighting the fight of faith. Hundreds of saints, such as St. Antony, St. Francis, St. Martin, St. Hilarion, and so on, would have been immeasurably preferable for such a purpose.

St. Germanus of Scotland leads a dragon to a deep pit, and throws it in (fifth century). When St. Germanus of Scotland reached Dieppe, he there saw a dragon of prodigious size ravaging the whole country. It had just killed a child, and was the terror of the neighbourhood. The saint first restored the child to life, and then, going to the dragon's lair, a deep cavern, threw his handkerchief about its neck, led it quietly to a deep pit, and pushed it in. This miracle so amazed the people, that five hundred of them were converted and baptized. (See note to ST. PAUL, etc., p. 115.)—Corblet, *Hagiographie d'Amiens*.

St. Hilarion commands the dragon Boa to walk into a fire, and be burnt to death. Dalmatia was troubled with a dragon called Boa, which destroyed all the country round about, devoured the oxen and other beasts, and killed the husbandmen and shepherds. St. Hilarion looked on the people with compassion, and bade them pile up a huge stack of wood. This being done, he commanded the dragon to go into the stack, which was then set fire to. The monster could not resist, and was therefore burnt to death in the sight of all the people.—St. Jerome, *Vita St. Hilarionis Eremitæ* (A.D. 390). See also Nicephorus Callistus (died 1350), *Ecclesiastical History*.

Probably this would be, in plain prose, St. Hilarion persuaded the people of Dalmatia to burn their national idol.

St. Honoratus, bishop of Arles, clears the isle of Lerins of serpents. The isle of Lerins in the fourth century was a mere desert, rendered inaccessible by the number of serpents which swarmed there. In 410 St. Honoratus landed on the island, and the serpents soon yielded to him. Hence, in Christian art, he is represented as expelling serpents from the isle with his pastoral staff.—St. Hilary, *Life of Honoratus.*

St. Hilary adds, the desert soon blossomed like the rose, the isle became peopled with angels, and grew into the city of God and colony of Jesus Christ. St. Honoratus changed the whole face of the island, and made what was once a wilderness a veritable paradise, rich in verdure, enamelled with flowers, filled with perfumes, and alive with a race of God-loving and God-fearing people.

St. Hilary, bishop of Poitiers, clears Gallinaria of serpents (A.D. 367). When St. Hilary set foot on Gallinaria, he found the island uninhabitable, from its great abundance of deadly serpents; but they all retired before the saint, fleeing as he chased them in the name of Jesus Christ. He then planted his stick in a certain spot of the island, and commanded them never again to pass that boundary, and they obeyed him.—Dom Constant, *Vita Sancti Hilarii Pictaviensis*, etc.

No doubt this is an allegory; the serpents being the aborigines of the island, who were confined to certain fixed limits.

St. Ilerius destroys the dragon of the Tarn (seventh century). St. Enimia, daughter of Clotaire II., king of France, being cured of leprosy by the waters of the Fontaine de Burle, constructed a monastery in the vicinity; but the devil, indignant at this new asylum for innocence and virtue, assumed the form of a dragon, and every Saturday night kicked down what had been constructed during the week. The princess told her grief to St. Ilerius, bishop of Mende, who promised his assistance. A few days afterwards the infernal dragon, more furious than ever, ran against the new building and utterly destroyed it; so the bishop went without further delay to encounter the demon. On his way he picked up two sticks, which he tied together in the form of a cross, and immediately the dragon saw this instrument of man's redemption, it retreated to a deep gorge and was never seen again.—*Propre du Diocèse de Mende* (1619).

There can be little doubt that the above is an allegory. The dragon is the spirit of opposition in the men of the neighbourhood, who kicked down the walls of the monastery as fast as they were built up. At length the bishop of Mende interfered, and by the influence of the doctrine of the cross allayed this spirit of opposition, so that the work was no longer interrupted

St. Lifard kills a huge dragon without touching it (sixth century). St. Lifard lived the life of a recluse in the ruins of an old chateau near the town of Mehun sur la Loire, a few miles from Orleans. Here was a dreadful dragon greatly feared by the inhabitants, but St. Lifard at once destroyed it. Urbicus had followed him to this retreat, and the saint told him to go and plant a stick near the mouth of the dragon's lair. Urbicus was greatly afraid, but nevertheless went, in obedience to his master, and stuck the stick in the ground where the monster could not help seeing it. Scarcely had he left the spot when the dragon came from his lair, attacked the stick, and, trying to pull it down, it snapped in pieces, wounding the dragon so severely that it bled to death. The demons which had made their abode in the dragon, and used it as their instrument of mischief, fled with hideous howls, crying aloud, as they flew into the air, "Lifard! Lifard!" The inhabitants of the neighbourhood heard the cries, knew that they were delivered from the monster, and thanked the saint with tears of gratitude.—*Acta Sanctorum* (Bollandists), June 3.

St. Marcel banishes from Paris a vampire dragon (A.D. 136). There was in Paris a dame of high rank who had lived a very abandoned life, and died in her sins. Being a Christian and not excommunicated, she was buried in consecrated ground; but the same night that she was interred, a dragon of monstrous figure and size came from a desert to Paris, hollowed out a great hole for its retreat, and began to feed on the dead body. It did not devour the whole at once, but returned to the hateful banquet over and over again. As the breath of the monster infected the air, those dwelling near the churchyard were so greatly alarmed that they left their houses; and the saint was petitioned to come to the rescue. St. Marcel, armed with arrows and spears, went to the churchyard; and when the dragon drew nigh knocked it on the head three times with his cross; then, throwing his cloak round the creature's neck, he led it four miles beyond the city gates, and said to it, "Either promise hereafter never to quit this wood, or I will cast you at once into the sea." The dragon made the required promise, and was never after seen in Paris or its neighbourhood. —Gregory of Tours.

This is without doubt an allegory. The dragon was aroused by burying a notorious evil-liver in consecrated ground, because she was of high rank. It was subdued by three blows of the cross, and commanded never again to enter Paris. Any one can apply the allegory and fill it up.

Martha, the sister of Lazarus, subdues the dragon of Tarascon (A.D. 84). Mgr. Guérin tells us that, after the Ascension, the Jews laid hands on Martha, the sister of Lazarus, and sent her adrift in a boat without sails, rudder, oars, or provisions; and that the boat carried her to Marseilles, where she landed, and introduced the gospel. About the same time a horrible dragon, half beast and half fish, caused dreadful havoc, for it used to hide under the waters of the Rhone, and upset the vessels, in order to prey upon the passengers and sailors. Sometimes it made incursions into the neighbouring forests, and devoured every one it encountered. The inhabitants being told about Martha represented their case to her, and Martha went at once into the forest indicated and saw the dragon eating a man. She made the sign of the cross (!!), she sprinkled holy water on the beast (!!), and the dragon became so submissive, that Martha led it like a lamb with her girdle, and gave it to the people, who forthwith killed it with lances and stones. "On dit que le nom de Tarascon" was given to the place, "à cause de ce dragon, parce que Tarasque, en provençal, signifie *une chose horrible*."—*Les Petits Bollandistes*, vol. ix. p. 96.

According to Greek mythology the place received its name from Taras, son of Neptune. As the river Rhone might be called "the son of the sea," there is just as much likelihood in this derivation as in the other, and no more. Holy water was unknown till A.D. 683, and the sign of the cross was probably not used in the first two centuries as a curative symbol. Eusebius tells us it was so used in the fourth century to his own personal knowledge.

St. Patrick expels the serpents from Ireland (fifth century). St. Patrick drove all the serpents out of Ireland; and hence he is represented in Christian art with a serpent coiled round a pastoral staff.

This probably was only an allegorical way of expressing his triumph over paganism; subsequently interpreted more literally.

Ireland exempt from venomous reptiles. It is said that Ireland is exempt from serpents and other venomous reptiles, because of St. Patrick's staff, called "The Staff of Jesus," given by St. Patrick, and kept with great veneration in Dublin.—Ralph Higden (1360), *Polychronicon* (published by Gale).

The isle of Malta is said to derive a like privilege from St. Paul, who was there bitten by a viper (Acts xxviii. 1-6).

St. Patrick overreaches a cunning old serpent. There is a current legend that when St. Patrick ordered the serpents of Ireland into the sea, one of the older reptiles refused to obey; but the saint overmastered it by stratagem. He made a box, and invited the serpent to enter in. pretending it would be a nice place for it to sleep in. The serpent said the box was too small, but St. Patrick maintained it was quite large enough. So high at length the contest rose, that the serpent got into the box to prove it was too small; whereupon St. Patrick clapped down the lid, and threw the box into the sea.

This story is only given as a legend, but it is marvellously like a story in the *Arabian Nights' Entertainments*. A fisherman, we are told, drew up in his net a box, and on opening it, an evil genius stepped forth, threatening the fisherman with death. Said the fisherman to the genius, "Where did you come from?" "Where did I come from?" said the genius; "why, out of that box, to be sure; where else should I come from?" "Nonsense," replied the fisherman; "you cannot gammon me, old fellow. You don't mean to tell me you came out of that box." "Yes, I did," rejoined the genius. "No, you didn't," persisted the man. "I say I did," exclaimed the genius, waxing in a rage. "I say you couldn't," retorted the fisher: "it is too small to hold half of you." "But I say I did," said the genius; and, to prove his point, he turned himself into smoke, and, entering the box, said to the man, "Who now is right, you or I?" but the moment the genius was fairly in, the fisherman slammed down the lid, and threw the box back into the sea.—*The Fisherman.*

St. Paul, bishop of Leon, commands a dragon to precipitate itself into the sea (A.D. 492-573). While St. Paul was at Witur, the count asked him to free the island of a terrible dragon which committed great ravages, and devoured human beings. The saint undertook the adventure, and passed the night in prayer with the priests of the island. Then, after celebrating mass, arrayed in his episcopal robes, he went to the dragon's cave, and commanded the beast to come forth. The dragon obeyed, and Paul, placing his stole about its neck, led it to the coast on the north side of the isle, and commanded the beast to precipitate itself at once into the sea. This did it, and in testimony thereof the place is called "The Dragon's Abyss" to this day, and the sea there always makes a terrible roaring noise like the howl of an angry dragon in agony. In reward of this great service, the count gave Paul his palace and its dependencies for a monastery; and there the saint lived with twelve priests and several laymen, who renounced the world and lived to God.—Mgr. Guérin (chamberlain of pope Leo XIII.), *Vies des Saints*, vol. iii. p. 359.

M. de Fréminville thinks this dragon was a crocodile or monstrous serpent. Dom Lobineau fancies the dragon means paganism which the saint extirpated. But neither of these suggestions will wholly satisfy the particulars of the legend, although the latter is far more likely than the former. The human beings devoured by the dragon would be men and women sacrificed to idols. (See ST. GERMANUS, p. 113.)

St. Pacomius trod on serpents and dragons without injury (A.D. 292–348). St. Pacomius was able to tread on serpents without injury; to crush scorpions under his feet; and when he visited the monasteries along the Nile, crocodiles took him on their backs across the river. Though he lived to the age of fifty-six years, he scarcely ever ate anything, and never went to bed; the only sleep he allowed himself was taken sitting on a stone. In Christian art St. Pacomius is represented as being carried across the Nile on the back of a crocodile.—His life, by a monk of Tabenna, his disciple.

In 1882 the Madhi, or False Prophet of the Soudan, who made war on the troops of the Khedive, was said to have been carried across the Nile on a crocodile's back.

St. Pavacius rids Cenomania of a monstrous dragon (époque unknown). A dragon of portentous size and prodigiously fierce appeared in Cenomania, and spread such terror in the neighbourhood, that the inhabitants fled, and sought safety in distant lands. This monster spared neither man nor beast, and its very breath was pestilential. The terror increased more and more every day, and none, not even the bravest of the brave, durst encounter it, or even show himself abroad. St. Pavacius resolved to rid the country of this plague; so, going to the dragon's lair, he terrified the beast by the sign of the cross, and entangled it in the folds of his garment; then he called together those who had followed him, but had hitherto remained far off, from fear. When they came up the look of the dragon curdled their blood; but the saint bade them take courage, and come forward to witness what would follow. He then knelt in prayer, the earth opened, and the dragon, falling into the chasm, never again made its appearance in Cenomania.—L'abbé Blin, *Vies des Saints du Diocèse de Séez.*

The apostle Philip kills the dragon of Hierapolis. In Hierapolis, a city of Phrygia, was a temple in which was a terrible dragon. It was a natural living creature into which the devil had entered, as he entered into the serpent in paradise. The people used to adore this reptile, and offer sacrifice to it as to a god. It was, however, the death of many innocent people, for when malefactors failed, innocent people were given it by lots for food. St. Philip, moved to indignation at this cruel idolatry, went up to the venomous beast, prayed to God, and the creature dropped down dead. A great crowd witnessed the miracle, and all rejoiced that the city was freed from the dreaded monster.—Simeon Metaphrastês, *Lives*, etc.

St. Romanus destroys a horrible dragon (A.D. 639). What renders the name of St. Romanus especially memorable in all France, is his victory at Rouen over a horrible dragon, of a shape and size hitherto unknown. It was a man-eater, and also devoured much cattle, causing sad desolation. Romanus resolved to attack this monster in his lair; but as no one would assist him in such a dangerous enterprise, he took with him, as assistants, a murderer condemned to death, and a thief. The thief, being panic-struck, ran away; but the murderer proved true steel. Romanus went to the dragon's den, and, making the sign of the cross, walked in, and threw a net over the beast's neck. The murderer, then taking the net in his two hands, dragged the monster through the town into the market-place, where was a huge bonfire. Into this bonfire he led the beast, there was it burnt to death, and then thrown into the Seine. All the people thanked the saint for delivering them from this pest, the murderer was set at liberty, and Romanus appointed a day of public thanksgivings.—*Propre de Rouen.*

St. Sampson of Wales destroys a dragon of Brittany (A.D. 480–565). St. Sampson delivered a village in Brittany of a very venomous dragon which had taken up its abode in a great cave. Near the spot he afterwards built a monastery, which he called Dole. His biographer tells us he had seen a cross sculptured on a very hard stone by the saint. In Christian art, St. Sampson of Wales is represented chasing a dragon.—Lobineau, *Lives of the Saints of Brittany.*

St. Simon and St. Jude make serpents obey their word. When the apostles Simon and Jude were at Babylon, the royal enchanters, Zaroes and Arphazar, who had been driven by St. Matthew out of of India, caused serpents to appear while they stood before the king. Their intention was to terrify the apostles, but the men of God commanded the serpents to fall on the enchanters. This they did, putting them to great torment. Zaroes and Arphazar, being thus shamed in the sight of the king, fled from Babylon, as they had done from India.—Edward Kinesman (1623), *Lives of the Saints*, p. 852.

A boa-constrictor submissive to St. Thecla Haimant. The Abyssinians believe in saints and miracles. Their calendar, in fact, is crammed full of saints; and the days of the year by no means suffice to honour them all. Among their saints are Balaam and his ass, Pontius Pilate and his wife, and many local celebrities who have from time to time astounded the Abyssinians with their miracles, particularly Thecla Haimant, who converted the devil, and induced him to become a monk. The devil continued a monk for forty days, but what then became of him we are not told. Thecla, wishing to ascend a steep mountain with almost perpendicular sides, like the Guimb, prayed for help, when a boa-constrictor took him on its back, and set him down safely on the summit.—Dufton, *Journey through Abyssinia.*

St. Theodorus of Heraclea slays a dragon (A.D. 319). St. Theodorus, general of the forces of Licinius, encountered a furious dragon in Thrace. This dragon lived in a cave, and used to issue forth every morning and devour any one it could find. Theodorus resolved to encounter the beast, trusting to the name of Jesus Christ and the power of the cross. Accordingly, he went boldly to the cave, and conjuring the monster in the name of God, bade it come out from its lair. When the beast came forth, St. Theodorus pierced it with his sword, and laid it dead at his horse's feet. Many Thracians by this act were converted to the faith of Christ crucified. In Christian art, St. Theodorus of Heraclea is represented on horseback with a dragon at his feet, like St. George.—Augard, *Life of St. Theodorus of Heraclea.* (See also Surius, vol. i.)

A dragon threatens to devour a recalcitrant monk (fifth century). A monk of Mount Cassino demanded of St. Benedict permission to leave the society, that he might return and live in the world. The abbot refused for a long time this sinful demand, but as the monk persisted, and was determined to have his own way, he lived so scandalously in the monastery he was of necessity turned out. Scarcely had he passed the abbey gates when he saw a huge dragon with open mouth waiting to devour him. The monk in terror shrieked for help. The brothers, running out, declared they saw nothing; but the monk, trembling and shrieking, requested them to take him back. They took him into the monastery, soothed him, and he ever after remained a consistent brother, most grateful to the abbot who had opened his eyes to see the dragon.—St. Gregory the Great, *Dialogues*, bk. ii.

No doubt many tales about dragons are allegorical, and probably "figures of speech" would go far to reduce the number of "miracles" ascribed to the saints. Many a wonder began in an allegory and ended in being received literally. Thus Mgr. Guérin, by no means chary of the miraculous gifts of saints, says of St. Rioc, "Il est censé avoir tué un dragon, image des efforts qu'a dû faire le christianisme pour déblayer le sol de la Bretagne de toutes les superstitions druidiques" (*Vies des Saints*, vol. ii. p. 480); and in his life of St. Anastase (vol. v. p. 55) he uses language which, taken literally, would make the saint a dragon-slayer: "Anastase, ayant vu le monstre de l'erreur lever sa tête funeste, se hâta de lui porter un coup mortel; il fit taire tous les sifflements de l'hydre." All that is meant by this grandiloquence is that Anastasius opposed effectually the heresy of Origen.

Dreams, Warning and Prophetic.

GEN. xli. 17-45 (*Pharaoh warned of famine*). Pharaoh dreamed that he was standing on the banks of the Nile, and suddenly there appeared before him seven kine, which seemed to come out of the river. They were fat fleshed and well favoured, and went to feed in a meadow. Afterwards came forth seven lean kine, as ill favoured as possible; and these lean beasts, falling foul of the fat ones, devoured them, yet remained as lean as they were before. That was the dream. Joseph, being asked the meaning of it, told the king it was an intimation from God that there would be in Egypt seven years of plenty, followed by seven years of famine. He told Pharaoh, therefore, to husband the corn of the seven years of plenty, to tide over those of scarcity. Pharaoh took the hint, and appointed Joseph to carry out the suggestion.

GEN. xl. 1-19 (*Pharaoh's butler and baker*). Pharaoh's chief butler and baker having offended the king were committed to prison, and had each of them a dream, which they told to Joseph their fellow-prisoner. The chief butler dreamt he saw a vine with three branches full of fruit of a most luxuriant kind. Plucking off some of the rich clusters, he squeezed them into the royal tankard, and handed it to the king. Such was the dream, which Joseph interpreted thus:—The three branches are three days, and as the king took the cup, it signifies that within three days he will restore the royal butler to his office again. The chief baker now told what he had dreamt. He thought he was carrying on his head three baskets full of cates for the king's table; but the birds pouncing on them devoured the contents of the uppermost basket. Joseph said this was an ill-omened dream, and that it foreboded the baker's death. "Within three days," said Joseph, "the king will hang you on a tree, and leave your dead body to the birds of prey." Both these interpretations proved true; the butler was restored to his office within the stated time, and the baker was hanged, as Joseph had said.

DAN. ii. 31-45 (*Nebuchadnezzar's dream*).

Nebuchadnezzar, in the second year of his reign, dreamt that he saw a great image, brilliant to look at, but of terrible aspect. The head was of gold, the legs of iron, the feet of clay, the arms and breast of silver, and the rest of brass. A stone, cut without hands from a quarry, fell on the image, and broke it to pieces, and the fragments were blown away by a strong wind, so that no part of the image remained. The stone, on the other hand, grew and grew, till it first became a mountain, and then filled the whole earth. Such was the dream, which Daniel pronounced to be an historical allegory. "The image," he said, "represents different kingdoms. Chaldea is the golden head; the silver arms and breasts represent the empire of the Medes and Persians; the brass part of the image represents the kingdom of Macedonia; the iron legs the Roman empire; and the feet, with ten toes, all of clay, are the ten parts into which the Roman empire, at its fall, will be subdivided: viz. (1) the Hungarians, (2) the Ostrogoths, (3) the Visigoths, (4) the Sweves and Alains, (5) the Vandals in Africa, (6) the Franks, (7) the Burgundians, (8) the Heruli, (9) the Anglish in England, and (10) the Lombards." Now for the stone which broke in pieces the image. It was cut without hands out of a mountain. The prophet tells us this stone allegorized the "kingdom of Christ." It was no part of the image of earth's monarchies, but wholly independent. No hand of man cut it out, but it came of itself from the mount of God; and grew and grew in power and extent, till it filled the whole earth.

This certainly is a most marvellous allegory. Said to have been made some six hundred years before the birth of Christ. Philip I. was king of Macedonia at the time, and the empire lasted four hundred and fifty years afterwards. Rome was almost unknown; it was just struggling into notice under its early kings. As for the ten kingdoms of clay, they were far remote, only looming, like the kingdom of the Messiah, in the dim obscurity of future history.

Porphyry maintains and St. Jerome admits that this marvellous vision was post-historic, written in the days of Antiochus Epiphanes: "Contra prophetam Danielem duodecimum librum scripsit Porphyrius; nolens eum ab ipso cujus inscriptus est nomine esse compositum; sed a quodam, qui temporibus Antiochi qui appellatus est *Epiphanes*, fuerit in Judæa." Antiochus died B.C. 164, and, of course, by that time most of the "prophecy" was history. As for the "stone cut out of the mountains without hands," it must be borne in mind that the kingdom of the Messiah was a general belief among the Jews, and a similar belief has existed in many nations, as Germany, England, Scandinavia, France, etc., etc.

Gen. xx. 2–16 (*Abimelech's dream*). When Abraham went to Egypt, he told his wife to say she was his sister, otherwise he might be slain in order that some Egyptian might marry her. Abimelech, king of Gerar, hearing that she was the sister of Abraham, sent for her, intending to make her his wife; but was warned in a dream not to do so, as the lady, though half-sister, was also the wife of Abraham. Abimelech now sent for Abraham, and reproved him for his equivocation; but gave him a royal present of sheep and oxen, menservants and maidservants, together with a thousand pieces of silver, and said to him, My land is before thee; dwell where it pleaseth thee.

Gen. xxxvii. 5–10 (*Joseph's dream*). Joseph dreamt that he and his brothers were in a field binding sheaves, and that his own sheaf arose and stood upright; while his brothers' sheaves, which were round about, bowed to his sheaf, and made obeisance. When Joseph told his brothers of his dream, they were very indignant, and cried in scorn, What! are you to reign over us? are you, the younger, to have dominion over us, who are your elders? And they hated him for his dream. Not long after he had another dream, which he told his brothers, saying, I dreamt that the sun, moon, and stars made obeisance to me. The brothers now reported what Joseph had told them to their father; and Jacob rebuked the lad, saying, Shall I and your mother, with all your brothers, bow down to you as our superior? But the time came when they did so, for Joseph rose to be viceroy of Egypt, and Jacob, with all his house, removed to Egypt, and gladly submitted to the rule of Pharaoh's favourite.

Matt. ii. 13–22 (*the dreams of Joseph, husband of the Virgin Mary*). Joseph had three dreams: one bidding him to flee from Judæa with his wife and child, because Herod the king was seeking to take the life of the young child; one when he was in Egypt, telling him that Herod was dead, and therefore he might return to his own country; and the third, which bade him not to take up his abode in Judæa, but in Galilee.

There are several other warning or prophetic dreams in the Bible; but these will suffice for the present purpose.

Dreams, among the Greeks, supposed to be sent by the gods. There were three words for dreams among the ancient Greeks: Chrēmatismos, Horāma, and Onīros. In the first of these the gods themselves, or some departed spirit, or some living being, came and conversed with men in their sleep. In the second, the sleeper saw the event about to occur performed before his sleeping eyes. In the third he saw a type, figure, or allegory of what was about to come to pass.

Agamemnon (*Iliad*, ii.) dreamed that Nestor came to him and bade him give the Trojans battle, on the assurance of success. Pindar dreamed that Proserpine appeared to him, and complained that, though he had written hymns to the other deities, he had written none in her honour (*Pausanias*). These are examples of the Chrēmatismos (a business matter, from *Chrēma*, a matter of business). Of this nature were the dreams of Joseph mentioned by St. Matthew (ii. 13–22), in which angels appeared to him, and told him directly what he was to do or to avoid doing.

Of the second sort, Horāma (a vision from *horāo*, to see), was the dream of Alexander the Great (*Valerius Maximus* i. 7), when he dreamed that he was murdered by Cassander. So was that of Crœsus, king of Lydia, when he dreamed that his son Atys would be slain by a spear (*Herodotus*, i. 34); and that of Penelopê concerning her son Telemachos, when searching for his father (*Odys.*, iv. 838).

The third sort was the Onīros, or dream-riddle (from *Onīros*, the god of dreams). These were typical dreams, allegories, and figures. Such was Hecuba's dream, that the child about to be born was a fire-brand. Of this nature were Pharaoh's dreams about the fat and lean kine; Joseph's dream about the bowing wheat-sheaves, and the sun, moon, and stars; the dreams of Pharaoh's butler and baker, which Joseph interpreted; the dreams of Nebuchadnezzar, etc.

The god of dreams, in Greek mythology, had three attendants, named Morpheus, Phobetor, Phantasos. The first counterfeited human forms; the second, the likeness of brutes; and the last, the forms of inanimate objects.

There were, among the Greeks, professional interpreters of dreams and a large dream-literature. Geminus Pyrius wrote three books on the subject; Artemon the Milesian, twenty-two books. There were also the dream-books of Achinês son of Scyrimos, Alexander the Myndian, Antipho of Athens, Artemidoros, Astrampsychos, Demetrios the Phalerean, Nicephoros, Nicostratos the Ephesian, Panyasis of Halicarnassos, Philo Judæus, Phœbos of Antioch, and many more.

Bruno (*Leo IX.*), *by a dream, is shown the ill condition of the Church, and its reform* (A.D. 1002–1054). One day Bruno, bishop of Toul, saw in his dream a deformed old woman, who haunted him with great persistency, and treated him with great familiarity. She was hideously ugly, clothed in filthy rags, her hair dishevelled, and altogether one could scarcely recognize in her the human form. Disgusted with her general appearance, the bishop tried to avoid her; but the more he shrunk from her, the more she clung to him. Annoyed by this importunity, Bruno made the sign of the cross; whereupon she fell to the earth as dead, and rose up again lovely as an angel. While pondering on the meaning of this vision, the abbot Odilo, lately dead, came before him, and said, "Happy man, you have delivered her soul from death." Wibert, the biographer of our saint, and his contemporary, informs us that the old woman represented the Church, which at the time was in a most deplorable state, but Bruno in his pontificate was employed by God to restore it to its original beauty.—Wibert, *Life of St. Leo IX.*, bk. i. chap. 1.

This was the time of the schism, when there were three concurrent popes: Benedict IX., Sylvester III., and Gregory VI.

Bruno (*Leo IX.*), *bishop of Toul, has a dream which symbolized to him his elevation to the popedom* (A.D. 1002–1054). One night Bruno, bishop of Toul, dreamt he was transported to the cathedral of Worms, where were assembled a host of persons clothed in white raiments. Bruno asked one of them who they were, and was told, "These are the saints who lived and died in the service of St. Peter." Scarcely had the words been uttered, when the apostle Peter, and Stephen the first martyr, led him to the altar, while the heavenly visitants sang "an ineffable melody." Bruno was ordered to administer the communion to all the assembly. This being done, St. Peter presented him with five gold chalices, "trois à un autre qui le suivait, et un seul à un troisième." He now awoke, and found he had been elected pope in the cathedral of Worms. —L'abbé Guillaume, *Histoire de l'Église de Toul.*

Constantine assured in a dream of the innocence of three men condemned. Three officers, named Nepotian, Ursus, and Herpilion, being falsely accused to Constantine, were condemned to death. At night, St. Nicholas appeared to the emperor and his judge Ablavius, and said to them, "Those three men are innocent; and, unless they are released in the morning, war shall desolate the land, and thou and all thine shall perish by the sword. I, Nicholas of Myra, forewarn you." So saying, he vanished. When the emperor and judge met next morning, they conferred together of the vision, and caused the three officers to be brought before them. "Tell me," said the emperor, "have any of you three any skill in necromancy?" They answered, "No." The emperor then rehearsed to them the vision; and the three officers, kneeling down, kissed the ground, and yielded hearty thanks to God for their deliverance. The emperor then sent them to St. Nicholas with a present, consisting of the four Gospels in letters of gold, and a gold thurible; and charged them with this message, "The emperor begs St. Nicholas not to threaten him, but to pray for him."—Metaphrastês, *Lives*, etc.

Sennadius's dream to prove that man has two natures. The dream of Sennadius was to prove that man consists of a material body and a something independent thereof, generally called a soul. The dream is told by St. Augustine to his friend Evadius, and is as follows:—Sennadius was a physician, who disbelieved the duality of man's nature, and consequently a future life; but one night, in a dream, an angel appeared to him, and bade him follow. The angel took him to the confines of a city, where he was ravished with celestial music, which, the angel told him, proceeded from the voices of spirits made perfect. Sennadius thought no more about the dream; but some time afterwards the angel appeared to him again, recalled to his memory the former visit, and then asked him if the vision had occurred while he was awake or during sleep. Sennadius replied, "During sleep." "Just so," said the angel; "what you saw and heard was not by your bodily senses then, for your eyes and ears were closed in sleep." "True," said the physician. "Then," continued the angel, "with what eyes did you see, and with what ears did you hear?" Sennadius could not answer this question; and the angel said, "It must be evident, if you see when your bodily eyes are shut, and hear when your bodily ears are closed in sleep, that you must have other eyes and ears besides those of your material body. When, therefore, your body sleeps, that other something may be awake; and when your body dies, that other something may live on. Yes, Sennadius, there is indeed a something in man which sleep cannot lull into oblivion, and death can never touch. Think of these things."—St. Augustine, *Epistles*, 159.

This argument is in a measure plausible, but would scarcely touch the difficulty which modern Sennadiuses feel. The eye does not see, nor does the ear hear. They are the mere telegraphs of the brain, which convey messages thereto; but the brain can both see and hear without this machinery; and although the eyes and ears often inform the brain, the brain not unfrequently informs the eyes and ears. Thus Macbeth saw a dagger, the creation of his brain, and we often hear sounds which proceed from within and not from without. This does not prove the existence of a second self, independent of the body, but only that the brain can act without its ordinary servants, called the senses. To a sceptic, the tale would be an argument to prove the very contrary of the duality of man.

An attempt to explain prophetic dreams. That succession of periods, called "time," is a part of mortality. With God there is no past or future, but all is known, all is visibly present. The history of man may be compared to a drama, or vast panorama. The spectator sees each scene and act gradually and successively developed, but God knows the whole drama, even before it is put on the stage, or the whole panorama before it is unrolled. To the spectator, who sees piece by piece, what he has seen or heard is past, what he now sees and hears is present, what he is about to see and hear is future; but to one who knows the whole drama or panorama there is no such succession; all is known, all is present to the mind, and he can tell exactly what actors are to come on, and what each is to say or do. In sleep, when the body is dormant, sights and sounds often present themselves distinctly; not sights of things present to the body, nor sounds which the bodily ears could hear, but sights and sounds perceptible to the "spirit man;" and if the "spirit man" could wholly shake off the body, it would see more of the drama of life, or panorama of history, about to be unfolded. This sight into the unfolded is what we call "prophetic," because it is a glimpse into the drama or panorama beyond that part which the spectators are looking at. Often at the approach of death this spiritual perception is very keen, and visions or sounds are present, wholly unrevealed to others. In fact, the "spirit man" is looking into the everlasting Now, and is no longer circumscribed to that order of succession which belongs to time. He is stepping into that state of being where "time shall be no more." This view of the matter will show how it is possible for God to see the future; and, in fact, what man calls "future" is no future with God, to whom the whole drama of life is known, the whole panorama of history is unrolled. It will also explain how men who have emptied themselves of earth by self-denial and holiness, may, as it were, stand on tiptoe and look over the wall of present time, so as to catch a glance of the panorama yet unrolled, or the drama not yet set on the stage of actual life.

Dry Bones restored to Life.

Ezek. xxxvii. 1-10. Ezekiel was taken by the Spirit into a valley full of dry bones, and was commanded to prophesy upon them, and bid them live; "and as I prophesied, there was a noise; and behold! a shaking; and the bones came together, bone to bone. And I beheld the sinews and the flesh come upon them, and the skin covered them. But as yet there was no breath." Then the prophet was commanded to bid the four winds to breathe upon these lifeless bodies; and, when he did so, they lived, and stood upon their feet, an exceeding great army.

The body of St. Stanislaus, bishop of Cracow, cut piecemeal, is restored. King Bolislaus sent officers to St. Michael's church to drag Stanislaus from the altar. The emissaries would have done their bidding, but a celestial light, shining on the bishop who was celebrating mass, so frightened them, that they drew back, and fell to the ground. Other officers were then sent, but they also were unable to lay hands on him. A third company met with no better success. Then the king himself rose up in a fury, and, rushing into the church, clave in two the head of the bishop, making his brains fly out against the wall. This done, the officers around the king hacked and hewed the body into gobbets, and flung them to the carrion-birds. Four eagles came, and watched over them till sunset, when bone came to bone, sinew to sinew, and limb to limb, till the whole body was pieced together, as if it had never been divided; indeed, says our author, "not so much as a scar or seam could be detected." Some Christians who had come to collect the fragments, saw this marvellous restoration, and, taking the body to St. Michael's church, buried it. Ten years afterwards it was removed to Cracow, and interred in the castle church with great solemnity (A.D. 1079).—Ribadeneira (died 1611), *Flower of the Lives of Saints.*

A child cut up and fried or roasted restored by St. Vincent Ferrier (A.D. 1357–1419). One of the most astounding miracles on record is that of St. Vincent Ferrier, who restored a child which its mother, in a fit of madness, had cut up into small pieces and roasted or fried. The father of the child lodged St. Vincent in his missionary visit; and one day, after attending the saint's sermon, returned home and saw this horrible sight. He was almost beside himself, but St. Vincent comforted him, by the assurance that God had suffered this frightful tragedy for His own glorification. Then, placing the pieces together, they united, and by the sign of the cross the body thus restored recovered life, and he handed the living child to its father. Father Ranzano, who relates this as a fact, adds, "so singular a prodigy is scarcely paralleled in Church history." The scene of this "miracle" is laid in Gascony.

Ranzano (*Life of St. Ferrier, Acta Sanctorum*, April 5, vol. i.) gives this marvellous tale as the eight hundred and sixtieth miracle brought forward at the canonization of the saint. It is recorded, "dans la quatrième antienne de Laudes de l'office St. Vincent Ferrier dans la liturgie Dominicaine.' Mgr. Guérin (1880), chamberlain of pope Leo XIII., repeats it as an undoubted fact in his *Vies des Saints*, vol. iv. p. 228. There is not an incident in Church history better attested, and its constant repetition shows it to have been a favourite "miracle."

The cooked pullets of the alcaydê of La Calzada restored to life. Some pilgrims, on their road to Compostella, stopped at a hospice in La Calzada. The daughter of the innkeeper solicited a young Frenchman to pass the night with her, but he refused; so she put in his wallet a silver cup, and, when he was on the road, accused him to the alcaydê of theft. As the property was found in his possession, the alcaydê ordered him to be hung. His parents continued their pilgrimage, and, after eight days, returned to La Calzada, when, to their amazement, they found their son still alive. The mother went instantly to inform the alcaydê, but he replied, "Woman, you are mad! I would as soon believe these pullets which I am about to eat are alive, as that a man who has been gibbeted for eight days is not dead." No sooner had he spoken, than the two pullets on the dish before him actually rose up alive. The alcaydê was terribly frightened, and was about to rush out of doors, when he was met by the heads and feathers of the two pullets scampering in to complete the resuscitation. The cock and hen thus restored to life were taken in grand procession to St. James's church of Compostella, where they survived for seven years, in which time the hen hatched only two eggs, a cock and a hen. These in turn lived also seven years, and did the same. This has continued uninterruptedly to this day, and pilgrims to Compostella receive feathers from these birds as holy relics; but no matter how many feathers are thus disposed of, the full plumage of the birds is never deficient.

This legend is seriously related by bishop Patrick, *Parable of the Pilgrims*, xxxv. 430–434. Udal ap Rhys repeats it in his *Tour through Spain and Portugal*, 35–38. It is inserted by the Bollandists in the *Acta Sanctorum*, vol. vi. p. 45; and pope Calixtus mentions it among the miracles of Santiago. Mgr. Guérin (1880) says, "Cette histoire !! a été raconté par un grand nombre d'auteurs. Les peintes-verriers du moyen âge l'ont souvent reproduite. On frappa des médailles commémoratives de l'évènent. Une de ces médailles a été retrouvée, de nos jours, dans la Seine, Paris" (vol. v. p. 504).

The subjoined is the Latin version:—"Gallum capiunt et gallinam, et in ecclesiam transferunt magne solemnitate. Quæ ibi clause res admirables et Dei potentiam testificantes observantur, ubi septennio vivunt; hunc enim terminum Deus illis instituit; et in fine septennii antequam moriantur, pullum relinquunt et pullam sui coloris et magnitudinis; et hoc fit in ecclesia quolibet septennio. Magnæ quoque admirationis est, quod omnes per hanc urbem transeuntes peregrini, qui sunt innumerabiles, galli hujus et gallinæ plumam capiunt, et nunquam illis plumæ deficiunt. Hac EGO TESTOR, propterea VIDI et interfui."—Lucius Marineus Siculus, *Rerum Hispanicarum Scriptores*, ii. 805.

(St. Dominic of Calzada (1109) is represented in Christian art with a cock and hen, which he holds in one hand, and a "corde de pendu" in the other. Of course, the allusion is to this most extraordinary "histoire," as the pope's chamberlain calls it.)

St. Aldebrand makes a roast partridge fly away (twelfth century). St. Aldebrand, bishop of Fossombrone, abstained from meat all his life. Being greatly reduced, and in failing health, a roast partridge was brought him for dinner. Without saying a word to those who brought it, the saint blessed the bird, and bade it fly away. So it flew from the dish through the window, and joined its companions in the open air.—*Acta Sanctorum* (Bollandists), May 1, p. 162.

Andrew of Segni restores to life some cooked birds (A.D. 1302). Andrew of Segni was extremely compassionate and kind-hearted. One day, being ill, some roast birds, killed in a chase [*à la chasse*], were brought for him to eat. "Poor birds," said Andrew, "how I pity you, who have been deprived of your life, in order to give me pleasure!" Then, making the sign of the cross over them, "les oiseaux commencèrent à s'agiter, battirent des ailes, et s'envolèrent."—*Breviaire*

Franciscain. (The same tale is told in the *Palmier Séraphique.*)

St. Francis of Paula restores some fried fish to life (A.D. 1416–1507). When St. Francis of Paula passed through Naples on his way to Tours, whither he was going at the invitation of Louis XI. and at the command of pope Sixtus IV., he was entertained in the palace of Ferdinand I. His highness asked the saint to breakfast at the royal table, but he refused, saying it would not be suitable. For dinner the king sent him some fried fish, but the saint, after blessing them, restored them to life, and sent them back by the page who brought them; "ce qu'il fit pour corriger sa défiance, sachant bien qu'il ne lui avait envoyé ce plat que pour l'éprouver."—Mgr. Guérin (chamberlain of pope Leo XIII.), *Vies des Saints*, vol. iv. p. 155 (1880).

St. Nicholas of Tollentino served with a boiled chicken which flew away (1307). St. Nicholas of Tollentino fell into a grievous infirmity, which brought him to the brink of the grave, whereupon his physicians told him, if he would recover his health, he must eat meat. Nicholas replied, this would be saving his body at the peril of his soul. The prior, being appealed to, commanded the sick man to obey the doctor, and sent him into his cell a boiled chicken. When the fowl was set before him, "the blessed man" prayed that God would help him out of his dilemma. If he ate the fowl, he broke his vow; if he refused to eat it, he disobeyed the prior, and also broke his vow. He was soon relieved of his perplexity, for the boiled chicken came to life, flew from the platter, and escaped out of the window. We are told that "all present were astonished, and the sick man was jocund and glad."—Antony (archbishop of Florence), *Life of St. Nicholas of Tollentino.*

This tale is repeated by half a dozen writers as a fact.

A young child boiled without injury (A.D. 117). The following must be given in the exact words of the historian, or the English reader might fancy the translation to be incorrect. When St. Julian was carried to his grave, "une femme qui lavait son enfant dans une chaudière placée sur le feu [!!], l'oublie, et court se joindre à la foule qui accompagne le corps de St. Julian. En son absence, la flamme grandit, enveloppe la chaudière, l'eau bouillonne, et déborde. La pensée de son fils, qu'elle a laissé exposé à un si grand péril, traverse le cœur de la mère. Elle accourt, et le trouve sans effroi et sans souffrance [!!]. Elle jette alors des cris, et attire un grand nombre de personnes pour être témoins de son bonheur, et de prodige."—D. Piolin, *Histoire de l'Église du Mans* (10 vols.).

Precisely the same tale is told of St. Antony of Padua (see next article).

A babe left in boiling water and not hurt (twelfth century). A "pious" woman, hearing that St. Antony of Padua was going to preach in her village, was almost beside herself with joy, and, being pressed for time, "au lieu de coucher son enfant dans son petit berceau, elle le déposa sans y prendre garde dans une chaudière pleine d'eau bouillante" (!!). When the sermon was over, some of the neighbours asked her where she had left her child, and instantly it flashed across her that something was not right. She ran home, and found the cradle empty; but what was her astonishment on finding she had put the babe in the boiler, the water of which was boiling furiously! Still greater was her surprise on finding the child laughing at the bubbling water, and holding out its arms to its mother. She fell on her knees, thanked God, and attributed the miracle to St. Antony.—L'abbé Gaudry, *Life of St. Antony of Padua.*

In some respects this tale is even more marvellous than the preceding one. In the preceding tale, the mother was washing the child and set it on the fire. In this case she intended to put it into the cradle, but made a mistake, and put it into the boiler. The tale is seriously told as a fact, and is repeated by right reverend authority.

A child rescued by St. Didacus from a heated oven (A.D. 1463). At Seville, a child, out of fear of its mother, concealed itself in an oven, and the woman, not knowing it, filled the oven with fagots, and set fire to them in order to heat it. The child was asleep, but the flames woke it, and it screamed dreadfully. The woman, in her terror, ran to tell her neighbours; but St. Didacus passing by, no sooner heard the woman's tale, than he went into the flaming oven, and brought out the child safe and uninjured. The neighbours formed a procession, and carried the child in triumph to the church, where the canons in their surplices received it, and took it to the lady's chapel, chanting and offering up thanks. —R. P. Cahier, *Caractéristiques des Saints.*

Dumb made to Speak. (See also under DEVILS.)

MARK vii. 32–35. When Jesus was in Decapolis, the people brought to Him a man deaf, who had also an impediment in his speech, and besought Him to cure him. Jesus took him aside, put His fingers into his ears, and He spit and touched his tongue, saying, Ephphatha [*Be opened*]; and straightway his ears were opened, and the string of his tongue was loosed, and he spake plainly.

MARK ix. 17-27. One of the multitude said, Master, I have brought my son which hath a dumb spirit; and wheresoever he taketh him, he teareth him: and he foameth, and gnasheth his teeth, and he pineth away. When brought to Jesus, the spirit tare the young man, and he fell on the ground, and wallowed, foaming. Then Jesus rebuked the foul spirit, saying to it, Thou dumb and deaf spirit, I charge thee come out of him, and enter no more into him. And the spirit came out of him; and the young man was as one dead, insomuch that many said, He is dead. But Jesus took him by the hand, and lifted him up; and he arose.

MATT. ix. 32, 33. They brought unto Jesus a dumb man possessed with a devil; and when the devil was cast out, the dumb spake.

St. Galla cures a child both dumb and deaf. St. Galla went into a house full of sick folk. Amongst others was a child both deaf and dumb. St. Galla took a glass of water, blessed it, and gave it to the child; whereupon its ears were immediately opened, and the string of its tongue was loosed.—*Les Petits Bollandists*, vol. ii. p. 200.

St. Maur gives speech to a child that was born dumb (A.D. 512-584). One day, while St. Benedict was absent, a child, dumb and lame, was brought to the abbey to be healed. The prior was referred to, but he rebuked the monks in anger, saying, "Am I God, to make alive, and to heal?" In this dilemma St. Maur, falling prostrate, said, "Thou God alone, it is true, can make alive and heal, bring down to the grave and bring up; I beseech thee, have pity on this child, and magnify Thy great name." Then, rising from his knees, he placed the corner of his stole on the child's head, and made the sign of the cross over the child's limbs, saying as he did so, "In the name of the blessed Trinity, and through the merits of my master St. Benedict, I command you to rise up in perfect health." The child obeyed, for it was cured, to the delight and wonder of the whole house.—Bollandus, *Acta Sanctorum*, Jan. 15.

St. Peter the martyr gives speech to a man who had been dumb for ten years. St. Peter of Gallia Cisalpina did many miracles. One day, preaching in Milan, some devout people brought to him a man who had been dumb for ten years. The holy man put his finger in the dumb man's mouth, touched the tongue, and cried, "Be opened!" whereupon the man spake plainly.—Thomas Lentinus, *Life of St. Peter the Martyr*.

St. Remi casts a dumb and deaf spirit out of a young girl. In the church of St. John the Baptist, at Reims, a damsel possessed of the devil was brought to St. Remi, that he might drive the spirit out. The holy man said to it, "Thou dumb and deaf spirit, I command thee, in the name of Jesus Christ, whose I am and whom I serve, to come out of her, and enter no more in." As the devil went out, he so tore and afflicted the damsel, that all present declared she was dead; but St. Remi, taking her by the hand, said to her, "Damsel, I say unto thee, in the name of Jesus Christ, arise, and go into thy house." And immediately the damsel arose in the presence of all, and went to her house.—Hincmar (archbishop of Reims, who died A.D. 882), *Life of St. Remi*.

St. Sebastian restores speech to Zoe, whose tongue had been paralyzed for six years (A.D. 303). St. Sebastian, commander of the first Roman cohort, was a Christian, and ventured to enter the house of Nicostratus, a Roman magistrate, to exhort sixteen prisoners to hold fast to the end. Zoe, the wife of the magistrate, was present, and knelt before the Christian soldier, looking steadfastly in his face, but without uttering a word, for her tongue had been paralyzed for six years. Sebastian, raising his hand, signed her mouth with the sign of the cross, saying, "If I am a true servant and soldier of God, He will restore thy speech to you, even as He opened the mouth of His prophet Zachariah." The words were hardly uttered before Zoe exclaimed, "Blessed art thou, and all who believe on the Lord Jesus!" When Nicostratus heard his wife speak, he fell at the saint's feet, and gave the Christian prisoners under his charge the free range of his house. Claudius, the jailer, had two sons of infirm bodies, one being dropsical and the other a cripple. When he heard of the cure of Zoe, he took his two sons to the house of Nicostratus, and besought of Sebastian that he and his two boys might be admitted by baptism into the Christian communion. Polycarp, who was present, baptized them, together with Tranquillinus, who suffered agony from gout. As the newly baptized rose from the water, all were healed of their several infirmities; and the prefect of Rome, whose name was Chromatius, being informed of these miracles, was also converted, laid down his high office, and retired into private life.—Baring-Gould, *Lives of the Saints*, Jan., pp. 300-302.

A dumb woman wishes three things, of which St. Vincent Ferrier accords two (A.D. 1357-1419). At Valentia a woman infirm and dumb presented herself to St. Vincent Ferrier, who made the sign of the cross on her forehead and mouth, and then asked her what he should do for her. "Grant me," she said, "three things—health to my infirm body, daily bread, and the use of speech." The man of God replied, "Two of these requests I will grant, but the third is not for thy soul's good." The woman said *Amen*, and went away dumb as before.—Peter Ranzano, *Life of St. Vincent Ferrier.*

The proverb gives point to this grant: "Remplissez votre bouche d'eau, et il vous arrevera ce qu'a dit St. Vincent" (*i.e.* silence). The tale is that a woman with a very irritating tongue asked St. Vincent what she could do to keep her husband at home, and moderate his ill temper. He replied, "Order your servant to bring you a cup of cold water, and when your husband returns take a mouthful and hold it in your mouth without swallowing it."

⁎ The dumb woman speaking is rather odd, but perhaps the saint communicated this power for the nonce.

An image of the Virgin Mary restores the voice of St. Peter Thomas (A.D. 1366). St. Peter Thomas reached the cathedral of Notre-dame du Puy, in Velay; but found himself so hoarse, that, when he rose to address the congregation, he was unable to utter a syllable that could be heard. Then, turning his eyes on the image of the Virgin, full of earnest entreaty, he immediately recovered his voice, and "never before was he so clear, so sonorous, and so eloquent."—*Les Petits Bollandistes*, vol. i. p. 167.

Election of a Bishop.

ACTS i. 24. The apostles prayed, and said, Thou, Lord, which knowest the hearts of all, show whether of these two Thou hast chosen.

Election of Nicholas as bishop of Myra. When Nicholas came to Myra, the bishops and clergy were assembled to chose a prelate for the see, and they made prayer to God to direct their choice aright. During the preceding night one of the aged bishops had a revelation, that the first person who entered the church would be the man sent by God. The convocation was in prayer, and the old prelate stood at the church door to see who would be the first to enter. St. Nicholas presented himself, and the old bishop, taking him by the hand, led him to the assembled clergy, and said to them, "Men and brethren, this is the man sent by God to fill the vacant see of Myra." So they consecrated him then and there; and all rejoiced that God had sent so eminent a saint to live among them.—Metaphrastês, *Lives*, etc.

Election of William to the archbishopric of Bourges (A.D. 1209). On the death of Henry de Sully, archbishop of Bourges, the clergy could not agree upon a successor; so Eudo, bishop of Paris, resolved to commit the choice to God. To this end the clergy were requested to write on slips of paper any names they thought proper, and the bishop, celebrating mass, asked God to show which of the names He had chosen. When mass was over, the bishop put his hand beneath the corporal, and drew forth one of the slips of paper which had been placed there. Then, opening the billet, he read the name of William, abbot of Challis; so this abbot was elevated to the vacant throne.—Baring-Gould, *Lives of the Saints*, Jan., p. 139.

Elijah and the Prophets of Baal.

1 KINGS xviii. 17-39. Elijah, being reproved by king Ahab for bringing a famine on Israel, replied that he did not bring the famine, but it was sent by God, because the king and the people had forsaken the Lord to worship Baal. In proof whereof he told the king to gather together on Mount Carmel the four hundred and fifty prophets of Baal and the four hundred prophets of the groves, and he would meet them there. So Ahab sent for the prophets, and Elijah said to the people, How long halt ye between two opinions? If the Lord is God, follow Him; but if Baal is God, follow Baal. He then proposed to prove experimentally which of the two is God indeed. The prophets of Baal were to offer a bullock to Baal, and Elijah would do the same to Jehovah, and the God which answered by sending fire to consume the sacrifice was to be received as the true God. The priests of Baal made their sacrifice, but no fire was sent from heaven to consume it. Elijah then offered a bullock to Jehovah, and fire was sent from the Lord to consume, not only the sacrifice, but the wood and the dust, and to lick up the water in the trench. When the people saw it they said, The Lord, He is God; the Lord, He is God.

St. Alexander proves to Rabbulus the truth of the story about Elijah and the prophets of Baal. Rabbulus often sent for St. Alexander; and one day, when Alexander was telling him the wondrous story of Elijah and the priests of Baal, Rabbulus said to him, "If the God of whom you speak wrought these wonders in the reign of Ahab, He can do the same now. Cry unto him as Elijah did, and bid Him send fire, that I may see and believe." At the word there fell fire from heaven, and consumed the mats that were in the room, but hurt nothing else. Then the governor bowed his head, and cried, "The Lord, He is God, and truly there is none beside Him." And he, with all his house, received baptism at the hands of St. Alexander.—Baring-Gould, *Lives of the Saints*, Jan., p. 229.

St. Pantaleon arraigns the priests of Rome. St. Pantaleon, being arraigned before the emperor Maximian, said, "My Lord, if it has been told you that I am a Christian, know you and all men that I worship Him who created heaven and earth, raiseth the dead, and cureth the leper. If you credit not what I say, cause a sick body, whose life is despaired of, to be brought into thy presence, and assemble hither the chief pontiff and all his priests. Let them call on their gods to restore the sick man, and I will call on the name of Jesus Christ; and let him that healeth the sick body be accepted as the true God." The proposal pleased the emperor; and a man sick of the palsy was brought forth. The priests called, some on Jupiter, some on Esculapius, and others on Diana; but all in vain. St. Pantaleon scoffed at them, and bade them call louder; but they retorted, saying, "Call you on your God Jesus." Then Pantaleon, lifting up his eyes to heaven, said, "O Lord, hear my prayer, and let my cry come unto Thee. Show this people that Thou art God, and there is none beside Thee." Having so said, he took the sick man by the hand, and said unto him, "In the name of Jesus Christ, stand on thy feet, and be ye whole." So the man arose, stood on his feet, and leaped, and went to his house joyful, for he was made whole.—Metaphrastês, *Lives*, etc.

Elijah and the Widow of Zarephath. (See FOOD MULTIPLIED.)

1 KINGS xvii. 8–16. After Elijah left Cherith, where he was fed by ravens, he went to Zidon. When he came to the gate of Zarephath, he saw a woman gathering sticks, and said to her, Fetch me, I pray thee, a little water in a vessel, that I may drink. And as she was going to fetch it, he called to her, and said, Bring me, I pray thee, a morsel of bread in thine hand. The woman said, As the Lord thy God liveth, I have not a cake, but [only] a handful of meal in a barrel, and a little oil in a cruise: and, behold, I am gathering two [or three] sticks, that I may go and dress it for me and my son, that we may eat it, and die. Elijah said to her, Fear not; go and do as thou hast said: but make me thereof a little cake first, and bring it unto me, and afterwards make for thyself and for thy son; for thus saith the Lord God of Israel, The barrel of meal shall not waste, neither shall the cruise of oil fail, until the day that the Lord sendeth rain upon the earth. So she went and did according to the saying of Elijah; and she, and he, and her house did eat many days. And the barrel of meal wasted not, neither did the cruise of oil fail, according to the word of the Lord, which He spake by Elijah.

St. Blaise and the poor woman's hog. A poor woman had a hog, which was all her earthly store, and a wolf stole it. The woman told her tale of sorrow to St. Blaise, and he said to her, "Woman, be of good comfort; the hog shall be brought to thee again." And so it was; for the wolf brought it back, and it had received no injury at all. When St. Blaise was in prison, the poor woman came to comfort him, and brought him a part of the hog, which had been killed for food. Blaise received it at her hands, and said to her, "Never from this day forth shall food fail thee;" and never from that day did she lack anything needful for her daily life.—Metaphrastês, *Life of St. Blaise*.

St. Isidore and the empty pot. St. Isidore was a farm labourer. One day, returning home after his day's work, he found a poor pilgrim at his cottage door, asking for food. Isidore told his wife to give the man something to eat, but the woman said sadly, "Alack, alack! there is nothing in the house." Isidore bade his wife look into the pot, but she replied, "It is quite empty; for I have just rinsed it, and set it by." "Go, wife, and fetch it," said the saint. So she went to fetch it, and found it very heavy. On taking off the lid, she was amazed at seeing the pot full to the very top of most excellent meat, cooked and hot, and fit for immediate use. So she gave liberally to the poor pilgrim, and set before her husband, but still the store was not diminished.—Edward Kinesman, *The Miraculous Life, etc., of St. Isidore, patron of Madrid, lately canonized by pope Gregory XV. Abridged from the Spanish. Authorized by Philip, king of Castile, etc., and signed by his minister, De Groote.*

St. Lupicin supplies the abbey of Lauconne with a sheaf of wheat which wasted not (A.D. 480). Sometimes the abbey grounds of Lauconne, in the Jura, always more or less sterile, would not supply corn enough for the monastery over which St. Lupicin presided. At such times the holy abbot used to lay his case before God, and always found that He who remembered the sparrows forgot not His own children. One year the abbey was unusually crowded, for a large number of seculars had sought an asylum there, so that scarcity had set in. The steward told the abbot that the resources would be utterly exhausted in fifteen days, but that the harvest would not be gathered in for three months at least. The abbot heard the announcement undisturbed, and said to his monks, "Come, my children, let us enter the granary, where we have still some sheaves left. Have we not renounced the world to follow Christ?" Then, having entered the granary and fallen on their knees, St. Lupicin said, "O Jesu Christ, Thou hast said, No one shall quit for My sake house, or brothers, or sisters, or father, or mother, or children, or goods, but shall receive a hundredfold in this world. Now send us Thy help. O God, who made that the barrel of meal should not waste, nor the cruise of oil fail, when Thy servant Elijah was with the widow of Zarephath, in Zidonia, now look upon us Thy servants, who have placed ourselves under the protection of Thy Son, our Lord; and as Thou hast given us freely the bread of life, vouchsafe to give us also the bread whereby we live." All the brothers cried *Amen*. Then, turning to the steward, St. Lupicin said, "Place these sheaves in one bundle; for thus saith the Lord God of Israel, The sheaves shall supply food, and shall not waste, till the harvest be gathered in." So the sheaves were piled together, and wasted not, and all the brothers and strangers fed thereon for more than three months. Many have testified to this miracle, amongst others St. Oyend, then a novice in the monastery, but afterwards abbot of Condat, from whom the historian of Condat was told the details given above. —*Acta Sanctorum* (Bollandists), March 21; Tillemont, vol. xvi. p. 142; St. Gregory of Tours, *De Vita Patrum*, ch. i.; Belley, *Hagiography;* Longueval, *History of the Gallican Church*, vol. ii. bk. 4; etc.

Two Christians fed by Rusticus on pork, and the pork diminished not. Two Christian pilgrims travelling in Poland came to the door of Rusticus, a heathen peasant who had just killed a fat hog, to celebrate the birth of his only son. The pilgrims, being invited to partake of the feast, pronounced a blessing on what was left, and this remainder of the hog never diminished in size or weight from that day forth, although all the family fed on it freely every day.—J. Brady, *Clavis Calandaria*, p. 183.

This reminds one of the hog Schrimner, in Scandinavian mythology, on which the gods and goddesses of Valhalla feed daily, yet the dish never decreases in quantity.

Elijah eats Angels' Food. (See MY FLESH IS MEAT INDEED, pt. iii.)

1 KINGS xix. 5–8. As Elijah lay under a juniper tree, behold, an angel touched him, and said unto him, Arise and eat. . . . And he arose, and did eat and drink; and he went in the strength of that meat forty days and forty nights unto Horeb the mount of God.

St. Aïbert, fed by the Virgin Mary, receives a force which lasted all the rest of his life (A.D. 1060–1140). A great flood of water having encircled the cell of St. Aïbert, he was for many days deprived of food. Then the Virgin Mary came to him, and put in his mouth a morsel of bread of such extraordinary virtue, that it imparted to him a vigour which lasted all the rest of his life, that is, twenty-two years, during all which time he had never more need of bread to eat, but only a few herbs and roots; and for twenty years he drank nothing at all.—Robert (archdeacon of Ostrevand), *Life of St. Aïbert.*

Elijah fed by Ravens.

1 KINGS xvii. 6. While Elijah was at the brook Cherith, in concealment, ravens brought him bread and flesh in the morning, and bread and flesh in the evening.

GEN. xxii. 14. Jehovah-jireh, "the Lord will provide."

A pigeon brings food to St. Auxentius (A.D. 470). While St. Auxentius was in Siope, near Chalcedon, the Christians, amazed at the tales told of his abstinence, determined to put him to the proof. With this intent, they placed in his cell baskets full of roots, dates, and other foods, lighted a candle, and set a child to watch him. After several days they found the candle still burning, and observed that it had not diminished. The food in the baskets had not been touched, and the child, being asked what the saint had lived on, replied, "A pigeon came daily and brought him food."—*Life of St. Auxentius*, by his disciple Vendimian. (There is an excellent MS. life of this saint in the Bibliothèque de la rue Richelieu, in Paris.)

Prince Cadoc and the rhetorician fed by

a mouse (sixth century.) Prince Cadoc went to finish his education under a famous rhetorician who had more pupils than money. Indeed, so poor was the learned scholar, that he often had no food in the house. One day, at the hour of breakfast, the prince observed a white mouse jump on the table, and deposit there a single grain of wheat. Cadoc watched the mouse, and followed it. He found that it ran into a cellar, one of those old Keltic subterranean granaries, remains of which are still to be seen in Wales. In this cellar Cadoc discovered a vast store of corn, which served to feed both master and pupils for many weeks. (See ST. GONTRAN.)—Rees, *Lives of the Cambro-British Saints.*

St. Calais fed by a sparrow (A.D. 545). One day St. Calais was working in his vineyard, and being very warm, hung his cloak on a tree. At sunset he felt fatigued and hungry, but had nothing to eat. He went to the tree to take down his cloak, and found that a sparrow had laid in it an egg. The egg afforded him sufficient nourishment, and more joy, for he felt it was a gift sent from God.—Dom Paul Piolin, *Histoire de l'Église du Mans.*

St. Catherine of Alexandria fed by a dove. Maxentius the emperor ordered St. Catherine of Alexandria to be scourged, and then confined without food in a dark dungeon. Here she remained twelve days. Angels came to heal her wounds, and a dove provided her every day with needful food.—Metaphrastês (died 911), *Lives*, etc.

St. Cuthbert, in the isle of Farne, fed by rooks (seventh century). When St. Cuthbert first retired to Farne, the isle was absolutely without inhabitant, without a tree, and without water. It was wholly barren of food, and provided nothing which could be converted into sustenance. It will be asked, how then did he exist? The answer is this: by prayer he obtained a spring of most delicious water, and rooks brought him food daily, till the barley he had sown was gathered in.—*Les Petits Bollandistes*, vol. iii. p. 550.

St. Cuthbert fed by an eagle. When St. Cuthbert was labouring to convert the Northumbrians, he was driven, on one occasion, by a severe snow-storm to the coast of Fife. "Never," said he to his despondent companions, "did man die of hunger who served God faithfully, for it is written, 'I will never leave thee, nor forsake thee.'" While he was still speaking, an eagle overhead dropped a large fish at his feet.—Green, *A Short History of the English People*, p. 25. (See p. 128.)

Another instance. At another time, being overtaken at sea by a terrible storm which kept them out in the deep for several days, food failed, and both St. Cuthbert and those with him must have died, if God had not sent them three large morsels of a dolphin, which served them well with food for three entire days.—*Les Petits Bollandistes*, vol. iii. p. 550.

God fed St. Didacus miraculously on a journey (A.D. 1463). While St. Didacus was journeying from Cerraya to St. Luc de Barramède he was unable to procure any food on the road, and both he and his companion were so faint with hunger, they were unable to continue their journey. They prayed for succour, and as they rose they found close by a cloth spread on the grass with bread, fish, citrons, and a bottle of wine. They looked about to see if any one was near; they waited awhile, but no one came; they felt certain that God had made them this feast in the wilderness; they ate, their strength was renewed, and they continued their journey, giving God thanks.—R. P. Cahier, *Caractéristiques des Saints.*

Brother Giles miraculously supplied with food (A.D. 1272). Brother Giles, making a pilgrimage to the Holy Land, was one day so overcome with hunger and fatigue, that he dropped on the ground and fell asleep. On waking, he found, close to his head, a mysterious loaf of bread. In fact, God had sent it him, as He sent bread and flesh to Elijah by His messengers, the ravens.—*Acta Sanctorum* (Bollandists), April 23.

Four hermits supplied daily with bread by invisible hands (fourth century). St. Paphnucius, having buried Onuphrius, the old anchorite, wandered four days till he came to a hill, where an old hoary recluse met him, addressed him by name, and said he was glad to have the honour of greeting the saint who had buried Father Onuphrius. Three other hermits came up, and greeted him warmly. They told him they had been sixty years in the desert, and that he was the only human being, except themselves, they had seen in all those years. Being asked how they obtained food, they replied that God sent it them miraculously, they knew not how, but every day they found in their cell four loaves of bread, very delicate and very white. They now led Paphnucius to their cavern, and lo! five loaves were deposited there, but no one had seen the bringer.—*Les Petits Bollandistes*, vol. vi. p. 591.

St. Marinus fed by two bears (A.D. 731). St. Marinus was a monk in the monastery sacred to the Virgin, in Moriana, in Italy. He left the monastery, retired to a cell on the edge of a rock, and sanctified it by a three days' fast. He would have continued his fast, but God sent two bears, each with a honeycomb full of honey, which they laid at his feet; then, crouching down, they proceeded to lick his feet, as if inviting him to taste the food they had brought him. This he did, and told the bears to come again another day. These bears ever after came daily to the cell, bringing to the hermit two little loaves of bread; and every day, for the space of four years, these wild beasts behaved like lambs, and showed the recluse every mark of reverence.—L'abbé Auber, *Vie des Saints du Diocèse de Poitiers.*

Dr. Moulins fed by a hen. During the dreadful Bartholomew slaughter, Dr. Moulins lay hid from the cut-throats for many weeks in a cave; but every day a hen came, and laid an egg there, by which means the doctor escaped starvation, and lived to record this marvellous interposition.

The old hermit of Sinaï fed by a lion (fourth century). When St. Simeon went to Sinaï, an old hermit told him that he and a brother hermit had come to live together in a cave on the mount. His companion having died, a lion had come daily ever since, bringing to the cave's mouth a bunch of dates.—Theodoret, *Philotheus*, c. 6.

St. Paul the hermit fed for sixty years by a crow (A.D. 341). When St. Antony was ninety years old he went to visit St. Paul the hermit, who was 113, and lived in the Lower Thebaïd. While conversing together, a crow settled on a bough, and presently alighting, laid at the hermit's feet a loaf of bread. "Ah!" said St. Paul, "the Lord is ever mindful and loving. For sixty years the bird has brought me daily only half a loaf, but now you are come God hath doubled the allowance."—St. Jerome (A.D. 375), *Life of Paul, the First Hermit of Egypt.*

It is a pity we are not told how much the loaf was heavier than the bird, and how the crow carried it. In the case of Elijah the same difficulty does not occur, for it is not one raven that carried a loaf, but [several] ravens which carried bread and flesh. No doubt the supply in both cases was miraculous, but the want of consistency in the latter case is certainly striking.

⁂ We are told in the *Acta Sanctorum* (Bollandists), vol. i. June 2, that St. Erasmus of Mount Liban was also fed by a crow.

St. Robert, abbot of Casa Dei, supplied with food by an eagle (A.D. 1067). While St. Robert, abbot of Casa Dei, was at Allanche, in the mountains of Auvergne, and was about to celebrate mass, the cook came to him to say there was nothing in the house for dinner. "Never mind," replied St. Robert; "serve the mass, and God will provide our daily bread." He had but just begun the "preface," when an eagle, passing over the church, let fall an enormous fish, which supplied the abbot and all his suite with an ample meal.—*Acta Sanctorum* (Bollandists), April 24. (See St. Cuthbert, p. 127.)

St. Simon Stock fed daily by a dog (A.D. 1164-1265). St. Simon Stock lived in the trunk of a hollow tree in the vast forest of Toubersville, in Kent. His food consisted of raw herbs, bitter roots, and wild fruits; his drink being water. God, ever watchful over His children, commissioned a dog to take him daily a piece of bread, as the ravens took bread and meat to the prophet Elijah.—*Life of St. Simon Stock* (by a contemporary, thirteenth century).

We are further told that St. Simon Stock lived for six years on Mount Carmel, as Moses lived on Mount Sinai. All these years he saw only angels, and his only food was manna, brought him from time to time by the Virgin Mary.

St. Stephen, third abbot of Cîteaux, has a fish brought him by a bird (A.D. 1134). On one occasion, when St. Stephen, abbot of Cîteaux, was very ill, and his stomach refused all food, a bird brought him a fish ready cooked, and fed him with it bit by bit, as it would have fed one of its own brood. In Christian art the abbot is represented being fed with a fish by a bird.—*Acta Sanctorum* (Bollandists), vol. ii. April 17.

St. Sorus and the stag (A.D. 520). Two young men, out of reverence to St. Sorus, attached themselves to him as servants. They loved their master dearly, and were in turn greatly beloved by him. The young men sought for him alms of food and raiment, and, of course, themselves partook thereof. One day the larder was quite empty, and the young men began to murmur. "My children," said the hermit, "why are ye of so little faith? The hand of God is not straitened that it cannot help. If God could feed five thousand in the desert with five loaves and two fishes can He not feed you two?

Be not faithless, my children, but believing. Jehovah-jireh, the Lord will provide." The two young men now left the cell, and found at the door a noble stag, which had fallen down before it and broken its neck. They ran back to tell the master; the stag supplied them with food for many days, and the hide made a garment for St. Sorus, which he wore, as the gift of God, to his dying day.—*Les Petits Bollandistes*, vol. ii. p. 192.

Wyat fed in prison by a cat. Henry Wyat was imprisoned by Richard III., and was so neglected that he was nearly starved to death. When reduced to the last extremity a cat appeared at his grating, and dropped into his hand a pigeon, which the warder cooked for him; and this was done daily till his release.

A weasel reveals to St. Gontran hid treasures for his charity (A.D. 525–593). St. Gontran, king of Burgundy, was extremely charitable. One day a weasel attracted his attention, and revealed to him enormous treasures, whereby he was enabled to indulge his charity without in any wise taxing his subjects. He fell asleep after a hunting expedition; his equerry was with him, and saw a weasel run out of the king's mouth towards a rivulet. As the weasel could not cross the water, the equerry laid his sword across the stream. The weasel ran over this bridge into a cleft in a mountain, whence it soon returned, and re-entered the king's mouth. When Gontran awoke, he told his equerry he had been dreaming a strange dream; he thought he crossed over an iron bridge, and came to a mountain in which was such a mass of money that he was quite dazed at the sight. The equerry then told the king what he had seen, and the coincidence induced Gontran to go to the fissure in the mountain and examine it, when he found treasures exceeding the wildest imagination. With a part of this hid treasure St. Gontran founded the celebrated abbey of Beaume les Dames. (See PRINCE CADOC AND THE MOUSE, p. 126.)—*Annales Hagiographiques de France*, vol. vi.

St. Vitus and his companions fed by eagles (A.D. 303). When Vitus, a lad only twelve years old, was threatened with death by Valerian, prefect of Sicily, and sent there by Diocletian to stamp out Christianity from the island, he fled, accompanied by his tutor Modestus and an attendant named Crescentius, to Naples; but, being wholly without provisions, they were fed by an eagle, till Diocletian sent for them to heal the prince his son, grievously afflicted with a devil.—Mgr. Guérin, *Vies des Saints*, vol. vii. p. 29, etc.

Elijah makes Rain to cease and to fall.

JAMES v. 17, 18. Elias was a man subject to like passions as we are, and he prayed earnestly that it might not rain: and it rained not on the earth by the space of three years and six months. And he prayed again, and the heavens gave rain, and the earth brought forth her fruit.

1 KINGS xvii. 1. And Elijah the Tishbite said unto Ahab, As the Lord God of Israel liveth, before whom I stand, there shall not be dew nor rain these years, but according to my word.

1 KINGS xviii. 1. And it came to pass that the word of the Lord came to Elijah in the third year, saying, Go, show thyself unto Ahab; and I will send rain upon the earth. (See *vv.* 42–45.)

St. Basil relieves Verzy of a great drought (A.D. 626). As in the time of Elijah the heavens overhead were brass, so, in the time of St. Basil, God, justly irritated with the sins of the people, refused rain, till most of the rivers about Verzy were dried up, man languished, and the herds and the flocks, the horses and other domesticated animals, were tormented with feverish thirst. In this necessity the inhabitants of Verzy had recourse to St. Basil; and the saint, touched with compassion, implored Jesus Christ to succour the people. At once there leaped from a rock a clear and plentiful spring of water, enough for both man and beast. This "miraculous" rock-fountain received the name of "Legit Ossa," because the waters were sanative. —Mgr. Guérin, *Vies des Saints*, vol. xiii. p. 603.

St. Bont, bishop of Clermont, intercedes for rain (A.D. 623–710). When all Auvergne was visited by a great drought, St. Bont ordered a fast and a religious procession for rain. Mass was scarcely finished, when rain fell in such great profusion that the congregation was unable to leave the church.—Bollandus, *Acta Sanctorum*, vol. i. Jan. 15.

St. Euthymius in a great drought intercedes for rain (A.D. 376–473). During a dreadful drought, when the "earth was iron and the heavens brass," the inhabitants of Melitena, in Armenia, went in procession, carrying the cross and chanting the *Kyrie Eleison*, to St. Euthymius, to crave his intercession with God to "water the earth and make it fruitful." St. Euthymius bade the procession fall with him on their knees, and pray to Him who says, "Ask, and ye shall receive." While they prayed the heaven grew black with clouds, and the rain fell in torrents. The earth revived, the hills clapped their hands for joy, and plenty crowned the year with fatness.—Cyrillus, *Life of Euthymius.*

St. Hilarion prays for rain, and the heavens give rain. After the death of St. Antony, there was no rain in Upper Egypt for the space of three years, and the people said it was because the elements lamented for the death of that holy man. And it came to pass, at the end of three years, the people of Upper Egypt besought St. Hilarion to pray for them, that God would be pleased to send rain. Hilarion did so, and rain fell in such abundance, that the earth was refreshed, and brought forth its fruits in their seasons.—St. Jerome, *Vita St. Hilarionis Eremitæ* (A.D. 390). See also Nicephorus Callistus (died 1350), *Ecclesiastical History.*

St. John Climacus causes rain to fall (A.D. 526–605). Soon after St. John Climacus was chosen abbot of Mount Sinai, the people of Palestine and Arabia applied to him in the time of a great drought, begging him to intercede with God on their behalf. The saint failed not to lay their misery before the Father of all mercies, and his prayer was immediately answered by an abundance of rain.—Daniel (a contemporary and monk of Raithu). *Life of St. John Climacus.*

The same is said in the *Propre de Bourges* of St. Eustadiola (seventh century).

St. Ouen commands rain to fall in Spain (A.D. 644). When St. Ouen passed into Spain, he found the country suffering greatly from a long drought. No rain had fallen for seven years ! ! vegetation was nearly parched up, few cattle survived, and the country was in a terrible state. St. Ouen, by his prayers, delivered the country from this great plague, which threatened a universal famine, and inevitable ruin. The effect of his prayers was a rich harvest, not only of temporal fruits, but also of spiritual graces ; for rain fell in abundance to render the land fecund ; and the people, grateful for the rain, promised to renounce their sins, which had called down upon them this divine wrath.—L'abbé Pécheur, *Annales du Diocèse de Soissons.*

St. Peter Thomas brings down rain from heaven (A.D. 1366). One day, while St. Peter Thomas was preaching, his voice pierced the clouds, causing them to open and supply the earth with abundance of rain, then greatly needed.—*Les Petits Bollandistes,* vol. i. p. 167.

St. Porphyry, at Gaza, prays for rain (A.D. 353–420). When St. Porphyry went to Gaza there was a very great drought, and as no rain fell for two months after his arrival, the Gazæans went to the temple of Marnas, their rain-god, to supplicate him to remove the calamity. For seven days they repeated their supplications, but no rain fell. The Christian women and children, to the number of 280, now fasted and prayed for one day, and then went with St. Porphyry, their bishop, to St. Timothy's church, singing hymns. On returning to Gaza, they found the gates shut against them, for the Gazæans insisted that their god Marnas was jealous of Jesus Christ. Here, before the gates, the bishop and the Christians with him prayed God in His mercy to send a gracious rain upon the land ; and while they prayed the heavens were black with clouds, and the rain fell in great abundance. The gates were now thrown open, and the heathen cried aloud, "Christ, He is God ; Christ, He is God !" 176 were baptized, and the Lord added to His Church daily such as should be saved. —Mark (a companion), *Life of St. Porphyry.*

St. Sabas, in a great dearth, intercedes for rain. When St. Sabas was at Jerusalem, there was a great dearth. No water could be found even to drink, so that the people were ready to perish. St. Sabas prayed, and the rain fell so abundantly that the cisterns were filled, and all the people had an ample supply. —Cyril (the monk), *Life of St. Sabas.*

St. Serenus brings down rain, and thus terminates a dearth and pest (seventh century). A great dearth prevailed in the vicinity of Mans, and a pestilence desolated the land. Men fell down dead while carrying the dead to their graves, and sextons were buried in the graves they were digging for others. In this dreadful calamity St. Berarius, bishop of Mans, went to consult Serenus, and Serenus advised a three days' fast. On the third day, a monk assured the bishop it had been revealed to him, that the country would be delivered from these calamities only by the prayers of St. Serenus ; the bishop, therefore, went at once to the hermit's cell, and told him what the monk had said. Serenus gave himself at once to prayer and fasting, and before sunset rain fell in torrents, purified the air, refreshed the ground, cleansed the drains, the plague ceased, and the earth yielded her produce most liberally.—R. P. dom Paul Piolin, *Life of St. Serenus*, etc. (1868).

The Thundering Legion. The twelfth legion of the Roman army under Marcus Aurelius, acting against the Quadi, A.D. 164, being shut up in a defile, was reduced to great straits for want of water, when a body of Christians, enrolled in the legion, prayed for relief. Not only was rain sent in abundance in answer to their prayer, but the thunder and lightning were so terrific that the foe was panic-struck; the legion then fell on them, and gained an easy but complete victory. The legion ever after was called the "Thundering Legion." It is almost incredible, but we are assured that these very Christians were all martyred not long after for being Christians, and the 10th of March is set apart in honour of the forty martyrs. —Dion Cassius, *Roman History*, bk. lxxi. 8; Eusebius, *Ecclesiastical History*, bk. v. 5; Metaphrastês, *Lives*, etc.

There may still be seen in Rome a record of this "miracle" on the bas-relief of the column of Antoninus. The Romans are represented with their arms in their hands, and the barbarians are stretched on the ground with their horses terrified at the thunder and lightning. Marcus Aurelius certainly wrote to the senate of Rome stating that his army, at the point of death, had been saved by the prayers of some Christian soldiers.

Elijah spirited away.

1 KINGS xviii. 12. Obadiah was sent by king Ahab to apprehend Elijah, and the prophet told him to go and tell the king, Behold, Elijah is here. Then Obadiah remonstrated with the prophet, and said, As soon as I am gone, the Spirit of the Lord shall carry thee whither I know not; and when Ahab comes and cannot find thee, he will slay me.

ACTS viii. 39. When Philip had baptized the eunuch, the Spirit of the Lord caught him away, and the eunuch saw him no more.

St. Antony carried from Padua to Lisbon and back again in one day. St. Antony wishing to attend the trial of his father, who was charged with murder, an angel carried him from Padua to Lisbon, where he was present at the trial, and then back again to Padua, in one day.—Edward Kinesman (1623), *Lives of the Saints.*

St. Maidoc of Ferns conveyed from Ireland to Rome and back again in one day (A.D. 632). On one occasion, St. Maidoc drove from Ireland to Rome and back again in one day. [We are not told *what* he drove, nor yet how he crossed the water. Probably "the Spirit of the Lord carried him."] — Baring-Gould, *Lives of the Saints*, Jan. 31.

St. Restituta carried during sleep from Rome to Sora (third century). St. Restituta was the daughter of a Roman patrician named Ethel, and was a Christian. The devil said to her, "Restituta, you think to escape from my hands; but know this shall not be, at least without blood." So saying, he drew a sword, and said, "This sword I shall entrust to one of my people, and I will bid him run you through with it, if you attempt to escape me." Restituta, somewhat frightened, made the sign of the cross, saying, "Let God arise, and let His enemies be scattered; let them that hate Him flee before Him." At these words the devil fled. Then said Restituta, "Arise, O Lord, and succour Thy servant who trusteth in Thee." Whereupon Jesus Christ came to her visibly, and said to her, "Why art thou disquieted, Restituta? Hope in God. He is thy Succour and Defender. Know you not that the devil is a liar, and the father of lies? Hear me. To-morrow, at daybreak, go to Sora, and there unite the creature with the Creator." Restituta replied, "I dare not venture alone from home, and know not where Sora is." "I will be with thee," said Christ, "and will send an angel for thy guide." Next morning, accordingly, she went to the Lateran, and there saw the angel waiting for her. He saluted her, and bade her sleep awhile, as Sora was forty miles off. So she slept; and while she slept, the angel transported her to Sora.—*Acta Sanctorum* (Bollandists), vol. vi. May 29.

Elijah's Chariot.

2 KINGS ii. 11. It came to pass, as Elijah and Elisha went on talking, that there appeared a chariot of fire, and horses of fire, and parted them asunder; and Elijah went up by a whirlwind into heaven.

2 KINGS vi. 13–18. The king of Syria sent horses, and chariots, and a great host, to encompass the city where Elisha was, in order to take him prisoner. Elisha's servant said to him, Alas, my master! how shall we do? Elisha replied, Fear not. And presently the servant beheld that the mountain was full of horses and chariots of fire, round about Elisha.

St. Germanus of Scotland crosses the British channel in a chariot (fifth century). St. Germanus of Scotland wished to go to France to see his namesake, bishop of

Auxerre. When he got to the coast, there was no vessel to carry him across, so he prayed God to send him the means of transit. As he was still praying, there appeared upon the sea a chariot and horses coming towards him. Having entered the chariot, he was lifted into the air, transported across the channel in a moment, and set down at Flammenville, close by Dieppe. The Dieppoise thought it was either Neptune or a magician; but certain miracles which the saint wrought among them convinced them of their mistake, and five hundred were soon converted to the Christian faith.—Corblet, *Hagiographie d'Amiens.*

Elijah's Translation. (See ANGELS CARRY SOULS TO HEAVEN.)

2 KINGS ii. 1–16. When Elijah was about to leave this earth Elisha was with him, and he tried to induce Elisha to tarry behind while he went forward to Bethel, Jericho, and the river Jordan. Elisha refused to quit the prophet, so they passed over the river together. Having come to the other side, "behold, a chariot of fire and horses of fire" appeared and "parted the two asunder, and Elijah went up by a whirlwind into heaven." Then cried Elisha, My father, my father, the chariot of Israel, and the horsemen thereof. And he took up the mantle which fell from Elijah, and went back again across the Jordan.

The translation of St. Paul, the first hermit, seen by St. Antony (A.D. 342). Paul the hermit was 113 years old, and Antony, the only other hermit, was ninety. Antony was led up by the Spirit to visit Paul a little before his death. Paul, wishing to get rid of his visitor, or to save him the pain of witnessing his death, entreated him to go and fetch the mantle of Athanasius which was preserved in a neighbouring convent. Antony made all the haste possible, and returned with the mantle, but as he drew near the hermit's cave, he beheld a company of angels, prophets, and apostles bearing up to heaven the soul of the departed hermit. "Paul, Paul!" cried Antony, throwing dust over his head and weeping, "why have you left me thus? So lately met, and so soon parted!" Then, entering the cell, he found the body of the deceased kneeling on its knees, with its hands uplifted towards heaven. He thought at first it was living, and in prayer; but, hearing no sigh, he felt assured that it was dead. He wrapped it in the mantle he had brought, and wished to bury it, but had neither strength to lift it nor means of digging a grave. In this perplexity he knelt in prayer, asking aid of Christ, and presently two lions appeared in sight. They came direct to the dead body, and, twisting their tails round it, carried it out of the cave; they then set to work to scratch a deep hole in the earth, lovingly lifted the body into it, and covered it decently with the soil. The work of interment being accomplished, the two lions approached St. Antony with heads abased, wagging their tails and shaking their ears. They licked the hands and feet of the old hermit, asking, as plainly as they could do so, for his benediction. St. Antony understood them, and holding his hands over their heads, said, "Saviour of the world, who allowest not a hair of the head to fall, nor sparrow to die, without Thy bidding, give to these lions what in Thy wisdom Thou seest best for them." Then, making in the air the sign of the cross, he dismissed them; and so they left him, roaring mournfully to express their grief. Antony returned to his cell, taking with him the raiment of leaves worn by the deceased, and this he continued to wear ever after till the day of his death.

This truly marvellous narrative is taken from St. Jerome, whose life of St. Paul the hermit has always been accepted as undoubtedly genuine. Paul died A.D. 342, and St. Jerome lived 345–420. The account may be read in almost any of the numerous compilations called "Lives of the Saints," "Acts of the Saints," and so on. St. Jerome concludes the life with these words: "If God gave me the choice, I would infinitely prefer the vile habit of Paul the hermit, could I be endowed also with his merits, to the most lordly robe of the greatest monarch of the earth."

Elisha and the Axe. (See GRAVITATION, etc.)

2 KINGS vi. 5–7. As one was felling a beam on the banks of the Jordan, the axe-head fell into the water; and the man cried, Alas, master! for the axe was borrowed. And the man of God said, Where fell it? And the man showed the prophet the place. Then Elisha cut down a stick, and cast it into the river, and the iron did swim. Then said he to the woodman, Take it up to thee. And he put forth his hand, and took it.

St. Benedict of Mount Cassino makes the head of an axe, which had fallen into a lake, float into its handle (A.D. 480–543). The monastery of St. Clement was situated on the bank of a lake. One day a novice, who was a Goth, was employed in clearing the banks of this lake, and used so much violence, that the head of his axe flew off into the water. St. Benedict went at once to the lake, and, holding the end of the haft in the water, the iron head rose to the surface, and fitted itself firmly into the handle. St. Benedict gave the axe to the Goth, and bade him go on with his work.—St. Gregory the Great, *Dialogues*, bk. ii.

St. Gerard makes a reliquary, which had been dropped into a river, rise again to the surface (A.D. 994). The emperor Otto II. of Germany sent for St. Gerard, bishop of Toul, respecting the affairs of the Church. While on the Moselle, opposite Dommartin, his clerk, wishing to wash his hands, leaned over the boat, and the reliquary (which he put upon the seat) rolled into the river. St. Gerard saw the emperor, accomplished his mission satisfactorily, and on his return stopped the boat opposite Dommartin. After a short prayer, he put his hand into the river, the reliquary rose to the surface, and he drew it in. This miracle, which was seen by all who accompanied the bishop, not a little amazed them.—Father Benedict, *Life of St. Gerard* (1700).

St. Leufredus makes an axe float in the river Eure (A.D. 738). One of the monks of La Croix, having dropped his axe in the river Eure, told Leufredus of the accident. The saint went to the river, put the end of his stick into the water, and forthwith the iron axe coming to the surface, fixed itself securely on the end of the stick, and was drawn out.—Mgr. Guérin, *Vies des Saints*, vol. vii. p. 188.

St. Wulfran makes a silver paten float on the sea (A.D. 647–720). As St. Wulfran was sailing from Caudebec to Frisia, St. Vando while at mass dropped the paten into the sea, while wiping it. St. Wulfran told him to put his hand in the sea, and immediately the silver paten was buoyed up into his hand, and he drew it out of the water, to the astonishment of all those in the ship with him. This "miracle" is quite certain, for the very paten was carefully preserved in the monastery of St. Vandrille till 1621 (above a thousand years), when it was stolen.—L'abbé Corblet, *Hagiography of the Diocese of Amiens*.

In Christian art, the parallel between Wulfran and Elisha is still more closely followed. Instead of St. Vando putting his hand into the sea, Wulfran is represented as casting a stick over the side of the vessel, and the paten floating. "Take it in, Vando," said the bishop, and then it was that Vando, like the woodman, put out his hand and took it in (2 Kings vi. 6, 7).

Elisha and the Moabite. (See Dead raised to Life.)

2 Kings xiii. 20, 21. And Elisha died, and they buried him. And it came to pass as the Moabites, who invaded the land at the coming in of the year, were burying a man, they spied a band of men, and cast the dead Moabite into the sepulchre of Elisha. And when he was let down and touched the bones of Elisha, he revived, and stood on his feet.

A young man, cast into the grave of St. Cyril (general of Mount Carmel), is restored to life (A.D. 1224). A young man who had come from Cyprus to the Holy Land, died aboard ship, and the pilot of the vessel gave the body to the monks of Mount Carmel to bury. Till the grave was ready, they laid the body on the tomb of St. Cyril, their late general; and immediately the dead body of the young man touched the saint's tomb it came to life, and cried with a loud voice, "Cyril has restored me to life, and reserved me for a better." The young man now joined the Carmelites, and lived with them for twelve years.—Mgr. Guérin, *Vies des Saints*, vol. iii. p. 202 (1880).

A blind man recovers his sight by touching the body of Edward the Martyr (A.D. 962–978). Edward, king of England, having reigned three years and a half, went out hunting in the forest near Wareham, in Dorsetshire; and, being somewhat weary, paid a visit to his stepmother, Elfrida, at Corfe Castle. Elfrida, pretending to be glad to see him, went out to meet him, and offered him a cup of wine; but while he drank, she stabbed him, and he died. Elfrida then dragged the body into the cottage of a blind man, thinking to hide her crime; but the moment the body came near the blind man his eyes were opened, and at midnight he saw a great light, which lightened the hut in which the body was. When Elfrida heard of this miracle, she threw the body into a swamp, but, as Alban Butler says, "it was discovered by a pillar of light, and honoured by many miracles" (March 18).—Baronius, *Annals*; Polydore Vergil, *English History*.

A boy who had been drowned restored to life by being placed on the tomb of St. Gertrude. A child fell into a well and was killed; but, being taken out, was laid on the tomb of St. Gertrude, late abbess of Nivelles. The mother did not believe that St. Gertrude could do anything for her, but a nun said, "O great saint, now make manifest the power of thy merits." No sooner were the words uttered, than the dead child recovered its life.—Surius, *Lives of the Saints*.

A dead girl reveals where the body of St. Fridian was buried (A.D. 810). St. Fridian died in the sixth century; but after a time the place of his interment was lost sight of. Some three hundred years afterwards a young girl died, and, being buried, cried out aloud, "Take me away, take me away; the body of St. Fridian lies here!" The girl was removed to another grave, and the bones of St. Fridian were thus miraculously discovered.—*Ecclesiastical History of Lucca.*

The dead body of St. Malachy restores a withered hand (1148). St. Malachy of Armagh died Nov. 2, 1148, at the age of fifty-four, and was buried next day. St. Bernard, who assisted in the ceremony, saw in the crowd a lad with a withered hand; and as the body of St. Malachy passed by, he touched the withered hand against the dead body, and forthwith it received its full vigour. Thus was it that the dead body of the saint gave life to a dead arm. St. Bernard himself has recorded this miracle; and he also mentioned it in his funeral sermon.—St. Bernard, *Life of St. Malachy of Armagh.*

A dead girl restored to life by touching the dead body of St. Virgilius (A.D. 610). When the funeral procession of St. Virgilius arrived at the grave, and the remains of the pontiff were about to be lifted therein, all of a sudden came persons carrying the body of one dead. It was that of a young girl, the only child of her mother, and she was a widow. The bearers, out of breath, implored the clergy to let the dead body touch that of the deceased prelate. The permission was granted, and at a given signal all the immense crowd fell on their knees, waiting to see what would happen. Forthwith the *Kyrie Eleison* was intoned; a thousand voices or more took up the chant, and at the seventh repetition, the young girl rose on her feet in the presence of the whole multitude. A shudder ran through the crowd, a silence ensued unbroken by a single sound, then a sudden reaction took place, a shout of joy burst forth, the funeral hymn was changed to a song of praise, the funeral procession to a march of triumph. The resuscitated damsel, pressed on all sides by the crowd, went homewards, crying as she went along, "O blessed bishop! O good and holy pastor! How am I thy debtor! How powerful thy merits! Well hast thou shown thy inheritance to eternal life in giving me back to life." Dinet, *Saint Symphorien d'Autun.*

The paralytic daughter of the baron de Nismes healed by touching the shrine of St. Wulfran, archbishop of Sens (A.D. 1687). St. Wulfran died A.D. 720. For 967 years "miracles" had honoured his shrine, and have not yet ceased. Father Giry says, "All Picardy knows about the miraculous cure of the daughter of Monchy, baron of Nismes. This young lady had been paralyzed for several months, and was wholly unable to move or speak. In this state she was carried to the shrine of St. Wulfran to pay her devotions. While thus employed her limbs recovered their full strength, and her tongue its speech, so that she returned to the convent of Bertaucourt in perfect health." Father Giry saw her himself, and relates this miracle.

At St. Wulfran's, Abbeville, there was formerly a tapestry hanging in twenty-five compartments, each compartment perpetuating a miracle of this saint, with a doggerel explanation. The following is the twenty-fifth tableau, and a fair specimen of the verses attached:—

> One who by headache lost her sight
> Is by the saint restored to light;
> The parents, greatly marvelling,
> Offerings to St. Wulfran bring.

This piece of tapestry in the fête of the Revolution was used to decorate the *autel de la Patrie*. It was then torn into tatters, thrown into a cemetery, and no one cared to gather up the fragments.

Elisha called Bald-pate.

2 KINGS ii. 23, 24. Elisha went to Bethel; and as he was going up by the way, there came forth little children out of the city, who said to him, Go up, thou bald head; go up, thou bald head. And Elisha turned back, and looked on them, and cursed them in the name of the Lord. And there came forth two she-bears out of the wood, and tare forty and two children of them.

St. Leufredus called bald-pate (A.D. 738). One day St. Leufredus was fishing in the Eure, which ran close by his monastery, when a woman muttered to herself, "This bald-pate will exhaust the river, so that there will be no more fishing." She never thought the saint would hear her, but God brought the words to the ears of the fisher, deeming every insult to His servants an insult to Himself. "Woman," said Leufredus, "why envy me a good common to all; and why mock me for baldness, which is no fault of mine, but a work of nature. Pray God that you and all your race be as bare of hair behind your head as I am on the pate." This curse immediately took effect: the woman was instantly bald on the hind part of her head, and the same disfigurement was hereditary.—Mgr. Guérin, *Vies des Saints,* vol. vii. p. 189.

Elisha heals the Water of Jericho.

2 KINGS ii. 19–22. When Elisha was at Jericho, and was told the water was not fit to

drink, he bade the man who told him to fetch a new cruse, and put salt therein. Then went Elisha to the spring of water, and cast the salt therein, and said, Thus saith the Lord, I have healed these waters. So the waters were healed unto this day, according to the saying of Elisha which he spake.

Francis Xavier heals sea-water and makes it fit to drink. "Many more and strange miracles were wrought of Xavier, as when, with the sign of the cross, he turned salt sea-water into fresh sweet water, that he and those with him might not perish of thirst, in a dry land where there was no water. . . . Many like things did he, as may be read at large in the narrative made in the Consistory."—Cardinal de Monté, *Speech before Gregory XV. at the Process of Canonization*, Jan. 19, 1622.

Eutychus restored to Life.

ACTS XX. 9–12. While Paul was at Troas, he preached to the disciples; and there sat in a window a certain young man, named Eutychus. As the sermon was very long, Eutychus fell asleep, and tumbled out of the window, which was in the third story, into the street. He was taken up dead; but Paul went to him, fell on him, and embracing him, said to the bystanders, Trouble not yourselves, for the life is in him. And the disciples brought the young man alive [into the house], and were not a little comforted.

St. Catherine of Sweden restores to life a coachman who had fallen from his box (fourteenth century). A man in the suite of St. Catherine of Sweden, overtaken with sleep, fell from his coach-box on his head, and the wheels of the carriage went over him. The princess, being told of the accident, went to the man, touched his hand, and he rose immediately, safe and sound.

At another time a workman fell from the roof of a house on the pavement, and was so mutilated by the fall that he could not be removed. St. Catherine simply touched the body, and the man was perfectly restored, insomuch that he was able to return to his work the same day.—Ulpho (a Brigittine monk), *Life of St. Catherine of Sweden* (written 1411; thirty years after her death).

St. Maur restores a broken arm, shattered by a fall from a high tower (A.D. 512–584). St. Maur was sent by St. Benedict, abbot of Mount Cassino, to found the monastery of Glanfeuil. When he reached Verceil, one of his companions, named Harderade, went to inspect a high tower, and fell from the top to the bottom. The biographers of St. Maur say, "No doubt he was pushed down by the malice of Satan." Dreadfully bruised, and more than half dead, he was taken to the town, and the physicians unanimously declared he must lose his arm, which was so fractured in several places as to be past all hope of remedy. St. Maur went to see his companion. He touched "with a morsel of the true cross, given him as a souvenir by St. Benedict," the several parts of his friend's arm and body which had received injury, and no sooner had he done so, than the wounds, bruises, and fractures were all healed, and Harderade rose to his feet perfectly cured. This miracle soon got blazed abroad, and so great was the crowd which assembled daily to see St. Maur, that he deemed it expedient to withdraw from Verceil without delay.—Odo of Glanfeuil, *Life of St. Maur* (A.D. 868).

St. Maur restores to life a boy who had fallen from a scaffold (A.D. 512–584). While the monastery at Bertulfe was a-building, a boy only eight years of age, the son of Florus, viscount of Austrasia, fell from a high scaffold on a heap of building stones. Every one thought he was killed, for blood poured from several parts of his mangled body. St. Maur, kneeling beside the lad, prayed, and made over him the sign of the cross; whereupon the lad rose up, perfectly restored. The father overjoyed, exclaimed, "O father, thou art indeed a worthy disciple of St. Benedict. We have never before seen the like of this."—Odo of Glanfeuil, *Life of St. Maur* (A.D. 868).

The restoration of life to persons who had fallen from a height was the speciality of St. Maur; as the multiplication of food was the speciality of St. Theodosius the Cœnobiarch; the reception of the eucharist from the hands of angels was that of Stanislaus Kostka; and so on. Besides the examples given, was the restoration of Sergius, who fell from his horse while crossing the Alps: St. Maur restored him to health instantaneously, merely by making over him the sign of the cross.

St. Tiburtius restores to life a young man killed by a fall. St. Tiburtius saw a young man who had fallen from a great height, and was so mutilated that his father and mother were about to bury him. St. Tiburtius coming up, said to the parents, "Give me leave to speak a word or two to your son; it seems to me that all hope of his recovery must not be abandoned." Then, saying the *Pater Noster* and the *Credo* over the young man, he had the satisfaction of seeing him revive, stand on his feet, and go to his parents in perfect health.—*Life of St. Sebastian* (from the public registers).

Fast of Forty Days or more.

(See My Flesh is Meat indeed.)

Matt. iv. 1, 2. Jesus was led up of the Spirit into the wilderness to be tempted of the devil; and when He had fasted forty days and forty nights, He was afterwards an hungered.

Exod. xxxiv. 28. And Moses was there [on the mount] forty days and forty nights. He did neither eat bread, nor drink water.

Deut. ix. 18. After the tables of the law were broken, Moses says, I fell down before the Lord, as at the first, forty days and forty nights: I did neither eat bread, nor drink water.

The possibility of fasting forty days and forty nights, without miraculous aid, was proved in 1880 by Dr. Tanner of New York, who undoubtedly took no food during all that time. After the fast he ate ravenously, and soon recovered his full strength. Of Moses it is said, he not only took no food, but also that "he drank no water." Dr. Tanner was allowed to drink water, but not to take food. It was a bet which he fairly won. The records of the Tower mention a Scotchman, imprisoned for felony, and strictly watched in that fortress for six weeks, who took no food whatever, and on this account obtained his pardon. The "fasting woman of Ross," described by Pennant, equals any of the saints in abstinence; and although Anne Moore, the "fasting woman of Tutbury," was detected by Dr. Alexander Henderson, yet the amount of nourishment she surreptitiously obtained was exceedingly small.

St. Francis of Paula fasts forty days and forty nights (A.D. 1416–1507). St. Francis of Paula always observed Lent with the prescribed rigour, but on one occasion at least he abstained wholly from food and drink for the whole forty days, in imitation of our Saviour, Moses, Elijah, and Simeon the pillar saint. The pope, in his bull of canonization, says of him, "he seems not to have had a body like other men, but to be only a pure spirit in human form."—Father Giry, *Acts of Canonization.*

St. Peter Celestine fasts forty days and forty nights (A.D. 1221–1296). St. Peter Celestine, before he entered into holy orders, lived in a cave, "et il observa en ce lieu un jeûne perpétuel durant trois ans."—*Les Petits Bollandistes*, vol. vi. p. 21.

After he was made priest he kept four Lents every year. In these 160 days he ate dry black bread once in three days.

Simeon Stylites fasts forty days and forty nights. Simeon, the pillar saint, retired to a hut in Telanassus, and tried to induce St. Blaise to close up the door, and leave him there for forty days and forty nights. St. Blaise warned him, that to die by one's own act is no virtue, but a crime. "Put, then, ten loaves and a cruse of water in the room; and if I find myself sinking, I will partake of them." At the end of forty days, the hut was opened, but the bread and water were untouched. Simeon lay motionless, unable to move or speak; but Blaise moistened his lips, gave him the eucharist, and he revived.—Baring-Gould, *Lives of the Saints*, Jan., p. 74.

Fig Tree withered.

Matt. xxi. 19. Jesus said to the fig tree, Let no fruit grow on thee henceforth for ever. And presently the fig tree withered away.

St. Leubais curses an alder tree and all the alders die (A.D. 540). One day St. Leubais, wishing to cross a river, entered a ferry-boat made of alder-wood. While he was in the boat the sides gave way, and the saint was thrown into the river. He was much incommoded by the accident, and said, "Let no alder tree grow in this neighbourhood henceforth for ever." And presently all the alder trees of the whole commune withered away. The abbot Rolland says this is "une tradition populaire," but adds, "ce qui est certain, c'est qu'on n'y voit un seul arbre de cette espèce dans tout le territoire de la commune, et que tous ceux qu'on a essayé d'y planter sont morts."—L'abbé Rolland, *Letter to Mgr. Guérin*, March 18, 1879.

At St. Valery's bidding a young monk touches a huge oak, and it falls with a crash (A.D. 619). Not far from Bresle St. Valery observed an enormous oak, on which were cut a number of pagan images, which were held in adoration by the people in the vicinity. St. Valery told a young monk who was with him to go and push the tree down. The young disciple had daily witnessed so many miracles performed by his master, that he went at once, and, touching the tree with his finger, it fell with a tremendous crash. The people in the neighbourhood were stupefied; but after a while, arming themselves with hatchets and sticks, they ran to assail the two Christians. St. Valery moved not, but stood perfectly quiet and composed. The fury of the mob subsided, and the saint, availing himself of this change of temper, preached to them Christ and Him crucified. His preaching was with power, the whole mob was converted, and a Christian church was forthwith erected on the spot where the oak had stood.—Besançon (1854), *Les Saints de Franche Comté.*

Fire Innocuous.

(See Shadrach.)

Isa. xliii. 2. When thou walkest through the fire, thou shalt not be burnt; neither shall the flame kindle upon thee

Fire innocuous to St. Catherine of Siena (A.D. 1317–1380). Once, when St. Catherine was sitting before a large fire watching the roast, she fell to the floor in an ecstasy. Her sister-in-law was by at the time, but, having often seen her in these fits, took no notice of her. In due time the meat was served in the refectory, and the sister-in-law, on coming back to the kitchen, saw Catherine sitting on the fire. She fully expected to find her dreadfully burnt; but, to her amazement, not only was Catherine uninjured, but even her clothes were not singed. Her biographer naïvely remarks, "The fire of holiness, which blazed in her heart, neutralized the heat of the burning fuel." —Raymond of Capua (her confessor), *Life of St. Catherine of Siena.*

One is wholly at a loss to understand how such an insane act as this, presuming it to be true, can be justified, much less commended as a proof of holiness.

St. Catherine of Siena, pushed into the fire, receives no injury (A.D. 1317–1380). One day Satan, in his rage against St. Catherine, pushed her into a roasting fire. All who saw it screamed with fright, and ran to pull her out; but St. Catherine, with the utmost calmness, walked from the flames, and even her clothes were not injured.—Raymond of Capua (her confesssor), *Life of St. Catherine of Siena.*

St. Francis of Paula, when a boy, carried about fire in his frock (A.D. 1429). One day the sacristan of St. Mark's sent St. Francis, then a boy of thirteen years old, to fetch fire for the censors, but gave him nothing to hold it in. Francis held out his frock, and carried it thus to the sacristan, and his frock received no sort of injury.—*The Bull and other Documents of the Canonization of St. Francis* (compiled by Father Giry).

St. Nofletta carries about fire in her apron (A.D. 653). St. Longis was a young man living at his monastery in Boisselière, and St. Nofletta or Agnefletta was a young woman who fled to him to escape being married to a young man selected by her parents as suitable. St. Longis took her in and heard her tale, "il encouragea sa résolution, et comme elle n'avait point d'asile, il la reçut dans son monastère." This, of course, soon raised a scandal, and king Clotaire sent for them to hear their defence. It was midwinter when they went to present themselves before the king, and when they reached the palace Clotaire was out hunting. While waiting for his return, St. Longis complained bitterly of the cold, and St. Nofletta ran to a baker's shop, asking him to give her a few live coals. The baker said, "Here is fire, but you have nothing to carry it in.' St. Nofletta told him to put it in her apron; and, wrapping it up, she took it to St. Longis, "et quand le froid qu'il ressentait fut soulagé, Noflette reprit dans son manteau les charbons encore brûlants, et les reporta au four." When Clotaire returned from the chase, and heard of this miracle, he not only quashed the charge, but gave large presents to St. Longis. "Après cela nos deux saints quittèrent le palais, et revinrent à leur monastère," and the mouth of scandal was for ever silenced.—*Vita Sancti Lenogisili*, No. 7 (from dom Piolin's version *Église du Mans*).

St. Francis of Paula holds fire in his hands without injury (A.D. 1416–1507). The many cures effected miraculously by St. Francis of Paula stirred up against him the physicians of the neighbourhood, who found their clients leaving them in all directions. They employed Father Scozetta to preach against him, and charge him with charlatanism. After preaching for a time against the saint, Father Scozetta determined to go to the saint's cell, and there charge him face to face with imposture. St. Francis received the reverend father with great courtesy, but the preacher was very violent and abusive. When he had done, St. Francis very quietly took two handfuls of red-hot coals in his hands, and, taking them to his visitor, said, "Father Antony, warm yourself, for you have great need." Father Scozetta was amazed to see the saint hold fire in his hand without being burnt, and, casting himself at his feet, begged pardon. St. Francis gave him his hand, bade him rise to his feet, and kissed him, saying, "Brother Antony, man of himself is but a feeble creature indeed, but, God helping, he can do all things."

Another instance. In 1469 pope Paul II. sent one of his chamberlains to ascertain if the wonderful things told of St. Francis were true or not. The chamberlain addressed himself to the archbishop of Cosenza, and the archbishop sent Charles Pyrrho, a canon of Cosenza, to attend the chamberlain to Paula. The saint was at work, as usual, with his workmen when the strangers arrived; and when the chamberlain was about to salute him by kissing his hand, St. Francis cried out "It would not be seemly for the pope's chamberlain, who has said mass for thirty years, to kiss the hand of such a humble individual as I am." The chamberlain was amazed that St. Francis knew him, and accompanied the saint into his cell. Here the chamberlain spoke very learnedly of the illusions of miracles and the danger of deluding one's self in such a matter. Then St. Francis, walking up to the fire, took two handfuls of hot burning coals to the chamberlain, and bade him warm himself. The chamberlain was wholly disconcerted at this; but St. Francis quietly remarked, "All creatures obey those who serve God with a perfect heart." Which golden words are inserted by Leo X. in the bull of canonization. The chamberlain returned to Rome, and told his holiness that the sanctity of St. Francis exceeded all that had been said of him, and that his gift of miracles could not be exaggerated. —*Acts of Canonization* (compiled by Father Giry).

St. Francis of Paula enters a kiln to repair it, while it was enveloped with flames (A.D. 1416–1507). A lime-kiln which had been lighted twenty-four hours, being out of repair, the flames burst through the chinks, and threatened to destroy the kiln. This would have destroyed the lime, and done considerable damage to the workmen's huts. The masons, greatly distressed, raised a cry of alarm, which brought St. Francis de Paula to the spot. Seeing the imminent danger, and knowing how important the lime was for the monastery he was building, he instantly set to work to repair the kiln, but for this purpose it was necessary to enter the burning furnace, and stop the holes from the inside. When the workmen returned from dinner, they found the kiln in thorough repair, and the saint washing his hands. To all appearances he was as fresh and uninjured as if he had come from his study. The bull of his canonization mentions this miracle; and the disciple who wrote his life, and the sixth witness of the process conducted at Cosenza, in connection with the canonization, not only mention the incident, but add that this lime miraculously renewed itself as fast as it was used, and lasted till the work was finished.—*Acts of Canonization* (compiled by Father Giry).

St. Martina, bound to the stake, was unharmed by the fire (A.D. 226). St. Martina, after having been subjected to unheard-of cruelties for her steadfast faith in Christ, was, by the order of Alexander Severus, tied to a stake in the midst of a fierce fire; but God sent a torrent of rain to quench the fire, and a high wind to disperse the fuel. As the burning fuel flew about in all directions, many of the heathen spectators were burnt to death, but the saint herself received no injury. The emperor insisted that St. Martina was protected by magic, and, fancying that the charm was lodged in her hair, commanded that every atom of it should be shaved off. After a lapse of three days she was conducted again to the temple of Diana, where she was locked in for three days and nights without food of any kind. Still she remained firm, and the emperor, tired of the struggle, commanded her head to be cut off.—Bollandus, *Acta Sanctorum*, vol. i. Jan. 1. (Surius wrote a life of St. Martina.)

A hermit stands unhurt on live coals during vespers. One day a solitary came to the cell of St. Palæmon, and asked permission to join his fraternity in vespers, and he proposed that they should all stand on live coals while at prayer. "Thou shalt not tempt the Lord thy God," said Palæmon; but the stranger persisted, and stood unhurt on red-hot cinders during the whole office. The writer ascribes the miracle "to the craft of Satan," but it is a dangerous distinction to introduce. (See PETER GONZALEZ.) —Baring-Gould, *Lives of the Saints*, Jan., p. 150.

St. Peter Gonzalez reproves a harlot by standing in a fire (A.D. 1190–1248). Some Spanish libertines hired a harlot to go and tempt St. Peter Gonzalez. She went to the saint, and begged to consult him on an affair of great moment; but when alone with him, she embraced his knees and pretended to weep; but all of a sudden threw off her mask, and employed all her artifices to seduce him. Gonzalez bade her follow him into an inner chamber. Here he lighted a fire, and placed himself in the midst thereof. The harlot screamed with terror—said he would burn himself to death; but the saint replied, "What is this to hell-fire, to which you would allure me?" The harlot, struck to the heart, was converted, and ever after remained a consistent Christian, who reverenced the very shadow of Gonzalez. (See above, A HERMIT STANDS, etc.)—*Acta Sanctorum* (Bollandists), vol. ii. April 14.

Fire would not burn the body of Leonard

Keyser. Leonard Keyser of Bavaria was one of the Reformed Church in the time of Zwingli and Luther. He was an ardent propagandist of the new views, and, being arrested by the bishop of Passau, was condemned to the stake. When he came to the fields outside the town, he bent over the cart, gathered a flower, and said to the judge, who rode on horseback beside the cart, "My lord, I have plucked this flower. If you can burn me and this flower in my hand, then believe you have condemned me righteously; but if you can burn neither me nor the flower, then reflect on what you are doing, and repent." When the procession reached the appointed place, the judge and his three officials threw an extra number of fagots on the pile, in order to increase its heat, and reduce the victim to ashes; but when all the wood was consumed, the body of the martyr was taken from the stake wholly unhurt. The three principals and their menials then brought fresh wood, and made a much larger fire; but still the body remained unburnt, the hair only being slightly singed, and the nails somewhat darkened. The ashes being brushed from the body, the skin was found to be smooth and of its natural colour, and the flower in the martyr's hand was unfaded, and wholly uninjured by the flames. The executioners then cut the body into pieces, and threw the gobbets into a fresh fire, but again the fire burnt out, and the pieces were not consumed. Lastly, they took the pieces and threw them into a running stream, called the Inn. The judge was so terrified, that he threw up his office, and the chief executioner joined the Moravian brethren. It was from the mouth of this convert that the narrative given above was taken down.—Van Braght, *The Bloody Theatre, or Martyrs' Mirror.*

Sebastian Frank, in his *Chronicle of the Roman Heresies* (letter Z), gives substantially the same tale; and Martin Luther, who records the martyrdom of Keyser, seems more inclined to credit the story than not. At any rate he does not deny it.

St. Lucy stands in the midst of a fierce fire wholly uninjured (Dec. 13, 305). Paschasius, governor of Syracuse, commanded that fagots, steeped in rosin, pitch, and oil, should be piled round St. Lucy, the holy virgin, and ignited; but she stood uninjured in the midst of the burning pile. Paschasius then caused a sword to be thrust down her throat, which wounded her mortally; but, before she died, she exhorted those spectators who were Christians to stand fast in the faith delivered to the saints, and those who were not, to flee from the wrath to come. —Ado (archbishop of Trèves), *Martyrology.* (The acts of St. Lucy find place in Bede, Sigisbert, the Roman Martyrology, etc.)

(One of the hands of St. Lucy is shown in the vestry of the church of Toledo; the rest of her body is said to be in Venice.)

Fire would not burn the body of St. Menas. Menas was a Roman soldier, in the army of Diocletian. Because he was a Christian he was put to death, and his body cast into a great fire to be consumed; but the fire refused to injure it; and some devout Christians obtained possession of it, and buried it.—Metaphrastês, *Lives.*

St. Polycarp stood unharmed at the stake (A.D. 167). In the sixth year of Marcus Aurelius, Polycarp, at the age of eighty-six, was seized by Herod, chief magistrate of Smyrna, and set in the midst of a pile of wood and other combustibles. The mass, being set alight, blazed up with great fury, but instead of attacking the body of the saint, formed a canopy "like the sails of a ship inflated by the wind." There stood the aged disciple of St. John in his canopy of fire, bright as silver purified in a furnace, while from his body there issued a fragrance sweeter than incense. The executioners, greatly exasperated at this spectacle, pierced him with spears, and the blood which spouted from the wounds of the martyr quenched the fire in which he stood.—*Roman Martyrology* (written by the Church of Smyrna, at the time of the martyrdom). See also Nicephorus Callistus, *Church History,* bk. iii. ch. 30–34.

Fire would not burn the bodies of the wise Roman converts. When Maxentius summoned the wisest men of the empire to a disputation with St. Catherine of Alexandria, they not only acknowledged themselves beaten in argument, but confessed themselves to be converted. Whereupon the emperor ordered them all to be burnt alive. They died in the flames; but the fire did not consume their bodies; nay, we are told not a hair of their heads was singed.—Metaphrastês (died 911), *Lives,* etc.

St. Sabas enters an oven without injury, while the fagots are blazing. St. Sabas of Cappadocia did a kind act to a baker. The baker had put his clothes in his oven to dry, but forgetting he had done so, stuffed the oven with fagots, and set fire to them to heat it. He then remembered he had left his clothes in the oven, and made great lamentation over his loss. St. Sebastian, being told of the mischance, went into the flaming oven, rescued the clothes, and returned wholly uninjured by the blazing fagots.—Cyril (the monk), *Life of St. Sabas.*

St. Silvester enters a blazing oven to rescue a baker's shovel (A.D. 1185). A similar legend to that of St. Sabas (p. 139) is told of St. Silvester. He entered a baker's furnace when fully heated "to scrape together the living embers"—for what?—because the baker had stupidly left his shovel in the furnace to be burnt up by the blazing fagots. It is to be presumed that the embers being "scraped together," the shovel was miraculously restored sound and whole, though Baring-Gould does not say so, but otherwise the incident would have no point at all.—Baring-Gould, *Lives of the Saints*, Jan., p. 37.

St. Thecla, set in the midst of a large fire, receives no hurt therefrom. St. Thecla, being converted by the preaching of Paul the apostle, refused to marry Tamarus, to whom she had been betrothed. So Tamarus told the proconsul that a foreigner was perverting the minds of the people, and bringing in strange gods. Paul, upon this charge, was scourged, and banished from Iconium; and Thecla, who still adhered to the new persuasion, was condemned to be burnt to death. The fire was kindled, and Thecla set in the midst of the burning fagots, in the presence of an immense throng of spectators; but, to the utter amazement of all, the fire did her no harm; and from a cloudless sky there suddenly fell such torrents of rain, amidst thunder and lightning, that the fire was extinguished and the crowd dispersed. Whereupon St. Thecla deliberately walked from the smouldering pile to the house of Onesiphorus, where she found Paul and some other Christians.—Ado (archbishop of Trèves), *Martyrology.*

St. Thuribius of Astorga proves his innocence of a charge by holding fire in his hand (A.D. 460). St. Thuribius, bishop of Astorga, was charged with an enormous crime by a deacon; but the bishop, to prove his innocence, took burning coals into his hand, and, placing them on his rochet, carried them to the church, and showed them to the people. As neither he nor his rochet received injury from the fire, his innocence was established by the judgment of God.—Tamayus-Salazar, *Spanish Martyrology.*

St. Tiburtius walks barefoot over live coals, and receives no injury. Fabianus, the Roman governor, commanded to kindle a great fire of coals on the ground, and said to Tiburtius, "Choose now which you will do: put incense on these coals to the immortal gods, or walk over them barefoot." Tiburtius made the sign of the cross, and then walked over the red-hot coals, as if they had been a carpet of rose-leaves and other flowers.—*Life of St. Sebastian* (from the public registers).

Fire shows reverence to Sister Benedicta's bed (A.D. 1850). Mgr. Depéry restored the cottage of Sister Benedicta; but on Jan. 28, A.D. 1850, a fire burnt down almost the whole village of St. Etienne. The flames attacked the cottage restored by Mgr. Depéry, destroyed the thatch, but stopped, "as if pushed back by some invisible hand," when they reached the alcove containing the bed of Sister Benedicta. The débris which the fire respected was carefully collected as relics, and used in constructing a new cottage. —*Les Petits Bollandistes*, vol. v. p. 228.

(Mgr. Barnadou, bishop of Gap, is collecting such data as these to effect the canonization of Sister Benedicta, 1884.)

The bed of St. Cunegunda caught fire but no mischief was done (1040). One night, after long prayer, St. Cunegunda, wife of Henry II., emperor of Germany, fell asleep and was lifted into bed. Her reader fell asleep soon afterwards, and, dropping her candle, set fire to the palliasse and bedclothes. The empress and her reader were roused from sleep by the noise and heat of the fire, and, making the sign of the cross, the fire instantly dropped out. Although the empress was lying on a bed blazing with fire, and the flames burnt fiercely all around her, yet her night-clothes were not touched, nor did she suffer any injury whatever.—*The Bull of Canonization by Innocent III.*, A.D. 1200.

Without going to miracles, allowing for a little exaggeration, the circumstance that Cunegonda's night-clothes did not catch fire may be accounted for. We are told she slept in a horse-hair gown, on a palliasse covered with a horse-hair quilt; so some of the articles on the bed might catch fire, but would not be likely to set fire to the horse-hair very rapidly.

St. Drogo uninjured by a fire which burnt down his cell (A.D. 1118–1189). St. Drogo lived for forty years against the church at Seburg, in Hainault. One day a fire broke out in the church, and burnt his cell to the ground, but though St. Drogo remained there all the time, he received no injury. Papebroch (p. 441) says,

"God repeated, in St. Drogo's favour, the miracle of the three children in the fiery furance of Babylon."—*Acta Sanctorum* (Bollandists), April 16.

A fire respects the house of St. Galla, and injures it not. A fire broke out in the house next to that in which St. Galla lived. It was very fierce, and spread so rapidly that all thought the saint's house must inevitably be destroyed. St. Galla, without leaving her room, fell on her knees in prayer, and the flames, starting back, gathered themselves together, and dropped out suddenly. A vast concourse had collected to assist in extinguishing it; and when they saw "the miracle," they stood stupefied with amazement.—*Les Petits Bollandistes*, vol. ii. p. 199.

St. Melanius's cerements uninjured by fire. When the church of Rennes was consumed by fire, the cerements of St. Melanius, although especially combustible, were wholly uninjured. So says St. Gregory of Tours, who lived only a century after the event.

Fire refuses to touch the statue of Minerva of Ilium. Many authors tell us that when the Fimbrians burnt Ilium, the statue of Pallas Minerva stood in the midst of a heap of ashes wholly uninjured. This prodigy was perpetuated on medals.

Fire quenched.

Numb. xi. 1–3. When the people complained, the Lord heard it, and His anger was kindled; and the fire of the Lord burnt among them, and consumed them that were in the uttermost parts of the camp. And Moses prayed unto the Lord, and the fire was quenched. And Moses called the name of the place Taberah, because the fire of the Lord burnt among them.

Heb. xi. 34. The time would fail me to tell of [those] who through faith quenched the violence of fire.

The ghost of St. Gertrude, abbess of Nivelles, quenches a fire in the monastery. Ten years after her death, the ghost of St. Gertrude "appeared visibly" in the refectory of the college of Nivelles, for the purpose of putting out a fire which threatened to destroy the whole pile of buildings.—Surius, *Lives of the Saints.*

St. Godeberta quenches a fire by the sign of the cross (A.D. 676). In A.D. 676 a violent fire threatened to burn down the whole city of Noyon. St. Godeberta was confined to her bed at the time. The fire spread rapidly, and reached the basilica of St. Mary, built by St. Medard. Godeberta caused herself to be carried in a chair into the very heart of the flames, and, making the sign of the cross, the fire instantly subsided, and the church was saved.—Radbod II. (bishop of Noyon, A.D. 1167), *Life of St. Godeberta.*

Fire extinguished by St. Lupus with the sign of the cross (A.D. 610). A horrible fire broke out in Chalons in the year 610, and destroyed half the city. No human means availed to arrest its progress, and the whole city must have been reduced to ashes, if the people had not sought the intercession of St. Lupus. Immediately the saint was solicited to interfere, he rose from his bed, and, placing himself right in front of the run of the fire, made the sign of the cross. The flames, as if by magic, stood upright and then sank into the earth, doing no more mischief; and thus the rest of the city was saved from destruction.—*Légendaire d'Autun.*

A fire walked out by St. Remi (A.D. 449–545). On one occasion, while St. Remi was at Reims, lodging in the house of the church of St. Nicasius, a great fire burst out, and destroyed a large part thereof, threatening the whole city with destruction. St. Remi made the sign of the cross against the conflagration, which approached towards him with rapid strides, but stopped suddenly, and then slowly retreated. The holy man followed it, and still it retreated. Thus did he till the fire came to the city gates, when it rolled itself into a ball, passed through the gates without injuring them, and rolling into the open fields was soon spent, to the amazement of the whole city which had assembled together, and were witnesses of this great miracle.—Hincmar (archbishop of Reims, 806–882), *Life of St. Remi.*

St. Wodoal's stick puts out a fire (A.D. 700). An angel gave St. Wodoal a staff, which was called his "crossillon," and which had the virtue of extinguishing fire. If, therefore, a fire broke out at Soissons or the neighbourhood, it was usual to hold up this rod and bid it cease to burn. Many and many a fire was put out in the monastery by this means. Mme. d'Harcourt, abbess of Soissons, tells us that a fire once broke out in the kitchen chimney with great violence, when she took up the crossillon, and made with it the sign of the cross on the chimney-place. Immediately the fire fell with a great thud upon the kitchen floor, and greatly alarmed those present; but, being dead, it was soon cast out into the yard. Ever after, it was customary on Feb. 5, after grand mass, for the head sacristan with the crossillon, followed by the second sacristan with a wax taper, and then by all the inmates of the house singing, to march through the abbey, when the kitchen chimney-place was first marked with a cross by the magic rod, and then other parts of the buildings.

Fire extinguished by St. Wodoal's hood. One day, a fire having broke out in the abbey, one of the monks, who was sick of a fever at the time, ran and told St. Wodoal. St. Wodoal gave his hood to the man, and told him to follow the fire till it retreated from the premises. This he did, and no mischief occurred.—L'abbé Pécheur, *Annales du Diocèse de Soissons.*

The fire which fell down the chimney with a thud, looks very much like a fall of soot dislodged from a foul chimney by the tap of the stick.

Fish Miracles. (See also Jonah.)

Matt. xvii. 27. Peter, being asked to pay tribute, told Jesus of the demand; and Jesus said to him, Go to the sea, and cast a hook, and take up the fish that first cometh up; and when thou hast opened his mouth, thou shalt find a piece of money: that take, and give for Me and thee.

St. Cadoc of Wales finds his lost Virgil in a salmon (sixth century). St. Cadoc was passionately fond of the Latin poet Virgil. One day, walking with Gildas the historian, he put his Virgil under his arm, and began to weep at the thought that his beloved poet might perhaps, at that very moment, be with Satan and his angels. A sudden gust of wind caused him to lift his arm, and his book was blown into the sea. The loss was an unspeakable grief to him; but next morning a fisherman brought him a fine salmon as a present, and in the fish was the very Virgil he had lost the previous day, and what completed his joy was to find the book wholly uninjured.—Rees, *Lives of the Cambro-British Saints.*

A fish restores to St. Egwin of Worcester the key of his fetters (A.D. 720). When St. Egwin of Worcester went on his pilgrimage to Rome, "to expiate his sins," he loaded his ankles with iron fetters, and, having locked the irons, threw the key into the Avon. As he neared Italy, a large fish floundered upon the ship's deck, and, being prepared for table, the key which Egwin had thrown into the Avon was found in its stomach. St. Egwin considered this as an intimation from God that he was to release himself of his fetters. Accordingly he unlocked them, and continued his pilgrimage foot free.—St. Brithwald (archbishop of Canterbury), *Life of St. Egwin.*

It would have been interesting to know what sort of fish this was to which the fresh water of the Avon and the salt water of the sea were equally congenial. It does not say a "salmon," which certainly is a stranger in the Avon.

Miss Elton of Stratford recovers a ring by a codfish (1696). A knight passing by a cottage heard the cries of a woman in travail, and knew by his skill in the occult sciences that the infant was destined to be his future wife; but he determined to elude his destiny. When the child was of marriageable age, the knight took her to the seaside, intending to drown her, but relented; and, throwing his signet-ring into the sea, he commanded her never more to see his face, upon pain of death, till she brought back with her that ring. The damsel then went as cook to a noble family, and one day, as she was preparing a codfish for dinner, she found the ring in the fish, took it to the knight, and thus became the wife of sir John Berry. The Berry arms show a fish, and in the dexter chief a ring, in record of this legend.

The arms of the city of Glasgow. The arms of the city of Glasgow show an oak tree with a bird above it, and a bell hanging from one of the branches. At the foot of the tree is a salmon with a ring in its mouth. The symbols are explained thus: St. Kentigern built the city, and hung a bell in the oak to summon the men to work. So much for the "oak and the bell." Now for the "salmon and the ring." We are told that a queen of Scotland formed an illicit attachment to a young soldier, and gave him the ring which her husband had presented to her as a betrothal or love gift. It coming to the knowledge of the king that the queen had parted with this ring, he contrived to abstract it from the soldier while he was asleep, threw it into the Clyde, and then asked the queen to show it him. The queen in consternation ran to St. Kentigern, and, confessing her crime, entreated his help. The father confessor went forthwith to the Clyde, and drew out a salmon with the ring in its mouth. He handed the ring to the queen, and by this means prevented a great scandal, saved the lives of two persons, and reformed the repentant lady. Jocelyn (bishop of Glasgow), in his *Life of St. Kentigern* (1125), mentions this; and in Christian art the saint is represented with a salmon and a ring in the foreground.

The keys of a reliquary discovered in a fish (A.D. 426). While St. Maurilius was bishop of Angers, a woman sent to him to come and baptize her child, who was dangerously ill. He was saying mass at the time, and no one durst interrupt him. When mass was over the child was dead, and not having been baptized, St. Maurilius accused himself of being the cause of the child's perdition. This so preyed upon his mind that he resolved to throw up his office, and live the rest of his life in private and in penitence. So, starting from Angers, he journeyed to the coast; and, while he waited for a vessel bound for England, wrote on a rock these words: "Here Maurilius, bishop of Angers, embarked. Quasimodo, A.D. 412." When he had got out of sight of land, he found he had taken with him the keys of the reliques of the church, and as he held them in his hand, thinking how to send them back, the devil knocked them into the sea. The saint was greatly distressed, and vowed he would never more return to Angers till these keys were restored. On reaching England, he hired himself out as a gentleman's gardener, and the crops he raised, his admirable industry, his modest behaviour, and saintly piety, made him a great favourite with his master and his family. When the people of Angers discovered that their bishop was gone, they were much grieved, and four of the monks were appointed to go in search of him. For seven years they searched without finding a trace, and then discovered the writing on the rock: "Here Maurilius, bishop of Angers, embarked. Quasimodo, A.D. 412." Hope dawned; they embarked for England, and had a capital passage; but as they ran through the sea, a fish leaped on deck, was caught, and prepared for dinner. As it was opened, the keys of the relics, labelled, were found in it. The monks first thought the bishop had been drowned, but an angel told them in a vision he was alive, and they would find him when they came ashore. Immediately they alighted, the angel guided them to the gentleman's garden, and there they discovered the lost bishop. Maurilius told them of his loss, and said he had made a vow never to return till he had found the lost keys. The monks then produced the keys, and informed the bishop how they had come by them. Maurilius, no longer doubting God's will, acquiesced in their desire. When he had again embarked, an angel appeared to him, and said, "Maurilius, return to your people, and in reward of your virtues God will restore to life the infant that died seven years ago unbaptized." The first thing the bishop did when he reached Angers was to go to the grave of this infant, and lo! it revived, and received the name of René (born again).—*Acta Sanctorum* (Bollandists), Sept. 13.

Fishes, called by St. Peter Gonzalez, came and gave themselves up to supply his table (A.D. 1190–1248). St. Peter Gonzalez built several religious houses, and was often at a loss to find food for the numerous workmen. On such occasions it was his wont to go to the nearest river, and tell the fishes, who immediately threw themselves on the banks in great numbers, and offered themselves voluntarily to death.—*Acta Sanctorum* (Bollandists), vol. ii. April 15.

A bell found in a fish given to St. Paul, bishop of Leon (A.D. 492–573). St. Paul, bishop of Leon, requested king Mark to give him a certain bell, but his demand was refused. Not long afterwards, being in the mansion of the count de Witur, a person made him a present of the head of a very fine fish. On preparing it for dinner, the very bell which the king had refused him was found in the fish, and is still preserved in the cathedral of Leon. It is quadrangular, but the sides are not all the same size, two being large, and two smaller. It is nine inches in height, and seems to have been beaten into shape by a hammer. The metal of which it is made is a mixture of copper and silver. Miraculous virtues are attributed to this bell.—Lobineau, *Lives of the Saints of Brittany*; and for description of the bell see *Antiquités de la Bretagne, Finisterre*, pt. i.

Polycratês, tyrant of Samos, recovers a ring from the sea. Polycratês was so prosperous in all things, that Amias advised him to part with some treasure dearly cherished in order to avert ill fortune. Accordingly, the king rowed into the open sea, and, pulling off a very valuable emerald signet-ring, threw it into the sea. The following week a fisherman presented the king with a fish of extraordinary size, and, on opening it, there was the signet-ring. Polycratês, thinking the circumstance of sufficient importance, and a memorable instance of divine interposition, wrote an account of it, and sent his narrative to Egypt. Herodotus, the Greek historian, was told it in Egypt, and from him it has come down to our knowledge.—Herodotus, *History*, iii. 40.

A cooked fish reproves Theodoric for murder (A.D. 526). Theodoric, suspicious of treason, and "blinded by heresy," put to death Boethius and Symmachus, two illustrious senators. Then, seizing upon pope John, he shut him in prison, and starved him to death. He then made a Jew his chief minister, and filled all the churches with Arians. Scarcely was this done, when, like Arius, he was afflicted with a bloody flux, and Procopius, the historian, says the officers of Theodoric happened to serve him one day with a cod's head and shoulders. Theodoric was terribly frightened. Nothing would persuade him that the cod's head was not the head of the senator Symmachus. He thought he saw the fish bite its lip, and glare at him furiously. He shuddered with fright, and was carried up to bed, trembling from head to foot. His physician was sent for, and found him crying like a child for the death of Symmachus and Boethius.—See *Liber Pontificalis*.

A crab brings to Francis Xavier his crucifix. As Francis Xavier was sailing from Ambionum, a city of the Molucca islands, to Baranula, he was overtaken with a storm, which threatened to wreck the vessel in which he sailed. Xavier took from his neck his crucifix, and held it in the raging sea in order to still the billows, but as the vessel lurched suddenly, he dropped it in the water. The ship next day arrived safely at Baranula; and when Xavier went ashore, a great crab leaped out of the sea, carrying the crucifix "devoutly, and in an upright direction between its fins." The crab made its way direct to Xavier, delivered to him the crucifix, and returned to the sea. Xavier was unspeakably thankful, and crossing his arms, he fell prostrate on the ground, where he remained for half an hour in devout prayer.—*Cardinal de Monte's speech before Gregory XV., on the canonization of Francis Xavier*, Jan. 19, 1622.

Flowers and Fruits from Paradise. (See Celibacy.)

Gen. ii 8, 9. And the Lord God planted a garden eastward in Eden, and there put He the man whom He had formed. And out of the ground made the Lord God to grow every tree that is pleasant to the sight and good for food.

Luke xxiii. 43. Jesus on the cross said to the penitent thief, This day shalt thou be with Me in paradise [or the garden].

The Virgin Mary brings flowers from paradise to Sister Benedicta (A.D. 1643-1718). Some workmen volunteered to dress the vineyard of Sister Benedicta's mother, who was very poor. The Virgin Mary filled the apron of Benedicta with roses from paradise, to distribute to these workmen in reward of their neighbourly kindness. There can be no doubt that the roses came from paradise, inasmuch as it was only the middle of March, when there were no roses in the alpine climate of the Valley of the Lake (Laus, 2 *syl.*).—*Les Petits Bollandistes*, vol. v. p. 226.

(Mgr. Barnadou, bishop of Gap, is collecting such data as these to effect the canonization of Sister Benedicta, 1884.)

Theophilus the lawyer receives flowers and fruits from paradise (A.D. 304). As St. Dorothy of Cesarea, in Cappadocia, was led to execution, Theophilus, a lawyer, who had been present at her examination, and heard her say to the judge, "I thank thee, for this day shall I be with my spouse in paradise," cried in ridicule, "Going to paradise, Dorothy? Well, send me some of its fruits and flowers; good-bye." "Gladly, Theophilus," said the martyr, "will I do what you request." She then knelt in prayer, and forthwith appeared a child, some four years old, who had in a cloth three different fruits, and three magnificent roses. "Take these," said Dorothy to the child, "to Theophilus, and say here are the fruits and flowers from paradise which you asked for." And so saying, her head fell to the sword of the executioner.

In the mean time Theophilus was telling his companions of his joke, and the maiden's answer. The laugh was loud, and the pleasantry applauded uproariously, when the child entered with the fruits and flowers. Going up straight to Theophilus, he said, "These are the fruits and flowers you asked the holy Dorothy to send you. I have brought them at her request from the garden of her divine spouse." So saying, the child vanished. Theophilus was amazed, and was at once convinced that the God of Dorothy is the only true God. The lawyer's boon companions tried to laugh him out of his conviction, but Theophilus replied, "It is midwinter. There are no fruits and flowers like these in February. Our gardens are barren, and our fruit trees leafless." The evidence was too strong to be gainsaid, and spoke irresistibly to the lawyer. Nothing could shake him, and, being accused before the judge of being a convert to the new religion, he witnessed a good confession and died a martyr's death.—*Acta Sanctorum* (Bollandus).

Food multiplied and reproduced.

(See ELIJAH AND THE WIDOW, etc.)

MATT. xiv. 15–21. When it was evening, the disciples said to Jesus, This is a desert place, and the time is now past; send the multitude away, that they may go into the villages, and buy themselves victuals. But Jesus said to the disciples, They need not depart; give ye them to eat. The disciples say unto Him, We have here but five loaves, and two fishes. Jesus said, Bring them hither to Me. And He commanded the multitude to sit down on the grass. And He took the five loaves and the two fishes, and blessed, and brake, and gave the loaves to His disciples, and His disciples to the multitude. And they did all eat, and were filled: and they took up of the fragments that remained twelve baskets full. And they that had eaten were about five thousand men, besides women and children.

(The total would not be less than fifteen thousand altogether.)

MATT. xv. 32–38. Jesus called His disciples unto Him, and said, I have compassion on the multitude, because they have been with Me three days, and have nothing to eat. His disciples say to Him, Whence should we buy bread in the wilderness, to fill so great a multitude? Jesus saith to them, How many loaves have ye? And they said, Seven, and a few fishes. And Jesus commanded the multitude to sit down on the ground. And He took the seven loaves and the fishes, and gave thanks, and brake them, and gave to His disciples, and the disciples to the multitude. And all did eat, and were filled. And they took up of the broken meat that was left seven baskets full. And they that did eat were four thousand men, besides women and children.

(The total would not be less than twelve thousand altogether.)

2 KINGS iv. 42–44. There came a man from Baalshalisha, and brought Elisha twenty loaves of barley; and Elisha said, Give unto the people, that they may eat. And the servitor said, What! should I set this before a hundred men? Elisha said again, Give the people, that they may eat: for thus saith the Lord, They shall eat, and shall leave thereof. So the servitor set the food before the people, and they did eat, and left thereof, according to the word of the Lord. (See ST. CLARA, p. 146.)

2 KINGS iv. 1–7. A widow, being in debt, told Elisha that her creditors had threatened to sell her and her children to satisfy their claims. Elisha asked the woman what she had in the house. Nothing, she replied, save a little oil in a pot. Go, said the propnet to her, and borrow vessels of all thy neighbours, empty vessels, not a few. And she did so. . . . Pour off thy oil now into all these vessels till they are full. And she did so. Now, said the prophet, go, sell the oil; and when thou hast paid thy debts, live thou and thy children on the rest.

St. Agnes supplies bread, and causes it to multiply (A.D. 1274—1317). St. Agnes built a convent on Mount Pulciano, where twenty sisters lived. For three days the house was wholly without food, and Agnes said, "O blessed Saviour, O tender Father, O my everlasting Spouse, at Thy command have I built this house, and wilt Thou leave Thy servants to die here for want of bread? Good Master, give us food, or we perish. Send us five loaves of bread. Our wants are not great, but great is Thy power, and infinite Thy love." One of the sisters now entered the cell, and Agnes told her to go into the tower, and bring out the bread which Christ had just sent. When the bread was set on the table, it multiplied as fast as it was eaten, and supplied the whole convent for many days.—La Vierge de Sienne, *Dialogue* 149.

St. Austregisil, bishop of Bourges, multiplies wine (A.D. 551–624). One vintage St. Austregisil went into the cellar of the monastery of the Château à Bourges to examine the vats, and take a register of their contents. He found all the tubs full, except one which held twenty gallons; this tub had a pint or so in it, but not more. St. Austregisil, making on it the sign of the cross, passed on. Next day the cellarer, on going into the vault, observed that the aforesaid cask was full to overflowing, and informed Austregisil; but the saint told the cellarer not to talk about the matter, for it was God's doing.

Another instance. On another occasion St. Austregisil, being in Geneva, saw on the borders of the lake a chapel half in ruins. There was neither priest nor clerk, guardian nor any other person to say mass there. The doors of the chapel were wide open, but the sacristy was fast locked. Austregisil bade his reader go and fetch some water; but the reader, being unable to find any, returned to the chapel, when he beheld the sacristy door open, and the bishop saying mass. Two cups were on the altar table, one of water and the other of wine.—*Legendes du Berry.*

St. Brigit of Kildare causes a cow to give three pailfuls of milk (A.D. 430–523). St. Brigit on one occasion was visited by several bishops, but had no food to give them. She sent to milk a cow which had been already milked twice that same day, but now gave freely milk enough to fill three large pails. Pilgrimages are made to Hamay, in Belgium, by cowkeepers, in honour of this saint, that their cows may be prolific. The peasants of Fosses, in the diocese of Namur, are accustomed, on Feb. 1, every year, "benir des baguettes avec lesquelles on touche les vaches malades pour les guérir."—Mgr. Guérin, *Vies des Saintes*, vol. ii. pp. 186, 187.

St. Clara feeds fifty nuns with half a loaf of bread. On one occasion there happened to be in the nunnery over which St. Clara presided only a single loaf of bread, and no other food whatever, for the fifty nuns. St. Clara ordered the loaf to be divided into two equal parts, one of which was given in alms to the begging friars. When dinner-time arrived, the fifty nuns took their seats, and St. Clara, holding the half-loaf in her hands, blessed and broke it. The broken bread was then handed to the nuns, and all ate thereof and were filled, declaring that they had never enjoyed so good a meal in all their lives.—*Life of St. Clara* (written by command of pope Alexander V.). See 2 Kings iv. 42–44.

St. Euthymius multiplies food to feed four hundred Armenians (A.D. 376–473). One day four hundred Armenians, who had lost their way, came to the monastery of St. Euthymius and craved food. There was not at the time food enough in the monastery to last the usual inmates a single day; but Euthymius ordered food to be set at once before the travellers. When the monks, in obedience to this order, opened the larder, it was literally piled up to the very ceiling with food; indeed, so full was it, they found it hard to open the door. The wine and oil were similarly multiplied, so that after the four hundred strangers had made a hearty meal, there was left a large store of provisions for the use of the monks.—Cyrillus, *Life of St. Euthymius*. (See also Surius, and the annotations of Bollandus.)

St. Francis of Paula feeds forty soldiers with two small loaves and one pint of wine. Ferdinand I., king of Naples, sent a captain with forty soldiers to arrest St. Francis of Paula. When the officer came into the presence of the saint, he was so awe-struck that he fell at his feet and craved pardon. St. Francis ordered a collation to be set before the captain and his band. There were but two small loaves and a single pint of wine at hand; but St. Francis blessed them, and there was not only enough to satisfy forty-one hearty soldiers, who ate and drank most liberally, but at the close there was more bread and wine left than there was before the meal began.—Father Giry, *Acts of Canonization*, etc.

St. Francis of Paula feeds nine men for three days with a morsel of bread (A.D. 1416–1507). When St. Francis of Paula was on his way to Sicily, he miraculously fed nine persons for three days with a little piece of bread left in the wallet of one of the travellers.—Father Giry, *Acts of Canonization*, etc.

St. Gerard reproduces the loaves he had given away (A.D. 994). St. Gerard retired to his cabinet just before dinner to pray, according to his usual custom. While there he heard the voice of beggars asking for bread; and, going into the refectory, took three loaves off the table, and handed them to the beggars through the window. When he came to dinner he saw the three loaves had been replaced, and asked the steward who had done it. The man protested that no one had touched the table since it was laid, and that no bread had been replaced at all. When Gerard told the steward he had given three of the loaves to some beggars, the steward replied, then God must have replaced them, for he was quite certain no one in the house had done so.—Father Benedict, *Life of St. Gerard* (1700).

The testimony of this steward is not worth much, for he evidently did not know that Gerard had taken three loaves off the table.

⁂ A somewhat similar incident is told of Albert d'Ogna in 1279. One day he gave everything on the dinner-table, provided for himself and family, to some beggars. His wife was very angry; but, on going into the dining-room, she found the table refurnished with everything afresh.—*Acta Sanctorum* (Bollandists), May 13.

Wheat multiplied by St. John Francis Regis (A.D. 1597–1640). St. John Francis Regis, the Jesuit, kept a granary of wheat for distribution to the poor, and placed it under the charge of Margaret Baud. One day Margaret announced that the granary was quite empty, but St. Regis, notwithstanding, sent a poor woman, who had a large family, with an order for wheat. Margaret, surprised at this, went and told St. Regis the chamber was quite empty, insomuch that it would not be possible to scrape together so much as a handful of corn, much less a pokeful. "Go," said Regis, "and fill the poke which this poor woman has brought." Margaret persisted there was not a grain left. "Do as I bid you," said

Regis. So she went to the granary, and, to her utter amazement, found it full of wheat even to the ceiling. This miracle was repeated several times afterwards.—Father Daubenton (Jesuit), *Life of St. John Francis Regis.*

Food placed by John Grandé before an image of the Virgin multiplied (A.D. 1546-1600). In 1579 a dreadful famine occurred in Spain; bread failed, and the distress was frightful. John Grandé was at Xerês, and exerted himself nobly in rendering assistance to the starving people; but so many presented themselves that all his resources were at length exhausted. Man's extremity is God's opportunity. John Grandé put a small piece of bread and meat before the image of the Virgin, and from that moment the more he gave the more he had to give. Neither bread nor meat failed him so long as the famine lasted. —*Les Petits Bollandistes*, vol. vi. p. 437.

Guilbert, founder of the congregation of Vallombrosa, creates pike for the entertainment of Leo IX. (A.D. 1049). While pope Leo IX. was visiting the Churches, he told Guilbert, founder of the congregation of Vallombrosa, he should dine with him in his monastery of Passigno. Guilbert found there was no fish, so he told two of the novices to cast their lines in the neighbouring lake and get some. The novices replied, "There are no fish at all in the lake;" but the abbot rebuked them, saying it was not their place to remonstrate, but to obey. So they went to the lake, and presently returned, bringing with them two magnificent pike, which amply supplied the pope and all his retinue.—Wibert, *Life of St. Leo IX.*, bk. ii.

St. Hermeland multiplies wine (A.D. 718). The count of Nantes et Rennes, doubting the miraculous powers of St. Hermeland, resolved to put them to the proof. So he called on the saint, and St. Hermeland, by his benediction only, multiplied a sip of wine presented to the count in a glass, and obliged him by this miracle to throw himself at the saint's feet and beg his pardon. After that, the count listened with more attention to the ghostly instructions of the saint.

Another instance. While on a visit at Coutances, in Normandy, a rich inhabitant of the place, named Launé, received the saint under his roof. There was only one pint of wine in the house, but St. Hermeland gave of it to a large multitude of persons who had assembled on all sides to see him. Hundreds and hundreds drank of this wine, and still it failed not; yea, after all had drunk and were satisfied, there was more left in the vessel than at first.—Bulteau, *History of the Monks of the East*, bk. i. ch. 37.

St. Hermeland produces a lamprey which feeds a whole monastery (A.D. 718). While St. Hermeland was at Aindrette on the Loire, a monk spoke to him of a little fish, called a lamprey, which he had seen in the bishop's palace at Nantes. Says St. Hermeland, "Do you suppose that God cannot send such fish here?" And while he was speaking a lamprey jumped out of the Loire, and threw itself on the bank close by the monk. St. Hermeland divided it into three pieces; one he kept for himself, and the other two he sent to the monastery, and they sufficed to feed all the brothers there assembled. —Bulteau, *History of the Monks of the East*, bk. i. ch. 37.

St. Hilarion feeds three thousand with a hundred measures of grapes, and has three hundred measures left. St. Hilarion, visiting his monasteries, came to one which was occupied by a very miserly man. This vineyard was attached to a monastery, and the tenant had placed watchmen in it to keep out the crowd. St. Hilarion, passing by this vineyard, went into another, and the crowd followed him. The saint blessed the vineyard, and the multitude ate. This vineyard usually yielded a hundred measures of wine annually, but this year, when about three thousand persons had eaten of the grapes as much as they wished, it yielded, within twenty days, more than three hundred measures of wine. The other vineyard yielded much less than usual, and the fruit it bore did not ripen, so that the grapes thereof were sour.—St. Jerome (A.D. 399), *Vita St. Hilarionis.* See also Nicephorus Callistus (died 1350), *Ecclesiastical History.*

St. Isidore feeds a great crowd with the portion of food set aside for himself. One night St. Isidore returned home later than usual, because he had entered a church on his way to pray there. When he reached the homestead of farmer Vargas, for whom he worked, supper was over, but a small portion had been set aside for him. Isidore took it to the door, where a great crowd of poor people and pilgrims was assembled, distributed to each as much as he would, and all went away filled and fully satisfied, so greatly had the food been multiplied.—From the Spanish *Life of St. Isidore.*

Another example. St. Isidore joined the confraternity of the Rosary of Our Blessed Lady, where, on certain days, a distribution of bread and wine was made to the "sodalês." Isidore always gave his quota to the poor. On one occasion it was larger than usual, so he invited all the poor round about to come and receive his dole of bread and wine. Above three hundred assembled; and, as he distributed, the bread and wine kept multiplying, so that all the three hundred were filled; and as they returned home, they blessed God for His miraculous liberality.

The life of St. Isidore is vouched for by the highest possible authority, and the version used in these extracts is a translation printed at Brussels, June 18, 1625, by John Heigham, by letters of authorization from Philip, king of Castile and Aragon, countersigned by his minister, Da Groote.

St. John Baptist de la Conception multiplies food (1561-1613). St. John Baptist de la Conception was head of the reformed Trinitarians in the new convent of Val de Pegnas. On one occasion, being wholly without food, a gift of twelve loaves was sent to the convent. Ten of these he gave to the poor, leaving only two for the convent, which contained some hundreds of inmates. He commanded the steward to break the two loaves into small pieces and hand round. All made a hearty repast, and there remained over and above sufficient for the evening meal.

On another occasion, being without food of any kind, the saint told the inmates they must perforce observe the day as a veritable fast. As he spoke two young men knocked at the gate, and gave in food of divers kinds "truly appetizing." When the porter demanded from whom the gift came, the young men made answer, "Take, take, and give God thanks." So saying, they departed, and were no more seen.—Godescard, *Vie des Saintes* (continued by Darras).

St. Jordanus feeds some fifty persons with two small loaves (A.D. 1237). St. Jordanus of Saxony on one occasion went to the village of Ursace, in the Alps, in company with two brothers and a secular clerk. Hungry and tired, they entered the village inn, and asked for something to eat. Mine host informed them he had nothing in the house but two small loaves, which he required for his own family. St. Jordanus requested the man to bring what he had, and set before them. He then invited the poor of the neighbourhood to come to the inn, and soon thirty poor folks gathered before the door. The host remonstrated; said it would not be possible to get food in that place; and wanted to send the poor away. But St. Jordanus distributed the bread first to the thirty poor folks, till all were filled; then to his three companions, till they were satisfied; then to the host and all his house; and lastly to himself. Mine host was stupefied, and exclaimed, "This man is a saint."—*Acta Sanctorum* (Bollandus), vol. ii. Feb.

St. Julian, bishop of Cuença, miraculously supplied with food (A.D. 1207). St. Julian, bishop of Cuença, used daily to give dinner to a large number of paupers, and God used to multiply his food miraculously to enable him to continue his charities. Sometimes he would find the corn in his granaries multiplied, especially in times of scarcity. On one occasion, having exhausted his provisions, a long train of mules, without a single driver, stood at his gates. Each mule was laden with corn, and, after being unloaded, departed, no one knows whither. As there was no driver, there was no one to pay, and St. Julian felt persuaded that the gift came from God.—*Acta Sanctorum* (Bollandus), Jan. 28.

St. Maur multiples wine to supply guests with it (A.D. 512-584). On one occasion St. Maur had to entertain unexpectedly the archdeacon of Angers and more than sixty strangers. He had no wine in the house, except a few drops in a bottle; but these few drops he multiplied so abundantly that all his guests had as much as they desired, and more was left than the original quantity. Faustus (a companion of St. Maur), *Life of St. Maur.*

St. Maidoc of Ferns reproduces six sheep, eaten by wolves (A.D. 632). On one occasion St. Maidoc fed six hungry wolves with six fat sheep, and then reproduced the sheep in their former state of life and fatness.—Baring-Gould, *Lives of the Saints*, Jan. 31.

Baring-Gould apologizes for the prodigies set down to St. Maidoc, saying "they are incredible;" but he ought to have told us where to draw the line between credible and incredible miracles.

St. Nicholas levies corn, and the levies are miraculously restored. During a great dearth in Lycia, St. Nicholas induced every ship laden with corn on its way to Constantinople to give him a hundred measures of the wheat (= four sacks), under promise that when the ship reached the docks the crew would find the gift replaced. With this voluntary levy, St. Nicholas kept the Lycians well supplied with food; for not only were the hundred measures miraculously restored to the various ships, but the quantity given was always miraculously increased according to the necessities of the people. There never was too little, and there never was too much. (See Exod. xvi. 17, 18.)—Metaphrastês (died 911), *Lives*, etc.

St. Odilo, bishop of Cluny, feeds a large number of visitors with a little fish (A.D. 962–1049). One day St. Odilo was in St. Martin's monastery when an unusual number of visitors arrived, and there was nothing in the house to eat except a little fish. Odilo caused it to come to pass that this little fish supplied a bountiful meal to all the guests, all the inmates of the house, and all the poor who came for alms.

Another instance. On another occasion he ordered that a number of travellers, who unexpectedly arrived at the monastery of Orval, should be served with the wine and food provided for the inmates. This was done, and though the hungry and thirsty travellers ate and drank to their hearts' content, yet the refection was not diminished, so that the wine-bottles and dishes seemed as if they had not been touched.—*Acta Sanctorum* (Bollandus), vol. i. Jan. 1.

St. Richard, bishop of Chichester, feeds three thousand poor folk with one loaf of bread (A.D. 1253). One day St. Richard, bishop of Chichester, distributing a single loaf of bread, all that he had, satisfied therewith three thousand hungry paupers, and after a hearty meal there was enough left to feed a hundred more. His biographer says he frequently multiplied food in a similar way.—J. Capprave, *Legends of England.*

St. Sorus, from three ripe grapes, makes three barrels of wine (A.D. 500–580). Gontran, king of Burgundy, with a large following went to Aquitaine, in the province of Perigord, to be cured by St. Sorus of leprosy. After the cure was effected, the saint invited the king and all his suite to a repast, and told his steward to spread a table suitable to such honoured guests. The steward told St. Sorus there was no wine, and that none could be procured in time. "Well," said he, "what of that? the hand of the Lord is not shortened. Go into the vineyard, and you will find three grapes plump and ripe; pluck them, and bring them to me." The steward did as he was bidden, and brought to the hermit the three grapes. "Now," said the saint, "bring hither three empty barrels, and squeeze the three grapes into the three barrels." This did he, and the barrels overflowed with most excellent wine. When the table was laid, the king and his courtiers commended the wine, greatly enjoyed the food set before them, and praised the hospitality of the hermit. King Gontran, to show his gratitude, built a monastery for poor travellers, which he endowed right royally, and placed under the charge of his saintly host. The monastery was built, endowed with immense revenues, and provided with everything necessary both within and without; for when kings acknowledge a benefit received, they acknowledge it like kings.—*Les Petits Bollandistes*, vol. ii. p. 194.

St. Theresa d'Avila multiplies food (A.D. 1515–1582). St. Theresa of Avila, founder of the barefooted Carmelites, found that the flour in her convent of Villeneuve would not last above a month longer, so she multiplied it into enough to last the whole community for six months, and at the end of that time there was more left than the original quantity.—*Les Petits Bollandistes*, vol. xii. p. 375.

St. Theodosius the Cœnobiarch feeds thousands in a famine (A.D. 423–529). During a great famine the monastery over which Theodosius presided was so crowded, that the porters closed the doors, and refused any further admittance. Still throngs crowded round the doors, craving bread. St. Theodosius ordered food to be distributed daily to all who applied for it, and God provided that the food given was as rapidly replenished. On the feast of the Virgin, the number of applicants was many thousands, but food was given to them all, as much as they liked; and after all had eaten and were filled, each took away as much as could be carried. It was a veritable repetition of our Saviour's miracle in the desert, when with five small loaves and two fishes He fed five thousand men besides women and children; or with seven loaves and a few fishes He fed four thousand men besides women and children.—*The Roman Martyrology.* (Cave tells us this life was written by Theodore, bishop of Pera.)

Another example. One day St. Theodosius and several of his disciples called on Marcian, a monk, and asked him to set food before them. Marcian brought forth a plate of lentils, and said he had no bread in the cell. St. Theodosius, observing a small crumb of bread on the monk's habit, said, "How say you, brother, there is no bread in the cell?" and handed him the crumb. The monk took it in his hand and carried it to the larder, whereupon it became bread sufficient to set before his guests; and next day it had so multiplied that it filled the larder and ran out through the door in great abundance.—*Acta Sanctorum* (Bollandus), vol. i. Jan. 1.

Food multiplied by St. Vincent Ferrier (A.D. 1357–1419). Time would fail us if we told of the sick folk healed by St. Vincent Ferrier, the blind he gave sight to, the deaf he gave hearing to, the dumb he gave speech to, the women he relieved from the pains of childbirth, the palsied he restored to strength, and the dead he raised to life; but we must not omit to mention that many a time and oft he multiplied bread and wine so prodigiously as to supply two thousand, four thousand, and even six thousand persons with a single loaf of bread and a single pint of wine; and after the multitude had eaten and drunk to satiety, the residue left was manifold more than the original quantity. This shows us that even our Lord and Saviour Jesus Christ "n'opère pas de moindres miracles par ses serviteurs que ceux qu'il a faits par lui-même."—R. P. Pradel, *Vie du Saint Vincent Ferrier*.

An incident mentioned by Raymond, the confessor of St. Catherine of Siena, on the life of that saint, will explain some of the "miracles" of the multiplication or supply of food. He says, "One day St. Catherine went to visit a poor widow woman confined to her bed, and moved to compassion by her extreme poverty determined to supply food without being seen or known. She filled her lap, loaded her shoulders, and her hands, with wine, corn, and oil, to the amount of a hundred pounds. On opening the cottage door one of the bags fell from her shoulder and woke the woman, who caught sight of Catherine's robe as she ran off, and recognized her." Had this not been the case, the food would have been put down to a miraculous supply instead of a secret private charity.

Garment touched or touching.

MATT. ix. 20, 21. A woman which was diseased with an issue of blood twelve years came behind Jesus, and touched the hem of His garment; for she said within herself, If I may but touch His garment I shall be whole. (See Numb. xv. 38, 39.)

MATT. xiv. 36. All the country of Gennesaret went to see Jesus, and brought to him all that were diseased, and besought Him that they might only touch the hem of His garment; and as many as touched were made perfectly whole.

ACTS xix. 11, 12. God wrought special miracles by the hands of Paul: so that from his body were brought unto the sick handkerchiefs or aprons, and the diseases departed from them, and evil spirits went out of them.

A paralytic cured by kissing the hem of St. Ambrose's garment. When St. Ambrose, at his sister's request, went to visit a great lady, he saw, sitting on a chair, a palsied woman. His sister called his attention to her, and as he approached the chair the paralytic kissed the hem of his garment, and was instantly made whole.—Paul the deacon, *Life of St. Ambrose.*

The touch of St. Angelus's cope restores a child to life (A.D. 1225). St. Angelus, at the age of twenty-six, went to Jerusalem to take priest's orders, and while there, a woman brought her dead son to him, laid the body at his feet, and implored him to restore it to life. Angelus resisted for a time, saying he was too young and too unworthy to ask so great a favour of God; but the woman persisted, and the young priest yielded to her importunity. He threw his cope over the child, and as he prayed, the child returned to life, publishing abroad the glory of the Almighty and the merits of the young priest.—*Les Petits Bollandistes*, vol. v. pp. 342, 343.

A demoniac cured as soon as the garment of St. Antony of Padua touched him (A.D. 1195–1231). St. Antony of Padua was called to see a brother monk who was ill; he was screaming horribly, laughing, and tossing himself about. It occurred to St. Antony that the man was possessed, so he threw his mantle over him. Immediately the garment touched the demoniac, the devil left him, and he was cured.

Another instance. When St. Antony was in the abbey of Solignac, one of the inmates, tormented by the devil, prayed him to intercede on his behalf. St. Antony took off his cloak and put it on the shoulders of the demoniac; whereupon the impure spirit departed, and never returned again.—L'abbé Guyard, *Life of St. Antony of Padua.*

A woman with a bloody flux healed by touching the hem of Aquinas's garment. William of Tocco tells us, that while Thomas Aquinas was coming out of St. Peter's church on Easter Sunday, a woman who was diseased of a bloody flux came behind, and touched the hem of his garment. No sooner had she done so than she was entirely cured. Alban Butler repeats this tradition as not too extravagant even for his expurgated calendar of saints (March 7).

A woman healed by touching the garment of St. Bernardin (1380–1444). A woman, suffering from a sore which was pronounced by physicians incurable, touched the edge of the garment of St. Bernardin, and was instantly made whole.

Another instance. St. Bernardin gave a pair of his shoes to a poor leper, and immediately the leper put them on, his leprosy left him, and he became as well as if he had never been afflicted.—Barnaby of Siena (a contemporary), *Life of St. Bernardin.*

St. Charles Borromeo's cloak cures Sister Candida of a disease pronounced to be incurable (the day of St. Peter and St. Paul, 1601). Sister Candida, of the convent of the Capucinesses, in Milan, had been sick for three years, and her disease was pronounced to be incurable. After receiving the "last sacrament," she made a vow to St. Charles Borromeo, and bade her attendants lay over her the deceased saint's gown, which he was accustomed to wear in his private cell. Immediately the gown touched the invalid she recovered, rose out of bed, and carried the gown in her own hands back to the church. This miracle is attested by all the sisters of the convent, and filled them with amazement.—Francis Penia, *Abridgment of the Life of St. Charles Borromeo.*

St. Giles's cloak cures a sick beggar. One day St. Giles saw in the street a sick man, who asked alms of him. St. Giles replied, "Silver and gold have I none; but such as I have, give I unto thee." So saying, he stripped off his outer garment and gave it to the beggar. No sooner had the beggar put on the cloak than he was entirely cured of his infirmity.—Gilbertus (bishop of Carnotum), *Life of St. Giles.*

St. Gregory's rochet kills a Jew (A.D. 261). Two Jews plotted together to overreach St. Gregory (Thaumaturgus), whom they saw approaching. One laid himself on the ground, pretending to be dead, and the other pretended to be bewailing the sudden death of his companion. When St. Gregory came up, the "live" man said to him, "O man of God, help me in my misery. This my companion has just fallen down dead, and I have nothing to wrap him in." St. Gregory, taking off his rochet, laid it over the man on the ground, and went his way. "Come along, old fellow," said the other Jew; "up with you; the man is gone, and we have not made a bad market;" but his companion stirred not. "Up, I say; no one is near, let us be off," persisted the "living" Jew. Still his companion answered not a word. In fact, he was dead. He died the moment the rochet touched him. Like Ananias and Sapphira, he consented to a lie, and the judgment of the Lord was upon him.—St. Gregory of Nyssa, *Life of St. Gregory Thaumaturgus.*

A leper healed by the touch of St. Hugh's cloak (A.D. 1024–1109). St. Hugh, abbot of Cluny, went one day to visit the monasteries of Gascony, and saw on the road a leper. This leper was once very rich and of excellent social standing, but he fled from society, and buried himself in solitude. Hugh entered his cabin, spoke kindly to him, and throwing his cloak over the man's shoulders, the leprosy left him.—Lorain, *History of the Abbey of Cluny.*

Two children cured by being touched with a rag cut from the garment of John Francis Regis, the Jesuit (A.D. 1597–1640). A woman of Marlhes, seeing the garment of St. Regis in holes, asked to be allowed to mend it; to which the saint readily assented. The woman had two sick children at the time; one was ill of dropsy, and the other of scarlet fever. She laid on each child a piece cut from the garment which she had repaired, and immediately both the children were restored to perfect health.—Father Daubenton (Jesuit), *Life of St. John Francis Regis.*

Touching the garment of St. John Joseph sanative (A.D. 1654–1734). Cardinal Wiseman says many were healed by merely touching the garments of St. John Joseph of the Cross, and many by touching St. John Joseph. For example, the mother of a madman held his mantle before her son, and the madman instantly leaped out of the window into the street. Every one expected he would have been crushed to death, for the window was in an upper story; but not only was he uninjured, he was actually restored to his right mind.

Again. Casimir Avellon healed his wife of spasms in the shoulders, which had resisted all the remedies hitherto tried, by simply placing on the part affected a small piece of one of the garments of St. John Joseph.

A lady suffering from neuralgia in the head was cured by touching the saint's hands. Similarly a blind man was cured, and an infant of three years old who was a cripple.—Migne, *Démonstrations Evangéliques*, vol. xvi.

A demoniac cured by touching the hem of St. Lubin's garment (A.D. 557). Among the many miracles wrought by St. Lubin, bishop of Chartres, we are told that a damsel, possessed of an evil spirit, was delivered by touching the hem of his garment.—Dupré, *Saints de Blois.*

A bloody flux staunched by touching the garment of St. Pacomius (A.D. 292–348). A woman, afflicted with a bloody flux, induced a monk to permit her to stand in the church where she could touch St. Pacomius when he went to the altar. As the abbot passed by the woman touched the hem of his garment, and was instantly made whole.—His life by one of the monks of Tabenna, a contemporary.

A woman with a cancer cured by touching the garment of St. Theodosius the Cœnobiarch (A.D. 423–529). One day, when St. Theodosius the Cœnobiarch was preaching in the church of Jerusalem, a woman with a horrible cancer waited for him outside the church; for she said within herself, "If I can but touch his garment I shall be made whole." When St. Theodosius passed by the woman, she touched his garment, and straightway was made whole.—*The Roman Martyrology.* (Cave says the life of St. Theodosius in this martyrology was written by Theodore, bishop of Pera.)

A woman cured of ague by her beads, which had touched against the tomb of St. Alfonso Rodriquez (A.D. 1526–1617). Some four days after the death of St. Alfonso Rodriquez, a woman sick of an ague sent her son, a boy of seven years old, to touch the tomb of the saint with her beads. The boy having done so, took the beads to his mother; and the woman placing them round her neck, the fever left her. She lived many years afterwards, and enjoyed far better health than she had before.—Michael Julian, *Life of St. Alfonso Rodriquez.*

A piece of the cassock of St. Alfonso Rodriquez cures an issue of blood (A.D. 1526–1617). Two days after the death of St. Alfonso Rodriquez, there came a woman afflicted with an issue of blood, whose life was despaired of, insomuch that a father had been sent for to assist at her expected death. Before the father arrived, a piece of the cassock of Alfonso Rodriquez was laid on her, and the moment it touched her, she cried out with a loud voice, "Praise be to God, I am cured!" The flux was staunched, and the ague from which she was suffering left her. The woman lived after this miraculous cure for many years.—Michael Julian, *Life of St. Alfonso Rodriquez.*

A cancer cured by a piece of the cloak of St. Alfonso Rodriquez (1526–1617). A woman suffering from cancer in the breast laid a piece of the cloak of St. Alfonso Rodriquez on the part affected. The moment the cloth touched her, a stream of corrupt matter ran from the breast; the wound healed in two days; and on the third day she had an abundance of pure milk to give her young babe. This miracle was sworn to by an eyewitness.—Michael Julian, *Life of St. Alfonso Rodriquez.*

A holy father of the Society of Jesus tells us that daily at the tomb of this saint miracles were wrought, and if he attempted to particularize each one, he might adopt the language of John the Evangelist, "I suppose that even the world itself could not contain the books that should be written;" or, in other words, that the number of books which would be required for the purpose would exceed all the books then extant.

Gates opening of their Own Accord.

Acts xii. 10. When they were past the first and second ward, they came unto the iron gate that leadeth unto the city, which opened to them of its own accord.

Acts xvi. 25, 26. At midnight Paul and Silas prayed . . . and suddenly there was a great earthquake . . . and all the doors were opened.

The gates of Paris open of their own accord to St. Geneviève. King Childeric had great respect for St. Geneviève, and was unable to refuse her when she preferred a petition. On one occasion, when the king was about to put to death a number of captives taken in war, he commanded the city gates to be closed, lest St. Geneviève should come and intercede for their liberation. When the saint heard thereof, she hurried to the city, and, touching the gates, they instantly flew open to her, though they were both locked and bolted. Going at once to the king, she fell on her knees before him, and refused to rise till she obtained her petition. So the captives were released, and the deed of blood was stayed.—Baring-Gould, *Lives of the Saints*, Jan., p. 50.

For other examples consult the index.

Gehazi.

2 Kings v. 20–27. When Naaman was cured

of his leprosy he wanted to reward Elisha with gold and other gifts; but the prophet refused to take anything. Gehazi, the servant of Elisha, resolved to profit by his master's independence, and ran after the Syrian captain, saying, My master hath sent me, saying, Behold, even now there be come to me from Mount Ephraim two young men of the sons of the prophets: give them, I pray thee, a talent of silver, and two changes of raiment. Naaman said, Be content, take two talents. So they bound for him two talents of silver in two bags, and sent two servants with him, bearing two changes of garments. Before they reached the tower, Gehazi took the garments himself, and sent the Syrian servants back again. When Gehazi showed himself to his master, Elisha said to him, Whence comest thou, Gehazi? And Gehazi answered, Thy servant has been no whither? Then said Elisha to him, Went not my heart with thee, when the man turned again from his chariot to meet thee? Is it a time to receive money, and to receive garments? The leprosy therefore of Naaman shall cleave unto thee and thy seed for ever. And Gehazi went out from the presence of Elisha a leper white as snow.

St. Benedict reproved one of his disciples for receiving a present from some nuns (A.D. 480–543). One day, when St. Benedict was engaged on a missionary tour, he sent one of his disciples to a nunnery to deliver the exhortation for him. The nuns begged the monk to accept some handkerchiefs which they had made, and he hid them in his bosom. On his return to the monastery, the patriarch met him, and said to him severely, "How is this, my brother, that you have suffered iniquity to enter into your bosom?" The monk was amazed at this reproof, and could not at once tell what the saint referred to. "Was I not with you when you received the handkerchiefs which you hid in your bosom? Is this the way you keep your vows of poverty and obedience?" These words fell on the monk like a clap of thunder, and, falling at the feet of the abbot, he demanded penance, and threw away the handkerchiefs which had been given him.—St. Gregory the Great, *Dialogues*, bk. ii.

John, the successor of St. Macarius, appropriated to himself the revenues of the abbey, and became a leper (fourth century). John succeeded Macarius, abbot of Alexandria, A.D. 394. St. Macarius, knowing his great foible, had said to him, "Brother, your great temptation is avarice. Resist it, or be assured the lot of Gehazi will be yours also." Instead of profiting by this advice, as soon as Macarius was dead, and John succeeded to the abbacy, he appropriated to himself the revenues which belonged to the poor, and became a leper, covered with elephantiasis, "qu'on ne trouvait pas en tout son corps la largeur d'un doight qui n'en fût gâté."—*Les Petits Bollandistes* (1880), Jan. 2.

A stolen bottle of wine converted into a serpent. A man of high condition sent St. Benedict two flagons of wine, but the valet stole one, and hid it under a tree. When he delivered the other at the abbey of Mount Cassino, the saint received it courteously, but said to the manservant, "On your return home, my man, don't forget the flagon under the tree; but before you put it into your mouth, look well into it. Adieu." When the man picked up the flagon which he had stolen, and looked into it, instead of wine, he found therein a deadly asp. This miracle had such an effect on the young valet, that he turned monk, and St. Benedict called him "Brother Exhilaratus."—St. Gregory the Great, *Dialogues*, bk. ii. ch. 1.

This "miracle" is repeated in the life of St. Dominic of Sora, about 540 years later. (See next two articles.)

Stolen fish converted by St. Dominic into a serpent (A.D. 1031). A certain person sent to St. Dominic of Sora some fish, but the man charged with the commission stole part, and hid it under a tree. When he delivered the residue at the monastery, St. Dominic said to the man, "Don't forget the fish under the linden tree." When the man arrived at the spot, he found, instead of a fish, a nest of serpents, and fled in fear of his life.—Cardinal Alberic II., *Life of St. Dominic of Sora*; also *Acta Sanctorum*, vol. iii. p. 56.

(See the articles above and below.)

Stolen bread and wine converted into poison and a serpent by St. Valery (A.D. 619). A pious lady sent by her son some food and wine to St. Valery of Luxeuil, but the lad hid a part, intending on his return to feast thereon. When he delivered the present to the saint, St. Valery said to him, "We thank God for the bounties sent by your hand; but when you return home, my son, take care how you put to your mouth what you hid in coming, for the food is poisoned, and a serpent is in the flagon." When the lad reached the spot where he had secreted what he had purloined, the food was quite uneatable, and a snake had crept into the flagon. The boy in terror ran back to St. Valery, fell at his feet, and begged pardon for his offence. (See the two preceding legends.)—Besançon (1854), *Les Saints de Franche Comté.*

A thief, having stolen some millstones, was punished by St. Leufredus (A.D. 738). A thief, having stolen some millstones from Leufredus's monastery, was taken by the saint before the magistrate of the district. Here he behaved like a man beside himself, and called Leufredus a liar and a slanderer. Leufredus simply answered, "May God judge between thee and me;" and at the selfsame hour all the teeth of the thief broke in his two jaws. As the leprosy of Gehazi was entailed on his posterity for ever, so were the broken teeth of this thief; for, as the chamberlain of pope Leo XIII. says, "toute sa posterité n'a point eu de dents." —Mgr. Guérin, *Vies des Saints*, vol. vii. p. 189.

One could well wish to know the chamberlain's proof of this toothless entail. The occurrence "took place" in the diocese of Evreux, somewhere about A.D. 730, say eleven hundred years ago. Does Mgr. Guérin know any of these teethless creatures? and has he any proof whatever that the race has been so for eleven hundred years? If so, the "miracle" might be regarded as something better than an old wives' tale.

Gideon's Stratagem.

JUDG. vii. 16–28. When Gideon went against the allied Midianites and Amalekites, he selected three hundred men, which he divided into three companies, and told the men to conceal a lamp in a pitcher, and to take a trumpet. His scheme was to surprise the foe, and spread a panic among them. So Gideon with the three companies, at the beginning of the middle watch, stole towards the camp of the foe, and all of a sudden every man blew his trumpet, brake the pitcher which concealed his lamp, and shouted, The sword of the Lord, and of Gideon! The Midianites and their allies rose in terror and fled, and the Lord set every man's sword against his fellow, so the overthrow was complete.

Michael, king of the Bulgarians, subdues an army of rebels by wax candles (A.D. 866). The Bulgarians revolted, because Michael their king had forsaken the national faith, and became a Christian. Marching against the rebels, the king obtained an easy victory, by availing himself of a panic. The rebels either saw, or thought they saw, seven clerks with wax candles setting fire to a house, and feared lest the burning house should fall upon them, and the king's cavalry trample them to death. Too terrified to flee, they lay on the earth trembling, and, of course, there was no difficulty in reducing them to submission.—Henschenius, *Lives of St. Cyril and St. Methodius* (March 9).

Gift of Tongues.

ACTS ii. 1–11. When the day of Pentecost was fully come . . . there were in Jerusalem devout men out of every nation under heaven . . . and they were confounded, because every man heard [the apostles] speak in his own language . . . Parthians, and Medes, and Elamites, and the dwellers in Mesopotamia, and in Judæa, and Cappadocia, in Pontus, and Asia, Phrygia, and Pamphylia, in Egypt, and in the parts of Libya about Cyrenê, and strangers of Rome, Jews and proselytes, Cretes and Arabians, heard in their own tongues the apostles speak of the wonderful works of God.

1 COR. xii. 4–11. There are diversities of gifts . . . to one is given the word of wisdom, to another the gift of healing, to another the working of miracles, to another divers kind of tongues.

St. Antony of Padua had the gift of tongues. St. Antony of Padua had, together with his other endowments, the gift of tongues, clear, pleasant, and shrill. Though thousands of every nation under heaven came to hear him, yet all understood him. As it happened in Rome: when a crowd of foreigners stood around him, and he preached in Italian, all affirmed that they heard him speak in their own native language. The same thing happened when the apostles, on the day of Pentecost, spoke in Jerusalem to the men there gathered together out of every nation under heaven.—Edward Kinesman (1623), *Lives of the Saints*, p. 367.

St. Bernardin preached to the Greeks in Italian, and what they heard was Greek (A.D. 1380–1444). St. Bernardin on one occasion had to preach to Greeks, but not knowing the Greek language, he preached in his native Italian, and was understood as well as if he had spoken in Greek the wonderful works of God.—Barnaby of Siena (a contemporary), *Life of St. Bernardin.*

St. Pacomius inspired in a moment with the Greek and Latin languages (A.D. 292–348). St. Pacomius knew only one language, his native Egyptian; but one day a religious from Italy came to consult him on a case of conscience; and Pacomius, kneeling in prayer, said, "O God, if the knowledge of languages is essential, in order that I may make known Thy will to strangers, why hast Thou not given me this gift? If it seemeth good in Thy sight give me now the gift of tongues, that I may be useful to this stranger." So saying, he rose from his knees, and found himself a perfect master of the Greek and Latin languages.—His *Life*, by a monk of Tabenna, one of his disciples.

When St. Vincent Ferrier preached, all

foreigners understood him (A.D. 1357–1419). St. Vincent Ferrier went about preaching. He was accompanied by fifty priests, a large number of Tertiaries of the order of St. Dominic, and a multitude of penitents. The audience of strangers amounted often to ten thousand, but though the crowd was so enormous, the persons furthest off heard him as distinctly as those near him; and although all nationalities were amongst the hearers, Frenchmen and Italians, Germans and English, Spaniards and Portuguese, all understood every word that was uttered, as if it had been spoken in their own tongue.—Peter Ranzano (bishop of Lucera), *Life of St. Vincent Ferrier.*

We are again told, in the same life, that St. Vincent went to Genoa in 1405, and though he preached in Spanish, the strangers of all nationalities, who had assembled at that important mart, understood him as well as if each had been addressed in his own native language. —Mgr. Guérin, *Vies des Saints*, vol. iv. p. 232.

St. Francis Xavier had the gift of tongues. As soon as Xavier came into any of those strange countries where he preached the gospel, he spoke the language of the people instinctively, were it ever so different from any other language of the globe. Not only so, but he spoke it as fluently and elegantly as if he had been a native brought up by the chiefs; so that every nation and tribe heard him in its own tongue; and if persons of divers languages hearkened to him at one and the same time, each one heard the sermon in his own mother tongue.—*Cardinal de Monte's speech before Gregory XV., at the canonization of Francis Xavier*, Jan. 19, A.D. 1622.

Glastonbury Thorn.

The legend of the Glastonbury thorn is, that it sprang from the staff of Joseph of Arimathæa, who was sent by the apostle Philip to preach the gospel in Britain. On reaching Yniswitcin, afterwards called Glastonbury, he stuck his staff in the ground, to indicate that he meant to abide there, and the staff put forth leaves and branches; and every year, on Old Christmas, it blossoms. This thorn, till the reign of queen Elizabeth, had two trunks, but a Puritan attempted to cut it down. However, he was punished; for not only did he cut his leg severely, but also lost one of his eyes, by a chip of the thorn striking it. The multilated trunk still flourished, and afterwards, when carted into a ditch, took root and bloomed. A year after it was cast into the ditch, half of it was carried off, but still the remaining part flourished, and the part stolen was carried into distant parts of the island and grew. In the reign of Charles I., the original tree was all cut down, but still there are several plants about Glastonbury reared from the old stock, and in mild winters, like that of 1881, they certainly flower.

The legend is told by William of Malmesbury, who died A.D. 1142.

In Withering's *British Plants*, vol. iii. p. 596, article "Cratægus," we read: "In a lane beyond the churchyard, on the opposite side of the street, near a pit, grows a very old tree [of the *Glastonburiensis* species]. A woman ninety years of age never remembers it otherwise than as it now appears.

"Another tree of the same kind may be seen two or three miles from Glastonbury. It has been reported to have no thorns, but that I found to be a mistake; it has thorns, like other hawthorns, but, as in other aged trees, they are few in number.

"There is also a full-sized tree of this kind in the garden at Piper's Inn. This variety blossoms twice a year: the winter blossoms, which are about the size of a sixpence, appear about Christmas-time; it may occasionally happen on Christmas Day, but it is sometimes sooner. This variety produces no fruit. The berries contain only one seed, and there seems to be only one pistil, but it was late in the season when I examined it (Oct. 1792). I was informed that the berries when sown produce plants nowise differing from the common hawthorn."

"Probably the tree which gave birth to the tradition of its having sprung from the staff of Joseph of Arimathæa grew within the abbey, and may have died from age, or been destroyed in the Reformation. However that may be, the existence of this *lusus naturæ* is unquestionable, and is not, as Dr. Hunter asserts, 'a sanctified deceit, sunk into discredit even with the meanest of the vulgar.'"—*Sylvia*, vol. i. p. 178.

The following is from the Rev. R. Warner, F.A.S. (*History of the Abbey of Glaston*, 4to, 1826):—"The Holy Thorn has been introduced into many parts, and is now found in various gardens of Glastonbury and its vicinity. Pilgrimages continued to be made to this wonderful tree even in Mr. Eyston's time (died 1721), and its scions were sought for with the greatest avidity both by the pious of the Romish Church, and the superstitious of other systems of faith, till within these eighty years."

In the *Evening Post*, London, Jan. 1753, we read: "A vast concourse of people attended the noted thorn on Christmas Day (new style); but, to their great disappointment, there was no appearance of its blowing, which made them watch it narrowly till Jan. 5 (Christmas Day, old style), when it blowed as usual."

Strype records that one of Henry VIII.'s "visiters" sent up, with various relics, "two flowers (wrapped in white and black sarcenet), which on Christenmass even, 1536, *hora ipsa qua Christus natus fuerat* will spring, and burgen, and bare blossomes."

We are furthermore told that the spot on which St. Joseph planted his staff was on the south ridge of Weary-all-hill, now called Werrall Park. The *Avalonian Guide* states that "about the year 1740 the stump of the original thorn was seen, but that nothing now remains except grafts from it, growing in different places. The oldest of these grafts stands near St. John's churchyard at Glastonbury, and is a large tree, which still blossoms twice a year."

The Cadenham Oak, near Lyndhurst, in the New Forest. The Cadenham Oak has been known for more than two centuries to bud every year in the depth of winter, or, as the foresters insist, on Old Christmas Day, and then only. Dr. Withering, vol. ii. p. 508, says, "Many leaves do certainly appear on this oak about Christmas-time, but the progress of germination is soon checked in inclement weather, and in summer its foliage resembles that of other oak trees."

In the same forest, near Rufus's monument, is another tree remarkable for its winter vegetation, and Camden assures us that the very tree against which the arrow of Tyrrel glanced is noted for the same peculiarity.

A tree in the churchyard of Ham burst into flower when St. Gudula was buried. St. Gudula was buried Jan. 8, A.D. 710. When her body reached Ham, a tree standing in the churchyard burst into flower, although it was midwinter. The body of the saint was subsequently moved from Ham to St. Saviour's, Moorsel; whereupon the tree transplanted itself, all covered with flowers, and rooted itself firmly in the earth right opposite the church door.—Nicholas of Durham, *Life of St. Gudula.*

An olive tree planted by St. Torquatus blossoms every year on May 15. St. Torquatus, the apostle of Cadiz, lived in the first Christian century, and planted an olive tree before the church dedicated to him in Cadiz. This tree is always in full bloom on the fête-day of Torquatus, May 15.—*Propre d'Espagne.*

God answering by Fire.

LEV. ix. 24. Moses having prepared a bullock and a ram for a peace offering, there came a fire out from before the Lord, and consumed upon the altar the burnt offering and the fat; which, when the people saw, they shouted, and fell on their faces.

1 KINGS xviii. 38, 39. When Elijah challenged the priests of Baal, and it was his turn to offer sacrifice, fire of the Lord fell, and consumed the burnt sacrifice; and all the people said, The Lord, He is God; the Lord, He is God!

JUDG. vi. 19–21. When Gideon wanted a sign that it was God who bade him go against the Midianites, he made ready a kid, and unleavened cakes. The flesh he put in a basket, and the broth in a pot. Then the angel touched the flesh and the cakes with the staff that was in his hand; and there rose up fire out of the rock, and consumed the flesh and the cakes.

1 CHRON. xxi. 26. When David bought the threshing-floor of Ornan the Jebusite, and built an altar to the Lord, because the plague was stayed, God showed his approval by sending fire from heaven upon the altar to consume the sacrifice.

2 CHRON. vii. 1. When Solomon dedicated his temple, fire came down from heaven, and consumed his burnt offering and the sacrifice.

When St. Theodosius the Cœnobiarch was seeking a site for a monastery, God indicated by fire the spot he had chosen. St. Theodosius the Cœnobiarch wished to build a large monastery, but requested God to point out to him a suitable site. So, taking a censer filled with incense and charcoal not lighted, he prayed that when he came to the right spot, God would indicate it by setting fire to the charcoal. St. Theodosius walked from place to place, censer in hand, but there was no sign. After reaching Gutilla, on the shores of the Dead Sea, he turned homewards, and, as he approached his own cave, the smoke of the incense showed that the charcoal was kindled. Here, therefore, he built his monastery, and it was soon filled with inmates.—*The Roman Martyrology.* (Cave says this life of St. Theodosius the Cœnobiarch was written by Theodore, bishop of Pera.)

God fights for His Saints.

EXOD. xxiii. 20–28. Behold, I send an angel

before thee, to keep thee in the way. . . . If thou obey his voice . . . then I will be an enemy to thine enemies, and an adversary to thine adversaries; for Mine angel shall go before thee.

JOSH. v. 13, 14. When Joshua was by Jericho . . . behold, there stood a man over against him with a sword drawn in his hand. Joshua said to him, Art thou for us, or for our adversaries? And he said, As captain of the hosts of the Lord am I now come. And Joshua fell on his face to the earth, and did worship.

DAN. x. 13. The prince of the kingdom of Persia withstood me one and twenty days; but, lo! Michael came to help me.

REV. vi. 2. I saw, and behold! a white horse; and He that sat on him had a bow; and He went forth conquering, and to conquer.

JOSH. x. 11. Five kings came up against Joshua, but they fled before Israel, and the Lord cast down great stones from heaven upon them. They were more which died with hailstones than they whom the children of Israel slew with the sword.

2 KINGS xviii. 13–37; xix. Sennacherib sent a vast army to invade the kingdom of Judah in the reign of Hezekiah; but the king prayed, and God sent His angel to destroy the Assyrian army. In one night the angel slew a hundred fourscore and five thousand (185,000). And when the men of Judah rose next morning, behold, the whole Assyrian army lay dead before them.

Castor and Pollux at the battle of lake Regillus. In the battle at lake Regillus between the allies, who wanted to restore Tarquin, and the Romans (B.C. 499), while victory was still doubtful, the Romans beheld two white horses, and they that sat on them went against the allies, conquering and to conquer. It was Castor and Pollux on their white chargers. Their arms were so mighty in fight that they broke the arrow and the bow, the sword, the shield, and the battle. The allies fled on all sides, and the victory rested with the Romans. In gratitude for this aid, the Romans reared a temple to the honour of Castor and Pollux; and there, ever after, gifts were made and sacrifices offered, on the anniversary of the battle, to the riders of those white horses.—*Roman Story.*

St. Isidore's ghost shows don Alfonso a path by means of which he could surprise the Moors and conquer them (A.D. 1211). In 1211, don Alfonso, king of Castile, making war on the Moors, in the defile of Navas de Tolosa, searched in vain for a path by which he could come upon them by surprise. The ghost of St. Isidore showed him a path unknown to his army; and the king, falling on the foe unawares, gained a signal victory. For this service, the kings of Spain interested themselves in the canonization of the saint, but a variety of circumstances caused its delay till March 12, A.D. 1622, when Gregory XV. added St. Isidore, with four others, to the calendar.—*Act of Canonization.*

Jesus Christ, St. Peter, and St. Paul, with a host of angels, win the battle of Lepanto over the Turks (Oct 7, A.D. 1571). Selim II., sultan of the Turks, met with a most disastrous naval defeat near the habour of Lepanto, Oct. 7, A.D. 1571. This great victory is always ascribed to pope Pius V., and is mentioned in his canonization, A.D. 1712. At the hour of battle, the procession of the Rosary began its march to the church of Minerva. The pope was there, and all of a sudden opened a window, stood for some time listening, then, returning to the cardinals, said to them, "It is now time to give thanks to God for the great victory He has granted to our arms." The time when this was spoken was compared afterwards with the official report of the victory, and was found to accord precisely. The prisoners avowed that they saw in the air Jesus Christ, St. Peter, and St. Paul, with a multitude of angels sword in hand, fighting against the Turks, and blinding them with the smoke of their own cannons. This "miracle" forms a conspicuous feature in the picture descriptive of the battle in the Vatican.—Père Giry, *Histoire de Saint Pie V.*

St. James the Elder, on his white horse, assists king Fernando in the siege of Coimbra (A.D. 1040-1099). When king Fernando lay before Coimbra, there came from Greece to Santiago a pilgrim named Estiano, who was a bishop. As the bishop was praying in the church, he heard certain of the townsfolk telling the pilgrims that St. James was wont to appear in the Spanish battles in their aid, and that he always appeared as a knight on a white horse. The bishop, on hearing this, said to them, "Friends, call not St. James a knight, but a fisherman." When Estiano fell asleep, St. James appeared to him, holding in his hands a bunch of keys, and said to him, "You think it a fable, bishop, that I come to assist the Christians in their battles against the Moors; but know I am a knight in the army of Christ Jesus." While he was speaking, a white horse was brought him; and the apostle, clad in bright armour, mounting thereon, said to the bishop, "I am going to the help of king Fernando, who has lain these seven months before Coimbra; and to-morrow, with these keys, will I open to him the city gates, and deliver Coimbra into his hands." Next morning the bishop heard that the gates of Coimbra had been opened to the king at the hour of tierce (nine o'clock in the morning).—Southey, *Chronicles of the Cid*, bk. i. 4.

St. James the Elder, on his white horse, wins for Spain the battle of Logrono (tenth century). The battle of Logrono was fought in the reign of Ramiro II., king of Asturias. It was in this battle that St. James of Compostella, mounted on his white horse, overthrew the Arabs under Abderrahman II. In consequence of this great victory numerous pilgrimages were made to Compostella, and the town became very celebrated.—Bouillet, *Dictionnaire d'Histoire*, etc.

St. James the Elder, on his white horse, in the battle of Mexico (A.D. 1521). In the conquest of Mexico, a mysterious rider on a white horse appeared amidst the Castilian troops, and led them on to victory. It was St. James of Compostella. Bernal Diaz, who was present in the battle, saw the mysterious rider, but calls the charger a "grey horse," and fancies the rider was Francisco de Morla, though he confesses it might be the glorious apostle St. James for aught he knew. Certainly many more believe the victory was due to St. James than to Francisco de Morla.

St. James the Elder, on his white horse, wins the battle of Xerês. In 1237, Alfonso, the "infant" of Ferdinand III., the saintly king of Leon and Castille, at the head of fifteen hundred men, won the famous battle of Xerês over Aben-hud, the formidable Moor, king of Seville. The Moors were above seven times more numerous than the Christians, but the victory cost Alfonso only ten men. The captive Moors being asked how it came to pass that so great a victory was won by so small a force, at so insignificant a loss, deposed that they saw the apostle James on his white horse, and in full armour, at the head of the Christian army, and they could not fight against God. Many of the Christian soldiers asserted that they also saw the same thing.—L'abbé Caillet, *Vie des Saints*.

Ferdinand II. wins the battle of Weissenburg by the good offices of St. John Nepomuck (A.D. 1620). St. John Nepomuck was martyred by Wenceslaus, in 1383; and in 1618 the Thirty Years' War began, by a revolt in Bohemia. This war was one between the "Protestants" of Bohemia and the [Roman] Catholics of Germany; and the first battle, generally called "the Battle of Prague," was won over the Bohemians by Maximilian, duke of Bavaria. The night before the battle the ghost of St. John Nepomuck appeared in the cathedral of Prague. It radiated light, like as it had been the sun, and promised victory. Maximilian, a relentless enemy of the Bohemian "heretics," felt confident of success after this vision, gained the battle, and recovered Bohemia.—*Acta Sanctorum* (Bollandists), May 16.

This victory was no great matter after all, for the contest still continued. In 1630 Gustavus Adolphus joined the Bohemians, and won battle after battle over the imperialists. In 1637 Ferdinard II. died; but the war continued till 1648, when the peace of Westphalia put an end to the war, and the holy Roman empire at the same time. It required no ghost to give so profitless and short-lived a victory to so vile an emperor as Ferdinand II.

Gabriel at the battle of Bedr, on his white horse, fights for Mahomet (A.D. 624). In the famous battle of Bedr, between Mahomet and the Koreishites, a white horse was seen, and he who rode on him was the angel Gabriel. He fought with Mahomet's three hundred against the enemy's thousand, and, as the Koran says, "one army fought for God's true religion, but the other was an army of infidels. The infidels thought their adversaries to be twice as numerous as themselves, for God had deceived them, and He can strengthen with His help whom He pleases, and whom He pleases He can bring low" (ch. iii.). The statement is not very logical, but no matter; there was a "white horse" in the ranks, no doubt, and the army of Mahomet was victorious; and as none can give victory but God, therefore the rider of the white horse must have been a messenger sent from God; and who could that messenger be but the archangel Gabriel? Q. E. D.

The Lombards driven from Valence by eagles dropping stones on them. About A.D. 566, an army of Lombards invaded Dauphiné in three armies, one of which besieged Valence. The invaders had scaled the walls, the gates were opened, the streets were filled with the foe. At this moment St. Galla entered the basilica; the inhabitants ran to her crying, "Save us! save us! Thou servant of the living God, save us, or we perish!" "Fear not," said the undaunted saint; "man's extremity is God's opportunity. St. Peter will defend you." As she so spoke, a flight of many hundred eagles appeared over the city, and dropped stones on the besiegers. They were struck down by hundreds, by thousands, and ran for shelter. "Pursue after them," cried St. Galla; "pursue and stop not. Let each take back his spoils. Drive them from the city. Close the gates, but spare the fugitives; for God hath given you the victory, and vengeance belongeth unto God." The city was cleared of the invaders. The gates were shut. The people were delivered. And all, in a transport of joy, gave glory to God and to St. Galla.—*Les Petits Bollandistes*, vol. ii. p. 200.

St. Marcellinus puts the Goths to flight (A.D. 433). When the Goths, in 433, invaded Gaul, St. Albin was archbishop of Embrun. They committed great atrocities, and although Embrun was concealed amidst mountains, it escaped not their irruptions. They laid regular siege to the city, and the consternation of its inhabitants was unbounded. All hope of preserving the city, nay, all hope of life, was abandoned. The archbishop Albin went in procession to the relics of St. Marcellinus, the first prelate of Embrun, who had died about a century before; and all falling devoutly before these relics, besought the saint to save them. The enemy carried on the siege vigorously; they had already gained the ramparts, when Marcellinus appeared in mid-air. His countenance was menacing; he carried in his hand a flaming cross, and advanced against the besiegers. An invisible legion cast down the assailants from the walls, the missiles hurled by the Goths returned on themselves with deadly slaughter; a panic seized them; they fled on all sides; and the city was saved. —Mgr. Guérin, *Vies des Saints* (7th edit. 1880), vol. iii. p. 80.

St. Theodosius went forth with the army of Cericus against the Persians. Cericus, captain of the Roman army, before starting on his expedition against Persia, went to pay his respects to Theodosius the Cœnobiarch, and to receive his benediction. The saint told him not to trust to the hand of man, but to God, who can give victory by many or by few. Cericus asked the abbot to give him the hair shirt which he wore, saying it would be a defence and a shield he should ever venerate as an inestimable treasure. Theodosius willingly gave him the cilice, and Cericus wore it on the day of battle. When his army was arrayed, and the onset sounded, Cericus saw the saint at the head of the Roman army, pointing out where the attack was to be made. This continued till the rout was complete and the victory was won. —*The Roman Martyrology.* (Cave says the writer of this life was Theodore, bishop of Pera, but others ascribe it to Cyrillus.)

St. Hilary went forth with Clovis against Alaric. About 146 years after his death, St. Hilary still showed himself the relentless adversary of the Arians; for when Clovis marched against Alaric the Arian, king of the Goths, he observed a great light proceeding from the church of St. Hilary of Poitiers, and advancing towards him. It was the pontiff Hilary come to help him in the impending struggle. He had spent his life in opposing the Arians, and now came from his grave to give the heretics their grace-stroke. As the light drew nearer a voice proceeded from the midst, which cried aloud, "Up, Clovis, and delay not, for as captain of the Lord's hosts am I come to thee this day, and the God of battles will deliver the foe into thy hands." Then Clovis advanced against the Arian Goths, fully assured of victory; and before the third hour of the day, contrary to the expectation of every man and all human probability, he had routed the foe, and won a victory second to none ever fought in this world.—Gregory of Tours, *Historia Francorum*, bk. ii. ch. 37.

The ghost of don Pedro Pacchi leads the Spaniards to victory over the Dutch "heretics" (A.D. 1585). The Dutch were fighting for their homes, their liberty, and their religion; the Spaniards for conquest, domination, and the [Roman] Church. The former were bent on relieving Antwerp, but their entrenchments were reached by the foe, and the grim play of slaughter was most horrible. At this moment the ghost of the commander of the old Spanish legion was seen charging in front. He was clad in his well-known armour, used his well-known gestures, but had been dead for several months. The wavering Spaniards rallied at once; they felt certain of victory, and nothing could resist their charge. The entrenchments were carried. The patriots retreated. The ghost had secured the victory.—Motley, *History of the United Netherlands*, vol. i. p. 211.

God talking with Human Beings.

GEN. iii. 8-19. After Adam and Eve had

eaten of the forbidden fruit, the Lord God called Adam, and reproved him for his disobedience; to the serpent He said, Upon thy belly shalt thou go, and dust shalt thou eat all the days of thy life. Unto the woman He said, I will greatly multiply thy sorrow and thy conception. And to the man He said, Cursed is the ground for thy sake; in sorrow shalt thou eat of it all the days of thy life.

Gen. iv. 6-15. When Cain had murdered his brother, the Lord said to Cain, What hast thou done? the voice of thy brother's blood crieth unto Me from the ground. Now art thou cursed from the earth. When thou tillest the ground, it shall not yield thee her strength. A fugitive and a vagabond shalt thou be in the earth.

Gen. vi. 13-21. God said to Noah, The end of all flesh is come before Me, for the earth is filled with violence through them [*i.e.* man], and behold I will destroy them with the earth. He then gives directions to Noah about the ark.

Gen. ix. 1-17. After the flood God spake to Noah again, and said, I will establish My covenant with you; neither shall all flesh be cut off any more by the waters of a flood: neither shall there any more be a flood to destroy the earth.

Gen. xii. 1-3. The Lord said to Abram, Get thee out of thy country, and from thy kindred, unto a land that I will show thee.

(A score of texts might be quoted in which God is said to talk with man.)

God talks with St. Coletta or Nicoletta (A.D. 1380-1447). St. Coletta lamenting for the sins of the world, God said to her, "My daughter, what would you I should do? Every day the sins of man cry unto me from the earth. They blaspheme My name and despise My commandments."—Douillet, *Vie de St. Colette.*

Goshen severed from the Plagues.

Exod. viii. 22. When God brought the plagues on the land of Egypt, He severed the land of Goshen in which His people dwelt.

The land of a prayerless man severed from God's protection. Eugippius, in his *Life of St. Severin* (A.D. 511), relates that a poor man, who went to drive locusts from his patch of corn instead of going to church to worship God, found next morning that his was the only crop devoured by the locusts; all the other fields having been protected from them by the hand of the Almighty.

Gravitation increased or diminished. (See Elisha and the Axe.)

Zech. v. 5-11. The angel that talked with me said, See what is this that goeth forth. And I said, What is it? And the angel said, This is an ephah. And, behold, there was lifted up a weighty piece of lead: and this is a woman that sitteth in the midst of the ephah. And the angel said, This is wickedness. And he cast it into the midst of the ephah, and the lead on the mouth thereof. And, behold, two women with wings lifted up the ephah between earth and heaven. Then said I to the angel, Whither do these women carry the ephah? And the angel said to me, To build a house in the land of Shinar.

St. Benedict exorcises a stone which a devil had made too heavy to lift (A.D. 448-543). The devil ceased not to annoy St. Benedict. It was not in visions or dreams that he showed himself, but face to face, besetting the saint persistently in all he did, and crying out, "Benedict! Benedict!" from time to time. If the saint pretended not to hear, this enemy of the soul would cry out, "Maledict not Benedict, cursed fool not saint, what is your business in these quarters? What right have you to interfere with me? What pleasure can it give you to annoy me?" When all these railings were without effect, his satanic majesty harassed the saint by obstructing the builders employed by St. Benedict in constructing his monasteries. One day the builders went to carry a stone prepared for a certain part, but when they attempted to lift it, they found all their united efforts wholly ineffectual. The stone could not be moved. No power of man could lift it. They went and told St. Benedict, who instantly knew that the devil was hanging on it; so he made on the stone the sign of the cross, and the stone which before was too heavy for six or eight men to stir, became so light that St. Benedict alone lifted it with ease, and carried it to the place required. This very stone is still shown at Mount Cassino, so there can be no doubt of the fact.—St. Gregory the Great, *Dialogues*, bk. ii.

All that the presence of this stone can prove is simply this, that the stone to which a certain tradition is attached is still at Mount Cassino, and that is all. It can no more prove any tradition attached to it, than our coronation chair can prove that Jacob saw a ladder reaching from earth to heaven, or that the Scone stone was the stone pillar on which he laid his head when the vision appeared to him.

Two pillars for a church in Constantinople become too heavy to be moved. A large church was being built at Constantinople in honour of the Virgin Mary. Two pillars intended for the church suddenly became so heavy that the workmen could not move them, to set them up in their places; but the Virgin Mary with two helpers came to assist the workmen, when lo! the massive columns became as light as two straws, and of course were set up without the slightest difficulty. (See below.)—Mariali Magno. (See *Notes and Queries*, June 25, 1881, p. 514.)

The devil makes two marble pillars too heavy to be moved (A.D. 610). While St. Virgile, bishop of Arles, was building his superb basilica, the workmen on one occasion found themselves unable to raise some magnificent marble pillars. In their perplexity they went as usual to the bishop, and the bishop at once perceived that the devil was in the pillars. So, going to the spot, he first offered up a short prayer, and then cried aloud, "Wretch! how dare you impede the work of God? Be off with you!" The workmen now lifted the pillars easily, and carried them to their respective places. (See above.)—*Les Petits Bollandistes*, vol. iii. p. 162.

The devil having seated himself on a stone to make it immovable, St. Francis of Paula compelled him to get off (A.D. 1416–1507). While St. Francis of Paula was building his monastery at Calabria, the devil seated himself on a stone designed for the main entrance of the church, and made it too heavy to be moved. St. Francis compelled the foul fiend to budge, and carry the stone himself to the required spot.

St. Christianna suspends a heavy pillar in the air (third century). Christianna was a Christian slave, who converted the king and queen of Iberia, who at once set about building a church. Three columns were to be placed in the façade. Two were erected, but the third was so heavy that neither men nor oxen were able to move it. St. Christianna, the captive maiden, knelt beside it, and besought God's help; when, presently, the column rose up, of its own accord, on its base, and then into the air, wholly unsupported, within a foot of the place where it was to be fixed. This was at midnight, and when the builders went to work in the morning they saw the pillar waiting to be guided by their hands. At a touch it descended slowly, and placed itself erect in the required spot. The Iberians saw it, and were confirmed in the Christian faith.—Rufinus, *History*, bk. i.

St. Francis of Paula arrests a rock which threatened to roll down upon his monastery and destroy it (A.D. 1416–1507). While St. Francis of Paula was building his monastery at Calabria, a huge rock, detached from the neighbouring mountain, came rolling down with prodigious velocity, threatening to destroy the building and crush the workmen employed. The danger was most imminent, and a cry of fright rose from the men; but the saint, quite calmly, arrested the rock with a word, then, going up to it, struck his staff in the ground before it, bidding it roll no further. There it stayed till hundreds had seen it, when it was split up and employed in the building.

St. Francis of Paula suspends a rock on a snag. St. Francis on another occasion, by the sign of the cross, suspended a huge rock on the projecting horn of a precipice. This rock is suspended in a situation and manner which seems a natural impossibility. It seems that it must fall, but there it hangs still.—*Acts of Canonization* (compiled by Father Giry).

St. Francis of Paula removes a rock which many men could neither stir nor split (A.D. 1416–1507). When St. Francis of Paula was building his great monastery, a huge rock stood in the spot designed for a dormitory. Many men together tried to push it out of the way, but could not stir it. They tried to cleave it that it might be moved piecemeal, but it resisted all their efforts. St. Francis himself took the task in hand, and carried the rock clean away.

He also carried into the spire a wrought stone which four strong men could not lift.

He drew, by his own unaided strength, trees from the forest where they had been cut down, and these trees were so large that many men, with their united efforts, could not move them.

He laid beams of enormous size on the backs of his workmen, and made it that the men were not even conscious of their weight. "It was as if angels had borne the weight, or at least had assisted in doing so."

He straightened trees which were twisted; shaped joists and fixed them in their proper places; hollowed ditches, dug foundations, "à sa seule parole, et sans y employer le travail des hommes, ni le secours des instruments."—*Acts of Canonization* (compiled by Father Giry).

A sarcophagus becomes light when employed for the body of St. Francis of Paula (A.D. 1507). St. Francis of Paula died at Plessis les Tours, and the duchesse de Bourbon gave a stone sarcophagus for his coffin. This sarcophagus was given to her by the commander of the commandery of Balan, but had been left on the road from its great weight, eighteen oxen (*dix-huit de bœufs*) being unable to move it. Immediately the duchesse communicated her intention to give it as a coffin to St. Francis, the sarcophagus became so light that a single yoke of bullocks drew it easily (*deux bœufs la traînèrent fort facilement*).—Mgr. Guérin, *Vies des Saints*, vol. iv. p. 166.

St. Francis of Paula sets a man with neuralgia in the thigh to carry a beam which two strong oxen could not draw (A.D. 1416–1507). The sixteenth witness in the process of canonization at Cosenza asserted that he was suffering from a stiff thigh brought on by neuralgia, and applied to St. Francis of Paula for a cure. The saint set him to carry on his back a beam of wood which two oxen could not move. The witness says he expostulated with the saint, urging the physical impossibility of the task. "Even if in robust health," he said, "with the aid of many men, I could not so much as lift the beam; how, then, can I be expected to do it alone, when my health is broken down?" "Do what I say," was the reply; "God will give the power in the day of His grace." Accordingly, he charged himself with the beam, carried it on his back to the place required, and his thigh was perfectly cured.—*The Bull and other Documents of the Canonization* (compiled by Father Giry).

We are told that "ce genre de miracle, de rendre les pierres et le bois légers, quelque pesants qu'ils fussent, et de les lever, ou de les faire lever sans difficulté, lui fut ordinaire dans tout le cours de cette construction [*i.e.* his church]."

St. Fridian lifts a stone which many men could not stir (sixth century). St. Fridian, bishop of Lucca, built twenty-eight churches. On one occasion, a large stone was required to be lifted on the wall of one of the churches he was building. Several men with their united strength tried to lift it, but were wholly unable to stir it in the least degree. The bishop then took it up without the least difficulty, and carried it with ease to the place required.—*Ecclesiastical History of Lucca* (1736).

The heavy slip of paper given to St. Gonsalvo. St. Gonsalvo, wishing to build a bridge over the Tamego, applied to a neighbouring count for a subscription. The nobleman, thinking the scheme visionary, in order to get rid of the importunate churchman, scribbled a couple of lines on a scrap of paper, and told Gonsalvo to take it to the countess, his wife. It was a long way he had to go, and when the lady opened the letter, she read aloud these words: "The poor fool, the bearer of this letter, wants to build a bridge. Let him have in cash the weight of this slip of paper." "So be it," cried Gonsalvo. Accordingly, the lady put the letter into a scale, but to her amazement found it balanced a very large sum of money, which she handed to Gonsalvo, and the bridge was built.—Didacus de Rosario, *Life of St. Gonsalvo.*

A small slip of paper weighs down a whole basketful of fruit (fifteenth century). An inhabitant of Florence presented St. Antonine, the archbishop, with a basket of fruit as a new year's gift, under the hope of receiving, in return, some substantial spiritual gift; but the saint only said to the giver, "May God reward you," and the man left, greatly and visibly disappointed. The archbishop, observing this, called him back, and putting the basket of fruit in one scale, and a slip of paper containing the words "May God reward you" in the other, found the slip of paper greatly outweighed the gift. The man, thoroughly ashamed, asked pardon, and was practically taught that it is not the present, but the mind and motive of the giver, which God considers and weighs in the balance of the sanctuary.—Surius, *Lives of the Saints*, vol. iii.

In Christian art, St. Antonine is represented holding a crozier in his left hand, and weighing the basket of fruit in the other.

A wooden statue of the Virgin Mary suddenly becomes too heavy to be moved (A.D. 1380). A merchant was transporting to Antwerp a wooden image of the Virgin Mary, but when he reached Schiedam the image made itself too heavy to be moved. All the inhabitants ran to see this "miracle," and every one came to the conclusion that it was the Virgin's wish to remain in Schiedam. The merchant was consulted, and sold the image to the people, who set it up in the church of St. John the Baptist.—*Life of Lidwina*, written by John Gerlac (cousin) and John Walter (confessor).

The dead body of St. Drogo makes itself too heavy to be moved from Seburg, in Hainault (A.D. 1189). St. Drogo died at Seburg, in Hainault, where he had lived six years as a shepherd, and forty years as a recluse. He was born at Epinoy, in Artois, and, at his death, his kinsmen living at Epinoy demanded his body. When the cart came to take it away, it was found too heavy to be lifted from the ground. Not all the power of several strong men could move it; the relatives were therefore obliged to leave it at Seburg, where it was buried. St. Drogo's tomb is shown in Seburg church to the present day. It is in the great nave, near the font. The place where the cart drew up to carry away the body is still called "Mount Joie St. Drogo."* In the thirteenth century his relics were removed to Binche, and an annual procession is still made to the place on Trinity Sunday.—*Acta Sanctorum* (Papebroke), vol. ii. April 16.

At Seburg persons are shown the "Fountain of St. Drogo," where the holy shepherd watered his sheep; "St. Drogo's Road," where stands a stone cross; and, close by the church, a spot called the "Cell or Cabin of St. Drogo."

The body of St. Fritz becomes suddenly too heavy to be moved (eighth century). St. Fritz fell in the battle of Lupiac, and his body remained for a long time undiscovered; but one day a herdsman was struck at seeing a cow licking a stone in the midst of some brushwood. He observed that this was repeated daily, and the cow was better liking and gave more milk than any other in the dairy. This singular circumstance soon attracted general attention, and persons went to examine the stone. On lifting it up, they were induced to dig about the spot, and soon came upon a body; it was that of a warrior in full armour, and no sooner was it raised from the ground than a miraculous spring of water issued from the spot. This is certain, inasmuch as the spring remains to the present day, and is well known for its healing virtues. The body thus discovered was the body of St. Fritz, and the monks resolved to remove it into the neighbouring town. When, however, they attempted to carry it away, it was found to be so heavy that several yoke of oxen were unable to stir the bier on which it was laid. At length some one suggested to try the cow, and immediately the cow was yoked in, she drew the bier along with the utmost ease to the top of a high hill, but then refused to move another step. Nothing would induce her to stir a step further, and the monks concluded that the saint did not wish to be taken into the town; so a chapel was built on the hill-top, and there the body of the saint was deposited in a marble tomb. In regard to the fountain, although its waters have healing virtues they can never be used for culinary purposes. Every one knows, says our authority, that "une femme d'Andreou, qui avait voulu employer l'eau de cette fontaine pour faire du pain, l'avait vue se changer en sang." (See AVENTINE, p. 167.)—L'abbé Guilhempey, *Histoire de Bassoues et de la Chapelle de St. Fritz*, 1858. This *brochure* is sold on the spot to visitors for the benefit of the chapel.)

* A funny combination, as Mount Joie is a corruption of Mount Jovis, the Mount of Jupiter.

The dead body of St. Gudula suddenly becomes too heavy to be moved (A.D. 710). When the dead body of St. Gudula was on its way to the village of Ham, a tree in the vicinity put forth leaves and flowers, although it was midwinter [Jan. 8]. It was the intention of the monks to convey the body to the college of Nivelle, but when the cortége reached Ham, it was found that no human power could bear the weight of the coffin. They then resolved to change their route, and instead of carrying the body to Nivelle, to deposit it in St. Saviour's chapel at Moorsel. On attempting now to lift the coffin, it was found to be light as a feather, plainly indicating the wish of the deceased. On reaching Moorsel, what was the astonishment of all to find that the tree which had put forth its leaves and flowers in honour of the saint, had removed from Ham, and planted itself before St. Saviour's chapel, right in front of the main entrance. It was completely covered with a rich green verdure, and full of beautiful flowers, the admiration of every one who saw it. This miracle was so "well attested" that Charlemagne built a religious house close by in honour of St. Gudula. To complete the "miracles," it must be added, that one day the king was out hunting, when a bear of prodigious size took refuge in this religious house. No sooner, however, had it done so than its whole nature was completely changed. It was no longer fierce and wild, but lived with the nuns as meek and playful as a pet lamb.—Hubert (1047), *Life of St. Gudule.*

St. John-Joseph of the Cross (A.D. 1654–1734). When St. John-Joseph was carried to the grave, cardinal Wiseman says, "Il semblait moins être porté par les porteurs que les porter euxmêmes."—Migne, *Démonstrations Evangéliques*, vol. xvi.

The coffin of St. Martin too heavy to be lifted (fifth century). The church built by St. Brice over the tomb of St. Martin being too small, St. Perpetuus, bishop of Tours (A.D. 461–494), built a much larger one. On the day of its consecration (A.D. 491) an attempt was made to remove the body of the saint into the new church; but it was found to be too heavy for men to lift. A young clerk suggested that two days later would be the anniversary of St. Martin's consecration as bishop of Tours, and probably the saint would not choose to be moved till then. Acting on this suggestion, the ceremony was deferred for two days. Another attempt was then made to carry the body into the new basilica, but it was equally unsuccessful as the former one. An old man, dressed like an abbot, now came forward and said, "Do you not see that St. Martin himself is ready to help you?" So saying, he threw his cloak on the ground, and lifting up the coffin without the slightest difficulty, carried it from St. Brice's church, and laid it solemnly and reverently in the place assigned for it in the new church, under the altar in the apse. The old liturgy of Tours adds, "Every one believes that the old man who carried the coffin from St. Brice's church was an angel sent from heaven for the express purpose." [It appears to me that the "old man" was St. Martin himself.] —L'abbé Rolland, *Life of St. Perpet* (bishop of Tours).

The bier of St. Medard refused to be moved till king Clotaire promised to give the whole borough of Crouy to the new church (A.D. 545). When St. Medard died, the king (Clotaire I.) was one of the bearers, and promised to build a new church at Soissons as a suitable monument to the saint, who died at Noyon. When the procession reached Aisne à Attichy, on the skirts of Crouy (about two hundred paces from Soissons), the bier became wholly immovable; no one could lift it on one side or the other. The king then promised to give half the borough of Crouy to the new church. On trying again to lift the bier, it was found that the half facing the part given to the church was loose and could be moved, but the other half was as fast as ever. Clotaire now promised to bestow the whole borough on the church, and the bier instantly became so light that it could be lifted and carried about without the slightest difficulty.—*Acta Sanctorum* (Bollandists), vol. ii. June 8.

These mercenary miracles are always suspicious. I was once supping with Mr. Guppy, a noted "spiritist," and during supper he called my attention to a spirit rapping. After the usual formula was gone through, the message received was, "Give Mrs. Guppy a new gown."

St. Patrick floats on a stone. St. Patrick, we are told, floated to Ireland on an altar-stone. Amongst other wonderful things he converted a marauder into a wolf, and lighted a fire with icicles.—James A. Froude, *Reminiscences of the High Church Revival* (Letter v.).

The dead bodies of Quirinus and Balbina too heavy to lift (second century). Pope Leo IX., at the earnest solicitation of his sister Pepa, abbess of Nuyss, gave her the bodies of Quirinus and Balbina (his daughter) to enrich her convent. When the mule bearing the dead bodies reached Dabo, it refused to stir another step, and the drivers were compelled to unload it. Next day they intended to continue their journey, but found the dead bodies so heavy that all their efforts could not raise them from the ground. Pepa, recognizing therein the hand of the Almighty, built a chapel on the spot, where she left the two bodies, but carried their heads to Nuyss.—Vagner (1847), *Conversion and Martyrdom of St. Quirinus and his Daughter Balbina.*

The dead body of St. Remi becomes too heavy to be lifted (A.D. 545). St. Remi died Jan. 13, 545, but his festival is kept on Oct. 1, for this reason: He was buried in the church of St. Christopher, in Reims; but as this church was small, and pilgrims to it very numerous, it was enlarged, and a costly shrine was provided for the saint. When all was completed, and the priests attempted to raise the body to deposit it in the new shrine, it was found to be so heavy that no human power could lift it; so the clergy and people betook themselves to prayer, and prayed till they fell asleep. While they slept, angels came and lifted the body into the shrine. This occurred on Oct. 1, so the "day" of St. Remi was removed from Jan. 13, the day of his translation.—Hincmar (archbishop of Reims, who died 882), *Life of St. Remi.*

Of course, it will occur to every one, if all were *asleep*, how could it be known that the body was lifted into its shrine by angels? It is the old question of the Roman guard and the stealing of the body of Jesus.

The dead bodies of three saints refuse to be moved from Amiens (sixth century). At the consecration of St. Honoré to the see of Amiens, Lupicin, a priest, gave out that he had been informed by revelation where the three martyrs Fuscian, Victorius, and Gentian were buried.

They had been dead above three hundred years, but Lupicin discovered the bodies in the place indicated; and the chant which was sung on the discovery was heard by St. Honoré six miles off. King Childebert II. sent commissioners to Amiens to remove the bodies to Paris, but they made themselves too heavy to be lifted, and were of necessity left at Amiens. The king, being told of this "miracle," sent rich presents to the cathedral of Amiens in honour of the new-found saints.—Morlière, *Antiquities of Amiens.*

St. Valery's dead body too heavy to be lifted (seventh century). St. Valery was buried at Leuconaüs, but Berchont, wishing to honour him, employed workmen to remove the body to Amiens. No strength of man could, however, lift the dead body from its grave. "Une puissance irrésistible paralysa tous les efforts; on ne put venir à bout de le soulever de terre." Thus was it that the saint showed he did not wish to be removed from the spot in which he was already interred.—Besançon, *Les Saints de Franche Comté.*

St. Macarius of Egypt overweighted (A.D. 304-394). St. Macarius of Egypt used to hire himself out as a porter. One day, being overweighted, he sat on the roadside and cried, saying, "O Lord, Thou knowest all things; Thou knowest now that the spirit is willing, but the flesh is weak." No sooner had he uttered these words, than he found himself with his burden at the place to which he was bound.—*Les Petits Bollandistes,* vol. i. p. 62.

Guide.

PSALM xlviii. 14. This God is our God. He will be our Guide even unto death.

MATT. ii. 9. Lo! the star, which the wise men saw in the east, went before them, till it came and stood over where the young child was.

According to an ancient commentary on Matthew's Gospel, the star had the form of a radiant child bearing a sceptre and cross; and it is so depicted in some early Italian frescoes.

> It was shaped, O wondrous sight!
> Like a radiant child of light,
> Holding sign of kingly might,
> With a cross combining.

NEH. ix. 12. Thou leddest them in the day by a cloudy pillar; and in the night by a pillar of fire, to give them light in the way wherein they should go (Exod. xiv. 19, 20).

St. William Firmatus of Tours guided by a crow (A.D. 1103). One day, St. William Firmatus having lost his way, God sent a crow to guide him into the right path. The bird went before, and by its voice and the clapping of its wings, induced the saint to follow.—Bollandus, *Acta Sanctorum,* Feb. 28.

Those seeking St. Gregory the Great guided by a pillar of fire. Nauclerus tells us, when St. Gregory the Great heard he was likely to be appointed pope, he fled to a certain mountain, and lay perdu. Persons were sent to hunt him up, and saw a pillar of fire descend from heaven, which led them direct to the mountain, and then stood over the place where Gregory lay concealed; so they found him, and conducted him to Rome, as it were by violence.—*Chronicles* (1501).

A heavenly light went before Jeanne Marie de Maillé to guide her in the dark. When Jeanne Marie de Maillé lost her husband, she was turned out of house and home by her late husband's relatives, and went as an assistant to St. Anne's chapel. Whenever she went in the dark of night to the chapel, or returned from it, a heavenly light went before her as a lamp unto her feet and a light unto her path.—Père de Boisgaultier (her confessor), *Life of Jeanne Marie de Maillé.*

St. Oringa guided by a hare (A.D. 1310). St. Oringa, having lost her parents, fell under the charge of her brothers, who tried to compel her to marry; as, however, she had vowed to be the bride of Christ, and her brothers would not relent, she fled from their roof. Ere long she came to a deep river; but, full of faith, she walked on, and the river, dividing, left her a dry path across. On, on she went, and came to a large meadow, when darkness overtook her, and she lay down to sleep. A timid hare came and cuddled beside her. Next morning she followed the guidance of her bed-fellow, and came to Lucques, where she entered the service of a good man.

Another instance. St. Oringa remained in the service of her employer a certain time, when the devil disturbed the peace of the house, and again she took herself to flight, intending to go on pilgrimage to Mount Gargano. Having lost her way, the archangel Michael, under the form of a young deacon, put her in the right road, supplied her with food, and then left her.—*Les Petits Bollandistes,* vol. ii. p. 575.

In this second legend we have a characteristic example of the mode of thought in the Middle Ages. Although the guide was, to all appearances, a young deacon, he must be transposed into the archangel Michael, because he does a good or kind act, and perhaps to prevent scandal.

Hair a Talisman.

JUDG. xvi. 17, etc. Samson said to Delilah, There hath not come a razor upon mine head, for I have been a Nazarite unto God from my mother's womb. If I were to be shaven, then my strength would go from me, and I should become weak, and be like any other man.

Ver. 22. Howbeit the hair of his head began to grow again after he was shaven [and with his growing hair his enormous strength returned].

Hence it is quite certain that the strength of Samson was in some mysterious way bound up with his hair, and not with his vow.

Hair supposed by the emperor Alexander Severus to be a talisman. St. Martina, being bound to the stake by order of the emperor Alexander Severus, was wholly uninjured by the fire, and the emperor, thinking this was due to magic, and that the charm was lodged in her hair, commanded every atom of it to be cut off. —Bollandus, *Acta Sanctorum*, vol. i. Jan. 1.

Many nations have supposed that some special virtue resides in the hair. The Nazarites vowed not to cut their hair (Numb. vi. 5, 9). In Greece and Rome the hair was cut at adolescence, and offered to the gods. The Greeks, just before marriage, cut off their hair, and offered it to their favourite deity; the hair of the dead was also hung on the door of the deceased before interment, as an offering to the infernals. Both Greeks and Romans supposed that no person could die till a lock of hair had been cut off; but this act was supposed to be done by Isis, Mercury, Thanatos, or some other divine messenger (Virgil, *Æneid*, iv. 694). The Syrians (we are told by Lucian) offered their hair to the gods. It was by no means unusual to make vows never to cut the hair till some stated object had been accomplished. Thus, Civilis vowed never to cut his hair till he had defeated the Roman legions (Tacitus, *History*, bk. iv.). Every one knows that three hairs of a dog which has bitten one will prevent any evil consequences from the bite.

> Take the hair, it is well written,
> Of the dog by which you're bitten.
> *Athenæus.*

Probably it was something more than a mere figure of speech when it was said that the strongest affirmation of Zeus or Jupiter was a shake of his ambrosial hair, and that the hair of Apollo gave light, heat, and pestilence.

Haman caught in his own Net.

ESTH. iv., vi., vii. Haman, the high steward of king Ahasuerus, hated Mordecai, uncle of queen Esther, because he refused to fawn on him and flatter him. He carried his hatred so far as to plot the death of all the Jews in Persia. The plot was revealed to Esther, who contrived to break it up in the following manner. She made a great feast, to which she invited the king and Haman. The steward was greatly delighted; and feeling sure of his game, had a gallows erected, fifty cubits high (seventy-five feet), to hang Mordecai on the day after the banquet. Now, it so happened that Mordecai some years previously had revealed to the king a plot by two eunuchs to assassinate him, and the affair was duly registered in the national records. The night before the feast, the king, feeling restless, had, for amusement sake, the records of his own reign read to him; and when he came to Mordecai, he said, How was that man rewarded? Being told he had received no reward at all, the king demanded who was in the court; and was told Haman, the high steward, was at hand. At this very moment Haman entered, and the king said to him, Haman, what shall be done to the man that the king delighteth to honour? Haman, feeling sure that he himself was the man referred to, replied, Let him be arrayed in royal apparel, set on the king's charger, and conducted through the city by the highest officers of the realm; while heralds proclaim from street to street, Thus is it done to the man whom the king delighteth to honour. The thing pleased the king, and he bade Haman on the morrow to honour Mordecai as he had said. This, of course, was gall and wormwood to the jealous favourite, but he durst not disobey; so Mordecai was arrayed in royal robes, set on the king's charger, and led through the city as the man whom the king delighted to honour. In the evening was the banquet, and Ahasuerus bade the queen ask of him whatever she liked, and it should be granted her. Esther modestly replied, Then I pray your highness that my life may be spared, that I may devote it to my lord and master. The king was thunderstruck. Life! spare your life! And who has threatened the queen's life? The queen then told him of Haman's plot to assassinate herself and Mordecai, and all the Jews of the whole realm. The king was so incensed that he rose from table, and went into the palace gardens. While he was absent, Haman fell at the queen's feet, beseeching her to spare his life. The king returned suddenly, saw Haman beseeching the queen, and exclaimed, The villain! What! will he force the queen also, before my very face? And, being directed to the gallows made for Mordecai, he commanded Haman to be hanged thereon. So Haman was hanged on his own gallows, and the king's wrath was pacified.

In regard to the general massacre of a whole race, we have a modern example in Turkish history. In 1770, the grand signior, in full council, decreed that the whole Greek race should be exterminated; but Hassan Pacha interfered, and obtained for them a general amnesty.—M. de Peysonnel, *Voyages au Levant.* (See also baron du Trott, p. 90.)

The steward of the emperor Martin caught in his own trap. The steward of the emperor Martin was jealous of Fulgentius, the emperor's nephew and cupbearer, and laid a plot for his destruction He told the emperor that Fulgentius had spread abroad a scandalous report, that his majesty's breath was so offensive it almost poisoned him; "but," said the steward, "this is a most shameful falsehood, the pitiful slander of disaffection and dislike." The emperor was certainly astonished at these remarks, but the steward said the truth of his observation was capable of very easy proof. "If, for example, your highness will be pleased to notice Fulgentius to-morrow, when he hands the cup to your highness, you will see that he turns his head on one side." Martin said he would not fail to watch his nephew when he handed him the cup. The steward now went to Fulgentius, and pretending great friendship for him, told him he heard the emperor say the breath of his cupbearer was so offensive, he hardly knew how to bear it, and he wished some kind friend would hint to his nephew to turn his head aside when he handed him the cup. Fulgentius thanked the steward; and, when he handed the king the cup on the morrow, turned aside his head, as the steward had advised him to do. The emperor, greatly enraged at the supposed affront, kicked Fulgentius on the chest, and exclaimed, "Out, caitiff! out of my sight; and let me never see you more!" When he was gone, the emperor asked the steward how he could contrive to make away with the slanderous valet without creating a scandal; and the steward replied, "Let your highness command him to go at daybreak to the brick-makers, and ask them if they have done my lord's bidding. The rest your highness may leave to me." So the steward sent a sealed order, bearing the royal signet, to the master of the brick-makers, commanding him to cast into the brick-kiln the person who first said to the brick-makers in the morning, "Have you done my lord's bidding?" Fulgentius was charged with the message, and rose up early to execute it. On his way to the brick-fields, he heard the church-bell calling to matins, and went to pay his devotions, saying to himself, "Nothing is ever lost by prayer;" and after matins he fell asleep, for in his distress he had not closed his eyes all night. Meanwhile, the steward, anxious to hear of the death of Fulgentius, made his way to the brick-fields, and said to the men, "Well, my friends, and have you done my lord's bidding?" No sooner were the words uttered, than they seized the speaker, and threw him into the kiln, where he was presently burnt to death. Not long afterwards Fulgentius presented himself, and said to the brick-burners, "His majesty has sent me to ask you, have you done my lord's bidding?" "Ay, ay," cried the man; "tell the emperor it is all right." When Fulgentius appeared at court, Martin was astounded, and asked if he had been to the brick-fields. "Yes, my lord," said Fulgentius, "and the brick-burners bade me say to your highness, 'Ay, ay, it is all right.'" He then informed his imperial uncle that the steward had gone to the fields first, and the men had cast him into the brick-kiln and burnt him to death. The emperor then asked his nephew if he had said what the steward had laid to his charge, and the whole truth came out. "The ways of the Lord," said the emperor, "are wonderful. The wickedness of the wicked hath come to an end. He made a pit, and digged it, and hath fallen into the ditch which he made. His mischief hath returned on his own head, and his violent dealing hath come down on his own pate. Praise the Lord for His righteousness; sing praises to the name of the Lord Most High."—*Gesta Romanorum*, ch. xcviii. (See also Scott's *Tales from the Arabic and Persian*, p. 53; and le Grand's *Fabliaux*, v. 74 (miracles of the Virgin).

Head carried after Death.

St. Aphrodisius, bishop of Beziers, walks away with his head after it was cut off (April 28, A.D. 69). St. Aphrodisius, the first bishop of Beziers, met with great success in his preaching, and converted many from idolatry to the Christian faith; but one day a number of pagans set upon him, and, after tossing him about from one to another, finished their sport by cutting off his head. St. Aphrodisius, raising himself up, took his head between his hands, and walking through the midst of the crowd, carried it to a certain chapel beyond the town, and buried it there.—Mgr. Guérin (chamberlain to pope Leo XIII.), *Vies des Saints*, vol. v. p. 61 (7th edit. 1880).

St. Aventine walks away with his head after it was cut off (A.D. 778–813). St. Aventine, apostle of Gascony, was beheaded by the Saracens. They had hunted him a long time, as one hunteth a partridge in the mountains, and were drunk with joy when they discovered him. They indulged all their rage upon him, and one of the barbarians drew his sabre, and cut off his head. The blood fell in pools upon the ground, and formed a long stream of blood; but what was their amazement when they beheld the saint, holding his head between his hands, walk off with it in the direction of the town. They were so scared that they ran away, telling the story to all they met. In the mean time, the martyred saint continued his journey till he came to a valley where he had often preached, when he laid himself down "and died." At night some of his converts buried him, and subsequently a little monument, which remains to this day, was erected on the spot where he fell. Over the portal of the church of St. Aventine is a group of soldiers disputing with a man who holds his head in his hands. Mgr. Guérin, chamberlain of pope Leo XIII., evidently sees nothing improbable in this story, for he adds, "La tradition la plus constante nous a conservé le récit fidèle de cette mort miraculeuse, et la reconnaissance du peuple la grava au xiie siècle sur la pierre et le marbre."—*Vies des Saints*, vol. vi. pp. 609, 610 (7th edit. 1880).

The discovery of the saint's body was also marvellous. Mgr. Guérin, the chamberlain of pope Leo XIII., says: "A bull was seen daily quitting the meadow, and withdrawing from its companions, in spite of the vigilance of the herdsman. It went always to the same spot, when it began to bellow, and kick the ground with his fore feet. It was difficult to drive him away, even at nightfall. At length this strange conduct excited attention, and the bull saw itself surrounded with a crowd of gazers, amongst whom were several priests. While all wondered what the bull meant, an angel cried aloud, 'In this spot lie the remains of Aventine of happy memory.' The crowd took up the cry of 'Aventine! Aventine!' The earth was removed, and the body and head of the martyr were both found. An unspeakable perfume filled the air—a perfume unlike any earthly fragrance—and the whole crowd was embalmed with it."

"Des procès-verbaux plus récents nous apprennent que la vérification des reliques fut faite par Mgr. Olivier Gabriel, en 1737" (only 928 years after the decease: this would bring us about 107 years before the Conquest); "une autre se fit en 1707, par Mgr. d'Osmond; une troisième en 1808 par M. Mengarduque, curé de la paroisse; la dernière en 1837, par Mgr. d'Astros, archevêque de Toulouse, qui fit placer les reliques dans une belle châsse en ébène que l'on porte aujourd'hui dans les processions solennelles." (Almost an identical tale is told of St. Fritz, p. 163.)

In so marvellous a narrative it is well to be fortified by good names, or "some" might doubt the possibility of walking off with one's head.

St. Desiderius, bishop of Langres, carries off his head after decapitation (A.D. 264). In the middle of the third century, a horde of Allemans invaded Gaul, under a chief named Chrocus. They besieged Langres, and spared neither age nor sex. Desiderius, bishop of Langres, went to Chrocus, and prayed him to spare the people; but the chief told one of his officers to cut off the fellow's head. As the head fell, Desiderius caught it in his hands; and he is usually represented in Christian art carrying his head in his hands. The martyr, at the time of his decapitation, was holding a book, which, of course, was saturated with blood, but, strange to say, the letters remained quite legible; and Vincent de Beauvais informs us that when he saw it, a thousand years afterwards, the letters were wholly "intact." The man who cut off the saint's head went mad, drove his head against the city gates, and dashed out his brains. The stains of this man's brains were suffered to remain on the gates as a standing testimony against him. As for Chrocus, we are told by St. Gregory of Tours he was taken prisoner at Arles, carried about for a time in an iron cage, and then put to death.—L'abbé Mazelin, ***Saints de la Haute Marne.***

Dionysius [*St. Denis*] *the Areopagite carries off his head, and hands it to Catulla* (A.D. 117). Dionysius the Areopagite did many great miracles, such as restoring sight to the blind, hearing to the deaf, speech to the dumb, and so on; but he is pre-eminently known for walking off with his head, after it had fallen to the sword of the executioner. The "historical" account is as follows:—Fescennius, governor of Gaul, having seized St. Dionysius and several other Christians, subjected them to many cruel torments in order to make them renounce the "Lord who bought them;" but, failing to shake their resolution, he ordered them to be executed on the Hill Mercury (now *Montmartre*). An immense crowd gathered together, for the victims were very numerous. Here St. Dionysius was decapitated; but immediately his head had fallen to the ground, he rose on his feet, picked up his head with his two hands, and walked off with it "in triumph." He carried it from Montmartre (near Paris) for about two leagues; then, giving it to a pious woman named Catulla, whom he met, fell to the earth at her feet. Catulla received the head with unspeakable joy, and hid it carefully in her house with those of St. Rusticus and St. Eleutherius. We are further told by the same writers that as Dionysius walked along with his head, angels hovered about him, some singing *Gloria tibi, Domine*, and others responding *Alleluia! Alleluia! Alleluia!*

This story is repeated as a fact in the Greek Menologies, and by Simeon Metaphrastês, Methodius, Hilduin, Hugh de St. Victor, Nicephorus Callixtus, Cœlius Rhodiginus, Suidas, Usuard, Michael Singelus, and others. Mgr. Guérin, in his *Vies des Saints* (1880), repeats it; and, indeed, no miracle of the saints has a greater crowd of attestators, nor any of higher authority.

The explanation sometimes offered that the legend arose from the device of some artist, who drew the body of the decapitated saint, and placed the head in front of the body between the martyr's hands, that his subject might be recognized, will not bear the slightest examination. Nothing can be more demonstrable than that the pictures represented the received opinions, and not that the legend sprang from any painting. Edward Kinesman (1623) writes thus, and his words, no doubt, will be in accordance with every faithful [Roman] Catholic who dares to be honest: "Although God permitted His servant to be put to death, yet was He not forgetful of him; yea, because He would the more glorify him, and not suffer his body to be dishonoured, His will was to worke a wonderfull miracle in that place. The headles body of the saint arose on his feet, and tooke up in his hands his owne head, and went, as it were, in manir of triumph untill it mett a vertuous woman coming out of her owne house, near what is now called St. Denis near Paris, and to her he delivered the head, which she received as a goodly jewell."

St. Chrysolius walks off with his cranium, which had been cleft from his skull by the sword of the executioner (A.D. 278). St. Chrysolius was a missionary in Belgium, and dwelt at Commines. He was unexpectedly seized by a company of soldiers, and ordered to lose his head for blaspheming the national deities. The man appointed to cut off his head missed his neck, and cut off the cranium from ear to ear. The body fell weltering in blood, and the soldiers marched off. No sooner was this the case than St. Chrysolius picked up his cranium, and returned to Commines, where he was seen by hundreds. On his way, feeling thirsty, he bade water spring from the ground, and forthwith a spring of delicious water welled up. This miracle cannot be gainsaid, inasmuch as the stream still flows to the healing of the nations.—J. Cousin, *History of Tournay.*

How the existence of a stream can prove its miraculous production must be left to the historian of Tournay. Some logicians would have us believe that the discovery of the word "Pharaoh" on some Egyptian ruins is a proof positive of the whole history recorded in the Book of Exodus; but all that such a coincidence can prove is that Pharaoh was a name or title known to the Egyptians, and connected with their history. Similarly, the discovery of the word "Cleopatra" on the Rosetta stone is no proof that she melted a pearl in drinking to the health of Antony.

St. Hilarian of Espalion carries his head to his mother, after it was cut off (eighth century). St. Hilarian of Espalion was Charlemagne's confessor, and used to cross the Lot every day to go to Levignac. One day his mother said to him, "My son, you will end by leaving your head behind you one of these days." "Well, mother," he replied, laughing, "if so, I will bring it to you." Not long after this he was seized by some of his persecutors, who cut off his head. The "valiant athlete of Christ" took it up in his hands, washed off the blood in a fountain, since called "Font-sange," and carried it to his mother, according to his promise. In the parish church of Espalion is a bas-relief representing this "fact."—L'abbé l'Servières, *Saints du Rouergue.*

St. Leo, archbishop of Rouen, walks off with his head after death (A.D. 900). St. Leo, having converted the people of Bayonne, greatly displeased the pirates, who plainly saw that Christianity and piracy could not exist in the same country; so they leagued together, waylaid the man of God, and cut off his head. Two miracles then ensued: (1) his blood, on touching the ground, caused a spring of water to well up; and (2) picking up his head, he carried it more than a mile, and buried it. A chapel was afterwards built to his honour on the spot.—*Vita Sanctorum* (Bollandists), vol. i. March.

St. Lucanus of Aquitaine, being beheaded, walks off with his head (fifth century). St. Lucanus raised up his voice in Aquitaine against idolatry. He was hunted from place to place, till at length he was apprehended at Orleans, and brought to Paris, where he was condemned to death. After various tortures, the judge ordered his officer to cut off the saint's head. As his head fell to the axe, Lucanus stooped, picked it up, and walked off with it, "entre ses mains, et la porta comme en triomphe à une demi-lieue de l'endroit où il avait été exécuté." He then laid it carefully on a stone, which, in memory of this miracle, has ever since been called *La Pierre de St. Lucain.* The remains were buried by the faithful with great care. In 1666 they were inclosed in a coffer covered with plates of silver, and placed on the high altar of the cathedral of Paris. The reliquary is carried in procession, in times of national calamities, with those of St. Marcel and St. Geneviève. At the present day Notre-Dame de Paris no longer possesses this treasure. [I suppose it was lost or destroyed in the Revolution.]—Mgr. Guérin (chamberlain of pope Leo XIII.), *Vies des Saints,* vol. xiii. p. 49 (7th edit. 1880).

St. Lucian, being beheaded, walks off with his head (A.D. 67). After the head of St. Lucian had fallen to the sword of the executioner, the detruncated body deliberately picked up the fallen head from the ground, and walked off with it towards the town of Beauvais. Crossing the river of Therain à Miauroy, the body stopped some four leagues from the town of Beauvais, to intimate the spot where he wished his body to be buried. Here it received honourable sepulture, angels assisting at the funeral, and filling the air with heavenly odours.—Bollandus, *Acta Sanctorum,* vol. i. Jan. 8. Also mentioned by Odo, *Life of St. Lucian;* Florus, *Martyrology* (ninth century); Louvet, *History of the Antiquities of Beauvais;* and many others.

It will be observed that this story is dated half a century earlier than the similar one about St. Denis or Dionysius (see preceding page).

St. Proba carries away her head after it had been cut off (fourth century). St. Proba was a native of Ireland, but to avoid a marriage arranged by her parents, she fled to Gaul. Her retreat being discovered, she was taken back to Ireland, and, as she persisted in leading a single life, her parents cut off her head. The saint, we are told, picked it up, and carried it on a stone to Old St. Peter's Church. The stone is still shown in proof of this "miracle."—Dom Robert Wyard, *History of St. Vincent's Abbey of Laon* (edition 1858, by the abbots Cardon and Mathieu).

The stone must have been a sort of pavement, which would serve the place of a dish or charger.

St. Solangia walks away with her head after it was cut off (A.D. 880). The shepherdess Solangia was very beautiful, and the count of Poitiers, Bourges, and Auvergne offered her marriage in honourable fashion. When, however, she declined the offer, he seized her, intending to carry her to his castle; but, as they approached a stream, Solangia contrived to throw herself to the ground. The count, greatly irritated, drew his sword and cut off her head; but Solangia caught it in her hands, and it thrice pronounced the name of Jesus. She carried her head from Villemont to St. Martin du Cros, where she was buried, and in 1281 a monument, in the form of an altar, was erected to her memory. In Christian art St. Solangia is represented walking off with her head in her hands.—Mgr. Guérin (chamberlain of pope Leo XIII.), *Vies des Saints* (1880).

(In the church of St. Solangia the life of this saint is represented in tapestry, in five compartments; and in St. Etienne de Bourges, in the nave, are five paintings of the same subject. Both represent her carrying off her head in her hands.)

⁂ Certainly the most strange legend under this group is that of St. Winifride, a Welsh woman. One day Cradorus, or Caradoc, the son of Alan, king of North Wales, finding her alone in her father's house, offered her violence; she fled, and the prince, pursuing, cut off her head. Where the head fell, a fountain sprang from the ground, called "Winifride's Well," or the "Holy Well," in Flintshire. St. Beno, her spiritual intructor, now came up, set the head adroitly on again, and St. Winifride returned home safe and sound.

Healed by Stripes.

ISA. liii. 5. With His stripes we are healed.

HEB. ii. 10. Perfect through suffering.

MATT. v. 30. It is profitable for thee that one of thy members perish, and not that thy whole body be cast into hell.

HEB. xii. 6. Whom the Lord loveth He chasteneth, and scourgeth every son whom He receiveth.

2 KINGS xx. 13-19. Hezekiah, in a spirit of worldly vanity, showed the ambassadors of the king of Babylon all his precious things—the silver and the gold, etc. Then came Isaiah and said to him, The days come that all that is in thine house shall be carried to Babylon. And Hezekiah said, Good is the word of the Lord.

PSALM cxix. 71. It is good for me to have been afflicted, that I might learn Thy statutes.

The falcon. A certain Roman lady, in the days of Pompey the Great, was courted by a knight, whose joy of joys was to be near his lady-love. One day he craved of her a falcon which sat on her wrist, and she gave it him. He was so taken up with this bird that he discontinued his visits to the lady, and she sent for him. The knight came with the falcon on his wrist, and the lady said to him, "Let me touch my old favourite;" but no sooner was it in her hand than she wrenched its head off, and said to the knight, "Grieve not at what I have done. That falcon weaned thy love from me, and caused thee to offend: now I have killed it, I shall again enjoy thy presence." And it was so.—*Gesta Romanorum*, lxxxiv.

This, of course, is an allegory. The lady is God, the knight a worshipper of God, the falcon some idol which weans his heart from God. God takes it away, and he says with the psalmist, "It is good for me to have been afflicted, that I might learn Thy statutes."

Herd of Swine.

MATT. viii. 28-32. In the country of the Gergesenes two persons possessed with devils met Jesus, and cried out, saying, What have we to do with Thee, Jesus, Thou Son of God? Art Thou come hither to torment us before the time? And they besought Him, saying, If Thou cast us out, suffer us to go away into the herd of swine. And Jesus said unto them, Go. And the whole herd of swine ran violently down a steep place into the sea, and perished in the waters.

At the command of St. Regulus a devil came out of a man possessed, and went into an ass (A.D. 130). St. Regulus was bishop of Arles and Senlis. One day he saw at Senlis a man possessed with a devil, and the devil besought him, saying, "If you cast me out, suffer me to enter into the body of this ass;" and the bishop said, "Go." When the devil was about to enter into the ass, the beast, being apprised of his intention, made on the ground with his fore foot the sign of the cross, and the devil was obliged to pass on, and leave the ass unmolested. In Christian art, St. Regulus, in allusion to this "miracle," is represented with an ass crouching at his feet.—L'abbé Corblet, *Hagiographie du Diocèse d'Amiens.*

Herod and the Innocents.

MATT. ii 16-18. Then Herod, when he saw that he was mocked of the wise men, was exceeding wroth, and sent forth, and slew all the children that were in Bethlehem, and in all the coasts thereof, from two years old and under. . . . Then was fulfilled that which was spoken by Jeremy the prophet, saying, In Rama was there a voice heard, lamentation, and weeping, and great mourning; Rachel weeping for her children, and would not be comforted, because they are not.

Albert of Swirnazew, in Podolia, crucified by Jews (A.D. 1598). Albert, a child of four years, "dont les yeux riaient toujours, et toujours disaient bonjour," was crucified by Polish Jews, in 1589. His body was laid in the Jesuits' college of Lubin.—*Les Petits Bollandistes*, vol. iv. p. 530.

Andrew, an orphan, crucified at Inspruck by Jews. Andrew lost his father when quite a babe, and was committed to the charge of his godfather. One day, while playing in the streets of Inspruck with his companions, some Jews who happened to be passing by, struck with his beauty, asked to be permitted to adopt him, and gave the child's godfather a good round sum of money in order to obtain his consent. Being in possession of the child, they conducted him to a forest, "et le circoncirent en proférant les plus horribles blasphèmes contra Jesus Christ." The child screamed to attract attention; the kidnappers opened his veins, and, having hung him to a tree with his arms extended in the form of a cross, took to flight. Soon as the murdered body was discovered it was buried at Rinn. M. Migne adds, "Les guérisons miraculeuses qui s'opérèrent à son tombeau y attirèrent bientôt un grand concours de pélerins." He was canonized, and July 12 was named as his day.—L'abbé Migne, *Encyclopédie Théologique*, vol. 40, p. 174 (1850).

No dates are given, and the whole tale seems most incredible.

St. Hugh of Lincoln, at the age of eleven, crucified by Jews (Aug. 27, A.D. 1255). Hugh was born at Lincoln in 1244, and in his eleventh year was seized by the Jews of that city, under the leadership of Joppin. These Jews, we are told, parodied on this child the whole tragedy of the sacred crucifixion of Christ. They spat in his face, they scourged him with rods, they slit his nose and cut open his upper lip, they knocked out his teeth, they crucified him; and, while he hung on the cross, they pierced his side with a spear. Joppin and seventeen others, all Jews of wealth and station, were arrested for this offence by order of Henry III., and brought before the parliament assembled at Reading. Being tied by the heels to young horses, they were dragged about till they were half-dead, and were then gibbeted.—L'abbé Migne, *Encyclopédie Théologique*, p. 1380, vol. 40.

There are several documents in Rymer's *Fœdera* relative to this event, and there seems no reason to doubt that eighteen of the wealthiest Jews of Lincoln were condemned to death for the offences alleged against them, before the parliament at Reading. The story is told by Matthew Paris in his *Chronicles*. It is the subject of the *Prioress's Tale* in Chaucer. Wordsworth has a modernized version of the Canterbury Tale.

St. Janot, a schoolboy, crucified by the Jews at Cologne (March 24, A.D. 1475). The French martyrology mentions the crucifixion of Janot of Sigeberg by the Jews, who, we are told, kidnapped him on his way to school, and, after scourging him, crucified him, out of hatred to the Christian religion.

St. Michael of Sappendelf, an infant three and a half years old, crucified by Jews (April 13, 1340). Michael was the son of a peasant, named George, of the village of Sappendelf, near Naumburg. He was stolen, at the age of three years and six months, by some Jews, on the Sunday before Holy Thursday, and reserved for their paschal ceremony on the eve of Good Friday, April 13, A.D. 1340. They cut crosses with knives on his wrists, the soles of his feet, and all over the body, till the poor babe bled to death.—Raderus, *Holy Bavaria.*

It is marvellous to see the horror with which Roman Catholic writers speak of these eight or ten cases of infanticide; but they seem wholly to forget the horrors of their own Inquisition, the sickening wholesale slaughter of St. Bartholomew, the Dragonades, the Albigenses, the Camisades, the reigns of Ferdinand II., emperor of Germany, Charles V. of Germany and Spain, Philip II. of Spain, and so on, when men, women, and children, all alike, fell in indiscriminate slaughter, not because they were Jews, but because they were Christians who differed from themselves on certain dogmas and practices. "O wad some power the giftie gie us, to see oursels as ithers see us!"

⁂ The tale of *Michel d'Heitingen*, or Heitingun, is so like the above that the authenticity of either is most doubtful. L'abbé Migne says this child also was three years and six months when it was roasted alive by Jews; he gives the date 1540 instead of 1340, and the date of the month March 25.—*Encyclopédie Théologique*, vol. 40, p. 502.

St. Richard of Pontoise, aged twelve years, crucified by the Jews (March 25, A.D. 1182). Richard of Pontoise was of good family, and was decoyed by the Jews, at the age of twelve years, to be offered up in sacrifice at their paschal feast. He was kept for several days beforehand in a cave. The chief of the synagogue asked the boy what was his creed, and Richard replied, "I believe in God the Father Almighty; and in Jesus Christ, His only Son, our Lord; born of the Virgin Mary; suffered under Pontius Pilate; was crucified and buried; but the third day He rose again from the dead; and now sitteth on the right hand of God." The rabbi commanded the boy to be stripped and scourged; and, while this was going on, the spectators spat in his face, mocked him, and uttered horrible blasphemies against Jesus Christ. When this part of the martyrdom was over, they crucified the poor boy, and pierced his side. He died, praying for his tormentors. This horrible crime was one of the chief causes that determined Philippe Augustus, king of France, to banish all Jews from his dominions, in April, the same year. The dead body of Richard, the infant martyr, was transferred to Paris, and enclosed in a shrine in the church of the Holy Innocents. His head is still there, but the rest of his body was carried to England, in the reign of Charles VI., by the English, who were then masters of the chief parts of France.—Gaguin, *History of St. Richard, the Infant Martyr*. (He is mentioned by Benedict XIV. in his *De Canonizatione*, bk. i. chap. 14, p. 103.)

L'abbé Migne says, "Le chef se trouvait encore dans cette église au commencement de la révolution Française." Meaning it is there no longer.—*Encyclopédie Théologique*, vol. 41, p. 879.

St. Simon crucified in infancy by some Jews of Trent (A.D. 1475). Simon was the infant son of Andrew and Mary, poor [Roman] Catholics living in the outskirts of the city of Trent, called the Fossé. Some Jews, who had recently arrived, employed Tobias to kidnap a Christian child for their paschal ceremony, and he laid hold of Simon, a babe "lovely as an augel, and only twenty-nine months and three days old." Tobias carried the child to the house of Samuel, where all the Jews of the neighbourhood were assembled, it being the eve of Good Friday, March 24, A.D. 1475. Samuel delivered the babe to an old man, named Moses, who stripped it naked, and stuffed a handkerchief in its mouth to stifle its cries; then, holding it between his knees, he cut small pieces out of the right cheek, put them in a basin, and handed them round to the company, each being expected to eat a small piece with the blood. When this part of the ceremony was over, Moses lifted up the child by the right foot, Samuel held out its arms in the form of a cross, and those assembled pricked the body from head to foot with awls and bodkins, till not a spot the size of one's finger could be found which was not punctured. The child had now been under torture a full hour, and the whole assembly sang in unison with a loud voice this chant—

May all thy foes, O Lord, be crucified,
As Christ, the Christians' god, was slain and died.

The child feebly raised its eyes to heaven during the chant; then Moses, still holding the right foot, dashed its head against the floor, and it died. The body was stowed under a wine-tub in the cellar; but, the child being missed, an inquiry was set on foot, and, for fear of discovery, the body was thrown into a stream of water which ran hard by the synagogue. The murderers, in order to cover their guilt, went to the chief magistrate, and told him, with feigned innocence, that they had discovered a young child in the river. It was picked out of the water, the truth came to light, and the bishop of Trent, assisted by all the neighbouring clergy, buried the body in St. Peter's church. Many miracles, we are told, wrought at the child's tomb testified to the power of God. As for the Jews concerned in this cruel butchery, they were tried, condemned, and suffered the extreme penalty of the law.—Surius, *Lives of the Saints*, vol. ii. (Surius borrowed his narrative from John Matthias Tiberin, M.D., who examined the body by order of the bishop of Trent, and dedicated his book, by express authority, to the senate and people of Brescia. The Bollandists have given the tale in March 24 of the *Acta Sanctorum*, and reference is made to it by Benedict XIV. in his *De Canonizatione*, bk. i. chap. 14, p. 103. L'abbé Migne gives 1472 as the date.)

It is no part of this book to give the pros and cons of these tales, but only to show that the [Roman] Catholic Church believes them.

St. William of Norwich crucified, at the age of twelve, by Jews (A.D. 1137). William of Norwich was twelve years old, and was apprenticed to a tanner at Norwich, when he was crucified, Good Friday, April 9, A.D. 1137. The Jews had inveigled him into their hands some time before the paschal week, and gagged him. When the day of sacrifice was fully come, they tortured him in divers manners, crucified him, and pierced his left side, in mockery of the spear-wound of Jesus Christ. After he was dead, they tied his body in a sack, and carried it through the city gates to Thorpe Wood, intending to burn it; but, being surprised, they left it hanging on a tree. A chapel was afterwards erected on the spot, dedicated to "St. William i' the Wood." In 1144 the body was removed to the churchyard of the cathedral of the Holy Trinity, and six years later was transferred to the choir.—Thomas de Monmouth, *History of the Martyrdom of William of Norwich* (a contemporary). See also Blomefield, *History of Norwich*. (Benedict XIV. refers to this "martyrdom" in his *De Canonizatione*, bk. i. chap. 14, p. 103.)

Two boys of tender age, those saints ensue
Of Norwich William was, of Lincoln Hue,
Whom th' unbelieving Jews (rebellious that abide),
In mockery of our Christ, at Easter crucified.
Drayton, *Polyolbion*, song xxiv. (A.D. 1622).

The Jews who murder St. Vernier discovered by a burning bush (A.D. 1287). Vernier was born in the village of Mammerath, not far from Baccarac, in Lower Germany. He lost his father, who was a vinedresser, while still an infant, and his mother married again. The father-in-law treated the lad so harshly, that he ran away, and reached the town of Wesel, where some Jews hired him, and gave him a little easy work to lull suspicion. At Easter-time they crucified him, with his head downwards, for their paschal sacrifice; but as he did not die, they beat him with rods, and opened several of his veins. At night they cast the dead body into a boat, and, "as Jews never bury Christians," they rowed as far as Winsbach, and thrust the corpse under a thick bush. At night the bush seemed to be on fire, but was not consumed. This strange phenomenon could not fail to attract attention, and all the people round about went to see the strange sight. The body of the boy was soon discovered, the crime searched into, and the Jews who had committed it were put to death. —*Vies des Saints de Franche Comté*, vol. iv. p. 566. (These volumes were written by the professors of the college of St. Francis Xavier.)

St. Werner (or Garnier), aged thirteen, crucified by Jews (A.D. 1214–1227). Werner of Oberwezel, in the diocese of Trèves, the son of poor parents, was noted for his early piety. He lost his father, and his mother, who married a second husband, treated him so brutally, that he ran away, and hired himself to a Jew. On Holy Thursday he was seized by a band of Jews, who crucified him in mockery of Christ, out of hatred to the Christian religion. We are told that God honoured the tomb of this lad with numerous miracles.—L'abbé Migne, *Encyclopédie Théologique*, vol. 41, p. 1288.

Mr. Weever says, "The Jews in the principal cities of the British Isles did use to steal away, circumcise, crown with thorns, whip, torture, and crucify their neighbours' male children in mockery and scorn of our Lord and Saviour Jesus Christ." This certainly requires proof; but one can understand how bitterly the Jews must have hated the [Roman] Catholics, who treated them with insufferable cruelty. Witness the scandalous persecution of these poor people in the reign of Richard II., when thousands were burnt or butchered in London, York, Norwich, and Stamford, merely because they were Jews. Witness, again, the still more horrible persecution begun in Germany in the autumn of 1348. At Mainz alone twelve thousand Jews were torn to pieces, or burnt alive, or butchered in the streets; at Strasburg two thousand were burnt by the populace in their own burying-ground, and those who attempted to escape were driven back into the flames with pitchforks. At Speyer the Jews set fire to their own houses, and consumed themselves, rather than fall into the hands of the people; and at Eslingen the entire Jewish population burnt themselves to death in their synagogue to escape the "tender mercies" of the Christian race. The wholesale butchery of the Jews is beyond a doubt; the retort of the Jews on Christian children is very doubtful indeed. The infamous persecution of the Jews in Russia in 1880–1881 roused the indignation of all Europe.

A boy (name unknown) crucified in Bohemia by Jews (A.D. 1287). Albert Krantze, in his *History of Vandalia*, gives an account of a boy crucified at Prague, on Good Friday, A.D. 1287. He says the Jews there seized by craft a young child, and "practised on him all the cruelties which their forefathers had shown to Jesus Christ our Saviour." This lad, he says, bore the agonies of crucifixion with admirable patience, and more than human courage. The butchery was discovered, and the crime punished with the utmost rigour. So certain is this, that two churches were erected in honour of this boy-martyr.

Hew of Mirryland stabbed, and cast into a well, by a Jewish damsel. This is a tale told in a ballad, inserted in Percy's *Reliques*, bk. i. 3, about a boy named Hew, whose mother was "lady Hew of Mirryland" (? Milan). He was decoyed by an apple, given him by a Jewish maiden, who "stabbed him with a penknife, rolled him in lead, and cast him into a well." Percy says, "It is founded upon the supposed practice of the Jews in crucifying and otherwise murdering Christian children, out of hatred to the religion of their parents—a practice which hath always been alleged in excuse for the cruelties exercised upon that wretched people, but which probably never happened in a single instance."

The rain rins doun through Mirryland toune,
Sae dois it doune the Pa [*Po*];
Sae dois the lads of Mirryland toune
Quhan they play at the ba' [*ball*].

Than out and cam the Jewis dochter,
Said, "Will ye cum in and dine?"—
"I winnae cum in, I cannae cum in,
"Without my playferes nine."

Scho [*she*] powd an apple reid and white
To intice the ȝong thing in;
Scho powd an apple white and reid,
And that the sweit bairne did win.

And scho has taine out a little penknife,
And low down by her gair,
Scho has twined the ȝong thing and his life;
A word he nevir spak mair.

And out and cam the thick thick bluid,
And out and cam the thin;
And out and cam the bonny hert's bluid,—
Thair was nae life left in.

Scho laid him on a dressing borde,
And drest him like a swine,
And laughing said, "Gae nou and pley
"With ȝour sweit playferes nine."

Scho rowed him in a cake of lead,
Bade him lie stil and sleip;
Scho cast him in a deip drawwell,
Was fifty fadom deip.

Quhan bells wer rung, and mass was sung,
And every lady went hame,—
Than ilka lady had her ȝong sonne,
But lady Helen had nane.

Scho [*i.e. lady Helen*] rowd hir mantil hir about,
And sair sair gan she weip;
And she ran into the Jewis castel',
Quhan they wer all asleip.

"My bonny Sir Hew, my pretty Sir Hew,
"I pray thee to me speik."—
O lady, rinn to the deip drawwell,
Gin ȝe ȝour sonne wad seik.

Lady Helen ran to the deep drawwell,
And knelt upon her kne;
"My bonny Sir Hew, an ȝe be here,
"I pray thee speik to me."

"The lead is wondrous heavy, mither,
"The well is wondrous deip,
"A keen penknife sticks in my hert,
"A word I dounae speik.

"Gae hame, gae hame, my mither deir,
"Fetch me my winding sheet,
"And at the back o' Mirryland toun
"Its thair we twa sall meet."
(*Here the ballad breaks off.*)

A list of children given by the Bollandists as Jewish victims:—

(1) At Bran, in Hungary, 1522, the murder of Christian children caused the expulsion of the Jews from that country.

(2) At Cracovia, in 1407, an infant of four years old, bought by the Jews for four florins, was crucified for their paschal victim.

(3) At Castille, in 1454, the ashes of an infant's heart, plucked out and calcined, were sprinkled by Jews on their paschal bread. This charge, followed by several others of the same kind, brought about the expulsion of the Jews from Spain, in 1459.

(4) At Dussenhof, in the canton of Turgovia, in 1401, an infant four years old, bought by the Jews of a peasant for three florins, was crucified.

(5) At Motta, in the Trevisan, in 1480, was a most savage butchery of an infant.

(6) At Pfortzhelm, duchy of Baden, in 1261, a young girl of seven was sold to the Jews. Her blood was drawn from her body with awls, and the body then thrown into a tank of water, where it was discovered. The dead body being taken to the town-hall, before the duke of Baden, seemed to recover life, and held out its arms for justice and vengeance. The Jews being taken up and brought into the court, blood spouted from all her veins, which was considered to be proof positive of their guilt.

(7) At Poland, in 1547, 1569, 1590, 1595, 1597, etc., children were crucified by Jews.

(8) At Turin, in 1459, a Jew tried to assassinate a Christian child in the open street. Not being able to complete the crime, he cut off a part of the child's calf, and fled.

(9) At Tyrnau, in 1494, three murders of Christian children, about the same time, brought about the expulsion of the Jews from Hungary.

(10) At Waltkirch, in Alsatia, a father sold his child, of the age of four, for ten florins to some Jews. The condition was, that the Jews were to draw a certain quantity of the blood, and then return the child to its parent. The child was bled to death, and the father was executed.

*** The Jews, we are told, after these horrible sacrifices, never buried their victims, because their law forbids a Jew to bury a Christian. Consequently, the crime came to light more frequently than it would otherwise have done.

Acta Sanctorum (Bollandists), April 20, after the name "Albert of Swirnazew." Here will be found all the details connected with these several instances of alleged crucifixion. The only reason for giving this list is to show that the charge was very widely credited in the fifteenth and sixteenth centuries. Indeed, hatred to a Jew was almost as much enjoined as charity to the poor.

The Jews of Tisza-Eszlar, in Hungary accused of murdering a Christian girl for a passover sacrifice in 1883. In 1882 certain Hungarian Jews were charged with murdering Esther Solymosi, a Christian girl, fourteen years of age, at Tisza-Eszlar, in Hungary, and the throwing the dead body in the river Theiss. The girl had been sent by her mistress to fetch some whitewash, but never returned, and the rumour got abroad that the Jews could, if they chose, throw light on this mysterious disappearance. The boy Moritz Scharf, aged fourteen, and the son of a Jewish butcher, now came forward, and asserted that he saw through a keyhole his father and several other Jews cut the girl's throat in the forecourt of the synagogue after the morning service, and he observed that the blood *trickled slowly* from the cut. The accused Jews were thrown into prison, where they were confined for a year, and some of them subjected to torture. The trial took place in 1883, and in August all the accused were set at liberty, even the public prosecutor saying "he wished the whole story could be erased from Hungarian history." The body of the girl was found in the river, but no wound could be detected on it. Many of the witnesses confessed to have taken bribes, and the girl had been seen alive some considerable time after that stated by the boy Scharf. What is so disgraceful is this, the vice-notary M. Bary (the examining judge), the deputies, public officials, and magistrates were all violent against the Jews, and would no doubt have given judgment the other way, if they could; indeed, they both sought evidence against the Jews, and browbeat the witnesses on the other side. Dr. Eötvös, chief counsel for the defence, was nearly murdered by the mob; but, in spite of all this prejudice, the Jews were fully acquitted, and the accusation was shown to be baseless and contradictory in every particular.

The girl disappeared April 1, 1882. The trial began at Nyiregyhaza, June 19, 1883, and the accused were acquitted Aug. 3, 1883. The object of the accusation was to drive the Jews out of the village.

Herod reproved.

Matt. xiv. 8–11. John the Baptist reproved Herod for living in adultery with Herodias, his brother Philip's wife. One day Salomê, daughter of Herodias, so pleased the king by her dancing, that he vowed he would give her whatever she chose to ask for, even to the half of his kingdom. Her mother told her to ask for the head of John the Baptist, their relentless enemy. The king was vexed at the request, but for his oath's sake he sent an executioner to cut off the prophet's head, which was brought on a charger to the maiden; and Salomê handed it to her mother.

St. Angelus loses his life for reproving count Berenger for living in incestuous intercourse with his sister (A.D. 1225). When St. Angelus came to Sicily, he was greatly shocked to find the count de Berenger living with his sister, as man and wife. He at first expostulated in private with the count, but producing no effect, he denounced him in public, and threatened him with divine vengeance unless he repented. The sister repented, confessed, and received absolution; but the count vowed that the insolent priest should pay for his interference with his life, and sent assassins to murder him. They attacked him while offering up mass, gave him five wounds, and he died repeating the fifth verse of the thirty-first psalm, "Into Thy hand I commit my spirit." As he breathed his last, all the assistants saw a ray of light, proceeding from his mouth, shoot upwards towards heaven, and a dove flew in the midst of the ray till it was lost to sight.—Mgr. Guérin, *Vies des Saints*, vol. v. p. 344 (7th edit. 1880).

St. Desiderius, bishop of Vienne, murdered by Brunehaut (A.D. 608). Thierry II., king of Burgundy, received into his palace his grandmother Brunehaut when she was driven out of Austrasia, and she exercised over her grandson unbounded influence; but his court was a nest of all unclean birds. St. Desiderius boldly said to the young king, "Chase these wicked women from thy court, and take to thyself a lawful wife, worthy of the throne of Burgundy." When Brunehaut heard thereof, she employed three assassins to waylay and murder the bishop. These ruffians fell upon him at Cormoranche, but he contrived to reach Prissignac, where he died from his wounds, May 23, A.D. 608, "comme un véritable imitateur de St. Jean Baptiste et du prophète Elie, dans la conduite qu'ils avaient tenue à l'égard d'Hérodiate et de Jézabel."—Mgr. Depéry, *Histoire Hagiologique du Diocèse de Belley*.

In Christian art St. Desiderius is represented reproving Brunehaut in the court of her grandson.

The duke Gosbert reproved by St. Kilian for living in adultery (A.D. 689). When St. Kilian carried the gospel tidings to Würtzburg, he reproved the duke Gosbert for living in adultery with Geilana, his brother's wife; and Geilana persuaded the duke to put the missionary to death.—Canisius, *Life of St. Kilian*, vol. iv. p. 628.

A don of Salamanca reproved for adultery by St. John of St. Facond (A.D. 1430–1479). When St. John of Sahagon was at Salamanca, he fearlessly reproved one of the nobles for his licentious mode of living. The don was so pricked by the words of the saint, that he dismissed his concubine; but the woman was furious, and swore to be the death of the meddlesome priest before the year was out. She contrived, accordingly, to give him a slow poison, which caused him several months of pain, and ultimately killed him, June 11, A.D. 1479. In allusion to this, St. John of Sahagon is represented in Christian art with a cup surmounted with a serpent.—*Acta Sanctorum* (Bollandists), vol. ii. June 12, p. 616.

The wise and the unwise cock. The wife of Gordian's guard was an adulteress, and one of her lady's-maids professed to be skilled in the language of birds. While her gallant was with her, a cock in the courtyard began to crow, and the adulteress asked her maid what it had said. "It exclaimed," quoth the maid, "'You insult your husband shamefully.'" "Wring its neck off this minute," cried her mistress. Presently another cock crowed, which the maid declared said this, "Hear and see, but always hold your tongue." "Run," said her mistress, "and give it a handful of corn."—*Gesta Romanorum*, lxviii.

Ovid, in his *Metamorphoses* (bk. ii.), tells a tale with the same moral. He says that ravens were once as large and white as swans; but one day a raven told Apollo that Corōnis, a Thessalonian nymph whom he passionately loved, was faithless. The god shot the nymph; but, hating the tell-tale bird, he blackened its plumage, and "bade him prate in swan-white plumes no more."

Herodias and the Head of John the Baptist.

According to tradition, when Salomê received from Herod the Baptist's head, she took it to her mother; and Herodias, in her spite, pulled out the tongue, and stabbed it through and through with her bodkin.

Fulvia and the head of Cicero. When the head of Cicero, the great Roman orator, was delivered by Mark Antony, his wife Fulvia seized hold of it, pulled out the tongue, and stabbed it over and over again with her bodkin.

Honour God's Saints. (See Violence offered to God's Servants.)

1 Tim. v. 17. Let the elders that rule well be counted worthy of double honour, especially they who labour in the word and doctrine.

Numb. xvi. 1–35. Korah, Dathan, and Abiram rose in rebellion against Moses and Aaron, the servants of God, and said unto them, Ye take too much upon you, seeing all the congregation are holy, every one of them, and the Lord is among them. Wherefore lift ye up yourselves above the congregation of the Lord? And the ground clave asunder under them, and the earth opened her mouth, and swallowed them up, and they perished from among the congregation.

King Clotaire punished with colic for making St. Germanus wait (A.D. 511). When Clotaire I. succeeded his brother Childebert on the throne of France, St. Germanus, bishop of Paris, called to pay his respects. Clotaire had been absent from Paris a long time, and not knowing anything about Germanus, made him wait so long at the door, that he left the palace without seeing the young king. The king was immediately seized with a violent colic, which racked him all night. He attributed his pain to his discourtesy to St. Germanus, and sent for him. When the bishop arrived, Clotaire fell at his feet, acknowledged his offence, and humbly kissed the bottom of the prelate's robe. St. Germanus touched the part affected, and the king was relieved of his pain.—Dom Ruinart, vol. i. (1708).

Nizon, bishop of Freisingen, struck dead for threatening Leo IX. (A.D. 1150). Leo IX., in his visitation, came to Ravenna, when Nizon, bishop of Freisingen, said, "May this my throat be cut with a sword from ear to ear, if I do not depose this meddlesome pope from his apostolate." No sooner had he uttered these words than he felt an intolerable pain in his throat, and died within three days.—Wibert, *Life of Leo IX.*, bk. iii. ch. 7.

A horse, having carried St. John of Tuscany once, refused to carry any one else (A.D. 526). St. John of Tuscany having to pass over the isthmus of Corinth, when he was pope, borrowed a horse; and the horse, which had been honoured by having a saint on its back, would never allow any other person to ride thereon.—*Acta Sanctorum* (Bollandists), vol. v. p. 239.

A far better tale is told of Rudolph I., kaiser and king of Germany. One day a poor priest, taking the holy elements to a dying man, was stopped by a brook, greatly swollen by recent rains. Rudolf, then a simple knight, happened to be riding by at the time, and seeing the difficulty, instantly dismounted, and placed his horse at the disposal of the priest. When the man of God had crossed the stream, and was about to return the steed to its owner, Rudolf begged him to accept it as a gift. "Take it, father," said he; "I am not worthy to use it now, seeing it has been consecrated to the service of God."

A novice, neglecting to ask the blessing of St. Benedict, died and was rejected from her grave. A novice, longing to see her mother, left the convent on leave, but neglected to ask the blessing of St. Benedict. This was so great a breach of reverence, that she died on the road, and was buried; but the very earth was so horrified at the offence, that it thrice tossed the body out of the grave. Her parents, in great distress, applied to the abbot, and he gave them a consecrated wafer to lay on the stomach of the deceased. This talisman was all-sufficient, for the earth could no longer refuse to receive a body so protected and sanctified.—St. Gregory the Great, *Dialogues*, bk. ii.

A team of horses kneel when St. Francis Hieronimus holds a crucifix before them (A.D. 1642–1716). St. Francis Hieronimus on one occasion took his position before a notorious brothel in Naples, and a great crowd gathered round him to hear him preach. While he was preaching, a carriage and pair tried to pass through the crowd, but was stopped. The gentlemen within called to the coachman to drive on, but the preacher, holding out a crucifix, cried aloud, "O holy Jesus, if these infidels have no respect for Thee, let their horses teach them better." As he spoke, the horses fell on their knees, and continued so till the sermon was over.—Cardinal Wiseman. (St. Francis was canonized in 1839.)

The emperor Valentinian punished for neglecting to show respect to St. Martin. St. Martin had been greatly honoured by the emperor Maximus, whose empress used to wait on him, and hand him water for his hands. Valentinian II., the successor of Maximus, was an Arian, and therefore disliked the orthodox prelate. One day St. Martin came into the royal presence, but the emperor rose not from his seat to show him reverence. The bishop came nearer and nearer, but Valentinian remained seated. Presently the throne was found on fire, and burnt his majesty severely. Then rose he, went to the bishop, knelt humbly before him, and promised to grant him whatever he desired.—Severus Sulpicius, *Dialogues*.

(St Martin would never sit in a church, but always knelt or stood. Being asked why, he replied, "Know ye not that the King of kings and Lord of lords is here; and is it meet, think ye, to sit in the presence of the Majesty of earth and heaven?")

Hospitality enjoined.

HEB. xiii. 2. Be not forgetful to entertain strangers, for thereby some have entertained angels unawares

MATT. xxv. 35–40. I was an hungred, and ye gave Me meat: I was thirsty, and ye gave Me drink: I was a stranger, and ye took Me in. . . . Verily I say unto you, Inasmuch as ye have done it unto one of the least of these My brethren, ye have done it unto Me. (See also ver. 45.)

GEN. xviii. 3, etc. Abraham entertained three strangers, who proved to be three angels or divine beings.

GEN. xix. Lot entertained two strangers, who proved to be angels, and these angels helped him to escape when the cities of the plain were overthrown.

GEN. xxiv. 31, etc. Laban entertained a stranger, who proved to be Abraham's servant, and this brought about the marriage of Isaac and Laban's daughter.

EXOD. ii. 20, 21. Jethro entertained a stranger, who proved to be Moses, his future son-in-law.

JOB xxxi. 32. The stranger did not lodge in the street: I opened my doors to the traveller.

St. Valery punishes a monk and a judge for refusing him hospitality (A.D. 619). One day, returning from Caldis (*i.e.* Cayeux), the cold was so intense that St. Valery asked a temporary asylum of a priest who dwelt on the road. As it happened, the judge of the district was there at the time. Instead of granting the hospitality asked for, these two "worthies" made the saint a subject of banter and obscene raillery. St. Valery sternly rebuked them, adding that for every idle word they would have to give an account in the day of judgment. This only increased the mirth of the two libertines. So, shaking off the dust of his feet, he left the house. On returning to their room, the priest discovered that he was blind, and the judge was stricken with a nameless malady. They now sent for the wanderer to come in and warm himself, but he refused to do so. The priest never after recovered his sight, and the judge died in agony from the "mal honteux qui l'avait atteint."—*Les Petits Bollandistes*, vol. iv. pp. 107, 108.

Idols shattered.

1 Sam. v. 2–5. The Philistines took the ark of God to Ashdod, and placed it in the house of Dagon (the fish-god). When the people of Ashdod rose on the morrow, behold, Dagon was fallen on his face to the earth before the ark of the Lord; and they took up Dagon, and set him in his place again. The morning after it had fallen on its face to the ground again, and the head, with both the hands, were knocked off on the threshold of the temple; only the stump of the idol remained.

The idol of Apollo broken, at the sign of the cross, by St. Martina (A.D. 226). St. Martina was the daughter of very honourable parents at Rome. Her father had been thrice consul, but was dead, when the emperor Alexander Severus set on foot his Christian persecution. The young maiden, being taken to the temple of Apollo to offer incense to the god, made the sign of the cross, and commended herself in prayer to Jesus Christ. Instantly the temple shook to its foundation, and the whole city felt the shock. A large part of the temple fell to the ground, and not only was the statue of Apollo broken to pieces, but all the priests and many of the idolaters present at the time were killed by the débris.

The sequel of this "legend" is worth attention. After being torn with iron hooks and scourged, St. Martina was conducted to the temple of Diana; but the moment she passed the door the devil rushed from the temple, bellowing horribly, and fire from heaven burned down a part of the magnificent building. The walls and roof, falling on the priests and the idolaters, crushed hundreds of them to death. The emperor Alexander Severus, thoroughly alarmed, left the precincts, bidding Justin, the president, to carry out his orders, and not suffer a mere girl to set the whole nation at defiance. Accordingly, Justin gave orders for the flesh of Martina to be torn to pieces with iron currycombs. While this was being done, the president stood over the martyr, saying, "Call on thy God, infidel, and let Him deliver thee, if He can." So horribly was Martina mutilated by these combs, that on her breasts alone she received 118 wounds. Justin thought she was dead, and was going away, when he saw her move. "Martina, have you had enough?" he said. "Will you now offer sacrifice, or will you wait for the apple?" "Christ is my salvation," cried the damsel, "and I will offer no sacrifice to devils." "Unbind her," roared the president, "and off with her to prison!" Little did he expect to see her rise on her feet, and walk steadily away, wholly unassisted. When the emperor was told of this, he commanded that she should be exposed in the amphitheatre to the wild beasts. First came a furious lion rushing towards her, lashing his tail, bristling his mane, and roaring with anger. Every one expected he would tear her to pieces, and devour her; but when he came near her, he stopped short, and his whole nature seemed changed. He dropped his mane, wagged his tail, crouched at her feet like a dog, and licked her hands; but, as he was led back to his den, he rushed on Eumenus, the emperor's father, who had instigated his son to this cruelty, and tore him to pieces.—Bollandus, *Acta Sanctorum*, vol. i. (This is one of the lives of Surius.)

The Cretan idol of Diana broken to pieces at the prayer of St. Titus (died A.D. 94). At the death of the apostle Paul, Titus went to Crete; and one day, discoursing on the subject of faith in Christ, he found great opposition to the doctrine. He then prayed that God would witness his word with power; and, at the same moment, the idol of Diana, adored in Crete, fell from its pedestal, and was broken to pieces. By this one miracle five hundred Cretans were converted, and, being baptized, were enrolled among the disciples.

Another example. On another occasion, passing before the palace of Secundus the proconsul, Titus saw the temple of Jupiter had been lately rebuilt. He cursed the temple, and it fell with a crash to the ground. Secundus went to St. Titus, and implored him to indemnify him for this great loss, saying the emperor would hold him responsible. St. Titus bade the proconsul rebuild the temple, and dedicate it to Jesus Christ. This he did, and Secundus himself was the first to receive the sacrament of baptism in the new edifice.—L'abbé de Maistre, *Lives of the Seventy-two Disciples.*

The idol of Mars shattered by the breath of St. Leo, archbishop of Rouen (A.D. 900). St. Leo, at Bayonne, preached in the temple of Mars on the folly and sin of worshipping idols. A great clamour arose, as when Paul was at Ephesus, when Demetrius and the craftsmen clamoured against him, because he asserted they be no gods which are made with hands (Acts xix.). Seeing the people would no longer listen to him, St. Leo ceased speaking, and began secret prayer, asking God to vindicate His honour and have pity on the people. Then, going up to the idol, he blew on it, and immediately it fell, and was reduced to powder. This miracle was the means of the conversion of many priests and not a few of the people in every rank of life.—*Acta Sanctorum* (Bollandists), March, vol. i.

The idol of Mars falls, and is broken at the word of St. Xistus. When St. Xistus was come to the temple of Mars, he said to the idol of the war-god, "Christ, the Son of the living God, destroy thee;" and all the Christians present cried, "Amen." Forthwith the idol fell from its pedestal.

and did considerable injury to the temple in so doing.—*Life of St. Lawrence.*

The idols of Sabinus, a maker of idols, crashed by a peal of thunder. Sabinus was a maker of idols. On the loss of his second child, he said, "If it is Thou, the Almighty, who reignest indeed in heaven and earth, as Christians tell me, destroy these idols which my hands have made, and which, although I have besought them by prayer and sacrifice, have been unable or unwilling to save my children from death." As soon as these words were uttered, a peal of thunder shook the building, and all the idols, falling to the ground, were broken to pieces. Sabinus was converted, and many who witnessed the incident were baptized with him, confessing their sins. —Defer, *Hagiology.*

St. Satyrus breathed on an idol and it was broken to pieces. St. Satyrus breathed on an idol, and, making the sign of the cross, the idol fell down and was broken to pieces. This is stated as a fact in most martyrologies, but some place the event in Achaia, and others in Antioch.

The idols of the great temple at Senlis shattered at the name of Jesus pronounced by St. Regulus (A.D. 130). St. Regulus entered the temple at Senlis. It was a magnificent edifice, most sumptuous, and full of idols. The moment he entered and uttered the word "Jesus," every idol fell to the ground and was broken to pieces. This disaster caused great consternation among the assembled worshippers; but the saint took advantage thereof to show that such fragile images could be no gods, and to direct the attention of the people to the one true God, invisible, omnipotent, the Creator of heaven and earth. The president and his wife were converted, hundreds presented themselves for baptism, and, what is more, even the idolatrous priests were unable to resist the force of truth. After three days' purification, the temple was converted to the Holy Virgin, and is still called "Notre Dame des Miracles."

Another instance. At Louvres, six leagues from Paris, St. Regulus entered the temple of Mercury, which was full of idolaters. He made the sign of the cross, touched with his staff the image, pronounced the name of Jesus, and the idol fell with a crash, and was reduced to powder. St. Regulus took occasion from this incident to teach the vanity of trusting to such creatures, which have neither eyes nor ears, nor hands to help, nor power even to save themselves. The word was with such power, that all who heard him were converted and baptized. —L'abbé Corblet, *Hagiographie du Diocèse d'Amiens.*

The idol of Serapis broken to powder when St. Felix spits on it. St. Felix was apprehended by order of the emperor Diocletian, and taken to the temple of Serapis to offer sacrifice. When he stood before the idol he spat on it, and the metal image, falling from its pedestal, was literally broken to powder. The same befell the idols of Mercury and Diana, when St. Felix was haled into the temples of these deities with the same object.—Archbishop Ado, *Martyrology.* (See also Bede.)

The idol of the sun turns to ashes before St. Faustinus and St. Jovitus (A.D. 121). The brothers Faustinus and Jovitus, of noble family, were Christians, and natives of Brescia, in Lombardy. The emperor Hadrian renewed the persecution begun by Trajan; and, being in Brescia, these two brothers were brought before him. He commanded them to be taken to the temple of the sun, where was a splendid idol of the sun-god, whose head was surrounded with golden rays. The two brothers, placed before the idol, invoked the name of Christ, and forthwith the face of the idol became black with soot, and the golden rays looked like expiring embers. Hadrian commanded the priests to clean the idol, but immediately they attempted to do so it crumbled to ashes. The emperor, furious with rage, ordered the two brothers to be thrown to the wild beasts in the amphitheatre, when four lions, with some leopards and bears, were let loose upon them; but the wild beasts lay down peaceably beside them, licking their feet. Men were sent to enrage the beasts by burning their flanks; whereupon they turned on their tormentors, and devoured them.—*Les Petits Bollandistes* (7th edit. 1880), vol. ii. p. 531.

The idol of the sun broken to dust at the prayer of St. Thomas. The king of India commanded St. Thomas the apostle to be taken to the temple of the sun, to do honour to the statue of brass. The apostle fell on his knees, and besought God to break the idol in pieces, that the people might know that such gods are no gods. As he prayed, the brazen statue fell from its pedestal, and was broken into dust. The priests in their rage rushed on the apostle, and killed him with their spears.—Metaphrastês, *Lives*, etc. (See also St. Isidore, Gregory of Tours, and others.)

The statue of Venus falls, and is broken, when St. Porphyry passed in procession before the altar (A.D. 353–420). When St. Porphyry returned to Gaza from Constantinople, all the Christians went out to meet him, carrying crosses and singing hymns. At Four-ways-end was a marble altar surmounted by a statue of Venus; this was held in considerable favour by the young women of Gaza, because it was supposed to give them oracles respecting their future husbands. As the procession passed this altar, the idol fell down, and was shattered into fragments. Whereupon thirty-two men and seven women joined the Christians, and were baptized.—Mark (a companion), *Life of St. Porphyry*.

Imposture.

1 KINGS xxii. 21–23. When God had determined on the death of king Ahab, He said to the spirits, Who will persuade Ahab to go to the war, that he may die there? One spirit suggested one expedient, and another spirit another. At length there came forth one and said, I will persuade him. And the Lord said, Wherewith? Then said the spirit, I will go forth, and will be a lying spirit in the mouth of the prophets. And God said, Thou shalt persuade him. Go, and do so. Accordingly, Ahab was persuaded, and fell dead by a random arrow.

Those who have read Homer's *Iliad* will readily call to mind the lying dream sent to Agamemnon, which assured him he should take Troy without further delay; but the object of this deception was to distress the Greeks and please Thetis. "Zeus woke from sleep, and mused how he could slay the Grecians at the ships. At lengtn this counsel pleased him best; viz. to despatch a lying dream to Agamemnon, assuring him that all the gods had at length consented to deliver Troy into his hands. Accordingly Oneiros was sent to deceive the king, and the Greeks at once arrayed themselves for battle; but instead of taking Troy, the Trojans everywhere distress the Greeks." —Bk. ii.

Bel and the Dragon. The Babylonians had an idol called Bel, and there were spent upon him every day twelve great measures of fine flour, and forty sheep, and six vessels of wine. And the king worshipped it, and went daily to adore it; but Daniel worshipped God. And the king said to him, "Why dost thou not worship Bel?" And Daniel answered, "Because I may not worship idols made with [men's] hands." Then said the king to him, "Thinkest thou not that Bel is a living God? Seest thou not how much he eateth and drinketh every day?" Then Daniel smiled, and said, "O king, be not deceived; for this [idol] is but clay within and brass without, and did never eat or drink anything." [Then the king sent for the priests of Bel, and told them what Daniel had said.] And the priests said, "Lo! we will go out, O king. Set on the meat, and make ready the wine, and shut the door [of the temple] fast, and seal it with thine own signet. And to-morrow when thou comest in, if thou findest not that Bel hath eaten up all, we will suffer death." Next morning betimes the king arose, and Daniel with him; and the king said, "Daniel, are the seals whole?" "Yea, O king." And as soon as the door was opened, the king [saw the meat and the wine were gone], and cried with a loud voice, "Great art thou, O Bel, and with thee is no deceit at all." Then laughed Daniel, and held the king that he should not go in, and said, "Behold the pavement, and mark well whose footsteps are these." And the king said, "I see the footsteps of men, women, and children." Then was the king angry, and took the priests with their wives and children, who showed him the privy doors [under the table] where they came in, and consumed such things as were upon the table. Therefore the king slew them, and delivered Bel into Daniel's power; and Daniel destroyed both Bel and his temple.

Etymology of the word "Arcy." With every desire to treat so important a subject with gravity, the reader of the *Acta Sanctorum* occasionally runs against a statement so astounding, so utterly defiant of even "miraculous" propriety, that the words of Gibbon seem the only ones appropriate: "If the eyes of the spectators have sometimes been deceived by fraud, the understanding of the readers has much more frequently been insulted by fiction." No doubt this is a hard thing to say, and, once admitting the possibility of miracles, it would be hard indeed to draw the line between the credible and the incredible; but the following statement is certainly a fiction "insulting the understanding." The body of St. Restituta remained at Sora till the middle of the ninth century; then the Saracens made an irruption into Italy, and this, with other relics, was carried to Rome. The pope applied to Lothaire for assistance, and the emperor sent an army which defeated the Saracens. The pope asked the general what reward would be most acceptable to him, and the general replied, "The body of St. Rest:

tuta." The request was readily acceded to, and the general intended to take the body to Moreuil, near Amiens. When he reached Florence, he lodged for a night in the house of a person whose son was just dead, and the body of St. Restituta was laid on the same bed; but immediately this was done, the dead man returned to life. The general made his way to France without needless delay, intending to go through Soissons to Moreuil; but when he reached Fère-en-Tardenois, a fountain of water burst from the ground in honour of the saint, and has never ceased to flow ever since. A dead infant was brought to touch the body of Restituta, and instantly gave signs of life; and when the body of the saint was taken up, to continue the journey, the resuscitated infant cried out in infant language, "Art-ci! Art-ci!" meaning *arrêtez ci* (stop here). At the same time, the body made itself too heavy to be lifted; so that the general had no choice left, and was obliged to leave his precious gift at Fère-en-Tardenois, where a church was erected over it. This church remains to this day, and is one of the most beautiful in the diocese of Soissons. The place has ever since been called Arcy from the infant cry "Art-ci" (stop here).

I will not insult the reader by suggesting that the etymology of Arcy is *Arx*, so called from the Roman fortress. In the French Revolution the relics of St. Restituta were burnt, but we are told that a few bones escaped, were carefully collected by the faithful, and authenticated, after the concordat, by Mgr. Leblanc de Beaulieu, bishop of Soissons.

Continued. The narrative given above is very circumstantial, but the inhabitants of Sora, in Naples, say it is all false, and that the body of St. Restituta never left Sora. They affirm that the body given to the general was not that of Restituta at all, but, like the body given by pope Nicholas to the monks of St. Germain (p. 186), was some one else. The Bollandists (vol. vi. May 29, p. 655, etc.) devote a long chapter to this subject, and side with the pretensions of Sora against Arcy, notwithstanding the attesting miracles in favour of the Soissonais. Father Cahier, in his *Characteristics*, throws the weight of his authority on the same side. Strange that these learned disputants do not see how utterly they discredit the value of miracles, and the integrity of their popes and prelates, by such controversies.

Boethius claimed to be a Christian, and several Christian treatises fathered on him (A.D. 470–526). Boethius, the great Roman statesman in the reign of Theodore the Goth, was doubtless one of the greatest geniuses of old Rome—a philosopher, mathematician, poet, and ripe scholar. He incurred the jealousy of Theodoric, and was kept by him in prison, where he wrote, in the form of a dialogue, his famous work *De Consolatione Philosophiæ*, in five books. The book, no doubt, is theistic, but affords no evidence whatever that the writer was a Christian, any more than Marcus Aurelius was. Boethius was called, in the Middle Ages, the "Augustine of Philosophy," but the Christian letters ascribed to him, on doctrinal points, are rejected by scholars as not authentic. Cassiodorus (A.D. 468–568), a contemporary, has given a list of the writings of Boethius, but says nothing about his theological works, and omits entirely the treatises entitled (1) *The Unity of the Trinity*; (2) *Are the Father, Son, and Holy Ghost substantially God?* (3) *A Brief Profession of Faith*; (4) *The Personality and the Two Natures*; and (5) *The Substances, so far as they are Substances, are Good.*" The *first* of these runs to nine pages, the *second* to two pages, the *third* to five pages, the *fourth* to sixteen pages, and the *fifth* to four pages. These are not treatises, but are said to be extracts from letters to Symmachus and John, afterwards pope; but Cassiodorus omits all mention of any such letters, and competent scholars deny that these five tracts are by Boethius at all. Most certainly his last work, *De Consolatione*, is not in harmony with these advanced dogmatical tracts. Well, not only does Cassiodorus, a contemporary, omit all mention of these theological tracts, but Isidore of Seville does so too. This Isidore died A.D. 636 (that is, sixty-eight years after Cassiodorus); he was the most profound scholar of his age, and carefully compiled a catalogue of "Ecclesiastical Writers." The first mention of any one of these tracts is by Honorius, bishop of Autun, in A.D. 1100 (that is, 574 years after the death of Boethius). Honorius says, "The consul Boethius wrote a book on *The Trinity*, and another on *The Consolation of Philosophy*." Now, *The Consolation* is a long work in five books, but no one pretends that the *De Trinitate* is a book at all. The utmost that is claimed for it is that it is part of a letter, and its whole extent is only nine pages. The insurmountable objection to these theological papers is this: that in the last and great work of Boethius, there is nowhere to be found the name of Christ, there is no mention direct or indirect of the incarnation and work of redemption, none of the existence of a Holy Ghost, nor the least hint of a Divine Trinity. So that, without doubt, the theological works of Boethius, like the decretals of Isidore, must be placed amongst the many "pious frauds" of the Middle Ages.

The twelve sibyls and their prophecies. The mediæval monks tell us there were twelve sibyls, and have given to each a distinct emblem and separate prophecy.

(1) The *Libyan* sibyl: "The day shall come when men shall see the King of all living things." *Emblem*, a lighted taper.

(2) The *Samian* sibyl: "The Rich One shall be born of a pure virgin." *Emblem*, a rose.

(3) Sibylla *Cumāna:* "Jesus Christ shall come from heaven, and live and reign in poverty on earth." *Emblem*, a crown.

(4) Sibylla *Cumæ:* "God shall be born of a pure virgin, and hold converse with sinners." *Emblem*, a cradle.

(5) Sibylla *Erythræa:* "Jesus Christ, the Son of God, the Saviour." *Emblem*, a horn.

(6) The *Persian* sibyl, "Satan shall be overcome by a true Prophet." *Emblem*, a dragon under the sibyl's feet, and a lantern.

(7) The *Tiburtine* sibyl: "The Highest shall descend from heaven, and a virgin be shown in the valleys of the deserts." *Emblem*, a dove.

(8) The *Delphic* sibyl: "The Prophet born of the virgin shall be crowned with thorns." *Emblem*, a crown of thorns.

(9) The *Phrygian* sibyl: "Our Lord shall rise again." *Emblem*, a banner and a cross.

(10) The *European* sibyl: "A virgin and her Son shall flee into Egypt." *Emblem*, a sword.

(11) Sibylla *Agrippina:* "Jesus Christ shall be outraged and scourged." *Emblem*, a whip.

(12) The *Hellespontic* sibyl: "Jesus Christ shall suffer shame upon the cross." *Emblem*, a cross.

Blondel, a French Protestant, pronounced these writings to be clumsy forgeries, 1649. They are manifestly a mere monkish invention of the sixteenth century, and never could deceive any one capable of judging such a matter.

The pretended blood of Christ proved to be only honey and saffron. Joseph of Arimathæa is said to have been the first to bring into Britain the blood of Christ, which he did in two silver vessels. King Henry III. had a glass vessel containing some of the blood of Christ, sent him by the master of the temple of Jerusalem; this treasure the king committed to St. Peter's church, Westminster. The college of Bonhommes, Ashridge, and the abbey of Hales had some of the blood of Christ given by Richard, duke of Cornwall, king of the Romans. In 1513 this blood, being analyzed, was found to be only clarified honey coloured with saffron, and was exposed by the bishop of Rochester at St. Paul's Cross. The like discovery was made of the "blood of Christ" found among the relics of the abbey of Feschamp, in Normandy; this "blood" was said to have been preserved by Nicodemus, when he took the body from the cross; it was given to William, duke of Normandy. This imposition was exposed by Speed, who gives a relation of it.

The devil shot. In 1824, in the village of Artes, near Hostabreich, about twelve miles from Barcelona, a constitutionalist sent to the parish priest to come and administer to him the last sacrament; but the priest refused, saying the man "is damned without hope of mercy." The brother of the sick man asked the priest who told him so, and the priest replied, "Who told me? why, God, to be sure." "What?" said the brother, "has God Himself come down from heaven to tell you this?" "Yes," said the priest; "He spoke to me during the sacrifice of the mass, and told me your brother was past the pale of absolution." The man died unabsolved, and when the brother requested the parish priest to bury him, he refused to do so, saying that God had told him devils would carry off the body that very night; "and in forty days," he added, "they will come and fetch you also." The Spaniard, armed with pistols, kept strict watch over his brother's body, and at dead of night a knocking was heard at the door. Being opened, "three devils, with horns, claws, and tails, entered the room." The Spaniard shot at them; one died immediately, another lingered a few minutes, and the third tried to escape. Being unmasked, the two men shot were found to be the priest and his curate, and the third man was the sacristan of the village church.—Bayley, *Family Biblical Instructor*.

Duprat and the sheriff's wife. The sheriff of Orleans, having lost his wife, who was a Lutheran, wished to have her buried in the family vault; but the Franciscans induced a young man to enter the vaults, and, without speaking, to make all the uproar he was able. At the hour of the funeral ceremony, while the service was going on, a terrible uproar was heard in the vaults; and the priests stopped short. An exorcist took his book and stole, and adjured the spirit to tell what troubled it. No answer. "Art thou a dumb spirit?" Three knocks; and the service was deferred. For three successive days this unseemly scene was repeated, and caused such a sensation that the church was crammed. On the third day the exorcist said, "Phantom or spirit, art thou the soul of [such and such a one]?" naming one of the buried dead. No answer. "Of such a one?" naming another. No answer. All the persons buried in the vaults being successively named, the exorcist then asked, "Art thou, then, the spirit of Margaret, the sheriff's wife?" Three tremendous raps were heard. "Art thou a goblin damned?" asked the priest. Three more loud raps with other noises. "Art thou doomed to everlasting fire, for having embraced the heresy of Luther?" Three knocks. "What is it you want?" No answer. "Do you wish the body of Margaret to be taken away, and cast out?" Three very loud knocks. The service was now broken off, the sacred vessels removed, and the host with them. Notice was given to the sheriff to remove his wife, as she was not in a condition to lie in consecrated ground. The sheriff now applied to the chancellor Duprat, and prevailed on him to appoint a commission to investigate this profane mockery. The young man, being apprehended, confessed the trick, and the two friars who employed him were sentenced to do public penance.—Paxton Hood, *World of Moral and Religious Anecdote*, p. 535.

The divine revelations made to St. Hildegardes (A.D. 1098-1179). Hildegardes had several revelations, and was commanded by the Holy Ghost to write them in a book. The book was shown to pope Eugenius III., and he sent the bishop of Verdun, with others, to investigate the matter. The deputation gave a favourable report, and St. Bernard, abbot of Clairvaux, was selected to lay the report before his holiness. "L'abbé Trithème dit, que St. Bernard alla la voir lui-même pour avoir le bonheur de l'entretenir; qu'il en fut pleinement satisfait, confessa hautement que Hildegarde était inspirée de Dieu . . . et qu'il lui écrivit plusieurs lettres. . . . Mais le Père Stilting, au tome v. de septembre des *Acta Sanctorum* a démontré que ce fait était tout à fait faux."—Mgr. Guérin, *Vies des Saints* (1880), vol. ix. p. 180.

The Isidorian decretals (A.D. 800). Decretals are the replies of popes *ex cathedra* to questions of Church doctrine and discipline put to them by bishops and others. They take, in the [Roman] Catholic Church, the position that reports take in our law courts. A man named Mentz composed a volume of forty-nine forged decrees or responses upon questions such as these: the infallibility of the pope; the rite of the chrism; the body and blood of Christ in the Eucharist; and other similar dogmas—always justifying the high "orthodox" party, exalting the clergy, and aggrandizing the Church. He pretended that these letters were all written between the first and fourth centuries, and signed them with the names of St. Anacletus (martyred A.D. 78); St. Alexander (martyred A.D. 109); St. Fabian (martyred A.D. 236), to whom he attributes the rite of the chrism; Julius (A.D. 337), to whom he attributes a letter to the Eastern Church against Arius; St. Athanasius (296-373), whose name he sets to a synodical letter; and so on. In order to give weight to these forged documents, our *Impostor Nequissimus* (who lived in the ninth century) palmed off his book as the compilation of the very learned and pious Isidore, bishop of Seville (570-636). It is positively certain that St. Isidore had no part nor lot in the matter, and probably never compiled a book of decretals at all. We say "probably," because André Marc Burriel, a Spanish Jesuit, professes to have found such a book in the archives of the Church of Toledo in 1749. Presuming, however, that Burriel's collection is genuine, it has nothing to do with the book in question, and seems to have been quite unknown; whereas the forged decretals of Mentz (made A.D. 800), according to Blondel (in his *Pseudo-Isidorus*), and Koch (in his *Notice of the Code of the Bishop of Strasburg, Rachion*), and many others, "have produced enormous changes in the Roman hierarchy, doctrine, and disciple, and have to an incalculable extent raised the authority of the pope." If this is so, it is a pity that the Church did not call to mind what the psalmist says (xl. 4), "Blessed is the man that maketh the Lord his trust, and respecteth not such as turn aside to lies."

"La réforme pseudo-Isidorienne, adoptée par St. Nicholas, en 865, par le huitième concile œcumenique en 870, confirmée par le concile de Trent en 1564, elle est depuis neuf siècles le droit commun dans l'église catholique . . . ce qu'il est impossible de justifier et même d'excuser, c'est le moyen employé par le pseudo-

Isidore pour arriver à ses fins."—*Études Religieuses*, No. 47, p. 392.

⁂ It certainly is passing strange how such an "impostor nequissimus" should be allowed to exercise the slightest influence on a Church, which is nothing unless true and above suspicion.

The liquefaction of the blood of St. Januarius. Edward Kinesman (in his *Lives of the Saints*, Sept. 19) says, "The most stupendous miracle is that seen to this day in the church of St. Gennaro, in Naples, viz. the blood of St. Januarius, kept in two glass vials. When either vial, held in the right hand, is presented to the head of the saint, the congealed blood first melts, and then goes on apparently to boil."

Alban Butler says, "The standing miracle is the liquefaction and boiling of the blood, when the vials containing it approach the martyr's head. In a rich chapel, in the great church at Naples, are preserved the blood in two very old glass vials, and the head of St. Januarius. The blood is congealed, and of a dark colour; but when brought in sight of the head, it melts, bubbles up, and flows down the sides of the vials."

Alban Butler says, "Certain Jesuits, sent by F. Bollandus, were allowed by cardinal Philamurini to see this prodigy; and the minute description of the manner in which it is performed is related by them in the life of Bollandus." The testimony of interested witnesses is quite worthless in such a matter. He furthermore informs us that "pope Pius II. mentions it, in 1450. Angelus Cato, a physician, and many others mention it in the same century;" but he does not say that Cato tested it in the modern acceptation of the word, nor indeed was the knowledge of any physician, in 1450, sufficient to make such a test of this liquefaction as would satisfy any but those predisposed to believe it.

Mgr. Guérin, chamberlain of pope Leo XIII., in 1880, thus describes the phenomenon: "On met la tête sur l'autel du côté de l'évangile, et les deux fioles renfermants le sang du côté de l'épître. On a quelquefois trouvé le sang liquide, mais en général il est solide. Lorsque les deux fioles sont vis-à-vis de la tête, le sang se liquéfie, ou dans le moment même, ou en quelques minutes. Cette liquéfaction est suivie d'une ébullition. Quand on a retiré le sang, et qu'il n'est plus en présence de la tête, il redevient solide. Quoiqu'il y ait plusieurs cierges sur l'autel, on trouve, en touchant les fioles, qu'elles sont presque entièrement froides. On les fait baiser au peuple en certaines occasions. Quelquefois le sang s'est liquéfié dans les mains de ceux qui tenaient les fioles, quelquefois aussi il est redevenu solide, de liquide qu'il était, aussitôt qu'on y touchait. La liquéfaction a lieu également lorsque les fioles sont en présence d'un ossement, ou de quelque autre partie du corps de St. Janvier. Il est arrivé quelquefois que la liquéfaction ne s'est pas faite; ce que l'on a regardé comme une marque de la colère céleste. On met ensemble les deux fioles sur l'autel, et le sang se liquéfie dans l'une et l'autre en même temps et dans le même degré, quoiqu'il y en ait peu dans la plus petite, et qu'il soit attaché aux parois du verre."

Januarius was put to death Sept. 19, A.D. 309. The head was given in 1036 by Charles II., duke of Anjou. The liquefaction takes place Sept. 19, the first Sunday in May, and Dec. 16. We are told that king Roger in 1140 venerated the relics of St. Januarius.—*Vies des Saints*, vol. xi. p. 244. (See *Acta Sanctorum*, Sept. vol. v.)

Mons. Neumann of Berlin performed the "miracle" of the liquefaction of dried blood, with all the circumstances of the Neapolitan experiment. Dr. Cumming did the same at Exeter Hall, London, and showed how the blood was made to flow. Dr. Cumming used ether, etc., to accomplish the liquefaction; but other agents will produce the same effect.

Now, we are told that Januarius was put to death on Sept. 19, and this is the great anniversary of the "liquefaction." When Murat was king of Naples the blood would not liquefy; whereupon the Frenchman planted two cannons opposite St. Gennaro, and told the bishop he would blow the church to pieces unless he performed the "miracle." The bishop protested it could not be done; but, seeing that Murat was in earnest, he produced the liquefaction as usual. There is something degrading in this paltering with religion. The show may bring money to the church of St. Gennaro, but surely imposition is very short-sighted policy, especially in these days of free investigation, when "audax omnia perpeti gens humana ruit per vetitum nefas."

The miraculous image of the mother of God, at Einsiedlen. J. Heinrich Zschokke, a well-known author (A.D. 1770–1848), tells us, in his *Autobiography*, that at Einsiedlen, at the celebrated place of pilgrimage, he was shocked at the desolation and poverty of this once most prosperous place. Wishing to do something towards its restoration, he was told that the most effectual way would be to restore the "miraculous image of the mother of God to the altar. 'But the image has been carried off to Paris,' I replied. 'Very true,' was the answer, 'yet the holy mother is still at Einsiedlen.' 'What!' said I, 'both here and at Paris at the same time?' 'Undoubtedly,' replied the capuchin; and, leading me to the sacristy, he unlocked a chest full of dolls, ready dressed, and lying side by side. All were exactly alike. All had the same bright black face; but every one had a distinct dress and special ornaments. I now learned that the image had to be presented to the people in a different costume for each holiday, and that a number of dolls were kept ready for each occasion. I allowed one to be set up on the altar, and pilgrimages were soon renewed. I now saw that miracles were nowhere less believed in than by those who lived by them."

Rose Tamisier and the bleeding picture of Christ (1850.) Rose Tamisier had been educated in a convent at Salon, Bouches du Rhone, where she made herself notorious. She gave out that she received constantly visits from the Virgin Mary, and that she was commissioned to convert infidel France. Having left the convent, she returned to her native village of Saignon, where she soon established a reputation as a miracle-worker, by causing the growth of a miraculous cabbage, sufficiently large to feed the whole village for several weeks. In the mean time she refused all food except consecrated wafers, which angels purloined from the sacred pyx, and brought to her. Her fame spread rapidly, and her body became marked with stigmata; not the usual nails and thorns, but a cross, a heart, a chalice, and sometimes a picture of the Virgin and Child. She now entered on her great achievement. There was in the little church of St. Saturnin a picture of Christ descending from the cross, and this picture she caused to emit real blood. Her first exhibition was Nov. 10, 1850. The "miracle" was examined into rigidly, and pronounced to be genuine. At length Mons. Eugène Colignon, a chemist of Apt, showed that human blood disgorged by a leech, having lost its fibrine, might easily be made to penetrate a picture, and produce the phenomenon of a bleeding picture. He imitated the "miracle" with perfect success in the presence of constituted authorities, and a large number of scientific men. Not a doubt remained that a leech was the miracle-worker, and Rose Tamisier, being tried at Nismes in 1851 for imposture, after a long and patient investigation, was pronounced guilty of *escroquerie et outrage à la morale publique et religieuse*, and condemned to six months' imprisonment, with a fine of five hundred francs and costs. (See index, BLEEDING).—*Any of the French journals of the period.*

The lives of saints. Mgr. Guérin accuses the Bollandists of foisting into their books false acts, and claims the right of private judgment in selecting the true from the false. These are very dangerous admissions and claims, which would go to the utter destruction of the whole work of the Bollandists and of Mgr. Guérin's *Lives of the Saints* also; for all who deny the possibility of miracles would claim the right of private judgment, and make a clean sweep of the legends of the saints, never forgetting that all miracles must be submitted to one and the same standard. Mgr. Guérin says, "Après avoir lu les 46 pages en folio que les Bollandistes consacrent à ces Martyrs [Alfio, Philadelphus, Cyrin, Thecla, Justina, and Isidora], notre conviction est celle de ces savants hagiographes: c'est-à-dire que les Actes qui les concernent ont été interpolés, et qu'on ne sait rien de certain à leur égard. Une seule chose est hors de doute, c'est la célébrité de leur culte chez les Siciliens et les Grecs. Il fut un temps [third century] où les Actes des Martyrs étaient un thème à romans!! ceux des saints Adelphe [Alfio], Philadelphe, et Cyrin, ont eu la mauvaise fortune de servir de trame à des broderies. De là, la difficulté de distinguer le vrai du faux. Nous l'avons essayé, et nous pensons qu'on peut s'en tenir à notre récit abrégé." This surely is wholly unjustifiable. Why should the judgment of Mgr. Guérin (in 1880) be preferred to that of the Bollandists? The saints referred to all occur in May, and the May series consists of seven folio volumes. Bollandus and Henschenius edited the first five volumes (January and February). The next thirty-nine volumes were under the charge of Henschen, Papebroch, Janninck, Baerts, Sollier, Pien or Pinius, Cuypers, Bosch, Stiltinck, Suyskene, Perier, and Stycker, and some eighty-eight years were spent by them on the work. The lives consulted were those usually accepted by the [Roman] Catholic Church, and their correspondence, like that of Mgr. Guérin, was with the dignitaries of their Church. If these men tampered with their documents, who are to be trusted? And if Mgr. Guérin is permitted to cull from their lives by private judgment, then hair by hair nothing will be left. The lives, such as they are, reflect the opinions of the times when they were written, and must be taken as they stand, for better or for worse. It is, however, not a little startling that Mgr. Guérin should call the third century the most untrustworthy of all. See *Vies des Saints*, vol. v. p. 443, note.

Cardinal Baronius avows, in his *Remarques*, that the acts of St. Venant, which he saw at Camerino, "sont remplis de choses apocryphes;" but he says he has left out the "lies," "et ne nous en a donné que ce qu'elle a jugé être conformé à la vérité." (See ST. VENANT.)

The relics of Job. Mgr. Guérin says, "Les prétentions de ceux de l'Occident sur les reliques de Job ne paraissent pas avoir plus de fondement. Ceux qui veulent qu'elles fussent à Rome dès le vii. siècle, ont négligé de nous dire quand et comment elles y étaient venues." The pope's chamberlain can see clearly enough the weak points when speaking of the Eastern Church, but admits relics of the Western Church utterly regardless of "the when and how they were procured." Let any one look over the few specimens here referred to (under the head of "Relics"), and say whether the evidence is one jot stronger than that of the Eastern Church for the bones of the patriarch Job. When and how were St. Peter's chains obtained, and how is it they are adorned with precious stones? How and when was the head of John the Baptist procured? How and when was the Virgin's milk obtained, so reverently shown at Souillac? How and when was one of the stones cast at St. Stephen picked up? The same may be asked respecting St. Paul's tooth, St. Peter's tooth, the girdle of Joseph the espoused husband of Mary, St. Luke's likeness of the Virgin, to say nothing of those marvellous relics mentioned by Brady, such as a lock of Mary Magdalene's hair, a ray of the star which appeared to the wise men, a rib of the *Verbum caro factum*, the rod of Moses, the sword and shield of St. Michael, the tear shed by Jesus over Jerusalem, and so on. Mgr. Guérin charges the Eastern Church with imposture in its relics; it would be well, however, if the Western Church had been able to show a clearer title, and some better apology for the two heads of the Baptist, the five legs of the ass ridden by our Lord, the multitude of nails employed in the crucifixion, and the quantity of wood said to be remnants of the true cross, than that very lame one, "He who fed five thousand men with five loaves, can multiply relics also." The tale about Job's bones is, that Rotharis, king of the Lombards, who reigned from A.D. 538 to 653, caused them, together with the bones of the two Tobies, the young Sara, and many others, to be transported from Rome to Pavia. They were deposited in the church of John the Baptist, and exposed to veneration in the chapel of St. Raphael, but suddenly disappeared; it is said that they were stolen. Mgr. Guérin adds that the thief was equally inexcusable, "sans que l'on eût pu savoir dans la suite ce qu'en firent les voleurs. Leur intention était de dérober de véritables reliques et de nuire à ceux qui les croyaient telles, et qui les honoraient de bonne foi. De sorte que ce ne serait rien diminuer de l'énormité de leur sacrilège de nous apprendre que c'étaient toutes fausses reliques, que jamais on ne vit à Rome les os ni de Job ni des deux Tobies; et que de plus, il est faux que le roi Rotharis ait jamais rapporté des reliques de Rome."—*Vies des Saints*, vol. v. p. 441.

St. Secundel works miracles by the aid of the devil (A.D. 559). Secundel fancied he was called upon to preach the gospel, and saw, as he supposed, Jesus Christ Himself, who said to him, "Secundel, you have now lived long enough in solitude; go into the high-roads, and compel men to come into my vineyard, that they may sit down at the feast which I have prepared." So he left his hermitage, went forth to preach, and did many wonderful things, so as to win the praise and glory of man. Success puffed him up more and more, and in his vain-glory he went to visit St. Friard, expecting great honour; but St. Friard said to him, "Alas! alas! my brother; the devil has deceived you. Go to your cell, humble yourself in the dust, and pray for forgiveness." These words struck Secundel to the heart. He felt he had been deceived, and prayed St. Friard to intercede for him at the throne of grace. "Let us pray," said the saint, "and God, who is infinite in mercy, will hear us." While they prayed, the devil stood before them in the likeness of Christ, but the two praying ones said to him, "If thou art Christ, make the sign of the cross, and we will believe thee." So saying, they both crossed themselves, and the devil fled howling and crestfallen.—Gregory of Tours, *Lives of the Fathers.*

Touching for the king's evil. The touched impostors. The Hon. Daines Barrington mentions the case of an old man he was examining as a witness, who stated that when queen Anne was at Oxford she "touched" him for the evil. Barrington asked him if he was really cured; upon which the old man waggishly replied, he did not believe he ever had the evil, but his parents were poor, and did not object to the bit of gold.—*Observations on the Statutes*, p. 107.

There cannot be a doubt that any number of similar miracles could be worked at the present day on the same terms, or even for a little local notoriety.

Relics of St. Urban I. not genuine. That relics are not "always" genuine is indubitable, at least in regard to the relics of St. Urban I. (A.D. 222-230). Pope Nicholas I., in A.D. 862, gave the body of St. Urban to the monks of St. Germain d'Auxerre; and the translation was attested by numerous miracles. Three years afterwards (A.D. 865) the monks of St. Germain gave the sacred deposit to the bishop of Chalon-sur-Marne, who placed it in his monastery in the diocese of Langres, and changed the name of his monastery from "The Holy Trinity" to "St. Urban." This seems very precise. Here is an infallible pope who gives the body, and numerous miracles to vouch for its genuineness. A better case does not exist in all the ten thousand relics of the Roman Church. Judge now of our amazement when we read, this was all a blunder from beginning to end. The body given by pope Nicholas to the monks of St. Germain was not the body of St. Urban I., pope of Rome, but of some one else. And the miracles, attesting the genuineness of the gift, were all deceptive. Papebroch has demonstrated this fact in his notes on the "Life of St. Urban" (*Acta Sanctorum*, vol. v. May 25). In 1599 the body of St. Urban I. was found entire in the church of St. Cecilia, and Clement VIII. separated its head from the body, and gave it to the church of "Our Lady of Ara Cœli;" other parts he sent to other churches, and the rest he deposited under the altar of St. Cecilia. Baillet says, "Pope Nicholas I., no doubt, thought the body he gave to the monks of St. Germain was the body of pope Urban I., and never knew that pope Paschal I. had removed the body forty years before to the church of St. Cecilia." Strange, that pope Nicholas, and all his cardinals, deacons, and notaries, should not know what had occurred in their own lifetime, only forty years ago! Stranger still, that numerous miracles should have attested the genuineness of the gifts! Strangest of all, that the mistake was never suspected till the seventeenth century, when a Flemish lawyer discovered it, and pope Clement VIII. ratified the truth of Papebroch's acuteness! There is not a shadow of doubt that the parish church of St. Urban, in the diocese of Langres, still believes that the body given to it by the monks of St. Germain, in 865, is that of pope Urban I., for in its archives is a "History of St. Urban I., pope," tracing the connection. In 1866 a *procès-verbal* was drawn up, attesting its genuineness. And on the coffer is a particular account of each of the eight bones contained in the reliquary, so that there can be no mistake there. If miracles often repeated are not to be relied on, if popes and all their notaries and court are ignorant of important matters in their own lifetime, we may well ask with Pilate, "Truth! What is truth?" nor care to wait for an answer.—Mgr. Guérin (chamberlain of Leo XIII.), *Vies des Saints*, vol. vi. p. 25.

The ghost of the royal palace of Woodstock (A.D. 1649). The commissioners of the Long Parliament took possession of the royal palace of Woodstock, and tried to efface from it every emblem of royalty, pulling down the insignia of royal state, turning the beautiful bedrooms into kitchens and sculleries, the council-hall into a brew-house, and the dining-room into a wood-house. They treated all persons connected with Charles Stewart about the palace with indignity, and one Giles Sharp apparently aided them. The first two days strange noises were heard by the commissioners in the house; then a "supernatural" dog howled, and gnawed the bed-clothes; the next day the "fun grew fast and furious,"—the furniture began to dance, the bells to ring, the plates and dishes to roll about; the pillows were replaced by logs of wood, and bricks came rattling down the chimneys. On the eleventh night the clothes of the commissioners disappeared; on the twelfth night their beds were filled with pewter plates; on the thirteenth the glass windows were all smashed; and the annoyances increased till the commissioners were obliged to leave. At the Restoration the whole was explained; Giles Sharp was the *primum mobile*. He knew all the secret passages, trap-doors, and blind doors about the place; and, with the aid of a few concealed cavaliers, produced the annoyances which the commissioners attributed to spirits.—Dr. H. More, *Continuation of Glanvil's Collection of Relations in Proof of Witchcraft.*

The devils confess there are four scourges which they cannot abide. In the examination of Sara Williams in 1602, before her Majesty's Commissioners for Causes Ecclesiastical, this extract was read to her out of Barnes's book, and she was ordered to declare if it was true or not. Barnes wrote that the devil in the examinate had declared, "There were foure scourges which the devils hated: holy water, halowed candles, frankensence, and the booke of exorcismes." To this Sara Williams replied, "that she said no such thing, and that the priests themselves, for the better gracing of those foure scourges, did proclaime them in her name, or rather in the name of the devil said to be in her, and did put it downe in theyr Miracle-booke as the devils owne words."—Samuel Harsnet (afterwards archbishop of York), *Popish Impostures* (1604), p. 103.

Confession of Richard Mainy, gentleman, avouched upon oath, June 6, 1602. Richard Mainy was a young gentleman of fortune, about seventeen years old, who had been sent, at the age of thirteen, to the English seminary of Reims, to prepare him for the priesthood. He remained there for two years, and entered, "out of boyish curiositee," the *fratres minimi* or *bonhommes*, as a probationer. Here he continued for three months, and then left for Paris. He quitted the *bonhommes* "because he found their rules too strict, and their diet confined to fish only." About this time the duke of Guise was preparing with the king of Spain to invade England, and all the English were commanded to leave France; so Richard went to Dieppe, and embarked for England. He landed at Rye, and after a few days joined his brother John in London. Being invited to dine with Lord Vaux at Hackney, he heard about the possessions of Marwood, who (he was told) "roared like a bull." Soon afterwards he visited Sir George Peckham of Denham, where the whole talk turned upon Edmunds [Weston] the Jesuit, and the persons possessed in the house of Mr. Edmund Peckham. He soon became known to the priests who frequented Denham, and they did their utmost to bring him back to join the priesthood. He was a merry, high-spirited boy, and partly from curiosity and partly from love of enterprise, he pretended to be possessed, and allowed the priests to take him in hand. Finding the part he played made him an object of notoriety, he increased his eccentricities, and drew crowds to see him. Barnes set down in his *Book of Miracles* all the lad did, and pretended to see in visions, as veritable facts; so he was arraigned, and examined in the ecclesiastical court by the royal commissioners, and was allowed to write down his deposition, which he afterwards ratified by oath. The whole of his "confession" is too long to reproduce here *in extenso*, but the following extracts bear upon the examinations of Sara and Friswood Williams, Anne Smith, and Antony Tyrrell:—

(i.) Richard Mainy suffered from *vertigo capitis*, accompanied with flatulence, and these gave the cue for the priests to pronounce him possessed. He willingly lent himself, at first, to their schemes, but says in his *Confessions*, "If I could have suspected they would have dealt with me as they did, I would certainly have avoyded them." He goes on to say, "At my first comming to Denham I was kindly used, and my brothers cooke told mee there was in the house greate walking of spirits, at which divers had been affrighted. I was, at the time, somewhat evill at ease, and this report made me worse, so that my old complaint did take hold of me againe. Maister Dibdale and Maister Cornelius came to me, and after sundry questions, they fell to be of opinion that I was possessed, (but I am fully perswaded they knew wel enough that neither I, nor any of the rest were indeede possessed). When they told me I was possessed, I answered that they were deceaved, and acquainted them with the nature of my complaint. They said I was mistaken, put me in minde of my leaving the *fratres minimi*, of my wild pranks, and youthfull follies, to prove that I was possessed, and finally perswaded me to submit myselfe to theyr triall, that I and they might know of a surety whether I was possessed or no. Soe I did yeeld myselfe to their perswasion, and then they told me about Sara Williams and her fits, and in what manner shee did behave, and how others who were possessed did behave. Being in one of my fits, Maister Dibdale came to me, and, when I recouvered, hee told me, it was because hee had applyed a holy relique to my bodie; and a day or two after, he with other priests told me it was necessary for me to be exorcised. Having submitted so farre, it was too late to draw backe, so I was bound fast in a chayre, and fell to theyr exorcismes with much solemnity. They gave me a holy potion to drink, which I found vastly unpleasant, and I told them to untye me, and let me lye downe uppon my bed; but they payd no heed to my words, and only answered, 'See, how the devill troubles him!' At other times when I was in the chayre, besides the drinke, they did burne brimstone under my nose. What I did and spake at such times I cannot remember. No doubt when I found myselfe soe entangled, that I could not rid myselfe from them, I spake many things which I should be ashamed of now. I was never left in peace all the time I was at Denham: eyther I was in the chayre, or I was called to witness what Sara Williams and her sister were doing, or I was confined to my chamber, or was otherwise tossed and turmoyled by them; at last I was informed that they had succeeded in casting out one of the devils, leaving me to infer that there were others left behind. By this time Christmas drew neere, and they gave me over for awhile, and sent me to Windsor to a maister Frittons were I remained till the end of the holy dayes, free from their vexations. I did much solace myselfe while I was there with merrie company, which, when the priests heard of, they gave out that I was possessed with a 'Merry Devil.' Others said, if I was possessed at all, it certainly was not with a melancolly spirit.

(ii.) "On Monday, Jan. 10, Sara Williams was said to have had a merveilous great fit at Hackney. The priest said to her, 'There is one here who hath the vertigo, what sayest thou of him?' Sara or her devill made aunswer, 'The vertigo indeede, that is all nonsense.' The priest sayd, 'Was any devill cast out of him?' And Sara or her devill aunswered, 'A very little one.' Then the priests tooke confidence, and told me I was certainlie dispossessed of one devill while I was at Denham. Saras devill furthermore told them there was stil in mee Modu the prince of devils. The priests asked her how this devill came into mee, and Saras deville aunswered, 'It was when he left the *fratres minimi*.'

(iii.) "When the priests had finished theyr busines at Hackney, they returned to mee, to cast out prince Modu. It fel out thus. I went to daunce, and daunced all night, which cast me in so great a sweat that I had a return of my old complaint. Som of the priests hearing of my attack, said it was no mervaile, as I had the prince of devils in me. Wel, the priests came and wrought upon me as before, but when they said they had cast the devill out, I found myselfe neither better nor worse than I was before, and this caused mee to think the whole thing an imposition. The priests now sent for one doctor Griffith who gave mee som physicke, but as it did mee no good, they declared I must needes be possessed. I was then caried back to Denham, and maister Edmunds [Weston] the chiefe of the priests was thought to be the meetest man to tackle so greate a devill. There was a great resort to the place where we were, and expectation was on tiptoe thinking to see som straunge sight. The course which maister Edmunds held with me was much more rigorous then that of the other priests. When I did not frame myselfe to his liking, hee gave me the most loathsome drinks, and filthy confections; and sometimes burnt under my nose the most stinking drugges; which heats and smels, together with their sack and oyle, made me talke and rage as if I had beene mad. Being thus dealt with, I became weake and sicklie, and to gain a little respite I resolved to frame myselfe to their liking: I omitted no occasion of going to confession; I pretended to see lights on the fingers of the priests; I shewed the utmost zeale at masse time; at the elevation I pretended to see extraordinarie lights, and sometimes fel backwards as if I could not abide the glare. I protest before God this was all a sham, but maister Edmunds would make long discourses about mee, and prove the real presence from these feints and words of mine, which were altogether untrue.

(iv.) "I furthermore found it did wel content the priests if I rayled against them sometimes, and praised the protestants, the ministers, the magistrates, and those in chiefe authoritie. So I set myselfe to fool them to their bent, and the catholiques present tooke great contentment at my speeches. By this means I did escape sometimes theyr loathsome drinks, and intolerable fumes. [He was now between sixteen and seventeen years of age.]

(v.) "I was next taken to the earle of Lincolnes house in Channon-row, and it soon got abroad that maister Edmunds was about to deale with mee. Soe I pretended to traunces and visions, having been told of such things by the priests, and read of them in their bookes. The very first sunday I was in Channon-row I fained to be in a traunce, and raved about purgatory, what I had seen and heard there. And I told maister Edmunds that these traunces and visions would occur every sunday at the same hour till Good Friday, when I should die, and be carried up to heaven. I also pretended to prophecy; I foretold great afflictions and persecutions to the catholiques in England, and of comming warres and national troubles. I confess, however, that my prophecies and forebodings were always framed on leading questions put to me by maister Edmunds. In some of my traunces I would make strange exclamations as if I saw Christ accompanied with angels, or the Virgin Mary attended with a trayne of virgins. At such times I would call on all present to fal downe upon theyr knees, and maister Edmunds with the rest would fal upon their [*sic*] knees, and lift up theyr hands as if Christ and the Virgin had been there indeede. I avowe that I never saw any thing more than usual, but only did frame myselfe to doe so; and I verilie believe that maister Edmunds saw through it all, and acted as he did only to induce the rest to follow his example. I am told that maister Edmunds [Weston] has filled a quire of paper with my traunces and visions, but if ever his booke doe come to light, I will not faile to give my aunswer to it. In the mean time I declare that all my traunces, and visions, and prophecies, and sufferings in purgatory, and all the rest, were entirely feigned by mee to please Father Edmunds, and gaine to myself a little notoriety; for I soon saw how eagerly the catholiques tooke it all in, and did seeme to wonder at me as a mervaile.

(vi.) "*The Good Friday when I was to die.* When Good Friday came there was an immense crowd collected where I was; but I must iet the priest tell what happened in his own words: 'Lying that day upon his bed, our brother Richard did make a most solemne exhortation, telling us that his houre was come. Hee exhorted all present to remaine constant in their profession, saying they had yet to beare the brunt of many persecutions, but hee who endureth to the end shall be saved. Then fel hee from exhortation unto prayer and desired all present to pray with him,—whereupon he began to recite the Litanie, all following the responses with great devotion. Hee then fell into a slumber, and after that into a traunce which lasted for two houres, when he awoke, fetched a great sighe, and said: "My hour is not yet come. Our blessed Ladie hath appeared to mee, and told mee there is yet worke for mee to doe." With that there began to be a muttering among the people, one asking another what hee could refer to. Whereuppon, maister Edmunds said, "It is not expedient to prolong the interview," and so the crowde dispersed.' What moved me to give out that I was going to die on Good Friday I cannot tell; but sure I am thee devise was both boyish and foolish. As far as I can gesse my whole drift was to make myself apparant. When maister Edmunds found out my trick, hee said it was all an illusion of Sathan, and that this must be made manifest out of hand by an exorcisme, but from Good Friday to St. Georges day I was left in peace. My old complaint then returned, and this gave occasion for him to take mee in hand againe.

(vii.) "*The seven deadly sins.* Mr. Edmunds and the rest did then deale very extreamely with mee, and I confesse that I did bend myselfe to all, under the hope of gaining my libertie. After maister Edmunds had exorcised and perfumed me, the devill, it is said, began to make his appearance; but I must set downe all that was done on that occasion in theyr owne wordes: 'By the commaund of maister Edmunds the devill confessed that his name was Modu, and that he had beside himselfe, seaven other devils, all captaines of great note, in the body of maister Mainy. Thereuppon, Father Edmunds commanded that all the seaven should come and shew themselves one by one; and as each one rose, that hee should make known his name and quality. Then maister Mainy did set his hands to his side, curled his haire, and used gestures of greate self approval; whereuppon Father Edmunds sayd aloud, "Lo! there the spirit of PRIDE." Then did the evill spirit exclaim, "I wil 'bide no longer with such rascall priests, but wil goe to Court, and brave it roundlie amongst the noble and mighty of the land." After which there was dead quiet, till Father Edmunds began his exorcismes againe; when suddenly maister Mainy began to swel himselfe out, to stare with his eyes, and cry excitedly, "Ten pounds per cent. Scrivener, make the bond, but harkye, I must have a pawne." Maister Edmunds asked the devill if he were the same as spake before, and hee aunswered, "Noe! but the former spirit is my deare companion." As the devill could only talke of money, loans, and usury, all the company agreed it was the spirit of COVETOUSNESSE. After awhile the exorcee recovering his fences, maister Edmunds began his exorcismes againe. He had not proceeded farre when a third spirit appeared. He manifested himself by singing filthy songs, and every worde he spake was ribaldry. Again the company cried with one voice, "It is the spirit of Lust or LUXURY." Maister Edmunds commanded the unclean spirit to be silent, and not to speak another word. Againe Father Edmunds did commence his exorcismes, and continued till one by one all the seaven devils had shown themselves. ENVY showed his qualitie by disdainfull lookes and contemptuous speeches. WRATH by furious gestures and doughty words. GLUTTONY by vomiting. SLOTH by gaping and snorting as if in sleepe. After all the seaven had shown themselves, Father Edmunds called up Modu himselfe. Whereupon this prince of darkness asked him how he liked his brethren? Then began hee to chafe, and declare hee would leave such scurvy dogges to goe to his good friends the protestants, who, he wel knew, would give him braver entertainment. On hearing this, Father Edmunds said aloud, "Feel assured, thou foul fiend, that I and all good catholiques are thy sworne ennemies, and will never make league with thee or any of thy kinde. I now command you all, by the power of my priesthood, to depart hence, and never to come back againe." Whereuppon Pride departed in the forme of a peacock; Sloth in the likenes of an asse; Envie under the similitude of a dogge; Gluttony as a wolfe; and so with all the rest.' I wel remember using some such gestures on St. Georges day, but I am perswaded the writer has dressed my words farre fairer than I spake them. In troth, the priests can make a faire tale out of anything. Of this be certaine, whatever I said or did it was lead up to, or suggested, or else I had beene before told of something similar. For as I was under seventeen yeeres of age, I doe not believe that such things would have come into my head unless I had beene instructed. Wee were always being told what this one or that possessed one had done or sayd, or some tale of exorcisme was read to us, to teach us how we ought to behave ourselves. As to the forme in which the seaven spirits departed, I am sure that this part of the description is eyther false altogether; or else I was led to my aunswers by the questions put to me; as, for example, 'whether Pride did not depart from me like a peacock,' and so of all the rest; or it may be that some of the priests said in my hearing that such and such devils assumed such and such formes. Pray God forgive them for their bad dealings with mee, but I have this comfort left, I am quite certaine I never was possessed, and that most of the things written or reported of mee are either highly coloured, or utterly untrue. Signed *Richard Mainy*."—Samuel Harsnet (afterwards archbishop of York), *Popish Impostures* (1604), Appendix, pp. 257–284.

Confession of Maister Anthonie Tyrrell, a Roman Catholic priest, written by his own hand and avouched upon oath, June 15, 1602. Many interrogatories being propounded to Antony Tyrrell respecting the casting out of devils by maister Edmunds (*alias* Weston) the Jesuit, and other seminary priests in the years 1585 and 1586 at Hackney, Denham, and other places, he set down his answers in writing, and the following are the most important:—

"*About the invasion of England.* In the yeere 1584 I and John Ballard, priest,* comming together from Rome, as we passed through Burgundy wee found there a great presse of souldiours, and were advertised that they were serving under the duc de Guise against England. Maister Crighton a Scotch Jesuit taken at sea the same year and brought to England, revealed the whole plot, and showed how far the pope and king of Spain were concerned therein. No doubt maister Edmunds (*alias* Weston), the chiefe of the Jesuits in England, was duly informed of the whole matter in which his owne societie was so deeply concerned. Soon after I reached England, in 1585, maister Martin Aray, a priest, met mee in Cheapside, and whispered in my eare, 'Be of good cheere, brother; for all is going on famously. The king of Spayne is almost ready with his forces, and wee shalbe sure of some good newes very shortly. Wherefore it standeth us now that be priests to further the catholic cause as much as lyeth in us.'

"*Exorcisms of Weston.* About the same time maister Edmunds (or Weston) was said to have cast out a devill from one Marwood, and Martin Aray said to me, 'The exorcismes of Father Edmunds will soon make the devils themselves confesse that theyr kingdom is come to an end.' Upon the dispossession of Marwood, many other priests, instigated to show their zeale in imitating him, did take in hand to cast out devils from Sara and Friswood Williams, William Trayford, Anne Smith, Richard Mainy, and Elizabeth Calthrop. The necke of this last named person was broken by a fall down some stayres. When I saw this course, it liked mee wel, and I became an actor therein. Our proceedings had for a time wonderfull success, and in the compasse of halfe a yeere the number reconciled to our church was three or foure thousand. In maister Edmunds his treatise hee sets forth that 'God permitteth some to be possessed that atheists may learne to acknowledge there is both a God and a Devill; and that the faith of the true church may be confirmed by the manifestation of the power left to her in casting out devils.' In the second part he says, 'Though protestants boast of being so neere the primitive church, yet can they not either discerne or cast out devils.' In the third part, speaking of the power of reliques and holy water,

* Ballard and Babington were both executed.

he tells us that 'St. Macarius by these means cured a woman who had been turned by magic into a mare, and that St. Peter hallowed bread, which averted the assault of certaine devils sent by St. Magus against him in the likenes of dogges.' He furthermore tells us how St. Martin 'put his finger into the mouth of a demoniack, and bade him bite it, but the devill durst not do it.' This brought us into great favor, credit, and repute, so it was no mervaile that some young gentlemen, like maister Babington, were allured to strange attempts which they tooke in hand.

"*Of the depositions of Williams, Smith, and Mainy.* I have read carefully the examinations and confessions of Sara Williams, Friswood her sister, Anne Smith, and Richard Mainy gentleman, and I am fully perswaded that they have deposed the truth respecting their possessions and dispossessions (!!). The effect whereof is—that they were allured by our cunning carriage of matters to seeme as though they were possessed, whenas in truth they were not so (!!). Nor were any of the priests ignorant of their own dissimulation in the matter (!!).

"*His opinion about exorcism.* After I had myselfe beene to one of theyr exorcismes, I chaunced to sleep in the Spittle with maister Thomson a maine actor in those matters. Falling into conversation about it, I said to him, I much doubted if any of the party was really possessed. Maister Thomsones answer was, 'I, being your friend, doe most earnestlie intreat you to cast forth to others no such words, whatsoever you may thinke. For the matter is judged to be veritable by Father Edmunds and others. And though I, for my owne part will not make it an article of my creede, yet I thinke that godlie credulitie doth much good for the furtherance of the catholick cause (!!), and tends to deface our common enemy the protestants, and their heretical proceedings.' St. Ambrose saith he never heard of any that could counterfeit to be a demoniack, but common experience hath taught us quite the contrarie (!!). The artificial skil whereunto priests have attained, makes it a very easy thing to bring a young girle or a youth, to doe and speake those things which any exorcist can readily colour and interpret as if it were done or spoken by devils (!!). I will give for a rule to all catholics that doe not wil to be deluded, doe but mark diligently what the parties said to be possessed doe eyther act or speak, and you shal readilie perceave there is nothing which may not be dissembled, or uttered under the influence of their loathsome potions, and violent fumigations (!!). But let those who see through these things keepe their owne counsel, or they wil be no welcome guests, I assure them. Let me recommend all curious in these matters to reade a French treatise by Martha Brossier on a counterfeit demoniack at Paris, and they will presently see how the exorcists would endure no question or doubt upon their work, and always pretended that idle curiosity did hinder them in their proceedings.

"*The knife-blade extracted from Anne Smith.* A chiefe objection to what I say about counterfeits wil be touching the piece of a knife, two and a halfe inches long, said to have come out of the bodie of Anne Smith, and to have been convaied into her by the devill. To explaine this matter wee are tolde that the devill would say, 'I am by creation a spirit, and have lost no part of my knowledge in the secrets of nature. I can therefore dissolve iron at pleasure into a liquid, and pour it into a porredge, so that Anne Smith should eat it and swallow it with her food. After she had so done I can restore it again to its original forme, and make it come out where I list.' To this I reply, the peece of the knife came out of the girles mouth without hurting her, —but answer me this, did it reallie come out of her mouth at all and that without shift or legerdemaine? But if it came out of her mouth, was it not first put there by the exorcist himselfe? Wee know that exorcists were in the habit of thrusting bigge bones and pieces of reliques into the mouthes of the possessed; and Friswood Williams deposed that shee verily believed they thrust a large rustie naile into her mouth, and then pretended that it came out of her stomack; and Anne Smith deposed that she was fully perswaded it has beene untruly reported that the priests did take out of her mouth a piece of a knife, howbeit, shee saith, though perswaded of the untruth, shee would not dare to contradict a priest. However, it is needless to argue on the matter, for it is so ridiculous that no man, I thinke, would be so mad as to take uppon himself to defend the report. When wee that were actors in these matters thought we had won our spurres, I wel remember that many older in yeeres, as maisters

Heywood, Dolman, Redman, and others, did shake their heads, and shew their mislike of it. Likewise many of the graver sort said, that howsoever for a time wee might be admired, yet in the end wee should marre all, and bring discredit on ourselves, and on our calling. We thought this was said in envie, but I verilie believe that they had seen these things done beyond the seas, and were truly greeved to see them introduced into England. Notwithstanding all that was said, maister Edmunds and the rest would needes proceede, and have proved to their shame, that their cautious elders were true prophets."

The Books of miracles by Maister Barnes. "The examinates were questioned from the bookes by the penn of maister Barnes, in which I myselfe tooke part. It was I who layd together those things that Sara Williams was pretended to have said and done. What I saw myself and what I heard from others I layd together with the best skill I had to make them seeme strange and wonderfull. For though I knew they were all false, yet forasmuch as we did gain great credit therefrom, and added thousands to the catholic church, besides heaping great discredit on the protestants, I held it lawfull and right so to doe, and soe did all those who acted with mee."

No faith to be kept with heretics. "It is a generall conceit with all priests that they may deny anything the confession of which would turne to the dishonour of their church or its administers. Besides, as the magistrates of England and the queen herselfe are all under excommunication, the examinations taken before them are idle and have no force to bind examinates. It is true that the apostle says 'we are not to doe evill that good may come of it,' but then we do not think it evill to deceive hereticks or to calumniate protestants by any devise whatsoever; nor doe we make it any conscience to tell and to publish abroad any untruthes which we thinke will defend or advance any doctrine or dogma or other matter which is for the honour of our church and for the dignitie of its priesthood."—Samuel Harsnet (afterwards archbishop of York), *Popish Impostures* (1604), Appendix, 246–256.

This letter, written by Antony Tyrrell, a Jesuit priest, is most astounding. Had it been written by any Anglican of the present century, it would be set down as a base calumny, but it so dovetails with the examinations included in the same appendix, and the whole is so verbally copied from the public records, that the mind is quite bewildered as it asks, "Can such things be, and be thought to be religion?"

Examinations of Friswood Williams, March 2, 1598, and May 17, 1602. "Friswood Williams was the sister of Sara Williams, and about seventeen years of age. She was taken into the service of Mistrisse Peckham, of Denham, Buckinghamshire, (daughter of Sir Thomas Jarret, Lancashire, and wife of Mr. Edmund Peckham) because her sister Sara was in the hands of the priests, because she was possessed. Many priests resorted to Denham under pretence of casting out devils, the chief of them were Maister Edmunds a Jesuit, and next to him was Maister Dibdale; others who acted under these two were maisters Driland, Middleton, Yaxley, Sherwood, Stampe, Tyrrell, Thomson, Thulice, Cornelius, Browne, Ballard, Blackman, Greene, Bruerton, and many others whose names she did not know or could not remember. Upon first coming to Denham, the examinate heard much of her sister's fits, and of those of William Trayford, Maister Peckham's man. Her own father was in the service of Sir George Peckham. Not long after her Mistris came from Fulmer, Marwood and Maister Richard Mainy were brought to Denham, both pretending they were possessed. Maister Ballard the priest brought Marwood to Denham, and in his [Ballard's] companie were twelve or thirteen others, as Maisters Babington, Tichburne, Dun, Gage, Tilny, and so on. Friswood Williams always went to the [protestant] church before she came to Denham, but then the priests laboured to perswade her to become a catholique. The parties that first dealt with her were her master, and one Alexander the apothecarie, (since then a priest). In about five or six weekes the priests began to perswade her that shee was possessed. The first occasion was this: Shee was washing clothes in Denham kitchen, when Alexander came in, and clapping her on the shoulder, said her mistrisse wanted her. Shee answered shee would go when she had done, which would be in a minute or so. Presently one of her fellowe servants filled a tub with water to rince the clothes, and as shee [Friswood] lifted the tub, her foot slipped and shee fel. The fal was so shrewd that shee hurt her hip, and was compelled to keepe her bed for two or three days. Heereupon Maister Dibdale came and told her it was the devill who had played her this jades trick, because shee had washed his [Dibdale's] shirt. The devill, hee said could not abide him, because hee was a priest; and spited any one who showed him any kindnes. Hee said the devill was specially spiteful, because the shirt shee had washed for him was fould with sweat, forced from him while exorcising different parties. Hee then most urgentlie exhorted her to become a catholique, and never ceased telling her that shee was possessed. All the other priests told her the same thing, and assured her shee would receive greate comfort if shee would doe as they told her. When maister Dibdale spoke to her about the ache in her hip, hee asked if ever before the fall shee had felt any sort of paine in her body. Shee confessed to him shee had sometimes a paine in the side; 'Ah!' quoth hee, 'I thought as much. Out of all question you are possessed, and have been soe for a long time. That paine in the side, you speak of, is undoubtedly from some evill spirit.' Being over perswaded that shee really was possessed, they next told her they could doe nothing for her unless shee became a catholick. That while shee remained as shee was, shee was in a state of damnation. They reminded her that shee herselfe said in her owne creede that shee believed in the 'holy catholick church,' and not in the protestant church which was heretical; in short, they induced her to join the [Roman] catholicks, and have her baptisme amended. In amending her baptisme, they cast over her head a white cloth with a crosse on it, put salt into her mouth, and annointed her lippes, nose, eyes, and eares. They changed her name from Friswood to Francis, which they told her was common to both men and women. As the paine in her hip continued, and they never ceased telling her it was certainly the devill, shee came to believe that shee was really possessed, but the doctors told her the paine was only a griefe of the spleene. After shee became a catholique the priests told her they would try to cast the devill out of her, and they proceeded thus: At the close of her first masse, maister Dibdale told her, they were going to make tryall of her, and shee must sit downe in a chayre. Shee did as they told her. Then they bound her with towells, whereat shee was cast into a great feare, not knowing what they meant to doe with her. Maister Dibdale then read from his booke of Exorcismes, and they forced on her their drinke, which was a pint of sack and sallet-oyle, mingled with spices. When shee had tasted their 'holy potion,' as they termed it, it did so much dislike her, that her stomacke turned against it, and shee refused to drink it; but the priests told her it was the devill in her which caused this mislike, for nothing the devill loathed so much as the holy potion. They then held her, and forced her to swallow the whole draught. Heereupon, shee was very sicke and giddie, her head reeled, and shee fel all over into a cold sweate, so terriblie bad did shee feele, that shee really believed it was the devill in her as they said, which caused her to be in such case; but when shee came to herselfe, shee felt perswaded it was the drinke that had made her so sicke and bad. Between Christmas and Whitsonday this abuse was often repeated, and when shee proved restive, they did burne brimstone in a chafing-dish and hold her face downe over the fumes, in which cases, no doubt, shee spake many things which shee could not recall to memorie. Whenever shee complained of their harde usage, the priests told her, It was not shee who spake, but the devill in her. If shee referred to the matter when shee was wel, they told her shee would by that meanes merit heaven, and gaine a crowne of glory. The priests, shee said, would often tell her about women possessed beyond the seas; how the devills in them never could abide the 'holy potion,' or hallowed brimstone, or the application of reliques, or the touch of a true priest, or holy water, holy candels, or the blessed sacrament,—they would always start at such times, say they burned, rage, rail against the priest, and praise all protestant practices. By this meanes shee learnt what to say, so as to please the priests; and accordingly, when they brought to her reliques, shee used to start, and sometimes shee pretended shee could not beare the presence of the sacrament; but after five or six weekes of this sort of thing shee got tired of it, and came to her senses.

"Shee said on one occasion when shee was in the chayre, Maister Sherwood thrust a pinne into her shoulder, whereat shee screamed, but maister Sherwood only said 'Doe you not heare the devill?' 'It is not the devill,' exclaimed the examinate, 'but myselfe who screamed.' Hee would not believe her, but persisted it was the devill in her which had cried out."

Needles in the leg. "In one of my fits, into which I was cast by the 'holy potion' and hallowed brimstone, needels were thrust into my legge. On coming to myselfe I complained of it, and one of the priests got some holy reliques, and tyed them about my legge. I was then taken to the gallerie, and Maister Dibdale bade me let down my hose. Hee then with others untyed the reliques, looked upon the woundes, washed them with holy water, and gently closed the flesh. Then holding up the needles, he said to all present (the number was very great), 'see what the devil has done to our sister here.' The people were in a greate maze, but as soon as this was done I was taken out of the gallerie, and my legge began to amend."

Relics thrust into the mouth. "The examinate further said, The priests have a custom of thrusting things into the mouthes of such as they say are possessed. I wel remember their thrusting a relique into my mouth. I cried out, 'Why doe you put this filthy thing into my mouthe?' 'Ah,' quoth they, 'hark how the devill hates a holy relique.' I was then asked if I knew what relique it was, I told them it was a piece of Campion's thumbe; whereupon maister Dibdale said to the people, 'See, how the devil knows all holy reliques.' But the truth is these reliques which they employed were daily in our sight, and we were taught to know one from another, so that I knew in a moment every one of them, and could say readilie, 'This is a peece of Father Campion; this of Maister Sherwin; this of Maister Brian; this of Maister Cottam; this of mistris Clithero;' and so on through all the lot. At another time I remember, when they thrust a relique into my mouth, they introduced a bigge rustie naile; and when they pulled out the relique, and I was almost choked with the naile, they made me open my mouthe, and taking out the naile, told the people it had been drawn out of my stomack by the vertue of the relique."

The knives and halter. "Alexander, an apothecarie, on one occasion, brought with him from London to Denham a new halter and two large knife-blades. These hee laid upon the gallerie floare in my maister-his house. Next morning hee took occasion to goe with me into the gallerie, when, espying the halter and blades, I asked him what they were for. Hee pretended not to see them, but I pointed them out to him, they were not a yarde of [off]. 'I cannot see them,' quoth the apothecarie. So I picked them up, and said, 'Look here.' 'Ah!' quoth hee, 'I see them now. No doubt the devill layd them there to worke some mischief.' Now, I know that Maister Alexander had brought them with him, for I noticed them in his pocket the night before, when hee drew out of it some wafer-cakes for masse. I told this to maister Dibdale, but hee replied, 'Ah! it is not you that speake, I know very well, but the devill in you, and the devill was a lyar from the beginning.' I was made to paye smartly for what I said, for they had me in the chayre, and exorcised me in somewhat a new manner. They bound me, sore against my will, in the chayre, forced down my throat the 'holy potion,' burnt brimstone under my nose, and pulling off my gowne, did whippe mee uppon my arms with 'St. Peter's girdle,' pretending it was to hunt the devill out of mee. They gave mee five blows in remembrance of the five wounds, seven blowes in honour of the seaven sacraments; and three in memory of the blessed Trinitie. Being constrained to cry out, they all said, 'It is only the devill that is crying out, because hee cannot abide the vertue of the holy girdle.' Certes, if it was the devill in mee that cryed out, I assuredly bore the smart, and my arms were blacke for a month after."

Hunting the devil upwards. "The examinate further said, The priests have another custome: At the end of every exorcisme, they would say, 'Ah! the devill is gone downe into the foote, or great toe.' Then in the presence of the congregation they would bring the partie againe to the chayre, and make the devill shew himself. I was once so hunted before a crowd of people. Being bound in the chayre, the exorcist, holding a relique in his hand, (such as a bone or some other hard substance) grasped my legge, and asked me if I felt any paine. I replied 'yes,' for the bone or other hard substance in his hand hurt me very much. 'Ah!' said the exorcist, 'so hee is beginning to stir, is hee?' Then hee went on pinching my legge two or three times; when hee came to my knee, he did wring it so hard that I screeched. Then all the priests exclaimed, 'Now then, wee have got the devill into her body, God be praised.' Then I was given the holy potion to abate the force of the evill spirit, lest it should teare mee a pieces."

Her complaint. "One day sitting at my worke, I complained to Maister Sherwood, who thrust the pinn into my shoulder, of the harde usages I was put to, and told him I mervailed greatlie how hee and the others durst so deale with mee; adding, if I were to complaine before a magistrate, they would all be hanged. Maister Sherwood was feared [frightened], and was for dismissing mee from the house, but Maister Dibdale said that would not doe. They then both came to mee, and said, 'The devil is not yet gone out.' Whereupon, they forced mee into the chayre, drugged mee horribly with their holy potion, and plagued mee with brimstone till I swound."

Maister Richard Mainies seaven devils. "I wel remember Maister Richard Mainie being exorcised on St. Georges day before a hundred people at the least. Hee certainly was the most dissembling hypocrite on Gods earth. The priests averred hee was possessed of the seaven deadly sins, and as hee was exorcised these seaven devils showed themselves thus: Maister Mainy being bound in the chayre, did first lift up his head, loking contemptuously, and making gestures with his hands as if tricking himselfe with bravery. When this had been played out sufficiently, the priests said, 'The devill now coming out of the possessed, is the spirit of Pride.' Hee next began to gape, and snort, and loll about, and the priests said, the devill now coming out is the spirit of Sloth. Then hee fell to vomiting, and the priests said, the devill now coming out of the possessed is the spirit of Gluttony. Again the said Maister Mainy began to prate of money, and about so much per hundred, of leases, and forfeyts, and the priests said the devill now coming out is the spirit of Covetousness. Thus hee and the priests went through all the seaven deadly sins. Then did Maister Mainy highly praise the protestants, especially the earle of Bedford (one that the priests greatlie abhorred), because they had all the seaven deadly sins; and hee railed soundlie on the catholiques because they would not tolerate any of these sins, but cut them all of [off] by the institution of confession. In conclusion hee said, 'This is a greate daye at court. I will stay no longer amongst you raskall half-starved priests; but will hence away to my fellows. I am loved at court. They all are mine at court.'"—Harsnet, *Popish Impostures*, Appendix, pp. 207-236.

Her examination upon oath, March 2, 1598, before the bishop of London, the dean of Westminster, Dr. Stanhop, and Dr. Swale. (See above, p. 190.)

The examination of Anne Smith on oath, March 12, 1598 (age about eighteen). Anne Smith had a sister in the service of lady Stafford, and some three weeks before Christmas she heard from her about Sara Williams and William Trayford being possessed, in Mr. Peckham's house. Her sister said she went down to Denham and saw both persons, but noticed nothing strange about either of them. On Christmas Eve Anne Smith went to Denham to call on her sister, and saw William Trayford, but "hee did not make any shew, as though hee was possessed; hee waited quite orderly on his maister. Sara Williams had gone to lord Vaux-his house, being taken thither by one Dibdale a priest. After I had beene at Denham about a moneth I attended upon Mistres Peckham to a churching, and had a return of my disease called the mother (*histeria*), and one White, a priest that used much the house told mee I was possessed, and the next day Cornelius, Stamp, Thomson, Christopher Tulice, and some other priests tooke upon themselves to exorcise me, and I was under their hands from morning till towards night. As I did not recover my health, I was sent to Mistris Mainy in Channon Row, where I remained til the beginning of Lent. Here I became acquainted with Eliza Calthrope who was said to be possessed, and was removed to Greenes Alley, where she was exorcised by maister Mainy. About three weekes after easter I consented to be exorcised hoping thereby to recover my health, but I always had a conceite in myselfe that I was not possessed. When, however, I told the priests so, they said it was the delusion of the devill within mee, who did not wish to be cast out. Maister Stamp carried mee to Denham, and wee were accompanied by one Harris, maister Mainyes man. I was under the hands of the exorcists from Easter to Whitsontide. About a fortnight after Whitsontide, pursuivants came and carried to prison maister Dryland the priest, Alexander the apothecary, Swythen Wells, James Stanborow (Maister Peckham's man), and two women. Soon afterwards Dibdale, Lowe, and Adams, were apprehended, and I was arraigned to give evidence, because it got wind that I did pretend to be possessed, and that the priests had dealt with mee. I was examined especially touching the devils which possessed mee, and touching a peece of knife which the priests averred came out of my body. When first I fell into the priestes hands I was about eighteen years old. The way I was exorcised was as follows: Cornelius and the rest did set mee in a chayre, and bind mee fast with towells. Then putting on his albe and stole, hee began to reade his exorcismes. I did greatlie shiver and quake at his words, and was strooke with a terrible feare lest the devill should teare mee a pieces, while I was fast bound. I thought if I could but have gotten under the altar-cloath, with a crosse in my mouth and a candel in my hand I should be safe, but I could not so much as move. They gave me some holy medicine which had rue and oyle in it to allay my fear. The drink was very ugly to behold, and they did burn brimstone under my nose, which did take away my senses. This was repeated some five or six times. My arms and body were so lamed by their holding, tying, and turmoyling of mee, that I was obliged to swathe my body for three yeeres afterwards. I mervail greatly how the priests can affirm that I said anything in my fits, seeing they always insisted that the devill in mee was a dumbe spirit, named Modion. After Cornelius had exorcised mee maister Edmunds the Jesuit [*i.e.* Weston] asked the devill in Mainy if I was possessed, and Mainyes devill answered that I was. Then quoth maister Edmunds, how is it hee could not be brought to speak the other day when Cornelius exorcised her? Mainyes devill replied because Modion was sullen and dumbe. Maister Edmunds then asked the name of Mainyes devill, and the devill answered, his name was Soforce.

"Finally, I wel remember the morning when Alexander the apothecarie went to London to fetch more priests. The day before I was exorcised, his horse praunced, and flung him. On his return backe hee insisted that it was the devill in mee which had troubled his horse, out of spite. When I laught at his words, he said, 'Ah, Anne, it is the devill in you that laughs at mee.'"—Samuel Harsnet (afterwards archbishop of York), *Popish Impostures*, Appendix, pp. 237-245.

It appears from the narrative that Alexander was executed at Holborn. Salisbury was also executed.

Examination of Sara Williams, said to be possessed with Maho and all the devils of hell, April 24, 1602. Sara Williams, aged about sixteen, in the service of Mistris Edmund Peckham of Denham, Buckinghamshire, was said to be possessed of the devil Maho. A number of priests, acting under Weston the Jesuit, undertook to exorcise her. She afterwards married William Trayford, Mr. Peckham's man, left the service of Mrs. Peckham, and returned to the protestant faith from which she had been converted, while she was in the service of Mrs. Peckham. She wholly denies that she ever was possessed, but Maister Dibdale, an exorcist, insisted that she was not only possessed, but that she lodged in her body all the devils of hell. The case was brought before her Majesty's Commissioners for Ecclesiastical Causes, and tried before the bishop of London, the dean of Westminster (Dr. Andrews), Dr. Stanhope, and Dr. Mountford, and the following items are copied from the records of the court. The person called the Examinate is Sara Williams. The trial began by reading to the examinate, from Barnes's *Booke of Miracles*, the way it was said she first began to be possessed, and how she was exorcised.

(i.) "It is stated in the book how Sara Williams had been diverse times scared with ugly visions: How sitting one night late by the fire three terrible cats sprauled about her, one of which leapt over her head, another crept betweene her legs: How a strange cat as big as a mastiffe stared uppon her with eyes as big as a saucer: And how afterward the same wicked spirit met her in the likenes of a cat, comming out of a hollow tree, as shee was seeking for eggs."

Sara Williams's reply. "All these things thus written of mee are most false. From a child I could never endure the sight of a cat, and when in the service of Maister Maynie, at Denham, going one day into a wood, near the house, looking for some hennes, I espyed a cat comming out of a hedge, which did fear [frighten] mee greatly, the more so as I was alone. I told this to my Mistris and to certaine priests. As for ugly visions I declare upon oath I never had any. It is wholly false that a cat ever did leape over my head, or runne betwixt my legges, or that I ever saw any cat as big as a mastiffe, with eyes as broad as a saucer."

(ii.) The next allegation in the book is as follows: "On Oct. 12, 1585, being at supper in the house of Mistris Peckham, Sara Williams did perceive a puffe of wind comming in at the doore; and saw a dog of two collours, blacke and greene: That therewith a spaniell of the house bayed once: Shee was then pulled by the eyes; and the thing that pulled her by the eyes, went into her mouth, and, resting at her heart, burnt her intolerablie: That thereupon shee cast away her knife, and would eat no more."

Sara Williams's reply. "O Jesus, that anyone should report so of mee. What happened was as follows: Being at supper, there was a great storme of thunder and lightning; and at one great clap of thunder, the dogges ran out of the hall barking. I was greatly alarmed, left my supper, and felt sick. More then this I deny upon oath to bee true.

"Shee further deposed, that after comming to Mistris Peckham, diverse men did attempt to offer her some injury, and among the rest Maister Dibdale the priest; insomuch that when her Mistris would send her with water to his chamber, or uppon any other busines, and shee shewed herself unwilling to go, they said her unwillingnes did proceed from a wicked spirit that was in her. Shee could never endure to be ever in Maister Dibdales company, or to goe into his chamber."

(iii.) The third allegation was this: "That shee could not abide Maister Dibdales presence for burning, especially when hee laid his hand upon her diseased place. That shee said, her master had commaanded her not to bless herselfe with the signe of the crosse; and that shee could not indure a casket of reliques. That shee knew shee was possessed; and that the devill was in her maister."

Sara Williams's reply. "When I came to live with Mistris Peckham, shee taught me to blesse myself in Latine, and at some words to make a crosse on my forhead, at others on my belly, at others on one of my shoulders, and with the last words upon my breast. Being dull to learne, it was a long time before I could doe these rightly. So that when my Mistris and Maister Dibdale wanted mee to blesse myself, and to use the signes of the crosse, being very evil at ease that night after the lightning, I could not hit upon the right words. Also in saying the Creed, I stumbled at the word 'Catholicke Church.' Otherwise I declare that all the particulars just read to mee are most false.

(iv.) "It was alleged in the book that shee said, Her father and mother were in a damnable state for going to the [protestant] church; and that it was dangerous for little children to goe to the church."

Sara Williams's reply. "These charges are most false. On Oct. 17, the day stated, I was not then a recusant, nor disliked going to the church. It was about this time they began to give mee things to drink, which I could not endure, as they made mee sicke; Maister Dibdale told mee, 'it was not I who disliked the "holy water," but the devil within mee.' About a fortnight after, they prevailed on mee to become a [Roman] catholic, altho' at the time the devill was within mee, as they said. When I attended mass, the first time they told mee, I should see a blacke man standing at the doore, beckning mee to come away; and that at the elevation I should see nothing but priestes fingers. What I myself said I really do not know, for I often told them things which were untrue, after I saw that it pleased them. On Oct. 30 they bound mee in the chayre, and applyed their reliques to mee; but whenever I came to the chayre, if I could have had my choice, I would rather have died than have gone into it."

[It will be here necessary to explain what she meant by "going into the chayre." Chap. 9, p. 30–45. At the end of the first mass that ever she saw, Mr. Dibdale said he would now make trial of her, and bade her sit down in the chair. Several priests bound her with towels, at which she was terribly frightened, not knowing what they meant to do with her. Mr. Dibdale then began to read his "Booke of Exorcismes," and handed to her a pint of sack and sallet oil, mingled with spices; but her stomach turned against the potion, and she declined to drink it. Then Dibdale told her, it was the devil in her which made her loathe the holy potion, for the devil hated nothing worse than this holy drink; so she was held, and made to drink it all up. Hereupon, she grew very sick, giddy in the head, and covered all over with a cold sweat. Dibdale assured her it was the devil that tormented her thus. This was the first part of the "chayre busines." The next was, while her stomach was full of the "holy drink" to make her take brimstone, burnt on a chafing dish. Her head was forcibly held over the fumes, and Richard Maynie says, when he looked on her, her face was blacker than that of a chimney-sweep. [Here six lines are lost in my copy, the paper not having received the impression of the type.] "The brimstone mixture is thus given in Flag. Dæmon. p. 173. *Accipiatur sulphur, galbanum,* etc. that is, 'Take brimstone, assafœtida, galbanum, St. John's wort, and rue. All these things are to be hallowed, and cast on a chafing dish, and the fumes thereof are to be received through the nostrils of the possessed.' This potion and these fumes did so intoxicate the examinate, that although two needles were thrust into her legs by one of the priests, she was not aware of it till after she had recovered. When she complained of this inhuman usage, they 'had her to the chayre again, and she swound.' On coming to herself, she told the priests if she had the devill in her, for God's sake to cast him out, or else kill her outright, for she could not bear it any longer. She told the commissioners she had no clear idea of the number of times she was set on the chair, but she added, 'I would much sooner have died, then have gone into it.' And she furthermore said, 'they used their holy brimstone so much, that the smell never got out of her chamber; and the loathsomeness of their potions and fumes did so stick in her mind, that to this very day she cannot endure the taste of any of the things with which she was then tormented.'"] She continued, "Being at Oxford a few days ago, one of my neighbours offered me a glass of sack, upon which I fell sick, and was obliged to goe to bed. While my head was held over the brimstone fumes, one of the priestes burnt feathers which made mee screame, and struggle to get away, till I fainted; no doubt, she added, I babbled many foolish things in my sufferings. Being unable to bear this persecution, I attempted to run away, but was captured while crossing a brook half-a-yard deep of water, and was taken back by my tormentors."

(v.) The next extract was this, p. 23. "Shee could not speake till Dibdale or some other of the priests had signed her throat with the signe of the crosse, and applyed holy reliques to it."

Sara Williams's reply. "I have no recollection whatever of any such thing, but I think it is altogether untrue. If, however, I was at any time unable to speake, it was by reason of the said waters and fumes which they forced upon mee. If again I was at any time silent, and did afterwards speake, it was not because the priestes did signe my throat with the signe of the crosse, or did apply reliques unto it. Whenever I did speak anything, the priestes always expounded my words according to their own liking, and either said they were the words of the devill, or that they were spoken by vertue of the holy potion."

(vi.) The next allegation read to her was this: "Shee did affirm that she saw the devill, in the form of a man, go out of her on Al Saints day; and when the devill left her, shee did use these words, 'Credo sanctam ecclesiam catholicam.'"

Sara Williams's reply. "God forgive them the falsehood! They well know it is all false; and this I would swear even if all the priestes were here present."

(vii.) The next extract read to her ran thus: "Shee, Sara Williams, did declare to Maister Dibdale and others, that a bird came to her: A blacke man at one time tried to persuade her to breake her necke downe a payre of staires, and at another time to cut her throat with a knife: That shee affirmed shee saw, on one occasion, the forme of a rough dog uppon the communion table: And that shee felt within her a grunting like of swyne, and a croaking like of a toade: That shee confessed to having receeved her sight by the touch of the priestes fingers, or by their breathing uppon her."

Sara Williams's reply. "It pittieth my hart that anyone who pretends to have any conscience should so write of mee. I confess that on one occasion a bird came suddenly flying in where I was, and I was scared; but I stroke the bird, which was a robin redbreast, with my beades; and it escaped through a hole in the boords. All the other statements are fabrications."

(viii.) "It is set down in the book that shee said, Shee wel remembered how William Trayford [the manservant] seemed one night to be greatly troubled; and afterwards pretending to be sodainly wel, Maister Dibdale the priest having catched him in his armes: That shee saw the devill in the forme of a mouse offer to come out of Trayfordes mouth, but, being hindered by the priestes mouth, it made its way out at his right ear."

Sara Williams's reply. "These things are all fained and false. Shee furthermore added, I wel remember when I was with them, they spake many things of mee, which I knew to be false, but I durst not say so, for fear of offending them."

(ix.) "It is written of her in the book that shee said,—By crying upon God and the blessed Lady, and by casting holy water upon William Trayford, shee made the devill leave hold of him; it was in the likenes of a toad, and shee catched it by the leg."

Sara Williams's reply. "Jesus have mercy upon mee! God is my witnes that all this is a shamefull untruth."

(x.) The following statement was then read to her: "The priests affirm that according to her own acknowledgment, they delivered her from these twenty-three devils, viz. Lustie Dick, Killico, Hob, Cornercup, Puffe, Purre, Frateretto, Fliberdigibet, Haberdicut, Cocobatto, Maho, Kellicocam, Wilkin, Smolkin, Nur, Lustie, Jolly Jenkin, Portericho, Pudding of Thame, Pourdieu, Bonjour, Motubizanto, Bernon, and Delicate."

Sara Williams's reply. "There were very strange names, said to be those of spirits, written on the wals of Sir George Peckhames house. When the priests told me it was the devill who spoke in mee, and asked mee the name, in order to content them I devised one of these names as near as I could remember, for they were always running into my head; I think, however, the priestes themselves must have amended my words. The name of Maho is very familiar to mee, from a tale in which the name occurs; the name of Lustie Dick is also mentioned in the same tale. As for the three captaine devils, that the priests say went out of my eares, every one of the captaines having three hundred devils under him, all lodged in different parts of my body, I declare upon oath it is an abominable untruth, and I mervail much what they can refer to."

(xi.) In regard to her running away from Mrs. Peckham's house, she said: "When I came to the brooke, meaning to run through it, I was catched and sent backe againe; I was very diligently watched, and never at any time allowed to goe out of sight. The pretence of this watchfullness was least I should make away with myselfe, which, thank God, never entered into my thoughts. Maister Peckham gave it out, after my return home, that I did runne all the way above ground, and the priestes insisted that devils carried mee through the air. This they make out to be a kind of miracle, but I know it is only a wicked lye. It is true I ranne home as fast as I could, but as to flying it is a meer fable."

(xii.) "Concerning Captain Frateretto, with his three hundred evil spirits, as is set down in the booke, under date of Nov. 21, the examinate deposed, It is the custom of the priestes to talk of persons possessed beyond the seas, and to tell us the manner of theyr fits, and what they say in them; also what sights they see, sometimes ugly, and sometimes joyfull. They also tel us how, when reliques are applyed to them, the persons would roare. Wee were often told that devills can never abide holy water, the sight of the sacrament, or an annointed priest of the true church. but that they love hereticks. They told us, whenever a priest touches a party possessed, the touch feels burning hot, and that devills know a priest by his smel. These things I heard so often that I learnt the way of pleasing the priests, and framed myselfe accordingly knowing well the reason why wee were told these things. At one time shee continued, the priests did thrust into my mouth a relique, which was a piece of one of Campiones bones. I loathed it, thinking it against nature to have a dead manes [man's] bone thrust into my mouth; but I could not help myselfe, as it was done by force."

(xiii.) To deposition p. 36, the examinate said: "I wel remember walking in the garden with one of the priestes, who led mee by the arme, because I was very weake. I began to complaine to himm of my hard usage, and told him I was no more possessed than hee was. Whereupon hee cast his head aside, and looking full into my face under my hatte, exclaimed, 'What! can this bee Sara, or is it the devill in her that speaketh thus? No, no! It cannot bee Sara, it must bee the devill.' I instantly saw I could expect no relief at his hands, and I fell aweeping. The priest said, 'Alas! these are the teares of the evil spirit in thee, Sara.' If I wept it was the devill, if I laught it was the devill. I was at my wits end."

(xiv.) "When I was at Denham, Maister Richard Maynie [a young gentleman seventeen years old] pretended to be possessed, and behaved himself in the presence of the priests, as though hee had been a sainte. It was mervaillous to see his pretended devotion. One time, at masse, at the time of the elevation, hee fel downe secretly backwards, and laye awhile as if in a traunce. When hee came to himselfe againe, hee said it was the glory hee saw about the altar which had struck him into the traunce. This young gentlemann tried to persuade mee to runn away with him in boyes clothing. At another time hee told mee to confess to him, and said hee had as good authority to hear confessions as the priestes had. I told Maister Dibdale of these things, and said if hee did not take good heed, Maister Maynie would bring them into trouble. Whereupon, Maister Dibdale said hee was sorry hee ever had any dealings with the youth."

(xv.) "Thee times they pretended I had fits, were either when the mother fits were on mee, or when I had been constrained to drinke their holy potions, or else when I was ill at ease by reason of their bad usage. They would then say, the wicked spirits had gone downe into my legges, and beginning with my foot they would hunt the devill upwards with their hands, pinching every inch of my body from my toe to my head, to make the devill goe forth from my mouthe, eares, or nose. As they ran their hands over mee I was put to much shame, especially when they desired to apply their reliques in a way no modest woman would allow. I perfectly loathe the memory of the way these priests treated mee [when only about sixteen years of age]."

(xvi.) "While I was at Denham one Haines was a suter to mee, but Maister Dibdale commanded mee in no sort to entertain him. My sister brought mee a jet ring from Haines as a token. I putt it on, but as it was too smal, it caused my finger to swel. Maister Dibdale said, as I had acted contrary to his commaund the devill had got under the ring. Hee then wetted my finger with holy oyle, and making crosses on it pulled the ring of [off] little by little, and told mee the devill had no power to keepe it on, after those crosses had been made."

(xvii.) "One night when I was in bedde, there was a scratching in the seeling of my chamber. I thought it was a ratt, but Maister Cornelius, a priest, who occupied the next room, came into my chamber in his gowne, and declared it was an evill spirit. Hee then charged the devill, upon paine of many torments, to depart. Hee flung holy water on the wals, and used much holy exorcisme. Albeit the scratching continued, nor did it cease till Maister Cornelius knockt uppon the seeling with a stick. I then thought, and doe still, that it was a ratt, though the priest insisted it was a devill."

(xviii.) "I was always obliged to tel the priests of a morning what I had dreamt about at night. They called the dreams visions, and interpreted them as they thought proper. Many were mere toyes, I am sure, which came into my head on waking, and I much mervailed how the priestes could make such mightie matters of them."

(xix.) "It is reported in the booke, that the examinate said, shee saw on Christmas night, at twelve o'clock, just as masse did begin, great beames of light issue from the sacrament; That uppon Newyeares day, shee saw fire flash in at the window; and a browne dogge, as big as a bullock: That on the Sunday after the sacrament, shee could not see the patten by reason of a greate brightnes; and that the priest seemed to her to be clothed in silver."

Sara Williams's reply. "I am perswaded these bee all false reports of mee, or otherwise I must have a recollection of som of them. I remember such things were reported of Maister Richard Maynie; but as for myselfe, I feel sure I never saw any such things."

(xx.) "It is reported that this examinate did say, On the 3rd Jan. shee saw Christ in his proper forme, when shee was receiving the sacrament: That shee received relief of pain by the application of a holy relique. And that shee flung away her beades, saying to the priestes, fie on you!"

Sara Williams's reply. "I wel remember on one occasion when a priest offended mee, I threw my beades at him. I deny that I ever was relieved of paine by any relique applied to the parte afflicted. I deny that I ever saw, or said I saw, Christ in the sacrament. I might have said to a priest, 'Fie on you,' knowing wel that they do not mislike such repremandes."

(xxi.) It is written of this examinate, that on Jan. 6 "shee said shee saw after consecration, a little heade in the challice; it was as it were the head of a child: That shee could tel a tale of a Mummerie which cam into herr chamber: That shee scoffed at the sacrament: That shee saw a propper man in a short blacke garment, girt about him, and having long turned-up haire, and great ruffes starched with blew starch: That shee complained the priestes hand did burne her, and his breath tormented herr."

Sara Williams's reply. "I remember no

part of all these things. I doe not believe I ever said that I saw a little childes heade in the chalice. As for the Mummery I believe it to bee a made-up tale of som of the priestes. If, however, I eve. said anything of thee kind, I am perswaded it must have been either in a dreame or in a christmas tale; but I have wholly forgotten it, if indeed I ever said it."

(xxii.) "It is reported of the examinate: That shee said shee knew a peece of the Holy Crosse by the smel. That a priest put his finger into her mouth, and bade the devill bite it if hee durst, and the devill answered, hee durst not bite the priest-his finger, because it had touched the Lord."

Sara Williams's reply. "I wel remember hearing the priests talk about theyr having a piece of the true cross; and if I said I should know it by the smel, I meant it would be kept in such fragrant spices, that the very perfume would tel how precious it was held to bee. No doubt I refused to bite the priest-his finger, for I well knew if I had done so, Maister Dibdale would have boxed my eares. I may have said, 'I would not bite the finger, because it has touched the Lord,' for I had been taught such reverence, but I do not remember to have said soe.

"In conclusion, shee said shee had been often examined about these possessions, but would confess nothing, in consequence of which shee was much made-of. The priestes told her never to take an oathe, and then shee might say anything, true or untrue. They warned her never to say a worde that would compromise a priest, or scandalize the true church. They told her of a woman that did dishonour the priests, and the devill entered her, and would never again leave herr, till hee had carried her into hell. Being married shee had got rid of her tyrants, and is very glad shee has now discharged her conscience, and unburdened her mind by telling the truth; and shee hoped that the devill will never draw her into such courses againe."—Samuel Harsnet (afterwards archbishop of York), Appendix to *Popish Impostures*, pp. 173–206.

The report of Mengus, and the unvarnished fact (1602). Mengus in his *Fustus*, or "Devil-mastix," speaking of Sara Williams, writes thus: "As she sate by the fire somewhat late with another maid-servant of the same house, both ready for bed, they fel into a slumber, and as they dozed over the fire, there approached them three cats, making a horrible noise, and sprawling about the young maid [Sara]. One of the cats leaped over her head, and another crept betwixt her legs. Whereat she looked suddenly behind her, and saw a strange huge catt as big as a mastiff, staring at her with eyes like fire, and of the bigness of a saucer." Such is the report, and the following is the fact. "I was looking one day for eggs in a bush, near masteres house, when a cat suddenly jumped out of the bush, and startled me, but it certainly was not big as a mastiff, nor had it eyes of the size of saucers." Harsnet shall tell the rest. "At supper," says Mengus, "the cat aforesaid was turned into a dogge of two colours, blacke and greene, and therewithall a spaniel bayed. At another time the devill came downe the chimney to her in a Winde, and blew the soote about the roome. Sometimes he appeared to her in the likenes of a Man; sometimes in the likenes of an Irish boy with black curlie locks; sometimes as a great Blacke Dogge; sometimes he came flying like a Sparrowe with a woodcockes bill; sometimes like a Toade with the nose of a moale; sometimes like a Mouse; sometimes like a Minister; sometimes like an Ey without a head; sometimes like a Ruffian with curled haire; sometimes like an Old Man with a long beard; and sometimes he came in with a drumme and seaven motly vizards dauncing about the roome." This last was at the lord Vaux-his house at Hackney at the end of Christmasse tide.—*A Declaration of Popish Impostures* (1604), pp. 138, 139.

When devils were cast out they were obliged to go in some visible form. Mengus, in his *Devil-mastix*, informs us, that when a devil is cast out, it is always obliged to depart in some visible form, and to leave some proof of its departure, such as a crack in a quarrie of a glass window, or the extinction of a candle. Harsnet remarks on this: "Breaking a square of glasse and blowing out a candel beeing two such supernaturall actions, as by a consorted conspirator with the exorcist, without the helpe of a cherrystone, or a suddaine puffe of some wenches breath, cannot cleanly be conceived, it is no marvell they be made a demonstration that the devil is surely gone. In regard to the visible formes of devils in theyr exits, the first devill disseised was called Smolkin, it was Trayfordes spirit, which Sara espied to goe out at his right eare in the forme of a mouse. The next devil dispossessed was Hilcho at Uxbridge, who appeared at his going out, like a flame of fire, which lay glowing in the stove in Trayfords sight, till it had a new change. The third devill was Haberdidance [Hoberdidance], Saras dauncing devil, who appeared in the likenes of a whirlwind, and his voyce was heard by a cooke, as hee flew over the larder. Captaine Filpot [a devil] went his way in the likenes of smoke turning round up the chimney. Lusty Dicke, the devill, did slippe a button, and went out in a stench. The devils Delicate and Lusty Jolly Jenkin went out, one whirling like a snake and the other like a vapour. Lusty Huffcappe went out in the likeness of a cat. Killico, Hob, and Anonymos, all of them devil-captaines, went out in a gust of wind. Purre went out in a little whirlwind, Frateretto in smoke." (See MAINY, p. 187.)—Harsnet, *A Declaration of Popish Impostures* (1604), pp. 140, 141.

It must not be supposed that these devil-forms, such as snakes, flames, whirlwinds, and so on, were visible to spectators, for this was not the case. The person dispossessed alone saw the form assumed, and declared it, as Mainy did, when he described the forms of the seven deadly sins. The person exorcised was asked by the priest in what form the devil made his exit, and he declared it openly, but no form appeared or disturbance took place cognizable by others (p. 196).

Effects of Popish imposture according to Samuel Harsnet. Samuel Harsnet, afterwards archbishop of York, writing at the close of the sixteenth century, gives a terrible description of the evil moral influence of the [Roman] Catholic teaching respecting apparitions, demoniacal possessions, exorcisms, and devilry. He writes of his own times, as one who lived and moved and had his being among the very persons he describes. He wrote not, as we should now, of what he had read in books, but of scenes passing before his eyes; and though it must be admitted he was a Protestant writing about Roman Catholics when the animosity between them was at fever heat, yet, all allowances being made, there is doubtless a broad basis of solid truth in his statements. In all the extracts I have made from him, I have carefully omitted his remarks of bitterness and irony, and have confined myself to his statements as an eye-witness or at least contemporary. "Heere in England," he says, in the early years of Elizabeth's reign, "what time the popish mists befogged the eyes of the people, how were our children, old women, and maidens afraid to crosse a churchyeard, or a three-way leet, or to goe for spoones into the kitchin without a candle? And no marveile: first because the devill comes from a smoakie house, and either he or some lewd frier was at hand, with ougly hornes on his head, fire in his mouth, a cowes tayle, eyes like a bason, fangs like a dogge, skinne like a neger, and a voyce roaring like a lyon,—then *boh!* in the dark was enough to make theyr haire stand upright. If a Peeter-penny or houzle-egge were behind, or a patch of tyth unpaid to the churche, then, Jesu Maria! ware where you walke for feare of bull-beggers, spirits, witches, urchins, elves, haggs, fairies, satyrs, pans, faunes, sylvans, Kit-with-a-candlesticke, Tritons, centaurs, dwarffs, giants, impes, calcars, conjurers, nymphs, changlings, scritchowles, the mare, the man in the oak, helwayne, the firedrake, the puckle, Tomthumbe, hobgoblin, Tom-tumbler, Boneles, and the rest. And what girl, boye, or olde wisard, would be so hardy [as] to step over the threshold in the night for a halfpenny worth of mustard amongst this frightful crue, without a dosen *Ave Maries*, two dosen crosses surely signed, and half a dosen *Pater nosters*; and without commending himself to the tuition of St. Uncumber, or els our blessed ladie?"—Samuel Harsnet, *Popish Impostures* (1604), pp. 134, 135.

For there as wont to walken was an elf,
There walketh now the Limitor himself;
In every bush, and under every tree,
There nis none other incubus but he.

Chaucer.

Phya personates in Athens the goddess of wisdom (B.C. 538). Pisistratos, being banished from Athens, remained in exile for six years, when Megaclês brought him back; and, to obtain the consent of the Athenians to his return, devised a plan to make it appear that the goddess Athenê or Wisdom was in favour of his restoration. His plan was this. He induced a woman of extraordinary stature and of handsome person, named Phya, to personate Athenê, the goddess of wisdom and patron goddess of Athens. Having well drilled her, she was arrayed in armour, placed in a chariot, and paraded through the streets, preceded by heralds, who cried aloud from time to time, "O Athenians, receive with favour Pisistratos, whom Athenê herself has vouchsafed to bring back to the Acropolis." The news flew abroad throughout all Attica that the goddess Athenê had brought back Pisistratos. Divine honours were paid to Phya; and Pisistratos, as the *protégé* of the goddess, was received with acclamations.—Herodotos, *History*, bk. i. 60.

Imputed Merit. (See Vicarious Suffering.)

Acts xxvii. 20–44. Neither sun nor stars for many days appeared, and no small tempest lay on us, so that all hope that we should be saved was taken away. But after long abstinence Paul stood forth, and said, Be of good cheer, for there shall be no loss of life, but of the ship only; for there stood by me this night the angel of God, saying, Fear not, Paul, for lo! God hath given thee all them that sail with thee. There were in all in the ship two hundred threescore and sixteen souls. The ship was wrecked and broken to pieces, but all in it escaped safe to land.

Gen. xviii. Three angels informed Abraham that they had come to destroy the cities of the plain, and Abraham intreated them to spare the cities out of consideration for the righteous ones that were therein; and one of the angels said to Abraham, If I find only ten righteous ones therein I will not destroy the cities for the ten's sake.

The merits of Brother Giles redeem many souls from purgatory (A.D. 1272). A Dominican promised a brother of the same order, if he died first, to come and tell him what his lot was. He happened to die April 23, A.D. 1272, the very day that Brother Giles died. God allowed the man to fulfil his promise, and when he made his appearance, his friend said, "Well, and what lot has befallen you?" "I am quite happy," replied the Dominican, "because I died the same day that Brother Giles died; and Christ, to recompense Brother Giles for his great sanctity, gave him leave to introduce into paradise all the souls he found in purgatory (!!). I was one of these souls, but have been delivered through the merits of Brother Giles."—*Acta Sanctorum* (Bollandists), April 23.

A crowd given to St. John of Therouanne, when a bridge fell in (A.D. 1130). Near the church of Merckem was a parvis, or fortified château, separated from the town by a deep foss, over which a bridge was thrown. St. John was in the château with his suite, for a grand ceremony had been arranged, and a vast crowd assembled in the church and parvis to witness it. The ceremony concluded with the consecration of the cemetery. As St. John went from the parvis, and was now in the middle of the bridge, some thirty-five or forty feet from the ground, he stopped a moment. The bridge was so crowded, it was difficult to move. All of a sudden it gave way with a terrible crash, and the whole of those on it were thrown into the foss below; bishops and priests, nobles and commoners, old and young, were all precipitated into the ditch, and with them fell the fragments of the broken bridge. Fortunately St. John was among the fallen; for as God gave to St. Paul the 270 souls that sailed in the ship with him, when it was wrecked off the coast of Malta, so God gave to St. John of Therouanne the crowd which fell with him into the foss, when the bridge of Merckem fell in; so that not one of all the vast crowd was even bruised, although the fall was some thirty-five or forty feet, amidst falling posts and rafters, masonry, and iron-work. St. John with a smile got on his feet again, shook off the débris, and thanked God for himself and those whom God had given him.—J. Colmieu (a contemporary), *Life of St. John, Bishop of Therouanne.*

St. Lidwina gives all her merits to her mother, and begins afresh (A.D. 1380–1483). The strongest example of the transference of merit which I have met with, is in the life of St. Lidwina of Schiedam. At the age of fifteen she fell on the ice while skating, and broke a rib. An inward bruise developed into a great imposthume in the womb. Soon ulcers consumed her lungs, and her whole body was covered with scorbutic sores. Besides these numerous ills, she suffered for nineteen years from dropsy, and was wholly unable to move in her bed; when others moved her, it was necessary to bind her with cloths to keep her together. For thirty years she lived thus, scarcely touching any food at all. During this period a horrible leprosy broke out in Schiedam. Her mother was laid low by the disease, and like to die. Lidwina, not content with praying for her mother, "elle lui céda aussi le mérite de toutes ses plaies, de toutes ses douleurs, de tous ses tourments, de toutes ses veilles, et de tous les autres exercises de vertu qu'elle avait pratiqués depuis qu'elle était sur la terre. Ainsi la mère, enrichie des trésors de sa fille, fit une très-belle fin; mais la sainte elle même, voyant qu'après avoir cédé son trésor [*i.e.* of merit] à sa mère, elle était obligée de travailler de nouveau, ajouta la mortification à la maladie, et s'entoura d'une grosse ceinture de crin rude et piquant, qu'elle ne quitta point jusqu'à la mort."—Mgr. Guérin (chamberlain of pope Leo XIII.), *Vies des Saints*, vol. iv. p. 403.

We read again, p. 404, "Elle avait un sentiment particulier de dévotion pour les âmes du purgatoire ; elle en a délivré plusieurs qui s'étaient recommandées à ses prières, et qui l'ont remerciée depuis. Elle a souffert pour cela des tourments horribles."

The merits of St. Patrick transferred to those who honour his memory. "Comme Dieu a promis à St. Patrice que ceux qui seraient dévots à sa mémoire, et qui feraient quelques œuvres de piété en son honneur au jour de sa fête, obtiendraient miséricorde à l'heure de la mort et ne périraient pas éternellement, il est extrêmement avantageux de se mettre sous sa protection."—Mgr. Guérin (chamberlain of pope Leo XIII.), *Vies des Saints* (1880), vol. iii. p. 475.

Edward III. and his queen Philippa of Hainault (A.D. 1347). After the siege of Calais, Edward granted mercy to the garrison on condition that six of the free citizens, with halters on their necks, would voluntarily surrender themselves to death. Six devoted men were found, and came to the king's camp. Then queen Philippa fell at the king's feet, and implored him to spare the lives of the six patriots. "Lady," said the king, "you pray so tenderly, I cannot refuse you ; and though much against my will, I give these men to you." So saying, he took the six citizens to the queen by the halters, and released them all for the love of her. The good queen ordered them to be well fed and clothed, and then set to go their way, just as they might list.

Infants in the Womb demonstrative.

LUKE i. 41. It came to pass that, when Elisabeth heard the salutation of Mary, the babe leaped in her womb.

St. Fursy, while in the womb, reproves his grandfather Ædfind (A.D. 650). Gelgês was the daughter of Ædfind, a king of Ireland, then divided into six kingdoms ; and married clandestinely prince Fintan, son of Finloga, king of Momonia, one of the six kingdoms. From this union sprang Fursy, afterwards canonized. Ædfind, perceiving that his daughter was about to give birth to a child, and learning by inquiry that its father was a Christian, was so enraged that he ordered Gelgês at once to be burnt to death, and went himself to see the sentence carried out. As Gelgês was led away to execution, the child in her womb reproved its cruel grandfather with a loud voice and intelligible words. Mgr. Guérin adds naïvely, "Au moins, entendit-on des paroles extraordinaires qui venaient du côté de la princesse, et l'on ne sait pas si ce fut un ange ou l'enfant même qui les prononça. Ce qui est plus certain, c'est que Gelgês fut delivrée des flammes par une pluie soudaine, et des sources miraculeuses qui les éteignirent."—*Les Petits Bollandistes* (7th edit. 1880), vol. i. p. 400.

The anti-climax in this paragraph is delicious. If it was not the child in the womb that cried out, it was some angel ; but be this as it may, it is quite certain that a shower of rain fell, and put out the fire.

Jacob's Ladder.

GEN. xxvii. 10–20. Jacob, fleeing from the wrath of Esau, came to Haran, where he dreamt that he saw a ladder set on the earth, and the top reached to heaven. On this ladder he saw the angels of God ascending and descending. And Jacob rose up early in the morning, and took the stone that he had put for his pillow, and set it up for a pillar, poured oil upon it, and called the name of the place Beth-el (*the house of God*).

St. Maur sees a pathway from earth to heaven by which St. Benedict ascended. On the day St. Benedict died, which was a Good Friday, St. Maur, at the hour of nine in the morning, was carried in spirit from Auxerre, in France, to Mount Cassino, and there saw a bright path carpeted, and bordered with innumerable torches. The path began from the cell of St. Benedict and terminated in heaven. While St. Maur looked on this vision, a venerable old man, all glorious, said to him, "By this pathway St. Benedict, the servant of the living God, is gone to heaven." Two companions who were with St. Maur also saw the vision.—St. Gregory the Great, *Dialogues*, bk. ii.

St. Perpetua sees a golden "Jacob's ladder." While St. Perpetua was in prison, she saw in a vision a ladder of gold reaching from earth to heaven. It was so narrow that only one person at a time could ascend its steps, and from top to bottom the sides were full of swords, lances, and hooks, ready to pierce and tear the flesh of those who ventured up it without due caution. At the foot lay a great dragon to deter those who wished to ascend from coming near the ladder. St. Perpetua saw her fellow-prisoners ascend this ladder; and, having reached the top, she saw them beckon to her to follow. By pronouncing the name of Christ she quelled the dragon ; and when she had set her foot on the first rung of the ladder she trod on the monster's head. Above, she found herself in a spacious garden, where she saw a shepherd, with white hair, milking his ewes, and thousands of angels, arrayed in white, were around him. The shepherd welcomed her, and gave her some curds, which she received with joined hands and ate, the white-robed angels saying "Amen." At the word "Amen" she woke, and the sweet savour of the curds still remained on her palate. The vision indicated that Perpetua and her companions were about to enter into glory by martyrdom.—J. C. Robertson, *History of the Christian Church* (1875), vol. i. p. 94. (This narrative was written by St. Perpetua herself.)

St. Romuald saw a "Jacob's ladder" on which monks ascended to heaven. When St. Romuald was 102 years old, he wished to pass the rest of his life in solitude, and accordingly retired to the Apennines. Here he had a dream, in which he saw a ladder that touched heaven and earth; and on this ladder the monks of his several convents, all arrayed in white, ascended to heaven. Next day he went to count Malduli to crave the site for a convent, a request which was instantly granted, the count assuring the saint that he also had seen the same vision. The convent, being built, was called Ca-malduli (*camp Malduli*), from the name of the count; and the society was called the Order of the Camaldulensians (A.D. 1009).—Ribadeneira, *The Flower of the Lives of the Saints* (died 1611).

St. Sadoth, bishop of Seleucia, sees a "Jacob's ladder" (A.D. 342). In the persecution raised by Sapor II., St. Sadoth with several of his clergy lay hid awhile, and during this retreat he had a vision which seemed to him prophetic of his death. "I saw," said he, "a ladder environed with light, and reaching from earth to heaven. St. Simeon my predecessor was at the top of it, in great glory. He looked on me as I stood at the bottom of the ladder, and said to me with a smiling countenance, 'Mount up, Sadoth, and fear not. I mounted yesterday, and it is your turn now.' This means," continued Sadoth, "that St. Simeon was martyred last year and ascended to heaven, and that I shall be martyred this year, and shall mount the ladder of life."—Alban Butler, *Lives of the Saints* (Feb. 20).

For other examples consult the Index, article JACOB'S LADDER.

Jacob's Pillar.

GEN. xxviii. 18, 19. Jacob had fraudulently obtained his father's blessing, and fled out of fear of his brother's vengeance. When he reached Luz he slept on the ground, and took one of the stones for his pillow. In his sleep he imagined he saw a ladder extending from earth to heaven, and angels seemed to him to be constantly ascending and descending this ladder. The dream made a strong impression on him, and he felt persuaded it was a divine vision of deep meaning. When he rose next morning he took the stone he had made his pillow, and, setting it up for a pillar, poured oil on it. He also changed the name of the place from Luz (*separation*) to Beth-el (*God's house*).

Arthur's Round Table. There is a table shown at Winchester, as "Arthur's Round Table;" but it agrees in no respect with the table made by Merlin, at Carduel, for Uther the pendragon. Merlin's table would seat 150 knights; was given by Uther to Leodegraunce of Camelyard; and passed to Arthur as a wedding gift, when he married Guinever, daughter of Leodegraunce. Round tables, however, were not uncommon. Thus, in the reign of Edward I., Roger de Mortimer established at Kenilworth a Round Table "for the encouragement of military pastimes." Some seventy years later, Edward III. had his Round Table at Windsor; it was two hundred feet in diameter. So enormous a table could only have been used in the open fields.

A table of two hundred feet in diameter would seat four hundred guests. Besides the military tables, we are told of John o' Groat's Round Table, made to accommodate his nine sons, to prevent their constant wrangling about precedency.

The Scone stone and coronation chair. A relic like Jacob's stone pillar was not likely to be overlooked in the early days of Christianity, when the fever for relics ran high; but it is passing strange that a fair traditional pedigree should connect this pillow-stone with our own coronation chair, and that actual history can trace the stone of our coronation chair up to A.D. 840, more than a thousand years. First, as to the traditional part, between Jacob and A.D. 840. According to tradition, Jacob's pillow and pillar-stone was carried into Egypt when Jacob went to reside there under the viceroyalty of his son Joseph; but Gathelus, son of Cecrops, who had married Scota, Pharaoh's daughter, carried it to Brigantia, in Spain, when he fled from Egypt out of fear of the man Moses. Here it remained, till Simon Brech, the favourite son of Milo the Scot, removed it to Ireland.* During a violent storm it was thrown into the sea to appease its rage; and, after the storm lulled, it was placed on the sacred hill of Tara, the capital of Bregia, and called the *Lia Fail*, or "Stone of Destiny." It was now used as the coronation chair of the Irish kings; and, it is said, a groan, like thunder, was always heard, if the person seated on it was only a pretender, who had no legal right to the crown, otherwise it was silent and uttered no sound. Fergus, the founder of the Scottish monarchy, removed the stone, as a palladium, to Dunstoffnage; and, when the Scots migrated eastwards, the stone was carried with them by Kenneth II., and set up at Scone, A.D. 840. From this point actual history takes up the tale. A stone called the "Fatale Marmor," on which the Scottish kings were crowned, was encased in a chair of wood, and set on the east side of the monastic cemetery; and at coronations it was the privilege of the earls of Fife to lead the new king up to the palladium-chair, and seat him thereon. Scone now became the *sedes principalis* of Scotland, insomuch that the kingdom of Scotland was called the kingdom of Scone, and Perth (not Edinburgh) was the metropolis. Edward I., by the battle of Dunbar, in 1296, conquered Scotland, and removed the stone to London. It is still in Westminster Abbey, and has been used, from the time of Edward I., as our coronation chair. All agree that the stone is the "Fatale Marmor" of Scotland, but it is by no means certain that this "Fatale Marmor" of Scotland is the "Lia Fail" of Ireland. And as for the wooden chair set over it, while some insist that it is the original chair brought from Scone by Edward together with the stone, others protest that it is the chair used by Edward the Confessor at his coronation. Whether it was the Scone chair or the Confessor's, it is quite certain it was decorated by Walter, the painter employed in beautifying the "Painted Chamber." A stone so venerable of course has also a prophetic virtue attached to it; this is incorporated in the Latin distich—

Ni fallat fatum, Scoti, quocunque locatum
Invenient lapidem, regnare tenentur ibidem.

[Where'er this stone may be, such is the fates' decree,
The sovereigns of that place shall be of Scottish race.]

Whether the accession of the Stuarts after Elizabeth satisfies this prediction must be left an open question, which every one must decide according to individual fancy. One thing is certain: Ireland once had the "Lia Fail," and had kings; Scotland once had the "Fatale Marmor," and had kings; both lost their palladium, and lost their kings. England has the Scotch stone now, and is the dominant power of both Ireland and Scotland.

The Celts erected a monolith, called a *Tanist Stone* or Heir-apparent Stone, at a coronation, as other early nations did. Thus we read in Judges (ix. 6) of Abimelech, that "a pillar was erected in Shechem" when he was made king. Again in 2 Kings (xi. 14) it is said that a pillar was raised when Joash was made king, "as the manner was." Besides these, there is the "Fatal Stone" or *Artizoe* of the Persians, mentioned by Pliny; the "Black Stone" of the Seids; the "Fatal Stone," described as a large mass of very rich grey silver ore, of an Indian South American tribe, removed from place to place, as the tribe fled before the Spanish invaders; the "Caaba" of the Mussulmans, which Mahomet removed to Mecca. Probably the idol of Diana at Ephesus was a meteoric stone and looked on as a palladium.

Another version. Mrs. G. A. Rogers tells a good story of the pillar of Bethel in her book entitled *The Coronation Stone.* The points of divergence are these:—

(1) Mrs. Rogers says, as the pillow-stone was Jacob's title-deed, he took it with him wherever he went, and erected another as a memorial of his dream. The title or pillow stone was carried from Egypt, with Joseph's bones, to the promised land. David intended to use it in the temple, but it was "rejected by the builders," and became a type of Christ. At the Captivity it was left behind, as Nebuchadnezzar saw "no beauty in it, that he should desire it;" but on the return from captivity, the princess Tephi, as princess royal of Judah, had a right to the title-stone, and carried it with her, under the leadership of Jeremiah and Baruch, to Ulster, in Ireland, where she married Eochaid, king of that part of Ireland, and was crowned on the stone, called by the Irish *Lia Fail*, or "Stone of Destiny."

Here we see a great divergence. The other tradition tells us it was not Tephi, the princess royal of Judah, who took it to Ireland, and married Eochaid; but that Gathe[r]us, son of Cecrops, who married Scota, Pharaoh's daughter, carried the stone to Spain, when he fled from Moses, and that Simon Brech, son of Milo the Scot, removed it to Ireland.

(2) Mrs. Rogers fills up the story thus: At the beginning of the sixth century, Fergus I., king of Ireland, sailed to Scotland, and conquered Argyleshire. He slew king Coilus, and the kingdom of the Scots was established on Fergus and his posterity. Fergus now sent to

* Instead of a "favourite son of Milo the Scot," many read "a favourite son of Milo, head of the Scoti," an ancient Celtic tribe. This occurred before the time of the founding of Rome.

Tara for the "Lia Fail," and, on its arrival, was crowned, sitting thereon.

(3) Mrs. Rogers says, all the monarchs of England, except Mary, have been crowned on this pillar-stone anointed in Bethel; and the present monarch of Great Britain, through the princess royal of Judah, is a lineal descendant of king David.

Of course, the great sticking place is princess Tephi. Mrs. Rogers fails to give her authority for this scion of the house of David, her voyage to Ireland under the conduct of Jeremiah and Baruch, and her marriage with Eochaid, king of Ireland. However, the other tale about Scota, daughter of Pharaoh, and Simon Brech, son of Milo the Scot, is even a worse invention, and would make our reigning monarch a descendant of the Pharaohs, a claim they would hardly wish to be allowed.

The Mahometans insist that the stone called Jacob's pillar is preserved in the mosque of Omar.

Regarding the "Lia Fail," it was a pillar nine feet high, not very easy for Jacob to raise up and move from place to place, and not easy to carry from Jerusalem to Spain, and Spain to Ireland, and Ireland to Scotland, and Scotland to London. It is, however, certain that the "Fatale Marmor" was not nine feet, but only twenty inches long, barely seventeen inches broad, and about ten inches thick. It is sienite, and accords with Pompey's Pillar at Alexandria. In Camden's time a tablet hung on the stone, now in Westminster, described it as "the stone on which Jacob lay his head at Bethel."

Jephthah's Rash Vow.

JUDGES xi. 29–40. When Jephthah went against the Ammonites, he vowed, if he returned victorious, to sacrifice, as a burnt offering, whatever first met him on his entrance into his native city. He gained the victory, and, at the news thereof, his only daughter came forth dancing to give him welcome. The miserable father rent his clothes in the fulness of grief, but the noble daughter would not listen to a violation of the vow. She craved a short respite to bewail her blighted hopes, and then submitted to her sad lot.

Idomeneus's rash vow. Idomeneus, king of Crete, on his return from Troy, made a vow in a tempest, if he escaped shipwreck and reached home safely, to offer to the sea-god the first living thing that met his eye on the Cretan shore. His own son was there to give him welcome, and he did unto him according to his vow.—Fénelon, *Télémaque*, bk. v. (This is a post-Homeric legend.)

King Oswi's rash vow. Oswi, king of Northumbria, in A.D. 655, met the pagan host in the field of Winwœd, by Leeds. The pagans were commanded by Penda, and costly gifts were offered him to avert his attack. Penda refused to accept the gifts. "Let us, then," cried Oswi, "offer them to One who will accept them;" and he vowed, if his arms were successful against Penda, to dedicate his daughter to God. Victory declared for Oswi. Penda's army fled. The river, swollen by rains, swept away the fugitives. And Oswi did unto his daughter according to his vow.—Green, *A Short History of the English People*, p. 24.

Jericho besieged.

JOSH. vi. 1–21. When Joshua besieged Jericho, according to the command of God, seven priests with trumpets went about the city before the ark of the covenant. Armed men went before as the advanced guard, and the rearguard went after the seven trumpeters with the ark of the Lord. The procession marched thus round the city for seven days, and on the seventh day at dawn they marched round the city seven times, and at the seventh time, when the priests blew the trumpets, Joshua said to the army, Shout; for the Lord hath given you the city. So the army shouted, when the priests blew the trumpets, and the wall of the city fell down flat, so that the people went up into the city, and they took the city, and utterly destroyed all that were therein, both men and women, young and old, ox, and sheep, and ass, with the edge of the sword.

JUDG. vii. 15–23. Gideon overcame the Midianites by surprising them in the middle night-watch. His three hundred men were furnished with pitchers which concealed lighted lamps, and at a given signal they all broke their pitchers and shouted, The sword of the Lord and of Gideon! The Midianites were panic-struck, and fled.

Avallon in Burgundy besieged, and its walls fall down as the "Agnus Dei" is chanted (A.D. 1022). King Robert besieged Avallon, in Burgundy, for three months without being able to take it. At the fête of St. Aignan he left the besiegers, and went to Orleans to keep the fête. While he was at the grand mass, dressed in a magnificent robe, and leading the choir, according to his custom, at the very moment the *Agnus Dei* was sung, the walls of Avallon fell down, and his army, marching into the city, took it. The king, in gratitude, made to the church of Saint-Croix, in Orleans, a present of a gold paten and chalice. He also rebuilt the church of St. Aignan, and greatly augmented its revenues.—Helgaud, *Life of King Robert;* and also S. Guyon, *History of the Church of Orleans.*

The Hallelujah Victory, or Victoria Alleluiatica (March 30, A.D. 430). This is given by several ecclesiastical historians as a fact. St. Germanus, bishop of Auxerre, and Lupus, bishop of Troyes, came to Britain to advise the British bishops how to act in respect to the Pelagian heresy which was greatly spreading. While in the island they headed a British army against the allied Picts and Saxons. They marched into Flintshire, saw the foe encamped at Mold, and rushed upon them so tumultuously, shouting "Hallelujah!" that the foe was panic-struck, and fled in the utmost disorder.

Jeroboam's Withered Hand.

1 KINGS xiii. 1–6. There came a man of God out of Judah unto Beth-el; and Jeroboam stood by the altar to burn incense. And the prophet cried against the altar. And when the king heard it, he put forth his hand from the altar, saying, Lay hold on him. And his hand dried up so that he could not pull it in again. The altar also was rent, and the ashes poured out. Then said the king to the prophet, Intreat now the Lord thy God that my hand may be restored me again. And the man of God besought the Lord, and the king's hand was restored him again, and became as it was before.

Aurelian's hand withered and restored by St. Vitus. St. Vitus, at the age of twelve years, was condemned by the emperor Aurelian to be scourged for worshipping Christ the crucified. The lictors appointed for the purpose no sooner began to scourge the child than their arms dried up; Aurelian also felt his arms and legs to be withered. Then said he to the father of St. Vitus, "Thy son is a magician, for he has taken from me the use of my limbs." The child made answer, "I am no magician, but a servant of the living God; and it is the God I serve who has chastened thee for thy sins." Said Aurelian, "If God will restore me the use of my limbs, I will own Him to be a great God, and Him only will I serve." Then Vitus made a prayer, and forthwith Aurelian was made whole, and would have no more to do with that just child, but released him and let him go.—Edward Kinesman (1623), *Lives of the Saints*, p. 381.

Timotheus blinded and restored by St. Januarius. When Timotheus, governor of Benevento, ordered St. Januarius and his companions to be beheaded, he suddenly lost the sight of both his eyes. He therefore sent for St. Januarius and implored him to deliver him from this state of misery. The saint restored him his sight; and the pagans being convinced of the power of God by this double miracle, five thousand of them were converted and baptized.—Edward Kinesman (1623), *Lives of the Saints*, p. 743.

Jewels.

One day a lady from Campania called upon Cornelia, the mother of Tiberius and Caius Gracchus, and, after showing her jewels, requested in return to see those of the famous daughter of the elder Scipio. Cornelia sent for her two sons, and, presenting them to the visitor, said, "These, madam, are my jewels."—*Roman Story.*

The treasures of the Christian Church. St. Lawrence was treasurer of the Christian Church in Rome, and the emperor Decius insisted on knowing where he had concealed the treasures. St. Lawrence begged three days' grace, and at the expiration of that time appeared before the emperor with all the Christians he could muster. Being asked if he had brought the treasures of the Church with him, he replied that he had; then, turning to the Christian throng, he said aloud, "These, Decius, are the treasures of the Church."—*Life of St. Lawrence* (from the public registers).

Jews converted.

JOHN xii. 11. Many of the Jews went away, and believed on Jesus.

ACTS xxi. 21. Thou teachest all the Jews to forsake Moses.

St. Vincent Ferrier converts a whole synagogue of Jews (A.D. 1357–1419). One day St. Vincent Ferrier, at the invitation of a Jew, went into the synagogue of Salamanca. He entered, crucifix in hand, which greatly troubled the assistants. The saint, however, soon tranquillized them, by saying he was going to speak to the congregation on a matter of great importance. They thought he meant some matter of public interest, so when he began to speak they were all ear. Using soothing and gentle words, he spoke of the Christian faith, and dwelt especially on the passion and death of the Messiah. As he spoke of the cross of Christ, a number of crosses appeared miraculously, and one attached itself to the dress of each one present, women as well as men; and, what is infinitely more important, every heart was converted to the Christian faith. St. Vincent, ravished at this outpouring of the Holy Spirit, baptized all present, and the synagogue became a Christian church, which went by the name of "The True Cross."—*Les Petits Bollandistes*, vol. iv. p. 241.

Jezebel devoured by Dogs.

1 KINGS xxi. 23; 2 KINGS ix. 30–36. Of Jezebel the Lord said, Dogs shall eat Jezebel by the wall of Jezreel. When Jehu was come to Jezreel, Jezebel heard of it, and looked out of a window to see him pass. She taunted him for treason, and Jehu told some eunuchs to throw her out of the window into the street, where she was trampled to death. Later in the

day, Jehu said, Go, see now this cursed woman, and bury her: for she was a king's daughter. So they went to bury her, but found only her skull, feet, and palms of the hand. And Jehu said, This is the word of the Lord, In the portion of Jezreel shall dogs eat the flesh of Jezebel.

Bolislaus, king of Poland, eaten by dogs (A.D. 1079). Bolislaus, king of Poland, was a very wicked man, who greatly persecuted the Church of Christ, and killed St. Stanislaus, king of Cracow, while serving at the altar, by cleaving his head in two with his sword. St. Gregory VII. excommunicated him for this atrocious crime; and, as he fled towards Hungary, he was thrown from his horse, and eaten up by dogs.—Ribadeneira, *The Flower of the Lives of Saints* (died 1611).

Job, the Story of.

JOB xlii. 10–16. The Lord gave, and the Lord hath taken away; blessed be the name of the Lord (Job i. 21). These were the words of Job, the man of Uz, when messenger after messenger announced to him some fresh calamity which had befallen him. One told him, The oxen were ploughing, and the asses feeding beside them, when the Sabeans fell upon them, stole them, and slew the servants with the edge of the sword. Another followed, and said, Fire of God has fallen from heaven, and hath burnt up the sheep and the servants, and consumed them. While he was still speaking, a third said, The Chaldeans have fallen on the camels, and have carried them away, and slain thy servants with the edge of the sword. A fourth said, Thy sons and thy daughters were eating in their elder brother's house, and lo! there came a great wind, and smote the four corners of the house, and it fell on them, and they are all dead. Oxen and asses, sheep and camels, sons and daughters, servants and all that he had, were taken from him; and Job fell to the ground and worshipped, saying, Naked came I into the world, and naked shall I return; blessed be the name of the Lord. And when the Lord saw that Job sinned not in his great sorrow, He gave him twice as much as he had before. For he had fourteen thousand sheep, and six thousand camels, and a thousand yoke of oxen, and a thousand she-asses. He had also seven sons and three daughters, and in all the land were no women so fair as the daughters of Job. And Job lived after this a hundred and forty years, and saw his sons, and his sons' sons to the fourth generation.

JOB ii. 10. Shall we receive good at the hand of God, and shall we not receive evil?

Sir Isumbras tried like Job. Sir Isumbras was informed by some of his household that his horses and oxen had been suddenly struck dead by lightning, and all his poultry killed by a swarm of adders. He received the sad intelligence with humble resignation, and commanded those who told him to bless the God of heaven, who bestows all good things, and in chastisement remembers mercy. Scarcely had he done speaking, when a page told him his castle was burnt to the ground, and many of its inmates had lost their lives, but that his wife and children had fortunately escaped. Sir Isumbras blessed the name of the Lord, who had thus tempered the wind to the shorn lamb, and bestowed on the page a purse of gold. When he came to his wife and children, he proposed to them a pilgrimage to Jerusalem, and cutting with his knife the sign of the cross upon his shoulder, he started at once for the Holy Land, resolving to beg his way. After they had passed through seven nations, they were stopped by a river. Sir Isumbras, taking up his elder son in his arms, carried him across, and set him under the shadow of a bush of broom, bidding him amuse himself with the flowers, while he went to fetch his younger brother. When half-way through the river, a lion pounced on the elder child and carried it off, while at the same moment a leopard ran away with the younger one. The mother was frantic; but sir Isumbras said, "The Lord gave, and the Lord hath taken away; blessed be the name of the Lord." It was now seven days since either of them had tasted food, and seeing a fleet at anchor not far off, they hastened thither to crave for something to eat. It was the soldan's fleet, and the two strangers were instantly seized as spies; but the soldan, after a time, convinced of his mistake, and struck with the beauty of the woman, offered sir Isumbras great riches if he would join his fleet, and give him his wife for a concubine. Sir Isumbras answered respectfully but firmly that he was the servant of the living God, and Him only would he serve; and as for selling his wife, the laws of Christ forbade it. However, while this parley was going on, the soldiers of the soldan contrived to carry the woman off, while others seized sir Isumbras and beat him till he was unable to move. Thus was he deprived of every earthly possession; but in all this the Christian knight sinned not.—Caxton's *Golden Legend.* (See also *The Metrical Lives of the Saints.*)

(We want the sequel to this story, which greatly resembles the legion of St. Placidus, p. 211.)

Grisilda afflicted and restored. One of the best imitations of the story of Job is that of Grisilda, in Boccaccio's *Decameron* (last tale). This very striking story has been copied by poets and novelists in all nations. Thus, Petrarch has left a Latin version, entitled *De Obedientia et Fide Uxoria Mythologia*. There is also a sixteenth-century ballad called *Patient Grissel*. Chaucer made it the subject of the Clerk's Story, in his *Canterbury Tales*. There is a mediæval prose version; and Miss Edgeworth's domestic novel, called *The Modern Griselda*. The general scope of the story is this :—

Grisilda was the daughter of a coal-burner, who became the wife of Walter, marquis of Saluzzo. [Grisilda is to take the place of Job, and her husband that of the Lord of Hosts. As God tried Job, and he exclaimed, "The Lord gave, and the Lord hath taken away; blessed be the name of the Lord;" so Walter, marquis of Saluzzo, tried the coal-burner's daughter, and she submitted without a murmur, saying, "Shall I receive good at the hand of my lord, and shall I not receive evil?"] Her lord put her to three trials. First he took her infant daughter from her, and conveyed it secretly to the queen of Pavia to be brought up, while the mother was made to believe that the child was murdered. Four years afterwards she had a son, which was also taken from her, and sent to be brought up with his sister. Eight years later Grisilda was divorced, and sent back to her native cottage, because her husband, as she was told, was going to marry another, younger and more beautiful than herself. When, in all this, lord Walter saw no mark of murmuring or jealousy, he bade Grisilda prepare to become the tiring-maid of his new wife. Without a frown, without a word of complaint, she went to her lord's castle, was introduced to the supposed bride, and was then informed that the beautiful maiden was her own daughter, and the youth, her brother, was her own son. Her heart was full, her cup of joy ran over, and she might have adopted the words of the psalmist, "Heaviness may endure for a night, but joy cometh in the morning."

St. Placidus, the Roman general, tried like Job. Placidus was very rich, and high in the favour of Trajan, the Roman emperor; but after his miraculous conversion (*vide* Index) he was tried like Job. A pestilence carried off all his menservants and maidservants, and all his sheep, horses, and cattle. Robbers despoiled him of his goods, and, for fear of the plague, he, with his wife and two sons, fled towards the sea. Here they found a vessel in which they intended to embark, but the captain, struck with the beauty of the woman, determined to make her his mistress; so, beckoning to his crew, they seized her, carried her aboard, and set sail, leaving Placidus and the boys behind. The general, finding all hopeless, took the boys, and wandered about till they came to a river. One he carried across, and as he was going back to fetch the other, he saw a wolf snatch up one child, and a lion the other. Having now lost everything, he hired himself to a farmer as a keeper of sheep, in which servile capacity he continued for fifteen years. In the mean time Rome was beset with foes, and the emperor sent messengers in all directions to hunt up Placidus. Two of the messengers arrived at the village where he lived as a hired labourer, recognized him, and told him the emperor desired him to lead his army to battle. So the shepherd was arrayed in the robes of a Roman general, returned to Rome, and once more headed the Roman legions.

His two sons were not devoured by the wild beasts, for certain husbandmen, who saw them, so alarmed the beasts that they dropped their prey to secure their flight, and the boys were brought up by the men who rescued them.

Placidus, finding the army under his command too small, had a new levy made, and his own two sons were amongst the recruits. After routing the foe, Placidus halted for three days in a town where his wife was living. She had been carried off by the sea captain, but, as she resolutely resisted all his advances, he put her ashore, and she earned her living as a poor peasant woman. The two young men happened to be billeted in her cottage. Here a sort of good fellowship sprang up between the two young soldiers, who were entire strangers to each other, and the elder told the younger the story of his life. When he came to the adventure at the river, the younger instantly discovered they were brothers. The woman, their mother, overheard the tale, went to the general, revealed herself, and introduced to him his two sons, who were thus marvellously lost, and as marvellously found.—*Gesta Romanorum*, cx. (See READER'S HANDBOOK, *Comedy of Errors*.

Job impleaded by the Devil.

JOB i. 6–12; ii. 1–6. Satan said to God tha

Job served Him from interested motives, and if God afflicted him, he would curse Him to His face. God gave Satan liberty to try what he could do by afflicting Job; but Job sinned not, and God restored him to health and prosperity.

When an Egyptian died he was tried before he was buried. A public accuser urged all that could be said against him, and another advocate defended the deceased. Judgment was then passed by the three judges, and the body was disgraced or honoured accordingly. The judges sat on the further side of a lake, which had to be crossed in a boat. Here we see the classic myths of Charon and his boat, the three judges of hell, and the river Styx.—Diodorus Siculus, i. 92. In the process of canonization the *Advocatus Dei* supports the motion, and the *Advocatus Diaboli* opposes it.

St. Bernard impleaded by the devil. Just before his death, St. Bernard was rapt in a trance, and presented before the Redeemer. The devil came among the sons of God, and accused him, saying he was unworthy to be admitted among the saints of light. St. Bernard fell on his knees before the throne of grace, and said, "I acknowledge, O most merciful Saviour, my unworthiness to receive any blessing at Thy hand. I plead not my merits, but Thy most precious blood-shedding which cleanseth from all sin. Washed in the blood of the Lamb, though my sins be as scarlet, they would be white as snow; though they be like crimson, they would be as wool." When the devil heard these words he left the leet, and angels carried the saint back into his cell.—William (abbot of Theodore), *Life of St. Bernard.*

The devil and the dying man. It is said that the devil came once to a dying man. He held in his hand a long parchment roll, in which was set down all the man's sins from birth to the passing hour; all the idle words he had spoken, all the falsehoods he had told, all the impure and profane words he had uttered, all his angry words, all his wanton words, all his vain and vaunting words, all his ungodly words, all his scandals, all his omissions. Next came his thoughts; and then his acts of sin, arrayed under the ten commandments. It was a frightful schedule indeed; and Satan said, "What have you as a set-off against this list of sins?" The sick man replied, "Put down this first: 'The blood of Christ cleanseth from all sin;' and underneath add this: 'Whosoever believeth in Me shall not perish, but have everlasting life.'" Whereupon the devil vanished; and the sick man died with these words on his lips, "Who shall lay anything to the charge of God's elect? It is God that justifieth. Who is he that condemneth?"

Jonah and the Whale.

JONAH i., ii. Jonah, the prophet, was commanded by God to go to Nineveh, and cry against it for its wickedness: but instead of obeying this command, he fled to Tarshish. While on his voyage to Tarshish a great storm arose, and the ship being almost wrecked, the mariners cast lots to ascertain which of the crew had provoked the gods to send this death upon them. The lot fell on Jonah; and when the sailors hesitated what to do, Jonah said to them, Take me up, and cast me into the sea, and so shall the waves be calm. The men were unwilling to do so, and rowed hard for land, but the storm was against them; so at length they cast the prophet into the sea, and the storm abated. Jonah was not drowned, for a great fish, called a "whale," swallowed him, and for three days and three nights he remained in the whale's belly, at the expiration of which time he was vomited alive on dry land.

Fish large enough to swallow a man have doubtless been found occasionally in the Mediterranean sea. The white shark swallows what it takes into its mouth whole. It is physically unable to divide its food piecemeal. Otto Fabricius tells us "its wont is to swallow down dead or living men at a gulp." In 1758 a sailor fell overboard in the Mediterranean, when a shark took him in its wide throat; but the captain shot the shark, and the sailor was rescued from his perilous condition without injury. The captain gave the man the fish, which was exhibited throughout Europe. It was twenty feet long, with fins nine feet wide, and it weighed 3924 lbs. Blumenbach makes mention of a white shark which weighed 10,000 lbs.; and he tells us that horses have been found whole in the stomach of these monsters of the deep. A writer of the seventeenth century, *On the Fish of Marseilles*, says the men of Nice assured him they once took a fish of the *Canis carcharias* family, 4000 lbs. in weight, in the belly of which a man whole was found.—Dr. Pusey, *Minor Prophets.*

Arīon, being cast into the sea, was swallowed by a dolphin. Arīon of Lesbos was very rich, and greatly beloved by Periander, king of Corinth. One day being out at sea, the mariners agreed to drown him, and take possession of his money; so they cast him overboard. But a dolphin, allured by the music of his lute, had followed the ship, and when the poet was cast into the waves, swallowed him up, and cast him forth alive on Tænaros, a town of Laconia.—Herodotus, *History*, i. 23, 24.

Herculês, being shipwrecked, was swallowed by a fish. Lycophron the Greek poet relates that Herculês, in his home voyage, after the adventure of the Golden Fleece, was shipwrecked; and, being swallowed by a monstrous fish, was disgorged alive on shore, after the space of three days.

Lycophron lived in the second century before Christ.

The daughter of king Ampluy, being shipwrecked, was swallowed by a whale. Anselm, emperor of Rome, had a son, and king Ampluy a daughter. This son and daughter being betrothed to each other, the princess was sent to Rome for her espousals. On the voyage a great storm arose; the ship was driven on a rock, and all hands except the bride were drowned. About three o'clock the storm lulled, and the lady, clinging to part of the wreck, was followed by a whale, which swallowed her. When she found out where she was, she took a knife, and wounded the whale so severely, that "according to its instinct" it made at once for land, and the spot it reached belonged to the earl Pirris, who happened to be walking at the time along the coast. Seeing the whale, the earl called together his men, and harpooned it; but a voice from the belly of the whale cried to them, "Have mercy, friends; I am a king's daughter." The earl was amazed, and, opening the whale carefully, found inside it the princess. He took her out, and she related to him her wonderful tale. The earl entertained her hospitably, sent to inform the two kings of the strange adventure, and after a few days the emperor sent an escort to conduct her to Rome.—*Gesta Romanorum*, cix. MS.

The dead body of St. Lucian, being cast into the sea, was brought to land by a dolphin. The body of St. Lucian, after his martyrdom, was cast into the sea, to the great grief of his disciples, who wished to bury it. But fifteen days afterwards a dolphin brought it ashore; and hence, in Christian art, this saint is often represented with a dolphin at his side.—Metaphrastês (died A.D. 911), *Lives*, etc.

St. Martinian saved by a dolphin (A.D. 830). St. Martinian, the hermit, first took up his abode in Cæsarea; but a woman named Zoa came one night to his cell, clothed in rags and drenched with rain, imploring shelter from the storm. St. Martinian took her in, but next day quitted his solitude, to find one more inaccessible. A mariner told him of a rock in the sea without inhabitant, and there he made his abode for six years, seeing no one, save only this mariner, who called thrice a year. One day a ship struck on the rock, and all the crew perished, except one young woman, who clung to a plank. Seeing St. Martinian on the rock, she cried out, "Help, help, or I perish!" The hermit gave help, and drew the woman on the rock. He took her to his cell, and said, "Here you may live, and here I leave you such food as I have; but I myself must quit this rock without delay. Farewell!" Then, going to the sea, he made the sign of the cross, commended himself to God, and threw himself into the waves. God sent a dolphin to bear him on its back to the nearest shore, and there he landed in safety. Martinian now saw that no place is free from temptation, so he lived the rest of his life as a wanderer, begging his daily food. After the space of two years, he reached Athens, where he died.—Metaphrastês (a personal friend), *Lives of Saints*. (Also Joseph Assemani, *Universal Calendar*, vol. vi. p. 145, etc.)

⁂ The young woman saved from the wreck was named Photina. Martin de Vos has a famous picture called "Photina saved from the Wreck," where she is represented climbing the rock with the help of the hermit.

Judas, the Death of.

ACTS i. 18. This man [Judas] purchased a field with the reward of iniquity; and falling headlong, he burst asunder in the midst, and all his bowels gushed out. (See 2 Chron. xxi. 15.)

Death of Arius, the heresiarch (A.D. 336). Constantine ordered bishop Alexander to receive Arius into the Church, and appointed the day following for the ceremony. Alexander prayed fervently that God would take his life before sunrise, if Arius was right; if not, that Arius himself might receive the reward of his iniquity before the Church was prostituted by receiving him into its bosom. The morrow came, and it seemed to promise a grand triumph to the Arians. Arius himself paraded about the city on horseback, with a large number of flowers. On coming, however, to Constantine's forum, a sudden disorder of the bowels seized him, and being compelled to dismount, he retired for relief behind the forum. Here he burst asunder, and all his bowels gushed out.—Athanasius, *De Morte Arii*, 3; Rufinus, *Ecclesiastical History*, i. 12, 13 (died 410); Socrates, *Ecclesiastical History*, bk. i. ch. 39 (died 439).

"Cum venisset juxta forum, quod dicitur Constantini, quo in loco statua porphyretica posita est, terror quidam ex conscientia scelerum ei subortus est; et cum terrore simul alvus relaxata. Percontatusque num in proximo essent latrinæ, cum post Constantini forum esse didicisset, illuc perrexit. Mox animo deficere cœpit, et unà cum excrementis anus ipsi delabitur; et id, quod medici vocant ἀπόφϑισμα, protinus per anum decidit. Subsecuta est sanguinis copia; ac postremo tenua intestina simul cum splene ac jecore effusa sunt. Et ille quidem continuò animam exhalavit. Latrinæ autem illæ Constantinopoli post forum Constantini, sicut antea dixi, et post macellum, quod est in porticu, etiamnum monstrantur; et cuntis prætereuntibus digitum ad eas intendentibus, genus mortis Arii perpetuo memorabile posteris reddunt."—Socrates, *Ecclesiastical History*, bk. i. ch. 38 (turned into Latin by Henry Valesius. Edition 1577).

Labour in Vain.

LUKE v. 5. Master, we have toiled all the night, and have taken nothing.

PROV. x. 2. Treasures of wickedness profit nothing.

JOB v. 12. He disappointeth the devices of the crafty, so that their hands cannot perform their enterprise.

A thief stole St. Eman's horse, but the horse moved not (A.D. 560). St. Eman, being invited to visit Bladiste, a grand seigneur of Chartres, was obliged to pass the night on the road, because the distance was too great for a single day's journey. He found entertainment for himself in a house on the road, but none for his horse. So, making on it the sign of a cross, he turned it adrift, bidding it not to stray. A fellow named Abbon mounted the horse, with intent of stealing it; but next morning, the horse and thief stood at the door of the house where the saint slept. St. Eman politely thanked the thief for bringing the horse to the door, and gave him a piece of money, that if he was in distress, the temptation to steal might be taken away. (See ODILO, below.)—*Acta Sanctorum* (Bollandists), vol. ii. May 16, p. 595.

The robbers who stole St. Hermeland's eggs (A.D. 718). Some villagers stole a lot of eggs from St. Hermeland's abbey, and walked with them all night long, expecting to find themselves many miles away; but what was their surprise, at sunrise, to find themselves still in the hen-house. Though they had walked all night, they had not stirred a single step, and, being found next morning, they were obliged to give back their plunder. —Bulteau, *History of the Monks of the East*, bk. i ch. 37.

The robbers who stole St. Laumer's ox, after driving it all night, found at daybreak they were still in the ox-stall (sixth century). One day some robbers stole an ox from St. Laumer's monastery; but after driving it all night, found, at daybreak next day, they had never quitted the ox-yard. As the servants and monks were all astir, they then decamped, leaving the ox behind in the shed.—*Les Petits Bollandistes*, vol. i. p. 472.

A robber who stole St. Odilo's horse remained immovable all night. One night a robber stole St. Odilo's horse, but no sooner had he reached the outer gates of the monastery of Orval than both he and the horse became powerless to move. There they stood, like living statues, all the night through. At daybreak St. Odilo saw them, and, going up to the robber, said to him quizzically, "Friend, you have put yourself to a vast deal of trouble to stand guard here all night." Then, casting towards him a small coin, he led the horse back into the stable. (See EMAN, col. 1.)—Bollandus, *Acta Sanctorum*, vol. i. Jan. 1.

The groom of Payen du Teil, having stolen his master's horse, travelled all night, and next morning found he had not left the yard (eleventh century). St. Bernard of Abbeville, with two companions, travelling from Nogent to Mortagne, met a chevalier named Payen du Teil, who invited them to sleep in his mansion. During the night, the groom stole his master's horse and rode off with it towards Bellesme, a town in the county of Perche, then at war with Mortagne. St. Bernard, who knew what was done, had recourse to prayer, and God led the groom a fool's chase; for after riding all night, and expecting to find himself at Bellesme, at daybreak he discovered he was still in his master's stables; and recognized at once that this was due to St. Bernard's prayers.—Corblet, *Hagiographie d'Amiens.* (The life of St. Bernard was written 1137–1148 by Geoffroy le Gros, one of his disciples.)

St. Vincent Ferrier journeyed eastwards from Vannes all night, and found next morning he had not moved (A.D. 1419). When St. Vincent Ferrier was about to die, the people of Valentia entreated that he would return thither, and lay his bones among them. He was then at Vannes, and started with his five companions, at sunset, to go to Spain. All night they travelled, taking a direction eastwards; but, at sunrise next morning, they found, after twelve hours' walking, they were still on the spot from which they started. St. Vincent understood by this "miracle" that God intended he should die at Vannes; and said to his companions, "You see, my brothers, God does not wish Valentia to have my bones, because that stiffnecked people rejected the word of truth which I preached to them." When the inhabitants of Vannes heard of this, the churches rang out their joy-peals, and ten days afterwards the saint died, at the age of sixty years.—Peter Ranzano (bishop of Lucera), *Life of St. Vincent Ferrier.*

Legion.

LUKE viii. 27–38. When Jesus arrived at the country of the Gadarenes, there met Him a certain man which had a devil, and wore no clothes, and abode in the tombs. When he saw Jesus, he cried out, What have I to do with Thee, Jesus, Son of God? I beseech Thee torment me not. Jesus asked him, saying, What is thy name? And he said, Legion. And they besought Jesus that He would not command them to go into the deep. Now, there was there a herd of many swine feeding on the mountain, and the devils besought Him that he would suffer them to enter into the swine; and He suffered it. Then went the devils out of the man, and entered into the swine; and the whole herd ran violently down a steep place into the lake, and there perished.

Orion, possessed of a legion, is delivered by St. Hilarion. Orion was a very rich man, but he was possessed of a legion. While St. Hilarion was preaching, Orion, slipping from his keepers, ran up to him, and, seizing him in his arms, hoisted him up into the air. All the congregation were terrified; but Hilarion said, "Let be! I will deal with this man." Then, taking him by the hair, he threw him on the ground, and set his foot upon him. The man howled and yelled; but the hermit said, "Ah! Lord, deliver this wretch, unloose him, for it is as easy for Thee to vanquish a legion as one." So saying, Orion opened his mouth, and there issued from it sundry noises, like the stir of a moving crowd. Presently the noise ceased, and the man was cured. Next day, Orion brought rich presents to the monastery; but Hilarion said to him, "Didst thou never hear what befell Gehazi and Simon Magus? The one sold the gift of the Holy Ghost, and the other thought to buy it; but both were severely punished. Go home, and do what you will with thy gifts, for I will in no wise touch them." Orion then besought the saint to take them in trust, as alms for the poor; but Hilarion declined to do so, for "many," he said, "under the guise of alms, indulge their own greed. We are not only to do no evil, Orion; we are not to let our good be evil spoken of, lest the name of Christ be blasphemed." Orion was vexed, but Hilarion said to him, "My son, grieve not at my words. Were I to accept thy bounty, I should be doing wrong, and devils would no longer be obedient to me. Then would they return to thee, fiercer and more numerous than before, and thy last state would be worse than thy first. Go to thy house rather, and give to the poor, even as thy heart bids thee; for whoso giveth to the poor, lendeth to the Lord." (See LUNATICS, etc., p. 223.)—St. Jerome, *Vita St. Hilarionis Eremitæ* (A.D. 390). See also Callistus (who died 1350), *Ecclesiastical History*.

Lifted up.

EZEK. viii. 3. He put forth the form of a hand, and took me by a lock of my head; and the Spirit lifted me up between the earth and the heaven.

JAMES iv. 10. Humble yourselves in the sight of the Lord, and He will lift you up.

PSALM cxlvii. 6. The Lord lifteth up the meek: He casteth the wicked down to the ground.

1 SAM. ii. 7. The Lord . . . bringeth low and lifteth up.

St. Agnes was often lifted from the ground in the ecstasy of prayer (A.D. 1274–1317). Even at the early age of fifteen, we are told, St. Agnes was often lifted five feet or more from the ground, in the ecstasy of prayer, and that "in the presence of all the inmates of the Convent del Sacco."—Raymond of Capua, *Life of St. Agnes*.

St. Angela of Brescia, founder of the Ursulines, lifted up (A.D. 1474–1540). On her return to Brescia, after the treaty of Cambrai, in 1529, St. Angela was at the "holy sacrifice," when she was suddenly and publicly entranced. Her body was lifted from the earth, in the sight of all the congregation, and remained suspended in the air a long time. "Ce prodige fut aperçu d'un nombre infini de persones. Elle eut souvent des ravissements semblables."—*Les Petits Bollandistes*, vol. vi. pp. 331, 332.

St. Antoinette of Florence often lifted up in prayer (A.D. 1400–1472). "Plusieurs fois on vit un globe de feu suspendu audessus de la tête de la Bienheureuse Antoinette, qui, dans l'obscurite, remplissait le saint temple de lumière; plusieurs fois aussi on la vit suspendue entre le ciel et la terre pendant qu'elle priait."—*Les Petits Bollandistes*, vol. iii. p. 71.

St. Arey, bishop of Gap, often lifted up in prayer (A.D. 535–604). Probus, a contemporary, tells us that St. Arey got a false key of the church, whereby he let himself in during the hours of sleep, and passed the time in prayer on the pavement of the church. Often and often, says Probus, during these vigils, the saint was ravished in spirit and carried before the throne of the Almighty, or lifted high into the air by the ministry of angels. At such times the whole church was a blaze of celestial light.—*Histoire Hagiologique du Diocèse de Gap.*

The spirits of St. Berard and his companions lifted up (A.D. 304). St. Berard and his companions tried to convert the Moors of Spain, but were cast into a dark dungeon. This dungeon was instantly illuminated with light from heaven, and the guards saw the spirits of St. Berard and his companions lifted into the air, "comme si elles eussent déjà monté au ciel." Forthwith they were miraculously set free, and again preached to the followers of the false prophet. Being again seized, they were scourged, dragged over broken glass and crockery till all their bodies were one vast wound. The wounds, being covered with salt and sprinkled with vinegar to irritate them, had boiling oil poured over them, but "au milieu de tous ces outrages, les saints montrèrent tant de constance qu'ils ne paraissaient pas être sensible aux douleurs."—*Les Petits Bollandistes* (1880), vol. i. p. 381.

Jamblichus lifted up in prayer (fourth century). Jamblichus, the Neo-platonist, when he prayed, was raised ten cubits from the ground, and his body and dress too assumed the appearance of gold.—Eunapius, *Jamblichus.*

St. Peter Celestine, saying mass, was lifted high into the air, and remained so through the whole service (A.D. 1274). When St. Peter Celestine went to Rome to obtain the pope's approval of the "Order of Celestines," he was ordered to say mass. The officers who waited on the priests handed him the gorgeous robes and ornaments, but Peter requested he might retain his hermit's cloak. He did so, but angels came and covered his cloak with precious ornaments; and, when he began mass, he was lifted by angels high in the air, where he remained suspended till the service was over. The pope, who was present, could not, after this, hesitate to confirm the new order, and accordingly granted the required bulls.

Another example. Celestine V., after his abdication, was imprisoned by his successor, Boniface VIII., in the castle of Fumone, and starved to death. No one was allowed access to him, and a strong guard was set over him. One day Boniface, being conscience-struck, sent three cardinals to console his prisoner. They found him saying mass for the dead; and were not a little astonished to see him surrounded with light, and suspended in the air. When the cardinals asked him why he was saying mass for the dead, he replied, "It is for the king of Hungary, who died this morning; by the mass just said, his soul has been delivered from purgatory."—*The Admirable Life of St. Peter Celestine, Pope,* etc. (from the press of the Celestines, Bar le Duc).

St. Clara of Rimini goes from Assisi to the church "de la Portioncule" without touching the ground (A.D. 1346). One day, as St. Clara went from Assisi to the church "de la Portioncule" about a mile off, her companions noticed that her feet never once touched the ground; in fact, "angels carried her to the church of their queen."—*Les Petits Bollandistes,* vol. ii. p. 439. See p. 200, xi.

St. Coletta or Nicoletta often lifted up by the Spirit (A.D. 1380-1447). One day, as St. Coletta was seated on the ground in the midst of her sisterhood, the twelve apostles, as twelve old men arrayed in white robes, stood round for some time, then rose into the air. St. Coletta rose with them, till she wholly disappeared from the sight of her companions. Often during her prayers was she lifted by the Spirit from the earth, sometimes so high as to be quite out of sight. At one time, "une flamme merveilleuse s'échappant de sa bouche illuminait son oratoire."—Douillet, *Vie de St. Colette.*

St. Francis of Paula lifted from the earth in prayer (A.D. 1416-1507). Louis XI. sent for St. Francis of Paula, and the pope (Sixtus IV.) commanded him to go. When he reached Naples, on his way to Tours, the whole city turned out to pay him honour, and the king (Ferdinand I.) entertained him in his palace. At night, his majesty, peeping through the crevices of the chamber door, saw the saint in prayer. He was encompassed with a great light, and was elevated many feet from the floor of the room. The king was greatly astonished, the more so as he thought the fatigues of the day would have overcome him; but he knew not the man, or he would have known that in the multitude of his thoughts he would say unto God, "Thy comforts refresh my soul."—Father Giry, *Acts of his Canonization,* etc.

St. Francis of Posadas often lifted from the earth in the sacrifice of the mass (A.D. 1644-1713). St. Francis of Posadas wept without ceasing during mass, and thought himself unworthy to touch his God. At the elevation of the host, his whole body trembled, and he could not restrain his sighs. One day he saw Christ Himself in the host, and his agitation was so great that his assistants were afraid he would break the host in his hands. Often he would fall into an ecstasy, and be caught up from the ground. When he came to himself he would say, "I cannot tell whether I left the earth or the earth withdrew from me." On one occasion, while pronouncing the words of consecration, his spirit left his body, and his body rose in the air, and remained suspended there. When he came down again, all the congregation saw he was encompassed with a great light, the wrinkles of his face disappeared, his skin looked transparent as crystal, and his cheeks were red as fire. On another occasion, while reading the Gospel of the day, rays of light issued from his mouth so as to lighten the missal he held in his hand. Twice, during Pentecost, such a brilliant light issued from his body that the whole altar was illuminated.—L'abbé Daras, *The Saints, etc., of the Eighteenth Century.*

St. John-Joseh of the Cross often lifted from the earth in his ecstasies (A.D. 1654–1734). St. John-Joseph of the Cross in his ecstasies was frequently lifted by the Spirit into the air, where he remained suspended. "Ses ravissements étaient parfaitement connus; plusieurs personnes qui assistaient à sa messe en furent témoins. La même chose arriva aussi d'une façon fort extraordinaire, dans le cours d'une procession."

Another instance. While St. John-Joseph was building his monastery, he used to assist in carrying materials, such as bricks, mortar, or timber. On one occasion he was missed, and searchers, going into the chapel, found him there in an ecstasy. He was entirely lifted off the ground; indeed, so high was he suspended upon nothing, that his head touched the ceiling.—Cardinal Wiseman, contributed to Migne's *Démonstrations Evangéliques*, vol. xvi.

St. Margaret of Hungary often lifted up by the Spirit (A.D. 1243–1271). One Good Friday, St. Margaret of Hungary was seen several times lifted by the Spirit more than a cubit's height from the ground. This has also occurred on several other occasions, especially on All Saints' days, and the days of the Assumption of the Virgin.—Bollandus, *Acta Sanctorum*, vol. iii. (Also Surius, *Lives, etc.*, vol. i.)

St. Mary of Egypt was lifted from the earth in prayer (A.D. 421). St. Mary of Egypt, in early womanhood, lived a most licentious life; but, being called to repentance, she retired to a desert in Palestine, where she lived on such herbs as she could find, and went about wholly without clothing. Father Zozimus one day came upon her accidentally, and after giving her his outer garment, learnt her history from her own mouth. He tells us he saw her retire a little distance, and turning to the east in prayer, she was lifted from the earth more than five feet. Father Zozimus tells us he was more than half afraid, and thought what he saw must be a ghost.—*Les Petits Bollandistes*, vol. iv. p. 123.

St. Monica lifted up from the ground in prayer. St. Monica, being confessed on the day of Pentecost, remained in a trance all that day. At another time she was seen in prayer lifted up by the Spirit at least three feet from the ground, and remained so, as if suspended in the air.—St. Augustine (A.D. 397), *Confessions.*

Philip of Neri lifted by the Spirit into the air (A.D. 1515–1595). Philip of Neri was ofttimes so rapt in spirit that he has been raised two feet or more above the ground, and has remained thus in the air for a considerable time, environed with light.—Antony Gollonius, *Life of Philip of Neri.*

St. Joseph Oriol often raised into the air in ecstasy (A.D. 1650–1702). While St. Joseph Oriol was sailing from Marseilles to Barcelona, the sailors declare they often saw him in an ecstasy lifted many feet above the deck, and supported in the air upon nothing.—*Les Petits Bollandistes*, vol. III. p. 615.

St. Stephen, king of Hungary, lifted into the air in prayer (979, 997–1038). The spirit of St. Stephen, king of Hungary, was often lifted up in communion with God, and sometimes his body followed, being buoyed into the air. One day, while praying in his tent, he was lifted into the air by the hands of angels, and so remained till his prayer was ended.—Chartruiz (bishop of Hungary), *Life of St. Stephen, King of Hungary.*

St. Theresa lifted by the Spirit into the air (A.D. 1515–1582). The body of St. Theresa has been seen many times elevated from the ground into the air; and there it has remained, "suspended on nothing," till she has desired of the Lord her Saviour the cessation of this miraculous favour. This occurred on one occasion in the presence of Dom Alvarês de Mondosa, bishop of Avila, who had come to converse with her on spiritual matters. He found her elevated above the window through which the sisters usually received the host. During the sacrifice of the mass, not only was her whole body radiant with light, it was not unfrequently raised from the earth, and suspended in the air.—Her autobiography and life, by Eather Bouix.

Francis Xavier lifted up into the air in prayer (A.D. 1506-1552). Francis Xavier, many and many a time, with his face on fire, was miraculously lifted above the earth, and raised by the Spirit into the air during prayer. On these occasions, wholly unable to contain his fulness of joy, he would exclaim, "Satis est, Domine! Satis est!" ("It is enough, O Lord; it is enough!"—Cardinal de Monte's speech before Gregory XV., at the canonization of Francis Xavier, Jan. 19, 1622.

Miscellaneous examples. The PRINCESS HEDWIGES (A.D. 1243) was often seen by her maidens elevated into the air during prayer, and encircled with light. —Surius, *Life of St. Hedwiges.*

ST. MARY FRANCES of the Five Wounds (1715-1791), on her dying bed, saw a cross lifted from the floor to the ceiling of her chamber. When she told this to her confessor, he said it was a warning sent from God that the days of her pilgrimage were drawing to an end.—R. P. Bernard Laviosa, *Life of Mary Frances.*

ST. JOHN OF ST. FACOND (1430-1479). St. John of St. Facond, in Spain, was often suspended in the air many feet above the ground, sometimes for a whole night.*—*Acta Sanctorum*, June 12.

Simon Magus ascended into the air and was cast down. St. Isidore says that Simon Magus died in the reign of Nero, and adds this tradition: He had proposed a disputation with the apostles Peter and Paul, and had, in accordance with his promise, risen high into the air; but, at the prayers of the two apostles, he was thrown down at noontime by the evil spirits who had carried him up.—Pinnock, *Analysis of Ecclesiastical History*, p. 47.

The Brahmin who sat on the air. In the *Asiatic Monthly Journal* (March, 1829) is an account of a Brahmin who apparently sat upon air. He could also remain under water for several hours. In the former case, when the fakir regained the *terra firma*, he looked like a sitting corpse, except that there was a swelling over the entire scalp. Hot water and cake being applied to this swelling, it subsided. It seemed as if "his whole life had been collected on the top of his skull."

If, as Milton says, the contemplation of divine things and the converse with angelic spirits etherealizes the body, and "turns it by degrees to the soul's essence," we have a solution of the legerity of those saintly bodies which in prayer rise into the air as if buoyed upwards. In Scripture we have the cases of Enoch, Elijah, and our Saviour, whose bodies had lost their earthly gravitation, and, though material still, were spiritualized and lighter than the air through which they rose.

Levitation of Mr. D. Home. Lord Lindsay describes the levitation of Mr. D. Home, and his floating in and out of a window seventy feet from the ground. I will give the account in lord Lindsay's own words. "I was sitting with Mr. Home, and lord Adare, and a cousin of his. During the sitting, Mr. Home went into a trance, and in that state was carried out of the window in the room next to where we were, and was brought in at our window. The distance between the windows was about seven and a half feet, and there was not the slightest foothold between them, nor was there more than a twelve-inch projection to each window, which served as a ledge to put flowers on. We heard the window in the next room lifted up, and almost immediately after, we saw Home floating in the air outside our window. The moon was shining full into the room; my back was to the light, and I saw the shadow on the wall of the window-sill, and Home's feet about six inches above it. He remained in this position for a few minutes, then raised the window, and glided into the room feet foremost, and sat down. Lord Adare then went into the next room to look at the window from which Home had been carried. It was raised about eighteen inches, and he expressed his wonder how Mr. Home had been taken through so narrow an aperture. Home said, still entranced, 'I will show you;' and then, with his back to the window, he leaned back, and was shot out of the aperture, head foremost, with the body rigid; and then, quite quietly, he returned. The window is seventy feet from the ground, and I very much doubt whether the most skilful tightrope-dancer would like to attempt a feat of this description, where the only means of crossing would be by a perilous leap, or by being borne across in such a manner as I have described." (July 14, 1871, signed "Lindsay.")

* Probably many persons have felt what is called levitation in bed. I myself have done so many and many a time. It is rather a pleasant sensation of walking on air, sometimes three or four feet above the earth, and sometimes above the trees, the higher the more agreeable. This is not in delirium, but in perfect health. It is hard, in the morning, to persuade one's self that walking on air is not possible.

Copied from Zöllner's *Transcendental Physics*, Appendix A, p. 249. Edition printed by W. H. Harrison, 33, Museum Street, London, 1882.

Lions.

2 TIM. iv. 17. I was delivered out of the mouth of the lion.

ECCLESIASTICUS xlvii. 3. He played with lions, as with kids; and with bears, as with lambs.

DAN. vi. 1–23. When Daniel was made chief minister of king Darius, the native princes were jealous, and leagued together to ruin him. With this intent, they went to the king, and pretending that they wished to honour him, asked him to pass an edict, that every one who wanted to petition for anything should ask it of the king only, and if any one disobeyed this edict he should be cast into the den of lions. The edict was proclaimed, and Daniel, as before, petitioned God in prayer three times a day. When Darius was told thereof he was very sorry, but as he could not ignore his edict, Daniel was let down into the lions' den. At daybreak Darius went to the cave, and found to his great joy that Daniel had received no harm, so he was drawn out of the den, and his accusers were cast in; and lo! the lions tore the men piecemeal ere ever they reached the bottom of the den.

BEL AND THE DRAGON i. 33–42. In the reign of Cyrus king of Persia, Daniel exposed the frauds of the priests of Bel, and destroyed the dragon which was held to be a god. By this means he provoked the anger of all those who worshipped this false god. Accordingly, the men of Babylon went to Cyrus, and said to him, Deliver Daniel into our hands, or we will destroy thee and thine house. So Daniel was given into their hands, and they cast him into a den containing seven hungry lions, and there left him for seven days; but the lions did him no harm. On the seventh day Cyrus went to the den, and saw Daniel sitting peacefully among the lions. The king commanded that he should be taken out, and his accusers be thrown to the lions. This was done, and the men were devoured by the hungry beasts, even before they reached the bottom of the cave.

Lions offer adoration to the Child Jesus. When Jesus was eight years old, He went into a cavern where a lioness was bringing up her whelps. When the beasts saw the true Prince they ran up to offer adoration. Jesus sat in the cavern, where the whelps frisked about His feet, while the two elder beasts stood reverently afar off, with heads bowed down, and meek faces. After a while, Jesus came out of the cave, and much people saw Him, with the lion and lioness marching before Him, and the young ones gambolling playfully around Him. The parents of Jesus were present at this sight; and Jesus said to the multitude, "Lo! the beasts of the forest are wiser than ye, for they recognize their Lord and Master; but ye see Me, and know Me not."—*Apocryphal Gospel* (pseudo Matthew).

"The lion will not touch the true prince" (1 *Hen. IV.*, Act ii. sc. 4) was a very common religious superstition in the Middle Ages. The "true prince" meant the Messiah, who is called "the Lion of the tribe of Judah." Loosely, however, it applied to any prince of the blood royal, and in this sense Falstaff applies the proverb to prince Henry. Similarly Beaumont and Fletcher say—

> Fetch the Numidian lion I brought over;
> If she be sprung from royal blood, the lion
> Will do her reverence; else he'll tear her.
> *The Mad Lover.*

No one pretends that the "Gospel" referred to is inspired; but it embodies a prevailing notion, no matter by whom written, and as such belongs to the data of the "Modes of Thought."

Androclus and the lion. Androclus, a Roman slave, was condemned to encounter a lion in the amphitheatre; but when the lion was let loose, it crouched at his feet and began licking them. The circumstance naturally excited the curiosity of the consul, and the slave, being brought before him, told him the following tale:—"I was compelled by cruel treatment to run away from your service, while in Africa; and one day I took refuge in a cave from the heat of the sun. While I was in the cave a lion entered, limping, and evidently in great pain. Seeing me he held up his paw, from which I extracted a large thorn, and the beast was soon able to use his paw again. We lived together for some time in the cave, the lion catering for both of us. At length, tired of this savage life, I left the cave, was apprehended, brought to Rome, and condemned to be torn to pieces by a lion. My enemy was my old friend, and he recognized me instantly." The consul, hearing the tale, pardoned the slave, and presented to him the lion, which followed him about the city like a dog.—Aulus Gellius, *Noctes Atticæ*, v. 15.

The extraction of a thorn from the paw of a wild beast is a common incident in the lives of the saints. (See GERASIMUS AND THE LION, p. 220; JEROME AND THE LION, p. 220; also under BEASTS CONFIDING IN SAINTS, pt. ii.)

St. Archelaa, being exposed to lions, is not injured by them (third century). St. Archelaa was exposed to lions, but was wholly unhurt by them. Boiling pitch was then poured over her body, but when she cried to God in her agony, a voice from heaven said to her, "Maiden, be not afraid, for I am with thee, and will give thee a crown of life."—Baring-Gould, *Lives of the Saints*, vol. i. p. 278.

St. Basilides, St. Cirinus, St. Nabor, and St. Nazarius, were first beheaded, and then thrown to hungry lions, but the lions touched not the dead bodies. St. Basilides, St. Cirinus, St. Nabor, and St. Nazarius, four Roman nobles, were put to death in the reign of Diocletian for being Christians. After being beheaded, their bodies were thrown to lions, bears, and other wild beasts; but the beasts, instead of devouring them, crouched reverently before them. Then some Christians came and buried the bodies in a place out of Rome, called *Catatumbe.*

Almost all general martyrologies contain this account. (See amongst others Bede's *Church History.*)

St. Faustinus and St. Jovita, being cast to four lions, received no harm. Claudius II. of Rome sentenced St. Faustinus and St. Jovita to be cast to four savage lions, for loving Jehovah more than Jove; but the beasts lay at their feet, like favourite dogs, and did them no sort of harm. Then leopards and bears, irritated with torches, were sent against them, but instead of attacking the saints, turned on their irritators, and tore them to pieces. Surius (1570), *Lives of the Saints.*

St. Gerasimus and the lion (A.D. 475). St. Gerasimus, being one day on the banks of the Jordan, saw a lion coming to him, limping on three feet. When it reached the saint, it held up to him its right fore paw, from which the saint extracted a large thorn, and the lion soon recovered the use of its paw. The grateful beast now attached itself to the saint, and lived with him in his monastery, following him about like a dog, without molesting any one. (See ANDROCLUS, p. 219; JEROME, below.)—*Vies des Pères des Déserts d'Orient.*

Sir Iwain de Galles. Sir Iwain de Galles was attended by a lion, which, in gratitude to the knight who had delivered it from a serpent, became ever after his faithful follower. The lion used to play with the knight like a dog, and would often rise on his hind feet and lick his face.

St. Jerome and the lion (A.D. 345–420). One day, as St. Jerome was reading with his disciples, a lion entered the room. Though lame and limping, the scholars were frightened and ran away. Not so the learned doctor: he waited quietly till the lion came near. As soon as this was done the beast lifted one of its fore paws into the doctor's hand, and showed him how it was bleeding from the wound of a thorn. The holy man extracted the thorn, washed the paw, and dressed it. When the lion was able to use its paw again, St. Jerome gave it his blessing, intending it to go into its wild haunts; but it refused to leave its benefactor, and lived in the monastery, following the doctor about like a dog, and offering violence to no one. In Christian art St. Jerome is often represented blessing a lion. (See ANDROCLUS, p. 219.)—Edward Kinesman, *Lives of the Saints*, p. 784.

St. John the Silent protected by a lion (A.D. 454–558). St. John the Silent, being obliged to quit his monastery in consequence of a sedition amongst the monks, betook himself to the desert of Rube, where he lived nine years in perfect silence, never in all that time speaking a word to any human being. Nothing would induce him to return to his monastery. A lion which prowled round his cavern effectually kept off the approach o strangers.—Cyrille, *Éloges des Évêques Illustres.*

St. Marciana was uninjured by a lion, but not by a bull and leopard (A.D. 300). St. Marciana was exposed in the amphitheatre in Mauritania to a lion, which did her no harm; but a bull gored her, and a leopard despatched her.—Baring-Gould, *Lives of the Saints* (Jan.), p. 120.

This is a valuable paragraph. The lion never injures a Christian, because it is the type of the Messiah, called "The Lion of the tribe of Judah." The bull of Basan and the spotted leopard are emblems of the devil, whose very nature is enmity against God's people. Death, like sickness, being considered the work of the devil, if Marciana was killed at all, it is quite in accordance with mediæval belief to kill her by some beast typical of sin and Satan. (N.B.—Sometimes bulls and leopards are represented as doing Christians no harm, in which case another idea is embodied, viz. that God makes every living thing subject to His saints.)

A fierce lioness sent against St. Myron does him no harm (A.D. 250). Antipater, having received the government of Achaia, determined to root out the Christians. St. Myron, priest of the Church of Achaia, was accordingly seized, and brought before the proconsul. He was first suspended on a beam, and his whole body cut with a scarifier, till the ground was one pool of blood. The savage governor then ordered a furnace to be lighted with pitch, oil, and dung, and when these were seething, the martyr was cut down and thrown thereon; but instead of receiving any injury, he walked about the furnace, singing hymns, as if it had been a bed of roses, while hundreds, who stood near the furnace, fainted from the heat or died. Antipater was stupefied with amazement, and ordered the saint back to prison. Next day, being brought forth again, he was flayed from shoulder to foot; but as a sheep before its shearers is dumb, so he uttered not a word. In the midst of his torture, he threw a piece of his skin to the proconsul, crying out, "There, dog, eat that." This so exasperated the governor, that he ordered the skinless body to be raked with iron hooks, till every morsel of flesh was torn from the bones. "Help me, O Christ," cried the saint, "to bear all, and make me a sharer of Thy glory." "A place of peace is prepared for you," said a voice from heaven; "because you have fought a good fight, and remained faithful unto death." Antipater heard the voice, and ascribed it to sorcery. "Cursed wizard!" said the governor, "sacrifice! sacrifice, I say, or you shall be cast to the wild beasts." "Never," said Myron. He was then ordered back to prison, while the stadium was prepared. Next day he was brought out again, and the proconsul was amazed to see the saint's body was not only sound and vigorous, without a single trace of all he had undergone, but his face was like an angel's, and he stood in the fulness of manly beauty. "Thy magic, Myron, I own, is marvellous," said Antipater, "and I should be well content if you would renounce your art, and sacrifice to god Bacchus." The martyr answered not. So he was cast into the arena, and a fierce lioness let out upon him. The beast ran up, but suddenly her whole nature was changed. She licked his feet with her tongue, as if wishing to kiss him; and having so done, she bit in twain the cords that bound him, and set him free. "The God of Myron is truly a great God!" shouted the spectators. "There is no god in all the earth but Myron's God, which can do after this sort!" Antipater, fearing an insurrection among the people, had the saint secretly sent to Cyzicus, with private orders to the governor to cut off his head.—*Actes des Martyrs*, by the Bénédictins de la Congrégation de France.

St. Paul of Ptolemaïs and his sister Juliana unharmed by serpents (A.D. 274). The emperor Aurelian, having tried various torments on Paul of Ptolemaïs and his sister Juliana to turn them from the Christian faith, which he regarded as mere sorcery, ordered them to be cast into a dungeon with serpents, adders, asps, vipers, dragons, and other venomous reptiles. Here they were shut up for three nights and three days. The creatures crawled and glided to the two martyrs, but did them no harm. They looked at the two saints fixedly, and then lay quietly at their feet, while Paul and his sister sang together psalms and hymns and spiritual songs. On the morning of the third day, Aurelian went to see if the martyrs were devoured, and, looking through the dungeon window, heard singing, and saw three persons seated amidst the venomous beasts, the face of the third being that of an angel. He immediately commanded his magicians to take away the serpents and set the prisoners free. When, however, the magicians opened the prison door to execute the emperor's bidding, the reptiles sprang on them with fury, killed them, and escaped to the deserts.—*Acts of the Martyrs*, by the Bénédictins de la Congrégation de France.

This is not a tale about lions, but it is so obviously like the story of Daniel and the lions that it is not out of place in this group.

St. Primus and St. Fœlicianus, after sundry tortures, were cast to two lions, but were delivered, and God was glorified. St. Primus and St. Fœlicianus, two Roman senators, seem to have been subjected to all the martyrdoms of the martyrology, in the reign of Diocletian, and by the command of judge Promotus. For example: Fœlicianus was nailed hand and foot to a post, which was then hoisted by pulleys. There was he left three days; but his constant song was, "In God put I my trust. I will not fear what man may do unto me." No, and he had no need of fear, for an angel was with him all the time to cheer and comfort him. After the third day he was taken down, scourged, and cast into prison.

It was now Primus's turn. He was first beaten with knotty clubs, then two lighted torches were applied to his sides. While thus tortured he sang, "Thou dost try me by fire as silver is tried, and thus shalt Thou purify me." Being then thrown on his back, molten lead was poured down his throat; but God converted the liquid metal to a refreshing draught.

Fœlicianus was brought out to see the torment inflicted on his brother, and both being taken to the theatre in the street Numentana, two hungry lions were let loose upon them; but the lions approached them like lambs, licked their wounds, and crouched lovingly at their feet. Then two terrible bears were sent against them, but they also fell at their feet, and offered them no violence. When the spectators saw these things, multitudes were converted to the Christian faith. Ultimately their heads were cut off, and their bodies, torn piecemeal, were thrown to wild dogs; but the dogs refused to touch what God had consecrated to Himself, and at night the Christians picked up the pieces, anointed them, wrapped them in fine white linen, and buried them in the arsenal near the Numentanian arches. A church was subsequently built on the spot, and June 9 was set apart by the Church in honour of these martyred saints.—Edward Kinesman (1623), *Lives of the Saints*, pp. 350, etc. (Kinesman informs us he took the account from an ancient MS., but the Venerable Bede and other authors sufficiently confirm the narrative.)

St. Placidus, the Roman general, was cast to a lion, but received no harm. Placidus, the Roman general, having obtained a great victory, the emperor Trajan appointed a day of thanksgiving, when he and all the army were to offer sacrifice to the gods. Placidus said he could take no part in the ceremony, as he was a Christian; and Trajan, interpreting this refusal as an act of rebellion or treason, commanded him with his whole family to be cast into the arena, and a ferocious lion to be let loose upon them. To the amazement of all the spectators, the lion did them no harm, but played with them, fawned on them, and held down his head to be patted by them.—*Gesta Romanorum*, cx. (See also Antonius, *Chronicon;* Metaphrastês, *Lives*, etc.)

St. Prisca, exposed to a lion, is not injured by it (A.D. 50). Claudius, the emperor of Rome, ordered Prisca, a maiden of consular birth, to be beaten by the hands of his lictors, for refusing to sacrifice to the gods of Rome. On the morrow she was again brought up, and, as she remained obdurate, was beaten with rods. The third day she was exposed to a lion, but the beast only crouched at her feet, doing her no harm.—*The Roman Martyrology.* (Alban Butler erroneously places this incident under Claudius II., A.D. 275.)

St. Sabas makes a covenant with a lion (A.D. 439–531). St. Sabas, having abandoned his monastery, retired to Scythopolis, in a desert, on the borders of the Gadara. Here he found a cavern, and resolved to make it his home. This cave happened to be the lair of a prodigious lion, and, while the saint slept, the lion returned, saw the stranger, and, taking him up by his clothes, carried him out of the cave. When St. Sabas awoke, he saw this terrible creature standing over him, and, without the slightest symptom of fear, began his matins. The lion retreated to a distance while the saint was at prayer, but when he rose and entered the cave, the lion entered also. "Dear lion," said the saint, "this cave is quite big enough for you and me; but if you prefer to live alone, look out for another lair, for it would not be seemly for one made in the likeness of God to yield to you who are not so formed." At these words the lion quietly walked away, leaving the cavern to the abbot. Here St. Sabas lived in peace for some time, but his reputation as a saint spread abroad, and many came to him as disciples.—*Les Petits Bollandistes*, vol. xiv. p. 71.

Two lions submissive to St. Simeon (fourth century). One day some travellers arrived at St. Simeon's cell, and begged to be directed to a certain fort which they named. The old hermit called two lions out of the desert, and bade them conduct the travellers to the fort; and they did so. This incident was told to Theodoret by one of the travellers.—Theodoret, *Philotheus*, c. 6.

Every one will call to mind the attendant lion of Una, in Spenser (*Faëry Queen*, bk. i.); but in this allegory Una is "Protestantism," and the lion "England." In the case of Simeon, the writer evidently believes the two lions were wild beasts submissive to the hermit.

St. Tropetius "of Cæsar's household" exposed to a lion and a leopard (first century). St. Tropetius is said to be one of Cæsar's household, referred to by St. Paul in his *Epistle to the Philippians.* Nero committed him to the tender mercies of Sattelicus to be put to death for daring to believe in the divinity of Christ. Sattelicus thrust him in prison for two days without food, then bound him to a pillar, where he was scourged so inhumanly, that his whole body was cut to shreds. The pillar to which he was bound suddenly staggered and fell, crushing the judge and fifty others in its fall. Sylvin, the son of Sattelicus, now took his father's place, and condemned the martyr to the wheel, then to the wild beasts. A lion was first let out upon him, but died at his feet. A leopard was then sent against him, but fawned on him and caressed him. Evellius, one of Nero's counsellors, seeing these things, was made a convert, and died a martyr. Sylvin, mad with rage, being thus foiled in his impotent power, commanded the executioners to take the victim beyond the city gates, and cut off his head. This was done on the third calends of May. In Christian art St. Tropez has for his attributes a lion and a leopard.—

Acta Sanctorum (Bollandists), vol. iv. May 17.

St. Vitus charms a savage lion by the sign of the cross. When the emperor Diocletian saw that the fiery furnace had no effect upon St. Vitus, he ordered him to be exposed to a savage lion, saying, "Here incantation will avail thee nothing." As the lion came rushing towards him, St. Vitus made the sign of the cross, and the lion lay at the martyr's feet as quiet and playful as a lamb. St. Vitus called aloud to the emperor, "Behold, Diocletian! the beasts of the forest acknowledge the Lord, but thou art blinder in folly than the beasts." The emperor rose like a fury at this rebuke, and commanded his lictors to put the insolent to the catasta (*vide* Index), and in this terrible torture he died.—Edward Kinesman (1623), *Lives of the Saints*, p. 383.

Locusts.

EXOD. viii. 22. I will sever in that day the land of Goshen, in which My people dwell, that no swarm of flies shall be there.

EXOD. ix. 20, 21. He that feared the word of the Lord among the servants of Pharaoh made his cattle flee into the house; but he that regarded not the word of the Lord left his cattle in the field. [The former was saved, the latter was destroyed by the plague sent.]

St. Severin and the locusts (A.D. 482). When the country about Vienne was devastated by locusts, the people implored St. Severin to intercede on their behalf. He commanded them to keep at home for the whole of the next day, and to pass the time in humiliation, fasting, and prayer. All obeyed except one poor husbandman, who spent the time in trying to drive off the locusts from his crops. The day following, when the people visited their fields, what was their astonishment to find all the locusts gone, and not a blade of corn or single tree-leaf injured, with one great exception, viz. the poor husbandman who would not obey the saint. Not a blade of grass remained in all his land; not a leaf on any of his trees. His whole produce was devoured. Weeping, and wringing his hands, he went about saying he was ruined, quite ruined. St. Severin had compassion on him, and commanded all the others to contribute to his support, till his fields had time to recover. The saint was obeyed willingly; and he said to the poor man, "Learn from the locusts this lesson: It is the Lord that maketh poor and maketh rich. He will keep the feet of His saints; but the wicked shall be silent in darkness; for by strength shall no man prevail."—*Les Petits Bollandistes*, vol. i. p. 218.

Lot's Wife.

GEN. xix. 26. Lot's wife looked back from behind him, and she became a pillar of salt.

Two worldlings converted by St. Vincent Ferrier into two marble statues (A.D. 1357–1419). One day, as St. Vincent Ferrier was preaching at Pampeluna, he suddenly stopped, seized with a trance. On coming to himself he said, "God bids me leave off, and go without delay into the city, to a house which He will show me." He instantly started forth, followed by an immense crowd, and came to a splendid mansion. He touched the doors, and they instantly flew open of their own accord. The voices of two persons were now distinctly heard in licentious conversation. St. Vincent, without entering the room, rebuked them, and threatened them with the vengeance of God unless they desisted and repented. The young libertines laughed at him, and bade him go about his business. Whereupon they were both changed into two marble statues. When St. Vincent entered the room, he saw the two statues, and, moved with compassion, breathed into their mouths, and they returned to life, confessed their faults, received absolution, and fell down dead at the feet of the saint.—*Les Petits Bollandistes*, vol. iv. p. 238.

Lunatics and Maniacs.

MATT. xvii. 15, etc. Lord, have mercy on my son, for he is a lunatic. And Jesus rebuked the devil, and he departed out of him, and the child was cured from that very hour.

JOHN x. 20. He hath a devil, and is mad.

St. Hilarion cures Marsitas, a maniac. Marsitas, the maniac, was so strong, he could carry on his back fifteen bushels of corn * (!!) Into this man the devil entered, and made him so fierce that he did much harm. It was in vain to bind him, for he broke his bonds asunder as if they had been pack-thread. One while he assailed this man, at another time he set upon that man. Sometimes he bit

* Fifteen bushels of corn would be the produce of half an acre, or an acre and a quarter in America. It would be 3¾ sacks of four bushels each. Taking 60 lbs. as the average weight of a bushel, 15 bushels would equal 900 lbs. The greatest average load a strong man can support on his shoulders is 330 lbs. We are told, in fable, that Milo could carry a bull calf. A Milo's bull calf would probably weigh about 600 lbs., giving about 340 lbs. of butcher's meat.

off a finger, sometimes a nose or ear. St. Hilarion commanded the keepers to unbind him, and then with a very gentle voice he said to the maniac, "Marsitas, Marsitas, come hither to me." The man trembled from head to foot, hung down his head, fell on the ground, and licked the feet of the man of God, like a spaniel. Hilarion kept him with him for seven days, making constant prayer on his behalf, and then dismissed him, perfectly cured, and gentle as a lamb. (See LEGION, p. 214.)—St. Jerome, *Vita St. Hilarionis Eremitæ* (A.D. 390). See also Nicephorus Callistus (who died 1350), *Ecclesiastical History*.

Malchus and Peter.

LUKE xxii. 50, 51. One of the disciples [Peter] smote [Malchus] the servant of the high priest, and cut off his right ear. And Jesus said [to Malchus], Suffer ye thus far. And He touched his ear, and healed him.

St. Julian heals the eye of the governor's officer by a touch (A.D. 313). Marcian, governor of Antioch, having summoned Julian to his tribunal, commanded his lictors to scourge him, because he refused to offer incense to Jupiter. As they were scourging him, the lash struck one of the officers and knocked out his eye. Julian stepped up to the officer and said, "Suffer me, I pray you." So saying, he touched the part affected, signing on it the sign of the cross, and immediately the eye was restored to perfect soundness. The officer was so affected by this miraculous cure, that he openly confessed the God of Julian to be the only God, for none of the idols could do after this sort. Marcian, greatly enraged, ordered his officer to be at once beheaded. Thus was he "baptized in his own blood;" and thus in a moment, like the dying thief, was he converted and taken to paradise. —*Les Petits Bollandistes*, vol. i. p. 236.

Hands cut off joined on again. The following is told by John Damascene, Simeon Metaphrastês, Nicephorus, and others. When the Virgin Mary was conveyed to the grave, a Jewish priest had the temerity to push the bier, in order to throw off the body, but his hands were instantly cut off at the wrists. The priest confessed his great fault, begged pardon, and St. Peter bade him put his stumps near the lopped-off hands. On so doing, the parts came together again, and the priest became a convert to the Christian faith.—See *Assumption of the Virgin Mary*, Aug. 15.

Metamorphoses.

Lucian tells us that he anointed himself all over with enchanted oil from Thessaly, and was turned into an ass, in which capacity he served for six or seven years under cruel masters who sorely ill treated him; he served, for example, under a "gardener, a tyle man, a corier, and such like." Ultimately he was restored into his proper shape by eating roses, and wrote his adventures.

St. Macarius, we are told, encountered an old woman that had been turned into a horse, and by sprinkling her with holy water he restored her to her proper shape. —See Harsnet, *A Declaration of Popish Impostures* (1604), p. 102.

Of course every reader will call to mind the tale of Circê, who changed the companions of Ulysses into pigs; Spenser's story of Acrasia, who turned her lovers into all sorts of monsters; and many others.

John Bodin, a Frenchman (1530-1596), in his *La Démonomanie*, maintains that devils can transform themselves into any shape they like; that witches can, at will, assume the form of bird, beast, or fish; fly in the air, transfer growing corn from one field to another, and bring down hail, rain, wind, and lightning as they list. He defends lycanthropia; believes in the objective reality of Circê's transformation of Ulysses' men into swine; and tells us, as a fact, of a woman who sold an Englishman an egg, and thereby transformed him into an ass, and made him her market-beast for three years, on which she rode to buy butter. This author was no fool, for he wrote a sufficiently learned work entitled *De la République*, "A Commentary on Oppian," and *Méthode pour Étudier l'Histoire*.

Micaiah and King Ahab.

1 KINGS xxii. 1–36. Ahab king of Israel allied himself with Jehoshaphat king of Judah to war against Ramoth-Gilead. Before starting on the expedition, the king of Judah asked Ahab to consult his prophets, and the prophets all declared that the kings of Israel and Judah would be victorious. Not quite satisfied with this unanimous declaration, Jehoshaphat asked Ahab if he had convened all the prophets. All but one, named Micaiah, replied Ahab; but him I hate, for he is a croaking prophet, always foreboding evil. However, at the request of Jehoshaphat, Micaiah was sent for, and told the kings plainly that they would be utterly defeated, and that Ahab would be slain. Ahab was exceedingly angry at this plain speaking, and ordered Micaiah to be thrust into prison, and fed on the bread and water of affliction till after the battle. The king of Syria proved victorious, as Micaiah had predicted, and Ahab was slain by a man "who drew his bow at a mere venture."

St. Isaac warns Valens not to wage war with the Goths, assuring him it would not be to his honour; and he was utterly routed by them at Hadrianople. St. Isaac, hearing that the Goths were ravaging Thrace, said to the emperor Valens, "Open, O emperor, the Christian churches which you have closed and God will prosper your expedition against the Goths." The king treated these words as the raving of a fool, and took no notice of them. A day or two afterwards, Isaac again encountered the emperor, and said to him, "Open, O emperor, the Christian churches you have closed, and God will give you victory over the Goths." Valens, struck with this repetition, consulted his council, who laughed at the words; and the emperor paid no further heed to them. A few days later, Isaac again said to the emperor the same thing, but Valens told his followers to throw the fellow into a thicket, and continued his way. Isaac, being extricated therefrom, again stood before the emperor, and said, "You thought to stifle my voice, O emperor, but the Lord has delivered me, and has commanded me to say in His name, 'Open the churches which you have closed, and He will deliver the Goths into thy hands.'" Valens now committed the prophet into the hands of two senators to keep till after the battle. Whereupon St. Isaac cried aloud, in the words of the prophet Micaiah, "If ever, O emperor, you return in peace, then the Lord hath not spoken by my mouth; but be assured of this, you will give battle, be put to flight, and be burnt to death." And so it fell out. He gave battle, was routed, fled, hid himself in a hut which the Goths set fire to, and was burnt to a cinder.—*Acta Sanctorum* (Bollandists), March 27.

Miracles not classified.

The walls of a church open that St. Antony of Padua may see the elevation of the host (1195–1231). One day St. Antony, who was born at Lisbon, was occupied on some humble work not far from the church, when he heard the bell ring to announce the elevation of the host. Instantly he fell on his knees; and at the same moment the stone walls of the church opened, and showed him the officiating priest standing on the steps of the altar, accomplishing the holy sacrifice.—L'abbé Guyard, *Life of St. Antony of Padua.* (See Sanctès of Urbino, p. 227.)

St. Baudil's head leaps up three times, and makes three fountains (second and third centuries). St. Baudil, the apostle of Nismes, was set on by a furious mob, and assassinated, praying with his last breath that his blood might prove the seed of the Church. It is said, when the head of the martyr fell, it leaped thrice from the ground, and at every bound a fountain of water sprang up. ["La tête du Martyr, abattue par la hache des sacrificateurs rebondit trois fois sur le sol, et chacun de ses bonds fit jaillir une source."] St. Baudil's spring still remains in testimony of this miracle, and a healing virtue has been always attributed to it; but the three fountains are now united, because the rock has been levelled, and a chapel been built on the spot, so that the three springs run underground till they emerge united into a single stream.—Mgr. Guérin (chamberlain of pope Leo XIII.), *Vies des Saints*, vol. vi. pp. 42, 43.

[*St.*] *Peter Celestine, sent to cut green wheat, brings it home quite ripe* (A.D. 1221–1296). When Peter Celestine was a lad he was visited by angels and the Virgin Mary. His mother, being told of these visits, in order to test the truth, sent the boy into a field of green corn, and bade him harvest it. Peter obeyed, and brought home the wheat not only fully ripe, but of the best quality.—*The Admirable Life of St. Peter Celestine, Pope, etc.* (from the press of the Celestines, Bar le Duc).

Two children, seven years old, harnessed to a full-sized cart, draw it up Mont des Cygnes. A dispute having arisen between the count of Laon and one Erchinoald respecting the relics of St. Fursy (seventh century), it was agreed between them to refer the matter to God. So two children, only seven years old, were harnessed to a cart; the relics of the saint were placed therein, and the children were told to drag the cart wherever they liked. This cart was no plaything, inasmuch as two strong oxen were unyoked from it to give place to the two boys. The children drew the cart to Mont des Cygnes, in Péronne; so the relics fell to the lot of Erchinoald.

There is some slight difficulty in this miracle, and that is how two children, only seven years old, could be harnessed to a great cart usually drawn by two full sized oxen. The needful strength may be accounted for by "miraculous interposition," but the size of the children must have puzzled the disputants. However, as Mgr. Guérin, the chamberlain of Leo XIII., vouches for the fact, and his holiness himself allows it, of course *cela va sans dire.*

St. Dunstan pushes a church round with his shoulder (A.D. 925–988). St. Dunstan, having observed that a church had been built not due east and west, pushed it with his shoulder into the true direction. By this and other miracles he acquired such high reputation in England, that the king, the prelates, and the peers called him the "Father" of the country.—Osbert of Canterbury, *Life of St. Dunstan.*

St. Francis of Assisi restores to its place the gable of a house which had started (A.D. 1182–1226). Two years before his death, St. Francis of Assisi was quite blind; he went to Rome, and the pope sent his own private physician to attend him. One day, in conversation, the doctor happened to say that the gable of his house had started, and he feared his house would fall. St. Francis told the doctor to cut off a lock of his hair, and put it into the chink. This he did, and the gable was restored to its place.—Chavin de Malin, *Life of St. Francis of Assisi.*

St. Gerard enlarges a silver coffer without mechanical force (A.D. 994). Theodoric, bishop of Metz, having restored Epinal monastery, invited St. Gerard, bishop of Toul, to perform the ceremony of the translation of St. Goëric, the previous bishop of Metz. Theodoric had ordered a double coffer for the occasion, one of iron and one of silver, the former to fit in the latter. When they were sent in, it was found that the workman had made both of the same size. Theodoric thought it would be necessary to defer the ceremony, which would have been very objectionable, as many of the nobles and gentry around had been invited to attend. St. Gerard came to the rescue. He prayed that God would honour his faithful servant Goëric, and not permit the ceremony to be put off for the carelessness of a workman; then, taking the two coffers in his hand, he found that one fitted into the other exactly. The outer one enlarged itself so as to contain the other, as Theodoric had designed it should.—Father Benedict, *Life of St. Gerard* (1700).

St. James of Tarentaise lengthens a water-pipe miraculously (fifth century). While St. James of Tarentaise was building a church, a gutter for carrying water from the roof was found to be five feet too short. This was very inconvenient, so St. James sprinkled holy water on it, and the gutter instantly stretched itself out to the required length.—Gui of Burgundy (afterwards pope Calixtus II.), *Life of St. James of Tarentaise.*

St. Germana carries water in a sieve without losing a drop (A.D. 451). St. Germana was carrying her pitcher to fetch water from a fountain, when some rough peasants took it into their heads to break the pitcher, and gave her an old sieve instead. Germana, without one word of reproof, took the sieve to the fountain, filled it with water, and brought it to the peasants without losing a drop. In allusion to this miracle, St. Germana is represented in Christian art with a pitcher, and a sieve lying at her feet.—L'abbé Blampignon, *Vie de Ste. Germaine.*

Travellers are still shown the road taken by St. Germana, and are told that no grass grows so rich and green, and no corn so vigorous, as there.

(St. Germana was more lucky than the daughters of Danäus, in classic story, who were compelled everlastingly to pour water into a sieve, *inane lymphæ dolium fundo pereuntis imo.*—Horace, *Odes*, bk. iii. ode 11, ver. 26.)

The ring of St. Hemetherius and handkerchief of Celedon fly up to heaven. St. Hemetherius and St. Celedon were two Spaniards in the Roman army, but being Christians were dreadfully handled. After undergoing divers torments, they were condemned to be beheaded. When taken to the place of execution, Hemetherius tossed his ring into the air, and Caledon his orarium (*i.e.* a handkerchief for wiping the face). A wind wafted the two objects into the clouds in the sight of a crowd of spectators, and the executioner, amazed at the spectacle, delayed for a time his office; but when the ring and orarium were shut from sight, he finished the triumph of the two martyrs.—*Acta Sanctorum* (Bollandists), March 3.

The lamp before the shrine of St. Isidore fed with water. The following "miracle," the biographers of St. Isidore assure us, "has been tested by thousands; and hundreds of thousands can bear witness to the fact: The lamp which hangs before his shrine has been over and over again lighted from heaven without fire. Nay, more; when oil fails, water will do as well. Hundreds of curious or incredulous persons have tried it, and have always found that the wick burns as brightly with water as with oil."—Ribadeneira and D. A. Villegas, *Extravagants.*

By means of burning glasses the Romans lighted the fire in the temple of Vesta when it went out. By the same means Archimedês burnt the Roman fleet. In regard to water instead of oil, there is not the slightest difficulty in obtaining a brilliant flame. If a small quantity of the oil of turpentine was left in the lamp, the hydrogen gas of water (decomposed) would generate a brilliant light. This is Dr. Hare's famous light. A company was organized in 1868 for lighting Paris and London with water, and failed solely because the speculation was not likely to prove a commercial success.

St. Ives multiplies oak trees (1221–1303). The seigneur of Rosternen gave St. Ives permission to fell some oak trees in a forest for building the cathedral of Treguier. The steward complained that St. Ives had made too great havoc with the trees; but when the seigneur was taken to see the devastation, he found two fine oaks growing for every one that had been felled. He severely reprimanded his steward, and told St. Ives he might have all the timber he required.—Dom Lobineau, *Lives of the British Saints.*

St. Lucian's vestments discovered. St. Lucian was beheaded in the first century. Eight hundred years afterwards, a few days before the feast of Pentecost, a brilliant light was observed to burst suddenly in the abbatial church of Beauvais; and some priests, on going to see the cause, found a part of the vestments of St. Lucian deposited under the altar.—Delettré, *History of the Diocese of Beauvais,* vol. i. p. 431.

(A disbeliever in miracles might suggest that the "light" proceeded from a lantern, and the clothes were deposited by some man who had access to the church. If so, probably they had not been laid by for eight hundred years, and certainly the proof that they belonged to St. Lucian is sadly required.)

St. Opportuna, the abbey ass, and the salted meadow (A.D. 770). One day St. Opportuna sent one of her servants with an ass to pick up wood in a neighbouring forest. The forester pounded the ass, and when the abbess demanded its release, the man replied he would release the ass when a meadow, which he pointed to with his finger, was covered with salt (meaning never). Next day, however, when the forester rose, he found the meadow was so covered. It was ever after called "The Salt Meadow," and at one time two processions were made to it every year. This tale has been represented in painting. —L'abbé Gosset (curé de Ste. Opportune), *Life of St. Opportuna.*

St. Paul of the Cross taught by miracle not to dance (A.D. 1694–1775). During carnival, Paul of the Cross was invited by a gentleman to lead off a dance, and accordingly selected a partner. But, just as he led his partner out, all the strings of the instruments snapped, and a stop was put to the dancing.—Father Pius, *Life of St. Paul of the Cross, Founder of the Passionists.*

The walls of a church open, to show St. Sanctés of Urbino the host (A.D. 1390). St. Sanctés had a special devotion for the sacrifice of the altar. One day, being prevented by his duties from attending mass, he fell on his knees, when he heard the bell announce the elevation of the host; and immediately the four walls of the church opened, so that he might see the altar and the host, which were radiant with light. When the office was over the walls closed again without leaving a trace of their miraculous disjunction.—*Annales Franciscaines.* The same tale is told in the *Palmier Séraphique.* (See Antony of Padua, p. 225.)

Why was it that "quatre murailles s'entr'ouvrirent"? If only one of the walls had unfolded it would have answered the purpose.

A woman struck dead for intruding into the close of the hermitage of Simeon Stylites (fifth century). Simeon, the pillar-saint, would not suffer any woman to enter within the precincts of his hermitage. One day a woman dared to set foot within this forbidden spot, but the very moment her foot touched the ground she fell down dead, in the presence of a large concourse of people. "Leaving a terrible example of the wrath of God against those who dared to violate the close of a religious sanctuary."—Metaphrastês, *Lives,* etc.

Miracles performed by the image of Mary and Child in Deols (twelfth century). In the parish church of Deols, in France, was an image of the Virgin and Child, of which Father Labbe says, "Astruunt miraculorum veritatem reges, et principes, et occidentalis Europæ fere universæ multitudo." The following is given in the *ipsissima verba* of Anseald of Brabançon, a famous highwayman:—"Four years ago, in an expedition under count Richard, I was wounded in the upper jaw by an arrow. The doctors could not remove it, and the pain I felt was horrible. On June 21, A.D. 1187, suffering like those in hell, I made my prayer to Our Lady of Deols, and said to the image, 'If you will heal me, and extract this cursed arrow, you shall be my queen, and I will give you every year a bit of silver.' Scarcely had I uttered this vow, when the arrowhead began to move; it then fell out of my jaw into my mouth without producing the least pain. I called for my horse, and with a little help, for I was weak, I got into the saddle and went to fetch my tribute. The monks requested me to deposit the arrowhead with them as a memorial of the 'miracle,' which, of course, I did willingly. Mounting the steps by the help of two comrades, I made my offering, and instantly my full strength was restored. I attended the next service, and told the people assembled this story, showed them the arrowhead, and handed it to the priests. I have renounced the high-road, and mean to take Mary for my suzerain."—Father Labbe, *Bibliotheca Nova.*

Father Labbe informs us that he has read in an ancient MS. of more than two hundred miracles performed by this image.

When St. Simplician was executed, his head made a great hole in the earth (second century). Simplician of Poitiers was the son of Justin, a man of high rank, and governor of Poitiers under the Romans. Much to the horror of his father, his son became a Christian, and was brought to the block. When his head fell to the axe, it made a great hole in the ground, which remained "jusque dans ces derniers temps," and numerous pilgrimages have been made to it. The faithful used to place their head over the hole, and were instantly cured of any malady they were afflicted with. More than twelve hundred cures are registered. The church built over the hole was destroyed in the Revolution.—L'abbé Auber, *Vie des Saints de l'Eglise de Poitiers.*

St. Wodoaldus assists two nuns to repair a cope (A.D. 700). One day, when St. Wodoaldus was about to celebrate mass in a convent, he met two nuns in great distress, because "elles avaient manqué la coupe d'une robe de grand prix qu'un seigneur de la cour avait prié l'abbesse de lui faire confectionner dans le convent." St. Wodoaldus made the sign of the cross upon the material, which immediately "reprit sa première forme, et put être taillée de nouveau avec de plus de précision."—L'abbé Pecheur, *Annales du Diocèse de Soissons.*

How Eligius shod a restive horse. St. Eligius was shoeing a restive horse, and as the horse would not stand still, he quietly took off the animal's leg, put the shoe on the foot at his leisure, restored the limb, and the horse was none the worse for the proceeding.—Baring-Gould, *Lives of the Saints.*

If for "took off" we were to read "took up," or "took off [the ground]," the miracle would disappear, but probably the truth would not be less.

Miracles of Doubtful Morality.

St. Antony of Padua by his prayers restores a woman's long hair (A.D. 1195–1231). A woman employed upon some commissions for the Minorites, got home later than she was expected. Her husband was extremely angry, beat her, and cut off her long hair, on which she greatly prided herself. Next day, St. Antony was miraculously told thereof by the Saviour; so he went to see the woman, whom he found weeping for the loss of her hair. He spoke comfort to her, exhorted her to resignation, and promised to intercede on her behalf. On returning to the convent, he assembled all the brothers in the chapel, and prayed. "Au même instant les cheveux de la femme renaissaient aussi beaux, et aussi longs que jamais."—L'abbé Guyard, *Life of St. Antony of Padua.*

This probably is the most frivolous miracle on record, and yet the actors are the Saviour, St. Antony, and a whole convent of friars. Prayer and miracle are added, and the object to lengthen a woman's hair and gratify personal vanity.

St. Hilary, by prayer, murders his daughter and wife (died 367). St. Hilary, bishop of Poitiers, had a daughter named Abra; and, when she was grown to marriageable age, he prayed that she might die, lest she should be corrupted by longer contact with this world. His prayer was heard, and his child died peaceably without pain. His wife, "jealous of her daughter's happiness," asked her husband to pray that she might join her daughter. This he did, and the wife died also. These two deaths, Mgr. Guérin, the pope's chamberlain, calls "miracles more extraordinary than raising the dead to life."—*Les Petits Bollandistes*, vol. i. p. 304.

St. Hilary ought to have remembered the Saviour's prayer: "I pray not that Thou shouldest take them out of the world, but that Thou shouldest keep them from the evil of the world." It must be presumed that St. Hilary believed his prayers would be efficacious to procure the deaths of his daughter and wife; if so, he might have poisoned them or cut their throats with equal right. In fact, he deliberately murdered both his victims.

St. Isidore gives away his master's corn to feed the birds (A.D. 1170). One day, in winter, when the earth was covered with snow, his master sent Isidore to the mill with a sack of wheat to be ground. On the road he saw a flock of birds perched in the trees; so, untying his sack, he gave the corn to the birds. Some neighbours coming up, bound also to the mill, laughed at him for what he had done, and all went to the mill together. On reaching the mill, Isidore set down his empty sack, but when the miller came up he found it full. All the corn of the different sacks was duly ground, but Isidore's flour required two large sacks to hold it.—John (the deacon), *Life of St. Isidore, the Farm Labourer* (1261).

Certainly this labourer had no right to give away his master's corn without leave. There is no charity in giving away what does not belong to you. Suppose a merchant sends his clerk with £1000 to the bank, and as he goes he gives the money to the poor; would this not be felony, and worthy severe punishment? Why are birds better than human beings? Our Lord says a man is better than man sparrows.

St. Nicholas and the pagan usurer. An army of Vandals, passing from Africa to Calabria, ravaged the country, and carried away great spoils. Amongst other things that fell into their hands, was an image of St. Nicholas. The Vandal to whom this image fell was a usurer, and on one occasion, being called suddenly from home, he said to the image, "Remember, Nicholas, to look well after the money-chests while I am away." When the usurer was gone, some thieves broke into the house, and stole his money; and, on his return, he rated the image soundly for not protecting his master's goods better; and told the image it should assuredly be burnt, if the money were not restored within three days. At sunset St. Nicholas showed himself to the thieves, and threatened to punish them unless they restored the money; so they took it back to the usurer, even to the uttermost farthing. When the man found his money restored, he was converted to the Christian faith, and baptized.

(All the ancient authors who have written the life of St. Nicholas mention this story; and this was the reason why St. Nicholas was chosen the patron saint of thieves.)

There are many moral objections against this tale. (1) Usury was itself illegal, and ought not to have been countenanced; (2) bribery and corruption are no instruments of God's grace; (3) St. Nicholas had no right to compound with thieves; (4) it is no part of God (represented by the image) to protect unlawful gains.

St. Zita gives away her master's goods in charity (A.D. 1218-1278). St. Zita was a servant in the house of Pagano, seigneur of Fatinelli. Once, when there was a famine, Zita, touched with pity for the half-starved wretches who applied at the house for food, gave them the beans from her master's granary, without asking his permission. Not long afterwards, the seigneur, taking stock, went to measure his beans. Zita was terribly alarmed, and hid herself behind her mistress. Pagano found the measure all right, and Zita thanked God for restoring what she had taken for charity.—Stolz, *Hagiography.*

I once heard an English clergyman, at a Church missionary meeting, extol his little daughter, a child of about seven years of age, for taking a shilling, which did not belong to her, to put into the Church missionary box. The charity of Zita, mentioned above, is of precisely the same character; but the miraculous replacing of the beans, to conceal the theft, is making God an accessory after the deed.

St. Zita neglects her work to attend matins (A.D. 1218-1278). It was the duty of Zita, who was servant in the house of Pagano, seigneur of Fatinelli, to make the bread and prepare breakfast. One day she stopped so long at church, there was no time to make the bread and cook it for breakfast. Zita hastened home, and found, to her inexpressible joy, that an angel had done her work for her; and the bread was both made and baked ready for use.—*Vita Sanctorum* (Papebroch the Bollandist), April 27, p. 497.

Prayer and attendance at church, no doubt, are duties which should be duly and diligently observed; but a servant has no more right to neglect her duty to her master, who pays for certain services, than she has to neglect prayer and public worship. If Zita neglected her duty, this angel taught her a very bad lesson by trammeling up the consequences. There are two tables of the law, and those who break either are equally guilty. It is passing strange that the words *Laborare est orare* (To labour is to pray) were so often in the mouth of Zita that they are called "Zita's Proverb." It seems from the above that the proverb would be more correctly written in Zita's case *Orare est laborare.*

Miracles of Special Saints.

It would be impossible in some hundreds of pages of this book to give even a list of the names of the workers of miracles in the Roman calendar. As Mgr. Guérin says, "Tous les grands prédestinés, l'illustre archevêque avait reçu d'en haut le don de miracles." Hence in the lives of saints miracles are spoken of in the most off-hand manner. Take, for example, St. William, by no means one of the great saints. Mgr. Guérin says of him, "Sans troubler les éléments, ses miracles salutaires assouplissaient les lois rigides de la Nature. C'était un enfant mourant qu'il remettait plein de vie et de force à sa mère charmée. C'était un paralytic dont sa bénédiction dénouait les membres; un énergumène auquel il rendait la paix du corps et de l'âme; un prisonnier dont il brisait les chaines. Au seul contact de sa main les aveugles, les sourds, et les muets, rentraient en possession de leur sons." This summary might be added to thousands of saints with equal applicability, but in this volume only those miracles are set down which have been recorded with sufficient circumstance to give them interest and speciality. All miracles which can be classified under some head are noticed in their respective categories. Those which the author of this book has been unable so to arrange will be found here, or under the title of "Miracles not classified."

What has been said of saints will apply also to relics and the tombs of saints. A saint can scarcely be carried to the grave without miracles accompanying the coffin, and adorning his tomb. Take, for example, the same St. William referred to above. Mons. Raynal (*History of Berri*, vol. ii. p. 165) writes, as an appendix of his living miracles, "Au seul contact de cette pierre sacrée [*i.e.* his tombstone] les maladies et les blessures mortelles sont guéries; les démoniaques délivrés; les insensés recouvrent la raison; les muets parlent; les sourds entendent; les aveugles voient; les prisons s'ouvrent; les chaînes tombent; des enfants ravis par des loups sont rétrouvés sains et saufs, jouant avec les petits, et dans la tanière des bêtes fauves..." etc. [Mons. Raynal has omitted to inform us how the "prisons" he refers to, the "chains," and the "infants ravished by wolves" came in "contact with the tomb of the saint." Undoubtedly the "pierre sacrée" means the tomb or tombstone, as the words immediately preceding are "innombrables miracles s'accomplirent sur le tombeau et par les mérites de saint Guillaume. Au seul contact de cette pierre," etc.]

Summary of the miracles of St. Aldric, bishop of Mans (A.D. 800-856). The contemporaneous historians and disciples of St. Aldric say that three quires of paper would not suffice for a mere catalogue of his miracles; and the prodigies which proceeded from his tomb indicated the glory to which he was advanced in heaven.

Our fathers have themselves seen a miraculous oil of healing virtues ooze from his marble statue, and run down it in streams.—*Les Petits Bollandistes*, vol. i. pp. 192, 193.

Summary of the miracles of St. Bernard of Abbeville (A.D. 1046–1117). Robert des Moteis, a near neighbour of St. Bernard's abbey of Tiron, was a chevalier, but very poor. St. Bernard went to visit him, and "par sa seule présence, fit affluer dans le modeste castel une inépuisable richesse."

Passing through St. Lubin de Chassant, he healed, with the sign of the cross, an infant born blind; and, with the same sign, delivered two of his own monks from malignant spirits.

One harvest-time a young novice was knocked down by a cart drawn by ten bullocks, and was terribly crushed by the wheels, which ran over her. She was carried to the infirmary, as it was supposed, quite dead; but St. Bernard, laying his hands on her, bade her arise; and she arose without the slightest trace of the late accident.

Louis le Gros, king of France, for being cured by St. Bernard of a dangerous malady, gave to the abbey of Tiron the territory of Centray.

At St. Bernard's death, all the monks of Tiron (except one) who had died since its foundation appeared round his bed, with glories ready to conduct his soul to paradise. The one exception was a monk who received the order of priesthood without passing regularly through the lower degrees first. For this offence the devils carried his soul to the bottomless pit.

St. Bernard's death was known the same day to the allied monks in England and to those on the banks of the Rhine. This, of course, was by divine revelation.

God, says his biographer, wishing to show by some signal prodigy His pleasure at the virtues of His servant, sent on him one day, when he was blessing the people, a shower of roses, "qui l'enveloppait de ses parfums." At another time, while he was celebrating mass, a white dew filled the air with a celestial odour. On another occasion, the saint, merely by a word, quenched a fierce fire, which had threatened to burn down all the cell.—Corblet, *Hagiographie d'Amiens*. (The life of St. Bernard of Abbeville was written in 1137–1148 by Geoffroy le Gros, one of his disciples.)

Summary of the miracles of St. Brigit, thaumaturge (A.D. 436–523). St. Brigit, or St. Bride, like St. Patrick, is patron saint of Ireland. She was the natural daughter of Duptac and a slave, and was a marvel of beauty. St. Brigit was a thaumaturge, and Baronius tells us he read a record of her miracles which ran through twenty-five chapters, folio. Alban Butler says, "There are five modern lives of her, which are little else than enumerations of her wonderful miracles." Some account is contained in Bollandus, *Acta Sanctorum*, Feb., vol. i. p. 99, etc.; and in St. Jerome's *Martyrology*.

A reference to the index of this volume will give the reader a few specimens of her miracles.

Summary of the miracles of Charles Borromeo (A.D. 1538–1584).

(The miracles wrought by the intercession and merits of St. Charles Borromeo are far too numerous to be given in detail; several are dispersed in the volume under the different heads. The following are also sanctioned and directly allowed by the bull of canonization.)

(1) He healed, by the virtue of prayer, John Pietro Stopano, archbishop of Matia, in the Valley of Telino, of a deadly disease, after being given up by his physicians.

(2) He preserved, by the sign of the cross, the abbot Bernardino Tarusi and Joseph Cavallerio from being drowned in the Ticino.

(3) He saved, by the force of prayer, Julio Homatto from being killed, when thrown from his horse over a steep precipice.

(4) He drove away, by the benediction of his hands, divers devils which had possessed a young man for a long time.

(5) He healed, by his benediction, Margaret Vertua of a double tertian ague, which had afflicted her for eight months. This miracle was instantaneous, though Margaret had been brought so low by the ague that she was unable to move.

(6) By his blessing, he healed a noble lady from a disease brought on her by witchcraft.

After his death. (1) Dame Paula Justina Casata, a nun in the great monastery of Milan, had been paralyzed for eight and a half years. Being given up by her medical attendants, she invoked the aid of St. Charles Borromeo, and was cured in an instant. This occurred on the day of St. John the Baptist, A.D. 1601.

(2) Philip Nava, of Milan, had a son born blind, and two strange tumours, as big as half-eggs, had sprung up under his eyes, so as wholly to bury those organs. The swellings increased daily

and his mother, Lucina, implored the aid of St. Charles, especially as the child was the saint's namesake. Instantly the ghost of St. Charles himself appeared in the chamber, and no sooner had he given his benediction, than the two tumours disappeared, sight was given to the child, and the boy was restored to perfect health (Oct. 1604).

(3) Martha Vighia, of Milan, had been afflicted in her eyes for six years. Her pain had been great, and her sight had wholly perished. She prayed to St. Charles for help, and the saint came to her in her sleep, told her to visit his tomb, and he would answer her there. Next morning, which was Friday, Martha was led by the hand to the tomb of the saint, and, after making her prayer, she kissed the stone which covered his sepulchre. As her lips touched the stone her sight was entirely restored, and she rose up in perfect health (Nov. 4, A.D. 1601).

(4) John Jacques Lomati, a gentleman of Milan, had his legs eaten full of holes by scrofula. He was wholly unable to stand; and the doctors said he could not possibly live the year out. One day the pain was so severe he begged to be taken to the tomb of Charles Borromeo, and there he earnestly implored the saint to send him some respite. As he made his invocation, he found himself completely healed, and all his sores were converted into sound flesh (Sept. 24, A.D. 1587).

(5) John Baptista Tiron, a child five years old, fell into the Ticino; but calling to mind the name of Charles Borromeo, to whose portrait he daily said his prayers, the saint came to his aid in a visible form, drew him out of the river, led him over its surface more than a hundred cubits, and set him safely on the bank. This was done in the sight of many who saw the accident.—Edward Kinesman, *Lives of the Saints* (1623), pp. 876–878.

(He says that the life given has been taken from the Italian abridgment set forth by the Very Rev. Prelate Francis Penia, translated into French by Charles de Canda, prior of Domp Martin.)

N.B.—The life of Charles Borromeo has been often written. For example, by Bimius (1585); Magnano (1587); Austin Valerio (1588); Possevino (1591); Bascapé (1592), *bis*; Guissano (1610); Withius (1611); Muñoz (1624); Godeau (1648); Touron (1761); Stolz (1781); Olcese (1817); Alban Butler (1835); Chenevières (1840); Dragoni (1844); Dieringer (1846); Alexander Martin (1847); Mgr. Guérin (7th edit. 1880); and many others.

St. Cuthbert, called the British Thaumaturge (seventh century). By the force of prayer only, St. Cuthbert quenched a fire which threatened to commit very serious damage. He also dissipated a fire in the air, which the devil had conjured up to deter the people from going to hear him preach. By prayer he quelled tempests and storms. By prayer he turned water into wine.

By his mere presence he caused an unchaste devil to quit the body of a woman which it had taken possession of.

With water, oil, or hallowed bread, he healed divers sick folk given over by the doctors, some of whom were plague-stricken. By water which he had blessed he cured the wife of a noble thane, who lay speechless and senseless.

By sending the girdle of a holy abbess, called Elfleda, he healed a contraction of the muscles, and performed many other remarkable cures.

When he retired to the Farne islands, never before inhabited by man, because they were so infested by serpents, and so many demons had made it their retreat, he found the island he selected afforded him neither corn, fruit, nor water. He first drove the serpents into the sea, and evicted the demons; then by prayer obtained a well of fresh water; and by sowing barley, though wholly out of season, he obtained an abundant crop.

During a plague at Lindisfarne he visited a poor woman who had just lost one of her sons, while another was on the point of death. St. Cuthbert took the child in his arms, kissed it, and said to the mother, "Be comforted; the child shall live." And so it did, for it recovered from the plague from that very hour.—Bede, *Church History*, bk. iv. ch. 27–32; *Acta Sanctorum*, March 20.

Summary of miracles attributed to St. Dominic (A.D. 1170–1221). One day, preaching before a church against the heresies of the day, St. Dominic found himself, with a brother from the Cistercian convent, suddenly transported into the church, without any one having opened the doors. At another time his valise and books fell into a river, and when, after several days, they were "fished up again," they were not even wetted. Often while travelling the rain fell in torrents, without one single drop falling on him, that he might reach his journey's end quite dry. As he never took money about with him, he had to ask free passage across ferries. On one occasion the boatman refused to ferry him across without his fare; so he lifted his eyes to heaven, and found at his feet the required money. In the convent of St. Vincent of Castres, the crucifix spoke to him, and told him to persevere in well-doing, and to remember that saints were made perfect by suffering. In the same place, while at mass, his fervour was so great that he was lifted into the air full five feet from the ground, of which fact the prior himself and the canons were personal witnesses. He saved miraculously from drowning forty English pilgrims going to St. James's, who had entered a boat too weak and had been thrown into the Garonne.—*Les Petits Bollandistes*, vol. ix. p. 284.

Summary of miracles of St. Francis d'Assisi (A.D. 1182–1226). The astounding miracles wrought by St. Francis d'Assisi would fill a large volume. He cast out devils, healed the sick, raised the dead, and commanded the elements. Many of his wonderful works are set forth in the bull of canonization, demonstrating that all true [Roman] Catholics believe them to be authentic and genuine. —*Life*, by Arrighetti, Peter d'Alva, St. Bonaventure, Chavin de Malan, etc.

St. Francis of Paula, thaumaturge (A.D. 1416–1507). Of all the saints, none but Vincent Ferrier have exceeded St. Francis of Paula in prophetic inspiration and miraculous gifts. In the acts of canonization we have this marvellous summary:—"He [Francis of Paula] made huge beams of timber and enormous stones light, that his workmen might carry on their works at Paterna more easily; he entered burning furnaces without himself or his clothes being burned; he stopped falling rocks, while rolling down the sides of mountains with impetuosity, or stayed them in mid-air from falling; he caused springs of water to well up from dry ground; he found brick earth in parts where there was none; he burnt lime and bricks instantaneously, without the aid of fire; he often fed all his workmen and disciples with food insufficient for the meal of one man; he commanded devils, and even made them work for him; he put seven chestnuts in the ground, and they instantly became seven large trees. This was done to appease the anger of a man who complained that St. Francis had cut down one of his chestnut trees without permission. The fact is, the man's wife had given the tree to the saint for his monastery. The fruit of these chestnut trees is sanative, and thousands have been cured of divers complaints by eating it. He made wild bulls draw his ploughs, and they were as docile as oxen which had been used to the yokes for ten years. An enormous tree, which stood in the middle of the road leading to his church, greatly incommoded the public; so he split the tree in two by his word alone, and caused each moiety to retire right and left for several feet, leaving a clear wide road between. These two half-trees stood on each side of the road, as two perfect trees, and neither lost their verdure nor showed any sign of injury. They stood for many years, but the branches being much used for crucifixes and rosaries, only the bare trunks now remain.

Then as for the healing of diseases. One of the witnesses examined in the consistory, at the canonization, affirmed that, to his own personal knowledge, St. Francis healed one hundred persons in one day. Other witnesses testified that he was always healing; and the numbers of persons so benefited could not be counted; they said, undoubtedly the saint held in his hands the keys of life and death. He brought down to the grave, and brought up therefrom. One day a child was born without eyes and mouth, but St. Francis marked with his spittle the places where these features ought to have been, and then, making the sign of the cross, the infant became possessed of two brilliant eyes and a model mouth. He gave eyes to the blind, hearing to the deaf, speech to the dumb; he made the halt to walk, the cripple to have the use of his limbs; and recalled six dead persons to life again. Thomas d'Yvre of Paterna he twice restored to life; once when he was crushed to death by a tree falling on him, and again when he fell from a steeple. This is the only instance on record of a person being raised from the dead twice. When he went to Messina on his cloak-raft (see p. 64), the first thing he did was to restore to life a man who had been hanged for three days on the public gibbet. Persons are shown at Milazzo, above the main entrance of his church, two huge stones which, we are told, the saint lifted without aid, and placed where they are now seen. They are also shown a pit, which once contained salt water, but which St. Francis made fresh till the cistern was completed.—Father Giry, *Bull of Leo X. and Acts of Canonization.*

Mgr. Guérin, chamberlain of pope Leo XIII., after recounting the great miracles of St. Francis of Paula, concludes thus: "Combien de fois a-t-il produit ou multiplié du pain, du vin, des figues, et d'autres aliments semblables, que la faim leur faisait demander! Combien de fois a-t-il fait cuire subitement, pour eus et pour d'autres personnes, des légumes que l'on avait oublié ou négligé de faire cuire! Combien de fois a-t-il remis en état de travailler ceux que des chutes et des blessures considérables avaient rendus incapables de faire la moindre chose! . . . Il rendit la vue aux aveugles, l'ouïe aux sourds, la parole aux muets, l'usage des pieds et des mains aux estropiés, la vie aux agonisants et aux morts; et, ce qui est encore plus considerable, la raison aux insensés et aux frénétiques. Les lépreux, les hydropiques, les paralytiques, les personnes affligées de la pierre, des écrouelles, de la colique, de la migraine, et de tout autre genre de douleur, de plaies, et d'ulcères, trouvèrent en sa charité un remède instantané. Il n'y eut jamais de mal, quelque grand et incurable qu'il parût, qui pût résister à sa voix ou à son attouchement."—*Vies des Saints*, vol. iv. p. 143.

The miracles ascribed to his relics after death are no less astounding. Mgr. Guérin says: Everything which belonged to St. Francis of Paula, and everything he had touched, received a miraculous virtue, as the handkerchiefs and aprons which had touched the body of St. Paul. A pair of spectacles that passed through his hands cured Angus Serra, an ecclesiastic, of blindness; his "discipline de fer," stained with his blood, healed a woman of heart complaint; a cord which he wore, being presented to a demoniac, constrained the foul spirit to quit the body of the possessed; a piece of his gown, subdivided into twenty parts, and given to twenty noblemen, multiplied into eighty parts, under the hands of seigneur Jean, comte des Arènes, and still seven parts were left for the count himself. These fragments were sources of countless miracles in France, Naples, and Calabria. The cap which St. Francis wore, and many which were placed on his head after death, became endowed with miraculous virtues, and cured many sufferers. "Il y en a de tous côtés des exemples fort authentiques, que je me dispense néanmoins de rapporter." If any one doubts, let him call to mind that water, chrism, and oil are the substances of three of the sacraments, and that God chooses the weak things of the world to confound the things which are mighty, and base things of the world, and things which are despised, hath God chosen . . . that no flesh should glory. Thus also St. Gregory the Great gave to certain ambassadors, who expected to receive from him some mighty relic of great value, a linen cloth which had touched the bones of martyrs, and when they complained of being deceived, he pricked the cloth, and blood fell from it.—Father Giry (1685), *Acts of Canonization*, etc.

St. Francis of Paula is sometimes drawn with an ass before a forge. The tale referred to is this: A farrier who had shod the ass demanded payment for doing so, but as the saint had no money, he could not pay the man, and the farrier began to curse and swear at the impostor. To put an end to this unseemly scene, St. Francis bade his ass give up the shoe, and the ass, kicking out his leg, shook the shoe off into the smithy.

Miracles of St. Francisca (A.D. 1384-1440). Amongst the miracles of St. Francisca, this summary is taken from her biographer and father confessor, John Mattiotti. She cured an infant, five years old, of the falling sickness, merely by laying her hand on its head. By the same means she healed another child of a rupture. A woman named Angela, who was a cripple from gout, happened to meet St. Francisca in the street, implored her succour, and was instantly restored to perfect health. One day she fed fifteen nuns with fragments of bread barely sufficient for three, and a basketful was left afterwards. On another occasion, when some nuns were chopping sticks, they felt extremely thirsty, but there was no water at hand; so Francisca bade some vines supply them with grapes, and this they did although the month was January. These are only a few of her numerous miracles; but these will suffice to show how greatly God honoured her.—John Mattiotti (her father confessor), *Life of St. Francisca.*

Her biographer adds, "These many miracles were brought to the notice of several pontiffs, as Eugenius IV., Nicholas V., and Clement VIII.; at length, in 1608, Paul V. canonized her; and Innocent X. commanded her fête to be celebrated with a double office."

Summary of miracles ascribed to St. Geneviève (A.D. 423-512). A mere catalogue of the miracles of St. Geneviève would fill several pages of this book. She gave hearing to the deaf, speech to the dumb, and sight to the blind. She healed the sick, and communicated sickness at her will. She raised the dead, commanded the sunshine and the rain, multiplied food and drink, and indeed did pretty well as she pleased with the laws of nature. Mgr. Guérin gives the following summary of the miracles ascribed to her relics:—"On y [at the church of St. Denis] une lampe, dont l'huile ne se consumait point, quoiqu'elle brûlât toujours, et qu'on prît continuellement de cette huile pour servir à la guérison des malades. Des aveugles y reçurent la vue; des muets, l'usage de la langue; des possédés, leur délivrance; des personnes tourmentées par la fièvre, une prompte et parfaite santé. Une femme, reprise de ce qu'elle travaillait le jour de la nativité de Notre Dame avait répondu impudemment que la Vierge était une pauvre femme comme elle,—en punition de ce blasphème, ses doights s'étaient si fort attachés au peigne avec lequel elle cardait la laine, qu'on ne pouvait les en séparer,—elle fut guérie en priant auprès de ce sépulcre. Un jour, la Seine, étant étrangement débordée, et ayant rempli toutes les églises et les maisons jusqu'à la hauteur des premiers étages, on trouva le lit sur lequel St. Geneviève avait rendu son esprit, et que l'on conservait dans un monastère de filles, tout environné d'eau comme d'un mur, sans qu'il en pût être inondé, ni même mouillé. Puis le débordement cessa, et la rivière rentra soudainment dans son premier état. Du temps de Louis VI., dit 'Le Gros,' il s'éleva dans Paris une cruelle maladie que les médecins nomment *feu sacré*,—un érysipèle gangréneux et épidémique. Plusieurs personnes en mouraient sans qu'on y pût apporter de remède. Cela obligea le clergé et le peuple d'avoir recours à St. Geneviève. . . . Tous les pauvres ardents . . . furent guéris à l'instant même, à l'exception de trois qui manquérent de foi, ou que Dieu ne voulut pas guérir pour des causes qui nous sont inconnues. Toute la France implore son assistance in temps de guerre, de peste, de famine, de sécheresse, d'inondation, et de trop grande abondance de pluie, et en toute autre sorte de nécessités. . . . Des guerres ont été ainsi apaisées, des pestes dissipées, la sérénité s'est changées en pluie, ou la pluie en sérénité, et la terre qui était stérile s'est vue changée d'une grand quantité de fruits. C'est ce que l'on a éprouvé l'an 1675, après la descente et la procession de la châsse qui s'était faite le 19th de Juillet . . . car quoque les pluies continuelles eussent mis toute la campagne dans la dernière désolation, et que les laboureurs fussent hors de toute espérance de récoltes, il se fit tout à coup un changement si merveilleux que l'année devint une des plus abondantes que l'on eût vue."—Vol. i. pp. 100, 101.

With such a patron, France should never be invaded, its harvests should never fail, and its rivers never overflow; but somehow these things do happen in France, as well as in countries not under the wing of such a "potent" protector.

Summary of the miracles of St. Germanus, bishop of Paris (A.D. 496–576). Fortunatus, bishop of Poitiers, after filling a whole volume with the miracles of St. Germanus, confesses he has left many unrecorded. The straw of his bed, the fragments and threads of his robe, his saliva, his tears, his words, the water in which he washed his hands, his look, his touch, his dreams during sleep, his letters, each and all carried miraculous remedies. When he went to church the sick were brought out, and ranged in two rows, that they might be healed. The inhabitants of Meudon, being afflicted with a contagious disease, were healed by some bread which he blessed. A monk of Tours, who had been ill for two years, was cured by simply kissing a letter written by the saint. Gertrude, the wife of Monsolis, who was blind, had her sight restored by invoking his name. A priest, paralyzed for doing some secular work on a Sunday, was cured by a little oil which St. Germanus had blessed. Attila, a favourite of king Childebert, having broken his arm, was blooded and died; but St. Germanus sprinkled on him a little holy water, and he revived. (Query: for *died* read *fainted?*) The daughter of a nobleman of Touraine, being at the point of death, was cured by him, and she became a nun. Two women, possessed of devils, were exorcised by rubbing them with oil and spittle. Queen Radegonde had retired from the world and taken the veil; but some evil counsellors advised the king to violate her vow. Radegonde wrote to St. Germanus, who dissuaded the king from his wicked intention, and "all his evil counsellors died horribly the death of Arius." When Germanus went to celebrate the fête of St. Martin, all the devils and demoniacs in alarm ran crying with loud and bitter lamentations, "O man of God, if you will not suffer us to dwell in human bodies, suffer us to dwell in these forests and mountain solitudes." One day, being at Avallon, he heard that many prisoners were confined for not paying the taxes. He asked count Nicaise to set them free; and, as the count refused, he appealed to God in prayer. Whereupon God sent an angel to open the prison doors, to break off the chains of the defaulters, and set the prisoners free. Being at Cervon he was told of a widow whose fields were infested by bears. St. Germanus went to the widow, made on her the sign of the cross, and all the bears died the same night (!!). One of them, trying to escape, was impaled on a hedge-stake. If St. Germanus went to any church, and found the doors locked, he had only to make the sign of the cross, and the doors flew open at once of their own accord.—Fortunat, *Lives* [of saints].

Chilperic's inscription on the tomb of Germanus was this: "St. Germain, un homme apostolique, le père, le médecin, le pasteur, et l'amour de son peuple."

The following miracles of St. Isidore of Madrid cannot be classed under any of the subjective heads of this book (1130–1170). (1) Women in childbirth, who applied to St. Isidore, never found him deaf to their prayers. Hundreds will bear witness that he has sustained them, when their medical attendants have pronounced their case hopeless.

(2) Once a man wanted to filch a relic of St. Isidore, and to this end secreted himself in the church where the saint was buried. When all was quiet, he broke open the shrine and cut off a finger. No sooner, however, had he done so, than he became transfixed, like a statue of stone, wholly unable to move either hand or foot. Fearing discovery, he put the finger back again, and it instantly adhered to the hand without leaving the slightest mark. The man, being released, fell on his knees, and thanked St. Isidore that no worse thing had befallen him.

The power of returning the finger came, I suppose, with the wish to do so; as the man with the withered hand was able to stretch it forth when bidden to do so by the Saviour.

(3) In times of drought the people of Spain are wont to carry the body of St. Isidore in solemn procession. When this is done rain never fails to come, the drought ceases, and the fields rejoice. Hence husbandmen take St. Isidore for their patron, if they hope for good harvests, and those who do so are seldom disappointed.

(4) On one occasion, some Spanish nobles were travelling down a steep hill, when their horses became unmanageable, fell down, and dragged the coach to a precipice. The danger was imminent, and the noblemen called on St. Isidore for help. Instantly the coach and horses stayed, hanging in the air, on the side of the rock, till all who were in the coach, to the number of eighteen, had got out, and saved themselves from further danger. This done, the coach was righted; and the horses, being drawn up, were found to have received no injury.

(5) The biographers of St. Isidore mention twenty instances of blind men cured of their blindness by his intercession; numerous instances of deaf and dumb persons who by his means recovered hearing and speech; many halt, lame, crooked, and deformed, made straight and comely; many paralytics healed, and a long list of promiscuous diseases cured by this favourite Spanish saint.

(6) Celestial music, we are told, is often heard at his tomb. And an angel tolled the church bell during his funeral march.—Ribadeneira and Villegas, *Extravagants.*

The history of St. Isidore is so marvellous that I subjoin the letter-patent for its publication. It is entitled "Le Privilege," and runs thus: "Philippe, par la grace de Dieu roy de Castille, d'Arragon, de Leon, etc. Auons accordé grace, octroy, et priuilege speciale à Jean Heigham, demeurant à S. Omer, luy seule et à l'exclusion de tous autres, d'imprimer ou faire imprimer, vendre, ou distribuer par tous les pays de nostre obeissance, là vie des Sancts [Isidore, Ignatius, Xauerius, Philip Nerius, S. Francisca, S. Teresa, B. Lewis Gonzaga, B. Stanislaus Kostka, and Alphonsius Rodriquez] en la langue Angloise, et ce pour l'espace de dix ans; defendant à tous imprimeurs et autres nos suiects quels qu'ils soient, d'imprimer, contrefaire, ou estant autre part imprimé, amener ès nos pays, à peine de trois florins d'amende pour chasque copie, et autre punition arbitraire mentioné en ledit priuilege. Fait à Bruxelles le 18 de Juin 1625. Signé De Groote."

(It is from this rare old book, in my possession, that every extract of the saint above mentioned has been taken.)

Summary of the miracles of St. Jeanne de Valois (died A.D. 1505). André Frémot, archbishop of Bourges, has *reduced* the number of miracles ascribed to St. Jeanne de Valois, the divorced queen of France, to 130, which are all set down in his book, printed A.D. 1618.—André Frémot (1575–1641).

Summary of the miracles of Jeanne Marie de Maillé (A.D. 1332–1414). Jeanne Marie de Maillé performed thirty-nine miracles during her life, and thirteen after her death. She healed lepers, gave hearing to the deaf, speech to the dumb, sight to the blind, the use of their limbs to the halt, and cured many diseases of other kinds; but she was never canonized.—L'abbé Rolland, *Life of Jeanne Marie de Maillé.*

We are told that Jeanne Marie died in 1414. In 1645 they opened her grave, but found only a stray bone or two. However, the bonnet which she was in the habit of wearing was recovered, "quoiqu'il fû tdepuis deux siècles enfoui dans la terre. Les fidèles avaient une grande dévotion a cette relique, et ils se la faisaient placer sur la tête pour obtenir le guérison de la fièvre et de la migraine." [An old hat which had been buried in the earth two hundred years and more would certainly be a curiosity, but its genuineness would be hard to prove.]

Ollivier Charreau, in his history in verse of the archbishops of Tours, asserts that he was himself miraculously cured of a violent headache from which he had suffered for forty years, by placing this bonnet on his head.

Summary of the miracles of St. Julian, bishop of Mans (A.D. 117). It would be quite impossible to give the miracles ascribed to St. Julian, first bishop of Mans, in a few pages. They would fill a volume. This one short paragraph will, however, suffice. After raising to life the son of Anastasius, the son of Priula-Leguilla, and Jovian, the biographer goes on thus: "Wherever he went crowds thronged around him. Many of the infirm and sick did not dare to ask him to heal them, but were content to follow in the crowd. The disciples spoke to him about these sick folk, and Julian, without uttering a word, turned round, and immediately all were cured of whatever infirmity they suffered from. To perpetuate the memory of this miracle, a chapter of canons was afterwards established on this spot. At Ruillé sur Loir, the only daughter of a man of great influence in the vicinity was presented to Julian. She was cruelly possessed of a devil, and the saint exorcised her. A church was afterwards founded on the spot where this occurred. A blind man being brought to him, he washed the sightless balls with a little water, and immediately they received sight."—Piolin, *History of the Church of Mans.*

Summary of miracles ascribed to St. Mathia or Mastidia (A.D. 1007). This is the off-hand way in which the miracles of St. Mathia are recorded in the *Propre de Troyes:* "Voici quelques-uns des miracles opérés par la sainte, en l'an 1007: Elle guérit une femme de la ville de Tonnerre, dont la main gauche était desséchée; elle guérit un enfant de trois ans, de la ville de Sens, malade et débile des jambes. Elle rendit la lumière à un aveugle. Elle redressa une femme qui était cul-d-jatte; elle rendit sain et dispos un paralytique, malade depuis déjà trente ans; elle rendit l'ouïe à une femme de Sens, et la vue à une autre femme. Elle fit marcher droit un enfant qui se traînait à la manière des bêtes; elle guérit deux petites filles âgées de cinqans; un homme de Toul, d'une contraction du visage; un jeune homme dont le côté gauche du corps était paralysé." These miracles were the work of only one year.

Summary of the miracles of St. Maurelius (A.D. 426). The sanctity of St. Maurelius shone forth in the following miracles:

(1) An inhabitant of Possonière, paralyzed in both hands, was told in a dream to go to St. Maurelius to be healed. Maurelius prayed, made the sign of the cross, and the paralytic instantly received the use of both his hands.

(2) A blind woman was brought to him; she was chained hand and foot, because she was possessed of a furious devil, which caused her blindness. Maurelius, fixing his eye on the woman, commanded the devil to come out of her. This it did immediately. Then the saint, going up to the woman, made on her eyes the sign of the cross, and she at once received her sight.

(3) A shepherd was bitten by a deadly viper; but, by the sign of the cross, St. Maurelius saved the man, so that the bite did him no harm.

(4) A woman of Angers was childless, and was of an age past the time of maternity; but St. Maurelius, by prayer, brought it to pass that she became the joyful mother of children.

(5) At Chalonne was an abominable temple, called Prisciacus, where were many idols. Maurelius resolved to destroy it. As he passed the doors, the devils cried out, "Why, Maurelius, do you persecute us thus? You leave us no place where we may abide in peace." The saint, paying no heed to these words, made the sign of the cross, and the devils fled. Then he burnt the temple to the ground, and built on the site the priory of St. Peter of Chalonne.

(6) A female captive, having escaped from a slave-merchant, implored Maurelius to save her. The saint offered to pay her ransom, but the merchant refused to part with her. Whereupon Maurelius prayed that Christ, who died to give liberty to the captive, would interfere, and immediately the merchant dropped down dead. The employés of the merchant, being terribly alarmed at this awful judgment, came to Maurelius in tears, and prayed him to take pity on them. He bade them release the whole of their slaves, which they did willingly, and also gave the saint handsome presents for his monastery. —*Acta Sanctorum* (Bollandists), Sept. 13.

Summary of the miracles of St. Odilo (A.D. 962–1049). St. Odilo, abbot of Cluny, gave sight to the son of one of his tenants born blind. He cured a nobleman whose eye had been knocked out by the branch of a tree; this cure was effected simply by making the sign of the cross. He healed a novice of Paternac, eaten up with scrofula. He cured Gerard of epilepsy, by giving him to drink some water which had been poured into St. Mayeul's chalice. He cured, by the sign of the cross, an ecclesiastic of Tours, who suffered grievously from a tumour, called in French *le charbon au bras*, a gangrenous carbuncle. He gave intelligence to a gentleman born an idiot, who used to break away from home, and run about the country naked, yelling most hideously. He often multiplied food. Twice he walked over a river which had overflowed its banks; the second time he did so without even wetting the soles of his shoes. On one occasion he dropped his *sac de nuit* into the river, but when he picked it out, he found its contents perfectly dry. (See DOMINIC, p. 231.)—Mgr. Guérin, *Vies des Saints* (1880), Jan. 1, p. 32, etc.

St. Patrick's miracles (A.D. 373–464). On the day of his baptism, he gave sight to a man born blind; the blind man took hold of the babe's hand, and with it made on the ground a sign of the cross. He made a spring of water leap from dry ground, and with this water he restored sight to several blind persons. He raised nine persons from the dead. On one occasion he performed a triple miracle: (1) he gave sight to one born blind; (2) he enabled the man, who had never seen a letter of the alphabet, to read fluently in a moment; and (3) he opened the eyes of the man's heart to receive the gospel. When he baptized a king of Ireland, he placed by accident his cross on the king's foot. Like a pastoral staff, the cross terminated in a sharp point, and as St. Patrick leaned heavily upon it, the point ran into the king's foot, and made it bleed. The king neither flinched nor stirred a muscle; in fact, he thought it a part of the baptismal service. When St. Patrick observed the wound, he miraculously healed it.—Messingham, *Florilegium Insulæ Sanctorum;* Jocelin, *Life of St. Patrick.* (J. H. Todd published a life of St. Patrick in 1863.)

Of course, the above epitome does not include all the miracles ascribed to St. Patrick; many are ranged under the different headings, and may be referred to in the index under the word PATRICK. In regard to the last, a very similar story is told of St. Areed, who went to show the king of Abyssinia a musical instrument which he had invented. His majesty rested the head of his spear on the saint's foot, and leaned with both hands on the spear while he listened to the music. St. Areed, though his great toe was severely injured, showed no sign of pain, but went on playing as if nothing was the matter.

Summary of miracles ascribed to St. Peter of Gallia Cisalpina. St. Peter of Gallia Cisalpina commanded a prater, who annoyed him with his tongue, to be dumb for a season, and the man lost the use of his speech. At Veronica he healed a girl that was on the point of death, by laying his scapular upon her. At Milan, when a deputation was held in the open air, he caused a thick cloud to keep off the sun, and temper the great heat. Being sick, and his physician being wholly at a loss to understand the nature of his disease, St. Peter laid on himself his own scapular, and he instantly vomited a hairy worm with two heads, and was presently quite well again. At Milan he cured Acerbus of the palsy, though he had kept his bed for five years. He healed Carasia, a woman of Caratre, of the same infirmity with which she had been inflicted for seven years. In Mantua he "healed a woman that would not make confession," and obtained health both of body and soul.—Thomas Lentinus, *Life of St. Peter of Gallia Cisalpina, Martyr.*

Summary of miracles ascribed to St. Placidus. Among the host of miracles ascribed to St. Placidus are the following:—He raised to life a child in the article of death. He cured a paralytic; a quartan ague; a man that could stir no part of his body, except his eyes; one afflicted with gout; a blind girl; a deaf woman; one blind, deaf, and dumb; restored sight to one who had been blind for eight years; and cast out many devils. In Sicily he cast out the devil from a man very sorely tormented; and in Africa throngs of sick folk were brought to him daily, and he healed them all. He was martyred at the age of twenty-six, and many miracles were performed by his relics.—Surius (1570), *Lives of the Saints.*

Summary of the miracles of St. Vincent Ferrier (A.D. 1357–1419). The number of miracles ascribed to St. Vincent Ferrier is incalculable. More than 860 are related of him in an inquest held at Avignon, Toulouse, Nantes, and Nancy. The same at Salamanca. Every morning, at the ringing of the miracle bell, crowds of impotent folk used to assemble, and he healed them. "N'eût-il fait dans le cours de ces vingt ans que huit miracles par jour, on arriverait au chiffre de 58,400. Mais ce calcul est évidemment trop faible!! puisque, c'est un fait constant, notre saint en opérait non seulement dans les assemblées publiques et en chaire, mais encore en marchant, en demeurant au logis, à tout instant, pour ainsi dire; d'où cette parole commune parmi les historians de sa vie, 'C'était un miracle quand il ne faisait pas de miracles, et le plus grand miracle qu'il fît était de n'en point faire.'"—Mgr. Guérin, *Vies des Saints*, vol. iv. p. 227.

St. Louis Bertrand (*Teoli*, bk. ii. tratt. i. c. 21) confirms this statement. "God," says he, "set His seal to the teaching of St. Vincent Ferrier by so many miracles, that from the time of the apostles to our own days no saint has operated so many God only knows their number, as He alone knows the number of the stars."

We are further told that St. Vincent employed miracle apprentices or assistants to carry on the work, when he himself was tired out. At such times he would turn to one of his assistants, and say, "To-day I have done miracles enough, and am wearied with fatigue. Go now, and do for me what is required. God who has bestowed this power on me will transfer it for the nonce to you."

Four hundred sick people recovered their health merely by placing themselves on the bed where St. Vincent died.

St. Cyprian's way of accounting for miracles. "The Holy Spirit," says St. Cyprian, "is poured forth without measure. As much of capacious faith as we bring, so much of abounding grace do we draw therefrom. Hence an ability is given to heal the sick, to neutralize the force of poison, to cleanse the filth of distempered minds, and to compel wandering spirits to quit their hold of men." Dr. Milner, who quotes these words, adds, "The testimony here given to the ejection of evil spirits, as a common thing among Christians, is a proof that miracles had not ceased in the Church in the third century. Indeed, the testimony of the Fathers in these times is so general and concurrent, that the fact itself cannot be denied without impeaching their veracity."

Of course, the following difficulties will strike every one: (1) Why should the age of miracles be limited to the first three centuries? (2) Are all the miracles vouched for by the Fathers in these times to be accepted? If so, some of the most incredible must be taken for granted, as a very cursory glance of this book will plainly show. (3) Is it not equally an impeachment of "the veracity of holy men" to doubt the miracles ascribed to saints since the first three centuries, as, for example, those of St. Bernard (1046-1117), Charles Borromeo (1538-1584), St. Francis of Assisi (1182-1226), St. Francis of Paula (1416-1507), St. Isidore (1130-1170), St. Vincent Ferrier (1357-1419), and many others? What further corroboration can the miracles of the first three centuries lay claim to than those of the saints referred to above, or indeed for those of the nineteenth century? The question is not one of veracity at all, but of credulity nursed by education and preconceptions. If anything the whole force should be in favour of more modern miracles, because more scientific investigation could be applied than in earlier ages, and deception would be more difficult.

Hindu method of acquiring complete command over elementary matter. The Yoga or Panjantala school of philosophy maintains the possibility and practicability of acquiring the entire command over elementary matter by ascetic privations. Yoga means, effecting a perfect union between the vital spirit in man and that which pervades all nature. When this union is effected, the Yogi is liberated from his body. He can then make himself lighter or heavier, larger or smaller, as he likes; he can traverse all space; animate dead bodies by transferring his own spirit into it; can render himself invisible; can become familiar with the past or future; and know all that is being done in any part of the earth. The way to acquire this power is by long-continued suppression of respiration; by inhaling and exhaling the breath in a particular manner; sitting in certain attitudes with the eyes fixed on the tip of the nose. H. H. Wilson, in the *Ayeen Akbiri* (vol. ii. p. 445), tells us he has seen many practising "assum," that is, sitting with the eyes fixed on the nose, and he says it is perfectly astounding what command they acquire over their muscles, nerves, and bones. He names four who could hold their breath for an incredible length of time.

Whether the saints by asceticism and constant contemplation acquired this union of their own spirit with the *anima mundi*, I cannot say, but certainly Milton believed it possible. He says angels speak to the [saints] in dream or vision—

> Till oft converse with heavenly habitants
> Begin to cast a beam on the outward shape
> (The unpolluted temple of the mind)
> And turns it by degrees to the soul's essence,
> Till all be made immortal.—But when lust
> By unchaste looks, loose gestures, and foul talk
> Lets in defilement to the inward parts,
> The *soul* grows clotted by contagion,
> Imbodies and imbrutes, till she quite lose
> The divine property of her first being.
>
> *Comus*

Moses and the Rock.

Numb. xx. 11. And Moses lifted up his hand and smote the rock twice, and water came out abundantly; and the congregation drank and their beasts also.

St. Francis of Paula brings water from a rock (A.D. 1416-1507). The third great miracle of St. Francis of Paula was to bring water from a rock in Calabria, simply by striking it with a rod. This miracle was performed to supply the workmen with water, which they much needed. Before this, the men had to go a considerable way to fetch water from the torrent. What renders the miracle still more striking is this: the saint caused the water to fall into a natural basin in the rock. This fountain has been examined, and no one has been able to discover any fissure in the rock, or whence the water proceeds; but one thing is certain, it never fails, summer or winter. If the reservoir is emptied from any cause, such as washing, in about five hours it is full again. Any one who goes to Paula may see the reservoir, the water of which is sanative. Thus, on one occasion, St. Francis threw into it a dead trout, and the fish instantly recovered its life; since then, cures without number have been effected by washing in it, or drinking it. Every year, on April 1, an enormous crowd visit the rock, so that it is well known.—*Bull and other Documents of his Canonization* (compiled by Father Giry).

Water trickling from a rock is by no means uncommon; but what requires proof is this: Did no water trickle from this particular rock before the fifteenth century? If this question can be answered, the next would be: Was nothing done to alter the physical condition of the rock?

Moses commissioned by God.

EXOD. iii. 7-14. God appeared to Moses near mount Horeb, told him He had seen the affliction of the Israelites in Egypt, and had appointed Moses to deliver them. Moses said, Who am I, that I should go unto Pharaoh, and bring forth the children of Israel out of Egypt? God said that He would Himself be with him, and when Moses asked by what name he should speak of the Almighty to his countrymen, God said He was to be called I AM THAT I AM. Thou shalt say, I AM hath sent me. And He assured Moses that his mission should be successful.

St. Angelus commissioned by God to preach the gospel (1669-1739). One day, while Angelus was at prayer, he heard a voice which said to him, "Fear not; I will give you the gift of preaching, and henceforth all thy labours shall be crowned with success." Astonished at these words, Angelus demanded, "Who art thou?" The voice replied, "I AM THAT I AM. Henceforth thou shalt preach with convincing words, and power of the Holy Ghost." Seized with alarm, the young friar fell to the earth; but, when he came to himself, he wrote down what he had heard, and went forth to preach. So powerful were his words, that the wisest heard him gladly, and the meanest understood him.—*Life of Angelus of Acri* (published at Rome in 1825).

Moses sweetens Water.

EXOD. xv. 22-25. Moses having brought the children of Israel to the wilderness of Shur, they went three days' march, and found no water. When they came to Marah there was water indeed, but they could not drink it, because it was bitter. The people murmured, but the Lord showed Moses a tree, which being cast into the water made it sweet.

It is well known that many waters unfit to drink may be purified by wood; thus—

Water in sandy districts corrupted by vegetable matters has an offensive taste and smell, but may be purified by chips of oak wood thrown into it. The foul matter in this case is of an albuminous nature, which the tannin of the oak chips neutralizes, and the coagulates falling to the bottom, the water becomes not only sweet but clear.

The marshy waters of India are purified by nuts of the *Strychnos potatorum*, of which travellers carry a supply. One or two of these nuts, rubbed to powder on the side of the earthen vessel into which the water is to be poured, will cause the impurities to subside.

In Egypt the muddy Nile water is clarified by rubbing the sides of the vessel with bitter almonds.

The waters of the sandy Landes of Bourdeaux are unfit to drink till purified by oak chips, which coagulate the albuminous matter, and carry all its impurities to the bottom as a sediment.

If the waters of Marah contained albuminous matter from decaying vegetables, an astringent plant would coagulate it, and purify the water.

Naaman the Leper.

2 KINGS v. The story of Naaman the leper.

MATT. viii. 2, 3. There came a leper to Jesus, and worshipped him, saying, Lord, if Thou wilt, Thou canst make me clean. And Jesus put forth His hand, and touched him, saying, I will; be thou clean. And immediately the leprosy was cleansed.

LUKE xvii. 12-14. As Jesus entered into a certain village, there met Him ten men that were lepers, which stood afar off, and said, Jesus, Master, have mercy on us. And when He saw them He said unto them, Go, show yourselves unto the priests. And it came to pass that, as they went, they were cleansed.

St. Ausonius cures Calfagius of a bloody flux (first and second centuries). Calfagius, a rich Gallo-Roman living in a sumptuous mansion in the suburbs of Angoulême, had been afflicted from boyhood with a bloody flux, which greatly reduced his strength and took away his energy. Medicines seemed powerless, although he was attended by the most skilful physicians of the day. Being told of St. Ausonius, he went to him in his chariot, taking a large sum of money with him. One of his servants, named Arcadius, tried to dissuade him from going, saying, "You have spent enormous sums of money already on physicians, and it is mere wasting of good money to squander it on this priest, who cannot possibly know anything of medicine." Scarcely had he spoken, when he himself became afflicted with his master's disease. Calfagius drove off immediately to the saint, and, throwing himself at his feet, said to him, "Ausonius, I crave baptism at thy hand, thou servant of the living God." Ausonius replied, "If you believe, Christ will hear your request." "I believe," said Calfagius, "that God is the Creator of the world, and that Jesus Christ, His Son, was crucified by Pontius Pilate, and rose again the third day." A profession so concise and exact was highly satisfactory, so water was brought, and Calfagius was baptized; and, as Naaman the Syrian was cured of his leprosy by the waters of the Jordan, so this rich young nobleman was cured of his bloody flux by the water of baptism. Just at this moment Arcadius came up, with a train of servants, and was led to the saint. "O man of God," said Calfagius, "I humbly beseech you to heal Arcadius also. He is my intendant." Then said Ausonius to the intendant, "In the name of Jesus Christ of Nazareth, be healed of thine infirmity." At these words he was cured, and, at a sign given by Calfagius, he laid great treasures at the feet of the saint. "These," said Ausonius, "I accept as an offering to the poor;" and he handed them to his archdeacon.—*Acta Sanctorum* (Bollandists), vol. v. May 22.

St. Brigit and the two lepers (A.D. 436–523). Two lepers came to St. Brigit to be healed of their leprosy. The saint made the sign of the cross over a basin of water, and told each of the lepers to wash the other therewith. When the first was washed by his companion, and found his leprosy gone, he refused to render the like service to his companion; but instantly his leprosy returned, and, at the same moment, his companion was cured.—Cardinal Baronius, *Roman Martyrology*.

St. Clare bids a beggar bathe in a neighbouring brook. He did so, and was clean (seventh century). St. Clare one day encountered a poor beggar completely covered with leprous sores. The saint bade him go and bathe in the neighbouring brook. No sooner had he done so, than his sores were healed, and his flesh came to him again, as fresh and healthy as that of a little child.—*Les Petits Bollandistes*, vol. i. p. 31.

St. Francis of Paula healed Marcellus Cardilla of leprosy (A.D. 1416–1507). Marcellus Cardilla of Cosenza was not only a leper, but a cripple in hands and feet, and his whole body was distorted. He had lost his speech, was black in the face, and indeed could scarcely be recognized as a human being. Being brought to St. Francis of Paula, the saint merely took him by the hand, and this terrible object stood on his feet, recovered his speech, became straight, and was made whole.—Father Giry, *Life of St. Francis of Paula* (chiefly taken from the bull of canonization and the original documents then brought forward).

St. Martin cures a leper by kissing him. When St. Martin, bishop of Tours, was in Paris, he observed at the city gates a leper full of sores. Going up to him, he kissed him, and immediately the leprosy was healed. This leper was well known to the whole city, and next day he entered the city to return thanks to God for his miraculous recovery.—Sulpicius Severus, *Dialogues*.

A leper healed with a kiss (tenth century). On his journey to Rome, one of his suite confessed to St. Mayeul that he had been guilty of a grave offence, and demanded absolution, with penance. "Are you in earnest," said the saint, "in your desire of penance?" "Doubtless," replied the erring brother. "Then," rejoined the abbot, "look on that leper there, who is seeking alms. Go to him, and give him the kiss of peace." The brother instantly went to the leper, and kissed him, and no sooner had he so done than the leper was healed.—*Les Petits Bollandistes*, vol. v. p. 463.

St. Romanus heals two lepers who had shown him hospitality (A.D. 460). St. Romanus, going to visit the tomb of St. Maurice, was overtaken by night near Geneva, and retired into a cabin occupied by two lepers, who showed him hospitality. Next morning, the lepers found themselves entirely cured, and proceeded towards Geneva, under the hope of finding their benefactor. This they failed to do; but, being well known in those parts, their miraculous cure caused a great sensation. When St. Romanus returned from the tomb of St. Maurice, and reached Geneva, all the magistrates, clergy, and people of the place went to meet him, and brought him into the city in triumph. The two lepers followed, as if they had been captives taken in war.—St. Gregory of Tours, the Bollandists, Mgr. Depéry (*Hagiographe of Belley*), and many others, have written the *Life of St. Romanus*, but are indebted to a life written by a contemporary monk.

St. Sorus heals king Gontran of leprosy (A.D. 500–580). Gontran, king of Burgundy, was a great man, but a leper. He prayed to God earnestly to heal him of his dreadful malady, and God sent an angel to say to him, "Rise, Gontran, and go at once to the blessed hermit who dwells in Aquitaine, in the province of Périgord, whose name is Sorus. Lo! God has given him charge to cure you of your leprosy." So the king rose, and departed at once, and came to the hermit's cell, where he prostrated himself to the earth, saying, "My soul is bowed down to the dust, and my body cleaveth to the earth. Arise to my help, and save me, O Lord, according to Thy word." St. Sorus, coming out of his cell, saw the king with his face to the earth, and said, "Arise; wherefore art thou come?" "An angel of heaven told me," said the king. "You see before you, O man of God, one grievously afflicted with leprosy, and he has no need to tell you what he desires at your hands." Then St. Sorus bade him fetch some water, which the saint blessed, and told the king to wash and be clean. Gontran obeyed the word of the man of God, and every part of his body which the water touched became fresh and healthy as the skin of a child. The king, overjoyed, blessed God and the saint who had shown him this grace, and returned to his own land.—*Les Petits Bollandistes*, vol. ii. p. 193 (7th edit. 1880).

A little maid said to Hermês, "Would God you had taken your son to St. Alexander, vicar of St. Peter's, for he would have cured him." Hermês, governor of Caput Tauri, had a son at the gates of death; and he carried the child to the temple of Jupiter, where he offered sacrifice; but his son died. A little maiden, nurse of the child, said to her mistress, "Would God my master had taken his son to St. Peter's vicar, for he would have recovered him." These words were told to the governor, who severely reproved the nurse; but so confident was she in her persuasion, that she herself took the dead child to St. Alexander, who prayed over it; and, before he had ended his prayer, the boy revived. Then Hermês fell at the feet of the man of God, and himself was baptized, with his whole house.—Edward Kinesman (1623), *Lives of the Saints*, p. 285.

Nathanael.

JOHN i. 47. Jesus saw Nathanael coming to him, and saith of him, Behold an Israelite indeed, in whom is no guile!

The prior Boisil's address to St. Cuthbert (seventh century). After St. Cuthbert had seen the soul of Aidan, bishop of Durham, carried by angels up to heaven, he resolved to quit the shepherd's life, and devote himself wholly to the service of God and his Christ. Accordingly, next morning, he went to the prior Boisil at Mailros, near Lindisfarne. When the prior saw the young man approaching, he exclaimed, "Behold an Israelite indeed, in whom is no guile!" Cuthbert told the reason of his coming, and Boisil admitted him at once into the priory. He received the monastic habit at the hands of Eätas, the abbot, and, on the death of Boisil, in A.D. 664, was appointed prior or provost in his place.—Bede, *Church History*, bk. iv. ch. 27–32.

Natural Marks ascribed to Miracles.

JOSH. iv. 9. When Joshua crossed the Jordan, he set up twelve stones in the midst of Jordan, in the place where the feet of the priests which bare the ark of the covenant stood; and they are there unto this day.

The sacred writer does not appeal to the pile of stones in proof of the stated fact, but simply says such is the fact, and the stones set up in memorial remain still. This is a very different thing from saying that Humber was certainly drowned near Hull, because the river is still called the Humber; or that Gog Magog was certainly brought in chains to London, because a statue of the giant stood at Guildhall till the great fire, and even still there is a stone effigy of him.

St. Antony's cross in Our Lady's Church, Portugal (A.D. 1195–1231). In Our Lady's Church, Portugal, is still preserved with religious care, a stone which served as one of the steps to the cathedral choir. It bears the mark of a cross, and we are told that St. Antony of Padua made this mark with his finger one day when the devil appeared to him in a formidable shape. This cross is as perfect now as it was in the twelfth century.—L'abbé Guyard, *Life of St. Antony of Padua*.

A footprint on the mount of Olives said to be that of Jesus Christ when He ascended into heaven. East of Jerusalem, on the flank of the mount of Olives, near the spot "where Jesus ascended into heaven," there is, on the ground, an impression of a footstep, which may still be seen. Here also in a grot, cut out of the rock, is shown where a dozen fishermen, by joining hands, formed a cross, "the immortal symbol of that faith which was to subdue the world."—*Les Petits Bollandistes* (1880), vol. v. p. 166.

The impression of St. Julian's footstep still shown in France. St. Julian died A.D. 117. When he was in Gaul his foot made a "miraculous impression on a stone in Champagne." As the footprint is still shown, of course *cela va sans dire*.—D. Piolin, *History of the Church of Mans* (10 vols.).

The foot-mark of St. Medard impressed on a boundary stone (A.D. 545). The farmers of Picardy, having quarrelled about the boundaries of their respective lands, applied to St. Medard to settle the dispute. Medard, having adjudicated the matter, had a large stone brought to mark the boundary; and, to give greater authority to his judgment, set his foot on the stone, and the impression remained as durable as if the stone had been soft wax.—*Acta Sanctorum* (Bollandists), vol. ii. June 8.

The Rats' Run in the Seine, a proof that St. Valentine cleared the peninsula of Jumièges of rats (A.D. 273). In the twelfth century, the peninsula of Jumièges was overrun with rats. The people invoked St. Valentine (once bishop of Terni), and the saint drove the whole of the vermin into the river Seine. Visitors are still shown the spot where the rats ran into the river. The "run" is called the "Rats' Run" (*chemin*), and the spot shown is called the "Rats' Hole" (*trou*). —*Les Petits Bollandistes*, vol. ii. p. 524.

This is not St. Valentine the letter-carrier's plague. The post-office St. Valentine was a Roman priest, and generally called "The Martyr." Both saints, however, are honoured on the same day, Feb. 14.

A fissure in a Scotch rock proves that Scotland was a fief of England. When Edward I. laid claim to Scotland, as the fief of England, his chief plea was a fissure in a basaltic rock, attributed to a sword-cut. The tale runs thus, and is taken from the *Life and Miracles of St. John of Beverley*. Adelstan went to drive back the Scots, who had crossed the border. St. John of Beverley appeared to him, and bade him cross the Tyne at daybreak. Adelstan obeyed the saint, and reduced the whole kingdom to submission. On reaching Dunbar, in the return march, he prayed that some permanent sign might be vouchsafed to him, to testify to all ages that God had Himself delivered the nation into his hands; whereupon the saint bade him strike the rock with his sword. Adelstan struck the rock, and his sword sank into it "as if it had been butter," cleaving it asunder "an ell or more." As the cleft remains to the present day, why, of course, no more can be said; and the wise council, consisting of the king, English and Scotch judges, prelates, noblemen, and lawyers, adjudged that Scotland was undoubtedly a fief of the English crown.—Rymer, *Fœdera*, vol. ii. p. 771.

The Devil's Dyke, Brighton. The following story will serve to show the tendency of man to ascribe natural marks to some known event, and raise them into importance by making them the basis of a tale. Near Brighton there is a gorge, called the "Devil's Dyke," the story of which runs thus: As St. Cuthman was walking over the South Downs one day, thinking to himself how completely he had rescued the whole country from paganism, he was accosted by his sable majesty in person. "Ha, ha!" said the prince of darkness; "so you think by these churches and convents to put me and mine to your ban, do you? Poor fool! why, this very night will I swamp the whole land with the sea." Forewarned is forearmed, thought Cuthman, and forthwith hies him to Sister Cecilia, superior of a convent which then stood on the site of the present Dyke House. "Sister," said the saint, "I love you well. This night, for the grace of God, keep lights burning at the convent windows from midnight to daybreak, and let masses be said by the holy sisterhood." At sundown came the devil with pickaxe and spade, mattock and shovel, and set to work in right good earnest to dig a dyke which should let the waters of the sea into the downs. "Fire and brimstone!" he exclaimed, as a sound of voices rose and fell in sacred song. "Fire and brimstone! What can be the matter with me?" Shoulders, feet, wrists, loins, all seemed paralyzed. Down went mattock and spade, pickaxe and shovel; and just at that moment the lights at the convent windows burst forth, and the cock, mistaking the blaze for daybreak, began to crow most lustily. Off flew the devil, and never again returned to complete his work. The small digging he effected still remains in witness of the truth of this legend of the "Devil's Dyke."

It would be an easy matter to fill a volume with such legends, but stories of this kind are no data of mediæval thought, but simply inventions to amuse. They are parodies to saintly legends, and therefore stand on very different ground. They bear about the same relation to legend and tradition proper, as historical romance to history. They would never have been invented if current thought had not favoured the invention; but no one believes them to be anything else than idle tales.

Nature disturbed at the Crucifixion.

MATT. xxvii. 50–53. Jesus, when He had cried again . . . yielded up the ghost; and behold! the veil of the temple was rent in twain . . . and the earth did quake, and the rocks rent; and the graves were opened; and many bodies of the saints which slept arose.

Earthquake at the death of St. Apian (A.D. 306). St. Apian, after being buffeted on the face, beaten and kicked, wounded on every part of the body, and cuffed on the mouth, had his sides torn open till his entrails were exposed. The executioners were then ordered to apply to his feet lighted flax dipped in oil; after which he was cast into the sea. What follows, Eusebius tell us, was seen by the inhabitants of Cæsarea. "The body was no sooner thrown into the sea, than the whole city was shaken with an earthquake, and the sea, unable to endure the martyr's corpse, cast it up at the gates of the city. All Cæsarea went to see the body, so that the prodigy cannot be gainsaid."—Eusebius (an eye-witness), *De Martyribus Palæstinæ*, ch. iv.

Earthquake at the martyrdom of St.

Boniface. When Simplicius beheaded Boniface in Tarsus, "there was a great earthquake in all the city, and every one said it was a judgment of God for the cruelty shown to Boniface, the stranger who had been put to death by Simplicius. The earthquake, however, was the voice of the Holy Ghost to many, who turned from their idols to serve the living God."—Ado (archbishop of Trèves), *Martyrology.*

Thunder and lightning disturbed the earth when the twenty martyrs fell. In the reign of Maximian, twenty Christians of Nicomedia (a city of Bithynia) were condemned to be burnt alive at the same time (Sept. 8, A.D. 306). When their bodies were bound to the stakes and the fagots were set on fire, the sky was suddenly overcast with thick darkness, thunder crashed dreadfully, lightning blazed, and thunderbolts killed many pagans busied in burning the martyrs. Many fled to save their lives; but the Christians, observing that the fire was extinguished by the heavy rain, took courage to rescue the relics of the martyrs, and convey them to Byzantium.—Ado (archbishop of Trèves), *Martyrology.*

Earthquake at the martyrdom of St. Philip the apostle. They took Philip the apostle, imprisoned, beat, wounded, and crucified him. They who committed this cruelty scoffed at him, wagging their heads, and rejoicing to see him suffer. But lo! on a sudden, the earth began to quake and open in divers places, swallowing up houses, public buildings, and inhabitants together, especially those who had been concerned in putting the martyr to death. The Christians crowded to the spot where the cross stood, and entreated the apostle to save them from this danger and death; so he prayed to God, and the earthquake ceased. His body, after death, was taken from Phrygia to Rome.—Edward Kinesman (1623), *Lives of the Saints*, p. 263. (See also Isidore, *Book of the Fathers*, ch. 75; St. Jerome, *De Vitis Illustribus*, ch. 6; Eusebius, *Ecclesiastical History*, bk. iii. ch. 30, 31; Dorotheus (bishop of Tyre); Metaphrastês; Usuand; etc.)

Earthquake, lightning, and thick darkness at the death of St. Vitus. St. Vitus was put to death in the catasta (*q.v.*), a machine of torture in which the victim is laid flat on the ground, and then every limb stretched till it is pulled from the socket. When the saint was put to this machine the sky was quite cloudless, but it was suddenly overcast, and a thick darkness came over the city, with thunder, lightning, and earthquake. The idols in the temples were overthrown, and many pagans perished.—Edward Kinesman (1623), *Lives of the Saints*, p. 383.

Nazarites.

JUDG. x. 17. A Nazarite was a person who vowed to abstain from wine; to let his hair grow without ever cutting it; to enter no house containing a dead body; nor ever to be present at a funeral. The best-known example is that of Samson.

James the Less was a Nazarite from birth. Eusebius Cesariensis, quoting from Egesippus, as an author close upon the times of the apostles, says of James the Less, "He was sanctified in his mother's womb. In all his life he drank neither wine nor other strong drink; he never ate the flesh of any animal, never cut his hair, nor was he ever anointed with any ointment. He was always clad in linen only, and always went to the temple crawling on his knees. Egesippus adds, that the knees of the Nazarite had become as hard as those of a camel. James the Less was so holy a man that he was allowed by the high priest to enter into the holy of holies, and was universally called 'The Just.'"

Obedience better than Sacrifice.

1 SAM. xv. 1–22. God told king Saul to go and destroy the Amalekites. Instead of doing so, he destroyed the refuse and mean, but saved alive the king Agag, and brought away with him the best of the cattle. When Samuel the prophet went to meet him on his return, Saul said boastingly, Blessed be thou of the Lord: I have performed the commandment of the Lord. But Samuel made answer, What then is this bleating of sheep and lowing of oxen which I hear? Saul said they were for sacrifice; and Samuel exclaimed, Behold, to obey is better than sacrifice, and to hearken than the fat of rams.

EPH. v. 22. Wives, submit yourselves unto your own husbands, as unto the Lord.

Cæsar bade Pharnăces return to obedience before he made offerings. Pharnaces, king of Pontus, was called "the friend and ally of the Roman people;" but when the civil war between Cæsar and Pompey broke out, he seized the opportunity of reinstating himself, and made himself master of Colchis and Armenia. Pompey being defeated in the battle of Pharsalia, Pharnaces sent Cæsar a golden crown, hoping thereby to conciliate him, and indicating that he acknowledged him the king of Rome. Cæsar sent back the gift, with this message: "Return first to obedience, and then come and offer thy gifts." No gift from a rebel could have any meaning but one, that of bribery to avert punishment; but gifts from the obedient are marks of love and gratitude.

Francisca miraculously taught the merit of wifely obedience (A.D. 1384–1440). It pleased the Lord, one day, to show, by an especial miracle, how acceptable to Him is wifely obedience. In saying the "Office of our Blessed Virgin," Francisca was called away four times by her husband, and four times she broke off the office at precisely the same verse. On returning to her chamber the fourth time, she found that her good angel had written out the verse, which was in common print before, in letters of gold; and St. Paul himself declared to her that God deemed obedience to superiors better than sacrifice, or any service to Himself. —John Mattiotti (her confessor), *Life of St. Francisca* (recited by Julius Ursimus, May 29, 1606, in the process of canonization).

Rita de Cascia set to water daily a dry stick (A.D. 1456). Rita is an abbreviation of Margarita. She was the daughter of respectable parents, and lived eighteen years in married life, when she craved to be admitted in the convent of St. Mary Magdalene, but was refused, because it was contrary to the rules of the convent to take in widows. However, the apparitions of St. Augustine (died 430), St. Nicholas de Tolentino (died 1306), and John the Baptist, came at night, opened the convent doors, and introduced her; after which, of course, she was admitted. To try her obedience she was sent to water, with great fatigue, a bit of dry stick in the convent garden. This she had to do daily, and did without a murmur.—*Acta Sanctorum* (Bollandists), vol. v. May 22.

Oil.

MARK vi. 13. The disciples anointed with oil many that were sick, and healed them. (James v. 14.)

1 KINGS xvii. 16. The barrel of meal [of the widow of Zarephath] wasted not, neither did the cruse of oil fail, according to the word of the Lord, which He spake by Elijah.

An empty muid or tun filled with oil by St. Benedict (A.D. 480–543). During a time of famine, Agapitus, a subdeacon of Mount Cassino, applied to St. Benedict for oil. It so happened that the monastery was out of oil at the time, there being only a few dregs at the bottom of a bottle. The patriarch commanded the cellarer to give what there was to the subdeacon; but the cellarer, fearing to be wholly without oil, neglected to obey the order. When St. Benedict heard thereof, he threw the bottle out of the window upon the rocks; but the bottle was not broken, nor was the oil spilled. He then assembled the whole house in full chapter, and reproved the cellarer severely for disobedience. When the chapter broke up, St. Benedict found a muid or hogshead quite full of oil of the best quality, and told the cellarer in future to remember that God's hand is not shortened; but, he added, "those who would receive liberally from Him must trust Him fully."—Gregory the Great, *Dialogues*, bk. ii.

The miraculous self-multiplying oil of St. Eugendus of Condat (fifth century). St. Gregory of Tours assures us that an oil of miraculous potency flows from the tomb of St. Martin. St. Eugendus, abbot of Condat, had a flask of this oil, which he miraculously multiplied according to exigencies; as, for example, when the lamps required filling, when he anointed the sick, or when it was required for any other purpose. On one occasion, his abbey caught fire at midnight, and was entirely consumed, with all its furniture, all its instruments, and all its relics; but, thanks to this *huile de saint Martin*, next morning everything was restored intact. This miracle so operated on the neighbours, that they subscribed freely to replace the wooden edifice, "not made with hands," by one of more substantial materials, and to furnish it throughout with richer vestments and many more conveniences.—Pragmacius (a disciple), *Life of St. Eugendus*. (This life is inserted in the *Lives of the Saints of Franche Comté*, by the professors of St F. Xavier.)

Respecting this self-multiplying oil of the abbot of Condat, it may be worth hinting that Condat is a great entrepôt of oil, and contains mines of natural oil. It would not require miraculous powers to supply the abbey from these mines.

Oil on Troubled Waters.

The notion that oil will smooth troubled water is very old indeed. The Syrian fishermen have been wont, time out of mind, to pour oil on the sea, when caught in a storm far from land. The boatmen of the Persian Gulf have always been in the habit of towing, astern their frail crafts, bladders filled with oil; these bladders are pricked so as to permit a gentle leakage of oil in the wake of their boats. Pliny tells us that, in his day, the Mediterranean sponge-divers used oil to obtain a smooth surface when they rose from the bottom of the sea.* And ever since whale-hunting has been followed, it has been noticed that when a whale is "being made off," that is, "the blubber flensed," the oily sea is smooth, no matter how rough the waters beyond the range of the oil. Professor Horsford, by emptying a vial of oil upon the sea in a stiff breeze, stilled the surface; and commodore Wilkes, of the United States, saw the same effect produced in a violent storm off the Cape of Good Hope, by oil leaking from a whale-ship. Among the herring-fishers of Shetland, the pilchard-catchers of Cornwall, in Northern Africa, in Samoa, and, indeed, all over the world, oil is used, more or less systematically, for soothing the sea. Sometimes a mop steeped in oil is hung in the water, sometimes pricked bladders. Mr. Shields laid perforated pipes under the dangerous bar across the mouth of Peterhead Harbour, and then pumped oil into them; the effect was that huge billows from ten to twelve feet high were reduced to petty waves, which any vessel could ride over in perfect safety. Two Italians crossing the Atlantic from Buenos Ayres, in 1881, were caught in a rough sea, but, by the use of oil, rode through the waves without shipping a bucketful. We are told of a captain who declared his steamer would have been lost in the Bay of Biscay had he not lulled the waves by pouring oil on them. Another case is on record of a schooner off Sable Island, which was seen tearing her way through a sea lashed into white foam by a violent storm, simply by ladling out oil; though otherwise she must have gone to the bottom. Once more, a vessel was caught in a hurricane, the breakers threatened to engulf the ship every minute, but oil was poured on the sea, and the vessel rode in safety. There seems to be no doubt of the fact, that oil does smooth the surface of troubled waters; let us now see what use hagiographers have made of this fact.

A stormy sea allayed by a cruse of oil. The devil, as prince of the powers of the air, is the evil principle that works mischief by storms and tempests, earthquakes and destructive gales. The devils hated St. Nicholas for throwing down the temple of Diana, in Lycia; and, when he was dead, used all their endeavours to prevent pilgrims from visiting his tomb. On one occasion a large number of pilgrims took ship for Myra; and Satan, in the guise of an old woman, coming on board, said to the pilgrims, "I also wish to go to the tomb of St. Nicholas, but cannot do so now. Oblige me, therefore, by taking this cruse of oil, and burning it in the lamps on the saint's sepulchre." This the pilgrims readily promised to do. When the ship was now in the middle of the sea, on the second day, a furious storm arose, and the crew expected the ship would be broken to pieces by the violence of the waves. Just at this juncture the spirit of St. Nicholas made its appearance, and said to the pilgrims, "Fear not, for none here shall be lost; but cast overboard the cruse of oil, for the 'old woman' who gave it you was the devil." As soon as the oil was thrown over into the deep, it blazed into a great flame, and sent forth an odious stench of sulphur and sin, proving to demonstration that it came from hell. The wind dropped, the sky cleared, the sea lulled, and the ship ran merrily into the Lycian port.—Metaphrastês (died 911), *Lives*, etc.

St. Germanus, bishop of Auxerre, lulls a storm at sea by some holy oil (fifteenth century). As Germanus, bishop of Auxerre, was sailing to Britain, a horrible tempest was raised by the devil, to drown the saint. He was fast asleep in the ship; but, being aroused by the shrieks of the perishing crew, he rebuked the storm. Then sprinkling, in the name of the Holy Trinity, a few drops of holy oil on the raging billows, immediately there was a great calm.—Dr. Jostin, *Dissertations*, ii. p. 73.

Vtta calmed a rough sea by pouring some holy oil on it. Before Vtta, a holy man, went to fetch the bride of king Oswin, he called on bishop Aida, who told him he foresaw a tempest, and gave him a cruse of holy oil for stilling the waves. All fell out as the bishop said. The winds arose, lashed the waves into fury, and the ship would have been wrecked, had not Vtta poured on them the holy oil, and bade them subside into a calm.—Bede, *Ecclesiastical History*. (Bede tells us he heard this story from Cymmund,

* Dr. E. Halley states that sponge-divers in the Archipelago descend to the bottom of the sea with a piece of sponge saturated with oil, and by squeezing a little from the sponge they obtain a clear surface, whereby they can see much more clearly at the bottom.

"a very creditable man," who was told it by Vtta himself.)

Paralytics healed.

MATT. iv. 24. His fame went throughout all Syria; and they brought unto him all sick people that were taken with divers diseases and torments, and those which were possessed with devils, and those which were lunatic, and those which had the palsy, and He healed them.

ACTS viii. 5-7. Then Philip went down to the city of Samaria, and preached Christ unto them . . . [and] unclean spirits, crying with a loud voice, came out of many that were possessed with them; and many taken with palsies, and [many] that were lame, were healed.

ACTS ix. 32, 33. As Peter passed throughout all quarters, he came to Lydda, and there found a certain man named Æneas, which had kept his bed eight years, being sick of the palsy. And Peter said to him, Æneas, Jesus Christ maketh thee whole: arise, and make thy bed. And he arose immediately.

St. Ausonius heals Caligia of general paralysis (first century). Caligia was the sister of Garrulus, count and prefect of Angoulême. One day, walking with her companions along the Charente, she caught cold, which brought on a general paralysis of all her limbs. The count applied to Ausonius, and said to him, "Thou man of God, my sister is grievously sick; come, I pray thee, and heal her." Ausonius went to the sick chamber, and saw that Caligia was at the point of death. Taking her by the hand, he said to her, "In the name of the Lord Jesus, damsel, I say unto thee arise." In an instant she arose in sound health, and Ausonius led her to her brother.—L'abbé Duchassaing (canon of Angoulême), *Life of St. Ausonius.*

St. Euthymius cures a paralytic (A.D. 376-473). Terebon, son of an Armenian chief, was paralyzed all down one side of his body, and neither medicine nor magic had availed to cure him. One night, in a dream, he was told, if he went to the cavern of Euthymius, he would be shown what he must do to be healed. Next day he started with his father to find the hermit, who made the sign of the cross upon the paralytic, and thus restored him to robust and perfect health. This miracle effected the conversion of the chief and all his tribe, who, being baptized, were one and all called Peter.—Cyrillus, *Life of Euthymius.* (See Surius and the annotations of Bollandus.)

St. Germanus of Scotland heals Petronilla of the palsy (fifteenth century). When St. Germanus of Scotland was in Lower Normandy, the daughter of the governor of Montebourg, a paralytic, blind from her birth, was brought to him. She entreated St. Germanus to baptize her. This he did, calling her Petronilla, in honour of St. Peter. Immediately the "water of regeneration" touched her, her eyes were opened, and her limbs received their normal strength. This miracle, wrought on one so considerable, was the cause of the conversion of the entire province.—Corblet, *Hagiographie d'Amiens.*

St. Laumer cures a paralytic (575). St. Laumer, by the sign of the cross and a little holy oil, restored to perfect health a nobleman whose whole body was paralyzed. He did the same also for Ulphrada, who in recompense gave him two farms for the use of his monastery.—*Les Petits Bollandistes* (7th edit. 1880), vol. i. p. 472.

Mary F. Pétitot cured of paralysis by St. Meinrad (1850). Mary Francis Pétitot of Neuchâtel, at the age of eleven, was paralyzed by sudden fright. His legs seemed glued together, and nothing that was tried would separate them or restore circulation. Dr. Marcou drove a pin up to its head in the flesh, but the child felt it not, and instead of blood there issued from the wound water slightly reddened. The paralysis resisted all medical skill. Thirty-two years after the stroke, the paralytic was taken in a pilgrim band to the hermitage of St. Meinrad, and arrived there May 11, 1850. Next day he was carried to the church, and immediately the host was elevated he felt his legs were free, that he could stand and walk, and, in short, that he was perfectly cured. The miracle could not but call to mind that performed by Peter and John on the cripple who was laid daily at the gate "Beautiful," in Jerusalem (Acts iii. 1-11). Francis Pétitot has now been eleven years enjoying the full free use of his limbs, and every year has repeated his pilgrimage to Einsiedeln on the anniversary of his miraculous cure.—R. P. Don Charles Brandes, *Life of St. Meinrad.*

St. Thecla cured of the palsy, and St. Justina of blindness, by the sign of the cross (A.D. 250). St. Thecla was a paralytic for six years, and St. Justina by accident lost the use of her eyes. One day Alfio, Philadelphus, and Cyrin came to Lentini to visit the two virgins. They prayed, and, making the sign of the cross, Thecla recovered the use of her limbs, and Justina received her eyesight.—*Les Petits Bollandistes*, vol. v. p. 443.

Paul and Elymas.

ACTS xiii. 7–12. Sergius Paulus, deputy of Cyprus, sent for Paul, desirous to hear the Word of God. But there was in the governor's suite a Jew named Bar-jesus or Elymas, who withstood Paul, and sought to turn away the governor from the faith. Then the apostle, filled with the Holy Ghost, set his eyes on the sorcerer, and said, O full of all subtilty and mischief, thou child of the devil, thou enemy of all righteousness, wilt thou not cease to pervert the right ways of the Lord? Behold, now, the hand of the Lord is upon thee, and thou shalt be blind for a season. Immediately there fell on him a mist and a darkness; and he went about seeking some one to lead him by the hand. Then the deputy, when he saw what was done, believed, being astonished at the doctrine of the Lord.

A mountebank struck dead for withstanding St. Amandus (A.D. 665). When seventy years of age, St. Amandus, preaching to the Basques, was mocked by a buffoon, who imitated his voice and manner, turning all he said into ridicule. Amandus took no notice of the fellow, but went on with his discourse. Not so God. To ridicule God's ministers is to mock God, and the hand of the Almighty was instantly stretched upon the buffoon. As he went on grimacing, suddenly his whole body was contorted. He writhed in agony, shrieking with pain; rolled to the earth; and, after most excruciating sufferings, died. The crowd was horror-struck, and many who had hitherto stood aloof were baptized.—Menjoulet (vicar-general of Bayonne), *Saint Amand, Apôtre des Basques.*

Paul and the Jailer.

ACTS xvi. 23–34. When Paul and Silas were at Philippi, they were assaulted by the people, and the magistrates sent them to prison for creating a street riot, and charged the jailer to keep them safe. The jailer, having this charge, thrust them into the inner prison, and made their feet fast in the stocks. At midnight there was a great earthquake, so that the foundations of the prison were shaken, all the doors of the prison flew open, and the bands of the prisoners were all loosed. The keeper, supposing the prisoners to have fled, drew his sword with intent to kill himself; but Paul cried aloud, Do thyself no harm; we are all here. Then the jailer called for a light, sprang in, fell down before Paul and Silas, brought them out, and said, Sirs, what must I do to be saved? On this, Paul and Silas spoke to him the Word of the Lord, and to all that were in his house. The jailer then washed their stripes, and both he and all his were straightway baptized.

St. Valerian and Maximus his jailer. Almachius, having apprehended Valerian and Tiburtius, his brother, for being Christians, caused them to be beaten with staves, and then delivered them to Maximus to be put to death. Now Maximus, being a mild man, felt pity for his noble prisoners, and tried to induce them to abjure the obnoxious faith; but they answered, "He who to save his life abjures the faith of Christ, the same shall lose it." Maximus, in admiration of this fidelity to Christ, took them to his house; and there Valerian opened up to him the Word of the Lord, and to all that were in the house. The result was that Maximus and all his house were converted and baptized.—Metaphrastês, *Lives*, etc.

Paul and the Viper.

ACTS xxviii. 1–6. Paul escaped from the wreck and came to Melita, where the barbarous people showed him no little kindness, for they kindled a fire, because of the cold. And when Paul had gathered a bundle of sticks and laid them on the fire, there came a viper out of the heat, and fastened on his hand. When the barbarians saw the venomous creature fasten on his hand, they said among themselves, No doubt this man is a murderer, whom, though he hath escaped the sea, yet vengeance suffereth not to live. Paul, however, shook the viper into the fire, and felt no harm. Now, the barbarians looked when he should have swollen, or fallen down dead suddenly; but when they saw no harm come to him, they changed their minds, and said he was a god.

MARK xvi. 17, 18. These signs shall follow them that believe: In My name shall they cast out devils; they shall take up serpents; and if they drink any deadly thing, it shall not hurt them; they shall lay hands on the sick, and the sick shall recover.

St. Hospitus supposed by the Lombards to be a murderer, then a god. In 575 the Lombards, a cruel and insolent race, invaded France, and put all to fire and sword. Having advanced to the tower of St. Hospitus, they were struck with the chains which were hung about the saint, and took him for a malefactor, either a parricide or other great criminal, cut off from the society of man. Questioning the saint, he avowed that he was indeed a wretched sinner, unfit to live; whereupon one of the barbarians raised his sword, intending to cleave his head asunder; but his arm became paralyzed, and he was wholly unable to move it. The barbarians, struck with terror, now thought the hermit was a god, and fell at his feet, imploring him to succour their companion. St. Hospitus, with the sign of the cross, restored the man's arm, and the man forthwith cut off his long hair, and became a faithful disciple of the saint. Gregory of Tours, who relates this story, says the man was alive when he wrote it, and was an excellent and most religious man.—*Historia Francorum*, bk. vi. ch. 6.

St. Julian and the serpent (A.D. 117). When St. Julian was at Artin, a crowd of idolaters gathered round him, with intent to kill him. Far from trembling at their rage, he walked deliberately into their temple, and, by simply naming the name of Jesus, the great idol fell from its pedestal, and was smashed into powder. Forthwith a serpent, falling on several of the idolaters, bit them severely, insomuch that they died. Then the barbarians changed their minds, and instead of threatening the apostle with death, implored his succour; whereupon St. Julian made in their sight the sign of the cross, and, commanding the reptile to do no further harm, it fled, in obedience to the word of the man of God. At this miracle all the people of Artin were converted and baptized, calling on the name of Jesus as the only Saviour.

As the barbarians gathered round St. Julian to be baptized of him, a serpent twined itself on a child, and all fled with horror; but St. Julian prayed, and forthwith the reptile burst asunder, and fell dead upon the ground.—D. Piolin, *History of the Church of Mans*.

Paul let down in a Basket.

Acts ix. 25. Paul escaped from the Jews at Damascus by being let down over the city wall in a basket.

St. Thomas Aquinas, let down in a basket, escapes from Rocca Secca. When St. Thomas Aquinas expressed his intention to join the order of St. Dominic, his mother, who was countess of Aquino, had him confined in Rocca Secca. During the temporary absence of the countess, the Dominicans of Naples went in disguise, and, with the connivance of his sister, let him out of the tower in a basket; and he made his escape to Naples.—Alban Butler, *Lives of the Saints* (March 7).

Carolstadt made his escape by being let over the city wall in a basket (A.D. 1524). Carolstadt, the image-breaker, would have been captured at Rotenberg by his persecutors, in 1524, but he was let down in a basket over the city wall, and made his escape.—Milman, *Ecclesiastical History*, vol. iv. p. 266.

Paul's Route assigned and changed by a Vision.

Acts xvi. 6–9. When they had gone throughout Phrygia . . . and were forbidden of the Holy Ghost to preach the Word in Asia . . . they assayed to go into Bithynia: but the Spirit suffered them not . . . So, passing by Mysia, they came to Troas, when a vision appeared to Paul in the night; There stood a man of Macedonia, and prayed him, saying, Come over into Macedonia, and help us.

St. Cyril is commanded by the apparition of St. Basil to go into Armenia (A.D. 1181). While St. Cyril, afterwards general of Mount Carmel, was living as an obscure monk on the mount, St. Basil, bishop of Cæsarea (who had been dead more than eight hundred years), appeared to him one night, and commanded him, on the part of Jesus, to go into Armenia to preach the gospel, and rekindle the fire of faith which was nearly gone out. St. Cyril communicated the vision to his superior, who instantly recognized it was from God, and not only gave Cyril permission to go, but also assigned to him Eusebius as a companion. So successful were the labours of these two missionaries, that all the Armenian nation, including the king, was converted, and submitted to pope Lucius III. in entire obedience.—*Les Petits Bollandistes*, vol. iii. p. 200.

Paul's Voyage.

Acts xxvii. 13–44. When St. Paul was on his voyage to Rome, as the ship drew near Crete, a tempestuous wind, called Euroclydon, arose, caught the ship, and nearly wrecked it. And when neither sun nor stars appeared for many days, all hope of safety was abandoned. Paul then told the crew to be of good courage, for an angel had told him, saying, God hath given thee, Paul, all them that sail with thee. On the fourteenth night, the seamen, thinking they were near land, let down the boat, intending to escape; but Paul said to the centurion, Except these abide in the ship, ye cannot be saved. So the soldiers cut the ropes of the boat, and let her fall off. At daybreak, Paul besought all on the ship to take food, and when they had eaten enough they lightened the ship by casting the wheat into the sea. The pilot then tried to run the ship into a creek; but she ran aground, and the hinder part was broken by the violence of the waves. The centurion then gave orders that all should save themselves who could; and some swam to shore, others were drifted there on boards or other parts of the ship. In fine, of the 276 souls on board, all escaped safe to land, and not one was lost.

The voyage of St. Amandus from Rome to France (A.D. 594–684). St. Amandus embarked at Rome for Gaul, but as the vessel drew near Civita Vecchia, then called Centumcelle, a great storm arose. The skies were covered with heavy banks of clouds, the sea surged, the waves rose in mountains, and the winds blew frightfully. The ship was blown about, and every moment it was thought it would be wrecked. In this terrible state the crew threw themselves at the feet of St. Amandus, imploring him to ask God to save them, for vain was the help of man. St. Amandus bade them be of good courage, assuring them that not one of them should be lost. "Now rest yourselves from your fatigues," he continued, "and take food." So they took food and retired to their hammocks, for it was night. St. Amandus took his place next the pilot, and when all was quiet St. Peter came to him, and said, "Amandus, God hath given thee all those who sail with thee." Then, turning to the sea, he said, "Peace; be still!" and immediately there was a great calm. At daybreak the sailors found the ship floating peacefully over the sea; she soon reached shore, and blessed God who had saved them in such imminent danger. As for St. Amandus, he went to the monastery of Elnon, preaching the Word and teaching in all the countries round about. — Menjoulet (vicar-general of Bayonne), *Saint Amand, Apôtre des Basques.*

Penitent Thief.

LUKE xxiii. 39–43. One of the malefactors which were hanged railed on Him, saying, If Thou be the Christ, save Thyself and us. But the other answering rebuked him, saying, Dost thou not fear God? . . . And he said to Jesus, Lord, remember me when Thou comest into Thy kingdom. And Jesus said to him, Verily I say unto thee, To-day shalt thou be with Me in paradise.

Dismas, the penitent thief (A.D. 33). The tale about the two thieves, in Longfellow's *Golden Legend*, is taken from St. Anselm, *Meditations*, xv., only he has changed the names from Dismas and Gestas into Titus and Dumachus. St. Anselm says, "Dismas lived in the forests of Egypt, and when the holy family fled to Egypt to escape from Herod, Dismas, with his band of robbers, started upon them from ambuscade; but seeing only an old man, a young woman, and an infant in arms, the brigand forbore to rob or molest them, and, being struck with the divine beauty of the infant Jesus, he conducted the three fugitives into his cave, and set before them water to wash in and food to eat. Mary assured Dismas that he should receive a recompense for his kindness before he died. This promise was realized on the cross, when Jesus said to him, 'This day shalt thou be with Me in paradise.'" Longfellow does not follow St. Anselm throughout. He says the holy family was set on by a band of robbers, one of whom, named Titus, said, "Let these good people go in peace;" but Dumachus, another of the band, insisted on being paid for their ransom. Whereupon Titus handed him the money, and the infant Jesus said to the good thief—

> When thirty years shall have gone by,
> I at Jerusalem shall die . . .
> On the accursèd tree.
> Then on my right and my left side,
> These thieves shall both be crucified,
> And Titus thenceforth shall abide
> In paradise with Me.

There was a mediæval charm, in Latin verse, which ran as follows:—

> Imparibus meritis pendent tria corpora ramis;
> Dysmas, et Gestas, media est Divina Potestas;
> Alta petit Dysmas, infelix infima Gestas;
> Nos et res nostras conservet Summa Potestas.
> Hos versus dicas ne tu furto tua perdas.

> Of differing merits from three trees incline,
> Dismas, and Gestas, and the Power Divine;
> Dismas seeks heaven, Gestas his own damnation,
> The Mid-one seeks our ransom and salvation.
> This charm your goods will save from spoliation.

Béziers, a great criminal, converted by St. Vincent Ferrier, and taken to paradise (A.D. 1357–1419). When St. Vincent Ferrier was in France, he met with one Béziers, a man who had committed many great crimes, amongst others that of incest, so that he utterly despaired of God's mercy. While the saint was preaching in the town, this great criminal went to hear him, and was so arrested by the fire of his words, that he went to him in great contrition, and, falling at his feet, cried in agony of spirit, "What must I do to be saved?" St. Vincent imposed on him a penitence of seven years. "What, my father," he exclaimed, "only seven years of penitence for crimes so many and so great as mine?" "Yes, my son," replied St. Vincent, "and I will reduce the seven years to three days on bread and water." The penitent was heart-broken with gratitude, he was wholly unable to utter a word, and St. Vincent added, "Go in peace, my son; repeat thrice the Lord's Prayer, and your sins, which are many, shall be all forgiven you." Scarcely had Béziers completed this easy task, when he fell down dead at St. Vincent's feet. At night, his glorified soul appeared to the saint, and said to him, "By the abounding mercy of God my contrition has been accepted, and I am admitted into paradise without passing through the flames of purgatory."—Father Teoli, bk. ii. tratt. 2, c. 4.

A courtesan, converted by St. Vincent Ferrier, dies suddenly, and is taken to paradise (A.D. 1357–1419). A woman, who led a most scandalous life, once went into a church where St. Vincent Ferrier was preaching. Her object was not to hear the preacher, but to show off herself, and attract the eyes of the audience; consequently, she was dressed in the height of fashion, and seated herself in the most conspicuous place of the church. St. Vincent took for his subject, "In like manner also I will that women adorn themselves in modest apparel, with shamefacedness and sobriety; not with broided hair, or gold, or pearls, or costly array; but (which becometh women professing godliness) with good works" (1 *Tim.* ii. 9, 10). He spoke strongly on the vanity of dress, and showed how dress bespoke the mind. He called it "the silent language of the heart;" and showed how utterly impossible it is to be vain in dress and sincere in good works. He then went on to show what are good works, without which none could hope for salvation. He was fervid, earnest, eloquent; and his words, sharper than a two-edged sword, pierced the heart and marrow of the harlot. She wept most bitterly; her sobs suffocated her; she fell dead. All the congregation said it was a judgment of God; but St. Vincent, addressing the crowd, said, "My dear hearers, this is, no doubt, an awful visitation, but not a visit of condemnation. I believe the contrition of our sister was so sincere and so bitter, that it broke her heart, and a broken heart God never can despise. Let us pray for her repose." At this moment a voice rang through the church, loud, clear, and awful, "It is not needful to pray for the repose of our sister's soul, for it is in paradise. Pray for your own souls, that your contrition for sins may be as sincere as hers."—L'abbé A. Bayle, *Life of St. Vincent Ferrier* (1855).

A dying infidel saved in spite of himself (fourteenth century). One day St. Vincent Ferrier stood beside a dying man whose blasphemies were shocking to hear. St. Vincent, confiding in the covenanted mercies of God, turned to the dying man and said, "I will save you in spite of yourself." He then invited those present to invoke the Virgin and recite their rosary. Before the rosary was finished the "Mother of God" appeared, bearing in her arms the infant Jesus covered with His wounds, all bleeding. The dying man saw the vision, demanded pardon of God and man, and was numbered with the elect. This forms the subject of a painting.—*Les Petits Bollandistes*, vol. iv. p. 237.

Peter's Denial of Christ.

MARK xiv. 66–71. During the trial of Jesus, Peter crept into the judgment-hall to see how it would all end. And, as he stood beneath in the palace, one of the maids of the high priest said to him, And thou also wast with Jesus of Nazareth. But Peter denied, saying, I know not, neither understand I what thou sayest. Shifting his place, he went into the porch, and the cock crew. A maid saw him in the porch, and said to the bystanders, This is one of them. And he denied again. A little time after some of the bystanders said to him, Surely thou art one of them: for thou art a Galilean, and thy speech agreeth thereto. Then Peter began to curse and to swear, saying, I know not this man of whom ye speak.

Cranmer, the archbishop, denies and recants. At the death of Edward VI., his half-sister Mary ascended the throne, and, being a rigid [Roman] Catholic, many Protestants were, by her instigation, subjected to torture and death. Cranmer, Ridley, and Latimer, leaders of the Protestant party, were committed to the Tower, and afterwards removed to the Bocardo, a common jail in Oxford. They were all condemned as heretics, and their execution at the stake was resolved on. Cranmer was frightened at the sentence, and, to avoid it, recanted, not three times, like Peter, but six times. It has been well said, that "the tender mercies of the wicked are cruel." The recantation of the archbishop availed him nothing, for the sentence of death was not revoked, but formally fixed for May 21, 1556. It is said, when Cranmer came to the stake, he held his right hand in the flame till it was burnt off, saying, "That unworthy hand! that unworthy hand!" He certainly underwent his sentence with undaunted resolution. It is not for us to condemn the weakness of Peter, Marcellinus, Jerome, and Cranmer, but, from their examples, to "take heed lest we also fall."

Jerome of Prague anathematizes the articles of Wiclif, but afterwards recants

(Sept. 11, A.D. 1415). Jerome of Prague, frightened at the terrible death of his friend Huss, retracted his "heretical" doctrines. His retractation was, at first, somewhat ambiguous, like that of Peter, who said to the damsel who charged him with being a disciple of Christ, "I know not, neither do I understand what thou sayest;" but when pressed by others, he "began to curse, and to swear that he did not even know the Prisoner." So Jerome's retractations, which were at first equivocal, became more and more explicit and circumstantial as he was harder pressed. He then not only denied belief in the new doctrines, but anathematized the articles of Wiclif and Huss, and professed to believe everything the council believed, adding these words, "If in future any word shall escape me inconsistent with this my recantation, may I be punished with everlasting perdition." The cock crew, and Peter, brought to himself, went out, and wept bitterly; so, a few days' reflection in prison brought Jerome to his senses, and when next he stood before the council, he boldly said, "I am not ashamed to confess my cowardice before this august assembly. I tremble when I think of it. I tremble when I think that the fear of the stake induced me to condemn the doctrines of Wiclif and Huss, which in my heart I most firmly believe." He then disowned his retractation, denouncing it as the greatest of crimes, and declaring that, come what might, he would with his last breath adhere to the principles of those two men. He was then sent back to prison, and, not long after, sealed his fidelity at the stake.—Milman, *History of the Church of Christ*, vol. iii. pp. 370-375.

(The comparison between Peter and Jerome is not in Milman's narrative.)

The pope Marcellinus offers incense to Apollo. In the reign of Diocletian, the Roman emperor, Marcellinus, the pope, was apprehended, and threatened with terrible torments unless he abjured the Christian faith by offering incense to Apollo. Being a very timid man, he yielded through fear, and offered sacrifice; whereupon he was set free; and the emperor greatly rejoiced that he had won over the chief pontiff of the pernicious sect. A council being called at Sinuessa, the renegade appeared before it. There were three hundred bishops and thirty priests present, and they all resolved with one voice that there resided no power in man to depose a pope. The case of Peter was brought forward for their guidance, and it was urged that the apostles did not cut off Peter from his apostleship for denying Christ, but left him to be dealt with as God thought fit. So Marcellinus was not deposed. Afterwards he recanted, and was put to death.—Damasus, *Life of Marcellinus.*

The judgment was no guide for future councils. Eugenius IV. was deposed by the Council of Basel in 1438. A still stronger case occurred in the reign of Kaiser Sigmund in 1414, when the Council of Constance deposed the three popes, John XXII., Gregory XII., and Benedict XIII. Surely it must be obvious that either the dogma of the pope being an overlord, and God's vicar on earth, must be abandoned, or else there resides no power in man to depose him. Not all the powers of the state, except that of the king himself, can depose his viceroys; and not all the powers of the earth, except that of Christ, can depose His delegate. If the pope, therefore, is God's delegate, as he claims to be, no body of men can depose him; if, on the other hand, a council can depose him, he is only an officer of the Church, and not God's delegate.

The position of king is radically different. A king is only a civil potentate, a chief magistrate of the state, just so long as the nation chooses to continue him in office. If we believe him to be "God's anointed," we must say with Shakespeare, "Show us the hand of God that hath dismissed us from His stewardship." A pope, if anything more than a president of brother bishops, cannot be deposed. Hence this dilemma: If the pope is God's delegate, man cannot depose him; if a council or king can depose him, he is only the officer of that council or king, and not "God's vicar" at all. The Council of Sinuessa was consistent, those of Basel and Constance suicidal to their own dogma.

Pharisee and Publican.

LUKE xviii. 10-14. Two men went up into the temple to pray, one a Pharisee, and the other a publican. The Pharisee stood and prayed thus with himself: God, I thank Thee that I am not as other men are, extortioners, unjust, adulterers, or even as this publican; I fast twice in the week; I give tithes of all that I possess. The publican, standing afar off, would not lift up so much as his eyes unto heaven, but smote upon his breast, saying, God be merciful to me a sinner. I tell you, this man went down to his house justified rather than the other.

Juno and her suitors. There is a legend or fable, no matter which, that Juno, on a grand festival, promised a great reward to the suitor who should bring her the most acceptable present. Amongst those who presented themselves were a physician, a poet, a merchant, a philosopher, and a beggar. The *physician* presented to her an elixir of life, whereby old age was restored to youth and beauty. The *poet* presented an ode on her favourite bird, the peacock. The *merchant* presented a rare and valuable jewel for an earring. The *philosopher* handed her a book, in which he had discovered certain secrets of nature hitherto unknown. The poor quaking *beggar* had nothing, literally nothing; and bending on his knees in abject humility, he cried with a broken voice, "Great queen, I have nothing,

nothing worthy of thy acceptance; but have mercy on me, O great queen, and accept me, as the humblest of thy slaves." Juno took the beggar by the hand, bade him stand upon his feet, put a crown upon his head, and said, "The gods delight to honour the lowly-minded, and he that humbleth himself most shall be most exalted."

The anchorite and the minstrel. A certain anchorite had passed a long life in a cave of the Thebaïd, remote from all communion with men. He fasted, and prayed, and performed many severe penances. Having thus lived for threescore and ten years, he was puffed up with the notion of his sanctity, and, like St. Antony, besought the Lord, if any saint on earth was holier than himself, to point him out, that he might emulate him. The same night an angel appeared to him, and said, "If thou wouldst be more perfect, seek out the minstrel who passes daily through the streets of Thebes begging, and learn of him." The anchorite, greatly amazed, nevertheless started, staff in hand, for Thebes, and soon found out the minstrel beggar. "Good brother," said the hermit, "what good works hast thou done, what time hast thou spent in prayer, and what penances have you performed, to make yourself so acceptable to God." The minstrel, amazed at these questions, hung down his head in great abasement. "I prithee do not mock me, thou man of God," he cried; "I have done no good works, miserable sinner that I am, but earn my bread with my viol and flute." "Nay, nay," rejoined the hermit, "but amidst this thy carnal life, no doubt you have found time to do some good works, pleasant and acceptable to God." "Alas! alas!" said the minstrel, "I know nothing good that I have done." The hermit, wondering more and more, said to him, "You are a beggar. Have you spent your substance in riotous living, like most others of your class?" "No," said the minstrel. "It is true that I once had a little, but I spent it to redeem the children of a poor widow, who had been sold to slavery to pay a debt; but any one would have done that for a fellow-creature in distress." The hermit, hearing this, wept bitterly, and exclaimed, "I have not done one-tenth so much as this poor beggar, and yet men call me the holy anchorite."—St. Jerome.

St. Theodulus a pillar-saint (fifth century). About a century after Simeon the pillar-saint, rose, in Edessa, Theodulus, who retired to a pillar as his hermitage. After living on his pillar many years, he said to Christ in prayer, "O Lord, if I have merited anything at Thy hand, let me know if there lives any one in the world who has done more than I have to earn eternal life." A voice said to him, "Yes, Theodulus, Cornelius the jester has." Theodulus immediately descended to hunt up this rival, and having found him, wrung from him in time this story: "A lady of fortune married; and her husband, who was a great libertine, wasted her fortune in riotous living. He was imprisoned for debt, and the wife set herself to work to earn money to pay off his debts. One day I asked her how much she required. 'Four hundred ecus' (£5 sterling), was the reply; so I sold everything I had, and raised thereby three hundred ecus. To complete the sum I sold my clothes, the collar which I wore round my neck, and a ring; and, having amassed the four hundred ecus, gave them to the lady, saying, 'There, lady, accept this offering, and redeem your husband.'" Theodulus returned to his column a better and a humbler man, but died in a few days.—*Acta Sanctorum* (Bollandists), vol. vi. May 28.

This seems to be simply another version of the preceding tale, which in my opinion is the better of the two.

Pinnacle of the Temple.

MATT. iv. 5–7. The devil took Jesus into the holy city, and setting Him on a pinnacle of the temple, said to Him, If Thou be the Son of God, cast Thyself down: for it is written, He shall give His angels charge concerning Thee; and in their hands they shall bear Thee up, lest at any time Thou dash Thy foot against a stone.

St. James the Less or the Just set on a pinnacle of the temple. The Jews came to James the Just, and desired him to speak unto the people on the day of the Passover. So he said he would do what was fitting for him to do. The day being come, an infinite crowd was assembled; and the scribes and Pharisees led James to the pinnacle of the temple, where all might see and hear him. Being there set, they propounded to him the question, "What thinkest thou of Christ?" Then spake James with a loud voice, saying, "He is the Son of man who now sitteth on the right hand of God, and He shall come hereafter to judge both the quick and dead." His voice was now drowned in the uproar, and the priests went in a body to the pinnacle, and threw him headlong to the ground. He was not killed by the fall, so they took up stones to cast at him; and St. James, getting on his knees, prayed God to pardon his murderers. His body was transferred to Rome, and laid beside the body of Philip, his fellow-apostle. His head, however, is in Galatia, in Spain.—Edward Kinesman (1623), *Lives of the Saints*, pp. 267, 268.

(Although Egesippus, Clemens Alexandrinus, Eusebius Cesariensis, and St. Jerome, all think that James, surnamed "Justus," is not the same as James the Less, yet the authority of pope Anacletus is sufficient to prove it, for he was pope of Rome, and who shall gainsay him?)

Plague stayed.

2 SAM. xxiv. 25. So the Lord was intreated for the land, and the plague was stayed from Israel.

JONAH ii. 4–10. Jonah was commanded to announce to the people of Nineveh the utter destruction of the city within forty days; but the king of Nineveh ordained a general fast, and bade that man and beast should be covered with sackcloth, and cry mightily unto God. So God repented of the evil, and the city was saved.

St. Peter Thomas intreated the Lord, and a plague in Cyprus was stayed (A.D. 1358). St. Peter Thomas stayed a plague which desolated the whole island of Cyprus. He commanded the people to make a public procession. He himself headed it, clothed in sackcloth, with ashes on his head, a cord round his neck, and barefooted. When God saw the procession, He was intreated for the land, and the plague was stayed.

Similarly, St. Peter Thomas arrested the plague in the island of Paphos.—Philip Mazzeri, *Life of St. Peter Thomas*.

Pool of Bethesda.

JOHN v. 2–9. There is at Jerusalem by the sheep-market a pool . . . called Bethesda, having five porches, in [which] lay a great multitude of impotent folk, blind, halt, and withered, waiting for the moving of the water. For an angel went down at a certain season into the pool, and troubled the water; whoever then first stepped in was made whole of whatever disease he had. A certain man was there who had had an infirmity thirty-eight years. When Jesus saw him, He said, Wilt thou be made whole? . . . Rise! take up thy bed, and walk. And immediately the man was made whole, took up his bed, and walked.

ACTS iii. 1–11. Peter and John went up together into the temple at the hour of prayer, and a certain man lame from his mother's womb was carried and laid daily at the gate of the temple, called Beautiful, to ask alms of them that entered into the temple. Seeing Peter and John about to go into the temple, he asked alms. Peter, fastening his eyes upon him, said, Silver and gold have I none; but such as I have give I unto thee: In the name of Jesus Christ of Nazareth rise up and walk. And immediately his feet and ankle-bones received strength, and leaping up he stood, and walked, and entered the temple, walking, and leaping, and praising God.

St. Marcian's porch. St. Marcian built a church dedicated to St. Isidore, which had a magnificent baptistery surrounded with five porches. This baptistery was more worthy of renown than the pool by the sheep-market in Jerusalem, in that greater miracles occurred there. To the pool in the sheep-market an *angel* descended, and that only once a year, and the water healed but one sick person at a time; but to St. Marcian's baptistery, not an angel, but Christ Himself was wont to descend; not once a year, but every day; not to heal bodies only, but souls as well.—Simeon Metaphrastês (died A.D. 911), *Lives*, etc.

Post-prophetic Intuition and Second Sight.

(We have not the words *Epiphetic* and *Epiphecy* to express the knowledge by inspiration of events just past; but we want them. The Hindû word is *yog-vidya*.)

ISA. xli. 22. Show them the *former* things what they be, or declare us things for to come *hereafter*.

JOHN xi. 1–17. Mary and Martha sent to tell Jesus that their brother Lazarus was sick; but, notwithstanding, He remained two days longer in the same place. After that He saith to His disciples, Our friend Lazarus sleepeth. Then said His disciples, Lord, if he sleep he will do well. Howbeit He spake of his death. When Jesus had come to Bethany he found that Lazarus had been buried four days.

St. Benedict in Mount Cassino sees the death of St. Germanus at Capua (sixth century). On the night of St. Germanus's death, Servantius, abbot of a monastery in Italy, went to Mount Cassino to confer with St. Benedict on spiritual matters. At night, Servantius retired to a chamber above that of St. Benedict, in the tower of the building. St. Benedict opened his casement to look at the starry heavens, and while he gazed, he beheld a light so brilliant, that the darkness was wholly chased away. It was lighter than mid-day, and the light was perfectly serene. And still he looked, rapt in admiration; when lo! he beheld the soul of St. Germanus, bishop of Capua, borne by angels to heaven in a globe or sphere of fire. He called to Servantius to come and see this marvel; but before he arrived, the vision was fading fast, and Servantius only saw the end of it. Next day, a messenger was sent express from Capua to announce the death of their bishop;

and the hour of his decease exactly corresponded with the time of the vision seen by St. Benedict from his chamber window.—St. Gregory the Great, *Dialogues*, bk. ii.

St. Bernard of Abbeville sees the death of the abbot Gervais by post-prophetic vision (A.D. 1096). Gervais was one of the abbots appointed by pope Urban II. to take part in the crusade of 1096. Mounted on his ass, and accompanied by numerous crosses, he was directing his course towards Jerusalem, when a lion sprang on him, and devoured him in the sight of his terrified companions. The very same day St. Bernard was apprised of the fatal event by revelation, and had funeral obsequies observed in his monastery. At the close of the war, when the crusaders returned to their country, St. Bernard was officially informed that the abbot had been killed by a lion on the very day that his obsequies had been observed.—Corblet, *Hagiographie d'Amiens*. (The life of St. Bernard was written 1137–1148 by Geoffrey le Gros, one of his disciples.)

St. Cuthbert knows of the death of king Egfrid by post-prophetic intuition. St. Cuthbert informed the queen of the death of king Egfrid on the very day that he was slain, fighting against the Picts. This he could have known only by inspiration, as he made the communication long before the swiftest messenger could have arrived from the field of battle (A.D. 685).—*Acta Sanctorum* (Bollandists), March 20.

St. Francis Hieronimus knows by epiphetic inspiration of the murder of François Cassier (A.D. 1688). François Cassier was a Protestant, who married a [Roman] Catholic, and had two daughters. When these daughters were grown up, the mother died, and the father resolved to go to Geneva, but insisted on his two daughters travelling in male attire. On the road, the two daughters shot their father with pistols, buried the body, and enlisted in the army of Charles II. of Spain. In an expedition against some brigands, one of the sisters was slain, and, to prevent exposure, the survivor buried her, enlisted in the army under the name of Charles Pimental, and after the extirpation of the brigands returned with the army to Naples. Here St. Francis Hieronimus saw her on guard in Chateau-Neuf, and made a sign to her to come and speak to him. "What in the world can that fellow want with me?" said the assumed Charles Pimental; but as the saint still beckoned her, she went and asked what he wanted. "I want you to confess your great sins," said the man of God. "Me! to confess my great sins?" she cried in bravado. "I have none to confess, so prithee go about your business, and don't trouble me." "No sin to confess?" said St. Francis. "Are you not a woman in soldier's attire? Is not your name Mary Cassier? Were you not born in Paris? Did you not, in conjunction with your sister, since dead, shoot your father François Cassier, and bury him? and did you not then assume the name of Charles Pimental, and join the army of Charles II. of Spain?" Seeing her secret so minutely known, she still tried to brazen it out, and cried, in seeming astonishment, "Who in the world can have told you so absurd a story? However, I will see you to-morrow." The saint waited the morrow, but no one came; he waited the next day, still "Charles Pimental" put in no appearance. On the third day he went, and said to her, "Is it thus you keep your word?" "Father," she replied, "believe me, I have not been able, and now we have marching orders for Tuscany." "No," said the saint, "you will not leave to-morrow; and if what I tell you is true, swear by the name of Christ you will call on me to-morrow without fail." Scarcely was the father gone, when the order for departure was revoked, and the "soldier" went to the church of *Gesù Nuovo* to fulfil her promise. Immediately the saint saw her he exclaimed, "So you thought to escape from the hands of God, did you? No bird can escape from that fowler." She then made her confession, received absolution, resumed her female attire, and was placed in a retreat by the marquis of Santo Stefano.—Cardinal Wiseman. (Mary Cassier gave these details "sous la foi du serment pour le procès de canonization de St. Francis Hieronimus," in 1839.)

St. Hermeland knows of the death of St. Maurontus, though it occurred sixty miles off (A.D. 718). While St. Hermeland was at prayers in St. Peter's church, he saw the soul of St. Maurontus, first abbot of St. Florent le Vieux, carried to heaven by angels, though his death had occurred sixty miles off. Hermeland told the monks of it, and they set down the exact moment. When messengers arrived to announce the saint's decease, the time stated by them exactly corresponded with what the monks had noted down.

Another instance. About the same time,

St. Hermeland saw the soul of one of his disciples, then in Aquitaine, eighty miles off, carried up to heaven by angels, and mentioned it to his monks. Some of the younger brothers thought the abbot was growing senile, but he opened their eyes to see the same vision, and reproved them severely for their want of faith.—*Acta Sanctorum* (Bollandists), March 25.

St. Hilarion knew of the death of St. Antony by epiphetic inspiration. A venerable matron came to visit St. Hilarion, and told him her intention of going to see St. Antony. St. Hilarion replied, "I also had the same intention, but it is too late; for two days ago the world was deprived of that shining light." A few days afterwards, a messenger came to announce to St. Hilarion that his friend St. Antony had been laid in the grave for four days.—St. Jerome, *Vita St. Hilarionis Eremitæ* (A.D. 390). See also Nicephorus Callistus (died 1350), *Ecclesiastical History.*

The death of St. Gertrude known to the abbess Modesta (A.D. 659). At the very moment that St. Gertrude died in the abbey of Nivelle, Belgium, Modesta abbess of the monastery of Rombach, in the Vosges, announced it to St. Cloud, bishop of Metz.—Surius, *Lives of the Saints.*

The murder of Kenhelm or Kenelm was known in Rome the same hour it was committed. When Kenelm was murdered by order of his sister Cwenthryth, at "the very same hour a white dove flew on the altar of St. Peter's, at Rome, and deposited thereon a letter containing full particulars of the murder." So the pope sent men to investigate the matter, and a chapel was built over the dead body. This chapel is still called "St. Kenelm's Chapel" (Shropshire).

St. Theresa, in Spain, announces the death of pope Pius V., at Rome, the very moment it occurs (May 1, A.D. 1572). Pius V. died at Rome May 1, A.D. 1572; and St. Theresa, in Spain, at the very moment of his decease, said to her Carmelites, "Be not astonished, sisters, at what I am about to announce, but weep with me; for the Church militant has just lost its holy pastor."—Père Giry, *Histoire de Saint Pie V.*

St. Vincent Ferrier knows of the death of his father and mother by epiphetic intuition. St. Vincent Ferrier knew by prophetic instinct what was going on in places far away. Thus, while he was preaching, he instinctively knew of the death of his father and mother, and commended their souls to the prayers of his audience.—Peter Ranzano (bishop of Lucera). *Life of St. Vincent Ferrier.*

With the telegraphic system in operation, this sort of knowledge, so common with the Brahmins, and called *yog-vidya*, ought to excite no astonishment. Probably the time is not far distant when we also shall be able to dispense with the clumsy wires and cables.

Prodigal Son.

Luke xv. 11-32. A certain man had two sons, the younger of whom, having received his patrimony, went into a far country, and wasted it in riotous living. Being reduced to want, he became a swineherd, and kept himself alive by the offal which the pigs were fed on. After a while he called to mind his father's wealth, his kindness, his affection, and resolved to return home and crave forgiveness. While still afar off the father saw him, ran to meet him, fell on his neck, and kissed him. Father, cried the young penitent, I have sinned against heaven, and in thy sight, and am no more worthy to be called thy son: make me one of thy hired servants. But the father clothed the penitent in the best of robes, put a ring on his finger and shoes on his feet, and set before him the fatted calf; for, said he, This my son was dead, and is alive again; was lost, and is found. While the feast was going on the elder brother returned, demanded of the servants the cause of this jubilee, and being told it was for the return of his younger brother, he was angry, and exclaimed in his wrath, Lo, these many years have I served thee, father, yet thou didst never give me so much as a kid wherewith to make merry with my friends; but as for this prodigal, who has wasted thy substance in harlotry, the moment he comes home, thou killest for him the fatted calf. The father made answer, Son, thou art ever with me, and all that I have is thine. It is meet that we should make merry for this thy brother: for he was dead, and is alive again; was lost, and is found.

The two sons of Diocletian's guardsman. One of the guardsmen of Diocletian had two sons, whom he loved most fondly. The younger married a harlot, and the infamy of his conduct was a sore grief to his father. In time a child was born, and the young prodigal sent it to his father to be brought up. Want weighed daily more heavily on the young scapegrace, and at last he was reduced to such abject distress, that starvation stared him in the face. He now sent to his father imploring alms, and the father bade him return home, and all should be forgiven. When the elder brother heard of the prodigal's return, he was extremely angry, and said his father must have lost his senses to take such a serpent into his bosom; but the father replied, "No, my son; this thy brother has craved forgiveness, and I have forgiven him; his heart is contrite, and I must heal it. It behoves me to relent, and take him to my bosom. Surely it would become you, too, my son, to welcome thy brother home, and rejoice that he has abandoned his evil ways. My son, my son, to err is human; to forgive, divine."—*Gesta Romanorum*, vii.

Prophetic Warnings.

MATT. xxiv. 1–28. Jesus foretold the destruction of Jerusalem, and said, Nation shall rise up against nation, and kingdom against kingdom; and there shall be famines, and pestilences, and earthquakes in divers places. All these are the beginning of sorrows.

MATT. xxiii. 37, 38. O Jerusalem, Jerusalem, how often would I have gathered thy children together, even as a hen gathereth her chickens under her wings, and ye would not! Behold, your house is left unto you desolate.

St. Benedict's prophetic warning to Totila. Totila, king of the Goths, to try St. Benedict, sent one of his servants arrayed in royal robes, with a great train of attendants, to the man of God; but St. Benedict said to the man, "Give back thy finery to Totila, and be content with thy calling." After this, Totila himself came, and St. Benedict told him to repent of his sins, for within ten years he would be numbered with the dead. And so it was.—St. Gregory, *Dialogues*, bk. ii.

St. Hilarion's prophetic warnings of Julian's future reign. St. Hilarion resolved to flee into some other country; but, when this was known, above a thousand persons came and besought him not to leave them. St. Hilarion, striking the earth with his staff, exclaimed, "I cannot bear it! I cannot bear that God should be accounted a deceiver. I cannot bear to see His temples overthrown, His altars trodden underfoot, and His children slain with the edge of the sword." These words he spoke in the spirit of prophecy, foreseeing the evils which would come on the land in the reign of the apostate Julian.

Another instance. When St. Hilarion was at Alexandria, he abode with certain religious men, but left suddenly. Being asked the reason, he replied, "To avoid the troubles which I see at hand." Next day the officers of justice came to arrest him, and when told he had left the city, they declared he was a sorcerer who knew things before they came to pass.—St. Jerome (A.D. 390), *Life of St. Hilarion the Hermit.*

The death of Julian the Apostate forewarned. When the emperor Julian was about to start on his Parthian expedition, he threatened, on his return, to smite the Christians hip and thigh, so as to wipe them entirely from the face of the whole earth. Libanius, the rhetorician, asked one of them scoffingly what the carpenter's Son was doing on their behalf. "Making a coffin," he replied, "for your master, the emperor." The event proved the answer to be prophetic; for the emperor was mortally wounded in a night skirmish; and, just before dying, tossed the blood, with which his hand was filled, into the air, saying, "Vicisti, O Galilee..." "Thou hast prevailed, O Galilean. Thy right hand hath the pre-eminence!"—Theodoret (A.D. 443–450), *Ecclesiastical History.*

Some say that Julian received his death-wound from an angel. Rosweyde, the hagiographer (vol. i. p. 416), in his *Life of Macarius*, asserts that Julian was slain by "Mercurius, the Christian martyr."

Peden's prophetic warnings. When Peden was a prisoner in the Bass, as he was engaged in public worship one Sunday, a young woman mocked him with loud laughter. Peden said to her, "Thou mockest at the service of God; but God hath said, 'I also will laugh at your calamity, and will mock when your fear cometh; when your fear cometh as desolation, and destruction cometh as a whirlwind.'" Soon afterwards this young woman was walking on the rock, and a sudden blast of wind swept her into the sea, and she was lost.

Another instance. One day, while walking on the rock, a soldier cried out to Peden, "The devil take you!" "Fie! fie!" said Peden, "you know not what you say, but will ere long repent it." At this reproof, the soldier went to the guard-room as one distraught, crying like a madman, "The devil! the devil!" Peden heard of the man's insanity, went to him, prayed over him, and he returned to his right mind.—*Martyrs of the Bass Rock.*

Reconciliation before Offerings.

MATT. v. 23, 24. If thou bring thy gift to the altar, and there rememberest that thy brother hath ought against thee; leave there thy gift before the altar, and go thy way; first be reconciled to thy brother, and then come and offer thy gift.

JOB xlii. 7, 8. The Lord then said to Eliphaz the Temanite, My wrath is kindled against thee, and against thy two friends: for ye have not spoken of Me the thing that is right, as My servant Job hath. Therefore take unto you now seven bullocks and seven rams, and go to My servant Job, and offer up for yourselves a burnt offering; and My servant Job shall pray for you; for him will I accept: lest I deal with you after your folly, in that ye have not spoken of Me the thing which is right, like My servant Job.

How St. John, the patriarch of Alexandria, taught reconciliation (A.D. 619). It must be borne in mind that it was customary, at least in Alexandria, at the time when St. John the Almoner was patriarch, for the priest to invite a certain number of lay assistants to accompany him in the prayers and canticles which come after the elevation of the host. Now, at Alexandria there was a man of wealth and family who, for a long time, had a deadly feud with another. They would negotiate nothing together, would not speak to each other, and all the efforts of the patriarch to reconcile them proved nugatory. At last he hit upon the following device: he invited the nobleman to assist him in the service of the mass, and as this was thought a very great compliment, it was readily accepted. The patriarch, however, had instructed all the other assistants beforehand what they were to do. Well, the assistants accompanied the patriarch as usual, and came to the Lord's Prayer, "and forgive us our trespasses," when the patriarch and those in the secret stopped suddenly, leaving the nobleman to say alone, "as we forgive those that trespass against us." The nobleman was utterly confounded and thoroughly ashamed; and at the close of the service came to St. John and said, "I confess my sin; come with me, and reconcile me to my enemy." St. John merely answered, "O God, forgive us our offences, as we forgive those who offend us," and went with the nobleman to witness his reconciliation.—Leontius (bishop of Naples), *Life of St. John the Almoner*.

Relics.

2 KINGS iv. 18–37. When the son of the Shunammite woman died, Elisha commanded Gehazi, saying, Gird up thy loins, and take my staff in thine hand, and go thy way, and lay my staff upon the face of the child.

2 KINGS xiii. 21. And Elisha died, and they buried him. And it came to pass, as the Moab ites were burying a man, they spied a band of men, and cast the dead body into the sepulchre of Elisha; and when it touched the bones of Elisha, it revived, and stood on its feet.

ACTS xix. 11, 12. And God wrought special miracles by the hands of Paul, so that from his body were brought unto the sick handkerchiefs or aprons, and the diseases departed from them, and the evil spirits went out of them.

ECCLESIASTICUS. He did wonders in his life, and at his death his body prophesied.

N.B.—The greatest collector of relics that ever lived was St. Boniface IV. On Nov. 1, A.D. 607, as many as twenty-eight waggon-loads of relics were brought to the church dedicated to the Virgin, which had been a heathen pantheon. It was then that "All-Saints' Day" was first appointed.

The baton of St. Cajetan. When St. John-Joseph of the Cross was on his deathbed, the Theatins came to visit him, bringing with them the famous baton of St. Cajetan, with which they touched his head. The behaviour of this relic was so remarkable, that it must be told in the very words of Father Michel, by whom the experiment was made. "En vertu de l'amour réciproque qui existait entre le Père Jean-Joseph de la Croix et moi, et aussi mon profond respect et de mes obligations particulières envers lui, je n'eus pas plus tôt appris qu'il avait été frappé d'une attaque d'apoplexie, et que l'on craignait pour sa vie, que je lui portai le bâton de St. Cajétan. Comme je lui en touchais la tête, il arriva un prodige qui n'a point eu de pareil, avant ni depuis, quoique la relique ait été continuellement et soit encore portée chez un grand nombre de malades. Lorsque je fus entré dans la cellule du susdit serviteur de Dieu qui était mourant, et que je lui eus posé la susdite relique sur la tête, le bâton, à l'instant même, fit certains sauts et certains bonds correspondant à un son mélodieux qui fut entendu de toutes ceux qui étaient présents; et, malgré tous mes efforts, je ne pouvais l'empêcher de remuer dans mes mains, à mon grand étonnement et à ma grande satisfaction, qui furent partagés de tous ceux qui étaient avec moi témoins d'un prodige si inouï. Au moment même où ce prodige s'accomplissait, on vit le serviteur de Dieu lever lentement la main, et indiquer de l'index le ciel. Frappé d'étonnement de ce qui se passait, et qui plus est, voyant que le saint, par la violence de son mal, était hors de lui-même, je me disposais à approcher une seconde fois de lui la relique, lorsque le bâton se mit à sautiller comme la première fois, et que le son mélodieux se fit de nouveau entendre; une seconde fois encore le serviteur de Dieu leva la main, et montra le ciel de l'index,—ce qui me fit comprendre que St. Cajétan l'invitait au paradis. Tout cela nous fut, à tous ceux qui étaient présents et à moi un grand sujet de consolation, et une surabondance de joie spirituelle. Le bruit de ce grand miracle venant à se répandre tout à coup dans tout le monastère, on vit arriver auprès du malade une foule de religieux et de personnes de distinction, qui joignirent leurs voix pour me prier de lui appliquer encore une fois la relique, afin qu'ils fussent aussi eux-mêmes témoins de ce prodige. D'abord je restai indécis, pensant que ce serait en quelque sorte tenter Dieu; mais, cédant enfin à leur importunité, je me prêtai à leurs désirs, me disant en moimême: Peut-être Dieu veut-il encore glorifier davantage son serviteur. Tirant donc la relique de son enveloppe, tandis que tous ceux qui m'environnaient examinaient avec une pieuse curiosité quel le résultat, j'appliquai la rélique sur le malade, à deux reprises différentes, et à chaque fois se renouvelèrent les sautillements, et les sons dont j'ai parlé; à cheque fois aussi, le serviteur de Dieu leva la main, et montra le ciel comme les premières fois; ce qui me confirma pleinement dans la persuasion que c'était une invitation par laquelle St. Cajétan l'appelait au bonheur céleste, et à laquelle le saint répondait par ce signe. C'est là un point digne d'une sérieuse attention, lorsqu'on réfléchit que le serviteur de Dieu avait été frappe d'apoplexie, et qu'il était privé de sentiment."

St. Cajetan died in 1547, this occurrence took place in 1734. There can be little doubt of the facts stated by Father Michel, but the object obtained by the mysterious behaviour of the baton is not apparent. Father Michel seems to think it was a call from St. Cajetan for Father John-Joseph to join the saints triumphant. We are told that he lingered on five days longer.

St. Peter's chains. St. Peter's chains and the Saviour's cross are the two most notable relics in the [Roman] Catholic Church, in celebration of which special days are set apart every year. St. Peter, we are told, was twice imprisoned and bound, once in Jerusalem and once at Rome. The former case is related in the Book of the Acts (xii. 1–12), where we read that Herod Agrippa, to please the Jews, seized Peter, and delivered him to four quaternions of soldiers, to keep till after Easter. The night before he was to be brought forth, while he still slept between two soldiers, bound with two chains, an angel came, and, smiting him on the side, said to him, "Arise up quickly." So Peter arose, and his chains fell off. Then said the angel, "Gird thyself, and bind on thy sandals." And he did so. Again the angel said, "Cast thy garment about thee, and follow me." And Peter went from the prison, following the angel, thinking it must be a dream. We are told that the apostles got possession of these two chains, and kept them religiously in the treasury of the church at Jerusalem. One would like to know how the apostles contrived to obtain them, for certainly they were not in favour with the authorities at the time; and it is not clear how the jailers could part with them. One would also like to know what is meant by the treasury of the church at Jerusalem, for the only places of assembly were private houses, and in the siege of Jerusalem there could be no opportunity for looking after relics, nor even personal property. Our Lord Himself said, "Let him that is on the housetop not come down to take anything out of his house; neither let him which is in the field return back to take his clothes" (*Matt.* xxiv. 17, 18). This was not a time for looking after chains and relics.

But let us turn to the second imprisonment, which is only traditional. It is supposed that St. Peter was at Rome in the reign of Nero, and that he was imprisoned there by that emperor during the Christian persecutions (A.D. 64). Probably he was also chained with two chains. We must now pass over fifty years, and come to the pontificate of St. Alexander I., who in the reign of Trajan (A.D. 118) was imprisoned in the house of Quirinus. While a prisoner in this house, he healed Balbina, his jailer's daughter, of the *king's evil*, by hanging his iron chains about her neck. The damsel being cured kissed the chains devoutly; but the pontiff said to her, "Daughter, kiss not my chains, but go and seek for the chains of the apostle Peter," meaning, we are told, the chains with which he was bound in Rome. Quirinus helped his daughter, the chains were found, and were carefully deposited in an oratory at Rome, which oratory was afterwards the famous church of St. Peter ad Vincula.

We must now pass over some 340 years, and come to A.D. 450, when Eudoxia, wife of Theodosius the Younger, emperor of the East, went to visit the holy places, and Juvenal, patriarch of Jerusalem, made her a present of St. Peter's chains, which were richly adorned "with pearls, and gold, and precious stones." We are not told if Herod was at this expense, or if the Christians had the bad judgment to tamper with what they deemed a priceless relic. If the latter, they were certainly to blame for raising a suspicion in a matter which ought to be above suspicion. One of the chains the empress of the East sent to Constantinople, and the other to her daughter Eudoxia, wife of Valentinian III., emperor of the West. This empress sent it to pope Sixtus III., who sent for the chains preserved in the oratory. Now follows a passage I cannot understand, and will quote the words of Mgr. Guérin (*Vies des Saints*, vol. ix. p. 188). "Le pape voulut lui [the empress] montrer les chaînes [*i.e.* the two chains] dont St. Pierre avait été lié à Rome. Il arriva alors un grand miracle: ces deux chaînes ayant été approchées l'une de l'autre, s'unirent d'elles-mêmes si parfaitement ensemble qu'elles ne parurent plus qu'une même chaîne forgée par un seul ouvrier." The difficulty I find is this. The pope's chamberlain speaks of *ces deux chaînes;* but there were three, the two chains from the oratory, and the one sent from Jerusalem. Nor does the following paragraph help the matter: "Eudoxia, amazed at this prodigy, did not demand back the chain her mother had sent to her, but left 'toute cette longue chaîne à l'Église,' and built a beautiful temple, afterwards called St. Peter ad Vincula, where the relic might be deposited, and shown to the faithful." Here evidently reference is made to one long chain, formed by the union of the Jerusalem chain with the Roman chain, and nothing is said of the second of the two Roman chains. On the next page (p. 189) the chamberlain returns to the subject, but only perplexes the reader more. He says, "On voit que les saintes chaînes (*plural*) ne sont plus entières. L'une d'elles se compose de vingt-huit anneaux, dont le dernier, en forme de S, soutient l'entrave qui serrait le cou de l'apôtre. L'autre chaîne, réunie à la première par le prodige que nous avons reconté, est formée de cinq anneaux" (so that the long chain is much the shorter now). Of the five links, he continues, "quatre plus petits que les autres, et le cinquième, en forme de S, auquel sont attachés un plus grand anneau rond, et une barre de fer qui réunissent les deux chaînes." Probably this iron bar went into the prison wall, and held the captive chained to the wall. Putting the two paragraphs together, the meaning seems to be this: The Jerusalem chain united miraculously with one of the Roman chains, leaving the number of chains two, as before; but at the present day the longer chain is the shorter, having only five links, while the other has twenty-eight; but nothing is said of the "pearls, the gold, and the precious stones" with which the Jerusalem chain was so richly studded.

St. Chrysostom, in his *Homily on St. Peter's Chains*, tells us that in his time the other chain was at Constantinople, where was also the sword with which Peter cut off the ear of Malchus.

I have done my best to piece together the sundry accounts of these chains, but such difficulties meet us at every turn, and the accounts of different writers differ so widely, it is by no means easy to unravel them into a consistent narrative. Alban Butler greatly increases the difficulty by his dogma, "Such was the veneration of the faithful for the relics, that [even] the popes themselves durst not presume to give away any part of the precious remains." This he corroborates on the authority of Gregory the Great and pope Hormisdas, and yet we are told that the long double chain contained only five links, while the other short one contained twenty-eight.

Authorities: Edward Kinesman (1623), *Lives of the Saints*, p. 549, etc. (authenticated by John Floyd, Soc. Jesu Theologus; Mgr. Guérin (chamberlain of Leo XIII.), *Vies des Saints* (7th edit. 1880), vol. ix. p. 186, etc.; L'abbé Maistre, *Histoire de St. Pierre; History of the Holy Chains*, published by the fraternity in Rome, established in their honour; Tillemont, *Memoirs for an Ecclesiastical History of the First Six Centuries*, vol. i. p. 185, etc.; Orsi, *Ecclesiastical History*, bk. i. p. 58, etc.; Monsacrati, *Discussion on the Chains of St. Peter* (1750); Alban Butler, *Lives of the Saints.*

A right hand sent from heaven (manus de cœlo missa). St. William of Oulx was a peasant with only one arm; but an angel, "guérit l'infirmite de Guillaume, à qui il manquait la main droite, en lui donnant une main miraculeuse, appelée *manus de cœlo missa.*" When St. William died this hand refused to be buried, and persistently pushed itself through the coffin. The archbishop of Embrun then ordered it to be cut off, and stored amidst the holy relics. This was done; and certain days were set apart when it was to be shown to the people. The number of miracles ascribed to this "Angelic Hand" are referred to as "incontestable evidence of the truth of this legend." Even pope Pius IX., so late as 1852, acknowledged the genuineness of the famous "manus de cœlo missa."—Mgr. J. I. Depéry (bishop of Gap), *Histoire Hagiologique du Diocèse de Gap.*

(See PELOPS' SHOULDER; ST. MELOR'S SILVER HAND.)

The hood of St. Francis of Paula given

him by an angel (fifteenth century). The tradition in the monastery of Calabria is, that an angel brought St. Francis of Paula his chaperon; and we are still shown there a hood which the angel is said to have put on the saint's head.—*Les Petits Bollandistes*, vol. iv. p. 139.

Lac Beatæ Virginis in the Crypta Lactea, near Bethlehem. A few minutes' walk south of the convent of Bethlehem, is the Crypta Lactea, or Grotto of Milk. The local tradition is, that the Blessed Virgin, alarmed at the threats of Herod, lost her milk; and never recovered it, till she found refuge in this grot, which offered an asylum more secure and less exposed than the "stable of Bethlehem."

According to another tradition the Holy Virgin used often to carry her babe to this grot, and suckle it there. A drop from her breast, on one occasion, fell on a stone, turned it to the whiteness of alabaster, and endowed it with the secret virtue of restoring milk to nursing mothers. "Ce qui est certain, c'est que toutes les femmes des enrivons, Juives, Chrétiennes, et Mahamétanes, ont une telle dévotion pour cette grotte, qu'il y en a toujours qui viennent y faire leur prière. La roche dans laquelle se trouve la grotte est une craie extrêmement blanche et friable; on la réduit facilement en poudre et on en fait de petits pains qu'on envoie dans tous les pays."—Mgr. Mislin.

Milk of the Virgin Mary at Souillac, in France. Catherine Emmerich, the visionary of Dulmen (1774–1824), says, "As soon as the Magi departed, the holy family, hounded by the emissaries of Herod, were obliged to quit the inn, and lie concealed in the tomb of Maraba. Here Joseph, fancying that his place of refuge was discovered, suddenly took to flight with the infant. Then saw I the Virgin, relieved of her disquietude, left alone in the cave for the space of half a day. When the time came for suckling the child, as the babe was gone, she pressed the milk which troubled her into a little hole of some stones lying by. She told this to one of the shepherds to whom the angels appeared; and he, going to the cave, found the milk as Mary had said, collected it with great care, and carried it to his wife, who happened to have an infant, but no milk. The woman took the sacred milk with reverence, and immediately her own breasts were abundantly supplied. I saw the stone," she continues, "which contained the milk," adding that it "possessed the same virtue as the milk itself; and even Mussulmans to the present day make use of it for the like purpose, and for other cures also."

The ring and cross of St. Coletta or Nicoletta (A.D. 1380–1447). St. John the Evangelist was sent from heaven with a gold ring, which he himself placed on the finger of St. Coletta, in token that Christ had accepted her as His virgin bride. Many persons saw this ring and touched it; and sometimes St. Coletta lent it to a sister as an amulet, when confided with a mission of more than ordinary danger.

St. Coletta also received from heaven a gold crucifix, which contained, in a small locket, a part of the true cross. This crucifix is still preserved in the monastery of Poligny. The upright is 0,035 millimètres, the crossbar 0,008 millimètres. The arms of the Saviour are almost horizontally extended, and the feet are fastened near each other with two nails. On one side are five precious stones, four of which are blue, and one red. Between each stone is a pearl. The stones are let in, but the pearls are simply nailed on by gold pins. The piece of the true cross is contained in a little box or locket just below the feet. The subjoined will be interesting to many:—

"St. Colette fût envoyé du ciel une petite croisette de fin or, en laquelle était enchâssé une petite portion de la sainte Croix, laquelle elle garda moult dévotement. Et plusieurs la voyaient et la maniaient, et affirmaient, que la dite croisette n'avait onques faite ni forgée de mains humaines."—Le Père Sellier, *Vie de St. Colette* (2 vols.), 1853.

One of the stones cast at St. Stephen broken without mechanical force (A.D. 994). St. Gerard, bishop of Toul, asked Theodoric, bishop of Metz, to assist at the dedication of his cathedral. Theodoric not being able to attend, Gerard went to Metz, and asked him to give him a piece of the stone which had been cast at St. Stephen, for which the cathedral of Metz was celebrated. Gerard took up the stone, kissed it, and let his tears fall on it. As he did so, the part he touched separated of itself from the rest of the stone; and Theodoric, looking upon it as the work of God, in honour of His saint, could not do otherwise than allow St. Gerard to take it away with him. This relic was enclosed in an image of St. Stephen given by Nicholas de Sane, archdeacon of Toul, and enriched by Antoine, duke of Lorraine, in 1540.—Father Benedict, *Life of St. Gerard* (1700). (See STONE, p. 264.)

Tooth of St. Paul. The Rev. Thomas Harmer says in his *Observations*, vol. ii. p. 306, "A gentleman once showed me a prodigious tooth, which apparently belonged to one of the monsters of the deep. It was found by one of his ancestors among the treasures of a Roman Catholic who was fond of relics, and who had evidently taken great care of this tooth. It was wrapped in silk, with two or three outer covers of paper, on one of which was written, '*A tooth of the holy St. Paul.*'" The person who showed it to Mr. Harmer was a Protestant, and as he held the monster tooth in his hand, quizzically remarked, "Don't you think that St. Paul had a fine set of grinders?"

St. Longis finds a tooth of St. Peter six hundred years after his death (A.D. 653). St. Longis, having built a monastery at Boisselière, started for Rome to obtain some relics for his basilica. One night St. Peter himself appeared to him, and told him to go to his tomb at daybreak, and he would find there a precious relic. St. Longis went to the apostle's tomb, and found there a tooth, which he took to Boisselière. St. Harduin and a great crowd of people flocked to the monastersy, "pour vénérer ce gage de la protection du Prince des Apôtres."—*Vita Sancti Leogisili*, No. 6.

If this is a specimen of the way relics are discovered, no wonder the supply is so abundant. We should like to know how this tooth came to be on the tomb of St. Peter. Had it been there some six hundred years and not noticed; or did St. Peter pull out one of his teeth to please St. Longis; or did the tooth somehow pass through the earth and tomb, and come to the surface at this exact juncture, when Longis was hunting for relics? After these difficulties are solved, it would be well to know how Longis knew the tooth to be one of St. Peter's, and whether he examined the dead body to see if this particular tooth was missing. Surely St. Longis and St. Harduin were easily satisfied.

Relics of Joseph the carpenter, the husband of Mary.

HIS GIRDLE. The Discalceati guard with great reverence St. Joseph's girdle in Notre Dame, Joinville sur Marne, diocese of Langres.

"Cette ceinture consiste en un tissu plat, de fil ou d'écorce, assez gros et de couleur grisâtre; elle est longue d'un mètre, et porte en largeur de 30 à 45 centimètres. Aux extrémités est attaché un fermoir en ivoire, jauni par le temps; une boutonnière se trouve aussi à l'un des bouts. Confectionnée, suivant la tradition, par les mains de la Ste. Vierge. On peut croire qu'elle lui resta, comme un souvenir bien cher, à la mort de son époux; et que plus tard elle fut remise à St. Jean ou à quelque autre apôtre." It was removed from Palestine to the château de Joinville in the thirteenth century.

HIS STICK is preserved in the monastery of angels, Florence.

ANOTHER STICK AND HIS HAMMER are preserved in the church of St. Anastasia, Rome.

THE CLOAK which St. Joseph is said to have thrown over the babe Jesus in the manger of Bethlehem, is also preserved in the church of St. Anastasia, Rome.

Relics of St. Paul, bishop of Leon (A.D. 492–573). St. Paul, bishop of Leon, was buried at Oxismor cathedral, but when the Danes ravaged Brittany, the body of the saint was removed to the monastery of Fleury sur Loire. At the Reformation, "the Calvinists," having got this monastery into their hands, burnt to powder the "holy relics," and scattered the ashes to the wind. After this positive statement, we are rather surprised to read in the next paragraph, "Nevertheless, the church of Leon still (1882) possesses the skull of the saint, the entire bone of the right arm, and one of his fingers, kept in a silver coffer." One naturally asks, if the "relics were burnt to powder, and the ashes scattered to the winds," how could such material parts as these have escaped? Of this we are not informed; but we are told that Mgr. Dombidau de Crousheilles, in 1809, "authenticated the relics."—Dom Lobineau, *Life of St. Paul, bishop of Leon*, edited, with notes, by Mons. Tresvaux.

As Paul died in 573, and his relics were burnt to ashes at the Reformation, how could these bones be authenticated in 1809? Probably the Calvinists, "who burnt the relics," would not feel satisfied with the authentication of the bishop of Quimper.

The relics of St. Trojecia strangely discovered and recognized. St. Trojecia was born at Poitiers, but no one knows when, and died at Ruthènes at a very advanced age. She was buried under a stone in St. Stephen's church, where she died. The troubles of the times made her quite forgotten, but in 1698 Philippe de Lusignan, bishop of Rodez, visiting St. Stephen's church, discovered, no one knows how, the body of this saint, the head being enclosed in an ivory casket. He ordered the relics to be removed to the cathedral with great pomp and ceremony, all the clergy of the diocese and an immense concourse of people being present.—L'abbé L. Servières, *Les Saints du Rouergue*.

Relics emit on St. Eloi a celestial balm (A.D. 659). St. Eloi, bishop of Noyon, kept in his chamber a number of relics, suspended from the ceiling in a bag. The bag hung over his head, and when he was abed he made his prayers under them. One night as he was so engaged, a man appeared before him and said, "Eloi, your prayers are heard, and you shall have the assurance you request, that God has accepted your penances and pardoned your sins." Forthwith a liquor flowed from the bag above his head; it fell on his head, it flowed along his robe, it anointed his feet. The odour itself was ravishing, surpassing all earthly perfumes. He knew his sins were forgiven, and he was placed again in the condition in which he was at baptism.—St. Ouen (archbishop of Rouen), *Life of St. Eloi.*

The relics of St. Briocus jump for joy (A.D. 1210). St. Briocus of Great Britain died A.D. 502. In 1210 the father superior of Angers wished to obtain some of his bones, and two ribs, an arm, and a vertebra were given him. When these bones entered the cathedral, they jumped for joy at the honour conferred upon them.—Dom Lobineau, *Lives of the British Saints.*

Relics made to bleed by St. Gregory the Great (A.D. 540–604). Certain ambassadors, on one occasion, besought Gregory the Great to give them some relics for their churches. The pontiff took a fine linen napkin, and touched with it the body of some deceased saints; then placing the napkin in a box, he sealed it, and handed it to the ambassadors. Being curious to know what it was that Gregory had given them, they opened the box, took out the napkin, and found nothing inside. Greatly astonished, and thinking a practical joke had been played upon them, they took the box and its contents back to the pope. St. Gregory laid the napkin on the altar, and falling on his knees, prayed God to open the eyes of the ambassadors that they might see the value of the napkin given as a relic. Then, holding the cloth out before them, he pricked it with a penknife; whereupon blood flowed from it in great abundance. The ambassadors, utterly confounded, took the napkin with many thanks, and prized the gift as a relic of inestimable value. (See Index, BLEEDING.)—John the deacon (twelfth century), *Life of St. Gregory the Great* (written by him at the especial command of pope John VIII.).

The custom of sending napkins and bandages which had touched relics was not unusual with the Roman pontiffs. The same Gregory told the empress Constance, when she asked him to give her the head of St. Paul, that it was not customary even to touch the relics except with great reverence, but in lieu of relics the church was accustomed to send a napkin or bandage which had touched a relic, and God operated miracles in virtue thereof.—See the *Epistle of St. Gregory.*

Relics join St. Gregory of Langres in psalmody (A.D. 541). One night a deacon watched, and saw St. Gregory rise from his bed, and leave his dormitory at midnight. The deacon followed unobserved, and saw him enter the baptistery, the door of which opened to him of its own accord. For a time, all was dead silence; and then St. Gregory began to chant. Presently a number of voices joined in, and the singing continued for the space of three hours. Gregory of Tours naïvely remarks, "I think the voices proceeded from the relics there preserved, which revealed themselves to the saint, and joined him in singing praises to God."—Baring-Gould, *Lives of the Saints,* vol. i. p. 59.

Of course echo had nothing to do with the "miracle."

Wonders due to the relics of St. Ignatius Loyola (A.D. 1491–1556). "At Sena the devils durst not look uppon his picture, but hung theyr heads in theyr bosomes for very pure shame. His picture in Malacia scared away a devill. His picture in paper at Madena, pinned closely uppon a wall, skared away a whole troupe of devils out of foure women possessed. The bare pronouncing [of] his name at Rome, skared out two legions of devils. A peece of his coife that hee wore, healed a woman of the phrensie. A peece of leather that he used at his stomack cured the plague. A peece of his hayre-cloth purged an holy nunne of a hundred stones in one yeere. A peece of a relique of his, close shut in a boxe, burnt a devill, and made him to roare the bredth of a chamber of [off]. A peece of a relique cast into the sea, calmed the waves, and stilled the windes. But the bare subscription of his name in a morsel of paper passeth all the rest: it healed the toothache, the crampe, the gowte, the sciatica, the leprosie, the skurvies,—and being laid uppon . . . a woman . . . in travaile . . . past all hope of life, tooke away her paine, facilitated the birth, and recovered her life."—S. Harsnet (afterwards archbishop of York), *Popish Impostures* (1604), p. 56.

Relics preserved in the abbey church of Savigny. At one time the abbey church of Savigny was said to contain—

The head of St. Vital, and his chasuble.

Part of the wood of the true cross.

Relics of the prophet Daniel; of St. Joseph, John the Baptist, St. Peter, St. Matthew, St. Bartholomew, St. James, St. Victor, St. Bernard, St. William Firmatus, and St. Thomas of Canterbury.

The chasuble of St. Peter (!!).

These were all contained in a costly casket, and carried in procession on Maunday Thursday. In 1793 the reliquaries were broken to pieces, and the relics thrown to the winds by the revolutionists.

Relics in Souillac church. Mgr. Doncy, bishop of Montauban, gives us a list of 111 relics of Souillac church, proved beyond a doubt to be genuine by the *procès-verbal* of May 25, 1856. Amongst them we find—

De vestimentis Domini.

De spinis coronæ Domini.

De tabula et pane Cœnæ Domini.

De terra ubi pes crucis [Domini] positus erat, quando Christus fuit crucifixus.

De velo, cingulo, vestimentis, et lacte [!!] Beatæ Mariæ.

De sangiune et vestimentis SS. Innocentium.

De vestimento S. Joannis, S. Petri.

De una uncia digiti S. Pauli, et duo dentes ejusdem.

Relics of S. Thomæ, S. Barnabæ, S. Timothæi discipuli Pauli, S. Stephani proto-martyris, S. Laurentii, S. Marci, S. Marcellini, S. Sixti papæ, S. Cæciliæ, S. Luciæ, S. Dorotheæ, and many others.

The relics are contained in a reliquary of copper, gilded and chased, evidently of the twelfth or thirteenth century.

That many of these relics may be traced back to the twelfth or thirteenth century may be readily admitted, but eleven hundred years is a long time from the Crucifixion; and such relics as the "milk of the Virgin Mary," "the bread of the Last Supper," the "mould where the cross stood," and the several garments of the Lord, ought to show an unbroken and incontestable legal instrument, far far clearer than that offered by "miracles" attributed to them. We know that the two tables of stone, inscribed by the finger of the Almighty, and religiously kept for some centuries in the sacred ark, though reverenced by the Jews, were nevertheless lost, and the loss of such relics is certainly most astounding, far more so than such relics as the above would have been.

A list of famous relics, given by John Brady, 1839.

(This list of relics is given on the authority of John Brady, who must be held responsible. It is a pity he has not given the whereabouts of each relic, that the accuracy of his statements might be verified.)

COAL. One of the coals that broiled St. Lawrence.

FINGER. A finger of St. Andrew; another of John the Baptist; one of the Holy Ghost; and the thumb of St. Thomas.

HANDKERCHIEFS (*Two*), stamped with the face of Christ. One was sent by our Lord Himself as a present to Agbarus, prince of Edessa; and the other was a cloth lent by Veronica to Jesus to wipe the sweat from His face on His way to Calvary. (See VERONICAS.)

HEAD. Two heads of John the Baptist (!!).

HEM. The hem of our Lord's garment touched by the woman who was healed of her bloody issue; the hem of Joseph's coat of many colours.

LOCK OF HAIR. A lock of the hair with which Mary Magdalene wiped the Saviour's feet.

NAIL. One of the nails used in the crucifixion was set in the "iron crown of Lombardy." [One nail is still preserved in the Santa Croce, at Rome; another at Siena; a third at Venice; a fourth in the church of the Carmelites, in Paris; a fifth in the Holy Chapel; a sixth at Draguignan; a seventh at Tenaille. One was thrown by the empress Helena into the gulf of Venice to allay a storm; another was inserted by Constantine in his helmet, as an amulet; one or two others were set in the emperor's horse's headstall.] (See CROSS DISCOVERED.)

PHIAL OF SWEAT. A phial of the sweat of St. Michael, when he contended with Satan (!!).

RAYS OF A STAR. Some of the rays of the guiding star which appeared to the Wise Men of the East (!!).

RIB. A rib of the *Verbum caro factum*, or the "Word made Flesh" (!!).

ROD. Moses' rod.

SEAMLESS COAT. The seamless coat of our Lord, for which lots were cast at the Crucifixion.

SLIPPERS. A pair of slippers worn by Enoch before the Flood.

SPOON. The pap-spoon and dish used by the Virgin Mary for Jesus when an infant.

SWORD AND SHIELD. The short sword of St. Michael, and his square buckler lined with red velvet (!!).

TEAR. The tear shed by Jesus over the grave of Lazarus. This relic was given by an angel to Mary Magdalene, and is preserved in a phial (!!).

TOOTH. A tooth of our Lord Himself.

WATERPOT. One of the wat rpots used at the marriage of Cana, in Galilee. —*Clavis Calendria*, p. 240.

Relics mentioned by Melancthon.

FACE. The face of a seraph without a nose (!!).

FLAME. A flame of the bush which Moses beheld burning. The bishop of Metz asserted that he was in possession of this relic (!!).

LEG. A leg of the ass on which Jesus rode in triumph to Jerusalem.

SKULL. The skull of St. Matthias,

said to have died A.D. 63. St. Helena (248–328) sent his body to Rome [John Eck says it was sent to Augsburg]. [Some bones of the head are at present in Santa Maria Maggiore; other parts of the skull were sent by the same empress to the archbishop of Trèves; and a part of the skull was preserved at Barbezieux, in Saintonge, till the Reformation, when it was burned.]

[Stone. In Soulac is preserved a bloody stone thrown at the martyr Stephen.]—*The Eclectic Review.* (See p. 260.)

Miscellaneous relics of remarkable character. Gregory the Great sent to his friend St. Leander the famous image of the Virgin Mary made by St. Luke the evangelist. It is preserved at Guadaloupe, in Spain.

In the crypt of the chapel of the Holy Sacrament are preserved not only some of the swaddling clothes of the infant Jesus, but also some of the hay on which He was laid in the manger of Bethlehem. Joseph's cloak, thrown over the child to keep it warm, is preserved in the church of St. Anastasia; and some of the hair of the infant in the basilica of the Holy Cross.

Harsnet says the following relics "are jewelled up in the popes Propitiatorie at Rome: viz. A sacred violl of our Ladies milke; a peece of St. Paules breeches and chaire; the tayle of the asse whereon our Saviour rode to Jerusalem, and the rest."—*Popish Impostures*, p. 118.

Cardinal Wiseman defends all relics as "precious treasures of the Church," and "insists on their genuineness." How could he do otherwise and be consistent? Miracles and relics are bound up in the Roman Catholic Church.

The makeshift of a relic suggested by Agazarius (1600). "Agazarius the Jesuit tels us, that hee having brought from Rome certaine halowed graines, which he gave to his holy children for their severall necessities,—they by misfortune lost them, but [he] comforts his shrivelings by telling them in honest terms, that any little prety peble taken up out of a gutter, will serve as well, if it be receaved and kept with humility and devotion."—Harsnet (afterwards archbishop of York), *Popish Impostures* (1604), p. 104.

Bruno (*Leo IX.*) *cures the plague by relics steeped in wine* (A.D. 1002–1054). Bruno used to make a pilgrimage every year to the tomb of some apostle. On one occasion he was accompanied by five hundred persons, and all were smitten by the plague, from the foul air of the country they had to pass through. Bruno, then bishop of Toul, "had the happy thought of dipping the relics which he carried about with him in wine, and gave the plague-stricken some of the wine to drink." Our biographer adds, "All those who drank in faith recovered," but he does not state the number that did so.—Wibert, *Life of St. Leo IX.*

Candida Francisca cured of a mortal disease by a picture of St. Charles Borromeo (June 22, A.D. 1600). Candida Francisca, a religious of St. Agnes, Milan, had been confined to her bed twenty-two months. She was lame in the left leg, and so afflicted in her whole body, that the doctors pronounced her case hopeless. She now requested that a portrait of St. Charles Borromeo might be handed to her, and as she held it, she earnestly invoked the saint to come to her relief. Presently all her pains left her; her leg, which was shorter than the other, was not only healed but elongated; and she rose up cheerful in spirits, and in perfect health.—*The Bull of Canonization.*

The relics of St. Desiderius, bishop of Langres, cure a woman at the point of death (A.D. 1657). Desiderius was a peasant in the third century, living at Bavari, and was chosen bishop of Langres. He was beheaded by Chrocus, an Allemand chief, in 264. In 1315 his relics were transferred from the little chapel on the Marne to the cathedral. In 1657 Mgr. Sebastian Zamet opened the reliquary to give the relics to the church of Avignon. They rested at Rosoy in the house of a woman confined to her bed, and supposed to be *in articulo mortis.* The relics were taken to her room, and the moment they touched her, she was restored to perfect health. "Ce miracle, le chroniqueur Clément Macheret, curé d'Hortes, dressa procès-verbal."—L'abbé Mazelin, *Saints de la Haute Marne.*

Miraculous cures effected by the relics of St. Germana Cousin of Pibrac (A.D. 1579–1601). Germana Cousin was a poor shepherdess of Pibrac, near Toulouse. She was very sickly and scrofulous, but is an object of considerable interest, because she was canonized so recently as 1854 by pope Pius IX., amidst such a concourse of people as have rarely been collected together. At Pibrac the Holy Communion was given to eight thousand persons, and hundreds were dismissed. At least seventy thousand persons were assembled in the little village of Pibrac to do honour to the shepherdess, crowding to kiss her cerements, and to cast eyes on her bones. Her elegy was made by Mgr. Pie, bishop of Poitiers, and R. P. Corail the Jesuit. On June 29, 1867, Pio IX., "après avoir approuvé de nouveaux miracles, l'inscrivit au livre des vierges."

The new miracles, all of the nineteenth century, are the following:—

(1) A young man of Mauvesin, in the diocese of Auch, named Dominic Gauté, having lost his sight, consulted the best oculists, but received the doleful assurance that nothing could be done for him, as the blindness arose from what is termed "the drop serene." His brother George advised him to apply to Germana Cousin (dead about two hundred years), and both went to Pibrac. Here the eyes of Dominic were bound with a cloth which had touched the dead body of the shepherdess, and on returning home he told his brother he could see the sails of the mill turning round.

We are not told whether Dominic Gauté ever recovered his full sight, or whether the miracle ceased with the incident mentioned above.

(2) Elizabeth Gay, aged eighteen, had long been blind "par suite d'une humeur qui s'était portée à son visage, et sur ses yeux." This young woman was cured at Pibrac, and lived many years without any return of her malady.

(3) Frances Ferrière, of Angoumer, was born blind, but received her sight simply by binding her eyes with a cloth which had touched the body of Germana. This miracle is avouched by Mons. le Castex, curé of Angoumer at the time.

(4) Aug. 1, 1839, an infant ten months old, born blind, the son of Antony Nous, "patron sur le canal du Languedoc," was entirely cured by the intercession of Germana Cousin. The abbot of Bourg, vicar-general, was appointed to investigate the case, and his deposition is preserved in the archives of Toulouse.

(5) Antoinette Estellé of Pibrac attested that her son, aged two years and six months, was quite blind; but, being taken to the tomb of Germana, received his sight. "Il a maintenant quarante-trois ans, et il a conservé la vue, et le souvenir de la grace qui Germaine a obtenue pour lui."

(6) Francis Lafon was born with a fatty tumour over his eyes. When the lids were opened, neither pupil nor cornea could be seen, but only "une matière informe comme un morceau de chair." This case was wholly cured by the intercession of Germana, and the child received his eyesight. The only remedy applied was to bind over the eyes a cloth which had touched the dead body of the shepherdess, when, "Bonté celeste! ce petit visage, auparavant si moine, est animé de deux yeux vifs et brillants qui se fixent sur elle."

(7) A paralytic, whose limbs were wholly powerless, was taken to Pibrac, April 29, 1840. This man was such a cripple that when held upright "ses jambes étaient flottantes comme celles d'un squelette." If set on his feet, his legs doubled under him. Well, he went to the parish church during mass, and at the moment of the elevation cried aloud, "Je suis guéri!" He knelt down, and remained kneeling to the end of the service, when he walked home, leaning gently on the arm of his grandmother, the baroness of Guilhermy. This was at nine o'clock in the morning; at five o'clock in the evening of the same day, "il parcourut à pied, sans être soutenu." He paid several visits, in which he walked upstairs and downstairs without the least difficulty.

(8) In 1845 the nuns of Bon Pasteur at Bourg, 116 in number, were reduced to the last extremity. Sister Mary of the Sacred Heart, superior of the convent, resolved to seek the aid of Germana Cousin, and accordingly placed a medal of the shepherdess in the pantry, and two of the sisters were appointed to provide forty large loaves of bread daily; but instead of twenty-four pounds of flour, only sixteen were provided. The flour lasted three days, and only eight pounds were left; but these eight pounds made forty loaves, and the flour diminished not. This occurred over and over again. The small dole of flour supplied the whole convent from day to day, and there was always more flour left when the bread was made than there was before. The miracle attracted great attention, and persons from all quarters ran to see "de leurs propres yeux le pain que Dieu leur avait donné. Le même prodige se renouvela deux autres fois."

(9) Jacquette, daughter of John Catala, when eighteen months old caught measles, and became more and more feeble every day. This was in 1828. The ankles and knees swelled to an enormous size, while the legs and thighs shrank, "que la peau était collée aux os." All medicines were ineffective, and at last her mother determined to take the child to Pibrac. The following is her deposition:—"I started on foot with a friend, and we drove before us a donkey with two panniers. Jacquette

was in one, and another child three years old was in the other. We reached Pibrac church on a Sunday, and attended the service with the children. Mass was celebrated, and when the *Sanctus* was rung, Jacquette cried out aloud; and I heard her bones crack. When I went to kneel, great God! judge of my surprise to see Jacquette leave her brother, and come and kneel beside me. She came all by herself, with no one to help her. I returned to my seat, and Jacquette followed me. Her legs had recovered; my vow was accomplished. We reached Toulouse at three o'clock; and when Jacquette saw her father she ran up to him, crying with joy, 'I am quite well now; take me in your arms, papa, and kiss me. See how I can run about. See what Germana Cousin has done for me!' Indeed, the cure was perfect."

(10) Philip Luc of Cornebarrieu, aged twelve, was suffering from a fistula, and was sent to the hospital of St. James, Toulouse, where he was two months, and was then dismissed as incurable. Cornebarrieu is about two miles from Pibrac, and Philip, starting with his mother on foot, arrived in time for mass. He went to the tomb of the shepherdess, and returned home without being cured. His mother put him to bed, and wrapped him in a cloth which had touched the dead body of Germana. After a short sleep he called his mother, who looked at the fistula, found it was quite dry, and the wound healed. M. Laurent Stevenet, one of the physicians of St. James's Hospital, came to see the cure. He expressed himself astounded, made a most careful examination, and pronounced the cure perfect. "Je dois indiquer le caractère de cette guérison: c'est la mobilité de la peau, et la reprise du tissu fibreux qui forme la cicatrice intérieure de la cavité fistuleuse."

Mons. L. Veuillot says of the above, "Nous allons signaler quelques miracles qui, après mûr examen, ont réçu l'approbation de la Congrégation des Rites, et ont été confirmés comme tels par le souverain pontife," and "Le souverain pontife Pie IX., après avoir approvée de miracles, inscrivit St. Germana au livre des Vierges."

A bone of St. Ignatius cures Drusilla Tursellina of a fever. Drusilla Tursellina, a Roman lady, being sick of a fever, was cured in a moment by laying one of the bones of St. Ignatius on her forehead.

Another example. Sir Francis Blasius of Nola was afflicted with ague and colic, so that his life was despaired of, but his mother Zenobia laid a bone of St. Ignatius upon his head, and he forthwith recovered.

A third example. The infant son of the baron of Belliboni of Lecha, when three years old, fell from the nurse's arms, and injured the right knee. A swelling ensued, which threatened to be fatal; but the baron took the child to the Jesuits' college of Lecha, and one of the monks touched the knee with a bone of St. Ignatius. The surgeons came next day to cut the swelling, and were not a little astonished to see it had subsided; and in a day or two the child was perfectly well. —*Authentic Relation made in the Consistory before Gregory XV. by cardinal de Monte*, March 12, 1622.

Writing of St. Ignatius cures Bartholomew Contesti of headache. Bartholomew Contesti of Majorca was a surgeon by profession. He suffered severely from headache and disease in one of his eyes. A slip of paper containing some writing of Ignatius being brought to him, he was instantly cured of his headache, and the eye, which before was stone blind, recovered its speculation. In order to prove that his recovery was due to the relic, it was removed two or three times, and immediately it was taken away the pain returned, and the eye lost its sight; but the remedy of both returned when the relic was brought back. So Bartholomew kept the paper about him, and his health and sight were permanently restored.

Another example. Olimpia Norina lost her sight for three months from acute pain; but, like Bartholomew Contesti, she was cured merely by laying on her forehead a slip of paper containing some writing of St. Ignatius.

A third example. The child of a nobleman, seven years old, named Geronimo Gabrielli, being sick, and like to die of black ague, called by the Spaniards *taberdillo*, was, in 1597, cured instantaneously by the same slip of paper.—*Authentic Relation made in the Consistory before Gregory XV. by cardinal de Monte*, March 12, 1622.

Donna of Aragon, etc., cured of a glandular swelling by a portrait of St. Ignatius (A.D. 1599). The donna of Aragon, who was also princess of Beltran and duchess of Terranova, suffered for four months with a swelling in her right breast. At length she laid a portrait of Ignatius upon the swelling, which instantly began to subside, and before sunset she was perfectly cured. So certain is this, that the princess went to Rome next year, and set up over the tomb of St. Ignatius a silver tablet as a thank-offering.—*Authentic Relation made in the Consistory before*

Gregory XV. by cardinal de Monte, March 12, 1622.

An image of St. Ignatius cures Ferdinand Pretel of ague (1603). Ferdinand Pretel of Mendoza fell ill, on Sept. 19, of a tertian ague, which developed into black ague, and his life was despaired of. On Dec. 3, an image of St. Ignatius was placed in his hands, when all of a sudden he became quite well; and was enabled, by Dec. 13, to make a nine days' journey in rain and snow, wind and frost, from Valladolid to Valencia.—*A statement made by cardinal de Monte,* March 12, 1622, *before Gregory XV., in claim of the canonization of St. Ignatius. The pope was satisfied of the truth of the statements, and Ignatius was added to the catalogue of the saints.*

The relics of St. Isidore cure Philip III. of a fever (A.D. 1619). Philip III. had been to Portugal in royal pomp; but, on his return to Madrid, was seized with *taberdillo*, a pestilential fever, and was given over by his physicians. His death was expected every hour, but *in extremis* he requested that the relics of St. Isidore might be brought him. No sooner was this done, than his highness began to amend, and in a day or two was restored to his usual health. The king greatly exerted himself to bring about the canonization of Isidore, but the death of the pope caused a delay. In the reign of Philip IV., however, the ceremony was performed by Gregory XV., March 12, A.D. 1622, in St. Peter's church, Rome, with a splendour wholly unequalled.—*Acts of Canonization.*

Diseases cured by the medal of the Immaculate Conception (eighteenth century). Crispino, the son of humble parents, entered the monastery of Paranzana, where he was employed as cook, and rose high in favour as a saintly man. A lady living at Tolfa requested that Brother Crispino might be allowed to visit her, as she was sick of an epidemic which then prevailed. When he entered the chamber, the lady said to him, "Brother Crispino, make on my head the sign of the cross with thy medal of the Immaculate Conception." This did he, and the lady was instantly cured. The experiment was subsequently tried on several others, and always with the same success.—*Vita del V. Servo di Dio Fr. Crispino da Viterbo,* etc. (1761).

St. John Francis Regis cures a woman with a medal (A.D. 1597-1640). St. John Francis Regis went to confess a woman given over by the physicians, and supposed by them to be at the point of death. The friends asked St. Regis to cure her, and the saint, putting the medal of his order into a cup, blessed the water, and gave it the woman to drink. No sooner had she tasted it, than the fever left her, "et elle se trouva dans une santé aussi parfaite que si elle n'eût point été malade."—Father Daubenton (Jesuit), *Life of St. John Francis Regis.*

Relics of St. John-Joseph of the Cross (A.D. 1654–1734). The hyacinths, cast on the coffin of St. John-Joseph of the Cross, healed the daughter of Girolamo Politi of a violent inflammation in the eye.

The pieces of his garments, seized eagerly by the throng on the day of his funeral, healed numbers of persons; amongst others, Anne di Matia and Pascal Christiano. The former of a violent stitch in her side which had obstinately resisted all sorts of remedies; and the latter of frightful colics from which he had suffered for six years.

During the funeral, Michel de San-Pasquale, trying to keep back the crowd, received a severe wound in the head from a halbert. The blood flowed abundantly, but, on touching the place with a piece of the saint's habit, the wound was instantly healed.

Charles Carafalo, an epileptic, vowed, during the funeral, if the saint would cure him of his fits, to which he had been subject for twenty-five years, he would publish the miracle throughout the world. He was cured; but not keeping his vow, his fits returned within a year. Then, repenting of his neglect, he begged pardon of the saint, repaired his fault, and was thoroughly cured.

Margaret di Fraja obtained, during the funeral of the saint, the cure of her nephew, who was dying of injuries received in a fall.

Vincenza Aldava was healed at the same time of a contraction in the knee, which prevented his walking. This cure was effected by simply sitting on the bier which had carried the saint to his grave.

After the inhumation, numberless miracles "attested the virtues of the saint." Fevers, spasms, attacks of apoplexy and epilepsy, and sundry maladies pronounced to be incurable, were cured by his relics. These "miracles" induced Pius VI. to inscribe him in the catalogue, May 15, 1789. Pius VII. recognized two new miracles, April 27, 1824. Leo XII.

decreed, Sept. 29, 1824, that the church might proceed with his canonization; and Gregory XVI. canonized him, May 26, 1839.—Migne, *Démonstrations Evangéliques*, vol. xvi.

The shroud of St. Landry quenches a fire (seventh century). St. Landry, bishop of Paris, died A.D. 650. Not long after his death a fire broke out in Paris in the Porte Royale, and the wind spread the flames in all directions, so that many houses caught fire, and a large part of the city was threatened with destruction. Dean Hervé bethought him of the late bishop; and, hoisting his shroud on a pole, he went with it where the flames were thickest and most violent. "Aussitôt le feu commença à se retirer, et à diminuer, et s'éteignit peu à peu, sans faire un plus dommage."—*Breviaire de Paris*, etc.

Archbishop Volcmar cured of a malady in his eyes by St. Maurin's tooth (tenth century). Volcmar was elected archbishop of Paris in 906; he soon afterwards suffered from a "malady in his eyes," and it was much feared that he would be unable to take part in the great Easter festival at Cologne. A sudden inspiration occurred to him—to try whether the recently discovered relics of St. Maurin of Cologne would do him any good. He sent a priest to go and fetch them. A tooth of the martyr was brought to his chamber; he touched his eyes with it, and the remedy was instantaneous. On Easter Day, at mass, he announced this "miracle" to the congregation.—*Propre de Cologne*.

If the "malady of the eye" was what is called a stye or stian, we all know the common "remedy" of rubbing it with a gold ring. There is no reason why a smooth tooth should not do as well. Whether the gentle pressure breaks the pustule or disperses the pus is beside the scope of this book. Suffice it to say, it was at one time generally believed that rubbing the stye with a gold ring would prove an effectual cure.

The chasuble of St. Peter cures a paralytic (eleventh century). When St. Hugh, abbot of Cluny, went to celebrate mass in St. Geneviève, a paralytic, named Robert, was brought to him. St. Hugh laid on him the chasuble of St. Peter, a relic most religiously preserved, and said to the man, "The Lord Jesus Christ has made thee whole; rise, Robert, and make thy bed." As he spoke the man was healed, and returned thanks to St. Peter and the abbot. Then follows this observation: "Il [*i.e.* St. Hugh] avait acquis une telle estime auprès de Dieu, que des pèlerins furent avertis, au sépulcre des Apôtres, par une vision céleste, d'aller à Cluny dont ils n'avaient jamais entendu parler."—Lorain, *Histoire de l'Abbaye de Cluny*.

St. Walbert's cup of miraculous virtues (seventh century). There was nothing which pertained to St. Walbert to which God did not attach miraculous virtues. Of this we have proofs which have come down almost to the present day. Thus Dom Grappin, in 1770, writes, "Un vase, de simple racine, qui a lui appartenu, a été l'instrument d'une infinité de guérisons: les fébricitants s'empressent encore d'y boire, et d'imiter à ce sujet la pieuse antiquité, et come elle, ils y éprouvent le pouvoir du saint abbé de Luxeuil. J'en ai vu des effets qui tiennent du prodige doi rendre ici témoignage solennel. C'est ainsi que les amis de Dieu sont honores et glorifiés."—*Mémoire Adressé à l'Academie de Besançon* (en 1770).

One of the bones of St. Walbert (who died 665, *i.e.* four hundred years before William the Conqueror) was authenticated Feb. 17, 1852, by his eminence Mgr. le Cardinal Matthieu. One would like to know how this was done. Similarly, a thigh-bone of St. Beat (who died in the third century) was authenticated recently by Mgr. de Simony bishop of Soissons and Laon. Probably, all the medical men of Great Britain would hesitate to vouch that a bone submitted to their inspection once formed part of the skeleton of Alfred the Great or William the Conqueror. May 4, A.D. 1854, Mgr. Crosnier, vicar-general of Nevers, verified the relics of St. Perelin, who died in 303.

All sorts of diseases cured by a medal of St. Francis Xavier. Pilgrims to the church where St. Francis Xavier is buried receive no small benefits. The blind receive their sight, the lepers are cleansed, and all other diseases are cured; yea, the very dead are restored to life. A greater wonder still remains to be told. A woman, called Lucy de Villanzan, above 120 years old, who had been baptized by Xavier, had a medal of the saint struck at Coccinum. For twelve years together, she touched with this medal all sorts of sick and diseased folk, and as many as she touched were instantly made whole. Ulcers and cancers, blains and boils, wounds and sores, were cured merely by washing them with water in which the medal had been immersed. Many other marvellous things were done by the virtue of this medal.—*Cardinal de Monte's speech before Gregory XV., at the Act of the Canonization of Francis Xavier*, Jan. 19, 1622.

This is no idle tale, but a relation made in full consistory by cardinal de Monte. The whole speech is still extant, and has been translated into French and English. Jean Heigham of St. Omer received the "privilege" of printing the French translation June 18, 1625, and every copy was signed and authenticated by De Groote. Edward Kinesman was authorized to publish the English translation May 27, 1623, and his "Approbatio" is signed by Joan. Floydus, Soc. Jesu Theologus.

The bandage with which Christ was blindfolded (*Mark* xiv. 65). The bandage with which Christ was blindfolded by the soldiers was given by Charlemagne to St. Namphasus, who built the abbey of Marcillac, where he deposited the relic. It is now kept in a little country church called St. Julian of Lunegarde. It is a linen bandage, stained in many places with blood. The historian Dominicy writes, "Asservatur in ecclesia St. Juliani de Lunegarde (cujus præsentatio ad abbatem Marciliacensem pertinet) tenue velum ex lino Ægyptio; idemque illud esse dicunt quo Christi faciem milites obduxere, dum per ludibrium colaphis cæderetur. Est et in eadem ecclesia, frustum arundinis, ei in signum regni affectati, pro sceptro traditæ."—*Sudario Capitis Christi*, p. 47.

One would have thought that the face of Christ was covered with a sudarium or pocket-handkerchief belonging to one of the soldiers or servants, and after the mockery was over that the cloth would be reclaimed by the owner. It is not the least likely that the Christians would buy up such relics, or even venture to pick them up at such a time of peril. There is no proof whatever that relics of such articles were diligently sought and preserved by the apostles and primitive Christians. The mania for relics set in during the reign of Constantine, when his mother Helena gave it an enormous impulse.

The blood of Jesus Christ. We are assured that some of the blood of Christ is preserved at Mantua. It is said to have been preserved by Longinus, when he pierced the side of Jesus with his spear; but it is more generally thought that this blood did not proceed from the body of the Saviour, but from crucifixes pierced in derision by Jews and other unbelievers. Alban Butler, in his *Lives of the Saints* (May 3), endorses this statement, and the chamberlain of pope Leo XIII. (1880) says, "Ces miracles" (that is, bleeding crucifixes) "si touchants sont racontés et établis d'une manière peremptoire dans des histoires fort authentiques."—See St. Thomas, bk. iii. p. 54, a. 2–5; and bk. v. 5.

The holy blood of Billom, in France. This relic consists of a spoonful of blood, said to be brought from Syria, in the first crusade, by two canons, named Durand Albanelli and Peter Barbasta. The blood had preserved its colour and fluidity. Several vouchers accompanied the vessel containing the blood, one dated in the reign of Tiberius, and another in that of Valens. A bull of Eugenius IV. (A.D. 1444) established a confraternity in honour of the blood of Billom. Paul VI., Calixtus III., Leo X., and Clement VII., all attest that a great number of miracles were performed by virtue of this blood, which, we are told, was a specific for dysentery, hemorrhage, sore eyes, etc. It was lost in the Revolution.—*Discours historique sur le sang précieux que l'on révère dans l'église collégiale et royale de St. Cerneuf de la ville de Billom, en Auvergne*, 1757.

The cross on which Christ was crucified discovered (A.D. 326). The cross of Christ is the great relic of the [Roman] Catholic Church, and ought to be authenticated by the most unimpeachable authority even from the day of the crucifixion to the present hour; but we hear nothing of it till the fourth century. And as it was made of deal, and buried in the earth, considerable decay must have taken place in three hundred years. The epoch of its discovery was as far from the time of the crucifixion as we are from Queen Elizabeth. But to the legend :—

We are told that it was found by the empress Helena, mother of Constantine the Great, May 3, A.D. 326. She was nearly eighty years of age at the time. Ancient authors do not agree upon the way she was led to the discovery. Thus Nicephorus Callistus and Cassiodorus assert that she was directed to the spot by revelation, but the Roman breviary and most other authorities maintain that one Judas betrayed to her the place where this and other relics connected with it were buried. Alban Butler tells us it was customary for the Jews to bury whatever was used in an execution in a hole near the place of execution; if so, it seems strange that the place was not generally known, and still more strange that the apostles and early Christians, who are represented to us by [Roman] Catholic Christians as great venerators of all relics relating to Christ, should have known this fact and not disinterred such inestimable treasures. The place of concealment was wrung from Judas involuntarily, but he told the empress to dig under a temple of Venus which stood close by the holy sepulchre. So the temple was knocked down, and men were employed to dig about the spot, and there were found three crosses, some nails, and a slab of wood which had been used for a title of accusation. St. Andrew of Crete, who died A.D. 722, in his *De Exaltatione Crucis*, adds, the spear also. The sponge, the crown of thorns, the cloth with which Christ was blindfolded, the whip, the reed, and the pillar at which He was scourged, were not buried in the hole under the temple of Venus, but have all come to light no one knows how, and no one knows when. The next question is obviously, what became of these relics? According to the same authorities there was a great difficulty in knowing which of the three crosses was the true cross. This perplexity was removed by Macarius, patriarch of Jerusalem, who advised the empress to test them by touching with them a body on the point of death. Writers differ as to the way this test was applied. Some say a sick woman was brought to the spot, and touched with the three crosses; when those of the two malefactors touched her no effect was produced, but immediately the true cross touched her, she was restored to perfect health. Others, amongst whom is Alban Butler, tell us the three crosses were carried to the house of a sick lady of high rank, and the test applied at her house. All agree that the miracle revealed which was the true cross. The right cross being thus determined on, the empress seems to have cut it into three unequal parts, one of which she enshrined in a rich silver casket, and gave to Macarius, the patriarch of Jerusalem, one she sent to Constantinople, and one to Rome, for the church built in that city by herself and Constantine, ever since called the Church of the Holy Cross; this part is now enclosed in one of the four huge pillars which support the dome of St. Peter's church. The part sent to Constantinople was given by Baldwin II., with other relics, to St. Louis of France, who had paid off a very large debt, and they are still preserved in Paris. It was given out, however, that Baldwin had sent these relics away, because it was no longer safe to keep them in a place so subject to spoliation as Constantinople. St. Paulinus (in his *Epistle to Severus*) tells us that chips were almost daily cut from the cross, and given to devout persons, and yet that "the wood suffered no diminution." Cyril of Jerusalem endorses this statement, and adds, that within twenty-five years of the "invention," pieces of the true cross were spread over the whole earth, "for its multiplication was like that of the loaves and fishes, when Jesus fed the multitude in the desert." Calvin says fifty men could not carry the wood of what is called "the true cross" scattered abroad. And Luther, a good authority, says there was wood enough to "build an immense house."

The following places are said to possess parts of the cross: Aix-la-Chapelle, Amiens, Angers, Arles Arras, Autun, Avignon, Baugé, Bernay, Besançon, Bologna, Bonifacio, Bordeaux, Bourbon Larchambault, Bourges, Brussels, Chalinargues, Chalons, Chamirey, Châtillon, Cheffes in Anjou, Chelles, Compiègne, Conques, Cortona, Coutrai, Denmark, Dijon, Donawert, England, Faphine, Fiume, Florence, Gand, Geneva, Grammont, Jaucourt, Jerusalem, Langres, Laon, Libourne, Lille, Limbourg, Longpont, Lorris, Lyons, Mâcon, Maestricht, Marseilles, Milan, Mont Athos, Montepulciano, Naples, Nevers, No way, Nuremberg, Padua, Paris, Pisa, Poitiers, Pontigny, Ragusa, Riel-les-Eaux, Rome, Royaumont, Saint Dié, Saint Florent, Saint Quentin, Saint Sepulc re, Sens, Siena, Tournay, Trèves, Troyes, Turin, Valcourt, Vamback, Venice, Venloo, and without doubt several others, and many parts are lost.

In 636 the part sent to Jerusalem was divided into nineteen parts, four of which were kept at Jerusalem, three were sent to Constantinople (!!), three to Antioch, two to Georgia, and one part to each of the five following places: Alexandria, Ascalon, Crete, Damascus, and Edessa.

Three were sent to Constantinople because the part sent there by the empress Helena had been transferred to France (see CROWN OF THORNS).

Without d ubt, the wood of the cross was sold at a good price, and this will account for its being cut up into so many pieces.

"Denmark." It was Urban V. who gave a part of the cross to Waldemar III. of Denmark, because he consented to assist in a crusade.

"Norway." King Sigur of Norway had a part given him for his services at the siege of Sidon. This part was deposited in the town of Konghell.

Ambrose, *Funeral Oration of Theodosius*; Cassiodorus, *Tripartite History*, bk. i. ch. 4; St. Chrysostom; St. Cyril of Jerusalem, *Lectures to Catechumens*, x.; Gregory of Tours; St. Isidore, *Missal*; Nicephorus Callistus, *Ecclesiastical History*, bk. viii. ch. 26; Rufinus, *Ecclesiastical History*, ch. 20; St. Paulinus, *Epistle to Severus*, 7, 12; Socrates, *Ecclesiastical History*; Sozomen, *ditto*; Sulpicius Severus, *Sacred History*; Theodoret; and scores of more modern authors.

⁂ Gretzer says the column of the cross was fifteen feet, and the crosspiece to which the hands were nailed was between seven and eight feet. Lipsius says the slab containing the accusations was three feet eight inches. The writing was in red letters. M. Rohault says the wood of the cross was deal or pine. Alexis Comnenus, writing to Robert, count of Flanders, in 1100, tells him there were preserved at Constantinople the column of the cross, the whip with which Christ was scourged, the purple robe, the crown of thorns, the reed given for sceptre, the dress that Christ wore, the nails, and the linen napkins found in the tomb.

The crown of thorns. The crown of thorns was not found in the hole with the cross, and there is no record or tradition extant of its discovery. In the thirteenth century Baldwin II., we are told, sent it for greater security to St. Louis, who built the Holy Chapel for its depository. In this chapel was also kept that part of the true cross which the empress Helena had sent to Constantinople. Alban Butler says, "Some of the thorns have been distributed to other churches, and some have been made in imitation of the real ones, but the imitation thorns are usually very long."

In the Hotel de Cluny, Paris, is a ring containing a small part of one of the thorns. Other like rings are probably known. One would like to know something of this relic before Baldwin, in the twelfth century, sent it to Paris. How was it obtained? How was it preserved during the siege of Jerusalem? Where was it during those troublesome times prior to the reign of Constantine? As the strength of a chain is only equal to its weakest link, so the authenticity of a relic is destroyed by any flaw in its history. Then there is the crown of thorns preserved in the Santa Maria della Spina of Pisa. In regard to the Paris crown, it is not a crown of thorns, but of "petits joncs réunis en faisceaux," eight inches in diameter. Besides this entire crown, there are 103 churches which profess to have parts of the true crown, especially Pisa, Trèves, and Bruges. The Trèves relic professes to have come direct from the empress Helena, and that at Pisa is exactly like it.

The cup or chalice of the Last Supper. The "Sacro Catino" is sometimes identified with the "Holy Graal" of the poets of the Middle Ages, but most Englishmen think the Holy Graal was the paten, not the chalice. The cup at Genoa, taken to Paris in 1816, was broken by its removals. It is of green glass, cast and cut with considerable care; has two handles, and is of hexagonal form. Its diameter atop is 326 millimètres, and it will hold three litres of liquor. Quaresmius says this was the cup used by our Lord in the Last Supper; but most [Roman] Catholics think the cup which served the Last Supper was the silver chalice at Valencia, in Spain.

Most certainly the Holy Graal of Arthurian romance was a golden vessel, not a green glass cup; and although the descriptions given are purposely obscure, there can be little doubt that it was either the consecrated bread converted into Christ, or the paten which held it. It seems, however, not to be any paten, nor all consecrated bread, for it is always brought in either by a dove, or by a miraculous light "more clear by seven times than the light of day," or by a celestial damsel, and immediately the bread has been distributed, the graal vanishes.—See *Morte d'Arthur*, pt. iii. ch. 3, 4, 35, 102.

The grave-clothes. I have not had time to invoice anything like all the places which claim to possess part or parts of the grave-clothes found in the rock sepulchre after the resurrection of the Lord; but the following are the best known:—

AIX-LA-CHAPELLE contains some of the grave-clothes.

BESANÇON. Here was, at one time, shown part of the grave-clothes, but the relic was cast away at the great Revolution. Cardinal Mathieu made great efforts to recover it or parts of it, but wholly without success.

CADOUIN, in the diocese of Périgueux, is said to possess "un suaire, de 2 m. 81, sur 1 m. 13. Il est l'objet d'une description détaillée, et nous offre un linge fort ornée."

CAHORS is especially rich in the grave-clothes. It claims to possess the cloth which covered the head of Jesus. It is of fine Egyptian linen, "trois doubles superposés." It was examined and verified (!!) by Champollion (1790–1832). It has many blood-stains; two in particular have penetrated through the folds.

CARCASSO, in Italy, contains some of the grave-clothes.

CHAMBÉRY. One of the cloths is deposited in a beautiful chapel at Chambéry; where is also a glass window recording its history (sixteenth century).

MAYENCE contains some of the grave-clothes.

ROME. Several churches lay claim to grave-clothes of the Christ.

TOULOUSE contains some of the grave-clothes.

TURIN. Here is a suaire of linen, somewhat yellow, "et rayé comme du basin." It is four mètres long. Has great spots of blood, some indicating blood from the head.

The nails of the cross. The number of nails employed in crucifixion is uncertain. Thus Gregory Nazianzen (329–390) asserts there were only three, one nail serving for both the feet, which were placed one above the other. St. Cyprian (200–258), who had been a personal witness to more than one crucifixion, says, in his *De Passione*, each foot was nailed with a separate spike, and that the number used was four. Of the nails found in the hole where the cross was buried, one of them, at least, was sent to Rome,* and deposited in what was afterwards the Santa Croce; two were sent by the empress Helena to her son Constantine, one of which was welded, as an amulet, to his helmet, and the other was set in his horse's headstall; † a fourth the empress Helena threw into the gulf of Venice to allay a storm. These were the four nails; but a nail, said to be one employed in the crucifixion, was set in the famous "iron crown of Lombardy," with which Charlemagne and Napoleon I. were crowned. Calvin enumerates fourteen or fifteen nails:—one in the Santa Croce, at Rome; another in Siena; a third at Venice; a fourth in the church of the Carmelites, in Paris; a fifth in the Holy Chapel; a sixth at Draguignan; a seventh at Tenaille; an eighth at Trèves; a ninth at Monza, etc.; and so on. Alban Butler, to explain this, tells us that nails made like the true nails were consecrated either by filings or by touching the genuine article; and, in corroboration of this statement, he says that the nail in the Santa Croce of Rome has been evidently filed, and is without a point. He

* Some say more than one of the nails was sent to Rome.

† Gregory of Tours says that two of the nails were set in the headstalls of Constantine's horse.

further says that Charles de Borromeo had many nails made like that at Milan, and distributed, after touching the true nail. One nail so touched he gave to Philip II. Whether a nail made by a common blacksmith can be called a nail employed in the crucifixion of our Lord, merely because it has touched one of the nails so employed, must be left an open question. I very much fear neither Calvin nor Luther would be satisfied with Butler's explanation. (For authorities, see under THE CROSS, p. 270.)

Mons. Rohault de Fleury assures us that "le cercle de fer de Monza, où il y avait du vrai clou, le clou de Trèves completé par celui de Toul, paraissent d'une authenticité incontestable;" but how can this possibly be, if one was thrown into the Adriatic, one was set in Constantine's helmet, one in his horse's headstall, and one was sent to Rome, the utmost number being only four? There can be no doubt that Magna Charta is a valuable relic, but I doubt very much if a copy of it could be called the original document, merely because it was made to touch it. The seal of the Golden Bull is a valuable relic, but its whole value would be destroyed, if the seal could be multiplied merely by touching it. Imitation relics, passed off as genuine articles, are neither more nor less than deceptions and impositions.

The reed placed in the hands of Christ for sceptre. We are told that the reed and sponge which was filled with vinegar, and offered to Christ on the cross, were sent to Constantinople in 614, when Jerusalem was taken by the Persians. St. Gregory of Tours (544–595) tells us they were objects of veneration in Jerusalem in his days; but their removal to Constantinople does not correspond with the statement of the Venerable Bede (672–735), who says he saw the sponge in Jerusalem, in a silver cup; unless, indeed, it had been sent back again. A part of the reed is said to be in Florence; a part in St. Julian's church of Lunegarde; a larger piece in the convent of Andeschs, in Bavaria; and a still larger piece in the convent of Watoped, on Mount Athos. We are left wholly to conjecture respecting this very fragile and perishable article. The cross, the slab of wood, and the spear, we are told, were buried in a deep hole, and discovered in A.D. 326 by the empress Helena; but no mention is made of the reed or the sponge. One would naturally suppose that the soldiers would throw the reed away after they had finished their practical joke.

There were two reeds connected with the crucifixion; one the reed sceptre, and the other the long reed which lifted the sponge (*Matt.* xxvii. 48). The reed relic is called "le roseau de la royauté derisoire de Jésus Christ," so that no shadow of doubt is left as to which reed allusion is made. Of the long reed I can find no mention, and know of no church, chapel, or religious house which makes any claim to this important instrument of the crucifixion.

The robe of our Saviour (*John* xix. 23). Two places lay claim to the seamless robe of Christ, Trèves and Argenteuil. The *holy robe of Trèves* is longer than that at Argenteuil, and we are told it was presented by the empress Helena to Ayvilius, then bishop of Trèves; but there is no document to show the authenticity of this tradition till the twelfth century. The archbishop John, in 1196, is said to have discovered the casket containing the holy robe. From 1512 to 1810 it saw many vicissitudes; but, at the latter date, it returned to Trèves. It is more delicate than the robe of Argenteuil, and intact. Its size is 1 m. 55 *before*, and 1 m. 62 *behind*. The width at the chest is 0 m. 73. At the lowest part, 1 m. 16.

The *holy robe of Argenteuil* has a far better register, which is given by St. Gregory of Tours, who tells us it was bought of the soldier to whose lot it fell; and was carried to a town in Galatia, where it was packed carefully in a wooden box. When Galatia was threatened by Persia, in 590, the relic was removed to Jaffa. In 594, it was taken in grand procession to Jerusalem. Twenty years later, it was carried by Chosroës to Persia; but, in 627, Heraclius recovered it, and took it, first to Constantinople, then back to Jerusalem, and then again to Constantinople. Irenê, empress of Constantinople, sent it, with other rich presents, to Charlemagne; and Charlemagne sent it to his daughter Theodrada, abbess of Argenteuil, A.D. 800. A curé of Argenteuil cut the robe into several pieces, so that now it is not possible to piece the parts together into the original form. It is a tissue of goat's hair without seam, and was originally 1 m. 35 long, by 1 m. 15 wide.

The holy robe of Moscow. Moscow claims to have a robe of Christ; and numerous other places make a similar claim, as St. Prasseda, St. Roch, Rome, etc. Venice is said to possess a part of the white robe in which Christ was arrayed by Herod's soldiers; and St. Francis of Philip Anagni, St. John de Lateran, and Santa Maria Maggiore are said to possess parts of the purple robe in which He was arrayed by the soldiers of Pilate.

The spear with which the side of Christ was pierced. A spear without a head is preserved in the basilica of St. Peter's, at Rome, said to be the shaft of the spear used by the Roman soldier Longinus, who pierced the side of our Lord, after his expiration on the cross. The emperor Baldwin II. sent the head of the spear to

Venice, as a pledge for money; and St. Louis, having redeemed it, took it to Paris, where it was kept, till the Revolution, in the Holy Chapel. Benedict XIV., wishing to know if the two fitted, sent for the head, and tried it on the shaft, when the fit was pronounced to be sufficiently satisfactory. The spear was first taken to Jerusalem; but the Venerable Bede (672–735) tells us, in his days, it was enclosed in a wooden cross, and kept in the porch of the church called the Martyr, built in Constantinople by the emperor Constantine. Gregory of Tours (544–595) speaks of its removal from Jerusalem to Constantinople in the reign of Heraclius (610–641). In 1492, the sultan Bajazet sent the shaft of the spear, in a costly case, to pope Innocent VIII., who placed it, as a precious relic, in one of the four huge piers which support the dome of the basilica of St. Peter's, where it is still an object of great veneration. Authors are not agreed where this spear was found. St. Andrew of Crete, who died A.D. 722, affirms, in his *De Exaltatione Crucis*, that it was buried together with the cross; but though, as Alban Butler tells us, it might be customary with the Jews to bury what was used in an execution in a hole near the place of execution, there seems no reason why a Roman soldier should cast his spear in the hole;* and certainly the spear is not included in any of the early lists of the relics discovered by the empress Helena. From the sixth century to the present time the register of the sacred spear is pretty satisfactory; but, after all, the interval between the first and sixth century is far more important, and this is just the period when our information is the most meagre and unsatisfactory.

That frauds were sometimes practised by the Christians, even the most zealous of the [Roman] Catholic Church freely acknowledge. Thus the chamberlain of Leo. XIII. (1880) tells us, "Mgr. Mislin a dénoncé une supercherie des Grecs. La cavité, qui est au sommet du calvaire, n'est pas celle où la croix fut plantée. Dans le bouleversement arrivé dans l'incendie de 1808, ils enlevèrent la pierre dans laquelle avait été enfoncée la vraie croix, pour la transporter a Constantinople, et mirent une autre pierre à la place, et la véritable fut perdue dans un naufrage."

The sponge. St. Gregory of Tours speaks of the holy sponge, as a relic publicly venerated at Jerusalem (together with the crown of thorns, the spear, and the reed), but he has omitted to state in what place they were preserved. The Venerable Bede assures us that he himself saw the holy sponge in a silver tankard, which he supposes was used by our Lord in the Last Supper. A part of this sponge is said to be preserved in France, with the other relics purchased by St. Louis. Other parts are shown at St. Jacques de Compiègne; at St. Sylvester, St. John de Lateran, St. Maria Maggiore, St. Mary in Transtevere, St. Mark, and St. Mary in Compitelli (all in Rome).

The staircase of Pilate's judgment hall. The staircase of Pilate's judgment hall was sent to Rome by the empress Helena in A.D. 326, and deposited in St. John Lateran. In 850 pope Leo IV. established the practice of mounting these stairs on one's knees, but they got so worn that they were cased with wood. The staircase consists of twenty-eight stairs of white marble.

The table used by Christ at the Last Supper. At St. John Lateran is preserved a table, said to be the one used by Christ at the Last Supper. Nothing is known about it, and probably very few believe it to be what it professes to be.

The title of accusation nailed to the cross of Jesus. The title of accusation was not paper or parchment, but a board nailed to the top of the cross. This board, we are told, was sent to Rome, and deposited, like the nail, in the Santa Croce. Bozio (1548–1610), in his *Tr. de Cruce*, bk. i. ch. 2, tells us that the title sent by queen Helena to Rome, and found in the hole with the three crosses, was deposited on the top of an arch; and was discovered, in 1492, in a leaden case. It was in Hebrew, Greek, and Latin, written in red letters on a slab of white wood. In 1492, the colour was not at all faded [though it had been buried in the earth for nearly three hundred years], but when Bozio saw it, some sixty or seventy years afterwards, the colour was greatly faded, and the wood so worm-eaten, that the words *Jesus* and *Judæum* were both gone. Lipsius (1547–1606), in his *De Cruce*, bk. iii. ch. 14, says the slab or board, when he saw it, was nine inches long, but must originally have been three feet longer.

Two other titles. We are told of two other slabs. Thus Father Durand (1232–1296), who lived in the reign of St. Louis, tells us that he saw in Paris the title of accusation, with the full inscription. The monk Antonine (1389–1459) asserts that he held in his own hands the slab bearing the accusation, when he visited

* A soldier's sword, spear, and accoutrements belong to the state, and no private could dispose of these articles at will; but if neither buried, nor sold, nor given away, how did the early Christians get it in possession? Galilean fishermen were not likely to stand high in favour with arrogant Roman soldiers.

the Holy Sepulchre, at Jerusalem. Perhaps the empress Helena divided the slab into three parts, as she did the cross, only Father Durand states that the Paris slab bore the full inscription. Or perhaps, like the nails, two of the slabs were imitations; or perhaps the slabs at Paris and Jerusalem were each a part of the real slab, and were supplemented, as we now restore churches.

The title at Rome is certainly not the whole "title." The words read from right to left, and the Latin words NAZARINVS RE[x] are quite legible in the lowest line. In the middle line we have ΝΑΖΑΡΕΝΟΥΣ. And the uppermost line, which contained the Hebrew inscription, is quite faded. Of course the entire Latin inscription was [*Jesus*] *Nazarenus Re*(*x*) [*Judæorum*], but the board being cut into three parts, *Jesus* and *Judæorum* were cut off, one being at Paris and one at Jerusalem.

Critics say that the little E in the Greek word is an anachronism, as well as the termination -ους for -ος. Others say that to read Greek and Latin from right to left is an error, which Pilate or his Roman officials would not have committed. Certainly an English mechanic would not print "Nazarenus" *sunera*-*aN*, and it seems unlikely that a Roman soldier would do so. That Gretzer and Montfaucon have discovered such examples of writing from right to left seems by no means to justify the case, unless they can show also that such was the usual custom in Pilate's time, for it may be taken for granted that the inscription was written in the ordinary manner of the time.

One of the most suspicious circumstances about these crucifixion relics is the astounding fact that they were all discovered by the empress Helena about three hundred years after the event. When a queen is known to be a relic-hunter, we all know that relics to any amount will be forthcoming, and an enthusiast of eighty is not exactly the person to discriminate between truth and fraud, especially when all her sympathies are one way.

The whipping-post of Christ. The post at which Christ was scourged used to be shown on Mount Sion, in the Holy Land, as St. Gregory Nazianzen informs us (*Oration* 1, *In Julian*). It is now at Rome, and is shown through iron railings in a little chapel in the church of St. Praxedês. Over the chapel is inscribed this information, that cardinal John Columna brought it to Rome in 1223; but the inscription does not state how the apostolic legate obtained it. The socle of the post is preserved in St. Mark's cathedral, at Venice. The post is of gray marble, one foot and a half long, by one foot in diameter at the bottom, and eight inches at the top, where there is an iron ring to which the victim was tied. The Jews scourged criminals first on their back, then on their belly, and then on each side. The post preserved at Rome, as the whipping-post of Christ, does not at all correspond with the description of St. Jerome.

The bed of St. Gertrude, abbess of Nivelles, multiplied. The abbess Agnes, who succeeded Wilfetrude, built a beautiful temple, in which she placed as a precious relic the little bed on which St. Gertrude, a former abbess, died. This bed was afterwards transported to another church, built by St. Beggha, her sister; but that the monastery of Nivelles might not be deprived of so valued a relic, God multiplied the bed, one for St. Beggha, and the other for the temple built by Wilfetrude.—Surius, *Lives of the Saints.*

The two heads of St. Agnes. The abbey of St. Ouen, at Rouen, glories in having the head of St. Agnes. The priory of St. Peter, at Abbeville, does the same.

John Brady, in his list of relics, mentions two heads of John the Baptist.

The church of St. Sylvester, at Rome, claims to have the "meilleure partie de son chef," says the chamberlain of pope Leo XIII., yet—

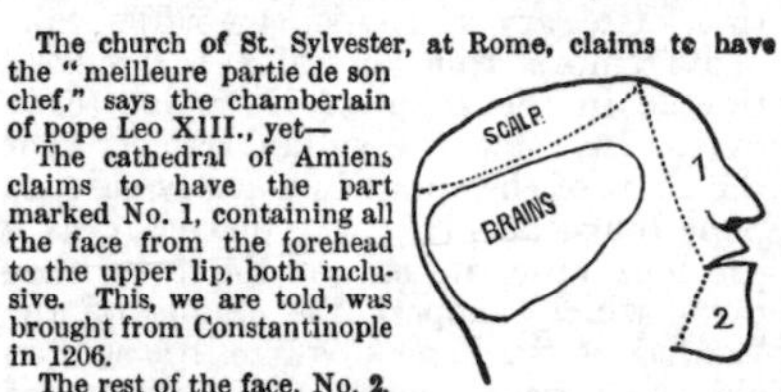

The cathedral of Amiens claims to have the part marked No. 1, containing all the face from the forehead to the upper lip, both inclusive. This, we are told, was brought from Constantinople in 1206.

The rest of the face, No. 2, from the upper lip to the chin, both inclusive, is said to be in the chapel of the chateau of St. Chaumont, in the Lyonnais.

The scalp was sold to St. Louis of France by Baldwin II. in 1247, and is deposited in St. Chapelle, Paris.

The brains are said to be in the abbey of Tyron. In 1515 they were placed in a skull borne by two angels.

Turin, Aosta, Venice, Lyons, Nemours, Nola, Bresse, all claim to have parts of the head; but how all these claims can be satisfied, and yet St. Sylvester, at Rome, have "la meilleure partie," is past understanding.

The five legs of the ass on which Christ rode. A Dutchman having received from a priest a "leg of the ass on which Jesus rode to Jerusalem," discovered that the priest had already sold four other legs. Father Ferund, being told of it, gravely assured the Dutchman it was all right, for God could multiply and reproduce as many legs as He thought proper for the edification of His chosen people. In fact, the more the legs the greater their value, as they must then be standing proofs of the productive power of the Almighty.—*Eclectic Review* (Melancthon).

The wood of the cross multiplied. A priest being asked how it was that almost every church of note possessed a piece of the original cross, and yet the cross at Jerusalem was in no wise diminished, made answer that the cross was no ordinary relic. It was true, he allowed, that if all the fragments of the cross scattered over Christendom were collected together there would be wood enough to build a man-of-war, but that Jesus, who could feed a multitude with a few loaves, could multiply relics of His cross for the benefit and consolation of the faithful over the whole Christian world.—Merryweather, *Glimmerings in the Dark.*

In this anecdote are several inaccuracies. It was not a priest, but St. Cyril, bishop of Jerusalem, who made this answer (see p. 270). Again, the entire cross never was at Jerusalem as a relic, but only one of the arms, about four feet in length. The column was sent by St. Helena to Constantinople, and one of the arms to Rome. St. Cyril, of course, did not say one word about "a man-of-war," but Luther said there would be "wood enough for a large house" (see p. 270).

Relics taken from Constantinople when it fell into the hands of Dandolo and the Crusaders in 1204.

(1) A piece of the true cross.

(2) An arm either of St. Gregory or St. George. [Rather funny there should be any doubt, as St. Gregory was sixty-one, and St. George was half that age at death.]

(3) Part of the head of John the Baptist. [A part of the cranium is in the Ville du Pay, the larger part of his head (*chef*) is in St. Sylvester at Rome, but the cathedral of Amiens glories in having also a large portion (with the upper lip, nose, eyes, and forehead). Baldwin, emperor of Constantinople, in 1247 gave or rather sold the upper part of the head (la partie supérieur du même chef), and it was deposited in Ste. Chapelle, Paris. The abbot of Tyron has the nape of the neck. A part of the jaws is preserved in the chapel of the chateau de St. Chaumont, in Lyonnais. Other parts of this wonderful head are in Turin, Aosta, and Venice; other parts in Lyons and Nemours, in France. St. Paulin deposited a part in his church at Nola, and St. Gaudence in his church at Bresse. The finger with which the Baptist pointed out the Messiah is in Malta, and some of his ashes are in Genoa.]

(4) A vial containing the blood of Christ, which flowed from a statue pierced by the Jews at Berytus.

(5) A fragment of the pillar at which Christ was scourged.

(6) A nail of the cross.

(7) A prickle of the crown of thorns.

(8) The bodies of St. Lucia, St. Agatha, and St. Simeon.

Ramusio, *Raccolta delle Navigazioni e Viaggi* (1550–59), bk. iii. p. 131.

Rent Garments.

1 KINGS xi. 30, 31. Jeroboam was clad in a new garment; and Ahijah caught the new garment, and, rending it into twelve pieces, said to him, Take thee [*sic*] ten pieces; for thus saith the Lord, the God of Israel, Behold, I will rend the kingdom out of the hand of Solomon, and will give ten tribes to thee.

1 SAM. xv. 27, 28. As Samuel turned about to go away, Saul laid hold upon the skirt of his mantle, and it rent And Samuel said unto him, The Lord hath rent the kingdom of Israel from thee this day, and hath given it to a neighbour of thine, that is better than thou.

JOHN xix. 23, 24. The coat [of Jesus] was without seam, woven from the top throughout. The soldiers said among themselves, Let us not rend it, but cast lots for it. [This may symbolize that there should be no schism in the Church (1 Cor. xii. 25).]

Jesus Christ, in a torn garment, appears to St. Peter of Alexandria. Arius, the heresiarch, wished to succeed St. Peter, bishop of Alexandria, and schemed to this end. St. Peter says, touching this succession, "I was in prayer, as my custom is, when Jesus Christ, my Lord and God, appeared to me, in the likeness of a little child. The glory of His face could not be seen, by reason of its exceeding splendour. He was arrayed in a long garment reaching to the ground, but it was rent from the top to the bottom, and He held it together over the paps with His two hands. Then said I, 'Ah, Lord, what is this I see? How is Thy garment torn!' He answering, said to me, 'Peter, thou talkest much of My torn garment, the Church, but doest nothing to repair the rent. Know, Peter, it is Arius that hath done this; he it is that seeketh to rend My people from Me, even My people purchased with My blood. Go and tell Achillas and Alexander what thou hast seen, and say they, and not Arius, are to succeed thee; and when they have so done, bid them anathematize and excommunicate that foul heretic, as thou hast done, that their souls may be saved.' So saying, He vanished out of sight."—St. Gregory Nazianzen (A.D. 363), *Orations against Julian.* (See also Eusebius, *Church History*, bk. viii. ch. 14, and bk. ix. chap. 6; Callistus, *Church History; The Tripartite History*; Usuard; Bede; Ado; *The Council of Ephesus*, and *Seventh General Synod.*)

Retributive Punishment.

PSALM vii. 14–16. He made a pit and digged it, and is fallen into the ditch which he made. His mischief shall return upon his own head, and his violent dealing shall come down on his own pate.

ESTH. vii. Haman, annoyed because Mordecai would not bow the knee to him, plotted the extirpation of the whole Jewish race, and raised a gallows fifty cubits high, on which he intended to hang Mordecai. His plot being betrayed to the king, Haman himself was hanged on his own gallows.

DAN. iii. 22. When Shadrach and his companions were condemned to be cast into the furnace, it was heated seven times more than it was wont, so that its intense heat slew those that took up the three servants of God, but those for whom it was heated walked about in the midst of the furnace, and received no harm.

DAN. vi. 24. When Daniel was let down into the cave of lions for praying to God, the lions did him no injury; but when his accusers were cast into the same cave, the lions had the mastery of them, and brake all their bones in pieces or [ere] ever they came to the bottom of the den.

Instances of this retributive punishment in the lives of the saints are so numerous they would fill a large volume. Only a few are here presented.

Abraham unharmed by a fire which consumed two thousand men. Nimrod commanded Abraham to be bound, and cast into a huge fire at Cûtha; but he was preserved from all injury by the angel Gabriel, and only the cords which bound him were consumed. Yet so intense was the heat of the fire that above two thousand men were consumed by it. —*Gospel of Barnabas*, xxviii. (See also Morgan's *Mahometanism Explained*, V. i. 4.)

St. Agnes uninjured by fire, but many of her tormentors burnt to death (A.D. 304). The son of Sempronius the Roman governor wanted to marry St. Agnes, who was only thirteen years of age. St. Agnes declined his suit; and said she had vowed to live and die the virgin bride of Jesus Christ. The governor, after many fruitless endeavours to make her change her mind, resolved to punish her on the plea of being a Christian, and commanded Aspasius his lieutenant to commit her to the flames. She was accordingly cast into the midst of a fierce fire, but "the flames parting asunder, she stood in the midst and received no harm." Not so those who clamoured against her, many of whom were burnt to death by the great heat. As St. Agnes stood, a flame on this side and a flame on that, she cried aloud, "O Almighty Lord, I give Thee humble and hearty thanks for that I am delivered from the hands of the wicked, and that the fire kindled to consume me has done me no harm. They only, O Lord, who sought my life have felt the fury of the flames. So may all thine enemies perish, that men may know that Thou whose name is JEHOVAH art the most high over all the earth." As St. Agnes thus spoke the fire dropped out, and there remained no trace that it had ever been kindled on the spot; but Aspasius, beside himself with rage, struck the damsel with his sword, and she was added to the army of martyrs.—Edward Kinesman (1623), *Lives of the Saints*, p. 76. (See also St. Jerome's *Epistle* viii.; St. Austin's *Sermon* 274; St. Ambrose; etc., etc.)

St. Barbara's father cut off her head, and was struck dead by a thunderbolt. Marrianus, governor of Nicomedia, commanded two lusty young fellows to tear the sides and breasts of St. Barbara with iron combs, then to set burning torches to both her sides, and beat her about the head with hammers. As these tortures did not shake her constancy to Christ, the governor bade his myrmidons cut off the nipples of her breast, and then lead her naked through the public streets, scourging her as she passed along. Still the beautiful but mutilated maiden remained unshaken, and the governor gave orders for her head to be cut off. Her father, who could not forgive her for being a Christian, begged that he might be commissioned to execute her, which request was readily granted. So she was led to the hill beyond the gates, the usual place of execution, and the father of the maiden cut off her head. No sooner had he done so, than he was struck dead by a thunderbolt. Angels came and carried the spirit of the martyr into paradise, but devils came and bore the spirit of the father into the bottomless abyss.—Peter Galesinus (apostolic protonotary); also archbishop Ado, *Martyrology*; Metaphrastês, *Lives*, etc.

St. Catherine uninjured by the wheel, but many others killed by it. The emperor Maxentius, being unable to make St. Catherine sacrifice to idols, was advised by a machinist to try a "wheel" which he promised to produce in three days. This machine consisted in reality of four wheels, armed with saws, knives, and teeth. Each of the four wheels turned "one against the other, so that the saws, knives, and teeth met." It moved with a hideous noise, and the whole affair was truly diabolical. When the holy maid was bound on the machine, an angel loosed her, and she fell to the ground: then striking the machine, it fell to pieces, and killed the inventor, with all those employed to work it, and many who had assembled to witness the novel torture. Those not killed ran away in consternation, crying aloud, "Great is the God of Christians; He doeth wondrously both in the heavens above and in the earth beneath!"—Metaphrastês (died 911), *Lives*, etc.

St. Catherine was not killed by the wheel, as most persons suppose—indeed, she was in no wise injured by it but, after being delivered from the diabolical instrument, she was beheaded.

Those who torment St. Faustinus and Jovita are themselves destroyed (A.D. 121). St. Faustinus and St. Jovita, brothers, were Christians of a noble family in Brescia, Lombardy. Hadrian commanded them to be thrown to the wild beasts in the amphitheatre; and when the lions, leopards, and bears lay down quietly beside them, men were sent to enrage them by burning their flanks with lighted torches; whereupon the beasts turned on their tormentors and devoured them. The martyrs were then taken to Milan. Here they were laid on their backs along the ground, and molten lead was poured through funnels into their mouths; but the lead, instead of rolling down the throats of the martyrs, rolled on the executioners and burnt them horribly. St. Faustinus and his brother were now conducted to Rome, and cast into the sea, but Jesus Christ Himself delivered them from this death. Ultimately they were sent back to Brescia, and beheaded.—*Les Petits Bollandistes* (7th edit. 1880), vol. ii. pp. 532, 533.

The forty martyrs, struck about the mouth with stones, receive no hurt, but the mouths of those who strike them lose their teeth. The emperor Licinius had in his army forty Christian soldiers of great valour; but while garrisoned in Capadocia, Agricolaus the governor, who hated all Christians, ordered them to be brought before him, that he might find matter of accusation against them. They defended themselves so boldly, that the governor commanded his officers to strike them on the mouth with stones. And now, we are told, "a strange thing happened: the forty martyrs who were struck received no hurt whatsoever, but the mouths of those who struck them became all bloody, and they spat out their teeth on the floor of the court." When the governor saw this, he took up a stone in a towering rage, and flung it at the martyrs; but the stone returned to Agricolaus, bruised his mouth grievously, and knocked out his teeth.—Metaphrastês, *Lives*, etc.

Certainly this is a very marvellous tale, and though there are no degrees in miracles, what Horace says of poets and painters may be applied to them:—

"Pictoribus atque poetis
Quidlibet audendi semper fuit æqua potestas."
Sinius, et hanc veniam petimusque damusque vicissim;
Sed non ut placidis coeant immitia, non ut
Serpentes avibus geminentur, tigribus agni . . .
Denique sit quidvis simplex duntaxat et unum.
Ars Poetica, 9, etc.

St. Januarius unharmed by fire which consumes many pagans. Diocletian commanded that a furnace should be heated for three successive days with a continual fire, and that St. Januarius, bishop of Beneventum, should be cast down bound into the midst of the flames. It was done according to the emperor's command, but the man of God walked amidst the fire, and received no harm. He was not alone, for angels walked with him, singing divine melodies. The soldiers reported this marvel to the emperor, and Diocletian ordered the mouth of the furnace to be thrown open, that it might be seen if the report of the guard was true; but immediately this was done, huge flames burst through the mouth of the furnace and killed many pagans. As for St. Januarius, he was taken out uninjured, and reserved in prison for other torments.—Edward Kinesman (1623), *Lives of the Saints*, p. 742.

St. Pantaleon's cylinder does him no harm, but kills many others. The emperor Maximian caused a most cruel engine of torture to be made. It was a large cylinder full of spikes. On this cylinder was St. Pantaleon bound, and it was then trundled down a steep hill, that it might keep rolling over the martyr, and the spikes be driven into his body. But God loosed the martyr from his bonds, and the huge cylinder, bounding down the incline, rolled over hundreds of idolaters assembled to witness the spectacle, and killed them most miserably.—Metaphrastês, *Lives*, etc.

St. Patricius of Prussia uninjured by scalding water, which kills his tormentors. St. Patricius, bishop of Prussia, was arrested and brought before Julian, the proconsul, for denying that Esculapius gave to the thermal waters of the place their medicinal qualities. Said the proconsul to the saint, "Do you mean to tell me that the man crucified by Pilate in Judæa communicates their hygeian properties to these waters?" "I mean to say," replied St. Patricius, "that the God I serve killeth and maketh alive; He bringeth down to the grave and bringeth up." "We will soon see as to the matter of that," said the proconsul, in a rage. Then, calling to his officers, he bade them cast Patricius into a cauldron of boiling water. The moment the martyr was cast into the water it rose in a jet, and pouring down upon the officers burnt them dreadfully; but Patricius, the man of God, enjoyed the bath, which he found of a delightful temperature; and, when taken out, was greatly refreshed. The rage of Julian was now unbounded, and he sent soldiers to cut off the enchanter's head.—L'abbé Migne, *Encyclopédie Theologique*, vol. xli. p. 651 (1850).

Penda's men, who set the city of Bamborough on fire, burnt to death. Penda, king of Mercia, was an irreconcilable enemy of all Christians. On one occasion he set fire to the royal city of Bamborough. "See, Lord," cried Aidan from his hermit's cell in the island of Farne, "what ill Penda is doing." Forthwith an adverse wind arose, which drove the flames from the city towards Penda's army. So sudden the wind and so violent the flames, that the men employed to fire the city had no time to escape, and they were all burnt to death. —Green, *Short History of the English People*, p. 23.

Salomê's head cut off by ice. Salomê, the daughter of Herodias, after pleasing Herod by her dancing, asked for reward the head of John the Baptist. The head was brought her in a dish, and she took it to her mother. Soon after this, Herod was dethroned, and Salomê, passing a river frozen over, fell through the ice up to her neck. Being unable to extricate herself, the ice gradually closed in, first throttling her, and ultimately parting her head from her body.—Nicephorus Cal'is-tus, *Ecclesiastical History*. (Metaphrastês tells the same story.)

St. Thyrsus subjected to the most horrible tortures (A.D. 250). [Of all the lives of saints none can exceed in marvels that of St. Thyrsus. I assure the reader that I have in no wise exaggerated the narrative; indeed, it would be difficult to do so. What is here transcribed is taken from *Les Petits Bollandistes*, vol. 2, pp. 90–92. The book bears the name of Mgr. Guérin, camérier de Sa Sainteté Leon XIII. It is most highly recommended by the chief dignitaries of the Catholic Church, and has the merit of being quite a modern book on the subject. The edition I quote from is the seventh, in seventeen massive volumes, A.D. 1880. It is needful to be thus precise, as the narrative subjoined is so startling it requires the sanction of pope and cardinals, archbishops and bishops, abbots and priors, "to make it credible."]

In the reign of the emperor Decius, one Leucius, who had committed the offence of being a Christian, was condemned to death. Thyrsus was one of the pagan officers employed to carry out the sentence; but, struck with the resignation and firmness of the martyr, he became a convert to the same faith, and dared boldly and publicly reproach the imperial proconsul for condemning Leucius to death; and now the words applied to Pharaoh (*Exod.* ix. 16) may be applied to the proconsul Combratius, "In very deed for this cause have I raised thee up, for to show in thee My power; and that My name may be declared throughout all the earth."

Irritated at this insolence, Combratius delivered Thyrsus to the executioner. In vain was he scourged with whips charged with lead. In vain was he hung by his thumbs to a tree with a fine cord. In vain were his arms broken and his eyelashes plucked out. Thyrsus, the new convert, remained unshaken, and, what is most marvellous, he seemed to acquire new force from his very torments.

Combratius would not be defied thus by one of his subordinate officers, and ordered the "rebel" to be stretched on an iron bed on his back, and lead, in a state of ebullition, to be poured down his throat; but the victim was invulnerable. The lead meant for Thyrsus rolled on his tormentors, and caused them excruciating agony. Mad with rage, the proconsul ordered the martyr to be cut to pieces; but the officer no sooner raised his sword to strike, than he was seized with vertigo, and the sword meant for Thyrsus stuck into the wall, where it remained fast; and at the same moment the place where the assembly was held shook so violently with earthquake, that the thongs with which Thyrsus was bound snapped asunder, and he was taken back to the public prison.

During the night an angel came to him, and having roused him from sleep, struck off his chains, and led him from his cell to the bishop Philias to be baptized. Having then administered to him the holy Eucharist, the angel conducted him back to prison, the gates and doors of which opened to them of their own accord.

In the morning the prisoner was again taken before the proconsul, who had summoned Silvanus to his assistance. They commanded the "traitor" to be taken to the temple of Apollo and made to offer sacrifice; but no sooner did he enter the temple, than the idol of the god fell to the ground and was smashed to pieces. This profanation was laid to the charge of Thyrsus, and the incorrigible Christian was ordered to be laden with the heaviest of chains; but no sooner did the chains touch him than they crumbled into dust. He was now scourged, and held head downwards in a butt full of wine; but the tub burst into a thousand pieces, and all the liquor was spilled. Not to be set at defiance, the two judges ordered their victim to be led to the brow of a steep cliff, and pushed down; but God gave His angels charge concerning him, and they bore him in their arms in safety; whereas Vitalicus, who pushed him from the rock, fell head foremost, and was dashed to pieces.

Combratius and Silvanus agreed that these things could not occur except by magic, and they ordered the supposed wizard to be laden with more chains of the strongest manufacture and greatest weight. But it was of no use; these chains fell to pieces and crumbled into dust. At the same moment the two judges were seized with a sudden fit, and taken to Apamea for medical aid; but nothing could be done. They both died, and their bodies were cast into a ditch. There they would have been left to the beasts and birds of prey, but Thyrsus prayed that they might be buried, and the earth of its own accord covered them.

It might be supposed that the vengeance of man was now exhausted; but Braudus, who succeeded Combratius, resolved to show that such conduct was not to be tolerated. Had not Thyrsus caused the death of Vitalicus, the proconsul Combratius, and his assistant Silvanus? Had he not caused the destruction of the god Apollo? Had he not by enchantment defied the strong arm of the law? Was he not a traitor to the emperor Decius, and must he not be made an example of? So thought Braudus, and accordingly commanded the rebel Christian to be sewn in a sack and cast into the deep sea. But God is God of the sea as well as of the land. Both land and sea obey Him. When thrown from the ship, angels caught him in their arms and brought him to land in safety. Here he was again seized by the new proconsul, and exposed in the amphitheatre to wild beasts; but the six bears and six leopards let out upon him walked gently towards him, licked his hands and his feet, fawned lovingly upon him, and crouched beside him as if they had been lambs.

Despairing of success by violence, the magistrate tried coaxing; and taking the martyr to the temple of Bacchus, entreated him to offer sacrifice. But the altar instantly fell down; the image of the god fell with it, and both were broken to pieces. The magistrates of Apamea, being thus foiled in every attempt, sent their prisoner to Apollonia, where he was whipped till the flesh fell from his bones. While this punishment was going on, Braudus was seized with racking pains, and the temples of the gods being shaken by earthquake, the idols were all broken. The inhabitants of Apollonia, panic-struck, confessed there were gods more mighty than their own; and the high priest, named Callinicus, renouncing paganism, reproved Braudus for his inhumanity. Nothing was able to shake the holy martyr, neither caresses, threats, nor tortures; so at last he was beheaded, with fifteen priests of Apollonia, who had been converted, like Callinicus, by his example, and resolved to imitate his unflinching firmness.—See *Roman Martyrology*, Jan. 28.

Rich Fool.

LUKE xii. 20, 21. Thou fool, this night thy soul shall be required of thee: then whose shall those things be which thou hast provided? So is he that layeth up treasure for himself, and is not rich toward God.

PSALM xlix. 16–19. Be not thou afraid when one is made rich, when the glory of his house is increased; for when he dieth he shall carry nothing away: his glory shall not descend after him. Though while he lived he blessed his soul, he shall go to the generation of his fathers, and shall never see light.

Bishop Hall's anecdote on his eightieth birthday. "There was a great lord who kept a fool in his house, as many great men did in those days, for their amusement and diversion. He presented his jester with a staff, and charged him to keep it till he met with a greater fool than himself. If such a one came across him, he was to deliver to him the bauble. Some few years afterwards his lord fell sick, and was indeed sick even unto death. His fool came to see him, and was told by the sick man that he must shortly leave him. 'And where are you going to?' asked the jester. 'Into another world, sirrah,' said the lord. 'And when will you come back again?' inquired the fool; 'within a week?' 'No,' said the lord. 'Within a month?' 'No.' 'Within a year?' 'No.' 'When, then?' asked the fool. 'Never,' said the lord. 'And what provision have you made for your well-being in the new world to which you are going?' 'None at all,' said the lord. 'What!' said the jester, 'none at all? Here, then, take my staff, for you are going away for ever, and hast laid up no store. Take my staff, I say. I may be a fool, but am not such a fool as that.'" (See "Golden Apple to the Greatest Fool," pt. ii., MAMMON OF UNRIGHTEOUSNESS.)

Rich Ruler.

LUKE xviii. 18-23. A certain ruler asked Christ, saying, Good Master, what shall I do to inherit eternal life? Jesus said unto him, Thou knowest the commandments? And the ruler said, All these things have I kept from my youth up. When Jesus heard this He said unto him, Yet lackest thou one thing: sell all that thou hast, and distribute to the poor, and thou shalt have treasure in heaven. When the ruler heard this, he was very sorrowful, for he was very rich.

The miser. (1) It is reported of a wretched rich man, when he heard that his sickness was fatal, that he sent for his money-bags, and hugging them in his arms, said, "Must I leave you? Oh, must I, must I leave you?" And so he died.

(2) Another on his death-bed called for his money-bags, and laid them next his heart. When any one attempted to remove them, he cried out, "It will not do! It will not do!"

(3) A third, being on the point of death, stole a guinea, and secreted it in his mouth, chuckling to himself, "I am wiser than some; I will take this with me; they will not see it; they will not take it from me." So saying, he swallowed the coin, it choked him, and he died.

Ruler of Capernaum.

JOHN iv. 46-53. A certain nobleman, whose son was sick at Capernaum, besought Jesus to come and heal his son, who was at the point of death. Jesus said to him, Go thy way; thy son liveth. As the father was returning home, his servants met him, and said to him, Thy son liveth. Then inquired he of them the hour when he began to amend. And they said, Yesterday at the seventh hour the fever left him. The father knew it was the very hour that Jesus had said to him, Thy son liveth: and himself believed, and his whole house.

St. Bernard says to a noble lady, "Go thy way; thy husband liveth." A great lady came to the monastery to see St. Bernard; and when St. Bernard had heard her request, she presented to him a large sum of money, and implored him to come to the house of her sick husband before he died. Bernard bade her go in peace, and added, "For thy husband liveth." And so she found it.—William (abbot of St. Theodore), *Life of St. Bernard.*

St. George says to a farmer, "Go thy way; thy ox liveth." While St. George was in prison, a farmer, named Glicerius, came to him, and told him his ox had just died. St. George, willing to help the poor in small troubles as well as in great, said to the farmer, "Go thy way; thy ox liveth." Glicerius returned home, and found it was so; and himself believed, with his whole house.—Pasicratês (an intimate friend, and witness of the miracles), *Life of St. George of Cappadocia.*

Sabbatic Rest.

EXOD. xx. 10, 11. The seventh day is the sabbath of the Lord thy God: in it thou shalt do no work; for in six days the Lord made heaven and earth, and rested the seventh day. Wherefore the Lord blessed the sabbath day, and hallowed it.

NUMB. xv. 32-36. While the children of Israel were in the wilderness, they found a man that gathered sticks upon the sabbath day. And the Lord said unto Moses, The man shall be surely put to death. And all the congregation stoned him with stones, and he died.

The sabbath-breakers in the diocese of Evreux (A.D. 738). One Sunday, as Leufredus went to celebrate mass, he saw some peasants tilling their fields, without any respect to the Lord's day of rest. "O wretched sinners!" cried the saint; "how can ye be guilty of so great a crime?" Then, lifting his eyes to heaven, he said, "May this land be evermore sterile, and never again bear fruit from this day forth for ever." As the fig tree, cursed by Jesus, withered away, so the produce of these lands withered from that hour, and ever since then these fields have borne only thorns and thistles, "et on n'a pu même y faire croître des noyers ni d'autres arbres."—Mgr. Guérin (chamberlain of pope Leo XIII., 1880), *Vies des Saints*, vol. vii. p. 189.

This assertion is capable of proof. Is any part of the diocese of Evreux hopelessly barren? What I remember of Evreux are its botanical gardens, its vineyards, and its very pretty garden-plots. I always thought the valley of the Iton was fertile and pleasant; but, of course, Mgr. Guérin, being a Frenchman and the pope's chamberlain, does not write thus positively without good authority.

A miller paralyzed for grinding on a Sunday (A.D. 645). When St. Ouen was returning from Spain, and had reached Anjou, he saw a miller, who was paralyzed in one hand for working his mill on a Sunday. St. Ouen remonstrated with the man on the sanctity of the Lord's day, and as he appeared penitent for his sin, the saint made the sign of the cross, and healed him.—L'abbé Pécheur, *Annales du Diocèse de Soissons.*

(See MIRACLES OF SPECIAL SAINTS, p. 234; a priest paralyzed for doing some secular work on a Sunday healed by St. Germanus.)

The sabbatic river. The Jewish rabbis tell us of a sabbatic river in Palestine, which ceases to flow on the Jewish sabbath. Pliny refers to this river, but says the very contrary, viz. that it flows on the sabbath only, and ceases to flow the other six days.* Josephus says, "Titus, passing between Arca and Raphăna, in the kingdom of Agrippa, came upon a river which flowed for six days in great abundance and a rapid course, but ceased to flow every seventh day. This it did incessantly, without ever deviating from the established order, and hence it was called the Sabbatic River." Calmet wants to make out that Josephus means the same as Pliny—that the river flows only on the sabbath, and ceases to flow the other six days. He translates thus: "Once in seven days it flows with a full stream into the sea, and hence is called the Sabbatic River." Mons. Arnaud d'Andilli translates the passage: "Après avoir coulé six jours en grande abondance, elle sèche tout d'un coup, et recommence le lendemain à couler durant six autres jours comme auparavant, et à se sécher le 7e jour, sans jamais changer cet ordre."

Samson and the Jawbone.

[It is with the utmost deference that I venture to suggest the following reading, which at any rate has the merit of grandeur, and is not without historic parallels. The reader must bear in mind the following Hebrew words and their meanings:—CHAMOR, an ass; LEHI, a jawbone.]

JUDG. xv. 3–19. While Israel was in bondage to the Philistines, Samson set fire to their cornfields, and provoked them to war. So they pitched in Judah, and spread themselves in LEHI. The men of Judah, to prevent war, bound Samson, and brought him from the rock Etam. When he came to LEHI, he broke the cords that bound him, and finding a *moist* "jawbone" of CHAMOR, he took it, and slew a thousand men therewith, and said, With the "jawbone" of CHAMOR have I slain a thousand. And it came to pass, when he felt thirsty, that God clave a hollow place in LEHI, and there came water thereout; and when Samson had drunk, he revived. The well thus made is in LEHI to this day.

All that is required is not to translate Chamor and Lehi, but to retain the words as proper names, and the following paraphrase will not be far-fetched:—

The men of Judah bound Samson, and brought him to LEHI, the summit of the hill called CHAMOR (the ass). Some thousands of the Philistines began to climb the hill with intent to take him captive; but Samson, seeing a great boulder *moist*, with his enormous and miraculous strength, straining every nerve, loosened the boulder, upheaved it from its bed, and rolled it on the ascending foe. Down it bounded, crushing the Philistines, who fell backwards, "heaps upon heaps, heaps upon heaps," till the hill CHAMOR was cleared of them, and Samson cried exultingly, "With the boulder of LEHI of CHAMOR have I heaped heaps upon heaps. With the boulder of LEHI of CHAMOR I have slain a thousand." Being thirsty with his Titanic effort, he sought for water, and going to the hollow whence he had torn up the boulder, he found water [it was *moist before*], and quenched his thirst. He called the hollow RAMATH-LEHI (the place of the lifted-out jawbone or boulder), but it was subsequently called En-hakkore (the well of him that cried for water), and the well remains to the present day.

The battle of Morgarten (A.D. 1315). Leopold, duke of Austria, being resolved to avenge upon the Swiss the insult offered by Tell in slaying Gessler, the governor set over them, entered the Forest Cantons at the head of fifteen thousand men. The Swiss could only muster some thirteen hundred to oppose this army; but, nothing daunted, they took up their position on the mountain slopes of Morgarten. At daybreak the Austrians, gleaming in purple and gold, began to climb the hill, in order to dislodge the mountaineers; when fifty of the Swiss rolled down upon them huge boulders and fragments of rock. The horses were terrified, the foremost men were crushed to death, and falling on those behind, heaps upon heaps were heaped in slaughter. Confusion followed surprise, and before order could be restored, the Swiss poured down upon them like an avalanche. Counts, knights, nobles of all ranks, and the rank and file, the pride of Austrian manhood, fell in one common ruin. In one half-hour the thirteen thousand Austrians had been slain by a few hundred Swiss peasants.—*History of Germany, Political, Social, and Literary,* p. 120.

Manlius saves the Roman Capitol (B.C. 361). The brennus of Gaul having laid siege to Rome, wished, if possible, to

* "In Judæa rivus omnibus septem diebus siccatur."

raise the siege with credit. At this crisis of affairs some of his soldiers informed him they had discovered footsteps which led to the rock, and they believed that these footsteps would guide them to the way of surprising the fort. Accordingly, a chosen body of men were told off for this dangerous night-attack. The Gauls, in single file, tracked the footsteps; the foremost actually reached the walls, and the watch-dogs gave no notice, but some sacred geese, hearing the footfalls, began to cackle, and alarmed the guard. Marcius Manlius was instantly on the alert, and, rushing to the rampart, thrust headlong two Gauls down the precipice, and these men, in their fall, bore down others to the bottom of the steep, so that the danger was averted, and the brennus was glad to arrange with the Romans terms of peace.—*Guide to Roman History*.

Saul's Conversion.

ACTS ix. 1–22. Saul, breathing out threatenings and slaughter against the disciples of the Lord, went to the high priest, and desired of him letters to Damascus, that if he found any of Christ's disciples there, he might bring them bound to Jerusalem. As he journeyed, and came near the city, suddenly there shone round about him a light from heaven; and he fell to the earth. A voice then addressed him, saying, Saul, Saul, why persecutest thou Me? And Saul said, Who art Thou, Lord? And the voice made answer, I am Jesus, whom thou persecutest. It is hard for thee to kick against the goad. Saul, trembling and astonished, then demanded what he should do, and was told to go into the city [Damascus] and there wait. In the mean time, Ananias was told to go to Saul. So he went, laid his hands upon his eyes, which had lost their sight in the vision for three days, and their sight returned. He was then baptized, and became the most active of all the apostles.

Conversion of colonel Gardiner (July, 1719). Colonel Gardiner had been spending the day with some roistering companions, and had made an assignation with a married woman. The company broke up at eleven o'clock; and, having some half an hour to spare, the colonel took up a book called *The Christian Soldier*, to while away the time. Suddenly he thought he saw a strong light fall on the book, and, lifting up his eyes, he beheld before him the Lord Jesus, and a voice said to him, "Sinner, did I suffer the shame and agony on the cross for thee? and is this thy gratitude?" Amazed, the colonel sank from his chair to the ground, insensible. When he came to himself, he abandoned his assignation, suffered great agony of mind, and became a new man, leading ever after a life consistent with a Christian soldier.—Doddridge (1747), *Life of Colonel Gardiner*.

This conversion is very graphically sketched by sir Walter Scott in *Waverley*. Dr. Hibbert, in his work *On Apparitions*, attributes the vision to concussion on the brain from a recent fall from his horse.

St. Hubert and the stag (A.D. 727). Hubert was the son of a nobleman of Aquitaine, and on one great Church festival, when all the faithful were gone to church, he went with his pack to hunt in the forest of Ardennes. Jesus Christ took this opportunity for his conversion. During the hunt a stag of great beauty showed herself to him, and as he looked at it, he was astonished to see a crucifix between the antlers. Presently a voice proceeded from the spot, saying, "Hubert, Hubert, how long will you spend your time chasing beasts in this forest, and neglecting the things which pertain unto your soul? Do you suppose that God sent you into the world to hunt wild beasts, and not rather to know and honour thy Creator?" Hubert was stupefied on hearing these words, dismounted from his horse, prostrated himself on the ground, worshipped the cross which the stag bore, and vowed henceforth to abandon the world, and give himself to God. Forthwith he went to St. Lambert, bishop of Maëstricht, who received him kindly, and from this point his remarkable life as a Christian saint begins.—L'abbé Bertrand, *Pèlerinage de St. Hubert en Ardennes*. (See PLACIDUS, next page.)

Sudden conversion of St. Norbert, archbishop of Magdeburg (A.D. 1080–1134). Norbert, son of the count of Genep, spent his youth like most other young German gentlemen of wealth, making the most of the pleasures and vanities of life, but at the age of thirty-three a change came over him like that which came over Saul of Tarsus in his journey to Damascus. Norbert was riding with his groom to Freten, in Westphalia, when all of a sudden the sky became overclouded, and a terrible tempest broke over them. The groom, greatly alarmed, entreated his master to return, as the hand of God was against him. At the same moment a voice in mid-air cried aloud, "Norbert, Norbert, why persecutest thou Me? I destined you to be a shining pillar in my Church, but your life is a scandal to the faithful." As these words were spoken, a thunderbolt fell at his feet, and made a great hole in the ground. Norbert was speechless for an hour; then, coming somewhat to himself, he said, sighing, "Alas! Lord, what wouldst Thou have me to do?" The voice replied, "Cease to do evil, learn to do well. Seek peace, and ensue it." Norbert resolved to quit the court, and returned home. Conon, abbot of Seigburg, came to him, taught him the rudiments of a religious life, and he became a shining pillar in the tabernacle of the Lord.—John Chrysostom Vande-Sterre, *Life of St. Norbert.* (There is a life in verse of this saint.)

Conversion of Placidus. Placidus, field-marshal of the emperor Trajan, was one day following a stag which had separated itself from the herd, and run into a thicket. Placidus followed, and as he drew near, saw a cross upon its brow, which seemed to shine like fire. While he gazed in astonishment, a voice seemed to proceed from the cross, and said to him, "Placidus, why persecutest thou Me?" Placidus, filled with terror, alighted from his horse at these mysterious words, and, kneeling on the ground, said, "Who art Thou, Lord?" The voice replied, "I am Jesus, whom thou persecutest. Jesus the Son of God, crucified for the salvation of man, but now exalted to the right hand of the Majesty on high." Placidus said, "Lord, I believe. What wilt Thou have me to do?" And the voice answered, "Be baptized straightway, thou, thy wife, and all thy house, and take up thy cross patiently, and thou shalt receive a crown of glory." So saying, the hart ran swiftly away, and departed out of sight. Placidus wondered greatly; but God had converted him. His wife also had seen a vision, and she with her two sons were baptized with Placidus by the bishop of Rome, who changed the name Placidus into Eustacius.—Antoninus (bishop of Florence), *Chronicon.* (See also *Gesta Romanorum,* cx.) This is very similar to the story of Hubert (see preceding page).

The stag, in Christian art, is a symbol of Jesus Christ, from the notion that it draws serpents by its breath out of their holes, and then tramples them to death. Pliny mentions this superstition in his *Natural History,* bk. viii. 50.

Conversion of St. Procopius of Jerusalem (A.D. 303). The emperor Diocletian gave Procopius two companies of soldiers to extirpate the Christians of Antioch. With these bands he departed for Antioch, and took his route through Alexandria. As he drew near the city, and was marching by night on account of the great heat, he felt suddenly the earth shake under him, and amidst thunder and lightning a voice said to him, "Neanius, whither goest thou, and against whom art thou marching with such fury?" "I am going on a commission of the emperor to hale to death the Galileans," said Procopius, "unless they consent to renounce Jesus Christ." "Then it is against Me," said the voice, "thou art going to make war." "And who, I pray, are You?" said Procopius; "I have not the honour of knowing You." At this moment a cross like crystal appeared to the captain, and the voice from the midst of the cross replied, "I am Jesus Christ, the Son of the living God, who was crucified." Procopius was astounded, but still had the hardihood to say, "I have heard from the emperor that the God of Christians never had a wife; how then can You be His Son? And if You are really so mighty and so noble, how is it You were condemned, scourged, crowned with thorns, and crucified?" Christ instantly inspired the infidel with the mysteries of His generation, incarnation, and death to take way the sins of the world. He changed his heart, and made him a true Christian. The same night the new convert went to Scythopolis, and, entering a jeweller's shop, ordered him to make for him a cross of gold and silver, according to the drawing which he left. The goldsmith refused at first, because crosses were the symbol of the Christian sect, and the emperor had strictly forbidden it; but on receiving the captain's word of honour that he would never betray him, he consented to execute the order; whereupon "par un grand miracle, l'image de Notre Seigneur se trouva gravée en haut, avec le mot *Emmanuel,* et aux deux côtés, les images de St. Michel et de St. Gabriel, avec leurs noms."—Mgr. Guérin (chamberlain of pope Leo XIII.), *Vies des Saints* (7th edit. 1880), vol. viii. p. 165.

This exaggerated parody of Saul's conversion is given by Mgr. Guérin as a fact, and appears in the *Acta Sanctorum* of the Bollandists. It is quite impossible to read it and not pity the bad taste of the writer who concocted the story, for notwithstanding the high and mighty names which vouch for it, no one can possibly believe it to be a fact. Alban Butler, with his usual want of fidelity, suppresses it, forgetting that his duty was to give the lives of the saints as he found them in books sanctioned by the pope and cardinals, and not to trim these biographies according to his own judgment, and pander to Protestant "prejudices."

St. Audaldus arrested from relapsing into the world by meteoric marvels (A.D. 423). St. Audaldus lived as a solitary in the Pyrenees; but, being weary of a hermit's life, he resolved to abandon it, and return to the world. Going to bid his adieux to St. Pancras, while his hand was on the cell door, he heard the old man praying for him, that his faith might not fail him, and that he might have grace to finish his course with joy. Just at the same moment a brilliant light, like a star, settled on the head of St. Pancras, and a peal of thunder burst over him. Greatly terrified, the illusions of the young man were scattered to the winds, and, casting himself on the ground, he implored the pardon of God for the thoughts of his heart; retired further into the desert, and disciplined himself with greater rigour.—L'abbé Authier, *Études Historiques et Religieuses sur le Pays de la Haute Vallée de l'Ariège* (1870).

The conversion of St. Francis d'Assisi (1182–1226). Francis d'Assisi, son of Pietro Bernadone, the rich merchant, was a gay worldling, who spent profusely, dressed fashionably, and fared sumptuously every day. He was fond of fun, lived in gay society, and was altogether a "rich man about town." When Walter de Brienne laid claim to the kingdom of Sicily, Francis d'Assisi took up arms, and with horse and suit of mail joined the war party. At Spoleto he had a fever, and while struck down with fever heard a voice which bade him go home. This did he, but only to return to his previous way of living. One day after a revel, while standing with his boon companions, he suddenly stood stock still, with his face turned to the sky, and his companions jestingly asked him if he was looking for a bride among the stars. "Yes," he said, "I am looking for a bride, but a bride past your imaginations even to conceive." And from this moment his whole course of life was changed. His father was extremely displeased, and Francis took refuge with a poor priest. Thither his father followed him, and Francis, pulling off the clothes he had on, threw them down at his father's feet, saying, "Thus I restore to Pietro Bernadone all that belongs to him. Up to this day I have called him father; henceforth I have only one father, God the Father Almighty." The bishop, who was present, threw his mantle over the young man, who was taken into the kitchen of the monastery, where he remained a short time, and then began a wandering life, barefooted, without staff or scrip, with a cord fastened round his waist. His preaching soon gathered round him a knot of followers, and his first abiding-place was the little church at the Portiuncula. Such was the early career, the conversion, and the first start in religious life of St. Francis d'Assisi, founder of the Franciscan Order, sometimes called Minorites or Gray Friars, and one of the most remarkable men that ever lived.—Mrs. Oliphant, *Life of St. Francis.*

Saul's Jealousy.

1 Sam. xviii. 6. After David had slain Goliath, and the army of the Philistines was routed, women came out of all cities of Israel, and cried, Saul hath slain his thousands, but David his ten thousands! Saul was very wroth, and the saying greatly displeased him. They have ascribed to David ten thousands, said he, and to me only thousands. And Saul was jealous of David.

Kaiser Leopold's jealousy of Sobieski. When the Turks laid siege to Vienna, and Sobieski overthrew them utterly, the Pole, writing to his mother, says, "Wherever I went the people shouted, 'Sobieski!' Mothers and children ran to touch me; old men covered my hands with kisses; and those who could not get through the crowd, waved their hats or handkerchiefs, shouting with one voice, 'God save thee, Sobieski! Welcome, Sobieski!'" But kaiser Leopold, who had taken no part in this great victory, greeted the conqueror with chilling politeness. He had deserted Vienna in the hour of danger, and felt humiliated that a minor king, Sobieski of Poland, should be more honoured than the kaiser of the Roman empire.—*History of Germany, Political, Social, and Literary.*

Sea obeys the Saints.

Matt. viii. 26, 27. Then Jesus arose and rebuked the wind and the sea, and there was a great calm; but the men marvelled, saying, What manner of man is this, that even the sea obeys Him?

Psalm lxxxix. 9. Thou rulest the raging of the sea: when the waves thereof arise, Thou stillest them.

Psalm cvii. 9. He maketh the storm a calm, so that the waves thereof are still.

Neptune stills a stormy sea. It is somewhat beyond the immediate scope of this book to refer to classic authors, but every one who has read Virgil must call to mind the beautiful incident of Neptune stilling the stormy waves, which had been lashed into fury by contrary winds:—

Interea magno misceri murmure pontum
Emissamque hyemem sensit Neptunus, et imis
Stagna refusa vadis. Graviter commotus, et alto
Prospiciens, summa placidum caput extulit unda.
Disjectam Æneæ toto videt æquore classem,
Fluctibus oppressos Troas, cœlique ruina.
Eurum ad se zephyrumque vocat. Dehinc talia fatur:
"Tantane vos generis tenuit fiducia vestri?
"Jam cœlum terramque, meo sine numine, Venti,
"Miscere, et tantus audetis tollere moles?
"Quos ego—— Sed motos præstat componere fluctus.
"Maturate fugam . . ."
Sic ait, et dicto citius tumida æquora placat,
Collectasque fugat nubes, Solemque reducit, etc.
Æn. i. 124, etc.

This, of course, is poetry, but may not a highly poetical imagination or diction help to account for some of the marvellous stories referred to in this section? No stories but those of the Bible demand implicit belief, and whatever helps to explain the rest is so much gain.

St. Castor saves from wreck a barge laden with salt (A.D. 389). A barge laden with salt, passing down the Moselle, came close to Cardon, where St. Castor dwelt. Castor asked the bargemen to give him a little salt, but they refused, whereupon a high wind suddenly sprang up, and every one expected the barge would be capsized. The bargemen implored Castor to help them, and the priest, making the sign of the cross, stilled the wind, and saved both the cargo and the crew.—*Les Petits Bollandistes*, vol. ii. p. 503.

When St. Clement, pope and martyr, was carried out to sea for three miles, and thrown overboard, the sea retired three miles for seven days (A.D. 102). Aufidianus, in the reign of Trajan, banished St. Clement, the pope, to the Chersonese, and afterwards commanded him to be taken out to sea for three miles and drowned. The Christians on the Chersonese prayed that God would show them the body of the saint; so the sea went back for three miles, and left the passage dry and firm. When the Christians went over this passage, they saw that a chapel had been raised, and in the chapel was found the body of the saint, with an anchor about his neck. The sea continued in this state for seven days, and then returned to its strength. What adds greatly to the marvel is this, that the phenomenon was repeated annually, at the same period, and showed the chapel with the body of the saint. Simeon Metaphrastês (who died seven hundred years afterwards) assures us that this miracle was seen annually even in his days.

No miracle is better attested than this most astounding one. Besides Metaphrastês, it is seriously given by Ephrem bishop of the Chersonese, the Venerable Bede, Gregory of Tours, Ado archbishop of Trèves, and Nicephorus Callistus in his *Church History*. But the wonder does not end here, for we are furthermore assured by Ephrem bishop of the Chersonese, and Gregory of Tours, that—

A woman, going with an infant in arms a pilgrimage to this chapel in the deep sea, placed her child beside the body of the dead saint. It so happened that this was the last of the seven days, and the sea coming in fast, the woman ran for her life, leaving her infant child behind. She was very sorry to abandon her child thus, and next year, when the sea retired as usual, she paid another visit to the chapel, and found her son quietly sleeping where she left him. She caught him up frantically, and asked him what had become of him all the past year, while the deep sea waves were rolling over his head. The child replied he could not tell, for he had only that minute woke up from sleep.

(St. Clement was drowned Nov. 23, A.D. 102. It is well these "facts" have been attested by eye-witnesses, by archbishops and bishops, confessors and historians, otherwise many of this incredulous age might halt to believe them.)

St. Gregory Nazianzen, being in danger of shipwreck, makes a vow. While St. Gregory Nazianzen was sailing to Athens, a great storm arose, and the ship was on the point of being wrecked; but Gregory made earnest prayer to God, and vowed, if the ship got safe to land, he would spend his whole life in His service. Forthwith "there came a fair season," and all the passengers confessed that the God whom Gregory had invoked had delivered them, and was far more powerful than the gods of Olympus.—Edward Kinesman (1623), *Lives of the Saints*, p. 312.

St. Hilarion commands the sea and it obeys him. While St. Hilarion was at Ragusium, the sea on one occasion swelled and rose out of all measure, insomuch that the people feared it would overwhelm the whole country. St. Hilarion, having made a cross in the sand, held up his hands, and immediately the swell ceased and the sea went back, to the utter amazement of the whole country. Fathers still tell their children how the winds and the waves were obedient to St. Hilarion.—St. Jerome (A.D. 390), *Vita St. Hilarionis Eremitæ*. (See also Nicephorus Callistus (died 1350), *Ecclesiastical History*.)

St. Hyacintha Mariscott calms a troubled sea (A.D. 1640). Some Italians, being overtaken by a great storm, invoked the aid of St. Hyacintha, saying, "Oh, Sister Hyacintha, help us or we perish!" Instantly one of the nuns of St. Clara, dressed in spotless white, stilled the waves, and guided the vessel safe to shore. The men went in a body to the convent to return thanks. The abbess sent for Hyacintha, but was informed that the sister, who had saved the crew, was not to be found. "Elle s'enfuit, comme un coupable poursuivi par la justice, et s'en alla rouge de honte se cacher dans sa cellule."—*Palmier Séraphique* (12 vols., 8vo).

St. Nicholas, bishop of Myra, commands the sea and it obeys him. St. Nicholas (afterwards bishop of Myra) embarked for the Holy Land, intending to visit the holy places. The sky was beautifully clear, and the sea as calm as possible; but St. Nicholas told the sailors to prepare for a great storm, as he had seen the devil, sword in hand, enter the ship. Soon after this warning the storm broke, and the crew implored Nicholas to save the ship from wreck. St. Nicholas prayed, the winds fell, the sea lulled, and there was a great calm. On the home voyage, the mariners wanted to drive the ship into Alexandria; but immediately St. Nicholas discovered this treachery he prayed, and, the wind shifting, the ship ran to Lycia, to which port St. Nicholas was bound, and where the master of the vessel had agreed to land him.—Edward Kinesman (1623), *Lives of the Saints.* (He tells us he has abridged the life of St. Nicholas from the lives given by John the Deacon and Leonard Justinian.)

St. Joseph Oriol stills a storm at sea by the sign of the cross (A.D. 1650–1702). The ship in which Joseph Oriol embarked at Marseilles for Barcelona was caught in a violent storm. The saint made on the sea the sign of the cross, and immediately the winds dropped, the waves abated, and there was a calm. (See PRAYER, pt. ii.) —*Les Petits Bollandistes*, vol. iii. p. 615.

Seven Candlesticks (The).

REV. i. 10–20. I was in the Spirit on the Lord's day . . . and I turned to see the voice [*sic*] that spoke to me. And being turned, I saw seven golden candlesticks; and in the midst of the seven golden candlesticks one like unto the Son of man. . . . The mystery of the seven stars which thou sawest in My right hand, and the seven candlesticks [is this]: The seven stars are the angels of the seven Churches [of Asia]; and the seven candlesticks are the seven Churches.

St. Francisca has a vision of seven candlesticks (A.D. 1384–1440). St. Francisca had ninety-three visions in twelve years. In the fifty-third vision she nursed Jesus, in the form of a little lamb, on her lap. Close by she saw an altar magnificently decorated, and on the altar was a lamb bearing the stigmata of the five wounds. At the foot of the altar were a number of golden candlesticks arranged in four tiers. That farthest off contained seven, symbolical of the seven cardinal virtues. The next tier contained twelve candlesticks, significant of the twelve articles of the symbol. The third range had seven, emblematic of the seven gifts of the Holy Ghost. And the fourth or nearest tier had seven candlesticks also, representing the seven sacraments of the Christian Church. (See SYMBOLS.) —John Mattistti, *Life of St. Francisca.*

Shadrach, Meshach, and Abednego. (See CAULDRON INNOCUOUS, p. 56; FIRE INNOCUOUS, p. 136; and RETRIBUTIVE PUNISHMENT, p. 275.)

DAN. iii. 22–27. When Shadrach, Meshach, and Abednego were cast by king Darius into the fiery furnace, the flame of the fire injured them not. The fire had no power upon their bodies, nor was a hair of their head singed, neither were their coats changed, nor had the smell of fire passed on them.

St. Alexander, Eventius, and Theodulus, being cast bound into a furnace, receive no hurt. Aurelian, one of the magistrates of Adrian, commanded Alexander and Eventius to be bound together, and cast into a great furnace, for being Christians. Pope Alexander was only thirty years old at the time, but Eventius was above eighty. They fell down bound into the midst of the flames, but felt no hurt. Theodulus stood by, and Alexander cried to him aloud, "Come, brother, come to us; the angel that walked with the three Hebrews is with us, and has kept a place for you." On hearing these words, Theodulus broke from his guards and ran into the furnace, where all three stood on their feet, singing praises unto God. Aurelian was mad with rage, and commanded Eventius and Theodulus to be beheaded, but pope Alexander he slew "with the pricks of needles."—The Roman Notaries, *Life of Pope Alexander*, May 3.

The blood of St. Blaise a talisman against fire. After St. Blaise had been carded with iron combs by order of Agricoläus, as he was led back to prison, his blood sprinkled the ground over which he walked. Seven Christian women gathered up his blood in napkins, and anointed their eyes therewith. Agricoläus, hearing thereof, commanded the women to be burnt to death. Accordingly, they were first beaten with clubs and then cast into a furnace; but the fire did them no harm, nay, it was even quenched by the blood which fell from their wounds. Agricoläus, beside himself with rage, then ordered them to be beheaded.—Metaphrastês, *Lives*, etc.

St. Faustinus and St. Jovita, being cast into a furnace, were uninjured. Claudius II. caused a great furnace to be heated exceedingly hot, and had St. Faustinus and St. Jovita cast into the midst thereof. But the fire did them no harm, and they sang hymns to God in the midst of the furnace. When the emperor saw that the fire did his victims no harm, he cried out in a great rage that the men were magicians, and must be put to death; so they were both beheaded.—Surius (died 1570), *Lives of the Saints*.

A young Jewish lad, after partaking of the Eucharist, was unharmed by a fiery furnace. Menas, bishop of Constantinople, in order to demonstrate the sacred character of the Eucharist, mentions the following "fact" from personal knowledge. A young Jew, the son of a glass-founder, seeing some of his schoolfellows going to church to take the sacrament, according to Greek custom, went with them and received the host. Being late at school, his father asked the cause, and the child innocently told him. The father, mad with rage, thrust the boy into his glass furnace, where he was shut up for three days. In the mean time his mother searched everywhere for the lad, filling the house with her cries. The boy, hearing them, answered from the furnace, and the mother, entering, rescued him. The boy told her that a beautiful lady, clothed in purple, had come to him in the furnace, quenched the flames, and fed him with delicious food. This prodigy was known to all the city of Constantinople. The mother and boy both embraced the Christian faith; but the father, who remained obstinate, was crucified by the order of Justinian the emperor.—Evagrius, *Church History*.

St. Mamas unharmed in the fiery furnace (A.D. 375). St. Mamas is ranked by the Greeks among their great martyrs. His death is placed under the emperor Aurelian and his minister Alexander, governor of Cappadocia. As Mamas refused to sacrifice to Apollo, Alexander ordered him to be thrown into a fiery furnace. Mamas made the sign of the cross, and abode in the furnace three days, not only without injury, but when, at the end of this period, he walked forth, he was more comely and lively than before. The president declared him to be a magician, and commanded him to be cast to the wild beasts. A bear and a leopard were let out against him. The bear laid itself down at his feet, and the leopard, putting its fore paws on his two shoulders, licked his face lovingly. He was now sent back to prison till a lion of unusual size and fierceness could be procured from the forests. The news of this capture brought to the amphitheatre an immense crowd of spectators. The famished lion was let loose, burst from the arena to the spectators; a panic spread on all sides, hundreds were trampled to death, some were torn to pieces by the lion. Men, women, children, tried to escape. The doors of the amphitheatre were shut, "et gardées par l'ange du Seigneur." Blood flowed on all sides. The arena was a pool of blood. Suddenly the lion stood still, "il salue le saint avec admiration et respect." Mamas told the beast to do no more mischief. It instantly obeyed, returned to its mountain lair, and was no more seen.—L'abbé Tincelin, *Vie de St. Mammès* (or Mamas).

St. Placidus uninjured in the brazen bull. St. Placidus having gained a great victory, the emperor Trajan appointed a day of thanksgiving, in which sacrifice was to be offered to the gods. Placidus, who was a Christian, said he could take no part in such a ceremony; whereupon Trajan commanded that he and all his family should be shut up in the brazen bull and baked alive. Three days were they in the furnace, but not a hair of their heads was injured, nor had the smell of fire come on their clothes.—*Gesta Romanorum*, cx.

St. Vitus uninjured in the midst of a fiery furnace. St. Vitus being in prison, a great light shone, and a voice bade him be of good cheer, as God was with him. The keepers told Diocletian, and the emperor sent for the young man. After the interview, Diocletian caused a great fire to be made in a furnace, filled with rosin, pitch, and lead; and when the ingredients were seething, Vitus was cast into the midst. "We shall see now," said Diocletian, "whether your boasted God can deliver you." St. Vitus, as he was let down into the furnace, made the sign of the cross, and an angel descended to drive back the seething mass, so that St. Vitus received no hurt. There stood the martyr in the midst of the furnace in the sight of the whole multitude. His face was cheerful, and he was singing praises to his God. At length he came forth as silver purified in the fire, not only uninjured, but ten times more beautiful than he was before.—Edward Kinesman (1623), *Lives of the Saints*, p. 383.

Dr. C. Wordsworth, bishop of Lincoln, on *Dan.* iii. 6, says: "When the kingdom passed into the hands of Persians, another mode of punishment [not the furnace] succeeded;" this, he says, is "evidence of the genuineness of the book." To this I cannot agree. Any one well-read in Persian history can cite many more examples of "casting men into a furnace," than of "casting them to lions," which was more a Roman than a Persian custom. It is bad form to press into Christian evidence anything which history will not corroborate.

Shibboleth.

JUDG. xii. 1–6. After Jephthah had defeated the Ammonites, the men of Ephraim, out of jealousy, complained that they had not been called to share in the enterprise. Jephthah answered with moderation; but the Ephraimites taunted the victorious men of Gilead so insultingly, that a war ensued between the men of Gilead and the men of Ephraim. The latter were discomfited, and guards were set at all the passes of Jordan to intercept their flight. If any man came to one of these passes, he was requested to pronounce the password "Shibboleth." If he pronounced it *Shibboleth*, he was allowed to go his way, but if *Sibboleth*, he was an Ephraimite, and was put to the sword. By this test 42,000 were put to death.

(In *Numb.* i. 33, the entire number of the tribe, when that census was taken, was only 40,500.)

The Danish Shibboleth on St. Bryce's Day (Nov. 13, A.D. 1002). In the great slaughter of the Danes on St. Bryce's Day, 1002, the test words were "Chichester Church." Those who pronounced the words in the ordinary way were allowed to pass; but the Danes betrayed themselves by pronouncing the words *Shish-shes-ter Sherch*, and were mercilessly put to death.

The French Shibboleth in the Sicilian Vespers. In the Sicilian Vespers, some dried peas (*ciceri*) were shown to fugitives. He who called them *che-cha-re* was allowed to go his way, for he was a Sicilian; but he who called them *sis-sa-re* was cut down, for he was an undoubted Frenchman.

Ship miraculously brought to Land.

JOHN vi. 18–21. The sea arose by reason of a great wind that blew. So when they had rowed about five and twenty or thirty furlongs, they see Jesus walking on the sea, and drawing nigh unto the ship; and they were afraid. But Jesus said unto them, It is I; be not afraid. Then they willingly received Him into the ship, and immediately the ship was at the land whither they were bound.

The ship in which St. Peter Thomas sailed transported by the Virgin from a stormy sea to a quiet lake (A.D. 1366). One day the ship in which St. Peter Thomas was sailing was caught in a sudden squall, and all thought it must go to the bottom; but the saint prayed to the Virgin, and instantly the ship was transported into a neighbouring lake, where it remained in perfect safety till the tempest had blown over.—*Les Petits Bollandistes*, vol. i. p. 168.

(We are told that on another occasion some Turkish pirates were bearing down upon this ship, when suddenly a thick cloud intervened, and hid the vessel from the pirates. See also PRAYER, pt. ii.)

Show me Thy Glory

EXOD. xxxiii. 18–20. And Moses said, I beseech Thee, show me Thy glory. And God said, I will make all My goodness pass before thee; but thou canst not see My face, for no man shall see Me, and live.

The woman who nursed St. Clara said to her, "Show me the queen of heaven." When St. Clara was dying, the woman who waited on her implored to be shown the queen of angels and mother of God. The dying saint replied, "If it pleases the lady mother to show herself, I shall rejoice with exceeding great joy." At these words a number of virgins, arrayed in white, with crowns on their heads, entered the chamber, and with them the queen herself, from whose face proceeded such ineffable splendour, that daylight was eclipsed by it. The holy mother bowed courteously to St. Clara, and bade the virgins of her suite give her the rich mantle brought from paradise. St. Clara well knew that her hour was come; and, as she breathed out her soul, the virgin train carried it with them into paradise. —*Life of St. Clara* (written at the express command of pope Alexander V.).

Jamblichus showed spirits to his disciples (fourth century). Jamblichus, the Neoplatonist, while he was at Gadara, drew from two fountains the guardian spirits, and showed them to his disciples.—Eunapius, *Jamblichus* (fourth century).

Simeon and the Child Jesus.

LUKE ii. 25–35. When Mary kept her purification, an old man, named Simeon, came by the Spirit into the temple at the same time, and taking the infant Jesus in his arms, blessed God, and said, Lord, now lettest Thou Thy servant depart in peace, for mine eyes have seen Thy salvation. He then prophesied that the Child would grow up to be "a light to lighten the Gentiles, and the glory of Thy people Israel;" but he told Mary that the Child would be "for a sign which shall be spoken against."

When St. Dunstan's parents offered presents in Glastonbury church for the birth of their boy, an angel took the child, and prophesied that he would be a light in the world. When Dunstan was able to walk alone, his parents took him to Glastonbury church to offer presents for his birth. They passed the whole night in prayer; and an angel, taking the boy's hand, led him through the church, and said to the parents, "This child will grow up to lead many into the way everlasting, and will become a great saint; but he will also be a sign which shall be spoken against."—Osbert of Canterbury, *Life of St. Dunstan.*

Sodom and the Dead Sea.

GEN. xix. 24, 25. Sodom, Gomorrha, Zeboim, and Admah were destroyed by fire from heaven, on account of their great wickedness. Afterwards, the waters of the Jordan overflowed the site of these cities, and made the present Dead Sea, sometimes called the "Lake of Sodom." The prophet Jeremiah alludes to this lake (iv. 38, 40).

The knight's castle overflowed by a dead sea. A poor knight fell in love with a rich lady; and, being told that his poverty was a bar to his marriage, murdered a rich duke, got possession of his wealth, and wedded the lady. For nearly thirty years all went smoothly; but eight days before the completion of that period of time the knight made a great feast. During the banquet a bird flew into the hall, the knight shot it, and in a moment the castle sank into the earth, and the site thereof became a spacious lake, on which no substance will float, and in whose waters no living plant or creature can live.—*Gesta Romanorum,* ch. lxxviii.

Solomon's Choice.

2 CHRON. i. 7–12. God gave Solomon the liberty of choosing what gift he liked best, whether wealth or wisdom, honour or dominion; and Solomon said, Give me wisdom and knowledge. And God replied, Because thou hast asked wisdom and not wealth, therefore wisdom and knowledge will I grant unto thee, besides riches and honour such as none of the kings have had before thee, neither shall there after thee have the like.

Ruod chooses wisdom in preference to wealth (eleventh century). Ruod lived in the court of the king of Egypt, and, in return for valuable services, was offered by the king a choice of gifts, wisdom or wealth. Ruod chose the former, and the Pharaoh appointed the twelve wisest men of the realm for his instructors. He also sent him, from time to time, valuable jewels concealed in manchets; so that Ruod was not only the wisest but also the richest man in all Egypt.—*The Ruodlieb* (eleventh century).

An apprentice chooses wise advice in preference to wages. A loving couple at Cantire had one son; but, being very poor, the man came to England, and took service with a farmer. Years rolled on, and the man resolved to return to Cantire. His master asked him which he would have, three bits of advice or wages, and the man chose the former. Then said the master, (1) "Keep on the highway; (2) lodge in no house where there is an old man married to a young wife; and (3) do nothing rashly." On his way to Cantire, the man overtook a pedlar journeying the same road, and the pedlar told him he would show him a short cut which would considerably shorten the way; but the highlander, recalling his master's advice, resolved to keep to the high-road. The pedlar, therefore, parted company, fell among thieves, and was robbed of everything he possessed. They met again, and at nightfall the pedlar advised his companion to put up at a tavern well known to him; but when the Scotchman found the landlord was an old man who had recently married a young wife, he passed on. In the night, the old man was murdered, and the pedlar was charged with the crime. At length our traveller reached Cantire, and saw his wife caressing a sturdy young man. In his rage, he would have killed the young man; but, being determined to do nothing rashly, he went to some of the neighbours, inquired who the young man was, and discovered it was his own son, who supported his mother with his daily toil. The father was greatly rejoiced, made himself known, and, on cutting up a cake which his master had sent as a present to the man's wife, he found therein the entire amount of wages due. The wise master had chosen this way of payment, to prevent the money being spent on the road before the man reached home.—Cuthbert Bede, *The White Wife, and other Stories.*

A beggar chooses three bits of advice in preference to three scudi. A poor man, not long married, started for Maremma to earn a living, and, after the lapse of several years, returned homewards. On his way he asked a publican for alms, and the publican said, "Which, now, shall I give you, three scudi, or three bits of advice?" The man thought awhile, and then chose the latter. "Well," said the publican, "my three bits of advice are these: (1) Never interfere in matters which don't concern you; (2) never quit the high-road for what is called a short cut; and (3) keep your wounded pride to cool till the sun has risen the next morning." On his way home, the poor man lodged for a night at a roadside house where a murder was committed; but, not interfering in the matter, he was suffered to depart. On he trudged till he overtook a traveller going the same way. The traveller recommended a short cut, but the man, recalling the second bit of advice, determined to keep to the high-road, and parted company. The traveller soon fell among thieves, who first robbed and then murdered him. At length the poor man reached home, and beheld his wife caressing a young priest. His anger was aroused, but he kept his wounded pride to cool till after sunrise next morning, and in the mean time ascertained that the young priest was his own son. The kind publican had given him a manchet for his wife, and, on opening it, three scudi were found concealed in the inside. —Nerucci, *Sessanta Novelle Popolari.*

The emperor Domitian saves his life by three sentences of advice, bought of a merchant. The emperor bought of a merchant a talisman consisting of three sentences of advice, for which he paid the good round sum of a thousand florins. These three sentences thrice saved the emperor's life from the plots of conspirators to assassinate him. Thus, in one of the plots, a barber, hired to cut the emperor's throat, read on the towel this sentence, "Think of the consequences," and refused to run the risk of a regicide; by keeping the high-road, the emperor escaped an ambush laid to take away his life; and by refusing to stay in a house where there was a young wife married to an old man, he again evaded a conspiracy to cut him off.—*Gesta Romanorum,* ciii.

There is a Turkish tale, called *The Sultan, the Sofi, and the Surgeon,* to the same effect. The sultan bought of an abdal a sentence of advice for which he paid a hundred dinaras. The sentence was, "Think of the end;" and this sentence the sultan had inscribed on his doors, his linen, and even on his crockery and plate. One day a barber-surgeon, hired to assassinate the sultan, read these words on the imperial basin, changed his mind, and putting back the poisoned lancet, employed another. The sultan, taking notice of this, asked the reason, and the barber-surgeon, on a promise of pardon, revealed the conspiracy.

Solomon's Judgment.

1 KINGS iii. 16–28. Two harlots came to Solomon for judgment. The case was this: The two women lived in one house, and both brought forth a male child within three days of each other, but one of the infants died. The mother of the dead child accused the other woman of stealing her living babe, and substituting the dead one. Solomon said, Bring me a sword. And they did so. Divide the living child, said the king, and give half to one, and half to the other. The mother of the dead child cried, Be it so. Let the child be neither mine nor hers. But the other woman cried, Not so, my lord; O give her the child, but in no wise slay it. Then answered the king, Hers is the child; give it to her. And all Israel approved the wise judgment of the king.

SUSANNA AND THE ELDERS. (See p. 299.)

MATT. xxii. 15–21. The Pharisees, wishing to entangle Jesus either with the Jews or the Roman government, artfully asked him whether in His judgment it was lawful for God's people to pay tribute to Cæsar. Jesus asked to look on the tribute-money, and demanded whose was the image struck upon it. Cæsar's, said the Pharisees. Then Jesus said to them, Render to Cæsar the things that are Cæsar's, and to God the things that are God's.

Charles V. decides a dispute of precedency. Two Spanish ladies of high rank disputed about a seat in church, each claiming "the higher room." Charles V. sent for the two dames, and listened patiently while each explained her right of precedency. The case being stated, the emperor said, "Let the greater fool go first." It is needless to state that neither lady contended for the honour. —Chevalier de Propiac, *Dictionnaire d'Émulation,* p. 230.

Rowland Hill, preaching a charity sermon, concluded thus: "Let no one who cannot pay his debts put anything in the plate."

St. Ives, the widow, and two swindlers. Two swindlers deposited a valise with a widow, which they asserted contained two hundred gold pistoles, and charged her not to give up the valise except they were both present. After the lapse of six days one of the men came for the bag, and carried it off, whereupon the other rogue brought the widow before the judge, and demanded either the bag or the two hundred gold pistoles. The case seemed straightforward, and sentence was just about to be pronounced for the plaintiff, when St. Ives interfered, and said his client could not produce the valise unless *both* the claimants were present. The plaintiff, therefore, must bring his fellow into court before the valise could be given up. The judge saw at once the justice of this, and commanded the plaintiff to produce his companion. This, of course, he would not and could not do; and he was so taken aback at the unexpected turn of affairs, that he confessed the valise contained nothing except a few old nails and bits of iron.—Dom Lobineau, *Lives of the Saints of Britain.*

This is the St. Ives of whom it was written—

> Sanctus Yvo erat Brito,
> Advocatus, et non latro,
> Res miranda populo.
>
> St. Ives was of the Land of Beef,
> An advocate, and not a thief,
> A stretch on popular belief.

The legitimate son of a king discovered by a wise judgment. A certain queen had four sons, three of whom were supposed to be illegitimate. When the king died, the question was, which of these four was the lawful successor. As they could not, of course, agree, they laid the case before a knight, in whose judgment they confided, and by whose award they swore to abide. The knight ordered the dead body of the late king to be disinterred, and bound to a tree; and then commanding each of the four sons to shoot at the body, promised to give his judgment. The first who discharged his arrow shot the right hand of the dead body; the second arrow pierced the mouth; the third, the heart. It was now the turn of the youngest to try his skill, but instead of shooting at the dead body, he burst into tears, and cried in agony, "Oh, father! Oh, my poor father, have I lived to see thee thus abused? Oh, my father, are we thy sons to make thee the butt of our ambition? Let who will take the kingdom, I can never consent so to insult the dead." "He is the son!" cried the knight; and all the people echoed the wise judgment, and him, with one voice, they elected to the throne.—*Gesta Romanorum*, xlv.

The judgment of the grand-vizier Cherluli. In the first quarter of the eighteenth century, a Turkish merchant lost a purse containing two hundred gold pieces, and sent the public crier to offer half the amount to any one who would restore it to him. A sailor brought the purse back, but the merchant, to elude his promise, affirmed that the purse also contained an emerald of great value, and insisted on its being restored. The case was brought before Cherluli, the grand-vizier, who said to the merchant, "You swear that the purse you lost contained two hundred gold pieces and an emerald of great value?" "Yes, I swear it," replied the merchant. "And you," said the grand-vizier to the sailor, "swear that the purse you found contained two hundred gold pieces, but no emerald?" "I swear it," said the finder. "Then," continued the judge to the merchant, "it is quite obvious that this purse is not the one you lost.—Take it back," continued he to the sailor, "and if within forty days it is not duly claimed, keep the money for your own use."

A similar judgment was made by Octaï-khan, emperor of Tartary.

Portia and Shylock. Doubtless the judgment of Portia is one of the shrewdest evasions on record. The Jew bargained with Antonio for a "pound of flesh;" whereupon Portia remarked that the Jew, in the first place, must cut neither more nor less than a pound; and, in the second place, it must be all flesh without one drop of blood. There are several similar tales.

(1) Amurat I. and the Turk (1360–1389). A Turk lent a Christian a hundred ecus, on condition that if the loan was not returned at a stated time, the Turk should cut off two ounces of the defaulter's flesh. The time expired, the Christian could not repay the loan, and was haled before Amurat. The sultan tried at first to conciliate the claimant, but not succeeding in that, he told the Turk to take his bond, but reminded him that the terms were two ounces, neither more nor less, and if he cut either more or less than two ounces, he would himself be subject to the same penalty. The Mussulman, being brought to reason, extended the time of payment, and the Christian was enabled to return the loan.

(2) Secchi and Samson Ceneda the Jew. A merchant of Venice, having been informed by private letter that admiral Drake had taken and plundered St. Domingo, sent word of the capture to Samson Ceneda, a Jewish usurer. Samson would not believe it, and bet a pound of flesh the rumour was not true. When the report was confirmed by the pope, his holiness told Secchi he might lawfully claim his pound of flesh if he chose, but that he must take no blood, and must also cut exactly a pound of flesh, neither more nor less; if either of these provisions was broken, the pope added that Secchi would be instantly

hanged on the nearest tree.—Gregorio Leti, *Life of Sixtus V.* (1666).

The forged transfer. In the reign of Maximian, a certain knight wanted to buy a piece of land contiguous to his estate, but the owner refused to sell it. Not long afterwards the owner died, and the knight drew up a forged instrument, purporting to be the transfer of the land for value received. The instrument was duly attested by three witnesses. The son and heir disputed the instrument, and the judge commanded the three witnesses to be kept apart, and examined separately. The first witness was called, but the questions put to him were of no importance. The second was then placed at the bar, and, taking it for granted that his companion had revealed the whole matter, made at once a clean breast of it. The third saw by the judge's face and manner that he knew all about it, and confirmed the statement of the previous witness. So the judge condemned the knight to death, and gave his estate to the young man he had tried to defraud. — *Gesta Romanorum*, cxxviii.

The stolen horse. A Spaniard in his travels overtook an Indian in a desert. Both were mounted, but the Indian had the better horse. The Spaniard wanted him to change, and as he refused, set upon, mastered him, and took possession of the steed. The Indian rode peaceably to the next town, and then laid his complaint before the cadi. The Spaniard insisted the horse was his, and that the claim of the complainant was simply ridiculous. The Indian, throwing his scarf over the horse's head, requested the cadi to demand of the defendant, which of the horse's eyes was the blind one. "The right eye," cried the Spaniard. "Neither," shouted the Indian, and the cadi at once adjudged the horse to its rightful owner.

Speaking without a Tongue.

Isa. xxxv. 6. Then shall the lame man leap as a hart, and the tongue of the dumb sing.

2 Macc. vii. 1–19. Antiochus took seven sons of one mother and commanded them to eat swine's flesh, and because they refused to disobey the law of Moses, they were scourged. Then one by one they were put to death. The first said to Antiochus, We are ready to die rather than to transgress the laws of our fathers. Then the king, being in a rage, commanded pans and cauldrons to be made hot, and, having cut out the tongue of his victim and lopped off his extremities, he was fried in the pan. The brethren looking on, exhorted each other to die manfully. When the turn of the third son came, he put out his tongue when required, and holding forth his hands, he said, These had I from Heaven, and from God I hope to receive them again. In like manner all the seven died.

Certain Christians of Constantinople spoke plainly, though they had lost their tongues. Humeric ordered the tongues of certain Christians, opposed to his Arian bishops, to be plucked out, to prevent their confession of the Trinity; but though they had no tongues, they spoke as well as they did before. "If any one doubts this statement," says Victor of Vita, "let him go to Constantinople, and he will there find the subdeacon Reparatus, who was so treated; but he speaks quite distinctly, and is much honoured by the emperor Zeno and the empress." Æneas of Gaza, who was at the time at Constantinople, says, "I myself saw these persons, heard them speak, and was amazed at their perfect articulation. I searched for their organs of speech, caused several to open their mouths, and saw with my own eyes that their tongues were plucked out even to the roots." Procopius, the historian, says, "When I was at Constantinople, I talked to many of those who were tongueless, but could detect no impediment of speech whatever, and they told me they felt no sort of inconvenience for the loss of their organ of speech." Count Marcellinus, in his *Chronicons*, says, "I have seen some of these tongueless persons, and can testify that they speak without the slightest imperfection of utterance." The emperor Justinian testifies the same thing in one of his constitutions.—Milner, *History of the Church of Christ*, vol. ii. pp. 287, 288.

Twenty Christians of Nicomedia speak after their tongues were plucked out. The emperor Maximian ordered a batch of twenty Christians of Nicomedia, a city of Bithynia, to be apprehended. They were first chained to wooden posts and beaten with raw sinews; and because they murmured not, but sang hymns in their torment, he had all their tongues plucked out by the roots, and their teeth knocked out with stones. Adrian was the name of the officer appointed to superintend this sentence. When he saw the resignation of these martyrs, he said to them, "I adjure you, by the God whom you adore, tell me for what reward you suffer thus." The twenty martyrs, who had lost both their tongues and teeth, made answer, "The reward we look for is so great that no eye hath seen, no ear hath heard, and no heart can conceive the glory God hath prepared for those that love Him." Adrian, hearing this, went to the notary and said, "Set down my name in the register of these soldiers of Christ, for I also will be enlisted under the same banner, and will fight the same battle with them, looking for the same recompense of reward."—Ado (bishop of Tours), *Martyrology*.

St. Ferreol and St. Ferrucius spoke eloquently after their tongues were plucked out (A.D. 212). Ferreol and Ferrucius were two friends or two brothers of Asia Minor, who were seized by Claudius the governor, in the reign of Marcus Aurelius, and set on the chevalet (see Index) for being Christians. While thus tortured they were also scourged unmercifully; but God made them insensible of pain, and surrounded them with a heavenly glory. Claudius blushed to see himself thus foiled, and ordered the martyrs back to prison. Three days afterwards they were brought again before him, and as they still refused to offer sacrifice to the gods of Rome, they were again placed on the rack, and their tongues plucked out; but after they had lost their tongues, the two athletes in Christ spoke eloquently to the people, and exhorted them to flee from the wrath to come. Claudius ordered his myrmidons to run thirty awls into their feet, hands, and breast; and then to hammer a wreath of nails into their skulls. As the martyrs bore all without the least indication of pain, the governor petulantly commanded their heads to be cut off. In Christian art they are represented holding their heads in their hands.—*Vie des Saints de Franche Comté* (by the professors of St. François Xavier de Besançon).

St. Leger spoke distinctly when deprived of his tongue and lips (A.D. 678). Ebroin, with a cruelty unparalleled, first pulled out the two eyes of St. Leger, bishop of Autun, then amputated his lips, and rooted out his tongue. Without tongue or lips he spoke distinctly, and for the space of two years ceased not to preach the Word of God in the abbey of Féchamp, and many were converted by his exhortations.—Dom Pitra, *History of St. Leger*.

Parmenius speaks after his tongue was plucked out (A.D. 251). St. Polychronus, bishop of Babylon, with Parmenius and four other Christians, were brought before Apollo Valerianus for contempt of the Roman gods. Valerian said to the bishop, "You are charged with contempt of the gods, and with disobedience to the commands of the emperor. What have you to say for yourself?" The bishop made no reply. The emperor, who was present, said to Parmenius and the others, "Why is your prince silent? why does he not answer to the charge?" Parmenius replied, "Cast not pearls before swine, and give not that which is holy unto dogs, lest they trample them under their feet, and turn again and rend you." The emperor, feeling himself insulted at this answer, commanded the tongue of Parmenius to be plucked out; but after he had lost his tongue, he cried aloud, "Father Polychronus, pray for me." The other saints, being hoisted on chevalets (see Index), cried aloud to Parmenius to pray for them, and the tongueless priest said in the hearing of all, "O God, the Father of our Lord Jesus Christ, comfort these Thy servants with the comfort of the Holy Ghost;" and they all answered, "Amen." The emperor, looking on the men as sorcerers, commanded them all to be thrown into the fire, but the fire did them no hurt. Finally they were beheaded.—Surius, *Lives of the Saints*, vol. iv., Aug. 10.

St. Raymond Nonnat speaks when his lips are locked (A.D. 1204–1248). St. Raymond Nonnat, when Setim was pacha, went to Algiers to redeem captives and carry the gospel of salvation. Setim ordered him to be impaled, but the ransomed captives interceded for him, and the sentence was commuted for scourging. His zeal was by no means abated by this punishment, and he still continued to preach the gospel. The pacha ordered him to be whipped, naked, at the corner of every street in the city, and then to have a red-hot iron padlock fastened through his lips, the key to be kept by the cadi, and never unlocked except when he took his food. One day, when the Moors entered his prison with his food, they were thunderstruck on hearing him say, "Take not the Word of truth utterly out of my mouth; for I have hoped in Thy judgments" (*Ps.* cxix. 43); their amazement was still more increased when he said aloud, "Thy Word, O Lord, endureth for ever." They thought he was a sorcerer, kicked him with their feet, and left him without unlocking his lips or giving him his food.—*Les Petits Bollandistes*, vol. x. p 360.

Speech ascribed to Dumb Animals.

NUMB. xxii. 21-30. Balaam was going to Moab, at the request of Balak son of Zippor, to curse Israel, that the Moabites might conquer them in battle. God's anger was kindled, because Balaam, a prophet of God, took service under an idolatrous king, to curse and destroy the very people that God had chosen for His own. So God sent His angel to obstruct the prophet. Though Balaam could not see the obstructing angel, the ass saw him, and turned aside. This was done three times, when Balaam smote the beast in his anger. Then was the mouth of the ass opened, and it spake with the voice of a man, and said to Balaam, What have I done to thee, that thou hast smitten me these three times? And Balaam said to the ass, Because thou hast mocked me: I would there were a sword in my hand, for then would I kill thee. The ass replied, Am I not thine ass, upon which thou hast ridden ever since I was thine; and am I wont to mock thee? Then the Lord opened the eyes of Balaam, and he saw the angel standing in the way with his sword drawn; and the humbled prophet fell on his face to the ground.

The dog Katmîr reproves the "Seven Sleepers." Seven young noblemen of Ephesus, according to Gregory of Tours, fled in the Decian persecution to a cave in Mount Celion. According to other authorities, the number of noblemen was six, and the seventh man was the shepherd Keschetiouch, whom they converted, and who showed them the cave, which "no one but himself knew of." The Korân tells us the shepherd had a dog, named Katmîr, which persisted in following the seven to the cave. They threw a stone at it to drive it back, and broke its left leg; but the dog, limping, followed them still. They then threw another stone at the dog, and broke its right fore leg; but the dog now followed, walking on its two hind feet. A third stone broke one of these legs, and the poor beast could no longer stand. Then was the mouth of the dog opened, and it said in human speech, "I, too, am the creature of God, and love Him as my Creator; and, loving God, I love thee also who love God. Sleep, masters, and I will keep watch over you." Hearing these words, the seven were astounded, and, taking the dog in their arms, they carried it with them into the cave, where they all survived for about three hundred years.—*Al Korân*, ch. xviii., entitled "The Cave revealed at Mecca." (See also *The Golden Legends* of Jacques de Voragine; Gregory of Tours, *De Gloria Martyrum*, bk. i. 9; etc.)

The horse Xanthos reproves Achillês for false insinuations. When Achillês sent Patroclos to the battle, he lent him his chariot and horses. The horses' names were Xanthos and Balios. Patroclos was slain, and the horses returned with the empty chariot to their master's tent. When Achillês had made up his mind to avenge his friend's death, he said to his horses, on mounting the car, "See that you leave not me, as you left my friend, dead on the battle-field." Then Xanthos, hanging its head till its mane touched the ground, said in human speech (for Juno gave it the gift), "This day, at least, will I bring thee safe home; but thy day of doom is not far off, most stormy chief. Not from fault of mine, the Trojans slew Patroclos, seeing it was Latona who slew him, in order to give thee glory. A far more inglorious fate is reserved for thee, O chief. He by a goddess fell, but human hand shall beat thee down." "Why, Xanthos," cried the hero, "are you foretelling thy master's death? It ill beseems thee, methinks, to speak thus unto thy lord. Perish or not, till Troy falls Achillês will never more cease from feats of arms." He spoke, and, shouting loudly, drove into the very van of the foe.—Homer, *Iliad*, bk. xix. (the close of it).

Arion (the horse of Adrastos) was said to be endowed with human speech; so was Fortunio's horse, named Comrade; Mahomet's beast, Al Borak; Sâ'eh's camel; the black pigeons of Dodona; Temliha, king of the serpents; the serpent which tempted Eve; the bird called Bulbul-hezar; the little green bird of princess Fairstar; the White Cat; and, indeed, in fable all animals, and all insensate things also, are possessed of human speech. Hence Cowper's lines—

> I shall not ask Jean Jacques Rousseau
> If birds confabulate or no;
> 'Tis clear that they were always able
> To hold discourse,—at least in fable.
> *Pairing-time anticipated.*

In the *Frithjof Saga* by Tegner, Ellida, Frithjof's ship, understood whatever its master said to it, and hence the son of Thorsten talks to it as to a companion.

Spider's Web.

Dr. Moulins protected in the Bartholomew slaughter by a spider's web. In the dreadful massacre of Huguenots in France on Bartholomew's Eve and the day following, Dr. Moulins took refuge in a cold oven. A spider wove its web over the oven's mouth, and when the cut-throats came up and saw the unbroken web, they passed on.

For David, Felix, and Mahomet, saved by cobwebs, see p. 75.

Spittle curative.

JOHN ix. 6, 7. When He had thus spoken, He spat on the ground, and made clay of the spittle, and He anointed the eyes of the blind man with the clay, and said to him, Go, wash in the pool of Siloam. The blind man went and washed, and came seeing.

MARK vii. 32-35. They bring to Jesus one that was deaf, and had an impediment in his speech. And Jesus took him aside from the multitude, and put His fingers into the man's ears, and He spit, and touched his tongue. And straightway his ears were opened, and the string of his tongue was loosed, and he spake plainly.

MARK viii. 22-24. Jesus cometh to Bethsaida; and they bring to Him a blind man, and besought Him to touch him. And He took the blind man by the hand; and when he had spit on his eyes, and put His hands upon him, He asked him if he saw ought. And the man said I see men as trees, walking. After that He put His hands again upon the man's eyes, and he saw clearly.

"Illa de sinu licium protulit varii coloris filis intortum, cervicemque vinxit meam: Mox turbatum sputo pulverem, medio sustulit digito, frontemque repugnantis signavit. Hoc peracto carmine, ter me jussit exspuere, terque lapillos conjicere in sinum, quos ipsa præcantatos purpura involverat, . . . Petronius."

Spittle used in baptism. After exorcisms, the priest [in Roman Catholic baptisms] puts salt in the mouth of the catechumen, saying, "M. or N., receive the salt of wisdom, that it may lead you to eternal life." The catechumen is then introduced into the Church, and the priest touches the ears and nose of the infant with spittle, saying, "Ephphatha, be opened." That is, may your ears be open to hear and receive the words of eternal life, and your nose to smell the sweet odour of sanctity. The Church, says St. Charles, "demands that every one who is baptized should hear the voice of God and His commandments, and that the doctrines of Christ, entering through the ears, should go down into the heart, and smell as a sweet perfume." The nose is touched with spittle, *ad discernandum bonum odorem a malo, sanam doctrinam a corrupta*, that it may know to discern a good odour from a bad one, that is, a sound doctrine from an heretical one.—Mgr. Guérin, *Vies des Saints*, vol. xvi. p. 519.

St. Attalus heals a cut thumb, and cures a child with saliva (A.D. 627). A monk working in a field about half a league from the monastery of Bobbio, cut off the thumb of his left hand, and applied to the abbot to heal the wound. St. Attalus sent a man to search for the thumb, and anointing it with spittle, replaced it on the hand. It instantly attached itself, and the monk used it as if it had never been cut at all. St. Attalus in the same way cured an infant which had been given over by the doctors. Jonas, a Scotchman, mentions both these miracles, and adds that he knows they are true, as he was himself an eye-witness of both of them.—Jonas, a Scotchman, and disciple of St. Attalus, *Life of St. Attalus.*

Spittle kills a dragon. Sozomenus tells us of a saint named Donatus (not St. Donatus, bishop of Arezzo, but another of the same name) who slew a dragon by "signing the sign of the cross, and spitting into the dragon's mouth."

St Francis of Paula makes two eyes and a mouth with his spittle (A.D. 1416-1507). One day a child which was born without eyes or mouth was taken to St. Francis of Paula. St. Francis marked with his spittle the spots where these features ought to have been, then making the sign of the cross, the infant became instantly possessed of two most brilliant eyes and a model mouth.

St. Hilarion cures a blind woman with his spittle. A woman who had been blind for ten years, and had spent all her substance on physicians without receiving any benefit from their prescriptions, was at last brought to St. Hilarion. "Woman," said the hermit to her, "if you had spent your substance on the poor, Jesus Christ would have cured you." He then anointed her eyes with spittle, and immediately her sight was restored.—St. Jerome, *Vita St. Hilarionis Eremitæ* (A.D. 390); Nicephorus Callistus (died 1350), *Ecclesiastical History.*

St. Peter II., archbishop of Tarentaise, cures with his spittle a blind boy (A.D. 1103-1174). When St. Peter II., archbishop of Tarentaise, was at Chaumont, on the confines of Normandy, he was met by Henry II. of England and Louis VII. of France. In the immense crowd was a woman, leading by the hand her son, who was quite blind. She tried in vain to force her way to the thaumaturgist; but, finding this impossible, she cried with a loud voice, beseeching him to heal her son. The saint bade the lad come forward; then, wetting his fingers with spittle, he rubbed them across the sightless eyes, making on them the sign of the cross. The kings and princes watched anxiously the result. All of a sudden the boy exclaimed, "Hurrah! hurrah! I see my mother, I see the trees, I see men and women, I see everything." All the crowd was ravished. The mother, beside herself with joy, fell at the saint's feet, kissing them, and bathing them with her tears. The king of France fell prostrate before the boy, adoring the power divine, kissed the boy on his forehead, eyes, and cheek, and then put into his hand a rich offering.—Geoffrey (abbot of Hautecomb), *Life of Peter II.*, etc. (written nine years after his death by order of pope Lucius III.).

St. Valery cures many with his spittle (A.D. 619). "On ne finirait pas si on voulait raconter combien St. Valery guérit de malades en faisant sur eux le signe de la croix, ou en les frottant de la salive."—Besançon (1854), *Les Saints de Franche Comté.*

Vespasian cures a blind man with spittle. Tacitus (*Annals*, bk. i. ch. 3) records many miracles done by the emperor Vespasian. "Many miracles," he says, "happened at Alexandria, manifesting the favour of the divine powers towards Vespasian. For example: a man of Alexandria, known to be blind, cast himself at the emperor's feet, begging him, with tears, to spit upon his eyes. Another, who was maimed, besought Vespasian to stamp upon his hand. Both these things being done, '*statim conversa ad usum manus, et cæco reluxit dies,*' the maimed man recovered the use of his hand, and the blind man the speculation of his eyes." Tacitus adds, "These things are testified to this day by eye-witnesses, to whom a falsehood could be of no advantage."—Tacitus, *History*, bk. iv. 81; Suetonius, *Vespasian*, vii.

There can be no doubt that spittle was considered a charm by Jews, Greeks, Romans, and many other ancient nations. We trace it among the Indians, Egyptians, Africans, etc., and find that it still exists among our own people. Probably the "eye-salve" referred to in *Rev.* iii. 18 is spittle. Theocritus says, "Thrice on my breast I spit to guard me safe from fascinating charms." Pliny tells us that spittle "averts witchcraft," and was "once deemed a specific for ophthalmia" (xxviii. 7), and sir Thomas Browne mentions among "vulgar errors" the notion that "fasting spittle will kill snakes, and is an antidote to the poison of serpents." Persius (*Satire* ii. 31) informs us that nurses were wont to spit on new-born infants for luck; when Mahomet was born, his grandfather Hassan "did spit in the child's mouth" (*History of the Saracens*, ii. 84); and Park tells us that the priest, when a Mandingo child is born, "spits three times in its face for luck." We all know that boys spit on gift-money for luck; fishwomen for the same reason "spit on their hansel," and boxers on the palms of their hands. Among the [Roman] Catholic ceremonies of baptism one of them is "to touch the nostrils and ears of the child with spittle."

Bale, in his *Interlude* (1562), makes Idolatry say—

> I can work wyles in battle;
> If I but ones [*once*] do spattle,
> I can make corne and cattle
> That they shall never thrive.

Star at Birth or Death; Guiding Star.

MATT. ii. 1-11. When Jesus was born, there came to Jerusalem certain wise men who had seen His star in the east.

A star seen at the birth of St. Ambrose of Siena (A.D. 1220). The same day that St. Ambrose of Siena was brought into the world, two other saints were born of great note, viz. St. Thomas Aquinas and St. James of Menavia. The day was marked by three bright stars seen at midday, "qui renfermaient chacun un religieux de St. Dominique, pour montrer que ces trois hommes étaient destinés du ciel à éclairer le monde par la lumière de leur doctrine."—Mgr. Guérin (chamberlain of pope Leo XIII.), *Vies des Saints* (1880), vol. iii. p. 553.

Ambrose was born at Siena in Tuscany; Thomas Aquinas at Belcastro in Calabria, according to Barrius and at Aquino in Calabria, according to the Bollandists; and James of Menavia was born at Bissignano in Calabria, April 16, A.D. 1220.

A flame of fire seen on the house-roof when St. Francis of Paula was born (A.D. 1416). St. Francis of Paula was the child of prayer, being born, like Isaac, Samson, Samuel, and John Baptist, when the mother was past the age of child-bearing. His parents invoked St. Francis of Assisi for this blessing, and when their prayer was answered they recognized the grant by calling his name Francis. At the moment of his birth a flame of fire, like a lamp, was seen burning on the roof of the house. And this house has since been converted into a chapel, where the Minims of Paula celebrate the "sacrifice of the mass."—*The Bull and other Documents of the Canonization* (collected by Père Giry).

Stars honour St. Theresa at death (sixteenth century). It pleased the Lord to show forth the holiness of St. Theresa by signs and wonders. For example: At the moment of her death, a certain religious woman saw two stars descend upon her cell. Another sister saw a bright star shining over the monastery, and one at the saint's chamber window. A religious woman of Valladolid saw the heavens open, and a glorious path prepared, reaching from earth to heaven, by which her soul ascended into paradise. A prioress of Segovia smelt at the same time an odour exceeding in sweetness any earthly perfume. Another sister saw a white dove issue from the mouth of the deceased, and fly upwards till lost to sight. All the convent saw a great light, and smelt a sweet odour.—John (of the Order of Jesus), *Life of St. Theresa.*

If the soul of St. Theresa flew out of her mouth in the form of a dove, and took its flight direct to heaven, what was the use of the path prepared, and reaching from earth to heaven? The light seen in the convent and the sweet odour may be accounted for by the custom of lighting candles and burning incense.

St. John the Silent sees and follows a guiding star (A.D. 454–558). St. John was bishop of Colonia, in Armenia, but, longing for retirement, his mind was greatly troubled between duty and inclination. One night while engaged in prayer, lifting his eyes to heaven, he saw a bright star in the form of a cross, and heard at the same time a voice in the air which said to him, "If you would be saved, follow this star." He instantly rose, followed the star, and was conducted to the cells of St. Sabas, in Palestine, called "The Great Laura." Here he was received, and employed at first in fetching water and carrying stones for the builders of a new hospital. Afterwards, he was promoted to the duties of receiving and entertaining strangers; and then he was allowed a separate hermitage.—Cyril (a monk), *Life of St. John the Silent.*

A *laura* is a kind of village of separate cells. The difference between a monastery and laura is this: in a *monastery* all the monks live under one roof, and meet together at meals and canonical prayers; but in a *laura* they live separately, each in his own hut, cave, or cell.

St. Solangia had a star night and day which directed her in all things (A.D. 880). Every night and day a star appeared over the head of St. Solangia to guide her in all her ways, "a lamp unto her feet, and a light unto her path." This star advertised to her the hour of orison or psalmody. In fact, it seemed "comme si la lumière, qui invitait autrefois les saints rois Mages à aller reconnaître et adorer Jésus-Christ, eût été reproduite pour favoriser cette sainte bergère, et lui indiquer les précieux moments auxquels le divine Epoux demandait ses adorations." In Christian art St. Solangia is represented as a shepherd with a star above her head.—Alet, *Vie de Ste. Solange*, p. 18, etc.

Stephen's Vision. (See Visions.)

Acts vii. 55, 56. When Stephen was about to be stoned, he looked steadfastly into heaven, and saw the glory of God, and Jesus standing on the right hand of God, and said, Behold, I see the heavens opened, and the Son of man standing on the right hand of God.

St. Attalus, at death, saw the heavens open (A.D. 627). When St. Attalus was dying, he cried out, "Behold, I see the heavens opened, and a seat prepared for me in the presence of the Majesty on high."—*Les Petits Bollandistes*, vol. i. p. 106.

St. Wulsin, bishop of Sherborne, Dorsetshire, saw Jesus standing at God's right hand (A.D. 983). When St. Wulsin was on the point of death, he exclaimed, saying, "I see the heavens open, and Jesus standing at the right hand of God." This he uttered without faltering, and then gave up the ghost.—Matthew of Westminster, *De Gestis Pontificorum Anglorum*, bk. ii.

Stones made Bread. (See "Bread made a Stone"—Churlishness.)

Matt. iv. 3. If Thou be the Son of God, command that these stones be made bread.

Psalm lxxviii. 25. Man did eat angels' food.

A flower converted into bread. A nobleman of Maillé, having lost his way in a chase, came to the cell of Jeanne Marie de Maillé, and asked if she could give him a morsel of food. "Messire chevalier," she replied, "of bread or other food I have none, but may it please you to accept this flower?" A flower, he thought, was but poor repast for a hungry man; nevertheless he took it graciously, stuck it in his bonnet, and rode on. He had not gone far when he was struck with the unusual weight of his cap, and, taking it off, perceived three small loaves of bread growing on the stem of the flower; they were very delicious in flavour, and on arriving at his château he recorded how Jeanne Marie had given him angels' food.—Père de Boisgaultier (her confessor), *Life of Jeanne Marie de Maillé.*

(See Rose, pt. ii., "Bread converted into Roses.")

Sun Submissive to the Saints.

Josh. x. 12. The sun and moon stood still, at the bidding of Joshua, that he might complete his victory over the five allied kings who made war against the Gibeonites.

2 Kings xx. 8. The sun went back ten degrees to lengthen the days of the life of Hezekiah.

Psalm civ. 4. His ministers a flaming fire.

Joshua's miracle of the sun and moon. I am well aware of the dangerous ground they tread who attempt to suggest any interpretation of Scripture different to what is usually received; but of late many inroads have been made, and though at first discredited, are now universally admitted: witness the movement of the earth, which brought Galileo into trouble, and the Mosaic cosmogony, which geology has compelled all men to modify. I have ventured to suggest a rendering of "Samson and the Jawbone" (p. 281), and would now, with all diffidence, hint at a rendering of the sun and moon miracle in the Book of Joshua. These new renderings in no wise touch upon the subjects of inspiration and miracles, but simply upon that of translation or interpretation. I admit, at starting, that ver. 14 is a difficulty, but probably not insuperable, as I hope to show.

What I would suggest is this: That the incident recorded in 2 *Kings* xviii. 17–40, respecting Elijah and the prophets of Baal, gives the true key of interpretation. The five kings mentioned by Joshua (ver. 3), like most if not all the people amongst whom the Israelites were about to dwell, were worshippers of the sun and moon, under the names of Astaroth, Astartê, Baal, or some other name; and Joshua might wish to show the Israelites, on their first entrance into the land, how powerless are such false gods. If this was his purpose, his words (ver. 12) might be paraphrased thus: "These men against whom you are fighting put their trust in the sun and moon, but I will show you the impotency of such a trust. I, a man, will command these gods of theirs to stand still, and not come to the aid of their worshippers. 'Sun and moon, stand still, I command you. Sun, stand thou still upon Gibeon. Moon, stand thou still upon Ajalon, while the children of Israel, the worshippers of the true God, pursue thy votaries to Beth-horon and Makkedah.' So the sun stood still, and went not to the help of his worshippers, and the moon moved not to succour her devotees, and all Israel saw how powerless were such false deities as Astaroth and Astartê (sun and moon); and when they saw the idolaters struck down on all sides, they could not but exclaim, as the people cried in the days of Elijah, 'The Lord, He is God! the Lord, He is God!'" By this rendering, an enormous difficulty, far beyond that of a mere miracle, is got over; and the people would be taught a most useful lesson—not to forsake the God which Moses taught them to worship, for the false gods of the people amongst whom they were henceforth about to live.

"So Astaroth and Astartê stood still, and came not to the help of the five kings, while Israel avenged themselves upon their enemies, who trusted to these false deities. Is not this written in the Book of Jasher?" This last clause and ver. 14 were not, of course, written by Joshua, but, like the close of ver. 9, ch. iv., and ch. xxiv. 29–33, etc., were added by some subsequent editor or commentator. Of course, Joshua could not have written the words (ver. 14) "there was no day like that before it or *after* it," for it would have been nonsense for Joshua to have said so. This verse, therefore, does not belong to the original text, and need cause no difficulty.

(As I said at the beginning, I do not wish to dogmatize—far from it; I merely wish to hint what appears to be a not improbable solution of an enormous difficulty.)

St. Deïcola, an Irish saint, hangs his cloak on a sunbeam (seventh century). Weifhardt cruelly ill-treated St. Deïcola, but soon afterwards fell sick; and his wife, thinking his sickness a punishment for his ill-treatment of the hermit, sent for him. Deïcola, mindful of the Christian precept of returning good for evil, hastened to the sick man. The day was very sultry, and the hermit stripped off his mantle. When the servants of Weifhardt offered to take it from him, Deïcola said to them, "Menservants and maidservants serve men and women, but the servants of God are served by God's servants." So saying, he threw his mantle on a sunbeam, and there it remained securely hung till he had finished his interview, and was about to leave the house.—Baring-Gould, *Lives of the Saints*, vol. i. p. 282. (See the *Roman Martyrology*, Jan. 18.)

St. Goar, the hermit, hangs his cloak on a sunbeam (A.D. 575). St. Goar was sent for by Rusticus, bishop of Trèves, who had assembled a large number of his clergy in his palace, with intent of reproving the recluse for violating the rules laid down for the observance of hermits. The first thing the hermit did on his entry into Trèves was to enter the church, and commend himself to the care of the Almighty. He then went to the bishop's palace, "avec une gravité et une modestie angéliques." Taking off his outer garment, he hung it on a sunbeam, "qu'il prit pour une barre ou une corde." The bishop, far from being influenced by this prodigy, accused the hermit of magic, and reproved him sharply for being in league with the devil. St. Goar appealed to God to vindicate him from this charge. At this moment a clerk entered the palace, bringing an infant which he found in the font. The bishop said if Goar would tell him who were the parents of this foundling he would believe him ; if not, he should treat him as a son of Belial, for eating before the canonical hours. St. Goar asked the age of the child, and the clerk said it was about three days old. Then, addressing the babe, the hermit said to it, "I adjure you, in the name of the Holy Trinity, tell this company who are your father and mother." The babe, pointing to the bishop, said distinctly, "My father is Rusticus and my mother Flavia." The bishop declared it was an infamous lie, but afterwards, being pricked to the heart, he confessed that the infant had told the truth. In Christian art St. Goar is represented hanging his cloak on a sunbeam.—*Acta Sanctorum* (Bollandists), July 6.

St. Gudula hangs a pair of gloves on a sunbeam (A.D. 652–710). St. Gudula, to render her prayers more efficacious, always imposed on herself some corporal punishment. Thus she went about with shoes without soles. One day a monk handed to her his gloves to set her feet on. Gudula thanked him for his kindness, but immediately his back was turned, she threw the gloves on one side ; when lo! a striking miracle manifested itself, for the gloves were "hooked up by a sunbeam which penetrated the church window, and there they hung for more than an hour." As all present saw the gloves suspended on the sunbeam, there could be no deception in the matter. The sunbeam caught up the gloves which St. Gudula cast aside, and held them suspended till the service was over.—Hubert (eleventh century), *Life of St. Gudula.*

St. Leonorus of Brittany hangs his mantle on a sunbeam (A.D. 509–560). One day king Childebert requested St. Leonorus to celebrate to him and his court the holy mysteries. The servant of God, before robing himself with the sacerdotal ornaments, pulled off his mantle, and, wanting to hang it up, could not find a peg unoccupied. At that moment a ray of the sun burst through the window of the vestry, and to the amazement of all present, the saint hung his cloak on the ray, and there it remained till he resumed it again. In Christian art St. Leonorus is sometimes represented hanging his cloak on a sunbeam.—Dom Lobineau, *Lives of the Saints of Brittany.*

St. Robert, abbot of Casa Dei, hangs a pair of gloves on a sunbeam (A.D. 1067), While St. Robert, abbot of Casa Dei, was preaching at Avignon, two giddy young men began tossing their gloves about as a ball, and distracting the attention of the audience. In one of the tossings, St. Robert caused the gloves to catch on a sunbeam, and hang there too high for the young men to reach them, till the service was over.—*Acta Sanctorum* (Bollandists), April 24.

This is a very favourite miracle of the saints, and recorded of the following, among others :—Alruna of Altaich, Amabilis (whose day is Oct. 19), Bridget (Feb. 1), Cunegunda (July 24), Cuthman (Feb. 8), David abbot of Sweden (July 15), Deïcola of Ireland (Jan. 18), Florence (Nov. 7), Goar (July 6), Gudula (Jan. 8), Hildevert of Meaux (May 27), Leonorus (July 1), Lucanus (Oct. 30), Odo of Urgel (July 7), Robert of Casa Dei (April 24), Utho of Metten, etc.

⁂ In all these cases there must of necessity be a double miracle. Not only the sunbeam sustains the cloak, but it also stays in the same place. Any one with the slightest observation must know that the sun shining through a window soon moves across it; but in these cases the miracle of Joshua, "Sun, stand thou still," was repeated, not to discomfit an allied army, but to act the part of an ordinary cloak-peg.

This very common "miracle" seems extraordinary to us Europeans, but any one who has been in India must have seen a man throw up a rope into the air, and then climb up the rope, dragging it after him, and disappearing at last in blue space. This "rope trick" is as common as the "mango trick" or "basket trick." It may be astonishing, but it is only a trick and not a miracle.

Susanna and the Elders.

Susanna and the elders. Susanna, the wife of Joacim, was very beautiful, and two elders fell in love with her. One day, as she went to bathe, they came upon her, and swore, if she refused to gratify their passion, they would accuse her of adultery ; and this, by the Jewish law, would be death to her. However, Susanna refused, and the two elders raised a great clamour, which brought her maidens to see what was the matter. Then said the elders, "We saw a young man enter the bath-room, and rushed forward to seize him, but he contrived to escape." When Susanna was taken before the Sanhedrim, and the elders had stated their charge, she was at once condemned to death ; but Daniel commanded to put the two accusers apart, and one being placed at the bar, Daniel said to him, "Under what tree did you say you saw the accused keeping company with a young man?" "Under a mastic tree," was the ready lie. Being put aside, the other elder was produced, and asked the same question. "Under a holm tree," was his answer. Then cried the seventy with a loud voice, rose from their seats against the false accusers, and put them both to death, for they had leagued together to take away the life of a virtuous woman. —*Apocrypha* (Susanna and the Elders).

St. Agnes protected by angels (A.D. 304). Procopius, the son of a Roman prefect, wanted to marry St. Agnes, a beautiful girl of thirteen, but Agnes told him she was Christ's bride, and could marry no other. Procopius fell sick, and the prefect, sending for Agnes, told her he would give her the choice of two things: to marry his son, or serve as a vestal virgin all the days of her life. Agnes replied she would do neither. As the bride of Christ she could not be given to another; and as the servant of the living God, she would not serve idols. The prefect then ordered her to be led naked through the streets, proclaimed as a strumpet, and left in a brothel to be abused by strangers. God sent His angel to avert all these evils. In the first place, He caused her hair to grow so long and thick that it covered her whole body like a mantle; and when she entered the brothel, an angel presented to her a white robe, whiter than any fuller could have whitened it; and the chamber was brilliantly illuminated with celestial light. Many entered the chamber with evil intent, but went away converts to the new faith. Last of all Procopius entered; and, walking up to St. Agnes, laid his hands on her; but instantly he fell down dead at her feet. When the prefect heard thereof, his heart was softened, and he implored Agnes to restore his son to life again. Agnes ordered all to withdraw, and then entreated God to resuscitate the young man. Her prayer was heard, and Procopius went home a chastened and a better man. —St. Ambrose wrote her acts. (See his *De Virginibus*, bk. i.)

A she-bear defends St. Columba from molestation (A.D. 274). Aurelian, finding that neither threats nor promises would induce Columba to forsake the religion of Christ, had her led in chains to the amphitheatre, to be confined there in a secret prison. Then, sending for a debauchee of a notoriously licentious character, he said, "Go to the secret prison of the amphitheatre, and there you will find a maiden whom I abandon to you." The young scapegrace went at once, and entered the prison. "Beware, young man," said Columba, "of the vengeance of God, and leave me, ere it is too late." Scarcely had she spoken, when a she-bear rushed into the prison, threw the young man to the ground, set its fore paw upon him, and looked towards Columba to know her will. Columba told it to do the man no harm; so, leaving him terribly frightened, it went and laid itself down at the door, to prevent any one from going out or coming in. Then said Columba to the young man, "Promise to become a Christian, or I will set the bear upon you." The young man promised to be baptized, and the bear allowed him to leave. (See ST. DARIA, below.)—L'abbé Brullée, *Life of St. Columba*.

This may be conversion in the eyes of the abbot Brullée, but I apprehend very few English readers will think so.

A lion defends St. Daria. The following is certainly one of the most romantic stories in the lives and martyrologies of the [Roman] Catholic Church. Numerian, emperor of Rome, gave orders for Chrisantus to be cast into the prison called "Tullianum," and his wife Daria to be sent to the common stews. God, however, changed the brothel into a holy chapel: and a lion, slipping his chain, broke from his den in the amphitheatre, entered the stews, and lay himself down at Daria's feet, making to her signs that he would be her guardian and defender. Presently a young Roman entered, a bold, insolent fellow; but immediately he set foot in the room the lion knocked him down, and, setting one of its paws upon him, looked towards Daria to learn her will. Daria bade the beast do the gallant no harm, and then addressing the young man, she converted him to the Christian faith; and he, on leaving the chamber, went about Rome preaching the gospel, and telling the people there was no god but the God of Christians. When the keepers of the lion entered the stews with the intent of capturing the lion, it fell on them with fury, cast them to the ground, and held them there till it had received instructions from Daria. The holy woman preached to the terrified keepers Christ and Him crucified, and they also became converts, and faithful preachers of the Lord Jesus. Celerinus, the prefect, being informed of all this, caused a fire to be kindled about the house to consume the saint and the lion; but the lion, having received Daria's permission and blessing, bowing down its head most reverently, passed through the flames, and walked peacefully through the crowded streets of Rome without molesting any one. [We are not told what ultimately became of this wonderful lion, nor how Daria escaped. That she did escape, however, is quite certain, as the biographer tells us she was at last buried alive under a pile of stones.] (See ST. COLUMBA, above.)—Verinus and Armenius (priests of St.

Stephen the pope) first wrote the lives of Chrisantus and Daria. Metaphrastês enlarged the biography, and both Usandus in his *Martyrology* and Surius in his *Lives of the Saints* (vol. v.) give full accounts of these favourite saints. They also stand in the *Roman Martyrology*.

St. Oringa delivered from evil men by St. Michael. St. Oringa, on her pilgrimage to Mount Gargano, was attacked at dusk by some men with a view of dishonouring her; but St. Michael flashed like lightning to her defence, and protected her till she arrived in safety at the place of her destination.—*Acta Sanctorum* (reprinted from the *Life of St. Oringa* by Silvanus Razzi).

Milton says—

> So dear to Heaven is saintly chastity,
> That when a soul is found sincerely so,
> A thousand liveried angels lackey her,
> Driving far off each thing of sin and guilt.
> *Comus.*

An angel protects St. Susanna from ravishers. Diocletian wanted Susanna to marry his adopted son Maximian; but she told him she had devoted herself to Christ, and could marry no man. Maximian, greatly disappointed, and determined to indulge his passion, introduced himself clandestinely into her chamber, intending to defile her; but an angel stood by her, and the chamber was lighted with such dazzling brightness that the prince fled aghast, and told the emperor. Diocletian treated the matter with ridicule, and sent Curtius to see into it; but Curtius returned more alarmed than the prince. The emperor declared the whole matter some devilish enchantment, and sent one of his lictors, named Macedonius, to put Susanna to death, if she refused to offer incense to Jupiter. Macedonius took an image of Jupiter with him, and commanded the damsel to offer incense to it; but the angel took the idol, and flung it out of the window into the street. So Macedonius, having scourged her as usual, cut off her head.—*Acta Sanctorum.*

It must be presumed, I suppose, that the lictor did not see the angel, but took it for granted that Susanna had thrown the idol into the street.

Temple a Den of Thieves.

MATT. xxi. 12, 13. Jesus went into the temple of God, and cast out all them that sold and bought in the temple, and overthrew the tables of the money-changers, and the seats of them that sold doves; and said unto them, It is written, My house shall be called the house of prayer; but ye have made it a den of thieves.

Old St. Paul's in the reign of Charles II. Besides booksellers, there were sempstresses, tobacco merchants, vendors of fruit and provisions, Jews and general dealers, all of whom had stalls within the cathedral, and all of whom were making preparations for the business of the day. Shortly afterwards, numbers who came for recreation and amusement made their appearance, and, before ten o'clock, Paul's Walk (as the cathedral nave was termed) was thronged with apprentices, rufflers, porters, water-bearers, higglers with baskets on their heads or under their arms, fishwives, quack doctors, cutpurses, bona robas, merchants, lawyers, and serving-men who came to be hired, and who placed themselves near an oaken block attached to one of the pillars, called the "Serving-man's Log," from the use it was put to. Some of the crowd were smoking, some laughing, others gathering round a ballad-singer who was chanting licentious ditties. Some were buying nostrums; while others were paying court to dames, many of whom were masked. Everything seemed to be got within the sacred edifice except devotion. Here, a man, mounted on the carved marble of a monument, bellowed forth the news of the Dutch war; while another, not far from him, announced from a bench the number of those who had died on the previous day of the pestilence. There, at the very font, was a usurer paying over a sum of money to a gallant, who was sealing the bond for thrice the amount of the loan. Elsewhere, a party of choristers, attended by a troop of boys, were pursuing one who had ventured into the cathedral booted and spurred, and were demanding spur-money. An admirable picture of this curious scene has been given by bishop Earle, in his *Microcosmographia*, published in 1629. "Paul's Walk," he writes, "is the land's epitome, or you may call it the lesser isle of Great Britain. It is more than this, it is the whole world's map, which you may here discern in its perfectest motion, jostling and turning. It is a heap of stones and men with a vast confusion of languages; and, were the steeple not sanctified, nothing could be liker Babel. The noise in it is like that of bees, a strange humming or buzzing, mixed of walking, tongues, and feet. It is a kind of still roar, or loud whisper. It is a great exchange of all discourse, and no business whatsoever but is here astir and afoot. It is the synod of all parts politic joined, and laid together in most serious posture; and they in parliament are not half so busy with the affairs of the nation as the praters in Paul's Walk. It is the general mint of all lies, which are here coined, stamped, and uttered. All inventions are emptied here, and not a few pockets. The best sign of the Temple in it is, that it is the thieves' sanctuary, who rob more safely in a crowd than in a wilderness, while every pillar is a bush to hide them. It is the other expense of the day, after plays and taverns; and men have still oaths left to swear here. The principal inhabitants are stale knights and captains out of service, men of long rapiers and short purses, who, after all, turn merchants here, and traffic for news. St. Faith's Chapel and the crypt, with many other secret chambers in the walls, are ordinary receptacles of stolen goods, and serve as brothels for the libertine." —H. Ainsworth, *Old St. Paul's*, vol. i. pp. 324–327.

Temptations.

Matt. iii. Before Christ began His public ministry, He fasted forty days in the wilderness of Judæa, and was then tempted by the devil. The temptations were: (1) to satisfy His hunger by turning stones into bread; (2) to establish His fame by casting himself down from a pinnacle of the temple in the sight of the people, who would at once acknowledge Him, if He received no injury by the fall; (3) to establish His kingdom by making a league with the devil as His overlord. Christ resisted all the temptations; whereupon Satan left Him, and angels came to minister to Him.

Eve was tempted: (1) By the "lust of the flesh:" she saw that the fruit "was good for food;" and to make stones good for food was Christ's first temptation. (2) By the "pride of life:" she saw that the fruit was good "to make one wise;" and the vain-glory of casting Himself down from the pinnacle of the temple was the second temptation of Jesus Christ. (3) By the "lust of the eyes:" Eve saw that the fruit "was pleasant to the eyes;" and Satan showed Christ the glory of the kingdoms of the world as His third temptation, and promised to give them to Him if He would fall down and worship him.

The three temptations of St. Antony the Great (fourth century). After Antony had sold all he possessed, and had given the proceeds to the poor, he retired into a wilderness, where he was tempted by the devil: (1) by the love of money; (2) by the lust of vain-glory; and (3) by carnal lust. In all these temptations he prevailed, as Christ had set him an example. In the first temptation Satan tried to impress upon the young recluse a vivid remembrance of the wealth he once enjoyed, and to stir up regret for its loss. In the second temptation the devil tried to arouse his self-conceit or self-complacency at the great sacrifice he had made for Christ. "I have left all to follow Thee." In the third temptation Satan stirred up the young man's blood, and tortured him with the lust of the flesh. Being foiled in all these temptations, the devil assumed the form of a black child, and said to Antony, "Young man, I have prevailed over many, but must confess myself discomfited by you." "Who art thou?" demanded Antony. "The Spirit of Impurity," was the reply. This was St. Antony's first contest and first victory over the powers of darkness. —St. Athanasius, *Life of St. Antony the Great*.

The three temptations of St. Julian, bishop of Cuença (A.D. 1207). Eve was tempted by the lust of the flesh, the lust of the eyes, and the pride of life. Being tempted, she fell. Jesus Christ was tempted by the same allurements, and, being tempted, resisted to the last. St. Julian was also tempted by the same three tests: the lust of the appetite; the pride of life; and the lust of the flesh. Being hungry, the devil set before him a table of the most appetizing foods and drinks; but St. Julian would none of them. Being very charitable, and in need of money to support his charities, the devil offered him gold and silver galore, and flattered him by the suggestion that the money was not for himself but for others, especially the poor and needy; but Julian saw at once through the sophistry, and manfully refused the offer. Then came the last temptation, the lust of the eyes. He was quite alone, no one would see him, and a troop of naked women appeared in his cell; but the man of God was proof against the seduction, and, holding up the cross, the phantoms fled.—Bollandus, *Acta Sanctorum*, vol. ii. Jan. 28.

The tempter was not very skilful, or he would have known that your true sportsman infinitely prefers the hare that has given him a good run, to the one that yields itself a voluntary sacrifice. The bishop in his *Choice of Hercules* was far wiser, who describes the enchantress Pleasure thus:—

> Her robe betrayed
> Through the clear texture every tender limb,
> Height'ning the charms it only seemed to shade.

St. Macarius, tempted in his hunger, resists the temptation (A.D. 306–395). St. Macarius being in the desert, extremely enfeebled and faint from long abstinence, the tempter came to him and said, "Since you are the favoured servant of God, ask Him to send nourishment to recruit your strength, that you may be the better able to serve Him." Macarius replied, "God Himself is my strength and my glory; and it is written, 'Thou shalt not tempt the Lord thy God.'" The devil then left him, but only to transform himself into a camel laden with loaves of bread. Macarius, suspecting the deception, fell to the earth in prayer, and immediately the phantom camel and its load vanished into thin air.—*Les Petits Bollandistes* (1880), vol. i. Jan. 2.

St. Waltruda tempted by the devil (A.D. 626-686). Waltruda was the wife of Madelgaire, count of Hainault, and the mother of four children. Two years after the death of her husband she retired from the world, and lived in a little cell at Castleplace, now Mons. Here the devil for a time greatly tormented her; sometimes setting before her eyes the luxuries and honours she enjoyed as countess of Hainault, and which she might still enjoy, if she would return to her proper home. At other times, he pictured to her the love of her children, the affection of her husband, the delights of social life, with plenty and rank, and all the domestic comforts she once enjoyed. Then again he would draw with exaggerated outline the horrors of solitude, its privations, its dangers, its temptations. Sometimes he would present himself before her as a man, and even touch her; but by prayer, by fasting, tears, macerations, and the sign of the cross, she firmly resisted, and finally overcame.—Molan, *Abridged Lives of the Saints of Flanders.*

James says (i. 14), "Every man is tempted, when he is drawn away of his own lust, and enticed." The devil, in this example, looks very like the lingering recollection of former times, mingled with regret. The human form seems to be some familiar acquaintance who tried to persuade Waltruda to return, perhaps even to marry again.

The Plague of Milan (A.D. 1630). A Milanese told Ripamonte, saying, "While I stood in front of the cathedral, I saw a chariot drawn by six white horses, and followed by a numerous attendance. In the chariot sat one of princely demeanour, though his dark, deep-burnt complexion, his long floating hair, the fire of his eyes, and the threatening expression of his lip, gave such an air to the countenance as I never saw before on any mortal face. The stranger stopped his chariot and bade me mount. I could not but obey, and the chariot carried me to a house where I saw many strange and wonderful things. In one part thick flashing lightning dispelled the darkness, and I saw a spectral senate holding their meeting. There were vast empty chambers and extensive gardens. The charioteer, after showing me many sights which well excited my curiosity, took me to his treasury, and promised to give me all I saw, if I would bow the knee to him and do his bidding. I positively declined, and was suddenly transported back to the spot where I was taken up."—Ripamonte, *De Peste Mediolani*, p. 17.

In this plague 140,000 had died in three months.

Tobit buries the Dead.

TOBIT i. 16-21; ii. 7, 8. Tobit was wont to give alms to his brethren; and if he saw any of his nation dead, and cast behind the walls of Nineveh, he buried them. He also buried those slain by Sennacherib. On the Feast of Pentecost, his son told him of a Jew who had been strangled, and cast out in the market-place. Then Tobit left the feast untasted, to go and bury the dead; but his neighbours mocked him, and said, This man is not afraid to be put to death for this matter. He fled away, but lo! he burieth the dead again.

Burying the dead, in the [Roman] Catholic Church, is one of the "Seven Spiritual Works of Mercy" (see Index); and this will account for the extraordinary care taken by mediæval Christians to bury martyrs. The ancient Egyptians made the want of interment a *post-mortem* punishment for crimes of unusual atrocity. The Jews treated dead bodies with marked respect, and Tobit evidently made it a special business and work of mercy. The ancient Greeks looked upon neglect to bury the dead as a crime of the deepest dye; and every one who has read Horace will call to mind the last two lines of his ode about the shipwrecked Archytas (bk. i. ode 28)—

Quanquam festinas, non est mora longa; licebit
Injecto ter pulvere, curras.

See also Virgil, *Æneid*, bk. vi. line 365.

The lords Abdon and Sennen bury many dead. St. Abdon and St. Senner were two Persian nobles, in the reign of Decius, emperor of Rome, and were Christians. Decius, having obtained a great victory, thought to show his gratitude to the gods by a sacrifice of their enemies, the Christians; so he put many of them to death, and forbade any one to bury them. The lords Abdon and Sennen, disregarding this prohibition, buried all who were put to death for the faith's sake. When Decius heard thereof, he was exceedingly angry, and commanded the two noblemen to be brought before him. "Why have you dared to break our imperial edict?" said Decius. "I have strictly charged that none shall honour those who suffer death for dishonouring our immortal gods. Your disobedience of my proclamation shows me you are yourselves in the same vile ways." Abdon and Sennen answered with firmness and modesty: "True, O king, we have buried those Christians put to death by thy decree, and we well knew your highness had forbidden any one to bury them. But we fear God, and honour Him above all the kings of the earth. Know, too, O imperial Cæsar, that we are Christians, and not ashamed to confess it." Decius ordered the two lords to be reserved in chains till he made his triumphal entry, and then to be led in his train as state prisoners, to deter others from following their example. This was done, and on the day of triumph, when Decius entered the senate-house, he commanded his two noble captives to atone for their offences by offering sacrifice to an idol of Mars placed before them by Claudius, the chief pontiff. This they refused to do, and were, therefore, cast to two fierce lions in the amphitheatre; but the lions offered them no sort of violence. Then the sword-players were set upon them, and hewed them to pieces.—Edward Kinesman (1623), *Lives of the Saints* (July 30, A.D. 253).

St. Odilo covers two dead children with his cloak (A.D. 962–1049). St. Odilo, abbot of Cluny, going one day to St. Denis, near Paris, saw two children lying in the road, killed by the cold. Dismounting from his horse, he stripped off his serge cloak, and, wrapping it round the dead bodies, buried them decently with his own hands.—Bollandus, *Acta Sanctorum*, vol. i. Jan. 1.

Tongues of Fire. (See Aureola.)

Acts ii. 1–3. When the day of Pentecost was fully come, [the disciples] were all with one accord in one place; and suddenly there came a sound from heaven as of a rushing mighty wind, and it filled all the house where they were sitting; and there appeared unto them cloven tongues like as of fire, and it sat upon each of them.

A globe of fire sits on the head of St. Aldegundis (A.D. 689). Three days before her death, a globe of fire descended from heaven, and sat on the head of St. Aldegundis; Christ also, with a troop of angels, was seen around the dying saint. When the globe of fire vanished, an admirable luminosity took its place, playing round the bed on which the saint was lying. All present saw it, and were astonished. At last the light hovered like a bird up into the sky; the soul of the saint had left her body, and her soul had returned to Him who gave it.—L'abbé Delbos, *Life of St. Aldegundis.*

A pillar of fire sits on the head of St. Brigit (A.D. 436–523). St. Brigit or Bride, the patron saint with St. Patrick of Ireland, was the natural daughter of Duplac and a slave. When she took the veil, the bishop Mel, who gave it her, declared that he saw a pillar of fire settle on her head. She had lost an eye, but when she fell prostrate and kissed the step of the altar, she recovered her eye, "et son visage reprit sa première beauté, à laquelle Notre Seigneur ajouta encore un nouvel éclat, ne voulant pas que celle qui avait désiré pour son amour perdre la beauté de son corps, afin de conserver la pureté de son âme, demeurât avec la moindre difformité corporelle." —*Les Petits Bollandistes* (7th edit. 1880), vol. ii. p. 184.

What Mgr. Guérin alludes to is this: St. Brigit was so very beautiful that she was solicited in marriage by many, but she had vowed herself the bride of Jesus Christ, and, to put a stop to these constant offers of marriage, she prayed God to make her ugly. Her prayer was heard, "et par la perte d'un œil, la sainte fille demeura si difforme qu'il ne se trouva plus personne qui parlât de l'épouser."

The Holy Ghost as a globe of fire descends on St. Gertrude (A.D. 626–659). One day, as St. Gertrude was in prayer before the altar of St. Sixtus, a globe of fire appeared on her head. It was seen by all the sisters, and signified that the Holy Ghost filled her soul with heavenly light.—Usuard, *Martyrology*, *Acta Sanctorum* (by one who was present at her funeral), March 17.

Jeanne Marie de Maillé was environed with a globe of fire (A.D. 1332–1414). When Jeanne Marie de Maillé ministered in St. Anne's chapel, she prayed that God would vouchsafe to bestow on her some small spark of that heavenly fire which was so freely poured on the apostles on the day of Pentecost. Her prayer was answered, and a globe of fire encompassed her whole body, "et elle fut comme embrasée d'un tel amour, qu'on s'aperçut extérieurement des merveilles qui s'opéraient dans son âme."—Père de Boisgaultier (her confessor), *Life of Jeanne Marie de Maillé.*

A pillar of fire descends on St. John of Matha at his ordination (A.D. 1160–1213). When St. John of Matha was ordained by the bishop of Paris, as the words were pronounced, "Receive the Holy Ghost," the Spirit of God was seen to descend on the young priest, and settle on his head, like a pillar of fire. And when the host was elevated, his face seemed on fire, his eyes fixed, and his head surrounded by an aureola most luminous. At the close of the service, the bishops present asked the young priest if he had seen a vision, when he replied, "I saw the angel of the Saviour, sitting on a cloud of glory. His face was brighter than the sun, his robes were white as snow, and he bore on his breast a cross of two colours, red and azure. At his feet I beheld two slaves laden with chains; one was a Moor, and the other a Christian. The hands of the angel were crossed, the right hand towards the Christian, and the left towards the Moor. That, father, is what I saw."—R. P. Calixte de la Providence, *Life of St. John of Matha.*

Flames of fire played round the cradle of [*St.*] *John Nepomuck at birth* (A.D. 1330). When John Nepomuck was born, marvellous flames of light played round him as he lay in his cradle, "presaging the gift of the Holy Spirit which would be bestowed on him, and that in due time he would be a light in the world, full of grace and truth."

Again. When he was thrown into the Moldau, by order of king Wenceslaus, for refusing to reveal the confessions of the queen, a fire played on the river, and a thousand stars lighted it. A stream of light also issued from the water, reflecting the glory of the martyr's soul. The body slowly drifted down the stream, throwing off rays of light in all directions. In fact, a "troop of light" went before and followed after the body, as a funeral procession. All the city ran to see the prodigy, and Wenceslaus, terrified almost to death, fled into the country, forbidding any one to follow him.—*Acta Sanctorum* (Bollandists), May 16.

St. Elmo's fire. St. Adelelm, bishop of Bruges, also called St. Elmo or Elesmo (1100, etc.), started one dark and stormy night to visit Ranco, bishop of Auvergne. To guide him on his way, he lighted a candle, which he handed to his companion to carry, and bade him lead on. The candle was wholly unprotected by lantern or other covering, but though the wind blew in gusts and the rain fell in torrents, it burnt with a bright and steady light, a lamp unto their feet and a lantern to their path. From this, the electric lights seen before and after storms about mastheads are called "fires of St. Elmo." It will be remembered that the Roman poets not unfrequently refer to these corpusants or comazants; a single flame they called Helen, and said it foretold that the worst of the storm was yet to come; if more than one luminous flame appeared, they called them Castor and Pollux, and said they signified that the worst of the storm was over. Horace refers to the latter—

> But when the sons of Leda shed
> Their star-lamps on our vessel's head,
> The storm-winds cease, the troubled spray
> Falls from the rocks, clouds haste away,
> And, on the bosom of the deep,
> In peace the angry billows sleep.
> *Odes*, bk. i. 12.

Thomas Chalkley, Dec. 1731, says he saw several of these corpusants in his voyage from Barbadoes to Philadelphia. —*Journal.*

In 1696 Mons. de Forbin saw more than thirty of them on the vessel in which he was sailing.

For the legend of St. Elmo, see St. Rudolf (who died 1130), *Life of St. Adelelm.*

St. Elmo's fires seen on land. Comazants are not unfrequently seen on land, also at the extremities of sharp metallic bodies, such as the lances of soldiers, the points of bayonets, and sometimes on the extreme branches of trees, the hair of the head, the ferules of umbrellas, the rims of hats; the clothes, the nose, ears, and fingers. Sometimes they assume the form of fiery jets, sometimes of globes of fire. Occasionally, a crackling or hissing noise accompanies the phenomenon. Pliny, in his *Natural History*, mentions it, but the most interesting example is that of Iulus, the son of Æneas, when about to flee from Troy—

> —— manus inter mœstorumque ora parentum
> Ecce levis summo de vertice visus Iuli
> Fundere lumen apex, tractuque innoxia molli
> Lambere flamma comas, et circum tempora pasci.
> Nos pavidi trepidare metu, crinemque flagrantem
> Excutere, et sanctos restinguere fontibus ignes.
> *Æneid*, bk. ii. v. 681, etc.

> Last night I saw St. Elmo's stars,
> With their glimmering lanterns all at play.
> Longfellow, *Golden Legend.*

> Sudden breaking on their raptured sight
> Appeared the splendour of St. Elmo's light.
> Hoole, *Orlando Furioso*, bk. ix.

A flame of fire on the lance of Poppo led to his conversion (A.D. 1048). When Poppo, in his youthful days, went to visit his intended bride, as he was riding with several retainers, night drew on apace, and suddenly a dazzling flash of light illumined him in a blaze of glory. As it faded away, he spurred his horse to greater speed, and then noticed that a flame burnt on the point of his spear. It was as though he rode bearing a tall church taper in his hand. Astounded at this "miracle," he reined in his steed, and, turning to his companions, said, "God calls me to another light." (See ST. ELMO'S FIRES, above.)—Everhelm, abbot of Hautmont (Poppo's contemporary), *Modern Roman Martyrology* (1669).

Touching for the King's Evil.

Lev. xiii. 9. When the plague of leprosy is in a man, then he shall be brought unto the priest.

Luke v. 12, 13. When Jesus was in a certain city, behold a man full of leprosy: who seeing Jesus fell on his face, saying, Lord, if Thou wilt, Thou canst make me clean. And Jesus put forth His hand, and touched him, saying, I will: be thou clean. And immediately the leprosy departed from him.

Leprosy, like scrofula, is a skin disease, which corrupts the blood. The Jews regarded it as a disease sent from God, and looked to the priest rather than to the physician for its cure. There are many points of resemblance between the two maladies. Probably the priestly character of kings gave rise to the notion that their touch would cure the malady, subsequently called the "king's evil," that is, the malady which kings cure, as a prerogative of their office.

Colquhoun, in his *Iris Revelata*, 1836, attributes the cure to animal magnetism; but this is absurd, for why then should it be the prerogative of kings more than of any other men?

The French generally attribute the virtue to a miraculous gift of St. Marcoul, abbot of Corbeny; but if so, how could our English monarchs have pretended to it?

Others attribute the grace to the holy chrism with which the French kings were anointed at their consecration. But this, again, will not apply to the kings and queens of Great Britain.

The writer in the *English Cyclopædia*, referred to below, ascribes the gift to the right divine of royal succession, and therefore excludes William III. from the divine prerogative. But surely William the Conqueror was not by right divine the successor of Edward who preceded him. His only right was that of stronger battalions, and not of blood succession.

It seems to me that scrofula takes the place of Jewish leprosy, and the priestly claim of the kings of France and England is the real solution of the question.

St. Benedict says, "The virtue resides in the kingly office, and is quite irrespective of the merits or demerits of the sovereign." This, however, can hardly be admitted, as Philippe I. and Louis XI. were deprived of the grace for their ill lives. Neither does an immoral life in all cases cut off the inheritance of the divine gift, for where can be found a more infamously immoral man than Louis XV.?

English history and statistics of the king's touch. Brompton (1198) is the first author to ascribe the gift of touching for the "king's evil" to Edward the Confessor (1042–1066). Stow, in his *Annals*, gives at length an account of the first "cure." It was that of a young woman who had a disease about the jaws and cheeks "like kernels which they termed Akornes." He tells us that the king sent for a basin of water, and, dipping his finger therein, he frequently touched the parts affected, every now and then forming with the tip of his finger the mark of a cross. The persons to be touched were selected by the king's surgeon, and the number went on increasing every year.

Edward I. (1272) introduced the practice of giving a gold or silver medal, called a touch-piece, to the persons he touched. This fact is distinctly stated in the *Records of the Tower*. It is an error, therefore, to suppose that this custom began with Henry VII., as most writers assert. Dr. Johnson, in 1714, was the last person to receive a touch-piece. (See Imposture, p. 186.)

Queen Elizabeth (1558–1603) touched, but discontinued, as superstitious, the sign of the cross.

Charles I., in 1650, by a pompous proclamation, invited all who stood in need of a cure to repair to him "for the heavenly gift."

Charles II., between 1667 and 1682, touched above four thousand persons yearly for the king's evil.

William III. (1694–1702) made some pretensions to this gift of the right divine, but met with no great success; probably he wanted faith in his sacred power.

Anne, on March 30, 1714, touched as many as two hundred persons, amongst whom was Samuel Johnson, the future lexicographer, then thirteen months old. He had been sent up by sir John Floyer, of Lichfield. Being asked, many years afterwards, if he had any recollection of the event, he replied, "I have a confused, but somehow a sort of solemn recollection, of a lady in diamonds and long black hood."

George I., in 1714, had the good sense to discontinue this foolery; but "The Office for Touching" remained in the book of "Common Prayer" till 1719, when it was quietly dropped out, without Act of Parliament.

It was still continued by the Pretenders. Thus Thomas Carte (1686–1754) tells us, in his *History of England*, that one Christopher Lowell went to the court of the Pretender, held at Avignon, and received a cure, in 1716; and that when prince Charles Edward was at Holyrood House, he touched a child for the king's evil, in Oct. 1745. This instance is somewhat remarkable, as Charles Edward was at the time only "prince of Wales," and not "king" even by pretence.

The writer of the article "Scrofula," in the *English Cyclopædia*, tells us that the power did not reside in Mary, William, or Anne, because they did not reign by right divine; but of all our sovereigns, the name of Anne stands out the most conspicuous for this silly superstition; and as for "right divine," one would have thought the absurdity had been buried in the tomb of the Capulet with the last Pretender, Charles Edward.

French history and statistics of the king's touch. The kings of France laid claim to the gift of touching for the king's evil, and that many years before the reign of Edward the Confessor. Probably it was Edward's residence in France which put this nonsense into his head, and introduced it into England. Respecting the origin of the prerogative, there are five persons pointed to by writers on the subject: Clovis, St. Marcoul [Marculphus], Robert the Pious, Louis le Gros, and St. Louis or Louis IX.

Mezeray distinctly asserts the gift was conferred on Clovis at his baptism, in 496, and adds that the first person he cured was his favourite Laninet.

In regard to St. Louis, we have proof positive that Louis le Gros (1108–1137), more than a century before his saintly namesake, touched for the distemper; for Guilbert of Nogent, who died in 1124, in his *Vows of the Saints*, writes, "I myself have seen our seigneur king Louis le Gros perform the usual prodigy. Yea, standing at his side, I have seen more than once, with my own eyes, persons suffering from scrofula in the neck, and others with similar sores in other parts of the body, come in crowds to be touched. The king made on them the sign of the cross, and that was all. His father, Philippe I. (1060–1198), possessed at one time the same gift, but was deprived of it on account of his evil living."

As Louis le Gros performed "the usual prodigy," of course the custom dated before his reign or that of his father, who "was deprived of the divine grace." The general opinion is that the gift was bestowed miraculously by St. Marcoul [Marculphus] in the sixth century.—See Benedict XIV., *De Canonizatione Sanctorum*, bk. iv. ch. 3, No. 21.

It is quite certain that all the kings of France. from Louis IX. to Louis XIII., both inclusive, made a pilgrimage to Corbeny before they attempted to touch any one for the malady. It was customary, after consecration at the cathedral of St. Remi, at Reims, to go on pilgrimage to the abbey of Corbeny, where the king was met by the monks bearing the head of St. Marcoul. This they placed reverently in the hands of the king, and the king, carrying it devoutly to the abbey church, placed it on the high altar. Next day, after mass, the scrofulous candidates were brought forward, and the king touched every one of them, making the sign of the cross, and saying, "Le roi te touche, Dieu te guérit." The persons touched then made a *neuvaine*, during which time they fasted, and in this manner "innombrables malades ont été guéris par les rois de France."

ST. LOUIS (1226–1270) certainly made a pilgrimage to Corbeny, after his consecration at Reims; and Guillaume de Nangis, a contemporary, in his *Life of Louis*, tells us that the pious king, whenever he touched for the evil, "pour la guérison desquels Dieu a accordé aux rois de France une grâce singulière," always used the sign of the cross as he uttered the prescribed words; but, he adds, some of his predecessors omitted the wholesome sign.

PHILIPPE IV., le Bel (1284–1314), on his death-bed, called his son, Louis le Hutin, to his side, and taught him how to touch; telling him at the same time that God would not hearken to him if he was an evil liver.—Dutillet, *Recuil des Rois de France.*

PHILIPPE VI., le Valois (1328–1350), "cured" fourteen thousand persons of the king's evil.

LOUIS XI. (1461–1483), like Philippe I., was deprived of the prerogative for his evil living. A pithy anecdote is told about this king. After his attack of apoplexy, he sent for St. Francis of Paula, who was very celebrated for his miraculous cures, but suffered himself from scrofula. The bargain was that St. Francis should cure the king of his apoplexy, and the king should touch St. Francis for his strumous disease. We are told that God, by special revelation, directed St. Francis to go to Plessis les Tours, but when he reached the royal palace, neither could the saint cure the king, nor the king the saint.

LOUIS XII. (1498–1515), who "reconciled himself to God seven times a year by confession," was accustomed, after confession, to touch those brought to him.—Seyssel, *Histoire de Louis XII.*

FRANÇOIS I., in 1515, touched for the distemper at Bologna, in the presence of the pope; and, in 1542, he gave this royal ordinance: "On our return from Reims, we went to Corbeny, where we and our predecessors have been accustomed to make oblations, and pay reverence to the precious relics of St. Marcoul for the admirable gift of healing the king's evil, which he imparted miraculously to the kings of France, at the pleasure of the Creator. The grace we exercised in the usual way by touching the parts affected, and signing them with the sign of the cross."

HENRI IV. (1589–1610) touched and healed above fifteeen thousand persons a year (*quınze mille*) !! so, at least, says André Larent, the king's physician and counsellor, in his book on this royal prerogative, published in 1609.

LOUIS XV. (1643–1715) was the first king since St. Louis (1226) who discontinued the pilgrimage to Corbeny. In the year of his consecration (1654) there was war in Picardy, and it was thought inadvisable to risk the life of the young king by so hazardous a journey. The relics of St. Marcoul were, therefore, brought to the abbey of St. Remi, at Reims; and, after mass, the young king touched, in the abbey garden, those presented to him to the number of two thousand and more. In 1686 he touched sixteen hundred sufferers.

LOUIS XV. (1715–1774). On the consecration of Louis XV., the relics of St. Marcoul were again brought to the abbey of St. Remi, at Reims.

LOUIS XVI. (1774–1793) thus writes: "Dear and well-beloved friends, we hoped to make our pilgrimage to Corbeny, after our consecration at Reims, following the example of our predecessors, but the intendant of the province of Champagne reports that the state of the roads and the great floods have rendered the journey impracticable. Unwilling, however, to omit any of the devotions observed by our predecessors, we have directed that the coffer containing the head of St. Marcoul be brought to the abbey of St. Remi; and we will be there, on the fourteenth day of the month, to fulfil all that piety and charity require of us."

CHARLES X. (1824–1830). Charles X. was consecrated in 1825, when the head of St. Marcoul was again brought to Reims; and, after the *neuvaine*, the king touched for the evil. (See the *procès-verbal* in the *Ami de la Religion*, vol. xiv., where every particular of the "cures effected" are set down in detail, and attested by Desgenettes of Notre-dame des Victoires.)

Every English work I have seen, on the subject of "Touching for the King's Evil," states that the practice was discontinued in England in 1714, but continued to be observed in France up to 1775. This is an error, as Charles X., in 1825, most certainly exercised the divine prerogative.

Trance, Ecstasy, etc. (See VISION.)

2 COR. xii 2–4. I knew a man in Christ (whether in the body, or out of the body, I cannot tell); such a one caught up to the third heaven, and heard unspeakable words.

REV i. 10. John, the divine, was in the Spirit on the Lord's day. And then was revealed to him the Son of man in His glory, and commanded him to write to the angels of the seven Churches of Asia what was told him.

REV. iv. 2. I [John] was in the Spirit, and behold there appeared the throne of God in heaven, with elders and the heavenly host in adoration. Then was opened the book with seven seals, and afterwards were sounded the seven trumpets.

The Greek ecstatici. The Greek ecstatici were diviners, who used to lie in trances; and, when they came to themselves, gave strange accounts of what they had seen while "out of the body." The Neoplatonist notion was, that men had a capacity of passing beyond the limits of their own persons; and, when so excorporated, that they could acquire knowledge of the infinite and absolute, even of absolute truth. Pilate refers to this belief, when he asked Jesus in the judgment hall, "What is truth?"—what is that absolute truth which is removed above and beyond the shades of human opinion and fallible doubt? Man thus carried out of the body was no longer himself, but a disembodied spirit, which could identify itself with the Eternal Spirit, and could then see and know things pertaining to the world of spirits. This ecstasy, however, was neither to be attained nor continued by the will of man; but was wholly a gift of inspiration, higher and holier than that of poet or prophet. Epimenidês, the Cretan, is reported to have remained entranced for seventy-five years. Plato (*Politics*, bk. x.) speaks of one Pamphilos, a Phærean, who lay entranced for ten days among the carcases of men, and on waking up related what places he had seen in heaven, earth, and hell, and what was being done at each while he was present. Plutarch (*Socratês' demon*) tells us it was reported of Hermodoros, the Klazomenian, that his soul would leave his body for several days and nights, travel over divers countries, and return. On waking he would give a minute description of all he had seen, and even hold discourse with persons far away. Unhappily, the body of Hermodoros was at last burnt, while his spirit was on one of its ecstatic wanderings. Many other stories of the same sort are mentioned in history.

St. Angelus of Acri had frequent ecstasies (1669–1739). Angelus of Acri had frequent ecstasies, but towards the end of his life they increased in frequency. Six months before his death he returned to the convent of the Capucins, and lost his sight. He recovered it when he celebrated mass, and lost it again immediately the service was over.—*Life of Angelus of Acri* (1825, Rome).

The ecstasy and vision of St. Barontius the hermit (A.D. 700). While Barontius was in the abbey of Lonrey he fell into an ecstasy, and for a time seemed terribly distressed. It seemed as if he was in great pain, and his respiration was very difficult. Afterwards he quieted down, and those about him thought he was dead. Next day he awoke and cried, "Glory be to Thee, O God!" He then recounted to those present what he had seen. He said two devils took him by the throat, and tried to strangle him. This lasted till the hour of tierce, when the archangel Raphael came to his help, and, taking his soul out of his body, carried it up to heaven. There he saw many of the happy ones which he knew, and was taken before St. Peter, patron of Lonrey. The devils came and accused him of sins, and claimed him as their subject; but St. Peter, in his defence, pleaded that he had expiated his sins by almsgiving, confession, and penance. The prince of the apostles then commanded the devils to leave his presence, and bade two white ones see that they were shut up in hell. After a few words of advice from the judge, Barontius was carried back to his cell, and woke from his trance.—*Les Petits Bollandistes*, vol. iii. p. 642.

The trance of Sister Benedicta (A.D. 1698). In the fifty-second year of her age, on the day of the Assumption, 1698, Sister Benedicta was carried up to heaven in a trance by the Virgin Mary, whether in the body or out of the body she never knew; but, buoyed upwards on waves of light, harmony, and perfume, she traversed the different phalanxes of the happy celestials. The trancist tells us: "The most elevated circle is that of martyrs, arrayed in red; then come the virgins, dressed all in blue; then the other happy ones of inferior rank, whose raiments vary in tint and tinge according to their respective merits." Benedicta recognized two directors who had been dead for several years, and her own mother. She was going to speak to her, but the Virgin Mary led her away to show her other visions. At the close, the same angelic host which had carried her up to heaven brought her back again to her own cell. She was quite intoxicated with what she had seen, and for fifteen days could neither eat, drink, nor sleep. —Mgr. Guérin (chamberlain of pope Leo XIII.), *Vies des Saints* (1880), vol. v. p. 226.

(Mgr. Barnadou, bishop of Gap, is collecting such data as these to effect the canonization of Sister Benedicta, 1883.)

St. Catherine of Siena was subject to frequent ecstasies (A.D. 1347–1380). St. Catherine of Siena, in her ecstasies, sometimes tumbled into water, and sometimes into fire, but escaped unhurt. When she was at Pisa she had an ecstasy, and all thought she was dead; but after lying in this state a whole day she returned to life, and the first words she uttered were, "O my soul, unhappy thou!" Catherine then told the sisters she had been shown all the mysteries of the life to come, the glories of the saints, and the confusion of the impenitent. She had seen the Deity; she had seen St. Peter, who told her that her hour was not yet come—she must still a little longer show God's judgments to man, and convert sinners from their evil ways. Not long after this she had another ecstasy, when she received in her body the five wounds of the Redeemer. (See STIGMATA.)—*Vita Sanctorum* (Bollandists), vol. iii. April 30.

Columba of Rieti had frequent ecstasies (A.D. 1477–1501). Columba scourged herself thrice every night: once for her own trespasses; the second time for the conversion of sinners; and the third time for souls in purgatory. She passed nearly the whole night in prayer, and God favoured her with constant ecstasies. Father Sebastian of Perouse, her confessor, makes the following statement:—"One day while in prayer, Jesus Christ went through all His passions in her sight. She saw Him in the olive garden; she saw Him before Annas and Caiaphas; she saw Him before Pilate. When, however, she saw the Redeemer's hands tied to the whipping-post, heard the sound of the lashes, and saw the blood flow, her anguish was so great, that she began to scourge herself in a similar manner. Her mother, hearing her screams, ran to her, and cried, 'My child, what is the matter? Why kill yourself thus?' But Columba, still in her ecstasy, neither heard the words nor made any answer."

At another time, during the sacrament

of the Eucharist, she saw Jesus above the chalice, nailed to the cross, pale and dead. His side was pierced with the spear, His head crowned with thorns. She fell fainting to the earth; and, on recovering, said to her confessor, "Pray for me, my father, that God will spare me these sad visions, or I shall die of grief."

Sometimes, in her ecstasies, her soul quitted her body. One day her mother entered her chamber, and saw her daughter sitting on her altar, like one asleep. She lifted her down, in order to lay her on her bed, when all her limbs and head fell as if the body was lifeless. The mother thought she was dead, and screamed. Some of her neighbours came, and they also thought she was dead. All blamed the confessor, and accused him of murdering his victim by enforced abstinence and austerities. No doubt, in their irritation, they would have committed some breach of the peace; but all of a sudden the damsel revived.

Greatly longing to see the holy places connected with the Saviour's history on earth, Columba had an ecstasy which lasted five days, during which she was "led by the Spirit" to Jerusalem, and Christ showed her all the places consecrated by His life and death. It was Christmas Day, and she saw the Babe in the manger between an ass and an ox; the Virgin was there, and Joseph, and many angels singing the *Gloria in Excelsis*. It was the Epiphany, and she saw the star guiding the wise men." Her confessor, seeing a globe of fire above the house, came to learn the cause, and Columba told him she had just been shown the star of the Magi; it had filled the chamber with its light, and left behind a most ravishing perfume.—*Life of the Beatified Columba of Rieti.*

The ecstasies of St. Flora (A.D. 1309–1347). St. Flora had frequent ecstasies, which often lasted a considerable time. One All-Saints' Day her soul was caught up to heaven, and remained out of her body for twenty-two days, but we are not told what visions were shown her in this long trance.—L'abbé Cyprien Lacarrière, *Life of St. Flora.*

The ecstasies of St. Francis of Assisi (A.D. 1182–1226). For the two years which St. Francis survived, after receiving the stigmata or marks of the passion on his body, he was very ill and very depressed in spirits. He was quite blind, but his mental vision was keener than ever, and God favoured him with frequent ecstasies, in which his spirit was caught up to the third heaven. Christ often came to bid him good cheer, showed him heavenly visions, and opened his ears to hear celestial music.

Again. On one occasion St. Francis went to dine with Sister Clara, and "made discourse so lofty and mysterious that all present fell into an ecstasy." The room where they were assembled seemed to be on fire. So the repast was a spiritual, not a corporeal one.—Chavin de Malin, *Life of St. Francis of Assisi.*

This looks very much like as if St. Clara had made a good blazing fire, and she, with all her guests, felt drowsy, and fell asleep.

St. Frodibert was caught up into the third heaven (A.D. 673). God accorded to St. Frodibert more than once to be caught up into the third heaven. On one of these occasions he was in conference with the abbot Theudecarius, when suddenly he was caught up, and heard the heavenly choir singing, "Holy, holy, holy, Lord God Almighty, which was, and is, and is to come." Ravished by the unspeakable melody, St. Frodibert implored that his companion might be permitted to share his divine ravishment, and it was granted him. It was by Theudecarius that this favour shown by God to St. Frodibert became known.—Camuzat, *Promptuarium Sacrarum Antiquitatum.* (Lupellus also wrote a *Life of St. Frodibert.*)

St. Fursy, during sickness, saw and heard the angelic choir. While St. Fursy was building his monastery at Burgh Castle, in Suffolk, he fell into a trance, and "quitting the body from evening to cock-crow, beheld the angelic choir, and heard them singing the celestial anthems."—Bede, *Ecclesiastical History*, bk. iii. ch. 19.

This might have been the delirium of fever, for Bede tells us he was "sick" at the time.

St. Fursy, in a trance, is shown the Holy Trinity (A.D. 650). St. Fursy, in a trance, was shown a revelation, like the apostle John in the island of Patmos. First several angels came and told him that the "four fires which consume the world and lose the souls of men, are: (1) infidelity to the promises made at baptism; (2) thirst for riches; (3) schism and the spirit of contention; and (4) disregard of the life to come." He then heard the trisagion sung: "Holy, holy, holy, Lord God Almighty, which was, and is, and is to come. . . . Thou art worthy, O Lord, to receive glory and honour and power. Amen." Then saw he, amidst the angelic host, the great Triune. It was a three in one, and a one in three—distinctly three, but with no shade of difference either in form, or voice, or brightness. St. Beodan and St. Meldan told him what the vision meant, and showed him things to come. Then saw he the spirit of a usurer from the bottomless pit, which God allowed to cast itself at the feet of St. Fursy, and to leave on his shoulders and jaw marks of fire, in punishment of his having accepted a garment which this usurer had in pawn.—Bede, *Ecclesiastical History*. (Reproduced by Ribadeneira in his *Flower of the Saints;* and many others.)

St. Fursy, we are told, prayed God that these marks might never be effaced, and they remained on him as long as he lived. Whenever he spoke to the monks about hell, he trembled fearfully, and the sweat rolled from him in a shower.

Gertrude of Ostend often entranced for several weeks together (A.D. 1358). Gertrude of Ostend was the daughter of a peasant, and was so fond of singing the hymn which begins, "The day He rose," that it is called by her name. Gertrude is famed for her ecstasies, in which she sometimes remained rapt for six weeks or more, during all which time "she was a stranger to this earth." When her spirit was caught up on these occasions, a ravishing "odour of sanctity" filled her chamber.—Bollandus, *Acta Sanctorum*, vol. i. Jan. 6.

The ecstasies of Brother Giles, companion of St. Francis of Assisi (A.D. 1209–1272). The spirit of Brother Giles held such frequent communion with God, that though *in* the earth he was not *of* it. His ecstasies were long and frequent. Whenever any one spoke to him about the elect of God, he fell into an ecstasy which lasted for hours, and sometimes days, on which occasions he lost all consciousness, and neither heard what was said to him, nor returned any answer. Gregory X. once sent for him, but he had scarcely entered into the presence of his holiness, when he fell into an ecstasy, and remained motionless, with his eyes raised to heaven. One day he said to the pope, a saint should always keep both eyes open—his right to look at things celestial, and his left to keep in order things on earth.—*Acta Sanctorum* (Bollandists), April 23.

The great trance of Ignatius Loyola (A.D. 1491–1556). Of all the divine favours bestowed on Ignatius Loyola, none were more remarkable than his ecstasy, which lasted eight days, beginning on Saturday evening and continuing till eight o'clock at night the Saturday following, during all which time his body was perfectly insensible. He was thought to be dead, and arrangements were made for his funeral; only a slight motion of the heart caused it to be delayed. He would never say what he saw in this ecstasy, and would never speak of it, except to his most intimate friends. His reticence greatly increased his reputation, for he was thought to be the possessor of a secret of the life to come unknown to others, which only his great modesty forbade him to make known.—*Acta Sanctorum*, July 31.

The trance or ecstasy of Jeanne Marie de Maillé (A.D. 1332–1414). One holy Thursday, as Jeanne Marie de Maillé was reading the Passion of Christ, she was ravished in ecstasy till the following morning. God transported her to paradise, and taught her to understand the greatness and the fall of Adam. She saw his return to paradise, and God revealed to her a perfect and clear knowledge of every event in the Old and New Testaments up to the time of the Passion. —Père de Boisgaultier (her confessor), *Life of Jeanne Marie de Maillé*.

St. John-Joseph de la Croix had frequent ecstasies (A.D. 1654–1734). St. John de la Croix had frequent ecstasies, in some of which his body was buoyed up as high as the ceiling of his cell. In others he was favoured with heavenly visions. In these ecstasies he was dead to all that passed around him; he neither saw, nor heard, nor felt anything; he remained as motionless as a marble statue, and his face grew bright as burning coals. Sometimes a glory of light encircled his head, and sometimes he held communion with the Virgin Mary. One Christmas Day Jesus Himself came to him as an infant, and was nursed in his arms for several hours. What is even more remarkable in these ecstasies is, that he was sometimes in two or more places at the same time.—Cardinal Wiseman, *Evangelic Demonstrations*, vol. xvi., of Mons. Migne.

The ecstasies of St. Joseph of Copertino (A.D. 1603–1663). The acts of the process of canonization refer to the ecstasies of St. Joseph of Copertino. He was constantly entranced. On one occasion the superior commanded him to return to himself, to leave the supernatural world for the world of this work-a-day life, and he instantly obeyed He seemed amazed that any one should think it strange to pass from earth to heaven, and from life to death, or back again. His ecstasies were a veritable absence from the body, a living death. He remained throughout in the same posture, whether sitting, kneeling, standing, or walking—his hands crossed, his eyes uplifted. No physical force had any effect on him. Sometimes he was pricked with needles, sometimes he was branded with hot iron, sometimes a torch or candle was held to his sides; but he showed no sign of feeling. One day he said to the cardinal of Lauria, "My brothers mock me for my ecstasies. They burn my hands, they break my fingers." And he showed the cardinal his blisters and broken fingers, but the cardinal only laughed. The cardinal asking him what an ecstasy was like, St. Joseph answered, "They seem like transportations into a gallery full of the new and the beautiful, where, as in a glass, one sees the wonders which it may please God to show."—Dominic Bernini, *Life of St. Joseph of Copertino.*

The ecstasies of Father Livier de Ripa Transona (A.D. 1556–1598). Father Livier de Ripa Transona would remain long hours in ecstasy, having foretastes of heaven. In these trances not unfrequently Jesus as an infant would appear to him, and sometimes the holy mother also. Father Livier often conversed with both freely, and felt how true it is that to die would be gain.—*Les Petits Bollandistes*, vol. xv. p. 16.

The ecstasies of St. Mary Magdalene of Pazzi (A.D. 1566–1607). Mary Magdalene of Pazzi, canonized by Clement X. (1670–1676), was noted for her ecstasies. After her novitiate she fell dangerously ill, and was taken to the infirmary, where she fell into an ecstasy, and her face became luminous and radiant as the sun. She remained an hour in this state; and for four successive days, after every communion, she was favoured with similar ravishments. Sometimes her ecstasies lasted an entire day, and the superiors appointed two sisters, as secretaries, to take down in writing what she revealed in these trances. Her revelations form a thick volume, which has received the approval of the Ordinary. In one of these ecstasies she cried out, "Lord, what wilt Thou have me to do?" and Christ replied, "Fast all Lent, and on other days take no nourishment except bread and water. Go barefoot, wear only one garment and a scapular. Pray six hours on the eve of communion." If ever her superior commanded her to take any other sustenance, she could never keep it down; and if she ever put shoes on her feet, they slipped off spontaneously. This great abstinence never enfeebled her, but rather gave her more vigour and energy.—Vincent Puccini, *Life of St. Mary Magdalene of Pazzi.*

The directions ascribed to Christ in this extract can need no comment.

St. Odilia at her death was in an ecstasy (eighth century). When St. Odilia was dying, she sent her nieces, who stood around, to go and pray. On their return, they found her in an ecstasy, and thought she was dead. Soon she came to herself, and told those about her that God had transported her to heaven, with St. Lucy, to give her a foretaste of paradise. She now greatly desired to receive the Viaticum, and an angel of light came down, in the presence of all those assembled, and presented to her the chalice "renfermant le corps et le sang précieux de Jésus Christ." When Odilia had received it, the angel vanished. The chalice, however, was left in her hands, and was preserved at Hohenburg till 1546. It was "enchâssé dans de l'or et de l'argent." The convent of Hohenburg has a chalice in its arms, and in Christian art St. Odilia is represented holding the cup in her hands.—St. Francis Xavier of Besançon, *Saints de Franche Comté.*

The venerable Anna Maria Taïgi noted for her ecstasies (A.D. 1769–1837). Anna Maria Taïgi of Siena was a tradesman's wife, the mother of seven children, and noted for her charity, self-denial, and piety. Cardinal Pedicini says the fire of her soul could not be suppressed, and it was truly marvellous to find her in some ecstasy, broom in hand, in the act of cleaning the house,—there she would stand immovable, as if petrified. Sometimes at table she would remain immovable as a statue, eyes fixed, and apparently asleep. Her husband would try to rouse her, but she would show no consciousness, nor give any sign of life. When the ecstasy was over she would appear joyous and happy, and her husband would chide her for sleeping at table, and sometimes he would prescribe her medicines.—L'abbé Richard, *Memoirs of Cardinal Pedicini.*

St. Theresa was caught up, in a trance, to the third heaven (A.D. 1515–1582). At one time St. Theresa was caught up to the third heaven, whether in the body, or out of the body, she could not tell; but she informs us, in her autobiography, that she saw in heaven such mysteries, such fulness of glory, and such joy, as pass all human understanding. While in the heaven of heavens, our Lord said to her, "Consider, daughter, what great joys worldlings deprive themselves of." This vision was afterwards repeated often and often. St. Theresa says she beheld, on one occasion, not in spirit only, but with bodily eyes, the blessed Trinity, the exalted Christ, the immaculate Virgin, St. Peter, St. Paul, and the angels round the throne.

St. Theresa saw both the Trinity and the exalted Jesus with her "bodily eyes." One could wish that she had described the former, and told us how the Son was both incorporated in the unity and yet alone, sitting on the right hand of the Father. Of course, if she saw these things with her bodily eyes, the whole mystery could be explained to human understanding. (See ST. FURSY, p. 310.)

On another occasion, while St. Theresa was singing the hymn *Veni Creator*, she fell into a trance, and heard the voice of Christ at the bottom of her heart say to her, "I do not wish you, My daughter, to hold any longer fellowship with man, but let your conversation in future be with angels only." From this moment all her love for every human being ceased, and she had no love which was not wholly absorbed by God and Christ.—*Autobiography* (edited by John of Jesus Maria).

St. Thomas Aquinas had frequent ecstasies (A.D. 1224–1274). Towards the close of life, St. Thomas Aquinas was more and more disengaged from all earthly thoughts; his eye was fixed on other horizons, and "angels' wings unfolded in him to bear his spirit up to things immortal." His ecstasies were frequent, and at such times his soul left his body, which remained like inert matter till the spirit returned. And when his soul returned to its house of clay, he would sigh, in the words of St. Paul, "Oh, who will deliver me from this body of death?"—*Les Petits Bollandistes*, vol. iii. pp. 260, 261.

The ecstasies of St. Thomas of Villeneuve (A.D. 1488–1555). In preaching, the spirit of St. Thomas of Villeneuve was so rapt by the inspiration of his text, that he would not unfrequently fall into an ecstasy, and remain so for hours. Thus, on one holy Thursday, after giving out the text, "Lord, dost Thou wash my feet?" he remained stock-still, with no movement of life, except indeed that tears rolled in floods down his cheeks. Again, on the day of the Transfiguration, after giving out the text, "Lord, it is good for us to be here," he was rapt in an ecstasy. But the most notable instance was on Ascension Day, when he was archbishop of Valentia. After giving out the text, "He was parted from them, and carried up into heaven," he remained in an ecstasy for five hours, without showing any sign of life. Generally, in preaching, he was most fervid and eloquent. He was called a St. Paul for the profoundness of his doctrine, the Elijah of the gospel dispensation for his zeal, and a seraph for his burning words of wisdom and grace. Charles V. admired him above all preachers, and when he went to hear him, always mingled with the general throng.—*Acta Sanctorum*, vol. v. Sept. 18.

St. Veronica of Binasco had frequent ecstasies (A.D. 1497). St. Veronica of Binasco, near Milan, was born in a very humble condition, but was rich in grace, and favoured with frequent ecstasies, in which were revealed to her both things past and things to come. Sometimes she saw Jesus Christ, sometimes the mother of God, sometimes the angels and the saints in light, and sometimes all together; and in these ecstasies were revealed to her the moral causes of events, and the secrets of God's providence. It is worth while to compare the visions of Veronica with those of Catherine Emmerich and Mary of Agreda. —Isidore of Isolano, *Life of St. Veronica of Binasco* (dedicated by authority to François I. and queen Claude).

St. Verulus leaves his body at Marcenay to go to Mussy to save a child from a fire (A.D. 591). Aganon, professor of Chatillon, in the ninth century, mentions the following incident in one of his homilies:— "King Gontran, having heard of the wonderful things done by St. Verulus, went to Marcenay to mass. While celebrating the communion, St. Verulus was taken in a trance, and remained silent and motionless for an hour, when he continued the service from the point at which he had broken off. When the service was over, the king asked Verulus why he had interrupted the sacrifice so long. Verulus replied, because he had seen a house on fire at Mussy, and went to rescue a child in danger of being burnt to death. The king instantly despatched a rider to inquire into the truth of this explanation, and the messenger brought word back that he found the people of Mussy all talking about the bravery of St. Verulus, who, they say, risked his life to save a child, who was fast asleep in a house on fire.—L'abbé Duplus, *Vie* [*sic*] *des Saints du Diocèse de Dijon.*

In Christian art St. Verulus is sometimes represented holding a child by the hand, and sometimes as rescuing a child from a house on fire.

St. Peter II. of Tarentaise went in duplicate to Lusanne to deliver three prisoners who invoked him (see p. 92).

The beatific vision of St. Victor of Plancy (sixth century). The lord of Queudes asked St. Victor to his castle. It was a Sunday, and St. Victor went first to assist in divine service. All of a sudden he was in an ecstasy, saw the heavens open, heard the angelic harmonies, such as no human ear except St. Paul's had ever heard, and beheld the beatific vision which Isaiah saw in the year that king Uzziah died (ch. vi.). In consequence of this, the church of Queudes selected St. Victor for its patron, and ever held him in the highest veneration.

Another instance. On another occasion, during prayer, St. Victor saw the heavens open, and in the midst a cross of gold, enriched with numberless precious stones more brilliant than the stars. As he gazed, enchanted at the sight, a voice said to him, "These precious stones which you see set in the cross are the souls of saints, who for the love of Christ have washed their robes and made them white in the blood of the Lamb."—St. Bernard, *Sermon on the Fête-day of St. Victor* (Feb. 26).

Tree of Knowledge.

Gen. i. 17; ii. 3. In the middle of the garden of Eden was the tree of knowledge, good to make men wise; but Adam and Eve were forbidden to eat the fruit of this tree, lest they should be as gods, able to discern both good and evil.

Buddha's Bo tree, a tree of knowledge. Buddha thought ignorance the source of all human ills, and that its removal would bring to nought the ills that flesh is heir to. Buddha himself attained to this perfect consummation while sitting under the tree of knowledge, called "Bodhidruma," or the Bo tree; and the Buddhists assert that this tree marks the middle of the earth.

Twelve hundred years after the death of Buddha, Hiouen-Thsang, the Chinese pilgrim, found the Bo tree; and in 1812 a peepul tree, planted on the spot of the original Bo tree, was in full vigour, and apparently about a hundred years old.

Unchaste and Unclean Spirits.

Luke viii. 2. Mary, called Magdalene, out of whom went seven devils.

Mark vii. 25–30. A woman, whose young daughter had an unclean spirit, came and fell at the feet of Jesus, and besought Him that He would cast forth the devil out of her daughter. And Jesus said, Go thy way; the devil is gone out of thy daughter. [And so it was.]

St. Antony the Great expels from a woman an unclean spirit (fourth century). When St. Antony came to the city gate, a woman called after him, saying, "Wait, thou man of God. My daughter is grievously vexed with an unclean spirit." St. Antony, hearing himself called after, stopped till the woman and her daughter came up to him, when the damsel dashed herself violently to the ground. St. Antony, moved with compassion, called on the name of Jesus, and said, "Thou foul and unclean spirit, come out of her, and enter no more therein." At the word the fiend came out, the maiden was made whole, and the mother blessed God that had given such power to His saints.—St. Athanasius, *Life of St. Antony the Great.*

St. Bernard casts out an unclean spirit from a woman of Pavia. When St. Bernard was in Pavia, a woman with an unclean spirit was brought to him. The devil cried insolently, "Thou muncher of leeks and onions, thou shalt not cast me out." St. Bernard ordered the woman to be taken to St. Syrus's church. Then the devil began to jest and to scoff, saying, "Ho, ho! Little Syrus could not cast me out, neither shall Bernard." St. Bernard replied, "Syrus cannot cast thee out, thou foul fiend, neither can Bernard; but Jesus Christ can, and in the name of Jesus Christ, I, Bernard, command thee to depart hence." Then the devil departed, and the woman was freed from her tormentor.—William (abbot of Theodore), *Life of St. Bernard.*

St. Bernard delivers a woman from an incubus. St. Bernard delivers a woman from an unclean spirit, called an incubus, which had kept carnal company with her for six months. The saint gave his staff to the woman, and she placed it in her chamber; after which the devil molested her no more.—William (abbot of Theodore), *Life of St. Bernard.*

"Incubes. Les demonographes ont imaginé des demons incubes, qui tourmentaient, par des images obscènes, et même des réalités, les personnes qui avaient fait vœu du chasteté." Unchaste dreams are called "Ephialtes."—Noël, *Dictionnaire de la Fable.*

St. Cyriacus chases an unclean spirit from a princess (fourth century. The daughter of the emperor Diocletian was grievously tormented by an unclean spirit, and while her imperial father was one day lamenting her sad state, the devil cried out aloud, "Ah! and I will continue to torment her, and will never leave her, unless Cyriacus compels me." The emperor then sent for the saint, and Cyriacus went to the royal palace, accompanied with Largus and Smaragdus. As Cyriacus approached the princess, he said, "Thou foul and unclean spirit, I command thee, in the name of Jesus Christ, to come out of her, and never more enter in." The devil answered, "If thou wilt have me leave this abode, assign me another where I may abide." Then said Cyriacus, "Enter into me, if you can." The devil answered, "You know very well I cannot, because you are a sealed vessel unto the Lord." Said Cyriacus, "Thou foul and unclean spirit, I now command thee a second time, in the name of my Lord Jesus Christ, to come out of this damsel, that she also may be a sealed vessel unto God." "O Cyriacus," cried the devil, "if you compel me to go out hence, I will compel you to go into Persia." Then said the saint a third time, "I tell thee, thou foul and unclean spirit, for the third time, come out, thou cursed devil, or suffer the penalty of your disobedience." The devil could parley no longer, and came out sullenly. The princess, being freed from her tormentor, fell on her knees at the saint's feet, and said to him, "Servant of the living God, I beseech you to baptize me, for my earnest desire is to be a Christian." St. Largus and St. Smaragdus lifted her up, and set her on her feet; and her father, the emperor, seeing his daughter perfectly recovered, rejoiced with exceeding great joy, and held in Rome a magnificent triumph in celebration of the event. The damsel was duly baptized, with the entire consent of her mother Serena, who was also numbered with the elect. Diocletian sent costly presents to Cyriacus, appointed him a commodious house, and gave him a suitable retinue.—*Life of St. Marcellus the Pope* (from the public registers).

This tale is also fathered on St. Vitus (see p. 316).

St. Cyriacus chases an unclean spirit from the princess Jobia (fourth century). Baharam, king of Persia, being informed of the cure by Cyriacus of the daughter of Diocletian, emperor of Rome (see above), sent for him to come to Persia to heal the princess Jobia, who was also possessed of an unclean spirit, which tormented her greatly. The emperor Diocletian broke the subject to the saint, and Cyriacus professed himself willing to undertake this long journey. Accordingly, the emperor of Rome provided for him a ship, fully equipped, and furnished with all things necessary. Largus and Smaragdus still bore him company. When the saint reached the shah's palace, he was very honourably entertained, and, being brought into Jobia's private apartments, the devil cried out to him, "Good day, Cyriacus. Are you tired with your long journey? I told you I would drag you to Persia, you remember, when you drove me from house and home in Diocletian's daughter. Well, well, so you are here now; and pray, what can I do to serve you?" Cyriacus said sternly, "Thou foul and unclean spirit, forbear this insolence. And I command you, in the all-powerful name of Jesus Christ, come out of this damsel, and never enter into her again." "With pleasure," said the devil, "will I oblige so kind a friend; but, of course, you will assign me a body where I may abide unmolested for the future." "I will assign you nothing of the kind," said the saint sternly, "nor will I make any terms with you at all; but I command you, now a second time, in the name of Christ, the ever-living God, leave this damsel without another word." Then the devil came out of her, and flew howling into the air, and crying as he went, "Terrible, dreadful name, that hath such power over me, and will never leave me at peace!" When the devil was departed, Cyriacus made the princess a catechumen, and in due time baptized her, with 450 other converts.—*Life of St. Marcellus the Pope* (from the public registers).

St. Hilarion casts out from a young woman an unchaste spirit. A young man of Gaza was enamoured of a damsel of high family, but found no encouragement; so, going to Memphis, he obtained from the sorcerers of the temple of Esculapius a love-charm. It consisted of a brazen plate filled with cabalistic signs; and was to be laid, with certain words, under the threshold of the damsel's house, wholly hidden from sight. This was duly done, and the result was that the maiden became shamelessly in love with the young man. Her father, quite shocked at her immodesty, took her to St. Hilarion, and the devil, howling, cried out, "I pray you, torment me not, for I was compelled by the priests of Memphis to take up my abode here." Hilarion commanded the unchaste and unclean spirit to depart, but the devil made answer, "I cannot, till the charm which binds me to obedience is removed from the threshold of the door." Hilarion demanded how the foul fiend had dared to enter into the body of a handmaid of the Lord; and the devil answered he did it to save the lady from evil. "Villain and liar!" roared Hilarion; "come out this instant, I say." When the devil again implored the saint that the charm on him might be removed first, Hilarion refused to interfere with it, to show that no charm or magic can resist the will of God. So, howling and yelling, the devil departed; and the damsel was restored to her right mind.—St. Jerome, *Vita St. Hilarionis Eremitæ* (A.D. 390). See also Nicephorus Callistus (who died 1350), *Ecclesiastical History*.

St. Vitus chases an unclean spirit from a princess (fourth century). The emperor Diocletian had a daughter possessed of an unclean spirit; and the devil said he would depart out of her, if Vitus commanded it. So the emperor sent for St. Vitus, and requested him to exorcise the princess, his daughter. The man of God laid his hands upon her head, and said, "I command thee, thou wicked spirit, in the name of the Lord Jesus Christ, come out of her, and enter no more in." Then the devil departed with terrible howlings, and hurt many pagans who had scoffed at the saint, not believing he had power over spirits of the other world. (See ST. CYRIACUS, p. 314.)—Edward Kinesman (1623), *Lives of the Saints*, p. 382. (See the collections of Papebroch, vol. ii. p. 1013.)

Edward Kinesman says, "This life of St. Vitus is taken out of an auncient MS., with which Venerable Bede accordeth, and other authours of martyrologes."

Urim and Thummim.

EXOD. xxviii. 30. The words Urim and Thummim mean "light and perfection." They were something in the breastplate of the high priest consulted by him on great national events. The high priest, when he consulted the Urim and Thummim, stood with his face to the curtain which divided the holy place from the holy of holies, and the king or his high officers stood at a distance, also facing the curtain, so the high priest, of course, stood with his back to the questioners. The question being put, the high priest consulted the Urim and Thummim, and gave his answer. Whether he obtained his response by drawing lots, or whether by some special sparkle of the precious stones in his breastplate, or whether by some other revelation, nobody knows.

The Urim and Thummim of Joseph Smith the Mormon. Joseph Smith, the Mormonite, called "Urim and Thummim" the spectacles which, he asserts, were given him by an angel, to enable him to decipher the "reformed Egyptian characters" of the plates containing God's revelation to him. These plates, we are told, were hidden at the foot of a mountain in Ontario. The Urim and Thummim spectacles are described as "two transparent stones set in the rim on a bow fastened to a breastplate." Not a very clear description, it must be confessed; however, Joseph Smith, by the aid of these spectacles, deciphered the plates, and Oliver Cowdery took down the words, "because Smith was no scholar."

There is literally no limit to the credulity of man on religious subjects. Wise men can be made to believe a block of wood or stone is a god; that a crazy woman is the Holy Ghost; that anything is anything, the more unlikely the better.

Veronicas.

A "veronica" is a cloth bearing a likeness. Gregory of Tours (*Vit. Patr.* c. 12) minted the word *iconica* from the Greek *icon*, an image, and the Latin *vera* (true). *Vera-iconica*, contracted into *veronica*, is applied especially to a kerchief or cloth stamped "miraculously" with the face of Jesus covered with sweat and blood, as He was led to execution.

The usual tale is this: A woman of position, living in the Via Dolorosa, broke through the procession, when it stopped a few moments to make Simon of Cyrenê assist in carrying the cross, and wiped the face of Jesus with a cloth. The name of the woman was Seraphia, but she is not unfrequently called Veronica, as much as to say, "The woman who had the veronica" or holy face of Jesus.

Some of the details of this story differ in different accounts. Thus some tell us Seraphia handed to Jesus the cloth, with which He wiped His own face and then returned the cloth to the woman with thanks. Some, again, say Seraphia did not live actually in the Via Dolorosa, but in the last house of a side street running into it.

[From the Bollandists we find that "St. Veronica" was quite another person to the woman referred to above. Seraphia, we are told, died A.D. 70, and was a native of Jerusalem of good station; whereas St. Veronica was a villager of Milan, who died A.D. 1497. Mgr. Guérin tells us that the "proper name" is a Latin form of the Greek Berenicê, as *venio* is from *baino* (Greek, to go). He, however, passes over the difficulty of the accentuated syllable and the changed vowel in the middle of the word, Berenicê, Veronica.]

St. Seraphia's veronica or holy face (A.D. 33). The following is a translation from *The Dolorous Passion* of Catherine Emmerich, a nun of the Augustine order in the convent of Dulmen (1774–1824). Of course, the tradition existed hundreds of years before the birth of this German visionary, and may be traced back to the sixth century, but the narrative of Catherine Emmerich is somewhat graphic, and has the merit of embodying the floating ideas of convent life upon the subject, presented under the form of a religious vision. How far the vision was a revelation must be left to the reader's judgment to determine. Speaking of the Saviour's passage to the place of execution, she says, "The procession which formed at the judgment hall entered a long street bearing to the left, into which ran several side streets. Many well-dressed persons, when they saw the crowd, retired, lest they should be defiled; but there were some who pitied the bearer of the cross, fainting under a load too heavy for His strength. The cortége had not proceeded above two hundred steps, when a man of Cyrenê, Simon by name, came up and assisted Jesus. As the procession stopped a few minutes to make this arrangement, a woman of tall stature and imposing aspect came from a large house on the left side of the street. She was closely veiled, had a cloth thrown over her shoulders, and led by the hand a little girl, not above nine years old. The child carried a small vase filled with aromatized wine, which the woman, whose name was Seraphia, had prepared. They made their way through the crowd, but were pushed back by the officers and archers. Nothing daunted, they persevered, passed through, and made their way straight to Jesus. Then, falling at His feet, Seraphia handed to the Man of Grief her cloth, saying, 'Suffer me to wipe my Saviour's face.' Jesus took the cloth, wiped His face covered with sweat and blood, and returned it with thanks. Seraphia, after kissing it, put it under her mantle, and rose to her feet. The little girl now timidly presented the wine. It was too late; the procession was ready to start again; the intruders were rudely pushed on one side, and Jesus, with a blow from the Pharisees, was commanded to move on. Seraphia hurried with her companion into the house, laid the cloth on the table, and fainted. While the child, terribly alarmed, bent over her, crying, a neighbour dropped in, saw the cloth on the table, and observed that it bore the impress of the face of Jesus. When Seraphia came to herself, and saw the likeness on the cloth, she wept bitterly, and, falling on her knees, exclaimed, 'Blessed be the name of God my Saviour, who has left me this memorial!'"

This probably is a pretty faithful picture of what is believed by "the faithful" of Seraphia and the veronica. Bernard de Breydenbach, dean of Mayence, went to Jerusalem in July 14, 1483, and passing down the Via Dolorosa, carefully measured the distances of the several "stations," and he informs us that the house of Seraphia, whom he calls Veronica, is a large house 550 paces* from the governor's palace. Adrichomius of Cologne says it was not in the row, but occupied an angle of a side street, the door of the house being round the corner. From this point to the spot where Jesus fell fainting the second time, he tells us, was exactly eleven feet more than 336 paces.

Whatever credit or discredit may be placed on this story, it cannot but be interesting to know somewhat of the future history of this mysterious cloth, and happily different writers have furnished us with the minutest details. Thus Philip of Bergamo informs us how it came to Rome. He says that Tiberius Cæsar, the emperor, sent his friend Volusian, a valiant soldier of the imperial guards, to escort Veronica to Rome. The emperor was ill at the time with a grievous malady, but the moment he set his eyes on the cloth he was completely cured. This miracle made a great impression on him, and he wanted to enrol Jesus among the Roman gods; but the senate would not listen to the proposal, so he was obliged to content himself with a statue of the Nazarene, which he placed in his palace.

Catherine Emmerich has described this interview between Tiberius Cæsar and Seraphia also, and the reader no doubt will be glad to see what she calls her vision. She says, "Three years after the Ascension, I saw the Roman emperor send a messenger to Jerusalem to collect together all that he could learn about the death, resurrection, and ascension of Jesus. When the imperial messenger returned to Rome, he took with him Nicodemus, Seraphia, and Epaphras, father of John Chuza. I saw Veronica introduced to the emperor. He was sick at the time, and confined to his bed. His bed was elevated on a dais, approached by two steps. The chamber was a large square one, with no window, light being admitted through the ceiling. Seraphia, when she entered the chamber, had with her the veronica or holy face, and another cloth impressed with the stripes of the flagellation. I saw her open the former, and show the emperor the impressed likeness. It was larger than life, because the cloth was moved about the Saviour's face, and wherever it touched the face it received an impression. The emperor never touched the cloth, but only

* 1000 paces = a mile.

looked at it; and as the children of Israel were healed by looking on the brazen serpent, the emblem and type of Christ, so Cæsar was cured by looking on the cloth impressed with the face of the Redeemer."

Calcaginus, cited by Sandini, and reproduced by Pamelius, says, "The cloth bearing the likeness of Christ exists still, and is held in high veneration, not only on account of the miracles with which it is honoured, but more especially because there cannot be the slightest doubt of its genuineness." Bollandus informs us that it is the unanimous opinion of all sacred historians and the firm belief of all true Christians that the *Veronica seu Vultus Domini*, now at Rome, is the identical and veritable cloth offered to the Redeemer on his way to Calvary. It was placed in the Vatican by John VII. in A.D. 707; and is enshrined in one of the four huge piers which support the dome of St. Peter's church.

The veronica is mentioned in an ancient ceremonial of St. Peter's of Rome, dedicated in 1143 to Celestin II., and published by Mabillon (*Museum Ital.*, vol. ii. p. 122).

In Matthew of Westminster's *Flowers of History*, mention is made of the same, under Innocent III., who died in 1216.

It is mentioned in a bull by Nicholas IV., dated 1290; in a bull by Pius IV., dated 1561; by Sixtus V., Benedict XIII., and Gregory XVI.

The sixth tableau of the Via Dolorosa is "Veronica wiping the face of Jesus." Several festivals, ostensions, and processions have been appointed by different popes in honour of the holy face, from the time of Celestin II. to Gregory XIII.

A book called *The Stations of the Churches of Rome* was published by Sixtus V., in which we read, "At the extremity of St. Peter's church, near the sacred door, is a chapel and altar of the holy cloth, in beautiful mosaics. The chapel was consecrated by John VII. to the Blessed Virgin. On the altar, in a marble coffer, is the holy cloth, called the veronica, with which Seraphia wiped the face of Jesus as He was led to execution. It was transferred to the Vatican in 1440, and is now enshrined in one of the huge pillars which support the dome of St. Peter's church." *

Benedict XIV. says, "In the basilica of the Vatican is preserved the lance which pierced the side of Jesus, and the veronica † or cloth which still bears faint traces of the Saviour's face, bedewed with sweat and blood."

The words of the hymn sung at the ostension of the veronica run thus: "All hail, thou holy face of our Redeemer, on which shone the light of heavenly splendour. All hail, thou holy face, imprinted on a cloth whiter than snow, in token of love. O God, who at the request of Thy servant Veronica hath left us this memorial of Thy likeness, vouchsafe to us, who now adore this symbol of Thy love on earth, to enter into Thy joy with the saints in heaven."

To the present day cloths with a veronica are manufactured and sold, each cloth being authenticated by the signature and seal of a canon

St. Brigit, who lived in the sixth century, reproved, we are told, many who doubted the genuineness of the holy face. Dantê, who lived 1265-1321, mentions the holy face in his *Paradise*. Jean Dorat (1507-1588) has a poem on the subject. And even to the present day the ostension of the veronica is one of the most popular of the sacred festivals.

It will be remembered that a statue of St. Veronica (*Seraphia*) stands in the basilica of St. Peter's, Rome. She is represented as holding the holy face. It was the work of Mochi, an Italian sculptor of the seventeenth century. Near it are St. Helena with a huge cross, St. Longinus with a spear, and St. Andrew. In the marble ciboriums below the statues are pieces of the true cross, the head of the sacred spear, and the veronica.

A copy of the veronica was sent by Urban IV. to the Cistercian nunnery of Montreuil, where his sister was an inmate. His letter is dated 1249.

The Rev. A. J. C. Hare, in his *Walks in Rome*, says, "When I examined the head on the veronica handkerchief, it struck me as undoubtedly a work of early Byzantine art, perhaps of the seventh or eighth century, painted on linen."

During the republican domination in 1849, it was rumoured that, about Easter, the canons of St. Peter saw the Volto-Santo turn pale when they looked on it!! It is exhibited for a few minutes to the people on Holy Thursday and Good Friday, but from such a height that nothing can be distinguished.

* It was moved from the altar either to the church of the Santo Spirito or to one dedicated to the Holy Virgin, and in 1440 it was carried back to the Vatican.

† The four pillars enshrine the spear, part of the cross, the head of St. Andrew, and the veronica.

Acheropites. Acheropites are likenesses not made by the hands of man.

The East boasts of an acheropite, which, we are told, "is a face of Christ, which the Saviour Himself sent, photographed on a cloth, to Abgarus, king of Edessa. It is twice referred to in the Greek Menology, on Aug. 16 and Oct. 11. In the former the cloth is held by an angel with outspread wings, with this inscription: "In memory of the likeness of Christ not made by the hand of man." In the latter case the inscription is, "In memory of the seventh synod of Nice," A.D. 787. This council was convened against the Iconoclasts, and the acheropite was presented by two Fathers who attended the synod, in testimony of their veneration for pictures and images. This holy face, mentioned by Nicephorus, Evagrius Scholasticus, and Procopius, was transported from Constantinople to Rome, and according to Carletti is the one now in the church of St. Silvester. Constantine Porphyrogenetus says of this acheropite, "All persons agree that the face of the Saviour has been miraculously impressed on this cloth, although it must be confessed all do not agree as to the time and details . . . but these are of very minor importance."

Emerich David, in his famous *History of the Paintings of the Middle Age* (1842), comparing the two "holy faces," says their traits are perfectly distinct, as well as their history. The acheropite he describes as "celle de toutes où la tête de Jesus a le plus de dignité." Raoul Rochette the archæologist (1789-1854) thinks it belongs to the sixth century and that it was placed by John VII. in the basilica of the Vatican.

The "holy face" of Jahen, in Spain. According to the *History of Christ* in

Persian, this face is not an acheropite, but a real veronica. We are told that Seraphia folded her napkin in three when she wiped the Saviour's face; and when the cloth was spread open, a veritable impression was found stamped on each of the three folds. One of the impressions is in the Vatican, and known as the veronica; another is at Milan; and the third at Jahen, in Spain.

The "holy face" of Lucca. Alban Butler speaks of the holy face of Lucca, which, he says, is a very ancient miraculous crucifix in the chapel of the Holy Cross, in the cathedral dedicated to St. Martin, at Lucca. This is all he says upon the subject.—*Lives of the Saints*, Jan. 13 (note to "St. Veronica of Milan").

The face of Charles I. impressed on a cerecloth. In 1813, while a passage was being constructed under the choir of St. George's chapel, Windsor, an aperture was accidentally made in one of the walls of Henry VIII.'s vault. Three coffins were seen, and it was supposed that one of them might hold the remains of Charles I. The vault was examined in the presence of George IV. and other distinguished persons, among whom was Sir Henry Halford, who published "An Account of the Opening of the Coffin of Charles I. 4to, 1813." On opening the aforesaid coffin, the body was found wrapped in cerecloth, and the damp folds about the face adhered so closely, that, on being detached, the cloth was found to retain an impress of the royal countenance—a circumstance which to ardent loyalists would doubtless recall the legend of the Santa Veronica.—*Notes and Queries*, March 3, 1883, p. 161.

Vicarious Suffering.

(See IMPUTED MERIT, and JUSTICE JUSTIFIED, pt. ii.)

ROM. ix. 3. I could wish myself accursed from Christ for my brethren, my kinsmen according to the flesh.

EXOD. xxxii. 32. And Moses said, Oh, this people have sinned a great sin; yet now, if Thou wilt forgive them——; if not, blot me, I pray Thee, out of Thy book.

1 PET. ii. 24. Who His own self bare our sins in His own body on the tree.

1 PET. iii. 18. Christ hath once suffered, the just for the unjust, that He might bring us unto God.

St. Abraham the hermit and his niece Mary (A.D. 360). The tale of St. Abraham and his niece Mary is one of the most touching stories in all the lives of the saints, and is told by St. Ephrem, deacon of Edessa, a contemporary and friend, with such simplicity and feeling that the reader feels there is unexaggerated truth in the painful narrative. The tale itself is not to be reproduced in this volume, but only such a brief outline as may suffice to illustrate the dogma of vicarious punishment.

St. Abraham the hermit was born at Chidana, in Mesopotamia, of wealthy and noble parents; but he abandoned the world and became a hermit. His brother dying, left an only daughter, Mary, to his charge, and Abraham built a cell next to his own for her, and here he brought her up most carefully to a religious life. She grew up very beautiful, extremely attached to her uncle, and most devout; but a monk fell in love with her, visited Abraham under sundry pretences, and ultimately seduced his niece. Mary, who was twenty years of age, now gave way to despair, quitted her cell, and for two years led a most abandoned life, trying to drown remorse in revelry. Abraham was inconsolable. "A wolf," he cried, in his agony, "has taken away my lamb. O Christ, the Saviour of sinners, restore my Mary, my lamb; bring her back to the fold, and let not my grey hair go down in sorrow to the grave. O God of all mercy, rescue my child from the mouth of the dragon." Being informed, after the lapse of two years, where his niece was living, Abraham dressed himself as a cavalier, and gained admission to her. When left alone he threw off his disguise, and was at once recognized. Mary was struck dumb, and the hermit cried with a breaking heart, "O Mary, my daughter Mary, my poor pet lamb, why—oh, why do you not speak to me? I am come to lead you into the fold again, my dear lost lamb. I will charge myself with all your sins, O my daughter, my child. I will bear them when called to judgment. I will suffer for them. On me, on me, my Mary, shall be all thy misdeeds, all thy shortcomings, and thou shalt be presented spotless before the throne. O Mary, Mary, though your sins be as scarlet, they shall be as white as snow; though they be red like crimson, they shall be as wool." It is needless to add that Mary returned with her uncle, and, like another Magdalene, became a distinguished saint, highly honoured and revered.—St. Ephrem, deacon of Edessa, *Works*, vol. ii. p. 1.

St. Catherine of Bologna promised to

bear in purgatory the penalties due to the sins of a novice (A.D. 1413–1463). St. Catherine one day observed a novice greatly tormented by a devil, and said to her, "Sister, keep up your courage; I am ready to satisfy for your sins in purgatory. I will take on me to do penance for you, and will hand over to you a part of my merits, provided you remain in the order." The novitiate, fortified by this assurance, continued in her vocation, and ultimately became the abbess.—Paleotti (about fifty years afterwards), *Life of St. Catherine of Bologna* (inserted in the *Ecclesiastical Annals*, vol. xvii.).

St. Emiliana takes on herself the infirmities of another (A.D. 1246). One day St. Emiliana went to visit a sick boy, and said to him, "My child, think not of your sufferings, but think what Christ suffered for your sake." "Ah!" said the child, "but I cannot help thinking of the pain I feel." "Will you give me your pain?" asked Emiliana. "Right willingly, if I knew how," replied the boy. Then said Emiliana, "O God, if this sickness is sent in mercy for the child's salvation, Thy will be done; if not, transfer it to me, and glorify Thy name." She then returned home, fell sick, and was told that the boy had perfectly recovered. The sickness she suffered from was erysipelas.—A. Stolz, *Acta Sanctorum*, May 19.

There really is no miracle in catching erysipelas from another—it is often epidemic; nor is it miraculous that the fever, which not unfrequently accompanies erysipelas, should abate.

St. John-Joseph de la Croix takes on himself the ulcers of Father Michel (A.D. 1654–1734). Father Michel, afterwards archbishop of Cosenza, suffered greatly from two ulcers in his legs. A painful operation was determined on, and Father Michel commended himself to the prayers of St. John-Joseph. John-Joseph prayed that the ulcers of Father Michel might be transferred to himself, and so it was; for Michel was at once delivered from his infirmity, and the ulcers broke out in the legs of John-Joseph. They were terrible sores, and caused much agony, but it was borne without a murmur.

Another example. One of the prince's household, who had led a very abandoned life, being struck with remorse, made his confession to St. John-Joseph. The confessor, moved at the penitence of the man, awarded him a very slight penance, and took on himself to work out the heavier penalty of the man's sins.—Migne, *Demonstrations Evangéliques*, vol. xvi. (Cardinal Wiseman is responsible for this life of John-Joseph, but a life of the saint had been already written by Father Diodato.)

Whipping-boys. Whipping-boys were boys kept in royal and princely houses to be whipped when a prince deserved chastisement. Barnaby Fitzpatrick stood for Edward VI.; D'Ossat and Du Perron, afterwards cardinals, were whipped by Clement VIII. for Henri IV. of France; Mungo Murray stood for Charles I.; Raphael was flogged for the son of the marquis de Lagenez, but, not seeing the justice of this vicarious whipping, he ran away.

Violence offered to God's Servants punished

(See HONOUR GOD'S SAINTS.)

1 KINGS xiii 1–6. There came a man of God out of Judah to Bethel, and Jeroboam stood by the altar of burnt incense. The man of God cried against the altar, and said, O altar, altar, behold, a child shall be born, Josiah by name, and upon thee shall he offer the priests of the high places that burn incense upon thee. When the king heard this, he put forth his hand, saying, Lay hold on him. And his hand dried up, so that he could not pull it in again; the altar also was rent, and the ashes poured out. Then said the king to the man of God, Entreat and pray for me that my hand may be restored me again. And the man of God besought the Lord, and the king's hand was restored him again. Then said the king to the man of God, Come home with me, and refresh thyself, and I will give thee a reward. But the man of God said to the king, If thou wilt give me half thy house, I will not go in with thee. So he went another way.

Barontus offered to strike the abbot Menelus, and his arm was paralyzed (seventh century). Barontus, a man of great wealth, wanted his daughter to marry Viance, the son of a serf; but when the day appointed for the nuptials drew near, the young lady fled to the abbey of Menat, and placed herself under the protection of Menelus. The father, in great anger, demanded that his daughter should be given up, and lifted his hand to strike the abbot, but it was instantly paralyzed. He would not ask Menelus to intercede for him, but he applied to Viance. So Viance prayed, and the palsied limb was restored to its former vigour. Barontus then gave to the abbey the dowry he had intended to bestow upon his daughter.—Herimbert, *Life of St. Vicentian* (written three months after the death of Vicentian, or Viance).

One of the servants of Barontus para-

lyzed for attempting to lay hands on St. Viance (A.D. 620–674). St. Viance, the son of a serf, was Barontus's groom; but, being ill-used by the rich man, he quitted his service, and retired to a desert, where he intended to live a hermit's life. Barontus, whose temper was most overbearing, tracked the fugitive to his retreat, and one of his retainers, rushing into the cell, was about to seize Viance, when his arms became instantly paralyzed. Barontus entreated his groom to restore the paralytic, but St. Viance replied, "Not yet, not yet. My day of death is not far off, and then will I entreat the Lord to show mercy on thy servant." Not long afterwards God took St. Viance to paradise, and the servant of Barontus was made whole on the selfsame day. —Herimbert (written three months after the event), *Life of St. Vicentian, or Viance.*

Eldebod lifted up his arm to strike St. Maximus, and it was paralyzed (A.D. 583–625). When St. Maximus succeeded to the abbacy of Limours, Eldebod the intendant sent for him, but the abbot sent word back, "If the intendant wants me, he must come to me, for I cannot leave my duties to wait upon Eldebod." The intendant, furious at this answer, went to the abbey, and was about to strike Maximus, but his hand became paralyzed. When Eldebod reached home, his household were enraged beyond measure with the abbot, and proceeded in a body to the abbey to take vengeance on the insolent Churchman; but no sooner had they reached the abbey court, than the whole party was struck blind. St. Maximus, coming out to them, exhorted them to repentance, and on their humiliation restored their sight. One of them, however, named Gontram, ran the abbot through with his lance; but vengeance was swift, for Gontram's whole body instantly became one universal putrefying sore, and the man died within three days, like Herod, eaten up of worms.—Bollandus, *Acta Sanctorum*, vol. i. Jan. 2.

Géronce, mother of St. Geneviève, slapped her child's face for crying to go to church, and was struck blind (A.D. 422–512). One day Géronce, the mother of Geneviève, dressed herself for church, and her young daughter begged hard to go with her. This being refused, the child began to cry, and Géronce slapped her face. Immediately she had done so she became blind, and continued sightless for twenty-one months. The bishop of Nanterre then interfered, and told the child to go to the river, and fill a bottle with clean water. When the water was brought to the bishop, he told the child to mark on the bottle with her finger the sign of the cross, and then bathe her mother's eyes with the water. This being done, Géronce recovered her sight straightway.—L'abbé Saintyves (1846), *Life of St. Geneviève.*

Visions and Revelations. (See STEPHEN'S VISION.)

ACTS x. 9–16. Peter went up upon the housetop to pray about the sixth hour, and fell into a trance, in which he saw heaven opened, and a certain vessel descending unto him, as it had been a great sheet let down to earth; in which sheet were all manner of four-footed beasts of the earth, and wild beasts, and creeping things, and fowls of the air. And there came a voice to him, Rise, Peter; kill, and eat. But Peter said, Not so, Lord; for I have never eaten anything common or unclean. And the voice spake unto him again the second time, What God hath cleansed, that call not thou common. This was done thrice; and the vessel was received up again into heaven.

JOEL ii. 28. It shall come to pass afterwards, that I will pour My Spirit on all flesh; and your sons and daughters shall prophesy, your old men shall dream dreams, and your young men shall see visions.

PSALM lxxxix. 19. Thou spakest in visions to Thy holy one.

ISA. i. 1; DAN. vii. 2; viii. 1; NAHUM i. 1; ACTS xvi 9; and many other texts.

REV. iv. 1. The voice which I heard was as it were a trumpet talking with me, which said, Come up hither, and I will show thee things which must be hereafter.

St. Aldegundis's vision of the devil (A.D. 689). God caused St. Aldegundis, towards the close of her life, to see the great adversary of man, under a most frightful form. St. Aldegundis demanded of him why he had appeared; and he replied, "My great vexation is to see daily so many of the human race going the strait and narrow road, while my broad and pleasant one is neglected." The truth of these words revealed the malignity of the evil spirit, and made Aldegundis long more and more to join the glorious company of saints and angels in the paradise of God. She prayed that God would come quickly and take her home. So He sent a cancer to her right breast, which she bore with patience for some time, and then changed her mortal for immortality, and her corruptible for incorruption. — L'abbé Delbos, *Life of St. Aldegundis.*

St. Anastasius sees in a vision the cup of

martyrdom (A.D. 628). One night St. Anastasius had a vision, in which he saw a man present to him a golden cup enriched with precious stones and full of red wine. The man, on presenting it, said to him, "Anastasius, take and drink." This did he, and his soul seemed filled with divine sweetness. The vision then left him, and he woke, feeling assured he had seen the cup of his martyrdom. — *Acta Sanctorum*, Jan. 22. (Metaphrastês wrote the life of this saint.)

Visions of Jeanne d'Arc, la Pucelle d'Orléans (A.D. 1412–1431). This is the statement given by Jeanne d'Arc herself: "Tout ce que j'ai fait de bien pour la France, je l'ai fait par la grâce et d'après l'ordre de Dieu, le roi du ciel, comme il me l'a révélé par ses anges et ses saints; et tout ce que je sais, je le sais uniquement par les révélations divines. C'est sur l'ordre de Dieu que je me suis rendue auprès du roi Charles VII. . . . J'aurais mieux aimé être écartelée par les chevaux que d'aller le trouver sans la permission de Dieu, dans la main duquel sont toutes mes actions. Sur Lui, et sur nul autre reposait tout mon espoir; tout ce que ses voix m'ont ordonné, je l'ai fait de mon mieux, selon mes forces et mon intelligence. Ces voix ne m'ont rien ordonné qu'avec la permission et le bon plaisir de Dieu, et tout ce que j'ai fait en leur obéissant, je crois l'avoir bien fait. Si je voulais dire tout ce que Dieu m'a ordonné, huit jours ne suffiraient pas. Il y a maintenant sept ans que les saints m'apparurent pour la première fois. C'était un jour d'été, vers l'heure de midi. J'avais à peine treize ans, et j'étais dans le jardin de mon père. J'entendis la voix à droite, du côté de l'église; je vis en même temps une apparition entourée d'une grande clarté. Elle avait l'extérieur d'un homme très-bon et très-vertueux; elle portrait des ailes et était environnée de tous côtés de beaucoup de lumière, et accompagnée des anges du ciel. C'était l'archange Michel. Il me parut avoir une voix très respectable; mais j'étais encore jeune enfant; j'eus grand peur de cette apparition, et je doutai fort que ce fût un ange. Ce fut seulement après avoir entendu cette voix trois fois que je la reconnus pour la sienne. Il m'enseigna, et me montra tant de choses qu'enfin je crus fermement que c'était lui. Je l'ai vu, lui et les anges, de mes propres yeux, aussi clairement que je vous vois, vous, mes juges; et je crois, d'une foi aussi ferme, ce qu'il a dit et fait, que je crois à la Passion et à la mort de Jesus Christ, notre Sauveur, et ce qui me porte à la croire, ce sont les bonnes doctrines, les bons avis, les secours avec lesquels il m'a toujours assistée. L'ange me disait qu'avant tout je devais être une bonne enfant, bien conduire; et aller souvent à l'église, et que Dieu me soutiendrait. Il me racontait la grande pitié qui était au royaume de France, et comment je devais me bâter d'aller secourir mon roi. Il me disait aussi que sainte Catherine et sainte Marguerite viendraient vers moi, et que je devais faire tout ce qu'elles m'ordonneraient, parce qu'elles étaient envoyées de Dieu pour me conduire, et m'aider de leurs conseils dans tout ce que j'avais à exécuter; St. Catherine et St. Marguerite m'apparurent ensuite, comme l'ange l'avait prédit. Elles m'ordonnérent d'aller trouver le sire Baudricourt, capitaine du roi à Vaucouleurs, lequel à la vérité, me repousserait plusieurs fois, mais finirait par me donner des gens pour me conduire dans l'intérieur de la France auprès de Charles VII., après quoi je ferais lever le siege d'Orléans. Je leur répondis que je n'étais qu'une pauvre fille qui ne savait ni chevaucher, ni conduire la guerre; elles répliquérent que je devoirs porter hardiment ma bannière, que Dieu m'assisterait, et que j'aiderais mon roi à recouvrer malgré ses ennemis, tout son royaume. 'Va en toute confiance,' ajoutèrent-elles, 'et, quand tu seras devant ton roi, il se fera un beau signe pour qu'il croire à la mission et te fasse bon accueil.' Elles m'ont dirigée pendant sept ans, et m'ont prêté leur appui dans tous mes embarras et mes travaux, et maintenant il ne se passe pas de jour qu'elles ne me visitent. Je ne leur ai rien demandé, si ce n'est pour mon expédition, et que Dieu voulût bien assister les Français, et protéger leur ville; pour moi, je ne leur ai pas demandé d'autre récompense que le saint de mon âme. Dès la première fois que j'entendis leurs voix, je promis librement à Dieu de rester une vierge pure de corps et d'âme, si cela lui était agréable, et elles me promirent, en retour, de me conduire dans le paradis, comme je les en ai priées." Thus spoke la Pucelle when she stood before Cauchon, bishop of Beauvais, appointed to be her judge. We are told this infamous judge "mourut subitement entre les mains de son barbier." Of her other persecutors,

Jean le Maistre "disparut d'entre les hommes sans qu'on pût savoir ce qu'il était devenu;" Joseph d'Estivet "fut trouvé mort sur un fumier devant Rouen;" Nicholas l'Oiseleur, the villainous ecclesiastic employed by Cauchon to pretend friendship in order to induce the maid to confide in him and criminate herself, died suddenly in a church at Bâle; Nicholas Midy, "qui avait prêché avant l'exécution, fut emporté par la lèpre." The duke of Bedford, regent of France, "mourut du chagrin et de honte dans ce même château de Rouen où Jeanne avait été enfermée;" Henry V. died suddenly at Rouen, whither he had gone to restore order, in the thirty-fourth year of his age, and the second of his marriage with Catherine the French princess; and Henry VI. his son, "au nom de qui la Pucelle fut immolée, se vit détrôné deux fois, passa la plus grande partie de sa vie en captivité, et périt massacré. Ainsi moururent ceux à qui Jeanne avait dit, 'Vous ne me ferez pas ce dont vous me menacer, sans en éprouver du dommage dans votre corps et dans votre âme.'" —See Quicherat, *Histoire de Jeanne d'Arc.*

St. Catherine of Bologna sees in a vision her own exaltation (A.D. 1413–1463). St. Catherine was chosen abbess of Bologna, but was unwilling to accept the honour, till the Saviour told her by revelation that it was His Father's good pleasure that she should do so. At the same time she saw the heavens open, and beheld two seats of resplendent glory, one of which was both larger and more resplendent than the other. As St. Catherine contemplated these things with admiration, and asked for whom they were reserved, a heavenly voice replied, "The larger and grander seat is reserved for Catherine of Bologna."—D. Paleotti (of the order of St. Francis), *Life of St. Catherine of Bologna.*

Vision of St. Catherine of Siena, aged six years (A.D. 1347–1380). One day, at the age of six, St. Catherine of Siena was sent with her brother Stephen, about a year older, to Sister Bonaventura. On their return, Catherine saw in the air, above the church of St. Dominic, a glorious throne, where sat the Lord Jesus, clothed in pontifical robes. St. Peter, St. Paul, and St. John the evangelist stood beside him. The Saviour fixed His eyes on Catherine, His face beaming with majesty and kindness. Stephen ran to his sister, asking her why she did not come on. Catherine replied, "If you had seen the beautiful things I have seen, you also would have been transfixed with ecstasy." When she raised her eyes again, the vision was gone; and she wept that she had ever taken her eyes off it.—Raymond of Capua (her confessor), *Life of St. Catherine of Siena.*

Revelation of St. Cyril, general of Mount Carmel (A.D. 1191). While celebrating mass in Armenia on St. Hilarion's Day (Oct. 21), an angel appeared to St. Cyril, holding in his hand a rod decorated with a lily, and two silver tablets inscribed with letters of gold in Greek characters. The writing was a revelation of things to come; it told of the ruin of the Greek empire, and of the faith in the Eastern provinces. History justified the revelation.—*Les Petits Bollandistes*, vol. iii. p. 201.

St. Dominic's vision about himself and St. Francis. St. Dominic had one night a vision in which he saw Jesus Christ. He was very angry for the sins of the world, and resolved to destroy it, as hopelessly bad. The virgin mother, kneeling before him to move His pity, presented to Him St. Dominic and St. Francis, saying to Him, "By these two instruments a great reformation will be made." At these words the Saviour relented. So distinctly did St. Dominic see St. Francis in this vision, that when he subsequently saw him in Rome, he recognized him instantly; and embracing him tenderly, recounted to him his vision. —St. Bonaventure, *Life of St. Francis d'Assisi.*

St. Felix de Valois sees the vision of a stag (A.D. 1127–1212). St. John de Matha was commanded to found an "Order for the Redemption of Captives," and to obtain the co-operation of St. Felix de Valois. Accordingly he went to confer with him. The night preceding St. Felix had a vision, which he could not then understand. Near the spring of water which he went to daily for his refection, he beheld a stag which came down to drink, and between its antlers was a red and blue cross. While Felix was pondering over this vision, John de Matha arrived, and imparted to Felix what God had told him about instituting an "Order for the Redemption of Captives." Felix, not doubting that his vision of the red and blue cross was connected with this foundation, instantly set to work with John de Matha to draw up rules for the new order. The two saints lived together for three years, when they went to Rome, and la d their plan before the pope, who ratified the institution, Feb. 8.—R. P. Ignace Dillond, *Vie des SS. Jean de Matha et Félix de Valois.*

The arms of the order are fleurs-de-lis without number; a red and blue cross "en abyme;" two stags for supporters.

Visions of St. Hildegardes (A.D. 1098–1179). Hildegardes was the daughter of the count of Spanheim, and from her girlhood had revelations, which the Holy Ghost told her to write down in a book. She neglected to do so for some time, but, being greatly afflicted in body and mind, she consulted a religious, who spoke to the abbot, and she was advised to keep a record of her revelations. These revelations, called "Scivias," fill three volumes; there is also a book of "Visions on Theological Dogmas" in three parts; a "Solution of Thirty-eight Knotty Points in Divinity;" an "Exposition of the Symbol [or creed] of St. Athanasius;" nine books of "Subtilties of Divers Kind," 145 letters, and some other works, all of which may be seen in Migne's *Patrologie Latine*, vol. cxcvii. It would be plainly impossible to give even a summary of these books in this volume, but it must be stated that they received the express sanction of pope Eugenius III.; and no less a person than St. Bernard, abbot of Clairvaux, was commissioned, with others, to examine into the "revelations," and they pronounced them to be undoubtedly genuine. Of course, they justify and corroborate the dogmas and practices of the Roman Catholic Church throughout. A selection from them, with the visions of Catherine Emmerich, and some others, would form a not unsuitable supplement to this volume. Although we cannot here produce the visions of St. Hildegardes, we can give what she herself says of the way they were communicated to her. "From infancy," she tells us, "to the present day, being now seventy years old, I have received without cessation visions and divine revelations. In these divine communications I seem to be carried through the air to regions far, far away, and I see in my mind's eye the marvels shown to me. I do not see them with my bodily eye, nor hear what is said by my bodily ears, nor do I discover them by the agency of any of my bodily senses, nor do they come into my thoughts, nor are they dreams, or trances, or ecstasies; but I see them with my eyes open, while I am wide awake, sometimes in the night, and sometimes by day. What I see, I see in my soul; and what I hear, I hear in my inner self." Her letters are addressed to Eugenius III., Anastasius IV., Adrian IV., Alexander III.; the emperors Conrad III. and Frederick I.; the bishops of Bamberg, Spire, Worms, Constance, Liége, Maëstricht, Prague, etc., the bishop of Jerusalem, all the bishops of Germany, and several prelates of other parts of Europe; to numerous abbots, to St. Elizabeth, and to all men of literary repute in Europe. These letters are full of the mysteries and secrets which the Holy Ghost revealed to her. The answers are also given by Mons. Migne, the originals being carefully preserved in the monastery of St. Rupert.—*Acta Sanctorum* (Bollandists), vol. v. Sept. 17; Thierry, *Life of St. Hildegardes;* Nicholas Serarius, *History of Mayence*, bk. ii. ch. 37, etc.

The visions of Ignatius Loyola (A.D. 1491–1556). Ignatius Loyola had frequent visits of angels, and frequent visions. On one occasion he was caught up by the Spirit, and saw a figure which represented to him quite clearly the mysterious Trinity. A little afterwards was shown him by revelation the design of Infinite Wisdom in the creation of the world, and in the special order of that great work, as recorded in *Gen.* i. In another vision he was shown the literal verity of transubstantiation, the Eucharist by consecration being verily and indeed changed into the body and blood of Jesus Christ. And in another vision, all the mysteries of the Christian faith were explained to him, especially those introduced since the times of the apostles, and therefore not mentioned in the New Testament Scriptures. All these were so clearly manifested to him, and received such certain vindication in these visions, that Ignatius declared he would lay down his life in defence of any one of them.—*Acta Sanctorum*, July 31.

Visions of Mary Magdalene of Pazzi (A.D. 1566–1607). (1) While Mary Magdalene of Pazzi was praying at the tomb of Mary Bagnesi, she saw a glorious throne covered with precious stones, and was told that this throne was the virginity which she had kept immaculate; and the precious stones thereon were the souls which had been brought to God by her means.

(2) She then saw a religious woman carried up to paradise, after having been fifteen days in purgatory. Her detention

in purgatory had been because she had done unnecessary work on festival days; had not informed the mother prioress of certain irregularities in the convent to which she had been privy; and had been too fond of her parents.

(3) Her next vision was a sister who had died with the reputation of sanctity. She appeared all luminous except in her hands, which were black. This was because she had accepted little presents from secular persons.

(4) Her fourth vision at the tomb was that of Lewis of Gonzaga, who shone in brilliant light. On seeing this vision, the saint cried aloud, "Oh, what glory, Lewis, son of Ignatius! I could not have conceived it possible, if I had not been shown it."—*Acta Sanctorum* (Bollandists), vol. v. May 23.

The vision of St. Patrick (A.D. 373–464). St. Patrick, in his *Confessions*, says, "One night I saw before me a celestial visitant, holding a book in his hand. He said to me, 'I am Victricius;' and he gave me the book, which was, in fact, a collection of letters. On the first page I read these words, 'A voice from Ireland.' As I read on, methought I heard the woodmen of Foclutum addressing me, and saying, 'We beseech you, O man of God, come back to us, and teach us about the Saviour.' I was moved to tears by this appeal, and the vision ceased. Next night I heard celestial voices singing the songs of heaven, but saw no one, nor can I at all tell where the voices came from. I fell to prayer, and heard a voice whisper in my ear, 'I am He who gave My life to redeem thine.' I felt as if some one had entered into me, and knew it was the Holy Ghost. Next day I told the vision to a friend, and he replied, 'One day you will be bishop of Ireland.' This remark threw me into a consternation, miserable sinner that I was; nevertheless, it came to pass."—*Acta Sanctorum* (Bollandists), vol. ii. March 17.

Alban Butler says that St. Patrick "saw all the children of Ireland from the wombs of their mothers stretching out their hands, and piteously crying to him for relief." But the account given above is a literal translation of the words of St. Patrick himself.

St. Porphyry's vision by which he was restored to sound health (A.D. 353–420). While St. Porphyry abode in his cave near the river Jordan, he fell sick with a complication of disorders, which obliged him to return to Jerusalem. There he visited daily the holy places, leaning on his staff, for he was too weak to stand without support. Mark, who afterwards wrote his life, here made his acquaintance; and one day, on offering him assistance, received for reply, "It is not right that I, who come hither in penance for my sins, should be relieved of the weight of that penance." Three months afterwards Mark saw him again. He was then quite well; and, on Mark's expressing surprise at his complete recovery, Porphyry said to him, "Forty days ago, being in extreme pain, I fainted away on reaching Calvary, and saw, in a kind of trance, the Saviour on the cross, and the penitent thief. I said to Christ, 'Lord, remember me when Thou comest into Thy kingdom.' Whereupon Christ ordered the thief to come to my assistance. He raised me from the ground, and bade me go to Christ; so I ran to Him, and He, coming down from the cross, said to me, 'Take up this wood [*cross*] into thy keeping.' Methought I laid it on my shoulders, and carried it some considerable way. When I came to myself, I found the pain had all left me, and I was as well as if I had never ailed anything."—Mark (a companion), *Life of St. Porphyry*.

Robert of Lyons is shown a vision of paradise (A.D. 1109). Robert, a student from Lyons, on a visit to Cîteaux, asked God to show him the path of heaven. So God showed him a vast table-land on the top of an exceeding high mountain. In this table-land was a magnificent city. The student wanted to enter it, but found it impossible so to do, in consequence of a large river which flowed between him and the city. Looking for a way across the river, he observed on the opposite bank twelve or fourteen poor men washing their garments. One of them had a robe of dazzling whiteness, and this shining One helped the others in their work. "Who are you?" said the student to the shining One. "These poor ones," He replied, "are monks washing away their sins by repentance, and making their robes white in the river of tears. I am Jesus Christ, ever ready to help the truly penitent. The city that you see is paradise, where I reign with those who have washed their robes and made them white. Behold the road to heaven which you wanted to see."—Vincent de Beauvais, *Speculum Majus*, bk. xxv. ch. 106. (See BEULAH (LAND OF) in the Index of this book.)

A monk sees the Virgin Mary and three

companies of virgins. Two monks went to administer the last rites to Pemena, a shepherdess, who was sick of a fever. One of them, overcome by fatigue, fell into a trance, and saw in a vision three companies of virgins. The virgins of the first troop were magnificently dressed in gold brocade; those of the second company were arrayed in dazzling white; those of the third wore robes whiter than snow, trimmed with royal purple. The first company saluted him, and he returned the salute. At the head of the third company was a virgin of surpassing beauty, whose robe was completely covered with white and red roses. He saluted the lady profoundly, and asked her name. "I am the queen of virgins," she graciously replied, "and accompany these troops of virgins from heaven. The first troop are those who debated in their minds whether they should marry or lead a virgin life, but decided upon the latter course. The next troop are those who vowed continence from the first, and kept themselves in chastity to the end. The third troop are those who have added the rose of martyrdom to the lily of chastity. We are now seeking the soul of a young shepherdess, which we are about to carry with us to heaven." The monk well knew the soul sought was Pemena's, and forthwith went with his brother monk to the cabin of the shepherdess. As they bent over the dying maiden, she said to them, "Oh, my fathers, that God would open your eyes to see the virgins from paradise which stand around me." The monks prayed that God would vouchsafe them this favour, and they saw the Virgin Mary place on Pemena's head a garland of flowers, which being done, the shepherdess breathed her last.—L'abbé Chapia, *Une Vie de Sainte par Jour.*

Voice from Heaven.

MATT. iii. 17. When Jesus was baptized, the Spirit of God was seen descending like a dove and lighting on Him; and lo! a voice from heaven, saying, This is My beloved Son, in whom I am well pleased.

JOHN xii. 28, 29. Father, glorify Thy name. Then came a voice from heaven, saying, I have both glorified it, and will glorify it again. The people that stood by said it thundered; but others said, An angel spake to Him.

ACTS ix. 4–7. When Saul [Paul] was on his way to Damascus, he heard a voice saying unto him, Saul, Saul, why persecutest thou Me? And Saul said, Who art Thou, Lord? And the Lord said, I am Jesus whom thou persecutest: it is hard for thee to kick against the pricks. And Saul said, Lord, what wilt Thou have me to do? And the Lord said to him, Arise, and go into the city, and it shall be told thee what thou must do. And the men that journeyed with him stood speechless, hearing a voice, but seeing no man. (See Exod. iii., and 1 Sam. iii.)

Apronius hears a voice from heaven, and is converted. Apronius the judge, who in the reign of Diocletian committed Sisinius to prison, heard a voice from heaven which said to him, "Come unto Me, all ye that labour and are heavy laden, and I will refresh you," and was converted. The emperor, being informed of the conversion, commanded the judge to be at once beheaded.—*Life of Marcellus the Pope* (from the public registers).

Jesus Christ speaks to St. Benezet, and commands him to build a bridge across the Rhone (A.D. 1165–1184). Benezet was a poor shepherd, born at Hermillon, in Savoy, wholly uneducated, and wholly ignorant of the world. On Sept. 13, A.D. 1177, he was sent by his mother, who was a widow, to look after her sheep, and an eclipse of the sun occurred. All of a sudden, Benezet heard a voice say to him three times, "Benezet, My son, hearken to the words of Jesus Christ." "Who art Thou, Lord?" replied the boy (then only twelve years old). "I hear Your voice, but see no one." "I am Jesus Christ," said the voice, "who by a single word created the heavens and the earth, the sea, and all that therein is." "And what, Lord," said the boy, "wilt Thou have me do?" "Leave these few sheep," rejoined the voice, "and go, build a bridge across the Rhone." "But, Lord, I never heard of the Rhone, and know not where it is. And as for the sheep, they are my mother's; and I dare not leave them." "Trust in Me," said the voice in reply; "I will gather the sheep into their fold, and will send one to conduct you on the way." "But, Lord," the boy objected, "I have only three oboli [= fourpence] in the world, and one cannot build a bridge with that." "Obey, My son, and I will furnish the means."

The sequel of this strange story is no less marvellous than the beginning, and what is more strange still is this, there is certainly some thread of truth in the story that Benezet, the shepherd boy of Savoy, did build a bridge across the Rhone. This is attested by public muniments drawn up at the time, and still preserved at Avignon, where the story is known to every one. Benezet died at the early age of nineteen, was buried on the bridge, and the body was twice disinterred. Once in 1669, when a large part of the bridge fell down; the body was then found entire, without any signs of corruption; "even the bowels being sound." And again in 1674, when the body was translated with royal pomp into the church of the Celestines. A full description of this grand pageant is in the *Acta Sanctorum* of the Bollandists, vol. ii. April 14, pp. 958, 959. Now to continue the story.

The boy started on his journey, not knowing whither he was going; and was soon joined by an angel, in the guise of a pilgrim, who said to the boy, "Come with me, and I will show you where Jesus Christ wants you to build the bridge." When the boy reached the river, he was aghast at its size and cried in terror, "It is not possible to build a bridge across such a big river." "Fear not," said the angel; "but go to yon ferryman, and get him to row you across the stream; then go to the bishop of Avignon, and tell him why you have come." So saying, the angel left him. Benezet made his way to the ferryman, who happened to be a Jew, and asked him to row him across the river for nothing, out of love to Jesus Christ and the Virgin. The Jew replied he cared nothing for Jesus Christ or the Virgin, and certainly would not unmoor his boat without being paid three oboli. This was every farthing the boy had, but he was obliged to part with them, in order to cross the ferry. Being set on the other side, he went at once to the cathedral, where the bishop was preaching; and cried aloud, "Listen to me, and hear what I have got to say. Jesus Christ has sent me hither to build a bridge across the Rhone." The bishop was most indignant at this unseemly interruption from a boy, evidently a rustic, and commanded the provost to punish him for his insolence. The provost was a hard man, named Berenger, who at once apprehended the boy; but the boy insisted that Jesus Christ had sent him to build a bridge across the Rhone. "Nonsense!" cried the provost; "how is a boy like you to build a bridge across this river, which even Charlemagne would not undertake to do?" Still the boy insisted that Jesus Christ had sent him to build the bridge. The provost laughed at the absurdity, and said, "I will believe it when I see you carry off that stone," pointing to a huge stone thirty feet long and seventeen broad. Benezet walked up to the stone, made the sign of the cross, lifted the stone on his shoulders, and carried it to the spot where the bridge was to spring from. The provost, the bishop, the whole people, were amazed. They no longer doubted the boy's tale. Money came in on all sides, for every one was anxious to be a fellow-worker with God, and the bridge was built.—L'abbé Truchet, *Histoire Hagiologique du Diocèse de Maurienne.*

This boy, who died at the age of nineteen, was a thaumaturgist, and wrought numerous miracles.

A voice from heaven addresses St. Catherine of Bologna (A.D. 1413–1463). A malefactor condemned to be burnt alive refused to confess, and rejected the services of the priest. St. Catherine of Bologna being informed thereof, prostrated herself before the Holy Sacrament for a whole day and night. After matins, she said in her orison, "O my God, I will not rise from my knees till You have granted me the soul of this malefactor, bought by Your precious blood." Then a voice from heaven answered, "I cannot refuse you this soul; thanks to your prayers it shall be saved." In the mean time, the malefactor sent for a priest to receive his confession; he was truly penitent, and though burnt to death, ceased not to invoke the name of Jesus.—Paleotti, *Life of St. Catherine of Bologna* (inserted in vol. xvii. of the *Ecclesiastical Annals*).

A voice from heaven speaks to St. Germanus, abbot of Granfel (A.D. 666). Catihe, duke of Alsace, greatly oppressed the monks and poor inhabitants of his dominion. St. Germanus remonstrated with him, and as the duke was one day plundering the people, at the head of a troop of soldiers, the abbot implored him to desist. Some of the soldiers afterwards met the abbot on his road to Granfel, and stripped him of his clothes. "I thank Thee, Lord of heaven and earth," said the saint, "that I am deemed worthy to suffer for Thy sake. Deign to admit me into the company of those who have washed their robes, and made them white in the blood of the lamb." A voice from heaven replied, "Come, faithful shepherd of My fold, the heavens are open to you; enter into the joy of thy lord." At this moment one of the soldiers pierced him with a lance, and he fell dead.—Bollandus, *Acta Sanctorum* (written by Babolen, a contemporary), vol. iii. Feb.

St. Henry of Northumberland strengthened in the right way by a voice from heaven (A.D. 1127). Henry of Northumberland resolved to serve God in solitude; so, leaving his home, he went to Coquet Island, off the coast of Northumberland. His parents went to fetch him back; but Henry, casting himself before his crucifix, implored God to direct him. Then came a voice from heaven, which said to him, "Stay here, Henry. Play the man; strengthen thy heart to resist, for I have called thee to My eternal purpose." So he remained in the island a solitary or hermit.—Capgrave, *Life of Henry of Northumberland.*

St. Hermylus of Belgrade hears in his martyrdom a voice from heaven (A.D. 315). St. Hermylus, being denounced to Licinius as a despiser of the gods of Rome, was arrested, and brought before the emperor. The emperor said to him, "Tell me, fellow, do you acknowledge yourself to be a Christian?" "I not only acknowledge myself to be a Christian," replied Hermylus, "but also a consecrated deacon in the service of Christ." Said the emperor, "Abandon this foolery, and save yourself from the penalties of the law." The deacon made answer, "It is no foolery to adore the Maker of heaven and earth, but it is indeed foolery to worship stocks and stones, the work of men's hands." "Not so glib with your tongue, fellow," said the emperor; "obey, or endure the reward of your obstinacy." "He that endureth to the end," said the deacon, "the same shall be saved." "Saved, i' faith!" laughed Licinius; "we'll soon see how your gods can save you." So saying, he ordered the lictors to scourge the rogue well, and teach him to reverence the gods of his country. Six men then stripped him, threw him on the ground, and scourged him soundly. "O Thou who didst endure before Pilate the mockery and the scourge," cried Hermylus, "strengthen me to endure, that I may finish my course with joy." Then was heard a voice from heaven, saying to him, "Verily, verily, Hermylus, in three days shalt thou be with Me in paradise." Hearing these words, the deacon was filled with comfort; but Licinius and his myrmidons were filled with consternation.—Metaphrastês, *Lives*, etc. (compiled from the original acts).

St. Lucian in his martyrdom hears a voice from heaven (eleventh century). When St. Lucian was led to execution, a great light encompassed him, and as his head fell to the axe, the executioners heard a voice from heaven saying to him, "Well done, good and faithful servant; receive the crown of glory prepared for you from before the foundation of the world."—*Acta Sanctorum* (Life of St. Lucianus).

Voices from heaven frequently heard by St. Margaret of Cortona (A.D. 1297). One day, as St. Margaret was praying for two artisans, whose apparitions had appeared to her, and told her they had been murdered by robbers, without being allowed time to confess, although they grieved for their misdeeds, the Saviour said to her, "Tell the Minorites to remember the souls of the dead. They are so numerous as to pass man's understanding, yet very few are taken from purgatory through any prayers or gifts of their friends."

At another time a voice told her that her mother had been delivered from purgatory after being there ten years, and her father would also be delivered, but his term was not yet ended.

One day, as she was praying for her dead servant, her guardian angel said to her, "Thy servant must remain in purgatory for a month, but her pains will be light, and then she will be transported to the choir of the cherubim."

Christ said to her, on a day set apart for the purification of the Holy Virgin, "The three dead persons for whom you prayed this morning have been acquitted by their judges from everlasting perdition, but they must suffer for their sins, and so great will be their torments, that unless their good angels sustain them, they will believe themselves outcasts. As on earth," He continued, "so in purgatory, there are separate cells. Some are purified in thick darkness, some in rapid torrents, some in ice, and others in devouring fire."—Bollandus, *Acta Sanctorum*, vol. iii. Feb., p. 298.

St. Peter Nolasco is encouraged to persevere by a voice from heaven (A.D. 1189–1256). St. Peter Nolasco, founder of the Order of Mercy, one Saturday night, being greatly distressed that his work progressed so slowly, cried aloud, "O Lord, how is it Thou art so bountiful to others, and so niggardly to Thy mother? If my demerits are the cause, remove me out of the way, and supply my place with one more worthy of the work which I have taken in hand." Then was heard in the church a voice which said, "Fear not, little flock; it is My Father's good pleasure to give you the kingdom." These words filled all who heard them with amazement; and Nolasco soon had the unspeakable consolation of seeing his order increase, and allied monasteries springing up in all directions.—R. P. F. Zumel, *Life of St. Peter Nolasco.*

St. Peter of Verona hears a voice from heaven (A.D. 1206–1252). While St. Peter of Verona was at Milan, he employed all his energies in the conversion of heretics. One day he found such obstinate resistance, that his heart failed him, and he resolved to abandon his work, which seemed quite hopeless. While praying, he heard a voice from heaven speak to him. It was the Virgin Mary, who said to him, "Peter, I have prayed for thee, that thy faith fail not. He who putteth his hand to the plough and looketh back, is not worthy of the kingdom of God." Then was his courage revived, and he resolved to continue the fight of faith even to his life's end.—T. Lentino, *Life of St. Peter the Martyr.*

St. Polycarp heard a voice from heaven, when led to execution (A.D. 167). As St. Polycarp was led to execution, a voice from heaven was heard by many, saying to him, "Polycarp, My faithful servant, be of good courage, and play the man."—*Written by the Church of Smyrna at the time of the martyrdom.*

St. Secundina hears at her execution a voice from heaven (A.D. 257). When St. Secundina of Anagni, in Italy, was led from her cell to martyrdom, she prayed for herself and her enemies. While she prayed, a resplendent light shone round about her, and the whole multitude heard a voice from heaven, saying, "Ye all were within a finger's length of hell, but the prayer of My servant Secundina has ascended to the ears of the Lord of hosts, and through her prayers your lives are saved. Daughter, be of good cheer, for I am thine, and thou art Mine, and all thine are Mine." Eighteen of the guard and many of the crowd, on hearing these words, were baptized, confessing their sins.—*Les Petits Bollandistes*, vol. ii. p. 247.

A voice from heaven determines which bones are Peter's and which Paul's. In the reign of Heliogabalus (A.D. 218–222), the bones of Peter and Paul were deposited by Christian converts in one tomb in the catacombs of Rome. This was some 130 or 140 years after their deaths. Two hundred years later, the two bodies were transported to a gorgeous shrine beneath the church of the Vatican. When pope Sylvester, at the consecration of the great church of St. Peter, wished to place the sacred remains of St. Peter in an altar, it was found impossible to distinguish which of the bones were those of Peter, and which were those of Paul. After fasting and prayer, a divine voice revealed that the larger bones were those of the preacher, and the smaller ones those of the fisherman. This being deemed conclusive, the smaller bones were placed in St. Peter's church, and the larger ones in St. Paul's.—Dr. W. Smith, *Dictionary of Christian Antiquities*, vol. i. p. 109.

This account is not strictly correct. The two heads are in the basilica of St. John Lateran. Under St. Peter's altar, thirty-eight feet from the ground, "on voit une tente de velours cramoisi rehaussé d'or. Ce pavillion recouvre une arche ou ciboire en marbre de Paros soutenu par quatre colonnes de marbre Egyptien avec des chapiteaux d'ordre Corinthien en bronze doré. Lá sont renfermées les têtes des apôtres St. Pierre et St. Paul. Deux fois chaque année, le Samedi Saint et le Mardi des Rogations, elles sont exposées solennellement à la vénération des fidèles."—Mgr. Guérin (chamberlain of pope Leo XIII.), *Vies des Saints*, vol. viii. p. 460.

Alban Butler says, "One half of the body of each apostle is deposited together in a rich vault in the great church of St. Paul, on the Ostian road, and the other half of both bodies in a more stately vault in the Vatican church."—June 29.

Anne Askew. Two views of the same phenomenon (A.D. 1546). Anne Askew was a Protestant of Lincolnshire, in the reign of Henry VIII. She was taken before "the Quest," and committed to prison. After being confined there above a year, she was brought before the council, and set upon the rack. With a savagery disgraceful to human nature, chancellor Wriothesley stripped off his robes of state, grasped the handle of the rack, and worked the torture till all thought the victim was dead. She was taken off the rack, and carried back to her dungeon, only to be burnt to death at Smithfield. When the torch was applied to the fagots, a few drops of rain fell, and a low peal of thunder was heard. "She is damned to all eternity," said some of the spectators. "God knows whether I may truly call it thunder," said one who was present; "but, for my own part, it seemed that the angels in heaven were singing their joy-song over another soul taken into bliss."—Dr. Wylie, *History of Protestantism*, vol. iii. pp. 406, 407.

Walking on Water.

MATT. xiv. 24–32. Jesus, having fed five thousand men, besides women and children, with five barley loaves, bade His disciples to pass over the sea. And when the ship was in the midst of the sea, it was tossed with the waves, for the winds were contrary. In the fourth watch of the night Jesus went unto them, walking on the sea. And when the disciples saw Him, they were troubled; but Jesus spake unto them, saying, Be of good cheer; it is I; be not afraid. Peter then got out of the boat to join him, but, his courage failing him, he began to sink, when Jesus caught him, saying, O thou of little faith, wherefore didst thou doubt?

St. Aldegundis walks across the river Sambre (A.D. 630-689). St. Aldegundis, daughter of prince Wabert, was solicited in marriage by Eudon, an English prince. Aldegundis told her father she could not accept the proposal, as she had already betrothed herself to Christ; but her father, unwilling to let slip so honourable an offer, promised the prince his daughter's hand. In this extremity Aldegundis had recourse to her celestial spouse, who told her to flee from her father's roof; so, in disguise, and covered by the shades of night, she made good her escape, and came to the river Sambre. There was no bridge, no boat, and the river was not fordable. Here, then, her flight was arrested; but she again appealed for help to Him whose ears are ever open to our prayers. Immediately two angels appeared, and bade her follow them; so she "ran over the surface of the river like a bird, without even wetting the soles of her shoes." Having crossed the Sambre, she continued her flight to the forest, where she built a little chapel, and resolved never to quit it, unless her parents promised not to force her into any marriage with man. Her father discovered her retreat, made the required promise, and the maiden returned home. (See St. Austrebertha, below.) —L'abbé Delbos, *Life of St. Aldegundis*.

Two angels, in the form of two young men, guided St. Benedict from Subiaco to Mont Cassino, a distance of eighteen leagues. (See Angel Visitants, p. 6.)

St. Austrebertha walks across the river Canche (630-704). Austrebertha was the daughter of prince Badefroy and Framechilde, both of royal blood. She vowed to make Christ her only spouse; and when she heard that her father had promised her in marriage to a young prince, she induced her brother to accompany her in her escape from her parents' house in Marconne to Thérouanne, where she hoped to hide herself till her father consented to the life she had chosen. When the brother and sister reached the river Canche, they found it so greatly swollen that it had swept away the bridge and no boat was at hand. Not to be deterred by this impediment, Austrebertha, taking her brother by the hand, walked on boldly, and they crossed over, walking on the water, and arrived safely at the monastery of Thérouanne, presided over by St. Omer. Austrebertha told her tale, and the bishop consented without delay to give her the veil. He then took her back to her parents, reconciled them to the choice which their daughter had made, and committed her to the care of Burgofleda, abbess of a nunnery called Port.—Surius, *Lives of the Saints*.

All this is a repetition, with a change of names, of the story of Aldegundis; and it is not a little remarkable that the date of the birth of both is 630. The very locality is about the same, the river Canche being in the Pas de Calais, and the monastery of Thérouanne in the same department.

The horse and hearse bearing the body of St. Julian cross the river Sarthe (A.D. 117). St. Julian died at Mans. When the funeral cortége reached the river Sarthe, it was so swollen with recent rains that it was no longer fordable. Never mind. Man's extremity is God's opportunity. The horses continued their route, dragging the funeral car; the procession followed, and all went safely on the surface of the water across the river, and reached without accident the other side. —D. Piolin, *History of the Church of Mans*.

St. Juvenal, hearing that a ship was in danger, went walking on the sea to save it. St. Juvenal, bishop of Narnia, in Africa, hearing that a ship, containing three thousand souls, was in danger of being wrecked during a severe storm, went to its relief, walking on the sea. When he came to the ship the tempest ceased, and was followed by a great calm.—St. Gregory, *Homily* 37. (See also Usuard's *Martyrology*.)

St. Mary of Egypt passes and repasses the river Jordan, walking on its surface (A.D. 421). St. Mary of Egypt, the anchorite, in her interview with Father Zozimus, appointed to meet him at the river Jordan the first Thursday in Lent, to receive from his hands the holy sacrament. Father Zozimus went to the place appointed "with the instruments of our salvation," but not finding Mary there, began to be filled with fear lest she should not come. Lifting up his eyes, he saw her in the distance, and wondered how she would be able to cross the river to come to him. She came to the brink, made the sign of the cross, and stepping on the water with confidence walked across it. The father and the penitent prayed together; he administered to her the holy communion, and she repeated the words of the aged Simeon, "Lord, now let st Thou Thy servant depart in peace, according to Thy word, for mine eyes have seen Thy salvation." Mary then told Zozimus to come again next year to the same place, and bidding him farewell, she repassed the Jordan in the same way as she had crossed it, and returned into the desert. Next year, when Zozimus returned to the Jordan, he found the body dead, with an inscription in the sand, to this effect: "Abbot Zozimus, bury the body of poor Mary, who died the same day that she received the holy Eucharist at your hands." She had been dead a year, but no corruption had taken place, and no wild beast of the desert had touched her. Zozimus buried her, and related her sad tale to his disciples.—*Les Petits Bollandistes*, vol. iv. p. 128.

St. Maurus runs on the surface of a river to save St. Placidus (A.D. 584). St. Benedict sent Placidus to fetch water from a river; but as he dipped the bucket into the stream, his foot slipped, and he fell head foremost into the water. St. Benedict, who saw the accident by revelation, bade Maurus run to his assistance. Maurus, coming to the river, saw the body carried down the stream, and, without stopping to reflect, ran on the surface of the river to rescue his companion. On drifted the body of Placidus, and on ran Maurus over the water to overtake it. He came up, he clutched hold of his friend, he pulled him out of the river, and took him safely to the abbey. Though Maurus had run nearly a mile on the surface of the stream, yet he sank not, nor were the soles of his shoes wetted. When Placidus told the abbot of his rescue, he said, "As I was lifted out of the water, I saw distinctly the hood of St. Benedict held over the head of my rescuer." Maurus modestly replied he had not himself seen it; whereupon the abbot replied, "Placidus, then, has won from God the greater grace, as his merits, in God's sight, are the more exalted."—St. Gregory, *Dialogues*. (See also Laurentius Surius, *Lives of the Saints*.)

St. Nazarius and St. Celsus being cast into the sea, walk to shore. St. Nazarius was a very old man, and St. Celsus was a child committed to his charge, as Samuel was committed to Eli by his mother. Nero commanded that they should both be put to death for being Christians; accordingly, they were taken to Ostia and put into a bark, and when several leagues from shore were both cast into the sea. Forthwith a violent storm arose, and the crew saw the two saints walking on the waves, and were sore afraid. In their terror the seamen implored the saints to intreat their God to save them. This did they; the storm ceased, and the ship rode safe to shore. The saints followed, walking on the sea. All the crew became converts, and were numbered amongst the disciples.—Simeon Metaphrastês, *Chronicon*.

St. Oringa, in flight, walks across a river (A. D. 1310). St. Oringa of Tuscany, being an orphan, was under the charge of her brothers, who wanted her to marry; and when she told them she was the betrothed of Jesus Christ, they ill-treated her, so that she fled from home. Coming to a river, "pleine de confiance, la jeune fille avance quand même, et avec le secours de Dieu la traverse à pied sec." On she went, not knowing whither. When night came on, she lay herself down in a meadow to sleep till daylight. A timid hare came and nestled beside her, and all but said, "Poor little dove! trust yourself as I do to the care of God." Next day Oringa followed the hare as a guide, and came to Lucca, where she took service as a domestic. After a time she started on a pilgrimage to Mount Gargan, and lost her way, when St. Michael, "sous la forme d'un jeune diacre," put her in the right road, served her with food, and then left her.—*Les Petits Bollandistes*, vol. ii. p. 575.

St. Wulfran walks on the water to save two children offered to idols (A.D. 647–720). The Frisons used to offer human sacrifices to their gods. These sacrifices were made sometimes by strangulation, sometimes by the sword, sometimes by fire, sometimes by water. One day the lot fell upon the two children of one mother, the ages of the children being five and seven years. St. Wulfran implored king Radbod to prohibit such cruelty, but Radbod replied he could not violate the laws he had sworn to preserve. The children were taken to a spot where two rivers disembogued into the sea, and the rush of water was very violent. St. Wulfran, amidst a crowd of idolaters, prayed God to save the children and magnify His name among the heathen. Then the waters of the two rivers stood like a wall round the two children, and Wulfran, walking on the sea, entered the precincts, and, taking up the two children, delivered them to their mother. All were amazed, and many "were regenerated by the water of baptism."—The abbé Corblet, *Hagiography of the Diocese of Amiens.*

One thing must strike every reader, and that is, the just horror of the [Roman] Catholic Church at these human sacrifices, and yet their more than wholesale slaughter in the Middle Ages of what they called "heretics." Here Wulfran very properly felt indignant that two children should be offered to the gods of the Frisons, but Charles V. and his son Felipe murdered ten times as many thousands, because they doubted some of the dogmas which they themselves believed.

Water supplied.

(See Elijah makes Rain, etc., p. 129.)

Gen. xxi. 17–19. When Hagar and her son were driven out by Abraham, they went into the wilderness, and the bottle of water being exhausted, Hagar laid her boy under a shrub, and went herself a good way off, and wept. God had compassion on her distress, and opened her eyes, and she saw a well of water. And she went and filled the bottle, gave the lad drink, and he revived.

Exod. xvii. 1–7. When the wanderers from Egypt reached Rephidim, the people were angry with Moses, because there was no water. And Moses cried unto the Lord. Then said the Lord to him, Go on before the people, and take with thee of the elders, and smite the rock Horeb with thy rod, and there shall come water out of the rock, that the people may drink.

Judg. xv. 18, 19. After the great slaughter of a thousand Philistines with a jawbone, Samson was athirst, and said, Now shall I die for thirst, and fall into the hands of the uncircumcised. But God clave a hollow place that was in the jaw, and there came water thereout. And when Samson drank thereof, his spirit came again, and he revived.

Isa. xli. 17, 18. When the poor and needy seek water, and there is none, and their tongue faileth for thirst, I the Lord will hear them, I the God of Israel will not forsake them. I will open rivers in high places, and fountains in the midst of valleys: I will make the wilderness a pool of water, and the dry land springs of water.

Psalm cvii. 35. He turneth the wilderness into a standing water, and dry ground into water-springs.

St. Antony the Great supplies water in the African desert (fourth century). While St. Antony was dwelling in the desert, near the Red Sea, he was requested by some monks to visit their monastery. A camel was employed to carry bread and water for the journey, for there was no drinking-water between the saint's cell and the religious house to which they were going. On the journey the supply of water failed, and the consequences would have been disastrous if St. Antony had not interfered. Going about a stone's throw from the caravan, the man of God knelt down in prayer, and forthwith the Lord caused a spring of water to bubble from the ground; and all drank, and filled their vessels, and continued their route without further incident.—St. Athanasius, *Life of St. Antony the Great.*

St. Benedict, in Subiaco, supplies a monastery with water. Some of St. Benedict's monasteries were built on the tops of hills. The monks of a monastery in Subiaco, being much troubled for want of water, all of which had to be fetched from a river in the valley below, went to St. Benedict, and begged to be removed into some place where water could be supplied with less labour. St. Benedict bade them return to their monastery, for God would supply them with water. Next night St. Benedict went with St. Placidus to the top of the hill, and laid in order three stones, one above the other, and then returned to their cells. When the monks saw him next day, he said to them, "Go to the top of the hill, and you will find three stones piled one above the other. Dig a small basin at the foot of these stones, and the water therein shall never fail." The monks went to the top of the hill, as St. Benedict told them, and dug a basin at the foot of the three stones, and it was instantly full of water, even to overflowing. From this fountain a stream of clear water ran at all times to the very bottom of the hill.—Surius (1571), *Lives of the Saints.*

St. Clement, pope and martyr, supplies two thousand Christians with water. St. Clement, being banished by order of Trajan to the Chersonese, found there two thousand Christians condemned to work in the quarries. These Christians suffered much from want of water, for there was none within two miles. St. Clement prayed God to consider this necessity; and, lifting up his eyes, he saw, on a hillock close by, a lamb which held up its right foot, and pointed to a certain spot. St. Clement knew the lamb was Christ, the Lamb of God; and, going to the spot indicated, he made a little hole, and there sprang up straightway a vein of pure water, clear as crystal and very abundant.—Metaphrastês, *Lives*, etc.

St. Donatus brings water from dry land. Sozomenus tells us of a St. Donatus (not St. Donatus of Arezzo, but another) who was travelling with many others, when they suffered severely for want of water. Donatus prayed, and forthwith a fountain of clear water rose in a dry field which before had shown no indication of moisture.

St. Dunstan, archbishop of Canterbury,

raised a spring of water by knocking the earth (A.D. 925–988). St. Dunstan, by rapping the earth with his pastoral staff, caused a fountain of water to well up. This fountain was ever afterwards called St. Dunstan's well or St. Dunstan's fountain.—Osbert of Canterbury, *Life of St. Dunstan.*

St. Florus makes water spring from dry land (first century). St. Florus was contemporary with Jesus Christ, and a disciple of St. Peter. He went to preach the gospel in Aquitaine, and coming with his companions to the top of a hill, they were parched with thirst, but there was no water to be found. St. Florus, in this emergency, stuck in the ground the staff which was in his hand, and instantly a spring of water burst through, which has never failed from that day to this.—*Propre de St. Flour et de Clermont.*

St. Firmatus brings a spring of water out of dry ground (A.D. 1103). When St. Firmatus returned to France, after his liberation from prison, he went to Vitré, in Brittany, where he stopped for a few days. At Dordenay he produced a spring of water merely by putting his stick into the ground. The inhabitants, out of gratitude, have ever since called this spring "The Fountain of St. Firmatus."

Another example. When St. Firmatus went in pilgrimage to Palestine, he was greatly distressed in a desert for want of water, so he prayed God to supply it, and forthwith a spring of delicious water bubbled from the dry sand.—Bollandus, *Acta Sanctorum*, Feb. 28.

St. Fursy, with his abbatial staff, brings water from dry ground to supply his monastery (A.D. 650). St. Fursy, having built at Lagny-en-Brie a monastery and three chapels, wanted a supply of water. In order to procure this, he drove his abbatial staff into the earth, and instantly there bubbled up a fountain of water possessing healing powers. "This miracle is beyond dispute, inasmuch as the fountain still exists, and is more than sufficient to supply the whole town with most excellent water, and thither go hundreds to be healed of divers diseases. On Ascension Day, after the *Magnificat*, a procession is annually formed, and the relics of St. Fursy are carried to the fountain."—*Les Petits Bollandistes* (7th edit. 1880), vol. i. p. 405.

We are told in Roman story that Romulus and Remus were placed in a cradle soon after birth, and exposed in the Tiber. The Tiber having overflowed, the cradle was drifted into the adjoining meadow, and when the water abated, the cradle was left on dry land. A wolf, hearing the cry of the two babes, suckled them, and brought them up. Now, what would the pope's chamberlain think, if any one were to say, "This story is beyond dispute, inasmuch as the river Tiber still exists, and is a river of considerable importance, being in some parts three hundred feet wide and eighteen feet deep; and that the very city, Rome (so called from Romulus), stands on its banks"?

St. Gangulfus transports a fountain of water from Bassigny to Varennes (A.D. 760). This certainly is the most marvellous "miracle" recorded under this head. Returning to Burgundy, St. Gangulfus stopped at Chaumont, in Bassigny, to rest, and was much pleased with the water of a fountain, which he found clear and refreshing. He asked the owner if he would sell it, and the man, supposing it quite impossible to carry off a fountain, readily consented, and named his price. Gangulfus paid the money, and next day left Chaumont, and came to Varennes, some twenty-five miles south-east of that place. Sticking his staff in the ground, the fountain which he had bought immediately left the neighbourhood of Bassigny, and threw up a magnificent spring at Varenne, on the very spot where the saint had planted his staff.—*Acta Sanctorum* (Bollandists), May 11.

Water and wine fetched out of a rock by St. Gentius (twelfth century). St. Gentius retired to the desert of Bausset. One day, when the neighbours came to visit him, he had neither wine nor water to give them; but by touching a rock close by, there came from it both water and wine. This miracle cannot be gainsaid, for persons are shown the fountain even to this day. The water thereof is very abundant, and is an excellent specific in fevers.—*Propre d'Avignon.*

That there is a fountain of water at Bausset is doubtless, but this fact does not prove that Gentius created it by touching a rock with his finger, nor does it prove that wine flowed from it.

St. Gertrude of Vaux-en-Dieulet brings water from dry land (fifth century). St. Gertrude retired to the Bois de Noé (now called the "Bout de Noé), west of Dieulet. Here still flows the "Fountain of St. Gertrude," the origin of which is thus accounted for. St. Gertrude, on arriving at the valley of Argonne, which terminates the territory of Vaux, could find no water in the neighbourhood. Having a stick in her hand, she touched with it the earth, and a fountain of clear water bubbled up, which still flows to perpetuate the saint's name. In Vaux-en-Dieulet is a painting of St. Gertrude touching the earth, and the water rising through it in obedience to her touch.—*Les Petits Bollandistes*, vol. v. p. 232.

St. Honoré supplies his disciples with water from a rock. When St. Honoré landed on the isle of Lerins, a large number of disciples followed him; but the island was deficient of water. Then St. Honoré repeated the miracle of Moses, and brought water from a stony rock."—St. Hilary, *Life of St. Honoré.*

St. Isidore brings water from dry ground with his ox-goad. One hot summer's day, Vargas the farmer, going into his fields, was overcome with heat and thirst. He asked [St.] Isidore, one of his farm labourers, if he knew of any spring in the vicinity. Isidore directed him to a corner of the field, but the farmer returned in great anger, thinking the man had befooled him. The saint said to his master, "Come with me, and I will show you the spring." So they went both of them together. When they reached the spot indicated, sure enough there was no water; but Isidore pricked the dry earth with his ox-goad. and forthwith there bubbled up a clear spring, not only refreshing, but of medicinal virtues. None can gainsay this miracle, inasmuch as the spring still flows near Madrid in a full stream, an infinite number of sick folk resort to it daily to be cured of their infirmities, and thousands of visitors have gone to see it.—*From the Spanish.* (This *Life of St. Isidore* is attested by the very highest authorities. Philip of Castile and Aragon, by letters patent, granted to John Heigham permission to print and publish it. The grant is signed by Da Groote, and the book was published June 18, 1625. I possess an original copy.)

Ribadeneira and D. A. Villegas tells us that "all persons in Madrid and its suburbs hold this fountain in reverence. In fact, you will not find a house which has not some of its water in a bottle in case of sudden sickness, especially ague, blue-spots, or plague. Every one knows there is no such remedy known for these complaints, as the water of St. Isidore's fountain."

St. James brings water from the rock Puppim to supply the village (fifth century). St. James of Tarentaise built his episcopal palace on the rock Puppim, and a chapel to St. Peter was annexed. A village in time sprang up around, but there was no water in the vicinity. So, as Moses struck the rock in Horeb, and supplied the Israelites with water for themselves and their cattle, St. James struck the rock Puppim and brought forth water for the service of the village St. Jacquemoz.—Gui of Burgundy (afterwards Calixtus II.), *Life of St. James of Tarentaise.*

St. Julian, first bishop of Mans, brings water from dry ground with his pastoral staff (A.D. 117). St. Julian, who was born at Rome, came to Mans during a siege. The inhabitants, making a sortie, drove off the besiegers, but were greatly exhausted for want of water. In this emergency, St. Julian planted his pastoral staff in the midst of a large plain, and forthwith there bubbled up a spring of water most abundant and refreshing. "This is the more remarkable, in that the spot selected by the bishop was wholly destitute of natural springs." This fountain, called "St. Julian's Spring," still flows; and in ecclesiastical art St. Julian is represented in pontifical robes, planting his staff; and at his foot is a damsel, filling her pitcher with water. —D. Piolin, *History of the Church of Mans.*

St. Lupus, bishop of Chalons, brings water from dry land with his pastoral staff (seventh century). St. Lupus, bishop of Chalons, stood one day with his pastoral staff watching the haymakers. The sun was exceedingly fierce, and the men greatly exhausted. There was no water in the neighbourhood, so the bishop struck the dry ground with his staff, and forthwith there issued from the ground a spring of the clearest water, which continues to this day.—See Canon Bright's *History of the Church* (1863).

St. Ursus brings a fountain of water from a rock (sixth century). St. Ursus was a native of Ireland, but quitted his native land and was made archdeacon of Aosta. One hot summer he heard the rustics of Busseia complaining of thirst, and lamenting the want of water in the neighbourhood. He called to mind the text that "all things are possible to him who believeth," and forthwith struck with his staff the rock on which he was standing. Immediately there flowed from it a spring of delicious water, which runs in a liquid stream even to the present day, and is called "St. Bear's Fountain." Mention is made of it in the archives of the chapter under the title of 1290, where it is stated that "one Jacquemet gave to St. Bear's church a parcel of land situate in the locality of St. Ursus' Fountain."—*Life of St. Ursus, Archdeacon of Aosta* (1868).

In Christian art St. Ursus is sometimes represented striking the rock. Thus, in the cloister of the Collégiale, he is represented on a marble column of the twelfth century, and below it is the inscription "FONS S. URSI."

St. Patrick and the triple miracle (fifth

century). A blind man, taking hold of St. Patrick's right hand, guided it into making on the ground a cross, when instantly three miracles ensued: (1) A spring of water bubbled from the dry ground; (2) the blind man, bathing his eyes with this water, received his sight; and (3) the man, who before could neither write nor read, was instantly inspired with both these gifts.—Thomas Massingham, *Florilegium Insulæ Sanctorum.*

St. Pharaïldis brings water from dry land with her distaff (A.D. 710). St. Pharaïldis produced a plentiful well-spring by striking the side of a hill with her distaff. This fountain had healing virtues, especially for children's complaints; and every Friday crowds come to Bruay to avail themselves of it.—Bollandus, *Acta Sanctorum*, vol. i. p. 170.

Simeon Stylitês brings water from dry ground (A.D. 459). Simeon, the pillar saint, made a fountain of water spring from dry ground to supply a certain locality where water was deficient.—Theodoret, *History of the Holy Fathers* (fifth century).

St. Vinebald, herdsman, brings a spring of water from dry ground (seventh century). When St. Vinebald was driving his oxen from Villeneuve la Lionne, he met a woman bringing water from the river, and asked her to give his beasts drink. She churlishly replied she had other duties in hand, and bade him look after his herd himself. A little further on he saw another woman who had been to the river to fetch water, and he asked her the same thing; whereupon she gave water to all the beasts. Vinebald then stuck his ox-goad into the ground, and said to the woman, "Henceforth this spring of water will save you the labour of going down to the river for water." A spring then issued from the ground, not only pure and excellent, but sanative also. In 1793, this spring was profaned by the villagers' washing their linen in it, and it nearly ceased flowing; whereupon the magistrates forbade any one to desecrate the water, and the spring recovered its full force. Now, a place for washing linen has been built lower down, "et l'eau est toujours très abondante."—*Les Petits Bollandistes*, vol. iv. p. 120.

Water supplied to a Christian army by the fountain of Elijah (thirteenth century). The river sources of the Ptolemaïd having been poisoned by the Saracens, the Christian army, as well as all the other dwellers in that district, were in danger of a cruel death. In this exigency, the chiefs of the Christian army sent a company of soldiers to protect the monks of Mount Carmel; for it was well known that the fountain of Elijah there never failed while the monks were on the mount, but the moment they were driven away by the infidel the fountain dried up. By protecting the monks on the mountain, the Christian army was abundantly supplied with wholesome water, and was thus in a condition at any time to meet the foe.—*Les Petits Bollandistes*, vol. v. p. 590.

Water turned into Wine.

JOHN ii. 1–11. The first miracle that Jesus did was to turn water into wine. This was at a marriage banquet in Cana of Galilee, to which Jesus, with His mother and disciples, was invited.

St. Adelm turns water into wine (eleventh century). Among the many miracles ascribed to St. Adelm, the following summary is mentioned in an off-hand manner by Mgr. Guérin, chamberlain of pope Leo XIII.: "He caused a serpent, which had glided into a man sleeping on the ground with his mouth open, to come out again; he cured the queen of England of an incurable malady by sending to her a piece of bread which he had blessed; he healed many sick of fevers in a similar way; and he changed water into wine."—*Les Petits Bollandistes*, vol. ii. p. 134.

St. Agnes converts a fountain of water into exquisite wine (A.D. 1274–1311). Amongst the many miracles of St. Agnes, one was to convert a fountain of water into exquisite wine.—Raymond of Capua, *Life of St. Agnes of Mount Pulciano.*

St. Aïbert turns water into wine of a healing virtue (A.D. 1060–1140). Count Arnoul, brother of Baldwin, count of Hainault, being attacked with a dangerous malady for which his physicians knew of no remedy, went to the hermitage of St. Aïbert. After confession, the count begged the saint to give him something to drink, as he was extremely parched with fever. St. Aïbert said there was nothing but water in the hermitage, and went to draw some from the well. He blessed it, and handed it to the count; but the saint's benediction was so potent, that the water was converted by it into a most generous wine, more delicious than any in the country. The draught made such a change on the count, that his fever left him, and he returned home in perfect health and spirits.—Robert (archdeacon of Ostrevand), *Life of St. Aibert.*

Water served to St. Gerard turned into wine (A.D. 994). St. Gerard, with twelve companions, made a pilgrimage to Rome, to visit the tombs of the two apostles, Peter and Paul. Here he made the acquaintance of Mayeul, bishop of Cluny, and Adalbert, the future bishop of Prague. Their interview was followed by a repast, but as it was a fast day with St. Gerard, he whispered to the servitor to bring him water to drink. The servitor went to the fountain to fetch some water, but when he handed it to the prelate it was found to be most excellent wine. The saint told the servitor he had bid him bring water, and the servitor protested he had brought it from the fountain. St. Gerard now confessed that God had turned the water into wine to honour his servants Mayeul and Adalbert; but Mayeul and Adalbert returned the compliment, and said the water had been converted into wine in honour of their guest.—Father Benedict, *Life of St. Gerard.*

A "miracle" of this sort is quite worthless. Every one knows how quick servants are in discerning an honoured guest, and how skilfully they humour the vanity of such a person. St. Gerard was the guest of honour, and no flattery could be so pleasing as to make him the subject of a miracle.

St. Gerlac the penitent turns water into wine (died 1170). One Sunday in Passion Week, the priest who usually said mass in a certain chapel, having brought with him some water to drink, found it thrice changed into wine. This miracle was the work of St. Gerlac the penitent, and it occurred a little before his death.—*Les Petits Bollandistes* (7th edit. 1880), vol. i. p. 149.

St. Guido converts water into wine (A.D. 1046). "C'était une chose assez ordinaire que l'eau qu'on lui servait à table se changeât en vin. Ce que de grands prélats ont même éprouvé avec admiration."—Mgr. Guérin, *Vies des Saints,* vol. iv. p. 77.

Martha, failing in wine to supply her guests, saw repeated the miracle of Christ at the marriage feast (first century). Eutropius, one of the seventy disciples of Jesus, was a native of Egypt, but lived in Antioch, and after the ascension was sent with Trophimus and Maximin into Gaul. Eutropius fixed his home at Orange, Trophimus at Arles, and Maximin at Aix. One day they all met at Tarascon to convert the house inhabited by Martha into a basilica. Martha was the hostess, and as her guests were very numerous, her wine failed her. At her prayer the water of the waterpots was converted into wine, precisely as it had been done at the marriage feast at Cana of Galilee.—Faillon, *Monuments inédits de l'Apostolat de Sainte Madeleine.*

Some water given to St. Odilo, abbot of Cluny, turned into wine (eleventh century). St. Odilo, abbot of Cluny, greatly reduced by fasting, was served by one of the brothers of Orval with a cup of water; but when it was handed to him, "God had changed the water into wine." The saint emptied the cup into the piscina, and told the brother to bring him water, not wine. This was done thrice; and then Odilo, perceiving it was God's doing, drank the draught, giving God thanks.—*Bollandus, Vita Sanctorum,* vol. i. Jan. 1.

Peter Celestine converts water into wine (A.D. 1221–1296). Peter Celestine, while dwelling as an anchorite in the desert of St. Barthélemy en Loge, changed water into wine for the celebration of the holy mysteries.—*Les Petits Bollandistes,* vol. vi. p. 24.

St. Peter the hermit turns water into wine (A.D. 1098). One day the lords of the Apennines being, on a hunting expedition, very hungry and thirsty, observed the roof of St. Peter's hermitage, and made towards it with all haste, in hope of obtaining something to eat and drink. "Hark ye, good hermit," said the huntsmen, "can you give us any refreshment?" Without answering a word, Peter brought forth what food he had, and, going to a fountain of clear water, he filled a large jug, which he changed to good wine, and set before the strangers. They ate and drank to their heart's content, and so pleased were they with the entertainment, that they gave the hermit all he required to build a monastery.—*Acta Sanctorum* (Bollandists), vol. ii. April 12, pp. 101, 102.

St. Vaast, bishop of Arras and Cambrai, turns water into wine (A.D. 540). St. Vaast performed many miracles, such as exorcising demoniacs, and turning water into wine. The usual drink of the people of the district was a kind of beer, called *cervisia,* very intoxicating, and drunk at festivals in large quantities. Sometimes the genial bishop would turn the water of a poor cottager into cervisia; but on one occasion he certainly set his face against the drinking habits of the people. Ocine was one of the chief leaders of Arras; and one day, when king Clotaire was invited to dine with him, the seigneur asked St. Vaast to meet him. On entering the hospitable mansion, the bishop, as usual, made the sign of the cross; whereupon every hogshead of cervisia burst, and the liquor was all spilt. The king asked St. Vaast the reason of this waste, and the bishop replied, "The devil, sire, could never abide the sign of the cross."—Surius (1570), *Lives of the Saints*, vol. i.

St. Victor of Plancy turns water into wine (sixth century). St. Victor of Plancy lived as a hermit near Saturniac, in the diocese of Troyes. His reputation induced Chilperic, king of France, to pay him a visit. St. Victor received the king with a kiss of peace, and invited him to take some refreshment. Now, the hermit had only a little water in a vessel, but falling on his knees, he said, "O Lord, bless this water, and fill the vessel which holds it with heavenly dew." Then he made on the vessel the sign of the cross, and lo! it was full to the brim of the most excellent wine. The king and all his suite drank thereof, and declared it to be of the very best quality. —Le sieur des Guerrois, *Histoire Ecclésiastique*. (See also St. Bernard's *Sermon on the Fête-day of St. Victor*, Feb. 26.)

The water, given by St. Zita to a pilgrim, turned into wine (A.D. 1218–1278). One day a palmer, parched with heat and thirst, asked charity of St. Zita. She had absolutely nothing to give, but all of a sudden she said, "Stop a minute," and ran to fill a vessel with water. When she handed the mug to the palmer, she made the sign of the cross, and the palmer, putting the mug to his mouth, drank the contents with great relish, for the water had been turned into most delicious wine.—*Vita Sanctorum* (Papebroch the Bollandist), April 27, p. 497.

A pot of virgin honey turned into gold (A.D. 616). Nicetas Patricius, subprætor of Africa, called one day on John, patriarch of Alexandria, when servants were bringing into the house some jars of virgin honey. "I wish," said the subprætor to the patriarch, "you would give me a taste of your honey." "With all my heart," replied John; and accordingly, when the subprætor was at dinner, a pot of the honey was brought in. What, however, was his astonishment, on opening the jar, to find it was full of gold.—Metaphrastês, *Lives*, etc. (John, patriarch of Alexandria).

Metaphrastês, who tells the story, says the "honey was miraculously converted into gold," but Leontius insinuates that the jars were really full of gold, labelled "VIRGIN HONEY," to prevent theft. This suggestion labours under a very serious difficulty, the difference of weight between honey and gold. No one could lift a firkin filled with gold and believe it to be honey. The false label would only attract attention to the deceit, and could not possibly delude any one. However, every one will call to mind the stratagem of Hannibal, who hid his gold in the hollow statues which he carried about with him as domestic gods. This he did because he knew the Carthaginians were great thieves, and by leaving these gods exposed no suspicion arose that they were full of gold. This tale is told by Cornelius Nepos; and the same objection might be urged against its probability as that urged above against the jars of honey.

St. Benet the Moor finds several water-tanks filled with fish (A.D. 1589). St. Benet the Moor was cuisier in the convent of St. Mary, near Palermo. One day, being snowed up, he was unable to buy food. Assisted by his brother cooks, he filled several large vessels or tanks with water, and passed the night in prayer. In the morning, on going into the kitchen, all the vessels were found full of live fish, and so abundant was the supply there was enough for the whole house till the snow cleared away.

Another instance. One Christmas Day, St. Benet the Moor was so absorbed in prayer, that he forgot to make preparation for dinner, and the archbishop of Palermo was going to be a guest. At the time appointed the table was laid, and well furnished with food. "Miracles of this sort were often repeated in favour of St. Benet."—*Acts of his Beatification.*

These acts of St. Benet the Moor differ from the "Multiplication of Food," (see p. 145), as the food in these cases is produced *ex nihilo.*

Waters divided or heaped up.

PSALM lxxvii. 16. The waters saw Thee, O God, the waters saw Thee, and were afraid.

EXOD. xiv. 22. When Moses came to the Red Sea, the Lord caused the waters to divide. And the children of Israel went into the midst of the sea upon dry ground; and the waters were a wall unto them on their right hand, and on their left.

JOSH. iii. 16. When Joshua crossed the river Jordan, which overflowed its banks all the time of harvest, the waters which came down from above stood and rose up in a heap; and those that ran into the sea failed, and were cut off, so that all the people passed over on dry ground.

2 KINGS ii. 8. Elijah took his mantle, and, wrapping it together, smote the waters, and they divided hither and thither. So Elijah and Elisha went over on dry ground.

2 KINGS ii. 14. Elisha did the same when he returned.

The Adige refuses to enter the church

where the body of St. Zeno was buried. St. Gregory the Great and several other "historians" relate the following tale as an historic fact. One day, when the clergy and people of Verona were assembled to celebrate the fête of St. Zeno, the river Adige overflowed its banks, and the waters rolled in a flood to the church itself; but "though the doors of the church were wide open, the waters were afraid to enter" (!!). They rolled up to the open doors, piled themselves to the windows, menaced the assembly with death, not by flood, but starvation; for as they formed a high wall round the church, no one could get out. Wonder followed wonder. This water-wall supplied needful drink for those shut up in the church; so that, adds St. Gregory, "it served as drink, but made no attempt to enter the sacred edifice" (!!). It arrested itself at the doors and windows, to demonstrate to all ages the merits of the saint there buried (!!). "It was a succour to the faithful, but reverenced the church, and did it no harm." St. Gregory then goes on to compare this flood of water to the fire mentioned by Daniel, which refused to injure Shadrach, Meshach, and Abednego.—St. Gregory, *Dialogues*, bk. iii. ch. 19. (See next column.)

Even Alban Butler is not afraid of repeating this story as a fact, and adds, "This prodigy had as many witnesses as there were inhabitants in Verona."

The Jordan divides to give a passage to St. Angelus (A.D. 1225). When Angelus was only twenty-six years old he was sent to Jerusalem to be ordained priest. He found the Jordan had so overflowed its banks that it was quite unfordable, but the duty of St. Angelus was to obey. To this end, he prayed to God that the river might not be allowed to prevent his keeping his vow, and commanded the waters, in the name of the Father, the Son, and the Holy Ghost, by the merits of Elijah and Elisha, and in consideration of his vow, to give him a passage. The river at once obeyed, by stopping the down current, and allowing the rest to flow on towards the sea. By this means a gap was made in the river, through which the saint and those with him crossed over to the other side, and continued their journey without further interruption to the city of Jerusalem, to which they were bound.—Baronius, *Ecclesiastical Annals.*

The river Sarthe divides to give a passage to St. Serenicus (seventh century). St. Serenicus wished to cross the river Sarthe, but had no boat. However, he had recourse to prayer; and then making the sign of the cross on the surface of the river, the waters divided, leaving a dry passage. The lad Flavart, who was following his master, stupefied with astonishment, let fall into the river the book he was carrying, but so bewildered was he that he was not conscious of the accident for some time. When he discovered it, he threw himself at the feet of the saint, imploring his forgiveness. Serenicus raised him from the ground, and, speaking kindly, said to him, "Be assured, Flavart, we shall find the book again sooner or later." And so it was, for six years afterwards the book was taken from the river wholly uninjured. Two hundred years later, this manuscript volume, preserved in the basilica built by St. Serenicus, was examined by the author of his life, who assures us he could see no indication at all that the book had ever been even wetted.—*Acta Sanctorum* (Bollandists), vol. ii. May 7.

The waters of the Seine afraid to enter the monastery where St. Geneviève's bed stood (A.D. 422–512). One day the Seine overflowed its banks, and so deep was the inundation that the houses and churches were filled with water some ten feet deep. When the flood came to the monastery where St. Geneviève died, and where her bed was carefully preserved, "it was afraid;" and, instead of inundating the place, stood on heaps, so as to form a wall of defence round the house; and the monastery not only was not flooded, it was not even moistened. When the waters had seen the bed on which the saint died, they reverently retired, and returned to their channel again.—Mgr. Paul Guérin (chamberlain of pope Leo XIII.), *Vies des Saints*, vol. i. p. 100 (7th edit. 1880).

This tale is very like that told by Gregory the Great of St. Zeno, who lived in the third century (see preceding column).

St. Adelelm and a whole army pass over the Tagus, when swollen with rain (eleventh century). Alfonso VI. of Castile and Leon told his wife Constance to write to St. Adelelm, and implore him to come to Spain to assist in putting down the Moors, who were Mahometans. On arriving at the Tagus, St. Adelelm found the king there with his army; and, as the river was very deep, and greatly swollen with rains, the king knew not how to transport his army across. St. Adelelm said to Alfonso, "Some put their trust in chariots, and some in horses, but we will remember the name of the Lord our God" (*Ps.* xx. 7). Then mounting his ass, he rode right into the river, and passed over, though the bed was deep and the current very strong. All the army followed, some on horses, some on foot, and all reached the opposite bank without accident of any kind. The king, ravished with admiration, fell at the feet of the holy man, kissed them, and implored him to take up his abode with them. This he consented to do, and Alfonso built for him, at Burgos, a monastery, which was dedicated to St. John.—*Les Petits Bollandistes,* vol. ii. pp. 134, 135.

(It does not, from the narrative, appear that the waters of the Tagus actually divided and left a dry passage; it seems rather to imply that the deep swollen river was miraculously rendered fordable so that an ass and men on foot could ford it.)

The river Ubaye divides to give a passage to St. Marcellinus (A.D. 374). The people of Seynes asked St. Marcellinus, bishop of Embrun, to come over and consecrate a church. The bishop left Embrun with a great crowd of followers, but when they reached the river Ubaye they found it so swollen with the late rains, that it was not possible to ford it. Marcellinus told the people not to be disheartened, for God would find them a way. Then, making the sign of the cross, he bade the waters remember how they had given a passage to Moses, Joshua, and Elijah. Instantly the down current stopped, and the river was divided, leaving a dry passage for the bishop and his followers. This miracle, says the biographer, was attested by a large number of eye-witnesses, and made a vast sensation in the province.—Mgr. Depéry, *Hagiographie de Gap.*

The waters of a lake retreat to give St. Blaise a dry passage (A.D. 289). Agricolaus, governor of Cappadocia, told St. Blaise, if he persisted in his refusal to sacrifice to the Roman gods, he should be thrown into a deep lake. St. Blaise replied, he would walk into the lake of his own free will, and show the governor how God can deliver those who trust in Him. So, making the sign of the cross, he walked into the lake, and the waters, retreating hither and thither, stood as a wall on both sides of him. St. Blaise cried with a loud voice in the midst of the lake, "Let any who are jealous of their gods come to me in the lake, and see if they can deliver after this sort." Whereupon eighty of the idolaters ventured to join St. Blaise in the lake; but the walled-up waters fell upon them, and drowned them. St. Blaise, in the mean time, had walked through the lake, and his face shone so brightly that no man could look upon him.—Metaphrastês, *Lives,* etc.

Occasionally rivers will divide from natural causes, as the Thames did in March 6, 1822. A gale of extreme violence blew that day on the river. It came from the south-west, and the entrance of the tide was thus interrupted for several hours. By the protraction of the ebb, and prevention of the tide, the water in the river at London Bridge sank so low that many persons walked across the river bed, between London Bridge and Gravesend. At twelve o'clock the tide returned suddenly and with great rapidity, but high water was delayed till 3 a.m.

*** Mgr. Guérin, in his *Lives of the Saints,* vol. ii. p. 228, makes several variations of this story. He says nothing about the piling up of the water into walls on each side of the saint, but states that Blaise "walked into the middle of the lake, and seated himself on the surface of the water." He gives the number that went into the lake at the invitation of St. Blaise as sixty-eight, not eighty; and he tells us that as soon as St. Blaise had passed over, he was seized by Agricolaus and beheaded.

St. Germana Cousin walks across a deep river, which divides to give her passage (A.D. 1579–1601). Germana Cousin of Pibrac, near Toulouse, was a shepherdess. One day, after a heavy rain, the river which she had to cross had greatly swollen, and some peasants who saw her from a distance wondered how she would manage to ford the torrent. Germana walked along the meadow, came to the torrent, took no heed of it, but walked on, apparently without even noticing the obstacle. On she went, and when her foot approached the river the waters divided, leaving her a dry passage, as the Red Sea divided for the children of Israel. Even the hem of her garment and soles of her shoes were respected. "À la vue de ce prodige, que Dieu renouvela dans la suite très souvent, les paysans s'entre-regardèrent avec crainte, et les plus hardis commencèrent à respecter celle dont ils avaient voulu se railler."—M. L. Veuillot, *Vie de la Bienheureuse Germaine.*

An inundation divides to give a passage to St. Thoretta and her flock (twelfth century). One day the stream at the foot of Nouzillers, swollen by rain, formed a barrier to St. Thoretta, who was keeping a flock of sheep in the opposite meadow, so that she could not fold her sheep or reach her cottage-home. Thoretta called to mind how Christ had said faith can remove mountains; and if mountains, why not floods? She made the sign of the cross on the overflow with her crook, and immediately the waters divided right and left, leaving a dry path for the shepherdess and her sheep to pass over.—L'abbé Boudant, *Légende de Ste. Thorette.*

"*Une autre fois*, c'étaient des étrangers, des ouvriers maçons se rendant du Bourbonnais dans la Marche, leur pays, qui se trouvaient arrêtés par la même difficulté. Dans leur impatience, ces hommes grossiers se laissaient aller au murmure, au blasphème. La jeune vierge les invite doucement à la résignation, les engage à faire la sainte volonté de Dieu, puis, dans la charité qui la presse, elle demande hardiment un miracle. Au tact de sa houlette, nouveau Jourdain, le ruisseau retourne en arrière, et laisse passer à pied sec ces hommes qui publient hautement les louanges et le pouvoir de la thaumaturge."—*Ibid.*

The water of a well rises at the bidding of St. John of St. Facond (A.D. 1430–1479). When St. John of St. Facond was at Salamanca, a child fell into a well. The saint laid his girdle on the coping of the well, and bade the waters restore the child. Whereupon they rose to the coping, buoying up the child, who was then taken safe and sound to his parents, in the presence of a host of persons who had come to the place when they heard of the accident.—*Acta Sanctorum* (Bollandists), vol. ii. June 12, p. 616.

St. Ursus, archdeacon of Aosta, commands the river Buthier to abate (sixth century). St. Ursus was a native of Ireland, and, like St. Patrick, prayed a hundred times every day and a hundred times every night. He quitted Ireland, and became archdeacon of Aosta. One day the river Buthier, which rises in the Apennines and passes Aosta, had so swollen, that not only it overflowed its banks, but it flooded all the houses in the vicinity, and even the church of St. Peter's, where the saint was wont to officiate. Many of the distressed had taken refuge in the church, and were held there prisoners by the deep water. St. Ursus, seeing the great danger, prayed that God, who had restrained the waters of the flood, and commanded the Red Sea to retire before Moses, would vouchsafe to deliver them in this their danger. While he still prayed, the clouds broke, the rain ceased, the sun burst out, the waters retired to their proper channel, and the banks were once more dry land. This event was commemorated for eleven hundred years every day at matins in the church of St. Ursus, but in 1608 a change took place, and this special "miracle" no longer formed part of the daily service.—*Life of St. Ursus, archdeacon of Aosta* (1868).

Wise Men of the East.

MATT. ii. 1–12. St. Matthew tells us, that when Jesus was born, a star appeared in the east, which induced certain of the Magi to start from their country and follow it. The star led them to Judæa; and, going at once to the king, they asked him where the royal infant was to be found. Herod did not know, but said he would make inquiries. As the wise men left the presence chamber they saw the star again, and were guided by it to a shed in Bethlehem, where Mary had taken up her temporary abode. The wise men entered the shed, saw the new-born babe, and made their offerings of gold, frankincense, and myrrh. This done, they returned home to their own country.

The Cologne tradition. In Cologne cathedral visitors are shown three heads, which they are assured are the heads of the three wise men. The names given to them are Gaspar, Melchior, and Balthazar, and they are generally called "The three kings of Cologne." The meanings attached to these three names are as follows: Gaspar, "The White One;" Melchior, "The King of Light;" and Balthazar, "The Lord of Treasures." The offerings, we are told, were symbolical: gold signified the kingly office of the Child; frankincense, His Godhead; and myrrh, that He would die.

Other names are given to the three men: as (1) Apellius, Amerus, and Damascus; (2) Magalath, Galgalath, and Sarasin: (3) Alor, Sator, and Peratŏras. Others say they were Shem, Ham, and Japheth, who had fallen asleep, and woke at the Nativity.*

Numbers differ. Klopstock, in *The Messiah*, says there were six wise men, whom he calls Hadad, Selima, Zimri, Mirja, Beled, and Sunith.

James, bishop of Edessa, says there were twelve wise men, all royal princes. He adds furthermore, that they left seven thousand soldiers at the Euphratês, and came to Judæa attended with only a thousand followers. Pope Leo spoke of them as *three*, and that is the orthodox number.

A Danish king receives three offerings from the three kings of Cologne. A Danish king, who had great reverence for the three kings of Cologne, used to invoke them in every trouble. One day he started for Cologne on a pilgrimage, intent on offering to the "kings" three golden crowns. He made his offering, and left besides six thousand marks for the poor. On his journey home, he saw the three kings; they were wearing their

* St. John Chrysostom tells us that St. Thomas baptized the three kings or wise men which came to Bethlehem to adore the infant Jesus, after which he went to India to preach the gospel.

crowns, and the oldest of them presented him a coffer filled with gold, saying, "Take this; it is the symbol of wisdom; and judge thy people with equity." The second gave him a coffer filled with myrrh, saying, "Take this; it is the symbol of prudence; and learn to master thyself." The third gave him a coffer filled with frankincense, saying, "Take this; it is the symbol of divine clemency; and learn to relieve the wretched." The king found the three coffers at his bedside when the vision had passed away, and when he reached his kingdom, he judged his people with equity, kept a mastery over himself, and relieved the poor and wretched in their afflictions.—*Gesta Romanorum.*

Witches and Familiar Spirits.

EXOD. xxii. 18. Thou shalt not suffer a witch to live.

LEV. xx. 27. A man or a woman that hath a familiar spirit, or that is a wizard, shall surely be put to death. They shall stone them with stones. Their blood shall be upon them.

1 SAM. xxviii. 3, 9. After the death of Samuel, Saul put away those that had familiar spirits, and the wizards, out of the land [*i.e.* he put them to death].

GAL. v. 19–21. St. Paul says witchcraft, like idolatry and heresy, adultery and drunkenness, is a work of the flesh, and no one who practises it shall inherit the kingdom of God.

Bible witches and familiar spirits. When the Philistines encamped against Saul in Shunen, he inquired of the Lord and His prophets what he should do; but receiving no answer, either by dreams, by Urim, or by prophets, he inquired of the witch who lived at Endor. She was very reluctant at first to answer him, because he had commanded all witches and wizards to be put to death; but when Saul swore not to punish her in any wise, she brought up Samuel from the grave to answer the king. The man thus called from the grave said to Saul, "Why hast thou disquieted me, to bring me up from the grave?" And the king replied, "I am sore distressed; for the Philistines make war against me; and I have called thee, that thou mayest make known to me what I ought to do." Samuel replied, "The Lord hath rent the kingdom out of thy hand, and given it to David. Thee He will deliver into the hand of the Philistines; to-morrow both thou and thy sons shall be with me" [among the dead].—1 *Sam.* xxviii. 7–19.

The whole of this narrative is very marvellous, the last remark not the least so: "To-morrow thou and thy sons shall be with me." It is generally supposed that Samuel, at death, went direct to paradise; but it can hardly be supposed that he meant, "To-morrow Saul and his sons would be with him in paradise." If not, how would they be with him? Comparing these words with those of our Lord to the penitent thief, involves the subject in great obscurity.

The account of the witch of Endor given in the *Book of Chronicles* (1 *Chron.* x. 13, 14) is not in accordance with that given in the *Book of Samuel.* The latter says, Saul inquired first of the Lord, but the Lord would not answer him, either by dreams, by Urim, or by prophets. And when Samuel asked why he had been called from the grave, Saul distinctly told him he had applied to the Lord, and had not been vouchsafed an answer. In *Chronicles*, the historian says that Saul was punished by death for "asking counsel of a witch, ***instead*** of inquiring of the Lord." (See p. 345, note.)

Manasseh dealt with witches and wizards. Manasseh, the son of Hezekiah, "did that which is evil in the sight of the Lord; for he used enchantments, and used witchcraft, and dealt with a familiar spirit, and with wizards."—2 *Chron.* xxxiii. 2, 6; 2 *Kings* xxi. 6.

Witches and familiar spirits in the New Testament. Elymas, the sorcerer, opposed Paul, and was struck blind for so doing.—*Acts* xiii. 8–11.

Simon Magus "used sorcery, and bewitched the people of Samaria."—*Acts* viii. 9.

Witches and sorcerers in heathen nations. The Thessalians were very famous for their sorceries. It is said they could draw down the moon to earth by their enchantments. The Egyptians, the Babylonians, the Chaldeans, the Hindûs, the Greeks, the Romans, the Teutons, etc., all believed in witches and familiar spirits. Indeed, so common was the belief, it would be very hard to find a nation that did not believe in them.

English laws against witches and wizards. The Scotch and English were for centuries, like other Christian nations, firm believers in witches and wizards. The Saxons of England, before the Conquest, punished them, sometimes by exile, but more often by burning them to death.—*Leges Alveredi*, folio 23; 2 *Ethelstani*, c. 7; *Canuti*, 4, 5.

Britton, in his *Compendium of English Laws* (before 1275), says, "Sorciers, sorciesses, etc., et miscreants, soient arses."

MARGERY GURDEMAN of Eye (Suffolk) was burnt to death for witchcraft, in October, anno 20 Henry VI.

JOAN OF ARC, usually called "The Maid of Orleans," was burnt to death for witchcraft, at Rouen, in 1431.

MOTHER SHIPTON, in the reign of Henry VIII., has immortalized her name by her witchcraft. Persons of all ranks and conditions consulted her. Her prediction of the downfall of cardinal Wolsey is one of the most notorious in traditional history.

Bishop JEWELL believed in witches; and in his sermon preached before queen Elizabeth, in 1584, says, "It may please your grace to understand, that witches and sorcerers, within these last four years, are marvellously increased within your grace's realm. Your grace's subjects pine away even unto death. Their colour fadeth, their flesh rotteth, their speech is benumbed, their senses are bereft."

In the Lambeth library is the "Examination and Confession of certain wytches at Chelmsford, Essex, before the Queen's Majesty's Judges, the 26th day of July, 1566, at the assizes holden there; and an account of one of them, put to death for the same offence, as their examination declareth more at large. Mother Fraunces learnt her art of her grandmother Eve, at Hatfield Peveril; and trained a whyte spotted cat with her own blood to be her sathan. And mother Waterhouse was hanged on her own confession of execrable sorcery, by her practised for fifteen years." *

JAMES I. was a great believer in witches, and hunted them to death with relentless vigour. This we are prepared to believe, for a more narrow-minded, conceited bigot never filled a throne. He was far too wise in his own opinion to be a wise man. Oh for the right divine to govern wrong!

GLANVILLE, the celebrated ecclesiastical writer in the reign of Charles II., and one of the leading members of the formation of the Royal Society, published a work entitled *Considerations on the Being of Witches and Witchcraft.* In this book he gravely examines the subject "theologically, historically, and philosophically;" and, with great array of argument, labours to remove all objections against the existence of witches, sorcerers, and familiar spirits.

The learned bishop Hall mentions a place where "there were more witches than houses;" and even the enlightened judge, sir Matthew Hale, in 1644, condemned Amy Dunny and Rose Callender, at Bury St. Edmund's, for bewitching children.

MONTESQUIEU was a believer in witchcraft, and in his *Spirit of Laws* devotes a whole chapter to this special "crime."

ADDISON and BLACKSTONE both thought that there was such a thing as witchcraft of old, although they admit there is no proof of any recent example.

Dr. John Fian, schoolmaster of Saltpans, near Edinburgh, mangled to death on the charge of witchcraft. The charge against Dr. Fian was that of raising a storm at sea to wreck that awkward pedant, James, when on his voyage to Denmark to visit his future queen. He was furthermore charged with having rifled the graves of the dead, to make hell-broth; and of running after a cat, because the devil wanted it to cast into the sea for the purpose of raising storms. These outrageous charges were made in Scotland against an intellectual schoolmaster, in the seventeenth century, in the Reformed Church; and nothing in the Inquisition was more absurd and diabolical than this proceeding. Well, Dr. Fian was arraigned by that mischievous bigot, our high and mighty James I., and as he would not confess, was put to the torture. First, a rope was tied slackly round his head, and between the head and the rope a strong stick, about two feet long, was inserted. Then the torture began. The stick was twisted round and round, shortening the cord, till the skull was crushed in upon the brain; and at every turn the victim was asked if he would confess. When the rope had cut through the scalp to the bone, and the whole skull was squeezed out of shape, for fear of death the rope was slackened, and the doctor was wheedled and coaxed to confess; but he resolutely refused to tell a lie, even to pander to the vanity of king James. Weak, pale, and in dreadful agony, the victim was now attacked on his other extremities, the feet. Each foot and leg was placed in a strong iron box reaching to the knees, and between the leg and the box wedges were loosely inserted. "Will you confess?" said the inquisitor. No answer; and the wedges were driven home by a huge mallet. A piercing shriek rang through the torture-chamber; but there was none to pity the unhappy victim. Down fell the sledge-hammer on another wedge, crushing the legs in the most fearful manner. But still the doctor would not confess that he had bewitched the sea to wreck king James. Down again and again fell the hammer upon the wedges, till skin and flesh, muscle and tendon, bone and marrow, were one mass of soft and bloody jelly. Nothing more could be done, so he was now released, and laid on his back, his

* We open our eyes with amazement in reading this, and ask, Could these be English judges in the reign of Elizabeth? We almost fancy it must be fable.

head swollen and lacerated, and both his legs crushed to a pulp. Raving mad, he was left till next day. Would he confess? No, not even yet would he lie; so they wrenched the nails off his fingers with pincers, and stuck pins through the parts which the nails had covered. Still no confession. They put his thumbs into thumbscrews till the bones were crushed into splinters. Still no confession. So they strangled him, and burnt him at the stake on the Castle Hill of Edinburgh, on Saturday, Jan. 26, 1591.

It behoves one to be modest when such brutality as this was tolerated in Protestant Britain, in the reign of a Stuart not three hundred years ago. Four times my present age would land us exactly on the year of this transaction.

The three witches of Belvoir (seventeenth century). March 11, 1618, two women, named Margaret and Philippa Flower, were burnt at Lincoln on the absurd charge of witchcraft; and three other women, named Anne Baker of Bottesford, Joan Willimot of Goodby, and Ellen Greene of Stathorne (all in the county of Leicester), were condemned to death by Sir Henry Hobbert, Chief Justice of the Common Pleas, as accomplices. This was in the reign of that wretched bigot James I., the greatest blot in the royal scutcheon of England. The Flowers were discharged servants of the earl and countess of Rutland, at Belvoir Castle, who out of revenge annoyed the family. The mother of the two Flowers professed to have a familiar spirit in the form of a cat, called *Rutterkin*, and the witchcraft of the three consisted in burning some of the hair of the earl and countess, and in plunging a glove of their son, lord Ross, into boiling water, after having rubbed it on the cat's back. Lord Ross died about this time, and his death was ascribed to witchcraft. When the three Flowers were taken up on the charge, the mother put a piece of bread in her mouth, saying, "May this choke me if I am guilty of this death." The bread, however, did choke her, and she died. Her daughter Margaret acknowledged she had stolen lord Ross's glove and had rubbed it on the cat's back, before plunging it into scalding hot water; and her sister Philippa confessed that she had a familar spirit, which sometimes sucked her flesh; so they were both condemned to be burnt alive.

In regard to the other three women, called the accomplices of the Flowers, Joan Willimot had an owl, which she called *Pretty*; Ellen Greene a kitten and a tame rat; and Anne Baker confessed she had once heard a voice in the air, and it was proved by credible witnesses that she had a white dog. So sir Henry Hobbert felt no doubt of their guilt. What can old women have owls, cats, and dogs for, but to work mischief? So he gravely put on his black cap, and condemned the three to death.—Nichol, *Leicestershire.*

Ruth Osborne and her husband, above seventy years old, murdered at Tring, in Hertfordshire, for witchcraft (Aug. 1751). Let us come down to the Georges, Aug. 22, 1751. Ruth Osborne asked a man named Butterfield for a sup of milk, which he denied her; so the poor creature went away, muttering that she wished the Pretender's army would loot the old hunks's cattle. The man fell ill, and his cattle "vix ossibus hærent." No doubt Ruth Osborne's was the "eye which scorched them up like a burning-glass," so a white witch was fetched from Northamptonshire to Tring, in Hertfordshire, to remove the spell. The wise woman employed six farm labourers with pitchforks to guard the farmer's house both day and night from evil spirits; but Butterfield got no better, nor did his lean kine grow fatter. So the town-crier was sent round the neighbouring villages to proclaim that Ruth Osborne and her husband (both over seventy years of age) were to be ducked in a pond on the following Monday for witchcraft. The overseers, in the mean time, lodged the poor old couple in Tring workhouse, and on the Saturday preceding the fatal Monday took them, for greater security, to the vestry of the parish church. On the Monday announced by the crier, a mob of above five thousand persons proceeded to the workhouse, demanding that the two Osbornes should be delivered up to them; and when the master of the workhouse assured them they were not on the premises, the rioters broke into the house, and searched every drawer, box, and cranny, even pepper-boxes, pots, and pans, to find the fugitives. Disappointed in their search, they demolished the building, and, making a bonfire of the lumber, they threatened to burn the master unless he told them where the Osbornes were concealed. The man, terribly frightened, revealed the place of concealment, and the mob, yelling and hooting, rushed to the church, seized the victims, and carried them to a neighbouring pond. The scene there enacted is too horrible and too indecent to be described; suffice it to say, the woman died, and the man, tied to the dead body of his aged wife, expired soon afterwards. Twelve of the gentry were appointed on the jury, and they brought in a verdict of wilful murder against Thomas Colley and twenty-one others of the ringleaders, names unknown. Colley was hung in chains, and thus ended this disgraceful outrage.—*The Universal Magazine*, 1751.

Bulls, edicts, provisions, etc., against witches and witchcraft. Pope INNOCENT VIII., in his celebrated bull *Summis Desiderantes*, 1484, charges all inquisitors and others to search out, and put to death, those who practised diabolical arts, such as witchcraft, magic, sorcery, and enchantment. Two special inquisitors (Heinrich Institor and Jacob Sprenger) were appointed for the purpose in Germany, and, with the aid of John Gremper, an ecclesiastic, drew up the infamous document called *The Witches' Hammer* ("Malleus Maleficarum"), in which the whole subject is systematized, a regular form of trial laid down, and a set of questions digested for the discovery of guilt in those suspected of the diabolical art.

ALEXANDER VI., in 1494; Leo X., in 1521; and Adrian VI., in 1522, supplemented the bull of Innocent VIII.,* adding to its severity, and feeding the witch-mania that for four centuries had raged in Christendom. The results of this scandalous persecution were dreadful. A panic-fear of witchcraft set in. If any one felt unwell; if any one suffered from cramp, lumbago, or rheumatism; if misfortune or loss befell any one; if a storm at sea occurred, or lightning injured man, cattle, or tree, or a high wind blew down some chimney or stack; if some foot-and-mouth disease broke out among the cattle, some rinderpest, some pleuro-pneumonia ill understood, it was sure to be attributed to the evil eye of witchcraft ("Nescio quis teneros oculus mihi fascinat agnos"); and to be accused was to be convicted of the charge, for *The Witches' Hammer* was sure to supply evidence sufficient for condemnation. If the accused pleaded "Not guilty," torture was applied, and the miserable wretch pleaded anything to escape the rack.

* Theoretically, popes speaking *ex cathedrâ* are infallible, but if any proof of their fallibility were needed, we need seek no further. I apprehend every [Roman] Catholic would wish that these bulls had never seen daylight. Protestants, no doubt, have been as great sinners, but then they never pretended to infallibility. Fallible laws may be repealed, but who shall reverse an infallible bull?

In GERMANY, the prosecutions were indeed frightful. In the small bishopric of Bamberg six hundred were burnt to death for witchcraft in four years; in Würzberg, nine hundred; in Lindhem, one in twenty of the entire population, in the same space of time.

In GENEVA, 1515, within three months, five hundred persons were burnt at the stake under the character of "Protestant witches."

In LORRAINE, the learned inquisitor Remigius boasts that he put to death nine hundred persons for witchcraft in fifteen years; and as many were banished.

In COMO, 1524, as many as a thousand persons were burnt to death for witchcraft in a single year; and at least a hundred per annum for many subsequent years.

In FRANCE, 1520, fires blazed in every town for the extermination of witches; and for a century the provincial "parlements" were ceaselessly employed in witch-trials.

In ENGLAND, during the Long Parliament, three thousand persons are said to have perished on the accusation of witchcraft; and witch-executions continued long afterwards. The last cases were those of Mrs. Hicks, in 1716, and her daughter, a child nine years of age (!!), who were hung at Huntingdon, for "selling their souls to the devil; and raising a storm, by pulling off their stockings and making a lather of soap" (!!).*

When JAMES brought home his bride from Denmark, in 1590, thirty persons were put to death for trying to raise the sea into a storm to drown him, "as he was the devil's worst enemy;" and the Scotch Assembly, between 1640 and 1649, passed five acts against witches, each more rigid than the preceding one. As many as seventeen persons in Stirling were burnt to death for witchcraft in 1659 and the last execution in Scotland on this charge was at Dornoch, in 1722. The entire number of victims in Scotland for this "religious crime" certainly exceeded four thousand.

The last execution for sorcery in Würzberg was in 1749; in Switzerland in 1782; in Posen in 1793.

The laws against witchcraft were repealed in England in 1736; in Austria not till 1766.

The entire number of persons put to

* Elspeth Rule was condemned for witchcraft by lord Anstruther, May 3, 1709. (See RUTH OSBORNE, p. 343.)

death for witchcraft in Christendom, according to Dr. Sprenger, is not less than nine millions (! !).

The name of MATTHEW HOPKINS of Manningtree, Essex, is infamously notorious, as the "Witch-finder" in the counties of Essex, Suffolk, and Norfolk. Dr. Z. Grey says that between three and four thousand persons suffered death through this villain between 1643 and 1661.

The following names stand out in honourable relief for resisting the prevailing credulity in witchcraft, and condemning its persecution:—

WIERIUS or WIER of Grars, in Brabant (1515–1588). He wrote *De Præstigiis Dæmonum*, and *Pseudo-monarchia Dæmonum*.

REGINALD SCOT (died in Kent, 1599) wrote *The Discoverie of Witchcraft* in 1584. This noble work, full of learning, humane feeling, and manly Christianity, was disgracefully burnt by the common hangman. James I., that contemptible prig, wrote his *Dæmonology* "chiefly against Wierus and Scot, the latter of whom," says our British Solomon, "is not ashamed to deny there can be such a thing as witchcraft."

HARSNET, 1599; THOMASIUS, 1700; HUTCHINSON, 1720.

The following Acts of Parliament disgrace our statutes:—33 Henry VIII. c. 8 (1541), which declares witchcraft exercised against the life of any one to be felony. But 5 Eliz. c. 16 (1563) and 1 James I. c. 12 (1604) go further, and declare it to be felony without benefit of clergy. Punishment of death for witchcraft was abolished by 9 George II. c. 5 (1736).

The Act of Parliament in the first year of James I. runs thus: "If any person shall use any invocation or conjuration of any evil or wicked spirit, or shall entertain, employ, feed, or reward any evil or cursed spirit, or shall take up any dead body to employ in witchcraft, sorcery, or enchantment, or shall practise any sort of witchcraft, sorcery, etc., whereby any person shall be killed, wasted, consumed, pined, or lamed . . ." [the penalty was death]. This statute was mere toadyism, like the preface which is still allowed to disgrace our English Bibles.

⁂ The belief in witchcraft is not yet wholly rooted out. Even in 1863 a man was drowned at Hedingham, in Essex, for being a wizard, his accusers and persecutors being village tradesmen.

Witch of Endor. There is not a tittle of proof that the writers of the Bible believed in witchcraft. Let us examine the point. First the laws made by Moses against witches and sorcerers, and then the famous case known as the witch of Endor. Suppose the British Parliament were to pass a law that any one who practises "table-turning" shall be put in prison—that would not imply that persons exist who can do that feat without mechanical force; but only that the law will not suffer knaves to practise on the credulity of fools, nor to rob them of their money under false pretences. So when Moses forbade the practice of witchcraft and sorcery, it does not imply that he believed in the possibility of such arts; but simply that the people under his charge were not to practise heathen arts, and arrogate to themselves superhuman powers. This prohibition was the more necessary, because the Egyptians among whom they had been brought up, and the Philistines among whom they were about to dwell, both practised magic. Moses virtually said, "The Egyptians and Philistines believe in magic, but it shall not be so with God's people, and if any of you pretend to magic or sorcery, he shall be dealt with as a traitor to God, and be put to death." The law should rather prove that Moses did *not* believe in such a power than that he *did* believe in it; as when Perkin Warbeck was condemned for passing himself off as Richard, duke of York, his trial and execution proved that his claim was *not* believed, not that he was supposed really to be the son of Edward V.'s brother.

The strong case is the "witch of Endor" (1 *Sam.* xxviii.). From ver. 12 it is certain that the woman did not know her visitor was Saul the king. From ver. 13 it is equally certain that the woman was terrified to see "gods ascending out of the earth;" and from ver. 14 it is certain that she did not know the form which appeared was that of Samuel, although she had been asked to call up Samuel. The whole incident, therefore, was to the woman alarming and unexpected; and the plain inference is that the woman knew she was a pretender, and did not for a moment suppose that her incantations had any efficacy. Why God permitted Samuel to appear to the king is quite another question. (See JOSHUA AND THE SUN AND MOON, p. 297; SAMSON AND THE JAWBONE, p. 281.)

A witch exorcised by whipping a cat (A.D. 1600). Harsnet says, "What man, judging according to wit, can imagine that a witch can transforme herselfe into a cat, mouse, or hare; and that shee, being hunted with hounds, or pinched by the breech, or whipped with scourges, in those forms, the same marks that were made by hounds, scourge, and so on, will be found on the witch in human forme; yet shal you see this sencelesse conceite verified in the practice of our conjuring priests. For example, in Fid Williams deposition before her Majesties Commissioners for Causes Ecclesiasticall you wil finde that twelve priests had a solemne assembly at the whipping of a cat, and they did whip the cat in a parlor at Denham, til shee vanished out of theyr sight. Sending next day to Bushie, to see in what plight the witch was, whose spirit they had cat-hunted over night, the witch was found in childbed, and the childe was newly dead. Whereby it plainly appeares, that the whipping of the cat is no jest, when it is done by catholique priests; and the hunting of a witch is no fabulous apprehension, but a good catholique sooth, agreable to the gravitie and wisedome of that venerable church."—*A Declaration of Popish Impostures* (1604), pp. 111, 112.

World all seen at once.

• MATT. iv. 8. The devil taketh [Jesus] up into an exceeding high mountain, and showeth Him all the kingdoms of the world.

Alphonsus Rodriquez saw in spirit the whole world (1526–1617). Alphonsus was very careful to pray daily for the conversion of the whole world. And once or twice God did so elevate him in spirit, that he saw all the men and women in the whole world. Then God assured him that, by his godly desires and daily prayers, he merited as much as if he had actually converted the whole human race.—Michael Julian, *Life of Alphonsus Rodriquez.*

Sospitra sees all the world at once. Sospitra possessed the omniscient power of seeing all that was done in every part of the whole globe.—Eunapius, *Œdeseus* (fourth century).

The mirror given to Cambuscan by the king of Araby and Ind showed him all that was being done in any part of his dominion, so that he might know whom to trust and whom to avoid.—Chaucer, *Canterbury Tales* (The Squire's Tale). Somewhat similar virtues were possessed by Dr. Dee's Speculum, Merlin's Magic Mirror, Prester John's Mirror, Vulcan's Mirror, and several other toys.

Zealous of the Law.

Acts xxi. 20, etc. When Paul, after his third missionary tour, came to Jerusalem, the Jews could not conceal their animosity against him for not insisting on circumcision. Seest thou, brother, said they, how many thousands of the Jews believe, but all of them are zealous of the law. A riot was soon organized against him, and the Jews fell on him, crying out, Help! men of Israel, help! This is the fellow that teacheth men to despise Moses and the temple. The rabble in their fury dragged Paul from the temple, and would have murdered him in the street, had not Claudius Lysias, the commanding officer of the Roman cohort, come to his rescue, and conducted him to the strong castle of Antonia. Having put him in chains, Lysias went forth into the street, and demanded of the people what offence the man had committed. Some cried one thing, and some another, so that the legatus could make nothing out. As he returned to the fort, Paul accosted him, and Lysias asked him if he could speak Greek, for he supposed him to be an Alexandrian. Paul replied, I am no foreigner at all, but a Jew of Tarsus in Cilicia; and prayed to be allowed to address the mob. Lysias gave him the required permission, and Paul, standing on the staircase of the fort, recounted to the people the whole history of his life. When he came to that injunction of the Lord, *Depart, for I will send thee to the Gentiles,* the whole rabble lifted up their voices and yelled forth, Away with him! away with such a fellow from the earth! Away with him! away with him; he is not fit to live! And so ungovernable was their fury, that they tore their clothes and threw dust into the air. Lysias, who did not understand Hebrew, the tongue in which Paul had been speaking, was unable to follow his discourse; but, seeing the mad fury of the mob, he very naturally supposed that the prisoner had said something extremely flagrant and offensive. Under this impression, he ordered Paul to be taken into the fort and scourged. The soldiers were about to bind him, when Paul said to the centurion in attendance, Is it lawful for you to scourge a Roman citizen, and that too uncondemned? The centurion instantly went to the superior officer, and advised caution; for, said he, the man is a Roman. Whereupon Lysias went immediately and asked Paul if it were true; and, being assured of the fact, feared he had gone too far in putting him in chains. [It must not be forgotten that this rabble was led by "believers," and their besetting sin was this, "they were zealous of the law."]

The Jews of Alexandria, zealous of the Unity of God, create a riot, and almost destroy the city (A.D. 249). In the middle of the third century, some Jews of Alexandria, zealous of the law, inflamed the people against the Christians. St. Francis of Sales calls them "magicians," but this simply means enemies of the Christians; and he tells us they were stirred up by the "powers of darkness" to provoke the people to riot, because the Christians worshipped the Trinity instead of the Unity, as Moses had commanded. The words of these Jews fell like sparks of fire on the mob; and the rioters rushed infuriated against the Christians, destroying their houses, pillaging their goods, and massacring all they encountered. The carnage was dreadful, the waste of property frightful. It seemed as if an invading army of barbarians had been let loose upon the city. Hundreds fled and hid themselves in the woods, abandoning all they possessed to the mad rioters. St. Apollonia refused to flee. This saintly virgin had no fear of losing her goods, for all her treasures were in heaven; she had no fear of death before her eyes, well knowing that to die would be her gain. What if she fell a martyr? To her would be granted "that she should be arrayed in fine linen, clean and white, which is the righteousness of saints." What if she changed her corruptible and mortal? Would it not be for incorruption and immortality? Her death would be the swallowing up of death in victory. The mob seized her like famished tigers; they glutted on her all their vengeance; broke her jaws; knocked out all her teeth; and then dragging her out of the city, lighted a bonfire of the *débris* and threw her into the midst. Her body, as a holocaust, was soon consumed by the fierce flames, and her spirit was carried by angels to the paradise of God.—St. Francis of Sales, *Treatise on Divine Love,* bk. x. ch. 8.

PART II.

REALISTIC MIRACLES,

OR,

MIRACLES FOUNDED ON THE LITERAL INTERPRETATION OF SCRIPTURE.

PART II.

Adulterers.

HEB. xiii. Adulterers God will judge.

The wife of St. Gangulfus punished for adultery (A.D. 760). The wife of St. Gangulfus was the daughter of a rich and noble family, but her conduct was so scandalous that her husband knew not how he ought to act. One day, walking together, they came to a rivulet of clear water, and Gangulfus said to his wife, "For a long time rumours have come to my ears derogatory to your honour, but I have hitherto said nothing; I would now remind you that a woman's honour is her most precious jewel, and she should guard it as the apple of her eye." The wife answered shamelessly, "Nothing can be more unjust than such a scandal. My honour I hold sacred, and ever will do so. It is a sad thing that virtuous women should be subjected to such calumnies." "Well," said the saint, "if so it is, plunge your arm in this water, and if you receive no harm I will firmly believe you innocent." "Right willingly," she replied, and plunged her arm up to the elbow in the stream; but, as she drew it out, the skin peeled off from her elbow to her finger tips. St. Gangulfus now separated from his wife, and she sent her paramour to murder him; but she herself died soon afterwards "par une incommodité honteuse."—*Les Petits Bollandistes*, vol. v. pp. 458, 459.

It will be remembered that the Jews had a beverage called "The Water of Jealousy," which they affirmed no adulteress could drink of without bursting.—*Five Philosophical Questions answered* (1653).

The legends about prince Arthur ascribe to him the possession of a drinking-horn, which no one unchaste or disloyal could drink out of.—*Lai du Corn*, and *History of Prince Arthur*, ii. 34.

Similar tests in ancient story were the Mantle of Matrimony, Alasnam's Mirror, Florimel's Girdle, the Grotto of Ephesus.

(The cuckolds' drinking-horn, the *coupe enchantée* of Lafontaine, Ariosto's enchanted cup, and Arthur's drinking-horn sent him by Morgan la Faye, are varieties of the same story.)

Afar off.

GEN. xxii. 4. Then, on the third day, Abraham lifted up his eyes, and saw the place afar off.

St. Antony the Great sees a man dying afar off (fourth century). Two monks, coming to visit St. Antony in the desert, were greatly distressed for want of water. One of them died; and the other lay himself down, expecting every hour to be his last. As Antony sat on the mountain, he called two of his monks, and said to them, "Go, take a pitcher of water, and run with all speed towards Egypt, for I see two men afar off who were coming hither. One has fallen on the way, and the other will die also, unless water be given him, and that quickly." So the two monks filled a pitcher, and hastened towards Egypt, and found the two men. One was lying dead, and the other was gasping in the throes of death. To him they gave water, and he revived. So, after burying the dead body, they went all three together to St. Antony. Though the distance was a day's journey, the Lord had opened the eyes of His servant to see things so far off.—St. Athanasius, *Life of St. Antony the Great.*

St. Benedict sees a man drowning afar off (sixth century). Placidus, being sent to fetch water from a river, accidentally slipped in, and was carried down the current, which was very strong. St. Benedict, sitting in his cell, saw the accident "afar off," and sent Maurus with all speed to render help. The accident must have been wholly invisible, at such a distance, to human sight; the Lord "miraculously" showed it to His servant Benedict; and Placidus, being plucked from the water, returned with Maurus to the abbey.—Surius, *Lives of the Saints.*

Almighty.

PSALM lxxxix. 6. Who among the sons of the mighty can be likened unto the Lord?

St. Cyprian is resolved to serve the mightiest only. St. Cyprian, before his conversion, was a magician, and by his art conjured up the devil. He promised to serve his sable majesty for ever, if he would procure for him the love of Justina. The devil used his utmost to do so, but without success, and told Cyprian he had no power over Christians, so long as they abided in Christ, and Christ in them. When Cyprian heard the devil make this humiliating confession, he thought to himself what an impotent power he must be to be foiled by a mere girl; so he resolved to quit the service of Satan for a stronger arm. Consulting a bishop on the subject, he was directed to Jesus, the almighty; and, being baptized, became a consistent saint and died a martyr.—St. Gregory Nazianzen (A.D. 360), *Orations*, 18. (See also Bede.)

The giant Offerus resolves to serve the most mighty. Offerus was a soldier and a heathen, who lived in the land of Canaan. He had a body twelve ells long, and loved only to command. He cared not what harm he did to others, and lived a wild life, attacking and plundering all who came in his path. He was merely a subordinate, but he resolved to serve only the mightiest master he could find. He heard that the emperor, the head of all Christendom, was by far the mightiest of the sons of men; so he offered him his services, saying to him, "Lord emperor, I am strong; will you have me in your service? for I am resolved to sell my heart's blood only to the most mighty." When the emperor looked on his huge stature and giant strength, his broad chest and mighty fists, he said to him, "Offerus, if thou wilt serve me faithfully, I will take thee into my service, and you shall serve me for ever." "Nay, nay, my lord emperor," replied the giant, "to serve you for ever is not so easily promised; but this I will engage to do—as long as I do serve you, no man from north or south, east or west, shall trouble you." So the emperor took the giant into his service, and was delighted with his bargain. Now, the emperor had a harper in his train, who sang to him. And whenever he was weary, the minstrel soothed him with sweet music. Once, at eventide, the emperor, who had pitched his tent near a forest, having eaten and drunk heartily, called for his minstrel. The minstrel came with his harp, and sang of the power of the cross; but whenever he spoke of the evil one, the emperor signed on his forehead the sign of the cross. Said Offerus aloud to his comrades, "What does this mean? What jest is this?" "Jest!" cried the emperor; "it is no jest, Offerus. What I did was to keep off the foul fiend, who goeth about like a roaring lion, seeking whom he may devour." These words seemed wondrous strange to the giant, who said sneeringly to the emperor, "I love a good lion-hunt most dearly; let us go together against this foul fiend, and I warrant we will prevail against him." "No, no, Offerus!" cried the emperor in a whisper. "No, no; that chase is better left alone, lest in battling with the foul fiend we lose our own souls." Then Offerus made a wry face, and said to the emperor, "Ah, ah! my lord emperor, I perceive the grapes are sour. If your highness is afraid of the devil, it is pretty plain he is the mightier of the two, and him will I serve." So saying, he coolly demanded his pay, quitted the emperor's service, and strode bravely into the forest to find this new master. The devil is never far to seek, though he is not always recognized. Offerus had not proceeded above a league, when he came to a wild clearing, and found there an altar built of coals; and on the altar, gleaming in the moonlight, lay bones, blanched and bare of flesh. Offerus was in no wise terrified, but quietly and deliberately examined the bones. Then, seating himself at the foot of the altar, he fell fast asleep. He thought, in his sleep, he saw the earth gape, and a coal-black horse come out of the chasm. The rider was as black as his horse; and, coming to Offerus, volunteered to take him into his service, if he would bind himself to him for ever. "Softly, softly!" cried Offerus; "not so fast, I prithee. I will engage to serve you for ever, unless I find a master mightier than thou." So the bargain was struck, and Offerus entered into the service of the foul fiend. The devil took his new recruit through the kingdoms of the world, and Offerus found him more to his liking than the emperor; but one day as they went on together, laughing and jesting, they came upon three posts—for so they seemed to Offerus—and the prince of darkness would not pass them, but turned another way. "How now?" cried Offerus; "it seems to me your majesty is afraid of that gibbet. Ha, ha!" And, drawing his bow. the giant shot an arrow, which lodged in the wood. "Gently!" said Satan. "You must not do so. Don't you know those three pieces of wood form what is called a cross?" "Well, and what of that?" cried the giant. "Why," said Satan, "the cross is the symbol of One with whom I once did battle, and He was slain on a cross." "If He was slain," persisted the giant, "what is there to fear. The slain are dead, and there's an end of them." "No, no!" cried Satan. "He is not dead, I can assure you; but liveth, and will live, too, for ever and for evermore." "Oh, oh!" cried Offerus, "I see it all. He died, but is alive again; and is mightier than thou. I serve none but the mightiest; so farewell, master; here we part." Satan did not dare pass the cross, but tried to cover over his chagrin with a loud laugh; and Offerus journeyed on, asking every one he met if he could direct him where to find Him who was crucified and rose from the dead. He met, however, no one who could tell him exactly. Some had heard speak of Him, and some thought they knew Him; but none could tell the giant where to find Him. At length came Offerus to a hermit's cell; and the man of God showed him that "faith" was the path he must go to find Christ, that "prayer" would give him strength for the journey, and "grace" would come to his help in time of need. The hermit then set the giant to carry pilgrims across a deep river, and told him Christ would know of his works, and his labours, and his patience; and in His own good time would show Himself to him. Offerus replied, "He did not mind the work, if he could find Christ." So he built himself a hut on the brink of the river, and carried pilgrims across; and if any offered him money, he would say, "Nay, nay; I work not for money, but to win Christ." Many and many a year did he serve this ferry, till his hair grew grey, and his strength began to wane; when, one night, he heard a very tiny voice calling to him. "Offerus," it said, "dear Offerus, carry Me across the river." The giant took his pine-stick, huge as a weaver's beam, waded through the river, and came to the other side; but could see no one. He thought he must have been dreaming; so he returned to his hut, and went to bed again. Scarcely had he so done, when he heard the same voice again, very small and very plaintive, but he distinctly heard it say, "Offerus, good Offerus, carry Me across the river." Again the giant waded through the stream, but yet saw he no one; and again he returned to his hut, that he might sleep till dawn. No sooner was he settled in bed than the voice came to him a third time, and still it said the same words, "Offerus, dear Offerus, carry Me across the river." It was a very small voice, but clear as a bell, and so plaintive that the giant had no heart to refuse; so he rose a third time, and waded through the river to the other bank. There he found a fair little Child, with golden hair. In His left hand He held a toy—it was the standard of a lamb; and in His right hand He had another toy, a little globe. The Child looked on the rough brawny giant with eyes full of love and trustfulness; and Offerus lifted the little wayfarer on his huge shoulders with only three fingers. On went he to the river, but when he entered the water, the Child seemed to weigh on him like a burden too heavy to be borne. Heavier and heavier grew the weight, heavier and still heavier, till the water well-nigh reached his chin. Great drops of sweat stood on the giant's brow, and he almost sank in the stream under the ever-increasing weight of that little Child. However, he struggled bravely on, contrived with tottering steps to reach the home shore, set the Child gently down, and said, "My little Lord, prithee come not this way again, for scarcely now have I escaped with my life." The Child spoke very little, but taking a handful of water in its hand, sprinkled with it the giant's face, saying, "Fear not, Offerus; the Child thou hast so bravely carried across the stream is the Lord Christ, whom thou seekest. Thy prayers are heard, and thy sins are forgiven thee. Plant now thy pine-staff in the earth, and it shall be a token unto thee. It shall no longer be dead and leafless, but shall send forth leaves and buds; and thou shalt be no longer called Offerus, but Christ-offerus shall thy name be;" and from that day he was called Christ-offerus, or Christopher. The Child left him; Christopher set his pine-staff in the earth, and on the morrow it had shot forth leaves and red blossoms like those of an almond tree. Three days afterwards the giant died, and angels came, and bore him up aloft into the bosom of good old Abraham, and there was joy in the presence of the angels of God.

This beautiful allegory has been taken mainly from *The Schönberg-cotta Family.*

Angels differ in Glory.

1 COR. xv. 41, 42. There is one glory of the sun, and another glory of the moon, and another

glory of the stars; for one star differeth from another star in glory. So also is the resurrection of the dead.

The orders of degrees among the angels of heaven. According to Dionysius the Areopagite, the angelic hierarchy of heaven is divided into nine orders—

1. Seraphim, 2. Cherubim, 3. Thrones, in the *first* circle;
4. Dominions, 5. Virtues, 6. Powers, in the *second* circle;
7. Principalities, 8. Archangels, 9. Angels, in the *third* circle.—*Hierarchia Cœlestis.*

Gregory the Great has a different arrangement in the third order—

Novem angelorum ordines dicimus, quia videlicet esse, testante sacro eloquio, scimus Angelos, Archangelos, Virtutes, Potestates, Principatus, Dominationes, Thronos, Cherubim, atque Seraphim.—*Homily* 34.

By this arrangement we have—

Seraphim, Cherubim, and Thrones, in the *first* order;
Dominions, Principalities, and Powers, in the *second* order;
Virtues, Archangels, and Angels, in the *third* order.

The seven holy angels are Michael (*the archangel*), Gabriel, Raphael (*these three are Scripture names*), Uriel, Simiel, Oriphiel, and Zachariel. The council held in A.D. 745 mentions with reprobation the names of Uriel, Raguel, Simiel, and others.

Raphael tells Tobias (*Tobit* xii. 15) that he is one of the *seven* angels who attend in the presence of God; and John, in the *Revelation* (viii. 2, 3), saw seven angels standing before the Lord.

The rabbins say Michael presides over the east, Raphael over the west, Gabriel over the north, and Uriel over the south.

According to the Koran, the throne of the Almighty is supported by eight angels (ch. lxix.), but Sale tells us, in a footnote, that "the number of those who bear it at the present is generally supposed to be four, and that other four will be added at the judgment-day, for the grandeur of the occasion." In ch. xxxv. we are told that the angels are furnished with two, four, or six pairs of wings according to their different orders.

Michael (*archangel*), Azrafil (*archangel which will blow the trumpet of the resurrection*), Gabriel, and Raphael are the four angels which now support the throne of the Almighty.

The orders of degree among the fallen angels. In one of the ninety-three visions of St. Francisca, she was shown the fall of the rebellious angels. When cast out of heaven some remained in the air, some fell upon our earth, and the rest fell into hell. The different degrees of demerit decided the region to be occupied. Lucifer, she tells us, is the monarch of all the hells, but he rules in chains of iron, and is supreme in misery as well as in power. Under him are three princes, each absolute in his own department. The first of these is Asmodëus, once a cherub, but now holding the "principality" of carnal sins. The next is Mammon, the demon of avarice, who holds the "throne" of this world. The third is Beëlzebub, who holds the "dominion" of idolaters. These three powers and Lucifer never leave their prisons, except under special permission from God; but they have legions and legions of subordinates on earth who are responsible to them. These subordinate demons have their ranks, like the angelic host; and so have the demons of the air and of the earth, but these last two are commonwealths, having no supreme head. The demons of the air cause storms, and injure men by diseases and breaking down their confidence in God. The demons of the earth ally themselves with all other demons to bring about the loss of souls. The best and surest safeguard against all demons is to pronounce the name of Jesus. When persons live in mortal sin, demons install themselves in the "temple of their body," which is otherwise the "temple of the Holy Ghost;" and when a sinner receives absolution from the Church, the demons quit his body, but loiter about near enough to suggest temptations to sin. Confession is an excellent armour; and those who go to confession most frequently are with the most difficulty beguiled.

Limbo. Limbo is contiguous to hell, but has no communication with it. An angel keeps guard over the gate. The only punishment suffered there is the privation of light. In limbo will be found all infants that have died unbaptized. In the first of its three regions are the infants of Christian parents; in the second region, the infants of Jews and pagans; and in the third or lowest region, children born out of wedlock. The darkness of this region is thicker than that of the other two.

Purgatory. Like hell and limbo, purgatory has three regions. Over the gate is this inscription, "This is purgatory, the place of hope." In the uppermost region are the souls of those who had not worked out the expiation of their sins before death; and seven years is the term of punishment for each mortal sin unobliterated at death, or after death by masses or other merits. The guardian angel of each soul collects carefully the masses said, the prayers offered, and the indulgences granted to each soul in purgatory. Pious legacies are accepted by God, whether executors pay the bequests or not. Prayers, masses, indulgences, and good works in behalf of those in bliss are scored to those who offer them on earth, and if there is any surplus it is placed to the credit of those in purgatory. The second region of purgatory is for the expiation of venial sins. The lowest region, which is the most burning, is for priests and nuns who have committed what are sins in the religious, but would not be accounted sins in seculars, such as indulging the appetite with food or wine beyond what is absolutely necessary to support life.—*Acta Sanctorum* (Bollandists), vol. ii. March. (See also Grimes, *Esprit des Saints*, vol. v., 3rd edit.)

St. Francisca sees in a vision the different orders of the heavenly host (A.D. 1384–1440). In one of her numerous visions, St. Francisca saw the orders of the saints in light, with their respective leaders. They all walked under their proper standards. First came the patriarchs, led by John the Baptist (*Matt.* xi. 11). Next came the apostles, led by St. Peter and St. Paul. The evangelists marched third, under St. John and St. Mark. Then the martyrs, under St. Laurentius and St. Stephen. The fifth company were the doctors of the Church, under St. Gregory and St. Jerome. The sixth were the monks, under St. Benedict, St. Bernard, St. Dominic, and St. Francis. The hermits, led by St. Paul the hermit and St. Antony, came next. Then the virgins, led by Mary Magdalene and St. Agnes. The ninth company was that of widows, under St. Anne and St. Sabina. And the tenth consisted of married women, led by St. Cecilia.—*Acta Sanctorum* (Bollandists), vol. ii. March. (See also Grimes, *Esprit des Saints*, vol. v., 3rd edit.)

St. Francisca sees her son in the second hierarchic choir of heaven (A.D. 1407). St. Francisca had a son John, who died of the plague at the age of nine, and was buried in St. Cecilia's church, beyond the Tiber. A year after his death, as St. Francisca was praying in her oratory, she saw her son John all brilliant in light, assisted by another angel more brilliant still. Her son showed her the different orders of the hierarchy of heaven, and their different degrees of glory. He himself was in the second range of the first hierarchy, and the other angel was more luminous because he was in a higher company.—John Mattiotti (her father-confessor), *Life of St. Francisca.*

Angels Ministering Spirits.

HEB. i. 14. [The angels] are they not all ministering spirits, sent forth to minister for them who shall be heirs of salvation?

Angels assist at the baptism of [*St.*] *Eusebius.* Before the pope baptized Eusebius, he had a revelation that the person he was about to baptize would be one day a great man. Angels, we are told, took Eusebius out of the baptismal font.—Surius (1570), *Lives of the Saints.*

Antediluvian Longevity.

GEN. v. And Adam lived 130 years. That was the age of Adam; but his offspring or dynasty, called his sons and daughters, continued *ab initio* 930 years (ver. 5).

Again. Seth lived 105 years. That was the term of Seth's own life; but Seth was the head of a tribe, and the sons and daughters of this sheik lasted 912 years altogether (ver. 8).

Enos lived 90 years. That was the span of this man's life; but Enos was a sheik, and his sons and daughters continued his sheikship 905 years (ver. 11).

Methuselah, the oldest man, lived 187 years. His sheikship was also the most enduring, extending to 969 years, when it died out (ver. 27).

This interpretation was suggested in the *Expositor*, December, 1878, and March, 1880. It is plausible, certainly, and preferable to the "lunar year" interpretation.

Similar examples in post-diluvian history. The most familiar example is that of Rome, where the first twelve emperors were all Cæsar; in imitation of Bible language, it might be said. Cæsar lived fifty-six, but all the days of Cæsar were 179 years; that is, dating from the birth of Julius to the death of Vespasian.

Pharaoh of Egypt would be very much longer. Josephus tells us all the kings of Egypt from Menês to Solomon were called Pharaoh, 341 kings. Menês, according to Lepsius, died B.C. 3893, and Solomon reigned 1015–975. This would make all the days of Pharaoh very much longer than all the days of Methuselah.

Bunsen places the death of Menês in B.C. 3643.

Ptolemy of Egypt, after the death of Alexander the Great, would give another example. It might be said that Ptolemy lived eighty-four years and begat sons and daughters; and all the days of Ptolemy were 272 years.

Similar examples familiar to Scripture readers are Abimelech, the common name of the Philistine kings; Agag, the common name of the Amalekite kings; Benhadad, the common name of the rulers of Damascus; and Candacê of Ethiopia. Darius also seems to have been a dynastic name in ancient Persia.

Leaving Scripture, we have Abgarus, the common name of the kings of Edessa; Augustus in the Roman empire; Cyrus in the Persian empire; Vladika in Montenegro; and Louis in France; with many more.

Age of the saints. The saints, as a rule, were long-lived, like the wise men of Greece. Very many of them passed fourscore years, but only ten reached a hundred. They are—

Years at death.

101. Lupicen, abbot of Lauconne (379–480).

102. Faust de Riez (391–493).

104. John the Silent (454–558).

106. Gilbert, founder of the Gilbertines (1084–1190).

108. Ortarius, abbot of Landelle (sixth century).

112. Grace of Valentia, who never had an illness (1494–1606).

114. Paul the Hermit; ninety of which he passed in the desert (229–343).

120. John de Réome; his eye was not dim, nor his strength abated (425–545).

120. Memmius, bishop of Châlons-sur-Marne (96–126).

120. Romuald, founder of the Camaldulensians (907–1027).

Ask, and ye shall receive.

MATT. vii. 7. Ask, and it shall be given you.

MATT. xxi. 22. All things whatsoever ye shall ask in prayer, believing, ye shall receive.

JOHN xiv. 14. If ye shall ask anything in My name, I will do it.

1 JOHN v. 14, 15. This is the confidence that we have in Him: that if we ask anything according to His will, He heareth us; and if we know that He heareth us in whatsoever we ask, we know that we have the petitions that we desired of Him.

St. Francisca asked God, in prayer, to give Vannosia a crab, and He gave it (A.D. 1384–1440). A gentlewoman, named Vannosia, a dear friend and kinsman of St. Francisca, being very sick, had an irresistible desire for some crab; but the season of crabs was over, and there were none to be got in all Rome. In this emergency Francisca "put herself in prayer, and desired one of God." Forthwith, in the sight of the whole household, there fell from the ceiling of the room a fine fresh crab, alive, and to all appearance just taken from the sea. Francisca gave it to her friend, who ate thereof, and not only allayed her diseased craving, but forthwith recovered her wonted health.—*Mentioned in the Acts of the Canonization of St. Francisca*, May 29, 1606.

St. John de Matha asked in prayer for money to redeem some slaves, and received the necessary sum (A.D. 1160–1213). St. John de Matha founded the "Holy Trinity for the Redemption of Christian Slaves." At Tunis, on one occasion, he paid to the governor the ransom he required, but found that the subordinates demanded black-mail. Not having the wherewithal to satisfy their greed, he laid the image of the Virgin under his scapular, and "conjured the good mother of heaven to have mercy on these captives." On lifting up his scapular he found the sum required, paid it, and brought home the captives.

The sequel. The Tunisians, greatly enraged, boarded the ship in which the captives had embarked, broke the rudder, cut down the masts, tore the sails, snapped in pieces the oars, and left the vessel a dead hulk. St. John de Matha was equal to the occasion. He stripped off his mantle and made a sail thereof, placed himself at the helm, crucifix in hand, and prayed God to grant a safe voyage. The vessel moved, it ran merrily over the calm sea, and in two days entered the Ostian port, amidst the loud acclamations of a vast crowd. The pope wept for joy, asked to see the captives, gave them his blessing, and sent them home to their respective countries.—R. P. Calixte de la Providence, *Life of St. John of Matha.*

A woman craved some peaches in February, and they grew on chestnut slips. In the month of February, about 1700, a Neapolitan merchant came to visit St. John-Joseph de la Croix, and on parting entreated his prayers in behalf of his wife, who was dangerously ill. On further inquiry, the merchant told him his wife had a craving for ripe peaches, but of course such things could not be obtained in winter. Being near a chestnut tree at the time, the man of God broke off three dry branches, and said to the merchant, "Plant these in three flower-pots, and ask St. Peter of Alcantara to give your wife her heart's desire." "What!" cried the merchant, "how can peaches grow on dry chestnut slips?" "All things are possible with God," said the saint. "Do as I bid you, and leave the result to God and St. Peter." The merchant planted the three dry chestnut sticks, made his prayer to St. Peter of Alcantara, and set the flower-pots on his window-seat. Next morning the sticks were covered with green leaves, and on each stick was a superb ripe peach. The sick woman had her heart's desire, and rapidly returned to perfect health.—Migne, *Démonstrations Évangéliques*, vol. xvi. (This life of St. John-Joseph of the Cross is from the pen of cardinal Wiseman. Father Diodato, in 1794, wrote the life of the same saint.)

Babes.

PSALM viii. 2. Out of the mouth of babes and sucklings hast Thou ordained strength . . . [to] still the enemy and the avenger.

MATT. xi. 25. Thou hast hid these things from the wise and prudent, and hast revealed them unto babes.

MATT. xxi. 16. Out of the mouth of babes and sucklings Thou hast perfected praise.

St. Augustine taught by a little child. While St. Augustine was composing his book *On the Trinity*, and was at Civita Vecchia, he saw a little child making a hole in the sea-shore, and asked him what he was doing. The child replied, "I am making a hole to contain the water of the sea." The doctor smiled, telling the child it would not be possible to do so; but the child made answer, "Not so, Augustine. It would be far easier to drain off the waters of the great deep, than for the finite to grasp the Infinite;" and so he vanished. Augustine then knew that the child was an angel of God, sent to warn him, and he diligently set to work to revise what he had written.—Possidonius (bishop of Calamentia), *Life of St. Augustine.*

An infant just born tells St. Brigit who was its father (A.D. 436–523). An unmarried woman, who had just given birth to a child, was asked to confess who was its father, and she declared it was bishop Broon, a disciple of St. Patrick. St. Brigit could not credit this scandal, and, making the sign of the cross on the babe's mouth, she asked it if it were true. "No," said the infant, "my father is no bishop, but a poor labourer." So the "truth" was discovered, the honour of the Church vindicated, and God defended the right.—*Les Petits Bollandistes*, vol. ii. p. 185.

A babe in arms picks out his father (fourteenth century). A woman who had recently given birth to a son, was accused by her husband of infidelity. The woman, greatly distressed, applied to St. Vincent Ferrier, and the saint said to her, "Come this afternoon and hear my sermon; bring your babe with you. Induce your husband to come also; not with you, but let him mix with the crowd." When St. Vincent had finished his sermon, he told the mother to set her infant on the ground, and then bade it go through the crowd and pick out its father. The babe, only a few days old, threaded its way through the dense crowd till it came to the husband of the woman, and laying its hands on him, said distinctly, "This is my father." "Un miracle aussi extraordinaire ne pouvait que faire rentrer la paix dans le ménage."—*Les Petits Bollandistes*, vol. iv. p. 237.

A child just born tells the apostles Simon and Jude that its mother told a lie. While the apostles Simon and Jude were in Babylon, they consecrated Abdias bishop, and ordained both priests and deacons; but the devil sought to bring discredit on the Church. It fell out thus: The daughter of a nobleman in Babylon became mother of a child, but was not wed. Her parents urged her to tell them who was the father of her child, and she (to screen her lover) charged one of the deacons of the new Church with the crime. When the apostles heard thereof, they went to the king's court, and requested that the deacon, with the mother and infant, might be brought before the judge. This was done, and the apostles asked the parents when the child was born. "This very day," they replied. Then, fixing their eyes sternly on the infant, they said, "We adjure thee, by the living God, and in the name of Jesus Christ, tell us truly if this deacon is thy father or not?" The infant answered, "This deacon is good and chaste, and never in his life committed any carnal sin. He is not my father." The apostles then asked the babe who his father was, and the wise infant made answer, "It is meet for me to clear the innocent, but not to disclose the guilty." And all the court was amazed at the answers.—Edward Kinesman, *Lives of the Saints* (1623).

The same answer was given by the dead man summoned by Macarius (see p. 77), and by the dead man summoned by St. Antony (see p. 75).

St. Vincent Ferrier speaks in infancy to

his mother (A.D. 1357). While St. Vincent Ferrier was an infant, a dreadful dearth desolated Valentia. The mother of the child was afflicted with the general calamity, and one day when she was lamenting the long drought, the infant in swaddling-clothes said to her distinctly, "Mother, if you wish for rain, carry me in procession." The babe was carried in procession, and the rain fell abundantly. ("Son enfant emmaillotté prononcer distinctement ces paroles: Si vous voulez de la pluie, portez moi en procession.")—Mgr. Guérin (chamberlain of pope Leo XIII.), *Vies des Saints*, vol. iv. p. 236.

A newborn babe declares that Abzenderoud is not his father. The imâm Abzenderoud excited the envy of his confraternity by his superior virtue and piety, so they suborned a woman to father a child on him. The imâm prayed Mahomet to clear him of this charge, and the newborn babe declared in a loud distinct voice, not only that the imâm was innocent of the charge alleged against him, but it furthermore said that one of his chief accusers was its father, and had suborned the woman to make this false charge to screen himself, and bring the imâm into trouble.—T. S. Gueulette (1723), *Chinese Tales*.

Mons. Gueulette's story is professedly a fiction; that of the two apostles Simon and Jude, and that of St. Brigit (see preceding page), are given as facts; but the parallels are striking enough to place them all in one category.

Infants at the breast announce the death of St. Agnes (April 20, 1317). When St. Agnes died, we are told by her biographer she received the most perfect praise this earth could afford, that of infants at the breast. The tongue of little infants was unloosed, "et ils se mirent dans les lieux voisins à publier la mort et les vertus d'Agnes; leurs parents s'éveillèrent en entendant ces voix."—*Les Petits Bollandistes*, vol. iv. p. 549.

It is not quite clear what the pope's chamberlain means. He tells us he is speaking of "des enfants à la mamelle." These "petits innocents se mirent à publier la mort d'Agnes" (announced the death of Agnes), and their parents woke on hearing their voices. Were these infants in bed when they made the proclamation? If so, does the chamberlain mean they spoke so loud as to be heard "dans les lieux voisins"?

St. Robert, in infancy, declined to suck the milk of any but religious wet-nurses (A.D. 1067). Robert, son of Gerard, baron of Aurillac, even from his birth showed signs of his future holiness. His mother, being for a time unable to give him suck, employed wet-nurses, but the babe positively refused to take the breast of any irreligious woman, and would only go to pious ones. When the mother was able to nurse the child herself, she dispensed with the services of strangers, and the infant was relieved of all further difficulty, for the baroness was an excellent Christian.—*Acta Sanctorum* (Bollandists), April 24.

St. Sigisbert, king of Austrasia, and his baptism (A.D. 636). When Sigisbert, the infant son of Dagobert I., was baptized, the church was so full of kings, princes, and nobles, there was no room for a clerk. In this difficulty the infant himself acted as clerk, and said "Amen" in the proper places, "pronouncing the word audibly and distinctly, to the great admiration of the nobles assembled on the occasion."*—R. P. Vincent, *History of Saint Sigisbert* (taken from the *Antiquités Austrasiennes*).

The monk Sigebert, who first wrote the life of king Sigisbert, says that a large number of miracles testified to the holiness of this favourite of God. He mentions many, and tells us he knows they are true, for he himself witnessed them with his own eyes.

John Stirling, the drunkard, reclaimed by his baby boy. When the drinking fit was on him, the will of John Stirling seemed to be wholly in the grasp of his master vice, which had well-nigh made an utter wreck of his conscience, honour, and affection; but help was at hand, and a little child was the David employed by God to slay the giant which held him captive. His wife had always been in the habit of observing family worship; the rest must be told by John Stirling himself. "I had been all day at the public-house, and when at night I came home my wife was reading from the twenty-fifth chapter of St. Matthew's Gospel: 'When the Son of man shall come in His glory . . . before Him shall be gathered all nations: and He shall separate them one from another, as a shepherd divideth his sheep from the goats: and He shall set the sheep on His right hand, but the goats on the left.' Our youngest boy, then about four years old, was sitting on a footstool, with his head on his mother's lap; and when he heard these words read, he looked up earnestly into his mother's face, and said,

* "Ce miracle (*AA. SS. Belgii*, vol. iv. p. 253, note 12) est rapporté par Baudemond, auteur contemporain, et répété par beaucoup d'autres."

A similar instance is recorded by Fleury, in his *History of the Church*, bk. xxxvi. n. 38, under date of Feb. 4, 1650, in the diocese of Strigonia, in Hungary. The case was severely investigated, and the archbishop recognized the undoubted fact.

"Will father be a goat then, mother?" This question cut me to the heart. It was a nail driven home. The earnestness of the child, the bewilderment of his mother, the home-thrust rankling in my heart, all told upon me. I spent a miserable night indeed. Next day was Sunday, but I was ashamed to go to church. While the family was at church, looking about for something to read, I laid my hand on Beecher's *Six Sermons on Intemperance*. I read, and read, and all I read seemed about myself. My future life was now determined. All the men on earth could not now have tempted me to drink. I loathed drink. The ale which yesterday was irresistible, was now gall and wormwood to me. I would have been cut to pieces rather than touch it. This was the turning-point of my life; and God, ever gracious, from that memorable moment led me in the way everlasting."—Wallace, *The Gloaming of Life*.

This is by far the best tale in this section. Monkish tales about babes are in all cases revolting. The prudery, the unwise wisdom, the immodest modesty of little children, is most unnatural, most prurient, and most repulsive. I know of no single legend of a child at all attractive, or bearing the least semblance to the beautiful innocence of young childhood; they are mere monks and nuns in small-clothes.

Beast of Burden.

PSALM lxxiii. 22. I was as a beast before Thee.

St. Marcellinus, bishop of Embrun, treated as a beast of burden. Returning from a long excursion, St. Marcellinus observed a large crowd of people at a short distance, and went to see what was the matter. He heard a great outcry, and found it was some strangers going to Embrun; but one of their pack-horses, being overladen, had fallen from fatigue, unable to advance any further. St. Marcellinus told the travellers to be patient, not to beat the poor beast, and above all things to refrain from their blasphemous language; whereupon the people, angry and tired, swore the bishop himself should be their beast of burden. Resistance was in vain, remonstrance would have been thrown away; so, bending his back, the mob, half in mischief and half in anger, piled on it the goods which had broken down their pack-horse. St. Marcellinus, with admirable patience and humility, lent himself to this insult, saying as he was being loaded, "My Saviour bore more than all this for me;" and then adding from the psalmist, "I was as a beast before Thee." When he reached the city, the people were greatly enraged to see their bishop thus insulted, and took up stones to cast at the strangers; but God Himself took it in hand to glorify His saint, by sending a "tourbillon of fire," which enveloped the most furious of the strangers, and caused him most frightful pain. Terribly frightened, he threw himself at the bishop's feet, craving his pardon; but the fire never left him till the bishop was disburdened, and had offered up prayer on the man's behalf. The man pressed St. Marcellinus to accept a present, but he refused to take anything, and after appeasing the people of Embrun, he retired to his own home.—Mgr. Depéry, *Hagiographie de Gap*.

Beasts, Birds, and Fishes preached to.

PSALM cxlviii. 7–10. Praise the Lord from the earth, ye dragons and deeps, beasts and all cattle, creeping things and flying fowl.

St. Antony of Padua preaches to the fishes (A.D. 1195-1231). When St. Antony was preaching at Rimini, he found the eyes of many obstinately closed to the words of light; and said from his chair, "Let those who list follow me to the seashore." He went to Marecchia, and raising his voice, cried aloud: "Ye fishes of the sea, hear; for man, though the image of his Maker, is like the deaf adder, and refuses to hearken to his God. To you, therefore, I announce the gospel of salvation." Instantly from the depths of the sea shoals of both little and great fish thronged to the shore. From all sides they came in countless numbers, crowding thick upon each other, their heads above the water, their big eyes turned to the preacher, who spoke thus: "What acts of thankfulness, O fishes, ought you not to render to Him who has given you to live in this mighty ocean? It is to God you owe those deep retreats, which protect you from the raging storm. When the great flood destroyed the families of man, that God preserved you. It is you who saved the prophet Jonah. It is you who brought the stater to St. Peter and the Lord of glory. You receive your life, your food, your protection, from God and God alone. Praise Him, seas and floods, bless ye the Lord; praise Him, and magnify Him for ever. Ye whales, and all that move in the waters, bless ye the Lord; praise Him, and magnify Him for ever." At these words the fishes seemed agitated, flapped their tails, opened their mouths, and testified in a thousand ways their wish to pay homage to the Almighty, and the tribute of their mute praise. The crowd on the shore could not restrain their admiration, and cried with one voice, "Come, let us laud and magnify God the Maker, the Redeemer, and the Sanctifier." And Antony, turning round, exclaimed, "Praise Him, ye children of men; praise Him, and magnify Him for ever. Let the fishes of the sea teach man to praise the Lord. Shall man, the image of his Maker, alone be mute in His praise?" The "heretics" were confounded, fell at the preacher's feet, and would not arise till he had given them absolution. The remembrance of this prodigy is perpetuated in Italy and France. Father Papebroch tells us he saw in 1660 an ancient chapel standing on the spot where St. Antony preached to the fishes. Many painters have represented it.—Guyard, *Life of St. Antony of Padua.*

I have myself seen the picture brought to Paris by marshal Soult, said to be by Murillo, of St. Antony preaching to the fishes.

St. Francis of Assisi used to preach to the beasts and birds (A.D. 1182–1226). St. Francis of Assisi wished to retire into solitude, but the Holy Ghost made it known to him that it was God's will he should continue to preach the gospel. "What, however, is very admirable is this: he often preached to the cattle of the field, and birds of the air, to the fishes of the sea, and even to the beasts of the forest, showing to them their obligations to God, and calling upon them to praise His holy name. These dumb creatures, without human reason, would listen attentively, and testify by their movements the joy they felt in his discourse, and after the sermon was over they would praise the Lord, each in his several way." —Chavin de Malan, *Life of St. Francis of Assisi.*

N.B.—St. Aventine, hearing that some fishers were coming to Vinzai, in Tourraine, warned the fishes to be on their guard, A.D. 538. This is strange, as the monks were always fishers.

St. Francis was a famous preacher, and nothing is more common than for preachers, who can find a spot sufficiently retired, to recite audibly their sermon in their walks. This might have been the practice of St. Francis, and accidental hearers might fancy he was preaching to the beasts and birds, instead of conning his sermon. All who have tried it will testify that sheep and oxen, birds and creeping things, are greatly charmed with the human voice, and will often run towards the speaker, and stand long listening to him, if his voice has any charm. I have myself seen it scores of times.

Birds accompany a monk of Mount Avernia to the tomb of St. Francis. The following beautiful legend is told by R. H. Busk in *Notes and Queries*, Oct. 20, 1883, p. 302, note. St. Francis of Assisi had received the stigmata in a retired and almost inaccessible spot which he had chosen for his meditations. After the death of the saint, the community adopted an annual procession to the spot where he was buried. It was a midnight procession, and not unfrequently the way was dark, cold, and stormy; but spite of dark, cold, and storm the procession went on, chanting solemn prayer and praise. After a time the attendance greatly diminished. The midnight hour, the darkness, the cold, the storm, told upon the monks, and at last the procession dwindled down to one single monk. Alone he stepped out into the midnight darkness. Alone he breasted the cold and storm. No sooner, however, had he left the monastery, than he saw before him a luminous road, and instead of cross-bearer, thurifer, acolytes with torches, and a choir of brown-habited monks, the road was filled with the birds of heaven. All the birds which made their dwellings in the shelving sides of the mountains had come forth to form a procession, and accompany the monk in his pious labour of love. On they went with slow and solemn wing. On with plaintive dirge and song. On with chirp as their "Amen." When the monk told his tale in the monastery next morning, the brothers were ashamed and mortified; but ever after, be the night as stormy as it may, be the wind biting and boisterous, be the cold nipping and eager, no matter how inclement the night, the monks in a body turn out to make their solemn procession to the grave of their holy founder.

"This I had from the lips of an enthusiastic son of St. Francis, whom I met when both of us were visiting Rome."

Beasts confiding in Saints.

JOB v. 23. The beasts of the field shall be at peace with thee.

HOS. ii. 18. In that day will I make a covenant for them with the beasts of the field, and with the fowls of heaven, and with the creeping things of the ground.

EZEK. xxxiv. 25. They shall dwell safely in the wilderness, and sleep in the woods.

A bear with a wounded paw comes to St. Aventine (A.D. 778–813). One day, when St. Aventine was praying in a wood, he heard a bear growling plaintively; and, raising his eyes, he saw a monster animal coming slowly down the mountain towards him. He was not the least alarmed, but waited patiently till the bear came up. It was docile as a lamb, and, holding up its fore paw, the saint saw it was swollen and bloody from a great thorn. Taking the wounded paw into his hands, he extracted the thorn, and washed the wound. The grateful bear licked the saint's hands, and showed in every possible way his thankfulness.—*Notice Historique sur St. Aventin d'Aquitaine* (Toulouse, 1850).

In St. Aventine's church is a sculpture of wood of the hermit dressing the bear's foot. (See ANDROCLUS AND THE LION, p. 219; GERASIMUS AND THE LION, p. 220.)

A wild boar, chased by hunters, takes refuge under the cloak of St. Basil (A.D. 620). One day, when Attila, count of Champagne, was out hunting, he came to Verzy, where stood the monastery of St. Basil. A wild boar, chased by the dogs, ran for refuge to the saint, who was sitting in the sun outside his cell; and Basil covered the terrified beast with his cloak. The dogs came up, but were at a standstill, not knowing what to do. Presently the count came to the spot, and recognizing in this incident the finger of God, gave St. Basil a large part of the forest, a part of Bouzy, and the town of Sept-Saulx.—Mgr. Guérin, *Vies des Saints*, vol. xiii. p. 603.

St. Calais protects a buffalo from the royal hunters (A.D. 545). St. Calais retired to Casa Gaiani, in the canton of Lavardin, then a profound solitude. Here a buffalo used to visit him often, and allow the saint to pat it, and pass his fingers between its horns or among the thick hair of its neck. One day king Childebert and his court came to Matovall to hunt, and hearing that a fine buffalo had been seen in the neighbourhood, prepared to hunt it. The buffalo ran for protection to the saint's cell, and there found a safe asylum. Soon the hunting party came up, but seeing the buffalo in the cell and the saint in prayer, knew not how to proceed. Says the king in a fury to St. Calais, "Where do you come from? And how dare you, without my leave, plant yourself in a royal forest? It is not for such as you to spoil the sport of a king?" "Most excellent prince," said Calais, suavely, "it was not to spoil your grace's sport that I came hither, but to commune more closely with God, both mine and yours." "Off with you!" cried the king, "and take care I do not catch you trespassing again." "Most excellent king, will it please your serenity, after your exertions, to take a draught of some excellent wine which I have made?" asked Calais. Childebert spurred his horse to run the saint down, but the horse started back, and remained immovable. One of the courtiers came up, and said to the king, "Sire, the man, doubtless, is a servant of God; let us not fight against God." Childebert was pacified, and Calais handed him a cup of wine. The king drank heartily, and passed the cup to his courtiers, all of whom drank, but the wine was not diminished. The king then made Calais a present of as much land as he liked to build a monastery on, and promised to endow it and become its patron.—Dom Paul Piolin, *Histoire de l'Église du Mans.*

A hunted wild boar seeks safety under St. Deïcola (A.D. 625). St. Deïcola lived in a monastery at Lure. One day its peace and quiet was broken by a royal chase. King Clotaire II. was hunting a wild boar, and the poor beast took refuge in the cell of St. Deïcola. The saint put his hand on the creature's head, saying, "As you confide in me, poor beast, I will defend you." The king, hearing that the wild boar was in the hermit's cell, came up to see the prodigy, and when he learned that Deïcola was a disciple of Columban, whom he greatly honoured, he inquired how he could serve the recluse. "It is written," said the Irishman, "he who fears the Lord shall want no good thing. We are poor, but we serve God." Clotaire gave large lands and endowments to the monastery, which hence became one of the wealthiest in the land.—Montalembert, *Monks of the East*, vol. ii. p. 608.

A goat, pursued by huntsmen, seeks the protection of St. Fructuosus (A.D. 605). One day, when Fructuosus, bishop of Braga, was wandering in a forest, a goat, pursued by some huntsmen, sought refuge under his cloak. The saint took the frightened creature, under his protection, to the monastery, and the goat, ever mindful of this kindness, never left him, but followed him everywhere like a dog, slept with him at night, walked with him by day, and ran to welcome him home whenever duty had called him away for a time. St. Fructuosus once and again took the goat to the forest, and offered it liberty; but it always returned to the cell. One day, when the saint was absent from home, some young man killed the goat, and Fructuosus was greatly grieved. Not long afterwards the young man was taken dangerously ill, and the saint, with noble Christian charity, whereby we are instructed to love our enemies, and do good to them that despitefully use us, went to the bedside of the sick man, and healed him.—*Patrologie Latine*, vol. lxxxvii. col. 1087.

St. Giles and the hind. St. Giles, seeking a solitary place to live in, wandered towards the mouth of the river Rhone, when a hind made signs to him to abide in the spot where he stood. Here he found a cave, in which he took up his abode, and the hind spontaneously offered herself to be milked by him every day. On one occasion the king of France, in a hunting expedition, came upon this hind, which instantly fled to the cave for succour. St. Giles was at prayer, and when the dogs saw him on his knees, not one of them would enter the cave, for fear of disturbing him. One of the huntsmen, however, discharged his arrow into the cave, and pierced the saint. The king having come up, the party entered the cave, but what was their astonishment to find the hermit on his knees, near the mouth of the cave, with the arrow still sticking in his body. The king offered to send the royal physician to him, and wanted to give him money; but St. Giles made answer, "I need no physician but God; and as for money, give it not to me, but spend it in founding a monastery to the glory of the Lord." This the king did, and appointed St. Giles its first abbot.—Gilbert (bishop of Carnotum), *Life of St. Giles.*

A hunted stag seeks refuge with St. Godrich of Norfolk (A.D. 1170). One day a magnificent stag, hunted by the parents of the bishop of Ramulfe, came panting to the cabin of St. Godrich, the hermit of Whitby, seeking refuge. St. Godrich took it into his cell, and the noble animal, looking into his face, pleaded silently, but eloquently, for protection. Presently the huntsmen came up and demanded the stag, but Godrich replied, "God has saved it." The huntsmen, recognizing an angel or saint in the poor hermit, called off their dogs, and left both Godrich and the stag unmolested. Next day the poor beast left the cabin, but every year it came to visit its deliverer, and show its gratitude by caresses. Godrich, in fact, had made himself the protector of the beasts of the forest, insomuch that hares and partridges, stags and goats, when hunted or in need of help, confidently went to him, and always found him ready to defend them.—Nicholas of Durham, *Life of St. Godrich.*

St. Gudula and the bears (eighth century). One day, when Charlemagne was hunting bears, a prodigious monster, which was so closely pressed that escape was impossible, fled into the church at Moorsel, where St. Gudula was buried. Here it found protection, and would never afterwards quit the church, but dwelt there "parmi ces sages vierges," not as a furious wild beast, but as a docile and playful lamb.—Hubert, *Life of St. Gudula.*

A hunted hare seeks refuge with St. Marculfus (A.D. 558). A hare, chased by hunters, ran to St. Marculfus for protection, and took refuge under his gown. The huntsmen commanded the saint to release the hare, which contrived to make good its escape, while Marculfus detained the huntsmen in angry conversation. When they discovered the trick, they were very angry, and one of them drew his sword to strike him, but, falling from his horse, was dangerously hurt. Marculfus, forgetful of injuries, and forgiving, approached the injured cavalier, made the sign of the cross, and cured him on the spot.—*Acta Sanctorum* (Bollandists, Papebroch), May 1.

Beasts Submissive to Saints.

HOS. ii. 18. I will make a covenant for them with the beasts of the field, and with the fowls of heaven, and with the creeping things of the ground. And I will make them to lie down safely.

JOB v. 23. The beasts of the field shall be at peace with thee.

ISA. xi. 9. They shall not hurt nor destroy in all My holy mountain.

EZEK. xxxiv. 25-28. I will make a covenant of peace, and they shall dwell safely in the wilderness, and sleep in the woods. The beasts of the land shall not devour them: and none shall make them afraid.

St. Agapitus, being cast to wild beasts, was not harmed by them. The emperor Aurelian commanded Agapitus to be cast to the wild beasts, after he had already been scourged, roasted with his head downwards, scarified, and douched with boiling water. When the wild beasts were let out upon him, instead of tearing him to pieces, they went up to him, wagging their tails, and then lay down meekly at his feet. The emperor, seeing that the beasts would not attack his victim, sent his lictors to cut off his head.—Ado (archbishop of Vienne), *Martyrology.*

St. Aldebrand forbade the rooks to make such a noise, and they obeyed him (twelfth century). One day, when St. Aldebrand was preaching, the rooks made such a noise that he could not be heard. The saint bade them be quiet, because they interrupted him; and they were instantly silent. (See Regulus, p. 365.)—*Acta Sanctorum* (Bollandists), May 1, p. 162.

Birds and beasts of prey respect the dead body of St. Andeol (A.D. 166–208). St. Andeol, first apostle of the Helvians, was put to death by Severus, and then his dead body, weighted with an enormous stone, was thrown into the Rhone; but Providence pushed it to the right bank, close to the spot where the saint wished to be buried. The chain which held the stone had snapped in two, so that the body was disencumbered. It lay for five days on the river bank, respected by the birds and beasts of prey, and without showing the slightest sign of corruption. Every night celestial sounds were heard about the spot, and a brilliant glory surrounded the body. A wealthy lady, being told of these wonders, went with her slaves and buried the body in her own private garden.—*Acta Sanctorum* (Bollandists), May 1, p. 39.

St. Antony the Great made the wild beasts submissive to him (fourth century). When St. Antony retired to the desert not far from the Red Sea, he made a garden of herbs, and at first the wild beasts, coming for water, greatly injured his crops; but one day, having caught one, he said to it gently, "Poor beast! why do you hurt my garden; I never disturb you? Now go in the name of the Lord, but don't come here again." And never afterwards did any of the wild beasts annoy him.—Bollandus, *Acta Sanctorum*, vol. ii. (St. Athanasius was the first to write a life of his contemporary, Antony the Great. St. Jerome inserted a Latin version in his *Lives of the Saintly Fathers of the Desert.*)

We are told in the *Acta Sanctorum*, vol. i. June 2, that beasts submitted to Erasmus, the recluse of Mount Liban, and did his bidding (A.D. 301). (See Firmatus, p. 362.)

A bear, having killed one of St. Arey's oxen, bent its neck to the yoke (A.D. 535–604). When St. Arey was crossing the Apennines, in a car drawn by two oxen, a bear fell upon one of them, and devoured it. "As you have killed my ox," said St. Arey to the bear, "you must take its place." The bear instantly submitted, was harnessed to the car, and drew it bravely as far as Gap, then retired to the mountains of Orcieres, where it remained till the death of Arey. It then quitted its retreat, came to Gap, went to the church to attend the funeral, and placed itself next the coffin while the funeral service was going on. Every year, on the 1st of May, the anniversary of St. Arey's death, this faithful beast, so long as Probus lived, never failed to come to Gap to be present at the fête, and he was such an immense favourite that all the people of Gap gave him something to eat. (See Gentius, p. 362; Sanctes, p. 365.) —*Histoire Hagiologique du Diocèse de Gap.*

A wolf brings back to St. Bernard of Abbeville a stray calf (A.D. 1046–1117). While St. Bernard was living in his monastery at Tiron, his herdsman, through neglect, allowed one of the calves to stray in the forest; but two days afterwards a wolf brought it back, and placing it at the feet of St. Bernard, returned peaceably into the forest. In fact, God had said, "I will make a covenant for those who serve Me, with the beasts of the field, and with the fowls of heaven, and with creeping things of the ground;" and this was a result of that covenant of peace.—Corblet, *Hagiographie d'Amiens.* (The life of St. Bernard of Abbeville was written 1137–1148 by Geoffroy le Gros, one of his disciples.)

St. Blaise dwells safely in the forests of Cappadocia amongst wild beasts (A.D. 316). Agricola, governor of Cappadocia, persecuted Christians, in obedience to the orders of the emperor Licinius, and sent his officers into the forest to capture wild beasts. When they came to Mount Argea, they made their way to the cavern of St. Blaise; and found the saint surrounded by lions, tigers, bears, wolves, and other wild beasts, all in friendly communion with each other and the saint. Returning to the governor, they told him what they had seen, and Agricola sent a band of soldiers to arrest St. Blaise, and bring him bound before his tribunal. In allusion to this incident, St. Blaise, in Christian art, is often represented as a hermit surrounded by wild beasts bearing him company, and sitting before a cavern in deep meditation.—*Les Petits Bollandistes*, vol. ii. p. 227.

St. Blandina, being exposed to wild beasts, was not injured by them (A.D. 177). St. Blandina was one of the martyrs of Lyons, towards the close of the second century. She was first stripped and tied to a post in the amphitheatre, her arms being extended in the form of a cross. Then hungry wild beasts were let loose upon her. She lifted up her eyes in prayer that her courage might not fail, but that she might be an example to others. It seemed like another Saviour crucified afresh, and the Christians who witnessed her heroism felt sure that those who suffered with Christ would hereafter reign with Him. The hungry beasts, lashing their tails, rushed into the arena with a roar; and, going straight to the victim, stopped short, bowed their heads, wagged their tails, and seemed more like lambs than wild beasts. It is no use. She is untied, and taken back to prison, reserved for new combats, "afin que, victorieuse de l'ennemi dans les attaques nombreuses qu'il lui livrait, elle rendît certaine la condemnation du dragon infernal."—P. André Gouilloud, *St. Pothin et ses Compagnons, Martyrs.*

A bear watched over the sheep of St. Eutychus, abbot of Florent (A.D. 540–548). St. Eutychus was a monk of Norcia, who lived the life of a hermit in a cave, which he never quitted except to preach and minister to the people. On the death of St. Spes, founder of the monastery of Castoria, Eutychus became his successor. Whenever he was absent, he left St. Florent in charge of the monastery, and if St. Florent was absent at the same time, a bear came from the neighbouring forest, lay down at the gate, and keep guard over the four sheep which constituted the whole flock of the monastery. Florent had perfect confidence in his bear-shepherd, and told him to fold the sheep at sunset. This bear used to come regularly to look after the sheep at their mid-day meal, and at three in the afternoon. Four monks, out of jealousy, killed the bear, but, being struck with leprosy, died. —Gregory the Great, *Dialogues*, bk. iii. ch. 15.

St. Firmatus reproves a wild boar for spoiling his garden (A.D. 1103). One day his clerk told St. Firmatus that a wild boar had broken into his garden and destroyed the vegetables. The saint went up to the savage beast, and taking it by the ear, led it into his cell, where it passed the night docile as a lamb. Next day he set the beast at liberty, but told it never again to trespass in his garden, or he should be obliged to punish it most severely. (See Antony, p. 361.)—Bollandus, *Acta Sanctorum*, Feb. 28.

St. Francis d'Assisi and the swallows (A.D. 1182–1226). One day, as St. Francis d'Assisi was preaching at Alviano, the twittering of the swallows was a considerable annoyance. So, breaking off suddenly, he said to the birds, "My sisters, the swallows, please keep peace while I am preaching." It need scarcely be added that they listened to his entreaty, and disturbed him no more. (See p. 361.)—Chavin de Malan, *Life of St. Francis d'Assisi.*

A swarm of wasps submissive to St. Friard (A.D. 511–557). St. Friard was a farm labourer, and one harvest-time, as he with his fellow-labourers were getting in the corn, a swarm of wasps proved very troublesome. Said his companions in mockery to him, "Friard, you are always making the cross on your eyes, ears, and mouth; why don't you drive away these devils with the sign of the cross?" Friard, thinking that this would be a good opportunity of directing his fellow-workmen to the power of God, and turning their hearts, knelt down in the field, and prayed in silence that God would remove the plague of wasps. Then rising to his feet, he said to his companions, "Work on now; these insects will no more trouble you." The wasps flew away. St. Friard followed them, saying, *Ajutorium nostrum in nomine Deum* ("Our help is in the name of God"), and, after chasing them afar off, they entered a hole in the earth, and were no more seen. This miracle made such an impression on the farm labourers that they nevermore laughed at him, but regarded him with the utmost reverence. (See Leufredus, p. 364.)—St. Gregory of Tours, *Lives of the Fathers.*

A bear brings wood to replenish the fire of St. Gall (A.D. 646). Gall was born in Ireland, of noble parents, and brought up in the monastery of Bangor. He with two companions went to a desert place near the river Stemaha, and while the two companions slept, St. Gall spent the time in prayer. Presently came a bear from the mountain, and carefully gathered up the crumbs left at the evening meal of the three recluses. St. Gall said to the beast, "I beg of you, in the name of Christ, to put a few logs of wood upon our fire." This the bear did, and St. Gall gave it a loaf of bread from his pouch. "Now go back to the mountain," said St. Gall, "and be sure to hurt neither man nor beast;" and the bear did as it was told.—Mgr. Guérin (chamberlain of Leo XIII.), *Vies des Saints*, vol. xii. p. 416 (1880).

St. Gentius makes a wolf, which had eaten one of his oxen, assist in ploughing (twelfth century). A wolf, having eaten one of the oxen employed by St. Gentius in ploughing his land, was made to take the place of the missing ox, and was yoked with the surviving beast to the plough. Hence, in Christian art, this saint is represented as ploughing with an ox and a wolf. (See AREY, p. 361.)—*Propre d'Avignon.*

St. Genulph reproves a fox for attempting to steal a hen (third century). St. Genulph retired to Berri, and took up his residence in a haunted cell; but he sprinkled it with holy water, and was never troubled by evil spirits. He kept a large yard of poultry, but the wild beasts never touched them, for God had made a covenant with them, so that they were at peace with His holy servant. One day a fox came into his poultry-yard, and was about to carry off a hen, but St. Genulph, aroused by the cackling, went out, and seeing the fox, said, "Reynard, that hen is not thine, and God hath commanded, saying, Thou shalt not steal." No sooner did the fox hear these words, than he dropped the hen and ran off.—Bollandus, *Acta Sanctorum*, vol. ii. p. 83.

Probably the fox would have done the same if the greatest sinner in the neighbourhood had cried, "Halloo!"

Wild beasts refuse to touch the dead body of St. Gregory of Spoleto (A.D. 303). Flaccus was appointed by Maximian to root out the Christian religion from Spoleto, and hearing that Gregory refused to worship Jupiter, Minerva, and Æsculapius, commanded him to be brought to his tribunal. "Will you sacrifice to the gods of Rome, I ask?" "No," said St. Gregory. "The gods of Rome are only devils." Flaccus, on hearing these words, commanded his minions to bring forth the "peignes de fer, et frappez-en ses genoux de toutes vos forces." "You serve devils, Flaccus, or you would tremble to provoke the wrath of God." "I serve devils, wretch?" roared Flaccus. "Bring hither the burning lamps, and burn his sides." "When my body," said Gregory, "is one vast wound, then Christ is my Physician, Flaccus, and will heal my wounds." "Tircan," cried Flaccus like a fury, "take this fellow, and fling him into the amphitheatre." "Blessed be the name of the Lord, who will take me this day to paradise!" said the saint. A voice from heaven answered, "Gregory, a crown awaits you. Your name is written in the Lamb's book of life." While the angel was speaking, Aquilinius struck off the martyr's head, and the body was thrown to the wild beasts; but instead of touching it, they adored it, and at night a Christian woman, named Abondantia, bought it for thirty pieces of silver, and buried it near the stone bridge of the Sanguinaire. — *Les Petits Bollandistes*, vol. xiv. p. 438.

St. Humbert makes a bear take the place of an ass which it had devoured (A.D. 682). While St. Humbert was on his voyage to Rome, a bear devoured the ass employed to carry the baggage; whereupon St. Humbert commanded the bear to carry his baggage in the ass's place. In Christian art St. Humbert is sometimes represented attended by a stag and a bear.—*Les Petits Bollandistes*, vol. iii. p. 641.

The stag is one pursued by hunters, which took refuge in St. Humbert's oratory, and was by him protected from its pursuers. (See AREY, p. 361; AVENTINE, p. 358.)

Wild beasts respect the bones of the martyred Ignatius (Sept. 20, A.D. 107). St. Ignatius of Antioch suffered martyrdom under the emperor Trajan, who, in the ninth year of his reign, visited Antioch, and made it his first business to look after the religious concerns of that important city. He soon found that the Christians had a strong footing there, and he resolved to stamp out the dangerous heresy. Ignatius, as the ringleader, was brought before him, and Trajan said to him, "Who are you, you devil, who dare to set yourself up against my authority?" Ignatius replied, "I am no devil, Trajan, but carry God in my heart." "And do not we also care for the gods? Who else assist us in our battles?" "The gods you worship, Trajan, are no gods. There is but one God, the Creator, and Jesus Christ is His only Son." "Do you mean Christ the malefactor, put to death by the governor Pilate?" asked the emperor. "Yes," replied Ignatius. "Though dead He liveth, and those who believe in Him carry Him in their hearts." "The man is a fool," said Trajan, "to talk of carrying a malefactor put to death in his heart. Take him to the amphitheatre, and cast him to the wild beasts." When taken to the arena he said to the spectators, "Think not, Romans, I am here for any misdeeds. No, I am here only because I love God, and Jesus Christ whom He sent for our salvation." The beasts, being turned out, soon despatched the old man; but though they ate his flesh, they broke no bone. As the archbishop of Vienne says, "They tore his flesh and fed on it in their rage, but touched not a single bone."—Ado (archbishop of Vienne), *Martyrology*.

St. James of Tarentaise makes a bear obey him (fifth century). While the monks of St. James were felling trees for the construction of a church, a bear killed one of the oxen employed in drawing the timber. The monks fled in terror, and told St. James; whereupon the man of God, going to the bear, said, "I, James, the servant of Jesus Christ, command thee, thou cruel beast, to bow thy neck to the yoke in place of the ox which thou hast slain." So said, so done. The bear was harnessed, and the work went on as before. (See HUMBERT, p. 363.)—Gui of Burgundy (afterwards pope Calixtus II.), *Life of St. James of the Tarentaise*.

St. Januarius and his companions unharmed by wild beasts. Timotheus, governor of Benevento, commanded St. Januarius and his companions to be cast into the amphitheatre, and the wild bears to be let out upon them; but the bears, forgetting their savageness, were gentle as lambs, and lay down lovingly at the saints' feet.—Edward Kinesman, *Lives of the Saints*, pp. 742–744. ("The life of St. Januarius as it is gathered out of the catalogue of saints and the Roman breviary.")

St. Leufredus and the flies (A.D. 738). One day, returning from the law-courts, where he had gone to demand certain lands which pertained by inheritance to his monastery, St. Leufredus stopped at a house on the way to pass the night. The weather was very hot, and the saint found the flies so troublesome that he could get no sleep; but the moment he bent his head on his hands in prayer, all the flies flew away; and, the chamberlain of Leo XIII. adds, "depuis, l'on n'en a pas vu une seule en cette maison." (See FRIARD, p. 362.)—Mgr. Guérin, *Vies des Saints*, vol. vii. p. 189 (7th edit. 1880).

It looks as if this house was still standing, but Leufredus died about eleven hundred years ago. Certainly this saint had the gift of cursing. He cursed a woman who called him "bald-pate," and she and all her posterity for ever were without hair on the back of the head. He cursed a thief who called him a slanderer, and the thief and all his posterity were without teeth from that day forth. He cursed some fields which some peasants were working in on a Sunday, and the land was ever after quite sterile. And now the flies felt the force of his terrible curse, and could nevermore enter the forbidden house.

A sea-cow, in submission to St. Maidoc, is yoked to a plough (A.D. 632). St. Maidoc, wanting to plough his fields, and having neither ox, horse, nor ass to help him, commanded a sea-cow to come out of the ocean, and yoke herself to his plough. This she did in obedience to his command, and his fields were ploughed. After this work was done, the sea-monster carried the saint on her back from Ferne to St. David's, in Wales, and back again. —Baring-Gould, *Lives of the Saints*, Jan., p. 31.

A wolf, having killed St. Malo's ass, is made to take its place (A.D. 630). St. Malo settled down near Saintes, where he built a monastery, and the neighbours made him a present of an ass, to carry wood and render other services. One day a wolf fell upon the ass and devoured it; whereupon St. Malo said to the wolf, "Since you have killed my ass, you must serve me instead." The wolf made no objection, and faithfully performed all the offices of the ass, and served the saint for many years. (See preceding column, ST. JAMES.)—*Les Petits Bollandistes*, vol. xiii. p. 416.

Dogs keep watch and ward over the dead bodies of Maximus and Olympias (A.D. 251). The emperor Decius, having made himself master of several of the provinces of Persia, determined to stamp out the Christian plague-spot therein. He laid his hands on Maximus and Olympias, men of high birth and great repute, and commanded them to be scourged till they renounced the new faith. This had no effect on them; and the emperor next resolved to confiscate all their goods. "Where is your wealth kept?" demanded the tyrant. "In our hearts, Decius," they replied. "Search, and you will find there the love of God." "Know you not, insolents," said the emperor, "that I have but to speak the word, and your lives are at my disposal?" "Do what you like, Decius," said the martyrs—"break us, bruise us, hack us, cut us, roast us, if you choose; but you shall not shake our faith, or separate us from the love of God our Saviour." Decius ordered them to be beaten with the flagra (see Index), and this was done till the scourgers fainted with fatigue. They were then set on the chevalet (see Index), then laid on iron beds beneath which fires were lighted. All devices being unavailing, Vitellius Anisius broke their heads with a crowbar, and flung their dead bodies into the fields. Here they were exposed for five days without being touched by bird or beast—for dogs kept watch and ward over them—till two noble Christians buried them honourably in their private garden.—*Acta Sanctorum Orientalium*.

St. Pantaleon, exposed to wild beasts, is

unharmed by them (A.D. 303). Maximian, greatly enraged against Pantaleon, not only for being a Christian, but more still for despising his threats, commanded that a number of wild beasts of all sorts should be collected together; then, showing them to Pantaleon, said to him, "Do you see these savage animals? I have commanded them to be brought hither. Having pity on your youth, I give you this warning; but be assured, if you remain obstinate, you shall be thrown into the midst of them, and where is the god who can deliver you?" Pantaleon made answer, "That God who quenched the fire you kindled upon me, that God who made innocuous the molten lead you poured upon me, that God who delivered me from the sea, will deliver me from the fury of these beasts, and in Him will I put my trust." The martyr was, therefore, cast to the wild beasts, and all the city went to behold the spectacle. Firm stood the saint, and every line in his face showed resolution. Certainly there was no distrust, no sign of fear. "Loose the beasts," said the emperor; and every one expected to see Pantaleon torn to pieces in a moment. But what says the psalmist? "Because thou hast made the Lord thy refuge, no evil shall befall thee; thou shalt tread upon the lion and the adder; the young lion and the dragon shalt thou trample under thy feet." The beasts came up with a rush, stood stock-still before him, sniffed at him, then lay down peacefully at his feet. There lay they, nor would one of them stir, till the martyr laid his hands upon them and blessed them. The whole theatre was amazed. "The Lord, He is God! the Lord, He is God!" rang like thunder through the crowded benches. But the cry pierced the emperor like a sword; his anger was increased tenfold, and it was now a duel of strength between the emperor of Rome and a young doctor of Nicomedia.—*Acta Sanctorum* (Bollandists), July 27.

St. Regulus makes a covenant with the frogs of Senlis (A.D. 130). St. Regulus, bishop of Arles and Senlis, found the croaking of the frogs greatly interrupted his preaching, and he made a covenant with them, if they would croak only one at a time, he would not drive them out. This covenant is represented in Christian art, and the chapel of St. Regulus at Rully is decorated with frogs in allusion thereto. (See Thecla, p. 366.)—L'abbé Corblet, *Hagiographie du Diocèse d'Amiens.*

Two savage dogs, set on St. Ronan, tamed by the sign of the cross (sixth century). A woman, named Keban, accused St. Ronan to Grallo, king of Quimper, of being a vampire, and Grallo, horrified at such a monster, said he would soon prove if the charge was true. "I have two dogs," he said, "extremely savage. Bring the man hither, and if he is guilty, these dogs will tear him to pieces; if not, God will protect His own." St. Ronan was produced, and the dogs let loose. As they rushed towards him, the saint raised his right hand into the air, made the sign of the cross, and said to the dogs, "Stop, in the name of the Lord!" Immediately they stopped, fawned on the saint, and licked his hands. Grallo at once released his prisoner, and declared him to be a servant of the living God; but the woman Keban was denounced as a vile calumniator, and was burnt to death in the public market-place.—Dom Lobineau, *British Saints.*

St. Sacerdos delivers Argentat from all birds of prey (A.D. 720). St. Sacerdos, bishop of Limoges, resigned his see, with intent of laying his bones in Calviac, the village of his birth. On reaching Argentat he was taken with his last illness, and one day expressed a wish for some eggs. Only one could be found in all the neighbourhood, because the hawks, kites, and other birds of prey were so numerous it was impossible to keep fowls. When told of this, the dying bishop said he would leave behind a benediction not to be forgotten, and pronounced these words, "Let no bird of prey henceforth touch the poultry of Argentat and its neighbourhood." All the historians of his life add this: "Cet arret a été inviolable jusqu'a ce jour."—Pergot, *Life of St. Sacerdos, Bishop of Limoges.*

In Christian art St. Sacerdos is represented banishing the kites, hawks, and other birds of prey from Argentat.

St. Samson drives off a flock of wild geese which troubled the monks of St. Iltut's monastery (A.D. 480–565). The monks of St. Iltut's monastery in Brittany were much disturbed by the noise of wild geese in the adjoining meadows of Dol. Their cries interfered with the quietude of the place, and spoiled the singing, so Samson purged the meadows of these noisy birds, and they never afterwards returned. — Dom Lobineau, *Lives of the Saints of Brittany.*

A wolf, having killed the ass of St. Sanctes of Urbino, takes its place (A.D. 1390). St. Sanctes, when he went to the forest to fetch wood, used to take an ass with him to carry it home. One day he forgot to drive it home, and when next morning he went in search of it, he saw the ass lying dead, and a wolf about to devour it. St. Sanctes said to the wolf, "As you have robbed me of my beast of burden, you must take its place." To hear was to obey; and for many years the wolf served the saint obediently and faithfully. (See AREY, p. 361.)—*Annales Franciscaines*, and also *Palmier Séraphique.*

Wild beasts obedient to St. Solangia (A.D. 880). St. Solangia was a shepherdess in Villemont. Her biographer says that by the mere act of volition she warded off both birds and beasts which devour or injure the fruits of the earth; and if any wild beast fell on a sheep or lamb, she had no need of dog or crook, but only to apply to her Divine Spouse to make the creature drop its prey, or bring it back so gently that no injury was inflicted.—Raynal, *History of Berry*, vol. i. p. 313.

St. Thecla was not harmed by the wild beasts turned out upon her. St. Thecla, having been first cast into a bonfire without receiving the slightest injury, was next exposed in the amphitheatre to the wild beasts. When the first lioness was let out, instead of tearing her to pieces, it crouched quietly at her feet without attempting to harm her. Other wild beasts, such as lions, bears, and wild bulls, followed the same example, as if they had made a league to do her no harm. St. Ambrose says, "The people were the savage beasts, and the wild animals, whose nature it was to be fierce, were humane. The people hungered and thirsted for blood, but the half-starved beasts could not be provoked to shed innocent blood." The judge, seeing that the wild beasts had made a covenant with the damsel, ordered her to be taken from the arena, and flung into the city sewer, where were serpents and other reptiles; but immediately St. Thecla fell into the ditch, fire came down from heaven to consume the reptiles and purify the foul air. So the holy virgin was delivered from this death also, as she had been delivered from the fire and the wild beasts; and she died many years afterwards, in the odour of sanctity, peacefully in her own bed.—Ado (archbishop of Vienne), *Martyrology.*

In the prayers said in the commendation of souls, occurs this sentence: "O Lord, deliver this soul as Thou didst deliver St. Thecla from the three most cruel torments." So that there cannot be a doubt that the narrative given by Ado, and referred to by St. Ambrose, is accepted as historically true.

St. Thecla of Moriana and the sparrows (sixth century). The oaks round the hermitage of St. Thecla of Moriana were so thickly crowded with sparrows, that their incessant clack disturbed the meditations of the saint; besides, they would fly round her in flocks, lighting upon her as she knelt in prayer, peeping, wrangling, and hopping about, distracting her contemplation. St. Thecla prayed God to deliver her from this annoyance, and forthwith they all left the neighbourhood. "Et, de fait, aujourd'hui encore, les moineaux ne vont pas à Sainte Thècle, bien que les environs de séminaire et toute la vallée en fourmillent." (See below, ULPHA.)—L'abbé Truchet, *Hagiologique du Diocèse de Maurienne.*

Two wolves act as dragomans to St. Trivier (sixth century). Theodebert, king of Austrasia, took Radignese and Salsufur, two princes, prisoners; and their calamity moved St. Trivier to pity them, so that he paid their ransom and set them free. St. Trivier then asked them if they wished to return to their own country, and they promised to give him a third of their patrimony if he enabled them to do so. The journey from Burgundy to the banks of the Saone was long and difficult, but the saint procured suitable raiment and food, and the three set out on foot. Having come to a thick forest, they lost their way, and St. Trivier prayed that God would vouchsafe to direct them aright. Whereupon two wolves made their appearance. The travellers were greatly alarmed at first, but soon discovered that the beasts meant them no harm, inasmuch as they wagged their tails, and began to fawn on them. Being reassured by these marks of lovingkindness, the wolves walked on, and the travellers, following, arrived safely at Lyons; then they pursued their journey to Dombes, the home of the two princes. The princes now offered to St. Trivier the promised third of their patrimony; but the saint would only accept from them a small hermit's cell, and a plot of ground for a garden. In this cell he lived all the rest of his life.—*Les Petits Bollandistes* (1880), vol. i. p. 410, etc.

St. Ulpha silences the frogs of the Paraclet (eighth century). St. Ulpha lived in a hermitage situate in the midst of a marsh called the Paraclet; one hot night in summer the frogs in this marsh kept such incessant croaking, that Ulpha could not sleep till towards midnight. When Domicus called for her she was sound asleep, and he, supposing she had already gone to the cathedral, hastened on, fearing he was late. When he reached the cathedral, he discovered that Ulpha was not there. This day she was absent from the early morning service, and prayed that Christ would impose silence on the frogs. "All the biographies of the saint agree that ever after the frogs were mute, and even to the present day no frog in the whole valley of the Paraclet is ever heard to croak." (See ALDEBRAND, p. 361.)—L'abbé Corblet, *Hagiographie du Diocèse d'Amiens.*

St. Vaast makes a savage bear obey him (A.D. 450). While St. Vaast was at Arras, he grieved to see every trace of the Christian religion had entirely vanished from the neighbourhood. The people showed him a ruin beyond the gates which was once a Christian church, but this church was now the haunt of satyrs and wild beasts. While he stood mourning over the ruin and desolation, a savage bear emerged from the thick underwood. St. Vaast conjured the animal, in the name of Jesus Christ, to leave the holy place and to retreat without delay beyond the river Scarpe. The bear obeyed, and was never after seen. On further search, St. Vaast found a broken altar of the Virgin. There built he a new church, and Mary the mother of God vouchsafed to become the patron of the diocese of Arras and Cambrai.—L'abbé Van Drival, *Trésor Sacré de la Cathédrale d'Arras.*

*** The more general tradition is that St. Vaast ordered the bear to follow him, and that it became his constant companion and faithful friend. Hence in works of art St. Vaast is represented with a bear following him, like a faithful dog.

Insect pests respect the garden of St. Valery (A.D. 619). St. Colomba was surprised to see the cabbages and other vegetables of St. Valery wholly uninjured by insect pests which commit such ravages in general, especially in kitchen gardens. He attributed it to the humility, obedience, and devotion of the saint. Valery repudiated this praise, and ascribed it to the merits of his brotherhood. Colomba admired the modesty of St. Valery, but knew that his conjecture was right, and that God had taken care of His servant's garden, because that servant had devoted his time to the service of God.—*The Saints of Franche Comté* (Besançon, 1854).

St. Wereburga of Chester makes geese submissive (seventh century). St. Wereburga was the daughter of Wulfer, king of Mercia, and took the veil at Ely. She died at Trentham, and was burned at Hambury, but the body, in A.D. 835, was transported to Chester. Her attribute is a flock of geese, in allusion to the following legend. A flock of wild geese, which had committed great devastation in the neighbourhood, followed her to the perron of her mansion, when she turned round and bade them cease from their devastations and leave the country. This they did, and Chester was freed from further ravages.—Mgr. Guérin, *Vies des Saints.* (Alban Butler gives a long life of this saint, in Feb. 3; but, as usual, omits the legend.)

Beaten with Many Stripes.

LUKE xii. 47. That servant which knew his lord's will, and prepared not himself, neither did according to his will, shall be beaten with many stripes.

Christ, armed with a whip, appears to St. Angela of Brescia (A.D. 1474–1540). When St. Angela was only twenty-two years of age, her heart was bent on establishing free schools for the education of girls, and on raising "l'étendard de la virginité si lâchement abandodé et trahi par Luther." A vision then appeared to her of virgins and angels ascending to heaven by a ladder, like that seen by Jacob. In 1535 (that is, forty-nine years afterwards) Christ appeared to her, while she was in prayer. His face was angry, His manner menacing, and He bore a whip in His hand, "prêt à la frapper." He asked, in manifest displeasure, how it was she had neglected the work He had set her to do for nearly fifty years. She craved pardon, and instantly calling together her companions, set about the work in good earnest. A society was organized, and called at first "Les Compagnes d'Angèle," its object being the gratuitous instruction of the young. The next question was the selection of a lady superior, and then the ghost of St. Ursula appeared to her, brilliant in glory, but frowning in anger. Ursula commanded Angela to take on herself the duties of lady superior, and not to arrogate to herself the name of founder by calling the society "Les Compagnes d'Angèle," but give to these companions the name of "Ursulines." So the name was changed, and great success followed; but Angela died in 1540, soon after the society was organized.—*Life of St. Angela of Brescia* (Montpellier, 1804).

St. Jerome beaten with many stripes for his love of "Cicero." St. Jerome, writing to Eustochium, says, "I, a wretched sinner, took pains in reading Tully's works, and his eloquence was a delight to me; but the prophets displeased me by their low and disordered style. About the middle of Lent, I was taken up and brought to the judgment-seat of God. Jesus Christ asked me of my quality, and I answered boldly, 'I am a Christian.' Then said Jesus, 'Nay, Jerome, thou seemest to Me to be a Ciceronian; for where thy treasure is, there is thy heart also.' At these words I was struck dumb, and the judge ordered me to be beaten with many stripes. 'Pardon me, O Lord; pardon me,' I cried, with many sighs and tears; nevertheless, my scourging went on. Many angels fell on their knees before the throne, imploring mercy, and pleading my youth. So at length Jesus ordered the scourgers to leave off, on my promise of amendment. Let none think this a vision or a dream!! The angels know it was no dream. Christ Himself is my witness it was no dream; yea, my whole body still bears the marks of that terrible flagellation." In his prologue to the Epistle of Paul to the Galatians, St. Jerome says, "It is now fifteen years since I took any book of secular learning in my hand." And, writing to pope Damasus, he reproves ecclesiastics for leaving Holy Writ for fables and other heathenish books. Such a deep impression was made on his memory by that celestial scourging.—*Letter beginning "Audi filia."*

Beauty of Holiness.

1 CHRON. xvi. 29. The beauty of holiness.
PSALM cxlix. 4. The Lord will beautify the meek with salvation.

St. Vincent Ferrier beautifies a very plain woman (A.D. 1357–1419). One day in Valentia, as St. Vincent Ferrier was passing down one of the principal streets, he heard a voice, tremulous with anger, uttering profane imprecations. He immediately entered, and the master of the house, evidently in a towering passion, passed him. He found the lady of the house no less excited than her husband, and still uttering blasphemies. St. Vincent soothed her passion, and asked the reason of such imprecations. The lady replied, still sobbing, "Father, this is not the first time by many that my husband has used me thus. Every day in the week he beats me, pulls my hair out, and abuses me, merely because I am plain. It is not life, my father, but a daily death, a damnation on earth. My home is a hell." "My daughter," said the man of God, "moderate your speech. It is not right to talk thus; and if, as you say, want of beauty is your only fault, we can soon remedy that." Then, raising his right hand to the woman's face, he added, "There, my daughter, you are no longer without beauty, but remember there is no beauty like that of holiness. And the Lord will beautify the meek with salvation." This woman was henceforth the belle of Valentia; insomuch that when any one saw a very plain woman, it was customary to say, "She wants the hand of St. Vincent;" and this became a proverb.—*Les Petits Bollandistes*, vol. iv. p. 239.

Bee-mouthed.

CANT. iv. 11. Thy lips drop as honeycomb. Honey and milk are under thy tongue.
PROV. xxiv. 13, 14. My son, eat thou honey, because it is sweet. . . . So shall the knowledge of wisdom be unto thy soul.

A flight of bees light on Plato while in his cradle. We are told that a flight of bees one day settled on the lips of Plato, the Greek philosopher, as he was sleeping in his cradle, to signify the eloquent and honeyed words which would drop from his mouth, and the knowledge of wisdom which would be unto his soul.

A swarm of bees lighted on Sophoclês in his cradle. Sophoclês, the Greek tragic poet, was called "The Attic Bee," from the great sweetness of his style. Sometimes the story told of Plato is told of him also, viz. that a swarm of bees lighted on his lips while he was sleeping in his cradle, a presage that words like honey would drop from him.

A swarm of bees flighted on St. Ambrose in his cradle. One day, while the infant Ambrose was in his cradle, there came upon him a swarm of bees, some of which entered the child's mouth. The nurse wanted to chase them off, but the father forbade her doing so. After a little time the bees took wing, and left the chamber, having done the little sleeper no injury whatever; whereupon the father said, "God shows us by this sign that this infant will be possessed of most admired eloquence hereafter."—Paulinus (deacon of St. Ambrose), *Life of St. Ambrose* (written at the request of St. Augustine). Alban Butler admits this anecdote in his *Lives of the Saints*, April 4.

A swarm of bees lighted on St. Isidore's mouth in infancy (A.D. 639). While St. Isidore was in swaddling-clothes, his nurse left him one day sleeping in the garden, when a swarm of bees lighted on him. Some entered his mouth and deposited their honey there. A presage this that his lips would drop eloquence as the honeycomb drops honey. In Christian art bees are his attribute.—*Acta Sanctorum* (Bollandists), April 4.

Bells and Clocks.

Eph. ii. 2. - The prince of the power of the air.

The bishop of Chalons christens a peal of bells. The bishop of Chalons not long ago christened a peal of bells, and said in his sermon, "The bells, placed like sentinels on the towers, watch over us, and turn away from us the temptations of the enemy of our salvation, as well as storms and tempests. They speak and pray for us in our troubles; they inform heaven of the necessity of earth." If this is anything more than "poetic fancy," there is more virtue in the clapper of a bell than in the tongue of the prelate.—*Quarterly Review* (Church Bells).

The bishop of Malta orders the bells to be rung in a tempest. In 1152, the bishop of Malta ordered all the church bells of the island to be rung for an hour, to frighten the powers of the air, and allay a heavy gale.—*Quarterly Review* (Church Bells).

In 1856, while I was living in Paris, I heard some of the church bells ringing during a thunderstorm. On inquiring of the head ringer the cause, he told me it was to exorcise the air, for every one knew that evil spirits were the cause of tempests. The wife of this man, a well-educated woman, was my *bonne*, and I had a long talk with her on the subject.

At the death of any one the parish tenor bell first "tells" the parish of the decease by tolling three times three for a man, and three times two for a woman (children are sometimes ranked with men and women, and sometimes three times one is told for a child). This is to bespeak the prayers of the parish on behalf of the dead. The bell is then "raised," and "told" to frighten away the evil spirits, that the soul may not be obstructed in its passage to heaven.

"Le pontifical Romain déclare que le bruit des cloches chasse les démons qui sont dans l'air, et qui font leurs efforts pour empêcher les fidèles de prier et de chanter les louanges de Dieu. C'est un acte de piété d'aider à la sonner."—*Mémorial de Chronologie*, etc. (1829), vol. i. p. 132.

The bells of Avignonet ring spontaneously a whole day (A.D. 1283). The "Protestants" or "Huguenots" of the thirteenth century in France were called Albigenses. They resisted the authority of the popes and the discipline of the Church of Rome. Peter of Castelnau, the papal legate, was sent to extirpate "the heretics" in the dominions of count Raymond VI. of Toulouse, and this led to the massacre of between twenty and forty thousand persons. Arnold, abbot of Citeaux, said to his satellites, "Kill all, whether Catholics or heretics, never mind; God will know His own." After hundreds of thousands had been slain on both sides, peace was concluded in 1229, but the "heretics" were put under the watchful eyes of the Inquisition. In May, 1242, the bailiff of Raymond VII. organized a band of a hundred men to murder the eleven inquisitors of Avignonet, and the persecution burst out afresh, the parish being laid under an interdict. This went on till 1283, when Alexander IV. removed the ban. The moment the pope did so, all the bells of the church of Avignonet set out ringing of their own accord, and continued pealing all night and all day, although they had not been heard to ring for forty years. This "fact" was attested by a declaration of the inhabitants of Avignonet, made in 1293. So *certain* is it, that mention is made thereof in a bull by Paul III., A.D. 1537, and in an *acte notarie*, Jan. 29, 1676.—L'abbé Carrière, *History of the Martyrs of Avignonet.*

The bull of Paul III. is carefully preserved in the parish church of Avignonet, and shown to any one who wishes to see it. We are also told that the church doors, which had been locked, barred, bolted, and nailed up for forty years, "s'ouvrirent d'elles mêmes, malgré les nombreuses serrures de fer dont elles étaient armées."

The bells of Madrid ring spontaneously when the body of St. Isidore is removed from the churchyard into the church. St. Isidore was only a day labourer, and when he died, he was buried in the churchyard. Forty years afterwards, the body was removed with great pageantry into Madrid cathedral. The moment his grave was opened, all the bells of the city began to ring of their own accord, and went on ringing till the ceremony was over.—*Life of St. Isidore*, by Ribadeneira and by D. A. Villegas, *Extravagants.*

The spontaneous ringing of bells may be accounted for thus: In some convents and churches the monks rang the bells, and in these cases a hut was attached to the tower, into which the bell-ropes were carried, or in some cases, "une corde attachée à une autre qui met en mouvement la cloche des offices." Persons hearing the bells, and seeing no ringers in the belfry, thought the bells rang spontaneously. It was a conclusion very natural in those who looked on miracles as a natural gift of the Church.

Bells of Fano refused to ring, but at Fossombrone rang spontaneously (twelfth century). St. Aldebrand gave a peal of bells to Fossombrone cathedral, which, after his death, were stolen by the people of Fano, who had made war on those of Fossombrone, and conquered them. St. Aldebrand said, "I gave these bells for the service of my own people, and not for the use of their enemies," and accordingly commanded them to be mute. The people of Fano, stupefied by this miracle, restored the peal to Fossombrone cathedral, and immediately they reached the pont du Métaure, near Fossombrone, all the bells began ringing of their own accord. (See below, STOLEN BELLS, etc.)—*Acta Sanctorum* (Bollandists), May i. p. 263.

The bells of Lanslevillard ring of their own accord (eleventh century). St. Landry, curé of Lanslevillard, was drowned in the Arc by the men who had undertaken to conduct him to Ecot. Christ Himself took in hand to announce this murder to the people. All of a sudden the church bells began to ring as if for some great Church festival. The population ran to church to see what was going on. No one was in the clock tower, but still the bells kept ringing. The church was crowded to see what would be next, and the great processional cross began of itself to move towards the door. The parish priest instantly followed, and the people fell into line. The cross led the way to the river, but no one carried it or so much as touched it. It stopped over a cavern hollowed in the rock. The priest entered, and the first thing he saw was the body of St. Landry. It was raised on a bier, carried to the church in procession, and buried in the sacristy, where it remained till 1765, when it was removed to the altar.—L'abbé Truchet, *Histoire Hagiologique du Diocèse de Maurienne.*

Stolen bells refuse to ring. When Charles Martel was mayor of the palace, he went to visit St. Rigobert, archbishop of Reims; but the primate refused to see him, because he was a usurper. So Charles Martel turned him out of his see, and gave it to Milo. St. Rigobert went to Gascony, and when he came to the church there, the bells refused to ring. The vicar, greatly perplexed, asked Rigobert if he could suggest the reason, and the saint replied, "The reason is not far to seek. These bells were stolen from St. Peter's at Reims." In proof of this assertion, when Rigobert laid his finger on the ropes, the bells sounded readily; so they were restored, and Rigobert was also reinstated. (See BELLS OF FANO.)—Bollandus, *Acta Sanctorum*, vol. i. Jan. 4.

St. Maidoc's bell transported through the air (A.D. 632). While St. Maidoc was in Ferns he wanted his bell which he had left in Wales. However, he called it to come to him, and, obedient to his call, it came without a moment's delay.—Baring-Gould, *Lives of the Saints*, Jan. 31.

Baring-Gould, with no great consistency, says the prodigies ascribed to St. Maidoc "are quite incredible;" but why should one prodigy be more incredible than another?

St. Fursy's clock transported through the air (A.D. 650). St. Fursy had a clock which an angel brought him from heaven. One day the monks of Lismore, in Ireland, observed a clock floating in the air, and asked St. Cuan, their abbot, what the prodigy meant. St. Cuan replied, "Oh, it is St. Fursy's clock, come from Bury St. Edmund's, in Suffolk. As St. Fursy cannot come himself to Lismore, he has sent his clock to represent him."—L'abbé Corblet, *Hagiography of the Diocese of Amiens*, vol. ii. p. 260.

This clock was shown in the abbey till 1468.

In the plague of Milan the bells of a Dominican convent ring spontaneously (A.D. 1630). Towards the end of September the plague began to abate. Now, attached to the Dominican convent in Milan was a church dedicated to the Virgin, and on the night of the 22nd, the monks being collected waiting for matins, the bells of the church began suddenly to ring of their own accord, "wholly without touch of mortal hand." Some were alarmed, some awe-struck, and presently a voice, far too awful to be human, was heard to say, "Mother, I will take pity upon My people." The Virgin had sought her Son and obtained from Him the remission of the plague. Next morning the oil which fed the lamp before the Virgin's image was found to possess a miraculous healing virtue, and was distributed drop by drop to high and low who crowded the church to receive it. The number of deaths continued to diminish, and by the close of the year the plague had ceased.—Ripamonte, *De Peste Mediolani.*

Birds telling the Matter.

ECCLES. x. 20. A bird of the air shall carry the voice, and that which hath wings shall tell the matter.

Lord Byron avails himself of this figure in the following couplet:—

I think I hear a little bird who sings
The people by-and-by will be the stronger.
Don Juan, viii. 50.

A little bird announces to the pope the murder of St. Kenhelm. When St. Kenhelm was murdered by order of his sister Kiventhryth, at the very same hour a white dove flew to the high altar of St. Peter's, Rome, and deposited there a letter containing a full account of the murder. The pope sent to investigate the matter, and a chapel was built over the murdered body, called "St. Kenhelm's Chapel" even to this day.—*Shropshire.*

Two ravens reveal the murderers of St. Meinrad (A.D. 797–861). St. Meinrad retired to Mount Etzel, where he built a cabin of branches, and lived a hermit's life. He brought up two ravens, and these birds were his constant companions. On Jan. 21, A.D. 861, two villains, named Peter and Richard, determined to murder the recluse, expecting to find hid treasures in his hut. Knocking at the door, St. Meinrad bade them enter, and said to them, "Friends, I know your mission. When you have slain me, place these two candles, one at my head and one at my feet, and make haste to escape." Unmoved by these words, the two villains knocked him on the head, and laid him dead at their feet. They then stripped the body and the hut, and made off to Wollerou, the two ravens following them. A carpenter recognizing the ravens, and struck with their angry looks, followed the two men to Zurich, and sent a companion to the hermitage to see if anything was amiss. Soon the murder was discovered, and the two ravens were observed flapping their wings, screaming, and pecking at the tavern window where the murderers had seated themselves. The alarm was given; the men were apprehended, confessed their crime, and were executed. After which, the two ravens flew back to the forest, and were no more seen.—R. P. Dom Charles Brandes, *Life of St. Meinrad.*

Three doves announce to St. Regulus the deaths of three martyrs (A.D. 130). St. Regulus was bishop of Arles, and one day, as he was celebrating mass, three doves flew on the altar, having the names of three martyrs, in letters of blood, on their white breasts. St. Regulus read the names; and when, in the office, he came to the names of St. Peter and St. Paul, he added, "and of the blessed martyrs Denis, Rusticus, and Eleutherius, who have just died at Paris;" and when the service was over he started for Paris to collect their relics.—L'abbé Corblet, *Hagiographie du Diocèse d'Amiens.*

A Basque legend about a little bird telling the matter. A king, having been deceived by envious sisters respecting the offspring of his wife, was informed of the real truth by a little bird. The sisters had assured the king that the firstborn of his queen was a cat, the next a dog, and the third a bear; but the little bird informed him that the first two were lovely daughters, and the third a son.

A little green bird tells the king about Chery and Fairstar. Queen Bondina had at one birth two sons and a daughter. On the same day her sister had a son called Chery (*Dear-one*). The queen-mother ordered Feintisa to strangle the four infants; but Feintisa, unwilling to go so far as this, set them adrift in a boat. The boat was discovered by a corsair, who took the four babes to his wife to bring up. In time, the four castaways get introduced to the king, and a little green bird tells him the whole truth.—Comtesse d'Aulnoy, *Fairy Tales.*

The last tale in the *Arabian Nights Entertainments* has a similar bird-story.

Blood-money.

MATT. xxvii. 3–6. When Judas saw that Jesus was condemned, he took the money he had received from the priests, and threw it down in the temple. And the chief priests took the silver pieces, and said, It is not lawful for to put them into the treasury, because it is the price of blood.

St. Francis of Paula refuses to accept the money of Ferdinand I., king of Naples, because it was the price of his subjects' blood (A.D. 1416–1507). When St. Francis of Paula passed through Naples on his way to France, he was lodged in the royal palace. The king, Ferdinand I., presented to him a bag of gold, to aid, as he said, the treasury of the saint's convents. St. Francis refused the gift, saying to the king, "It is not lawful to put them into the treasury, because they are the price of thy subjects' blood." To prove this, he took up one of the gold pieces and broke it in two, whereupon several drops of blood fell from the money. This terrible miracle, "qui est attesté par les plus anciens écrivains de sa vie," greatly alarmed the king, who confessed his faults, and wept bitterly.—Mgr. Guérin (chamberlain of pope Leo XIII.), *Vies des Saints*, vol. iv. p. 155 (1880).

Blood of Christ cleanseth from all Sin.

1 JOHN i. 7. The blood of Jesus Christ cleanseth from all sin.

REV. i. 1. Unto Him that loved us, and washed us from our sins in His own blood.

Longinus the Roman soldier converted by the blood of Jesus (first century). According to tradition, the soldier who pierced the side of Jesus with his spear was named Longinus. It is said that some of the blood which spurted from the wound fell on the soldier's face; and as the blood of Christ cleanseth from sin, it purified the soldier's heart, and opened his eyes to the beauty of holiness.—*Acta Sanctorum* (Bollandists). This life is from an ancient MS. in the Vatican library.

Bodies of Saints Incorruptible.

PSALM xvi. 10. Thou wilt not suffer Thy Holy One to see corruption.

Body of St. Bertha incorruptible (seventh century). St. Bertha was cruelly murdered by her nephew and cousin, but a hundred years after her death, her coffin being opened, the body was found to be "aussi beau et aussi entier, et ses plaies aussi fraîches, que le jour de son martyr. Il en sortit même du sang, lorsque celui de St. Gombert [her husband] en fut approché."—D. Morlot, *Histoire du Diocèse de Reims*.

The body of St. Cuthbert preserved from corruption. St. Cuthbert died, March 20, A.D. 687, in the isle of Farne, but was buried in the monastery of St. Peter, in Lindisfarne, on the right side of the high altar. Bede* says, eleven years afterwards his body was taken up, and instead of being turned to dust, was whole and fresh, the joints all pliable, and even the clothes uninjured. The whole being put into a new coffin was placed above the pavement, over the former grave. William of Malmesbury† writes that 415 years later the body was again examined and found incorrupt. In the Danish invasions the monks carried the body from Lindisfarne to Durham, and the present cathedral was built in 1080. When the shrine of St. Cuthbert was plundered and demolished by order of Henry VIII., the body of the saint was still found entire, as Harpsfield testifies, and was not burnt like that of other British saints, but privately buried where the shrine stood.

St. Cuthbert's ring, in which a sapphire is enchased, was given to the bishop of Chalcedon by the viscount Montaigne.‡

* Bede, *Church History*, bk. iv. ch. 30.
† William of Malmesbury, *English Pontiffs*, bk. iv.
‡ Smith, *Flores Historiæ Ecclesiasticæ*, p. 120.

The copy of St. John's Gospel found in his tomb was given to Mr. Thomas Philips, canon of Tongres, by the earl of Lichfield.

The body of St. Daniel, merchant, has never seen corruption (died 1411). St. Daniel, the merchant, died in 1411. Centuries afterwards it was exhumed, and not only found entire, but "exhaling an agreeable odour." Hundreds saw it, and bore testimony that it showed no indication at all of corruption. It was removed into the church, and an altar was erected over it, where many miracles were performed. It was afterwards placed in a noble coffin, where it is still, and we are assured that it is this day as free from any taint of corruption as ever. Augustine Fortinius says he saw it recently, and can warrant this statement to be correct. —Augustine Fortinius, *Histoire de l'Ordre des Camaldules*.

No corruption had passed on St. Fursy in twenty-five days (seventh century). Twenty-five days after the death of St. Fursy, the new church of Péronne was to be consecrated. One Leutsinde, out of curiosity, stole into the church to look at the body of the saint, but was instantly struck blind. Having repented of his fault, the bishops, at the consecration, prayed that he might be forgiven, and his sight returned. He then looked with reverence on the dead body, and devoutly remarked that God had not suffered His holy one to see corruption.—L'abbé Corblet, *Hagiography of the diocese of Amiens*, vol. ii., from p. 260.

The bodies of St. Gervasius and St. Protasius, three hundred years after their martyrdom, were both sound and fresh. St. Gervasius and St. Protasius were martyred in the reign of Nero, A.D. 64. Some three hundred years afterwards, the ghost of St. Paul appeared to St. Ambrose, archbishop of Milan, and bade him go to a certain spot, and he would there find the bodies of the two martyrs, and a book containing their names and history. St. Ambrose says, "I then called together the bishops of the cities thereabouts, and told them what St. Paul had said to me, and we went together to the place indicated. I was the first," he says, "to ply the mattock and throw up the earth, but the rest helped me, and at length we came on a stone chest (twelve feet underground), in which was found the bodies of the two martyrs whole and perfectly sound, as if they had been laid there only that very day. Their limbs were entire, their blood fresh, and the bodies emitted a sweet odour, which spread through the whole city. At their heads was the book containing an account of their lives and martyrdom." St. Ambrose built a church on the site, which he dedicated to the two saints.—St. Ambrose, *Epistle* 22 (written to his sister Marcellina).

That two bodies and a book were found may be granted; but had the earth been recently disturbed, and was the character of the book critically investigated?

The body of St. Hilarion saw no corruption in ten months. Hilarion was buried on the day of his death on the top of a hill in Cyprus; but ten months afterwards his disciple Isichius, who had buried it, disinterred it secretly, and carried it into Syria, where he buried it in the presence of an immense concourse of people. The body was then as fresh as on the day of decease, and so were all the clothes. A very sweet odour also issued from both. St. Jerome tells us, even in his day there was a great dispute about the body of this saint; the Syrtads insisting that they have it, and the Cypriots as stoutly maintaining that it is with them. Miracles, we are told, proceed from it in both places, which St. Jerome accounts for thus: the body is in one place, and the spirit in the other. —St. Jerome (A.D. 390), *Vita St. Hilarionis Eremitæ.*

The spirit in this case does not mean the soul, which, of course, was in paradise, but the ghost, which for the most part bides below till the resurrection of the body. The explanation of St. Jerome is ingenious, if no ingenuous.

The body of St. Isidore, forty years after his death, showed no sign of decay. St. Isidore was a farm labourer who worked for Juan de Vargas, a farmer on the outskirts of Madrid. Being a mere peasant, he was buried, at death, in the churchyard; but forty years afterwards a matron of Madrid had a revelation from God that the Lord desired the saint to be honoured according to his transcendent merits; and, therefore, the body was disinterred, and removed into the church. The historian says, "When the body was taken from the grave, it was found to be as perfect as if it had but just died, although it had been lying in the earth for forty years. Not only no sign of decay was perceptible, but a sweet and ravishing odour proceeded from it, an odour which all extolled. The moment the grave was opened, all the bells of the church began to ring of their own accord, and kept on ringing in perfect time and tune till the body was laid in the modest shrine prepared for it. Furthermore, while the ceremony was going on, all the sick folk of Madrid were healed of their several infirmities."—*The Life of St. Isidore*, by F. P. Ribadeneira and by D. A. Villegas, in their *Extravagants.*

Bells ringing. This spontaneous ringing of church bells is a favourite prodigy in the lives of the saints. Thus, at the death of St. Toretta, the abbot Boudant says, "Elle a entendu la voix du Bien-Aimé qui lui disait: *Viens du Liban, ma Colombe, mon épouse, ma toute belle; viens, tu seras couronnée.* Elle n'a pu résister à une invitation si pressante, et ses liens se sont à l'instant brisés. En ce moment, O prodige! toutes les cloches des églises environnantes, à Murat, à Villefranche, à Montcenoux, s'ébranlent d'elles-mêmes pour annoncer qu'une créature privilégiée venait de quitter la terre."

*** See p. 369, note, col. 2, where this spontaneous ringing of bells is accounted for.

The body of St. Isidore, exhumed 450 years after his death, was sound and fresh as if he had just died (A.D. 1622). The body of St. Isidore, of Madrid, a day labourer, was exhumed for a second time in 1622, to be placed in a splendid tomb. He had been dead for 450 years, but no mark of decay was perceptible. Not only was the body sound and fresh, but there issued from it a heavenly odour quite ravishing. Many are now alive who were present at the canonization, and will bear willing testimony to the fact here stated.—History of the canonization of St. Isidore, printed and published by letters patent from Philip, king of Castile, etc., by John Heigham of St. Omer (signed by his minister, "De Groote," June 18, A.D. 1625).

The tongue of St. John Nepomuck knew no corruption. St. John Nepomuck was martyred by king Wenceslaus in 1383, because he refused to reveal the secrets of the confessional. In 1719 (*i.e.* 336 years afterwards) the coffin was opened, and the skeleton was quite fleshless, but the tongue, "which God wished specially to honour, for having so faithfully guarded the seal of confession," was as red and fresh and supple as that of a living man. It was placed in a rich reliquary, and is still venerated as a precious relic. In Christian art St. John Nepomuck is represented holding his tongue in his hand. [Qy. Allegory?]—*Acta Sanctorum* (Bollandists), May 16.

St. Oringa. St. Oringa, a villager of Tuscany, died in 1310, and 204 years afterwards (A.D. 1514), the body being disinterred was found perfect, and wholly exempt from corruption. It was then consumed in a fire which accidentally broke out in the church where she was buried.

--Mgr. Guérin, *Vies des Saints*, vol. ii. p. 576.

The body of St. Romuald was found whole and fresh 440 years after his death. St. Romuald, founder of the Camaldunenses, died A.D. 1027, in the 120th year of his age, and was buried in the monastery of the valley of Castro. Four hundred and forty years afterwards (A.D. 1467), the body was found "whole and entire, without the slightest trace of corruption. The countenance was pale and venerable, and the body arrayed in a hair shirt, over which was a white robe." It was moved to the church of St. Basil, where it now is.—Ribadeneira (died 1611), *Flower of the Lives of the Saints.*

The body of St. Stephen was not corrupted in four hundred years. More than four hundred years after his death the body of St. Stephen was discovered, with three others; it had not corrupted in the least, and the "sweet odour of sanctity" was quite perceptible when the coffin was opened.—Edward Kinesman (1623), *Lives of the Saints* ("Invention of St. Stephen").

Charles V. of Spain and Germany saw no corruption in eighty years. Charles V. of Spain and Germany certainly was no saint, and even though he abdicated his throne, and lived a sort of recluse for two years, his time was spent in writing useless despatches, and eating Estremadura sausages, sardines, omelettes, eel-pies, partridges, fat capon, intermixed with iced beer, flagons of Rhenish, senna and rhubarb. A more unsaintly man it would be hard to find in the respectable classes. His bigotry was unbounded, his self-conceit intolerable, his slaughters sickening; yet in 1654 his coffin being opened, when the body was removed from the Escurial to the Pantheon, the corpse, says sir W. Stirling-Maxwell, in his *Cloister Life of Charles V.*, p. 279, "was quite entire, and even some sprigs of sweet thyme, folded in the winding-sheet, retained all their vernal fragrance, after the lapse of four-score winters."—See *Notes and Queries*, March 3, 1883, p. 161.

Stirling-Maxwell and Mignet exhibit Charles V. in his cloister life very differently to the picture drawn of him by Sandoval and Strada; but Stirling-Maxwell and Mignet have dared to be true to facts, while Sandoval and Strada have made an ideal recluse, no more like Charles V. than David's picture of Napoleon on his cream-white charger is like the real Napoleon, with his greatcoat and comforter, toiling doggedly over the Alps on a patient mule.

The bodies of the eight hundred martyrs of Otranto remain uncorrupted and unviolated (A.D. 1480). Of all the tales under this head, none equal the marvels of the eight hundred martyrs of Otranto. We are told that when Mahomet II. took Otranto in 1480, he put to death eight hundred ecclesiastics. Francesco Maria di Asti, archbishop of the see, assures us in his *Annals* that a priest, named Stephen, was slain at the altar, and as his head fell from his body, a portrait of the Virgin, from the pencil of St. Luke, was snatched up to heaven and saved from desecration. The other ecclesiastics were taken without the walls and slain. The first one put to death was Antonio Primaldo, the abbot. His head rolled along the ground, but his body remained upright notwithstanding the many attempts of the Turks to overthrow it. All the eight hundred were now put to the sword, but their dead bodies, though left unburied for thirteen months, showed no signs of corruption, nor were they once violated by birds or beasts of prey. Afterwards they were interred at Naples; but when Solyman the Magnificent, in 1537, threatened Otranto with assault, the ghosts of these martyrs, with an innumerable company of angels, appeared on the walls, and saved the city. Again in 1644 the same ghostly army averted another Turkish assault. Some Christian galley-slaves who rowed the Ottoman galleys avouched their inability to see the ghosts, and were put to death for their short-sightedness.—*In Memorabilibus Hydruntinæ Eccl. Epitome;* Burmann, *Thesaurus Antiq. Hist. Ital.*, vol. ix. p. 8.

Bonds bind not the Word of God.

2 Tim. ii. 9. I suffer trouble as an evil-doer, even unto bonds; but the Word of God is not bound.

St. Savinian was bound, but not the Word of God (A.D. 275). St. Savinian was arrested in Champagne by order of the emperor Aurelian, and was placed under the guard of forty-eight soldiers. His crime was being a Christian, for which offence he suffered as an evil-doer, even unto bonds; but, as St. Paul said, "the Word of God was not bound," for the whole guard became converted by the preaching of the prisoner, were baptized, and sealed the confession of faith by their blood. All the forty-eight soldiers were beheaded in the presence of St. Savinian, under the hope of making him recant; but neither bonds, nor imprisonment, nor death could separate him from the love of God his Saviour.—

Bollandus, *Acta Sanctorum*, vol. ii. Jan. 29. (See also Nicolas des Guerrois, *Saintеté Chrétienne de l'Église de Troyes.*)

Braying to Death in a Mortar.

PROV. xxvii. 22. Though thou shouldest bray a fool in a mortar among wheat with a pestle, yet will not his foolishness depart from him.

A Turkish custom of braying to death in a mortar. Baron de Tott says, "Fanaticism has enacted in Turkey that the goods of the ulemats or lawyers shall never be confiscated; nor shall any ulemat be put to death, except by being pounded in a mortar."

The guards of the tower who suffered prince Coreskie to escape were some of them impaled, but others were pounded to death in great iron mortars used for braying rice.

Royal criminals, in Siam, brayed to death in a mortar. Mr. Hamilton, in his *Scripture Elucidations*, speaking of the king of Siam, who, in 1688, made war on Cambodia and Cochin China, says, "In the land army was a Siamese fruit-seller, who by his daring rose to be commander-in-chief, and soon brought the war to an end. Returning to Siam, he discovered that the king was wholly under the control of the Jesuits, and so he picked a quarrel with him; and, as the army was devoted to his service, he was soon enabled to seize the king, and put him to death. This he did after the custom observed in Siam towards royal criminals, viz. by putting him in a huge iron mortar, and braying him to pieces with wooden pestles. This was done, that none of the 'sacred blood' of the king might fall to the earth, and mix with it, calling for vengeance on the traitor who put the king to death."

Broad and Narrow Way.

MATT. vii. 13, 14. Wide is the gate and broad is the way that leadeth to destruction . . . strait is the gate and narrow is the way that leadeth unto life.

The two knights. Two knights, one wise and one foolish, swore eternal friendship, and set off together on their adventures. They came in time to the crown of two roads, leading to two large cities. The path of the one which led to the imperial city was narrow, stony, and difficult. It was also well guarded by three men-at-arms, named the World, the Flesh, and the Devil, with all of whom every traveller that ventured that way had to do battle. If overcome, he lost his life; but if victorious, he was crowned with honour by the emperor, and dwelt in a paradise of delight for ever. The other road was broad and smooth, pleasant to the eye, and easy for travellers. The same men-at-arms had this road also under their charge, but instead of harassing travellers and doing battle with them, they befriended them, directed them on the way, and did what they could to flatter and please them. The way certainly was all that one could wish, but the city was detestable; it was, in fact, no better than a mass of dungeons of the foulest and worst character. The wise knight was for going to the imperial city; but the foolish knight objected, as the road was so bad. The wise knight, being over-persuaded, went with his companion along the smooth broad road, and both agreed that it was delightful. When they reached the city gates, they were both seized as felons, and taken before the seneschal. The wise knight pleaded that he had greatly wished to go the other road, but was over-persuaded by his companion. The foolish knight pleaded that he could not be blamed for following the steps of the wise, and that if his friend had insisted on going the other road he should certainly have given in to him. The seneschal replied, "Both stand self-condemned. The wise man gave up his wisdom to be the companion of a fool, and the foolish man refused to hearken to the words of wisdom. Both have gone in the way of folly, and must receive the reward of their foolishness. Those who sow the wind must reap the whirlwind; for what a man soweth that also must he reap."—*Gesta Romanorum*, lxvii.

(Why is the way of destruction broad, and that of salvation narrow? Not because God delighteth in the death of sinners, not even because God hath made it so; but simply because truth is one, and error manifold. There is but one path to life eternal, viz. faith in Jesus Christ, a narrow straight path from earth to heaven—narrow because it admits no widening, no addition. Faith is the one way to rich and poor, learned and unlearned, old and young, male and female, Greek and barbarian, bond and free. But the road of error is very broad, because every walk except the narrow one of faith belongs to it. Every road of sin, every road of error, every road of wrong doctrine, all the ten thousand ways of straying from God and His righteousness, are but parts and tracts of the wide, well-beaten high-road of destruction; and if all these tracts are added together, they would make a very wide road indeed.)

Burden of Sin.

PSALM xxxviii. 4. *David weighed down with the burden of sin.* David says, Mine iniquities are gone over my head. As a heavy burden, they are too heavy for me.

Christ weighed down with the burden of sin. Christ was once offered to bear the sins of [the] many (*Heb.* ix. 28); but so great was the burden, His agony in the garden caused the sweat to pour from Him, "as it were great drops of blood;" and He prayed earnestly, "O My Father, if it be possible, let this cup pass from Me." But He was to be made a perfect Atonement, and that could be done only by suffering; and as He hung on the cross, His cup ran over, and He cried aloud, "My God, My God, why hast Thou forsaken Me?" So great, so grievous, was the burden of sin laid upon Him.

The burden of sin allegorized by a heavy bundle on Christian's back. When Christian fled from the City of Destruction, he was weighted with a heavy burden on his back, which nearly dragged him under the water of the Slough of Despond. This bundle weighed heavily upon him, till he had passed the little Wicket Gate, and reached the rising ground where stood a cross. Then, says Bunyan, "I saw in my dream that just as Christian came up to the cross, his burden loosed from off his shoulders, and fell from off his back, and began to tumble, and so continued to do, till it came to the mouth of the sepulchre, where it fell in, and I saw it no more."—Bunyan, *The Pilgrim's Progress*, pt. i. (An allegorical dream.)

Christopherus weighed down with the burden on his back. Offerus was a ferryman, a giant in strength and stature, who ferried wayfarers across a deep river. One day a little Child presented Himself, and begged the giant to carry Him across the ford; so Offerus took the Child on his back, and began to wade through the river, according to his wont; but every step he took was the more difficult, because the Child seemed to grow heavier and heavier, till at last it was well-nigh more than he could bear. As the giant sank beneath his load, the Child told him He was Christ; and Offerus replied, henceforth Christ should be his master, and Him only would he serve. He now received a new name, and was called Christ-offerus, shortened into Christopher.—James de Voragine, *The Golden Legend.*

This is a similar allegory to that of Bunyan's pilgrim (see above). Offerus knew not the burden of sin till Christ came to him. He tried to "put on Christ," but then felt he the burden of sin, which grew heavier and heavier till Christ revealed Himself to him. Being then "born again," he had a new name given him, and was called "The bearer of the Christian Cross," Christ-opher (the Christ-bearer).

(We are told that the body of Christopherus is at Valencia; one of his arms at Compostella; one of his jawbones at Astorga; one of his shoulders at St. Peter's, Rome; and one of his teeth at Venice. We are not told where any of the relics of Bunyan's "Christian" are preserved.)

Caiaphas's Counsel to the Sanhedrim.

John xviii. 14. Caiaphas was he who gave counsel to the Jews, that it was expedient that one man should die for the people (see xi. 50).

Without, in the remotest way, touching upon the vicarious death of our Redeemer, which cannot possibly have a parallelism, there can be no doubt that history supplies many noble examples of the expediency that Caiaphas talked of. The following are examples of voluntary self-sacrifice, for what is termed patriotism, and no names in history or fable stand higher in honour, or stir more deeply our love and veneration. They acted out the counsel of Caiaphas, "It is expedient for us [the nation] that one man should die for the people, and that the whole nation perish not."

Codros the Athenian gives his life to save his country. When the Dorians invaded Attica, an oracle declared that they would be victorious, "if the life of the Attic king was spared." Codros, the Attic king, on being told of this response, went to the Dorian camp in disguise, provoked a quarrel with the soldiers, and was slain in the dispute. When the invaders heard thereof, they drew off their forces and returned home, being fully convinced that it was vain to hope for victory. The Athenians lost their king, and would never after elect another; for "no one," they declared, "could be worthy to fill the throne of Codros." (See Decius Mus, below.)—Pausanias, *History of Greece*, i. 19; vii. 25.

Mettius Curtius gives his life to fill up a chasm in the Roman forum. The earth of the Roman forum from some unknown cause gave way, leaving a vast chasm, which the soothsayers declared could never be filled up till the Romans threw into it their greatest treasure. On hearing this, Mettius Curtius mounted his charger in full armour, declaring that Rome's greatest treasure is a brave patriot; and so saying he leaped into the chasm, which immediately closed upon him. Of course, the truth of this story in no wise affects the lesson taught by it. The Romans thought with Caiaphas, "It is expedient that one man should die for the people, and not that the whole nation should perish."—Valerius Maximus, *Memorable Acts and Sayings*, v. 2.

Decius Mus gives his life for his country. In the great Latin war, B.C. 340, each of the consuls had a dream, that the general of one side and the army of the other were devoted to death. Decius Mus, who had the command of the left wing of the Roman army, rushing into the thickest of the fight, devoted himself to death, and thus fell the consul on one side. The other side was to be the army of the Latins, which, according to the announcement of the vision, strewed the plain like broken glass. (See Codros, p. 376).—Valerius Maximus, *De Factis Dictisque Memorabilibus.*

Leonidas and his three hundred Spartans give their lives for their country. When Greece, B.C. 480, was invaded by Xerxes, king Leonidas was sent to Thermopylæ with a forlorn hope of five thousand men to make a stand against the Persian host. The Persians, finding it impossible to force the pass, entered Greece by another route. When Leonidas was informed thereof, he sent away all his army except three hundred, who were Spartans. This little band was cut down to a man, but no victory could have commanded more reverence and honour than the self-devoted Leonidas and his three hundred. —Valerius Maximus, *Memorable Acts and Sayings*, i. 6.

Arnold von Winkelried gives his life to save his country. The Austrians, in 1386, wishing to stamp out the spirit of the Swiss and reduce them to bondage, sent a large army under duke Leopold to subdue them. The Austrians consisted of four thousand horse, and a mixed multitude of infantry; the Swiss had only fourteen hundred in all to oppose this force. The Swiss occupied the higher ground; and Leopold commanded the horsemen to dismount, and join the infantry in climbing the steep to dislodge the foe. On marched they with pikes advanced. It was a solid wall of brass, a *chevaux de frise* of pointed pikes with no opening. Arnold von Winkelried, seized with a noble inspiration, rushing forwards, caught in his arms all the pikes he could grasp, and flinging himself on the ground, bore with him the pikes sheathed in his own body. A gap was made in the iron wall, the Swiss rushed in, a dreadful havoc ensued, the result of which was a complete victory over the assailants. Arnold von Winkelried felt it was "expedient that one man should die for the people, and not that the whole nation should perish," and thus with patriotic self-devotion did he effect his country's safety.—Brewer, *History of Germany*, p. 132.

Candle and Lamp.

(See Consumed but not Diminished, p. 67.)

Prov. xxiv. 20. The candle of the wicked shall be put out (Job xxi. 17).

Prov. xiii. 9. The light of the righteous rejoiceth; but the lamp of the wicked shall be put out.

On the day of Cinedrita's purification, her candle is lighted by a flame from heaven (A.D. 925). Cinedrita (or Cynethrith) was the mother of St. Dunstan, and she went to return thanks for the birth of the child on the day of the purification of the Virgin Mary. The ceremony was held in Glastonbury with great pomp and circumstance; many nobles and a numberless crowd of others carried wax tapers, and the church was a blaze of light. All of a sudden, without any known cause, every taper went out, and a minute afterwards a flame from heaven kindled Cinedrita's candle, and from this all the rest were relighted. This was looked on as a sign that the child Dunstan would grow to be a great light in the world of darkness; and the future history of the saint proved that it was so.—Osbert of Canterbury, *Life of St. Dunstan.*

The candle of St. Genovefa [Geneviève] put out and rekindled (A.D. 423–512). As the sabbath drew towards Sunday morning, St. Genovefa [or Geneviève] left home to go as usual to the church of St. Denis with the virgins which were her fellows. The lantern which was carried before them was put out by a sudden puff of wind, and the maidens were alarmed at the pitchy darkness, the more so as there was a great storm. St. Genovefa took the lantern into her hand, and the candle instantly relighted of itself; and the saint holding the lantern on high, it gave a brilliant light to all till they had entered into the church.—Bollandus, *Acta Sanctorum* (Vita St. Genovefæ).

In allusion to this "miracle," St. Genovefa is represented in Christian art with a devil blowing out her candle, and an angel lighting it again.

A storm, accompanied with wind and rain, failed to extinguish lighted candles exposed to their violence (A.D. 994). St. Gerard maintained a large number of refugees from Ireland and Greece, who had come to Toul. One stormy night, after he had retired to rest, he was told that one of these strangers had just died. He immediately assembled the clergy, and had the body carried to the grave. The wind was high and gusty, rain fell in torrents, it was a most stormy night, but the lighted candles, though undefended and in the open air, burnt steadily; neither wind nor rain had any effect on them. (See St. Elmo, p. 305.)—Father Benedict, *Life of St. Gerard* (1700).

The candle of St. Gudula blown out and relighted (died A.D. 670). One wild night the prince of the power of the air blew out the lantern which a servant girl carried before St. Gudula, leaving them both in utter darkness in the midst of a barren heath. St. Gudula, falling on her knees, prayed God to lighten their darkness, and immediately the candle was rekindled, affording them a light to their feet, and showing them the way that they should go.—Hubert, *Life of St. Gudula.* (Hubert died A.D. 1047.)

St. Hermeland rekindles a lamp by making the sign of the cross (A.D. 718). One day St. Hermeland rekindled, by simply making the sign of the cross, a lamp which a gust of wind had blown out; and though the wind continued to blow fitfully with great violence, the lamp continued to burn with a steady flame till the monk who carried it arrived at his place of destination.—Bulteau, *History of the Monks of the East*, bk. i. ch. 37.

The candle of St. Laumer thrice blown out by the devil and relighted. One night, as St. Laumer was praying in his cell, the devil, hoping to frighten him by leaving him in the dark, thrice blew out his candle, and thrice was it miraculously relighted.—*Gallican Martyrology.*

Mgr. Guérin says, "Toutes les fois que le démon, ennemi de la lumière, lui éteignait sa lampe la nuit, elle se rallumait aussitôt."—*Vies des Saints*, vol. i. p. 471.

It is really amazing that such an ordinary incident as this should be thought wonderful. What so likely as the draught of an ill-built cell to blow out a candle?—and if the wick is long and incandescent, another puff of wind would relight it. When candles were in common use it was a game of fun with children to blow out a candle, and by a sudden jerk upwards, or a puff of the breath, to relight it. I have done it many a time.

All the candles of John Liquillic of Dinan burst spontaneously into light (April 5, A.D. 1419). Every one of the many historians of St. Vincent Ferrier mention the following incident. John Liquillic of Dinan had in his keeping the candles which had been used at the mass of St. Vincent Ferrier. The 2nd of February being the festival of the purification of the Virgin Mary, he went to his store-room to fetch these candles, but they were all gone. He searched everywhere, but could find no trace of them. He asked all who could have had access to the store-room if they knew what had become of them; but no one could solve the mystery. What, then, was his astonishment, on April 5, at finding all the candles in his store-room, and all standing upright and burning! He asked the woman who kept the stores if she could explain the mystery; but the only solution she could offer was this—the candles were those employed at the mass of St. Vincent, and April 5 was the day of his death.—*Les Petits Bollandistes*, vol. iv. April 5.

St. Servan's fire being wantonly put out relights itself. In olden times it was no easy matter to kindle fires; so it was usual to keep them burning all night and all day. In St. Servan's cell it was the duty of the boys to rise by turns at night to mind and mend the fire. Kentigern, the favourite of the old saint, was an object of jealousy with the other boys; and one night, when it was his turn to attend to the fire, he found the boys had mischievously put it out, and scattered the live brands about the floor. Kentigern carefully scraped together the ashes, laid the brands above them, and, invoking the Holy Trinity, blew upon the embers, when lo! they revived, a flame burst forth, and the fire was "miraculously" rekindled.—St. Asaph, *Life of St. Kentigern.* (Jocelyn, in 1125, wrote a longer and more detailed memoir.)

This tale is told by St. Asaph and bishop Jocelyn of Glasgow as a miracle; but those who have lived in Paris, as I have done, must be quite familiar with these rekindlings. It is a daily practice, when the servants rise, to rake together the wood embers and top them with charred wood; if then the *rideau* is drawn down, and a little puff of breath is applied, the fire soon revives. Even in our coal fires, who has not been amazed occasionally at the recovery of a fire apparently quite dead, especially if light cinders are carefully piled in cells above each other? Kentigern was an intelligent lad, and managed his fire skilfully, not trusting wholly to his invocation.

St. Severin causes the candles of Christians to light of themselves (died A.D. 482). One day St. Severin was in a town half-Christian and half-pagan. He told the people to enter the church on a given day, each holding an unlit candle. The saint appeared before the congregation and prayed; whereupon all the candles of the Christian party burst into flame, but those of the pagans remained unlit. This "miracle" carried conviction to the hearts of the idolaters, who forthwith abandoned their idols, and served the living God.—*Les Petits Bollandistes*, vol. i. p. 218.

At the death of St. William of Paris, God sent a torch from heaven to attest his sanctity (A.D. 1105–1202). God honoured the decease of St. William of Paris by sending from heaven a lighted torch, which came to the tomb of the saint through the roof of the church.—Surius, *Lives of the Saints*, vol. iii. (The life, we are told, was written by a disciple of St. William.)

The candle of St. Zita is not extinguished by wind or rain (A.D. 1218–1278). Every Friday St. Zita went to San Angelo in Monte, some four miles off. On the eve of St. Mary Magdalene, she wished to burn a candle before her altar. She arrived so late that the doors of the church were locked; nevertheless she lighted her candle, and fell asleep. The night was very stormy, the wind blew, and the rain fell in torrents; still St. Zita slept. When she woke next morning her candle was burning steadily; neither the wind nor the rain had put it out, and Zita herself was quite dry. In fact, when the curé came to unlock the doors, he found Zita in the church, though the doors had certainly not been opened.—*Acta Sanctorum* (Papebroch the Bollandist), April 27.

It does not seem quite clear what Papebroch means by the words "She was not touched by a drop of rain, and her candle burnt still," and a line or two afterwards, "The curé found her in the church, though the doors had not been opened." If Zita was *in the church*, how could she be wet with rain, and how could the rain and wind have any effect on her candle?

A woman with a bloody flux cured by presenting a candle to St. Rigobert (A.D. 743). St. Rigobert was buried at St. Peter's of Reims, and numerous miracles attested his sanctity. Three lame men were cured; a blind woman received her sight; a multitude of impotent folk were restored to health. But one of the most conspicuous of these prodigies was that of a woman with a bloody flux, who simply sent a candle to be burnt before the tomb of the saint, and immediately it was lighted, the flux was staunched.—Bollandus, *Acta Sanctorum*, vol. i. Jan. 4.

Captives and Prisoners set Free.

ISA. lxi. 1. The Lord hath anointed me to proclaim liberty to the captives, and the opening of the prison to them that are bound.

ISA. xlii. 7. I the Lord have called thee . . . to bring out the prisoners from the prison, and them that sit in darkness out of the prison-house.

The prisoners in the tower of Angers set free by the prayers of St. Aubin (A.D. 470–550). Many prisoners being confined in the tower of Angers, St. Aubin, bishop of the city, entreated the magistrates to set them free. This, of course, they refused to do, and the bishop said, "God is less inexorable than man." He now prayed God to have pity on the captives, and continued all night in prayer. In the mean time, a large part of the tower wall fell down, and the prisoners made their escape. They went immediately to St. Aubin to render thanks, and promised him to abandon their evil ways.—Fortunatus (bishop of Poitiers, a contemporary), *Life of St. Aubin, Bishop of Angers.*

St. Evermode, bishop of Ratzburg, releases the captive Frisons (A.D. 1168). Henry, count of Ratzburg, had taken some Frisons captive in war, and St. Evermode demanded their freedom, which the count refused. On Easter Sunday the prisoners were brought to church in their chains. The pontiff, taking the stoup in his hand, went to the captives and sprinkled holy water on them, saying, "Dominus solvit compeditos" (*The Lord delivers you from your bonds*); whereupon their chains were loosed and the captives free. The chains were preserved for a long time in the treasury of Ratzburg church "in proof of this miracle."—L'abbé Destombes.

It is not very clear how a number of chains kept in a church can prove anything more than that there are chains in the church. Registers carefully kept and well authenticated may go to prove that the chains have been in the church for a certain number of years, but the mere presence of chains can no more prove the miracle referred to, than the existence of the Severn proves the truth of the fable about Locrin's daughter, or the existence of the Humber proves that the king of the Huns was drowned in the river Abus.

Chains fall from the prisoners when the body of St. Gregory of Langres passed the prison door. When the body of St. Gregory of Langres was carried to the sepulchre prepared for it, the bearers set down the bier for a little rest before the prison, and immediately the chains of every one of the prisoners fell off, and the prisoners were free.—Baring-Gould, *Lives of the Saints*, Jan., p. 59.

At the prayer of Jeanne Marie de Maillé the prisoners of Tours are set free (A.D. 1332–1414). While the king was at Tours, Jeanne Marie de Maillé solicited him to release the prisoners. He promised to do so, but amidst the gaieties of court life the promise was forgotten. "Put not your trust in princes, nor in the son of man, in whom there is no help." Having no help from the king, Jeanne Marie addressed the King of kings, and immediately the prison doors flew open, the chains fell to the ground, and the prisoners were free. One of the prisoners went back to his cell to fetch a book, called "Heures de Vierge," but was allowed to go out again without obstruction. When the king heard thereof, he instantly called to mind his promise, and said no measures were to be set on foot to recapture the escaped prisoners.—Père de Boisgaultier (her confessor), *Life of Jeanne Marie de Maillé.*

St. Julian delivers from prison six malefactors (A.D. 117). Passing by the prison of Artin, where six malefactors were confined, St. Julian heard them cry to him for pity. Forthwith he went to the magistrates, and begged that they might be released; but the magistrates told him they were malefactors, and must abide the sentence of the law. St. Julian then vowed that he would not break bread till they were set free. The same night an angel broke off their chains, opened the prison doors, and bade the prisoners escape for their lives.—D. Piolin, *History of the Church of Mans.*

Chains fall from the prisoners when the body of St. Lupus of Châlons passed the prison door (seventh century). St. Lupus, on his death-bed, entreated the governor of Châlons to release the prisoners sentenced to death. This he refused to do; so St. Lupus ordered that, when his body was carried to the grave, the bearers should rest awhile before the city prison. This they did, and immediately the chains fell from the prisoners, the doors flew open, and all the prisoners made their escape.—Canon Bright, *History of the Church* (1863).

In the *Légendaire d'Autun* the tale is slightly varied. It says, "When the funeral procession came in front of the prison, the bier became so heavy that the bearers were obliged to rest, and while the bier thus rested, the chains fell off," etc. It is added, "This miracle is the origin of the privilege for a long time enjoyed by the bishops of Chalons, viz. a jail delivery on Feb. 19, the 'day of St. Lupus.'" This privilege was allowed up to the year 1844, and may have been since, for aught I know.

Carried and Delivered.

ISA. xlv. 4. Even to your old age I am He; and even to hoar hairs will I carry you. I have made, I will carry, and will deliver you.

A child carried and delivered by St. Nicholas from captivity. The young son of Cerrone and Euphrosina, two devout persons under the patronage of St. Nicholas, was stolen away by the Agarenes and carried to Babylon. One day, on the feast of St. Nicholas, the child was unusually sad, and the king asked him why his eyes were filled with tears. When the child told him, the king said jestingly, "If Nicholas is so mighty, bid him carry thee away, and deliver thee." The child had the king's cup in his hand at the time; but before he could set it down, he was carried by the hair of his head from the king's palace, in Babylon, to the church of St. Nicholas, in Lycia. There were his father and mother, come to keep the feast of the saint, and mourn over their lost son. Great indeed was their joy when they saw him borne through the air, and set down at their feet.

This tale is told by all the authors I have seen who have written the *Life of St. Nicholas.*

Cast thy Bread on the Waters.

ECCLES. xi. 1, 6. Cast thy bread upon the waters. . . . In the morning sow thy seed, and in the evening withhold not thy hand: for thou knowest not whether shall prosper, either this or that, or whether they shall be alike good.

The travelling pedlar who sold a book to Baxter's father. The visit of a travelling pedlar to the door of Richard Baxter's father led to the purchase of a little book, and that book led to the conversion of Richard Baxter. This Richard Baxter wrote *The Saint's Rest*, which was blessed to the conversion of Philip Doddridge. Doddridge wrote *The Rise and Progress of Religion in the Soul*, which led to the conversion of Wilberforce. Wilberforce wrote *Practical Views*, which was the instrument of the conversion both of Dr. Chalmers and of Legh Richmond. Dr. Chalmers by his burning piety, and Legh Richmond by his *Dairyman's Daughter*, handed on the good seed, the leaven went on leavening, and who shall tell whether of the two has done the most good, this or that, or whether they have both alike prospered? Truly the bread cast by the street pedlar upon the water was found to spring up and bear fruit after many days.

Changelings.

JUDG. xx. 13. Deliver us the men, the children of Belial, that we may put them to death.

ACTS xiii. 10. O full of all subtilty and all mischief, thou child of the devil.

[It is not evident upon what authority the prevailing notion of changelings is based, but it is quite certain that even to the present hour the superstition has not wholly died out. The general belief was, that children were liable to be changed till they were baptized, and hence they were most carefully watched till that rite had been performed.]

Luther believed the absurd superstition of changelings. In his *Table Talk*, Luther says, "Eight years ago I saw at Dessau a changeling twelve years old. This child did nothing but feed; it would eat as much as two farm labourers. It cried if any one touched it, and was never happy but when mischief was abroach

I told the prince of Anhalt if I were in his place I would throw the child into the Moldau; and I exhorted the villagers to pray God to take away the cursed thing out of the land. They followed my advice, and their prayers were heard, for the creature died within two years."—*Colloquia Mensalia.*

It is almost past credibility that a man like Luther should have written such horrible stuff as this; but we must bear in mind that the belief in witches prevailed amongst the wisest men and women long after the Reformation.

A changeling thrown into a river. In Saxony, near Halberstad, was a man who had a *killcrop*, which required six women to satisfy it; so the man resolved to take it to Halberstad "to be rocked by the Virgin." As he was crossing the river, a devil below the water called out, "Killcrop! Killcrop!" and the child, which had never spoken before, answered, "Ho! ho! ho!" "Whither away?" asked the devil. "To the Virgin Mary to be rocked," said the infant. The father, in alarm, then threw the babe into the river, and the two devils [that is, the river devil and the infant] floated down the stream, crying "Ho! ho! ho!" To this Luther adds, "The devil hath the power of changing children, and of laying imps in cradles in the place of human beings; but such changelings never survive above eighteen or nineteen years."—Luther, *Colloquia Mensalia.*

A changeling boiled to death. The following tale is more revolting still, and is given on the authority of R. G. Haliburton, 1875, who says he was told it by colonel Tydd of the 76th regiment, then stationed in Ireland. A man and woman named Mahoney were tried for the murder of their child, which they believed to have been a changeling. It was a delicate child; and the parents felt certain it had been substituted for their own healthy infant. They wanted to compel the real mother to come forward and save her child; so when it was between four and five years of age they put the poor wee thing into a pot of boiling water, and set the pot on the fire. The little fellow screamed in its agony, "I'm Johnny Mahoney! I'm Johnny Mahoney! Indeed, indeed, I am. I am no changeling." But there was none to hear, none to take pity. And the child was boiled to death. I know not, in all the history of man, a more pitiable story; but if Luther had been by, his heart would not have relented, for he would have thought it meritorious to kill a child of the devil. O religion, religion! how many sins are committed in thy name! Verily there is no habitation of cruelty equal to religion "falsely so called."

Charity brings its own Reward.

MATT. x. 42. Whosoever shall give to drink unto one of these little ones a cup of cold water only, in the name of a disciple, verily I say unto you, he shall in no wise lose his reward.

MATT. xxv. 40. Verily I say unto you, Inasmuch as ye have done it unto one of the least of these My brethren, ye have done it unto Me.

TOBIT xii. 9. Alms doth deliver from death, and shall purge away all sin.

St. Isidore's charity to a pilgrim rewarded. Isidore of Madrid, the farm labourer, returning from work, found at his door a poor pilgrim, who craved bread of him, which Isidore, with his usual liberality, freely bestowed. At night the pilgrim returned, and, putting on his benefactor a pilgrim's weeds, took him from Madrid to Jerusalem, and showed him all the places of note connected with the life and ministry of our Redeemer. He showed him Bethlehem, the place of birth; Nazareth, where He was brought up; Jordan, where He was baptized. He showed him the wilderness, where Christ was tempted; the mount of transfiguration; the spot where He was scourged; Calvary, where He was crucified; the tomb in which He was laid; and the hill from which He rose through the air. Having showed him all, he carried him back to Spain, and left him sleeping peacefully in bed.—John of Madrid (140 years after his death), *Life of St. Isidore of Madrid.* (See also cardinal Lambertini, *De Canonisatione Sanctorum*, vol. iii.)

Christ before All.

MATT. x. 37. He that loveth father or mother more than Me is not worthy of Me; and he that loveth son or daughter more than Me is not worthy of Me.

LUKE xiv. 26. If any man come to Me, and hate not his father, and mother, and wife, and children, and brethren, and sisters, yea, and his own life also, he cannot be My disciple.

St. Sorus refuses to see his mother (A.D. 500–580). The mother of St. Sorus called at his hermitage to see him, but when told who was at the door he resolved to show the world an example of abnegation, and refused to see her. Neither her tears nor her words of grief moved him. "Why, why is this, my son, my son?"

exclaimed his mother. "Will no prayers touch thee? Will you not show this small courtesy even to your aged mother, who has come all this way to see you? O my son, my son!" But the saint spoke not; he only removed further into his cell, saying, "O my God, Thou art my father and my mother." The grief of the aged woman having somewhat abated, she said, "Ah! my son, your faith has triumphed over your maternal love. Though you refuse to see me on earth, may we meet in heaven." "L'ange de Dieu eut à écrire ce jour-là dans le livre de vie, un sacrifice sublime à côté du nom de la mère et à côté du nom du fils."—*Les Petits Bollandistes*, vol. ii. p. 192.

Christ's Sorrows.

LAM. i. 12. Behold, and see if there be any sorrow like unto My sorrow.

Christ describes to Camille Baptiste Varani his seven sorrows (A.D. 1458–1527). Camille Baptiste Varani is her own biographer, and writes in the first person singular. Her father, Julius Cesar Varani, built her a monastery, and she entered it with seven other religious women in January, 1484. Here she had many very remarkable revelations, of which the following is an example:—One day Jesus Christ came to her in person, and said to her, "Behold, My daughter, and see if any sorrow is like unto My sorrow," and He then goes on to explain to her the seven sources of His great grief: (1) As the federal Head of the whole family of man, He feels acutely that His grace is not as widespread as original sin; (2) As Head of the body, the Church, He feels that all who fall away from grace are members cut off from His own body; (3) He feels by sympathy the great disappointment His mother feels at the slow progress of his work; (4) He feels the repenting anguish of all true penitents; (5) He feels the sorrow of His disciples who grieve at the great sufferings He has endured for their redemption; (6) He feels the sorrow of ingratitude when any reject His free salvation; (7) He feels most acutely that the Jews, God's chosen people and His own fellow-countrymen in the flesh, refuse to be grafted into the true olive, but persist in being castaways. It would occupy several pages to reproduce what Christ is said to have told Varani in illustration of these seven sorrows, but the following illustrations employed may be here repeated. *First Sorrow:* "Imagine the pain a felon feels when he is torn limb from limb; such suffering I f el when souls are torn from My hands. Only My pain is as much more acute, as spirit is more sensible than matter." Varani asks if He feels the torments of the damned. No, He replies; a man feels pain in losing a leg or arm, but after the limb is off, you may cut it, or burn it, or torment it in any other way without his feeling it. So the Son of man feels pain when a soul is plucked from Him, but when that soul is cast into hell He feels not its torment, because it is no longer of the body. *Second Sorrow:* "The falling away of the elect, like Judas, is even a worse grief, as the loss of a beloved child is felt more than the loss of a stranger. Judas was a chosen disciple, in whom was My hope; and when such a one lifts up his heel against Me, My love, My hope, My sympathies, are crushed. It is touching the apple of Mine eye, wounding the most sensitive part. Those who die and go to purgatory fill Me with suffering, as burning My hand or side would do. They are not cut off from the body, like those in hell, and all they suffer I suffer also." Passing over the next two sorrows, that of sympathy with His mother, and that of the penitence of the repentant, we come to the *Fifth Sorrow*, the grief of His disciples at the sorrows He Himself endured in His great passion. He says, "I felt the crown of thorns, the buffeting, the scourging, the crucifixion, as any other would have done; but over and above this, as My disciples are one with Me, their grief was My grief; and when afterwards Peter was crucified, Paul beheaded, Bartholomew was flayed alive, James cast down from the temple, or any other member of My mystical body is martyred, their suffering is My suffering, their sorrow My sorrow." *Sixth Sorrow:* The sorrow of ingratitude may be passed over, so come we to the last or *Seventh Sorrow*, the obduracy of the Jews, God's own chosen people, Christ's own countrymen; this He says is a standing grief. To be rejected by the heathen, by strangers, is bad enough, but to be rejected by one's own people is far worse. A king who has done all that king can do to make his people happy, to be reviled by foreigners is a grief, but to be dethroned, insulted, misunderstood by his own subjects, is a far deeper sorrow.—L'abbé P——, *Vie Spirituelle de la Bienheureuse Varani* (from her own autobiography).

Coals of Fire ("Overcome evil with good").

ROM. xii. 20. If thine enemy hunger, feed him; if he thirst, give him drink; for in so doing thou shalt heap coals of fire on his head.

The baron and the malefactor. A certain malefactor was sentenced to death by a baron, and heaped curses on his head. The baron reprieved the man, but he ceased not his invectives. Next leet-day, the same man was brought again before the baron, who asked him if his choler was expended; whereupon he renewed his railings with even greater bitterness. The baron, still resolved to win him if possible, again dismissed him without punishment. Before the third leet-day, the baron sent for the man, and asked him if his temper had yet cooled down. But no; the man was obdurate and sullen with secret rancour. "God forgive thee, my man, as I do," said the baron; and so saying, he handed to him his pardon. The man was melted, burst into tears, and even fainted with emotion. On coming to himself, he refused to receive his pardon, unless the baron would take him into his service. This he did, and he proved the very best of servants, so diligent, so loving, so obedient, that the baron at death bequeathed him a large portion of his estate. He had indeed overcome evil with good.

This looks like an allegory of God and man. Man, the self-willed, wicked servant, melted into love and obedience by the unremitted goodness of God.

Contentment.

PHIL. iv. 11. I have learned, in whatsoever state I am, therewith to be content.
MATT. vi. 10. Thy will be done.
MATT. xxvi. 39. Nevertheless, not as I will, but as Thou wilt.

The contented beggar (fourteenth century). One day when St. Tauler had been preaching in Cologne, as he left the church he encountered a poor man covered with rags, and so full of sores as to be most revolting. One half of his head was a mass of ulcers; he had lost an arm and one of his legs, and his whole body was covered with blains. Tauler gave him a piece of silver, and as he did so, said to the man, "Good day, friend." "Thank you, sir," replied the man, "but all my days are good days, sir." Tauler, thinking the man misunderstood him, rejoined, "I wished you good day. I wish you to be happy, friend." "Yes, I hear, sir," replied the man, "and thank you, but your wish has been long accomplished." Tauler, thinking the man either an idiot or deaf, said in a louder voice, "I fear you have not heard me; I wished you happiness." "Yes, yes, sir, I heard you; and I repeat, I am always happy, and every day with me is a good day." Tauler, struck by the man's words and manner, asked the man to explain what he meant. "Sir," said the man, "from early childhood I knew that God is wise and just and good. From early childhood I have suffered from a disease which has preyed on my whole body. I was always poor. What then? Nothing happens to man without the will and permission of God. The Saviour, who died for me, must know better than I do what is good for me. So, though I suffer, I know I am being made more perfect by suffering. I have taught myself, through grace, to wish nothing but what my God and Saviour sees fit to give me. If He sends me sickness, I receive it with joy; ay, even as if it were my sister. If He gives me health, I accept it with thanks. If He gives no food to eat, I am content to fast for my sins. If I am without raiment, I remember that Christ, my Saviour, gave up heaven itself, to become a naked infant in a manger. If I am houseless, I call to mind that the Son of man said, 'The foxes have holes, and the birds of the air have nests, but the Son of man hath not where to lay His head.' If I suffer on this earth as Lazarus, I remember that Lazarus, at death, was taken into Abraham's bosom. What shall I say more? I am content with my lot, and feel I have more than I deserve. If I weep with one eye, I laugh with the other, because I wish only what God wishes for me. Hence, sir, I said, each day is to me a good day, and I am always happy." Tauler wept in silence, and declared he had never heard such a sermon as that of the poor beggar.—*History of the Illustrious Men of St. Dominic*, vol. ii. pp. 334, etc.

All weathers pleased the shepherd of Salisbury plain. A gentleman, travelling on a misty morning over Salisbury plain, asked a shepherd what he thought of the weather. He replied, "I am sure the weather will please me, sir." Being asked if he meant the mist would lift by'n'-by, and the sun break out, the shepherd made answer, "Well, sir, I give no heed to my own opinion; but I am sure of this, what pleaseth God will please me."

Pythagoras conforms himself to the will

of the gods. When Pythagoras embarked from Sicily to sail to Greece, his friends assembled to embrace him, and bid him farewell. One of them, in taking leave, said to him, "May such things befall you from the gods, O Thymaridas, as are most in accordance with your own wishes." "Say rather," replied the sage, "may my wishes conform minutely to such things as may, by the will of the gods, befall me."—Iamblichus, *Life of Pythagoras*, ch. xxviii.

Covetousness is Idolatry.

COL. iii. 5. Inordinate affection, evil concupiscence, and covetousness, which is idolatry.

COL. iii. 2. Set your affection on things above, not on things on the earth.

MATT. x. 37. He that loveth father or mother more than Me is not worthy of Me.

EPH. v. 5. A covetous man is an idolater.

Inordinate affection may prevail in a hermit's cell. A hermit asked God in prayer what recompense he would receive who had forsaken all for Christ. A voice said to him, "The same recompense as is due to the poverty of pope Gregory." "Strange," thought the hermit; "then all my poverty is nothing worth, if it weighs no more in the estimation of God than that of the pope, the greatest and richest potentate of all the earth." As he thus reflected, the voice addressed him again, saying, "Inordinate affection is idolatry, and not the possession of wealth. You love your cat more than pope Gregory, called the Great, loves all his wealth and all his honours. You in your poverty have set your heart on a cat, but Gregory in the midst of wealth despises it."—John the deacon, *Life of St. Gregory the Great* (written in the twelfth century, at the command of pope John VIII.).

Crucify the Son of God afresh.

HEB. vi. 6. [Those who fall away from grace] crucify to themselves the Son of God afresh.

The Virgin Mary shows St. Coletta how the sins of the world had crucified the Son of God afresh (A.D. 1380–1447). One day, when St. Coletta was praying to the Virgin, and begging her to intercede with God in behalf of the poor, the Virgin appeared to her, bringing in her hand a beautiful platter full of little pieces of flesh, the body of Christ mutilated and broken. Showing it to St. Coletta, she said to her, "How can you ask me to intercede with my Son for those who live in daily sin, and crucify their Lord afresh, cutting up the body into little pieces such as you see on this platter?"—Father Ignatius, *Histoire des Maïeurs d'Abbeville*, p. 814.

Darkness turned to Light.

ISA. xlii. 5–7. I the Lord have called thee in righteousness, to open the blind eyes, and bring them that sit in darkness out of the prison house.

ISA. xlix. 9. Say to them that are in darkness, Show yourselves.

LUKE i. 76–79. Thou, Child, shalt be called the Prophet of the Highest: for Thou shalt give light to them that sit in darkness.

St. Valentine turns the darkness of Asterius's child into light (A.D. 268). St. Valentine almost persuaded the emperor Claudius II. to become a Christian, but, fearing the people, he delivered the saint to the judge Asterius, to deal with as he thought proper. St. Valentine prayed that God would give light to them that sat in darkness and in the shadow of death; and he told the judge that Jesus Christ was the true Light, which lighteth every man that cometh into the world. "What is that you say?" demanded Asterius—"that Jesus Christ is the true Light?" "Even so," replied the saint. "He is more. He is not only the true Light, but the only light, which can give life and light to them that sit in darkness." "Say you so?" said the judge. "I will soon put your words to the proof. I have here, in the house, a little adopted daughter who has been blind ever since she was two years old. If you can turn her darkness into light, by restoring her eyesight, I will believe that Jesus Christ is indeed the true Light, that giveth light to them who sit in darkness." So saying, he went into the house to fetch the blind girl. St. Valentine, laying his hand upon her eyes, said in prayer, "O Thou who art the true Light, give light to this Thy servant." Instantly sight was restored to the blind child. Asterius and his wife, falling at the feet of Valentine, prayed that they might be admitted into the Christian fellowship; whereupon St. Valentine commanded them to break their idols, to fast for three days, to forgive their enemies, and to be baptized. Asterius and his wife did all the saint told them to do, and Valentine baptized them and all their household, to the number of forty-six in all.—*Les Petits Bollandistes*, vol. ii. pp. 510, 511.

Day for a Year.

EZEK. iv. 6. I have appointed Thee each day for a year.

It was revealed to St. William of Paris that in seven days he should die, but the seven days meant seven years (A.D. 1105–1202). Seven years before his death, a venerable old man appeared to St. William of Paris, and said to him, "Your life will be extended yet seven days." The saint supposed that he would die in a week's time, but seeing no indication of death at the close of seven days, he supposed the prophet meant seven weeks, then seven months, then seven years—a day for a year. And so it was. Just seven years after the announcement he died, aged ninety-seven.—Surius, *Lives of the Saints*, vol. ii.

Death at the Door.

1 Sam. xx. 3. There is but a step between me and death.

The citizen and the sailor. Said a mariner to a city burgher, "All my ancestors have been sailors, and all died at sea. My father, my father's father, and my great-grandfather, and, for aught I know, his father and grandfather before him, they all died in their ships, and were buried at sea." "Methinks," said the the citizen, "you can never embark, then, without thinking of the uncertainty of life, and committing your soul to God." "Well," says the seaman, "there is sense in what you say. And where, pray, did your father die?" "In bed," said the burgher. "We are a peaceful race, that has followed trade from generation to generation; and all my ancestors, as far as I know, have died in their beds." "Ah?" said the seaman; "it was so, was it? Then, methinks, you can never go to bed without thinking of the uncertainty of life, and committing your soul to God."

Death-terrors.

Psalm cxvi. 3. The sorrows of death compassed me, and the pains of hell gat hold of me. I found trouble and sorrow.

Psalm lv. 4, 5. The terrors of death are fallen upon me; fearfulness and trembling are come upon me. The terrors of death are fallen upon me.

1 Cor. xv. 56. The sting of death is sin.

Prov. i. 24–29. Because I have called, and ye refused, I also will laugh at your calamity, and will mock when your fear cometh; when your fear cometh as desolation, and your destruction as a whirlwind; when distress and anguish cometh upon you. Then shall they call upon me, but I will not answer; they shall seek me, but they shall not find me.

Death-terrors of Charles IX. of France. Charles IX. inaugurated with his mother, Catherine de Medicis, the slaughter of the Huguenots, begun on St. Bartholomew's Eve, 1572, and even assisted in shooting down fugitives, as he watched, like a spider, from the windows of the Tuileries. In 1574 his health gave way. He was extremely restless. His complexion became flushed, his eyes fierce, and his slumbers disturbed by ugly dreams. He complained of internal heat and dreadful colics. A blood-stained foam rose frequently to his mouth, and a bloody sweat oozed from every pore of his body. His physicians thought that arsenic must have been given him; and strong suspicions rested on his mother. During his last night he moaned and wept without ceasing. "Ah! nurse, nurse, nurse! What blood! What murders! What evil counsels have I followed!" These were his dying words. He was but twenty-four years old, and had reigned fourteen of them.—*Political, Social, and Literary History of France.*

Death-terrors of the emperors Decius and Valerian. Decius and Valerian were great persecutors of the Christians, and, amongst other atrocities, roasted St. Lawrence alive on a gridiron, but soon met with their own deaths. The devil, we are told, seized on them while they were sitting in the amphitheatre. First Decius screamed aloud in agony, saying that Hippolitus, a Christian he had put to death, was binding him in chains of iron. Then Valerian exclaimed that St. Lawrence was burning him alive with fire. Valerian died in agony in the province of Decius, and Decius, after three days, ended his life in like misery. All the time of their death they kept incessantly calling on Hippolitus and Lawrence to take pity on them; but the fire within them ceased not to torment them. Distress and anguish came upon them, but the Lord laughed at their calamity. They called for succour, but there was none to help them.—*Life of St. Lawrence* (from the public registers).

It does not appear historically true that Decius and Valerian died within three days of each other. Decius died A.D. 251. It is not certainly known when Valerian died, but it is quite certain he was alive in A.D. 260.

Death-terror of sir John Guise. Several Quakers having met together in worship in Stoke Orchard, sir John Guise entered the place with a file of musketeers, and abused them roundly. John Robarts warned him; but sir John, regardless of the expostulation, sent twelve of them to

Gloucester Castle. Robarts said to him, "God will plead our cause, and with Him we are content to leave it." Next night but one, sir John went to bed in his usual health, but in the morning, as he did not ring his bell at the usual time, his housekeeper went to see the reason, and found him dying. "Pray, sir," she said, "what's the matter?" But all he answered was, "Oh, these Quakers, these Quakers! Would to God I had never had a hand against these terrible Quakers." And so he died.—*Memoirs of John Robarts, the Quaker.*

Death-terror of Giovanni Maretti. Savonarola was burnt alive at the stake, May 22, A.D. 1498. Giovanni Maretti, one of the chief persecutors, perished miserably soon afterwards, crying out in terrible anguish, "Oh, this hand! this hand! the friar is torturing it."—*Eclectic Review* (on Savonarola).

Death-terrors of the priest who burnt St. Vitalis at the stake. St. Ambrose gives a death-scene very similar to that of Charles IX. of France (see p. 385). It is to be found in his *Life of St. Vitalis of Ravenna*, martyred in the reign of Nero. A priest, he says, mainly instrumental in the saint's death, was possessed of the devil immediately afterwards, and dreadfully tormented. In his agony he howled, saying, "Vitalis, thou burnest me! Vitalis, thou consumest me! I burn! I burn! I burn! Vitalis! Oh, Vitalis!" In this state he continued for seven days, and then, unable to bear the agony longer, he threw himself into a river, and was drowned.

Desert made Fertile.

ISA. xxxv. 1. The wilderness and the solitary place shall be glad, and the desert shall rejoice and blossom as the rose.

St. Clare restores a vineyard to fertility by prayer (seventh century.) The vineyard of the monastery of Vienne, in France, was one year so injured by hail, that all the fruit was cut off. St. Clare prayed, and passed the whole night in earnest supplication. Next morning the vines were crowded with rich clusters, and the produce of the vineyard far exceeded that of the average yield.—*Les Petits Bollandistes*, vol. i. p. 31.

St. Giles converts a wilderness into a garden by prayer. When St. Giles sojourned for a few days with Veredemus, the hermit, on the banks of the Rhone, he found the solitary place a barren wilderness; but by his prayers he converted it into a garden, which rejoiced in its fertility, and blossomed as the rose.—Gilbert (bishop of Carnotus), *Life of St. Giles.*

St. Honoré made the isle of Lerins a fertile garden (fifth century.) The isle of Lerins was filled with serpents; it was wholly uncultivated and without inhabitant, when St. Honoré landed there, and determined to make it his abiding-place. The serpents soon yielded to him, and ere long a multitude of disciples gathered round him. In an incredibly short time the whole face of the island was changed. Instead of the thorn, there came up the fir tree; and instead of the briar, there came up the myrtle tree. The desert became a paradise, and the solitary place was glad. The island was watered with streams of water, enamelled with flowers, rich in pasture, and abundantly fruitful.—St. Hilary, *Life of St. Honoré* (or Honoratus).

There needed no miracle to effect this change, nor indeed does the biographer affirm that the transformation was miraculous. A very similar change occurred in Brandenburg, during the wise rule of Frederick William, the great elector. Louis XIV. had driven from France the most industrious and peaceable of his subjects by his insane revocation of the Edict of Nantes. Twenty thousand of the fugitives went to Brandenburg, where the wise elector gave them allotments; and by their industry and frugality they soon converted the waste lands of Berlin into potherb gardens. It was no miracle, beyond that of steady industry, which made either of these places "blossom as the rose."

Destruction of the Temple.

MATT. xxiv. 1. 2. His disciples came to Jesus to show Him the buildings of the temple. And Jesus said unto them, See ye not all these things? Verily I say unto you, there shall not be left here one stone upon another that shall not be thrown down.

1 KINGS ix. 7. Then will I cut off Israel out of the land which I have given them; and this house, which I have hallowed for My name, will I cast out of My sight.

(The temple referred to in the *Book of Kings* was Solomon's temple, that referred to in *Matthew* was Herod's temple.)

Julian's effort to rebuild the temple abortive. [Julian's abortive attempt to rebuild the temple is generally quoted by Christian writers as a most triumphant proof of the truth of prophecy; but our Lord does not say it shall never be restored, but that it shall be utterly destroyed. In the *Book of Kings* we read of Solomon's temple, "I will cast it out of My sight," not that it shall never be restored; and in the Gospels we read of Herod's temple, "One stone shall not be left upon another which shall not be thrown down," not that it shall never be built up again. Solomon's temple was cast out of God's sight, and rose again twice, once in the days of Nehemiah, and again in the days of Herod; analogy, therefore, would be better carried out if Herod's temple, having been utterly destroyed, should, after a time, be rebuilt.—See Warburton's *Dissertation on the Project of Julian to rebuild the Temple;* Ambrose, *Letter* xl., A.D. 388; Rufinus; Theodoret; Socratês, *Ecclesiastical History;* Sozomenês, *ditto;* Philostorgius; Chrysostom; etc., etc.]

We are told that "Julian, by a letter full of hypocritical flattery," assembled the Jews at Jerusalem, stating that, from a careful examination of prophecy, the fulness of time was come, when the Jews should be gathered in. He put at their disposal a host of workmen, and immense sums of money, and appointed Alypius, his friend, to superintend the restoration of the city and temple. The Jews from all quarters flocked to the holy city, and ill-treated the Christians. For the foundations of the new temple, the materials of Herod's temple were employed. Never work went on so merrily. The people worked both day and night. Some Jews actually used silver trowels and hods to show honour to the work in hand, and express their enthusiasm therein. Women the most delicate assisted by carrying materials for building in their robes, and gave freely of their ornaments, jewellery, and wealth. One mind and one spirit animated all. The foundations were laid, but while count Appius pressed on the work, flames burst out from the ground contiguous to the foundations, burning the workmen and rendering the place inaccessible. St. Chrysostom, Sozomenês, and Theodoret say the flames issued from the new foundations, and so persistent were they, that the workmen were obliged to abandon the work. These are the words of Ammianus Marcellinus, bk. ii. ch. 1. Marvellous as this statement is in itself, the ecclesiastical writers have embellished it with marvel upon marvel. They tell us that, besides the fire, there were earthquakes and storms; that thunderbolts fell; that crosses were miraculously impressed on the garments of those who laboured in the work; that a luminous cross, enclosed in a circle, appeared in the clouds; that many pursued by the flames would have taken refuge in neighbouring churches, but were repelled by invisible hands. St. Gregory of Nazianzen says it was universally believed, and all the world acknowledged, that when the builders fled from the destructive elements, fire leaped from the ground, mutilating some and killing others (*Against Julian*, orat. iv.). These earthquakes, eruptions, and lightnings were repeated every time any attempt was made to continue the work, which was therefore of necessity abandoned. This tale is told by a host of writers, who agree in the general scope of the narrative, though they differ in details. Libanius, a pagan, devoted to the service of Julian, speaks of the earthquake, and Ammianus Marcellinus was also an idolater and admirer of Julian.

Devil a Liar.

JOHN viii. 44. The devil is a liar, and the father of lies.

The devil, by a lie, tries to disturb St. Antony while preaching. Once when St. Antony was preaching, a messenger entered the place, and whispered to a noble lady that her son had just died. St. Antony said from the pulpit, "Woman, believe it not. Thy son is alive and well; but the devil is a liar from the beginning, and the father of lies." The devil, seeing himself foiled in disturbing the congregation, "vanished away in the sight of the whole assembly."—Edward Kinesman (1623), *Lives of the Saints.*

Devil Man's Adversary.

EPH. iv. 27. Neither give place to the devil.

EPH. vi. 12. We wrestle not against flesh and blood, but against principalities, against powers, against the rulers of the darkness of this world, against spiritual wickedness in high places.

2 TIM. ii. 26 If God peradventure will give them repentance, and that they may recover themselves out of the snare of the devil, who are taken captive by him at his will.

JAMES iv. 7. Resist the devil, and he will flee from you.

1 PET. v. 8, 9. Your adversary the devil, as a roaring lion, walketh about, seeking whom he may devour: whom resist steadfast in the faith.

1 JOHN ii. 13. I write unto you, young men, because ye have overcome the wicked one.

St. Francisca's encounters with the devil (A.D. 1384–1440). The devil, who witnessed with regret the virtue of St. Francisca, resolved to go against her, and employ all his efforts to get her into his snare. For this purpose he presented himself to her in a thousand disguises, some horrible, others ridiculous, and others, again, immodest. He was fond of attacking her at prayer-time, when he would roll her face along the ground, drag her by the hair, beat her, and whip her cruelly. One night, as she was taking a little repose, he carried into her chamber the body of a man who had been dead a long time, the stench of which never left her. It would not be possible to set down all her combats with this adversary of her soul, in all of which she came off more than conqueror through Him who loved her, and gave Himself for her. Even her ghostly confessor, being one day attacked by the devil, was delivered by her prayers, and many abandoned women were reclaimed by her, after she had driven the devil out of them.—John Mattiotti (her father confessor), *Life of St. Francisca.*

The devil, to ruin the monks of Mount Avernia, sends daily offerings to the convent. A certain rich man entertained no friendly feeling towards the monks of Mount Avernia; but one day the community was amazed at receiving from him a present of some dainty production of his garden. Their astonishment was increased when next day a fresh supply was received; and this continued for many days. At last some of the older monks began to feel suspicious, and called on the rich man. Being questioned about the matter, he replied he had acted on the urgent advice of his gardener, the best servant he ever had in his service, and one only lately engaged. The monks asked to see this paragon of a servant, but the servant positively refused to come forward. The monks, accordingly, went into the garden, fixed their eyes on the gardener, and instantly recognized him to be a spirit of evil, who, to corrupt the monks, had hit upon the device of alluring them to habits of luxury. Unable to endure the gaze of these holy men, the devil instantly vanished; but the rich man never after met with so good a servant.—R. H. Busk, *Notes and Queries*, Oct. 20, 1883, p. 302.

Disfigurement for Christ's Sake.

Matt. v. 29, 30. If thy right eye offend thee, pluck it out, and cast it from thee: for it is profitable for thee that one of thy members should perish, and not that thy whole body should be cast into hell. And if thy right hand offend thee, cut it off, and cast it from thee: for it is profitable for thee that one of thy members should perish, and not that thy whole body should be cast into hell.

St. Angadrema, to avoid marriage, prays to be made hideous (seventh century). Angadrema was the daughter of Robert comte de Renty, in the diocese of Arras, keeper of the seals in the reign of Clotaire III. She was very beautiful, well educated, and deeply religious. When of marriageable age her father promised her in marriage to Ansbert, son of Siwin, seigneur of Chaussy, near Mantes. Angadrema was greatly surprised to hear of this arrangement, and was placed in this dilemma: If she consented to the marriage, she would break her vow, for she had vowed her virginity to Christ; if she refused, she would disobey her father, whom she dearly loved. In this perplexity she threw the burden of the solution on God, and prayed that He would render her such an object of abhorrence that the marriage must be abandoned. During the night before the marriage she was struck with leprosy, and, of course, the marriage was broken off. She now told her father what she had done, and with his consent she took the veil, which she received from the hands of St. Ouen, archbishop of Rouen. The moment she received it the leprosy left her, and she was more beautiful than ever. The archbishop then placed her in a monastery, and in due time she became abbess of Oroir des Vierges, in the diocese of Beauvais.—L'abbé Sabatier, *Vie des Saints de Beauvais.*

St. Angela of Merici, that she might not be vain of her beautiful hair, washed it frequently with sooty water (A.D. 1474–1540). St. Angela was the youngest of five children, and was very pious even from her earliest childhood. This she showed by her disregard of finery, and all the appliances usually resorted to by the female sex to set off their personal advantages. She was a very beautiful child, with long curling blond hair, very glossy and extremely fine. As everybody admired and praised its gloss and colour, she used to wash it frequently with soot and water, even when she was a mere child, saying, "If thy right eye offend thee, cut it off, and cast it from thee; and if thy hair is a temptation to sin, mar its beauty, lest it should feed vanity, and wean the heart from God."—*Life of St. Angela di Merici* (published at Montpellier, 1804).

I do not believe any child ever existed who was such a religious prig as this. And only a monk could see any merit in such abnormal childhood.

St. Enimia, to escape marriage, prays

that she may be despoiled of her beauty (seventh century). St. Enimia, daughter of Clotaire II., king of France, was full of grace and beauty. At the age of fifteen she vowed her virginity to Jesus Christ. One so nobly born and so richly endowed would be sure to have suitors, and at an early age her hand was solicited by a young nobleman, whose addresses were accepted readily by the king, her father. The day of espousals was duly fixed, and every preparation was made for the royal marriage. But Enimia felt that the force of her vows prevented her obedience to her father in this particular; so she prayed that God would so disfigure her, that she might escape the sin of marriage without the sin of disobedience; and that very night she was covered with a hideous leprosy. Of course, all thoughts of marriage were now abandoned, and physicians were sent for to cure the disease; but as it was sent by God, only God could remove it. After several years of suffering, an angel came and said to her, "God now wishes to restore you to health; you are therefore to go to Gevaudan, and wash in the fountain of Burle." Accordingly, next day, the king supplied her with a suitable escort and all things necessary, and she started for Gevaudan. Having reached Gevaudan, she made inquiries about the fountain of Burle, but no one had ever heard of it. An elderly lady said there was a fountain celebrated for its healing waters at a considerable distance from Gevaudan, but the name was "Bagnols les Bains." The princess felt certain that this could not be the fountain mentioned by the angel, and again prayed to be directed aright. The angel came and said to her, "No, the waters of Bagnols are not those which God has designed for your cure. The fountain of Burle is close by." After diligent search in the immediate vicinity, some shepherds were heard to speak of the Fontaine de Burle, and, being asked about it, they directed the princess to the place. Immediately she plunged into this fountain, the enormous rock which dominated opened its hundred chinks, and sent forth streams of water in great abundance, and immediately they reached the princess, her leprosy left her, and her skin became clean and fresh and wholesome as that of a little child. The princess now resolved to take up her abode in this neighbourhood; and here she built a monastery, which was duly dedicated to the Virgin Mary, and St. Enimia was its first abbess.—*Propre du Diocèse de Mende*, 1619.

St. Eusebia and her companions, called the martyrs of Marseilles (seventh century). Not far from Marseilles, on the borders of a little river called the Huveaune, once stood a monastery of St. Cassian, which has won immortal renown by the heroism of its abbess and her sisterhood. The lady referred to was St. Eusebia, who had been abbess for fifty years. The times were troublous times, for the Saracens had invaded Europe, and wherever they marched, they pillaged, they sacked, they devastated, they destroyed with fire and sword. The cross paled before the crescent. Spain had succumbed to them, and they had crossed the Pyrenees to ravage France. The monasteries were spoiled, devastated, burnt; massacre without pity was the order of march. The churches were thrown down, the priests put to the sword, disaster followed disaster, and all was hopeless despair, for there was none to help. The monastery of Eusebia stood isolated and alone, and one day a number of Saracenic soldiers were observed upon the walls. No time was to be lost. Eusebia called her companions about her, and addressed them thus: "Courage, my companions! Courage, virgins! Still some little time is left us, and victory is in our hands. Death before dishonour be our word. Torments, suffering, a martyr's death, before shame. Pray God to give us a glorious death, but to protect our innocence. Pray Christ, whom we have chosen for our Spouse, may fly to our aid in the moment of our need. Christ sustain you! Christ fortify you! He speaks by me; hear Him, sisters. Sacrifice your beauty, sisters, but spare your souls. Immolate your charms, but save your innocence. Tear from your faces those graces which attract the ravisher, and where they seek for beauty, let them behold sights to affright their souls. Follow my example, sisters, and ere long, I promise you, we shall all join the chorus-song of the saints in light." So saying, she drew a knife across her face, and mutilated her nose and lips. Blood covered her face, blood reddened her garments. Her example inspired the other sisters; and when the soldiers entered, they were horrified to behold these bleeding saints. In their rage and disappointment they fell upon them without mercy, and put them all to the sword;

but now they behold the face of God, and bear His name in their foreheads, in that New Jerusalem, where every tear is wiped away for ever and ever. Amen.—L'abbé J. B. Magnan, *Conseiller Catholique* (Marseille).

Isberga, to avoid marriage, prays to be deprived of her beauty. Isberga, daughter of Pepin le Bref, was very beautiful, and was first asked in marriage by the emperor of Constantinople; but this alliance was declined by the advice of all the grandees of the nation, and even of the pope himself. Her next suitor was the prince of Wales—handsome, rich, young, and manly. Every one wished Isberga to accept this suit, but she herself had vowed to remain single, and, that she might not violate her vow, she prayed that God would mar her beauty. Forthwith a violent fever seized her, and covered her with a sort of hideous leprosy, insomuch that she became an object of disgust to all who saw her. The prince took leave of king Pepin, and, returning to his own country, left Isberga unmolested. Ultimately she recovered her beauty, by eating an eel picked out of a dead body thrown into a ditch, and embraced a religious life.—Vandrival, *Life of St. Isberga.*

St. Syra, to prevent marriage, prays that she may become blind (A.D. 640). St. Syra, of the royal house of Scotland, was the daughter of Eugenius IV., and was brought up by her mother according to the religious notions of the time. When of marriageable age, she had a great number of suitors, but having vowed her virginity to Christ, she prayed earnestly for the "grace of blindness," in order to resist the demands for her alliance more effectually. Her prayer was granted, but she was told by revelation that she would recover her sight, if she went to Troyes, and made her prayers to St. Savinian. So she went to Troyes with some chosen companions, discovered the tomb of the saint, then unknown, prayed that her sight might be restored, recovered it, and lived the rest of her life as a religious recluse.—Boitel, *Beauties of the History of Champagne.*

Divided Kingdom.

MATT. iii. 24. If a kingdom be divided against itself, that kingdom cannot stand.

"Divide and conquer."

Examples: Divisions among the Trojans brought in the Greeks to their destruction;

The divisions of the Greeks brought in the Macedonian Philip;

The divisions of the Assyrian monarchy brought in the Persian;

The divisions of the Persian monarchy brought in the Macedonian;

The divisions of the Macedonian monarchy brought in the Roman;

The divisions of the Roman empire brought in the Turks;

The divisions of the Jews brought about the destruction of their nation;

The divisions of the Britons brought in the Saxons; etc., etc.

Cyrus, by dividing the Euphrates, was enabled to ford it. When Cyrus came near Babylon with his great army, he found the river, which he wanted to pass, so deep that it could not be forded; so he caused it to be divided into numerous channels, whereby it was soon so reduced in depth, that his men passed over almost on dry land, and took the city.—*The Bundle of Sticks.*

Dumb Idols.

1 COR. xii. 2. Ye know that ye were Gentiles carried about unto these dumb idols [*i.e.* these idols now dumb, according to the subjoined quotations].

As soon as the apostles Simon and Jude entered a country, all the idols became dumb. The apostle Simon preached in Egypt, and Jude in Mesopotamia, and, as St. Isidore and St. Ado say, "as soon as they came into these countries, all the idols, which before gave lively oracles, became dumb." The two apostles went together into Persia, and there also the oracles ceased to give responses. When Baradach (called *Xerxes*) went to consult an oracle respecting a great war which he had taken in hand, the priests told him he must look for no responses so long as Simon and Jude remained in the land. Baradach then sent for the apostles, and told them he acknowledged their God to be mightier than his, inasmuch as He had silenced the oracles. He then asked them what would be the issue of the war he had in hand. The apostles replied, "That you may see, O king, the impotency of your gods and the falsehoods of your oracles, we will give them leave to answer you." So Baradach sent for his priests, and they said to the king, "The war in hand, O king, will be both long and bloody." The two apostles laughed, and Baradach asking why they laughed, they answered, "Never fear, O king; to-morrow, at three o'clock, ambassadors will come from the Indian rebels with overtures of peace." Baradach said he would keep both apostles and priests in safe custody till sunset next day, and those who should then prove to have spoken falsely should be put to death. Next day, at three o'clock, the Indian ambassadors arrived, according to the words of the two apostles, and Baradach concluded peace with them. He would have put the priests to death, but the apostles interfered, and they were simply dismissed in disgrace. The king was then baptized, and the apostles were allowed to preach freely to the people; so they went through all Babylon, healing the sick, and bringing many to the knowledge of Christ. They also consecrated Abdias as bishop of Babylon, and ordained both priests and deacons.—Edward Kinesman (1623), *Lives of the Saints*, pp. 853, 854.

Enemies turned back or scattered.

PSALM lxviii. 1–3. Let God arise, let His enemies be scattered: let them that hate Him flee before Him. But let the righteous be glad; let them rejoice before God; yea, let them exceedingly rejoice.

PSALM xxxv. 4. Let them be confounded and put to shame that seek after my soul: let them be turned back and brought to confusion that devise me hurt.

PSALM xci. 3. Surely He shall deliver thee from the snare of the fowler.

Attila saw two angels standing beside St. Leo. When Attila threatened Rome, St. Leo, with his ecclesiastical dignitaries, went to him in all their bravery to plead for the city. To the amazement of every one, Attila forthwith removed his army; and being asked the reason why, replied, "While pope Leo was speaking, I distinctly saw two shining beings of venerable aspect, and manifestly not of this earth, standing by his side. They had flaming swords in their hands, and menaced me with death if I refused to withdraw my army." The writer continues, "The Church has ever held it for certain that the two beings alluded to were St. Peter and St. Paul."—Damasus, *Lives of the Popes.*

St. Geneviève delivers Paris from Attila (A.D. 450). Attila, king of the Huns, called "The Scourge of God," entered Gaul in 450, and spread desolation wherever he went. It was expected he would pass through Paris, and lay it waste. The people were in a terrible state of consternation, but St. Geneviève exerted herself to allay their terror, to persuade them to remain, and to place their trust in God. Her influence was very great, and many obeyed her words; but others doubted, and fled for safety elsewhere. Attila, instead of marching to Paris, went from Champagne to Orleans, and then turned suddenly back again. The people of Paris could hardly believe it possible, but they all ascribed their deliverance to the prayers of St. Geneviève. Next year (A.D. 451), a combined army of Romans, Franks, and Visigoths overthrew Attila at Chalons-sur-Marne, and the victory was considered to be a miracle, also ascribed to the holy virgin of Nanterre. —*Les Petits Bollandistes* (Life of St. Geneviève), Jan. 3.

The Badagars, who were about to attack St. Francis Xavier, confounded and put to confusion. The Badagars, a very ferocious people, came in hot haste over the mountains, intent to kill Xavier, and destroy the Christians of Trauancor and Comorinum. Xavier was informed of their approach, and went forth all alone to confront them. No sooner did he show himself, than the army came to a sudden halt, wholly unable to advance. They were spellbound; and when their leaders bade them advance, they declared they durst not encounter the lightning of his eyes, nor face the terrible giant that stood beside him. When the leaders of the host observed these things, they also were confounded, and sounded a retreat; so that it was literally fulfilled that they who devised his hurt were put to shame, and they who sought after his soul were turned back and put to confusion.—Cardinal de Monte, *Speech before Gregory XV. at the canonization of Francis Xavier* (Jan. 19, 1622).

Engraved on the Heart.

PROV. iii. 3. Write them upon the table of thine heart.

JER. xxxi. 33. I will put My law in their inward parts, and write it in their hearts.

2 COR. iii. 2. Ye are our epistle written in our hearts, not with ink, but with [? by] the Spirit of the living God.

The word CALAIS engraved on the heart of queen Mary (1516, 1553–1558). When Calais was lost, queen Mary was so vexed that she declared the word CALAIS would be found written on her heart at death.

The name FELIPE written on the heart of Montpensier. Montpensier said, if his body were opened at death, the name

FELIPE [II. of Spain] would be found imprinted on his heart.—Motley, *Dutch Republic*, pt. ii. 5.

The name JESUS engraved on the heart of St. Ignatius (A.D. 116). Ignatius was exposed to lions in the amphitheatre of Rome. Being asked why he had always the name of Jesus in his mouth, he replied, "Because it is graven on my heart." And so indeed it was; for after death, when his body was opened, the word JESUS was found written on his heart in letters of gold. Ribera, a Spanish painter, has a picture representing this. A lion is tearing open the martyr's heart with his claws, and exposes the letters of gold written thereon.—Antoninus; Metaphrastês, *Lives*, etc.

Margaret of Metola carried in her heart three intaglios of Christ (fourteenth century). Margaret of Metola was born blind, and forsaken of her parents. She was brought up by a poor cottager with a large family, and ultimately received into the sisterhood of the Tiers Ordre de St. Dominique. Her love for Christ was so great, that at death three little intaglios of Christ on small stones were found in her heart; and in Christian art she is so represented.—Father Marchèse, *The Dominican Year.*

The name MARY written on the heart of St. Peter Thomas (died A.D. 1366.) St. Peter Thomas "could eat nothing, could drink nothing, could do nothing, without pronouncing or invoking the name of Mary," and we are assured that at his death the word MARY was found graven on his heart.—Philip Mazzeri, *Life of St. Peter Thomas.*

St. Henry Suzo cuts on his breast the word JESUS (A.D. 1365.) One day St. Henry Suzo took a knife, and "love guiding his hand," he punctured on his breast the five letters of the name Jesus, and said, "O Jesus, the only love of my soul, may the name I have written on my breast be engraved in my heart." The name thus punctured by the knife remained till death.—Pustet of Ratisbonne, *The Life and Writings of Henry Suzo, surnamed "Amandus."*

The Virgin Mary shows the Cistercian Order written in her heart (A.D. 1109). One day a Cistercian monk saw heaven open. The angels were seated on shining thrones, amidst patriarchs, prophets, and apostles. With the heavenly host he recognized the monks of the several religious orders, but failed to discover any of his own brotherhood. "How is this, O holy Virgin?" he cried in affright. "I cannot see a single Cistercian among all the celestial denizens. Can it be possible that the Cistercians, who honour thee above all other orders, are not admitted into paradise?" The queen of heaven, seeing her servant greatly troubled in spirit, replied, "No, no; the Cistercians are so dear to me that I carry them in my bosom." So saying, she opened her robe, and showed him how she carried about with her at all times these devoted brothers of the Cistercian Order. Transported with delight, the monk to whom this revelation was made recounted to his brothers of Cîteau what he had seen, and all the brotherhood gave thanks to God and the ever-blessed Virgin.—*Acta Sanctorum* (Bollandus), vol. iii. Jan. 26.

Falls inflict no Injury on Saints.

MATT. iv. 6. The devil, having set Jesus on a pinnacle of the temple, said to Him, If Thou be the Son of God, cast Thyself down: for it is written, He shall give His angels charge concerning Thee: and in their hands shall they bear Thee up, lest at any time Thou dash Thy foot against a stone.

St. Agatha Hildegardes, thrown from a dungeon-keep, receives no injury (A.D. 1024). Agatha Hildegardes was the wife of count-palatine Paul, who for some motive best known to himself chose to suspect her of infidelity, and locked her up in the castle *donjon.* After a long imprisonment, the count one day went to visit her, and pretending penitence, induced her to walk with him on the keep, and then pushed her from the top of the tower into the foss below. Supposing her dead, he began to wail, and cry for the servants, to whom he said their mistress had fallen over the tower. The servants ran to the foss, fully expecting to find a dead body horribly mangled, but to their amazement they found the countess wholly uninjured; and they thanked God that He had given His angels charge concerning her. The count made the best of the matter he could, confessed his crime, and expiated it with a long penitence.—Bollandus, *Acta Sanctorum.*

Fasts observed by Infants.

JOEL ii. 15, 16. Sanctify a fast; gather the people; assemble the elders; gather the children, [even] those that suck the breast.

Marianne de Jesus fasted when an infant

in arms (A.D. 1618–1645). Mgr. Guérin, chamberlain of Leo XIII., assures us that Marianne de Paredes, who at the age of eight changed her name to Marianne de Jesus, practised fasting from the hour of her birth. She would take the breast only twice a day, at noon and midnight. On Wednesdays and Fridays, only once a day. Her mother thought that the milk was not to the child's liking, and got a wet-nurse. But no; the child would never change her hours—twice a day five times, and once a day twice in the week.—*Vies des Saints*, vol. vi. p. 230.

If this tale is credible, it will be easy to believe what Schöneich tells us about Christian Heinrich Heinecken. That a babe at the breast should know anything of the [Roman] Catholic fast-days, Wednesday and Friday, is rather too much to expect. The chickens of Compostella may stand beside this fasting babe.

Marianne wrote her life, but with unusual good taste her confessor burnt the manuscript when she died. One can only regret that Godescard and Mgr. Guérin did not follow the same example. Some may say the same of this recital, but they will wholly mistake the difference of the two standpoints.

[*St.*] *Nicholas of Myrrha fasted when an infant.* St. Nicholas of Myrrha, afterwards bishop and confessor, knew "when to draw nourishment from the breast, and when to abstain." On Wednesdays and Fridays he would never take the breast more than once a day, and on the great fasts he abstained altogether, so that the Spirit was given to him even from his very birth.—John (the deacon), *Chronicles of the bishops of Naples* (sixteenth century). See also Methodius, Metaphrastês, etc. He is also mentioned by St. Clement of Alexandria, *Stromates* vii. p. 877.

[*St.*] *Simon Stock fasted when an infant* (A.D. 1164). Simon Stock was the child of an English baron of Kent in the reign of Henry III. Even from birth he showed signs of his future holy life, for on Saturdays, and all the vigils of the Virgin Mary, he refused the breast, and kept unbroken fasts.—*Life of Simon Stock* (thirteenth century.)

Wednesday is a fast-day in remembrance that Christ was taken prisoner on that day; Friday as the day of His crucifixion; Saturday as the day of His entombment. Why Simon Stock fasted on Saturday and not on Friday is not explained. (For the twenty fête-days of the Virgin Mary, see pt. iii.) Seventy-two fast-days in a year for an infant may seem all very well to a monk, but to any one who knows about children practically the thing is utterly absurd.

Fire a Test.

1 COR. iii. 12, 13. If any man build upon this foundation gold, silver, precious stones, wood, hay, stubble; every man's work shall be made manifest: for the day shall declare it, because it shall be revealed by fire; and the fire shall try every man's work of what sort it is.

St. Dominic tries the doctrines of the Albigenses by fire. St. Dominic bade the Albigenses write down their doctrines and religious opinions in one book, while he wrote in another the true Catholic doctrines. The two books were then thrown into a huge bonfire in the public market-place, which was crowded with spectators. The Albigensian book was consumed in a moment; but St. Dominic's book remained unhurt, and leaped three times out of the fire, having been thrice cast in. Although this "miracle" brought some to the truth, yet others remained obstinate in their errors.—John Gerzonius (orator of Bologna); confirmed by Theodore of Apoldia (of the Order of St. Dominic). They were not present, but they wrote the *Life of St. Dominic.*

Presuming the legend to be true, it is a pity that the book was not carefully preserved, that the material thereof might be tested. Every one knows how paper, muslin, etc., can be made fire-proof; and asbestos is fire-proof, thin lamina of which might pass for paper. The "miracle" is worth nothing unless the materials of the books were identical in every respect.

Ordeals by fire and water. "When thou passest through the waters, I will be with thee; and through the rivers, they shall not overflow thee: when thou walkest through the fire, thou shalt not be burnt; neither shall the flame kindle upon thee." Here, then, was a test of guilt and innocence: if water and fire did no harm to the accused, God was with him to assert his innocence; if not, God left him alone to reap the reward of his unrighteousness. In the Middle Ages, this class of vindication was very general, the fire ordeals being reserved for the free and well-to-do, the water ordeals being confined to serfs, slaves, and minions.

In the fire ordeals, the accused was required to hold a ball of red-hot iron in one hand, or both hands, for an allotted time; or he had to walk barefoot and blindfold among nine red-hot ploughshares. If innocent, he received no injury; but if guilty, the iron burnt him. As the priests had the management of the ordeals, and a certain length of time transpired before the accused was put to the test, those who paid well were taught how to escape injury, and the test was more a gauge of fees than of anything else.

In the water ordeals the accused were required to plunge one or both arms into boiling-hot water; or, being bound hand

and foot, were cast into running water. If uninjured by the scalding water, or buoyed up on the river, like a cork, God testified to their innocence, by not permitting the water to harm them, and *vice versâ.*

Oaths in legal transactions. Oaths, still exacted in many legal transactions, are a relic of the same custom. The person now kisses the New Testament; in former times he laid his right hand on some relics, saying, "So help me God." Of course the idea is, that God will interpose to punish the swearer if he speaks falsely, and will protect him if he speaks the truth. The sooner this rag of the obsolete ordeals is done away with the better, for however such a ceremony may restrain the ignorant, it is false teaching and mischievous. If there is a shadow of truth in it, then by all means be consistent, and return to the ordeals at once.

Thanksgivings for victories. Thanks offered to God for a victory is another relic of the same notion. The very fact of a victory is thus supposed to prove the righteousness of the cause, just as the fact of passing through an ordeal unscathed proved innocence. No one believes that God interposes in ordeals or wagers by battle to defend the right, and no one can possibly believe that all victories have been on the side of right. It was blasphemous, after the massacre of the Poles by the Russians, to sing a *Te Deum*, as if the God of battles could possibly approve such treachery and wanton barbarity. Can any one in his senses believe that the victories of Alexander, Julius Cæsar, Bonaparte, those of Montfort over the Albigenses, those of Felipe II. of Spain over the Netherlanders, or those of the Zulus over our own troops, were due to the interference of God? The notion is preposterous in the extreme. Victories are no proofs of a righteous cause. More than half are wholly unjustifiable, and not a few are a disgrace to the history of man.

Fool.

1 COR. iii. 18. If any man among you seemeth to be wise in this world, let him become a fool, that he may be wise.

St. Isidora of Tabennes was accounted a fool. In a female convent at Tabennes, in Egypt, was a sister that all the rest of the convent treated as a fool, and was employed to wash up dishes, and for other menial works of the humblest kind. She wore a patchwork turban, and her dress was one of rags, patched with sundry bits of cloth. The house contained four hundred inmates, none of which ever saw the scullion eat, or drink, or sit at table. She was ill-treated by every one, but never complained; and she rarely uttered a word. Not far from this convent lived a holy man, named Pyoterius, to whom an angel appeared, and bade him go to the convent of Tabennes, and look up a sister there whom he would know by her head-gear, a kind of crown. "That sister," said the angel, "is holier than thou art. Though always in tribulation, both night and day, she is always with God, and never troubled in mind; while you, though living alone, are troubled with a thousand distractions." Pyoterius went to the convent, and requested to see the sisters. They were all brought before him; but the old saint said, "One is still missing." "My father," said the lady superior, "all are here except a poor scullion, who is a fool." "Let me see her," said the hermit. Immediately Isidora entered, Pyoterius fell at her feet, and cried, "Bless me, my sister, beloved of the Lord!" The four hundred were amazed, but Pyoterius said to them, "Pray that you may find as much favour in the day of judgment as this despised one. I tell you, the Lord hath said, you think yourselves wise, but let those who think themselves wise become as this fool, that they may be wise." So saying, he left the convent. A few days after this, St. Isidora, unable to endure the altered treatment which she received, left the convent, and was never heard of more. —Rosweide, *Vies des Pères.* (This is told by St. Basil.)

Foolishness of Preaching.

1 COR. i. 21, 29. It has pleased God by the foolishness of preaching to save them that believe. For God hath chosen the foolish of the world to confound the wise, that no flesh should glory in His presence.

Philetus, the rhetorician, vanquished by the foolishness of preaching. Philetus, a disciple of Hermogenês the rhetorician, coming to maintain a disputation with St. James the Elder, relied much on his casuistry and sophistry; but the apostle, with all simplicity and faithfulness, preached to his antagonist Christ and Him crucified. When Philetus returned to his master, he told him, saying, "I went a sophist, but have returned a Christian."—Spencer, *Things Old and New.*

Fountain becomes a River.

ESTH. x. 6. A little fountain became a river.
ECCLESIASTICUS xxiv. 31. I said, I will water my best garden, and will water abundantly my garden-bed. And lo! my brook became a river, and my river became a sea.

St. Bertha makes a little fountain a river (seventh century). The town of Avenay was so badly supplied with water, that the monks of the abbey of Val d'Or implored their holy mother St. Bertha to help them by her prayers. While she was at her orison to this end, St. Peter, in the form of a venerable old man, came to her, holding in his hands two golden keys, and told her to buy a little spot of land near the abbey, where was a fountain of water, which she might utilize for the town. St. Bertha bought the piece of land for a livre of silver (£2 present value of money), but had now to cause the water to flow in a perpetual stream to the town of Avenay. To this end, she traced on the earth with a stick from the fountain to the town the course which the water was to take; the water made a channel along this trace, and never after deviated from it. This river is still called the "Livre," from the price which St. Bertha paid for the purchase. —L'abbé Flodoard, *History of the Church of Reims.*

Fruitful Harvests.

PROV. iii. 9, 10. Honour the Lord with thy substance, so shall thy barns be filled with plenty.

DEUT. xxviii. 1–8. If thou shalt hearken diligently unto the voice of the Lord thy God, to observe and do all His commandments . . . blessed shall be thy basket and thy store. . . . The Lord shall command the blessing upon thee in thy storehouses.

Two farmers put the promise of God to the test (thirteenth century). St. Peter of Ravenna, preaching at Como on the text, "Honour the Lord with thy substance, so shall thy barns be filled with plenty," excited the attention of two farmers. One scoffed at the notion, and declared that whether he honoured the Lord or the devil, his harvest would depend on his own farming; the other commended his labours to God, and vowed to dedicate to Him a tenth of his gains, if He vouchsafed to bless his crops. The days of harvest came; the fields of the former did not produce "one single ear of corn," while those of his next neighbour produced a hundredfold. However, the failure of the former farmer brought about his complete conversion, and ever after he hearkened diligently to the voice of the Lord, and was blessed in his basket and his store.—Ambrose Tægio, *Life of St. Peter the Martyr.*

Frustation of Wicked Devices.

PSALM lii. 1–5. Why boastest thou thyself in mischief, O mighty man? the goodness of God endureth continually. . . . God shall destroy thee for ever; He shall take thee away, and root thee out of the land of the living.

PSALM ii. 1–4. Why do the heathen rage, and the people imagine a vain thing? . . . He that sitteth in the heavens shall laugh: the Lord shall have them in derision.

St. Martina sees the devices of Alexander Severus frustrated (A.D. 226). The emperor Alexander Severus commanded St. Martina to be taken to the temple of Apollo to offer incense; but no sooner did she make the sign of the cross, than the image of Apollo fell to the ground, and was shattered to pieces. Alexander, greatly irritated, commanded his officers to box the maiden's face, and then ordered her to be stripped, and lacerated with iron hooks. Four men were appointed for the work; but the Lord held them in derision, and sent four angels to turn the instruments of torture from the damsel to her tormentors. The emperor, seeing this, sent eight other officers to take their places. They hoisted their victim in the air for the purpose of tearing her flesh with strong iron needles; but the tormentors were struck to the earth by an invisible power, and were, like Saul, converted to the new faith. Alexander, beside himself with rage, commanded them all to be beheaded, and their names were enrolled amongst the martyrs and confessors of Jesus Christ.—Baronius, *Ecclesiastical Annals* (1588–93).

St. Martina. Next day St. Martina was taken again to the temple of Apollo, and the emperor told her if she refused to offer sacrifice he would hack every inch of her flesh from her bones. Still she persisted, and was then stripped, laid with her face towards the earth, tied hands and feet to four posts, and scourged by seven strong men till they dropped with fatigue. The father of Alexander, named Eumenius, advised his son to send the damsel back to her dungeon and to pour scalding hot oil over her wounds; but immediately she entered her dungeon she found it lighted with light from heaven, and heard angels singing the praises of the Most High. At the same time, all her sufferings were assuaged, and all her wounds were healed.—Surius, and Bollandus, *Acta Sanctorum*, vol. i.

Gifts from Heaven and Miracles of Convenience.

1 KINGS xv. 4. For David's sake did the Lord his God give him a lamp in Jerusalem.

GEN. xliii. 23. God hath given you treasure in your sacks.

PSALM lxviii. 18. Thou hast received gifts for men.

ECCLES. iii. 13. It is the gift of God.

1 COR. i. 7. Every man hath his proper gift of God.

JAMES i. 17. Every good gift and every perfect gift is from above.

An angel gives St. Fursy a clock (A.D. 650). St. Fursy, having built a monastery in Bury St. Edmund's, wanted a clock for the use of the monks, but could not afford to buy so expensive a luxury. Happily an angel brought him one from heaven:

and this clock remained in the abbey till the year 1468.—L'abbé Corblet, *Hagiography of the Diocese of Amiens*, vol. ii. p. 260.

Jesus Christ sends St. Jane-Frances Fremyot de Chantal a silver pyx (A.D. 1512–1641). Jane-Frances Fremyot was baroness of Chantal, and founded "The Religious House of the Visitation of St. Mary." At first the convent had only a tin pyx; but Jane-Frances prayed Christ to exchange it for a silver one, and next day a stranger brought to the house a silver pyx gilt, but left no message.

On one occasion the community was wholly destitute of food as well as money. Whereupon, St. Jane-Frances repeated the Lord's Prayer up to the words "Give us this day our daily bread," and there stopped. At that moment a knocking was heard at the door, and a stranger delivered in a parcel for Madame de Chantal. On opening it, the parcel was found to contain twenty-four gold écus. —L'abbé Bougaud, *History of St. Chantal*.

God gives St. Peter Nolasco a clock for his church (A.D. 1189–1256). St. Peter Nolasco built in Spain the church of St. Mary del Puche. For four Saturdays seven strange lights were seen at night over a certain spot, and looked like seven stars. They were observed to drop from heaven seven times, and disappear in the earth in the same place. St. Peter Nolasco felt certain that this strange phenomenon announced something; so he commanded men to dig about the spot. They had not gone far into the earth, when they came upon a clock of prodigious size, bearing a beautiful image of the Virgin Mary. Nolasco took it up in his arms as a valuable gift from heaven, and built an altar on the spot where it was buried. This altar became very celebrated for the number of miracles performed there.—R. P. F. Zumel, *Life of St. Peter Nolasco*.

In Christian art Nolasco is drawn with a clock at his feet, and a beam of light from seven stars resting on the image of the Virgin Mary. We are told that the Virgin Mary herself gave him the scapular of the Order of Mercy, and this incident is also seen portrayed in paintings.

St. Servasius receives a silver key from St. Peter (A.D. 384). The prince of the apostles gave St. Servasius, in proof of his affection, a silver key made by the hand of angels, and this key has worked many miracles.—Father Gilles Buchère, *Gestes des Évêques de Tongres*, etc., ch. iv.

Some authors have hinted that this key was given by the pope, and was one of those many keys given to pilgrims; their great value being that they had touched the chains, or contained some of the filings of the chains, of St. Peter. This conjecture is, however, scouted by most people, who say there is no proof; and certainly the suggestion "ne peut être aussi forte que la tradition des eglises de Maëstricht et de Liége, qui porte que cette clef est un présent de saint Pierre." This key was found in the coffin of St. Servasius when the body was disinterred in A.D. 732 (nearly 350 years afterwards), and was taken to Rome.

St. Gildas miraculously supplied with windows for his oratory (A.D. 494–570). St. Gildas made his home in a rock, partly hollowed out by nature, but enlarged by the hermit himself. When he had hollowed out his oratory, God miraculously supplied him with glass windows, and also gave him a spring of water for his daily use.—*Les Petits Bollandistes*, (7th edit. 1880), vol. ii. p. 106.

Giving to the Poor. (See Lending to the Lord.)

MATT. xiv. 16. Give ye them to eat.

MATT. xix. 21. If thou wilt be perfect, go and sell that thou hast, and give to the poor; and thou shalt have treasure in heaven.

LUKE xi. 31. Give alms of such things as ye have.

2 COR. ix. 7. Give not grudgingly, or of necessity; for God loveth a cheerful giver.

St. Oswald, king of Northumberland, fed the poor (A.D. 642). King Oswald, sitting at table, was served on one occasion with regal delicacies in a silver dish. He was just about to begin his repast, when his almoner whispered in his ear that a crowd of mendicants were at the gate clamouring for food. The saintly king bade his steward take the dish provided for himself, and distribute it among the beggars, and, having so done, to break the dish up and give them each a piece.

Glass and Pottery Miracles.

EZEK. xxxiv. 16. I will bind up that which is broken.

St. Benedict, abbot of Mount Cassino, mends a broken jar by prayer (A.D. 480–543). Cyrilla, the nurse of St. Benedict, first abbot of Mount Cassino, when fleeing with him from Rome, came to Afidum,* about thirty miles from Rome, where the saint performed his first miracle. Cyrilla had borrowed of a villager an earthen jar, and accidentally broke it. Benedict, by the virtue of his prayers, re-joined the broken pieces, and restored the jar so perfectly mended that no eye could detect the slightest crack or flaw in the vessel. In memory of this miracle, the jar was attached to the church door, where it

* Alban Butler calls this town Afilum.

remained till the irruption of the Lombards.—St. Gregory the Great, *Dialogues*, bk. ii. ch. 1. (St. Gregory assures us he received the several items of St. Benedict's life from four abbots who were his disciples.)

St. Donatus miraculously mends a glass chalice (A.D. 365). One day, as St. Donatus was saying mass, a pagan broke to pieces the glass chalice. Donatus had the fragments carefully gathered together, and laid on the altar. Then he prayed, and gradually piece came to piece, and fragment to fragment, till the chalice was restored whole as at the first.—Edward Kinesman (1623), *Lives of the Saints*, p. 590. (He tells us he compiled the life of St. Donatus from Bede and the Roman martyrology.)

St. Marcellinus miraculously mends a glass goblet (A.D. 374). St. Marcellinus, bishop of Embrun, met with such great success, that all the people of his diocese, except one man of high position, were converted and baptized. The bishop gave a great banquet, at which this man was present, and the bishop expressed to him his great desire to see him follow the example of his countrymen, and avouch himself on the Lord's side. The man replied, "I have heard speak of your miracles, but have never witnessed one, nor have I seen anything yet to induce me to leave Apollo." Just then the bishop's cupbearer dropped a valuable glass goblet, which broke into a thousand pieces. "There," said the man, "mend that goblet, and I will believe." Marcellinus groaned in spirit, but conjured God to come to his assistance, and not confirm this doubter in his unbelief. Immediately the pieces of broken glass came together, and the goblet was perfectly restored. The man, struck with the miracle, confessed before all that he could no longer doubt, and begged to be baptized. That this cup was actually mended is quite certain, inasmuch as Marcellinus used it always to the end of his life.—Mgr. Depéry, *Hagiographie de Gap*.

That Marcellinus used a glass chalice may be readily allowed, but this would be no proof that it was broken and mended as the legend describes.

St. Odilo miraculously mends a glass goblet (A.D. 1049). On one occasion, says Albert bishop of Como, St. Odilo came to the court of the emperor Henry. A goblet of glass, being placed before the emperor, was handed to the saint, and after Odilo had inspected it, he passed it on to other guests. As it passed from hand to hand, one of the monks let it fall, and it was broken to pieces. St. Odilo was much vexed, and said to his monks, "Lest the innocent suffer for the carelessness of one, let us now all go and crave God's mercy, that He may vouchsafe to repair this mischief." This was done, and then Odilo commanded all the pieces of the goblet to be picked up carefully, and laid on the altar. The holy man looked at the pieces very earnestly, and the fragments glided gradually into their proper places. When all had come together, the saint took the goblet in his hand and examined it most minutely, but could find no scar or flaw at all. "My brothers," said he to the monks, "behold the glass." And they returned it to the emperor.

Baring-Gould, who mentions this miracle in his *Lives of the Saints* (Jan. 1, p. 20), says, "The story comes to us on good authority." But it would be hard indeed to assign any satisfactory reason for miracles to exonerate acts of mere carelessness, or to save a monarch from the petty annoyance of injury to one of his curiosities. For the grandest of all effects miracles will always be a difficulty to many, but wanton miracles are an insult to man's understanding.

Several glass vessels roll from the top to the bottom of Mount Jura without receiving the slightest injury (eleventh century). On one occasion St. Odilo was crossing the Jura, and a man followed, bearing several glass vessels. The man having tripped let the glasses fall, and they rolled from the top to the bottom of the mountain. They were found at the foot of the Jura next day, wholly uninjured, neither cracked nor chipped. The historian is very precise, and adds, "St. Odilo les trouva le lendemain aussi entiers et aussi beaux que s'ils avaient été conservés soigneusement dans une chambre."—*Les Petits Bollandistes*, vol. i. p. 39 (1880).

God protects His Saints.

PSALM xci. 3. Surely He shall deliver thee from the snare of the fowler, and from the noisome pestilence.

PSALM cxxiv. 7. Our soul is escaped as a bird out of the snare of the fowlers. The snare is broken, and we are escaped.

MATT. x. 30. The very hairs of your head are all numbered.

The pyx placed by St. Clara on the nunnery wall saves it from the Moors. When the army of Frederick, kaiser of Germany, was passing through Assisum, some Moors scaled the nunnery wall with intent to rob the house, and dishonour the nuns. St. Clara placed the pyx on the outside wall; and when the Moors attempted to scale it, some of them fell headlong to the bottom, some were stricken with blindness, and the rest fled in terrible alarm. Thus by the sacred pyx was the nunnery preserved, and the nuns delivered from the snare of the fowler.—*Life of St. Clara* (written at the express command of pope Alexander V.).

God protects St. John of St. Facond from assassins (A.D. 1430–1479). St. John of St. Facond, in Spain, one day declaimed loudly against the sin of stifling conscience. A Spanish don, thinking St. John referred to him, employed two assassins to murder the saint. They came upon him suddenly, but were panic-struck, and their horses, turning round, galloped with all speed home again. The don heard the story which the cut-throats had to tell, felt convinced it was God's doing, repented, and became both a wiser and a better man.—*Acta Sanctorum* (Bollandists), vol. ii. June 12, p. 616.

St. Martin protected by God from assassins. Olympias was hired by the emperor Constans to murder pope Martin while saying mass. The assassin went, accordingly, to do his bidding; but when about to attack the holy father, he was suddenly struck blind, so that he could not see to do the deed of blood.—*The Pontifical*, or *Lives of the Popes*, kept by the notaries.

God will provide.

MATT. vi. 25–33. Take no thought for your life, what ye shall eat, and what ye shall drink; nor yet for the body, what ye shall put on. Is not life more than meat, and the body than raiment? Behold the fowls of the air: they sow not, neither do they reap, nor gather into barns; yet your heavenly Father feedeth them. Are ye not much better than they? Take no thought, saying, What shall we eat? or, What shall we drink? or, Wherewithal shall we be clothed? But seek ye first the kingdom of God, and His righteousness; and all these things shall be added unto you.

God helps St. Franchy to make bread (seventh century). St. Franchy was employed in making bread for the monastery of St. Martin de la Bretonnière, but some of the brothers, out of envy, wishing to bring him into disgrace, concealed the several articles which he used in bread-making. St. Franchy was not in the least disconcerted, but making the sign of the cross, began to knead nothing with nothing, and at the time required produced his batch of bread in perfect condition.—*Hagiography of Nevers.*

In answer to prayer, William Huntington is supplied with a new pair of breeches. By riding, William Huntington, S.S., tells us his breeches got worn out, but he had no money to buy new ones. "I often make very free in my prayers with my invaluable Master, and laid this want duly before Him. Well, calling on Mr. Croucher, a shoemaker in Shepherd's Market, the same morning, he told me he had a parcel left for me. On opening the parcel, there I found the very things I wanted, with a note, as follows:—'Sir, I have sent you a pair of breeches, and hope they will fit. I beg your acceptance of them.—I.S.' I tried them on, found the fit perfect, and wrote the following reply:—'Sir, I thank you for your present. I was going to order a pair, for I did not know my Master had bespoken them of you. The fit is perfect, but no wonder, as God guided your hand, and He knows my measure exactly.—S.S.'"—*The Quarterly Review*, vol. xxiv. p. 483, *Life of the Rev. W. Huntington.*

In *The Bank of Faith*, written by W. Huntington, we have a large number of similar anecdotes. The gift, in this case, may seem to some below the dignity of prayer; but our Lord Himself gives sanction to it, when He warns His disciples against anxious care about food, drink, and wearing apparel, reminding them that God knows they want such things, and will duly provide them.

St. Mayeul, abbot of Cluny, finds a purse of money when reduced to great extremities (A.D. 906–994). St. Mayeul gave so largely to the poor, that he did not reserve enough to provide for his own daily wants. He was severely reproved for this imprudence, but quietly answered, "God will provide. Whoever saw the righteous forsaken, or their seed begging bread?" His faith was soon recompensed, for the same day he found near his chamber a purse containing seven silver pieces. He made every inquiry, and advertised throughout the town for the owner, but no one came forward to reclaim it. He then distributed the silver among the poor. Next day there came to his door a cart full of provisions, but no name of the sender could be ascertained.—*Les Petits Bollandistes*, vol. v. p. 460.

St. Theodosius the Cœnobiarch, though neglected by man, was not forgotten by God (A.D. 423–529). One day a man of great wealth bequeathed alms to a very large amount to the poor, but neglected to state what houses were to have the disposal of his bounty, or to what class of poor his alms were to be distributed. The executors sent no part thereof to the monastery presided over by Theodosius the Cœnobiarch, and the monks advised him to apply for his share. "No," said the abbot; "God will provide. He never abandons those who trust in Him." About an hour afterwards, a man stopped before the abbey. He was on horseback, and was laden with provisions for the poor. His intention was to carry these alms to another house, but the horse refused to go any further; and the rider considered this as a hint from God that he was to bestow his alms on the religious house before him. So he stopped at the abbey, and deposited his alms with Theodosius. This gift was found to be much larger than the share which would have fallen from the "rich man's bequest," had the executors awarded a proportionate share to the monastery under him.

God provides food for Theodosius and his monks. One Easter Eve, no food of any kind was left in the monastery presided over by Theodosius the Cœnobiarch. The monks complained to him, and he replied, "Take no thought for your life, what ye shall eat, or what ye shall drink. Is not life more than meat? Behold the fowls of the air: they sow not, neither do they reap and gather into barns; yet your heavenly Father feedeth them. Are ye not much better than they? Go, provide for the Holy Communion to-morrow, my brethren, attend to the altar, seek the kingdom of God and His righteousness, and He who feeds the sparrows will provide the rest." While he was still speaking, two mules, laden with provision, arrived at the monastery, and the drivers said others were on the road, and would come up soon. So abundantly had God provided, that there was enough to last till Pentecost; ay, and though all had their fill for those forty days, many a basketful remained when Pentecost was over.—*Roman Martyrology.* (Cave tells us the *Life of St. Theodosius the Cœnobiarch* was written by Theodore, bishop of Pera.)

Hand sent from Heaven.

EZEK. ii. 9. And when I looked, behold! a hand was sent me.

Pelops, lacking a shoulder, had one sent from heaven. The tale is that Pelops was served up by Tantalos, his father, in a banquet to the gods, and Cerês [or Demeter] ate his shoulder. Jupiter perceived that Tantalos had set before him a human being for food, and restored Pelops to life, but the restored body lacked the right shoulder; so either Jupiter or Cerês gave him an ivory one in its place. This ivory shoulder, like the *manus de cœlo missa* of St. William (see p. 400), had the power of working miracles, for every one who touched it was cured of whatever complaint he suffered from.—Pausanias, *History of Greece*, bk. v. 1.

Pythagoras had a golden thigh given him by the gods. Pythagoras had a golden thigh, and showed it to Abaris the Hyperborean priest during the celebration of the Olympic games.—Jamblicus, *Life of Pythagoras*, ch. xix.

St. John Damascene had a hand sent him from heaven (A.D. 780). The caliph cut off the right hand of John Damascene, and fastened it to a post in a public market. When in his oratory, John prayed thus to the Virgin Mary: "O pure and holy Virgin, mother of God, thou knowest why the caliph has cut off my right hand, and thou canst, if it please thee, restore it to me again. I pray thee grant me this grace, that I may employ it, as before, in celebrating the praises of thy Son and thee." During his sleep the Virgin came to him, and said, "Thy prayer is heard, and thy hand restored. Go on composing hymns and writing my praises, according to thy promise." Next morning he found his hand had been restored, and no indication was left of his ever having lost it, except a thin red line round his wrist. When the sultan heard of this, he felt assured that John was an innocent sufferer, and restored him to his honours and office.—*Acta Sanctorum* (Bollandists), vol. ii. May 6.

In Christian art St. John of Damascus is represented prostrate at the feet of the Virgin, who is restoring his hand.

St. Melor had a silver hand and brazen foot (A.D. 411). St. Melor was the son of Melian, duke of Cornwall. His uncle Rainald, having put the duke to death, cut off the right hand and left foot of Melor, to prevent his succession, because maimed princes were disqualified from becoming rulers. The mutilated boy was sent to a Cornish monastery, and was there miraculously supplied with a silver hand and brazen foot. One day, as the monks went out nutting, the abbot was amazed to see prince Melor using his silver hand as freely as if it were made of flesh and blood—clasping the boughs, plucking off the nuts, and handling them like any other boy. Subsequently, he saw him throw a stone; and, where the stone fell, there instantly welled up a fountain of pure water.—Baring-Gould, *Life of the Saints*, Jan., p. 44.

(See RELICS, "A right hand sent from heaven," p. 259.)

In mediæval times, no one either maimed or blind was allowed to reign, because such a person would not be qualified to lead an army. Thus, in Moorish history, Witiza blinded Theodofred, heir to the Spanish throne, in order to cut off the succession. Witiza was himself subsequently blinded by Roderick (son of Theodofred). King John put out the eyes of prince Arthur with the same object. Mediæval history teems with similar examples.

St. William of Oulx receives a hand from heaven (twelfth century). St. William was a poor shepherd, born with only one hand. As he was keeping his sheep, an angel one day appeared to him, and bade him go and tell the abbot of Notre Dame de Calme to quit his abbey, and fix his abode at the foot of Bouchet, now called Mont Dauphin. It so happened that the abbot was at the time contemplating the enlargement of his abbey, and paid no heed to the shepherd. The angel appeared a second time to William, and sent him with the same message; but the abbot was too busy to attend to him. The angel came a third time, and gave him a miraculous hand (*manus de cœlo missa*), which he was to show the abbot as his credential. William said to the abbot, "You know I had only one hand; now, behold! I have two. Art thou now convinced that God hath sent me?" The abbot could no longer resist, and proceeded at once to build a new monastery at the foot of the rock of Bouchet. Scarcely was the building finished, when the river Durance overflowed its banks, and swept away Notre Dame de Calme, and ever since the spot presents to the traveller the appearance of a vast plain, arid, stony, and sterile. The monastery was never rebuilt, but a wooden cross marks the spot where it once stood. Afterwards, William "with the angel's arm" was made prior of Oulx. When he died, the monks of Eygliers saw, the day after his funeral, a hand raised above his grave. It was the right hand brought by the angel from heaven. "Ils se contentèrent de la recouvrir. Le jour suivant le même prodige eut lieu; ils recouvrirent la main comme la première fois. Le troisième jour le miracle se reproduisit. Alors, craignant de résister à la voix du ciel, ils consultèrent l'archevêque d'Embrun, qui leur ordonna de couper la main, de la conserver, et de la transmettre à leurs successeurs, comme une sainte et précieuse relique." This *manus de cœlo missa* operated numerous miracles, especially in the cure of fevers, in the perils of childbirth, and in gangrenous disorders; in 1653 the relic put out a fire which threatened to destroy the whole town of Eygliers. It is still carried in grand procession on Easter Monday and Quasimodo Suuday through the parishes of Guillestre, Eygliers, Risoul, Mont Dauphin, St. Clement, and Réotier. "Une statue fort ancienne qu'on voit dans la chapelle du saint Guillaume représente notre saint avec son seul bras gauche, comme il est peint dans deux tableaux de l'église d'Eygliers, ne laisse point de doute à cet égard." Mgr. Jean-Irénée Depéry, bishop of Gap, in his pastoral visit in 1847, requested to be shown this *manus de cœlo missa*, and describes it in his process-verbal. He says the hand is entire, but it has only one nail, that on the little finger, the other nails "ont été enlevés par des personnes pieuses, et aussi par quelques archevêques d'Embrun." The skin has the discolouration of great age, and has been injured by the dampness of the sacristy in which it is kept. In his ordinance, dated Feb. 2, 1852, the archbishop writes, "Parfaitement renseigné sur l'authenticité de la relique, et voulant respecter une tradition aussi antique, après avoir lu tous les documents qui nous ont été diligemment fournis par M. Barthélemy, curé de la paroisse d'Eygliers, après avoir pris l'avis de notre conseil, et celui de plusieurs canonistes, permettons que la main de saint Guillaume, qui existe dans l'église d'Eygliers, soit rendue désormais à la vénération des fidèles de la paroisse d'Eygliers, et de ceux des paroisses voisines." The archbishop adds, "The hand shall not be exposed on the rock of Mont Dauphin till the chapel is rebuilt, and this is to mark his displeasure at the impiety of not restoring that chapel." Pope Pius IX., by a brief dated May 10, 1852, accords in perpetuity plenary indulgence to all who visit the angelic hand on Easter Monday and the following eight days. "Cette indulgence est applicable aux ames du purgatoire."—Mgr. J. I. Depéry (bishop of Gap), *Histoire Hagiologique du Diocèse de Gap*.

How the ancient statue and two paintings of St. William, with only one hand, can help to establish the fact that an angel brought him another hand from heaven, is by no means self-evident. If they prove anything it must surely be this, that he had only one hand and not two. The "piety" of the archbishops of Embrun in stealing the nails from the hand is at least dubious. And the examinations of Mgr. Depéry, seven centuries after the event, would scarcely satisfy an English jury. Many great names testify to the authenticity of this *manus de cœlo missa*, but probably there will be many who doubt the fact notwithstanding.

Happy in Suffering.

(See ANGELS SENT TO CONSOLE, p. 9.)

1 PET. iii. 14. And if ye suffer for righteousness' sake, happy are ye; and be not afraid of their terror, neither be troubled.

MATT. v. 10-12. Blessed are they which are persecuted for righteousness' sake. . . . Rejoice, and be exceeding glad: for great is your reward in heaven.

St. Mennas bore the most cruel tortures with equanimity (Nov. 11, A.D. 301). Mennas, a Roman soldier, was tortured most grievously for refusing to burn incense to idols, but was neither afraid of the terrors nor troubled by them. He was first laid flat on the ground, and beaten with the fresh sinews of beasts. He was then subjected to the "torture of the cord;" that is, he was suspended on high by cords. "These are but light afflictions," said the Christian soldier—"light indeed to the eternal weight of glory prepared for those who serve God; and the God I serve hath sent His angels to cheer and comfort me." He was then scourged still more severely, and his gashed and bleeding body was rubbed with cloths of harsh horsehair. Still the martyr showed no signs of suffering, insomuch that Pyrrhus, who superintended the punishment, greatly marvelled, and said, "Why, Mennas, how is this? It seems that the body subjected to these tortures is not your own body, but one borrowed for the nonce." "Pyrrhus," replied the martyr, "I do not even feel your tortures; not because this body is not my own body, but because Christ gives me strength to bear all you choose to inflict, and His strength is sufficient for me." Then said Pyrrhus, "We will soon see how that is.—Bring the torches," he cried to the executioners, "and set them to his sides." This was done for the space of two hours, and still the martyr winced not. "Dost not feel that, Mennas?" cried Pyrrhus. "No," said the martyr, "I feel it not; and I now know what the prophet Isaiah meant, when he said, 'When thou walkest through the fire thou shalt not be burnt, neither shall the flame kindle on thee.'" "Well, well," cried Pyrrhus, "that is mere vain babbling, Mennas. Either offer sacrifice, or see if the fire I have in store will not burn." "Never, Pyrrhus, will I sacrifice to devils, come what may. I fear not them that can kill the body, but not the soul; Him I fear that can kill both body and soul in hell." Then Pyrrhus caused caltrops (see Index) to be set thick on the ground, and Mennas to be dragged backwards and forwards over them. "Try again, Pyrrhus," said the martyr; "this has not force enough to separate me from the love of God my Saviour." Pyrrhus, having exhausted all his resources and his patience also, roared aloud to the executioners, "Take the magician to Potemia, and off with his head." So he was beheaded, and slept in the Lord.—Metaphrastês, *Lives*, etc.

St. Perpetua, tossed and gored by an infuriated cow, was unconscious of being hurt. St. Perpetua and her companions were exposed in the amphitheatre to wild beasts; the men to lions, bears, and leopards, the women to infuriated cows. After Perpetua had been tossed and gored, she seemed to be in a celestial trance, and was so insensible of any pain, that she asked when the beasts would be let loose on her, and could hardly be persuaded that this part of her martyrdom was already over. A gladiator then came forward, and cut off the heads of all the victims which still survived.—J. C. Robertson, *History of the Christian Church* (1875), vol. i. p. 98.

St. Theodore rejoiced and was exceeding glad under torture. St. Theodore of Armenia was a soldier in the Roman army during the reign of Diocletian, but, being a Christian, he was apprehended, and subjected to most cruel tortures. St. Gregory of Nyssa, in his sermon preached on the anniversary of the saint's martyrdom in St. Saviour's church, Venice, where the body was buried, says, "They bound him to a post, and whipped him; then rent his flesh with iron hooks, and burnt his sides with torches; but the more diligent the executioners to increase his torments, the more cheerful seemed the sufferer. You would have thought, had you seen him, he had been in a pleasure-garden, and not under torture. Not a groan, not a sigh, escaped him; but he sang sweetly unto the Lord, 'I will always bless the name of the Lord; His praises shall be ever in my mouth.' When the officers took him back to his horrible dungeon, the voices of angels were heard there, and it was filled with celestial fragrance. Next day he was sentenced to be burnt alive, and he stood in the midst of the fire, praising and glorifying God. No mark of pain was to be seen. True, God took his spirit into paradise, but the fire touched not his body, nor so much as scorched a hair of his head. Eusebia, a Christian woman, afterwards wrapped the body in linen and buried it; and we all know that miracles, almost daily done, show how greatly God doth honour him. By recourse to his intercession, out of this man devils are cast; another is loosed from his infirmities; here tempests are stilled by him; orphans find him a father, pilgrims a haven of rest; the afflicted find in him a comforter, and the needy a present help." (The sermon concludes with a prayer and invocation to the saint.)

St. Triphon was happy in suffering (Nov. 10, A.D. 250). Quilinus, a Roman governor, apprehended Triphon for being a Christian, and subjected him to the following tortures. He was first impaled on the equileus (see Index), and while thus tortured his flesh was torn from the bones by iron hooks; then burning torches were held to his raw sides, and he was beaten with sticks; this over, red-hot nails were driven through both his feet. In all this the martyr showed no marks of pain; his countenance remained cheerful, and his voice was steady and melodious. Respicius the tribune, seeing this, said to himself, "Flesh and blood could not endure such agony, and he who could undergo such torture with cheerfulness must be sustained by a power divine. Triphon must be in favour with his God, and his God must be a God indeed which can sustain after this sort." These reflections brought forth fruit, and Respicius was added to such as believed. When this came to the ears of the governor, he ordered both Triphon and the tribune to be beaten with flagra or leaden plummets (see Index) till they were dead.—Ruinart (A.D. 1689), *Acta Primorum Martyrum.*

Harm warded off.

ISA. xliii. 2. When thou passest through the waters, I will be with thee; and through the rivers, they shall not overflow thee: when thou walkest through the fire, thou shalt not be burned; neither shall the flame kindle on thee.

ISA. liv. 17. No weapon that is formed against thee shall prosper.

LUKE x. 19. Nothing shall by any means hurt you.

1 PET. iii. 23. Who is he that shall harm you, if you be followers of that which is good?

St. Agatha, being frightfully tortured, was miraculously restored (A.D. 251). St. Agatha was horribly tortured by Quintianus, consul of Sicily. She was suspended on a chevalet (see Index), had her two breasts cut off, and was torn from head to foot by iron hooks. When conducted back to her dungeon an old man [*St. Peter*] and a little Child [*Christ*] visited her; and, when they left the dungeon, not only were all her wounds healed, but her breasts were restored. The prison cell being filled with an intense light, the jailers in alarm fled, leaving the prison doors open; but St. Agatha refused to escape, saying, as Christ had healed her wounds, He could take care of her life, if so it pleased Him. —Bollandus, *Acta Sanctorum*, vol. i. Feb. 5.

The tortures to which St. Anthimus was subjected (April 27, A.D. 303). St. Anthimus, being brought before the emperor Maximian, told him it was unreasonable to suppose that he would barter for the pleasures of this life those of heaven and eternity. Maximian, supposing that this was mere bravado, ordered his lictors to beat the man's head with stones. St. Anthimus said, "These blows kill not me, but will help to destroy thy false gods." The tyrant now commanded his myrmidons to pierce the saint's heels with long red-hot awls, and, having thrown him down on caltrops (see Index), to whip him without mercy. Being scourged, his feet were thrust into brazen boots made red hot; but God stood by him to console him in his tortures, and whisper promises of everlasting joy. Instead of succumbing, therefore, the martyr seemed to gain new strength, and his whole face was lighted up with joy. "It is pure folly," he cried, "to suppose I shall be driven to acknowledge your false gods by torture. Fear not those who can kill and torture the body, but Him who can cast both body and soul into hell." These words only exasperated Maximian the more, and he bade his officers bind the insolent on a wheel, and, while it turned slowly round, to burn with lighted torches each part of the body in succession. This was done; but when the executioners expected to reduce the body to a cinder, they were felled to the earth by an invisible hand; their torches went out, their wheel broke, and they themselves were paralyzed in every limb. Maximian scoffed at his myrmidons, threatened them, and declared they were trifling with him; but the men replied, "We lack not courage, O great Cæsar, to obey your orders, but there are three persons full of majesty, and of dazzling light, standing over Anthimus to protect him, so that all our efforts to injure him are in vain; our blows touch him not, our torches scorch him not, our boots of brass and burning awls are powerless to harm him." "Load him with chains, and off with him to prison," roared the tyrant; "we will soon see if Jupiter is to be defied by a man like this." As the officers attempted to bind him, the chains crumbled to powder, and fell like dust to the ground. The officers, terribly frightened, fell to the earth; but St. Anthimus went of his own accord to the prison. His fellow-prisoners were so delighted to see him, that they were all converted and baptized. Maximian, unable to endure this contest any longer, sent executioners to behead his victim.—*Acta Sanctorum* (Bollandists, from a Greek MS.).

St. Audaldus preserved from harm under most revolting cruelty (A.D. 450). The whip employed by the Goths was a kind of *knout*, consisting of a long straight leather handle strengthened with metal wire, so as to make it both stiff and heavy. The lash was made of slips of leather braided with iron wire, and terminating in a little iron hook. The victim was bound to what was called the *kobila*, *i.e.* two boards one above the other; the head being bound to the higher board, the feet to the lower one, and the hands made to embrace the *kobila* by bonds. The bare back of the victim is thus hollowed, and in this state the public scourger administered 101 lashes, unless the sufferer died before the number was completed. Audaldus went to preach the gospel to the army of Attila, and being seized by the Hun's brother Wuillielm, was ordered to be scourged or knouted. The lash cut through his flesh like a knife, and being swept across the back horizontally, made long furrows by means of the iron hook, detaching huge gobbets of flesh at each blow. Wuillielm himself was present, and thinking his victim dead, gave orders to cease the scourging. Being unbound from the *kobila*, the martyr was left for the nonce as a dead body, to be buried at some convenient leisure; but he had only fainted, and being miraculously healed, went and preached to the Ostrogoths. He was now seized by Valamir, who ordered him to be knouted again, and blamed Wuillielm for not having given the pestilent fellow the full number of blows. Valamir made a public exhibition of his victim, and said, if he survived the scourging, he should drink to the health of the gods in a cup of liquid lead. The day of the "spectacle" arrived. St. Audaldus was bound to the *kobila*, and received the 101 lashes; but life not being extinct, he was unbound, set on his feet, and handed the cup of molten lead to drink. He took the cup, made the sign of the cross, and (our author says) "l'avala (*i.e.* the lead) comme une confortable liqueur." There was a sort of rough justice in these Goths. Audaldus had received the awarded punishment, and was set free. The Goths scorned to follow the Roman fashion of cutting off the head of their victim who happened to survive. Being released, the sufferer was warned to leave the place, and never again attempt to corrupt the soldiers of Attila, lest a worse thing should befall him.—L'abbé Authier, *Études Historiques et Religieuses sur le Pays de la Haute Vallée de l'Ariège* (1870).

St. Peter Balsam, being tortured, felt no pain (A.D. 311). Peter Balsam, being brought before the emperor Severus, was commanded to sacrifice to the Roman gods, and as he refused to do so, he was gibbeted on the chevalet (see Index); and while he was thus racked, he was torn with iron combs. As his blood flowed in great profusion, the spectators implored him to offer sacrifice to put an end to such horrible torture. "How torture?" cried the martyr. "I protest that I feel none. I am persuaded that nothing which can be done unto me can in any wise harm me; for has not the prince of the apostles said, 'Who is he that shall harm you, if you be followers of that which is good?'" The martyr was then taken down from the chevalet, and crucified.—Dom Ruinart, *Life of St. Peter Balsam.*

St. Chrisantus found that no instrument of torture hurt him. St. Chrisantus was cast into a stinking dungeon, but immediately he entered it, the foul stench was converted into a delicious perfume. He was bound with gyves and fetters, but the chains crumbled into dust when they touched him. He was then packed in a fresh bull's hide, and laid in the hot sun; but the hide, instead of shrinking, and squeezing him to death, proved only a pleasant garment from the heat. Then was he bound with heavier chains, but they also fell into powder. The dungeon in which they thrust him had no window, and was usually pitch dark, but while St. Chrisantus was there, it was beautifully illuminated with celestial light. The officers now bound him to a whipping-post, but the iron bullets with which the whip was laden became perfectly soft, and instead of breaking through the skin, relieved the force of the lashes. He was next put upon the armentarium (see Index), a cruel instrument of torture; but the cords which bound him fell from him like tow; the post snapped asunder; and the torches which were to burn his sides went out. The tribune Claudius and all the officers of the prison, amazed at these miracles, came to the saint, and kneeling at his feet, prayed to be baptized. So the saint embraced them; and that day were added to the Church the tribune Claudius, his wife Hilaria, their two sons Iaso and Maurus, all the household slaves, the whole band of soldiers, and all the prison officials. (See *Acts* xvi. 25-34.)—Verinus and Armenius (priests of St. Stephen, pope and martyr), *Life of St. Chrisantus.* Metaphrastês enlarged this life. See also the Roman martyrology, Usuandus, and Surius, vol. v.

St. Eugenia unharmed by fire, water, and other tortures (A.D. 183-250). St. Eugenia was the daughter of Philippus and Claudia. Her father, as augustral prefect of Egypt, when Eugenia was ten years old, took up his abode in Alexandria; but ten years later suffered a martyr's death, after which Eugenia and her mother returned to Rome. During the reign of Decius, Nicetius the prefect arrested Eugenia for being a Christian, and his sentence was, that she should be taken to the temple of Diana, and if she refused to sacrifice to the goddess, to be put to death by tortures. She was, accordingly, dragged to the isle of Lycaonia, when the lictor said, "Sacrifice, Eugenia, and live." "My God," cried Eugenia, "Thou knowest the secrets of the heart, and hast promised to be a present help to those who call upon Thee. Now glorify Thy name, and cover with confusion those who serve idols and put their trust in graven images." As she thus spoke, the isle trembled as with an earthquake, the temple was shaken to the ground, and the image of Diana was broken to pieces. The immense crowd was divided in their opinion; some declared Eugenia was innocent, but others that she was a magician. The emperor, being told of what had happened, gave orders for the witch to be thrown into the Tiber, with a large stone round her neck. Now was God's opportunity. The stone loosed from the martyr's neck, and Eugenia seated herself on the surface of the river, as if upborne by the hands of angels. As the water had spared the victim, the emperor ordered her to be cast into a fiery furnace. She was, accordingly, taken to the Porta Capena, where were the Thermes of Severus, and was cast into the hypocaust; but the fire instantly went out and lost its heat. It was in vain that the attendants tried to light it again; the wood piled on the hypocaust smoked, but would not burn. The martyr was now thrust into a dark dungeon, and was to be allowed neither drink nor food; but God lightened the dungeon, and Christ Himself came to His servant, holding bread in His hand of dazzling whiteness. "I am thy Saviour," said He, "and will receive you this day into paradise." It was Christmas morning, and at daybreak the executioner entered the dungeon, and cut off her head.—L'abbé Toursel (canon of Arras), *History of St. Eugenia.*

St. Felix, St. Fortunatus, and St. Achillëus miraculously protected under torture (A.D. 212). Cornelius treated the saints Felix, Fortunatus, and Achillëus with diabolical cruelty. They were first scourged with ox sinews, and when the scourging was over, the brute said to them, "There, where were your gods, that they could look on and not succour you? The Christ of which you prate so bravely, you see, could not rescue you." "If you were not bat-blind," said St. Felix, "you would see with your own eyes that all your scourging has not left a mark upon us." "Off with the traitors to the dungeon!" roared Cornelius; "we will soon see who is to be master, Cornelius or Christ." At night an angel came, delivered them from prison, and commanded them to go into the temples and break with hammers the amber statue of Jupiter, with the idols of Mercury and Saturn. The rage of Cornelius was now unbounded, and he ordered them to be bound with their hands behind their backs, their legs and ribs to be broken, and then, being fastened to a wheel, to be enveloped in stinking smoke; after that they were to be impaled on the equileus (see Index) for a day and night. Seeing all his cruelty unavailing, in a spirit of desperation Cornelius ordered the lictors to cut off their heads.—L'abbé Nadal, *Histoire Hagiologique du Diocèse de Valence.*

The marvellous "history" of St. Julian under torture (Jan. 9, A.D. 313). Marcian was sent by Maximinus II., emperor of Rome, to extirpate the Christian religion in Antioch. One of his first acts was to summon St. Julian before him, and command him to offer incense to the gods. As Julian refused to do so, Marcian ordered the lictors to load him with chains, drag him through the streets, and at each turn to torture him with a different kind of punishment. Celsus, the only son of the governor, seeing the martyr pass, was touched with pity, and, running up to the man of God, prayed to be admitted one of his disciples. Marcian, out of all patience at this untimely sympathy, ordered his son to be thrust into Julian's dungeon; and as soon as the two entered it, the darkness of the horrible cell was dispelled by celestial light, and its foulness by odours from paradise; so that the twenty warders were all converted. Next day the emperor commanded the governor to put Julian and all his fellow-Christians to immediate death. Accordingly, Marcian ordered his officers to fill thirty large jars with burning oil, resin, and pitch, and thrust Julian and his companions therein. As the martyrs were led from the dungeon, the bearers of a dead man happened to pass by, and Marcian, in mockery, told Julian to restore the dead man to life. This he did; and the dead man, rising on his feet, cried with a loud voice, "Jesus Christ of Nazareth is the true God, and it is He who has given me life." Marcian, beside himself with rage, ordered his officers to seize the resuscitated man, and put him to death with Julian and his gang. So Julian, with thirty others, were all thrown into the burning oil. But God converted it into a refreshing bath, as saith the psalmist (lxvi. 12): "We went through fire and through water, but we found there only refreshment." Marcionella, the governor's wife, hearing of these things, went to see her son Celsus in the dungeon, hoping to turn him, but was herself converted and baptized. Marcian, in a paroxysm of rage, ordered the twenty warders to be put to instant death, but remanded back to prison Julian, Celsus, Marcionella, and Anastasius (the man resuscitated), till he could make up his mind what to do next. He was advised to proclaim a grand festival to be held in the temple of Jupiter, and to assemble there all the priests of the city to offer sacrifice. The four Christians were brought into the temple, and told to pit their god Christ against the god Jupiter. The four fell on their knees in prayer, when suddenly the earth opened, and swallowed up all the idols and all their priests. Metaphrastês adds, "Even to the present day, flames of fire issue from the earth where these slaves of Satan went down alive into the pit." The four Christians were taken back to their prison, when lo! the twenty warders who had been beheaded, Basilissa the wife of Julian, and a vast throng of the heavenly host, filled the dungeon. Basilissa told Julian he should join her on the morrow in heaven. Well, on the morrow a huge fire was kindled by the order of Marcian, and the four Christians were cast bound into the midst of it; but the fire only burnt their bonds, and did the saints no harm. They were then cast to the wild beasts; but the wild beasts only fawned on them, and licked them lovingly. Every device he could think of thus failing him, the governor ordered the four martyrs to be beheaded, with several felons, murderers, and other malefactors, that no one might be able to distinguish the bodies of the saints from those of the criminals; but even in this he was foiled, for at night the souls of the saints appeared visibly, each sitting on its own dead body, and the Christians, who came at night to bury them, were guided by an unerring sign to the bodies of the four martyrs. So they buried them honourably, and if any shadow of doubt remained respecting their identity, it was soon removed by the many miracles wrought by the holy relics. Amongst other miracles, ten lepers were healed by these relics in one day.—Mgr. Guérin (chamberlain to pope Leo XIII.), *Vies des Saints*, vol. i. pp. 236, 237 (7th edit. 1880).

St. Macra subjected to frightful tortures without harm (third century). Rictiovarus was sent by the emperors Diocletian and Maximian to root out Christianity from Gaul. His first victim was St. Macra of Reims, and as she refused to renounce the hated religion and worship the "divine emperors," she was put to the torture. Rictiovarus now asked if she would repent. "Know, tyrant and child of the devil," she replied, "it is not in the power of man to shake my faith." The judge then ordered her to be burnt alive; so she was taken to

Fismes, stripped of all her raiments, and tied to a stake. As she showed no sign of fear, the judge commanded his executioners to cut off both her breasts; this was done, and she was taken back to prison. Here God restored her breasts, and healed all her wounds, so that not even a scar could be seen. When brought next morning before Rictiovarus, he asked her who had cured her wounds. "Jesus Christ, my Lord," she replied. "Fool!" said the judge. "I ask if you will obey the divine emperors." "I obey God," said the maiden, "and Him only will I serve." She was now thrown on broken potsherds and fagots. The fagots were set on fire, and the victim rolled backwards and forwards over the potsherds; but God was with her, and she felt no pain. After a time, however, God sent His angel to bring her soul to paradise, and her body returned to the earth, earth to earth, and dust to dust.—*Acta Sanctorum* (Bollandists), vol. ii. June 11).

The marvellous story of St. Prisca under torture. St. Prisca was only thirteen years old, when she was taken before Claudius I., and accused of being a Christian. The emperor commanded her to be taken at once to the temple of Apollo, and compelled to worship the god of her fathers. Prisca said she would only worship the Maker of heaven and earth, and Jesus Christ whom He had sent to redeem sinners. The emperor hereupon commanded the malapert little minx to be stripped to the skin, and whipped, till she knew better than to insult the gods of ancient Rome. When the child was stripped naked, God clothed her body in a raiment of light, so dazzling as to blind those who ventured to look at her. Limenius advised the emperor to smear her body with oil to destroy the light which issued from it; but the oil, instead of dimming the light, only diffused a most ravishing odour through all the prison. Claudius, being thus thwarted, grew very angry, and bade the prefect tear the young witch's body to pieces with iron hooks; but the hooks never touched the delicate skin, nor dimmed its lustre. Prisca was next day cast naked into the amphitheatre, to a famished lion, but the lion crouched at her feet like a lamb. She was then impaled on the equileus (see Index), but received no hurt. Next day she was thrown into a brasier, but the fire scorched her not. Being foiled in every way, the emperor in desperation commanded the young sorceress to be conducted beyond the city walls, and there to be beheaded. This was done, Jan. 19, A.D. 54.—*Roman Martyrology.*

St. Restituta unharmed by tortures (third century). Restituta, the Christian daughter of a Roman patrician, was carried by an angel from Rome to Sora (about forty miles), and left in the house of a widow, whose son had been a leper for two years and eight months. The saint offered a prayer, and the young leper was instantly made clean. The miracle came to the ears of Agathius, the proconsul, who sent for Restituta. "Tell me, damsel," said the proconsul, "your name, parentage, religion, and what motive brought you to Sora." "My name," she replied, "is Restituta, my father is a Roman patrician, my religion is the Christian faith, and I was brought here by an angel to win souls to Christ." "My pretty maiden," said Agathius, "leave off this nonsense, obey the law, and you shall be my bride." "Judge," she replied, "I hate frivolity. I will never forsake Christ for dumb idols; and as I am the bride of the great Creator, neither will I nor can I be thy wife." The proconsul, angry at this answer, ordered the maiden to be laid on the ground and beaten with scorpions (see Index). She uttered no groan, but sang sweetly and softly, "Blessed be the Lord God of Israel, who has visited His servant. I rejoice in the *parure* of my Spouse. Alleluia." "What is that you say?" said the proconsul. "Do you call these stripes your *parure?*" "Yes," said the Christian maiden; "and I reckon the present sufferings as nothing to the glory which shall be revealed hereafter." The judge, more and more incensed, ordered the young damsel to be confined in the prison dungeon, to be heavily laden with chains, and to be kept seven days without food or drink. This order was strictly carried out; but an angel came into her dungeon, healed all her wounds, filled the prison with celestial light, broke the chains to powder, relieved her hunger and her thirst, and made her beautiful as a saint in light. The guards were terribly alarmed, ran into the dungeon, and, casting themselves at the maiden's feet, prayed to be admitted into the Christian communion. Restituta sent for a priest named Cyril, who baptized the new converts, to the number of nine souls. When Agathius heard thereof, he ordered his apparitors to bring Restituta, Cyril, and the neophytes to his tribunal, and said to the converts, "Is it true, what I am told, that you have forsaken the immortal gods, whom all the princes of Rome adore, to worship a crucified malefactor?" "It is true, O judge, that we avouch ourselves to be the servants of Jesus Christ, the Creator of all things, the true God, and the Redeemer of man." "Take these fellows at once," cried the judge, "to the golden temple, and if they refuse to offer incense, off with their heads." They refused to offer incense, and were all beheaded. When the persecution ceased, this golden temple was razed to the ground, and a Christian Church was built on the site, in honour of the mother of Christ, and St. Peter prince of the apostles. Cyril and Restituta were now condemned to have their bodies burnt with torches; but they felt no sort of pain, because the Holy Ghost lighted within them the flame of God's grace. Nay, more; the torches were extinguished as often as they were lighted, and the executioners, blinded with the smoke, fainted. When they came to themselves, they said to Cyril and Restituta that the God of Christians is the only true God, and they also became converts; but Agathius ordered both the men to be beheaded. Restituta was then again brought before the proconsul. "What are we to do with this sacrilegious enchanter?" said Agathius to his officers. "She melts iron by her witchcraft, sows light in darkness, quenches fire with a word, and corrupts the imperial soldiers. She first befooled nine of the guard, then two; and is not afraid to blaspheme our immortal gods." Then, turning to the maiden, he said, "In virtue of the imperial edict, we condemn Restituta as a sorcerer, and order her to be taken to the river Caruellus, there to be beheaded, with Cyril and the two others, their heads to be flung into the river as food of fishes, and their bodies left a prey to dogs and wolves and the birds of heaven." After their execution, the four bodies were buried by some pious Christians. The end of this tale is not yet. What follows is in harmony with same marvellous antecedents. After a few days, the murdered Restituta, with her three companions, all resplendent in glory, and surrounded with angels innumerable, appeared to the venerable Amasius, bishop of Sora, and said to him, "Up, father, and go without delay to the spot of our martyrdom. There you will find our heads, thrown by the executioners into the Caruellus. The waters have now left them on the river bank. Go, pick them up, and place them with our truncated bodies." The bishop rose, went to the river bank, and found the four heads, as the apparition had said. He brought them to Sora, placed them with the bodies, and gave the martyrs a glorious sepulture.—*Acta Sanctorum* (Bollandists), vol. vii. May 29.

St. Sabas, the Goth, unharmed by divers tortures (A.D. 372). Athanaric, king of the Goths, in A.D. 370, raised a fierce persecution against the Christians, in which fifty-seven martyrs fell, the principal of which were Nicetas and Sabas. The persecution began by compelling all men to eat meat offered to idols, and was at its height about Easter, 372. It was then that Atharidus, son of Rothestes, entered unexpectedly into the chamber of Sabas, with an armed troop, and dragged him naked over thorns and brambles which had been set on fire, driving him on with whips and sticks. At daybreak, Sabas said to his persecutors, "You have dragged me naked over burning thorns and rough roads, but see! my body is unharmed, my feet unbruised. You have whipped me with all your might, but see! not a wale, not a mark, is to be found on my whole body." This, indeed, was quite true, but only enraged his persecutors the more; so they laid the axletree of a cart on his neck, and, stretching out his hands, fastened them to the end thereof; in a similar manner, they bound his feet to another axletree, drawing them asunder as far as possible; then, pushing him violently, they left him in this improvised rack for the night. When they were gone, the woman of the house where he lodged cut the thongs and bade him escape, but this he refused to do; and next morning, Atharidus, seeing him free, had him bound again, and hung by one finger to a baulk of the prison-cell. He then sent for some meat which had been offered to idols, and commanded the Christian athlete to eat thereof; but he stoutly refused, saying, "This meat is impure and profane, as Atharidus himself, who tempts me with it." One of the slaves of Atharidus now struck him against the breast with the head of his javelin, with such force that all present believed he was killed; but St. Sabas said to the slave, "Did you think you had slain me? Why, man, I no more felt your blow than if you had flung a lock of wool at me." Atharidus, beside himself with rage, ordered the magician to be thrown into the Musæus, now called the Mussovo. As Sabas came to the river-side, "I see," said he exultingly, "what you cannot see. Lo! there, on the other side, stand angels, waiting to carry my soul to paradise." The executioners again bound the axletree about his neck, and threw him into the river. Thus died he, "by water and by wood, symbols of baptism and the cross," say his acts, "at the early age of thirty-eight, April 12, A.D. 372." In Christian art he is represented suspended by one finger to a beam or a tree.—St. Ascholius (bishop of Thessalonica), *A Letter written to the Church of Cappadocia by the Church of Gothia.*

St. Savinian unharmed by a variety of tortures (A.D. 275). The martyrdom of St. Savinian by the emperor Aurelian, in Champagne, is one of those marvellous accumulations met with in the lives of the saints. Not quite so wonderful as that of St. Thyrsus (*q.v.*), but sufficiently so to merit a separate mention.

He was first scourged naked, with ropes' ends, till not a spot in his whole body could be found which had not its proper gash. While this scourging was going on, Aurelian stood by mocking his victim, and saying, "This flagellation is nothing to what I have in store for you, if you persist in your blasphemous obstinacy." The martyr seemed as if his body had been made of brass, and replied, "The earth, the more it is laboured, the more fertile it becomes; and the true Christian, like Christ, is made perfect by suffering." Aurelian, irritated by this answer, had a burning helmet forced on the martyr's head; but the red-hot metal did him no harm, and was the means of the conversion of three persons present at the spectacle. St. Savinian, rejoicing to see the blood of the servants of Christ made the seed of the Church, chid the emperor for the folly of his malice; and the emperor, more and more annoyed, commanded the rebel to be laid on a catasta or iron grating (see Index), under which fires in brasiers were placed; but the God who preserved His three servants in the fiery furnace, preserved St. Savinian from injury in this case also. Aurelian, not to be foiled by the God of Christians, now commanded his soldiers to bind the traitor to a post, and every one "in his whole army" to discharge an arrow at him; but again Jehovah interposed, and turned aside the arrows. Not one reached the body of the saint; one, however, turning aside and wounding the emperor in the right eye. St. Savinian was then taken back to prison, while Aurelian racked his brain to find out some new torments. The emperor might have saved himself the trouble, for at night the chains which bound his victim snapped asunder, the prison doors flew open, and St. Savinian, passing the guards unchallenged, fled towards the Seine. In the morning, Aurelian was informed of the escape of his prisoner, and sent a squadron of soldiers after him, with orders to cut off his head. They followed the saint to the river, which had overflowed its banks. St. Savinian walked across the water, as Jesus walked on the sea, but the soldiers were unable to pursue. Now followed one of those strange marvels only to be met with in lives of the saints. No sooner had St. Savinian crossed the flood, than he prayed God to give a passage to the Roman soldiers also. His prayer was heard, for God intended to take the martyr to Himself. The squadron soon overtook the fugitive, and cut off his head as the emperor had commanded. This occurred Jan. 24, A.D. 275.—Bollandus, *Acta Sanctorum*, vol. iii. Jan. 29. (See also Nicolas des Guerrois, *Saintété Chrétienne de l'Église de Troyes.*)

It would be absurd to subject the above to criticism, as professed miracles are beyond the pale of criticism; but one or two points of a purely historic character may be noticed. In the first place, the narrative seems to assume that Aurelian's army carried bows and arrows, which was not the case. Bows and arrows were not used in the Roman army at all, but only by hunters. Auxiliaries accustomed to the bow were allowed to use their national weapon, but the Roman soldier was never so armed. Again, no doubt Aurelian persecuted Christians, but the wanton barbaric cruelty here ascribed to him is quite out of character. The narrative does not say that one of his proconsuls or lieutenants was guilty of these diabolical acts, but the emperor himself in person. What is worst of all is this: Aurelian was not in Gaul in 275. He left the year preceding, and was himself assassinated somewhere between Byzantium and Heraclea, Jan. 29, 275, the very day he is said to have sent his soldiers to behead Savinian. The "miracles" must stand on their own bases, but history is a fair subject of criticism.

St. Thomas was not hurt by burning iron or a fiery oven. St. Thomas went to the city of Calamina, in India, where the king held his court; but, although the apostle wrought many miracles in his presence, he would not believe. Being angry because Thomas denied the sun to be a god, the king ordered him to be tortured with sundry kinds of torments. Amongst others, he had red-hot iron plates laid on his naked body, but they harmed him not. He was also cast into a burning oven, but the oven burnt him not.—St. Isidore, Metaphrastês, St. Gregory of Tours, etc., give a life of this apostle.

St. Victor was subjected to all sorts of tortures, but received no harm (second century). St. Victor of Damascus was summoned to the tribunal of Sebastian for being a Christian, and as he refused to abjure his faith, his fingers were first broken, his skin flayed, and then was he cast into a fiery furnace. Having remained here for three days, he was taken out, having suffered literally nothing. He was then compelled to swallow poison, but the deadly draughts did him no harm. His nerves were then drawn from his body, his body douched with boiling oil, flaming torches held to his sides, and chalk and vinegar poured down his throat. His eyes were plucked out, and he was hung to a tree head downwards; but in all this, which lasted three days, so far from suffering any pain, he did not even feel the tortures. "He was well called Victor, for he was victorious over the feebleness of nature, the rage of demons, and the savagery of man."—*Les Petits Bollandistes* (1880), vol. v. p. 537.

St. Vitus of Sicily, amidst horrible tortures, preserved from harm (A.D. 303). Vitus was the son of an illustrious family in Sicily, and was but twelve years old, when Valerian arrived in the island, with a commission from Diocletian to stamp out the pestilential rebels called Christians, who never obeyed the emperor, nor reverenced the gods. One of the first persons apprehended was Vitus, and the governor sent for the child's father, bidding him correct the boy, and teach him his duty better. The father tried all in his power to induce the boy to abandon "the pestilential sect," but without avail; whereupon Valerian had him brought to his tribunal. "Boy," said the governor, "how dare you resist the authority of your father and the emperor?" "Sire," said the boy, "whether I ought to obey man rather than God, judge ye." The father, who was present, exclaimed, "Ah me! unhappy in such a son!" "Nay," said the boy, "happy you should call yourself to have a son which is also a son of God." The prefect, hearing these words, ordered the boy to be beaten; but the boy received the blows so quietly, that he seemed not to feel their force. The prefect cried out, "Why don't you scourge him harder, as he deserves to be? Fools! your arms are like those of a girl." The officers, on hearing this, lifted up their arms to obey; but they were dried up like a stick, and lost all power. "The boy is a sorcerer," cried Valerian. "No," said the boy, "not so. Christ is my all, and in Him do I put my trust." Then, going up to the men, he touched their arms, and they returned to their strength. Valerian, touched with this miracle, delivered the boy to his father, with strict injunction to use his best endeavours to bring him to a better state of mind. The father, thinking the best plan would be to surround his son with every sort of pleasure and self-indulgence, fitted up a room for the purpose; but the boy rejected every allurement, and prayed with earnestness, "O Saviour, leave me not, nor forsake me." The chamber was forthwith filled with celestial light and a delicious perfume, and twelve precious stones of marvellous brilliancy appeared in the midst. The domestics set to wait on the boy saw the light, and confessed they had never seen the like in any of the temples of the gods. The father came to see it, when twelve angels of unearthly splendour and beauty met his view; but he was blinded by the excess of light. Being in great pain, he was led to the temple of Jupiter, and prayed the god to help him; but no help came. He then went to his son, and asked him to restore his sight; whereupon the boy put his hands on the blind eyeballs, saying, "O Saviour, the Light of the world, give light to these sightless orbs," and immediately sight was restored to them again. Valerian, being informed of these things, resolved to put the boy to death; but an angel appeared to Modestus, the boy's tutor, and ordered him to take the lad to Italy. Modestus, therefore, accompanied with Crescentius, took him to Naples. Here the three exiles were fed by an eagle, but the boy performed so many miracles that his whereabouts could not lie hid. It so happened that the son of Diocletian was possessed of a demon which cruelly tormented him, and all sorts of superstitions were employed for his deliverance, without effect. The devil in every case cried out, "It is of no use; only Vitus shall dislodge me." The emperor, hearing this over and over again, sent for St. Vitus, and brought him, with Modestus and Crescentius, to Rome. Diocletian asked Vitus if he could cure the prince.

"No," replied Vitus; "but God can by my means." Diocletian implored the young saint to do something for the prince; so, putting his hands on the prince's head, he said with a loud voice, "Thou wicked spirit, I command you, in the name of Christ, come forth." This did he with a horrible noise, and "beaucoup d'idolâtres qui avaient insulté les saints, furent frappés de mort." Diocletian offered St. Vitus apartments in the palace, a seat at the imperial table, and even a share of the empire, if he would accept these proofs of his gratitude; but St. Vitus replied, "These offers, if accepted, would deprive me of far better. It would be bartering heaven for earth, the Lord of lords and King of kings for an earthly monarch, eternity and its glory for time and its uncertainty." The emperor replied, "You talk like a child; but if indeed you reject my favours, you shall feel my displeasure." "I neither accept your bribes, O emperor, nor regard your threats," said Vitus. At these words, Diocletian ordered St. Vitus, with Modestus and Crescentius, to be laden with chains of forty pounds weight, and to be cast into prison. While in prison angels, and even Jesus Christ, came to comfort them, and bade them be of good courage, for a crown of everlasting glory was prepared for them. Diocletian, being told that the prison had been converted into an earthly paradise, commanded Vitus to be cast into a cauldron filled with rosin, pitch, and molten lead; but the saint made the sign of the cross, and invoking Him who delivered the three Hebrew youths, received no sort of harm, not even a hair of his head being singed—nay, more; the deadly bath seemed to give him new life and new beauty. Diocletian came to see him, and Vitus said to him, "Is it possible, miserable wretch, that you cannot see your own blindness, and that it is useless to fight against God?" But this new Pharaoh only hardened his heart, and commanded Vitus to be cast to a terrible lion, "dont le rugissement seul épouvantait toute l'assemblée." The lion, however, instead of tearing the martyr to pieces, crouched at his feet, licking them lovingly; "ce qui fut cause de la conversion d'un grand nombre d'idolâtres." The emperor looked on Vitus as a magician, and ordered him, together with Modestus and Crescentius, to the rack. By the violence of this engine, not only were all their joints pulled from their sockets, but their bones were forced through the skin of their bodies, and their entrails came out. The weather at the time was brilliant and serene, but all of a sudden thick clouds came rolling on, thunder and lightning terrified the people, and thunderbolts falling on the temples crashed the idols to pieces. "L'empereur même s'enfuit plein de confusion, et de dépit de se voir vaincu par un jeune enfant." An angel now came and unbound the martyrs from the racks, healed their bodies, restored their strength, and carried them miraculously from Rome to Silaro. Vitus prayed that God would take him, and a voice from heaven replied, saying, "This day shalt thou be with Me in paradise."—Mgr. Guérin (chamberlain of pope Leo XIII.), *Vies des Saints*, vol. vii. pp. 26–29 (7th edit. 1880).

This is the most outrageous life I know. In this lad is accumulated all the wonders of all the martyrs. He is the quintessence of martyrdom. All children drawn by monks are frightful prigs.

Heart and Treasure go together. (See IDOLS SHATTERED, pt. i.)

MATT. vi. 21. Where your treasure is, there will your heart be also.

St. Antony proves that a miser's heart is in his money-bags. St. Antony of Padua, preaching a funeral sermon over a rich man of very penurious habits, took for his text, "Where your treasure is, there will your heart be also." He said, "This is obviously true, inasmuch as the heart of the deceased would not be found in his dead body, but in his money-bags." Search being made, sure enough there was no heart in the dead body, but in one of the largest of the money-bags there was the dead man's heart, as fresh as if it had only that moment been removed from the carcase.—Edward Kinesman (A.D. 1623), *Lives of the Saints*, p. 368.

Heathen Gods are Devils.

LEV. xvii. 7. They shall no more offer sacrifice unto devils.

DEUT. xxxii. 17. They sacrificed unto devils, not to God.

PSALM cvi. 36, 37. They served their idols, which were a snare to them. Yea, they sacrificed their sons and their daughters unto devils.

1 COR. x. 19, 20. What say I then? that the idol is anything, or that which is offered in sacrifice to idols is anything? I say, that the things which the Gentiles sacrifice, they sacrifice to devils.

REV. ix. 20. The men repented not of the works of their hands, that they should not worship devils, even idols of gold, and silver, and brass, and stone, and wood, which neither can see, nor hear, nor talk.

Apollo confesses he is no god, but only a devil, to St. George of Lydda (A.D. 280–303). The emperor Diocletian had put St. George of Cappadocia to many great tortures for being a Christian, without being able to wean him from the new faith. He then tried to wheedle him back by smooth words and great promises. St. George promised to go with the emperor to the temple of Apollo, and Diocletian, supposing he had made a convert, commanded the senate and the court to be present in the temple, and witness St. George's renunciation. The Christian took his stand directly before the idol, and said with a loud voice, "Apollo, tell me, art thou a god?" The fiend in the statue answered, "No, George, I am not a god. There is but one God, and that is the Maker of heaven and earth." "Who are ye, then?" demanded St. George. "We are the angels who lost their first estate, and were cast out of heaven for rebellion." "If so," said St. George, "why do ye deceive men? and how dare you remain in my presence, seeing I serve the living God?" So saying, he made the sign of the cross before the idol, and immediately was heard a tremendous uproar, the devils howling, and the idol of Apollo falling to the ground. Away flew the devils out of the temple, and the idol of Apollo, with many others, was ground to powder.—Baronius, *Roman Martyrology; Acta Sanctorum;* and Dr. Heylin, *History of St. George.*

Lipomannus tells us, in all the East the life of St. George is read in the manner he has given it. Pasicratês, who wrote the life of the great saint, informs us that he was an eye-witness of the scene above described; and Usuardus is very minute in his details, telling us where and when it occurred, A.D. 290. We are taught to look upon devils as false-tongued, but surely St. George himself could not have spoken more truthfully than these fiends are said to have done.

The devils driven out of the temple of Apollo by St. Gregory the thaumaturgist (A.D. 261). As St. Gregory was on his way to his see, he got benighted, near a temple of Apollo, famous for its oracles. He entered the temple, intending to pass the night there; but, that he and his attendants might do so securely, he made the sign of the cross as he entered in. Forthwith "a huge throng of devils flew out of the temple," unable to abide the presence of the saint. These devils had taken up their abode there, and were accustomed to give responses to those who consulted the oracle. Being driven out, the responses, of course, ceased. St. Gregory and his companions passed the night peacefully, and no mischief befell them.—St. Gregory of Nyssa, *Life of St. Gregory Thaumaturgist.*

St. Nicholas pulled down a temple of Myra, and ejected a nest of devils. In Myra was a notable temple of the great goddess Diana, which none durst lay hands on. St. Nicholas, however, having collected a band of lusty young fellows, pulled the temple to the ground, and, we are told, "devils were heard roaring and yelling, because they were thus forcibly evicted from their ancient and favourite haunt."—Simeon Metaphrastês, *Lives,* etc. (Methodus tells the same tale.)

Heaven of Heavens.

DEUT. x. 14. Behold, the heaven and the heaven of heavens is the Lord's thy God.

1 KINGS viii. 27. Behold, the heaven and the heaven of heavens cannot contain Thee.

PSALM cxv. 16. The heaven, even the heavens, are the Lord's.

PSALM cxlviii. 4. Praise Him, ye heavens of heavens, and ye waters that be above the heavens.

2 COR. xii. 2. I knew a man . . . caught up to the third heaven.

St. Francisca is shown in a vision the three heavens (A.D. 1384–1440). St. Francisca had ninety-three visions in twelve years. The fourteenth vision was heaven, which, she says, was divided into three. The firmament, or starry heaven, in which are the stars, called the host of heaven; the crystalline, a luminous heaven brighter than the firmament; and the empyrean, or heaven of heavens, the place of God's residence, and where the angels and spirits of the just made perfect dwell in everlasting joy. She says the "wounds of Jesus are the light of the empyrean."—John Mattiotti, *Life of St. Francisca.*

The Jews believed in three heavens, as we see by St. Paul, who was "caught up to the third heaven," but the three were these: the aerial, in which the birds fly, the winds blow, and the rain is housed in clouds; the starry heaven; and the heaven of heavens. In regard to the first heaven, read *Gen.* i. 6–8. Ptolemy taught the existence of three heavens, called the starry heaven, the crystalline, and the empyrean; but in his system the crystalline, which divided the empyrean from the starry heavens, was noted for its trepidation or shimmering. The idea that the "wounds of Christ produce the light of heaven" is based on *Rev.* xxi. 23, "The city had no need of the sun, neither of the moon, to shine in it: for the Lamb is the light thereof."

Dante's paradise and heaven of heavens. Dante divides heaven into ten spheres, each of which, he tells us, is appropriated to its proper order. The first seven are the seven planets, viz. (1) the moon for angels; (2) Mercury for archangels; (3) Venus for virtues; (4) the sun for powers; (5) Mars for principalities; (6) Jupiter for dominions; (7) Saturn for thrones. The eighth sphere is that of the fixed stars for the cherubim; the ninth is the *primum mobile* for the seraphim; and the tenth is the empyrean for the queen of heaven and the triune Deity. The empyrean, he says, is a sphere of "unbodied light," or, as Milton expresses it, "bright effluence of bright essence, uncreate." This empyrean is what the Jews call the heaven of heavens.

The Mahometan's heaven, and heaven of heavens. Mahomet, in the *Koran*, ch. xxiii., says, "We have created [one over another] seven heavens." Of these the *first heaven* is of pure silver, and here the stars are hung out like lamps on golden chains. Each star has its angel for warder. It was in this heaven the prophet found Adam and Eve. The *second heaven* is of polished steel, and dazzling in splendour. It was in this heaven the prophet saw Noah. The *third heaven* is studded with precious stones too brilliant for the eye of man. Here the angel of death (Azrael) is stationed, and, as Mahomet says, "is for ever writing in a large book, and erasing what he has written." What he writes is the birth of man, what he erases is the name at death. The *fourth heaven*, like the first, is of the finest silver; and here dwells the angel of tears, whose height is "five hundred days' journey," and he sheds ceaseless tears for the sins of man. The *fifth heaven* is of the purest gold; and here dwells the avenging angel, who presides over elemental fire. It is here the prophet saw Aaron. The *sixth heaven* is composed of hasala (a sort of carbuncle); and here dwells the guardian angel of heaven and earth, half snow, half fire. It is here the prophet saw Moses, who "wept with envy." The *seventh heaven* is formed of divine light. Each inhabitant of this sphere has seventy thousand heads, and all the tongues of all the heads are employed day and night in singing the praises of the Most High. It is here the prophet saw Abraham.

Hell.

ISA. lxvi. 24. The righteous shall go forth, and look upon the carcases of the men that have transgressed against me; for their worm shall not die, neither shall their fire be quenched; and they shall be an abhorring unto all flesh.

REV. xxi. 9. The fearful, and unbelieving, and the abominable, and murderers, and sorcerers, and idolaters, and all liars, shall have their part in the lake which burneth with fire and brimstone. Where their worm dieth not, and the fire is not quenched (Mark ix. 48). There shall be weeping, and gnashing of teeth (Matt. viii. 12).

St. Francisca's vision of hell (A.D. 1384–1440). One day St. Francisca, having shut herself in her cell, was in an ecstasy about four o'clock in the afternoon, and the archangel Raphael came to conduct her through hell. Having come to the gates, she read over them this inscription: "Hell, without hope, without cessation of torment, without repose." The gates opened of themselves, and St. Francisca saw an abyss so deep, so terrible, and from which came such shrieks of anguish, and such a stench, that she could never afterwards speak of it or think about it without her blood freezing in her veins. It was divided into three regions—upper, intermediate, and lower. In the lower region the torments were greatest, and in the upper the least. In the upper region she saw the Jews who rejected Christianity, but were not guilty of great moral offences; here, too, she saw those Christians who neglected confession, and who died without receiving the last offices of the Church. In the lowest region she saw the people of Sodom, and all others who had committed sins contrary to nature. These wretched demons were pierced incessantly with fiery darts. Here, too, she observed usurers stretched on tables of red-hot brass, while demons poured into their throats buckets of liquid metal. In this region were blasphemers, whose tongues were held by hooks. Traitors and hypocrites were here, and their hearts were being torn out of their bodies, but replaced again to endure for ever the same agony. Homicides were here, and women who made away with their own offspring; these wretches wander for ever in a bath of boiling blood to another of thick-ribbed ice, and back again. Apostates were being sawn asunder. The incestuous lay imbedded in stinking ordure. Enchanters and sorcerers were pelted with burning quoits. The seven capital sins were punished here—violators of their vows, women who idolized their own beauty, calumniators, and licentious widows.

The whole is too long to transcribe, but those who care

to see this Dantesque *Inferno* of St. Francisca may read it in the *Acta Sanctorum* of the Bollandists, vol. ii. March 9.

The Valley of Hinnom. Ge-hinnom was a gorge south and west of Jerusalem, with steep rocky sides, famous for idolatrous rites. Here Solomon built a "high place for Moloch" (1 *Kings* xi. 7). Here Ahaz and Manasseh made children pass through the fire, "according to the abomination of the heathen." The south-east extremity of the gorge was called Tophet (or *the place of burning*). King Josiah "defiled the valley" by making it the common cesspool of the city, into which its sewage and offal was conducted, to be carried off by the Kidron. And here all the solid filth of the city was cast. Hence it became a huge nest of insects, whose larvæ or worms fattened on the corruption. Fires were kept constantly burning to consume the offal, the refuse of sacrifices, and the bodies of criminals which were thrown there, with the filth and offscouring. Among the latter Jews, this gorge was regarded as a symbol of hell, and the constantly burning fire, with the perpetual breed of worms, are referred to in the Gospels as symbolical of the state of outcasts from God in the life to come. As criminals were cast into the laystall of Tophet, where fire was for ever burning, and worms ceaselessly battened on corruption, so unbelievers shall be cast out as the offscouring of the human race, as the carcases of criminals and the offal of the city are cast into the Valley of Hinnom.

De Croly's description of Ge-hinnom. "The vapours that rose hot and sickly before me were the smokes from fires kindled in the Valley of Hinnom, where the refuse of animals, slaughtered for the use of the city, and the other pollutions and remnants of things abominable to the Jews were daily burned. The sullen and perpetual fires, the deadly fumes, and the aspects of the degraded and excluded beings, chiefly public criminals, employed in this hideous task, gave the idea of the place of final evil. Our prophets, in their threats against national betrayers, against the proud and the self-willed, the polluted with idols, and the polluted with that still darker and more incurable idolatry, the worship of the world, pointed to the Valley of Hinnom. The Pharisee, the Essenes, the Sadducee, in the haughty spirit that forgot the fallen state of Jerusalem, and the crimes that had lowered her—the hypocrite, the bigot, the sceptic, alike mad with hopeless revenge, when they saw the Roman cohorts triumphing with their idolatrous ensigns through paths once trod by the holy, or when driven aside by the torrents of cavalry and the gilded chariot in which sat some insolent proconsul fresh from Italy, and looking down on the noblest of our people as the beaten slaves of the stranger —pointed to the Valley of Hinnom. How often, as the days of Jerusalem hurried towards their end, and, by some fatality, the violence of the Roman governors became more frequent and intolerable, have I seen groups of my countrymen hunted into some byway of the city by the hoofs of the Roman horse, consuming with that inward wrath which was soon to flame out with such horrors, flinging up their wild hands as if to upbraid the tardy heavens, gnashing their teeth, and, with the strong contortions of the Oriental countenance, the stormy brow and flashing eye, and lips scarcely audible from the force of their own convulsion, muttering conspiracy. Then, in despair of shaking off that chain which had bound the whole earth, they would appeal to the vengeance of the endless future, and, shrouding their heads in their cloaks, stand like sorcerers summoning up demons, each with his quivering hand stretched out towards the accursed valley, and every tongue groaning 'Gehenna!'"—*Salathiel.*

Dante's Inferno. Dante divides his hell into nine regions. Of these, the seventh, called Dis, contains three circles; the eighth, called Malebolgê, contains ten abysses; and the ninth contains four pits.

Region 1. Is a vast meadow, in which roam Electra, Hector, Æneas, and Julius Cæsar; Camilla and Penthesilēa; Latinus and Junius Brutus; Julia (Pompey's wife) and Cornelia; and here apart was Saladin. Linos and Orpheus were in this canton; Aristotle, Socratês, and Plato; Democritos, Diogenês, Heraclitos, Empedoclês, Anaxagoras, Thalês, Dioscoridês, and Zeno; Cicero and Seneca; Euclid and Ptolemy; Hippocratês and Galen; Avicen and Averroes.

Region 2 (*for sinful love*). Here sits Minos in judgment on the ghosts brought before him, and here are heard groans and blasphemies. This canton is the hell of carnal and sinful love; and here the poet places Semiramis, Dido, Cleopatra, and Helen; Achillês and Paris, Tristan, Launcelot, and Francesca.

Region 3 (*for gluttons*). Here fall in ceaseless showers hail, black rain, and sleety flaw; the air is cold and dun, and a foul stench rises from the soil. Cerberus keeps watch over this canton, set apart for gluttons.

Region 4 (*for misers*). This canton, presided over by Plutus, "hems in all the woe of all the universe;" and here are gathered the souls of the avaricious, who made no good use of their wealth.

Region 5 (*for unrestrained anger*). This is the Stygian lake of inky blue. It is a miry bog, the abode of those who put no restraint on their anger.

Region 6. Here Phlegyas was the ferryman; and here was Filippo Argenti.

Region 7. "The city of Dis," subdivided into three circles: one for those who by force and fraud have done *violence to others;* one for those who have done violence to *themselves*, as suicides; and one for those who have done violence to *God*, as heretics, atheists, and so on.

Region 8. "Malebolgê," subdivided in ten abysses. In the first he saw Jason; the second was for *harlots;* in the third was Simon Magus; in the fourth was pope Nicholas III.; in the fifth the ghosts had their heads turned the wrong way—this abyss was for *witches* and *sorcerers;* in the sixth was Annas and Caiaphas; the seventh was for *robbers of churches;* in the eighth was Ulysses and Diomed; in the ninth was Mahomet and Ali, "horribly mangled;" the tenth was for *alchemists*, *coiners*, and *forgers*.

Region 9. "The lowest hell," in which was the river Cocytus. Here Lucifer and Judas were confined in thick-ribbed ice.

The Tartaros of the Greeks. This is described by Homer and Hesiod as an underground region, vast, dark, and subdivided into four districts. One of them is terrible with its infected lake, its river of fire, its burning furnaces, and its furies, whose office is to torment the tormented. The other three are fields, of more or less enjoyment, for the dead of the better sort. Later poets placed hell proper under Tenaros, and described it as a dark region, encompassed with thick forests, and with labyrinths of sewers. Here, they tell us, the souls of the wicked are held in bondage in lakes of ice, or wander in everlasting fire, or are taken from one to the other to aggravate their torment. Tartaros, strictly speaking, is not the hell of the Greeks, but a region beyond; the prison, in fact, of the infernal gods, where the offspring of the Cyclops, Uranus, Saturn, and the Titans, are confined.

The Roman Avernus. The Romans placed hell under the lake Avernus, and divided it into seven regions: (1) The paradise of infants, who knew no evil and have done no good: (2) the paradise of those who have been unjustly condemned to death; (3) the hell of suicides; (4) the "field of tears" for the perjured and faithless; (5) the hell of heroes stained with crimes; (6) the place of torment by fire and torture; and (7) the Elysian fields.

Hell according to the Korân. They who believe not shall have garments of fire fitted to their bodies. Boiling water shall be poured on their heads. Their bowels shall be dissolved thereby, and their skins also; and they shall be beaten with maces of iron. And as often as they shall attempt to get out of the place of torment, they shall be dragged back into it again (ch. x.).

(Dante seems to have borrowed from the Korân; but has still further piled up the agony with poetic licence.)

Ifurin of Celtic mythology. The Celtic hell was not a place of everlasting heat, so much as of agonizing cold. The heat was said to be that internal heat which arises from fever, the effect of poison. The region is described as sombre, sunless, infected by venomous insects and reptiles, by roaring lions and ravening wolves, by which the tormented were for ever bitten and torn, without suffering death. Those who, like infants and idiots, died neither good nor bad, were said to be doomed to a mitigated hell of perpetual fog, above the other region.

The hell of the native Floridians. The natives of Florida think that criminals are transported at death to mountains in the far north, where they are exposed to wild bears and severe cold.

The hell of the people of Laos, in Asia. According to the teaching of the people of Laos, the wicked are punished in six regions, differing in suffering; but no punishment is for ever. After a certain term, varying according to the degree of wickedness, the souls pass into the bodies of other animals, more or less vile; and gradually mount upwards till they reach again the human state.

The hell of the Parsees. The Guebres believe that the wicked, after death, are tormented by fire, which burns but consumes not. One of the torments they endure is the "stench of sin." This and the sweet "odour of righteousness" are [Roman] Catholic tenets. Some of the damned, according to the Parsees, are confined in dungeons, where they are for ever choked with thick smoke, and bitten by innumerable insects and reptiles. Others are plunged to the neck in thick ice, while demons tear their flesh with their teeth. Others, again, are hung by the heels, and constantly stabbed with daggers.

The hell of the Santos of Japan. The hell of the Santos is one of envy and disappointment, rather than of elemental fire and cold. The wicked are doomed to wander round and round paradise, that they may see the happy state of the heavenly host, and ever regret the blessings they have lost.

The hell of the Siamese. The Siamese, like Dante, subdivide their inferno into nine regions, but do not hold the doctrine of the eternity of hell-punishment.

The hell of the native Virginians. The Indians of Virginia believe in a hell somewhere in the west. It is a deep ditch filled with devouring flames, and called Popoguno.

Paduma Hell is a most ingenious conception of horrors. The wicked are said to be "beaten with iron hammers, and boiled in iron pots in a mixture of blood and matter; they are fed on food resembling red-hot balls of iron, and plunged in the accursed river Veterani, difficult to cross, and flowing with streams of sharp-edged razors. The torments, though not eternal, are to endure 512,000,000,000 times as long as it would take to clear away a large heap of tiny sesamum-seed, at the rate of one seed in a hundred years."

Holiness better than Rubies.

PROV. iii. 15. Wisdom is more precious than rubies; and all the things thou canst desire are not to be compared to it.

MATT. xiii. 45, 46. The kingdom of heaven is like unto a merchantman seeking goodly pearls, who, when he had found one pearl of great price, sold all that he had and bought it.

PROV. xx. 15. The lips of knowledge are a precious jewel.

JOB xxviii. 18. The price of wisdom is above rubies.

Simeon Stylitês was so holy that a maggot which fell from him became a pearl (A.D. 459). The body of Simeon Stylitês was full of sores covered with maggots. One day a maggot fell from the pillar-saint at the foot of Basilicus, king of the Saracens, and the king, picking it up, laid it on his eye, whereupon it was instantly converted into a magnificent pearl, so large, so beautiful, and of such fine water, that Basilicus valued it more than his whole empire.—Theodoret (fifth century), *Church History.*

Honi soit qui mal y pense.

TITUS i. 15. Unto the pure all things are pure: but unto them that are defiled is nothing pure; but even their mind and conscience is defiled.

ROM. xi. 14. To him that esteemeth anything unclean, to him it is unclean.

1 COR. xiii. 5. Charity thinketh no evil.

The prurient modesty of St. Angela of Brescia (A.D. 1472–1540). St. Angela of Brescia was between sixty-five and sixty-six years of age when she died; but even at that advanced age, the religious ceremony of washing her dead body was revolting to her modesty. "Elle imagina de se rendre à elle-même cet office, pour épargner à son corps virginal la honte d'être découvert, même lorsqu'il ne serait plus le tabernacle de son âme sainte."—*Life of St. Angela of Brescia* (Montpellier, 1804).

This appears to me a most prurient sort of modesty indeed. The dead body of an old woman of sixty-five could conjure up no immodest thoughts in waiting-women of a middle age, any more than the chickens, rabbits, hare, and game which a cook has to handle, clean, and dress. The very notion shows an immodest and perverted imagination, and not a mind pure as purity, chaste as the driven snow, purged of all earthly thoughts and carnal imaginations. These examples of mock-modesty are quite revolting to read about.

The immodest modesty of St. Francisca in infancy (A.D. 1413). The modesty of St. Francisca was innate. Even from her cradle she had a horror of immodesty, insomuch that she would not allow either of her parents to nurse her till she was dressed, nor would she allow any of the other sex, not even her own father, to kiss or fondle her, although such a liberty is authorized by nature to all parents.—John Mattiotti (her ghostly father), *Life of St. Francisca,* recited at her canonization, May 29, 1606.

No one can for a moment doubt that this manifestation of prudery was the record of a monk. No father could ever have dreamt of such a thing. It is a pity that Mattiotti did not call to mind that beautiful instance of real modesty recorded of Adam and Eve in paradise—they did not even "know that they were naked." The squeamishness of St. Francisca, instead of proving her innate modesty, can only prove that her impure thoughts were far above her age.

A fellow who insulted St. Galla fell to the earth in convulsions. One day when St. Galla, with her handmaids, entered a house of low reputation on a mission of charity, a fellow cried out after her, saying, "You call yourself a saint, do you? A pretty saint indeed! I warrant you, no saints ever enter into a house like that." No sooner had the fellow uttered these base insinuations than he fell to the earth in horrible convulsions. As to the pure all things are pure, so unto them that are defiled is nothing pure.—*Les Petits Bollandistes*, vol. ii. p. 199.

St. John the Silent would never bathe or wash his body (A.D. 454-558). St. John the Silent was a native of Armenia, of such wonderful "modesty" that he would never wash his body or bathe, "lest he should offend his modesty by looking on his naked body."—Cyrille, *Life of St. John the Silent.*

The only inference one can draw from this is that St. John the Silent must have had a most depraved mind, if he could not even wash himself without calling up unchaste and impure thoughts. So far from this being a mark of modesty, it was the self-condemnation of a most immodest mind.

Households set at Variance by the Gospel.

LUKE xii. 51, 53. Suppose ye I am come to give peace on earth? I tell you, Nay; but rather division . . . for the father shall be divided against the son, and the son against the father; the mother against the daughter, and the daughter against the mother; the mother-in-law against the daughter-in-law, and the daughter-in-law against the mother-in-law.

St. Barbara delivered up to torture by her own father. St. Barbara, daughter of Dioscorus, a wealthy noble of Nicomedia, was a Christian, but her father was an idolater. Dioscorus had ordered a bath of white marble to be made for his daughter's use. When Barbara first entered it, she crossed it with her finger, and the mark she made remained enduringly on the marble. Hundreds saw the cross on the white marble, and many by kissing it were healed of their infirmities. When it caught the eye of Dioscorus it instantly flashed into his mind that his daughter must be a Christian, and so great was his anger, that he handed her over at once to Marrianus to be punished as the law directed. She was accordingly stripped and beaten with ox sinews, after which the raw flesh was irritated by being rubbed with a coarse hair-cloth. She was then led back to her dungeon under the hope that she would recant, but lo! her dungeon was brilliantly illuminated with celestial light, and Jesus Christ was waiting there to strengthen and comfort her. He healed her wounds, assuaged their pain, spoke to her of the reward in store for her, and having filled her heart with heavenly ravishment, left her with the promise that He would come again, and take her to dwell with him for ever in paradise.—Simeon Metaphrastês, *Lib r dictus Paradisus*; and Ado's *Martyrology.*

Hundredfold returned.

MATT. xix. 29. Every one that hath forsaken houses, or brethren, or sisters, or father, or mother, or wife, or children, or lands, for My name's sake, shall receive a hundredfold now, in this life, and in the world to come life everlasting (Mark x. 29, 30).

St. Briocus gives his cruse to a leper, and God rewards him (sixth century). While Briocus of Cardigan was a child only ten years old, and was going to fetch water from a fountain, he saw a leper, and having nothing to give him, gave the cruse he was carrying in his hand. As this cruse was not his own, God "miraculously sent him" another, a hundredfold more beautiful than the one he had given to the leper.—Dom Lobineau, *Lives of the British Saints.*

The custom of giving what is not one's own, so frequently recorded in the lives of the saints, and always held up to imitation, is most censurable. It is no act of self-denial, it is undoubtedly dishonest, and if indulged in extensively would be the ruin of society. Let a journeyman give away his master's goods, let a clerk give away his employer's money, let children give away what is in the house, without permission, and no one would be trusted. It is perfectly amazing how any one can commend and hold up to imitation such obvious dishonesty, yet is this practice most common, and most highly commended in hagiography. Robin Hood might salve his conscience by saying he robbed the rich to give unto the poor; but Robin Hood was a "base, dishonest robber," and not a saint.

St. John the almsgiver felt assured that the Lord returns all charities a hundredfold (A.D. 616). A nobleman having been reduced to the utmost poverty, John, patriarch of Alexandria, gave an order on his treasurer for fifteen pounds of gold. The treasurer, thinking the sum exorbitant, crossed off the "tens," and gave the man five pounds. During the day, a wealthy lady sent St. John an order for five hundred pounds of gold, as a contribution towards his charities. The almsgiver begged the lady to call on him, and in conversation she remarked, "I wrote the order originally for fifteen hundred, but this morning I observed that the ten of *your* order was erased, so I crossed off the ten of *mine.*" The patriarch now sent for his treasurer, and learnt what had been done. "I knew it, I felt sure of it," cried he, "when I asked the lady to call on me. The Lord has assured us He returns all charities a hundredfold, and I felt sure that the Lord well knew that five hundred is not a hundredfold of fifteen."

Another instance. Going to matins one day, St. John the almsgiver saw a beggar in rags, and gave him his mantle. Scarcely had he so done, when a stranger put into his hands a purse containing a hundred pounds of gold.

Another instance. St. John, patriarch of Alexandria, finding himself short of money and corn, during a time of dearth, borrowed a large sum of money for distribution in alms. Soon afterwards two ships from Sicily, laden with wheat, arrived, for the almoner to distribute as he thought fit.

Another instance. At another time three barges laden with corn were wrecked by the fault of the seamen, who, greatly alarmed, took refuge in the church of Alexandria. St. John, the patriarch, spoke kindly to them, and gave them money. As he left the church, a messenger informed him that three barges, double the size of those lost, had just come into harbour for him.

Another instance. Nicetas, in the Persian war, under pretext of public necessity, took from Alexandria all its treasures, leaving only a small pittance for present necessities. The patriarch bore the loss without a murmur, merely saying, "God will provide." The very same hour, some men brought to the church two jars for the patriarch, one labelled "EXCELLENT HONEY FOR THE BISHOP," and the other "UNADULTERATED HONEY." These two large jars were, in reality, filled with gold for the almoner. St. John sent one of the jars to Nicetas, and Nicetas sent back to the patriarch everything he had taken from the Church, and added to this restitution a gift of a hundred pieces of gold, with a note, "Pray God to pardon my sacrilege."—Leontius, *Life of the Patriarch John of Alexandria.*

St. Helen of Troyes gives water to a beggar, and finds her earthen jug converted into silver. St. Helen of Troyes certainly strikes us as a very marvellous coincidence; and it becomes still more strange when we are informed that the king of Corinth was her father, but nothing is known about the year of her birth and death. She is, however, the patron saint of the diocese of Troyes. We are told this marvellous story about her, at the early age of twelve years. Going one day to a fountain to fetch water, a beggar asked her to give him drink. The damsel instantly handed him her jug, and when she received it back again, she was not a little surprised to find her earthen vessel had been converted into silver.—L'abbé Defer, *Saints du Diocèse de Troyes.*

Idol-makers confounded.

ISA. xlv. 16–18. They shall be ashamed, they shall go to confusion together, that are makers of idols. For thus saith the Lord, I am the Lord, and there is none else.

An idol-maker made ashamed and put to confusion by St. Lucy. St. Lucy, laden with chains, was dragged through the streets, but as she passed by the warehouse of Germinian, a noted image-maker, all his idols fell to the ground, and were broken to pieces. Germinian was confounded at the miracle; and, being convinced that it was God's doing, became a convert to the faith of Jesus, and was beheaded with St. Lucy the selfsame day.—Metaphrastês (died A.D. 911), *Lives*, etc.

Innocency protected by God.

JOB iv. 7. Remember, I pray thee, who ever perished, being innocent?

St. Cyriacus, being falsely accused, is defended by an angel (fourth century). St. Cyriacus, wishing to avoid vainglory, performed his religious exercises secretly, in the night, but was accused to St. Maximin of neglecting them. The bishop suspended judgment, and prayed that God would give him wisdom to judge righteous judgment. As he was preparing to celebrate mass, an angel appeared to him, and assured him that Cyriacus was wholly innocent of the charges brought against him. "Ces choses," says our author, "répandues par la voix puissante de la renommée chez tous les peuples anciens, et transmises jusqu'à nous, méritent de trouver place ici. Elles sont vraies. Les peintures des églises nous l'attestent."—Sigehard, *Miracles of St. Maximin.*

Inspiration promised to the Saints.

MATT. x. 19, 20. When men deliver you up, take no thought how or what ye shall speak; for it shall be given you in that same hour what ye shall speak. For it is not ye that speak, but the Spirit of your Father which speaketh in you.

St. Catherine of Alexandria before the

wise men of the empire. St. Catherine, wishing to convert the emperor Maxentius, who had ordered a hecatomb to be offered to the gods of Rome, went to the imperial palace, and had an interview with him. Maxentius, being wholly unable to cope with her in argument, sent for all the wisest men in the empire to come and hold a disputation with the Christian maid, whom he called "the second Plato." On the eve of the disputation an angel appeared to St. Catherine, and said to her, "Fear not, thou beloved spouse of the Lamb of God, nor take thought how or what you shall say on the morrow; for it shall be given you at the time what you shall say. Be of good courage, for you shall surely prevail, seeing it is not you who speak, but the Spirit of God who speaketh by you."—Metaphrastês (died A.D. 911), *Lives*, etc.

Justice justified in Forgiveness.

PSALM lxxxv. 10. Mercy and truth are met together; righteousness and peace have kissed each other.

The adulteress forgiven. A certain king had a son and four daughters. The names of the daughters were Justice, Truth, Mercy, and Peace. The son married the daughter of the king of Jerusalem, who was guilty of adultery, repudiated, and reduced to abject poverty. The king, moved with pity, sent messengers to invite the fallen woman back; but she declined to return, unless the prince himself gave her the kiss of peace and forgiveness. When the king heard this, he consulted his family what should be done. The eldest daughter, Justice, said the adulteress could not be recalled without doing dishonour to the law. The second daughter, Truth, said that she was of her sister's opinion; for if the king said one thing and did another, his word would never be depended on, and sin would abound. The third sister, Mercy, pleaded for the wife, and said compassion is the brightest jewel in the crown. The youngest sister, Peace, terrified at the family jar, fled into the wilderness. The king's son was now appealed to, and he was asked to state what was his advice. The prince replied, "The woman is my spouse; I am willing to take her back. On my head be all her sins, and on me fall what punishment she deserves." Justice and Truth said they were satisfied, the law was honoured, and so be it. Mercy kissed her brother, and her tears fell fast. The wife returned, and Peace came with her. Mercy and Truth then embraced each other. Justice and Peace did the same, and all were reconciled.—*Gesta Romanorum*, lv.

Zaleucus the Locrian loses an eye on behalf of his son. Zaleucus, the Locrian lawgiver, enacted that any citizen of Locris proved guilty of adultery should be deprived of both his eyes. His own and only son was the first person convicted of the offence, and Zaleucus vindicated the law by giving his own right eye, and plucking out his son's left eye. The whole kingdom extolled the justice and wisdom of this act, and the law was more honoured in consequence of this vicarious punishment than if the whole weight of the law had fallen on the guilty son. If Zaleucus would not spare his own eye, there could be no hope that he would spare a stranger's.—Valerius Maximus, *Memorable Acts and Sayings*, bk. vi. ch. 5, 3.

Lending to the Lord. (See GIVING TO THE POOR.)

PROV. xix. 17. He that hath pity upon the poor lendeth unto the Lord; and that which he giveth will He pay him again.

LUKE vi. 38. Give, and it shall be given unto you; good measure, pressed down, shaken together, and running over.

Putting the text to the test. A certain Jew, resolving to see if God would really return the money given to the poor, distributed in alms all that he possessed, except two pieces of silver, and then waited to see the result. Nothing occurred for several days, and the Jew, being disappointed, went to Jerusalem, resolving to lodge a complaint against Solomon for falsehood before the high priest. On the road he saw two men quarrelling over a stone which they had picked up; so he offered to give for it his two silver pieces. The offer was accepted, and each man took a piece. When the Jew reached the city, he showed the stone to a jeweller, and was told it was one of the precious stones dropped from the ephod of the high priest. He took it to the pontiff, and received in value many times the sum of money he had distributed in alms.—Cedrenus (1061), *Chronicle from Adam to Isaac Comnenus.*

St. Elizabeth of Hungary gives her state robe to a beggar (A.D. 1207–1231). One day, when the landgrave was entertaining at his table the grand-seigneurs of his estate, Elizabeth, the landgravine, was importuned by a beggar for alms, and having no money at hand, she gave her state mantle to the woman. God set His seal of approval to this act, by sending an angel to the landgravine with another robe, precisely like the one she had bestowed on the beggar, "et peut-être était-ce-lui-même qui l'avait reçu." The count de Montalembert, *History of Elizabeth of Hungary.*

If "angel" means messenger in this extract, then the "miracle" turns out to be this—a messenger brought the robe back again. As, indeed, one would expect; for what could a beggar do with a robe of state, as pawnbrokers were not yet known?

St. Francisca gives some corn sweepings to the poor, and the gift is restored (A.D. 1384–1440). St. Francisca, during a time of great dearth, gave to some poor people the corn swept from the rafters and beams of her husband's granary. Returning to the chamber to see if she could scrape together a little more, she found forty measures of fine wheat, in lieu of the sweepings she had given to the poor.—*Process of Canonization*, May 29, 1606.

St. Francisca gives the wine of Andreas to the poor, but the wine so given is spontaneously restored (A.D. 1384-1440). During a famine in Rome, Andreas, the father-in-law of St. Francisca, laid in a tun of wine. Francisca, being importuned by the poor, gave all who came some of this wine, till the tun was empty. When Andreas found all his wine gone he was exceedingly angry, but his daughter-in-law said, "Have you never heard, that he who hath pity on the poor, lendeth unto the Lord; and that which he giveth, the Lord will pay back again? The wine given is still in the barrel." And so it was. Andreas found the tun quite full of the very best wine, and confessed that God is as good as His word. —*Process of Canonization*, May 29, 1606.

See note under ISIDORE, next column. What is there said applies to this case also. St. Francisca had no right whatever to give away this wine without her father-in-law's consent. It was no charity at all; not in the case of Francisca, for she made no personal sacrifice, but was liberal at another's expense; not in Andreas, for he gave nothing, and was angry that Francisca had squandered his wine. To reward Francisca was to reward a selfish and dishonest act; to reward Andreas was to reward him for nothing at all but ill-temper and a grudging disposition.

St. Francis Hieronimus steals bread for the poor, but the bread is miraculously restored (A.D. 1642-1716). One day, in boyhood, St. Francis Hieronimus was detected by his mother stealing bread to distribute to the poor. She reproved him for taking what was not his own, and forbade him to do so again. The boy blushed scarlet at the reproof, and said, "Mother, do you suppose we shall ever be the poorer for lending to the Lord? Look on the shelf, and see if any loaf is missing." The mother counted the loaves, and found they were all there. Then, throwing her arms round the boy's neck, she told him he was free to dispose of anything in the house in charity.—Cardinal Wiseman. (St. Francis was canonized in 1839.)

This is wretched teaching altogether. The boy steals the bread, and gives what is not his own; the mother is angry at the loss of her bread, and finding the loss restored, not only condones the offence, but is willing, on similar terms, to allow its repetition. If the theft was wrong, the "miraculous" restitution of the loaf or loaves could not make it right. The mother was offended at her loss and not at the peculation.

St. Isidore gives his master's corn to feed some stray pigeons. John da Vergas, a farmer of Madrid, sent his man Isidore with a sack of wheat to the mill to be ground for family use. It was midwinter, and the ground was thickly covered with snow. On the way, Isidore was joined by other labourers bent on similar errands. So, on they trudged together, talking and toiling, till they came to a tree literally covered with pigeons. The poor birds were starving, for the snow was deep. Isidore removed the snow for a yard or so, and almost emptied the sack. Down flew the pigeons in a body, but before they touched the corn, they flew to the feet of the holy man, and lovingly caressed them with their bills. One of the companions reproved Isidore for wasting his master's goods, but he replied, "I am lending to the Lord, and that which I give He will surely repay me again." And so it was. He deposited his sack well-nigh empty in the mill; but the flour which it made was so multiplied between the millstones, that he took back twice as much as any of his companions whose sacks were full of grain. —John the deacon, *Life of St. Isidore.*

This is certainly very unsound morality. It was no charity in Isidore to give what was not his own, and the mere accident that the theft was miraculously restored does not alter the character of the deed. Take the following illustration: A merchant sends his clerk to the Bank of England with £500 cash. In going through some of the London slums, he sees a host of poor folk, meagre women, children crying for food, and men lounging about for want of work. The clerk distributes amongst them £400 o his master's money, and deposits only £100 instead of £500 in the bank. Stop there. What would be thought of this transaction? It really has not one redeeming feature. The clerk makes no personal sacrifice, and if such conduct were tolerated, honesty and confidence would be destroyed. If the banker's clerk accidentally put down £500 instead of £100, so that the master never detected the robbery, so much the worse. No restitution of the money could possibly justify the theft, although it might save the clerk from its evil consequences. Such teaching is wretched indeed.

St. Medard gives one of his father's horses to a poor man, and yet his father lacked not one of his horses (A.D. 545). St. Medard was of royal blood, both on his father's and on his mother's side. One day his father, returning from the country with a large cavalcade, charged his son Medard, then a boy, to conduct the horses to the meadow, and look after them, as the grooms were all fully occupied. As he went to the meadow, he saw a man carrying a bridle and saddle on his head, and asked him why he did so. The man replied, his horse had just died, and the loss was very great, as he had no money to buy another. On hearing this, Medard gave the man one of his father's horses. As he returned home it began to rain heavily, and God, in reward of his gift, sent an eagle to ward off the rain from him with outstretched wings. Not only the grooms saw this, but his father, mother, all the guests, and all the domestics. When the groom saw one of the horses was missing, he complained of it to his master. Medard explained the matter, and his father went with him to the stables. What, however, was his amazement to find his whole tale of horses quite complete; not one was missing. The father now gave his son liberty to give in alms whatever he thought proper, feeling assured that whatever he gave would be given him again.—*Acta Sanctorum* (Bollandists), vol. ii. June 8.

It was a dishonest act, wholly without the merit of self-sacrifice, for young Medard to give what was not his own. And the principle on which his father permitted him in future to give alms was most reprehensible.

Peter Vellius gives Francis Xavier the key of his cash-box. Xavier takes from it three hundred crowns, but Vellius finds his cash in full tale. Francis Xavier went to Peter Vellius, a wealthy merchant of Machai, to ask for a subscription to some charity. As Vellius was absorbed at the time in a game of chess, he gave the key of his cash-box to Xavier, bidding him help himself; so, taking out three hundred crowns, he brought back the key, and went his way. When Vellius examined his cash-box to see what had been taken, he found all his money in full tale, just as he had left it. The next time he met Xavier, he told him about it, and Xavier replied, "Just so; he that giveth to the poor, lendeth to the Lord; and that which he giveth, the Lord will pay him again."—Cardinal de Monte, *Speech before Gregory XV. on the canonization of Francis Xavier*, Jan. 19, 1622.

Liars frustrated.

ISA. xliv. 25. [God] frustrateth the tokens of the liars.

St. Gregory the thaumaturgist falsely accused (A.D. 212-270). The great chastity and moral life of Gregory when a young man stirred up the envy of some fellows of his own age, who suborned a woman to father a child on him in a public lecture-room. No sooner, however, had she done so, than the devil took possession of her, and so terribly tormented her that life was unendurable. St. Gregory, moved with compassion, exorcised her, and she freely confessed that the young men had suborned her to utter the false slander.—St. Gregory of Nyssa, *Life of St. Gregory Thaumaturgist.*

Life more than Food.

LUKE xii. 23. The life is more than meat, and the body than raiment.

GEN. xxv. 29-34. Esau sells his birthright for a mess of pottage.

Lysimachus barters his crown for a draught of water. Lysimachus, king of Thrace, being besieged by the Getæ, was, with his soldiers, reduced to the greatest straits for want of water, and actually consented to give up his kingdom and crown to Dromichætês for a draught of water. No sooner, however, had he slaked his thirst than he repented of his folly, and cried in his grief, "Oh, that for a drop of water I should have sold my crown and kingdom, and be debased from the state of a king to that of a slave for a moment's gratification! For a draught of water have I sold liberty and dignity, royalty and life." Lysimachus, however, is not alone in this. How many are there, in this our own day, who sell their inheritance of eternal life and eternal glory, their golden harps and golden crowns, their kingship and priesthood in heaven, for the pleasures of sin for a season, no better than a mess of pottage and a draught of water!

Light. (See AUREOLA, pp. 39-41.)

MATT. v. 14. Ye are the light of the world.

JOHN v. 35. John the Baptist was a burning and shining light.

ACTS xiii. 47. I have set thee to be a light to the Gentiles.

MATT. xiii. 43. Then shall the righteous shine forth as the sun.

EXOD. x. 22, 23. There was a thick darkness in all the land of Egypt for three days; but all the children of Israel had light in their dwellings.

PSALM xcvii. 11. Light is sown for the righteous.

PSALM cxii. 4. Unto the upright there ariseth light in darkness.

St. Fillan's hand shines forth as the sun. St. Fillan was educated by Munna, an abbot, and as candles were forbidden in the cells after a certain hour, he used to hold up his left hand, which shone brilliantly, and yielded him quite sufficient light for him to go on with his writing after curfew time. Hence St. Fillan wrote with his right hand by the light shed from his left.—Baring-Gould, *Lives of the Saints*, Jan., p. 127.

St. Hilary's chamber, at his decease, filled with light (A.D. 368). St. Gregory of Tours assures us that, when St. Hilary died, a brilliant light filled all the chamber where the body was lying. Of course, these words leave it an open question whether the light was miraculous, or whether, according to [Roman] Catholic custom, the chamber was artificially illuminated. Those who know St. Gregory's writings cannot but feel assured he meant to intimate a miracle and not a custom.

At the death of St. Patrick the nights in Ireland were for twelve months less dark than usual (A.D. 464). At the death of St. Patrick there was no night and no cloud in Ireland for twelve successive days; and for a whole year the nights in the island were less dark than usual. —*Acta Sanctorum* (Bollandists), vol. ii. March 17.

When St. Veronica was dying her chamber was illuminated (A.D. 1497). Sister Thaddæa assured Benedetta (from whose notes Isidore wrote the life of St. Veronica), that going to the cell of Veronica at the hour of nones, she was amazed to see a brilliant light shining through the chinks of the cell door. Peeping through the crevices, she saw Veronica dying; but she was chanting the nones, and a dazzling light shone round about her.

Of course Thaddæa believed the light to be miraculous, but a lamp would suffice to deceive one who only peeped through the chinks of the door.

Love your Enemies.

MATT. v. 43, 44. Ye have heard that it hath been said, Thou shalt love thy neighbour, and hate thine enemy. But I say unto you, Love your enemies; bless them that curse you; do good to them that hate you; and pray for them which despitefully use you, and persecute you.

PROV. xxv. 21, 22. If thine enemy be hungry, give him bread to eat; and if he be thirsty, give him water to drink; for thou shalt heap coals of fire upon his head, and the Lord will reward thee.

EXOD. xxiii. 4, 5. If thou meet thine enemy's ox or his ass going astray, thou shalt surely bring it back to him again. And if thou see the ass of him that hateth thee lying under his burden, thou shalt surely help with him.

St. John the almoner's counsel to his nephew, who wanted to avenge himself. George, the nephew of St. John, patriarch of Alexandria, fell out with a publican, who insulted him and even struck him. Boiling with rage, the lad laid his complaint before his uncle, fully expecting the patriarch would make the fellow an example. St. John replied, "Well, George, I must take this matter in hand, and will so avenge the insult, as even you shall be astonished." The young man fully expected his uncle would order the insolent publican to be publicly scourged, but the patriarch said, "You are proud, George, of your relationship to the patriarch of Alexandria, and near kinsmen should be like each other, not in feature only, but more especially in spirit and disposition. Now come with me to the man who insulted you." So saying, he went to the publican, who was also a farmer, greatly indebted to the patriarch. "Friend," he said, "Jesus Christ has told me to love my enemies, and to do good to those who hate me; you have offended and insulted my nephew, now bring me the agreement for your rent, due in a few days." The farmer brought the paper, and the patriarch, tearing it to pieces in the sight of his son, said to the publican, "There, I forgive you that debt; and as I forgive offences against me, may God forgive me." When the neighbours heard thereof, they were ravished with admiration, and loved the patriarch more than ever.—Metaphrastês, *Lives*, etc.

St. John, patriarch of Alexandria, and the swindler (A.D. 619). A swindler, who knew the character of St. John, patriarch of Alexandria, borrowed of him a large sum of money, saying he had heard this scripture, "And from him who would borrow of thee, turn not thou away." The patriarch handed over the money, and the rascal, being asked to repay at the time due, stoutly maintained he had never received it. The patriarch was advised to lay the matter before the judge. But St. John replied, "St. Paul said to the Corinthians, 'Surely this is utterly a fault, that ye go to law one with another. Why do ye not rather take wrong? Why do ye not rather suffer yourselves to be defrauded?'" When his advisers remarked that the money thus swindled by a rascal might be distributed to the poor, the patriarch replied, "He maketh the sun to rise on the evil and on the good, and sendeth His rain on the just and on the unjust."—Leontius (bishop of Naples), *Life of St. John the Almoner.*

Luke the Evangelist an Artist.

There can be no doubt that the [Roman] Catholics generally suppose that St. Luke the Evangelist was an artist of considerable note. There is no authority, direct or indirect, in the New Testament to confirm this notion, but in early ecclesiastical writers several allusions are made to it, and several pictures and images are ascribed to his handiwork. Theodorus lived about A.D. 518, and on his authority Nicephorus, in 980, states that St. Luke left several paintings of Christ and also of the Virgin. Nicephorus is followed by several modern Greeks, as may be seen in Gretzer's dissertation on the subject. Theodorus states that Luke sent a portrait of the Virgin to the empress Pulcheria, who placed it in the church at Constantinople. In the "Via lata" of Rome, near St. Mary's church, we are told that an ancient inscription was found on a portrait, in these words: "This is one of the seven paintings of St. Luke." Of the portraits ascribed to St. Luke, now existing, the principal one was placed by Paul V. in the Borghesi chapel of St. Mary the Greater. The inhabitants of Lyons affirm that St. Pothin, who died A.D. 177, brought with him from the East "an image" of the Virgin Mary, attributed to St. Luke. Mgr. Guérin tells us the portraits ascribed to St. Luke are very numerous. His words are, "St. Pothin aurait apporté de l'orient une image de la Vierge. Peut-être était-ce un de ces nombreux portrait attribués à St. Luc."

If any one is curious enough to know what sort of face and stature are ascribed to the Virgin Mary, it is as follows: Medium height, face long, complexion brownish, hair blond, eyebrows black, eyes a dark olive grey very glistening, nose Italian, cheeks rather full, lips a bright vermilion, expression very modest and maternal, deportment stately, dress neat, poor, and wholly without ornament. (See ANGEL OF DEATH, "Gregory the Great," p. 5.)

In Saragossa is the famous picture of the Virgin and Child given by the Virgin herself to St. James, who was preaching the gospel there. It is ornamented with a profusion of gold and jewels, and illuminated with a multitude of lamps.

Mammon of Unrighteousness. (See RICH FOOL, pt. i.)

LUKE xvi. 9. Make to yourselves friends of the mammon of unrighteousness; that, when ye fail, they may receive you, etc.

Dionysius, the son of the king of Syracuse, made to himself friends of the mammon of unrighteousness. A marvellous illustration of this text occurs in the life of Dionysius, king of Syracuse. His son of the same name stored up such vast hoards of silver and gold that the father grew suspicious and asked him with what object this was done. The son replied that he meant to make friends with it, that when the king, his father, died, the Syracusans might receive him into the inheritance.

The golden apple to be given to the greatest fool. A certain king, on his death-bed, gave a golden apple to his son, and told him to bestow it on the greatest fool. The son travelled through many regions, and although he found many foolish ones, he found no one that quite answered the condition of being the greatest of all fools. At length he came to a large province, and saw one conducted through the streets in royal apparel, with every demonstration of honour, and asked the cause. He was told that the man was a king for the year being, but as soon as his year of office was ended, he would be degraded and banished from the province. The young prince immediately drew near, and said, "My lord, the king my father commanded me on his death-bed to present your grace with this golden apple." "How so?" said the magnate. "I never even knew your father." "My lord," rejoined the prince, "my father's injunction to me was to give the apple to the greatest fool. I have travelled through many lands, and found many foolish men, but never till to-day found I one willing to endure a lifelong banishment for a twelvemonth's splendour." "Right," said the receiver of the apple; "but I will labour in my year of splendour to make to myself friends, that when my year of office ends, I may be received with welcome in the land to which I shall be exiled."—*Gesta Romanorum*, lxxiv.

Marks of the Lord Jesus.

GAL. vi. 17. I bear in my body the marks of the Lord Jesus.

(This observation has given rise to what the Roman Catholics call *stigmata*; that is, prints in the hands, feet, side, and temples, of the wounds of Jesus Christ, sometimes complete, and sometimes only in part.)

The following persons claim to have been so marked :—

I. MEN.

Angelo del Pazzi (all the marks).
Benedict of Reggio (the crown of thorns), 1602.
Carlo di Saeta (the lance-wound).
Dodo, a premonstratensian monk (all the marks), died 1231.
Francis d'Assisi (the five wounds), Sept. 15, 1224.
Leo (marked from birth with red crosses), 1002.
Nicholas of Ravenna.

II. WOMEN.

Blanca de Gazeran.
Catherine Emmerich of the Tyrol (crown of thorns, and marks on the hands and feet), 1774–1824.
Catherine of Raconigi (marks on the hands and feet), 1486–1547.
Catherine of Ricci (crown of thorns, 1547), 1522–1589.
Catherine of Siena (the five wounds), 1346–1380.
Cecilia di Nobili of Nocera, 1655.
Clara di Pugny (marks of the spear), 1514.
Dominica Lazzari of the Tyrol (nineteenth century).
"Ecstatica" of Caldaro (all the marks), 1842.
Gabriella da Piezolo of Aquila (spear-marks, which bled afresh every Friday).
Gertrude of Ostend (the five wounds), died 1358.
Joanna Maria of the Cross.
Lidwina (all the marks), 1380–1433.
Louise Lateau (all the marks), 1850–1868.
Maria Morl of the Tyrol (nineteenth century).
Maria Razzi of Chio (the crown of thorns).
Maria Villani (the crown of thorns).
Mary Magdalene de' Pazzi (all the marks), 1566–1607.
Mechtildis von Stanz.
Oxanna (the cross, crown of thorns, and spear), 1449–1505.
Petronilla (all the marks), died 1472.
Rita de Cascia (the crown of thorns), 1452.
Rose Tamisier (special marks. See IMPOSTURE, p. 184), 1850.
Sybillina of Pavia (crown and thorns and whip-wales).
Ursula of Valencia.
Veronica Giuliani (all the marks), 1660–1727.
Vincenza Ferreri of Valencia, 304.

Pagan Stigmata. It was by no means unusual for the pagans to make incisions in their skin in honour of their gods. Sometimes the marks were burnt in with hot irons, and sometimes a black or violet pigment, rubbed into punctures made in the skin with some sharp instrument, like a needle, made abiding marks. Many Arabian women are so marked on the arms and legs; and probably tattooing is a similar sacred marking of the skin. Lucian tells us that all Syrian women were marked either on the hands or on the neck.

St. Catherine Emmerich of the Tyrol had all the marks (A.D. 1774–1824). St. Catherine Emmerich of the Tyrol, generally called the "nun of Dulmen," is a modern example of the same phenomenon. Catherine Emmerich had from early youth an intuitive faculty of discerning the qualities of plants, and also of interpreting people's thoughts. This sickly abnormal visionary was marked on her head with the wounds of the crown of thorns, in her side with the wound of the spear, and in her hands and feet with the impress of the nails. These wounds, we are told, were as plain as if they had been painted by an artist, and bled regularly every Friday. There was also a double cross on her breast. When the blood was wiped away, the marks looked like the punctures of needles. Catherine was a poor uneducated cow-keeper, but in her ecstasies talked like one inspired. She could see in the dark just as well as in daylight, and frequently made clothes for the poor at night without either lamp or candle.—*Ecstaticas of the Tyrol.*

N.B.—Maria Morl and Dominica Lazzari are two other modern instances.

St. Catherine of Raconigi marked in the hands and feet (A.D. 1486–1547). Jesus one day came to St. Catherine of Raconigi, and said to her, "Thy great faith, daughter, merits a reward, and therefore will I make you participate in the pains

I myself endured in My hands and feet." So saying, He reached out His hands, placing His palms in those of St. Catherine. As He did so, there leaped from the wounds "a dart of blood," which pierced the hands of the maiden, and left there a perpetual stigma. A similar shooting pain darted through her feet, and there also was left the stigma of Christ. These stigmata on the hands and feet continued all through life, and when she was dead, hosts of persons came to see them, and bore witness of the fact which their own eyes had seen. In the convent of St. Margaret, at Chieri, St. Catherine of Raconigi is represented with the stigmata, a great cross on the left shoulder, a little one on the breast, a lily in her hands, and three rings on the ring-finger. — Mgr. Guérin, *Vies des Saints*, vol. x. p. 513 (7th edit. 1880).

St. Catherine of Ricci receives the marks of the Lord Jesus (A.D. 1522–1583). An extraordinary number of graces were vouchsafed to St. Catherine of Ricci in Florence. She vowed herself the virgin bride of Christ, and the Saviour Himself placed on her finger a betrothal ring, and marked her body with the sacred stigmata. She also experienced habitually "all the torments of the Redeemer, one after the other, in due order during Passion Week." In Christian art St. Catherine of Ricci is represented as receiving from Christ the engagement ring, and crowned with thorns. Sometimes she is represented "recevant dans la bouche un jet du lait de la Sainte Vierge."—Mgr. Guérin, *Vies des Saints*, vol. ii. p. 506.

St. Catherine of Siena had the five wounds (A.D. 1346–1380). St. Catherine of Siena called herself the virgin spouse of Christ. One day, meditating on the passion of Christ, she was stricken in the hands, feet, and side with the marks of the Lord Jesus; and, as St. Antony assures us, actually felt the wounds as acutely as if she had been really crucified. In fact, they were so painful to her, especially the wound in the side, that she declared she must have sunk under the agony, if God had not relieved the pain. —Surius, *Lives of the Saints* (A.D. 1570).

St. Francis d'Assisi had the five wounds impressed on him by a seraph with six wings (Sept. 15, 1224). St. Francis d'Assisi had all the marks of the Passion impressed on him. Not only many who conversed with him, as St. Clara, saw and touched the wounds, but St. Gregory IX., who canonized him, affirms that he himself saw them also. The marking fell out thus. Being in a solitary place during his "Michaelmas Lent," in Auvergne, two years before his death, early one morning, about the exaltation of the cross, he saw a seraph with six wings. His face burned with fire, and radiated light in every direction. Between the wings of the seraph was the figure of a man crucified. The uppermost wings were held above his head, the two middle ones were spread abroad so as to form a cross, and the other two were gathered up together so as to cover the whole body. When St. Francis saw the seraph, he fell into an ecstasy; and, during the trance, was transformed into the exact similitude of Christ crucified. There were the prints of the nails in his hands and feet, and the print of the spear-wound in his side. The heads of the nails appeared in his two palms; they were round and black, the points being long and bent. So also was it in the feet. The spear-wound was in the right side, and the mark was both wide and red. — St. Bonaventura, *Life of St. Francis of Assisi.*

The spear-wound in Veronica Giuliani was in the left side, but artists generally represent the soldier piercing the right side. (See p. 426.)

St. Gertrude of Ostend had the five wounds (A.D. 1358). On the evening of Tuesday in Holy Week, A.D. 1340, St. Gertrude of Ostend felt all of a sudden five punctures, two in the hands, two in the feet, and one in the side. From these wounds blood flowed abundantly. Next day, and for several following days, blood flowed from these stigmata seven times a day, at the seven canonical hours. Crowds went to witness the spectacle. St. Gertrude, "fearing she might grow vain," prayed that the flux of blood might cease, and her prayer was heard; but the marks of the Passion remained till death.—*Vita Sanctorum* (Bollandus), vol. i. Jan. 6.

Louise Lateau had all the five marks (born 1850–1868). Annie Louise Lateau was the daughter of Gregory Lateau, a workman of one of the foundries of Hainault. The father died in 1850, the year of his child's birth. Annie Louise became a sempstress, but when the cholera broke out in 1866 she distinguished herself greatly by nursing the sick in the village of Bois d'Haine. Next year she was taken ill, and received the last sacrament in September; but, taking a few drops of a miraculous fountain, contrary to all expectation, she suddenly recovered. On April 24, 1868, she suffered from great pain in the localities of the five wounds, and an abscess appeared on her left side. Next day it wholly disappeared, but the following Friday blood flowed from the hands, feet, and side. In August, the same year, the archbishop of Mechlin appointed a committee to examine the marks, one of the gentlemen being Dr. Lefebvre, professor of medicine at the university at Louvain, and the next Friday "the crown of thorns" made its appearance on her head. In Aug. 29, 1878, *The Times* says that Anne Louise Lateau the stigmatic still works in the house, and has been visited by above a hundred doctors of all nationalities, none of whom have detected the slightest malady. The stigmata make their appearances on Fridays, between the hours of one and two, and four and five.—See *The Lancet*, April 22, 1871; *The British Medical Journal*, 1871, and Oct. 1875; Dr. Bourneville, *Science and Miracle;* etc.

St. Leo marked at birth with red crosses (A.D. 1002). Bruno (the baptismal name of St. Leo) was born in Alsace, and his body at birth was marked all over with red crosses, attributed to the intense meditation of his mother on the passion of Christ, and a token that the child himself would carry the cross to his life's end.—Wibert, *In vita Leonis IX.*, bk. i.

Without doubt, the imagination of the mother sometimes impresses visible marks on the offspring. Jacob acted on this principle when he told Laban he would take the speckled and spotted sheep for his hire (*Gen.* xxx. 37-43). And he took rods of green poplar, hazel, and chestnut, and pilled white strakes in them, and set the rods in the watering-troughs where the flocks came to drink; and the ewes brought forth cattle ring-straked, spotted, and speckled.

St. Lidwina had the marks of the Lord, but they were not visible (A.D. 1380-1433). Angels, in human forms, often appeared to St. Lidwina she conversed with them, and called them by their names. She was also granted interviews with her "celestial Spouse," who appeared to her personally, and on one occasion impressed on her body the sacred marks of His passion; but, to avoid vanity, St. Lidwina intreated the Saviour to render these stigmata invisible, a favour readily accorded to her.—*Life of St. Lidwina* (compiled by her cousin John Gerlac and her confessor John Walter). See *Acta Sanctorum* by the Bollandists, April 14, vol. ii. p. 287.

St. Mary Magdalene of Pazzi marked with all the stigmata (A.D. 1566-1607). Catherine, allied by blood to the Medici, changed her name to Mary Magdalene, on taking the veil. She was noted for her visions, and Christ Himself put on her head a crown of thorns, and marked her body with all the marks of His passion. In Christian art she is represented as receiving "the instruments of the Passion and the stigmata, as a safeguard against the temptations of the devil."—Vincent Puccini (of Florence), *Life of St. Mary Magdalene of Pazzi.*

St. Oxanna marked with the five wounds of Jesus (A.D. 1449-1505.) The signal favours of Jesus and Mary, shown to St. Oxanna from early childhood, continued as she grew in years and stature. Before she was fifteen years old she was honoured by the stigmata of the cross, the crown of thorns, and the spear. More than once she received the Eucharist from the hand of angels; and God often revealed to her the secrets of the future, and gave her the power of working miracles.—L'abbé Chapia, *La Vie d'une Sainte pour chaque Jour de l'Anneé* (June 18).

Rita of Cascia marked with the crown of thorns (A.D. 1452). Rita of Cascia, after hearing a famous missionary preach on the passion of Christ, prayed that she might be a partaker of the Saviour's grief, and forthwith felt in her forehead the punctures of the crown of thorns. From these punctures proceeded a most offensive pus, and worms cráwled from the sores. This lasted four years, and then she died, when rays of glory issued from the punctures. This we are told by an artist, who says he was a personal witness, and knew Rita from her first introduction to the convent to the hour of her death.—*Acta Sanctorum* (Bollandists), vol. v. May 22.

The pimples on the forehead, the pus, the offensive smell, and the contagious nature of these "marks," look very much like smallpox or variola. The account is not stated with sufficient accuracy to know whether the pimples were running sores for four years, or whether only "pock-marks" remained. We are distinctly told she was "separated from her companions for fifteen days, during all which time she spoke to no one." This would be about the length of time that smallpox runs. The scabs begin to fall off on the fourteenth or fifteenth day. In some cases smallpox is followed by sloughing sores and erysipelatous inflammation, and this may have been the case with Rita.

N.B.—Rita is a contraction of Margarita.

Sybillina of Pavia had the marks of the crown of thorns and the whips (fourteenth century). Sybillina of Pavia was blind from the age of twelve years, and was received into the sisterhood of the Tiers Ordre de St. Dominique. Her sufferance impressed upon her the crown of thorns and the marks of the scourging. "Aussi porta-t-elle dans ses membres de vierge les marques cruelles de la passion de son divin époux."—*Les Petits Bollandistes*, vol. iii. p. 538.

St. Veronica Giuliani has all the marks (A D. 1693, 1697). St. Veronica Giuliani, at the age of thirty-three, felt persuaded that the Saviour intended to make her an associate in His passion. In 1693 she felt in her forehead the pains of the crown of thorns, and any one might have seen the marks by a circle of pustules round her head. The physicians tried caustic, but only added to her suffering without removing the marks. Other remedies being also tried with no better success, the physicians abandoned all hope of removing the marks. In 1697, on Good Friday, while contemplating the crucifixion, the Saviour Himself appeared to her; He was nailed to the cross, and five rays darted from his five wounds, into the hands, feet, and side of Veronica. The pain of the wounds was very great, and she felt exactly as if she were crucified. She was obliged to reveal this "extraordinary favour" to her confessor, and the confessor informed the bishop of Citta di Castello, who, in turn, consulted the pope. The bishop received from the holy office of Rome a reply to take no further notice of the affair, and not to talk about it; but in the course of the year "the miracle" was repeated over and over again, and the stigmata were apparent to all the sisterhood. The bishop, to assure himself of the fact, selected four persons to accompany him to the church attached to the nunnery; and Veronica, being placed in the grille, was examined with care. There could be no doubt about the matter; the wounds were evident, and Veronica said sometimes they were wet with blood, and at other times scabbed. The wound of the spear was in the left side; it was between four and five inches long, by half an inch in breadth, and had all the appearance of a wound made by a spear. This wound never closed, and therefore the linen of the saint was always bloody. "Les incrédules regarderont ces prodiges comme imaginaires, et les témoins qui les ont rapportés, comme des gens simples, que l'on pouvait facilement tromper. Nous ne craignons pas d'assurer que toutes les précautions que la prudence humaine peut inspirer pour bien connaitre la vérité furent prises par l'évique, guidé par les instructions qu'il avait reçues du tribunal du Saint-Office. Véronique elle-même cherchait si peu à en imposer, que, dans toutes les circonstance, elle témoignait la crainte que ce qui se passait en elle ne fût une illusion du demon."

The marvel does not end here. Veronica asserted that the stigmata were not confined to her body, but were also marked on her heart. She drew a map of her heart, marking the spot of each instrument of torture, and also that in which the cross was fixed. At death a post-mortem was held in the presence of the bishop, the governor of the town, several doctors and surgeons, and seven other witnesses. All these testified to the wounds in the body and the marks on the heart corresponding with the map drawn by Verońica. — Mgr. Guérin (chamberlain of Leo XIII.), *Vies des Saints*, vol. viii. pp. 222-224 (7th edit. 1880).

N.B.—The spear-wound in Francis of Assisi was in the right side.

One would like to see the report of the medical men; but I cannot find it either in the original Italian or in the French translation of this life. Alban Butler does not even mention the name of this saint.

Thomas the apostle's reply when the disciples said, "We have seen the Lord." In the life of St. Thomas the apostle, written by Gregory of Tours, Isidore, Metaphrastês, and others, the sentence, "We have seen the Lord," and the reply of Thomas are thus paraphrased: "O brother, whilst thou wert absent we saw the Lord; the same that was beaten and crowned with thorns; the same that was nailed to the cross and died; the same whose side was pierced with the spear; the same that was taken down from the cross and laid in the tomb. He is risen, brother, and we have seen Him. He showed us His hands and His feet, and there saw we the prints of the nails, not stained with blood, but wonderfully adorned, and blazing like diamonds and rubies set in gold. Even now He parted from us, brother." Thomas made answer, "It was a mere vision. For my own part, I tell you plainly, I will not believe it, till I not only see the prints in His hands, feet, and side, but actually put my fingers into the wounds to be assured that my eyes have not deceived me. Till this is the case, I say, I can neither believe that you have really seen the Master, nor yet that He is risen from the dead."

The bad taste and extravagance of this paraphrase is very valuable as a lesson in hagiography. The supposed embellishment, but real tinsel, about the "diamonds and rubies set in gold" is in the worst possible taste, and when we read it, we can only feel thankful that these men were not the evangelists of the four Gospels.

Three children fell into a pit, but were unharmed, in answer to the prayers of St. Porphyry (A.D. 353–420). Three children of Gaza, between the ages of six and seven, fell into a deep pit. St. Porphyry, having heard of the accident, fell to the earth, and remained an hour in fervent prayer. In the mean time, a man descended into the pit, and found the children safe and sound, sitting on a stone. What is more wonderful still is this—they were all marked with a red cross, one on the forehead, another on the shoulder, and the third on the hand. —Mark (a companion), *Life of St. Porphyry.*

An attempt to explain the phenomenon. The fact that certain bodies have been marked with strange impressions is beyond dispute, and without in any wi e attributing these marks either to miracle or imposition, they can be accounted for by the mystical action of thought upon the body. Every one knows that thought may produce local pain, disease, and even death. Let any one, for example, fix his thoughts on any part of the body, and imagine that he suffers pain there, and the pain will assuredly follow; so, if a person will strongly imagine that he is ill, he will undoubtedly become so. All know that fright will produce birth-marks, and in some cases marks when the body is full-grown. Any very strong emotion that vitiates the secretions will affect the skin; and by fixing the thought strongly on any particular part of the skin, the vicious effect may be determined. Suppose a nun of delicate health and extreme excitability is worked up by imagination to a state of morbid frenzy, her secretions will become vitiated, and her skin diseased. Suppose, now, her whole soul is fixed on the crown of thorns—so firmly fixed that she believes her forehead to be scarred with the punctures; this centralized thought may determine the *locus* and character of the skin disease, and it may in extreme cases assume those pustules or pimples round the brow which are called "the crown of thorns." The same diseased thought that made Macbeth see a dagger in the air, and Banquo's ghost sitting on an empty chair, may make a religious visionary see an angel, and believe that the angel gave the marks to which reference has been made. Such false creations often proceed "from the heat-oppressèd brain;" and vivid fancy, especially with the superstitious, will often "inform thus to the mind." It is certain, however, that mechanical means were sometimes employed to produce the mark. Thus Laurent of the Benedictine Order seared his forehead with hot iron to produce the semblance of a crown of thorns (see p. 430).

Self-deception is a common occurrence with hysterical women. Dr. Du Saulle, physician to the Salpétrière, Paris, has found many of his patients labouring under the delusion that they had been struck or stabbed, though they had inflicted the injuries on themselves. A wife was found lying on her bedroom floor, with her face covered with blood. She said she had been attacked by armed men; but the story proved to be a mere delusion. A girl wounded herself with a pistol, and then described an attempted assassination in the most minute detail. Another young woman was found in a railway carriage with a knife-wound in her side. This injury was proved to have been self-inflicted. A housemaid, found behind a door, gagged, bound, and bruised, swore she had been attacked by burglars, but was believed to have been her own burglar. Then comes the most striking case of all, which occurred in the practice of Dr. Tardieu. "A young lady, living at Courbevoie, wished to make herself an object of public interest by passing as a victim of a political conspiracy, which she pretended to have discovered. One night she was found in a state of the greatest mental perturbation at the door of her apartment. She could not talk; but stated, in writing, that she had been attacked outside her own house by a man, who had attempted to garotte her, at the same time striking her twice with a dagger. Only the lady's clothing was injured, and the body of her dress and her corset were found to be cut through, but at different levels. She tried to make out that the attempt at strangulation had caused dumbness. M. Tardieu remarked, in her hearing, that this infirmity rapidly disappeared when produced under circumstances of this kind. She soon managed to regain her speech, and in a short time admitted that the whole narrative had been developed out of her inner consciousness."—*British Medical Journal,* 1883.

Men like Trees.

Mark viii. 24. I see men, as trees.

St. Gregory the thaumaturgist and his deacon mistaken for two trees. During a dreadful persecution, Gregory the thaumaturgist and his deacon retired to a mountain, where they lay *perdue.* The governor of Neocæsarea, being informed of their whereabouts, sent officers to apprehend them. While these officers were on their way, St. Gregory said to his deacon, "You pray here while I go yonder and pray." When the officers came to the mountain they could see no man, and returned to the governor, saying, "We found no one, but we saw two trees a little apart from each other." The governor then went himself to the mountain, fell at the feet of St. Gregory, and begged to be baptized, saying, "Verily, none can deliver after this sort but the Lord thy God; the Lord thy God He is God, and there is none beside. Blessed be His name."—Nicephorus Callistus, *Ecclesiastical History,* bk. vi. ch. 17.

More than Conquerors.

Rom. viii. 35–39. Who shall separate us from the love of Christ? Shall tribulation, or distress, or persecution, or famine, or nakedness, or peril, or sword? Nay, in all these things we are more than conquerors through Him that loved us. For I am persuaded that neither death, nor life, nor angels, nor principalities, nor powers, nor things present, nor things to come, nor height, nor depth, nor any other creature, shall be able to separate us from the love of God which is in Christ Jesus our Lord.

2 Cor. xi. 24–27. Of the Jews five times received I forty stripes save one. Thrice was I beaten with rods, once was I stoned, thrice I suffered shipwreck, a night and a day have I been in the deep; in journeyings often, in perils of waters, in perils of robbers, in perils by mine own countrymen, in perils by the heathen, in perils in the city, in perils in the wilderness, in perils in the sea, in perils among false brethren; in weariness and painfulness, in watchings often, in hunger and thirst, in fastings often, in cold and nakedness.

St. Juliana of Nicomedia tortured by Evilatius (A.D. 299). Evilatius asked

Juliana of Nicomedia to be his wife, but she told him she had vowed to be the bride of Christ only. The young nobleman afterwards became prefect, and under Diocletian was commanded to extirpate the Christian heresy. Juliana was brought to his tribunal, and the torture he inflicted on her was almost unparalleled. She was first suspended in the air by four leather thongs, and beaten with whips made of the sinews and hide of a bullock; this beating went on till the officer employed could no longer continue from fatigue. When taken down, the prefect said, "This punishment is only the shadow of what will follow;" but the damsel made answer, "As is thy day, so shall thy strength be." She was then hung by her hair to the branch of a tree so long that every hair of her head was rooted out, and straw was set on fire beneath her; her eyebrows and eyelashes were plucked but also, and her hands pierced with hot irons. Being sent back to prison, the devil came to her as an angel of light, and said, "God is satisfied with what you have endured. Your courage is proof of your enduring love, and you may now bow yourself in the house of Rimmon, and be free." St. Juliana felt convinced this could not be the counsel of God, and prayed earnestly that God would speak unto her soul. Immediately she heard a voice from heaven, which said, "Juliana, be of good courage; for I am with you, and will never leave you nor forsake you." As these words were spoken, she not only felt comforted in spirit, but perceived that she was healed of her wounds, that her hair, eyebrows, and eyelashes were restored, that her strength was renewed like an eagle's, and that the devil lay at her feet chained and helpless. The maiden "le garrotta derechef, et le chargea de coups. Cet infâme monstre fit voir qu'il les sentait et se plaignit de ce que, après avoir triomphé de tant de fidèles, il se voyait maintenant vaincu par une fille." When Juliana was next taken before the prefect, he was amazed to see her in excellent health and more beautiful than ever. He now ordered her to be cast into a fiery furnace; but no sooner was this done than the fire was quenched and the furnace without heat. The people shouted, "There is no god like Juliana's God!" and more than five hundred were converted to the Christian faith. The prefect, finding himself foiled, became mad with rage, and ordered the sorceress to be cast into a cauldron of boiling oil; "mais elle y trouva du rafraîchisement, et cette liqueur toute enflammée rejaillit sur les bourreaux et les ministres de l'injustice." The prefect now commanded that her head should be cut off. "Le démon la voyant aller au supplice, excitait les exécuteurs à la tuer vivement pour être délivré de ses mains; mais la sainte vierge, le regardant d'un visage sévère et terrible, le fit trembler de crainte et aussitôt il disparut; ce qui montre la puissance de la croix de Notre Seigneur Jésus Christ."—Mgr. Guérin (chamberlain of Leo XIII.), *Vies des Saints* (7th edit. 1880), vol. ii. pp. 548, 549. (The life and martyrdom is given in Bollandus.) Brautius wrote her life in verse. The following four lines are quoted by the chamberlain:—

> Fusa viget plumbo; ludit suspensa capillis;
> Robur ferventi mersa resumit aqua.
> Virgo, palam forti cum dæmone prælia gessit,
> Nec cessit donec victa trophæa tulit.
>
> The boiling cauldron but new strength supplies,
> Hung by her hair she laughs; fused lead defies;
> War with the devil wages day and night,
> Nor ceases till she joins the saints in light.

Alban Butler says, "Her acts in Bollandus deserve no notice;" but what does he mean? He cannot mean that they were not credited by the general. Bollandus was a far better authority on what the people were taught to believe and what they did believe than Alban Butler; and Mgr. Guérin, chamberlain of Pope Leo XIII., evidently believes the acts, and his book is dated (7th edit.) 1880. It is historically dishonest to look at the third century in the light of the nineteenth. Alban Butler does not dare to deny that some of the saints "performed miracles;" but this admitted, who is to draw the line between credible miracles and incredible? All an historian of modes of faith has any right to do is to collect painsfully from every available source evidence of what was believed. Comparative belief would form a most interesting subject; but writing the lives of saints and expurgating whatever is not in accordance with your own judgment and education is mere abortion, most misleading and dishonest. It is no portrait of times gone by, but simply a fancy portrait of yourself, and wholly worthless.

Mortify the body.

COL. iii. 5. Mortify your members which are upon the earth.

GAL. v. 24. They that are Christ's have crucified the flesh with the affections and lusts.

ROM. viii. 13. If ye live after the flesh, ye shall die; but if ye, through the Spirit, do mortify the deeds of the body, ye shall live.

1 PET. ii. 11. Abstain from fleshly lusts, which war against the soul.

1 COR. ix. 27. I keep under my body, and bring it into subjection.

Illustrations of these texts in the lives of the saints are so numerous that it would be easy to fill a volume with examples. In fact, every saint would furnish an example. All, therefore, that is attempted here is to bring together some few examples as specimens of the rest.

St. Aïbert mortifies his body (A.D. 1080-1140). St. Aïbert fed only once a day, and that on bread and water, with sometimes a few vegetables; never took he meat, fowls, fish, butter, cheese, or milk. He slept on a board; wore an old dress full of holes; never threw off his hair shirt, and never changed it, either to cleanse it or repair it. He went through daily the 150 psalms before matins; said 150 *Ave Marias*, some on his knees, and some prostrate on the earth; chanted the vigils of the dead; made numerous genuflexions; and was the model of a true monk.—Robert (archdeacon of Ostrevand), *Life of St. Aïbert.*

However much one may admire the self-denial of such men as St. Aïbert, it is hard to see how dirty habits and ragged clothes, living on bread and water, and repeating daily before breakfast the 150 psalms, can be the service which Christ enjoined upon His disciples. There may be as much rivalry and vanity in monkish rags as in the dandyism of men about town. And as for gabbling through 2462 verses and 300 doxologies before matins, it is no better than a Ceylonese praying-mill, after all.

St. Benedict of Anian mortifies his body (A.D. 750–821). This one example is given at random to show the usual mortification practised by the saints; many hundreds of similar examples might be quoted, but *ex pede Herculem.* St. Benedict of Anian mortified his body, crucifying the flesh with its affections and lusts. He lived solely on bread and water, and partook of these only in quantities sufficient to support life. He looked on wine as a veritable poison. His only bed was the bare ground, and he never indulged in sleep except after long vigilance. The whole night was for the most part passed in prayer, and often in mid-winter he sat with bare feet on the church pavement chanting the psalms, or reflecting on the mercies of God. He possessed in a remarkable degree the gift of tears, and they flowed in torrents at the thoughts of sin and the judgment to come. His occupations in the monastery were of the most menial kind—to clean the shoes of travellers, to sweep the rooms, to wash dishes, and light fires. The clothes he wore were of the poorest sort, full of patches of divers colours. In appearance he was like a skeleton, thin and dry. He preserved continual silence, and was looked on as a fool; but he thought the reproach of Christ greater glory than the honours of men.—Bollandus, *Acta Sanctorum.*

Self-mortifications of Benet-Joseph Labre of Artois (A.D. 1748–1783). Besides the usual methods of semi-starvation, exposition to cold, ragged clothes, and so on, we are told, "Il avait de plus, sur sa chair, comme un cilice vivant qui le dechirait sans cesse, comme St. Thomas de Cantorbéry, chancelier d'Angleterre, dont l'historien dit: 'Après qu'il eut subi la mort du martyr, on trouve son cilice tellement plein d'insectes pédiculaires, que l'on jugea ce martyr antérieur, au milieu du luxe et de la mollesse d'une cour, bien plus insupportable que le dernier.'" Not only did Benet-Joseph not seek to be delivered from these vermin, he actually prided himself on this humiliating affliction.—R. P. Desnoyers, *De Bienheureux Benoît-Joseph Labre.*

How such filthy ways can be called Christianity it would be hard to say. Sancho Panza might share, with Thomas of Canterbury and Benet-Joseph, such a "martyrdom." Most undoubtedly the Bible is no advocate of uncleanness. Even "when thou fastest, anoint thine head and wash thy face" (*Matt.* vi. 17), were words which both Becket and Labre should have known and observed.

St. Clara's ingenious method of mortifying her body (A.D. 1346). St. Clara tried to imitate all the sufferings of Jesus Christ. With this view, on Good Friday she was accustomed to put a cord round her neck, get her hands tied behind her back, and then be dragged through the streets of Rimini, as Jesus was through those of Jerusalem. She could not nail herself to a cross, but she went as near to this degrading death as she durst; for she employed persons to bind her to a pillar and lash her with whips, amidst the jeers of the rabble. She tried to drink of the cup which Christ drank of, and repeated year after year "cette scène, plus digne de l'admiration du ciel, qu'imitable pour les enfantes de la terre. En récompense, elle eut le bonheur de contempler, dans une vision qui dura quinze jours, tous les détails des souffrances de son Époux, comme si elle eût assisté à cette sanglante tragedie."—*Les Petits Bollandistes*, vol. ii. p. 439.

Self-mortifications of St. Gregory of Armenia, bishop of Nicopolis (eleventh century). Gregory of Armenia constructed for himself a cell just the length and height of his own body, where he shut himself up, and seldom stirred abroad. He fasted entirely every Monday, Wednesday, Friday, and Saturday. On Tuesday and Thursday he ate three ounces of food after sunset. On Sunday he did not fast, but he ate very sparingly. He never ate meat or butter, but his chief food was lentils, steeped in water, and exposed to the heat of the sun. His rule was to eat as many as he could take up in his left hand. Sometimes he had barley bread, and sometimes raw roots found in the desert.—*Acta Sanctorum* (written by an anonymous contemporary).

Such examples as these, and the pillar-saints, seem a practical satire on the words of Christ: "Take My yoke upon you, and learn of Me; for My yoke is easy, and My burden light.'

Self-mortifications of Jeanne Marie de

Maillé (A.D. 1332–1414). The austerities of Jeanne Marie de Maillé are incredible. It is difficult to form an idea of her self-inflicted mortifications. If such is the yoke of Christianity, how are we to understand those memorable words of Micah, "Shall I give the fruit of my body for the sin of my soul"? Jeanne Marie always wore "un cercle de fer dentelé, et les pointes aiguës dont il était armé dessus et dessous, pénétraient fort avant dans sa chair. Un rude cilice en crin lui servait de chemise." She always fasted every Monday, Wednesday, Friday, and Saturday; her only food was a morsel of black bread, and a little cold water. Besides the fasts prescribed by the Church, she observed Advent, from St. Martin's to Christmas Day. She fasted in honour of the Virgin Mary; she fasted in honour of St. Michael and all angels; she fasted thirty days before All Saints, and fifty-two days before Pentecost. Her whole life was one of extreme rigour. She slept on the bare ground, and gave herself very frequently "the discipline."—Père de Boisgaultier (her confessor), *Life of Jeanne Marie de Maillé*.

Monsieur l'abbé tells us that "dans l'octave de la Pentecôte, elle s'enfonça dans la tête une longue et forte épine, qui y demeura jusqu'à la fin du carême suivant."

St. Julian of St. Augustine mortifies his body in divers ways (A.D. 1606). Every day St. Julian of St. Augustine devised some new torture wherewith to afflict his body. He lived in a little cabin. He covered his body with instruments of torture. Ate only once a day, and then only a little bread and a few herbs. He slept at no regular time, but passed the nights in church; and if sleep oppressed him, he tied himself to the wall, or to some confessional, and so slept for a few hours. He preached to the birds, which would gather round him, attentive to his words, and disperse singing, when he dismissed them. Sometimes he would preach to the beasts of the field also. He was beatified by Leo XII., and his reputation has spread throughout the whole length and breadth of Spain.—*Les Petits Bollandistes*, vol. iv. p. 295.

Self-mortifications of St. John-Joseph de la Croix (A.D. 1654–1734). The furniture of St. John-Joseph consisted of one stool, and one table of the most ordinary make; a bed made of two boards, with a sheepskin next the boards, and a sheepskin and woollen quilt for covering. As his legs were ulcered he had a foot-rest, and his library was his breviary. He wore the same garment for forty-six years, and had no other. For sixty years he never looked on the face of girl or woman; and if his vocation called him to visit any nun, he always took a companion with him, and never lifted his eyes from the ground. When dying, one of the monks was about to turn down his bedclothes to dress his ulcers, but his modesty was shocked, and he forbade the brother to do so. Though his legs were so ulcerated, yet his holiness spread a sweet and delicious odour over the room where he happened to be. He never wore any covering on his head. Next his skin he wore a hair shirt, and divers chains, which he changed according to the amount of penance he awarded himself. He gave himself frequent rough "disciplines." His sandals were covered inside with little nails; and over his shoulders he wore a cord about a foot long stuck full of needles; at his breast he wore a similar cord formed into a cross. He slept little; almost entirely abstained from drink; fasted often, and never ate but once a day, his food consisting chiefly of dry bread.—Cardinal Wiseman, contributed to Migne's *Démonstrations Évangéliques*, vol. xvi.

Self-mortifications of Laurent of the order of St. Benedict (A.D. 1248). Laurent, a native of Naples, was noted for his austerities. He never ate more than once a day, and his food was bread and water, with a few herbs. Often he fasted entirely. He wore an iron cuirass, rings of metal on his arms, thighs, and legs, and carried on his head two iron rods in the form of a cross. In order to impress on himself the "marks of Jesus," every Friday he burnt his forehead to represent the crown of thorns. He seldom spoke, and never uttered a single word on a Monday, Wednesday, and Friday all Lent, and all days of fast.—Godescard, *Monastic Breviary*.

Self-mortifications of Marianne de Jesus, at the age of twelve years (A.D. 1618–1645). We are told by Mgr. Guérin, chamberlain of pope Leo XIII., that Marianne, the daughter of don Jerome of Quito, fasted twice a week when a babe in arms. At the age of twelve years she wanted to live as a recluse, and was allowed to live in an empty chamber by herself. We are then told that this child never left her chamber except to go to church. That she allowed herself only three hours' sleep, and that "sur des pièces de bois triangulaire." The only furniture of her room was a skeleton in a coffin, which was surmounted with a "death's head," whips for discipline, hair body-clothes, a few crosses, and an altar with statues of the infant Jesus and the "divine Mary." Every Friday the child strewed the coffin with thorns and slept in it, taking the place of the skeleton. She rose at four every day, and began the day with "discipline," then gave an hour to meditation, recited "les heures canoniales," and at six attended church for confessions, attended mass, and partook of the Holy Communion. At eight "elle s'efforçait de gagner les indulgences pour les pauvres âmes du purgatoire," then recited the chapelet, and at eleven returned to her solitude. At two she recited vespers, and "travaillait ensuite en la présence de Dieu jusqu'à cinq heures;" from five to six came spiritual reading and complins; from six to one next morning came prayer and reading the lives of saints. She denied herself meat, fish, and milk, restricting her food to bread, vegetables, and fruits. Later in life she gave up the fruits and vegetables, eating dry bread only once a day, and that at eleven o'clock; and later still in life "l'euchariste fut sa seule nourriture," Mgr. Guérin adds, "ce fait n'est pas rare dans la vie des saints et des saintes." A glass of water at nine o'clock was "son repas du soir," but this she dropped after a time, and the last years of her life she endured a horrible torment of thirst; but, says Mgr. Guérin, she added to this horrible torment by having the glass of water approach her burning lips, "et qu'elle avait ensuite le courage de rejeter." She also waited at dinner on her cousins while they dined, to see them eat, and to deny herself the more by not tasting anything herself. This sort of life made her very thin and pale; but when she found herself an object of pity, she prayed that her pallor might be removed; her prayer was heard, and her face became plump and exquisitely beautiful.—*Vies des Saints*, vol. vi. p. 232.

One can only sigh at the thought that such a life in a child of twelve can be held up for imitation. Whether true or only ideal, it seems such an utter perversion of the teaching of Christ, who deemed the ceremonial law of the Jews too heavy, and gave no countenance to the Pharisee who boasted of his weekly fastings and his self-denial.

St. Patrick's purgatory. St. Patrick's purgatory is a cave in a little isle in the lake Dearg, in the west of Ulster. St. Patrick had the walls "decorated" with the torments of the damned. Here he often retired to practise austerities, and to meditate on the judgments of God. Many others resorted to the same cave. On the verge of the isle were erected little huts for pilgrims. What were called "St. Patrick's pits" were six small round lodges, three feet in diameter, where those who wished to anticipate in this life the penalties of purgatory were shut in to practise austerities for nine days. They were allowed to come out three times a day to go to chapel. Their only food for eight days was bread and water, and on the ninth day they were allowed neither food nor drink. The popularity of this institution was extraordinary, and traces continued of it even to the middle of the seventeenth century (1645).—Messingham, *Florilegium Insulæ Sanctorum*; Wright, *St. Patrick's Purgatory* (1844).

Peter Damian, cardinal, mortifies his body (A.D. 1072). Cardinal Damian retired to the monastery of Font Avellane, in a desert, where he occupied the worst of the cells. His only food was barley bread and water, and the water was always stale by long exposure to the air. The vessel he used for his food was the same as that in which he washed the feet of beggars. He slept on wood, and wore night and day rings of iron, whipped himself daily, and crucified his body with its affections and lusts by studied torments. Later in life he omitted the barley bread, and took a few herbs cooked in water. He fasted wholly for the three days preceding Lent, and in Passion Week inflicted on his body tortures in imitation of those endured by Christ.—John of Lodi (a disciple), *Life of Peter Damian.* (See also Henschenius, one of the Bollandists, Feb. 23, p. 406.)

One is puzzled to know what religion there can be in kneading bread in a foot-bath. We sow vegetables on a muckheap, it is true, but not with a view of increasing our merits, but solely with a view of increasing our crops; but nastiness for nastiness' sake is not religion, but only nastiness.

St. Simeon Stylitês (died A.D. 459). In order to mortify his body, Simeon Stylitês elevated himself on a pillar, first of six cubits, then of twelve, then of twenty-two, and finally of forty cubits in height, and there stood he for thirty-seven years with a chain round his neck, a spectacle to men and angels. The pillar top on which he stood was surrounded with a balustrade, and had a diameter not exceeding three feet, so that he could neither lie down nor even sit to rest. There was neither cell nor covering to ward off the weather; but he was exposed to the sun by day and the moon by night, the rigours of winter, the rain, the snow, and the tempest. Theodoret, an eye-witness, asserts that the pillar-saint took food only once in forty-one days, except indeed the Eucharist, which was administered to him every eighth day. His orison lasted from sunset to daybreak, during which time he made 1244 genuflexions or inclinations of the body. In prayer he lifted his eyes and hands towards heaven. Another eye-witness tells us he stood one whole year on one foot, and that this was done by way of penance. The fault was this: the devil came to him as an angel of light, and told him that God had sent him with a chariot of fire to take him, like Elijah, into glory. Simeon, believing the announcement without trying the speaker, raised his left leg to step into the chariot. As he did so he signed himself with the sign of the cross, and the devil, chariot, and horses all vanished. It was for this want of vigilance he condemned himself to stand on one foot for 360 days. St. Simeon used to preach from the pillar twice a day to immense crowds of people. Even before he hit upon the extraordinary device of standing day and night on a pillar, his mortifications were very extraordinary. He took food only once a week, and he bound his body with thongs, made of wild myrtle, so tightly, that the thongs pierced to the bones, so that from the loins upwards his body was one universal sore, covered with blood, worms, and maggots. The slough of the wounds was most offensive, and the abbot commanded him to leave off this discipline. It took three days to pull away the thongs and cleanse his body of the corrupt matter. Even before he took to the pillars he fasted all the forty days of Lent, and for nine years never once quitted his cell.—Theodoret (fifth century), *Ecclesiastical History*.

Simeon died on his pillar at the age of seventy-two. It was observed that he remained immovable for three days, his head bowed forwards and his hands crossed over his breast. On the third day, one of his disciples mounted the pillar by a ladder, and found that the saint was dead. Probably he had been dead for three days. (N.B.—A ladder of forty cubits' length was itself extraordinary, and to carry the saint down it would require no little strength, management, and nerve.)

St. Valery's way of living (died A.D. 619). St. Valery slept on a hurdle; his only dress was a frock with a hood; he never wore linen. He never took any sort of nourishment except on Sundays. He never touched wine, beer, or any other fermented drink. He recited two offices complete every day, and all the rest of his time he employed in preaching, lectures, prayer, or work. His charity was unbounded. More than once he stripped himself of his frock to give it to a beggar.—Besançon, *Les Saints de Franche Comté*.

Mons. Besançon says of St. Valery, "Il n'avait pour vêtement qu'une grossière tunique, il s'interdisait l'usage du lin." He then goes on to say, "Plus d'une fois il se dépouilla de son propre vêtement, pour en revêtir quelque membre souffrant de Jesu Christ." Does he mean us to understand that St. Valery went about wholly naked occasionally?

St. Wulfilaïc, the only pillar-saint of the West (died A.D. 595). St. Wulfilaïc was a native of Lombardy, and the scene of his austerity was a mountain in the valley of Chiers, in Belgium. Gregory of Tours went to see him, and wrote down the following account from the saint's own mouth:—"I came to this mountain, because here was erected the gigantic statue of Diana, which the inhabitants worshipped as a divinity. Beside this idol I built a pillar, on the top of which I placed myself barefooted, and my sufferings defy description. In winter the cold froze my feet, and all the nails of my toes mortified, and the rain which saturated my beard turned to icicles, which glistened like candles [*ut . . . in barbis aqua gelu connexa, candelarum more, dependeret*]. My only food was a little bread and a few vegetables, and my only drink was water. Though my sufferings were so great, I felt no little satisfaction in my austerities. When I saw the people come to my pillar I preached to them, and told them Diana was no goddess, and that the songs which they sang in her honour ought to be addressed to the Creator of heaven and earth. Often and often did I pray that God would overturn the idol, and snatch the people from the error of their ways. The people hearkened to my words, the Saviour lent an ear to my prayers, and the people were converted. I appealed to some of my converts to assist me in overthrowing the colossus of Diana. We broke away some of the medals at the base, but we were not able to overturn the idol. We tried to do so with ropes, but it resisted all our efforts. I now went to church, prostrated myself on the earth, prayed earnestly, wept, and groaned in spirit, imploring Christ to destroy by His almighty power that which the power of man could not move. My prayer being ended, I went to rejoin my workmen. We seized the ropes, and with a vigorous pull succeeded in overthrowing the gigantic image. I broke it to pieces and reduced it to powder with a huge sledge-hammer. This done I was about to retire to rest, when I found my whole body completely covered with pustules, so thick and numberless one could not have laid a finger on a spot between them. Again I went to the church, and anointed myself from head to foot with some oil which I had brought from the tomb of St. Martin, and fell asleep. At midnight, when I woke to recite the sacred offices, I found my body sound, and without the slightest trace of an ulcer. I knew that the devil had sent me the pustules out of revenge for having destroyed the image of Diana; but stronger was He that was for me, than he who was against me. I now mounted my pillar again, but the bishop* interfered, and told me I should never rival Simeon of Antioch as a pillar-saint, and that the climate of Belgium was wholly unsuited for such a life. He commanded me to enter a monastery and live with the brothers assembled there. Next day the bishop sent a number of workmen to knock down my pillar. I wept bitterly, but durst not disobey, and ever since I have lived where you now find me."—Gregory of Tours, *History of the Francs*, bk. viii. n. 15.

This narrative is truly touching, from its simplicity and manifest truthfulness. There is no exaggeration, no astounding wonders. The colossus was overthrown by mechanical force, the people were converted by the force of moral suasion, and the saint having done his task retires to a monastery, in obedience to authority.

Music heard at Death.

JER. xlviii. 36. Mine heart shall sound for Moab like pipes, and mine heart shall sound like pipes for the men of Kir-herês, because the riches that he hath gotten are perished.

AMOS v. 16. Wailing shall be in all streets. They shall call the husbandman to mourning, and such as are skilful in lamentation to wailing.

MATT. ix. 23. When Jesus came into the ruler's house, He saw the minstrels, and the people making the noise [*i.e.* the wailing for the dead].

REV. xiv. 2. I heard the voice of harpers harping on their lips.

Nothing is more common than the sound of music in the air at the death of saints. Thousands and tens of thousands of examples might be easily given, and accounted for simply as the reverberation of the requiem sung at death. Thus, when St. Pacomius died (A.D. 348), we are told by his biographer, "His disciples passed the whole night in singing, without intermission, psalms and hymns till the next morning, when the body was interred. In cases where several religious houses were under one head, and requiems were sung in each, these "airy sounds" or reverberations would be heard in places "far apart."

Sometimes the dying saint hears the music. This is the disease called *hedonia*. I have myself been at deathbeds where the person dying has heard these musical sounds, and even joined in them with feeble but musical voice.

Bunyan's pilgrims welcomed into heaven with the sound of music. There came to meet Pilgrim and Hopeful several of the king's trumpeters, clothed in white and shining raiment, who with melodious and loud noises made even the heavens echo with their sound. These trumpeters saluted Christian and his fellow with ten thousand welcomes, and this they did with shouting and sound of trumpet. This done, they compassed the newcomers round about on every side. Some went before, some behind, some on the right side and some on the left, continually sounding as they went with melodious noise in notes on high; so that the sight was as if heaven itself was come down to meet them. Thus Christian and Hopeful walked on together; and, as they walked, ever and anon these trumpeters, with joyful sound, signified to them how welcome they were. [As they approached nearer the celestial city] the two pilgrims thought they heard the bells of heaven ringing to welcome them. Thus came they to the gate.—*Pilgrim's Progress*, pt. i. (an allegory).

St. Martin welcomed to heaven with music (A.D. 397). When the agony of death came, St. Martin distinctly saw the devil, and said to him, "What dost thou here, thou cruel beast?" and, having so said, he rendered up his spirit to the Lord, being eighty-one years of age. His blessed soul was borne to heaven by many angels, who made much joy, and sang melodiously. This heavenly music was heard by many in places far apart, as by Severinus archbishop of Cologne, and by St. Ambrose archbishop of Milan, who said, on hearing it, "Our brother Martin of Tours has fallen asleep, and his spirit is being carried to heaven with shouts, and a great noise of melody."—Severus Sulpicius (a contemporary), *Epistle to Bassula*. (The life of St. Martin was also written by Paulinus, bishop of Nola; Fortunatus, a priest; Gregory of Tours; Odo, abbot of Cluny; Hebernus, bishop of Turin, and many others.

Celestial music proceeds from the spot where St. Julian and his companions were burnt to death (A.D. 313). St. Julian was

* It was the archbishop of Trèves.

at the head of a monastery of more than ten thousand religious men. When Maximinus II. was emperor, he sent Marcian to extirpate the whole Christian population of Antioch. One of the first acts of the lieutenant was to summon Julian before him, and command him to abandon the Christian faith, and offer incense to the gods of Rome. St. Julian replied, "Neither I nor any of my disciples will forsake the God whom we adore, nor will we offer incense to stocks and stones, the work of men's hands." Marcian, blind with rage, set fire to the four corners of Julian's monastery, and all were consumed. This holocaust was so pleasing to God, that for many and many a year persons who passed the spot where this monastery stood heard celestial music proceeding from the ground, whereby many that were sick were made whole. —*Les Petits Bollandistes*, vol. i. p. 235.

(Does the pope's chamberlain mean that "plus de dix mille religeux" "furent tous consumés"? Ten thousand is a large holocaust indeed.)

Celestial music heard at the death of St. Servasius (A.D. 384). When Servasius died, an angel brought from heaven a silk pall to cover over him. Celestial music was heard in the air, celebrating the victories obtained over the powers of hell. All the sick in Maëstricht and Tongres who attended the convoy were cured of their infirmities whatever they were, and other miracles were wrought so as to spread his fame throughout all Gaul.—Gregory of Tours, *Glory of the Confessors.*

The body was disinterred in A.D. 732 (nearly 350 years afterwards), and not only had no corruption set in, but the face shone so brilliantly as to light up the whole vault. The silk pall was found in the coffin, and a silver key, the gift of St. Peter. Another marvel is told of his grave. No snow ever fell on it; it fell around in great abundance, but never on the tomb. So we are told in the Roman martyrology, and also by Gregory of Tours. This, however, need be no miracle, unless the tomb was covered with grass like the parts around. Even the airy music might be reverberation of the requiem sung in the church; but these suggestions, like that of the key being the gift of the pope, take from the romance, and of course will be received with small favour by those who love to multiply miracles. (See p. 396.)

Nakedness of Man.

JOB i. 28. Naked came I out of my mother's womb, and naked shall I return thither.

1 TIM. vi. 7. We brought nothing into this world, and it is certain we can carry nothing out.

PSALM xlix. 16, 17. Be not afraid when one is made rich, when the glory of his house is increased; for when he dieth he shall carry nothing away.

Alexander the Great and Diogenês the cynic. Alexander was much interested with the snarling wit of Diogenês the cynic, and on one occasion asked him what boon he could grant him which would be acceptable. Diogenês replied, "Well, grant me this—'tis but a small thing—that I may carry my tub with me into the world of spirits." Alexander replied it was not in his power to grant such a request. "What!" cried the cynic, "cannot the great Alexander insure me so much as that? Then what, pray, will Alexander himself take with him, who has made himself master of the whole world?"

St. Chrysostom makes light of Eudoxia's persecutions of him (A.D. 347–407). St. Chrysostom was greatly persecuted by Eudoxia, the wife of Arcadius, emperor of the East. Cyricus, his friend, condoling with him on the subject, Chrysostom replied he had laid up his treasure where neither moth nor rust can corrupt, nor thieves break through and steal. "Be it the empress banishes me from the empire, there is the world before me. Be it she confiscates my goods, naked came I unto the world, and naked must I return. Be it she condemns me to be stoned to death, the martyr Stephen entered thus into everlasting glory. Be it she condemns me to the headsman's axe, the Baptist joined the blessed company of martyrs when he was released from prison. Eudoxia can take from me only that which perishes in the using; she cannot even touch that better part which is the heart's true measure."

Nature subjected to Faith.

MATT. xvii. 20. If ye have faith, ye shall say to this mountain, Remove hence to yonder place; and it shall remove; and nothing shall be impossible unto you.

St. Gregory Thaumaturgist removes mountains. A priest of Apollo came to St. Gregory the wonder-worker, and asked to be instructed in the Christian religion. St. Gregory said the mysteries of the Christian religion, being past human understanding, are confirmed by miracles. The priest made answer, "Show me a miracle, that I may believe." And Gregory, pointing to a huge rock, as big as a mountain, said to him, "I will command this rock to remove hence to yonder place, that you may believe." He gave the command, and the rock obeyed. The priest, fully convinced, was at once baptized, with his wife, his children, his servants, and a number of his neighbours and acquaintances.

Another instance. When the thaumaturgist came to Neocæsarea, he gave orders for the building of a church, but a mountain or huge hill stood in the way. So he prayed, and commanded the mountain to move elsewhere; and it removed at once to another place.

St. Gregory raises the bed of a lake. A father, at death, divided his estate between his two sons; each was to have an equal moiety. But a lake full of fish was on the estate, and the brothers could not agree about it, for both wanted to have it. St. Gregory, hearing of this dispute, caused the lake to dry up while men slept, and when the brothers rose next morning the bed of the lake was raised to the level of the land around. The cause of quarrel being thus removed, the brothers became friends.—St. Gregory of Nyssa, *Life of St. Gregory Thaumaturgist.*

A volcano stops its eruption in honour of St. Januarius. When Januarius was beheaded, his body was taken to Naples, and buried in the cathedral there. Just prior to this removal, Vesuvius was in such fierce eruption, that the Neapolitans feared the whole country would be destroyed; but no sooner had the body of Januarius entered into the city, than the volcano became utterly extinct,—"quenched," we are assured, "by the merits and patronage of the saint."—Edward Kinesman (1623), *Lives of the Saints*, p. 742.

Alban Butler places the removal of the body to Naples "about the year 400," and again in 1497, neither of which years was memorable for an eruption. The years of disturbance were 203, 472, 512, 685, 993, 1036 (very violent), 1049, 1138–39, 1306, 1580, 1631, 1660, etc. Most certainly the *eruptions have been more frequent since* 1497 than before. In 1631 the town of Torre del Greco, with four thousand persons, was destroyed. The eruption of 1707 is described in the *Philosophical Transactions*, No. 354. There was a violent eruption in 1707, and another in 1797, when five thousand acres of land were inundated with lava. Alban Butler does not go the length of Edward Kinesman in stating that "the volcano became extinct" after the removal of the body of Januarius to Naples, but he does say that the procession of the shrine of Januarius has caused eruptions, in the very torrent of their violence, suddenly to cease. He refers in proof to the eruptions of 1631 and 1707, as notable instances, and cites F. Putignano (vol. iii. p. 153; ii. p. 61) in confirmation of this statement. "In 1707, while cardinal Francis Pignatelli, with the clergy and people, devoutly followed the shrine of St. Januarius to the chapel at the foot of Mount Vesuvius, the fiery eruption ceased, the mist was scattered, and, at night, the stars appeared in the sky." Alban Butler furthermore says, but does not give his authority, that in 1631 "the terrible eruption was extinguished by invoking the patronage of this martyr" (Sept. 19).

St. Laumer removes a great oak tree (A.D. 575). "Par le seule force de l'oraison, St. Laumer fit changer de place un gros chêne qui nuisait au plan de ses batiments."—*Les Petits Bollandistes*, vol. i. p. 471.

Nothing that defileth shall enter in.

REV. xxi. 27. There shall in no wise enter into it anything that defileth, neither whatsoever worketh abomination, or maketh a lie.

ISA. xxxv. 8. A highway shall be there, called the way of holiness. The unclean shall not pass over it.

NAHUM i. 15. The wicked shall no more pass through thee.

Mary the Egyptian unable to pass through the church doors where the holy cross was shown to the people (A.D. 421). Mary the Egyptian told Father Zozimus her sad story. "At the age of twelve," she said, "I quitted my father's roof, and went to Alexandria, where I abandoned myself to all sorts of licentiousness, having no fear of God or man. I lost my native modesty, and lived seventeen years in the basest impurity. One day, seeing a number of persons embark for Jerusalem to solemnize the fête of the exaltation of the cross, I went on board too, with the intention of luring to carnal crime some of these pilgrims, and succeeded by selling myself to pay my passage and living. Reaching Jerusalem, I revelled deeper in sin than even at Alexandria, and when the day of the exaltation arrived, I went with the crowd to see the holy tree. I intended to slip in unnoticed, but when at the door I was unable to pass through, 'il m'était impossible de passer plus avant, parce qu'une force secrète m'empêchait d'y entrer.' After using all my efforts over and over again to force my way through, I began to ask myself why it was that I alone should be unable to cross that threshold, and I called to mind the words, 'A highway shall be there, called the way of holiness. The unclean shall not pass over it.' Was I then too unclean to pass the way of holiness? My heart smote me, tears ran in torrents from my eyes. Seeing an image of the Virgin Mary, I fell before it in passionate humility, and cried with a broken heart, 'O glorious virgin, chaste and pure, pity me, pity me, base unworthy sinner that I am. Is there no balm in Gilead for such as me? Is there no physician for such as me? O glorious virgin, let me, let me see the cross of salvation; let me, let me look upon Him who died for sin, and suffered a Mary Magdalene to wash His feet with her tears.' I rose from the ground; I again went to the church. I could enter it now. I saw the holy cross. I shrank into myself with shame. I ran back to the image of the Virgin, and vowed henceforth, with God's help, to lead a new life. I heard a voice say to me, 'Mary, pass the Jordan, and you will find peace for your soul.' I instantly directed my feet to the river, I washed my face in the water sanctified by the baptism of Jesus, I confessed my sins, received in the monastery of St. John the Baptist the divine mysteries which give life, entered this desert, and here have lived for forty-seven years, hoping by penance to do away with the sins of my evil life."—L'abbé Faillon, *Monuments inédits de l'Apostolat de Marie Magdeleine*.

Oil and Wine as a Medicament.

Luke x. 30–35. A man going from Jerusalem to Jericho fell among thieves, which stripped him of his raiment, wounded him, and left him on the wayside half dead. A Samaritan, as he journeyed, came to the spot, and seeing the man, had compassion on him, went to him, bound up his wounds, pouring in oil and wine; and then, setting him on his own beast, he took him to an inn, and paid the innkeeper to take care of him.

A man wounded in the battle of Salamanca. Mr. Brackenbury says, a relation of his was wounded at the battle of Salamanca, and applied every recognized specific to the wound, without any beneficial result. A year and more passed, but the wound would not heal. The fact was incidentally mentioned to a Spanish nun, who immediately said to Mr. Brackenbury, "Why does not your brother try the Samaritan remedy?" "What is that?" asked Mr. Brackenbury. "Why, oil and wine, of course," was the reply. "Mix olive oil and sherry to a proper consistency, and apply the mixture to the wound. It is a common remedy with us in Spain." The mixture was tried, and the wound healed rapidly.—William Brackenbury.

I myself heard this anecdote told by Mr. Brackenbury at a Bible meeting, in 1838.

Paper.

Exod. xxxii. 16. The writing was the writing of God graven upon the tables.

It is sometimes said that Elijah wrote a letter from heaven to king Jehoram. In 2 *Chron.* xxi. 12, it is said, "And there came a writing to him [*i.e.* to Jehoram king of Judah] from Elijah the prophet." Now, Elijah was translated to heaven B.C. 896, and Jehoram king of Judah reigned B.C. 885–881. So that this letter came to the king fourteen years after the translation of the prophet, and "was therefore sent to him from heaven." So say the Roman Catholics Lyran, Sanchez, Bellarmin, Salian, and A. Lapide.

No doubt there is great difficulty in this passage; and the difficulty is increased by ver. 2, where Jehoshaphat, the father of Jehoram, is called "king of *Israel*," whereas he was king of Judah (see 1 *Kings* xxii. 41), and Ahab was king of Israel.

In the marginal Bibles it is said that the letter of Elijah was written before his death, and was delivered to Jehoram fourteen or more years after it was written; but there is no text of Scripture to confirm this hypothesis, and "guesswork" is much to be deprecated in elucidation of Scripture, and indeed of history in general. I frankly acknowledge that I know of no satisfactory solution of the difficulties, and think it far wiser to leave it as it is, than to try to accommodate the words to our own notion of what they ought to be.

St. Vincent Ferrier receives from heaven a paper containing the writing of God (A.D. 1357–1419). One day, when St. Vincent Ferrier was preaching in Spain, he was called to attend the dying bed of a great sinner. All the exhortations, "de cet ardent chasseur des pécheurs," were unheeded by the dying man. "God will pardon you, if you ask Him," said the saint; "yea," he added, "I will myself take your sins on me, and if I have any merit in God's sight I will transfer it to you." "I will confess my sins," said the dying man, "but you must first give me in writing an assurance of absolution." St. Vincent wrote on a slip of paper the required assurance, put it in the hands of the dying man, who "dans une douce agonie" and a peaceful sigh gave up the ghost. Scarcely was he dead, when the slip of paper with the man's spirit left this earth for the judgment seat of God. Some time after this, St. Vincent went to preach; some thirty thousand persons (*plus de trente mille personnes*) were assembled to hear him. In the midst of his sermon a piece of paper fell from the skies into his hands. He opened it. It was the slip he had given to the dying man. He explained the case to the congregation, and our author adds, "Qu'on juge de l'impression produite sur la foule par le récit de ce miracle surprenant."—Mgr. Guérin (chamberlain of pope Leo XIII., 1880), *Vies des Saints*, vol. iv. p. 238.

St. Vincent Ferrier receives a letter from the Holy Trinity (A.D. 1357–1419). Perhaps it will be more satisfactory to give this narrative in the words of the pope's chamberlain. "Appelé à Pampelune, près du lit de mort d'une pécheresse publique endurcie, St. Vincent Ferrier lui dit ferait venir du ciel son absolution, si elle promettait de se confesser. 'S'il en est ainsi, je le veux bien,' répondit la courtisane. Alors il traça ces mots: 'Frère Vincent supplie la très-sainte Trinité de daigner accorder à la présente pécheresse l'absolution de ses péchés.' L'écrit s'envola au ciel, et revint quelques instants après, portant tracé en lettres d'or l'engagement suivant: 'Nous, très-sainte Trinité, à la demande de notre Vincent, nous accordons à la pécheresse dont il nous a parlé, le pardon de ses fautes; nous la dispensons de toutes les peines qu'elle devait endurer, et si elle se confesse, elle sera dans une demi-heure portée dans le ciel.'"—Mgr. Guérin, *Vies des Saints*, vol. iv. p. 238 (7th edit. 1880).

The pope's chamberlain gives us plenty of vouchers for this "fact," and the names of fourteen living prelates who approve and recommend his book.

Passing Away.

Job xxx. 15. My welfare passeth away as a cloud.

Luke xii. 16–20. The ground of a certain rich man brought forth plentifully; and he said, I will pull down my barns, and build greater; and will say to my soul, Take thy rest. . . . But God said to the rich man, This night thy soul shall be required of thee; then whose shall those things be which thou hast provided?"

A Ceylonese custom to teach the uncertainty of life. When the sultan of Serendib (i.e. Ceylon) went abroad in state, the vizier used to cry aloud from time to time, "This is the great monarch, the mighty sultan of the Indies; greater than Solima, or the grand Mihragê." An officer behind the monarch then exclaimed, "This monarch, though so great and powerful, must die, must die, must die."—*Arabian Nights* (Sindbad, sixth voyage).

An Egyptian custom to show the fleetness of life. Plutarch tells us that, towards the close of an Egyptian feast, a servant was wont to bring into the banquet hall a skeleton, and, as he drew it through the room, to cry aloud to the guests, "Eat, drink, and be merry; for to-morrow you die." Herodotus refers to this custom, and says the skeleton was made of wood, about eighteen inches long.

Like skulls at Memphian banquets.
Byron, *Don Juan*, iii. 65.

The stranger feasted at the board;
But, like the skeleton at the feast,
That warning timepiece never ceased,—
"For ever!—Never! Never!—For ever!"
Longfellow, *The Old Clock on the Stairs.*

Roman customs teaching the transitory nature of mundane glory. (1) It was a Roman custom, when the emperor went in state through the streets of Rome, for an officer to burn flax before him, crying out as the flax burnt away, "Sic transit gloria mundi." This was done to remind the emperor that all his honours and grandeur would soon vanish, like the smoke of burning flax.

(2) When a Roman conqueror entered the city in public triumph, a slave was placed in the chariot to whisper from time to time in the conqueror's ear, "Remember, thou art but a man."

(3) Vespasian, the Roman emperor, employed a slave to say to him daily, as he left his chamber, "Cæsar, bear in mind thou art a man."

Guerricus converted by the reflection, "In the midst of life we are in death." Guerricus was a man of the world who had heaped up many stores, and said to himself, "Soul, thou hast much goods laid up for many years; take thine ease; eat, drink, and be merry." At church he happened one day to hear *Genesis* xv. read: "And all the days Adam lived were 930 years, and he died. And all the days of Seth were 912 years, and he died. And all the days of Enos were 905 years, and he died. And all the days of Methuselah were 969 years, and he died," and so on. This invariable repetition of the words "and he died" so riveted his mind on the uncertainty of life, and the certainty of death, that he became a new man, most devout, charitable, and given to all good works, fully resolved to make to himself friends of the mammon of unrighteousness, that when flesh and life failed he might be received into everlasting habitations.

Plague.

Exod. xiii. 23. The Lord will pass through [Egypt] to smite the Egyptians. (See vers. 12, 13.)

1 Chron. xxi. 15. And God sent an angel unto Jerusalem to destroy it.

Numb. xi. 33. And while the [quails] were yet between their teeth . . . the Lord smote the people with a very great plague.

Smiting with plague. "Some I have talked with have ingenuously confest to me that, when first infected, they felt themselves distinctly stricken, being fully sensible of an actual blow suddenly given them either on the head or neck, back or side. Sometimes so violent was the blow they have been knocked down by it to the ground, remaining insensible for some time. In some cases the stricken have died instantly from the blow, and in others they have died in a short time afterwards."—Richard Kephale, *Medela Pestilentiæ*, p. 49.

Richard Kephale says, "There are two sorts of plague, the one simple and the other putrid. The simple plague arises from an angel's striking the victims in execution of the vengeance of God [as in the case of David, when he numbered the people]; the other kind ariseth from putrefaction of humours, the influence of stars, or distemper of the blood."

Plague described by Procopius. Procopius tells us of a great plague in the reign of Justinian, which ravaged nearly the whole known world. When Evagrius wrote his *Ecclesiastical History*, this plague had lasted fifty-two years, with alternate fits of relaxation and fierceness; but during all that long period the earth was never wholly free from its ravages. Procopius says, "No one could account for it, except by referring it to a stroke of God. For it fell on no particular portion of the earth or race of men, nor was it confined to any season of the year, but it spread over all the earth, and ravaged all nations, no matter what their habits, their diet, their locality, or constitutions. Sometimes in summer, sometimes in winter, spring, or autumn. It began in Egypt, among the inhabitants of Pelusium, and, dividing there, passed to Alexandria on one side and Palestine on the other, and from these two centres spread over all the earth, missing no cave or island, no mountain summit or valley inhabited by man, and never quitted a spot till the tale of the dead had reached its full measure. It always began at the seaside, and spread thence into the interior. It reached Constantinople, where I then happened to be living, at midsummer in the second year of its devastation. The manner of its attack was this: Visions of spirits [φάσματα δαιμόνων] in all sorts of human shapes were seen, and these spirits struck with a blow the victim, who was forthwith taken ill. At first men tried to turn away the demons by uttering holy names and hallowing themselves as best they could; but they gained nothing by so doing, and even those who fled into churches for protection perished at the very foot of the altar. Most persons shut themselves indoors for fear of being struck, and would not open their doors, lest the demon should enter and give the fatal blow. Not a few saw the phantom demon in their dreams at night; it stood over them, and struck them, and they were numbered with the dead. No one, however, fell sick from contact with the sick or dead. There was no danger of contagion. Those who suffered were struck, and those who were not so struck escaped. The plague lasted in Constantinople four months; at its height it carried off five thousand daily, went on to ten thousand, and even more, and then gradually declined."—Procopius, *De Bello Persico*, bk. ii. ch. 22, 23.

Plague of Florence (A.D. 1346). In the plague of Florence those who shut themselves up in solitary places where the air was healthy, where the inmates were furnished with every comfort, and where there could be no suspicion of infection, could not shut the door against God, who entered the privacy and struck down the inmates, just as He had done others who had taken no thought for themselves.—Matteo Villani, *Istorie Fiorentine*.

Pepys in the plague of London (June 17, 1665). "It struck me very deep this afternoon, going with a hackney coach down Holborn, from the Lord Treasurer's. The coachman I found to drive easily and easily, at last stood still . . . and told me he was suddenly struck very sick. So I lighted and went into another coach with a sad heart for the poor man, and for myself also, lest he should have been struck with the plague."—*Diary*.

Here the same language is used—"struck with the plague;" but Pepys does not probably mean anything more than that the attack was sudden and unexpected, without any premonitory symptoms.

Poison Innocuous.

MARK xvi. 17, 18. These signs shall follow them that believe . . . if they drink any deadly thing, it shall not hurt them.

St. Antony of Padua eats and drinks poison without injury (A.D. 1195–1231). St. Antony of Padua had many enemies, for he would make no league with sin. On one occasion they mixed poison both with his food and with his drink. Antony was warned of it by the Saviour. "Fear not," said the Lord; "remember I have said, if ye drink any deadly thing, it shall not harm you." The poisoners knew they were detected, and impudently exclaimed, "Eat and drink; for it is said, no deadly thing shall hurt those who love God." Antony made the sign of the cross, and cried in the hearing of the poisoners, "It is not, Lord, because Thou canst avert the evil of poison that I take this meat and drink, but to give a new occasion to manifest Thy love and power." So saying, he ate the soup and drank the wine, and felt no sort of pain or ill effects. The poisoners were pricked to the heart, acknowledged their sin, and were received into the bosom of the Church.—L'abbé Guyard, *Life of St. Antony of Padua*. (See *Matt.* iv. 7.)

St. Austrebertha takes poisoned food without ill effects (A.D. 630–704). When Austrebertha was appointed abbess of Pavilly, she found the whole establishment in dreadful disorder, and set at once about restoring a stricter discipline. Her severe rule caused the greatest dissatisfaction, and some of the sisters combined to poison her food. When the food was set before her she knew that it was poisoned, but nevertheless partook of it, saying as she did so, "Christ hath promised His disciples, saying, if they take any poisoned thing, it shall not hurt them; but nevertheless, my daughters, I pray God to pardon the malice of your hearts, and lead you to repentance." This mild rebuke had no effect, and the devil resolved to make the best of it; so a few days afterwards, while the sisters were at matins, he so shook the convent that part of the dormitories were thrown down. The sisters, in alarm, were about to rush out of the church, when the stern abbess forbade them to move. One disobeyed, and part of the building, falling on her, crushed her to death. She was dug out, and taken to the infirmary. Austrebertha went to see the mangled corpse, took a little oil from the lamp, blessed it with the sign of the cross, anointed the dead body, and immediately it was restored to life and health.—Surius, *Lives of the Saints*, vol. i.

St. Benedict has poisoned wine given him, but the poison is spilled. St. Benedict was chosen abbot of Vicovara, but his discipline was so rigid, that some of the monks resolved to poison him, and, accordingly, drugged his wine. When, however, St. Benedict made, as usual, the sign of the cross over the cup, the glass broke asunder, and the wine was poured out. "God forgive you, brethren," said the abbot; "you see plainly what I told you, that your manners and mine do not agree." So saying he left the abbey, and returned to his cave at Sublacum.—St. Gregory the Great, *Dialogues*, bk. ii.

Politeness of the Dead.

ROM. xii. 10. Be kindly affectioned one to another with brotherly love; in honour preferring one another.

PHIL. ii. 3 Let each esteem other better than themselves.

Politeness of the three Magi, when in the grave (A.D. 54). The wise men who came from the East, and made offerings to the infant Jesus, were (according to the Catholic Church) Melchior king of Arabia, Balthazar king of Saba, and Gaspar king of Tarshish and the Isles (*Ps.* lxxii. 10). They all died in Jan., A.D. 54, at Servan. Melchior died first, Jan. 1, at the age of 116; Balthazar died next, Jan. 6, at the age of 112; and Gaspar died last, at the age of 109. They were all buried in the same vault. When the body of Balthazar was lowered into the grave, the dead body of Melchior budged on one side, to give the place of honour to him; and when Gaspar died, the two other bodies moved to the right and left, that the king of Tarshish and the Isles might occupy the middle place.—*Les Petits Bollandistes* (7th edit. 1880), vol. i. p. 159.

Two dead bishops make room for St. John the almsgiver (A.D. 619). St. John the almsgiver, patriarch of Alexandria, was buried in a vault containing the bodies of two other bishops. When the patriarch was lowered into the grave, the two bishops moved right and left to give the almsgiver the post of honour; not forgetting the apostolic precept, "Let each esteem other better than themselves."—Leontius (bishop of Naples), *Life of St. John the Almsgiver*.

The dead wife and daughter of St. Severus make room for the saint (A.D. 389). "St. Sévère sentant approcher la fin de sa vie, un peu après avoir achevé l'office de la sainte messe, il se mit en route pour le tombeau de sa femme et de sa fille, mortes avant lui. Arrivé là, il se fait ouvrir le tombeau, et commande qu'on lui fasse une place. À sa voix le sarcophage se meut de lui-même, et se déplace miraculeusement. Le saint évêque, descendu vivant dans ce tombeau, s'y endormit dans le Seigneur tout en priant."—Mgr. Guérin (chamberlain of pope Leo XIII.), *Vies des Saints* (7th edit. 1880), vol. ii. pp. 205, 206.

This extract is given in the exact words of the writer, and as his book is highly recommended to "all the faithful" by the chief dignitaries of the papal Church of the present day, it may be presumed that "votre refus à ajouter foi à cette vérité" would be to strain at a gnat, while you swallow a camel.

Portions.

ECCLES. xi. 2. Give a portion to seven, and also to eight; for thou knowest not what evil shall be upon the earth.

St. Nicholas, bishop of Myra, portions

off three damsels. There was in the city of Patara a decayed gentleman with three marriageable daughters. Not having the wherewithal for providing daily food, he implored his daughters to earn for him the wages of unrighteousness, but this they refused to do. The father of St. Nicholas was just dead, and his large inheritance came to his only son, who resolved to make this case his special care. So, filling a bag with gold, he went to the gentleman's house at night, and slipped it through an open window. Next day the man found the money, thanked God, and provided for one of his daughters. When St. Nicholas heard how his device had succeeded, he repeated his gift, and the second daughter was married. The man now watched to find out who was his benefactor, and when St. Nicholas came with the third portion, ran after him, and falling at his feet, thanked him with many tears, for that he had raised the poor out of the mire and the needy from the dunghill. St. Nicholas bade him keep the matter secret, but the news soon spread, and the man ceased not as long as he lived to blaze abroad the praises of the saint.—Edward Kinesman (1623), *Lives of the Saints*, p. 976. (He tells us he has taken his life of St. Nicholas from John the Deacon and Leonard Justinian.)

Prayer.

Matt. xxi. 21, 22. Jesus said, If ye have faith, and doubt not, ye shall say unto this mountain, Be thou removed, and cast into the sea; and it shall be done. And all things, whatsoever ye shall ask in prayer, believing, ye shall receive.

St. Armentarius, bishop of Pavia, on the force of prayer (A.D. 730). "La prère eteint la violence du feu; ferme la bouche des lions; termine les guerres; chasse les démons, les maladies, et les orages; brise les liens de la mort; détourne de nous la colère de Dieu."

Putting the God of Jacob to the test. A merchant of Leeds told the Rev. Edward Parsons this fact:—"I am a Scotchman, and went with my wife to London, where I soon found work as a skilled mechanic. In time work grew slack, and I was obliged to sell some of my furniture, and live in a cheaper house. Circumstances grew worse and worse. My health failed, more furniture was sold, and at length I was compelled to live with my wife and family in a wretched cellar in St. Giles's. One day, after parting with my last article of furniture for bread, I resolved to drown myself. It was Sunday; and as I passed down Tottenham Court Road, on my way to the New River, a little before seven o'clock, I found myself moving on with a throng of persons who were bent to the Tabernacle. In a sullen mood I entered with the stream. Mr. Parsons was in the pulpit; and when he came to the sermon, he took for his text, 'When the poor and needy seek water, and there is none, and their tongue faileth for thirst, I the Lord will hear them, I the God of Jacob will not forsake them.' It seemed so exactly to suit my case, that I stopped to the close, spellbound. Towards the conclusion of the sermon, the preacher paused, and then said, 'Have you put the God of Jacob to the test?' The question was repeated more than once; the nail was driven home, and I said to myself, 'No, I have not put the God of Jacob to the test.' I returned to my cellar, and found my wretched wife and starving children crying for food, but I had none to give. In a few minutes I said to my wife, 'I think we will read a chapter.' Poor woman! she burst into a flood of tears. No Bible was left. We had pawned our Bible for bread. An old bit of a Bible was, however, discovered, from which I read, and then said, 'Wife, shall we pray, and put the God of Jacob to the test?' We knelt down; I laid my case open, casting my cares upon Jesus. Next morning a letter was brought by the postman, stating that a large London firm had made extensive contracts, and was seeking skilled hands, and I was advised to apply for employment. It also contained a pound note, as a loan. I instantly purchased food, took my best coat out of pawn, applied to the firm, and obtained employment. I rose to be foreman, was taken in as under partner, and, when one of the brothers of the firm died, I took his place. In a few years the other brother retired, leaving the whole business to me. I have well thriven, and the God of Jacob has fulfilled the test with both hands open, and has supplied me amply with the nether and the upper springs, so that I can set to my seal that it is true to the very letter, 'When the poor and needy seek water, and there is none, and their tongue faileth for thirst, the Lord will hear them, the God of Jacob will not forsake them.'"—Phillips, *Remarkable Answers to Prayer*.

Difficulty of fixing one's thoughts on the words of prayer. A man scoffing at the merit of prayer, St. Jerome said to him,

"I will give you my horse, if you can repeat even the short Lord's Prayer slowly, without allowing your thoughts to wander." The man laughed at the notion, and began: "Our Father, which art in heaven——" but then breaking off exclaimed, "You did not say if the saddle was to be included in the bargain."

St. Apollo supplies an Easter feast by prayer. One Easter Day, the community over which St. Apollo presided, in Upper Egypt, being wholly without food, the abbot said, "Be of good cheer, brothers; let each one ask God for what he likes best, and be sure He will give liberally, and upbraid not." But the monks could not be induced to do so; whereupon St. Apollo prayed for them. As the monks shouted "Amen," a knocking was heard at the door, and there stood at the monastery several men, and asses laden with food: there were new loaves of the best white bread, there were citrons and pomegranates, honey and the honeycomb, nuts and dates, grapes and figs, with plenty of fresh milk.—Palladius (a personal acquaintance), *Historia Lusiaca.*

It would have been more satisfactory if Palladius had informed us who paid for these provisions. If St. Apollo paid for them, the arrival was well timed, but there was no miracle.

St. Benedict, by prayer, coins money (A.D. 480-543). St. Gregory the Great assures us he heard the following story from some of the disciples of St. Benedict, who vouched for its truth. A poor man owed a considerable sum of money, but had not wherewithal to pay it. In great distress he applied to St. Benedict, abbot of Mount Cassino, for aid. St. Benedict said, "I have not so large a sum of money in the house, but come again in two days' time, and God will supply your want." The man returned at the time appointed, and the saint, having made his prayer, went to his coffer, and found not only all the money required to pay the man's debt, but a good deal more, although no human hand had put a single coin into the box. St. Benedict gave the whole to the man, some to pay his debt, and the rest for present wants.—St. Gregory the Great, *Dialogues*, bk. ii.

St. Benedict, by prayer, stops the devil from molesting his workmen. In the year of grace 529, St. Benedict, with two of his disciples, went to Aureola, near Hercularia, when it was revealed to him that God desired him to build a monastery in that spot, and another in Mount Cassino. These doings greatly annoyed the devil, who manifested himself to the saint in sundry shapes. The builders heard the roaring and howling of the foul fiend, but did not see his shape. However, the devil did all the mischief he could, by disturbing the work, making the stones heavy, throwing down the walls, and raising up false alarms of fire. St. Benedict suffered these obstructions for a time, but finding that they ceased not, had recourse to prayer, and so effectually delivered the workmen from any further annoyance.—Surius (1570), *Lives of the Saints.*

St. Bont stills a tempest by prayer (A.D. 705). When St. Bont was returning from the Holy Land to Rome, a terrible tempest arose, which wrecked one of the ships, and menaced that in which the saint was sailing; but he prayed, and the rage of the storm immediately lulled. — Bollandus, *Acta Sanctorum*, vol. i. Jan. 5.

The potency of the prayers of St. Catherine of Siena. The prayers of St. Catherine were of marvellous power. Thus, when her father died, she desired God to liberate him from the pains of purgatory, and to award her some pain instead. This was instantly done, for she suffered a grievous pain in her bowels, which continued till death—"a sure and certain token that her prayer was heard." A few days later, her mother died without confession, but St. Catherine, by fervent prayer, restored her to life, and she lived many years after. Again, Andreas Naddino of Siena, a man of most evil life, being sick and at the point of death, at the earnest prayer of St. Catherine confessed his sins, and obtained absolution. Two malefactors, while led to execution, were exhorted in vain by the monks who accompanied them, to repent and confess their sins; but they continued to blaspheme, till St. Catherine prayed for them, and then they became new creatures, confessed their sins with great contrition, received absolution, and died true penitents.—In 1374 a great pestilence ravaged Siena; but St. Catherine, by prayer, delivered many from death, amongst others Raymond, her confessor, and Stephen, a Carthusian. Those who were wicked she prayed over and turned from their evil ways.—Stephen (prior of Pavia), *Life of St. Catherine of Siena.*

St. Clare, when a boy, lays a furious tempest by prayer (seventh century). One day, in early childhood, [St.] Clare went with his mother to the church of St. Ferreol, on the Rhone, and their hearts were so stirred within them they quite forgot how the day was passing, till the shades of evening warned them to hasten home. They made all the haste they could, but had to cross the river in a boat. The night turned out very tempestuous, with thunder and lightning, wind and rain, so that the boatman despaired of getting them across. In this sad plight, the boy began to cry bitterly, and, stretching out his hand towards the church, he said, "O God, in whose name the glorious martyr St. Ferreol suffered death, deliver us from this great danger." In a moment the tempest ceased, and the boat was on the bank, where Clare and his mother wanted to land.—*Les Petits Bollandistes*, vol. i. p. 30.

St. Eusebius, bishop of Versailles, opens the cathedral doors by prayer. The Arians, knowing that Eusebius was named bishop of Versailles, endeavoured to hinder his entrance into the cathedral church, by shutting and barring the doors; but Eusebius kneeling at the porch, the doors flew open of their own accord, and Eusebius, entering in, took possession of the church.—Surius, *Lives of the Saints*, vol. iv. (See also Vincent of Beauvais, *Historical Mirror*.)

St. Giles lays a storm at sea by prayer. While St. Giles was sailing from Greece to France, a great tempest arose, so that the sailors every moment expected the ship would be wrecked; but St. Giles prayed, and the storm ceased. So convinced were the sailors and passengers that they owed their lives to St. Giles, they came to him in a body to thank him for his intercession.—Gilbert (bishop of Carnolum), *Life of St. Giles*.

Every one knows that the Mediterranean Sea is subject to what are termed "levanters," sudden winds which blow in all directions from N.E., round by E. to S.E. Probably the wind called (*Acts* xxvii.) Euroclydon, which means *south-east wind wave*, was a levanter.

When [*St.*] *Isidore fell into a well, the water, in obedience to prayer, restored him* (A.D. 1170). St. Isidore, when a little boy, fell into a well, but his parents made fervent prayer for his restoration. "Whatsoever ye ask in prayer, believing, ye shall receive;" and so it proved in this case, for the water heaved itself to the top of the well, bearing up the body of the child, not only uninjured, but in perfect health. In corroboration of this miracle, the very well is still shown in Madrid, and it was doubtlessly the property of St. Isidore's master, John de Vergas, for it has continued in the family even to the present day.—John the Deacon, *Life of St. Isidore* (1261).

Of course the fact that a certain well has been in the family of de Vergas for seven hundred years or more, and that it is still pointed out as the well into which St. Isidore fell in boyhood, does not prove the truth of the legend, though it may prove the existence of such a story.

St. Laumer extinguishes a fire by prayer (A.D. 575). "Par ses seules prières, St. Laumer éteignit le feu, qui avait pris à des paniers d'osier remplis de blés pour la provision du monastère."—*Les Petits Bollandistes*, vol. i. p. 471.

Fire quenched by the prayers of St. Mamertus (A.D. 477). On Easter Eve a fire broke out in Vienne, and threatened to destroy the whole city. St. Mamertus, the archbishop, threw himself before the altar in prayer, and the fire suddenly ceased. St. Avitus mentions this (490–570), and distinctly attributes the extinction of the fire to a miracle.—*Les Petits Bollandistes*, vol. v. p. 455.

Marianne de Jesus, when a child, heals a sore finger by prayer (A.D. 1618–1645). One day, in childhood, Marianne, the daughter of don Jerome of Quito, hurt her finger. She said nothing about it, "afin de pouvoir souffrir davantage." A gangrene was the result, which threatened her life, and her cousins, children also, advised her to consult the family doctor. "Wait a bit," said Marianne; "you shall see how I cure myself." She then knelt before the image of the Virgin; and "lorsqu'elle se releva, toute trace du mal avait disparu."—Mgr. Guérin, *Vies des Saints*, vol. vi. p. 231 (1880).

We are told that Marianne was seven years old at the time, and "peu de temps après, elle fit le vœu de chasteté perpétuelle." In my opinion she ought to have been whipped for even knowing what "chastity" meant.

St. Martin puts out a fire by prayer. One winter, when St. Martin went to visit his diocese, the priests prepared him a bed in the vestry, and lighted a fire. Being too warm, he threw the coverlet off, and it fell by accident into the fire; but Benedict, being drowsy with sleep, knew it not. Presently the whole vestry caught fire, and the flames, spreading to the roof, threatened to burn down the whole church. St. Martin, starting up, ran to the door, but could not open it. What was to be done? He fell on his knees in the midst of the flames, and prayed for help; when lo! the fire suddenly went out.—Severus Sulpicius, *Dialogues*.

St. Patrick prays, and a herd of swine instantly appears to give food to a starving crew. When St. Patrick fled from captivity in Ireland at the age of twenty-two, he was taken on board a pirate's skiff, which ran to a desert place, where the crew was detained for twenty-seven days. St. Patrick, in his *Confessions*, says, "While here both food and water failed us, and the hunger of the men was frightful. The pilot said to me, 'You tell us you are a Christian, and that your God can do anything. Ask Him to help us in this our necessity.' 'I will, if you will become Christians, and God will interpose and save us.' Scarcely had I spoken, when a great herd of swine ran by. All praised the name of the Lord, and treated me with great reverence. But griefs, trials, and temptations were not ended here."

St. Peter Thomas stills a tempest by prayer (A.D. 1358). St. Peter Thomas appeased the fury of a storm at sea by prayer. All the sailors expected the ship would be lost; but St. Peter Thomas laid his crucifix on the rough water and prayed, and in a moment there was a perfect calm.—Philip Mazzeri, *Life of St. Peter Thomas.*

Wesley, by prayer, lays a storm at sea. Wesley and Dr. Adam Clarke, coming from Guernsey, were overtaken by a storm at sea. Wesley was in the cabin reading; and, hearing the noise and bustle, put his head above deck to inquire what was amiss. Being told that the ship was in great danger, he quietly said, "Then let us pray:—Almighty and everlasting God, who hast sway everywhere, and holdest the winds in Thy fist, command these winds and waves, in obedience to Thy word, to take us safely into haven." Then rose he from his knees; made no sort of remark; but, taking up his book again, went on with his reading. Dr. Clarke went on deck, and what was his surprise, when he found the vessel running smoothly in the right course, with a favourable breeze, which brought them safely near St. Michael's Mount, in Penzance Bay. Mr. Wesley made no remark on this sudden change, so fully did he expect, and take for granted, that God would hear and answer prayer.—*Life of Dr. Adam Clarke.*

Any one who has crossed over to Guernsey or Jersey, or back therefrom, will remember the Caskets. Here prince William, the son of Henry I., and his suite, perished in 1119; and here H.M.S. *Victory*, of 110 guns, went down in 1744. I have seen the sea from Southampton calm and tranquil till the vessel has reached this dreadful spot, and then Eolus seems to have let all the winds out of their prison-house to flourish red flags at sea. Immediately the Caskets are passed all goes merrily again.

Preparing the Way.

Isa. xl. 3, 4. The voice of him that crieth in the wilderness, Prepare ye the way of the Lord, make straight in the desert a highway for our God. Every valley shall be exalted, and every mountain and hill shall be made low. The crooked shall be made straight, and the rough places plain. (See Matt. iii. 3.)

March of Semiramis into Medea and Persia. Marching towards Ecbatana, Semiramis came to the mountain Zarkeum, which extended many furlongs, and was full of craggy precipices and deep hollows. She ordered the precipices to be cut down, and the hollows to be filled up with earth; and thus made she a plain open road, which is to this day called the "Road of Semiramis." Afterwards, she made a royal progress through Persia, and all her other dominions in Asia; but, wherever she went, she ordered the mountains and craggy rocks to be cut down, and made all the ways level and plain. On the other hand, in low valleys she raised mounds, on which she built monuments to her deceased generals.—Diodorus Siculus, *The Historical Library*, bk. ii. pp. 44, 47.

Rain, etc., obedient to the Saints. (See Sun warded off.)

Isa. iv. 6. There shall be a tabernacle for a shadow in the daytime from the heat, and for a covert from storm and from rain.

Isa. v. 6. I will command the clouds that they rain no rain upon it.

St. Antony of Padua, preaching, commanded the rain not to molest his congregation. One summer's day, as St. Antony of Padua was preaching at Bruges in the open field, the sky became suddenly overcast; but St. Antony told the people not to stir, for the rain should not fall on them to wet them. Down came the rain in torrents on the surrounding parts, but "not one single drop fell on the congregation, and not one of those who heard the words of the preacher were wetted by the shower."—Edward Kinesman (1623), *Lives of the Saints*, p. 367.

Rain does not wet a woman sent by St. Antony of Padua to get vegetables (A.D. 1185-1231). St. Antony went to found the convent of Brives, and arrived at a time when there was no food. St. Antony sent to a woman in the neighbourhood to give him a few onions out of her garden. It rained in torrents, and the garden was a considerable way from the house, yet the woman told one of her female servants to go and get the onions for the convent. The maidservant obeyed, and great was the astonishment of her mistress to find that not one drop of rain had fallen on her, though it had not ceased raining for a single moment, and the servant had been exposed to it for more than half an hour.—L'abbé Guyard, *Life of St. Antony of Padua.*

A heavy rain refused to touch St. Aubin (A.D. 470–550). One day the abbot of Cincillac, near Angers, sent St. Aubin with a message to the neighbouring town; and while he was in a house where a large number of people were assembled, a heavy rain fell, which penetrated through the roof and drenched all who were gathered together, except St. Aubin. Not one drop fell upon him. His clothes were as dry after the downfall as before. The historian says, "The rain had respect to the holiness of the saint, and no more attempted to annoy him, than did the flames of the furnace attempt to burn the three faithful ones in Babylon."—Fortunatus (bishop of Poitiers, a contemporary), *Life of St. Austin, Bishop of Angers.*

St. Bernard, writing a letter in the open air, commands the rain not to fall on it to blot it. St. Bernard, on one occasion, was writing a letter to a monk who had quitted his order. He wrote in the open air, and not under shelter. Presently the sky was black with clouds, and the rain came pelting down both fast and furious. St. Bernard simply bade the rain not to fall where he was sitting, and went on writing. The rain obeyed the man of God, and not one single drop of the shower fell on him or on the letter he was writing. (See ST. MAIDOC, next column.)—William (abbot of Theodore), *Life of St. Bernard.*

A heavy fall of snow respects the cottage of St. Eumachus of Perigord (sixth century). One rigorous winter day, while St. Eumachus was occupied in prayer for the clergy and people of Perigord, a heavy storm of snow fell on all the surrounding country, but not a single flake fell on the cottage or in the little garden plot of St. Eumachus. We are told that an eagle with outstretched wings brooded over the cottage and garden, and protected them. —*Les Petits Bollandistes*, vol. ii. p. 414 (1880).

St. Geneviève commands rain not to fall on a field under reapers (A.D. 422–512). One harvest-time, clouds black with rain threatened to inundate a field in which reapers were employed. St. Geneviève commanded the clouds not to drop their burden there, so as to spoil the fruits of God's bounty; the clouds, accordingly, rolled away; and though rain fell in great abundance in the neighbourhood, not a drop fell on the corn or the reapers protected by the saint.—Bollandus, *Acta Sanctorum* (*Vita St. Genovefæ*).

The elements obedient to Hugh of Poitiers (A.D. 928). Hugh of Poitiers not only wrought the usual miracles ascribed to saints, such as giving hearing to the deaf, eyes to the blind, and speech to the dumb; he also gave fecundity to seed, and, with the sign of the cross, or the relics of saints, he dispelled clouds, averted storms, changed hail into dew, and had full command of Nature and all her works.—Mabillon, *Acta Sanctorum*, vol. vii. April 20.

The elements obedient to St. John-Joseph de la Croix (A.D. 1654–1734). The elements, says cardinal Wiseman, were obedient to St. John-Joseph de la Croix. The rain, at his command, ceased to fall. On one occasion, being on a journey into the country with a companion, an incessant rain fell all the time, but at their journey's end they found their garments as dry as if they had been indoors. In fact, all nature was submissive to him, and did exactly what he desired. "L'air lui rapporta sur ses ailes son bâton qu'il avait laissé derrière lui, et les plantes poussaient surnaturellement pour seconder les vues de sa charité."—Migne, *Démonstrations Évangéliques*, vol. xvi.

A heavy downfall of rain refuses to wet St. Maidoc's book (A.D. 632). St. David once called his pupil Maidoc, while he was in the fields reading. The young man promptly obeyed, but left his book behind him. A heavy shower fell, but when Maidoc ran back to fetch his book, great was his joy to find that not a drop of rain had touched it. (See ST. BERNARD, preceding column, and UBALDUS, p. 445.)—Baring-Gould, *Lives of the Saints*, Jan. 31.

Queen Margaret's book of the Gospels uninjured by the water of a river (A.D. 1046–1093). Queen Margaret of Scotland had a book of the four Gospels with intaglios of the four evangelists, and all the initial letters illuminated with much gold. One day she charged a page with this book, who let it fall into a river, and never knew it till he was about to hand the book to the queen. Search was instantly made for it, and it was ultimately seen at the bottom of the river, wide open, with the leaves apart. Every one thought it would be ruined, its illuminations washed out, and its binding spoiled. It was drawn out, and not the slightest injury could be detected; not a spot could be seen, the pages were not discoloured, the binding was not disturbed, the gilding was not tarnished; in a word, the book had sustained no harm at all. The queen acknowledged the miracle, and loved the book the more.—Thierri, monk of Durham (the queen's confessor), *Life of Margaret, Queen of Scotland.*

St. Scholastica brings down rain to prevent her brother leaving her (A.D. 543). St. Benedict came to visit his sister Scholastica. They spent the day in talking about heaven, for Scholastica knew she was soon about to die. After taking a refection, Scholastica pressed her brother to continue his discourse; but St. Benedict, unwilling to transgress the rules of his order, told her he could not pass the night out of his monastery. Scholastica, finding her brother resolved to leave her, laid her hands on the table, and bent her head in prayer; whereupon such a downfall of rain, mingled with thunder, lightning, and wind, burst over the house, that St. Benedict was compelled to stay. "What have you done, sister?" said St. Benedict. "I asked my brother a favour," she replied, "and he refused me; I asked the same of God, and He granted it me." So St. Benedict continued his discourse on the eternal happiness of the saints, and three days afterwards Scholastica died.—St. Gregory the Great, *Dialogues*, bk. ii. 33, 34.

A heavy downfall of rain wets not Thoretta nor her sheep (twelfth century). One day, when St. Thoretta was in the open fields with her sheep, and no sort of shelter was near at hand, a great storm gathered over her. "Fear not, holy shepherdess! though rain falls in torrents around, and inundates all the neighbourhood, it shall not come nigh thee. Round thee and thy sheep the weather shall be fine and peaceful. New flock of Gideon's wool, thou shalt be dry while all around is wet. Fear not, thou child of grace; for what tempest can harm thee whose trust in God is so great?"—L'abbé Boudant, *Legend of St. Thoretta.* (The whole of this life is written in this pastoral semi-poetical style.)

A heavy fall of rain refuses to wet the book of St. Ubaldus (A.D. 1084–1160). St. Ubaldus left his book behind him under a tree, where he had been sleeping with his companion. It was his book of rules, and here it remained during a heavy fall of rain. Recollecting where he had left it, he returned to the spot, expecting to find it ruined; but, to his great joy, he discovered that though the rain had been very heavy and of long continuance, not a drop had fallen on his book. (See ST. MAIDOC, p. 444.)—L'abbé Hunckler, *Les Saints d'Alsace.*

Repetitions Vain.

MATT. vi. 7. When ye pray, use not vain repetitions, as the heathen do.

LUKE xviii. 5. Because this widow troubleth me, I will avenge her, lest by her continual coming she weary me.

LUKE. xi. 8. Though he will not rise and give him, because he is his friend, yet because of his importunity he will rise and give him as much as he needeth.

The Jewish repetition of the word "Elijah." (1) At the close of the sabbath Elijah sits under the tree of life, and records the merits of those who have kept the day holy. Those Jews who reverence the day, and are very strict, write the words "ELIJAH THE PROPHET" 130 times.—*Talmudic Miscellany*, p. 340.

(2) One of the most curious repetitions is the cabalistic transpositions of the letters in the word "Elijah." Of course, the English word, having six letters, can be transposed in 720 ways, as 720 changes can be rung on six bells; but in Hebrew the word contains only five letters, as in the Greek form "Elias," and five letters can be transposed only 120 different ways: thus—

Elias, Elisa, Elsai, Esail, Saile,
Liase, Liaes, Licsa, Lesai, Esail,
Iasel, Iasle, Iales, Ilesa, Lesai, etc.
(120 changes).

Elijah might run—

Elijah, Ehlija, Ejahli, Eijahl, Elhija,
Elahij, Eljahi, Elhaji, Eljiah, Ealijh
Eahlij, Eajhli, Eaijhl, Ealhij, Ehalij,
etc. (720 changes).

Repetitions in the [Roman] Catholic prayers. In a "Rosary," the *Ave Maria* is repeated 150 times, besides thrice in the preliminary prayers. The *Pater Noster* is repeated fifteen times, and once in the preparation. (See Introduction.)

The Church of England has not escaped this fault. The Lord's Prayer is much too often repeated, especially in the full morning service. And it is doubtful whether the Litany does not err in the same direction, even to weariness:—

Desine deos . . . obtundere . . .
Ut nihil credas intelligere, nisi idem dictum sit centies.
Terence, *Self-tormentor.*

A Mahometan prayer. The Rev. Thomas Harmer, in his *Observations*, says, "The following is the commencement of a Mohammedan prayer now lying before me:—

"O God! O God, O God, O God! O Lord! O Lord! O Lord! O Lord! O thou living, O thou immortal! O thou living, O thou immortal! O thou living, O thou immortal! O thou living, O thou immortal! O Creator of the heavens and the earth! O Creator of the heavens and the earth! O Creator of the heavens and the earth!" . . . (vol. i. p. 56).

The Trisagia is repeated thrice in acknowledgment of the doctrine of the Trinity—at least, so it is said by Christians. Probably Isaiah's idea was a sort of double superlative, like "most highest," two repetitions being equivalent to a superlative. The Mahometans repeat four times, once to each quarter of the universe.

Resist the Devil.

JAMES iv. 7. Resist the devil, and he will flee from you. (See Luke x. 17.)

St. Clare resisted the devil, and he fled (seventh century). St. Clare, going round the monastery of Santa Blandina, on one occasion encountered the devil in person. He was in human form, but of gigantic size and hideous aspect. St. Clare fixed his eyes on the monster, never blanched with fear, but boldly demanded the object of his coming. "To drive you hence," was the ready answer, "for without your interference I should be master here." "Aroint thee, Satan!" cried the saint. "The earth is the Lord's, and the fulness thereof." Then making the sign of the cross, the foul fiend fled howling, and vanished from his sight.—*Les Petits Bollandistes*, vol. i. p. 31.

St. Patrick resisted a legion of devils, and they fled from him (fifth century). When St. Patrick drew near the coast of Ireland, the devils, knowing what a formidable enemy he would prove to be, determined to resist his landing, and accordingly formed a cordon round the coast to bar his passage. "Off!" cried the man of God; and, raising his right hand, he made in the air the sign of the cross. Instantly the whole legion fled, leaving the coast clear. The men with him heard the noise of the howling fiends in their precipitate retreat, but only St. Patrick could see their forms.—Jocelinus the monk, *De Furnesio apud Lancastriensis.*

Returning not Evil for Evil.

1 PET. iii. 9. Not rendering evil for evil, but contrariwise, blessing.

MATT. v. 39. Resist not evil; but whosoever shall smite thee on thy right cheek, turn to him the other also.

ISA. l. 6. I gave My back to the smiters, and My cheeks to them that plucked off the hair.

St. Benet-Joseph Labre being insolently struck, rejoiced in the affront (A.D. 1748-1783). One night, going from Notre Dame des Monts, Benet-Joseph, in the dark, ran against a young man, who struck him with his stick, and then boxed his ears. Benet-Joseph spoke not one word of reproach. At another time, in the Corso, he was insulted by some peasants, but instead of quickening his pace, he walked along more slowly than before, rejoicing that he was thought worthy to be insulted and persecuted.—R. P. Desnoyers, *Life of Benet-Joseph Labre.*

St. Gertrude of Ostend returned good for evil (died A.D. 1356). St. Gertrude of Ostend was affianced to a young man whom she dearly loved; but, shortly before the day of espousal, the lover jilted her for one with a better dowry. The new wife in due time had a son, and both mother and child were expected to die; but St. Gertrude by fervent prayer obtained their restoration to health, not rendering evil for evil, but contrariwise, blessing.—*Vita Sanctorum* (Bollandists).

Reviled and Persecuted.

MATT. v. 11, 12. Blessed are ye, when men shall revile you, and persecute you, and shall say all manner of evil against you falsely, for My sake. Rejoice, and be exceeding glad: for great is your reward in heaven.

St. Peter reviled and persecuted because St. Agnes, St. Catherine, and St. Cecilia appear to him in his cell (A.D. 1206-1252). While St. Peter of Verona was in the monastery of St. John the Baptist, in Como, St. Catherine, St. Agnes, and St. Cecilia visited him in his cell, and conferred so familiarly with him, that a man passing by heard them, and laid an information against him for admitting women into his chamber. The case was heard before the whole chapter, and St. Peter was banished to Ancona, and forbidden to appear any more in public. The man of God grieved sore at this unjust sentence, and cried, "Why, oh why, my God, hast Thou suffered this? Thou knowest my innocence; remove, then, this great scandal, which is an offence to thy holy Church." Christ said to him, "And I, Peter, was I not innocent, when men said I was a drunkard, and in league with the devil? Learn of Me to suffer patiently, and remember what I said, 'Blessed are ye, when men shall revile you, and say all manner of evil against you falsely: for so persecuted they the prophets which were before you.'" Then was St. Peter comforted; and in due time, his innocence being established, he was recalled from banishment, and his fame stood higher than ever. —*Acta Sanctorum* (Bollandists), April 29.

Rivers dried up or diverted.

PSALM lxxiv. 15. Thou driedst up mighty rivers.

ISA. xlii. 15. I will make the rivers islands, and will dry up the pools.

ISA. xliv. 27. The Lord saith to the deep, Be dry, and I will dry up thy rivers.

Sinvaldus commands the river Bobbio to change its course (A.D. 627). When the mill of Bobbio monastery was in great danger of being swept away by the river Bobbio, which had overflowed its banks, St. Attalus sent his deacon Sinvaldus with his abbatial cross, and charged him to make the sign of the cross, and command the river to flow in another course. Sinvaldus did as he was directed, and the river obeyed. It not only drew back the water which threatened the mill, but made for itself a new channel further away. Sinvaldus, amazed at this obedience, told the abbot, and was commanded not to talk of the miracle during the lifetime of St. Attalus.—*Acta Sanctorum* (Bollandists), vol. ii. March. (See Bede, vol. iii.)

The life of St. Attalus was written by Jonas, a Scotchman, one of his disciples.

Roses from the Blood of Saints.

The Adonis flower. The flowers of the Adonis plant, especially before they are expanded, being globular and deep scarlet, resemble small drops of blood; hence French peasants call the plant the "Blood-drop" (*Goutte de sang*). The poetic Greeks, tracing the same resemblance, connected these blood-drops with young Adonis, who, they say, was gored by a wild boar. When Venus heard of this mishap she flew to the boy's succour, and her tears, mingling with the blood, converted the blood-drops into flowers, which still bear the name of the young huntsman.—Bion.

A few conceits about flowers springing from blood will show what a favourite the notion is with imaginative minds.

Anacreon's conceit respecting the origin of the red rose. The erotic poet Anacreon says, when the goddess of Love and Beauty first arose from the briny waves, and set foot on dry land, the earth produced the rose in commemoration of that happy event.—Anacreon, *Ode* 55.

Gesner's conceit of the origin of the blush rose. Gesner says that Bacchus was enamoured of a nymph, who fled at his approach, and hid herself among some bushes in which she became entangled. The wine-god approached, saying, "Fear not; I am Bacchus, god of wine, of joy, of youth." So saying, he seized the maid, who kissed the eyes of the amorous god, and blushed. Bacchus, in acknowledgment, touched the bush which had detained the fugitive, and commanded that it should ever after be covered with the flowers of love and beauty; accordingly it became the blush-rose bush.

Rapin's conceit of the origin of the rose and its suitors. Father Rapin, in his poem called *The Garden*, says, Rhoda queen of Corinth, whose beauty exceeded that of the sea-nymphs, being distracted by her many suitors, shut herself up in the temple of Diana. Three of her lovers, more importunate than the rest, intruded into this sanctuary, and tried to force her thence. A scuffle ensued, when Apollo interfered, changed Rhoda into a rose, and her three suitors into a worm, a fly, and a butterfly.

A new suggestion of the origin of the rose and its thorn. The queen of Beauty one day strayed with Love till both were tired; when they stepped into Flora's bower to rest awhile. Here they found Adonis asleep; and while the queen stooped to kiss the boy, young Love drew his bow and pierced her to the heart. The ichor which flowed from Beauty's wound became a rose; and in order to perpetuate the story of its origin, the goddess decreed that the shaft which wounded her should grow for ever on its stem.—E. C. B.

(The author apologizes for introducing this conceit.)

Moslem tradition of the white and yellow rose. According to a Mussulman tradition the white and yellow roses are thus accounted for: When Mahomet took his journey to heaven, the sweat which fell on the earth from the prophet's forehead produced *white* roses, and that which fell from Alborak (the animal on which he rode) produced *yellow* ones.

The blood of Zillah the origin of white roses. Sir John Mandeville says that a Jewish maid of Bethlehem (whom Southey names Zillah) was beloved by Hamuel, a brutish sot. Zillah rejected his suit; and Hamuel, in revenge, accused her of offences for which she was condemned to be burnt alive. When brought to the stake, the flames burned Hamuel to a cinder, but did no harm to Zillah. There she stood in a garden of roses; for "as the fyre began to brenne about hire, she made her preyeres to oure Lord, and anon was the fyre quenched and oute, and the brondes that weren brennynge becomen white roseres . . . These werein the first roseres that ever ony man saughe."—Sir John Mandeville, *Voiage and Traivaille.*

The blood of St. Lucian engenders roses (first century). No one will for a moment suppose that the seven conceits of blood-flowers given above have any pretence beyond poetic fancy, but the legends which follow claim to be historic facts. The first shall be given in the *ipsissima verba* of the "historian" himself: "C'est une chose véritable" (dit Mons. Louvet), "que les gouttes de sang du chef de notre martyr [St. Lucian] dont la terre fut empourprée, engendrèrent telle quantité de rosiers garnis de roses vermeilles, qui ont paru jusqu'à présent, que le lieu du martyre s'appelle encore *La Rosière*, pour signifier, comme dit Tertullien, que le sang des martyrs est une graine et une semence des belles fleurs du paradis."—Louvet, *History and Antiquities of the Diocese of Bouvet*, vol. i. p. 387.

St. Francis, by the sign of the cross, converts thorns and brambles, covered with the blood of St. Benedict, into roses (sixth century). When St. Benedict, afterwards abbot of Mount Cassino, first retired to the cavern in Subiaco, he was not more than fifteen years of age, and was greatly harassed by the recollection of a young woman with whom he had been in love. He felt sometimes that he must perforce return to the world; but when the heat on him was greatest, he would wallow naked for hours among thorns and brambles, till his whole body was one vast bleeding wound. It was thus by his blood that he quenched the heat of his carnal passion. When, at a future period, St. Francis went to visit the rocks of Subiaco, where Benedict had his cavern, he made the sign of the cross over these thorns and brambles, so often covered with the blood of the young solitary, and they were converted into roses, which have given health to many a pilgrim.—St. Gregory the Great, *Dialogues*, bk. ii.

St. Benedict is sometimes represented rolling in a bramble bush; and the monks of Subiaco show a thorny bush, the leaves of which are marked "d'un petit serpent noir," which they say is a souvenir of the triumph of St. Benedict when a youth over "that old serpent the devil."

Jesus Christ sends St. Agnes of Mount Pulciano a rose in midwinter (A.D. 1274–1317). One winter, two hermits, who had heard of the wonderful things told of St. Agnes, came to pay her a visit. After a long conversation on the spiritual life, Agnes invited them to dine with her. Before any food was brought in, all of a sudden there appeared a plate, in the middle of which was a beautiful rose. "Fathers," said St. Agnes, "Jesus Christ has been kind enough, in the very middle of winter, when the frost has cut off all earthly flowers, to send us this rose from the garden of paradise. This, fathers, is a symbol of how greatly your words have refreshed my soul." The hermits went away enchanted, each saying to the other that the words of the holy Agnes dropped like manna into their souls.—Raymond of Capua, *Life of St. Agnes.*

The bread of Germana Cousin of Pibrac turned to flowers (A.D. 1579–1601). Germana Cousin of Pibrac was a poor shepherdess, but very charitable. She gave so much to the poor, that her mother-in-law felt certain she must rob the larder. One day, in the depth of winter, the mother-in-law fancied she saw Germana hide food in her apron, and ran after her with a stick, intent on chastising her severely. Two of the neighbours happened to see her, and followed to screen the shepherd girl from the angry woman, whose dislike to Germana was well known. They joined the woman just as she reached her daughter-in-law, and commanded her to show what she had in her apron. On doing so, the apron was full of nosegays tied in bunches. It was midwinter, but even in summer-time no such flowers grew in the neighbourhood of Pibrac. They all felt convinced the flowers were from paradise. The incident spread in all directions, and even the hard heart of the mother-in-law was softened. (See the next two articles.)—M. L. Veuillot, *Vie de la Bienheureuse Germaine.*

Bread turned to roses in the lap of St. Rosaline (A.D. 1263-1329). One day the poor, pressed by hunger, crowded round the door of the chateaux of Villeneuve, begging bread. Rosaline, the daughter of the squire, heard them, but her father paid no attention to their importunity. Rosaline went secretly into the larder, and filled her apron full of food to distribute to them, but the squire came across her, and said sharply, "Rosaline, what have you got in your apron?" "Only roses," said the girl; and opening her apron, it was full of the most magnificent roses. God, to show His approval of her charity, screened her from the anger of her father by a miracle. The squire, ravished by this testimony of God to Rosaline's sanctity, told his servants they were never more to oppose her wishes, but were to give her full liberty to do what she thought proper. (See the article before and after this.)—Count H. de Villeneuve-Flayose, *Life of St. Rosaline de Villeneuve.* (See also *Acta Sanctorum*, vol. ii. June 11.)

This is a mere repetition of the tale told of Elizabeth of Hungary (1207–1231) a few years previously. Both are open to the same grave objections. Rosaline knew she was doing wrong, because she told a lie to cover her wrong-doing. That the lie was covered by a "miracle" did not alter its character, though it induced the father to condone the offence.

Bread turned to roses in the lap of Elizabeth of Hungary (A.D. 1207–1231). Elizabeth of Hungary was very profuse in her alms to the poor; her husband thought her too lavish, and she knew it. One day, when the landgrave was out hunting, Elizabeth and a favourite domestic went to the larder, and filled the skirts of their gowns with bread, eggs, and other food, to distribute to the poor. Just as they came out of the house, the landgrave met them; and astonished to see them so heavily laden, said, "Heyday, Elizabeth, what have you got here?" "Only roses," said the landgravine; and opening her lap, behold, it was filled with the most exquisite red and white roses. This was the more surprising, seeing it was not the season for flowers. The landgrave was amazed, and went up to salute his wife, but stopped short on seeing a luminous cross upon her head. He told her to do what she thought proper, and continued his way to Wartenburg, taking one of the roses with him.—Count of Montalembert, *History of St. Elizabeth of Hungary*, etc.

Precisely the same tale is told of Rosaline of Villeneuve a few years later. (See THE SCHÖNBERG COTTA FAMILY, below.)

(See the converse, flowers turned into bread—STONES MADE BREAD, p. 297.)

Practical application of St. Elizabeth's example. In the *Schönberg-Cotta Family* Elsè tells us they had a picture of St. Elizabeth and the roses, of which all the children were very fond, because the landgravine was their neighbour. She lived in the old castle of Wartburg, "not above three hundred years ago," and often walked through the streets of Eisenach, where the Schönberg-Cotta family lived. She says, "There is one thing in St. Elizabeth's history which once brought Fritz and me into great trouble and perplexity. When we were little children, our grandmother told us about the holy landgravine emptying her husband's larder to feed the poor. Now, we thought what was right for the saint must certainly be right for us; so we resolved to imitate St. Elizabeth. There was in the next street a poor old woman, with a great many orphan grandchildren, and her we determined to help, like St. Elizabeth. Christmas Eve was close at hand, and for a rarity there were some meat and apple-pies in our store-room. We crept into the room in twilight, as St. Elizabeth did, and I filled my pinafore with the pies, meat, and cakes, and stole out to give our booty to the old woman. Next morning was Christmas Day, and the larder was empty. There was no Christmas dinner. The younger children cried, mother looked distressed, and father was very angry. He thought it was the cat or else rats, but our grandmother said very quietly, 'I never heard of cats and rats eating pie-dishes.' Fritz and I looked at each other, and began to fancy we had somehow done wrong, when little Christopher said, 'I saw Fritz and Elsè carry away the pies last night.' 'Elsè, Fritz,' said our father, 'what does this mean?' I would have confessed, but remembering the answer of St. Elizabeth, replied, 'No, Christopher, they were not pies, but roses.' 'Roses,' said mother very gravely, 'at Christmas?' I hoped the pies would reappear, but they did not, and everything went against us. 'Fritz,' said father, 'tell the truth, or I will flog you soundly.' This was different to the legend, but I instantly cried out, 'It is my fault, father; we took the things to the poor woman in the next street.' 'Then you are no better than thieves,' said father, 'and shall have no dinner for your pains. As for you, Elsè, go to your room at once, for telling a lie.' All this was very different to the history of St. Elizabeth. While I sat shivering in my room, aunt Ursula entered. She had divined in a moment the mistake, and said, laughing, 'My poor Elsè, you are too young yet awhile to imitate our patron saint. What may do for St. Elizabeth will not do for you, any more than it will do for me to wander to Rome with eleven thousand young ladies, like my namesake.' Ever after I understood it was not for us to follow the example of the saints, but to try and keep the ten commandments. And yet to think that St. Elizabeth, a real canonized saint, whose picture is over the altar of our church, whose bones are laid up in reliquaries—I could not make it out, and concluded it must be because she had lived three hundred years ago, and that if I had lived in those times it would have been all right."—*Elsè's Story*, ch. i.

The rose-girl of Salency (sixth century). St. Medard, bishop of Noyon, established in the sixth century a beautiful institution for good conduct, which continues to the present day. It is known by the name of the "Fête de la Rosière," held every third year. The prize given is a chaplet of roses and a purse of £25 to the girl selected by the parish as the best deserving. The following rules are indispensable: the girl herself must be irreproachable; so must her father, mother, sisters, and other near kinsfolk to the fourth generation. A mere scandal will suffice to disqualify a competitor. Three girls are presented, a month in advance, to the seigneur of Salency, who has the choice of selecting one as the Rosière. The decision is publicly announced, and the two competitors with their friends are invited to investigate the choice, and either confirm it or dispute it. June 8 is the day of the fête, at two o'clock. The Rosière is dressed in white, powdered, her hair curled and falling on her shoulders; and accompanied by her parents, brothers, and sisters, and twelve girls all in white and blue ribbons and sashes, she goes in procession to the hall with a band of music. The seigneur or his son and heir, with his steward and a band of music, goes to meet her, and lead her to the parish church to attend vespers. The clergy then form a procession, and all follow to the chapel of St. Medard, when the curé places the chaplet on the girl's head, and gives her the purse of gold. This ceremony was interrupted at the Revolution, but was reinstituted in 1812, and the corporation guarantees three hundred francs.—Godescard, *Année Litteraire*, 1766, No. 19.

The lily of Quito (A.D. 1645). Marianne de Jesus, daughter of don Jerome of Quito, lived a life of almost unparalleled abstinence and self-denial. She allowed herself only three hours' sleep, and that on a hard triangular board, drank nothing at all, and took no food except the Eucharist. Mgr. Guérin says, "Le Seigneur, pour augmenter les mérites de sa fidèle servante," caused her to suffer from dropsy, and goes on to say, "elle fut saignée cent cinquante fois en deux ans!!" The blood drawn from her was thrown into a ditch, and after her death this blood was the bed of "d'un lis d'une beauté admirable," which was called "The lily of Quito."—*Vies des Saints*, vol. vi. p. 233.

Satan as an Angel of Light.

2 Cor. xi. 14. Satan himself is transformed into an angel of light.

The devil in the guise of Jesus Christ and also in that of the Virgin Mary appears to St. Catherine of Bologna (A.D. 1413–1463). One day, when St. Catherine of Bologna was rudely assaulted by the devil, she said to him, "You cannot deceive me." God, in order to humble her, resolved to show her that Satan was, after all, more habile than she was. He presented himself to her in the form of Jesus Christ, and not long after he appeared disguised as the Virgin Mary, and suggested to her thoughts of insubordination. The resentment she felt interfered with her prayers and reading. She grew less vigilant, and almost succumbed to the adversary, when God by His grace came to the rescue; for He would not suffer her to be tempted above what she could bear, but with the temptation made a way of escape. The Saviour showed her that the temptation she had suffered was the wile of the devil, permitted by God for a little time to teach her diffidence, humility, and self-abasement.

St. Catherine afterwards wrote a book, in which she recounts her temptations, and the graces whereby she was enabled to overcome them. This book she afterwards burnt, but she then wrote *The Seven Spiritual Arms*, in which she speaks of herself under a pseudonym. The object of the book is to warn against self-confidence, and the wiles of the devil.—Paleotti, *Life of St. Catherine of Bologna.* (This life, written about fifty years after the death of St. Catherine, is inserted in the seventeenth volume of the *Ecclesiastical Annals.*)

Satan falling.

Luke x. 18. I beheld Satan, as lightning, fall from heaven.

St. Zeno saw a devil tumble into a ditch

(third century). Between the age of thirteen and fourteen, Zeno one day accompanied the bishop of Verona, whose clerk he was, down the street of the city, and burst into an uncontrollable fit of laughter. The bishop rebuked the boy for his unseemly conduct, and demanded the reason. Zeno replied "qu'il venait de voir un diablotin dormant tranquillement sur la queue de la robe d'une dame qui marchait devant eux ; mais que cette dame, ayant ramené sa jupe avec une prestesse toute féminine, le diable était tombé dans l'eau fangeuse du ruisseau, ce dont il faisait pitoyable mine." In Christian art Zeno is drawn with a background representing a devil falling into a slough.—*Les Petits Bollandistes*, vol. iv. p 351.

Sea giving up the Dead.

REV. xx. 13. The sea gave up the dead which were in it.

The sea gives up the dead bodies of Peter, Gorgonius, and Dorothëus. When Peter, Gorgonius, and Dorothëus were martyred, by order of the emperor Diocletian, their bodies were buried by some Christians; but when the emperor heard that certain devotees visited these bodies to offer up their prayers on the spot of their interment, he commanded them to be disinterred, and cast into the sea. God would not, however, suffer these holy relics to be lost, for the sea threw them up again, and the Christians again buried them. The body of Gorgonius was afterwards carried to Rome, and buried in the "Via Lavicana," between two bay trees. —Eusebius (bishop of Cæsarea, A.D. 630), *Ecclesiastical History.*

(For other examples consult the Index.)

Sell all thou hast.

MATT. xix. 21. Jesus saith to him, If thou wilt be perfect, go and sell that thou hast, and give to the poor, and thou shalt have treasure in heaven: and come and follow Me.

Roger Crab sold all he had and gave to the poor (A.D. 1680). Roger Crab served seven years in the parliamentary army, but was imprisoned two years for breach of discipline. At his discharge he set up in Chesham, Buckinghamshire, as a "haberdasher of hats," but having got together property, he resolved to follow the injunction given by Christ to the rich young man, and accordingly sold all he had, distributing the proceeds among the poor. He now retired to a shed or hut, situated on a rood of land (quarter of an acre), near Ickenham, Middlesex, where he limited his expenses to three farthings a day. He ate no meat, and drank only water. His quarter of an acre of land supplied him with all his food, which consisted of bread, bran, herbs, roots, dock-leaves, mallows, and grass. He dressed in a sackcloth frock, and wore nothing round his neck. This, he said, was consistent with the injunction of Christ, and in accordance with the habits of the Rechabites (*Jer.* xxxv.), highly commended by the Lord, because they "neither planted vineyards, nor built houses, nor drank wine." Roger Crab wrote a memoir of himself, and calls the *natural* man the "old man," meaning his body. He says, "Instead of strong drinks I gave the old man a cup of water; and instead of roast mutton and rabbit, I gave him broth thickened with bran, or bran-pudding relished with chopped turnip-leaves. The law of my members had a shrewd skirmish with the law of my mind; but the wonderful love of God, well pleased with the battle, filled the new man full of love, peace, and content; and he has now become more humble, for he will eat dock-leaves, mallows, and grass, and yet give God more thanks for it than formerly for roast meat and wines." This "Old English Hermit" of the Commonwealth not only thus afflicted himself, but he was also greatly persecuted by his neighbours and others. Some thought him a wizard, some tore his few rags, some whipped him. If this "mad fellow" had been a Roman Catholic, living in a Roman Catholic country, he would probably have been canonized; but being a Protestant, living in a Protestant kingdom, he is ruthlessly rebuked as an insane old fool. He died Sept. 11, 1680, and was buried in Stepney churchyard.—See Chambers, *Book of Days*, and the *Harleian Miscellany.*

St. Serapion the Sindonite sold all he had, and himself too (died A.D. 388). St. Serapion, an Egyptian, not only sold all that he had, but himself too, several times for the benefit of the poor. This made St. John the almsgiver say, "Can we flatter ourselves on our gift to the poor, who have given to them of our abundance? Here is one who gave them not only all he had, but himself also; not once, but again and again." The first time he sold himself was to a comedian for twenty pieces of silver.

The comedian was an idolater, and Serapion became his slave that he might teach him the truth as it is in Jesus. Having converted his master and all his family, and having induced him to quit the stage, Serapion had his liberty given him. His master offered him the twenty pieces of silver he had bargained for, but Serapion refused to take it. He had not been long free when, wishing to relieve a distressed widow, he sold himself a second time, and gave the price to the widow. After having served this second master a term of years, he again obtained his liberty, and received from him a cloak, a tunic, an under-garment, and a book of the Gospels. He was scarce gone from the door, when he gave his cloak to one poor man, and his tunic to another. He was now reduced to a single garment, and that of linen. A stranger coming up asked him who had stripped him of his clothes, and left him thus. Serapion replied, "This book," showing the stranger the Gospels. Not long afterwards, he sold his book to relieve a man in distress. Scarcely had he so done when an old acquaintance asked him what had become of his book; and he replied, "It cried unto me so incessantly, 'Sell *all* thou hast, and give unto the poor,' that I sold it, and gave the money to Christ's poor brethren." He then sold himself a third time. The fourth time he sold himself was to a Manichee, at Lacedæmon, whom he served for two years. Him also and all his family he converted to the faith as it is in Jesus. Several other times he sold himself, and at length died in Egypt, in a desert, at the age of sixty years, March 2, A.D. 388.—Alban Butler, *Lives of the Saints*, March 21.

Examples of persons selling all they possessed and giving to the poor are extremely numerous, but the case of Serapion is the most striking, and that of Crab is a good practical example. If every one sold all he had and gave to the poor, no one would have anything to give; for the poor must give of their poverty as well as the rich of their abundance, and no one would have anything at all.

Separation from Christ Impossible.

Rom. viii. 35–39. Who shall separate us from the love of Christ? Shall tribulation, or distress, or persecution, or famine, or nakedness, or peril, or sword? . . . I am persuaded that neither death, nor life, nor angels, nor principalities, nor powers, . . nor any other creature, shall be able to separate us from the love of God, which is in Christ Jesus our Lord.

Not all the malice of Satan could separate St. Antony from the love of Christ (fourth century). St. Antony, resolved to live as much as possible out of the world, retired to the tombs; but Satan, terrified lest he should turn his empire upside down, brought with him a legion of devils, resolved to bring him to submission. Life and death are not in the power of Satan, but disease and persecutions are. The devils could not take away his life, but they beat him till he was speechless, and was found next day apparently quite dead. Being carried to the village church, he was laid on the floor, but at vespers he revived, and begged to be taken back to the tombs. This was done, and as he lay prostrate, wholly unable to kneel, he cried out with a shout, "Here am I, Antony. I will not fly; so come and do your worst. Neither tribulation, nor distress, nor famine, nor stripes, nor peril, nor sword, shall separate me from the love of Christ." Then he sang, "Though a host were laid against me, yet shall not my heart be afraid." During the night the devils made such an uproar, that all hell seemed to be let loose. The walls broke in; the shapes of every sort of wild beast and noxious reptile stood staring at the prostrate saint. Lions roared, and spread their bristly manes; bears growled, wild bulls bellowed, snakes hissed; leopards and wolves, asps and scorpions, each in its native fashion, showed its wrath. There lay the man of God unmoved by terror, and said, "Fools and idiots, if there were any power in you, any one of you would suffice to destroy me; but seeing ye are weak, ye hope to frighten me." Being thus mocked, the devils gnashed their teeth, and howled horribly. Suddenly a light gleamed; angels came down, and the demons fled. "Why," said Antony, "did ye not stop this unequal contest?" "There has no temptation happened to you, O man of God, beyond what you were able to bear," said the angels; "and we were ever by. We waited to see the end; and, seeing thou hast fought a good fight and prevailed, henceforth the Lord will be thy shield and place of defence." St. Antony now stood on his feet; his strength was renewed; and, in the fulness of his new life, he gave praise and glory to God. He was only thirty-five years old when he endured this conflict, and won this victory, wrestling not against flesh and blood, but against the rulers of the darkness of this world, and spiritual wickedness in high places.—St. Athanasius, *Life of St. Antony the Great.*

This is very like the combat of Christian in *Pilgrim's Progress.*

Serpent Cursed.

GEN. iii. 14. The Lord said to the serpent, Because thou hast done this, thou art cursed above all cattle, and above every beast of the field. Upon thy belly shalt thou go, and dust shalt thou eat all the days of thy life.

Tradition. The punishment of the serpent was twofold: (1) Michael was commanded to cut off its legs; and (2) the serpent was doomed to feed on human excrements ever after.

"Y llamô [Dios] a la serpiente, y a Michael, aquel que tiene la espada de Dios, y le dixo; Aquesta sierpe es acelerada, echala la primera del parayso, y cortale las piernas, y si quisiere caminar, arrastrara la vida per tierra. Y llamô a Satanas, el qual vino riendo, y dixole; Porque tu reprobo has engañado a aquestos, y los has hecho immundos? Yo quiero que toda immundicia suya, y de todos sus hijos, en saliendo de sus cuerpos entre por tu boca, porque en verdad ellos haran penitencia, y tu quedaras harto de immundicia."—*Gospel of Barnabas.*

Sheep Obedient.

JOHN x. 3. The sheep hear his voice.

The sheep of Benedicta Rencurel hear her voice and obey it (A.D. 1647–1718). One day St. Benedicta was told of a woman who had lost all consciousness, and was on the verge of the grave. Without delay she ran to the church, collecting as she went all the children she met with on the way, and with these children she recited the rosary with great fervour. Before she started, however, she said to her sheep, "Be good while I am absent. You are not to touch that meadow, nor yet that one yonder, nor yet this one, remember." The sheep heard her voice, followed her directions, and remained browsing on the spot where she left them.—*Les Petits Bollandistes*, vol. v. p. 218. (See also *Notre Dame de France.*)

St. Thoretta's model sheep (twelfth century). While St. Thoretta was engaged in her devotions, her guardian angel took care of her sheep. One day, seeking for better pasture, a severe storm gathered in the horizon, but a voice said to her, "Fear not, virtuous maiden; though the rain falls in torrents, and floods the whole country, the sky over thy head shall be ever calm, and the pasture of thy sheep shall be ever fresh. As Gideon's fleece was dry when all around was wet, so shall it be with thee." The sheep recognized the sanctity of their shepherdess, and while she was occupied with divine meditations they would group around her, nibbling the grass close by; and if she went to confession or church, she had only to plant her staff amidst her flock, and the sheep would take care of themselves during her absence, and no wolf or other savage animal would attempt to molest them. One day the river overflowed so that the sheep could not go home, but St. Thoretta calling to mind that promise, "If ye had faith, even as much as a grain of mustard seed, you should be able to move mountains," made the sign of the cross, touched the water with her staff, and immediately a dry path was made for her and her sheep to pass over.—L'abbé Boudant, *Legende de Sainte Thorette.*

Silence.

JAMES i. 26. If any man among you seem to be religious, and bridleth not his tongue, this man's religion is vain.

JAMES iii. 2. If any man offend not in word, the same is a perfect man, able to bridle his whole body also.

ISA. liii. 7. He was oppressed, and He was afflicted, yet He opened not His mouth: He is brought as a lamb to the slaughter, and as a sheep before her shearers is dumb, so He openeth not His mouth.

MATT. xxvi. 63. When Jesus was brought as a malefactor before Caiaphas, and the false witnesses had stated their charges against Him, the high priest arose, and said to Him, Answerest Thou nothing? What is it which these witness against Thee? But Jesus held His peace.

MATT. xxvii. 13, 14. Again, when arraigned before the Roman proconsul, and accused by the chief priests and elders, He answered nothing. Then said Pilate to Him, Hearest Thou not how many things they witness against Thee? But he answered him to never a word, insomuch that the governor marvelled greatly.

PSALM xxxix. 1, 2. I said, I will take heed to my ways, that I sin not with my tongue: I will keep my mouth with a bridle, while the wicked is before me. I was dumb with silence, I held my peace, even from good words.

St. Andronicus and his wife Anastasia dwell together in speechless silence. St. Andronicus was a banker of Alexandria, and he married Anastasia, a banker's daughter. They had two children, who died, and then Andronicus and his wife resolved to lead the life of recluses. After visiting the Holy Land, they retired to the laura of the Thebaïd, and occupied two separate cells; but Anastasia assumed male attire, and called herself Athanasius. In this retirement they vowed to observe perpetual silence. After living separately for some years, "Athanasius" proposed to her husband to build a cell in which they both might live together. This was done, and they lived together in absolute silence, neither speaking to the other to the day of their death. "Athanasius" died first, and not till then did the other solitaries of the laura know she was a woman, and the wife of Andronicus. The religious, not only of the laura, but of all Alexandria, attended the funeral, and gave great praise to God, that she had so triumphed over the world, the flesh, and the devil.—*Acta Sanctorum* (Bollandists), Oct. 9.

A laura is an assemblage of huts or cells, each occupied by its own inmate; a monastery is a religious house with several cells under one roof. A laura resembles a block of almshouses, a monastery resembles a workhouse.

St. Arsenius asking God, "What he must do to be saved," was answered by a voice from heaven, "Flee the society of man, and preserve inviolable silence" (A.D. 450). St. Arsenius was a native of Rome, of an opulent and noble family, in the fifth Christian century. Praying to the Saviour to know what he must do to be saved, he was answered by a voice from heaven, "Arsenius, the foundation of the edifice of salvation consists in these two things: Flee from the world and the society of man, and keep thy tongue in inviolable silence." St. Theodore tells us that, having heard this direction, Arsenius observed it to the letter. He lived in a desert far from the haunts of man, and even when strangers came to visit him, observed the strictest silence. On one occasion several hermits from Alexandria came to see him, and being told of their visit by his disciples, Arsenius said, "Entertain them hospitably, but leave me to contemplate heavenly things." On another occasion a hermit took some brothers to see the famous solitary. Arsenius sent word by one of his disciples that the visitors were welcome to eat and drink, but that he saw no one. One of the strangers, thinking to force him to speak, intruded into his private cell; but Arsenius uttered not a single word.—Michel Ange Marin, *Lives of the Fathers of the Eastern Deserts.*

St. Benet-Joseph was surnamed the Silent (A.D. 1748–1783). It was a favourite maxim of Benet-Joseph, "Keep your mouth under doors and bolts," and his biographers tell us it was quite impossible to be more guarded than he was not to be taxed for speech. He was never the first to break silence, except from some motive of charity, and not unfrequently he answered by some motion of the head, in preference to open speech. For whole months he never uttered a word, so that he was usually called Benet-Joseph the Silent.—R. P. Desnoyers, *Life of St. Benet-Joseph.*

St. Catherine of Siena observed unbroken silence for three years (A.D. 1347–1380). When St. Catherine of Siena was admitted into the order called "The Sisters of Penitence," she imposed upon herself inviolable silence for three years, during all which time she never uttered a word except in confession to her father-confessor.—*Acta Sanctorum* (Bollandists), vol. iii. April 30.

Silence one of the vows of the abbey of Cluny. Odo, abbot of Cluny in the tenth century, observed almost absolute silence, and demanded the same of the religious under him. In fact, the chief conversation carried on by the brothers was by signs, and when two of the monks were taken prisoners by the Normands, who devastated Poitiers and Tours, they observed the same unbroken silence even when beaten and wounded, although their obstinate silence increased the irritation of the conquerors.—P. Giry, *History of the Abbey of Cluny.*

St. Emiliana of Florence kept annually the fast of the tongue (A.D. 1246). St. Emiliana was always careful to abstain from uttering a single unnecessary word; during Lent she kept absolute silence for forty days, and for the rest of the year observed the fast of silence three days a week. When on Saturdays she went to receive the communion, her companion had most strict orders not to speak to her a single word on any subject whatever. She used to say, "When God is speaking to the soul, it is unmannerly to interrupt Him."—A. Stolz, *Acta Sanctorum* (May 19).

St. Euthymius lives three years in speechless silence (A.D. 824–886). St. Euthymius retired to Mount Athos, as a solitary, with a monk named Theocteristês; but Theocteristês soon left him, not being able to endure the austerities of his companion. Euthymius then found another companion, named Joseph, and went to live on Hagion-Oros with the Athonites. Here he agreed with Joseph to live on herbs "to expiate their sins." Succeeding in this, Euthymius proposed that they should live three years without speaking a word. At the end of a year Joseph, tired of this absolute silence and diet of herbs, left his companion, but Euthymius persevered to the end. He then retired to a tower in Thessalonica, "like a new Simeon Stylitês," and having lived as a pillar-saint for some time, he returned to Mount Athos.—St. Basil (archbishop of Thessalonica), *Life of St. Euthymius.*

St. John the Silent lived four years in his cell without speaking a single word to any one (A.D. 454–558). After John the Silent left the Grand Laura, and was allotted a hermitage, he lived four years in his cell without speaking a word to any one, except once, and that was to the patriarch when he dedicated the church of the Grand Laura (see p. 454, *n.*). In A.D. 503 the monks of the Grand Laura revolted, and John the Silent, that he might in no wise be dragged into this unhappy rebellion, withdrew into a neighbouring wilderness, where he lived six years in absolute silence. On one occasion a man named George, who seems to have gauged the idiosyncrasy of the hermit, brought his son, who was possessed of the devil, and, without speaking a word, laid the child at the door of the hermit's cell. St. John saw the child, and, without a single word, made on its forehead the sign of the cross. All was dumb-show, but the child was exorcised, and the father received it perfectly restored and in his right mind.—Cyril (the monk, a disciple), *Life of St. John the Silent.*

We are told that a lady, who had her finger severely bitten by a parrot, called on Abernethy, and knowing his idiosyncrasy, held out her finger without speaking a word. Said Abernethy, "Bite?" The lady replied, "Parrot." "Poultice," said Abernethy, and the interview ended. When the finger was healed, and the lady offered Abernethy his fees, he put the money away from him, and said, "No, you are a sensible woman. Good morning."

Absolute silence was enjoined by John-Joseph de la Croix (A.D. 1654–1734). John-Joseph de la Croix not only gave to his monastery at Afila a simple undecorated exterior, with rooms of small proportions, he also required of its inmates absolute silence, the most profound retirement, and an exact submission to orders without any right of private judgment.—Cardinal Wiseman, *Evangelic Demonstrations*, vol. xvi., of Mons. Migne.

St. Pacificus was noted for his restraint over his tongue (A.D. 1653–1721). St. Pacificus had well learnt that difficult task of bridling the tongue. His superior, wishing to put him to the proof, called him a hypocrite, who thought to break into heaven, like a burglar. Pacificus made no reply; but thought of those words of the Lord Jesus, "Blessed are ye, when men shall revile you, and say all manner of evil against you falsely, for My sake. Rejoice, and be exceeding glad: for great is your reward in heaven." One day a man, who hated him, spouted a mouthful of wine in his face, and called him a drunkard. Pacificus wiped his face quietly, but spoke not a single word. So was it when the soldiery spat on the face of Jesus; as a lamb before its shearers is dumb, so He opened not His mouth.—L'abbé Daras, *The Saints, etc., of the Eighteenth Century.*

St. Peter of Alcantara lived for three years in speechless silence (A.D. 1499–1562). St. Peter of Alcantara was noted for his long silence. For three years he carried pebbles in his mouth to prevent his speaking; "for," said he, "life and death are in the power of the tongue."—Father Talon, *Life of St. Peter of Alcantara.*

St. Poma was noted for her silence (first century). St. Poma was contemporary with the apostles, her conversion being placed in the year A.D. 53, when Dionysius the Areopagite received the faith, and Paul preached on Mars' Hill. She was very beautiful and of an illustrious family, rich and held in great honour. After her conversion she renounced all the pomps and vanities of the world, and went clad in humility. She imposed on herself the law of silence, "the guard of virginity;" and made a compact with her tongue, regulating the hours when she might talk, and when to observe absolute silence. As a rule she never opened her lips except when obliged to speak, or when her heart overflowed with a sense of the love of God.—L'abbé Boitel, *Beauties of the History of Champagne.*

Silence enjoined, even at meals, among the Tabennites. The Tabennites were founded by St. Pacomius (A.D. 292–348). Every moment of the day was occupied, and silence most rigorously enjoined. If at any time one of the monks wanted anything, he indicated it by signs. When they moved from place to place, they were required to meditate on some passage of Scripture; and at meals every one drew his hood over his head that he might not even see his neighbour.—His life by a monk of Tabenna, one of his disciples.

St. Vincent de Paul was especially famous for the restraint he put upon his tongue (A.D. 1576–1660). St. Vincent de Paul was complete master of his tongue, which St. James calls indomitable: "Every kind of beasts, and of birds, and of serpents, and of things in the sea, is tamed, and hath been tamed of mankind: but the tongue can no man tame; it is an unruly evil, full of deadly poison" (iii. 7, 8). Vincent de Paul never uttered a superfluous word; boasting, flattery, mockery, impatience, sallies of passion, were wholly unknown in him. He knew well how to bridle his tongue, and to impose on himself the most rigorous silence. Being accused of injuries, being slandered and maligned, when the heart of another man would burn with the sense of injustice, and would leap to justify itself, St. Vincent de Paul imitated his Divine Master, who, "being reviled, reviled not again," and overcame the malice of evil speakers simply by his silence.—L'abbé Maynard, *St. Vincent de Paul: his Life, his Times, his Works, and his Influence* (1860).

Besides these, the following saints were noted for keeping fast the door of their mouths: Domenic, Edward the Confessor, Eugenie, Felix, Friard, Giles of Portugal, John Baptist de Sala, Kostka, and Pemena.

Sins forgiven.

Luke vii. 47. Wherefore I say unto thee, Her sins, which are many, are forgiven.

Sister Frances murdered her paramour and produced abortion, but was forgiven (fourteenth century). While St. Vincent Ferrier was celebrating mass at Valencia, a woman appeared to him on the altar, surrounded with flames, and holding a dead infant in her arms. It was Sister Frances, who had married a rich merchant, and had committed adultery with one of her servants, during the absence of her husband. Covered with shame, she poisoned her paramour, "et fit périr le fruit de ces entrailles, avant qu'il vînt au monde." To add to her crimes, she feared to go to confession, but meeting by chance a stranger in priests' orders, she told him everything, and died within three days. Some time after her decease, she appeared to her brother, and implored him to obtain for her an abridgment of her pains in purgatory. The brother referred the case to St. Vincent, and St. Vincent prayed on her behalf. At the expiration of three days Sister Frances appeared to the saint, crowned with flowers; and, surrounded by angels, she ascended up into heaven.—*Les Petits Bollandistes*, vol. iv. p. 239.

Sleepers in Death.

Acts vii. 60. [Stephen] kneeled down, and cried with a loud voice, Lord, lay not this sin to their charge. And when he had said this, he fell asleep.

1 Cor. xv. 6. The greater part remain to this day, but some are fallen asleep.

1 Cor. xv. 17, 18. If Christ be not raised, then they which are fallen asleep in Christ are perished.

The Greeks thought it ill-ominous to mention the words *death* and *die*; hence they called *death* "sleep," *to die* "to sleep," and a *graveyard* a cemetery or *sleeping-place*. Thus Lycophron speaks of (*Cassandra*, ver. 583) the sleeping-place of Sithon's daughter.

The seven sleepers. The seven sleepers were seven noble youths in the household of the emperor Decian, who fled from his court to a cave in Mount Celion. They were Christians, and the emperor had set on foot a Christian persecution. The mouth of the cave was blocked up, and they fell asleep. Some 230 years afterwards the cave was opened, and the "youths" awoke; but they died soon afterwards, and were taken in a large coffin to Marseilles. Visitors are still shown the stone coffin in St. Victor's church.—Gregory of Tours, *De Gloria Martyrum*, i. 9 (died 595).

See the Korân, "The Cave Revealed at Mecca," ch. xviii. There is considerable difference in several particulars on minor points. Thus Al Seyid, a Jacobite Christian of Najrân, says the sleepers were three, others say five, but the more general account is that there were six noble youths, a shepherd, and his dog. The number of years, according to the Korân, was three hundred, and nine over. The names of the seven youths were, according to Gregory of Tours: Constantine, Dionysius, John, Maximian, Malchus, Marcian or Martinian, and Serapion. The names are not given in the Korân; but the dog is called "Kratimer" in Sale's *notes*. (See also Jacques de Voragine, *The Golden Legends.*)

(N.B.—If there is any truth at all in the legend, it amounts to this: In A.D. 250 some youths (three, five, or seven) suffered martyrdom under the emperor Decius—"fell asleep in the Lord"—and were buried in a cave or vault in Mount Celion. In A.D. 479, during the reign of Theodosius, their bodies were discovered, and, being consecrated as holy relics, were removed to Marseilles.)

Arthur not dead, but only asleep, till the fulness of time is come. King Arthur, we are told, is not dead, but sleeps in Avillon, till the fulness of time; when he will wake up, twice as fair, to rule over his people, and make Britain the head and front of all the kingdoms of the earth. Cervantês refers to this legend in his *Don Quixote* (pt. i. bk. ii. ch. 5), where he says, "According to tradition, Arthur never died, but only fell asleep; and he will, in the fulness of time, appear again, as a giant refreshed with wine, and recover his kingdom." Another legend says he is metamorphosed for the nonce into a raven, and hence the people of Britain never kill a raven.

Barbarossa not dead, but only asleep. It is said that kaiser Frederick I., surnamed Barbarossa or Red-beard, is not dead, but only asleep in Kyffhaüserberg, in Thuringia. There he sits at a stone table with his six knights, waiting the fulness of time, when he will come from the cave to rescue Germany from bondage, and give it the foremost place in all the world. His red beard has already grown through the table slab, but must wind itself thrice round the table before the ravens will quit the mountain and the sleeper awake. A peasant declared he had actually seen the red-bearded king sitting at the table, leaning on his elbows. He looked up and asked, "Is it time?" "Not yet, not yet," was the mysterious answer of some unknown voice; and the venerable kaiser closed his eyes again, till the world requires his aid to set it right.—*Political, Social, and Literary History of Germany*, p. 81.

Bobadil et Chico is not dead, but only fallen asleep. Bobadil et Chico, last of the Moorish kings of Granada, lies asleep, spellbound, near the Alhambra; but the day appointed will come, when he will return to life, and restore the Spanish government in Spain.

Brian, king of Ireland, is not dead, but only fallen asleep. Brian, surnamed "Boroimbe," king of Ireland, who conquered the Danes in twenty pitched battles, and was supposed to have been slain in the battle of Clontarf, in 1014, was only stunned. He still sleeps in his castle of Kincora; and the day of Ireland's necessity will be Brian's opportunity.

Charlemagne not dead, but only fallen asleep in Jesus. According to legend, Charlemagne is not dead, but has only fallen asleep; and waits, crowned and armed, in Odenberg or Untersberg, near Saltzburg, till the advent of Antichrist, when he will wake up and deliver Christendom, that it may be prepared to receive the second advent and personal reign of Christ.

Charles V., kaiser, is not dead, but only fallen asleep. Kaiser Charles V. of Spain and Germany is not dead, but only asleep, waiting his time. When the fulness of the time is come, he will return to earth, resume the monarchy of Germany, Spain, Portugal, Belgium, the Netherlands, and Denmark, putting all enemies under his feet.

Elijah the prophet was taken up to heaven alive, and will come again. Elijah the prophet sleeps in Abraham's bosom till Antichrist appears, when he will return to Jerusalem, and restore all things.

Knez Lazar of Servia is not dead, but only fallen asleep. Knez Lazar of Servia, supposed to have been slain by the Turks, in 1389, is said to be not really dead, but to have put on sleep for awhile; and, at the allotted time, he will reappear in his full strength, leading captivity captive.

Elijah Mansur is not dead, but only fallen asleep. Elijah Mansur, warrior, prophet, and priest, in Asiatic Russia, tried to teach a more tolerant form of Islam, but was looked on as a heretic, and condemned to imprisonment in the bowels of a mountain. There he sleeps, waiting patiently the summons which will be given him; when he will awake, and wave his conquering sword to the terror of the Muscovite.—Milner, *Gallery of Geography*, p. 781.

Mahommed Mohadi is not dead, but only fallen asleep. Mahommed Mohadi, the twelfth imân, is, according to Arabian legend, only sleeping till Antichrist appears, when he will wake up in his strength, and overthrow the great enemy of all true believers.

Sebastian I. is not dead, but only fallen asleep. Sebastian I. of Brazil, who fell in the battle of Alcazarquebir, in 1578, is not dead, but sleeps, patiently abiding the full time, when he will return, and make Brazil the mistress of the whole earth.

Three of the family of Tell are asleep, waiting their country's call. Three of the family of Tell sleep a semi-death at Rütli, waiting for the hour of their country's necessity, when they will wake up and deliver it.

Olaf Tryggvason of Norway is not dead, but only fallen asleep. Olaf Tryggvason, king of Norway, who was baptized in London, and introduced Christianity into Norway, Iceland, and Greenland, being overthrown by Swolde, king of Sweden, in A.D. 1000, threw himself into the sea, swam to the Holy Land, became an anchorite, and fell asleep at a greatly advanced age. He is not dead, but only sleeping, and waiting his opportunity, when he will sever Norway from Sweden, and raise it to a first-class power.

Miscellaneous examples. The tale of RIP VAN WINKLE is based on the same general idea. Rip was a Dutch colonist of New York, who slept for twenty years in the Kaatskill mountains of North America.—Washington Irving.

DESMOND OF KILMALLOCK, in Limerick, supposed to have perished in the reign of queen Elizabeth, is only sleeping under the waters of Lough Gur. Every seventh year he reappears in full armour, rides round the lake early in the morning, and will ultimately return to waking life, and restore the family estates.—Sir W. Scott, *Fortunes of Nigel.*

ENDYMION, a beautiful youth, sleeps profoundly in Latmos. Selēna fell in love with him, kissed him, and still lies by his side. In the British Museum is a beautiful statue of Endymion asleep.

EPIMENIDES, the Cretan poet, was sent in boyhood to search for a stray sheep. Being heated and weary, he stepped into a cave, and fell asleep for fifty-seven years.—Pliny, *History*, vii. 12.

GYNETH slept five hundred years by the enchantment of Merlin. She was the natural daughter of king Arthur and Guendolen; and was thus punished because she would not put an end to a combat in which twenty knights were mortally wounded, including Merlin's son.—Sir W. Scott, *Bridal of Triermain.*

MERLIN, the enchanter, is not dead, but sleeps and sighs in an old tree, spellbound by Vivien.

NOURJAHAD, wife of Geangir the Mogul emperor, is only in a temporary sleep, waiting till her time of waking has fully come.

ST. DAVID was thrown into an enchanted sleep by Ormandine; but after sleeping for seven years, was roused from his sleep by Merlin.

The French slain in the SICILIAN VESPERS are not really dead, but only sleep for the time being, waiting the day of retribution.

THOMAS OF ERCELDOUNE sleeps beneath the Eildon hills, in Scotland. One day, an elfin lady led him into a cave in these hills, and he fell asleep for seven years; when he woke up and revisited the upper earth, under a bond that he would return immediately the elfin lady summoned him. One day, as he was making merry with his friends, he heard the summons, kept his word, and has never been seen since.—Sir W. Scott, *Minstrelsy of the Scottish Border.* (See *Castle Dangerous.*)

Sores and Blains cured.

JER. xxx. 17. I will restore health unto thee, and will heal thee of thy wounds, saith the Lord.

Constance, daughter of the emperor Constantine, cured of her sores by St. Agnes. Constance, the daughter of Constantine the Great, was covered with sores from head to foot, but, being told about St. Agnes, went to the tomb of the saint to crave her aid. While she knelt in prayer, St. Agnes appeared to her in a vision, and said, "Constance, forget not thy name, but embrace the faith of Jesus Christ, and remain constant therein. You must be baptized, and you shall be cured of your infirmities. No longer shall your sores be an offence, no longer shall they give you pain. Now arise, and do as I have told you." Then she arose, and her body was as healthy as a child's. In gratitude, she built a magnificent church to St. Agnes, at which many miracles were repeated every day. Constance was baptized, remained a virgin to the end of her life, and when she slept in Jesus was a shining light amongst the redeemed.—Mgr. Guérin (chamberlain of Leo XIII.), *Lives of the Saints*, vol. i. p. 511.

Soul of Man. (See ANGELS CARRY, etc. p. 7; DOVES, p. 107.)

ECCLES. xii. 7. Then shall the dust return to the earth, and the spirit shall return to Him who gave it.

LUKE xvi. 22. And it came to pass that the beggar died, and was carried by angels into Abraham's bosom.

MATT. x. 28. Fear not them which kill the body, but are not able to kill the soul.

1 THESS. v. 23. I pray God your whole spirit and soul and body be preserved blameless unto the coming of our Lord Jesus Christ.

HEB. iv. 12. The Word of God is quick and powerful, piercing even to the dividing asunder of soul and spirit.

St. Cuthbert sees the soul of bishop Aidan carried from Lindisfarne to heaven. One night, as Cuthbert was watching his father's sheep in the valley of Lauderdale, he saw the soul of St. Aidan, late bishop of Durham, carried up to heaven by a company of angels, at the very moment that the holy man departed this life. He woke his companions, and asked them to join him in singing praises to God.—Bede, *Life of St. Cuthbert* (*Church History*, bk. ix. ch. 27–32).

The soul of Alcuin, in the form of a dove, conveyed to heaven (May 19, 804). On the eve of Alcuin's death a mysterious light enveloped the whole monastery, which many thought was a fire. Next day, at dawn, a globe of fire ascended up to heaven. An Italian recluse, who happened to be at Tours, asserts that he saw St. Stephen and St. Laurentius, with a crowd of angels, escort the spirit of Alcuin to heaven. Two young cenobites, pupils of Alcuin, walking together in the monastery close of Hirsauge, distinctly saw a dove mount to heaven, and heard celestial music in the air. "There goes the soul of our dear master, to receive the crown of everlasting life," said one of the young men to the other. Two days afterwards the news was brought to Hirsauge of the death of the great scholar, and the time of decease minutely corresponded with the flight of the dove.—Corblet, *Hagiographie du Diocèse d'Amiens.*

The following suggestion is made with all possible deference. The frequent mention of the flight of doves at the death of great men, might it not be the despatch of carrier pigeons to convey the intelligence to some associated monastery? The globe of fire, might it not be a rocket used as a telegraph? The fire or light was probably due to the candles lighted on such occasions, and the celestial music to the requiem sung by monks.

St. Antony of Padua sees the soul of a Franciscan like a white bird ascend to heaven (A.D. 1195–1231). On one occasion when St. Antony, who was born at Lisbon, was helping the priest at the altar, he distinctly saw the soul of a Franciscan flit out of purgatory. It was like a white bird. He saw it ascend to heaven, and enter the kingdom of the elect.—L'abbé Guyard, *Life of St. Antony of Padua.*

Marcan sees the soul of St. Briocus carried up to heaven (A.D. 502). When St. Briocus died, the chamber was filled with a delicious odour, and a religious, named Marcan, saw his soul, in the form of a dove, carried up to heaven. Another religious, named Siviau, saw the saint mounting to heaven by a luminous ladder, on which was a vast number of angels.—Dom Lobineau, *Lives of the British Saints.*

It seems that the soul went first in the form of a dove, the saint afterwards by the ladder, and the body, of course, remained behind. The "saint" must mean the spirit, making man to consist of body, soul, and spirit, all independent of each other.

A dove issued from the mouth of St. Devota, at death (A.D. 300). St. Devota was a Christian handmaid in the service of Eutyches, a Roman senator, when Diocletian issued his edict for the extermination of the whole Christian sect. Eutyches was living at the time in Corsica, of which Barbarus was governor. Of course Devota was seized by the governor, and ordered either to sacrifice to the Roman gods or to suffer the penalty of her disobedience. The maiden stoutly refused to honour as gods idols made of wood, clay, and stone, the work of men's hands; and Barbarus commanded her to be dragged by her feet over the rocky ground, and hung on a chevalet (see Index) till she was dead. As she breathed her last, a white dove was seen to issue from her mouth, and take its flight straight up into the deep blue sky, where it was lost to sight. Barbarus had ordered the body to be burned; but two Christians came by night, and embarked with it for Africa. Immediately the skiff loosed from shore the white dove again appeared to guide it on its way. It skimmed the water for a few yards, and then waited till the skiff came up, when it flew off again, skimming the water as before. In this way it guided the skiff to the port called Hercules Monecus (*Monaco*), when it flew away, and was no more seen. Here the two men debarked, and buried the body. In 1687 the Corsicans obtained from Monaco some relics of the Christian maiden; and these relics are still held in veneration in the island.—*Acta Sanctorum*, vol. ii. Jan. 27.

The soul of St. Engelbert appears to St. Hermann as a moon (A.D. 1230). One night, as St. Hermann was contemplating the starry heavens, he saw two moons—the natural moon, and one below it infinitely more beautiful. A voice told him this second moon was the soul of St. Engelbert, archbishop of Cologne. St. Hermann could not think this was true, because Engelbert was still alive; but the event showed the truth of the revelation, for Engelbert had been murdered by his own kinsmen; and, as a martyr, he entered into paradise without passing through purgatory. In punishment of his incredulity, St. Hermann was afflicted for a season with bad eyes, which were not healed till he sent an offering to the tomb of St. Engelbert.—*Life of St. Hermann* (Bollandists), April 7.

St. Eulalia of Barcelona being martyred, her spirit ascends to heaven as a dove (A.D. 304). St. Eulalia, a mere child, conceived the idea of reproving Dacian for persecuting the Christians of Spain. With this view she called on the governor, who said to her, "Well, child, what do you want with me?" "To reprove you," said the maiden, "for your cruelty to the Christians." "Heyday!" said Dacian, "and who are you that dare speak thus to me?" "I am a Christian," said Eulalia. "Don't be insolent, child," said the governor. But as the child continued, Dacian ordered her to be hoisted on the back of a soldier, and whipped with a birch rod like a naughty girl.

He soon found she was not to be silenced thus; and at last he commanded her to be cast into a bath of quicklime, to which boiling oil was added. She died in her horrible bath, and the assistants saw her spirit, in the form of a white dove, fly through her mouth straight up to heaven.—*Les Petits Bollandistes*, vol. ii. p. 473.

The soul of St. Germanus of Scotland ascends to heaven like a dove (May 2, A.D. 480). When St. Germanus reached Vieux Rouen, one Hubault, who heard of his arrival, rushed upon him, and cut off his head with his sword. His soul in a visible form, like a dove whiter than snow, left his body, and ascended to heaven. Next day, the dead saint told a young maiden to go to Senard, the seigneur of Senarpont, and bid him bury his body. Senard went to the spot indicated, but angels had carried the body further on. There the seigneur embalmed it, placed it in a beautiful sarcophagus, and buried it. This was the origin of the name St. Germain-sur-Bresle, given to a town which afterwards sprang up upon the site.—Corblet, *Hagiographie d'Amiens.*

The soul of St. Norbert resembled a lily (A.D. 1134). When St. Norbert died, a religious saw his soul change in a moment into a lily, and saw angels come and carry it into heaven. Another religious saw the saint come down from heaven with an olive branch in his hand. The religious said to him, "Whence comest thou, and whither goest thou?" The saint replied, "I come from paradise, and am going to Premontré to plant this olive slip, as a pledge of everlasting peace between God and my disciples." Hugh, the abbot of the order, saw him in a most magnificent palace, filled with brilliant rays of light, and having asked him what had become of his soul since death, the saint replied, "Venez, ma chère sœur, reposez vous."—Mgr. Guérin, *Vies des Saints*, vol. vi. p. 498.

The reply of St. Norbert to the abbot is certainly noteworthy, and proves the duality of man, in the chamberlain's opinion, beyond all doubt. Norbert calls his soul "his sister," and bids her rest, so that Norbert himself was soulless at the time. Very strange!

The soul of St. Robert, abbot of Casa Dei, ascends to heaven visibly (A.D. 1067). At the moment of death, a religious saw the "Mother of God" come to console St. Robert, abbot of Casa Dei; and immediately he had breathed his last, another religious distinctly saw the soul of the man of God leave his body, and ascend to heaven as a globe of fire.—*Acta Sanctorum* (Bollandists), April 24.

The soul of St. Scholastica ascends to heaven in the figure of a dove (A.D. 543). While St. Benedict was on Mount Cassino, he saw the soul of his sister Scholastica ascend to heaven in the shape of a dove. Filled with joy, he thanked God and announced the fact to his brethren. St. Scholastica died in the nunnery of Plombariola, in the neighbourhood of Mount Cassino.—Gregory the Great, *Dialogues*, bk. ii. ch. 34.

The soul of William Wallace and of Edward I. (A.D. 1305, 1307). Sir William Wallace was beheaded and quartered, in 1305, by Edward I.; but Bower tells us, in his continuation of Fordun, that on the testimony of many credible Englishmen, a holy hermit saw, at the moment of the patriot's death, a company of innumerable souls delivered from purgatory, and that of Wallace, marshalled by them, was borne by angels up to heaven.

Not long afterwards, in 1307, Edward I. died on his march to Scotland; and an English knight, named Bannister, saw the soul of the late king surrounded by a host of devils, who were mocking it with much laughter. Bannister distinctly remembers their saying—

En! rex Edwardus, debacchans ut leopardus!
Olim, dum vixit, populum Dei male flixit.
Nobis viæ talis comes ibis, care sodalis,
Quo condemneris, dæmonibus socieris.
Te sequimur voto prorsus torpore remoto.

Behold, Edwardus rex O, once wont the Church to vex so,
As raging leopard now, sir, to the infernal slough, sir;
Where dæmons fleer and titter, with us, dear friend, you'll flitter,
And company for ever henceforth we will not sever.

While thus they sang in leonine doggerel, they drove the ghostly king before them with whips and scorpions. Edward cast a piteous look upon the knight, so full of heart-broken sorrow, so helpless and woebegone, that Bannister says he can never forget it to his dying hour. The earth opened, and as the kingly ghost was about to enter the yawning gulf, he cried aloud—

Heu, cur peccavi? fallor quia non bene cavi.
Heu, cur peccavi? perit et nihil est quod amavi
Heu, cur peccavi? video, quia littus aravi
Cum sudore gravi mihimet tormenta paravi.

Why did I sin indeed? And take of death no heed?
Why did I sin indeed? Vile dross my only greed.
Why did I sin indeed? The barren sand my seed,
Now, in my hour of need, torment my only meed.

[In these doggerels I have endeavoured to imitate the Latin leonine doggerels. Those who prefer trochaic rhymes to the latter quatrain may add "ah!" to each half-line.]

Spider's Web.

JOB viii. 13, 14. Bildad the Shuhite tells Job that the trust of those who forget God shall fail; and the hope of the hypocrite shall perish. Their hope shall be cut off, and their trust shall be a spider's web.

The work of the spider. "It is a great deal of care and a great deal of pains that the spider takes in weaving her web. She runneth much and often up and down; she fetcheth a compass this way and that, and returneth continually to the same point. She spendeth herself in multitudes of fine threads, to make for herself a round cabinet. She disembowels herself to make an artificial and curious piece of work, which, when it is made, is apt to be blown away with every puff of wind. She hangeth it up aloft; she fasteneth it to the beam; she tries its strength; she increases it with many a thread, wheeling often round and round about, not sparing her own bowels, but freely spending them upon her work. And when she hath done all this, spun her fine threads, weaved them one into another, wrought herself a fine canopy, hung it aloft, and thinks all sure, suddenly, in the twinkling of an eye, with a little sweep of a broom, all falls to the ground, and so her labour perisheth. But this is not all, poor spider! The weaver is killed in her own web, or taken in her own snare, or trodden underfoot. She wove diligently and painsfully, but the web she wove was her own winding-sheet. She strengthened her cords and made them fast, but only to be her own death."—Spencer, *Things Old and New.*

Spoiling the Egyptians.

EXOD. xii. 35, 36. The children of Israel did according to the word of Moses; and they borrowed of the Egyptians jewels of silver, and jewels of gold, and raiment; and the Lord gave the people favour in the sight of the Egyptians, so that the people lent unto them such things as they required; and they spoiled the Egyptians. (See Exod. iii. 22.)

St. Francis of Assisi spoils his own father (A.D. 1182–1226). The father of St. Francis d'Assisi was Pietro Bernadone, a wealthy merchant. When the young man, who had hitherto lived a very worldly life, declared for the cross, and determined to follow in all things "the example of Christ, and walk in His steps," he changed his fine clothes with a beggar, and then going to his father's warehouse carried off on a pack-horse several bales of cloth, which he sold, and presented the proceeds for the repairs of the church of St. Damian.—Mrs. Oliphant, *Life of St. Francis.*

It is passing strange that any right-minded man, let alone a religious man, cannot see this, that thieving to give in charity is wholly without excuse. (1) It is the violation of a positive law, "Thou shalt not steal;" (2) it is no personal sacrifice to give away another man's property; (3) such gifts are mere vanity or gross self-deception; (4) if once permitted, the whole fabric of commercial society would be broken down. A reference to the Index, article "Theft for Gifts of Charity," will bring to notice a number of these strange delusions, such as stealing bread to feed the hungry, stealing corn to feed birds, lending what does not belong to one, stealing a horse to indulge the vanity of giving.

I know of no religious delusion more mischievous and blameworthy, yet is it always set down in all hagiographies as a merit. A somewhat similar delusion is the constant practice of releasing prisoners utterly regardless of the offences for which they are detained (see Index, "Prison"). It is true that Christ came "to preach deliverance to the captive" (*Luke* iv. 18), but we hear nothing about His delivering from prison the Barabbases, merely because they were prisoners. This is one of those wretched realistic interpretations which not only the Roman Catholic Church but our own Puritans mistook for godliness, and even to the present day there are not wanting Protestants led away by the same delusions.

Standing fast; Immovable.

PSALM xvi. 8. I have set the Lord always before me. Because He is at my right hand, I shall not be moved.

ROM. xiv. 4. God is able to make him stand.

PSALM x. 30. The righteous shall never be removed.

PSALM cxxv. 1. They that trust in the Lord shall be as Mount Zion, which cannot be removed.

St. Brigit renders immovable a mounted escort, in pursuit of a young lady, in flight (A.D. 436–523). A young lady, on the eve of her marriage, stole secretly from her father's house, and fled to the convent of St. Brigit. The father, with a large mounted escort, went in pursuit of the fugitive; but when St. Brigit saw it in the distance, she made the sign of the cross, and every horse and rider became instantly immovable as statues. After a certain interval, the father confessed he was wrong in pursuing his daughter, and allowed her to take the veil. Whereupon St. Brigit removed the ban, and the father with his escort returned home.—*Les Petits Bollandistes*, vol. ii. p. 185.

St. Lucy, who set the Lord always before her, could not be moved. St. Lucy, being brought before Paschasius, governor of Syracuse, for refusing to marry, was asked if she were a Christian. Said the governor, "How standeth this together, that a god should suffer an ignominious death?" Lucy replied, "Nay, rather, how standeth it together, that Jupiter, Apollo, and Venus should be gods and goddesses, and yet commit sins which it would be death in mortals to indulge in?" "You are pert," said Paschasius, "and talk like a child." Said Lucy, "It is not I who answer, but the Holy Ghost within me that tells me what to answer." "What!" exclaimed the governor, "does one of your gods live in your body?" Said Lucy, "Every one who leads a chaste and holy life is a temple of the Holy Ghost." "We'll soon drive this god out, then," said Paschasius; and so saying, he ordered one of his officers to conduct Lucy at once to a notorious brothel. When this got wind, many went thither to dishonour her; but she stood like a rock in the middle of the room, and no one could move her. All the servants of the house tried to push or drag her from her moorings, but without effect. Ropes were thrown around her, and many hands haled at the ropes with all their might and main, but she stood fast. Several yoke of oxen were attached to chains and cables, but could not stir her. The governor declared it to be witchcraft, but St. Lucy replied, "I have set the Lord always before me; and because He is at my right hand, I shall not be moved."—Ado (archbishop of Trèves), *Martyrology*. (Bede, Sigisbert, the Breviary, the Roman martyrology, etc., have accounts of St. Lucy and her deeds.)

An Egyptian idol becomes quite immovable. St. Apollo, having heard that a grand idolatrous procession was about to take place in a village of Upper Egypt, prayed God to prevent it. Whereupon the idol became quite immovable, insomuch that neither the priests, nor yet the combined strength of all their attendants, availed to lift it from its pedestal. So the procession was perforce abandoned.—Palladius (a personal friend of St. Apollo), *Historia Lausiaca.*

Some soldiers having looted Vermandois, are unable to make their pack-horses stir (sixteenth century). Some of the soldiers of Clotaire I., having made great ravages in Vermandois, piled their loot on baggage waggons; but, by the virtue of St. Medard, the horses refused to stir, and nothing could make them move even when the plunder was restored, till St. Medard came forward and gave his benediction.

Another instance. A thief broke into St. Medard's vineyard and made great spoil, but could not find his way out. He wandered about all night with the grapes on his arms and shoulders, till half-dead with fatigue and fright. Next morning he was caught with his spoil, and taken before St. Medard. St. Medard refused to commit him, cautioned him, dismissed him, and even allowed him to carry away the grapes.—*Acta Sanctorum* (Bollandists), vol. ii. June 8.

The sword of Uther, the pendragon, stuck fast in a steel anvil, immovable except to Arthur. At the death of the pendragon, all the states and lords of the realm assembled, long ere it was day, in the great church of London. And when matins were over, there appeared in the churchyard, against the high altar, a huge stone, four square; and in the midst of the stone a steel anvil a foot in height, in which was a naked sword, bearing in letters of gold this legend, "Who can pull forth this sword from the anvil, he and he only is the rightful king of Britain." After mass all the states went to look at the sword, and one after another assayed to pull it out, but without avail. "The rightful man," said the archbishop, "is not here. This, then, is my counsel, that we let purvey ten knights of good report to keep the sword, till God shall make the right-born king appear." This advice was followed, and the crier cried in the streets that he who claimed the crown must win it by removing the sword. On New Year's Day the barons rode to joust and tourney, and it fell out that sir Ector was amongst the barons, with sir Key and young Arthur. Now, sir Key had left his sword at home, and asked young Arthur to go and fetch it for him. "That will I, with right good will," said Arthur, and hasted to fetch it; but no one being in the house, he could not open the doors. He was much vexed, but resolved to take instead the sword in the churchyard. Coming to the place, he tied his horse to the stile, and went to the knights' tent; but all the knights were gone to the jousts, so he took the sword by the handle, gently wrenched it from the anvil, and took it to his foster-brother. Soon as sir Key saw it, he recognized it; and, riding up to his father, said, "Sir Ector, here is the sword of the churchyard, so I must be king of Britain." Then went sir Ector, with his son and Arthur, to the church; and sir Ector made his son take oath how he came by the sword. "Arthur brought it me," said sir Key. "Well," said sir Ector to Arthur, "put the sword back into the anvil, and let me see thee pull it out." "There is no mystery in that," replied Arthur, and instantly replaced the sword in the anvil. Then sir Ector and sir Key tried to pull it out, but were unable. "Come, Arthur," said sir Ector, "let us see you try." And Arthur pulled it forth right easily. Then did sir Ector and sir Key kneel before Arthur; but Arthur cried, "Alas! my father and my elder brother, it is not meet that you should kneel to me." "Nay, nay, my lord," said Ector, "no son of mine art thou. I wot well you are of higher blood than mine, but wist not you were of royal blood." Then all three went to the archbishop, and told him how the sword had been achieved, and the archbishop proclaimed on the feast of the Epiphany that the barons should again assemble and try to draw the sword; and so it was, but none was able to move it but only Arthur. So Arthur was acknowledged king by the judgment of the sword.—Sir Thomas Malory, *La Mort d'Arthur*, bk. i. ch. 3-6.

St. Wulfstan's pastoral staff fixed fast in solid stone. William the Conqueror, wishing to fill all the seats of dignity with his own followers, ordered Wulfstan, bishop of Worcester, to yield up his staff and ring to Gundulf, because he could not speak Norman. Wulfstan had been appointed by Edward the Confessor, and when he heard that he was deposed, he went to the tomb of the deceased king, and said, "Thou knowest, O my master, how reluctantly I received this staff at thy bidding; but now we have a new king, a new law, and a new archbishop, who found new rights, and declare new sentences. They convict thee, O saintly king, of error, in appointing me to the see of Worcester, and me of presumption in accepting the dignity. Not to them, but to thee only, can I resign my staff; not to those who walk in darkness, but to thee who hast escaped from the region of ignorance and error." So saying, he stuck the pastoral staff into the sepulchral stone; and, laying aside his episcopal robes, seated himself among the monks. All were amazed to see the staff fixed firmly in the solid stone, and some ran to tell Lanfrac of the miracle. The archbishop would not believe the report, and sent Gundulf to go and fetch the staff; but Gundulf found it so embedded in the stone that he could not pull it out. Then the king and archbishop both went to the chapter-house to wrench out the staff, but were unable to move it. Lanfranc, convinced that this was God's doing, went at once to Wulfstan, and said to him, "Verily, God resisteth the proud, but giveth grace to the humble and meek. Thy simplicity, brother, was scorned by us, but thy righteousness is exalted. Keep the bishopric over which God Himself hath made thee overseer, for God hath sealed thee by miracle to the holy office." Then Wulfstan put his hand on the staff, and lifted it from the stone without the slightest effort.—Roger de Wendover and Caprave.

Stones crying out.

LUKE xix. 40. I tell you, that if these should hold their peace, the stones would immediately cry out.

HAB. ii. 11. The stone shall cry out of the wall, and the beam out of the timber shall answer it.

EZEK. xxvi. 26. A new heart will I give you. I will take away the stony heart, and will give you a heart of flesh.

Bede preached to a heap of stones (A.D. 672-735). On one occasion, we are told, the Venerable Bede preached to a heap of stones, thinking himself in a church; and the stones were so affected by his eloquence, that they exclaimed, "Amen, Venerable Bede!"

Stones Obedient. (See GRAVITATION, etc., p. 159.)

JOB v. 23. Thou shalt be in league with the stones of the field.

St. Francis of Paula arrests a huge stone which threatened to knock down a monastery which was in construction (A.D. 1416-1507). While the celebrated monastery of Calabria was under construction, a stone of prodigious size, detached from a neighbouring mountain, came rolling down with great impetuosity towards the new building, threatening great danger to the work, and to many of the workmen. A general cry of alarm rose on all sides, but St. Francis of Paula, with perfect calmness, lifting his hand, said "Stop!" and the stone stopped instantly in its course. Then, going to the rock, he planted his staff before it, and the rock remained immovable for many days. At last it was broken up and used in the walls of the building.—Le P. Giry, drawn chiefly from the witnesses in the process of canonization and the bull of Leo X.

St. John Baptist de la Conception stays a man carrying a stone who overbalanced himself (A.D. 1561-1613). While the convent of Cordova was a-building, one of the masons, carrying a huge stone, and climbing a ladder, lost his balance and fell. St. John Baptist de la Conception happened to be on the spot, and, extending his hand, cried aloud, "In the name of the Holy Trinity, stop!" Instantly the stone ceased from falling, the workman adjusted himself, and both came slowly and deliberately to the ground. "A miracle! A miracle!" shouted the workmen; but the saint quietly withdrew, and returned to his cell.—Godescard, *Vie des Saints* (continued).

Strength according to thy Day.

ISA. xl. 31. They that wait upon the Lord shall renew their strength. They shall run, and not be weary; they shall walk, and not faint.

1 SAM. ii. 4. They that stumbled are girded with strength.

PSALM xxix. 11. The Lord will give strength to His people.

DEUT. xxxiii. 25. As thy days, so shall thy strength be.

St. Francis of Paula carries away a huge rock which many men were unable to stir (A.D. 1452). While the monastery of Spezza was under construction, it was necessary for a huge rock to be removed, as it obstructed the approach. Many men tried by a united effort to loosen it, but without avail; they tried to break it, but with no better success. At length St. Francis took it up in his hands and carried it away without help of any kind.

A few days afterwards he carried on his shoulder to the top of the clock-tower a coping-stone which four strong men were unable by their united strength to lift.

About the same time he dragged from a wood by the river-side two pieces of timber which a number of workmen with their united strength were unable to move.

During the same building operation he carried on his own shoulders, and enabled his workmen to lift and carry about, heavy weights which no human beings could have lifted, "if God Himself had not girded them with strength, or sent His angels to assist them in supporting the loads."

Finally, crooked trees were made straight, rough joists were worked into shape and carried to their places, sawpits were sunk, and other work done by the mere word of command of the saint, without instrument or the aid of man.—All these instances are mentioned in the *Act of Canonization.*

St. Francis of Paula commands a paralytic to carry a huge stone (A.D. 1452). While St. Francis of Paula was building his monastery at Spezza, in the diocese of Cosenza, a woman from Cortona, who had been paralyzed for thirty years, was brought before him. St. Francis bade her get from the carriage and carry a great stone to the builders. The woman made the required effort. She that stumbled was girded with strength; she lifted the stone, carried it to the builders, and was perfectly cured of her disease.—Process made at Cosenza before Leo X., at the canonization of St. Francis of Paula.

St. Francis of Paula gives strength to a lame man to carry a rafter (A.D. 1452). While St. Francis de Paula was building his great monastery, the seventeenth witness of the process made at Cosenza stated that a lame man, suffering so severely from sciatica that he could not move, was brought to him. The patriarch told him to carry to the building a huge rafter, which two strong oxen could not lift. The man said, "How can you desire me to carry this huge rafter?" "They that wait on the Lord," said St. Francis, "shall renew their strength, and the Lord will give strength to His people." The man charged himself with the beam, carried it to the building, laid it in the place required, and was perfectly cured of his malady.—Le P. Giry, *Life of St. Francis of Paula,* drawn from the witnesses called in the process of his canonization.

Sun warded off. (See RAIN WARDED OFF.)

PSALM cxxi. 6. The sun shall not smite thee by day.

REV. vii. 16. Neither shall the sun light on them, nor any heat.

ISA. iv. 6. There shall be a tabernacle for a shadow in the daytime from the heat, and for a covert from storm and from rain.

St. Peter of Verona wards off the sun from a public assembly (A.D. 1206–1252). St. Peter of Verona had a disputation at Milan in the open air with certain heretical bishops. The assembly found the heat of the sun quite intolerable, and St. Peter prayed, saying, "O Lord, Thou hast promised that the sun shall not smite Thy servants by day, nor the moon by night; bring now the clouds to be unto us a tabernacle for a shadow from this great heat." No sooner had he spoken than a thick cloud formed a canopy over the heads of the assembly till the disputation was brought to a close.—T. Lentinos, *Life of St. Peter the Martyr.*

Taught of God.

JOHN vi. 45. It is written in the prophets, They shall be all taught of God.

MATT. x. 20. It is not ye that speak, but the Spirit of your Father which speaketh in you.

JAMES i. 5. If any of you lack wisdom, let him ask [for it] of God, that giveth liberally, and upbraideth not.

2 PET. i. 21. St. Peter says that prophecy came not in olden time by the will of man, but holy men of God spake as they were moved by the Holy Ghost.

2 SAM. xxiii. 2. David in his last address confesses that the psalms he sung were not his own words, but "that the Spirit of the Lord spake by me, and His word was in my tongue."

ACTS iv. 8. When Peter was arraigned before the Jewish Sanhedrim, his answer was dictated to him by the Holy Ghost.

St. Aldegundis taught by St. Peter personally (A.D. 689). St. Aldegundis, the daughter of prince Walbert, was in the direct line of the kings of France, and was born in Hainaut, A.D. 630. God interposed in her childhood to lead her in the way everlasting, by sending the apostle Peter to teach her what to believe and how to live. She was often visited by other heavenly visitants, and sometimes by the King of angels, whom she had chosen to be her Spouse.—L'abbé Delbos, *Life of St. Aldegundis.*

St. Ambrose told by an angel how to convict the Arians. When St. Ambrose, on one occasion, preached against the Arian heresy, one of the leading "heretics" was converted. Being asked why he had gone over to the other side, he answered, "Because I distinctly saw an angel whispering in the ear of St. Ambrose the words that he spoke, so that it was not Ambrose that convicted me of error, but the Spirit of God."—Paulinus, *Life of St. Ambrose.*

St. Bernard told the exact hour of Christ's birth by Christ Himself. St. Bernard, being in a church on Christmas Eve, had a great desire to know the precise hour of the Nativity. He prayed earnestly that the Holy Ghost would inform him. Whereupon Christ Himself stood by him in the form of a little child, and informed him minutely of the day and hour when He was born in Bethlehem.—Godfrey (St. Bernard's secretary), *Life of St. Bernard.*

St. Gregory the thaumaturgist taught the mystery of the Trinity by the Virgin Mary (A.D. 270). St. Gregory wrote his *Symbol of Faith*, and received his inspiration direct from the Virgin Mary in the following manner:—One night, while the saint was meditating on the subject, an old man was sent by God to instruct him fully in the verities of the Christian faith. Beside the old man was a lady of celestial beauty, who addressed the old man as John the Evangelist, and told him to instruct the young Gregory in all the mysteries of the true faith. The old man expressed his pleasure in obeying the mother of God, and at once explained the whole subject to Gregory, who wrote down what St. John taught him; and when all was written, the old man vanished. St. Gregory has left this treatise for the benefit of the Church, and it has always preserved the Church from falling into heresy, especially that of the Arians and semi-Arians. The original was extant in the archives of the Church of Neocæsarea in the time of Gregory of Nyssa, and is cited by Gregory Nazianzen, Rufinus, and many others.—St. Gregory of Nyssa, *Life of St. Gregory Thaumaturgist.*

St. Leo's manuscript corrected by St. Peter himself. When St. Leo was writing his treatise against Nestorius, "the heretic," he left his manuscript one night on the relics of St. Peter, and prayed if anything in it needed amendment, that the holy apostle would make the necessary correction before the treatise was made public. When Leo rose next morning and examined his manuscript, he found several words had been blotted out and others substituted in their place. In fact, the whole manuscript had been carefully corrected throughout; and he gave God and St. Peter his hearty thanks. —Damasus, *Lives of the Popes.*

St. Savinian taught by an angel (A.D. 275). St. Savinian was a Greek, born in Samos, and brought up in the Greek mythological religion. But one day the psalms of David fell into his hands, and he was greatly struck with the verse, "Purge me with hyssop, and I shall be clean; wash me, and I shall be whiter than snow" (li. 7). He pondered over these words for many an hour and many a day, but could not make out what they meant. At length an angel was sent to him, and told him it was by baptism that man was cleansed from sin, and though those sins were as scarlet, yet by baptism the Christian in God's sight was whiter than snow. Leaving his native land, he wandered into Champagne, and there a stranger conferred on him "the grace of baptism." Some say the stranger was St. Parre, a citizen of Champagne, others think it was an angel.—Bollandus, *Acta Sanctorum*, vol. iii. Jan. 29. (See also Nicolas des Guerrois, *Saintété Chrétienne de l'Églisc de Troyes*.

Whether the exeges's of the angel was right or not, be it distinctly understood that it is no part of this book to determine.

Veronica of Milan taught by an angel (A.D. 1497). It was a great disappointment to Veronica that, being unable to read and wholly uninstructed in singing, she was disqualified from taking part in the choir offices; and she prayed often and earnestly that God would help her. One day, as she was praying, an angel came into her cell, holding a psalter in his hand. Then opening the book, he bade her read, and she found she could do so without difficulty. He then bade her sing, and she chanted the psalms correctly, she and the angel taking the antiphons and responses alternately. Thus was fulfilled what was spoken by St. James, "If any of you lack wisdom, let him ask [for it] of God, that giveth to all liberally, and upbraideth not, and it shall be given him."—Isidore of Isolani. (Said to be taken from the notes of Benedetto, who was intimately acquainted with Veronica, and received the above from her own mouth.)

Thoughts discerned.

MATT. ix. 4. Jesus, knowing their thoughts, said, Wherefore think ye evil in your hearts?

1 COR. iii. 20. The Lord knoweth the thoughts of the wise.

HEB. iv. 12. The Word of God is quick and powerful . . . a discerner of the thoughts and intents of the heart.

St. Vincent Ferrier could discern the thoughts and intents of the mind (A.D. 1357–1419). St. Vincent Ferrier knew what was in the mind even of a stranger, and would put searching questions touching the very quick of their secret sins, so that men said, "This man knows our thoughts, and the secret intents of our mind." Suppose it was a usurer, a fornicator, a thief, an assassin, no matter what, the word addressed to him by St. Vincent went right home, and struck at the besetting sin. God gave such an insight to Ezekiel, that he might reprove the people for their sins. So was it with St. Vincent Ferrier; wherever he went he knew by revelation the besetting sins of the people, and directed his words point-blank thereto. Thus he convinced of sin, and thus was it he led men to repentance. —Peter Ranzano (bishop of Lucera), *Life of St. Vincent Ferrier.*

Thus far and no further.

JOB xxxviii. 11. Hitherto shalt thou come, but no further; there shall thy proud waves be stayed.

St. Fridian arrests the river Auser (*or Serchio*), sixth century. Gregory the Great assures us that the river Auser, in Lucca, frequently overflowed its banks, and caused great damage to the inhabitants. On one occasion, when the flood was greater than usual, and threatened to lay the whole country under water, St. Fridian prayed that the river might in future take another channel less dangerous to the inhabitants. Accordingly, it changed its bed, and the country was no longer subject to inundations.—Gregory, *Dialogues*, bk. iii. ch. 9.

We are told the truth of this miracle cannot be gainsaid, inasmuch as a rock which St. Fridian made to retire is still showed in proof thereof. But how this can prove any such thing I am wholly at a loss to understand. (See Mgr. Guérin, *Les Petits Bollandistes*, vol. iii. p. 498.) The chamberlain calls the river the Arno.

St. Gregory the thaumaturgist restrains the river Lycus. The river Lycus having overflowed its banks, threatened to destroy the village and flood the fields. St. Gregory, called the Thaumaturgist, planted his staff between the river and the village, saying to the torrent, "Thus far may be thy overflow, but no further." Next morning the staff had become a green tree; and whenever the Lycus in its overflow came up to this boundary, it stopped, and did the villagers no harm.—St. Gregory of Nyssa, *Life of St. Gregory Thaumaturgist.*

St. Hilarion said "Thus far" to some pirates, and stopped pursuit. When St. Hilarion was sailing from Dalmatia, and the ship was well away from land, some pirates bore down upon them; and the sailors fully expected the whole crew would be either cut down, or sold to slavery. St. Hilarion, standing on deck, prayed; and then, stretching out his hands towards the pirates, cried with a loud voice, "Thus far, but no further." Instantly the pirates' vessel veered about, and sailed away as if driven by a strong gale. —St. Jerome, *Vita St. Hilarionis Eremitæ* (A.D. 390). See also Nicephorus Callistus (died 1350), *Ecclesiastical History.*

St. Remi said to a fire at Reims, "Thus far, but no further." A fire broke out in the church of St. Nicasius, at Reims, threatening to spread and destroy the whole city; but St. Remi, making the sign of the cross against the fire, cried with a loud voice, "Thus far, but no further." The fire instantly retreated, and St. Remi advanced, backing the element through the city gates into the open fields. "There let thy proud waves be stayed," said the prelate, and the fire died out.—Hincmar (archbishop of Reims, died A.D. 882), *Life of St. Remi.*

St. Sabinus restrains the overflow of the river Po (fourth century). The river Po, having overflowed its banks, was devastating the Church lands in the neighbourhood, when St. Sabinus told one of his deacons to say to the river, "The bishop commands thee to cease thy rage, and to return at once to thy proper channel;" but the deacon refused, thinking it would be a fool's errand. So St. Sabinus wrote on a tablet, "I, Sabinus, servant of the Lord Jesus Christ, command thee, O river, to return at once to thy proper bed, and do no more injury to the Church lands in thy vicinity." Then giving this tablet to the deacon, he bade him throw it into the stream. This being done, the river instantly drew back its waters, confined them to the channel, and acknowledged by its obedience that God was master of the floods, and that both rivers and seas obey Him.—*St. Gregory the Great*, bk. iii. ch. 10.

St. Severin sets a bound to the overflow of the Danube. Eugippius relates how the Danube durst never rise above the mark of the cross which St. Severin cut on the posts of a wooden church.—Eugippius (a disciple), *Life of St. Severin*, A.D. 511.

Tongue of Man.

JAMES iii. 8, 9. The tongue is an unruly member. Therewith bless we God, and therewith curse we men. Out of the same mouth proceedeth blessing and cursing.

JAMES iii. 8. The tongue can no man tame. It is an unruly evil, full of deadly poison.

PSALM xxxix. 1. I said, I will take heed to my ways, that I sin not with my tongue.

Alured the philosopher called the tongue man's best and worst member. Alured, the Christian philosopher, being asked which is the best member of the body, replied, "The tongue, for it is the trumpet of God's glory." Being then asked which is the worst, he replied, "The tongue, for it is the firebrand of hell."

Pambo's first lesson in Christian ethics (about 400). Socratês, the ecclesiastical historian, tells us that one Pambo went to a Christian missionary, and asked him to teach him something from the Bible; whereupon the man of God opened the thirty-ninth psalm, and read the first verse: "I said, I will take heed to my ways, that I sin not with my tongue." "That will do for the present," said Pambo; and he took his leave, saying, "I will go, and learn that first." A month rolled past, but Pambo returned not; two months, three months, when the missionary happened to encounter him in the city, and asked him if he would go on with his Bible lessons. "Not yet," said Pambo; "I have not yet mastered my first lesson." Forty-nine years afterwards he gave the very same answer to one who asked him the like question. Hear what St. James saith, "If any man among you seems to be religious, but bridleth not his tongue, this man's religion is vain."

Tormented by Devils.

Christian's progress through the Valley of Humiliation and that of the Shadow of Death.

The points of resemblance between Bunyan's allegory of Christian in the Valley of Humiliation and that of the Shadow of Death, with the legends of some of the saints, are so striking that they may be profitably placed side by side, and may throw some light upon each other.

Early in his career Christian came to the palace Beautiful, where he was hospitably entertained, and before he left he was furnished with the whole armour of God. Discretion, Piety, Charity, and Prudence conduct him down the hill, and bid him farewell. Then Christian entered the Valley of Humiliation, but he had not gone far when Apollyon met him, and began to question him about his antecedents. He represented to the wayfarer the dangers of the way, and promised many delights if he would go back. As Christian stood firm to his purpose, the tempter told him he had no ground of hope that God would accept him, seeing he had already so often broken His laws, and wandered from His ways. Christian freely admitted his great unworthiness, but pleaded the abounding mercy of God, which (he said) had already pardoned him. Then Apollyon broke out into a grievous rage, and bade Christian prepare to die, for "I swear thou shalt go no further." So saying, the great adversary threw a flaming dart; but Christian caught it on his shield of faith, and drew his sword in self-defence. The encounter was long and dangerous. Christian fell, and his sword flew out of his hand. "Now am I sure of you," cried Apollyon, and pressed him almost to death; but as the foul fiend lifted up his hand to give the death-stroke, Christian contrived to regain his sword, and gave Apollyon such a deadly thrust, that he flew off and was no more seen. "Rejoice not against me, O mine enemy; for when I fall, I shall arise. Nay, in all these things we are more than conquerors through Him that loved us." Bunyan says, "No man can imagine, unless he had seen and heard, as I did, what yelling and hideous roaring Apollyon made all the time of the fight, and what sighs and groans burst from Christian's heart." When the battle was over there came to him a hand with some of the leaves of the tree of life, which Christian applied to his wounds, and immediately thep were healed. Christian now addressed himself to his journey, but alas! the Valley of Humiliation only led to another valley, called that of the Shadow of Death, if possible more fearful and dangerous still. The path was very narrow, with a deep ditch on one side and a dangerous quag on the other. It was so dark withal, that ofttimes when Christian raised his foot he knew not where to set it down next. In the midst of the valley was the mouth of hell, through which ever and anon burst flame and smoke. As the pilgrim journeyed on through the valley, with his weapon "All-prayer" in his hand, he was assailed by most hideous noises, doleful voices, and rushings to and fro, so that sometimes he expected to be torn to pieces or trodden down like mire. This continued for several miles, so that sometimes Christian thought he really must turn back; but, when the fiends came nearest and his case seemed most desperate, he cried with vehemence, "I will walk in the strength of the Lord God;" whereupon the fiends gave back, and he heard before him a voice which said, "Though I walk through the valley of the shadow of death, I will fear no evil: for Thou art with me; Thy rod and Thy staff they comfort me." So he knew that some one who trusted on the Saviour was in the valley besides himself, and hoped in good time to find a companion to keep him company.—Pt. i. ch. ix., x.

St. Antony of Padua tormented by the devil. One night the devil tried to throttle St. Antony of Padua; but the man of God commended himself to the "glorious Virgin," and the foul fiend flew away. (See Antony, p. 452.)—Edward Kinesman, *Lives of the Saints* (1623).

St. Hilarion tormented by devils. St. Hilarion lived as a hermit, and one night, while at his prayers, he heard the crying of children, the mourning of women, the alarums of armies, the bleating of sheep, the bellowing of bulls, the roaring of lions, the hissing of serpents, and sundry other noises. Calling to mind the craft of the devil, he fell flat on the ground, and made the sign of the cross. Then, raising his eyes, he saw a chariot drawn by furious horses, which seemed to kick him and scamper over him. The holy youth called on Jesus with a loud voice, and in an instant the earth opened and swallowed up the chariot. The noises ceased at the same time, and Hilarion cried in rapture, "Sing unto the Lord a new song, for He hath triumphed gloriously; the horse and his rider hath He thrown into the abyss."—St. Jerome, *Vita St. Hilarionis Eremitæ* (A.D. 390).

St. Nicholas of Tolentino tormented by the devil. St. Nicholas of Tolentino was much vexed and tormented by the devil, who used all his wiles to draw the man of God from his abstinence and penances by scoffs and threats; sometimes beating him, and otherwise ill-treating him in such sort that the friars, hearing the uproar, would run to his defence. They always found him on the floor of his cell utterly exhausted, like a dead man, and would gently lift him on his straw pallet.—St. Antonius of Florence, *Chronicon.*

St. Romualdus in the Valley of Humiliation, etc. (A.D. 907–1027). Not long after St. Romualdus had entered on his monastic life, the spirit of darkness, which seems to have slept for awhile, rose in full strength to oppose his further progress in the way of holiness, and attacked him with terrible assaults. He set strongly before the pilgrim the pleasures he had abandoned, and the rugged ways of the new life he had chosen. The more Romualdus tried to lean upon God, the more his mind was troubled. When now he was well-nigh distracted, the malignant tempter assaulted his body with fiery darts; scared him at nights with horrible voices and unearthy noises, and seemed to threaten him under most frightful forms, troubling his imagination with revolting thoughts. This contest continued for five years. Sometimes the foul fiend, assuming the form of a hideous human being, would hurl the recluse to the earth, kneel on him with his knees, kick him with his feet, and try to strangle him; but the saint would only mock his assailant, saying, "O my enemy, being chased out of heaven, resort you to this desert? Avaunt, I say, vile serpent!" Then would the devil flee, and Christ Himself come to the cell to bring comfort to His disciple. "Thy heart has been sore pained within thee, and the terrors of death have fallen upon thee; fearfulness and trembling have come upon thee, and horror hath overwhelmed thee; but cast thy burden upon the Lord, and He will sustain thee. He will never suffer the righteous to be moved."—Bollandus, *Acta Sanctorum*, Feb., vol. ii. (Jerome of Prague and Peter Damien also wrote the life of this saint.)

Touch not Mine Anointed.

PSALM cv. 15. Touch not Mine anointed, and do My prophets no harm.

St. Catherine of Sweden, being molested, was miraculously defended. A nobleman wanted to marry St. Catherine, daughter of prince Ulpho of Sweden, but seeing no hope, determined to abduct her. Accordingly, as she was going with other ladies to St. Sebastian's church, he waylaid her. A stag happened to attract his attention, and while he was thus engaged, St. Catherine secured her retreat. On her return home, her mother congratulated her on her escape, and said to her, "Blessed be God, my daughter, who sent His stag to deliver you from the snare of the fowler."

At another time, going to the church of St. Laurent, a cavalier was about to lay his hand on her, when he was instantly struck blind, and a voice said to him, "Touch not Mine anointed, and do My prophets no harm." Repenting of his fault, the cavalier threw himself at the feet of the saint, begging pardon; and St. Catherine offering up her prayers on his behalf, God gave him back his sight. The cavalier told this story to the pope himself.

This "miracle" was repeated not long afterwards at Assisa, as Catherine was going with her mother to St. Mary's church. Some brigands tried to seize her, but were struck with instantaneous blindness, and the holy maiden escaped from their hands.—Ulpho (a Brigittine monk), *Life of St. Catherine of Sweden.* (Written 1411, only thirty years after her death.)

Trees Symbolize Man.

DEUT. xx. 19. The tree of the field is man's life.

ISA. lxv. 22. As the days of a tree are the days of My people.

EZEK. xxxi. 3–12. The Assyrian was a cedar in Lebanon, with fair branches, and of high stature; fair in his greatness and in the length of his branches. But the terrible of the nations cut him off; his branches fell, and his boughs were broken off. Lebanon mourned for him, and all the trees of the field fainted for him.

St. Honoré symbolizes himself in a bay tree (thirteenth century). When St. Honoré told his mother he was about to take a journey to Thenezay, she tried to dissuade him from going, having a presentiment that she would never see him again. They were sitting together at the time under a bay tree, and Honoré said to his mother, "See this tree, planted by my father on the day of my birth. This tree will always represent me. If I am well, it will be vigorous; if I am ill, it will droop; if I die, it will wither." St. Honoré left Buzançais, taking two brothers, named Gabidier, with him. For a time the bay tree remained green and vigorous, but one morning it was found withered to its roots. The anxious mother felt persuaded her son was dead; and, giving the alarm, several of the neighbours went in search of their fellow-townsman. They came to a spot smeared with blood, and soon found the body of the murdered man, whose head had been severed from the body, and thrust under some bushes. The brothers Gabidier had murdered him. They were both executed, and St. Honoré was buried with due honours.—J. Veilliat, *Pious Legends of Berri.*

Triads.

ST. PAUL. "Now abide these three, faith, hope, and charity; but the greatest of these is charity" (1 Cor. xiii. 13).

DANTE. Dante's regeneration triad is —light, grace, and mercy.

MATTHEW ARNOLD. Matthew Arnold's three regenerating virtues are — light, sweetness, and culture.

Two-edged Sword.

HEB. iv. 12. The Word of God is quick and powerful, and sharper than any two-edged sword . . . and is a discerner of the thoughts and intents of the heart.

REV. i. 16. Out of His mouth went a sharp two-edged sword.

PSALM cxlix. 5, 6. Let the saints be joyful

in glory. Let them sing aloud upon their beds. Let the high praises of God be in their mouth, and a two-edged sword in their hand.

St. Flora, greatly harassed by the devil, is given a two-edged sword (A.D. 1309–1347). St. Flora was greatly annoyed by the devil, who was no sooner resisted in one temptation than he tried another. God, who had sufficiently tried her fidelity, sent an angel to give her a two-edged sword. It was very sharp, and would pierce even to the dividing asunder of soul and spirit, and of the joints and marrow. The young virgin took this sword into her hand, and then felt herself armed against all the attacks of the devil. —L'abbé Cyprien Lacarrière, *Life of St. Flora.*

There can be no doubt that this was originally mere figure of speech, subsequently perverted into a realistic and miraculous incident.

Ubiquity.

1 COR. v. 3. Absent in body, but present in spirit.

COL. ii. 5. Though I be absent in the flesh, yet am I with you in spirit, beholding your order.

1 THESS. ii. 17. We, brethren, being taken from you for a short time, [yet] present, not in heart, endeavoured to see your face with great desire.

St. Benet-Joseph, like St. Druon (see below), *was often in two or more places at the same time* (A.D. 1748–1783). The author of the life of Benet-Joseph says, "Benoît fut aussi l'objet d'une faveur que Dieu semble avoir réservée pour nos temps, afin de mieux confondre l'incrédulité par ce miracle le plus inexplicable de tous: On le vit souvent en plusieurs endroits différents, juste à la même heure." Thus while he was confined in the "hospice des pauvres," where he was all the last years of his life, and from which no inmate was on any account to absent himself, he was seen by many in adoration before the Holy Sacrament, at different hours of the night, and even after midnight. He was also seen on Christmas night, 1782, in Notre-Dame des Monts, both at matins and also at the night mass, kissing the feet of the infant Jesus.—R. P. Desnoyers, *Le Bienheureux Benoît-Joseph Labre.*

Perhaps in the opinion of many this "miracle," which seems to the biographer both more "inexplicable," and more limited to these later days, is neither the one nor the other. The mind informing the eyes, as in dreams and illusions, is as old as man himself, and it is no more "inexplicable" that persons should see the sick man where he was not, than that Macbeth should see Banquo on hi own stool in the banquet-room.

Je ne puis pas être, comme St. Druon en deux lieux en même temps. St. Druon (A.D. 1118–1189) was born at Epinoy in Artois, and hired himself out as a shepherd in Hainaut. In this occupation he greatly regretted that he could never leave his sheep to go and receive the Eucharist. This privation, however, was removed by an angel, who assumed the form of the shepherd, and kept watch over his flock, whenever he went to the sacrifice of the mass. Hence arose the proverb, "I cannot be in two places at the same time, like St. Druon."—L'abbé Destombes, *Saints d'Arras.*

St. John-Joseph de la Croix was often in two places at the same moment (A.D. 1654–1734). Cardinal Wiseman says, God refused not to St. John-Joseph the singular prerogative sometimes accorded to the saints of being present in two or more places at the same moment, or at least of going from one place to another with the rapidity of thought. Thus, while he was confined in his cell grievously ill, "une dame l'envoya chercher pour venir l'entendre à l'église." "You see," said the saint to a lackey, "in what a state I now am. I cannot stir." But when the lackey reported these words to his mistress, she would not believe him; "for," said she, "I have just seen him, and conversed with him."

Again: Francisco Viveros, the domestic of a duchess, went to the cell of St. John-Joseph, and asked him to accompany him to the duchess, who greatly desired to see him. The saint replied, "You see I am unable to move from my bed." Francisco Viveros hastened back to inform his mistress, but on entering the chamber of the duchess, there was the saint at her bedside, administering consolation.

Another instance. Madame Artemisia, mother of the marquis de Rugiano, being seized with excruciating pain, and having no one at hand whom she could send to St. John-Joseph, exclaimed in her agony, "O Father John-Joseph, how I wish I could see you! O Father, why are you so far off in my distress? There is no one I can send to fetch you. O Father John-Joseph, would God that you were here!" She had not finished speaking when the saint was at her bedside, and said cheerfully, "Courage, lady. It is nothing. It is nothing." Then he gave his benediction, the pain ceased, and the saint vanished in a moment.—Migne, *Démonstrations Evangéliques*, vol. xvi.

Mary Magdalene of Pazzi had the gift of being in two places at the same time

(A.D. 1566–1607). Mgr. Guérin says, "Non seulement notre sainte [*i.e.* Mary Magdalene of Pazzi] eut de ces visions, mais on l'a vue aussi elle-même, bien qu'encore vivante, en des lieux d'où elle était fort éloignée: Car elle apparut à Catherine de Rabatta, sa sœur, qui avait mal à l'œil, et la guérit en lui touchant seulement la paupière."—*Vies des Saints*, vol. v. p. 170.

The chamberlain does not tell us where Mary Magdalene was at the time, nor yet where her sister Catherine was. The sentence quoted is every word he tells us about the matter.

St. Philip of Neri was often in two or more places at the same time (A.D. 1515–1595). St. Philip of Neri was often seen in several different places at the same moment. At one time, while he was in the house of St. Jerome, he was seen in St. Mary's church of Vallicella. At another time, while he was at Rome, he showed himself to Catherine, a nun of the Order of St. Augustine, in Tuscany. On another occasion, while he was at Rome, one of his penitents, going from Rome to Naples, was taken by pirates; and, to save himself from captivity, he threw himself into the sea, calling on the name of Philip of Neri. Instantly Philip was at his side, caught him by the hair, and drew him safe to shore.—*The Bull of Canonization by Gregory XV.*

Wants supplied.

PSALM xxiii. 1. The Lord is my Shepherd; I shall not want.

PSALM xxxiv. 10. They that seek shall not want any good.

St. Dominic, wanting to cross a ferry, finds the fare at his feet. St. Dominic, according to the precept of Christ, never took money about with him; and if he required a ferry, he had to ask for a free passage. On one occasion, the boatman refused to put him across a river unless he paid his fare, like others. St. Dominic lifted up his eyes to heaven as if in prayer, then stooping down, picked up the necessary coin from the ground, and was ferried across the river.—*Les Petits Bollandistes*, vol. ix. p. 284.

The Virgin Mary deposits money on a stone for Hermann (A.D. 1075). One day Hermann, while still a boy, entered into Cologne cathedral barefoot; this was in the depth of winter. The Virgin Mary appeared to him, and asked why he went barefooted. "Alas!" said the boy, "the poverty of my parents constrains me." The Virgin then pointed to a stone, and told him to go and see what he could find there. He went, and found four pieces of silver, and, returning, thanked the Virgin for her benevolence. She kissed him, and said, "When in want, return to the stone, and you shall always find sufficient for your daily bread." This occurred often; and what makes the miracle especially surprising, is that other boys from time to time went with him, but none of them, except he himself, ever saw the deposit. "Celui qui a écrit le premier cette histoire assure l'avoir apprise de sa propre bouche, un peu avant qu'il mourût."—*Les Petits Bollandistes*, vol. iv. p. 272.

Water Innocuous.

ISA. xliii. 2. When thou passest through water, I will be with thee; and through rivers, they shall not overflow thee.

St. Cosmus and St. Damian, cast bound into a river, were not drowned. Lisias, governor of Egeas, commanded Cosmus and Damian to be bound hand and foot, and cast into the river. The sentence was obeyed, but an angel unbound them, and brought them safe to land; for God was with them, and would not suffer the river to overflow them.—Ado (archbishop of Trèves), *Martyrology;* and Metaphrastês, *Lives*, etc.

St. Godrich uninjured by a flood of water (A.D. 1170). St. Godrich was a native of Walpole, in Norfolk, who earned his living as a pedlar. Being converted, he turned hermit, and lived at Whitby, then called Finkley, in a cabin on the bank of a river. On one occasion the river overflowed, and inundated the whole country round about, including the hermitage. The neighbours, fearing the hermit was drowned, ran to the meadow, but could find neither hermit nor hut. All supposed the hut had been swept away by the flood, and that the hermit was dead. When the waters subsided, the neighbours were amazed to see the monk alive and the hut still standing, wholly uninjured. Godrich, being asked about the flood, expressed surprise, and declared that no water had come nigh his dwelling. "It is thus that God never forgets those who forget not Him."—Nicholas of Durham, *Life of St. Godrich.*

White Stone and a New Name.

REV. ii. 17. John the divine was commanded to write to the Church of Pergamos, "To him that overcometh will I give a white stone, and in the stone a new name written, which no man knoweth, save he that receiveth it."

Explained: In primitive times, when travelling was difficult for want of places of public entertainment, hospitality was exercised by private individuals to a great extent. Persons thus entertained often contracted friendship with the entertainers, and both Greeks and Romans had marks in recognition of this mutual regard, which were given to guests, and which were kept as heirlooms in the family. A very usual mark was a white stone cut in twain. On one of the halves the host wrote his name, and the guest on the other. The host's name was handed to the guest, and the guest's name to the host. To produce this tessera would always suffice to secure a welcome to remotest descendants. Of course, the stones were kept private, and the name written on them was sacred. Look now at the application: "I will give him that overcometh to eat of the hidden manna," for he shall be My guest, and eat at My table, and "I will give him a white stone, on which shall be written a new name, that no man, but he who receives it, knoweth."—Blunt, *Exposition of the Epistles to the Seven Churches of Asia.*

St. Angela of Brescia sees angels carrying white stones (A.D. 1474–1540). Angela of Brescia lost her father and mother when she was only ten years old. Her uncle Biancosi took charge of her, but he also died when she was twenty-two. Angela was much distressed at the bad education of Italian girls, and bent her mind to devise a remedy. One day, when she was in the country with some companions, she saw a ladder, like that seen by Jacob, reaching from earth to heaven. A great number of virgins were mounting it two and two, their heads ornamented with rich crowns. They were accompanied by angels dressed in white, and all carried on their foreheads a white stone, with something written on it, which Angela could not read. As she looked and admired, a voice from the ladder said to her, "Angela, take courage. Before you die, you shall establish in Brescia a society of virgins, like those you see here; and Christ shall give them white stones, in which shall be written the new name." It was twenty years before God opened a way to the fulfilment of this promise, and then she founded the society called the Ursulines.—*Life of St. Angela of Brescia* (Montpellier, 1804).

In Christian art St. Angela is represented with a Jacob's ladder, up which her virgins are ascending two and two.

Wings.

ISA. xl. 31. They that wait upon the Lord shall mount up with wings as eagles.

St. Vincent Ferrier had wings occasionally when he "waited on the Lord" (A.D. 1357–1419). "Chose qui semble incroyable, un public entier a vu St. Vincent Ferrier au milieu de sa prédication prendre subitement des ailes, s'envoler dans les airs, disparaître pouraller très-loin consoler et encourager une personne malade qui réclamait son assistance, et puis revinir de la même manière après avoir rempli cet acte de charité, pour continuer sa prédication." Hence St. Vincent Ferrier in Christian art is often represented with wings like an angel.—Mgr. Guérin (chamberlain of pope Leo XIII.), *Vies des Saints* (1880), vol. iv. p. 239.

Wolves.

ISA. xi. 6–9. The wolf shall dwell with the lamb, and the leopard shall lie down with the kid; and the calf and the young lion and the fatling together; and a little child shall lead them. . . . They shall not hurt nor destroy in all My holy mountain; for the earth shall be full of the knowledge of the Lord.

ISA. lxv. 25. The wolf and the lamb shall feed together, and the lion shall eat straw like the bullock.

HOS. ii. 18. In that day will I make a covenant for them with the beasts of the field, and with the fowls of heaven, and with the creeping things of the ground: and I will break the bow and the sword and the battle out of the earth, and will make them to lie down safely.

Andrew Corcini converted from a wolf to a lamb (A.D. 1302–1373). Andrew Corcini was the son of wealthy parents in Florence. Shortly before his birth, his mother dreamt she had brought forth a wolf, and that her wolfish offspring ran into a church, and became transformed into a lamb. As the boy grew up he proved a very wolf indeed, worldly, selfish, impious, fond of persecution, and given to cruelty. One day his mother said to him, "Andrew, you are in very truth the child of my dream," and when the young man inquired of his mother to what she referred, she told him. He was greatly struck with what he heard, spent the night in solitude and prayer, and next day went to the church of the Carmelites, and prostrating himself before the image of the Virgin, uttered these words: "Glorious Virgin, see the wolf full of iniquity at thy feet. Thy offspring, O mother, was a Lamb without blemish. Make me also a lamb of God, and receive me into the fold." For three hours he continued thus, when the prior saw him, and asked him what he craved. Andrew told him, and implored to be taken from the wicked world into the Carmelite order. In due time his request was granted, and he became transformed into the humblest, most industrious, self-denying, and self-abased of all the brotherhood. He was ultimately bishop of Fiesolê.—Surius, *Lives of the Saints* (1570).

St. Blaise dwells peacefully with wild beasts. When St. Blaise fled from Sebastê, in Syria, through fear of Agricolaus, he lay concealed in a cave "in a craggy mountain called Argeus." Here savage beasts visited him daily; and if, by chance, they happened to drop in while he was in prayer, "they would reverently wait till he rose from his knees." Sometimes the wolf and the sheep would meet in the cave, the lion and the lamb, tigers, bears, leopards, and kids, yet none would hurt another; but there would they bide in friendly intercourse, till the holy man gave them his blessing, and bade them go in peace. Some of them he quite transformed, so that those beasts which before preyed on each other, ate grass like oxen; and whenever he saw any defiled with blood, he never failed to chide them for their cruelty, and told them to abandon their evil ways.—Metaphrastês, *Life of St. Blaise.*

We have all seen what are called "happy families," in which will be cats and mice, birds of prey and canaries, dogs and rats, with other small deer. In exhibitions we have seen wild beasts associating with those on which they prey; but for carnivorous beasts to eat grass and hay is quite another matter; and before they could do so their whole animal structure must be remodelled, from their teeth to their claws.

St. Laumer and the wolves. One day a troop of wolves were pursuing a hind, when the terrified creature ran to St. Laumer, and crouched at his feet for protection. St. Laumer patted the panting beast most lovingly, and commanded the wolves to be off; whereupon the savage beasts went peacefully away, leaving the hind unharmed.—Surius, *Lives of the Saints* (6 vols. folio).

This tale looks like an allegory, in which the hind symbolizes the Christian Church, and the wolves the powers of evil. "Saul, Saul, why persecutest thou Me?" said a voice from heaven to the future apostle. "Wolves, wolves," said St. Laumer, "why persecute the poor hind?" and many found protection in caves and woods, when driven from their native dwelling-places by the savagery of man.

Torello, by prayer, rescues a child from the mouth of a wolf (A.D. 1282). Torello of Poppi, in Tuscany, saw a wolf seize a child, while its mother was washing linen in the river Arno. He immediately offered up a prayer to God, and commanded the wolf to drop its prey. The wolf obeyed; whereupon Torello healed the teeth-marks of the savage beast, and returned the child safe and sound to its mother. He then forbade the wolves in future to injure any inhabitant of Poppi; and from that day to this his command has been rigidly obeyed. In Christian art Torello, in remembrance of this act, is represented with a wolf at his side.—*Acta Sanctorum* (Bollandists), vol. ii. March 16.

St. William of Aquitaine converted from a wolf to a lamb (A.D. 1157). William, count of Poitou and duke of Guyenne, was a giant in stature and a wild beast in disposition. He lived in adultery with his brother's wife, and was so violent in temper that no man was hardy enough to resist him. He is described as overbearing to his vassals, cruel to strangers, without pity to his enemies, quarrelsome with his equals, debauched with self-indulgence, and revengeful. A more hopeless subject for God's grace could not be imagined, but this Saul the malignant persecutor became a Paul in humility, zeal, and Christian love. The wolf became a lamb, and the leopard a kid. The lion which no man durst encounter, became the gentle fondling that a child might lead; and the veriest infant might play unharmed on this cockatrice's den. St. Bernard reasoned with him, but to no effect; but one day, after celebrating mass, St. Bernard took with him to the duke's palace "the body of Jesus Christ on a paten." He went straight to the duke, and said, "We have called, but ye have refused; we have stretched out our hands, but ye have not regarded. Ye have set at nought all my counsel, and would none of my reproof; behold, now the Son of the Virgin is come to you, the chief among the ten thousand, the Lord of the kingdom of God. You may mock at His counsel, you may laugh at His reproof, but know, O man, He will call you into judgment. Then ye shall call, when fear cometh as desolation, and destruction as a whirlwind; but He will not answer.

Then shall ye seek, when anguish is come upon you; but ye shall not find Him. If now ye turn your back upon your Saviour, then the Judge will turn His back upon thee, saying, 'I never knew you. Depart from Me, ye cursed, into everlasting fire, prepared for the devil and his angels.'" These words were uttered with unspeakable solemnity, and a fearlessness superhuman. They went right home by the power of the Holy Ghost, and the duke trembled, fell at the bishop's feet foaming, but unable to utter a word. Some of his household picked him up, but again he fell to the ground. St. Bernard touched him with his foot, and demanded what answer he made to the call of God. The bold rebel, rebel now no longer, burst into tears, and cried in anguish of spirit, "What must I do to be saved?" St. Bernard then told him what he ought to do; and from that moment the count was an altered man, whose one concern was the salvation of his soul, and whose whole study was to crucify the body with its affections and its lusts. Leaving his court, he betook him to a desert, where he lived as a hermit, and called himself "the chief of sinners." He used to say, "Many souls, now in hell, have sighed for the hair shirt of Jerome, the tears of Arsenius, the pallet of Eulalius, the nakedness of Paul, and the food of Elijah, but their sighs never led them to repentance and good works."—Thibault, *Life of Guillaume of Aquitaine* (abridged by Surius).

Women's Apparel.

1 Tim. ii. 9. In like manner also I will that women adorn themselves in modest apparel. Not with broided hair, or gold, or pearls, or costly array.

St. Paul of the Cross causes a lady, immodestly dressed, to turn black (A.D. 1694–1775). In Orbetello, St. Paul of the Cross reproved the women for immodesty of dress; but a French lady, determined to show her independence of spirit, planted herself just under the missionary's eyes in an exaggerated low costume. St. Paul stood gazing on her with a fixed stare, and gradually her face, hands, arms, neck, shoulders, all became as black as charcoal. The congregation was horrified. The lady fell at the saint's feet, imploring pardon; but she was not suffered to recover her former looks for two or three days.—Father Pius, *Life of St. Paul of the Cross, Founder of the Passionists.*

Words spoken by Saints spread Far and Wide.

Rom. x. 18. But I say, Have they not heard? Yes verily, their sound went into all the earth, and their words unto the ends of the world.

The sermon of St. Antony of Padua heard three miles off (A.D. 1195-1231). St. Antony of Padua was a most popular preacher. And one day, when he went to Bruges to preach, the crowds were so great he was obliged to preach in the open fields. A woman living about three miles off wished much to hear the preacher; but her husband, being indisposed and by no means a religious man, would not consent to her leaving the house. Very vexed, she went to her chamber, and, opening the window, was astonished to find she could hear every word as distinctly as if she had been on the spot. Her husband asked why she did not come down, and she said she was listening to the sermon. He laughed at the notion, but, going upstairs, found he could hear the words spoken quite plainly. The chronicler adds, "Que ce seul fait décida de sa conversion, et que, dans la suite, au lieu de contrarier son épouse dans ses exercices de piété, il voulut assister avec elle à tous les sermons du missionnaire franciscain."—L'abbé Guyard, *Life of St. Antony of Padua.* (See also Edward Kinesman (1623), *Lives of the Saints*, p. 367.)

St. Gregory the thaumaturgist hears the prayer of Fedimus three miles off. Fedimus, bishop of Amasia, wanted to consecrate St. Gregory the thaumaturgist over Neocæsarea, and went in search of him; but, not finding him, said, "O Lord, Thou seest both Gregory and me. I desired to lay my hands upon him, and consecrate him; but let my words now spoken serve the same end. I do now consecrate him unto Thee, and give him the oversight of Neocæsarea to the honour of Thy holy name. Amen." Though St. Gregory was three miles off when these words were spoken, he heard them as plainly as if they had been spoken in his presence, and went at once to Fedimus, who forthwith made him bishop with the usual ceremonies.—St. Gregory of Nyssa, *Life of St. Gregory Thaumaturgist.*

Wounds healed.

Psalm cxlvii. 3. He healeth the broken in heart, and bindeth up their wounds.

Jer. xxx. 17. I will restore health unto thee, and will heal thee of thy wounds.

St. Francis of Paula miraculously cures a cut leg (A.D. 1416–1507). A young monk of the order of St. Augustine, named Francis, was sent to cut wood in a forest, and gave himself with his hatchet a dreadful cut on the right foot; the blood gushed out, and the wound was very serious. St. Francis of Paula happened to be in the forest at the time; and immediately he was aware of the accident, went to the young man, and by his mere touch healed the wound in an instant. So complete was the cure, that the young man was able to continue his work just as if nothing had happened. —Father Giry, *Life of St. Francis of Paula* (chiefly taken from the witnesses examined, the speech made, and the bull issued at canonization).

The wounds of St. Christina healed (A.D. 300). The following tale by Ado, in the *Acta Sanctorum*, is wholly unparalleled. Christina was a child not above ten years old, living at Tur, in Tuscany, on the borders of the lake Bolsena. It no longer exists, having been swept away by an inundation. Her father, Urban, was prefect and governor of the town. It appears that this child, as Ado says, "was moved by the Holy Ghost to become a Christian," and showed her conversion by stealing her father's idols, made of gold and silver, breaking them up, and giving the pieces to the poor. Urban was naturally very angry at this, and whipped her soundly, and so far no blame can be attached to him—probably any sensible man under the same circumstances would have done the same; but the sequel is a Pelion upon Ossa of diabolical cruelty. Having whipped the child, he scourged her with scorpions, and while her body was covered with blood, tore the flesh with iron claws till the bones were bared. Says Ado, "This savagery, far from causing the child to relent, only confirmed her resolution to stand fast in the faith into which she had been called;" and, picking up the gobbets of flesh at her feet, she handed them to her father. Of course, this insolence only irritated him the more, and he sent the child to prison, laden with heavy irons. When in prison, she was first bound on a wheel drenched with oil, the oil set alight, and the wheel being turned racked all her bones out of joint. But the oil, refusing to burn the child, "tournant ses flammes sur une troupe d'infidèles que la curiosité et le plaisir avaient fait accourir à ce spectacle, il en consuma un grand nombre." The father, seeing this, was frightened, and ran home; while an angel, coming into the prison, comforted the child, healed her wounds, and inspired her with new courage and resolution. Urban, though alarmed, would not relent, and accordingly sent an officer to tie a great stone round the child's neck and to throw her into the Bolsena. Here again the angel was at hand to keep her from harm. He allayed her terror, bore her in his arms, and carried her to the bank. The father, mad with rage, fell down in a fit, and "le lendemain on le trouva mort dans son lit." He was succeeded in office by Dion, who resolved to carry on the same vindictiveness, and threw the child into an iron chest filled with boiling pitch and oil; but Christina, with the sign of the cross, reduced the boiling elements into a refreshing bath, saying to the men around, "You have placed me in this font that I may be born again by the baptism of regeneration by the grace of God." The men, irritated by these words, dragged her naked by the hair of her head to the temple of Apollo, and commanded her to burn incense to the god. No sooner were the words uttered than the idol fell from its pedestal, and was dashed into a thousand pieces, at which sight "trois mille de ces infidèles, qui y étaient présents, se convertirent à la foi." Well, Dion died suddenly as Urban had done, and the next governor was Julian, who determined to revenge the death of his two predecessors. This third doughty giant cast the child into a furnace; but the flames touched her not. Here she remained five days the companion of spirits and angels. Having failed in this, Julian next applied to a magician, who shut up the child in a dark cave, filled with adders and serpents, asps and vipers; but they played lovingly with Christina, and did her no harm. Julian then plucked her tongue out by the roots; but her voice was as sweet and her words as articulate as they were before. Having lost all patience, the governor then bound her to a post, and set a band of soldiers to discharge their arrows at her till she died. "Cette précieuse mort arriva le 24 juillet, comme il est marqué dans tous les Martyrologes."

In some copies of St. Augustine's *Psalm* cxx., the word Christina has been substituted for Crispina. Pilgrimages are made to her tomb, monasteries and churches have been dedicated to her honour. Her relics are still carried twice a year in procession through the parish of Viserny, and many pictures have represented her martyrdom, so that there can be no doubt that the tale is accepted as an unvarnished truth. Yet is it not amazing, is it not indeed lamentable, that such palpable romance should be set forth with authority, taught as veritable history, held up for our example, and honoured with the halo of canonisation?

Filumena, the nineteenth-century thaumaturgist (third century). The discovery of this new saint has been recorded in the first part of this volume (p. 21), and as nothing was known about her, her ghost came to three different persons in 1836, to reveal the mystery of her life and death. It first appeared to a young artisan, then to a priest, and then to some nuns at Naples. These nuns had an image of the hypothetical saint, which they carried in solemn pomp to their chapel and set on the high altar. Then, greatly longing to know all about the stranger, the image began to roll its head about, open and shut its eyes, and at length said with touching sweetness, "Dear sisters, it was the 10th of August on which I changed my mortal for immortality; and it was my everlasting Spouse who brought me to Mugnano, not to be buried in obscurity, but to be set before the universal Church, that henceforth the day of my martyrdom may be a great and holy festival." The abbot Darche says, "Ces paroles portaient avec elles des preuves de la vérité." In my judgment they bear on the surface the proof of imposition; but let that pass. They were duly reported to Dom Francis, who "les trouve parfaitement d'accord avec la vérité;" and his reply comforted the nuns and encouraged them to go on further. Accordingly, not many days afterwards, the ghost visited them again in their oratory, and told them, saying, "My mother was of the blood royal, and had for neighbour one Publius, a Christian, who taught my parents the new faith, and baptized them. I was born after their conversion, and they called me the 'child of the Light of Life,' *Filia Luminis*, contracted into *Fi-lumen*, whence I was called 'Fi-lumena.' When I was thirteen years old, the emperor Diocletian asked me in marriage. Both my parents urged me to accept so great an honour; but I told them I had vowed to be the spouse of Christ, and would be the bride of no other. They told me I was far too young to know my own mind; but I replied that I was not too young to remember my Creator in the days of my youth, not too young to have a heart and to give it to the Lord. When the emperor was informed of my resolution his anger burst forth in terrible fury, and he ordered me to be confined in the palace donjon, well laden with chains. Every day he visited me to shake my obstinacy; but he could not separate me from my love of Christ my Saviour. For forty days I was kept a prisoner, when the blessed Virgin, holding her divine Son in her arms, entered the donjon, and told me in three days I should be released. The announcement made my heart leap with joy, when the mother of God added, 'My daughter, after your release you will pass through much anguish into paradise, having been made perfect by suffering. Remember you are called 'The Daughter of Light,' and my Son was 'The Light of the World,' and I am 'The Mother of Light.' He is the Sun, I am the Moon, and you the Morning Star. In all your anguish the angel Gabriel will be with you, to console you and strengthen you. Farewell.' Scarcely had the queen of heaven left me, when Diocletian, with his officers, entered the donjon. Said the emperor, 'I will teach you what it is to insult me, by preferring an infamous malefactor to the emperor of the world.' I was then stripped, tied to a pillar, and scourged till my whole body was a bleeding wound. When I fainted, and my persecutor thought me dead, he and his myrmidons withdrew, and two shining ones came and healed my wounds with balm from paradise. Next day the emperor, being informed that I was more beautiful than ever, came to me, looked on me with unfeigned amazement, and told me to return thanks to Jupiter for having healed me, and promised to make me the empress of Rome. When I rejected his advances, he commanded his men to bind an anchor round my neck and cast me into the Tiber. His order was executed, but two angels caught me in their arms, loosed me from the anchor, and carried me to the banks of the river in the sight of thousands. By this miracle 'un grand nombre de spectateurs se convertirent à la foi;' but Diocletian called it magic, and commanded me to be dragged naked through the streets of Rome, and a shower of arrows was discharged at me. Again I fainted, and, being taken to my donjon, was thought to be dead; but I fell asleep, and during sleep all my wounds were healed. Next day I was cast into a furnace, which burnt to death six of my tormentors; but, happy for me, Christ Himself came and carried my soul to paradise, where He placed on my head the crowns of virginity and martyrdom."

PART III.

DOGMATIC MIRACLES;

OR,

MIRACLES TO PROVE ECCLESIASTICAL DOGMAS.

PART III.

Apparitions.

The ghost of St. Anastasius reproves Areta for not paying honour to his relics (A.D. 628). When the relics of St. Anastasius were carried to Cæsarea, in Palestine, all the city went in procession, except one woman, whose name was Areta. This women was one of the aristocracy of the place, and said she saw no reason why she should trouble herself about the relics of a Persian; but she was soon taught otherwise. At night, the ghost of St. Anastasius came to her. It was dressed in the usual habit of a monk, and reproved her severely for her impiety. Areta, being seized at the same moment with violent pains, wholly lost her power of speech. She was advised to recommend her petition to St. Anastasius, and accordingly went to the place where his relics were deposited, and again the ghost appeared to her. She paid it the honour required, and immediately lost her pains, and recovered her speech. The relics of the saint were subsequently removed to Constantinople, and the empress Irene built a church there in their honour.—*The Fourth Session of the Second Council of Nice.*

While St. Simon was imprisoned in the Luxembourg, his ancestor Charlemagne appeared to him, and said, "Since the world began, no family has produced a hero of the first magnitude. This honour has been reserved for my house. My son, thy success in philosophy shall equal that of mine in war and politics." St. Simon was at the time thirty-eight years of age, and from that moment began the study of science, of which he was then profoundly ignorant. So he invited to his house the most renowned professors, and by conversation obtained the information he longed for.

St. Angela's sister shows herself after death (fifteenth century). John Merici of Desenzano, in the diocese of Verona, had two daughters, the younger of whom was named Angela. Her father and mother died when she was only ten years old, and an uncle, named Biancosi, took charge of the two sisters. Ere long the elder sister died suddenly, without having received the sacraments of the Church, and Angela was greatly troubled in mind to know how this affected her sister's state in the world to come. A fortnight after her sister's death, Angela was sent by her uncle into the country to distract her mind and restore her health; and on the road she saw a luminous cloud. She stopped, and in the cloud she beheld her sister, radiant in glory, in the midst of a multitude of angels, and accompanied with the queen of heaven. "Persevere, Angelica, in the way you have begun," said the sister out of the cloud, "and you also will share the same glory."—*Life of St. Angela of Brescia* (Montpellier, 1804).

This shows that "the sacraments of the Church" are not needful for the dying, if it shows anything.

An angel appears to St. Dosithëus, and he is converted (sixth century). St. Dosithëus was an officer in the army of the emperor of the East; and, being one day in Jerusalem, he asked permission to go and see the sights of the city. Amongst other things he saw a picture representing hell and its torments, which greatly terrified him. While wondering what the picture referred to, a stately lady of great beauty came, and explained it to him. He listened with silent attention, for he never before had heard of a judgment to come. The strange lady now spoke to him of monastic life, and told him those who lived to God often fasted, abstained from meat, and gave themselves to assiduous prayer. Having so said, she vanished. Our author naïvely remarks, "Celle qui lui parlait ainsi n'était pas une créature mortelle, car après cette leçon elle disparut."—*Vies des Pères des Déserts d'Orient.*

The ghost of Apollinaris appears to St. Romuald (A.D. 907–1027). Romuald, being present at a duel in which his father killed his antagonist, was so struck with terror, that he vowed to retire from the world for forty days, and went as a penitent to the monastery of St. Apollinaris in Ravenna. At the expiration of the forty days he was about to leave the monastery, when one of the monks to whom he was much attached tried to persuade him to join the society; but Romuald would not listen to such a proposal. "What would you say," said the monk to him, "if St. Apollinaris himself came and asked you?" "Why, then," replied the young man, "I should feel it my duty to obey." "Watch with me," said the monk, "this night in the church." To this Romuald agreed. That night, and the night following, at cock-crow, St. Apollinaris showed himself to the watchers, in the midst of a great light, and Romuald at once resolved to retire from the world, and devote the rest of his life to the service of God.—Bollandus, *Acta Sanctorum*, Feb., vol. ii. (Jerome of Prague and Peter Damien both wrote the life of this saint.)

Christ appears and speaks to Agnes de Jesus (A.D. 1602–1634). One day Agnes de Jesus entreated that she might be taken at once from this vale of tears; whereupon Christ came, and said to her, "I want your services still to sanctify souls to My glory." About the same time the Virgin Mary appeared to her, and said, "Implore my Son on behalf of Olier, abbot of Pibrac." Mons. Olier was at the time wholly unknown to Agnes, but from that moment became an object of great solicitude to her, and she daily interceded with Christ for three years on his behalf. God, who always answers prayer, sent His grace on the abbot. Mons. Olier says, "I was one day in my chamber, when the vision of a lady appeared to me. She held a crucifix in one hand and a chaplet in the other. Her guardian angel carried the end of her mantle in one hand and a handkerchief in the other. The vision said to me, 'Olier, I weep for thee,' which words caused me much distress. I thought it was the holy Virgin, but found afterwards it was Agnes de Jesus, whom I met not long afterwards at Auvergne, and we both recognized each other, being familiarized by visions."—*Life of the Blessed Agnes de Jesus* (by Mons. Lantage and the abbot Lucot).

This Mons. Olier established at Vaugirard, in 1641, an order of priests for the gratuitous instruction of young ecclesiastics.

Jesus Christ, with several saints in glory, appear to St. Columba (A.D. 1477–1501). When St. Columba was only twelve years old, Jesus Christ appeared before her, seated on His throne of glory; beside Him were St. Peter, St. Paul, St. Dominic, and St. Jerome who held a book in his hand. Transported with joy, the young girl cried with fervour, "Lord, give me Thy blessing;" and after Christ had so done, she vowed to preserve perpetual virginity as His espoused.

Another instance. On another occasion Jesus Christ came to her, and represented His earthly passion. She saw Him in the garden of Olives; she saw Him before Annas and Caiaphas; she saw Him before Pilate; but when she heard the whips of the scourging, and saw the blood which followed the blows, she became so excited that she began to scourge herself unmercifully. Her mother, hearing the noise, ran to her; but Columba was in an ecstasy, and neither saw her nor heard her.—Father Sebastian of Perousa, *Life of St. Columba of Rieti.*

Columba was the fond name of this saint, because when she was baptized a dove perched upon her head. Her real name was Angeletta or Angetella, because two angels appeared at her birth, holding over her a bow of gold with seven flames.

Apparition of Christ to Emily Bicchieri (A.D. 1238–1314). Emily Bicchieri asked Christ to inform her which of the several pains of His passion was really the most agonizing; and Christ assured her that the three hours He hung on the cross His sufferings were wholly unequalled. He then promised Emily "to grant the gift of the three theological virtues (see Introduction) to all those who at the third hour of the evening repeated three *Paters* and three *Avês* in memory of His crucifixion."—*Acta Sanctorum* (Bollandists), May 3.

Apparition of Christ to Margaret Mary Alacoque of Burgundy for the devotion of His "Sacred Heart" (A.D. 1648–1690). Few women have met with more opposition, been more ridiculed, but by dogged perseverance have risen superior to all, than Margaret Mary Alacoque, a French nun of Paray-le-Monial, in Burgundy, who instituted the festival and confraternities of the Sacred Heart of Jesus,* which received the sanction of pope Clement XII. in 1732, 1736, and of Clement XIII. in 1765. Her visions were for many years frowned down as the dreams of a sick

* The festival of "The Sacred Heart of Mary" was established in 1661

fancy, but were ultimately credited as revelations from heaven.

We are told that Jesus Christ often appeared to her. Thus in the year after her profession, "il lui fit part de sa vie crucifiée." One day, going to communion, He put a crown on her head, saying as He did so, "My daughter, take this crown in token of that which will be given you in the Church triumphant." After this, she had intense headaches, and it seemed as if some one was piercing her head with sharp-pointed bodkins. Christ over and over again said to her, "To carry My cross in your heart, is to be crucified entirely; to carry it in your arms, is to embrace lovingly every cross sent as a token of My love." The next step was to teach her the mysteries of His passion, and then it was she understood what the apostle meant by "Our God is a consuming fire." Sometimes she endured this "consuming fire" for the souls in purgatory, and sometimes for sinners on this earth. It was about this period of her life she began to observe "The Holy Hour." Every Thursday and Friday throughout the year she rose from her bed to recite five *Paters* and five *Ave Marias*, and she prostrated herself in adoration five times to the earth, in homage of the agony of Christ on the night of His passion. She now began to introduce the "Devotion of the Sacred Heart of Jesus," but it took twelve years to establish it. It was in 1674 that the idea was first broached to her. She was at mass. Jesus had long allowed her to repose her heart on His bosom, and He now revealed to her the secrets of His sacred heart. "My sacred heart," said the Saviour to her, "is full of love to man in general, and for thee especially, to whom I enjoin the privilege of making known the treasures of love which it contains--those treasures of sanctification and salvation which alone can redeem from hell." Then, taking His heart, He put it into hers. She saw it with her eyes, and says it was like an atom heated red hot in a furnace. Every Friday the Saviour repeated this, till the sacred heart appeared to her as the sun shining in its glory, and the rays falling on her own heart set it on fire, and seemed to reduce it to ashes. Whenever Margaret Mary mentioned these visions to any one they always laughed at her, and she was greatly puzzled how to proceed. Christ came to her in this perplexity, showing His five wounds blazing with light, while floods of flame flashed from his heart. He spoke of His great love to man, and of man's ingratitude to Him. He told her how fully He trusted in her to carry out His wishes; and He announced to her that every Thursday and Friday He would allow her to participate in His agony in the garden. To this end she was to rise an hour before midnight, and remain prostrate on the ground for a full hour, to defy the devil, and obey the commands He gave her. Margaret Mary after this vision was in a raging fever; but all the three Persons of the Godhead appeared to her: the Father placed on her shoulders a heavy cross bristling with thorns; the Son announced to her His love for this cross; and the Holy Ghost announced to her that He would sanctify her love thereto. It happened that the Père de la Colombière came to visit the nunnery this very year (1674), and to him the visions of Margaret Mary were told. He recognized at once the voice of God therein. During his stay, on Christmas Eve, Margaret Mary had another ecstasy, in which Christ more fully developed His design. The sacred heart of Jesus appeared to her as a throne of fire and flames, radiant, but transparent as crystal. The wound which it had received on the cross was visible. There was a crown of thorns around it, and a cross above it. A voice from the midst said to her that Christ's great love for man had induced Him to show His heart, and that He would take a signal pleasure "d'être honoré sous la figure de ce cœur de chair, dont il voulait que l'image fût exposée aux regards afin de toucher les cœurs insensibles." On the recently established fête of the "Heart of the Virgin Mary" (Feb. 8, 1661), the Saviour again appeared to Margaret Mary, and announced to her that He had chosen the Père de la Colombière to assist her in establishing His wished-for fête. He again showed her His heart, saying, "There, daughter, is the heart whose love to man is so great, but for which I receive nothing but ingratitude. I now command you to establish a fête in honour of my heart 'le premier vendredi d'après l'octave du St. Sacrement,' * and thus to make the *amende honorable* for this long neglect; and I promise that My heart shall shower abundant grace on all those

* The fête of the Saint Sacrement or of Fête Dieu is the Thursday after Trinity Sunday; in France it is held the first Sunday after Trinity. Its object is to celebrate the Real Presence in the Eucharist.

who observe this fête. When the Pere de la Colombière heard that he was chosen of God to carry out this design with Margaret Mary, he set about the work in good earnest; but he lost character by so doing, was removed, and packed off to England.* The object was to stamp out the project: but, strange to say, the Father contrived to establish the "Devotion of the Sacred Heart in England." Margaret Mary suffered all sorts of indignities; but her enthusiasm was infectious. Several religious houses adopted the new office, and at length, in Sept. 7, 1668, a chapel in the garden of Paray-le-Monial was dedicated to the Sacred Heart. The attendance was crowded, the success complete. Margaret Mary was now the heroine of the day; but she did not long survive her triumph, as she died Oct. 17, 1690, aged forty-two years, two months, and four days. Her funeral attracted a most extraordinary concourse of people. Not only has the "Fête of the Sacred Heart" been sanctioned by Clement XII. and XIII. (1732–1765), but Margaret Mary's sacred hour has received the sanction of Gregory XVI. (1831–1846); and Margaret Mary was herself beatified by Pius IX., June 24, 1864.—*Life and Works of Margaret Mary Alacoque* (a publication of the monastery of Paray le Monial).

To most English readers these rhapsodies will seem more than half profane, and it will be a matter of amazement how they could be received in 1864 as divine revelations, literally and verbally true. Yet pope after pope *ex cathedrâ* have pronounced them to be so. It is somewhat strange, too, that the day appointed "by Jesus Christ Himself for the Fête of the Sacred Heart was to be the first Friday after the octave of Fête Dieu," but the day fixed by the Church was first "the third Sunday after Pentecost," and then "the second Sunday in July."

In the great plague of Marseilles, 1722, Mgr. de Belzunce organized a grand procession of the Sacred Heart, in which the magistrates and the whole town joined, "et le fléau disparait aussitôt, à tel point que pendant six semaines dans une ville aussi vaste et aussi peuplée que Marseille, on ne vit ni morts, ni malades d'aucune sorte." —Breton, *Instruction sur le Sacré Cœur de Jésus.*

Apparitions of Christ and of Mary Magdalene to Martha (A.D. 84). Martha was the sister of Mary and Lazarus. Mgr. Guérin says she was the daughter of Theophilus the Syrian, a wealthy seigneur, and that her mother was Eucharis, a Jewish noble of the blood royal. "Elle avait pour sœur utérine Ste. Marie Madeleine, et pour frère utérin St. Lazarus." By this account Mary the sister of Lazarus was Mary Magdalene. The pope's chamberlain says, after the Ascension, the Jews seized Martha, and placed her in a boat without sails, oars, or provisions, and set her adrift. That the boat carried her to Marseilles, where she introduced the Christian faith, and then went to Aix, Avignon, and other neighbouring parts. She ultimately took up her abode at Tarascon, where she lived in great austerity; went about barefooted, dressed in a coarse woollen robe, and wore a "tiare blanche en poil de chameau" for head-dress. "Son corps portait une ceinture de crins de cheval, remplie de nœuds, et un cilice qui lui déchirait les chairs (! !). One day St. Maximin quitted Aix to visit Martha, and at the same time Trophimus bishop of Arles, and Eutropius bishop of Orange, without concert, started on the same errand. So the three bishops met at Tarascon, and consecrated Martha's house for a Christian church (! !). As Martha had no wine to give her guests, Jesus Christ Himself came and changed some water into wine, which the bishops greatly commended. When the bishops left Tarascon, Martha asked Maximin to request her sister Mary to call and see her before she died. This he promised to do. Soon afterwards, "Notre Seigneur, pour la purifier davantage, et lui donner le moyen de mériter une couronne plus glorieuse," sent on her a fever which lasted for twelve months; and during this time her sister Mary died. "Les historiens racontent," that Jesus Christ Himself, accompanied with angels, visited Martha in her illness, and during this visit Martha saw angels carrying her sister's soul to heaven. "Dear sister," she cried, "why did you not give me a parting visit according to my request?" As her end drew nearer a vast number of Christians encamped around, and Mgr. Guérin says the following miracles are established on the highest possible authority: "ces prodiges que les historiens des premiers siècles nous racontent, ont donc eu pour témoins non pas trois ou quatre fidèles privilégiés, mais tout un peuple" (! !). At nightfall Martha had seven candles and three lamps lighted, "ce nombre avait-il quelque chose de symbolique." Forthwith a great gust of wind filled all the house. It was not the descent of the Holy Ghost, as on the day of Pentecost, but the devil who had come to blow out the lights. Martha armed herself with the sign of the cross, and waking her guardians, who were asleep, she told them to light the candles and lamps again. As they went out to

* We are told in Hamlet "They are all mad here."

seek for a light, the chamber was filled with celestial light, and Mary her sister appeared, relighted the lamps and candles miraculously, and coming to the bed, said to Martha, "Dear sister, I am come to see you before your death, as you wished me to do. But see here; Christ Himself is come to fetch you home. Come, sister, and tarry not." Then Christ came to the dying saint, and said to her, "Here am I, Martha; as you served Me with so much devotion, and showed Me such hospitality in Bethany, I am now come to redeem you from exile, that where I am thou mayest be also. He then added, "Farewell, Martha, for a little time, while I go and prepare a place for you." Then Christ disappeared, and Mary, with a loving smile, disappeared also. The companions of Martha, on their return, found all the candles and lamps burning, and Martha requested to be carried into the open air. She was laid under a tree, "et on y traça une croix avec de la cendre." At sunrise, by her command, a crucifix was held before her (! !). "Come, Lord Jesus, come quickly!" she cried, and yielded up the ghost. Seven bishops (Parmenas, Germanus, Sosthenes, Epaphras, Marcellus, Evodius, and Synticus) led the multitude in singing the dirge, and celebrating the funeral rites, which lasted three days. "Ils chantaient nuit et jour autour de ce saint corps, allumant des cierges dans l'église, des lampes dans les maisons, et des feux dans les bois." She was buried on Sunday, and St. Front, the first bishop of Perigueux, was in his church, and waited in his chair for the people who were to join him in the sacrifice of the mass. Jesus Christ came to him, and said, "My son, come with Me to celebrate the obsequies of Martha, My host." "Il dit, et sur-le-champ, tous deux en un clin d'œil apparurent à Tarascon dans l'église, tenant des livres dans leurs mains:" Christ at the head and the bishop at the feet, "et eux seuls placèrent le corps dans le tombeau, au grand étonnement de ceux qui étaient là presents." When the funeral was over, and the assembly dispersed, one of the clerks asked Christ who He was, and whence He came. Christ made no reply, but handed the book He held in His hands to the clerk. On opening the book, he found on every page these words, "The memory of Martha, the hostess of Jesus, will be everlasting.' The book contained nothing else. Meantime the deacon at Perigueux came and reminded St. Font that the congregation was waiting for him to begin mass; and the bishop said he had been to Tarascon to assist in the funeral obsequies of Martha, whether in the body or out of the body he did not know—God knows; he then added, "Send some one for my ring and gloves which I left in the church, when I lifted the body into the grave." A messenger was sent at once to Tarascon, and brought back the ring and gloves. These gloves were carefully preserved in the church at Tarascon till 1793.—Mgr. Guérin (chamberlain of pope Leo XIII.), *Lives of the Saints*, vol. ix. pp. 101, 102 (7th edit. 1880). Faillon, *Monuments inédits sur l'Apostolat de St. Marie-Magdeleine* (1858). The chamberlain refers us to Peter de Natalibus, Raban Maur, Vincent de Beauvais, and others, and assures us that the above are facts beyond question, witnessed to not by three or four faithful witnesses, but by "tout un peuple."

A tale so full of anachronisms can scarcely be matched; but be it remembered that this biography is recorded in the nineteenth century as a history worthy of all men to be received and believed.

There is no Scripture proof that Mary the sister of Lazarus was Mary Magdalene, and the general opinion of Protestants is that they were different persons. Without doubt Mary the sister of Lazarus anointed the Lord with ointment, and wiped His feet with her hair (*John* xi. 2; xii. 3). Luke (vii. 37, 39) also tells us of a woman who did the same, and in the heading of the chapter this woman is called "Mary Magdalene," but upon what authority I know not. The next chapter (viii.) introduces Mary Magdalene by name, not as the woman referred to at the close of the previous chapter, but as a new subject. Look at the last verse of chap. vii., "And Jesus said to the woman, Thy faith hath saved thee; go in peace." And the next chapter opens thus: "And certain women which had been healed of evil spirits and infirmities, [viz.] Mary Magdalene, Joanna wife of Chuza, Susanna, and many others . . . were with Him." There seems no connection between the woman, without a name, who anointed the feet of Jesus, and the women mentioned by name who ministered to Him. Matthew (xxvi. 7) and Mark (xiv. 3) mention another woman, who anointed the *head*, not the "feet," of Jesus. It seems probable that Mary, Martha, and Lazarus were natives of Bethany, a suburb of Jerusalem. Certainly they lived there, and certainly Lazarus died and was buried there, but Mary the Magdalene was probably a native of Magdala in Gadara, near the Lake of Tiberias, quite another place. On the whole, there seems to be three anointings: (1) The woman mentioned by Matthew and Mark, who anointed the *head* of Jesus; (2) the woman "who was a sinner," mentioned by Luke, and called in the heading "Mary Magdalene;" and (3) Mary of Bethany, the sister of Lazarus and Martha, mentioned by John.

The apparition of Dinocratês appears to St. Perpetua. While Perpetua was in prison, a few days before her martyrdom, her brother Dinocratês (a boy who had died at the age of seven) appeared before her. He came from a place of dismal darkness, and was both dirty and livid. He had died of cancer, and his face was still disfigured with a terrible sore. The boy tried to reach some water to drink, for his tongue and mouth were parched. Being unable to raise the water to his mouth, he groaned mournfully. Perpetua was greatly troubled at the sight, and prayed that the Saviour would take compassion on her brother. As she prayed, the darkness grew light, the pallor of the boy turned to a roseate hue, the skin became clean and healthy, the sore on the face healed, and he was enabled to lift the water to his lips. Having drunk most heartily, he went away as blithe as a lark. "Then," said Perpetua, "I know the boy has been taken from purgatory, and has been translated to the communion of the saints in light."—J. C. Robertson, *History of the Christian Church*, vol. i. p. 96 (1875).

(This account was written by Perpetua herself.)

The "Immaculate Conception" appears to Bernadetta Soubirous (A.D. 1858). Every one has heard of Notre-Dame de Lourdes, and knows that the village of Lourdes is situated in the Hautes Pyrénées, at the meeting of the seven valleys. It is here that one of the most astounding events of modern days is reported to have occurred, and the following account is extracted from a pamphlet sold on the spot.

Feb. 11, A.D. 1858, was Thursday in Shrovetide, called in French *Jeudi gras*. It was on this day that three girls went to gather sticks in the direction of Massabielle. Two of them crossed the river, but the third, named Bernadetta Soubirous, a sickly child, fourteen years of age, hesitated for some minutes to encounter the cold, but at length made up her mind to join her companions. Sitting on the bank of the river, she had pulled off the shoe of one foot, when a sudden gust of wind induced her to raise her head. The air seemed quite calm, and not a leaf was stirring. She now proceeded to strip her other foot, when another gust of wind arose. She thought it very strange, and looking towards the rock saw a honeysuckle gently waving. There is a cave or grot in this rock, and the child noticed that the opening of this cave, usually quite dark, was brilliantly luminous. In the midst of the light appeared a lady, young, of pleasing aspect, and arrayed in white. A long white veil fell from her head to her feet, and a blue sash floated to her knees. Her feet were naked, but on the instep of each foot was a full-blown rose. The child rubbed her eyes, and thought she must be dreaming; but no, she was wide awake, and there stood the lady in the mouth of the cave, smiling at her incredulity. Falling on her knees, Bernadetta would have made the sign of the cross on her face, but found her hand paralyzed. The apparition, taking a crucifix of gold, now made on itself the sign of the cross, after which the child was enabled to sign herself also. The lady crossed her hands, and told off between her fingers the white beads of her rosary. The child did the same, and repeated her *Ave Maria*. The lady beckoned the child to come near, but she was afraid, and then the vision vanished. Bernadetta now crossed the canal, and told her companions what she had seen; and, on reaching home, she told the vision to her mother. Her mother, greatly alarmed, thought it a trick of the devil, and forbade the child ever again to go to the *rive de Massabielle*. Meantime, the news of the vision spread in all directions. On Sunday, Feb. 14, a party of girls obtained permission to accompany Bernadetta to the grot, and her mother allowed her to go; but told her, in passing the church, to supply herself with a phial of holy water, in case the vision was a wile of the devil. When the girls reached the spot, there stood the lady as before, and Bernadetta, throwing the holy water towards her, exclaimed, "If thou comest from God, draw near; but if from Satan, avaunt!" The lady smiled, especially when the holy water wetted her feet, and coming near the child, bent over her. Bernadetta had already fallen on her knees, and her face seemed to her companions luminous and beautiful as that of an angel. By sunset, all the neighbourhood had heard of the vision. Well, Thursday, Feb. 18, arrived, and two of the gentry followed Bernadetta, unknown, to the grot. It was early day, before sunrise. They saw the child go to the usual spot, and there, as before, stood the beautiful lady, resplendent in her glory. One of the girls had brought paper and pencil, and told Bernadetta to ask the lady to write her name down. The lady smiled at this request, and said, "Child, it is not necessary. Come hither for fifteen successive days." Next day the parents accompanied their daughter to the grot, and a number of the neighbours went with them. They all saw the supernatural change which came over the face of the child, but only the child saw the vision. The crowd increased every day, and thousands of persons assembled before the grot in the early dawn. The child now always came accompanied by her mother, and carrying a candle in her hand. She saluted the lady reverently, signed herself, crossed her hands, and recited her chapelet [or rosary]. The crowd looked on in silence, every eye directed to the child, and all saw her transfigured. Her eyes glistening, her cheeks white and shining, she gazed fixedly at the vision, and sometimes a tear rolled down her face. This went on till March 4, the fifteenth day, and the police had directions to disperse the crowd. Still Bernadetta repeated her visits. By the direction of the lady, she had made a little hole in the earth near the rock, and saw every day the stream of water which ran from this hole increase in volume. It was found to possess sanative virtues, and numberless are the cures ascribed to it. On Lady Day (March 25, 1858) the crowd which had assembled was greater than ever, thousands upon thousands assembled, and this day the child asked the vision her name. The vision replied, "I am the IMMACULATE CONCEPTION," and at once vanished. The same year, Mgr. Laurence, bishop of Tarbes, instituted a commission of ecclesiastics and men of science to investigate the matter, and report upon it; the grot, in the mean time, being guarded by a barrier. In 1862, Jan. 18, the commission having already given in their report, the bishop issued his mandement, pronouncing it to be an undoubted fact that the lady of the Immaculate Conception had appeared to Bernadetta Soubirous; that the lady who so appeared was Mary, mother of God; and, accordingly, he authorized her worship by the faithful under the title of NOTRE-DAME DE LOURDES. The bishop published at the same time the recital of "seven undoubted miracles" in the year 1858, strictly investigated by the commission. He furthermore announced that a chapel would be erected forthwith in honour of the lady of Lourdes, according to her express command, and he invited liberal subscriptions. The chapel was completed in 1866, and Bernadetta retired to a convent. A statue of white marble was erected in the grot in 1862, amidst an immense concourse of people. It represents the Virgin at the moment of her saying, "I am the Immaculate Conception." This was four years after Pius IX. had enunciated by public proclamation the dogma of the "Immaculate Conception." — Lassere, *Notre-Dame de Lourdes* (sold on the spot).

Here "I am the Immaculate Conception" makes this dogma a real person. Only the child Bernadetta saw the vision, and we are told she was a sickly child, and the vision occurred soon after the dogma was enunciated by pope Pius IX. Put these things together, and the solution seems ready at hand.

The Virgin Mary appears to St. Alfonso or Ildefonso (A.D. 606–669). St. Alfonso, or, as he is called in the Roman Breviary, Ildefonso, was archbishop of Toledo, especially noted for his devotion to the Virgin Mary, whose virginity he defended against the Helvidians; and several miraculous visions of Mary were made to him in testimony of her approval of his zeal.

December 9, St. Leocadia came out of her grave to discover to him where to find her relics, for a long time lost sight of. She took him by the hand, and said, "O Ildefonse, per te vivit Domina mea quæ cœli culmina tenet" (*By thee, O Ildefonso, my queen, who reigns in the heaven of heavens, lives*); that is, "By thee she is defended against heretics who deny her on earth." In order to have a proof of this visitation, Ildefonso seized the sword of king Receswinthe who accompanied Leocadia, and cut off a part of her long veil before she could get back into her grave. This relic was carefully preserved in the church of Toledo.

Ildefonso established the fête called "The Expectation of the Lying-in of the Virgin," Dec. 18, and before matins he went with his clerks and several others to chant songs in her honour. When they came close to the church they found it lighted with such a dazzling light that they were frightened; and all fled, except Ildefonso and his two deacons, who entered the church, and went to the altar. Here they saw the Virgin Mary seated on the bishop's throne, surrounded by a troup of virgins, singing the songs of paradise. Mary beckoned Ildefonso to draw near, and fixing her eyes on him, said, "You are my chaplain and faithful notary. Receive from me this chasuble, which my Son sends you from His treasury." So saying, the Virgin herself invested him with it, and told him to wear it only on the fête-days held in her honour. This apparition is so indubitable, that a council of Toledo ordained that a fête, with special rites and a special office, should be kept yearly to perpetuate its memory. The fête is still observed on Jan. 21, and called "The Descent of the Holy Virgin and of her Apparition" to St. Ildefonso. It is certainly deserving of notice that the fête is observed by the Copts in Egypt.—*Acta Sanctorum.* (See also *Les Petits Bollandistes*, vol. i. p. 562.)

Apparition of the Virgin Mary to Antony of Padua in proof of the Immaculate Conception (twelfth century). St. Antony of Padua was a staunch supporter of the dogmas of the Immaculate Conception and the Assumption of Mary. He was shocked to find that Usuard throws doubt on these dogmas; and, falling on his knees in his cell, he prayed God to pardon the sins of those who dared to doubt. All of a sudden his cell was filled with celestial light, and there appeared before him the queen of heaven, surrounded with seraphin and cherubin. "My son," said the Virgin, "feel assured that I was born without sin, and that I ascended into heaven both body and soul. Fail not to preach this great truth, both in season and out of season." And the vision vanished.—L'abbé Guyard, *Life of St. Antony of Padua.*

These visions of the Virgin Mary to prove her immaculate conception and assumption are certainly an "insult to common sense;" and if these dogmas rest or are propagated by such dreams, they are indeed baseless fabrics.

The Virgin Mary appears to St. Benedicta (A.D. 1664). One lovely day in the month of May, St. Maurice appeared to Benedicta, and told her to drive her flock on the morrow to St. Stephen's valley, and there the Virgin Mary would visit her. Next day her flock went of its own accord to St. Stephen's valley, instead of St. Maurice's downs as usual. When the shepherdess came to the grotto, she saw a lady of surpassing beauty, holding in her arms an infant more beautiful than its mother. Benedicta could not persuade herself that the vision was the Madonna, but thought it was some human being, and offered her a piece of bread. The lady smiled, but spoke not. Every day for four months Benedicta saw the vision in the same place, and the countenance of the young shepherdess seemed wholly spiritualized, her beauty became divine, and her speech like that of an angel. When the young shepherd girl was familiar with the vision, the Virgin broke silence, instructed her in divine things, encouraged her, prayed with her, and taught her certain litanies wholly unknown in those parts. These litanies were subsequently adopted in all the Valley of Laus (2 *syl.*), and were called the litanies of Loretta. The rumour of this visitation soon got wind, and Mons. Grimaud, judge of the district, requested Benedicta to ask the apparition if she was not the mother of God, and if it was her wish to have a chapel built on the spot. When Benedicta asked the visitant these questions, she replied, "I am Mary, the mother of God. My Son wishes to be honoured in this valley, but not in this spot." She then told the young shepherdess to bring to the grot the girls of St. Stephen in procession. Benedicta replied, "But perhaps they won't believe me, unless you write——" "Nay, nay," said the vision, "that is not necessary." On Aug. 30, the girls of St. Stephen, led by Mons. Fraisse, pastor of the parish, went in procession to the grot. The *juge de paix* went with them to mark attentively all that transpired, and to prepare a *procès-verbal.* The Virgin Mary appeared to all, and when the procession had left, and Benedicta was alone, she said to her, "You will see me here no more." In 1640, a little chapel was erected in this spot, and dedicated to "Notre-Dame de Bon-Rencontre." Here the Virgin frequently appeared, and here it was she told the shepherdess, "que nulle offrande ne lui était plus agréable que celle de la couronne mystique du rosaire; que nulle prière n'était plus efficace pour arracher les pécheurs de l'abîme du mal, et les âmes souffrantes de l'abîme du purgatoire;—aussi prit-elle depuis lors la résolution à laquelle elle ne faillit jamais, de réciter chaque jour, en outre de plusieurs autres prières, quinze rosaires et quinze chapelets pour honorer doublement le nombre sacré des mystères du rosaires; et, comme le jour ne lui suffisait pas pour tant de prières, pendant le sommeil de ses maîtres, elle quittait sans bruit la maison, et, malgré les ténèbres, le froid, et la pluie, elle allait s'agenouiller sur le seuil de l'église du village où les premiers rayons du jour la trouvaient souvent encore." Sometimes, we are told, St. Dominic came from heaven to open the church door for her, and sometimes angels did her work for her, while she was engaged in her religious duties. One day, in the autumn of 1664, her masters sent her to cut grass near Valserre church. She entered the church intending to say a short prayer, and then attend to her appointed duties; but when she entered the sacred building, her soul was lifted to heaven in an ecstasy, and when she returned to herself the sun had sunk behind the mountains. She was greatly distressed, but what was her joy to find that some angel had cut the grass for her, tied it together with a rope, and brought it to the church door! In 1665, Benedicta resolved to replace the little chapel with a church, and this the young shepherdess achieved in four years, and called it "Notre-Dame du Laus."* It was consecrated Dec. 25, A.D. 1669, and after the midnight mass a vast number of the heavenly host made three times the tour of the church, singing the "Gloria in Excelsis," Sister Benedicta following. A great crowd was gathered outside, and were almost blinded by the light which shone through the windows; and the vicar-general declares that the sweet odours gave to the crowd a foretaste of heaven.—Mgr. Guérin (chamberlain of pope Leo XIII.), *Vies des Saints* (1880), vol. v. p. 224.

(Mgr. Barnadou, bishop of Gap, is collecting such data as these to effect the canonization of Sister Benedicta, 1883.)

The Virgin Mary appears to St. Gonsalvo (A.D. 1259). St. Gonsalvo, having retired to a wild spot near Amarante, erected there a little oratory to the Virgin Mary; and here he laboured hard to instruct the neighbouring peasantry in the Christian faith, and to kindle in their hearts the love of God. Not satisfied with this small field of operation, he prayed to be guided by the Holy Spirit in the right way. The Virgin Mary came to him, as he knelt before her altar, and said, "Rise, Gonsalvo, and enter that religious order in which you shall hear the *Ave Maria* both open and close the daily office." After great search he found at Vineraua a Dominican house which began the morning service and ended it in the way indicated, and knew at once that he had found his haven. The sequel is certainly somewhat strange, for though "directed by the Virgin herself, and fully persuaded in his own mind that this Dominican house was the lot of his inheritance," nevertheless he left it after a while, returned to his little oratory near Amarante, and there remained till he died.—Didacus de Rosario, *Life of St. Gonsalvo.*

The Virgin Mary brings John Grandé a hermit's cloak (A.D. 1546–1600). John Grandé was apprenticed to a draper of Seville, but wished to be a monk. When he was twenty-two years of age, he entreated the Virgin Mary to tell him what was his duty to do. The Virgin came to him, brought him a hermit's cloak, and said to him, "John, put on this dress, and enter at once into the service of my Son. So only will you please me." John Grandé put on the cloak, left the house, and turned hermit.—*Les Petits Bollandistes*, vol. vi. p. 435.

The Virgin Mary appears to St. Jourdain of Saxony (A.D. 1237). One night St. Jourdain, having risen from his bed for prayer, saw the blessed Virgin pass with a company of celestial maidens through the dormitory, and sprinkle holy water on the sleepers. One of the brethren she passed by without aspersing him, whereupon St. Jourdain threw himself at her feet, and asked why she had omitted to sprinkle this brother. The mother of God replied, "Je n'ai point aspergé celui-ci, parce qu'il n'est point assez couvert; dis-lui donc qu'il se couvre, car j'aime votre Ordre (*Dominican*) d'un amour spécial, et ce qui m'est surtout agréable, c'est votre habitude, quoi que vous fassiez ou disiez, de le commencer et de le finir par ma louange. Aussi j'ai obtenu de mon Fils que personne ne puisse longtemps rester dans votre Ordre en état de péché mortel, sans qu'on le couvre, qu'il se repente ou qu'on le chasse, de peur qu'il ne trouble mon Ordre favori."—Mgr. Guérin (chamberlain of pope Leo XIII.), *Vies des Saints* (7th edit. 1880), vol. ii. p. 541.

The Virgin Mary and Christ appear to St. Lutgardes (A.D. 1246). One day the Virgin Mary appeared to St. Lutgardes with sorrowful countenance and much disfigured. Her dress was neglected, and was all black. Lutgardes demanded how it came to pass that the queen of heaven, bright as the sun and fair as the moon, was so cast down. She replied, "The cause of my affliction is those vile heretics the Albigenses, who crucify my Son afresh. In vengeance of this great crime God will send unheard-of evils on the earth. To avert this wrath, Lutgardes, fast for seven years, taking no nourishment but bread and water, and for all those years let your eyes be never dry of tears." Lutgardes observed this long fast, and at the close thereof Christ came and told her to observe another seven years' fast, but allowed her to eat vegetables. "This fast I enjoin," said Christ, "for the sins of the world, to

* "Laus" (2 *syl.*) means a lake. "Notre-Dame of the Lake"

reconcile God." Lutgardes observed this fast also. Mary d'Oignies assured Lutgardes that no one on earth had such power as she had to deliver souls from purgatory. We know that the abbot Simon of the Cistercian order, who was condemned to eleven years of purgatory, had his term shortened by the intercession of Lutgardes; and that the prior of Oignies, named Baudoin, was rescued from purgatory altogether, because Lutgardes said to Christ, "Either erase my name from the book of life, or rescue this man from purgatory at my intercession."—Thomas de Cantimpré, *Life of St. Lutgardes.*

The Virgin Mary appears to St. Nicholas of Tolentino, and gives him bread. St. Nicholas of Tolentino, being very sick for want of sufficient nourishment, was commanded to eat meat, but replied that by so doing he should save his body at the peril of his soul. In this dilemma the Virgin Mary, accompanied by St. Augustine, brought him a loaf of bread, and told him, having soaked it in water, to eat thereof in the name of Jesus Christ. This did he, and he recovered. Hence rose the custom of distributing in the Augustine convents what is called "the bread of St. Nicholas of Tolentino," that is, consecrated bread, given away on the feast of St. Nicholas, and said to be a specific against tertian fever, the fever from which the saint was suffering when the Virgin came to him.—Antony (archbishop of Florence), *Chronicon.*

The Virgin Mary appears to St. Peter Thomas (A.D. 1362). There was much jealousy about the order of Mount Carmel, because of the many favours bestowed on it from heaven. St. Peter Thomas appealed to the Virgin for protection, and the Virgin came to him in person, and said, "Peter Thomas, be of good cheer, for the order of Mount Carmel shall continue to the end of the world, in honour of Elijah, its founder." So saying she vanished, leaving the saint full of the sweetest consolation.—*Les Petits Bollandistes*, vol. i. p. 170 (7th edit. 1880).

The Virgin Mary appears to a widow of Velaune, and hence the cathedral of Notre-Dame du Puy (in France). A widow of Velaune, the ancient capital of Velay, being sick of a fever which resisted all the skill of the physicians, addressed herself at length to the Virgin, who directed her to go to Mount Anis to have her health restored. Mount Anis is the summit of a conical mountain on which the church of Notre-Dame du Puy * was subsequently erected. The widow arrived at the place indicated, and placed herself on a square stone formed like an altar. Here she dozed, and saw a company of angels surrounding a queen in royal robes, from whom proceeded rays of glory. "That," said one of the angels to the widow, "is the mother of God, who has selected this spot for a sanctuary; and, that you may not mistake this vision for a dream, you will find yourself restored to perfect health." The vision then vanished, and the widow rose completely cured. St. George, governor of the church of Velay, being told of this vision, climbed the Mount Anis, and observed that a part of the plateau was covered with snow, although it was the middle of July, the time of summer heat; he also observed that footprints of a stag in the snow marked the ground plan of a church. The bishop had a hedge thrown up to perpetuate the plan, selected the square stone on which the widow saw the vision as the spot for the high altar, and left there a shoe of the Virgin which he had brought with him from Rome. Nothing more was done till the episcopate of St. Vosy, A.D. 220, when a dame from Ceyssac, paralyzed, was laid on the stone, had a similar vision, was cured of her palsy, and reported the whole to St. Vosy. After fasting for three days, St. Vosy visited the spot, and found the enclosure of St. George still covered with snow. "This," said he in transport, "is no other than the house of God and gate of heaven;" and he resolved to transfer the episcopal seat thither from St. Paulien, where it then was. As the consent of the pope was necessary for this transfer, he at once started for Rome, obtained the required authorization, and brought back with him Scrutarius, a young architect of senatorial family, whom he employed to superintend the buildings. The design of the church was extremely simple, with few ornaments, and the whole edifice was finished within seven years, when it was deemed expedient to consecrate it. As Scrutarius and the bishop went to Rome to lay the matter before the pope, two old men, arrayed in white, met them, each bearing a gold casket, which at the consecration the bishop was requested to present to the church of Mount Anis; and so saying they disappeared from sight. The prelate, and all with him,

* "Puy" means *elevation.*

instantly drew off their shoes, returned with the caskets, and reported what they had seen. The news spread like lightning, throngs flocked to the place, a grand procession was formed, and the march to Mount Anis began. As they came to the church the doors flew open of their own accord, the building was illuminated with thousands of torches, and the altar sprinkled with an oil the perfume of which filled the whole building. The bishop intoned the service, and, when it was over, collected three hundred of the torches to keep as relics. Two of them remain still in the church treasury. The new church drew a large concourse of people to the place, which soon numbered many thousands of inhabitants. — Hamon, *Notre-Dame de France; Le Triomphe de Marie, ou Relation du Jubilé de* 1842; and *Relation du Jubilé de Notre-Dame du Puy*, 1853.

Tasso the poet and the apparition (A.D. 1544-1595). [A better example of the power of imagination cannot be given than the following, which will explain very many of the apparitions referred to in this volume. It is taken from the life of Tasso by Giambattista Manso.] Tasso, he tells us, constantly saw a spirit which conversed with him on theological and other subjects; and the poet declared that the things he learnt from this spirit surpassed his own understanding, and anything he had ever read. Manso being invited to come one evening, Torquato suddenly exclaimed, "See, see! there is my spirit-friend. Look at him well, and be convinced." The poet then entered on some abstruse disquisition, now propounding questions, and anon answering arguments, after the manner of a man in deep converse with another. Manso, however, saw nothing but the rays of the sun shining on the wall, and heard no voice but that of Tasso himself.—*Notes and Queries*, Nov. 24, 1883, p. 401.

This probably will explain the legends of St. Augustine (the Trinity), p. 355; Catherine of Bologna, p. 28; Theresa, p. 21; and scores of others.

Body and Blood of Christ.

JOHN vi. 51. I am the living bread which came down from heaven. If any man eat of this bread, he shall live for ever; and the bread that I will give is My flesh, which I will give for the life of the world.

JOHN vi. 53-57. Verily, verily, I say unto you, Except ye eat the flesh of the Son of man, and drink His blood, ye have no life in you. Whoso eateth My flesh and drinketh My blood, hath eternal life; and I will raise him up at the last day. For My flesh is meat indeed, and My blood is drink indeed. He that eateth My flesh and drinketh My blood, dwelleth in Me, and I in him. As I live by the Father, so he that eateth Me shall live by Me.

MATT. xxvi. 26-29. As the apostles were eating, Jesus took bread, and blessed it, and brake it, and gave it to the disciples, and said, Take, eat; this is My body. And He took the cup, and gave thanks, and gave it them, saying, Drink ye all of it; for this is My blood of the new testament, which is shed for many for the remission of sins. But I say unto you, I will not drink henceforth of this fruit of the vine, until that day when I drink it new with you in My Father's kingdom.

1 COR. x. 16. The cup of blessing which we bless, is it not the communion of the blood of Christ? The bread which we break, is it not the communion of the body of Christ?

Transubstantiation proved by miracle. Father Giry, in his *Discourse on the Fête du Très-saint Sacrement*, after citing the usual texts of Scripture, and giving in confirmation quotations from St. Cyril of Jerusalem, St. Ambrose, St. Augustine, and St. Chrysostom, refers to the corroboration of the dogma by five general councils—that of the Lateran, under Innocent III.; that of Vienne, under Clement V.; with those of Constance, Florence, and Trent. He then goes on to say, "le pape Urbain IV. fut excité à établir la fête du Saint Sacrement par un miracle arrivé à Bolsena, non loin d'Orvieto." The miracle was this: A priest, saying mass in St. Christina, felt incredulous about the transubstantiation of the elements; but no sooner had he uttered the words of consecration, than the wafer host began to stream with blood, "comme si elle eût voulu pleurer l'infidélité de ce ministre." It shed such a profusion of blood, that the corporal, the napkins, and even the altar, were completely covered with it. The pope, informed of this "miracle," had the blood-stained articles sent to Orvieto, where they were received with great pomp, and a procession containing a vast number of cardinals, archbishops, bishops, and other Church dignitaries. They were duly deposited in the ancient church of Orvieto, till a magnificent church was erected for their reception, the first stone being laid by Nicholas V.

Blood from the host proves the dogma of transubstantiation (A.D. 1608). St. Andrew Avellin was a staunch advocate of the dogma of transubstantiation. One day a communicant who disbelieved it, after receiving the wafer, wrapped it in his handkerchief, with intention of analyzing it when he reached home.

When he opened his handkerchief he found it saturated with the blood which had flowed from the host. He ran back to St. Andrew, confessed his "sacrilege," and recounted the "miracle." St. Andrew took advantage of this to prove the verity of the mystery, and the bloody handkerchief was carried in procession as a proof which could not be gainsaid.—Mgr. Guérin, *Vies des Saints*, vol. xiii. p. 305.

A host bleeds profusely from the knife of a Jew. In A.D. 1290, under the reign of Philippe le Bel, a poor woman pawned her best gown to a Jew. Easter Sunday being at hand, she asked the pawnbroker to let her have it for that one day, and the Jew replied he would let her have it entirely, if she would bring him the consecrated wafer which the priest gave her in the communion. This she did, and the Jew, placing it on the table, stabbed it over and over again with his penknife. Blood in great streams flowed from the wounds, splashing the woman and her children. "La même chose arriva lorsqu'il la pendit avec un clou (!!), la frappa à coups de fouet (!!), et la perça avec une lance (!!)." Then casting it into the fire, it fluttered among the flames, but received no harm. "Enfin, sa rage l'ayant porté à la plonger dans une chaudière d'eau bouillante, à l'heure même l'eau prit la couleur de sang, et l'hostie se fit voir en la forme de Jesus Christ crucifié, élevé au-dessus de la chaudière (!!)." The Jew, in affright, hid himself in the coal-hole. A woman passing by, entered the house, and saw "Notre-Seigneur en cet état; et alors cette hostie, reprenant sa première forme, se vint mettre saine et entière dans un petit vase qu'elle avait entre les mains (!!). Elle reçut ce trésor avec beaucoup de révérence, et le porta aussitôt à l'église de St. Jean-en-Grève, où on le conservait encore très-précieusement avant la Révolution, et d'où on le portait tous les ans en procession, je jour de l'octave du St. Sacrement." The king and bishop of Paris were informed of this prodigy, and the house where it occurred was converted into a church.

This tale is given as a sober fact by Father Giry, in his discourse on the "Fête du Très-saint Sacrement," to persuade Christians to observe the feast and honour it. Mgr. Guérin, chamberlain of pope Leo XIII., repeats it with full approbation in his *Vies des Saints*, vol. xvi. p. 472 (7th edit. 1880), and introduces the tale with the following words:—"Pour l'autre hostie [the other was about the "stolen host which flew into the air," p. 493], le miracle en est plus tragique, mais il n'est pas moins célèbre, ni moins authentique (!!)." For my own part, one of the greatest marvels of this "authentic story," is the simplicity of the woman in asking the pawnbroker to give her back her Sunday gown for nothing.

Blood issues from the host which was pierced by some Jews (A.D. 1370). (1) Some Jews, in 1370, took from St. Gudula's, in Brussels, some consecrated wafers, which they pierced with penknives. Blood issued from the wounds. Happily the wafers were rescued from their hands, and safely deposited in the church of St. Gudula, where every year, in the month of July, they are carried in sacred procession.

(2) At Dijon, the capital of Burgundy, there was, before 1791, a miraculous host in St. Chapelle, sent from Rome, in 1433, by pope Eugenius IV. to Robert Anclou, canon of the Church. This wafer had been stabbed by a Jew, and a vast stream of blood issued from the wound. King Louis XII., being cured of a distressing malady by the virtue of this wafer, sent to the church his coronation crown. On Feb. 10, 1794, this sacred host was thrown into a brazier and burnt to atoms, "aux applaudissements de la démagogie et de l'enfer." No vestige of St. Chapelle now remains.—Father Giry, *Discourse on the Fête Dieu or Holy Sacrament.*

The truth of the dogma of transubstantiation proved by actual conversion. At the Augustine's, in Louvain, part of a wafer is still shown, which was brought from Middelburg, the capital of Zeland, where it was actually turned into flesh, in the mouth of a young man, named John of Cologne, who came to the sacrament of the Eucharist unworthily.—Father Giry, *Discourse on the St. Sacrament.*

The host appears in the likeness of the Child Jesus. The bishop took a wafer, made in the likeness of bread, and at the lifting up [*i.e.* the elevation of the host], there came a figure in the likeness of a child, whose visage was as red and as bright as fire; and He smote Himself into the consecrated bread. So they all saw that the bread was formed of a fleshly man; and then the bishop put the corporal into the holy vessel again. And sir Galahad, as he kneeled down, received his Saviour.—Malory, *History of Prince Arthur*, pt. iii. 101, 102.

This *History of Prince Arthur* is, of course, romance, but there would be no point in the transubstantiation unless it pictured forth the general belief. It seems, however, to favour the doctrine of consubstantiation more than transubstantiation, for the Child Jesus "smote Himself into the bread," and did not transmute the bread.

Christ rises, in the form of a child, from a sacred host. At Braine, in the diocese of Soissons, there was, up to the first quarter of the eighteenth century, a miraculous host shown in the Premonstratensian church. At the commencement of the twelfth century, in the presence of the archbishop of Reims and the bishop of Soissons, a beautiful young child rose out of the sacred host, and was the cause of the conversion of several Jews, who had sworn to believe in transubstantiation when they saw with their own eyes the God of the mass. This host, with the chalice, and chasuble worn on the occasion, and even the tools employed in making the bread, were long preserved in the church. The host was seen by Dom Marten in 1718. The chalice has quite disappeared, but the box in which it was kept remains still. The chasuble was sold by the prior for some ecclesiastical ornaments. The annual procession is still made.

St. Antony proves the doctrine of transubstantiation by Boniville's mule. St. Antony of Padua had a disputation one day with Boniville on the sacrament of the mass. Boniville denied the transubstantiation, and Antony maintained its truth. To convince his adversary of his error, St. Antony told Boniville to shut up his mule and give it no food for three days. At the end of this fast, St. Antony held out to the mule a consecrated wafer, and Boniville threw towards it a feed of oats. The mule took no notice of the oats, but fell on its knees before the holy wafer, adoring it as its Creator and Lord (! !). This "miracle" greatly comforted the Catholics, but infuriated the heretics. Boniville, however, was converted by it.—Edward Kinesman (1623), *Lives of the Saints*, p. 365. (He adds, "It shalbe vnbeliefe not to geue credit to the manifest verity of St. Anthony's miracles. Euen so to deny the due honour vnto the merits of the saint, shalbe a kind of enuy.")

As a supplement to this legend may be given one told by St. Optat, bishop of Milah, in Africa. Some Donatists threw the consecrated bread to some dogs; but the dogs, instead of touching the sacred food, turned on the Donatists in great fury, and tore them to pieces.

⁂ The "Mule Miracle," as it is called, is given somewhat differently by the abbot Guyard. He says the disputant was one Guiald (not Boniville), that he was one of the Albigenses, and that the proposal to try the mule was made by him and not by St. Antony. He says the mule not only knelt "to his creator" (the host), but "plaçant sa tête sur les pieds d'Antoine, reste immobile dans cette position." The Albigenses were covered with rage and confusion, but the joy of "the Catholics" was unbounded. Guiald was converted, and a great number of "heretics." This occurred at Toulouse, and a nephew of Guiald made a tableture of the "Mule Miracle," and below it is a Latin inscription, which may still be seen over the chapel:—

> . . . celso statuere loco spirantia signa:
> In foribus stat equus, supplex ante ora dicati
> Corporis, effigies cultus monumenta verendi
> Illi spreta fero calathis portatur avena.

> Above the door in living sculpture wrought,
> The host and oats before the hinny brought.
> The beast in worship kneels, and scorns to nibble
> The tempting bait beside him in the cribble.

St. Gregory proves the reality of transubstantiation (A.D. 540–604). St. Gregory the Great, celebrating one day the "holy sacrifice of redemption," offered the bread to a woman, and in so doing uttered these words, "The body of our Lord Jesus Christ preserve thy body and soul to everlasting life." Observing the woman smile as he spoke these words, he took away the bread, and placed it on the altar. When mass was over, he asked the woman why she had smiled at the solemn moment of receiving the body of Jesus Christ. She replied, because he said the little piece of bread was the body of the Lord Jesus. St. Gregory, on hearing this, fell on his knees at the foot of the altar, and began praying that the Father of lights would illuminate the soul of this benighted woman. On rising from his knees, he showed the woman that the piece of bread he had taken from her, and placed on the altar, was real flesh, with all the ingredients of meat. The woman saw it was so; she could not disbelieve her eyes, and was converted. St. Gregory then prayed again, and the flesh was reconverted into bread. These miracles greatly confirmed the Church in the doctrine of transubstantiation.—John the deacon, *Life of St. Gregory the Great.* (Written in the twelfth century, at the express desire of pope John VIII.)

St. Odo, archbishop of Canterbury, proves the real presence (A.D. 875, 942–958). Alban Butler tells us that some of the clergy at Canterbury doubted the real presence of Christ's body in the Eucharist. St. Odo prayed that God would demonstrate to them the truth of this mystery; and while he was saying mass in the cathedral, at the breaking of the host, blood was seen by all present distilling from it into the chalice. The saint called up to the altar those who doubted, and they joined the archbishop in a solemn thanksgiving to God for having vouchsafed this miracle to remove their doubts. —*Lives of the Saints*, July 4.

Surely this is not very logical. This is an axiom of the [Roman] Catholic Church: "Totus Christus in toto sacramento, et totus in qualibet parte sacramenti." So that whether you cut or break the bread after consecration, each individual part contains the *whole Christ.* If so, no incision can possibly divide the Saviour's body or make it bleed, any more than cutting off an arm can divide the soul. It must be obvious, if by cutting the host in two you make it bleed, then you have so divided it that each part does *not* contain the entire Christ, you have *cut* the Christ; but every fragment contains *totus Christus*, it is a physical impossibility to *cut* Christ and make Him bleed.

Tilman's book in proof of transubstantiation. Tilman wrote a book entitled *De Miraculis veri Sacramenti*, which is divided into forty-four chapters, to prove the real presence.

Ch. i. Tells us of a farmhouse freed from the haunting of evil spirits by celebrating mass therein.

Ch. ii. Tells us of a duke of Saxony who, at the time of mass, saw in the Eucharist the form of an elegant young child.

Ch. v. Tells us of one whose shackles fell off at the time when a mass was said for him.

Ch. vi. Tells about one Baraca, a seaman, who escaped shipwreck by "the salutary host of the Eucharist."

Ch. xx. Tells us how one Satyrus (brother of St. Ambrose) was saved in shipwreck by having the Eucharist hanging about his neck.

Ch. xxix. Is about a Eucharist flying through the air to an altar, and there appearing in the form of a most beautiful child upon the paten.

Ch. xxxvi. Tells us of a host which skipped thrice from off the altar, because it was defiled by a little fly.

The Latin titles of this interesting book are subscribed.
(i.) De prœdio ab infestatione malignorum spirituum liberatio, per oblationem sacrificii corporis Christi.
(ii.) De Saxoniæ duce, qui sub sacrificio Missæ vidit speciem elegantis pueruli in eucharistia.
(v.) De quodam cujus vincula solvebantur tempore, quo pro illo offerebatur sacrificium Missæ.
(vi.) De Baraca nauta per salutarem Hostiam eucharistiæ a naufragio liberato.
(xx.) Quomodo Satyrus, divi Ambrosii frater, eucharistiam collo appensam habens, in naufragio incolumis servatur.
(xxix.) De eucharistia, quæ a terra suapte virtute sublimata per aera ferebatur ad altare, ibidemque in specie venustissimi pueri apparuit.
(xxxvi.) De Hostia tertio ab altari divinitus projecta, eo quod cimice esset contaminata.

Transubstantiation proved on the testimony of devils (A.D. 1602). When Sara Williams was examined by her Majesty's Commissioners for Causes Ecclesiastical, April 24, 1602, we are told that her devil proved the real presence thus: (1) The devil was commanded by the priestly exorcists to kiss the sacrament. He durst not disobey; but, being asked what he had kissed, replied, "The body of Christ, and it has eyes in it." (2) On another occasion the priests held to the devil the blessed sacrament, and bade him adore his Lord and God; whereupon the devil answered, "He is thy God indeed; and if you believe it not, cut it with a knife, and you will see it bleed." (See note, p. 491).—Samuel Harsnet (afterwards archbishop of York), *Popish Impostures* (1604), p. 130.

In the *Book of Miracles*, Dibdale asks the devil, "What sayest thou of the sacrament of the altar?" And the devil replies, "It is the very body of Christ."

The Eucharist, impatient to enter the mouth of St. Catherine of Siena, leaps from the paten to the lips of the saint (A.D. 1317–1380). Raymond of Capua, the confessor of St. Catherine of Siena, assures us, as a solemn fact, that "the Eucharistic victim, as if impatient of going to reside in that temple of purity, Catherine of Siena, actually placed itself, one day, on the paten, at the moment the priest advanced towards the saint to administer it to her." He furthermore affirms that many persons have borne witness, from their own personal knowledge, that the holy host, at the moment of communion, sometimes jumped from the hands of the officiating priest into the mouth of Catherine.—*Life of St. Catherine of Siena.*

Mgr. Guérin, the pope's chamberlain, quotes this paragraph, and his French translation runs thus: "La victime eucharistique, comme si elle eût été impatiente d'aller résider dans ce tabernacle de pureté et de sainte adoration, vint un jour se placer d'elle-même sur la patène au moment où son confesseur s'avancait pour donner la communion à son illustre pénitente." From which it would seem that the change of the bread does not take place at the moment of consecration, but at the moment of communion.

St. John of St. Facond often saw Christ visible in the Eucharistic elements (A.D. 1430–1479). John of St. Facond, in Spain, had often the advantage of seeing with his eyes the visible Saviour in the eulogie or consecrated bread, and this visible manifestation of Christ took from him all difficulty in understanding this sacred mystery. The bread might appear to be bread to unbelievers, but he saw with his eyes Christ there, Christ visible, and it would be more mysterious that his eyes should see clearly what is not, than that the consecrated bread should be changed into the sacred Person of our salvation.—*Acta Sanctorum* (Bollandists), vol. ii. June 12, p. 616.

This argument is wholly worthless, as our eyes are perpetually seeing "what is not," as in dreams, visions, trances, delirium, fever, and fifty other abnormalities. False sights and false noises are phenomena known to all medical men, and are treated as symptoms of diseased action.

Laurentius of Brindisi saw Christ in the Eucharist (A.D. 1559–1619). "One day," says his chief biographer, "the blessed Laurentius, during the sacrifice of the mass, immediately after the consecration, saw the Saviour Himself, visibly, in the sacred host. He was under the form of a little child, who caressed Laurentius, and smiled on him lovingly. Brother Adam de Rovigo, who was officiating, says he also saw the infant Jesus, and fell as if dead at the foot of the altar, where he lay for fifteen minutes. On coming to himself, he fell in adoration before the divine Infant. What were his emotions 'il n'y a qu'un habitant du ciel qui pourrait les décrire.'"—Mgr. Guérin, *Vies des Saints*, vol. vi. p. 127. (He does not tell us who was "son principal biographe," but subjoins, as a colophon to the life, *Palmier Séraphique*.)

St. Leo brings blood from the sacred wafer. If any one of note required a relic, St. Leo was wont to say mass, and then dividing the corporal, give part of it for a relic. If the receiver seemed dissatisfied, Leo would prick the wafer with a knife, and blood would issue from the wound. (See Bleeding Relics, p. 262.)—Damasus (died A.D. 380), *Lives of the Saints*. (See Blood of Jesus, etc., p. 269.)

(See St. Odo, p. 491, *note*.)

St. Theresa of Avila often saw Christ Himself in the host (A.D. 1515–1582). Christ often showed Himself to St. Theresa in the consecrated wafer, sometimes as a child of surpassing beauty, sometimes in His passion, sometimes in His resurrection. Once on Palm Sunday, after she had received the host into her mouth, it bled so profusely she could not swallow it. The blood was warm, as if it flowed from living veins. Her terror was unspeakable, but Christ whispered to her not to fear, for His blood was the fount of grace.—*Her Autobiography*.

Fire respects the Holy Eucharist (May 26, 1608). In A.D. 1608 a fire consumed the abbey of Notre-Dame de Faverney, in Franche Comté; but though the monstrance, which contained two hosts and a finger of St. Agatha, was exposed to the full force of the flames, it remained miraculously suspended in the air, without anything to support it, and continued so for thirty-three hours. More than ten thousand persons witnessed the miracle, and fifty-two of the principal witnesses signed the *procès-verbal*, which was sent to the archbishop of Besançon, who carefully examined into the matter, and, being satisfied of its truth, commanded the account to be published. In the bull of Paul V. all the chief points of the marvel are duly rehearsed. "L'éclatante vérité du dogme catholique confondit les hérétiques, qui travaillaient alors à introduire leurs erreurs dans la province. Nul d'entre eux n'osa élever publiquement la voix contre les faits racontés dans les relations authentiques; et leur silence est une preuve de plus de l'évidence du miracle."—Fanny de Poinctes Gevigney, *Faverney et sa Sainte Hostie*.

Sister Benedicta receives her Well Beloved, at the hand of an angel (A.D. 1643–1718). While the Jansenists were masters of the Valley of the Lake (Laus, 2 *syl*.), an angel offered "to give Sister Benedicta her Well Beloved." The tabernacle opened to them of its own accord, and immediately the angel took up the pyx, the "blessed Jesus entered into the heart of the saintly shepherdess, while another angel assisted at the holy ceremony."—*Les Petits Bollandistes*, vol. v. p. 227.

(Mgr. Barnadou, bishop of Gap, is collecting such data as these to effect the canonization of Sister Benedicta, 1883.)

An angel brings to St. Columba "the sacred body of Jesus Christ" (A.D. 1477–1501). Not unfrequently St. Columba received the Holy Communion from the hands of Christ Himself. One day her confessor went to say mass in another church, and Columba entreated the Virgin Mary to satisfy her ardent desire "to unite herself to Christ." In a few seconds an angel came to her, "holding between his fingers the sacred body of Christ," and gave it her. Her confessor, missing the wafer, was greatly distressed, and the next time he saw St. Columba, told her of his trouble. "Grieve not, my father," she replied; "an angel brought the missing fragment of the host to me, and it now reposes in my heart." "In that case, my daughter," said the confessor, "I rejoice, and thank God. Blessed be the name of the Lord."—Sebastian of Perousa, *Life of St. Columba of Rieti*.

A stolen host flies into the air, when the pyx is opened (A.D. 1274). In 1274, under the reign of Phippe le Hardi, a thief stole the pyx from the church of St. Gervais, in Paris, and carried it to the Champ du Landit, near St. Denis. Here he opened the vase to throw away the sacred host which he expected to find; but the moment the pyx was opened, the host flew upwards, and began to flutter about the man. Some peasants who saw it went and told the abbot of St. Denis, whose name was Mathieu de Vendôme, and the abbot told the bishop of Paris. These two Church dignitaries at once organized a large procession, which proceeded to the place, singing sacramental hymns. When the procession reached the Champ du Landit, all saw the host fluttering in the air, and immediately the curé who consecrated it appeared, the host placed itself in his hands in the sight of an infinite numbe of people. The abbot and bishop ordained that every Friday the church of St. Gervais should chant a canticle in memory of this miracle, and that once a year a special office should be held on Sept. 1. This host disappeared at the Revolution, but the office is still rehearsed.

The consecrated wafer converted into a serpent (sixth century). St. Melanius administered, at one time, the eulogie or sacred bread to four bishops. One of them (Mars of Nantes), instead of eating it, hid it in his bosom, that he might not break his Lenten fast. When the service was over, the bread thus hidden had been converted into a serpent; whereupon the bishop returned to St. Melanius, confessed his sin, obtained absolution, and was delivered from his tormentor.—Dom Lobineau (contemporary), *Life of St. Melanius.*

The consecrated wafer converted into a stone. A disciple of St. Chrysostom induced his wife, who was an Arian, to accompany him on one occasion to St. Chrysostom's church. When, at the mass, the woman received the eulogie, she held it in her hand till she reached home, and then put it into her mouth to eat as a morsel of ordinary food. When, however, she tried to bite it, she found it had become "a veritable petrifaction, hard as a flint." Alarmed at this prodigy, she went without delay to the saint, showed him the stone with the marks of her teeth, and implored absolution. "C'est un historien contemporain, et vivant à Constantinople, qui nous raconte ce miracle, en ajoutant que l'on conservait dans l'église de cette ville le pain eucharistique pétrifié."—Mgr. Guérin (chamberlain of pope Leo XIII.), *Vies des Saints*, vol. ii. p. 16.

Punishments sent for dishonouring the host or eulogie. (1) In A.D. 1277, at Maëstricht, a number of young lads and lasses were dancing on the bridge over the Meuse, when the curé happened to pass, carrying the sacrament to a dying man. The young giddy-pates pretended not to see him, and went on with their dance; but, in a moment, the bridge broke under them, and above two hundred were drowned in the river, or crushed to death by the débris.—Father Giry, *Discourse on the Fête du Très-saint Sacrement.*

(Father Giry has omitted to state whether the curé was one of the two hundred submerged, or, if not, how he escaped.)

(2) In A.D. 1348, a somewhat similar judgment occurred at Friburg, in Brisgau. A number of young folk were amusing themselves with dancing, and in the midst of their dance the curé happened to pass, bearing the Holy Sacrament. The young people pretended not to hear the bell; but one of the giddy girls exclaimed, "My father's cows and sheep carry such a bell." This caused a loud laugh, but when the laugh was loudest, a thunderbolt fell on the whole party, "qui emporta tous les hommes, et tous les biens de cette vallés, sans que, depuis, on ait pu savoir ce qu'ils étaient devenus."—De Sponde, *Annals.*

(Here again we ask, What became of the curé? But the whole tale should be compared with that of Dathan and Abiram, *Numb.* xvi.)

(3) In A.D. 1420, Thomas de Walden, provincial of the Carmelites, in England, says he was eye-witness of the following incident. The archdeacon of London was examining a tailor, who denied the dogma of transubstantiation, and said, "A spider is more worthy of adoration than the wafer shown him." As he uttered "these blasphemous words," a great black, villainous-looking spider, deformed and horrible, fell from the ceiling into the mouth of the "blasphemer, to carry its poison into his heart." The duke of Ossuna was also present, and several other persons, all of whom bore witness to this divine judgment.

(4) In A.D. 1556, Dorothy Lazesque, a Christian servant of Sachazet, in the diocese of Posen, was induced by her master, who was a Jew, to bring home the sacred wafer given her by the priest. The Jew took it to the synagogue, where he and three others cut it with their penknives, when lo! blood in such great abundance fell from the wounds, that the "parricides" were obliged to collect it in a basin. This miracle was known through all Poland. "Elle produisit de très-bons effets dans toute la Pologne; elle convainquit les Juifs de lèse majesté divine; elle confondit les hérétiques sacramentaires qui combattaient la vérité du corps de Notre-Seigneur en l'eucharistie; et elle ferma la bouche aux Luthériens qui se plaignaient de ce qu'on avait ôté aux laiques l'usage du calice, comme si le sang de Jésus Christ n'était pas tout entier, et aussi véritablement sous les espèces du pain que sous celles du vin."—Father Giry, *Discourse on the Fête du Très-saint Sacrement.*

In reply to this last remark it may be asked, If it is really believed that the bread contains everything *tout entier*, and the wine is wholly superfluous, why is the cup given to the clergy? Why not apply to them the remark made by Father Giry to the laity: "Why administer the cup, as if the bread did not contain every grace, or as if every blessing possibly to be obtained was not 'sous les espèces du pain que sous celles du vin'?"

The duke of Buckingham's way of disproving the dogma of transubstantiation. When Viliers, duke of Buckingham, was unwell, James II. sent an Irish priest to convert him to Popery. The duke received the priest most courteously; but before entering on the religious discussion, requested that the priest would join him in a glass of wine. After the priest had tasted the wine, the duke took up the cork of the bottle, and stroking it with great gravity, asked him how he liked the horse. The priest was utterly amazed at the duke's words; but Buckingham continued patting and stroking the cork, which he insisted was a beautiful racer of the very best breed. "Your grace," said the priest, "has chosen an unseasonable time for jesting." "Jesting?" said the duke; "jesting? I was never further from jesting in my whole life than at this moment." "Say not so, your grace," rejoined the priest; "you should compose yourself, and consider." "Consider?" said the duke; "what, I pray you, should I consider? I again say, can you not see how fine a horse this is?" "Oh!" exclaimed the priest, "don't be foolish. It is surely but a poor joke to call a wine-cork a horse." "What!" rejoined the duke with great gravity, "would you persuade me this magnificent courser is only a cork?" "Certainly," said the father; "it is nothing but a cork." "Well," replied the duke calmly, as if recovering from a dream, "I will not be positive; my illness may have unsettled my mind. But how can you prove to me that I am wrong?" So saying, he looked as if his mind was wandering. "Why, my dear duke, your eyes must convince you that a cork is not a horse. Your hands must convince you of the same. Common sense must convince you that you could not draw a racehorse out of a wine-bottle. Look at it, your grace, feel it, examine it, and you cannot but know that what you are pleased to call a horse is only a little cork." "Ah! just so, just so; well, well," said the duke, "your reverence may be right. Let us talk no more about it. To what do I owe the honour of this visit, your reverence?" The priest then entered upon the points of difference between Papists and Protestants, and continued till the duke said, "If your reverence will prove to me the doctrine of transubstantiation, I can easily believe all the rest." This the priest proceeded to do, and concluded by asking the duke if he did not think the doctrine both scriptural and true. The duke listened very attentively to all that was said, and then replied, "You thought me foolish, perhaps insane, when I spoke of a cork as being a horse; but your assertion that bread and wine are the actual body and blood of Christ is every whit as absurd, and a little more profane. You told me to use my senses in proof of my error—my eyes, my hands, my common sense. Out of your own mouth I will judge your words. You told me I had taken the cork out of the bottle, and it could not be a horse. I tell you, that you take a piece of bread out of a little box, and it cannot be a body of flesh and blood. I patted and stroked the cork, but though I used it like a horse, it remained a cork; and you pronounce certain words, and touch the bread, but that cannot alter its nature. You must see that the thing is absurd, if not worse than absurd. If you are not bereft of your senses, it must be evident to you that your bread is bread, and your wine, wine; and nothing else. Good morning, father, and remember the cork—remember the cork."—Bagley, *Family Biblical Instructor.*

Of course, the weak part of the duke's argument is his ignoring the virtue of consecration. The priest does not say that bread is the body of Christ, as the duke said a cork is a horse, but that by a special grace the bread by consecration becomes transubstantiated; and he ought to have proved that consecration has no power to change a material substance even by miracle. The duke allowed the creative fiat of the Almighty and the miracles of the Bible, and he ought to have proved that neither the creative power of the Almighty nor the gift of miracles accompany the act of consecration; and this he does not prove. Therein lies the weakness of the jest. After all, the subject is too serious to be confronted with a jest.

Celibacy and Married Celibates.

1 COR. vii. 32, 33. He that is unmarried careth for the things that belong to the Lord, how he may please the Lord; but he that is married careth for the things that are of the world, how he may please his wife.

REV. xiv. 1–5. I looked, and lo! a Lamb stood on the mount Sion, and with Him a hundred forty and four thousand. . . . These are they which were not defiled with women, for they are virgins . . . they are without fault before God.

ECCLESIASTICUS xix. 2. Wine and women will make [even] men of understanding to fall away. In French, "Le vin et les femmes font apostasier [même] les sages."

St. Cecilia and Valerian. St. Cecilia told Valerian on their bridal night that an angel was set over her to preserve her in chastity. Valerian asked to see this angel, but Cecilia made answer that it would be impossible to do so unless he was baptized. As Valerian questioned her further on the subject, she directed him to go on the morrow to the Appian Way, and talk to pope Urban. This did he, and Urban baptized him. The same night, when Valerian entered his chamber, he beheld the angel with Cecilia. He held in his hand two garlands, one of roses and the other of lilies. The roses he gave to Valerian, and the lilies to Cecilia, saying as he did so, "These garlands I brought from the garden of paradise; they will never wither, for there is no death there. To you they are sweet and beautiful, but to those whose virginity is soiled they not only yield no perfume, but they are not even visible." So saying, he left the chamber, and vanished from their sight.—Metaphrastês, *Lives*, etc. (See FLOWERS, ETC., OF PARADISE, p. 144.)

St. Gombert and St. Bertha, celibates in married life (seventh century). When Gombert was of a marriageable age, his parents urged him to take Bertha to wife. The young prince hesitated, because he wished to live to Christ; but a voice from heaven said to him, "Fear not, Gombert, to take Bertha for thy wife, for God designs great things from this union." So they were married, but vowed to God, by mutual consent, to live together as brother and sister, and to love each other only with platonic love.—D. Morlot, *History of the Diocese of Reims.*

Jeanne Marie de Maillé and Robert de Sillé. Jeanne Marie de Maillé was constrained to marry Robert de Sillé, a young gentleman whom she had saved when he fell into a water-tank. When the marriage was consummated, Marie told her young husband she had made a vow to Christ of perpetual virginity. Robert was not a little annoyed at this avowal, but as the bride had the stronger will, she won over the bridegroom to comply with it, and they lived together for sixteen years without "once sullying their angelic purity."—L'abbé Rolland, *Life of Jeanne Marie de Maillé.*

St. Julian and Basilissa. When St. Julian was eighteen years of age, his parents urged him to marry, and he requested to be allowed seven days to think the matter over. He spent these days of grace in prayer and fasting, and on the seventh day Christ appeared to him in a vision, and said to him, "Fear not, Julian, to take to thyself a wife, for as virgins ye shall still serve Me." So he married Basilissa; but when they entered the bridal chamber, both were struck with the sweet odour of roses and lilies which pervaded it, and clasping their hands together, they vowed to serve the Lord in virgin chastity. Then was the chamber filled with celestial light; and Jesus, with Mary and many saints, entered. Christ said, "Julian, thou hast conquered, and I have reserved for thee a crown of glory." The Virgin Mary, then addressing the bride, said, "Blessed art thou above women, Basilissa; and to thee shall be given to eat of the hidden manna." Then came two arrayed in white robes, and, raising Julian and Basilissa from the ground, they placed on their heads crowns of flowers, and showed them an open book seven times more lustrous than silver, and bearing letters of gold. Four elders also stood by, with vials of gold in their hands; and they said to Julian and the bride, "In these vials your perfections are carefully preserved, and their odour ascends as a sweet savour to the Lord of hosts. Blessed are ye, in that ye have vowed to abstain from carnal lusts, and to dedicate your virgin bodies to the glory of God." Julian, lifting up his eyes, looked on the book which the four elders showed him, and saw there his own name written with that of Basilissa his bride; and beneath them he read these words, "Every one that hath forsaken houses, or brethren, or sisters, or father, or mother, or wife, or children, or lands, for My name's sake, shall receive a hundredfold, and shall inherit everlasting life" (*Matt.* xix. 29).—*Les Petits Bollandistes*, vol. i. p. 234. (See FLOWERS, ETC., OF PARADISE, p. 144.)

St. Thierry, abbot of Mont d'Or, married and lived in celibacy (A.D. 533). St. Thierry was the son of a peasant named Marquard, living in the village of Menancourt, near Reims, a man of bad character, who supported himself and family by theft and depredation; his mother was not so bad as his father, and kept a dame's school. When Thierry was old enough, they compelled him to marry; but Thierry resolved, even in his married state, to preserve his virginity. When he told his bride of his determination she was extremely angry, and Thierry next morning went to consult the abbess Suzanne of Reims, who advised him to call on the archbishop, and lay the matter before his grace. The archbishop told him a married man had no right to live as a celibate without the consent of his wife, but advised him to explain to the bride that the King of heaven and earth has promised a crown of everlasting glory to those who have the courage and self-denial to preserve their chastity unspotted, and that the vow of virginity is the most glorious sacrifice that can be offered to God. When Thierry reported these words to his wife, she seemed pacified, and both of them made a vow to consecrate their virginity to Jesus Christ. In order to remove all danger, Thierry kissed his wife, and left her to live the life of a solitary in the desert.—Billy (almoner of the abbey of St. Thierry), *Life of St. Thierry.*

St. Vulphy of Ponthieu breaks his vow of celibacy in married life (died A.D. 643). St. Vulphy married and had three daughters, but ordered his house so wisely and well that St. Riquier appointed him to a missionary tour, and obtained the consent of his wife, binding both from that moment to a vow of perpetual continence. This vow being taken, St. Riquier ordained Vulphy priest, and his preaching was with great power of the Holy Ghost. "Mais, O faiblesse de notre nature! O inconstance de notre cœur! O misère de notre condition mortelle! Vulphy, oubliant la sainteté de son ministère, eut un commerce . . . avec sa femme, qu'il ne devait plus regarder que comme une sœur." Repenting of his crime, he abandoned his cure, and went on pilgrimage to the Holy Land, with no companion except his guardian angel. He watered the road with his tears, and visited the holy places. "Il ne se contenta pas de laver de ses pleurs les endroits que Notre Seigneur a teints de son sang." He wished to remain in the Holy Land, but the Holy Ghost bade him return to France "pour faire pénitence au même lieu où il avait péché;" so he returned to Ponthieu, and retired to a desert, where his austerities were so severe "qu'il est surprenant qu'un corps humain ait pu les supporter. On pouvait presque dire qu'il ne mangeait point, qu'il ne buvait point, et qu'il ne dormait point."—*Les Petits Bollandistes*, vol. vi. p. 511. (See *Acta Sanctorum*, vol. ii. June 7.)

Crucifixes, Images, Relics, etc., acting. (See pp. 184 and 501.)

MATT. xvi. 24. If any man will come after Me, let him . . . take up his cross and follow Me.

MATT. xxiv. 3. The sign of the Son of man.

LUKE xiv. 27. Whosoever doth not bear his cross . . . cannot be My disciple.

LUKE xix. 40. I tell you, that if these should hold their peace, the stones would immediately cry out.

HAB. ii. 11. The stone shall cry out of the wall, and the beam out of the timber shall answer it.

ISA. lv. 12. The mountains and the hills shall break forth before you into singing, and all the trees of the field shall clap their hands.

HEB. vi. 6. They crucify to themselves the Son of God afresh, and put Him to an open shame.

In an image representing the Virgin and Child, the Child Jesus leaves the arms of the Virgin, and associates with some boys (about A.D. 1265). This is a most astounding story told in the life of Bernard, the Dominican of Santarem, in Portugal. After performing mass he used to collect the acolytes together and teach them their catechism; not unfrequently the fathers of the boys attended also. They met in a chapel, where they took their breakfast, and were allowed to play; and in this chapel was an image of the Virgin, holding in her arms the infant Jesus. Jesus, delighted at the happy faces of the acolytes, often left His mother's arms, and went to partake of the boys' breakfast. The servants, feeling aggrieved because Jesus contributed nothing towards the meal, complained to Bernard, and the pious catechist advised them to say to Jesus, "Seignior, how is it You so often breakfast with us, and yet contribute nothing to the meal? You ought, in turn, to invite our master and his acolytes to Your Father's table." The Child Jesus said, "Be it so. I invite them for Ascension Day." The servants told their master, and he looked forward with a longing heart to the heavenly feast. Ascension Day arrived. Bernard and his two acolytes went to mass in good time; they completed the service, and—ceased to live. All three were buried in the same tomb in the king's chapel, where a tablet told this tale of their death.—*Acta Sanctorum* (Bollandists), vol. ii., May 8.

An image of the Virgin Mary takes an apple from a little boy (A.D. 1230). One day Hermann, coming from school, stopped before the image of a Virgin and

Child, and offered an apple which had been given him; praying the Virgin to accept this little gift as a token of his love. "Chose étonnante! aussitôt la Reine des anges, pour ne point contrister cet aimable enfant, et pour rendre recommandable à toute la postérité l'innocente simplicité avec laquelle il agissait avec elle, rendit son image flexible, et étendant sa main de pierre comme si c'eût été une main de chair, elle reçut favorablement le present de son petit serviteur. 'O bienheureuse enfance d'Hermann!' s'écrie l'abbé qui a composé sa vie, laquelle a mérité d'être si tôt consolée par des signes et des révélations célestes."—Mgr. Guérin (chamberlain of pope Leo XIII.), *Vies des Saints*, vol. iv. p. 272 (7th edit. 1880).

This is a valuable token of the ready credulity of the age. This abbot had no doubt upon the subject, and even the chamberlain of pope Leo XIII., in 1880, expresses no misgiving, but cites the incident as an undoubted fact. The tale is accepted by the great Bollandists, and the *petits Bollandistes*. It has the highest authority that can be accorded to it by man, and only wants one thing to make it credible—that is, credulity.

Image of the Virgin moves its hands to bless the congregation (1882). On Sunday evening, Aug. 20, 1882, while a large congregation were at worship in the Franciscan Church, at Athlone, in Ireland, and just as the priest, the Rev. Father McDermott, had concluded his sermon, a brilliant light shone from the roof immediately above the figure of the Virgin Mary. Showers of stars descended on the head of the figure, the eyes opened and rolled from side to side, the hands moved, and the figure assumed the attitude of blessing the congregation; after which it resumed its former appearance. Those who saw the sight moved from their seats in different parts of the church, and pushed to the altar. A scene of the greatest excitement ensued. The religious services were suspended, but the church remained crowded until a late hour at night, and even then it was with difficulty cleared. This morning the thoroughfares near the church had become impassable. Much credence is attached to the accounts of the "wonder," as numbers of persons who witnessed it all give the same version of what took place.—Newspaper paragraph, Aug. 22, A.D. 1882.

The image of Virgin and Child at Déols, in France, shows by certain movements it wishes to change its place (A.D. 1187). In the parish church of Déols, in France, was an image of the Virgin and Child, which stood against the north door. On the last day of May, 1187, at the hour of vespers, Mary broke the collar round her neck, and moved about on her pedestal so uneasily, that the priests were convinced the image wanted to be moved into some other place. It was, accordingly, shifted into the middle of the church, and Rigord, the historian of Philippe Auguste, living at the time, informs us how it was done. "The priests," he says, "stood at the bottom of the church singing hymns and canticles, while workmen moved the image." A little afterwards, a high chapel was constructed above the main entrance, and hither the image was ultimately removed with great pomp and ceremony, amidst an enormous crowd of spectators.—Thomas de la Thaumassière, *History of Berry*.

The old Bourges breviary refers to this "miracle" in these words: "Dominica pridie calendas Junii, circa vesperam, visa est eadem imago moveri, quasi vellet se inde transferre," etc.

The crucifix of Annecy sheds rays of light over St. Francis of Sales (A.D. 1567–1622). When St. Francis of Sales arrived at Annecy, he retired to the Jesuits' college to prepare his sermon. He began his station in the church of St. Dominic, in the presence of a crowd of senators and others. It was a cloudy day, but the moment he began to preach, the crucifix shed such rays of light upon him that his person seemed dazzling, and his face was brighter than the stars. All the audience cried out in surprise and admiration, but the preacher stood unmoved. He preached with such power of the Holy Ghost that many were converted, and his success only increased as he went to the other churches.—Hamon (curé of St. Sulpice), *Life of St. Francis de Sales*.

A crucifix speaks to and blesses Mme. de Bermond. Mme. de Bermond entered one day into a lady's house with the view of inducing her daughter to join the Ursulines. She there met a hermit, who said to her significantly, "Many are called, but few chosen." Mme. Bermond understood the hint, shortened her visit, and entering the church at Avignon, fell on her knees before the crucifix, crying, "Alas! my Saviour, is it possible that Thou shouldest have given me such a strong desire to be Thine entirely, and yet that I should not be one of Thy chosen ones? Forbid it, Lord, I beseech Thee." Then the crucifix before which she knelt lifted up its hand, gave her its benediction, and said, "Continue, My daughter, in thy well-doing, and I will bless thee and thy order."—*Les Petits Bollandistes*, vol. vi. p. 336.

The crucifix of St. Camillus moved and spoke often to him (A.D. 1614). St. Camillus wanted to organize a body of hospital nurses, who would attend the sick without fee or reward, and thought, if persons would carry a crucifix on their breast, many would be induced to join his corps. He spoke of his plan to several persons, and they fitted up a little chamber with an oratory, but met with great opposition from the hospitals. One night his crucifix spoke to him, and nodded its head to encourage him in his work. "Fear not," said the crucifix; "I am with you, and I will be your help in the time of trouble." This prodigy was often repeated. In fact, whenever he felt himself downhearted, the crucifix used to say to him, "Why art thou cast down, My son? Hope in God, thy Succour and Defender. Thy work is Mine, and the gates of hell shall not prevail against it." Thus assured, he persevered, and founded the "Order of Canons Regular for the Service of the Sick."—Cicatello (his disciple), *Life of St. Camillus*, etc.

The crucifix in St. Damian's church speaks to St. Francis of Assisi (A.D. 1182–1226). One morning St. Francis of Assisi wandered into St. Damian's, an old church almost a ruin, and falling before the crucifix, prayed thus: "Great God, and You, my Saviour Jesus Christ, dispel the darkness of my soul, give me pure faith, lasting hope, and perfect charity. Let Thy will, O God, be my will, make me and keep me Thine, now and for ever." The crucifix said to him thrice mysteriously, "Go, Francis, and repair My church falling into ruins." Francis thought he was to go and repair St. Damian's, where he was kneeling, but the crucifix spoke of the Holy Catholic Church, the Church universal.—Chavin de Malan, *Life of St. Francis of Assisi.*

The cross in the monastery of St. Dominic speaks audibly. St. Thomas Aquinas was a staunch defender of the religious opinions of St. Dominic. The Franciscans opposed him, headed by Duns Scotus; and the Church was divided between Thomists or Nominalists, and Scotists or Realists. We are gravely told, even by such a "protestant or reformed view of the saints" as that of Alban Butler, that while the dispute ran high, the crucifix or cross in a monastery of St. Dominic, Naples, spake and said, "Thomas, thou hast written well of Me; what recompense dost thou desire?" "None but Thyself," said Thomas.—*Lives of the Saints* (March 7).

The image, of course, spoke in orthodox Latin: "Bene scripsisti de me, Thoma; quam mercedem accipies?" "Non aliam nisi te, Domine."

A crucifix speaks to Emily Bicchieri (A.D. 1238–1314). One day, when Emily Bicchieri was meditating on the sacred mystery of the crown of thorns, she implored the Saviour to let her feel in her own person what He suffered when He was so tortured. Christ answered her by the mouth of her crucifix, and told her He would grant her what she requested. Forthwith she felt an excruciating headache, and was confined to her bed for three days, at the end of which Mary Magdalene and St. Catherine appeared before her, and gave her a draught of something like water, which instantly cured her headache and feverish thirst.—*Acta Sanctorum* (Bollandists), May 3.

A crucifix nods approval to St. John Gualbert (A.D. 1073). John Gualbert was the son of an officer in the Italian army. His brother had been slain, and John was the avenger of blood, whose duty was to avenge his brother's death. He found the murderer in Florence, in a place where all hope of escape was taken away. Drawing his sword, he was just on the point of running it through the murderer, when the man threw himself at the feet of Gualbert, with his arms extended in the form of a cross, and conjured him by "the passion of Christ" to spare his life. Gualbert's arm was arrested, as if by magic, and he said to the prostrate foe, "I cannot refuse what you ask in the name of Christ; go in peace." John Gualbert then continued his way to St. Miniat's abbey, and entering the church, he fell before the crucifix devoutly; whereupon the crucifix bowed its head approvingly, and thanked him for having accorded pardon to his enemy so heroically. This was the turning-point of his life, for without delay he abandoned the army, and became a monk.—*Acta Sanctorum* (Bollandists), vol. iii. July 12.

The crucifix of St. Thomas of Villeneuve speaks words of encouragement to him (A.D. 1555). St. Thomas of Villeneuve was made archbishop of Valence, but was so distressed by the thought that this worldly advancement should peril the interest of his soul, that he would run constantly to his confessor, who slept close by, and cry in terror, "My father, my father, can I be saved and hold this dignity?" He applied to the emperor to release him, but the emperor paid no attention to his supplication; he then applied to the great King of kings, and conjured Him to deliver him from the danger of perdition. On the day of the Purification (Feb. 2), while he was in his oratory, his crucifix said to him, "Thomas, afflict not yourself, but be patient. On the day of My mother's nativity (Sept. 8) you shall receive the recompense of all your troubles." As an incontestable proof of this revelation, the mouth of the crucifix, which before had sweated blood in his sight, now remained open, although it was shut before; and what was more surprising still, it showed a set of teeth, made of copper, so perfect and so exquisite that no art of man nor human instrument could possibly have constructed them.—*Acta Sanctorum* (Bollandists), vol. v. Sept. 18.

The crucifix said the archbishop would die on the 8th of September, but he died on the 18th, or ten days later.

The crucifix of St. Vincent Ferrier turns its head and speaks (fourteenth century). One night, as St. Vincent Ferrier was praying before the *Crucifix des Martyrs*, and meditating on the sorrows of Jesus, His wounds in the hands, feet, and side, he was moved to tears, and exclaimed involuntarily, "O my Saviour, how great were Thy sufferings on the cross!" The crucifix turned its head over its right shoulder towards the saint, and replied, "Yes, Vincent, I suffered all you say, and more, much more." The crucifix, which still retains the position of the head which it turned towards the saint, is preserved as a precious relic.—Father Teoli, bk. i. tratt. ii. c. 3.

The crucifix called St. Sauf, at Amiens, turns its head round (A.D. 600). When St. Honoré died, his body was buried with great honour, and reposed under the high altar till the irruption of the Danes. It was then transferred to the church of St. Peter and St. Paul, formerly called the church of St. Firmin, confessor, where it remained till it was carried to the episcopal church of Amiens. As the body entered the church, the crucifix turned its head, following the bearers. All present saw and wondered, and glorified God. This "miracle" is quite beyond gainsaying, because "on voit encore aujourd'hui ce crucifix dans la cathédrale d'Amiens."—Mgr. Guérin, *Vies des Saints* (1880), vol. v. p. 576.

The foot of a crucifix, being poisoned, drew back when Pius V. was about to kiss it (A.D. 1504–1572). All the contemporaneous historians recount the following:—One day pope Pius V. was about to kiss the foot of a crucifix, according to custom, when the crucifix drew back its foot. In fact, some ill-disposed person had poisoned the crucifix, as was proved to demonstration by rubbing the crucifix with bread, which was afterwards thrown to some dogs. The moment it was eaten, the dogs died. "Le Saint ne voulut pas même qu'on recherchât ces assassins. Les arts ont souvent reproduit l'événement du crucifix."—Père Giry, *Histoire de Saint Pie V.*

The bleeding image of Déols (A.D. 1187). In the twelfth century France was overrun with highwaymen and cut-throats, many of which were enrolled as soldiers. On May 29, A.D. 1187, a number of these villains were playing before one of the gates of the church at Déols, where was an image of the Virgin Mary, holding in her arms the infant Jesus. One of the fellows, who had lost in play, lost his temper also, and, taking up a stone, flung it at the image, and broke off the arm of the child. Now, says Rigord, the historian of Philippe Auguste, a contemporary, "A stream of blood poured from the arm of the broken image and made a pool on the earth below. The fellow who flung the stone was seized with madness, and dropped down dead on the spot. John Lackland, and Adhemar viscount of Limoges, carefully collected the blood, and deposited it in a rich chapel, erected in England and dedicated to the Virgin." Rigord, who recounts this "miracle," adds that numberless cures were effected by this blood. A confraternity was established, in 1187, in memory of this blood-shedding; it flourished till the Revolution, and was reorganized in 1830, and May 31 is set apart to commemorate "The Miracle of Notre-Dame de Déols."

Rigord, the historian, calls this fellow who threw the stone "a new Judas."

The cross of Piagaro bled bluish blood (eighteenth century). St. Paul of the Cross (A.D. 1694–1775), preaching for the last time in the church of Piagaro, said, "When I am gone this crucifix will preach," pointing to a large crucifix on one of the altars. He gave the blessing and left; but hundreds remained kneeling, expecting every moment to witness a miracle. In a short time a stream of bluish fluid oozed from the figure on the cross, and all shouted, "A miracle! a miracle!" The priest called out aloud, "My people, my sins are the cause of this miracle;" and then he wiped off the "sacred fluid" with a white napkin. Messengers were despatched to inform St. Paul, and a chapel was afterwards built for the "miraculous cross." (See IMPOSTURE, p. 184.)—Father Pius, *Life of St. Paul of the Cross, Founder of the Passionists.*

A relic of St. Philip di Neri both moves and speaks (sixteenth century). Stephen Calcinard used to carry about him a relic of St. Philip di Neri; and one day, being tempted to sin by a licentious woman, he felt the relic very restless, moving about his bosom in a most unaccountable manner. Presently he heard it say to him, "Stephen, Stephen, if sinners entice thee, consent thou not." He took the word of warning, and fled from the tempter.—*The Process of the Canonization.*

The rood at Boxley, in Kent. At Boxley there stood an image, the eyes of which "did stir like a lively thing." The body bowed, the forehead frowned. It drooped its lower lip, as if to speak. The people looked on this "Jesus on the cross" with the utmost reverence, and offerings to it poured in abundantly. One day a commissioner, looking closely, discovered mechanism at the back of the head, but the abbot and his monks professed both ignorance and unbelief of anything of the sort. However, the commissioner had the image removed to Maidstone, and there, on market-day, exposed the fraud to the people. It was then exhibited in London, and performed before the court; and lastly it was set on a platform before St. Paul's cross, where it was made to go through its paces while the bishop of Rochester lectured on the imposition in a sermon. The sermon over, the platform gave way, the image was thrown down, and the angry mob tore it to pieces.—J. A. Froude, *History of England*, etc.

Simon Magus made statues act like human beings. St. Clement tells us that Simon Magus made statues walk and fly in the air, and made pots and pans in a house move about spontaneously, and minister to persons' wants. The whole passage about this famous "sorcerer" is worth transcribing: "Legimus apud B. Clementem, eum [*i.e.* Simon Magus] ex aëre novum hominem creasse;—quibus volebat invisibilem factum;—saxa quasi lutum penetrasse;—statuas animasse;—et in ignem positum [these statues] non arsisse." He furthermore says, "In ovem aut caprano se immutasse;—in aërem sublatum volasse [like Mr. Home, p. 218]; . . . Statuas faciebat ambulare . . . ; ex lapidibus panes faciebat;—serpens fiebat, et in aliquas alias tertias transformabatur in conviviis exhibebat spectra omnis generis . . . ; efficiebat, ut multæ umbræ eum precæderent, quas dicebat esse animas defunctorum." Menghi says that he made dogs speak and sing with human voices. To prove his power superior to that of the apostles, he floated in the air across the Forum. He always insisted that his power was divine, and that he himself ought to obtain divine honours. Justin Martyr states that a statue was actually erected to him in Rome, where he was worshipped as a god.—See *Notes and Queries*, Nov. 24, 1883, p. 402, for the exact references.

The veneration for crucifixes must have received a great shock in the plague of Malaga, 1803–4. The governor of Malaga ordered all the effects of those who had died of the plague to be burned in a field outside the town. It so happened that a wooden crucifix was brought to be cast into the fire, when the officer in charge interfered, crying out, "Poor Christ! is it not enough that the Jews crucified Thee on Calvary; must we also burn Thee here in Malaga?" The people, greatly moved, implored that the sacred image might not be cast into the fire and burned; so the crucifix was rescued, and set in a balustrade for public veneration. Five men went and kissed it, "contractent la contagion, et en deviennent bientôt les victimes."—*Mémorial de Chronologie,* 1829, vol. ii. p. 887.

Dr. Pinnock, in his *Analysis of English Church History* (p. 55), says, "To uphold the credit of particular monasteries, recourse was had to fraud, tricks, and lying miracles. At a synod held at Winchester in 968, to settle the dispute between the Seculars and Regulars, when it was found that the argument was in favour of the Seculars, mysterious sounds were heard coming from a crucifix on the wall, exclaiming, "God forbid it should be done!" upon which Dunstan and his party came off triumphant. The king was wholly in the hands of the monks, who engaged to defend him from the devil and his imps, on his promise of protecting Dunstan and his party against their opponents.

Again. A synod was convened at Calne, in Somersetshire, and met in an upper chamber, A.D. 978. The advocate of the Seculars was a Scotch prelate, who had the best of the argument; but Dunstan simply replied, "I commit the cause of Christ's Church to Christ Himself," and immediately, by previous arrangement, part of the floor gave way, and precipitated the Secular party to the ground floor, while the Regulars remained unhurt (p. 56).

Dress prescribed. (See CHASUBLE, DEVICE, etc., in Index.)

DEUT. xxii. 5. The woman shall not wear that which pertaineth unto a man, neither shall a man put on a woman's garment.

1 TIM. ii. 9. I will that women adorn themselves in modest apparel; not with broided hair, or gold, or pearls, or costly array.

EXOD. xxviii. 40. For Aaron's sons thou shalt make coats, and thou shalt make for them girdles, and bonnets shalt thou make for them, for glory and for beauty.

EXOD. xxviii. 4–43. These are the garments

thou shalt make for Aaron: a breastplate, and an ephod, and a robe, and a broidered coat. a mitre, and a girdle. And they shall make the ephod of gold, blue, purple, scarlet, and fine twined linen. . . . And thou shalt make the robe of the ephod all of blue, and upon the hem of it thou shalt make pomegranates of blue, and purple, and scarlet; and bells of gold between them round about.

The Virgin Mary appears to St. Alberic to change the colour of the Cistercian dress (A.D. 1109). The Cistercians dressed originally in grey or black; but one day in the nones of August, while the monks were chanting matins, the Virgin Mary came amongst them; and going up to the abbot, St. Alberic, threw over his shoulders a white robe, and as she did so, the vestments of all the monks present became white in a moment. This being done, the "spotless Virgin" reascended to heaven, with all the saints and angels which formed her cortége. This miracle has been commemorated by the order ever since, on Aug. 5, under the title of "The Descent of the Blessed Virgin Mary at Citeaux, and the Miraculous Change of the Black Habits for White Ones, while Alberic was Abbot." White is the livery of the Virgin, and since this event all Cistercian monks have dressed in white.*—Bollandus, *Acta Sanctorum*. (See also *The Annals of the Cistercians*, vol. i.)

Mgr. Guérin, chamberlain to pope Leo XIII., says, "Cette apparition n'est pas un fait isolé. Souvent la Mère de Jesus se montrait aux frères du désert de Citeaux, pour les défendre et les consoler."—*Vies des Saints*, vol. i. p. 630.

The Virgin Mary appears to St. Norbert, and prescribes what dress the Premonstratensians are to wear (A.D. 1080–1134). The bishop of Laon, very desirous that St. Norbert should settle in his diocese, promised to build him a monastery. The bishop first showed him a place called Foigny, but St. Norbert was told by revelation that God had set aside this spot for the Cistercians. The bishop then showed him Thenaille, but St. Norbert was told by revelation that this was not the site which God had chosen. The bishop then showed him a dale called Premontré, and Norbert cried out aloud, "That's the place the Lord has chosen." There was a small chapel here, and in that chapel Norbert passed the night in prayer. During the night he was visited by a host of angels all in white, who made a procession with crosses and candles. The Virgin Mary also came, showed him the exact site he was to select, gave him the pattern of the dress his disciples were to wear, and prescribed white as its colour. In allusion to this vision, St. Norbert is represented in Christian art with the Virgin presenting to him a white garment, and the devil called him "The White Hound."—John Chrysostom Vande-Sterre, *Life of St. Norbert*.

The Virgin Mary prescribes the dress of the order of the Servitors of Mary (thirteenth century). Alexis Falconieri founded the order of the Servitors of Mary, on Mount Senario, and entreated the bishop of Florence to draw up the rules. While this was being done, the Virgin Mary appeared to Alexis, and showed him the dress which the order were to wear. It was to be black, "in memory of the passion of her Son." At the same time she presented to Alexis the rule of St. Augustine. In memory of this vision, every Good Friday the brothers of this order observe a ceremony called "The Obsequies of Jesus Christ;" and the day following they celebrate "The Coronation of the holy Virgin."—*Les Petits Bollandistes*, vol. ii. p. 566.

Not only is the dress of certain orders thus prescribed by revelation, but even the rules to be observed. Thus St. Pacomius, when, in the third century, he founded the Tabennites, received from an angel "The Book of Rules." —His life by a monk of Tabenne, one of his disciples.

Scallop-shells enjoined as a pilgrim's badge by a voice from heaven. All know that scallop-shells used to denote a pilgrim, but all do not know the reason why. The legend is this: When the marble ship which bore the headless body of St. James approached Bouzas, in Portugal, it happened to be the wedding day of the chief magnate of the village; and, while the bridal party was at sport, the horse of the bridegroom became unmanageable, and plunged into the sea. The marble ship sailed over the horse and its rider, and when they emerged from the sea, the cloak of the bridegroom was thickly covered with scallop-shells. All were dumfounded. They knew not what to make of these marvels; but a voice from heaven exclaimed, "It is the will of God that all who henceforth make vows to St. James, and go on pilgrimage, shall take with them scallop-shells; and all who do so shall be remembered in the day of judgment." On hearing this, the

* We in England call the Cistercians "White Friars," and the Benedictines "Black Friars." In Christian art St. Alberic is represented with the Virgin changing his black habit for a white one.

lord of the village, with the bride and bridegroom, were duly baptized, and Bouzas became a Christian village.—*Sanctoral Portugues* (copied into the Breviaries of Alcobaça and St. Cucufate).

*** The following Latin hymn refers to this legend:—

Cunctis mare cernentibus,
Sed a profundo ducitur;
Natus regis submergitur,
Totus plenus conchilibus.

In sight of all the prince went down
Into the deep sea dells;
In sight of all the prince emerged,
Covered with cockle-shells.
Hymn for St. James's Day.

St. Simon Stock receives a scapular from the hands of the Virgin (July 16, A.D. 1251). Soon after St. Simon Stock was promoted to the dignity of general of the order of Carmelites, the Virgin Mary, in the dress of a Carmelite, brought him a scapular, and directed him to institute the confraternity of the Scapular to unite all her devout clients in certain regular religious observances. This occurred on July 16, A.D. 1251, and St. Simon set apart that day as the anniversary of the confraternity. The object of this association was to invite all its members, while living in the world, and employed on their daily duties, to wear a small emblem, called a scapular, to recite certain prayers, and practise certain religious exercises out of devotion to the holy Virgin.

The scapular is a portion of the dress worn on the shoulders (Latin *scapula*, the shoulder). It consists of a long stripe of serge, the centre of which passes over the head; one flap of the scapular hangs down in front, and the other on the back. The scapular worn by monks generally reaches to the feet, but that worn by lay brothers only to the knees. The scapular of the confraternity of Simon Stock was much less pretentious, not being conspicuous at all, and very small. It was a little badge worn by persons engaged in the ordinary duties of life, binding them to certain observances consistent with their occupations, whatever they might be; as a strip of blue ribbon is a badge of temperance worn by men and women.

Guardian Angels.

Psalm xxxiv. 7. The angel of the Lord encampeth round about them that fear Him, and delivereth them.

Matt. xviii. 10. Take heed that ye despise not one of these little ones; for I say unto you, that in heaven their angels do always behold the face of My Father which is in heaven.

Acts xii. 15. Then said they, It is his angel.

Heb. i. 14. Are not the angels all ministering spirits, sent forth to minister for them who shall be heirs of salvation?

Hesiod, the Greek poet, says—

Aerial spirits, by great Jove designed
To be on earth the guardians of mankind;
Invisible to mortal eyes they go,
And mark our actions, good or bad, below;
Th' immortal spies with watchful care preside,
And thrice ten thousand round their charges glide.
They can reward with glory or with gold;
Such power divine permission bids them hold.
Works and Days, bk. i.

Mme. de Bermond and her guardian angel (A.D. 1562–1628). Mme. de Bermond was always in great intimacy with her guardian angel. If she feared the loss of any important letter, she commended its care to her angel, and she was sure to receive an early reply. Her feebleness made her cough at almost every footstep that she took; so she would invoke her angel, and used to say, "Without the help of my angel I should die many times a day." At whatever hour of the night she wished to wake, her angel was sure to call her, by rapping on the table. If she wished to speak to any one absent, she told her angel, and the person was sure to come to her. This often occurred with the mother superior, to whom Mme. de Bermond would say, "God be praised, my mother; I sent my angel to ask you to come." She always saluted her angel when she entered or left a room, and would stop awhile at the door, to give her angel time to pass first.—*Les Petits Bollandistes*, vol. vi. p. 337.

One of the guardian angels of St. Francisca was visible to her (A.D. 1384–1440). Besides her own special guardian angel, God allotted St. Francisca a second, which accompanied her everywhere in a form visible to her. If at any time the devil assumed the guise of a spirit of light in order to deceive her, this visible angel exposed the tempter, and delivered her from his wiles. If at any time a word escaped her which was superfluous, or a thought crossed her mind not according to grace, or a desire of food came on more than was needful for bare subsistence, this visible angel became invisible, and recalled her to her right mind. Hence is it in works of art that St. Francisca is represented with a companion angel.—John Mattiotti (her father-confessor), *Life of St. Francisca.*

A guardian angel conducts St. Onuphrius to a desert place (A.D. 303–400). Onuphrius was a monk in a monastery of the Thebaïd, but was inspired to become a hermit, left the monastery, and took his way towards the desert, praying God to guide him. Presently he saw a light moving on before him, and, being alarmed, thought of turning back; but a voice said to him, "Fear not, Onuphrius; I am thy guardian angel; I have defended you since your birth, and will always be your protector." The angel then made himself visible, and conducted him seven miles to the cell of an old recluse. Here he remained to learn the way of living as an eremite, and then retired further into the desert, to a spot more secluded still.—*Les Petits Bollandistes*, vol. vii. p. 589.

St. Opportuna conducted to the altar by her good angel (A.D. 770). Opportuna entered the little solitude of Montreul, and received the veil at the hands of her brother Chrodegand. When she entered the solitude, all the sisters saw her good angel visibly walking at her side, and telling her what to do; so that none of them were surprised that she made such rapid strides towards perfection, and that she soon outstripped even her mistress in the "science of Jesus Christ." In Christian art St. Opportuna is represented with a guardian angel walking at her side, and turning over the leaves of her missal. —L'abbé Durand, *Life of St. Opportuna.*

St. Paul the Simple was able to see the ministering angels (fourth century). St. Paul the Simple had the special grace of reading the heart of those who entered church, and could discern the conscience of men and women as distinctly as other persons see their faces. Being one day in a monastery where many brothers were assembled for a conference, Paul scrutinized those who came, saw if they had a clean conscience, and were attended by their angels. After a time, one entered whose conscience was soiled by sin, and a demon waited on him. Paul, seeing the man's angel hold back dejected and weeping, wept and prayed. He saw the sinner during the sacrifice of the mass repent. He saw the blackness of the man's conscience gradually fade away: "Though your sins be as scarlet, they shall be white as snow; though they be red like crimson, they shall be as wool." He saw the demon slink off, and the good angel rush to the penitent; and he cried in the fulness of joy, "O the unspeakable mercy of God! How great is His compassion, and His love past finding out!" Then rushing into the church, he cried with a loud voice, "Come, come and see how the Lord is gracious. He willeth not the death of a sinner, but that all should be saved. Come worship the Lord in the beauty of holiness, and bow before Him, for He only can forgive sins." When the brothers gathered round him, curious to know what had occurred, Paul told them; and the monk he referred to, coming forward, confessed what Paul had said was true. "O God," he added, "who came into the world to save sinners, give me the grace of repentance not to be repented of. I here vow that from this moment I renounce the devil and all his works, and will no more fall into sin, but will walk in Thy laws and commandments blameless for the rest of my life." This public confession gave great joy to all the brothers; they thanked God and took courage.—*Vies des Pères des Déserts d'Orient* (see *Roman Martyrology*, vol. i. March 7).

Rosana, called "Sister Humility," had two guardian angels (A.D. 1310). Rosana, the daughter of noble parents of Faenza, had two guardian angels, one named Sapiel and the other Emmanuel. "When I think," said Rosana, "of the exalted rank of my celestial guardians, my heart is exalted; when I muse on their incomparable beauty, it is ravished; but when I call to mind that they stand before the throne of the Almighty, my joy is ecstatic. With two such guardians I can fear no evil; they are a fortress, a buckler, a rock of defence. They direct me with their counsel, protect me with their love, keep the keys of my heart and the door of my lips. O Emmanuel, O Sapiel, my angels, my beloved, conduct me into the presence of the queen of heaven, and place me in the arms of her divine Child Jesus."—*Acta Sanctorum* (Bollandists), vol. v. May 22.

St. Vincent Ferrier speaks to the guardian angel of Barcelona (A.D. 1357–1419). Angels often visited St. Vincent Ferrier. On one occasion he spoke to the guardian angel of Barcelona. He was about to enter the city gates, when he observed a young man environed in light sitting near the gates. He had a naked sword in one hand, and a buckler in the other. St. Vincent asked him who he was, and what he did in that place, thus armed as he was. The angel made answer, "I am the guardian angel of Barcelona. This city is under my protection." In the sermon which he preached at night, he told the congregation of this vision, felicitated them on their good fortune, and exhorted them to render themselves worthy of such an honour. An enormous statue of the angel was subsequently erected on the spot, and stands there still. —Mgr. Guérin, *Vies des Saints*, vol. iv. p. 236.

This guardian angel has not succeeded in guarding the city, which has always been taken whenever it has been attacked. Thus in 1640 it was taken by the French, who continued masters of the city till 1652. In 1697 it was again taken by the French, but restored at the peace of Ryswick. In 1705 the governor was obliged to surrender up the town to the English and Dutch. In 1713 the town, after a siege of sixty-two days, was taken by assault. But this is not the place for a history of this city.

Holy Water.

NUMB. xix. 18. A clean person shall take hyssop, and dip it in the water, and sprinkle it upon the tent, and upon all the vessels, and upon the persons that are there.

St. Clement, in his *Constitutions* (bk. viii. ch. 25), asserts that St. Matthieu was the institutor of holy water, but this nowhere appears in the *Gospel* ascribed to that evangelist. The most probable origin is the Greek and Roman lustral water.

Greek and Roman lustrations. The Greeks and Romans, as well as the ancient Jews, were accustomed to purify cities, camps, houses, persons, and implements of war, etc., by sprinkling them with water. When a person died, the house was swept and sprinkled. Newly married people were sprinkled by the priest with water. Scarcely any undertaking was begun without lustration. Sacrifices were never made without it, and what is far more striking, after numbering the people, lustration always followed. As a census was taken by the Romans every five years, a lustration, of course, was made every five years, and hence a period of five years was called a lustrum.

There was a lustration by fire as well as by water, and the ghost in Hamlet speaks of his sins being burnt and purged away.

The ancients placed lustral water in a vessel at the door of their temples, and all persons who entered the temple dipped their fingers in this sacred water and sprinkled themselves, that they might present themselves ceremonially clean before the gods. Lustral water was also placed at the entrance door of a house where a person was dead.

The Roman Catholics follow this custom of the ancient Greeks and Romans.

St. Achard warded off the devil with holy water (A.D. 687). St. Achard, abbot of Jumièges, in the diocese of Rouen, used to go over his abbey every night when the inmates had retired to their cells, and visit the dormitories with cross and holy water to drive away evil spirits, which often hid themselves in these places to scare the sleepers in their sleep. —Surius, *Lives of the Saints.*

The worm in wheat destroyed by St. Gunthiern by sprinkling the fields with holy water (sixth century). Guerech I. of

the Pays du Vannes, seeing his vassals menaced by famine, because the worm had eaten up the wheat, and ruined the hopes of harvest, applied to St. Gunthiern, who gave the royal messengers some holy water, and bade them sprinkle a few drops over the fields. Immediately this was done the worm disappeared and the corn recovered. The count, in gratitude, gave St. Gunthiern a plot of meadow land on the banks of the Blavet, called Vegnac, and subsequently Ker-vegnac. —Dom Lobineau, *Lives of the British Saints.*

St. Sampson by holy water cures the deadly bite of a venomous serpent (A.D. 565). One day St. Sampson, with other school-boys, was sent by St. Iltut to pull up weeds in a wheat-field, and while they were thus occupied, a deadly serpent crept under the clothes of one of the boys and bit his leg. The death of the boy was imminent; but Sampson poured into the wound some oil, and sprinkled the leg with holy water. The venom exuded drop by drop, and the boy suffered no injury.—Dom Lobineau, *Lives of British Saints.*

St. Vincent Ferrier cures the vineyards of Montcallier by sprinkling them with holy water (A.D. 1357–1419). Being in Piedmont, the inhabitants of Montcallier complained to St. Vincent Ferrier that every year a tempest had ruined their vine-harvest. The saint gave them some holy water, and told them to sprinkle a few drops on their vineyards. The effect of this remedy was most marvellous, for when the tempest came, it did no harm whatever to the vines which had been sprinkled, whereas those vineyards which had not been sprinkled were ruined.—Peter Ranzano (bishop of Lucera), *Life of St. Vincent Ferrier.*

St. Willibrod dispels with holy water a fever which had broken out in St. Irmina's convent (seventh century). At the close of the seventh century, a dreadful fever broke out in St. Irmina's convent. Many had died from it, and almost all the establishment was affected by it. St. Willibrod was just at this crisis led by the hand of God to visit this convent, and Irmina implored him to lay his hands on the sick, that they might be restored to health. St. Willibrod offered the sacrifice of the mass, and then sprinkled the sick with holy water, or gave it them to drink, and ere night the fever entirely abated, and all the sick inmates were restored to health.—L'abbé Hunckler, *Histoire des Saints d'Alsace.*

Incense.

PSALM cxli. 2. Let my prayer be set forth before Thee as incense.

REV. viii. 3, 4. Another angel came and stood at the altar, having a golden censer; and there was given unto him much incense, that he should offer it with the prayers of all saints upon the golden altar which was before the throne. And the smoke of the incense, which came with the prayers of the saints, ascended up before God out of the angel's hand.

Incense was used by the Jews, Greeks, Romans, etc., in their temples to cover the offensive smells of their sacrifices. The Jews consumed half a pound of incense morning and evening.

St. Hermann sees two angels incensing the choir. When St. Hermann joined the choir, he often saw two angels incensing the choir during the canticle *Benedictus*. Some they incensed joyfully; these were the religious fervents, who sang the praises of God from the heart, as well as from the mouth. Others they pretended not to see; these were the careless negligents, who either failed to sing, or sang without attention and reverence. Others, again, they hurried past with scorn and horror; and these were those whose lives were a disgrace to their profession: though God might be on their tongues, the devil ruled in their hearts. —*Life of St. Hermann of Steinfeld* (Bollandists), April 7.

Monastic Life and Monasteries.

Defence of monastic life from Scripture is too shadowy to require notice. In the Old Testament is the extremely doubtful case of Jephthah's daughter, and in the New Testament the instance of John the Baptist, which was very far indeed from a monastic life. Then we have the two texts, *Matt.* xix. 21 exhorting to voluntary poverty, and 1 *Cor.* vii. 37 in commendation of celibacy. The Essenes seem to have approached nearer to the point. According to Josephus, they lived in union, abandoned all the pleasures of life, never married, despised riches, and had all things in common. Oil and perfumes were prohibited; they dressed only in white, were very hospitable, took great care of the sick, and were most patient under suffering. Before any one was admitted into their society, he had to undergo a year's probation. There were both male and female Essenes. The primitive Church imitated the Essenes in their community: "No one said aught of the things which he possessed was his own, but they had all things in common." This, however, is communism, not monachism.

A far nearer pattern is to be found in the "Triple Basket" of Buddhism than in the Bible. The five precepts for those who would live a religious life are: (1) Abstinence from food after midday; (2) abstinence from dances, theatres, songs, and music; (3) abstinence from all personal ornaments and perfumes; (4) abstinence from a lofty or luxurious bed; and (5) abstinence from the accumulation of gold and silver. Buddhist monks dress in rags; eat only the simplest food; possess no property, except what they distribute in alms, and which has been obtained for the purpose by begging from door to door. These contributions they carry in a wooden bowl. They eat only one meal a day; and they live for a part of the year, at least, under a tree, where also they sleep on a rug. Their greatest merit consists in almsgiving, chastity, patient endurance, and contemplation; but charity and self-abnegation are their royal virtues.

Confession is a Buddhist institution. Twice a month every good Buddhist confesses—at the new and at the full moon. Penance and humiliation are with them the only means of atonement for sin. A Bikshu vows to lead a life of self-denial, celibacy, and mendicity; is forbidden to converse with or even look at a female; and passes the day in contemplation and almsgiving.—Wilson (the Orientalist).

The archangel Michael bids St. Bertrand build a basilica near his monastery (A.D. 503). When St. Bertrand had finished his abbey, known under the name of La Couture, as he was praying, one morning at daybreak, the archangel Michael appeared to him, and bade him build a basilica in a place called Vivereus, near his abbey, adding it was God's wish he should do so. St. Bertrand could not but obey, and put the work in hand at once. He dedicated the basilica to St. Peter and St. Paul with great pomp, and deposited there some relics of the two apostles.—Dom Piolin, *History of the Church of Mans.*

An angel marks out the ground-plan, etc., of the church and monastery of Blangy. St. Bertha, the widow of Sigefroy, son of the duke of Douai, built a monastery at Blangy, but it fell down in utter ruins, and Rictruda, her sister-in-law, suggested that most likely the site selected was not acceptable to God. All the sisters put themselves in prayer for three days, and then an angel showed Bertha in a dream a spot on the same estate, in the midst of a green meadow near the Ternoise. The ground was covered with dew, and the angel with a Latin cross marked out in the dew the ground-plan of a monastery and church. Next morning Bertha went to visit the meadow, and found four stones disposed at the four angles, marking the length and breadth of the projected building, and thanked God for revealing to her His will. She employed skilful architects, and the new church and monastery were the admiration of every one.—L'abbé van Drival, *Légendaire de Morinie.*

The monastery of St. Francis of Paula laid out by the ghost of St. Francis of Assisi (A.D. 1452). St. Francis, at the age of fifteen, retired to a lonesome solitude near Paula; and soon afterwards chose for his abode the cave of a rock nearer the sea-coast. Two neighbours joined him, and they then built three cells and a chapel. About seventeen years afterwards their numbers increased considerably; and, with the consent of the archbishop of Cosenza, a monastery and church were begun. When the walls of the church were a few feet high, a stranger in the habit of a cordelier presented himself, and remonstrated with St. Francis on the dimensions of his church, which, he said, were far too small. St. Francis replied he would willingly have designed a more ambitious edifice, but could not see his way to cover the expense." "Fear not," said the stranger, "pull down these walls, and let us lay out a plan of a nobler house of God." The walls were duly demolished, and the stranger showed St. Francis the design of a much grander church, and laid out the ground-plan. This done he disappeared, as mysteriously as he first appeared. The question arose, who was this stranger and architect? Leo X., in the bull of canonization, says it was St. Francis of Assisi, who had been dead 226 years, and this is the orthodox belief.—*The Process of the Canonization of St. Francis of Paula* (on the testimony of an eye-witness).

An angel directs St. Marculfus to apply to king Childebert for the site of a monastery (A.D. 558). While St. Marculfus was leading the life of a hermit near Coutances, an angel told him to go to king Childebert I., son of Clovis, and ask him to give the spot called Nanteuil, near Coutances, on the sea-coast, for the site of a monastery. Marculfus, without delay, obeyed the angel and went to Paris, where he arrived just as the king and queen Ultrogotha were hearing mass. Not liking to appear before royalty in his hermit's dress, he hid himself behind the pillars, when all of a sudden some devils screamed out, "Marculfus, thou servant of Christ Jesus, have pity on us. Thy presence is a torment to us." These words amazed the king and court; and, search being made, the saint was presented to the king, to whom he told his message. Childebert not only made the grant, but also promised his patronage and protection. Marculfus, having thanked God and the king, made the sign of the cross, and commanded the devils to depart. This they did, leaving the possessed half-dead; but they soon recovered, and returned home well and in their right minds.—*Acts of St. Marcoul* (with notes by Father Papebroch).

An eagle sent by God to point out the site of a monastery (A.D 533). St. Remi, wishing to found a monastery on Mont d'Or, imparted his wish to St. Thierry, then quite a young man. St. Thierry consulted Suzanne, the abbess, and the two went to Mont d'Or to look out for a suitable site. While thus employed, an eagle "descendit miraculeusement du ciel," and lighted in the forest, then fluttered round a certain spot several times, intimating unmistakably the place most agreeable to God. The archbishop accepted the omen, and built his monastery there; and that this "miracle" might not be gainsaid or be lightly considered a mere coincidence, the same eagle came every Christmas Day for four successive years, and hovered "tout autour et sur toute l'étendue du monastère." The monastery was dedicated to Bartholomew.—Billy (almoner of the abbey of St. Thierry), *Life of St. Thierry.*

An angel draws the plan of the monastery of Val d'Or (seventh century). Bertha, the widow of St. Gombert, wished to build a monastery in memory of her late husband, and, while she was pondering over the subject, an angel of light appeared to her, and led her to the foot of a hill, where was a large flat sandy plateau which seemed to be made expressly for the purpose. Here he drew out the ground-plan in full size, the elevations, and the whole architectural design. With this as her guide, she built the abbey of Val d'Or near Avenay, and richly endowed it. The Virgin Mary commanded Bertha herself to be the first abbess, and though unwilling, she was unable to withhold her consent. —D. Morlot, *History of the Diocese of Reims.*

My Flesh is Meat indeed, and My Blood is Drink indeed.

(See ELIJAH EATS ANGELS' FOOD, p. 126; see also pp. 489–495.)

JOHN vi. 48–55. Jesus said, I am the bread of life. A man may eat thereof, and not die. I am the living bread; if any man eat of this bread, he shall live for ever; and the bread that I will give is My flesh. For My flesh is meat indeed, and My blood is drink indeed.

JOHN vi. 35. Jesus said to the people, I am the bread of life. He that cometh to Me shall never hunger; and he that believeth on Me shall never thirst.

JOHN iv. 13, 14. Jesus said unto the woman of Samaria, Whosoever drinketh of the water [of this well] shall thirst again; but whosoever drinketh of the water that I shall give him shall never thirst.

St. Catherine Fieschi of Genoa supported by the Eucharist (A.D. 1447–1510). All through Advent and all through Lent, Catherine Fieschi took no food at all except that administered to her in the mass. In fact, for twenty-three years, from St. Martin's Day (Nov. 11) to Christmas Day, and from Quinquagesima Sunday to Easter Day, she took no food except "this heavenly manna," administered to her daily, and her only drink was a glass of water mixed with vinegar and salt. If ever she attempted to swallow any other food or drink, her stomach rejected it. Sometimes she made great efforts to retain what she had thus swallowed, especially before her confessor, but in these cases her efforts were followed by alarming illness, almost to the verge of death.—*Acta Sanctorum,* Sept. 14.

St. Gerasimus, a recluse of Palestine, ate nothing but the bread given him in the Eucharist all Lent (A.D. 475). St. Gerasimus was noted for his extraordinary abstinence. He fasted always all Lent, taking no nourishment of any kind, except the eulogie or sacred bread administered to him in the Eucharist.—*Lives of the Fathers of the Eastern Deserts.*

St. Joseph of Copertino lived for five years on the Eucharist only (A.D. 1603–1663). St. Joseph of Copertino lived five years without eating, and fifteen years without drinking. In these long abstinences he was sustained by the eulogie, which was administered to him daily. It was often noticed that before the sacrament he looked pale and haggard, weary and spiritless; but when he left the altar he was brisk, animated, and full of vigour. The body of Christ was food indeed, and the blood of Christ was drink indeed. On one occasion the superior insisted on his taking a little food; he took it in obedience to the superior, but the moment he swallowed it his stomach rejected it again.—Dominic Bernini, *Life of St. Joseph of Copertino.*

St. Nicholas de Flue for twenty years ate and drank nothing but the Eucharist (A.D. 1417–1487). This must be given in the *ipsissima verba* of John de Muller himself, Protestant historian of the Swiss Confederation: "Nicolas de Flue, pendant les vingt ans qu'il vécut [in Ranft], ne prit plus d'autre aliment, ni d'autre boisson, que la sainte eucharistie qu'il recevait tous les mois. Cela se fit par la grâce du Dieu tout puissant qui a créé de rien le ciel et la terre, et peut les conserver comme il lui plait. Ce miracle fut examiné pendant sa vie, raconté au loin, livré à la postérité par ses contemporains, et tenu pour incontestable" (1487).—John de Muller, *Histoire de la Suisse,* vol. v. p. 248.

Oswald Isner, curé at Kerns, writes in 1488, "When Father Nicholas began his life of total abstinence, and had reached the eleventh day, he sent for me, and asked me privately if he should take food or continue to abstain. He wished to live wholly without food, that he might more sever himself from the world. I felt his members, and found only skin and bone; all the flesh was dried up entirely, the cheeks were hollow, and the lips wonderfully thin. I told him to persevere as long as he could without endangering life. For if God had sustained him for eleven days, He could sustain him eleven years. Nicholas followed my advice; and from that moment to the day of his death, a period of twenty and a half years, he took no sort of food, and drank nothing. As he was more familiar with me than with any other person, I often spoke to him on the subject. He told me he received the sacrament once a month, and felt that the body and blood of Christ communicated vital force which served him for meat and drink, otherwise he could not sustain life without nourishment.

The magistrates, wishing to verify the fact, sent guards for an entire month to surround the retreat of the saint both night and day, to see that no one brought him food.

The prince-bishop of Constance sent his suffragan, the bishop of Ascalon, with strict orders to unmask the imposture, if he could detect any. The suffragan took up his abode in a chapel adjoining the cell of Nicholas, and entering the cell, asked him, "What is the first duty of a Christian?" "Obedience," said Nicholas. "If obedience is the first duty of a Christian, I command you to eat these pieces of bread, and to drink this wine," said the bishop. Nicholas besought the bishop not to insist on this order, but the bishop would not give way. Nicholas was obliged to obey; but the moment he swallowed a mouthful of bread, his agony was so great, that the bishop pressed him no longer, and said he only wished to prove whether Nicholas was possessed with a devil; but his obedience had shown him to be a child of grace.

The archduke Sigismond of Austria sent the royal physician, Burcard von Hornek, to examine into the case, and he remained in the cell several days and nights.

The emperor Frederick III. sent delegates to search into it, but one and all confessed it was a real fact, wholly without delusion.'

The following note is written in the archives of Saxlen:—"Qu'il soit fait savoir a tous et a chacun, que, dans année 1447, vivait un homme du nom de Nicolas de Flue, né et élevé près de la montagne, dans la paroisse de Saxlen; il a abandonné père et frère, femme et enfants, cinq fils et cinq filles, et s'en est allé dans la solitude qu'on nomme le Ranft, où Dieu l'a soutenu sans nourriture ni boisson jusqu'aujourd'hui où le fait est écrit, c'est-à-dire pendant dix-huit ans. Il a toujours été d'un esprit éclaire, d'une vie sainté, ce que nous avons vu et savons en vérité. Prions donc afin que délivré de la prison de cette vie, il soit conduit là où Dieu sèche les larmes aux yeux de ses saints."

He took part in the service of the parish church every Sunday, and in the great annual procession at Lucerne; and he tried to be as little different from other men as possible.

St. Sabas and his Armenian disciples live on the Eucharist (A.D. 430–531). St. Sabas and several Armenians retired to a desert, where they lived in what is called a laura—that is, a number of separate huts (p. 454, *n.*)—but every Saturday and Sunday they met in a common oratory. All Lent they lived in the desert in absolute solitude till Palm Sunday, without seeing a soul, or taking any food except the Eucharist, which they received twice a week.—Father Giry, *St. Sabas*, etc.

St. Silvinus, bishop of Régionnaire, lived for forty years on the Eucharist (A.D. 718). St. Silvinus was noted for his austerities, and for forty years ate no bread except that which he received in the Eucharist. Sometimes he took a few herbs or a little fruit. He never slept in a bed, but always on the bare ground, wholly without covering, even in winter. He treated his body as a slave, surrounded it with bands of iron, macerated it with scourges, and carried enormous stones, which he deposited as a trophy before the doors of the basilica of St. Peter.—Bollandus, *Acta Sanctorum*, Feb. 17, p. 23.

Grace of Valencia used to live all Lent on the Eucharist only (A.D. 1494–1606). For seven years Grace of Valencia drank nothing, not even one drop of water; this was before she entered the order of St. Francis of Paula; and for the last twenty-one years of her life she abstained wholly from drink of any kind. She often went four or five days on "angels' food;" that is, the eulogie or sacred bread of the Eucharist.—R. P. d'Attichy, *Histoire Génerale de l'Ordre des Frères Mineurs.*

(There must be some mistake in the dates, but it is quite certain that the words run thus: "Cette humble servante de Jésus Christ naquit a Mançanera en 1494."... "Elle rendit son esprit à Dieu le 16 Janvier 1606." This would give 212 years; but her age apparently was about 112, for we read, "Depuis l'âge de quatre-vingt-onze ans jusqu'à sa dernière maladie, ce qui fait encore vingt et un ans, elle s'abstint tout a fait de boire.")

Miscellaneous examples of saints going for long periods on the strength afforded by the Eucharist. Father Sebastian of Perouse says, in his *Life of Colomba of Rieti,* "The holy Eucharist was well-nigh her only food; but this sacred bread sustained her forces and her courage."

ELIZABETH OF WALDSECH, IN SUABIA (A.D. 1386–1420). Her biographer says that Elizabeth of Waldsech often lived a whole day on the bread she received in the Holy Sacrament.

JOHN THE GOOD OF MANTUA (A.D. 1222). John the Good of Mantua fasted from Easter to Pentecost; the days prescribed by the Church before Easter and before Christmas; besides every Monday, Wednesday, and Friday throughout the year. On the first of these fasts, between Easter and Pentecost, he took no food except that supplied in the Holy Communion. On Ash Wednesday he took three ounces of bread, which lasted him for three days. On the Christmas fast-days his daily allowance of food was three beans. His weekly fasts were restricted to bread and water. He never touched meat from year's end to year's end.—*Histoire des Hommes Illustres de l'Ordre des Ermites de St. Augustin.*

MARIANNE DE JESUS (A.D. 1645). Marianne at first restricted her diet to bread, fruit, and vegetables; she then gave up the bread, and at last confined herself to the eulogie or sacred bread as her only food. This, says her biographer, is by no means unusual in the lives of saints. Her drink was a glass of water at noon, but later in life she dropped this luxury, and suffered dreadful thirst. On one occasion a cup of water was brought her; she raised it to her feverish lips, and then suddenly put the cup down without touching a drop. She entreated to be allowed to serve the table at the daily meals, that she might mortify her flesh by seeing and handling food without touching a morsel. —*Les Petits Bollandistes*, vol. vi. p. 232.

RITA OF CASCIA (A.D. 1456) took scarcely any nourishment, and the sisters of the convent always believed it was the Holy Eucharist which supplied material aliment to her.—Augustin Cavalucci, *Life of the Beatified Rita de Cascia.*

ST. MANUTIUS OF BAYEUX (A.D. 480). For forty-seven days before his death the only aliment taken by Manutius of Bayeux was the Holy Eucharist. He died May 28, A.D. 480.—*Propre de Bayeux.*

ST. MARY FRANCES OF THE FIVE

WOUNDS (A.D. 1715–1791). This was the name taken by Anna Maria Rosa Nicoletta of Naples when she joined the Society of St. Francis d'Assisi. She was a great invalid, and lived for some considerable time on the eulogie or sacred bread alone. —R. P. Bernard Laviosa, *Life of Mary Frances.*

No Faith to be kept with Heretics.

Harsnet tells us in his *Popish Impostures*, p. 118, that Cottam, Brian, and Campian, executed at Tyburn for high treason in 1582, were at once canonized. For queen Elizabeth, whom they sought to dethrone and assassinate, being a Protestant, was excommunicated; in consequence of which all persons were absolved from allegiance to her, and it was a positive merit to kill her, if possible. In this, the future archbishop of York is corroborated in part by Mengus's book, the *Devils-mastix*, where we read the following:—"The holy sacrament being brought, and invocation made to the blessed Lady, with *Ave maries, salve reginas*, the application of relics, and calling upon blessed martyrs, especially Father Campian, Father Brian, and the rest who had been martyred at Tiburn, hell itself quails, the devils roar, and the prince, with all his commanders and assistants, are finally cast out" (p. 48).

Mengus, on p. 17 of his *Devils-mastix*, makes the devil tell a priest that "he himself [*i.e.* the devil himself] is a heretic, and that heresy came first into England in the reign of Henry VIII." He goes on to say, that he [the devil] "teaches Protestants to call themselves Catholics, and that he caused Sara Williams to weep for her father and mother, because they went to the English church."

Odour of Sanctity.

(By the "odour of sanctity" is meant not only that the dead bodies of saints exhale a sweet perfume, and those of sinners a disagreeable smell, but that even when alive the holy smell sweet and the unholy offensively.)

PSALM xvi. 10. Thou wilt not suffer thy Holy One to see corruption.

REV. v. 8. The four beasts and four and twenty elders had every one golden vials full of odour, which are the prayers of saints.

REV. viii. 3. Another angel came, having a golden censer; and there was given unto him much incense, that he should offer it with the prayers of all saints.

Bragadino, governor of Cyprus, exhales the odour of sanctity (A.D. 1571). Bragadino, governor of Cyprus, was no saint, but, like other Cypriots, was a Roman Catholic, and maintained at great odds an heroic resistance against the Turks, under the command of Mustapha. When resistance was no longer possible, he surrendered to Mustapha the keys of the city, and was received with well-dissembled courtesy. A cause of complaint was soon invented, and Bragadino being seized was brutally flayed alive. His head, being cut off, was hung to the bowsprit of the admiral's galley, a spectacle of mockery to Turkish soldiers. Pietro Justiniani, an eye-witness, asserts that the head for three nights was "engloried with rays like those of the sun, and diffused a most marvellous fragrance."—Bk. xvi. p. 451.

The ill savour of sinfulness. "Then they smote off the head of sir Corsabrin, and therewithal came a stench out of the body, when the soul departed, so that might nobody abide the savour. So the corpse was had away, and buried in a wood, because he was a panim. Then the haughty prince said to sir Palomidês, 'Here have ye seen this day what savour there was when the soul of sir Corsabrin departed from his body; therefore, we require you to take the holy baptism upon you, [that when ye die, ye may die in the odour of sanctity].'"—Sir T. Malory, *History of Prince Arthur*, vol. ii. ch. 133.

The extract given above, of course, is not meant for history, but a romance may serve quite as well as history to illustrate a popular belief. If the odour of sanctity and ill savour of sin had not been a general belief, there would be no point in the story. As a sequel to the above, we are told in the same romance, "When sir Bors and his fellows came to sir Launcelot's bed, they found him stark dead, and the sweetest savour about him that ever they did smell."—Vol. iii. ch. 175.

The odours of sanctity differ both in quality and degree. St. Benedicta tells us from "personal observations" she finds that the odours of the angelic hierarchy differ as much as the perfume of flowers. All angels exhale odour, but none of them so ravishing and so powerful an odour as the queen of men and angels. The perfumes which exhale from our Saviour Jesus Christ surpass, however, in an infinite degree every other odour. St. Benedicta, we are assured, while still on earth, was greatly distinguished for her odours; her breath, all that she touched, her clothes, all were sweet with perfume—a perfume which suffused on those near her the love of God, and in her ecstasies the odour was so potent as to be overpowering. The perfumes of Jesus Christ, the Virgin Mary, the angels of heaven, and Sister Benedicta, compose what is called "The Bouquet of the Lake" [Laus, 2 *syl.*]. This bouquet is perceptible at a great distance.—Mgr. Guérin (chamberlain to pope Leo XIII.), *Vies des Saints*, vol. v. p. 224.

(Mgr. Barnadou, bishop of Gap, is collecting such data as these to effect the canonization of Sister Benedicta, 1883.)

The dead body of St. Clare, late abbot of Ferriol, exhaled a sweet odour (A.D. 660). St. Blandina told St. Clare, abbot of Ferriot, that within three days she and St. Marcel would come to carry his soul into paradise. St. Clare ordered prayer to be made without ceasing both day and night for him; and on the third day, as the choir was chanting the last words of the last psalm—"Let everything that hath breath praise the Lord. Praise ye the Lord"—he gave up the ghost. The chamber was instantly filled with a celestial light, and a fragrance of marvellous sweetness. The body was buried in St. Blandina's church before the high altar, and the odour which pervaded the chamber at the death of the saint continued with the body till its interment. —Mgr. Guérin, *Vies des Saints*, vol. i. pp. 31, 32.

St. Hermann exhaled from his body sweet perfumes (A.D. 1230). Every time St. Hermann of Steinfeld said grace at table, when he was sacristan, he exhaled "des odeurs si ravissantes, qu'il lui semblait être dans un jardin plein de roses, de lis, de violettes, d'œillets, et de toutes sortes de fleurs les plus agréables." His humility was so great he never knew that the odours proceeded from himself, but used to say each brother of the community smelt sweet with the odours of sanctity. "De plus, toutes les fois qu'en prononçant le nom de Marie, il se prosternait la face contre terre, il sortait de la terre même un autre parfum inestimable qui lui ravissait tous les sens."—*Les Petits Bollandistes*, vol. iv. p. 275.

When St. Hubert of Brittany died, the whole province was filled with sweet perfumes (A.D. 714). St. Hubert died on May 24; and, when he gave up the ghost, there was diffused over all Brittany an odour so sweet, that it seemed as if God had combined all the perfumes of all the sweet-scented flowers of spring, to symbolize the sanctity of His servant whom He had taken up to paradise.—*Acta Sanctorum* (Bollandists), vol. vii. May 30.

It was by no means strange that Brittany at the end of May should smell sweet with spring flowers.

When St. Patrick died, the whole room was filled with a ravishing odour (A.D. 464). The funeral of St. Patrick was not without many marvellous incidents: (1) Angels were heard chanting from his death to his interment; (2) an odour of ravishing sweetness filled the room where the body was laid out; (3) for twelve days there was no night, no twilight, no darkness at all through the whole province; nay, for a whole year the nights were more luminous than usual, and the clouds less heavy!! and (4) God promised that they who placed themselves under the charge of St. Patrick, and who kept his fête-day, should obtain mercy in time of need, and at the hour of death.—*Les Petits Bollandistes* (1880), vol. i. p. 475.

St. Peter Thomas died in the odour of sanctity (A.D. 1366). "Son corps exhala, après son décès, comme un excellent parfum, et son visage devint vermeil et beau comme celui d'un ange. Des rayons de lumière furent aperçûs sur son corps, qui en fut tellement échauffé, qu'il en coula une certain sucur de toutes les parties; il fallut les essuyer avec du coton qui a servi depuis à plusieurs guérisons miraculeuses. On conserva ce dépôt sacre six jours entiers, exposé dans le chœur du couvent des Carmes, où il était décédé, sans que l'on y aperçût en tout ce temps-là la moindre trace de corruption."—Mgr. Guérin (chamberlain to pope Leo XIII., 1880), *Vies des Saints*, vol. i. p. 173.

When St. Polycarp was at the stake, a smell of incense issued from his body. As Polycarp entered the arena, a voice from heaven said to him, "Be strong, Polycarp, and play the man," and many of the brethren heard it. On his appearance, the spectators broke into loud clamours. The proconsul exhorted him to purchase liberty by renouncing his faith; but he replied, "Fourscore and six years have I served Christ; how, then, can I now blaspheme my King and Saviour?" The fire was then kindled. In compliance with his own request, the aged martyr was not fastened to the stake with iron cramps, but was tied with cords. The flames, instead of touching him, swept round his body, "like the sails of a ship filled with wind," and the hoary saint appeared in the midst of this fiery tent, like gold glowing in a furnace; and a perfume sweeter than frankincense issued from him, filling the whole air. One of the executioners, to hasten his death, stabbed him with a sword, and the blood from the wound put out the fire.—Robertson (1875), *History of the Christian Church*, vol. i. pp. 42–44.

The dead body of St. Severin did not corrupt, but it exhaled a sweet odour. When Onulf was sent to fetch away the dead body of St. Severin, that had been buried six years, it was not only undecayed, but it gave out a most exceedingly sweet fragrance, "though no embalmer's hand had ever touched it."—Eugippius (A.D. 511), *Life of St. Severin.*

St. Valery from his sanctity, even in life, exhaled a sweet odour (A.D. 619). One day St. Colomban was explaining to his monks the subject of a lecture, when all of a sudden the room was filled with a celestial odour. The abbot asked who it was that had just entered, and being told it was Brother Valery, he cried in transport, "O my beloved, it is you, not I, who are the veritable head of this monastery."—Besançon (1854), *Les Saints de Franche-Comté.*

The dead body of St. Francis Xavier exhaled a sweet perfume. As soon as Xavier was dead, his body was laid in a coffin filled with pure lime to consume the flesh. Four months afterwards, when the coffin was opened, it was found that the grave-clothes were wholly uninjured, and the flesh was as fresh as if the body had but just died. No sort of effluvia was perceptible, but, on the contrary, an agreeable odour. Putting the body back with more lime, the coffin was taken to Malacca, which at the time was troubled with plague; but the moment the coffin arrived, the plague ceased. A new coffin was made, but it was too small, and as the dead body was forced down, blood issued from the shoulders, and stained the shroud. The coffin was buried in the churchyard of Our Blessed Lady, and in nine months was again opened, when the body was still fresh, and the blood on the napkin moist. The body was now laid in a most sumptuous coffin, and carried to the Indies. It was received at Goa with great pomp, the viceroy himself taking part in the ceremony. No ointment, spices, or balm had been used; but the body "had a ravishing fragrance," and was laid on the right side of the high altar.—*Cardinal de Monte's speech before Gregory XV., in the Act of Canonization*, Jan. 19, A.D. 1622.

The brothers of the Sodality of the Blessed Sacrament gave out that their sense of the odour of sanctity was so nice, they could detect a Jansenist by the smell (seventeenth century).

An attempt to explain the phenomena. The constant recurrence of *light and odour* at the death of saints must of necessity have some basis of truth; but probably the custom of lighting candles and swinging the censer gave rise to numerous legends. It must be further borne in mind, that embalming dead bodies and washing them with powerful perfumes was not unusual. This would be done to those honoured and beloved, but not to the dishonoured and despised. Hence the bodies of the one would smell sweet with strong perfumes; but in the other case, putrefaction would soon emit its offensive smell. Mark and Luke tell us of certain women, by whom Jesus was greatly beloved, who took spices to anoint His body after the crucifixion; and it will be remembered the box of precious ointment poured on Jesus was "against His burial." There certainly was nothing unusual in this. In regard to washing the body with strong perfumes, Homer (*Iliad*, xxiii.) mentions it, and says Hector's body was washed with rose water. Maillet (*Letters*, x. p. 83), speaking of the modern Egyptians, says, when persons of position die their friends wash the dead body several times with rose water, and then perfume it with incense, aloes, and other sweet-smelling substances, of which they are not sparing; and they carefully plug up all natural apertures with cotton wool, well saturated in the strongest perfume. Herodotus (*History*, ii. 86–90) gives us a pretty full account of the Egyptian treatment of dead bodies in his and in previous times. (See p. 459 first note.)

The rose water of the East is immeasurably more powerful than that sold in Europe. If these suggestions are accepted, the origin of the "odour of sanctity" must be sought in the love and reverence of survivors, rather than in odour-yielding virtue of holiness. The person died honoured and beloved, and his body was washed with perfumes costly and powerful. The accretions which grew out of this basis had for their objects the exaltation of the Church, and the justification of monastic or conventual life. It would be an insult to ordinary experience to remind the youngest of our readers that sanctity or unsanctity makes no difference whatever on the odour or decay of a dead body, except that riotous living will sometimes sow the body with diseases which are offensive; but at the same time the holiest saint may suffer in life or die of diseases so offensive that no amount of love can help knowing it.

Prayers for the Dead.

2 MACC. xii. It is a holy and wholesome thought to pray for the dead, that they may be loosed from their sins.

MATT. xii. 32. Whosoever speaketh against the Holy Ghost, it shall not be forgiven him, neither in this world, neither in the world to come. [Whence some sins are forgiven in the world to come, but not blasphemy against the Holy Ghost.]

1 COR. xv. 29. Else what shall they do which are baptized for the dead, if the dead rise not at all? Why are they then baptized for the dead? [Here St. Paul says persons were baptized for the dead, and in virtue thereof the dead rose.]

How far the two texts from *Matthew* and *Corinthians* corroborate that of *Maccabees* is no part of this book to determine. The Roman Catholics think there is a connection, which is confirmed by the practice of the Church, certainly in the second and third centuries, as Clement of Alexandria, Tertullian, St. Cyprian, St. John Chrysostom, Cyril of Jerusalem, and St. Augustine undoubtedly prove. Besides, all liturgies contain prayers for the dead.

and assuredly the text quoted from the *Maccabees* was a Jewish doctrine, whether the book quoted from is canonical or not. (See DINOCRATÊS, p. 483.)

The prayers of St. Evrard deliver Mangold from purgatory (A.D. 1075). Mangold was an abbot of St. George, at Stein, near Schaffaüsen, who abandoned the religious life, and returned to the world. St. Evrard met him one day, and severely rebuked him. He repented, and prayed to be admitted into the house, where he had been abbot, as one of the lowest of the brethren. His request was granted, but he soon died. Evrard prayed for the repose of his soul; and one day the ex-abbot appeared to him, and thanked him for having delivered his soul from purgatory by his prayers and good works. Mangold told the saint at the same time how agreeable his works were to God, and that he would go on growing in grace, till he arrived at the fulness of the stature of a perfect man.—*Acta Sanctorum* (Bollandists), April 7.

St. Gregory the Great redeems a soul from purgatory by masses for the dead (A.D. 540–604). A monk noted for his medical skill died, leaving three gold pieces behind him. The possession of personal property being forbidden by the vows of the monk, this was looked on as a sin; and, when the body was buried, St. Gregory threw the three gold pieces into the grave, saying, "Thy money perish with thee!" However, they were not buried with the dead, but, being picked up, were paid for masses in behalf of the monk. On the thirtieth day the ghost of the monk showed itself to one of the brethren, and told him that he had been in purgatory for thirty days, enduring great torment, but, thanks to the masses offered for his soul, this very day he was delivered, and he was now on his way to paradise.—*Acta Sanctorum*, vol. viii. 20; Gregory the Great, *Dialogues*, vi. 55.

Prayers to Saints.

PSALM cxxxii. 10. For Thy servant David's sake turn not away the face of Thine anointed.

JOB xlii. 8. My servant Job shall pray for you: for him will I accept.

GEN. xx. 17. So Abraham prayed unto God, and God healed Abimelech, and his wife, and his maidservants.

JAMES v. 16. The effectual fervent prayer of a righteous man availeth much.

Almost all nations have deified their popular heroes, given them a power over nature, and made them the objects of prayer. Probably most heathen gods are only deified human beings. The Roman Catholics not only canonize their favourites, but suppose them to be possessed of superhuman powers, able to answer prayer, to command nature, to heal diseases, to protect those who confide in them, and by their intercessions with the Virgin Mary, Christ, and God the Father, to reconcile them to man. As on earth we get an influential friend to plead for us, if we want to obtain a favour; so in heaven, the Roman Catholic enlists on his side the power of some saint, if he wishes to obtain a special favour of God. Protestants do not pray to saints, because they do not believe that they possess any supernatural power at all, and the only intercessor they believe in is Jesus Christ. If Christ is for us, who can be against us? if Christ is against us, who can change the unchangeable? The efficacy of saintly intercession implies (1) either that God will listen to saints in preference to the pleadings of His own Son; or (2) that Jesus Christ is less willing to help us than a saint is; or (3) that He requires to be informed of some palliative on our behalf known to a saint, but not to Himself; or (4) that He may be importuned by saints to do something contrary to His judgment and justice; or (5) that God will give to a saint a favour to be bestowed on a friend, irrespective of the merits or demerits of the applicant, the right or the wrong of such a grant.

St. Bernard the Great, apostle of the Alps, prays to St. Nicholas (A.D. 923-1008). St. Bernard was born at Savoy, and was the son of Richard, seigneur of Menthon. When a young man his father arranged a marriage for him with Margaret, daughter of the baron of Miolans, but Bernard had vowed to live in perpetual celibacy, and the night before the wedding was to have taken place, addressing St. Nicholas (died A.D. 342), he said, "O great saint, refuse me not your aid to remain a virgin, I pray you. It is you who made me know that I must give myself wholly unto Christ, and it is you who will aid me to preserve my body and soul in purity." Bernard then heard a voice commanding him to flee from home. As the doors were locked, he made his escape through the chamber window, by breaking an iron bar. The window is still shown from which he escaped. After a while he reached Aosta, and in due time he resolved to carry the gospel to the ferocious brigands of the Alps, and to build a hospice on the summit of those mountains.—Mgr. Guérin, *Vies des Saints*, vol. vii. p. 37.

A large part of this volume is in illustration of the power of saints to hear prayers, and obtain an answer thereto.

Purgatory.

(An article of the [Roman] Catholic Church says, it is an undoubted verity that there is a purgatory. Protestants cannot but be interested in knowing on what Scripture texts this "undoubted verity" is founded.)

ISA. iv. 4. When the Lord shall have washed away the filth of the daughters of Zion, and shall have purged the blood of Jerusalem from the midst thereof by the spirit of judgment, and by the spirit of burning. [*Rendered thus by Roman Catholics:* Our Lord shall wash the uncleanness of the daughters of Sion, and the blood of Jerusalem in the spirit of judgment, and in the spirit of burning.—Alfonso de Castro, *Against Heresies.*]

MAL. iii. 3. He shall sit as a refiner and

purifier of silver. [*Rendered thus:* He is a fire in which the silver is molten and purified.—St. Augustine.]

ISA. i. 25. I will turn My hand upon thee, and purely purge away thy dross, and take away all thy tin.

MATT. xii. 32. I say unto you, whosoever speaketh against the Holy Ghost, it shall not be forgiven him, neither in this world, neither in the world to come. [Whence both St. Gregory and St. Bernard maintain, it is obvious that some sins are forgiven "in the world to come;" but as nothing that defileth shall enter heaven, there can be no forgiveness of sin *there*. So also it is impossible to conceive that there can be forgiveness of sin in hell, where the punishment is everlasting. Hence there must be a third place, where sin may enter, where punishment is not everlasting, and where it may be forgiven. This third place is purgatory.]

1 COR. iii. 13-15. Every man's work shall be made manifest; for the day shall declare it, because it shall be revealed by fire. The fire shall try every man's work of what sort it is. If a man's work shall be burned, he shall suffer loss; but he himself shall be saved, yet so as by fire. [*Rendered thus:* The works every man hath done the fire shall try. He whose works have need of this trial shall suffer detriment, so that such a one shall not be saved except by fire.—Origen.]

REV. xxi. 27. There shall in no wise enter into heaven anything that defileth, neither whatsoever worketh abomination, or maketh a lie.

EPH. v. 27. Christ gave Himself for the Church, that He might present it a glorious Church, not having spot, or wrinkle, or any such thing; but that it should be holy and without blemish. [As many men die with venial sins, but have no time to do the penance enjoined by the Church, it is obvious that they must complete their penance after death. Else we are reduced to this dilemma: The persons with sins unatoned are taken to heaven, where there is no spot or stain; or else these venial sins are punished in hell like mortal sins, which is revolting to suppose.—Edward Kinesman, *Lives of the Saints*, p. 864.]

1 PET. iii. 19. Christ went and preached unto the spirits in prison.

1 PET. iv. 6. For this cause was the gospel preached also to them that are dead. [Not, of course, to them already in paradise; not, of course, to them in hell, where hope never enters; but to them in purgatory.]

The flames of purgatory put out by the water abstained from by Cecily Margaret (thirteenth century). Emilia Bicchieri was the superior of the convent of St. Margaret, and compelled the sisters on fast-days to abstain even from drinking water, in remembrance of Christ's thirst. One of the sisters, named Cecily Margaret Avogadro de Quinto, died. Three days afterwards she showed herself to Emilia, and said she had been in purgatory for three days to efface the taint of birth, and on the third day her guardian angel appeared to her, and said, "With this water you abstained from on earth, in memory of Christ's thirst, the flames of purgatory are extinguished. Enter, therefore, now into the joys of paradise."—*Acta Sanctorum* (Bollandists), vol. vii. May 3.

Durand of Bridon redeemed from purgatory by the monks of Cluny (eleventh century). St. Hugh, abbot of Cluny, had often reproved a monk named Durand for his pleasantries and levities, so unsuitable in an ecclesiastic, and had often told him that God would surely chastise him for them. The man died, and his ghost appeared to one Seguin. His mouth was horrible to look at, for that unruly member had been set on fire by hell. He implored Seguin to report to St. Hugh how terrible were his sufferings in purgatory. Hugh commanded a strict silence to be observed, by way of penance, throughout the whole abbey, for the redemption of Brother Durand. At the end of the seven days the ghost again appeared, and complained that the penance of silence had been broken by one of the brothers, and therefore he was still in purgatory. Hugh enjoined, therefore, another term of silence for seven days. After this second penance Durand appeared for a third time, but now he was a saint of light. He had been redeemed from purgatory, and taken to paradise.—Lorain, *History of the Abbey of Cluny*.

The Virgin Mary, at the intercession of Sister Benedicta, delivers a "cloud of souls from purgatory" (A.D. 1698). On All Saints' Eve, A.D. 1698, Sister Benedicta remained long at the cross of Avançon, praying for the souls in purgatory; when suddenly she beheld coming out of the valley a cloud, three quarters of a mile in length, composed entirely of human souls, conducted by the Virgin Mary and two angels. One of the souls, detaching itself from the immense cohort, said to her, "We are souls coming out of purgatory. In our days on earth we commended ourselves to the Blessed Virgin, and now, instigated by thy prayers, dear Sister Benedicta, she has come to deliver us before our time; but before we enter paradise, the holy Virgin wishes us to return our hearty thanks to God in His sanctuary at Laus (2 *syl.*)." Sister Benedicta saw the souls enter the church, and saw them leave it. In fact, "la familiarité des anges et de notre pieuse sœur était comme celle qui existe sur la terre entre des frères et sœurs bien unis, tant sa pureté sans tache la rapprochait des esprits angéliques."—*Les Petits Bollandistes* (7th edit. 1880), vol. v. p. 226.

(Mgr. Barnadou, bishop of Gap, is collecting such data as these to effect the canonization of Sister Benedicta, 1883.)

St. Francisca sees purgatory in a vision (A.D. 1384–1440). St. Francisca had ninety-three visions, in the fifty-third of which she was shown purgatory. It is divided, she says, into three regions; and over the gates is this inscription: "THIS IS PURGATORY, THE PLACE OF HOPE." The lowest region is assigned to those who have died without having made satisfaction for their sins in life. The highest region is for the purification of imperfections. The intermediate region is for the purgation of venial sins. Francisca tells us that the hottest part of the lowest region is for priests and nuns who have not made satisfaction for their sins. Here she noticed a very excellent priest, who nevertheless did not mortify his body as he ought to have done, but ate and drank more than was absolutely necessary to sustain life. She tells us that the guardian angel of each soul posts up daily all the credits from prayers, masses, indulgences, and gifts in behalf of the soul under his charge. If there is no credit, each sin is punished with seven years of purgatory. She says money given by the living for a soul is credited in full, but money in a legacy is discounted, a part being placed to the general account of all the souls, though the major part is posted to the credit for the soul specified.—*Acta Sanctorum* (Bollandists), vol. ii. March 5.

Death of Brother Giles celebrated by a general delivery from purgatory (A.D. 1272). Brother Giles, having been a monk for fifty-two years, died in the odour of sanctity, and was buried in a marble sepulchre. A Dominican, who died on the same day, appeared to a brother of the same order, according to promise; and being asked how he fared in the land of spirits, replied, "I am happy in paradise because I died on the same day as Brother Giles died; and Jesus Christ, in recompense of his great merits, allowed him to clear purgatory, and take with him to paradise all the souls therein, amongst which number was I one."—*Acta Sanctorum* (Bollandists), April 24.

St. Malachias of Armagh and his sister in purgatory (A.D. 1148). The sister of Malachias of Armagh was not a religious woman, which was a cause of great distress to her brother. She died, however contrite, and masses were said for her repose. In time these masses were discontinued, and one night Malachias heard a voice saying to him, "Your sister stands without, craving food; she has had none now for thirty days." Malachias could not imagine what food to give the dead, but after a little reflection he remembered it was just thirty days since he had discontinued saying masses for her repose. So he at once began them again. A day or two afterwards the ghost returned to him again; she was dressed in black, and was standing near the church door, unable to enter the house of God. Malachias continued saying masses, and in another week the ghost returned again, clad this time in half-mourning. She was able now to pass through the church doors, but not to approach the altar. Malachias still continued the masses, and in another week the ghost showed herself again, arrayed in spotless white, and accompanied with angels. St. Bernard says this history is very profitable, as it proves the degrees of suffering in purgatory. At first this sister was in the blackness of darkness, then by the aid of the Church her sufferings were greatly mitigated, and ultimately she was received amongst the saints in light.—Bernard, *Life of Malachias of Armagh*, and also his *Discourse* upon the same saint.

A nobleman named Peter, being raised to life, refused to live again (A.D. 1030–1079). St. Stanislaus bought a parcel of land of a nobleman named Peter, without deeming it needful to have a legal document of the purchase duly drawn up and signed. Lord Peter died, and his heirs disputed the purchase. The case was brought into the law courts, and Stanislaus, to prove his right, summoned lord Peter from the grave. Lord Peter, of course, acknowledged the purchase, and Stanislaus asked him if he would like to live awhile, or would prefer to return to the grave. He replied, "I am now in purgatory, and prefer to return at once, to being exposed to the temptations of sin. All I ask is that my term of purgatory may be abridged." He then walked back to his grave, followed by Stanislaus and an immense concourse of people.—*Acta Sanctorum* (Bollandists), May 7.

St. Thomas Aquinas is told that his brother Landolph is in purgatory (A.D. 1224–1274). The sister of Thomas Aquinas, abbess of St. Mary of Capua, died before him, and after death appeared to him. He inquired of her about his two brothers, Landolph and Raynald, both of whom were dead. The sister told him that his brother, count Landolph, was still in purgatory, but that Raynald was in heaven. Raynald had been especially bitter against the monastic life of Thomas, so derogatory to the family, but since his death Thomas had never ceased praying for the repose of his soul, so that it was especially gratifying to find his prayers were answered, and that Raynald had already passed from purgatory into paradise.—L'abbé Bareille, *History of Thomas Aquinas.*

Supererogation.

St. Catherine offers her surplus merits to redeem souls in purgatory. The souls in purgatory had a large share in the solicitude of St. Catherine. "Elle offrait à Dieu pour elles le mérite de ses bonnes œuvres, et exhortait ses sœurs à en faire autant."—(See IMPUTED MERIT, p. 204.) Mgr. Guérin, *Vies des Saints*, vol. iii. p. 324.

Tonsure. (See Introduction.)

1 COR. xi. 14. Doth not even nature itself teach you, that, if a man have long hair, it is a shame unto him?

Homer speaks of the "long-haired Greeks" by way of honourable distinction. Subsequently, the Athenian cavalry and all Lacedæmonian soldiers wore long hair. The Parthians and ancient Persians of rank wore long flowing hair. The Franks and ancient Germans considered long hair a mark of high birth. Hence Clodion the Frank gloried in being called "the long-haired;" and his successors are spoken of as *les rois chevelures*. The Goths looked on long hair as a mark of honour, and short hair as a mark of thraldom; so did the Gauls, for which reason, when Julius Cæsar subdued them, he obliged them to cut their hair short in token of submission. Absalom was noted for his long profuse hair (2 *Sam.* xiv. 26), and Samson, as a Nazarite, had long hair till he was enslaved to the Philistines. Something of this distinction survives in our own country. Our judges, the Speaker of the House of Commons, and formerly our bishops, wore long-haired wigs, while paupers and criminals have their hair cropped short. The Jewish priests, on the other hand, during their time of service, cut their hair once a fortnight, and Roman slaves wore their hair and beard long, but shaved their head when manumitted. Sailors also, who escaped from shipwreck, shaved their heads, as if manumitted from the sea.

St. Anicet's defence of the tonsure, from 1 Cor. xi. 14 (A.D. 150–164). St. Anicet, in his ordinance, makes allusion to St. Paul's precept about short hair, and it may be inferred from his words that Christian ministers shaved their heads, or at any rate wore short hair. This might be in conformity with the Roman custom in manumission. St. Paul says (2 *Cor.* iii. 17), "Where the Spirit of the Lord is, there is liberty;" and in *Gal.* iv. he represents Christians as being manumitted from the bondage of the law; and exhorts them to "stand fast in the liberty wherewith Christ had made them free." As we have shown already, Roman *slaves* wore long hair, but shaved their heads when manumitted. St. Germanus, patriarch of Constantinople (A.D. 715–740), relates the following tradition on the subject:—"The crown or tonsure of the priest, besides its signification of the renouncement of the vanities of the world, recalls a fact in Church history. When St. Peter was sent by the Saviour to announce the advent of the Messiah, the Jews, incredulous of his words, seized him, and in derision cut off his hair from the crown of his head. On his return, Christ blessed him, and thereby changed the bald place into an aureola." If there is any truth in this tradition, the idea of cutting off the hair seems to have been suggested by the custom of manumission, out of disgust to the boast that Christ had made him free from the law of Moses.

St. Amand's explanation to St. Maurant of the symbolical character of the tonsure is given thus by Mgr. Guérin: "La tonsure, en mettant à nu le haut de la tête, nous rappelle que rien n'est caché aux yeux du Seigneur, pas même les pensées les plus intimes; et par le retranchement des cheveux, souvent renouvelé ensuite, elle nous apprend qu'il faut retrancher de même sans relâche les désirs superflus et criminels. Cette forme de couronne nous exprime, et la tiare du souverain prêtre, et le diadème du grand roi; elle nous dit que nous appartenons désormais à un sacerdoce royal, et qu'après les combats et les épreuves de cette vie, endurés avec patience, Dieu réserve dans l'autre, à ceux qui l'aiment, une couronne de gloire immortelle et infinie."—Vol. v. p. 336.

From such authority there is no room to doubt what the symbolical meaning of the tonsure is understood to mean by the [Roman] Catholic priesthood; but certainly the symbolism seems forced and not very pertinent. The last idea is common to all Christians, male as well as female, and is therefore not special to the priesthood; while the notion that a bare or bald head can teach us that God sees our thoughts, and that the growing of the hair can teach us watchfulness in curtailing our desires, seem to be too far-fetched for a practical symbolism.

Virgin Mary.

The position held by the Virgin Mary in the [Roman] Catholic Church may best be understood by a few quotations from standard authors:—

(1) St. Ambrose says, "Thy sweet name is a balm which breathes forth the odour of grace. Ah! what divine effluence of grace does it diffuse into our souls." [a]

(2) Father Pelbart says, "As the five wounds of Christ have given salvation to man, so the five letters of the word Maria procure pardon for all sins. It heals the sinner, refreshes the soul, and surrounds it with divine love." [b]

(3) Richard de St. Laurent exhorts all sinners to invoke the powerfulness of Mary, as it alone suffices to deliver man from all evils; for there is no evil can befall man which will not give way to the name of Mary. [c]

(4) Thomas à Kempis assures us that all devils, the moment they hear the name of Mary, queen of heaven, will flee away as from a burning fire.[d]

(5) St. Brigit says, "The moment the name of Mary is uttered, not only do all foul spirits flee affrighted, but all good spirits approach and bring the heart nearer to the just."[e]

(6) St. Germanus says, "As respiration is a sign of life in the body, so the repetition of the name of Mary is a sign of life in the soul."[f]

(7) Richard de Laurent says again, "The name of Mary is a fortress and strong tower; it not only delivers sinners from the punishments they have deserved, but it protects the good from the assaults of hell."[g]

(8) St. Bernard says, "In all dangers, difficulties, and doubts, invoke Mary. Let it be ever on your lips; let it be ever in your heart."

(9) Jesus Christ said to St. Brigit, "Those who honour the name of Mary are precious to Me, and whoever invokes her name shall receive three graces—perfect repentance, perfect justification, and perfection hereafter; for so sweet to Me are the words of My mother, I can refuse her nothing."[h]

(10) St. Ephrem says, "The name of Mary is the key of heaven to those who invoke it devoutly."[i]

(11) St. Bonaventure calls Mary the salvation of those who invoke her, procuring grace in great abundance here, and glory in the highest hereafter.

(12) Thomas à Kempis says again, "If you wish to be consoled in all your troubles, have recourse to Mary, invoke Mary, honour Mary, commend yourself to Mary, rejoice with Mary, mourn with Mary, pray with Mary, walk with Mary, seek Christ with Mary, live and die with Christ and Mary."[j]

(13) Father Sertorius Caputo exhorts all on their death-bed to repeat often the name of Mary; for this name alone pronounced in the hour of death will suffice to put to flight demons, and fortify the dying in the agony of death.

(*a*) Unguentum, nomen tuum; descendat istud unguentum in animæ præcordia, sancta Maria, quod divina gratiæ spiramenta redolet.

(*b*) Sic Maria, suo sanctissimo nomine, quod quinque litteris constat, confert quotidie veniam peccatoribus. Ægrotantem sanat, odorem parit, flammam nutrit.

(*c*) Peccatores, ad Mariæ nomen confugias; ipsum solum sufficit ad medendum; nulla enim pestis quæ, ad nomen Mariæ, non cedat omnino.

(*d*) Expavescunt cœli reginam spiritus maligni, et diffugiunt, audito nomine ejus, velut ab igne.

(*e*) Omnes dæmones verentur hoc nomen, et timent; qui, audientes hoc nomen, Maria, statim relinquunt animam de unguentibus, quibus tenebant eam; et angeli boni, audito hoc nomine, statim appropinquant magis justis.

(*f*) Quomodo corpus vitalis signum operationis habet respirationem, ita sanctissimum nomen tuum, O Virgo! quod in ore servorum tuorum versatur assidue, vitæ et auxilii non solum signum est, sed etiam ea procurat et conciliat.

(*g*) Turris fortissima, nomen diminæ; ad ipsam fugiet peccator, et liberabitur; hæc defendit quodlibet et quantumlibet peccatores. Non est in aliquo nomine tam potens adjutorum, nec est aliquod nomen datum, post nomen Jesu, ex quo tanta salus refundatur hominibus.

(*h*) Quicunque invocaverit nomen tuum, et spem habet in te, ista tria dabuntur ei, insuper et regnum cœleste. Tanta enim mihi dulcedo in verbis tuis, O Mater! ut non possim negare quæ petis.

(*i*) Nomen Mariæ est reseratorium portæ cœli. Devota invocatio nominis hujus ducit ad virorem gratiæ in præsenti, et ad virorem gloriæ in futuro.

(*j*) Si consolari in omni tribulatione quæritis, accedite ad Mariam, Mariam invocate, Mariam honorate, Mariæ vos commendate; cum Maria gaudete; cum Maria dolete; cum Maria orate; cum Maria ambulate; cum Maria Jesum quærite; cum Maria et Jesu vivere et mori desiderate.

The following are the fête-days of the Virgin Mary:—

		Founded
1. The Annunciation, or Lady Day	March 25	Before 492
2. The Assumption	Aug. 18	5th century.
3. The Immaculate Conception	Dec. 8	1854, by Pius IX.
4. The Marriage with Joseph	Jan. 23	
5. The Maternity	3rd S. of Oct.	431, Council of Ephesus
6. The Name of Mary	Sept. 9	1683
7. The Nativity of Mary	Sept. 8	? 11th century
8. Notre Dame des Ardents	May 21	1109
[Notre Dame de Deols	May 31	1187]
[Notre Dame des Miracles	Local	The 1st Thursday of the year, 1283]
9. Our Lady Auxiliatrix	May 24	1814, by Pius VII.
10. Our Lady of Mercy	Sept. 24	1223
11. Our Lady of Mount Carmel	July 16	1251
12. Our Lady of the Seven Sorrows *	July 15	1200, by l'abbé Roland.
13. The Patronage of Mary	5th S. of Oct.	
14. The Preparation for the Lying-in	Dec. 18	654.
15. The Presentation in the Temple	Nov. 21	1372, by Gregory XI.
16. The Purification	Feb. 2	541
17. The Purity of Mary	4th S. of Oct.	
18. The Sacred Heart of Mary	Feb. 8	1661, Father Eudes
19. The Translation of the Virgin's House, or Santa *Casa*	Dec. 10	1294
20. The Visitation of the Virgin	July 2	1263

ANNUNCIATION OF THE VIRGIN MARY, OR LADY DAY, MARCH 25.

Lady Day commemorates the announcement of the angel Gabriel to the Virgin Mary, that she was to be the mother of the Messiah, and was to call His name Jesus, that is, Saviour (*Luke* i. 26–28).

The first mention of the festival is by pope Gelasius I., in A.D. 492.

* It is somewhat surprising that no festival has been devised for the Seven Joys of the Virgin Mary.

According to the Bollandists, the seven days of creation were seven days in the month of March, and on the 25th man was made in the likeness of his Maker. In this month the children of Israel were led from Egypt by the passage of the Red Sea. In this month Joshua crossed the Jordan to enter the promised land. In this month Christ died on the cross. In this month, say the Bollandists, we believe will be the general resurrection. In this month, on the 25th of the month, the pious believe that St. Michael triumphed over Satan and his angels. In this month Adam was buried in Calvary. In this month Cain slew his brother Abel; Melchisedek offered tithes to Abraham; Abraham offered up his son Isaac on Mount Moriah; St. Veronica died; John the Baptist was beheaded by Herod; the apostle James was put to death; St. Peter was delivered from prison; etc.—*Acta Sanctorum*, March 25.

If Christ was crucified in March, it could not have been A.D. 33, for then Good Friday was in April. In A.D. 34 and 36 Good Friday would fall in March; but in 33, 35, and 37 it fell in April.

The Annunciation on the 25th would make Christmas Day Dec. 25; but December being the rainy season, no shepherds would be watching their flocks by night in the open fields.

ASSUMPTION OF THE VIRGIN MARY, AUG. 15.

There are, in reality, three assumptions of the Virgin Mary:

1. At her death, when her soul ascended to heaven;
2. At her resurrection, three days afterwards, when her body was taken to heaven, and reunited to her soul;
3. At her coronation in heaven, when she was inaugurated queen of angels, and lady of the universe.

"It is very remarkable that the evangelists make no mention of these important events; but Juvenal, archbishop of Jerusalem, told these things to the emperor Martian; St. John Damascene has inserted them in his writings; they may be read in the Breviary of pope Pius V.; and the Church receives them as [Roman] Catholic verities, which no true Christian ought to doubt."

(1) The first of these assumptions, of course, depends on the death of the Virgin Mary; but great diversity of statement and opinion prevails on this point. St. Epiphanius, bishop of Salamina, in Cyprus, asserts that she lived twenty-four years after the Lord's ascension. Raphael Volaterranus maintains that she lived forty-nine years after that event, and that he found it so written in an ancient roll. St. Elizabeth of Sconeugia was told by a personal revelation, in A.D. 1166, that the Virgin lived only one year after the ascension. Nicephorus Callistus says she lived eleven years after the crucifixion. And Eusebius affirms that she died fourteen years after the ascension, being at the time sixty-three years old. Some affirm that she never died at all, but this belief is not considered orthodox.

(According to Eusebius, the Virgin was sixteen years old at the birth of Jesus, forty-nine at His crucifixion, and sixty-three at her own death; but it is quite evident that nothing is known about the subject.)

(2) The second assumption, we are told, occurred three days after the decease. St. John Damascene and Juvenal, archbishop of Jerusalem, assert that Adam and Eve, the prophets, all the apostles (except Thomas), and many angels, were present at the death of the Virgin Mary, and attended the funeral procession to Gethsemane. On the third day after her interment came St. Thomas, and entreated that he might be allowed to look upon the deceased lady; so the grave was opened, when lo! the body was gone. It had been taken to heaven. The odour of sanctity remained in the place where the body had lain, and the linen clothes, in which it had been wrapped, had been carefully folded together. The apostles were amazed, but they knew the body had been taken to heaven to be united to its living soul. Juvenal, archbishop of Jerusalem, continues, "There can be no doubt about this fact; for not only the apostles saw that the body was gone, the same was seen by St. Timothy, bishop of Ephesus, Dionysius the Areopagite, the divine Hierotheus, and many other saints."

(If all the apostles were at the funeral, St. James must have been there, and as St. James was executed by Herod A.D. 44, or eleven years after the crucifixion, St. Epiphanius, who says she lived twenty-four years, and St. Raphael Volaterranus, who says she lived forty-nine years after the crucifixion, are manifestly wrong; so also is Eusebius, who says she survived the ascension fourteen years. St. Elizabeth, who says she survived one year, and Nicephorus Callistus, who says it was eleven years, are within the limit. How the body being gone from the grave was any proof that it had been taken to heaven, must be left.

St. Bernard's demonstration may satisfy those who wish to believe, but can hardly convince others. He says: (1) God has revealed the spot where the bodies of many saints have been buried, but never revealed where the body of the Virgin was interred, therefore her body was not hidden in any part of the earth; (2) certain relics of the body have been preserved in divers places, but not her body, or any part thereof, therefore her body must be in heaven. Well, St. Bernard was no great logician, if this is a specimen of his ratiocination, that is certain.)—See Nicephorus Callistus, *Ecclesiastical History*, bk. xvii. ch. 28.

⁎ The parallelisms between the assumption of Mary and the resurrection of Christ are noteworthy. (1) Our Lord rose the third day, and the assumption of the Virgin Mary was on the third day; (2) when the disciples visited the tomb of Jesus the body was gone, and when the apostles visited the tomb of Mary the body was gone; (3) the grave-clothes of Jesus were left behind, so was the linen in which the Virgin Mary was wrapped; (4) Thomas in both cases was the absentee.

(3) The third assumption was the coronation. In the *Revelation* (xii. 1) we read, "And there appeared a great wonder in heaven; a woman clothed with the sun, and the moon under her feet, and upon her head a crown of twelve stars." This woman, we are told, "without doubt is the Virgin Mary." So says St. Bernard, and the other fathers and doctors of the Church, and therefore "the coronation of the Virgin is placed beyond the possibility of a doubt." St. Epiphanius calls her *sponsa Trinitatis*, the bride of the Holy Trinity. Others call her "The Bride of the Holy Ghost." Father Poiré says the crown of twelve stars means the crown of excellence, which contains the twelve stars of perfection; the crown of power, which contains twelve prerogatives; and the crown of goodness, which contains twelve operations. Her crown, therefore, is a triple crown, each of which has its twelve stars. St. Bernard sums up thus: "If the winds of temptation blow fiercely upon you, look to these stars. If you find yourselves in a sea of trouble, look to these stars. In all the storms of life implore the aid of Mary. If you are tossed on the waves of pride, ambition, envy, look to these stars, and invoke the name of Mary. O holy Virgin, no man is saved, but by thee alone! O thou pure Virgin, no one escapes from evil, but by thy help! O chaste Virgin, no one receives the joys of life eternal, but by thee! God takes pity on no man, but by thy mediation! Mother of eternal benediction."

IMMACULATE CONCEPTION OF THE VIRGIN MARY, DEC. 8.

The dogma that Mary, the wife of Joseph the carpenter of Nazareth, was free from original sin was introduced by Pope Pius IX. in 1854. The logic of this dogma is as follows:—If Mary inherited the taint of Adam's transgression, she must have imparted the taint to her Son Jesus, for it is impossible to bring a clean thing out of an unclean. As Jesus, however, was without sin, it follows that His mother must have been without sin also, and was therefore free from original sin. It is acknowledged that the ancient fathers did not hold this dogma, but the logic of the argument seems sound. In reply to this it is objected that Mary died, and death is the penalty of sin. Christ, it is true, died also, but the death of Christ was vicarious; not so the death of Mary. To get rid of this difficulty some maintain that Mary never died, but, like Enoch and Elijah, was taken up to heaven without dying; this, however, is not considered orthodox. The orthodox faith is that God cut off the entail. This, we are told, God either could do, or could not do. If He could not do it, then we deny His omnipotence. If He could, and did not, then Jesus did not honour His mother, and was not born immaculate. Logic is of very little value in theology. Tried by the rules of logic, the whole scheme of the Christian religion must fall to pieces. If Mary was an offspring of Adam, it was a *fact*, and not even omnipotence could make it otherwise. But see the evil of the dogma. St. Paul says Jesus was in all points like as we are, sin only excepted. His recurring wants, His growth in grace, His bodily infirmities, all go to prove His real humanity. But if Mary was exempt from original sin, its penalties of temptation, sickness, and death, then Jesus was in no wise like as we are, except in bodily form. He was not tempted, like as we are; He was not touched with the feelings of our infirmities; His humanity was not the humanity of the son of David and the seed of a woman. Mary and Jesus did not belong to the family of man, except only in outward fashion. Without doubt there is a logical difficulty, but we lose more than we gain by admitting the new dogma.

In the *Book of Miracles*, p. 16, Dibdale says to the devil, "What sayest thou of the Virgin Mary?" To this the devil replies, "Oh, she had no original sin. I had no part of her, either within or without." Whether the testimony of the devil, the father of lies, is worth anything "non nostrum tantas componere lites."

MARRIAGE OF JOSEPH AND MARY JAN. 23. (See BUDDING ROD.)

The fête and office of the marriage of Joseph and Mary date from the fifteenth century. A canon of Chartres made a dying request that the day of his death should be honoured by a special devotion of Joseph the carpenter of Nazareth. Gerson, the chancellor of the university of Paris, suggested that the best way of honouring Joseph would be by celebrating his marriage with Mary. So a suitable office was prepared; but it was only the office of the Nativity with the word "marriage" substituted for "nativity," and a different Gospel. Afterwards, Peter Doré composed a special office; and in 1725 pope Benedict XIII. made it obligatory on all Churches to recite this office.

The wedding ring of the Virgin Mary, we are told, was discovered by Gregory V. (A.D. 996–999), in the village of Clusium, and was given to the church of Perousa. "L'authenticité de cette relique s'appuie sur des preuves propres à porter la conviction dans l'ésprit. Les actes de Sixtus IV. et d'Innocent III. prouvent cette authenticité, mais ne la définissent pas."—Mgr. Guérin, *Vies des Saints*, vol. xvi. p. 147.

(It would be interesting to know how Gregory V., nearly a thousand years after the event, identified this ring, and how it got to Clusium, now called Chiusa in Veronese, Italy. Besides, wedding rings formed no part of a Jewish marriage.)

Maternity of the Virgin Mary, Third Sunday in Oct.

This fête is not to commemorate the motherhood of Mary in the ordinary acceptation of the word "maternity," but the dogma that Mary, in giving birth to Jesus, was the mother of God. The dogma was established in the Council of Ephesus, A.D. 431, and was provoked thus: Nestorius, patriarch of Constantinople, an eloquent preacher of most exemplary life, took up the teaching of Anastasius, that though Mary was the mother of Jesus, she was not, strictly speaking, the "mother of God." Jesus, he said, had two natures, a divine nature, which existed before His advent, and His human, which He received at His incarnation. By His divine nature He was God, by His incarnation He was man. Mary was not the mother of His divine nature, and therefore she was not the "mother of God;" but she was the mother of His incarnate nature, and therefore she was the mother of "the man Christ Jesus." Cyril, patriarch of Alexandria, condemned this teaching in "twelve anathemas;" and Celestine, bishop of Rome, threatened Nestorius with excommunication unless he withdrew the obnoxious doctrine. Nestorius would not withdraw it; nay, more, he confirmed it *ex cathedrâ* at Constantinople in these words: "If any one says that Mary is the mother of God, let him be accursed;" so a council was called at Ephesus, when it was voted that "Mary was the mother of God" amidst considerable opposition, and Nestorius was banished. Ever since, it has been made a fundamental doctrine of the [Roman] Catholic Church, that when Mary became the mother of Jesus she became also the mother of God.

There cannot be a doubt that the phrase "mother of God" is very objectionable, and has led to much error. As God, Jesus Christ is one and inseparable from God the Father and God the Holy Ghost, and to make Mary the "mother of God" is to make her the mother of the Trinity. And then we are involved in this utter absurdity: Mary, the descendant of David and of Adam, is the mother of the Creator who existed, not only thousands and thousands of years before Mary had even birth, but from all eternity. Mary was the "mother of Jesus;" this the Gospels tell us, and no dogma of a Church ought to go beyond the words of the law, or give an inferential interpretation to those words. Certainly Mary was not the mother of the Trinity in any ordinary acceptation of the words, though she was the mother of Jesus, and Jesus, as the Son of God, is the Second Person of the Godhead.

Name of the Virgin Mary, Sept. 9.

The fête of "The Name Mary" was ordained by Innocent XI., by a decree bearing date Nov. 20, 1683. It arose thus: Vienna, in 1683, was threatened by the Turks. Their army numbered two hundred thousand men, and on they marched, destroying everything in their path, almost to the walls of the city; and then pitched their tents. The siege began. It went on from week to week. Probably the grand-vizier intended to starve the defenders into a capitulation. The people of Vienna were in despair. They felt that at any moment an assault would lay their city at the mercy of the foe, when every one would be put to the sword, or reduced to slavery. The kaiser had deserted them, and sent no relief. We are told that the Christian Churches of Rome, France, and other parts of Christendom, offered prayers on behalf of Vienna, and implored especially the aid of the Virgin Mary. On Sept. 12, early in the morning, a booming of cannon was heard from Mount Kalen. It was Sobieski, king of Poland, come to the rescue of the besieged. He threw himself on the Turks with the fury of a hurricane. The cry went forth, "Sobieski! Sobieski to the rescue!" In hot haste Mustapha mounted his horse, and gave orders for battle. It was too late. Sobieski was within the camp. The grand-vizier galloped off; the Turks fled in disorder, leaving everything behind—the money for the siege, the soldiers' pay, the baggage, tents, cannons, chariots, even the sultan's standard. It was a brilliant victory. The rout was perfect. The people of Vienna attributed their rescue to the Virgin Mary, and the pope instituted a perpetual souvenir of this grand victory by establishing the fête of the "Name of Mary."

Respecting the Virgin's name. We are told she was not called Mary till she was so saluted by the angel Gabriel. St. Ambrose, St. Bernard, and St. Anselm all agree in this. We are further told that the name means "Lady" (*Maria Hebræo sermone, Latine Domina nuncupatur*); and St. John of Damascus says she was well called *domina*, "when, by her maternity, she became the sovereign of the universe, and the mother of the Creator of the world." Christ is King of kings and Lord of lords, but Christ "was subject to Mary and Joseph, and therefore Mary was, in fact, the *lord* or ruler of the Lord of lords and King of kings." *

St. Bonaventure, St. Isidore, and the venerable Bede tell us that the name Mary means "light," or the "illuminator" (*Maria idem est quod illuminata et illuminatrix*), and may be interpreted, "I am the light of the world." The Roman Breviary says it means "star of the sea" (*maris stella*), and St. Bernard says she is referred to in *Numb.* xxiv. 17, "A star shall come out of Jacob, and a sceptre shall rise out of Israel." He goes on to say, *Ubi nomen Mariæ invocatur, dæmonum nocumentum effugatur, quia Maria terribilis ut castrorum acies ordinata.*† St. Anselm says, *Velocior est nonnunquam salus, memorato nomine Mariæ, quam invocato nomine Jesu unici filii sui.*‡

"Mary" cannot possibly mean *light*, nor yet "*star* of the sea," nor yet *lady*. These are pure fancies. It may mean "bitterness." It may mean "woman of the sea." It may mean "the bitterness of the sea;" but the other meanings are wholly indefensible. It is exactly tantamount to "Oceana," unless indeed we derive it from *Marah*, "bitterness" (*Exod.* xv. 23).

NATIVITY OF THE VIRGIN MARY, SEPT. 8.

This festival was unknown to St. Augustine (A.D. 354–430), for he distinctly states in one of his sermons that only two nativities were recognized in the Christian Church, that of John the Baptist and that of Jesus Christ. The nativity of Mary was not celebrated till the year 1250, and came about in this manner. A religious man said he heard every year, on Sept. 8, angels making melody. On seeking the reason thereof, one of the angels told him they were celebrating the nativity of the mother of God; and, on the credit of this story, the feast of the Nativity was instituted.—Edward Kinesman (1623), *Lives of the Saints*, p. 707.

Alban Butler tells us the nativity of the Virgin was celebrated long before the time of Charlemagne, although no mention is made of it in the *Capitulars* of that monarch. Thomassin did not find the feast of the nativity of Mary mentioned by any author before Fulbert of Chartres, A.D. 1000; but Alban Butler says it is mentioned in the famous manuscript calendar kept in the treasury of the cathedral of Florence, dated A.D. 813. He says also it is spoken of by Walter, bishop of Orleans, in 871.—Alban Butler, *Lives of the Saints*, Sept. 8.

St. Jerome says that Joachim and Anna were man and wife for twenty years without a child, and that Issachar the priest not only refused to accept their offerings on the feast of *Encenia*, but ordered them out of the temple, under the conviction that God had refused them an offspring in punishment of *secret sin*. Gregory Nazianzen and Simeon Metaphrastês assure us that Anna then went to the temple of Jerusalem to lament her barrenness, and vowed, if God would grant her a child, she would devote it to His service. God heard her prayer, and granted her a daughter, which became the queen of angels and the mother of God.

Notre-Dame des Ardents (May 21, A.D. 1105). In 1105 a frightful disease burst out in Arotis, called the "Feu Ardent." This was a terrible scourge indeed, which decimated a part of Europe. It visited equally the mansions of the rich and cabins of the poor, old and young, male and female. The parts attacked grew black as coals, and fell into powder; the hands rotted from the wrists, the feet from the ankles, and then other parts of the body mortified. In many respects it resembled the "Black Death" of the fourteenth century. On May 21 the Virgin Mary appeared to two men, named Itier and Norman, sworn enemies to each other, and bade them go to the bishop of Arras, and tell him to go with them into the church, and watch all night till cock-crow, when she would come to them. This did they, and, on the night appointed, the Virgin came through the roof of the choir with a lighted candle in her hand. "Here," she said, "I confide this taper to your charge; take it as a gage of my compassion. It shall be for the healing of the people." Then she departed, and the three chosen ones dropped three drops of the celestial taper into three large vessels of water, and gave of it to the sick to drink, or as a lotion for their wounds. In one day 144 were healed. Only one of those who tried it died, and he was an infidel. A *Te Deum* was appointed, and Itier and Norman founded the society called "La Charité de Notre-Dame des Ardents." The holy candle is "an incontestable fact," and was celebrated throughout all the country. St. Bernard saw it in 1131, and has attested it. It is the subject of a bull of Gelasius II. and Sixtus IV. In the thirteenth century the counts of

* This certainly is bad logic. St. Luke says, "He [Jesus] was subject to *them*," not to Mary. And if this gives Mary pre-eminence to Christ as the Ruler of the universe, it gives Joseph the same pre-eminence.

† "Where the name of Mary is invoked, the evil influence of devils is averted; for Mary is terrible to them as a tented army."

‡ "Salvation is sometimes more speedily obtained by invoking the name of Mary, than by invoking the name of her Son Jesus."

Flanders built an elegant shrine for it; this shrine was a pyramid forty feet in height, and under it was a small chapel and sacristy. The sacred candle is kept in the upper part, locked in by several doors, the keys of which are deposited with different persons, one being held by the mayor and another by the deputy mayor. When shown to strangers, it is let down into the chapel by the mayor and the chief officers of the prince. In 1793 the shrine was knocked to pieces. The mayor, however, had taken charge of the candle, and it was guarded by different persons through all the revolution. At the restoration a new shrine was constructed for it at Arras, where it is now.—*Notre-Dame de France*. See the charter dated May 21, 1201, with six seals, and registered by the notaries of the pope in 1482, under the commands of Sixtus IV. (Those who deny this statement must perforce deny the authority and truth of the [Roman] Catholic Church.)

Our Lady the Auxiliatrix, May 24.

This fête was instituted to commemorate the return of pope Pius VII. to Rome, May 24, 1814, after his release from Fontainebleau, where he had been held the virtual prisoner of Napoleon since the June of 1812. The history of this captivity is as follows:—Napoleon resolved to restore the religion which the revolutionists had abolished, and with this view entered into negotiations with the pope, who was Pius VII. The concordat was ratified in Paris on Easter Sunday, 1802. In 1804 Napoleon resolved to be called emperor, and invited Pius VII. to crown him; accordingly the pope went to Paris to crown the usurper. Napoleon from this moment began to encroach on the pope's dominions and prerogatives, till in May 17, 1808, Rome and all the other dominions of the pope were annexed to the French empire. Pius VII. now excommunicated Napoleon; and Napoleon removed the pope from Rome to Fontainebleau (1812), where he was made to sign a paper recognizing the annexation of his dominions to France. In the mean time occurred the dreadful Moscow catastrophe, and the star of Napoleon was setting fast. Pius VII. revoked his consent; Napoleon tried to compromise matters; but the pope refused to yield unless he was suffered to return to Rome. Matters went on thus till Jan. 22, 1814, when Pius was suffered to return, and he entered Rome May 24, 1814. In commemoration of this event, he instituted on the 24th of May a grand festival, under the title of "Our Lady Helper," or "Our Lady Auxiliatrix," and appointed a suitable office for the day.

Our Lady of Mercy, Sept. 24.

The order of Our Lady of Mercy was founded in 1223, by Peter Nolasco, its object being the redemption of slaves and captives. While thinking over the subject, the Virgin Mary came to him, and told him it was God's good pleasure that he should found the order, and call it the order of "Our Lady of Mercy." "Who am I," said Peter, "that God should honour me thus? And who art thou, who knowest so well the secrets of the Most High?" "I am Mary," was the answer, "the mother of God. My Son, the Redeemer of the world, who came to give liberty to the captive, has much people bound in captivity, and wishes the order to be established." As soon as Nolasco heard this he was transported with joy, and went to tell the king of Aragon what the Virgin had said to him. He then learned that the Virgin had appeared to the king and to St. Raymond de Pennafort of the order of St. Dominic on the same mission; so, without delay, he summoned the bishop of Barcelona with his chief ministers, and laid the first stone of the new monastic edifice, Nolasco being arrayed in the robe and scapular of the new order. The king authorized the order to bear the royal arms, which were quartered with those of the bishop of Barcelona. Peter Nolasco, being thus invested Grand Master of the order, had frequent visits from Jesus Christ, in which he received instructions how he was to act; and the new foundation prospered wonderfully.—R. P. F. Zumel, *Life of Peter Nolasco*. (Not yet canonized.)

Our Lady of Mount Carmel, July 16.

The order of Our Lady of Mount Carmel was founded in 1251. The reasons given are the following:—

(1) The little cloud that rose out of the sea, like a man's hand, which foreboded to Elijah (who was on the top of Carmel) abundance of rain (1 *Kings* xviii. 44), was a type of the Virgin Mary, her prerogatives, her humility, and her exaltation. St. Bernard says her humility is typified by the smallness of the cloud, no bigger than a man's hand; her prerogatives are

typified by the abundant rain, which refreshed the earth, and gave new life to man and beast; her exaltation is typified by the spread of the cloud, which covered the whole heavens.

(2) The second reason is this: The first and principal church built on Mount Carmel was dedicated to the Virgin Mary. And if a lord takes the name of the place where he dwells, surely the Virgin Mary should be called by the name of the place where her honour dwelleth.

(3) Without doubt Elijah, who was a prophet, foresaw the coming of Mary and of Christ, and informed his disciples of the mystery. Even the Druids had an altar "to the parturient Virgin."

For these "cogent" reasons the order of Our Lady of Mount Carmel has been founded, and many miracles have testified that God has pleasure therein.—Mgr. Guérin, *Vies des Saints*, vol. viii. pp. 375–385.

If these reasons can satisfy the pope's chamberlain in 1880, he must be very easily convinced.

Our Lady of the Seven Sorrows, July 15.

St. Roland, abbot of Chezery, showed great devotion to the Virgin Mary, and wished her to be held in special honour in his abbey. To this end he built a chapel to "Our Lady of the Seven Sorrows" in 1200, in the city of Confort, where the abbey had its chief landed property; and to this chapel many pilgrims resorted. Leo XII., in 1828, accorded, by a brief, plenary indulgence to all who visited the chapel on the fête of the Conception (Dec. 8), the Nativity (Dec. 25), the Annunciation (March 25), and the Assumption (Aug. 15), or on the octave of the festivals. He also accorded an indulgence of forty days to all the priests and their assistants who administered mass on Saturday in this chapel.

Patronage of the Virgin Mary, Fifth Sunday of October.

St. Alphonso de Liguori, in his treatise called *Les Gloires de Marie*, divides his subject into these six heads: (1) Mary our hope; (2) Mary our succour; (3) Mary our mediatrix; (4) Mary our advocate; (5) Mary our guardian; (6) Mary our salvation.

In regard to the first—*Mary our hope*—he says, "Heretics tell us Mary is only a human being, and cursed is he who places his hope in man; yet the true Christian will still cry daily, *Maria, spes nostra, salve!* God the Father calls her 'My well-beloved daughter,' God the Son calls her mother, God the Holy Ghost calls her His spouse, and man calls her his hope." St. Basil says, *Ne diffidas, peccator; sed in cunctis Mariam sequere et invoca, quam voluit Deus in cunctis subvenire.** And St. Bernard is very bold: *Non dubito quod, si ad te, Maria, venerimus, habebimus quod volemus. In te, ergo, speret, qui desperat.*†

In regard to the second—*Mary our succour*—Alain de la Roche says, "Satan flees, hell trembles, when I say, *Ave, Maria.* Glorious and admirable is thy name, O Mary; he who calls on thee shall never fear death." We read in *Exodus* (xl. 30), "The cloud of the Lord was upon the tabernacle by day, and fire was on it by night." Richard de St. Laurent says, this cloud and this fire was a type of Mary, who covers our sins with a cloud from divine justice, and defends us from Satan as a fire.

The third head is *Mary our mediatrix.* "Si un Jérémie, après sa mort, prie pour Jerusalem; si Vieillards de l'Apocalypse présentent à Dieu les prières des saints; si un St. Pierre promet à ses disciples de se souvenir d'eux après sa mort; si un St. Etienne prie pour ses persécuteurs; si un St. Paul prie pour ses compagnons et ses amis; en un mot, si les saints peuvent prier pour nous, pourquoi ne pourrions-nous pas supplier les saints d'intercéder en notre faveur? C'est un impiété de nier que Dieu se plaise à octroyer ses grâces en ayant égard à l'intercession des saints, et surtout de Marie, mère du Sauveur, elle que son divin Fils désire tant de voir aimée et honorée de nous." He then goes on to say Mary "non pas mediatrice de justice, mais mediatrice de grâce et d'intercession, *mediatrix nostræ salutis,*" the salvation of sinners, the refuge of the destitute, the help of believers, *vita nostra et nostra spes. Qui me invenerit, invenerit vitam, et hauriet salutem.*‡ St. Bernard says, *Nulla gratia venit de cœlo ad terram, nisi transeat per manus Mariæ.*§ And St. Bonaventure goes a step further: *Nullus potest cœlum intrare,*

* "Be not faithless, sinner, but follow Mary, and invoke her name; for God has ordained she should be your succour in all things."

† "I doubt not, Mary, if to thee we come, we shall obtain whatever we desire. Therefore he who puts his hope in thee shall never be disappointed."

‡ "Mediatrix of our salvation; our life, our hope. Who findeth me, findeth life, and drinketh in salvation."

§ "No grace comes down from heaven upon earth, but what passes through the hands of Mary."

*nisi per Mariam transeat, tanquam per portam.** The evangelist says, "You will find the boy [Jesus] with Mary His mother," and the Seraphic Doctor adds, "You will never find Christ but with His mother, and through Mary."

Mary our advocate is the fourth head. As Christ chose Mary for His mother, He is obliged, as a son, to obey her. Hence St. Germanus says, "O Mary, thou art all-powerful to save sinners. Thy advocacy is all-sufficient, for thou art the life of life." St. Bernardin says, *Omnipotens auxilium tuum, O Maria. Te Deus exaltavit, et omnia tibi secum possibilia esse donavit.*† Bonaventure compares her to Noah's dove: *Tu enim es illa fidelissima columba Noe, quæ inter Deum et mundum, diluvio spirituali submersum, mediatrix fidelissima extitisti.*‡ Vitalis calls her the rainbow of the covenant: *Iris in circuitu sedis est Maria, quæ mitigat Dei judicium et sententiam contra peccatores.*§

Mary our guardian is the fifth idea. According to St. Bernard, "Mary is our all in all. She opens to all her bosom of mercy, and gives redemption to the slave, health to the sick, comfort to the afflicted, pardon to the sinner. Christ Himself said to St. Gertrude, 'Of My omnipotence I give all power to My most honoured mother of pardoning sins, and granting whatever she pleases to those who ask her.'"

Mary is our salvation. St. Anselm says, "It is impossible for any one to be saved who loves not thee, O Mary, and no less impossible for any one to perish who honours thee." St. Bonaventure says, "Whoever neglect Mary, must die in their sins;" and again, "Those who neglect Mary in this life, can never enter into the kingdom of God." Ignatius says, "Impossibile est aliquem salvari peccatorem, nisi per tuum, O Virgo, auxilium et favorem; quia, quos non salvat Dei justitia, salvat sua intercessione Mariæ misericordia infinita." || St. Bonaventure exclaims, "In thee, O Mary, have I placed my hope. Let me never be brought to confusion." The Virgin Mary said to St. Brigit, "I am the mother of all the souls in purgatory, and all the sins unatoned for in their life are daily diminished by my intercession." St. Ambrose says, "Open to us, O Virgin, the gates of heaven, for to thee hath God given the keys of eternal life." St. Fulgentius calls her "the ladder by which God descended to earth, and by which man ascends to heaven." Again St. Bonaventure says, "To know thee, Mary, is the root of immortality, and to talk of thy merits is the way of salvation." "Sainte Mère de Dieu, tous ceux qui participeront à la joie éternelle, habitent en vous, et vivent sous votre protection."

The tractate from which this is extracted is very long, and the extracts given can give but a faint idea of the adoration expressed in the original, but may serve feebly to show what is meant by the "Patronage of the Virgin Mary." Many of the quotations are in the original Latin or French, that none may suppose them to be garbled or misquoted.

Preparation for the Lying-in of the Virgin Mary, Dec. 18.

This fête-day was established in the tenth council of Toledo, held A.D. 654. It is the octave previous to the birth, and is called "Our Lady of the O," because the Vespers begin with the fifteen prayers all beginning with the letter "O" (*Horæ Beatissimæ Virginis Mariæ*).

Presentation of the Virgin Mary in the Temple, Nov. 21.

This does not mean the presentation of the Child Jesus by His mother Mary, but the presentation of Mary herself in early childhood. It is said that she was presented at three years old, and lived twelve years in the temple, being left there by her father Joachim to be educated in the girl's college. When Joachim took his child to the temple he set her down on the lowest of the fifteen steps leading up to the temple, and the priests went down to assist her up; but Mary refused all help, and ascended all the fifteen steps sustained only by the hands of the Holy Ghost. Having accomplished the ascent, she proceeded at once to the altar; so that the priests, and they who were with the child, were filled with amazement, and confessed that she was destined to become the mother of the Messiah.—Lippomani (bishop of Venice, and secretary to pope Julius II.). See also George, archbishop of Nicomedia; Metaphrastês, archbishop of Constantinople; etc.

* "No one can enter heaven, except by passing through Mary, the door of heaven."

† "Omnipotent thy help, O Mary. God hath exalted thee, and hath given all things possible to thee, as with Himself."

‡ "Thou art that most faithful dove of Noah, which flew as a most faithful mediator between God and a world drowned in a spiritual flood."

§ "Mary is God's rainbow, which mitigates God's judgment and sentence against sinners."

|| "It is impossible for any sinner to be saved, except by thy help and favour, O Virgin. The infinite mercy of Mary can by her intercession save those whom the justice of God would otherwise condemn."

Purification of the Virgin Mary, Feb. 2.

"The Purification," or at full length "The Feast of the Purification of the Virgin Mary," called in Scotland "Candlemas Day," is fixed to Feb. 2, which is forty days from Christmas Day of the preceding year. Jewish mothers, after the birth of a son, were ceremonially "unclean" for forty days, and were debarred from the privileges of religious communion. In all this time, says the law, "she shall touch no hallowed thing, nor come into the sanctuary. . . . But when the days of her purifying are fulfilled . . . she shall bring a lamb of the first year for a burnt offering, and a young pigeon for a sin offering, to the door of the tabernacle of the congregation." The officiating priest was to take the offerings, make an atonement for her, and she was accounted ceremonially clean. In the case of poor women, the lamb was commuted for a pigeon, so that two pigeons were offered instead of a lamb and a pigeon. At the birth of a daughter the time of uncleannesss lasted another week (*Lev.* xii.). We read in St. Luke that the Virgin Mary complied exactly with these directions: first, the Child was circumcised on the eighth day (*Lev.* xii. 3; *Luke* ii. 21); secondly, the mother waited till the "days of her purification according to the law of Moses" were accomplished; thirdly, she then brought the young child to Jerusalem, and presented two young pigeons, one for a burnt offering, and the other for a sin offering (*Luke* ii. 24). This being done, she was restored to all the privileges of religious communion.

In the [Roman] Catholic Church, a "papal chapel" is held on the day of Purification in the apostolic palace of the Vatican. The pope, who is always present, makes the blessing, and distributes candles, symbolical of Christ, "the Light of the world." From this distribution of candles, and the unusual number employed in the service, the day was called Candlemas Day ("Candelariæ," "St. Mariæ Candelariæ," "Candelosæ," "Candelarum," and "Luminum"); in primitive times, "The Fête of Simeon and Anna;" and it is still often called "The Presentation of Jesus in the Temple." The fête was instituted in A.D. 541, by the emperor Justinian, though some think it had then only fallen into disuse, and was re-established, the immediate occasion being a plague which desolated and threatened to depopulate Rome. Justinian vowed, if the Virgin would avert the plague, he would establish this fête to her honour. The plague ceased, and the fête was established. Baronius gives quite another account: he says the Roman *Lupercal* was held on Feb. 2, and that pope Gelasius converted it into the Christian observance.

Purity of the Virgin Mary, Fourth Sunday in October.

The word "purity" in the fête means chastity and virginity. St. Augustine says the "battles with chastity are the hardest of all; the fight is daily, but the victory seldom." St. Thomas says "the beauty of the blessed Virgin excites those who behold it with the principle of chastity;" and St. Jerome tells us "that Joseph lived in perpetual chastity by living in the company of Mary." This was his argument to Helvidius, who denied the virginity of Mary.* We are told by Bellarmin that the way to preserve chastity is by prayer, fasting, and fleeing from youthful lust, all which practices he ascribes to Mary.

In fasting he includes the lust of the eyes, and both St. Epiphany and St. John of Damascus tell us that the Virgin always went with her eyes looking on the ground; but they do not tell us how they obtained this information. In regard to food, Philebert declares it was revealed to Felix the hermit that Mary, when an infant at the breast, would take its nourishment only once a day; and Gregory of Tours caps his assertion by the words *nullo tempore Maria non jejunavit* (she ceased not to fast all the days of her life). A gratuitous assertion without one iota of proof.

The other two ascriptions are proved by similar *dicta*, and without the slightest attempt at historic evidence. They may, therefore, be passed over in silence.

Translation of the Santa Casa.

The Santa Casa is the reputed house of Mary and Joseph in Nazareth, where Jesus was brought up. We are told that angels carried this house bodily in 1291 to Fiume, in Dalmatia, and on Dec. 10, 1294, removed it from Dalmatia to Recanati. At last, after twice more shifting its place, it was permanently fixed in

* "Tu dicis Mariam virginem non permanisse; ego mihi plus vindico etiam Joseph virginem fuisse per Mariam."

Loreto. The house is 32 feet long, 13 feet wide, and 18¾ feet high. Towards the east end, separated now by a silver grating, is the sanctuary, and here stands the image of the Virgin, in a silver niche. It is made of the cedar of Lebanon, and was carved, we are told, by St. Luke. The image has a triple crown on the head, holds the image of Christ, now covered with diamonds; bearing in His left hand a golden globe, while the first two fingers of the right hand are held up, as if in the act of benediction. At the lower end of the house is a window, through which, we are told, the angel entered at the annunciation. The sanctuary is now crowded with sixty-two great lamps of gold and silver. One of the gold lamps weighs thirty-seven pounds. One of the angels about the image is of massive gold, two others are of silver. The walls are covered with plates of silver. In this splendid house is preserved the sacred bowl, out of which the sacred family are said to have eaten. The treasury is invaluable for its vestments, lamps, candlesticks, goblets, crowns, crucifixes, images, cameos, pearls, gems of all kinds, in prodigious numbers and varieties. Such is the Santa Casa. Now for its history, as told by Rohrbacher in his *Life of the Saints*, and believed in by [Roman] Catholics, if we may trust the chamberlain of pope Leo XIII.

First translation (A.D. 1291). Towards the close of the thirteenth century the Holy Land was lost to the Christians; but the house occupied by Mary, when she conceived the Word which was made flesh, was rescued from the infidels, by being removed bodily, by angels, May 10, 1291, at the second watch of the night, from Nazareth to Tersatz or Fiume, in Dalmatia. At daybreak some of the inhabitants of Fiume were not a little amazed, to see a new edifice had sprung up as if by magic. The rumour soon spread, and people from all sides flocked to see the mysterious house. It was built of little red square stones, cemented together. The people were puzzled at the singularity of the building, its air of antiquity, and its Eastern style of architecture. No one could guess where it came from, how it got there, or how it could hold together without a foundation. When they went inside their amazement was increased tenfold. The chamber was a parallelogram; the roof was surmounted with a little clock-tower made of wood, and painted azure sown with gilt stars. The walls were about a cubit thick, but the bricks were not set in lines. The door was in the side. To the right was a small window, opposite to which was an altar of square stones, and the altar was surmounted with an antique Greek cross, ornamented with a crucifix made of cloth glued on the wood, and the legend over it was—"Jesus of Nazareth, King of the Jews." Beside the altar was a little cupboard filled with domestic articles, and several for the use of a baby. On the left of the altar was a fireplace, and close by was an image of cedar, representing the Virgin Mary bearing in her arms the Infant Jesus. The faces looked like silver somewhat blackened with smoke, as if candles had been burned before the image. A crown of pearls was on the Virgin's head; her hair was long, and parted in the Nazarene fashion. She was dressed in a robe of gold, girded with a large belt, and the robe fell in folds over her feet. Over her robe she wore on her back and shoulders a blue mantle. The Child Jesus was larger than ordinary children of the same age; His hair was also long, parted in the middle and flowing over His shoulders. He held up the first two fingers of His right hand, as if in the act of giving a benediction, and in His left hand was a globe.—The above is taken from the *Histoire Critique et Religieuse de Notre-Dame de Lorette*, by A. B. Caillau, 1843.

The mystery explained. While all the neighbourhood was pondering on the marvellous house, so strange in appearance, so wonderfully transported, so manifestly connected with the religion of Christ, bishop Alexander, the pastor of St. George, made his appearance. This only added to the mystery, as it was well known that the bishop was confined to his bed with a fever. Now, when he was told of the Santa Casa, he made a vow to the Virgin, and all of a sudden the heavens opened, and the Virgin, surrounded by angels, came to him and said, "My son, you called me, and I am come to help you to unravel the secret which has so perplexed the people of Fiume. Know, then, that the house just transported to Fiume is my house, where I was born and brought up. It was there that the archangel Gabriel saluted me, and there I conceived by the Holy Ghost the divine Infant. It was there that the Word was made flesh. The altar in the house was made by St. Peter. The cedar image was made by St. Luke, and he has caught the likeness exactly, and expressed them as nearly as it is possible to express living faces in wood. This house, loved by the angels of heaven, has been taken from Nazareth for its better security. It has been done by God, to whom nothing is impossible. Now, be cured of your fever, and make known to the people the mystery which they cannot understand." So saying, she rose again into the clouds, and was no more seen. The bishop rose from his bed in perfect health, and went without delay to see the Santa Casa. The governor of Dalmatia was Nicholas Frangipane, who was at the time away, having been called by Rodolph of Habsbury to the wars; but immediately he was told of the strange prodigy, he sent four honourable men, of great wisdom and prudence, to Nazareth, to investigate the matter minutely, and report upon it. The commission said that the house at Nazareth was undoubtedly gone; the foundation was there, but not the house. On minutely examining the foundation stones, they were certainly of the same character as the stones of the Santa Casa, and precisely of the same dimensions. The report was committed to writing, and confirmed by oath. The people of Bosnia, Servia, Albania, and Croatia went in crowds to see the mysterious house, and the governor, for its better security and the convenience of visitors, surrounded it with solid posts and rails. Offerings poured in from all sides, and the Santa Casa proved a veritable mine of wealth.

The second translation (Dec. 10, A.D. 1294). The Santa Casa remained at Ternatz or Fiume for three and a half years, and was then transported by angels through the air from Dalmatia to Loreto. The governor built a chapel on the site, and in this chapel may still be read this inscription: "*Here is the spot where formerly stood the house of the blessed Virgin of Loreto, now removed to the territory of Recanati.*" The people of Fiume still chant the hymn of the Santa Casa; and numbers go annually from Dalmatia to Loreto, to lament their irreparable loss, and pray for its removal back again. In 1559 the number of pilgrims from Dalmatia exceeded three hundred. They went bearing wax candles in their hands, and fell prostrate at the door of the house, saying, "Return, return to Fiume, O Mary, Mary. Return to Fiume; return, return." Respecting this second translation Paul della Selva thus wrote to Charles II., king of Naples: "On Saturday, Dec. 10, 1294, at midnight, a great light from heaven was observed on the banks of the Adriatic, and a celestial harmony was heard by many. Hundreds were roused from sleep, and got up to gaze on the mysterious light, and listen to the music. All of a sudden they saw a house in the air, blazing in light, and supported by the hands of angels. Those who saw were stupefied with wonder. The angels set the house down in the midst of a wood, and the trees bent in reverence to it. Even to this day the trees in the vicinity are still bent. The spot chosen by the angels was once occupied by a heathen temple, which was surrounded by a laurel grove [*laureto*], whence the name of the place, 'Loreto.' At daybreak the rumour had spread in all directions, and all the inhabitants of Recanati went to see the mysterious house. Hundreds and hundreds entered it, and fell prostrate before the cedar image of Mary and Jesus. The crowd increased daily; but in eight months the house left the forest, which was infested with brigands, and was set by angels on the hill, the property of count Stephen and count Simeon Rainaldi. Offerings poured in, and a scandal arose that the offerings were misappropriated. In four months' time (1295) the house again shifted its place from the hill to a heap of stones near the high-road leading to Recanati, near the sea coast, and there it is still. The house has no foundation, and the situation is exposed to most violent winds and torrents of rain; so a strong wall, with a most solid foundation, has been built round the house, and the walls have been decorated by celebrated painters. Father Riera tells us that soon after this wall was made, as a sort of lean-to to support the house, the Virgin Mary pushed it away from the house so far that a child with a flambeau could walk between the house and the wall. This was done to show the world that the house did not require the help of man to support it."

In the fourteenth century the inhabitants of Recanati built a temple to enclose the Santa Casa. In 1464 pope Pius II. offered a gold chalice to Notre-Dame of Loreto; and Paul II., in a bull dated Oct. 15, says, "There cannot be a doubt of the miracles which proceed from the Santa Casa, for we ourselves have proved it in our own person." Sixtus IV., Leo X.,

Clement VII., Sixtus V., Clement VIII., Clement IX., have all issued bulls respecting this wonderful house, and no more doubted the "history" given above than they doubted that Mary was the mother of Jesus.

Visitation of the Virgin Mary, July 2.

This fête commemorates the visit of Mary to her cousin Elisabeth, the future mother of John the Baptist (*Luke* i. 39–56). St. Bonaventure was the first to establish this fête, in 1263; and Urban VI., in 1389, issued a bull making the observance thereof compulsatory. The Council of Basle, in 1441, fixed the day to July 2.

Our Lady of Caravaggio.

Our Lady of Caravaggio and the son of the duke of Norfolk (1883). The son of the duke of Norfolk made a pilgrimage to Lourdes under the hope that the Virgin would restore him to a *mens sana in corpore sano;* but the hope was disappointed, and the pilgrimage in vain. He is now recommended to visit the holy shrine at Caravaggio, on behalf of the sorely afflicted child. The *Court Journal* says that "the number of pilgrims who have visited the shrine this year exceed a hundred thousand." An eye-witness tells us that "every day, at noon, the vision of the Virgin Mary rises from a dark recess behind one of the pillars of the aisle, and the struggles of the thousands of eager devotees to catch a glimpse of the apparition are most extraordinary. The shrieks and screams of the victims who are knocked down and trampled on amid the confusion are appalling. Those who cannot approach near enough to the shrine throw handfuls of copper coin against the iron grating which encloses it, and the shock of the metallic sound, amid the deep monotonous intoning of the priests, seems to produce a frenzy in the crowd, many of whom rush wildly about, shrieking and tearing their hair, and treading without mercy on the limbs of the paralytics outstretched on the pavement. The simple village church, which is capable of containing only a few hundred people, is made to hold ten thousand, who, although packed, suffocating, perspiring, and trembling beneath the stifling atmosphere, yet contrive to howl out their invocations. Outside, on the piazza, the scene is still more astounding. Around the fountain stand groups of devotees of every grade of life. The paralytic, with the maimed and crippled, are laid on the bare stones under a burning sun, and in due time are lifted into the fountain; while others, filling their little tin mugs with water, drink greedily, without heed of the pollution it has undergone from the sick who have been immersed therein. This year (1883) the pilgrimage has been swollen by many families of the highest rank in North Italy . . . and when the dismal howlings of the pilgrims within the church announce the appearance of the misty vapour which precedes the apparition of the Virgin, the whole crowd fall to the ground, and literally shriek forth the litany composed for the occasion. The cripples fall back upon the pavement; the tin mugs are left to float upon the fountain; and the litany is succeeded by a dead silence."

"Pepper's ghost" was seen under great disadvantage compared with this. The crowd, the accessories, the difficulty of catching a glance, and that only in a prostrate condition, the religious fervour prepared to believe and not to doubt, are all in favour of this, the latest vision of our Lady; but if this is religion, and this the way that God or the Virgin is revealed to man, then "turn tears to fires," for who can approve the text?

Miracles ascribed to the Virgin Mary.

The Virgin Mary rescues a knight from going down into the pit, because he made her a handsome present. Matthew Paris, one of the most respectable of the Middle Age chroniclers, and by no means pinned to the priesthood, tells us of a knight who was on the point of being carried off to perdition for "frequenting tournaments" rather than the services of the Church; but the Virgin Mary, out of gratitude for a handsome donation made by him, saved him, and carried him safely to Abraham's bosom (p. 290).—Hallam, *Middle Ages*, vol. iii. p. 350, cites this tale.

The Virgin Mary rescues a man suspended on a gallows. A certain highwayman always addressed a prayer to the Virgin Mary when he started on one of his expeditions. He was at last taken, and condemned to death. Being led to the gallows, when the cord was round his neck he made his usual prayer to the Virgin, and his prayer was answered; for the mother of God came from heaven to support his feet with "her white hands," and thus she kept him alive for two entire days, to the no small surprise of the executioner, who, to complete his work, struck the man with his sword. The same invisible hand which held up the feet of the thief turned away the sword from injuring her votary, and the executioner was compelled to release his victim. The thief retired to a monastery, and ended his life in the odour of sanctity.—Hallam, *Middle Ages*, vol. iii. p. 349.

The Virgin Mary rescues a monk from the hands of Satan. At St. Peter's monastery, near Cologne, there lived a monk utterly dissolute and wholly without one spark of holiness, but this carnally minded monk was nevertheless very devout towards the apostle Peter. Unluckly, the man died so suddenly there was no time for confession, and none for absolution. Like Hamlet's father, he was

> Cut off e'en in the blossoms of his sin;
> No reckoning made; but sent to his account
> With all his imperfections on his head.

Of course, the fiends came at once to seize on his soul. St. Peter was much vexed to lose so faithful a votary, and besought the Almighty to admit his friend into paradise. His prayer was refused; and though the whole body of saints, angels and archangels, apostles and martyrs, joined in the petition, it was of no avail. In this extremity the prince of the apostles had recourse to the mother of God, the fountain of all mercy. "Fair lady," said the Galilean fisherman, "my dear monk is lost, if you do not at once interfere on his behalf. We have all knelt before the throne to avert this dreadful doom, but to no purpose. The high and holy One is inexorable. In thee only is hope, fair lady; thy voice is never heard in vain. Your Son cannot choose but yield, if you speak to Him. Your wishes are commands, your petitions fiats which even the Father cannot gainsay." So spake the head of the apostolic college, and the queen-mother consented to interfere. She at once went to her Son, with all her attendant virgins, and He who had given the precept, "*Honour thy father and thy mother*," no sooner saw her approach than He rose to greet her. Taking her by the hand, He begged to know her request, adding politely, "To ask is to receive." The Son heard, went to the Father, promised to take on Himself the sins of the monk, and to wash him clean with the blood of Calvary. "Be it with you, My Son," said the Eternal Father, "even as you list." The doors of heaven flew open, the monk was welcomed amongst the saints in light; and there was joy in heaven for half an hour.—See Hallam, *Middle Ages*, vol. iii. p. 349, where this tale is substantially recounted.

The Virgin takes on her the personal presentiment of a nun which had eloped from a convent. A nun, having eloped with a paramour, gave full fling to a libertine life for ten years; but this nun was a devotee of the Virgin Mary, and never passed the image of the holy mother without repeating an *Ave*. To prevent a scandal, and shield her votary, the immaculate Virgin took on herself the semblance and personal presentiment of the recalcitrant nun during her long absence. When tired of sin and its wages, the nun returned to the convent, and not a soul there suspected their erring sister.—Hallam, *Middle Ages*, vol. iii. p. 349.

The Virgin Mary induces a soiled dove to marry and cancel her offences. A gentleman fell in love with a handsome young widow, and they lived together, loving each other not wisely but too well, for both were under the spell of a wicked sorcerer, an imp of Satan. All this time the erring widow never omitted her *Ave*, morning, noon, and night, being fully persuaded, if she kept hold of the Virgin Mary, she would surely find grace to help in time of need. And so it fell out, for the young widow inspired her keeper with a truer love than mere carnal affection; he declared his passion, and they were duly married, received absolution, and their sins, which were many, were all forgiven.—See Hallam, *Middle Ages*, vol. iii., where the substance of this tale is given.

Hallam adds this observation: "These tales, it may be said, are the production of ignorant men, and circulated among the populace. Certainly they would have excited contempt and indignation in the more enlightened clergy. But," says Hallam, "I am concerned with the general character of religious notions among the *people*; and for this purpose it is better to take such popular compositions, adapted to what the laity believed, than the writings of comparatively learned and reflecting men." Just so. If we would know the popular belief of the ancient Greeks and Romans, we must seek for it in the popular literature, and not in the "atheistic" writings of Cicero and the doubts of Socratês. After all, these tales are the outcome of the popular religion, and without doubt were by no means confined to the ignorant and credulous. Every book of the saints of any authority abounds in such tales. Lords and ladies, abbots and bishops, cardinals and popes, set their seals to them, encouraged their circulation, and at one time they were the popular literature of all Christendom. Even to the present hour there is a constant cropping up of some such tale; and that man who doubts cannot have travelled far from his own door, or looked into the hagiographies of Spain, Italy, France, Russia, or Greece.

These articles about the dogmas of the [Roman] Catholic Church, and the adoration of the Virgin in particular, may be concluded with the memorable words of the abbot, in reply to a monk who consulted him respecting the demon of fornication (Δαιμων πορνειας), who interrupted him daily in his prayers to a picture of the Virgin hung in his cell. The question was, Ought he to abstain from these prayers in order to quit himself of the demon? The abbot replied, "Συμφερει δε σοι μη καταλιπειν εν τῃ πολει ταυτῇ πορνειον εις ὁ μη εισελθῃς, η ἱνα ἀρνυησῃ το προσκυνειν τον κυριον ἡμων καὶ θεον Ιησουν Χριστον μετα της ἰδιας ἀυτου μητρος εν εικονι:" *i.e.* "Rather than forbear from adoring Christ and His mother in their holy images, it would be better for you to enter every 'cage of unclean birds,' and to visit every 'nymph' in the whole city."—*Actio* iv. p. 901, and *Actio* v. p. 1031 (Second Nicene Council).

(These two items, crowded out of pt. ii., are of sufficient interest to be added here.)

Voice from Heaven.

John Bunyan hears a voice from heaven. John Bunyan was very fond of dancing on the village green, and of a game called "cat," till a sermon against dancing and games drew him for a time from these youthful diversions. The temptation, however, again "shook the sermon out of my mind," he says, "and to my old custom of sports and gaming I returned with great delight. But the same day, as I was in the midst of a game of cat, and having struck it one blow from the hole, just as I was about to strike it the second time, a voice did suddenly dart from heaven into my soul, which said, 'Wilt thou leave thy sins and go to heaven, or have thy sins and go to hell?' At this I was put in an exceeding maze; wherefore, leaving my cat upon the ground, I looked up to heaven, and was as if I had with the eyes of my understanding seen the Lord Jesus looking down upon me, as being very hotly displeased with me, and as if He did severely threaten me with some grievous punishment for those and other ungodly practices."

This is a most instructive example of the religious phenomenon referred to. Bunyan actually heard "the voice from heaven," but his mind or conscience created it and uttered it to his ear. It came from within to the auditory nerves, and not from without, but it was no less real on that account. As Macbeth's "bloody purpose" informed his mind of the dagger he was about to use, so Bunyan's uneasy conscience informed his mind of what he dreaded, but strove to stifle.

Yoked with Unbelievers.

2 COR. vi. 14. Be ye not unequally yoked together with unbelievers.

[The two following historic facts are patent violations of this precept.]

Venice forms an alliance with the Turks (A.D. 1480). Soon after the Turkish war, a Venetian ambassador was despatched to Constantinople to invite Mahomet II. to make a descent on the coast of Apuglia, to weaken the power of Ferdinand of Naples. Accordingly, a hundred Turkish ships were assembled in the ports of Albania, and sixty Venetian galleys aided them in the sack of Otranto. The result was most calamitous. Within a fortnight eleven thousand souls perished in the assault, and at least as many were reduced to slavery. Among the victims of this infamous alliance were eight hundred ecclesiastics who were all put to the sword.—*Venetian History*, vol. ii. p. 133 (Murray, 1838).

Pope Alexander VI. leagues with the Turks against the eldest son of the Church!! (A.D. 1494). When pope Alexander VI. was alarmed at the approach of Charles VIII., son of Louis XI., that "most Christian king, and eldest son of the Church," he actually made a league with the Turks to achieve the ruin of Charles. Here the head of the Christian Church, the vicar apostolic, the representative of Christ Himself, allies himself with a horde of infidels, to overrun Italy—infidels against whom crusade after crusade had been organized. The proof of this alliance is beyond all contradiction, for the instructions of Alexander to his nuncio in Constantinople, and the letters of sultan Bajazet II. in reply, are all extant and in print.—*Preuves et Illustrations aux Mémoires de Philippe de Comines*, p. 293 (Haye, 1682).

INDEX.

INDEX